The Middle East

A History

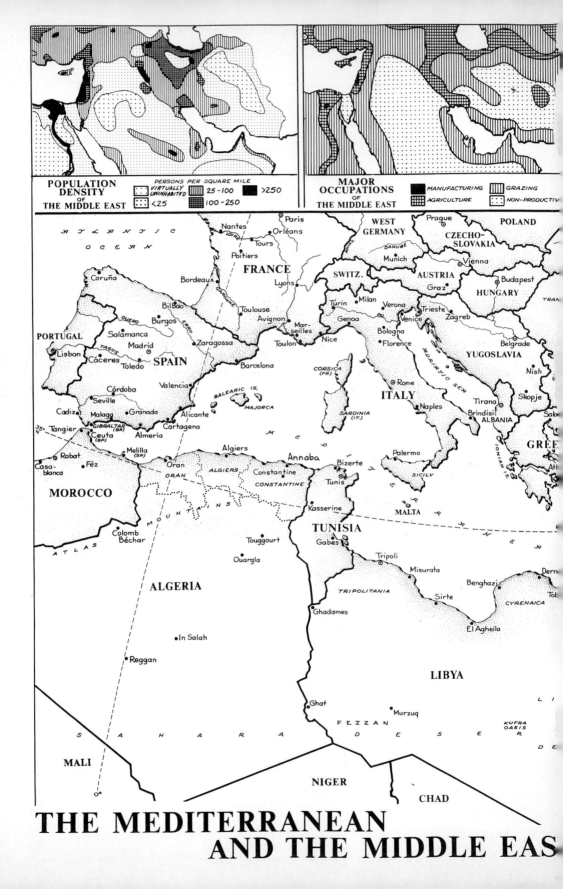

THE MEDITERRANEAN
AND THE MIDDLE EAS

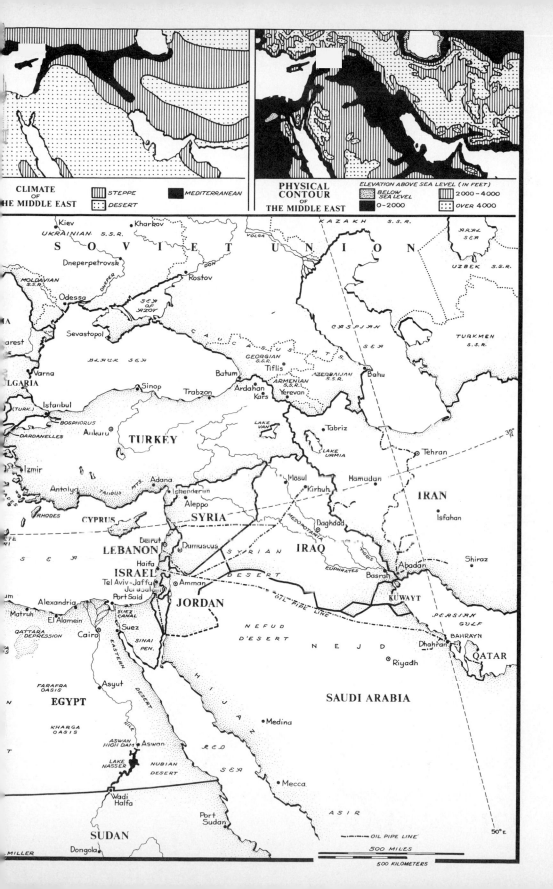

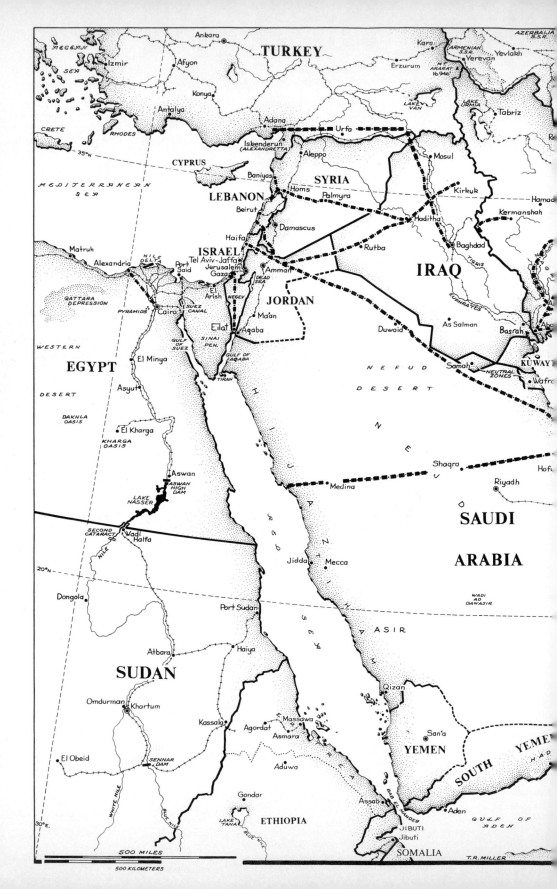

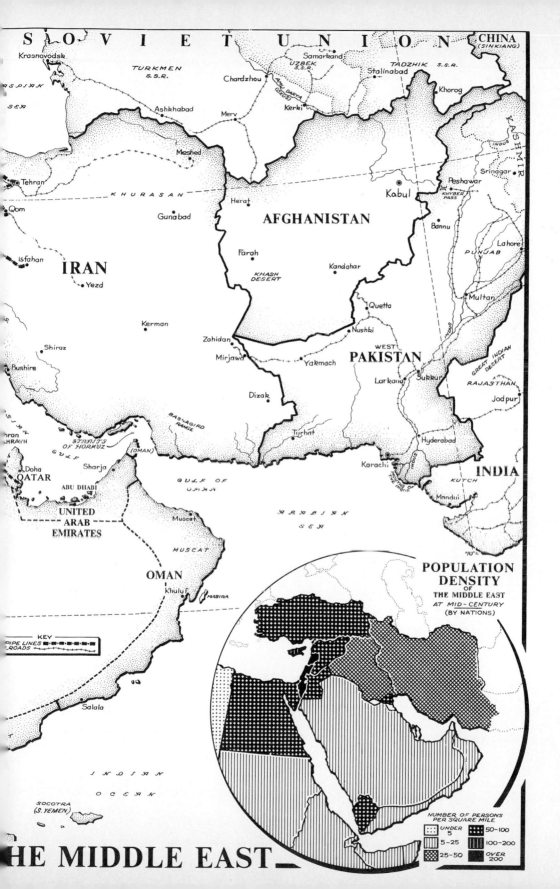

SOVIET UNION CHINA (SINKIANG)

Krasnovodsk
CASPIAN SEA
TURKMEN S.S.R.
Ashkhabad
Chardzhou
AMU DARYA (OXUS)
Kerki
UZBEK S.S.R.
Samarkand
TADZHIK S.S.R.
Stalinabad
Khorog
KASHMIR
INDUS
Srinagar
Peshawar
KHYBER PASS
Merv
Meshed
Tehran
KHURASAN
Qom
Gunabad
Herat
Kabul
Bannu
PUNJAB
Lahore
Isfahan
IRAN
Farah
KHASH DESERT
Kandahar
Multan
Yezd
Kerman
Zahidan
Mirjawa
Yakmach
WEST PAKISTAN
Quetta
Nushki
INDUS
GREAT INDIAN DESERT
RAJASTHAN
Jodpur
Shiraz
Larkana
Sukkur
Bushire
Dizak
Tirhat
Hyderabad
BASHAGIRD RANGE
Karachi
INDIA
KUTCH
Mandui
tehran
BAHRAYN
STRAITS OF HORMUZ
GULF
(OMAN)
Doha
QATAR
Sharja
ABU DHABI
UNITED ARAB EMIRATES
GULF OF OMAN
Muscat
ARABIAN SEA
OMAN
MUSCAT
Khulu
MASIRA

KEY
PIPE LINES
ROADS

Salala

POPULATION
DENSITY
OF
THE MIDDLE EAST
AT MID-CENTURY
(BY NATIONS)

INDIAN OCEAN

SOCOTRA
(S. YEMEN)

NUMBER OF PERSONS PER SQUARE MILE
UNDER 5
5-25
25-50
50-100
100-200
OVER 200

HE MIDDLE EAST

The Middle East

A History

Fourth Edition

The Middle East

A History

Sydney Nettleton Fisher

The Ohio State University

William Ochsenwald

Virginia Polytechnic Institute and State University

McGraw-Hill Publishing Company

New York   St. Louis   San Francisco   Auckland   Bogotá
Caracas   Hamburg   Lisbon   London   Madrid   Mexico   Milan
Montreal   New Delhi   Oklahoma City   Paris   San Juan   São Paulo
Singapore   Sydney   Tokyo   Toronto

This book was set in Garamond by the College Composition Unit
in cooperation with Ruttle, Shaw & Wetherill, Inc.
The editors were Christopher J. Rogers and Fred H. Burns;
the designer was Chuck Carson;
the production supervisor was Valerie A. Sawyer.
R. R. Donnelley & Sons Company was printer and binder.

THE MIDDLE EAST

A History

1 2 3 4 5 6 7 8 9 0   **DOH DOH**   8 9 4 3 2 1 0 9

ISBN   0-07-557262-1

Library of Congress Cataloging-in-Publication Data

Fisher, Sydney Nettleton.
    The Middle East: a history/Sydney Nettleton Fisher, William
Ochsenwald.—4th ed.
        p.   cm.
    Includes bibliographical references.
    ISBN 0-07-557262-1
    1. Middle East—History.   2. Middle East—History—20th century.
I. Ochsenwald, William.   II. Title.
DS62.F5   1990
956—dc20   89-12155

About the Authors

Sydney Nettleton Fisher was born in Warsaw, New York, in 1906 and attended Oberlin College (A.B., M.A.) and the University of Illinois (Ph.D., 1935). He was a member of the faculty of the Ohio State University from 1937 to 1972, except for leaves of absence to accept visiting professorships and grants for foreign travel and study. In addition, Professor Fisher worked with various branches of the U.S. government as a specialist in Middle Eastern problems. He was a member of Phi Beta Kappa, a Fellow of the Royal Historical Society, and a member of the Accadèmia del Mediterràneo. He served as Director of Publications of the Middle East Institute and as editor of *The Middle East Journal* and contributed articles to numerous journals and encyclopedias. He was the author or editor of several books, among them *Foreign Relations of Turkey, 1481–1512* (1948), *Social Forces in the Middle East* (1955), and *The Military in the Middle East* (1963). He died on December 10, 1987.

William Ochsenwald attended the Ohio State University (B.A., M.A.) and the University of Chicago (Ph.D., 1971). He has been a member of the faculty of Virginia Polytechnic Institute since 1971, with occasional leaves for research in Lebanon, Syria, Jordan, Israel, Egypt, Turkey, Britain, and France. He has received grants from the Fulbright-Hays program, the American Research Institute in Turkey; the former United States Department of Health, Education and Welfare; and the Social Science Research Council and American Council of Learned Societies. In 1979–1980 he was an Associate Fellow of the Middle East Centre, University of Cambridge. He is the author of two books, *The Hijaz Railroad* (1980) and *Religion, Society, and the State in Arabia* (1984); co-editor of *Nationalism in a Non-National State: The Dissolution of the Ottoman Empire* (1977); and has published many articles, among them essays appearing in *The Middle East Journal, International Journal of Middle East Studies, Die Welt des Islams, The Muslim World, Arabian Studies,* and the *Encyclopaedia Britannica.*

Contents

29. Unrest in Iran and the Revolution of 1907 and 1908   *358*

Muhammad Shah; Babism; First Years of Nasir al-Din Shah; The Age of Concessions; The Tobacco Concession and Its Aftermath; Muzaffar al-Din Shah and the Constitution; Muhammad Ali Shah and the Counterrevolution; Muhammad Ali Shah Abdicates; Constitutional Government, 1909–1911; The Strangling of Persia; References.

Part IV *THE CONTEMPORARY MIDDLE EAST*

30. Impact of World War I Upon the Middle East   *379*

Turkey Enters the War; Gallipoli Campaign; War Operation; The Armenians; Arab Movements; The Secret Treaties; The Balfour Declaration; The Fourteen Points; Allied Victory; References.

31. The Middle East at the Paris Peace Conference   *392*

Allied Claims and Promises; San Remo Agreement; The Treaty of Sèvres; Allied Occupation of Turkey; Turkish Nationalists; Mustafa Kemal; Turkish-Greek War; Lausanne Conference; References.

32. The Turkish Republic Under Atatürk   *403*

Establishment of the Republic; Secularization; Populism; Nationalism; Statism; Continuing Reform; Turkish Politics; International Affairs; References.

33. The Fertile Crescent Under the Mandate System: Lebanon, Syria, and Iraq   *416*

French Occupation of Lebanon and Syria; Mandate for Lebanon; French Imperialism in Lebanon; Local Lebanese Government; Mandate for Syria; Local Syrian Government; British Occupation of Iraq; The Kingdom of Iraq; Anglo-Iraqi Affairs; The Government of Iraq; Minority Problems in Iraq; Social Problems; Iraqi Oil; Politics in Iraq; References.

34. Palestine and Transjordan   *432*

Zionists, Arabs, and the British; British Mandate; Immigration Policies; Land Policies; Industrial Progress; Social Developments; Finances; British Administration; The Jewish Agency; The Passfield White Paper; Economic Advances; Peel Report; Civil War; Transjordan; References.

35. Egypt and the Sudan   *450*

The British Protectorate; Egyptian Nationalism and the Wafd; Egyptian Independence; The Constitution of 1923; Egyptian Politics; The Constitution of 1930; The Anglo-Egyptian Treaty of 1936; Social and Economic Problems; Education and Intellectual Life; The Anglo-Egyptian Sudan; References.

June 1967 War; The Arab-Israeli War of October 1973; Continuity in the 1980s; Kingdom of Iraq; Republic of Iraq; Ba'thist Rule in the 1970s; Saddam Husayn and the War with Iran; The Arab League; References.

List of Maps

List of Charts
and Genealogies

Preface

to the Fourth Edition

Sydney Nettleton Fisher and I first discussed a joint revision of his classic *The Middle East: A History* in 1985–1986. We began in early 1987 to work on the fourth edition, agreeing on major deletions in the entire volume. I had revised the first eight chapters with the approval of Professor Fisher before he became ill and had to cease work on the project. He died December 10, 1987. Because of this tragic loss, I am solely responsible for all other aspects of the fourth edition.

The changes made for this new edition reflect the extraordinary flood of scholarly work on the subject of the Middle East since 1977. The high quality and great diversity of books and articles has resulted in a number of new interpretations, analyses, and data that have been incorporated into the text. Bibliographies have been brought up to date; more information on cultural, economic, and social matters has been included; many minor names and dates have been deleted and more space has been devoted to broader themes and topics. Highly dramatic developments took place in the Middle East between 1977 and 1988. As a result, the later chapters have been considerably changed so as to incorporate recent events. In the book the following sections have been changed the most—Chapters 7–10, 15, 18, 19, 24, 27, 28, 33, and 35–45. Chapter 46 is almost entirely new except for part of the discussion of the old imperial powers, which is drawn from the second edition. About one-third of the total volume is new; the large degree of revision indicates the importance of new works and contemporary developments.

A book of such scope must inevitably owe much to the help and resources provided by many persons. I acknowledge with gratitude the advice and encouragement extended by my students who have read several drafts of this new edition. They made many valuable suggestions for improvements. Several of my colleagues critically read sections of the manuscript, and my thanks go to David Burr, Richard Hirsh, Burton Kaufman, Ann LaBerge, David Lux, Albert Moyer, and Joseph Wieczynski. I am especially grateful to Glenn Bugh, whose tactful help on ancient history was invaluable. The Virginia Tech History Department provided time for writing and, most importantly, an environment conducive to undertaking such a task. Mrs. Dorothy McCombs, the Interlibrary Loan Office, and others at Newman Library assisted cheerfully and diligently in bibliographic work.

My general approach to the history of the Middle East rests upon foundations established with the help of dedicated teachers and scholars with whom I have studied. They are Sydney Fisher, William McNeill, Marshall Hodgson, William Polk, Richard Chambers, Reuben Smith, Leonard Binder, and Marvin Zonis. Arthur Goldschmidt, Jr., has provided a challenge and set a high standard for writers of surveys of Middle Eastern history. In the last several years I have gained many insights about general surveys of the history of the Middle East from discussions with Jere Bacharach, Karl Barbir, Herbert Bodman, Lynne Rienner, and Marilyn Waldman. My thanks go to all these people, while they of course bear no responsibility for this work.

Friends and family have provided me the support needed to write this edition. I am very grateful to them, and especially to Elizabeth Fisher, Peggy Dean, Donald Miller, and Larry and Marcia Shumsky.

I can only hope that this fourth edition will be as useful to students and the general public as preceding versions have been. In this way the memory of Sydney Fisher, an inspiring teacher, writer, and friend, will be commemorated.

WILLIAM OCHSENWALD

Preface
to the Third Edition

In the ten years since the publication of the second edition of this work, major events have transpired in every one of the Middle Eastern states that affect their internal political, social, and economic patterns. These developments have had their impact on the relations between and among these states. At the same time, international forces in distant sectors of the world have had a bearing on Middle Eastern life. To attempt to record these changes in any meaningful and intelligent way has required the addition of a number of pages in chapters dealing with the history of the several countries since the end of Word War II. In turn, the increased coverage has necessitated cutting and eliminating material throughout the entire volume in order that its length not become too unwieldy.

The chapters embracing the long period prior to World War II were not touched in the second edition, published in 1969, and, consequently, stood as originally written, largely in 1954 and 1955. The amount of new scholarship that has appeared in the last twenty-five years is almost beyond belief when one begins to review it. No field or period of history has been ignored in research, study, and writing by the increasing number of scholars. Therefore, a full revision was demanded. Updating the contents of the previous edition in the light of new knowledge and understanding has been enjoyable though challenging.

In view of the growing importance and influence of Iran over the last two decades, it seemed fitting to develop more of the historical growth of that country between the fifteenth and the twentieth centuries. Sections have been added to chapters covering those years as well as a new chapter dealing with the decades from the middle of the nineteenth century to World War I. Likewise the material on Egypt from the time of the British occupation to World War I has been expanded into a separate chapter. Also the old chapter on Arabia has been divided into two: one on Saudi Arabia, and the other on all the other states of the Arabian peninsula.

In all the varied aspects of this revision, students and colleagues have been generous and helpful in their corrections and suggestions. Without all their aid and encouragement this revision could not have been completed. The forbearance of my family has been wonderful throughout this seemingly unending task.

SYDNEY NETTLETON FISHER

Preface

to the Second Edition

Since 1959, when this text first appeared, the Middle East has experienced many events and developments of considerable significance for the world and for the area. Furthermore, new evidence and information of the past have been revealed by documents, memoirs, statements, and scholars.

In this revision, an attempt has been made to update the material since 1958, to include some of the details of the crisis of the summer of 1967, and to change and correct other statements as required by recent studies and publications.

I wish to thank the various individuals who over the past decade have pointed out errors and omissions and have offered other views for consideration. Some of these have been incorporated in the several reprintings of the first edition and others are included in this revision. I am especially indebted to Mr. James Saeger of Lehigh University for aiding in the preparation of additions to the bibliographic references.

SYDNEY NETTLETON FISHER

Preface
to the First Edition

For the last two thousand years and more the West has been drawn to, involved in, and fascinated by the culture, religion, resources, and politics of the Middle East. First the Greeks, then the Romans, later the Western Europeans, and now the Americans are discovering the Middle East and its peoples. Historically, the area has been labeled the Orient, the East, and Levant, or the Near East; at present the most widely used term is the Middle East.

The United States, because of her great power and world position since the end of World War II, finds herself concerned with the contemporary problems of the Middle East. In general, Americans of today, many of whom have just become cognizant of the existence of the Middle East, find numerous aspects of its life and affairs quite unintelligible. This is particularly true when these complexities are expressed in the various and often conflicting pronouncements of propagandists for the Arabs, the Israelis and Zionism, the imperialists, the oil companies, the internationalists, the isolationists, the various nationalisms of the Middle East, and all sundry interests.

The attempt of this volume has been to present a brief account of the contemporary Middle Eastern scene so that the beginning college student or general reader can place the area in its proper setting and perspective. Many of the present situations and problems cannot be appreciated or evaluated properly without a knowledge and comprehension of the past, since the contemporary civilization of the Middle East probably has deeper and more significant roots in its past culture and experience than many other civilizations.

With this in mind, it was deemed advisable to begin the story, after a short introduction, with the life of the prophet Muhammad and the revolutionary changes that he made upon the society of his time. From this point the narrative has been carried forward, changing the central locus of the scene from Medina to Damascus to Baghdad to Asia Minor to Istanbul and back to the Arab lands as the fortunes of the area have developed, and at the same time examining each era more in detail as the present is approached.

Certain technicalities have been simplified for the beginner. The titles of many positions, past and present, have been translated into English equivalents in order not to confuse the reader with strange words or tire his eyes with unfamiliar combinations of letters and words. The transliteration of Middle Eastern proper names has always presented difficulties. In Western literature pertaining to the Middle East, one can find the name of the Prophet rendered as Muhammad, Mohammed, Mohammad, Mohamed, Mahomet, Mehmed, Mehmet, Mehemet, and several other ways. In this book, Muhammad has been used for Arabs, Mehmed for Turks, and Mohammed for some others when individuals spelled the name in that fashion. For most words a spelling has been employed that would render them and their pronunciation most easily adopted by American readers. Where names of places or people have acquired a widely accepted Western spelling, those forms have been used.

Since almost every volume concerning detailed or specialized aspects of Middle Eastern life and affairs contains considerable bibliographical material, and because of the excellent and wide coverage provided in Richard Ettinghausen's *A Selected and Annotated Bibliography of Books and Periodicals in Western Languages dealing with the Near and Middle East with Special Emphasis on Mediaeval and Modern Times* (The Middle East Institute, Washington, D.C., 1952 and 1954), the inclusion of an extensive bibliography has not been felt necessary. The bibliographical entries at the end of the chapters have been supplied to indicate to the beginning student where easily accessible additional material on particular subjects may be obtained. These titles are suggested to serve as second steps for inquiring students who wish to dig more deeply into the many topics discussed only summarily in this text.

In gathering material for this volume it has been necessary to refer to a wide range of books, produced after years of diligent research and study by several generations of scholars in various lands. All will recognize my debt to these; students familiar with the literature of the diverse aspects of Middle Eastern history will appreciate my indebtedness to scholars of other years. This text could not have been written without their labors.

Through the years it has been my good fortune to obtain a closer knowledge of many aspects of Middle Eastern affairs and society through personal conversations and correspondence with many individuals concerned with that area of the world. Without mentioning names, I wish to thank them for the contributions they have made, sometimes unknowingly, to this text. Specifically I desire to pay tribute to inspiring teachers and mentors who have given me a better understanding of general and detailed problems and periods of Middle Eastern history. They are Frederick B. Artz of Oberlin College; Dr. Edgar J. Fisher of Amherst, Virginia; the late Albert Howe Lybyer of the University of Illinois; Philip K. Hitti and the late Walter Livingston Wright, Jr., of Princeton University; and Paul Wittek of the University of London.

In addition to these I am under deep obligation to my colleagues Professors William F. McDonald and John R. Randall for their criticism and aid in regard to certain chapters. Also, Dr. Halford L. Hoskins of the Library of Congress and Professor George G. Arnakis of the University of Texas read the entire volume, offered valuable suggestions, and caught numerous errors and slips. Dr. J. Merle Rife, State University, Indiana, Pennsylvania, was most helpful in assisting in the compilation of the bibliographical references.

However, any faults in fact or judgment which remain are my sole responsibility. Further recognition is due The Ohio State University Graduate School for assistance in the preparation of the manuscript.

This text could not have been prepared without the tolerance and cooperation of my entire family, which has lived with the manuscript for several years.

SYDNEY NETTLETON FISHER

The Middle East

A History

1

Geographic Prologue

GEOGRAPHY

Since the end of World War II the term *Middle East* has referred to that area of the world comprising the present political states of Lebanon, Syria, Israel, Jordan, Iraq, Saudi Arabia, Kuwayt, Bahrayn, Qatar, the United Arab Emirates, Oman, South Yemen, Yemen, Egypt, Sudan, Turkey, and Iran. In addition, *Middle East* is employed as a cultural designation for a society and civilization found not only in that region but also to a certain degree in a number of adjacent localities such as Afghanistan, Pakistan, Libya, Tunisia, Algeria, and Morocco. Many people in the modern Middle East use this term to designate their region even though the term originated in the United States and therefore reflects a geographical definition of world regions as seen from Washington and Europe. In earlier times, the peoples of the Middle East viewed this region as the center of the world, while the lands to east and west, including Europe and later the Americas, were seen as the peripheries.

Two geographic features of the Middle East have been significant in all periods of history. Its location has given it an important, sometimes strategic, central position between Africa and Eurasia, and between the Mediterranean world and the Asia of India and China. Nations, tribes, traders, armies, and pilgrims—peoples on the move have traversed the Middle East, finding the land bridge convenient and along the way discovering the wealth of the area and the civilization of its people.

The second important geographic feature is the relative magnitude of the Middle East. Arabia, the central land mass of the Middle East, embraces an area about the same size as that of the United States east of the Mississippi River plus Texas and California. The southern shore facing the Indian Ocean from Aden to Muscat spans the same distance as that between Boston and New Orleans; on the west, the Red Sea is as wide as Lake Erie is long, and the distance from Aden to Port Said is nearly the same as that from New York to Denver. Northward from Arabia proper to the Turkish frontier is another 400 miles, or 644 kilometers. When Egypt, Iran, and Turkey are added, the area becomes equivalent to that of the continental United States.

Stretching out 2,000 miles (3,218 km.) westward in a narrow band from the mouth of the Nile River to the Atlantic Ocean lies North Africa, culturally a part of

I

the Middle East since the end of the seventh century. Moreover, this delimitation of the Middle East has omitted Turkestan, Afghanistan, and Pakistan, with such historic cities as Bukhara, Samarkand, Kabul, and Lahore. Thus, the physical size of the Middle East becomes impressive to Europeans and Americans who are accustomed to seeing these areas in the framework of maps of Asia and Africa.

PHYSIOGRAPHY

The geologic characteristics of the Middle East show a wide variety of land features, ranging from great bodies of water to low-lying land and swampy regions to rough mountain areas. Over the past 7,000 years or so there seems to have been no important physiographical change except that the deltas of most of the rivers have grown and extended the land seaward. In western Turkey, for example, camels and cattle now graze on the flood plain of the Meander River in front of the ancient walls of Miletus and Priene, in the exact spot where the Persian fleet vanquished the Greeks five centuries before Christ.

Arabia, in general, is a tilted plateau, slanting upward from the northeast to the southwest with a sharp drop in Yemen from 12,000 feet (3,657 meters) down to the Red Sea. Central Turkey and central Iran are elevated plateaus, in places reaching an altitude of 8,000 feet (2,438 meters). Rugged mountains dominate Middle Eastern geography. From a high center in northwestern Iran in the neighborhood of Mount Ararat, mountain ranges up to 18,000 feet (5,486 meters) in altitude branch out in several chains: the Elburz group, running eastward south of the Caspian Sea; the Zagros system, a wide series of ranges protruding in a southeasterly direction to Afghanistan and India; and the famed Taurus mountains, pushing southwestward to the Mediterranean and separating the Anatolian plateau from Arabia.

Rivers have played an important role in society in fostering settled agriculture and have deeply influenced the development of civilization in the Middle East. Two river systems are fabled and basic in the history of the area: the Nile and the Tigris-Euphrates. Flowing from central Africa and Ethiopia, the Nile passes through a relatively flat region in the Sudan until it reaches the cataract zone north of Khartoum, where a gorge has been cut. Below Aswan, the Nile flows through a well-developed valley about six miles (10 km.) wide to Cairo, where the delta begins. In August the river starts to rise in Egypt, reaching its peak in September, eighteen feet above the low of April and May. Annually some 110 million tons of sediment, rich in mineral substances, are carried into Egypt, and until the completion of the Aswan Dam in 1970, more than half of this silt reached the delta.

The other great river system, the Tigris-Euphrates, rises in the highlands of eastern Turkey. Winter snowfall feeds both streams, which turn and twist through precipitous and narrow defiles emptying out upon the plateau plains of Syria and Kurdistan. Rushing southward, they converge upon Baghdad but meet only about 230 miles (370 km.) farther on where they form the Shatt al-Arab, which flows gently for about 75 miles (121 km.) to the Persian Gulf. The fall in the river beds between Asia Minor and Baghdad is very marked, producing a swift current with strong erosive powers. The rivers are at their lowest in September and October but begin to rise appreciably in December, reaching a flood stage in April for the Tigris and, until recently, in May for the Euphrates. The Tabqa Dam in Syria, completed in 1973, and the Turkish Keban Dam on the Euphrates control much of the flooding, generate electric power, and extend the arable lands in both countries. Within historic times silt from the Tigris and the Euphrates and two Iranian tributaries of the former—the Karkeh and the Karun—filled in the Persian Gulf from near the site of Baghdad to the present shoreline. No longer a tributary, the Karkeh is dissipated at the present time in the marshes of lower Iraq.

One of the most renowned and romantic geographic spots of the Middle East has been the straits that form the waterway from the Black Sea to the Aegean Sea. At the northern end is the present-day Bosphorus, a sixteen-mile (26-km.) strait varying in width from nearly two miles to one-third mile at the narrowest point. Everywhere the channel is deep, and the drop-off at the edge is so sharp that vessels requiring considerable draft may tie up at many places along the shore and unload directly upon the adjacent road. On a point of land where the Bosphorus empties into the Sea of Marmara stands one of the great cities of the Middle East— variously known as Byzantium, Constantinople, or Istanbul. Dotted with a number of islands, the Sea of Marmara is 60 miles (97 km.) wide and extends some 125 miles southwestward to the Dardanelles. This historic passage, often called the Hellespont, is 25 miles (40 km.) long and is wider than the Bosphorus, varying from 2.5 miles to 4.5 miles at its southern end, where it empties into the Aegean. These three bodies of water, collectively known through the years as the Straits, separate Europe from Asia yet serve as a strong connecting link between East and West. Economically, politically, and strategically, the Straits have been important throughout all history in controlling passage between the Mediterranean and the Black seas.

CLIMATE

During the fourth glacial period, some 25,000 years ago, when much of Europe and northern Asia was covered with an ice sheet, the southern Middle East and the Sahara regions were moist and dotted with lakes and seas, a well-watered wooded land abounding with game. As the ice receded, the desert area between the tropic and the temperate zones appeared. Compared to these major events, little change, however, has occurred in the climate of the Middle East in the last 5,000 years.

Rainfall along the shores of the Mediterranean, Black, and Caspian seas comes for the most part during the winter months. Many areas receive an average annual fall of thirty inches (762 mm.). (As one progresses inland, however, the average drops appreciably; Egypt and the plateaus of Arabia, Iran, and eastern Turkey have a desert climate.) Moreover, the rains are not only seasonal but almost capricious. Damascus has an average annual rainfall of about ten inches (254 mm.), but four inches have been known to fall in one morning. The mountainous areas of eastern Turkey and Iran receive more moisture, but here, too, winter is the wet season, with much of the precipitation occurring in the form of snow. The one exception to the winter rain pattern is the monsoon region of southern and southwestern Arabia, which gets most of its rainfall in the months of July, August, and September.

Temperatures depend upon latitude and altitude, and winter in the mountains of Arabia can be quite bitter. Summer temperatures in Egypt, Arabia, Iran, and the interior of Turkey are hot, over 100°F. (38°C.) during the day, but nights are cool everywhere except in some of the lower valleys and along some coasts where the humidity is high.

FLORA AND FAUNA

Wood has been a prized building material and, along with animal dung, the principal fuel in the Middle East from the beginning of history until the advent of coal and oil. Over the last 5,000 years a process of deforestation has denuded most of the land. Some stands of oak, beech, pine, juniper, and boxwood remain on the slopes of the Elburz Mountains, in east Asia Minor, and the Lebanon Mountains. Elsewhere the land would be bare but for cypresses in cemeteries and gardens and poplars along streams and irrigation ditches.

It has been estimated that unconcern about land conservation over the last 5,000 years has resulted in the destruction of 90 percent of the forest and topsoil resources of the Middle East. But absence of concern cannot be said to exist with respect to the cultivation of edible flora of the area. Wheat, barley, rye, broad beans, lentils, onions, leeks, garlic, figs, grapes, melons, pomegranates, pears, plums, apples, peaches, apricots, almonds, walnuts, olives, and dates are the principal foods developed from the vegetation of the area.

Domestication of native animals of the Middle East probably began about the same time that the land was beginning to be cultivated. It is difficult to tell in what order, but at some very early time the dog (probably first), sheep, goat, pig, ox, and ass were tamed and used for work or to provide food and clothing. Domesticated horses and camels were introduced into the area from farther east in Asia in the second millennium before Christ. As the forests became scarcer, the pig was replaced by more economical all-purpose animals like the ox, goat, and sheep; and the arrival of the camel made habitation in the desert possible and facilitated Middle Eastern nomadism in Arabia proper.

The waters teem with fish. The Caspian has long been noted for its sturgeon and caviar. The Black Sea and the Bosphorus abound in tuna, mackerel, and herring of many excellent varieties. And the eastern Mediterranean, fed by the vegetable matter of the Nile, has been through the centuries an attractive and productive spot for fish of all kinds.

RESOURCES

The significant natural resources of the Middle East have been, and still are, the availability and interrelationship of water, soil, sun, plants, and animals, allowing for a propitious agricultural life. Other natural resources are the excellent clays with which the bricks, pots, and finer ceramics of many cultures have been fashioned. Mountains, lava extrusions along the geologic faults, and rock formations laid bare by river erosion have provided extensive quarries for basalt, granite, marble, porphyry, sandstone, and limestone.

Gold, silver, copper, and iron are extracted in easily workable ores, and their ready utilization marked the end of the Neolithic age. The presence of other metals such as tin and nickel with copper led the way to the development of bronze and brass. Deposits of these metals have been worked almost continuously up to the present, and the output has been of considerable value in the economy and life of the area. In the twentieth century other metals have come to the fore. Chromium and manganese are found in sizable deposits; and small amounts of antimony, molybdenum, mercury, and cobalt are available. Coal and lignite exist in considerable amounts in Turkey and Iran, but only in recent years have these beds been exploited.

The greatest of the natural resources of the Middle East of the twentieth century, beyond land and water, is oil. Small fields have been located in Turkey, Egypt, Syria, Yemen, and Israel, but the large ones are those of Khuzistan in Iran, Mosul-Kirkuk in Iraq, along the Persian Gulf in Saudi Arabia, Kuwayt, Bahrayn, Qatar, the shaykhdoms of the Persian Gulf, and Oman, and in Libya and Algeria. No one yet knows the full extent of the oil reserves of the Middle East; but its known reserves alone far outstrip those of any other oil-producing region, and the presence of this natural resource has changed the world importance of the Middle East.

PEOPLE

The Middle East, despite its large deserts, was blessed with a warm climate, a fertile soil, native animals and plants suitable for food, waters available for controlled irrigation, and varied mineral resources, and was thus an area of the world favorable for the propagation of the human race, for the increase in standards of living, and for the growth of an organized society.

Although anthropologists, archaeologists, and geneticists have yet to unravel the twisted and indistinct story of life and the wanderings of prehistoric *Homo sapiens* in the Middle East, it seems quite certain that around 15,000 B.C., as the fourth glacial period terminated, the well-watered regions of Arabia and the Sahara were inhabited by people of a Mediterranean race. Then, through ten millennia of the Mesolithic age, as the ice cap was retreating to Scandinavia, Arabia and the Sahara became desiccated and their inhabitants moved northward and seaward. Some in east Africa became the ancestors of the Egyptians; others in Arabia clung to the shores of the Persian Gulf or moved to the southern highlands. The latter became known to the world as Semites. In addition, significant pockets of Mediterranean peoples remained along the shores of that sea, and evidences of their settlements are being found in Israel, Lebanon, Syria, and Turkey. Another branch of the Mediterranean group lived on the Iranian plateau, where much domestication of plants and animals took place. As these peoples moved with their advanced cultures into other parts of the Middle East and into Europe, the Neolithic age was born.

With the advent of Neolithic *Homo sapiens* into the chief river valleys, Middle Eastern civilization had its beginnings. Because the annual flooding of rivers renewed the soil with the silt they deposited, Neolithic agriculturalists could continue to cultivate the same fields year after year, generation after generation. Even a partial nomadism became unnecessary; a stable, stationary society evolved. Records accumulated and history in the Middle East began.

REFERENCES

Bacharach, Jere L. *A Middle East Studies Handbook*. Seattle: University of Washington Press, 1984. Invaluable not only for its maps, but also for chronology, dynastic tables, and lists of recent heads of state. Excellent for the beginning student and also highly useful for specialists.

Beaumont, Peter, *et al. The Middle East: A Geographical Study*. London: John Wiley and Sons, 1976. Covers physical and social geography for the whole region and country-by-country.

Brice, William C., ed. *The Environmental History of the Near and Middle East Since the Last Ice Age*. London: Academic Press, 1978. Specialized studies of regions, including discussions of climate and geology.

————. *An Historical Atlas of Islam*. Leiden: Brill, 1981. Valuable for its extensive coverage.

Coon, Carleton S. *Caravan: The Story of the Middle East*. New York: Holt, 1951. An excellent anthropological introduction to the Middle East, written in a style easily understood by the beginning student.

Drysdale, Alasdair, and Gerald H. Blake. *The Middle East and North Africa: A Political Geography*. New York: Oxford University Press, 1985. Shows the relationship between recent political and diplomatic issues and geographic factors.

Fisher, W. B. *The Middle East: A Physical, Social and Regional Geography*. London: Methuen, 1978. Authoritative yet easily read; seventh edition of a classic.

————, ed. *The Cambridge History of Iran*. Vol. 1. *The Land of Iran*. Cambridge: Cambridge University Press, 1968. A complete study of Iranian geography, broadly defined.

Robinson, Francis. *Atlas of the Islamic World Since 1500*. New York: Facts on File, 1982. Filled with beautiful illustrations, maps, and a historical narrative that is comparative and informative.

Survey of Israel. *Atlas of Israel: Cartography, Physical and Human Geography*. 3rd ed. Tel Aviv: The Survey of Israel, 1985. The geography of Israel through maps.

2

Pre-Islamic Politics
and Society
in the Middle East

THE RISE OF CIVILIZATION

Scholars have debated for two centuries whether Western civilization began first in the Nile valley or in Mesopotamia along the Tigris and Euphrates rivers. However, archaeologists are now discovering that significant Protoneolithic cultures were independently developed in north Syria at Ras Shamra and in Palestine in the Jordan valley, especially at Jericho about the year 9000 B.C.; in northern Mesopotamia around 8900 B.C.; and in the south-central plateau of Asia Minor north of the Taurus range in the general region around Konya some time before 7000 B.C. There is general agreement that these Protoneolithic and Neolithic populations of the Middle East were descended from Paleolithic and Mesolithic inhabitants of the area. Botanists and geneticists have shown that in these upland regions and perhaps in other foothills of western Asia between the Mediterranean and the Himalayas, edible grasses, like wheat and barley, and herd animals, such as sheep, goats, and cattle, had their natural habitats. Small sheltered groups of people learned to cultivate and domesticate these natural resources and established settled societies. Eventually, large towns were built and defended, and civilizations with art forms, religious practices, foreign trade, and social and political norms appeared.

Only when agricultural skills and social techniques had been developed adequately could the complex problems of living on great riverine plains be solved. Just how and where the transitions occurred has not yet been determined, but they undoubtedly took place slowly over several millennia. In any case, in two centers of highly evolved urban civilizations along the Nile and the Tigris-Euphrates it can be shown that each culture arrived in the area already in a transitional stage from the Neolithic age to the Early Bronze age, that each brought with it domesticated plants and animals (many of which were of common origin), but that each in its new habitat independently developed an urban civilization.

Somewhat after the year 4000 B.C. the Sumerian people arrived at one of the mouths of the Tigris and Euphrates rivers. Where they came from has not been determined with any exactitude, but they spoke a language wholly unrelated to any known tongue. There in the Tigris-Euphrates valley, Sumerian city-states evolved around 3000 B.C. with society divided into technological-social classes—bureaucrats, priests, traders, farmers, and artisans—divisions that have persisted as factors in Middle Eastern civilizations. Shortly thereafter, other peoples from the shores and watered places of Arabia were drawn to the prosperous Sumerian cities. They spoke a language belonging to the Semitic family, the basic tongue arising in the Arabian peninsula. Thus, very early in history, the Sumerians became a mixed people.

Farther north along the middle Euphrates about the beginning of the third millennium B.C., Semites, probably from the desert, began to become sedentarized in Kish and other cities of the region. For a thousand years the Sumerian and the Semitic states were ardent rivals, although internecine conflict among the cities in each group was the norm. In some of the city-states Semites and Sumerians intermingled. Cities such as Lagash, Akkad, and Ur each had its day and then passed the scepter to another. The Sumerian element in the area, however, was again politically submerged by the union of all of Mesopotamia under the Amorite (Semitic) Hammurabi of Babylon about the year 1700 B.C. Western Syria, first under Ebla, then the kingdom of Yamkhad, was an alternative center of power, rivaling both Mesopotamia and Egypt.

At approximately the same time that the Sumerians appeared in Mesopotamia, Hamites began to develop a civilization along the Nile. Some came from eastern Africa, and others from North Africa; the Hamitic tongue of the early Egyptians was a blending of the two. The nature of the land, the annual flooding of the Nile, the local presence of copper (which began to be worked about 3000 B.C.), and the relative isolation of the Nile valley by the surrounding deserts were conducive to the establishment of an absolute monarchy and a flourishing culture.

Early in the second millennium B.C. Indo-Europeans from eastern Europe and western Asia began a southward movement, exerting population pressures upon the whole of the Middle East. In a succession of thrusts, these intruders, first equipped with bronze and then with iron weapons, and accompanied by horses and camels, pushed ahead into the Middle East. The Kassites came down with horses from the Zagros Mountains to rule Mesopotamia through most of the second millennium B.C.; and the Hyksos came with their horse-drawn chariots to rule Egypt for two centuries beginning about 1800 B.C. Later, genuine Indo-European waves brought Hittites, Armenians, Achaean and Dorian Greeks, Philistines, Medes, Persians, Macedonians, Parthians, Romans, and Sasanids. Between these invasions and conquests of the northmen, Hamite rulers reappeared in Egypt, and Semitic tribes such as Amorites, Assyrians, Arameans, Canaanites, Phoenicians, Hebrews, Nabateans, Palmyrenes, and Ghassanids moved from the Arabian peninsula to establish states in Mesopotamia, Syria, or Palestine.

Each group of invaders, at the time of its arrival upon the Middle Eastern scene and in its first contact with Middle Eastern civilization, was leading a nomadic or pastoral life. The transition to an organized life with greater specialization and division of labor produced turmoil and strains, but the transition was usually made

THE EARLIEST CIVILIZATIONS
OF THE MIDDLE EAST
AND THE
MIGRATIONS OF PEOPLES, 1500-200 B.C.

successfully. Each group added something in religion, the art of writing, metallurgical skills, political organization, transportation, irrigation, or astronomy, and within a brief period the knowledge was disseminated over the entire area.

ANCIENT EMPIRES

By the beginning of the first millennium B.C. the Middle East was rapidly becoming one cultural region, and a number of efforts were made to unite the area politically. Throughout the second millennium B.C. the Egyptian pharaohs sought and from time to time held control of Syria and Palestine. Anatolian kings such as the Hittites, however, vied with the pharaohs for these provinces; and from that age until the present the Syrian coast has been able to maintain its independence only when both Egypt and Anatolia/Mesopotamia have been weak or evenly matched.

One of the great empires controlling a major part of the Middle East was that of the Assyrians, whose capital was at Nineveh on the upper Tigris in Mesopotamia. Iron weapons, a disciplined army, a tight bureaucracy, and iron battering rams mounted on wheels gave the Semitic Assyrians such an advantage in the seventh century B.C. that Nineveh held sway from Sinai to the Caspian Sea and from the Persian Gulf to the plains of central Asia Minor. However, overextension of the empire and exhausting battles, coupled with luxury, indolence, and unwise taxation, weakened the army and the government, with the result that Nineveh with its palace and great library was sacked by Iranians in league with another Semitic group which established its capital at Babylon on the Euphrates. Comprising the full Fertile Crescent from Sinai to the Persian Gulf, this new Chaldean empire won fame for its "hanging gardens," the Babylonian captivity of the Hebrews, and such names as Nebuchadnezzar and Belshazzar.

Upon the fall of Nineveh, the unity of the Middle East was destroyed until the Persians, a small group of Iranians from the southeastern end of the Zagros range, reunited the areas of the previous Assyrian empire and added Greek Asia Minor, Byzantium, Thrace, the Nile valley to the Sudan, Afghanistan, Baluchistan, the Punjab, Bactria, and Sogdiana. With the establishment of the Persian Empire in the sixth century B.C. Semitic rule in the Middle East was crushed for over a thousand years. It was not until the rise of the Arabs under the banners of Islam that the Indo-Europeans lost their hegemony.

Despite being checked by Greeks at Marathon in 490 B.C. and at Thermopylae a decade later, the Persians maintained their power in the Middle East by an imperial system of government that skillfully combined local autonomy with centralized authority and responsibility. This form of government fashioned by the Persians was adopted in most essentials by succeeding rulers for over 2,000 years and established a governmental pattern that became accepted as a part of Middle Eastern civilization. The twenty-three provinces, or satrapies, of the Persian Empire were organized along ethnic lines and local autonomy was real to a considerable degree. Taxes and loyalty were the important requirements; a governor (satrap), a general, and a secretary, each reporting independently to the royal residence (Susa, Babylon, or Persepolis), preserved Persian rule.

Another secret of Persian success was the advancement of communications and transportation. Good roads from the frontier to the heart of the empire were kept open under constant repair and surveillance. The old canals between the Nile and the Red Sea were repaired so that the Phoenicians, the stalwarts of the Persian fleet, could sail directly from the Persian Gulf to the Mediterranean. In the end, however, the old story was repeated: the emperors grew decadent; the traveling inspectors of the empire became careless; and corruption, inefficiency, and incompetence developed.

Alexander and the Greeks

In the fourth century B.C. a new Indo-European people related to the Greeks began their ascent to power under Philip of Macedon. By the use of heavier armor and the integration of cavalry and the Macedonian phalanx, Greece was subjected to his rule. But Greece captured the mind and spirit of his son, Alexander, perhaps through his private tutor, the famed Aristotle. The campaigns and conquests of Alexander the Great and the creation of his vast Greek empire have been retold through the ages by countless poets, romantics, and historians of many lands and races.

After defeating the Persian army in 334 B.C., the young Alexander, only twenty-two years old, swept all before him. Asia Minor, Syria, Palestine, Egypt, Mesopotamia, Persia, and India to the Indus had been conquered and consolidated into an empire before his death in 323. Alexander had hoped to unify the entire Middle East into one lasting empire. He married an Asian princess and commanded his army officers to follow his example. But his untimely death left only his chief generals to battle for the empire, which they eventually divided: Ptolemy in Egypt, Antigonus initially in Asia Minor and then his successors in Macedonia and Greece, Seleucus in Syria and Asia, and a number of lesser officers in scattered corners of the Middle East.

Following the breakup of Alexander's empire, the Middle East fell heir to a century of international political anarchy and intermittent wars; yet it enjoyed a period of vast trade and wealth as well as many decades of important intellectual and artistic activity. It was the apogee of the brilliant Hellenistic age, which persisted for two centuries more until the last vestige of Ptolemaic rule in Egypt had ended with Cleopatra's suicide and the Nile valley became a Roman province.

The Roman Empire and Its Successors

At the invitation of Egypt, Rhodes, and Pergamum, Rome became the arbiter of Middle Eastern affairs, as the Mediterranean was turned into a vast Roman lake. Except for the Tigris-Euphrates and Iran, the Middle East was transformed into Roman provinces, and was subjected to rule from Rome until the emperor Constantine transferred his capital eastward to Constantinople, on the shores of the Bosphorus. From the establishment of Constantinople in A.D. 330 to the defeat of Emperor Heraclius by the Arab armies in 638, the Roman provinces of the Middle East were important parts of the Byzantine Empire.

The eastern Seleucid provinces—Mesopotamia and Persia—fell away from the state, and early in the second century B.C. the great Parthian Empire was established in Iran by Mithridates I. Seleucia-on-the-Tigris was taken; and before the century closed, all territory east of the Euphrates had been seized by the Parthian King of Kings, who built his royal palace at Ctesiphon on the east bank of the Tigris opposite Seleucia. The Parthian power rested on its nomadic cavalry and on the reaction against Hellenism, even though the kings knew Greek and had Greek tragedies performed at their court. The Parthians defeated the Romans, who recognized Parthian dominion over all of Mesopotamia.

Early in the third century internal weakness brought the downfall of the Parthian kings at the hands of a new Persian family, the Sasanids. The founder of the dynasty was a devotee of Zoroaster, and the fire cult was vigorously advanced, becoming the official religion of the empire. Wars with the Romans and Byzantines found the religious differences to be as important as the political ones.

From their main residence at Ctesiphon the Sasanids time and again harried the Byzantine provinces of Syria and Asia Minor. After the fifth century, when Christianity was tolerated and the Nestorian Church had become widespread in the Sasanid Empire, particularly in Mesopotamia, the conflicts with Constantinople were more imperial in nature. Justinian checked the Sasanids temporarily, but they sacked Aleppo and Antioch and forced upon the Byzantine emperor a peace treaty whereby no Christian proselytizing would be permitted within the empire. Peace, however, was not realized and exhausting campaigns were resumed under Justinian's successors. Bubonic plague and the decline of urban life further weakened the Byzantine lands.

A powerful Sasanid army erupted into Syria in 613, destroying the Church of the Holy Sepulcher in Jerusalem, pillaging Damascus, and plundering and massacring everywhere. A Sasanid army conquered Egypt in 619, and another captured the cities across from Constantinople. Evil days appeared for the Byzantines, but the tide turned. Between 622 and 628 Heraclius, the new Byzantine emperor, conducted three brilliant campaigns and even succeeded in driving the Sasanids from Egypt and Syria. But the wars, ensuing destruction, and internal changes left both empires weakened. Syria, Egypt, and Mesopotamia were ripe for picking by the new vigorous Muslim Arabs in the next decade.

PRE-ISLAMIC CIVILIZATION IN THE MIDDLE EAST

For nearly a thousand years the Semitic and Persian Middle East had been subjected to the influence and the forced cultivation of Greek, Hellenistic, Roman, and Byzantine civilizations. Although it would be possible to point out distinguishing characteristics of each of these four civilizations and to show how each evolved from its predecessor, they form one continuous cultural experience and development in the history of the Middle East.

First and foremost among the changes was the adoption of Greek by the educated and by the leaders of society as the language of government, philosophy, literature, and sophisticated communication. Greek colonists—merchants, soldiers, and government officials—settled in most of the Middle Eastern cities and founded many new Greek cities like Antioch in Syria and Alexandria in Egypt. Intellectually and artistically, the Middle East appeared as one world. Greek philosophies and Greek science became universal throughout the area, although many leaders were not of Greek stock, and much of the philosophy and science was not Greek in origin or inspiration.

Roman and Sasanid rule ended the internecine warfare of the Alexandrian successor states and brought a more bountiful material life to the cities of the Middle East. The remains of the almost countless theaters, temples, baths, and public buildings that dot the Middle East today are silent witnesses of the populous, thriving, and wealthy cities of that age. However, in governing the Middle East the Romans were more crassly materialistic, more ruthlessly extortionate, and more heedlessly arrogant than previous foreign rulers.

Even Roman military might, genius for efficiency, and administrative skill could not always control the Middle East. Natives who adopted Greek and Roman ways in speech, dress, food, religion, and manners were detested and shunned by the others. As the years passed, the Hellenistic states became less and less Greek, conforming more faithfully to the age-old patterns of life in the Middle East. The Ptolemies appeared as pharaohs, and the Seleucids lived as Assyrian and Persian monarchs. Jesus of Nazareth spoke Aramaic, not Greek. St. Paul was a learned Jew with a Greek and Roman education, but his conversion to Christianity exemplified a rejection of foreign ideologies.

For all the show of Greek and Roman civilization in the cities of Syria and Egypt, Hellenism and Romanism rested very lightly on the common peoples of the Middle East. Under the rule of the Byzantine emperors the reassertion of Middle Eastern patterns was accelerated in Syria and Egypt. Asia Minor, which had participated in Greek cultural development long before the age of Alexander, had not been a part of the empires of the Middle East except that of the Persians. Thus, the Roman province of Asia (western Asia Minor) exhibited a Hellenistic life more Greek and Roman and less Oriental than did Syria or Egypt.

CHRISTIANITY

The new contribution that came to the cultural stream of the Middle East with Byzantine dominion was Christianity, which received recognition as the official religion of the empire. In Hellenistic and Roman periods people were groping for a philosophy of life and a religion that would answer some of the problems of those rapidly changing and turbulent days. Faith in the power or protection of the Olympian gods had largely disappeared by the time of Alexander. The educated neglected the gods and pursued the philosophies fashioned by Plato and Aristotle. Other philosophic systems followed: Cynicism, Epicureanism, Skepticism, and Stoicism. Each of these had its advocates and its followers, but each was more negative than positive. They were intellectual shelters where sensitive and distressed souls might take refuge from a materialistic and heartless society.

To the masses these philosophies were meaningless. The formation of a world state deprived one of a sense of identity with a city-state and its protecting god. As helpless individuals in a large empire, people needed a savior. They therefore turned to the mystery cults of Asia, which spread widely and had a devoted and numerous following.

Magic and astrology were so popular that the latter quite destroyed astronomy for many centuries. By some secret formula a person might force the hand of a god to alter one's fate or open a shortcut to fortune. But the mystery cults were far more influential. Here the individual, by witnessing and participating in an esoteric ritual, was initiated into the mysteries of life and death, god and immortality. As the savior-god had lived and died and risen again, so the lonely and helpless individual, living in a tumultuous and materialistic world, might win eternal salvation by personal union with the god.

The most important of these religions of the Hellenistic world was that of the triplex of Sarapis-Osiris, Anubis-Horus, and Isis. Sarapis was a Greek Osiris, ruler of all, and his son Anubis led the souls of the dead to immortal life. Isis, however, was above Fate and she freed her adherents from the dominion of Fate and of death. Moreover, being a woman—one who was a wife and a mother and one who had suffered—she appealed to the female half of the population. The ritual of initiation comprised a purification by water, a journey through dark places of the underworld comparable to that of Osiris between the time of his death and resurrection, and a final appearance in holy robes and in a full panoply of light before the whole congregation. From that moment onward the member's soul was godlike and secure from earthly forces.

In the second century A.D. under Roman rule, the greatest change in the Middle East came with the rise and spread of Christianity. Taking many of the positive and uplifting tenets of Judaism, of the Greek philosophies, and of the Oriental cults, Christianity added two vital factors which were largely absent in Hellenism and Romanism: Christ offered immortality to all; and His creed was based on love of humanity.

Early Christianity appealed almost solely to urban Hellenistic society, the language of the church being Greek exclusively. After Christianity obtained official favor and adoption, the Byzantine state rapidly developed into a synthesis of Hellenism, Orientalism, and Christianity and a syncretism of the political power of the state and the religious authority of the church.

The union of autocracy and theocracy in the Byzantine state—the so-called Caesaro-papism of Constantinople—ensured the permanent alienation of the masses in the Middle Eastern provinces. As new doctrines from the Middle East were branded heresies by the state-dominated church councils—Nicaea (325), Ephesus (431), and Chalcedon (451)—separate native Christian churches evolved. Aramaic, its Syriac dialect, and Ethiopic became liturgic languages. Byzantine Constantinople could not force her type of Christianity upon the Middle Eastern peoples.

The Nestorian Church presented a dualism of good and evil not far distant from Zoroastrian doctrines, a fact which may explain its acceptance in Mesopotamia and Iran. Monophysite Christianity certainly embodied some of the Egyptian ideas of human divinity. Heresies flourished in non-Greek areas of the Byzantine Empire and served as basic factors in the almost complete lack of resistance and even passive cooperation of the Middle Eastern provinces at the time of the conquests by the Muslim Arabs. Links with the Semites from the desert proved stronger than those with Christian Constantinople.

THE ARABS

In the first half of the seventh century, the Arabs, a Semitic group under the banners of a new religion, descended upon Syria, Egypt, Mesopotamia, and Persia. Coming from an area little touched by the mainstreams of Middle Eastern life, the Arabs seemed to be a new and different force to the peoples of that age.

The chief difference between the Arabs and other Semites lay in the fact that they did not sever their connections with their past abode. The Arabs lived along the shores of Arabia, in the southern highlands where there was some rainfall, and in the scattered oases and around the meager water holes that remained in Arabia as the fourth glacier receded. These desert inhabitants—farmers and shepherds—were numerically small and insignificant until the advent of the camel about 1200 B.C. The peculiar characteristics of this beast made nomadic life in the desert possible and profitable. The camel was as revolutionary to life in Arabia at that time as oil and the motor vehicle have been in the twentieth century. The camel people became lords of the desert. Above all, the camel welded town and desert life in Arabia into one integrated society, each dependent upon the other.

The use of the camel, moreover, eased many difficulties of the transit trade between India and the Mediterranean. Camel caravans began to carry spices and incense from Yemen to Mecca, the Hijaz, Damascus, and the Mediterranean. Other trade routes connected Mecca with towns on the Euphrates and the Persian Gulf. Cities prospered, small kingdoms were established, and civilization advanced, as demands of the Hellenistic, Roman, and Sasanid worlds expanded. Arabia in the sixth century, the time of the birth of Muhammad the Prophet, was being affected increasingly by events in surrounding states.

ARABIAN SOCIETY

In order to understand Muhammad and the people's response to his preaching, it is profitable to examine briefly the economic, political, social, and religious forces current in his day in the Hijaz and in Mecca.

Mecca, Muhammad's birthplace, was near the caravan routes from Yemen to Syria. Possessing a permanent spring and an ancient sacred shrine, Mecca dominated the Hijaz. It was a commercial city and a growing financial center. Mecca had originated as an entrepôt, but by the end of the sixth century Meccan merchants were buying and selling wares (especially leather and perfume) in all of the markets from Yemen to southern Syria. Mercantile wealth was turning to financial

THE MIDDLE EAST

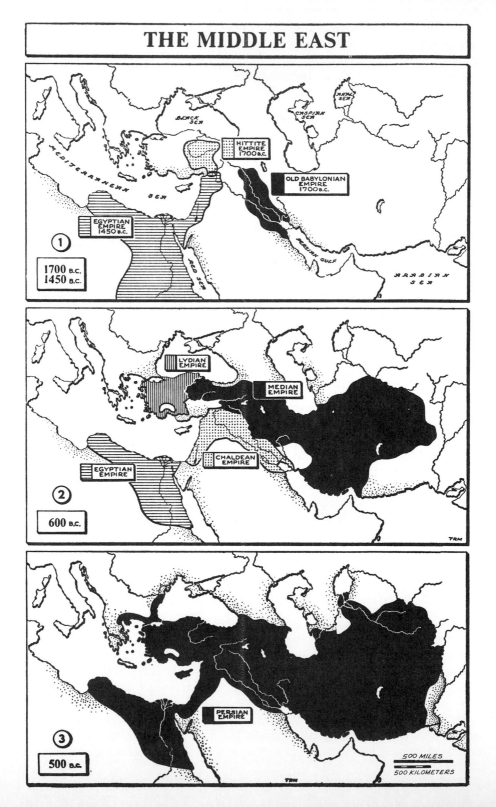

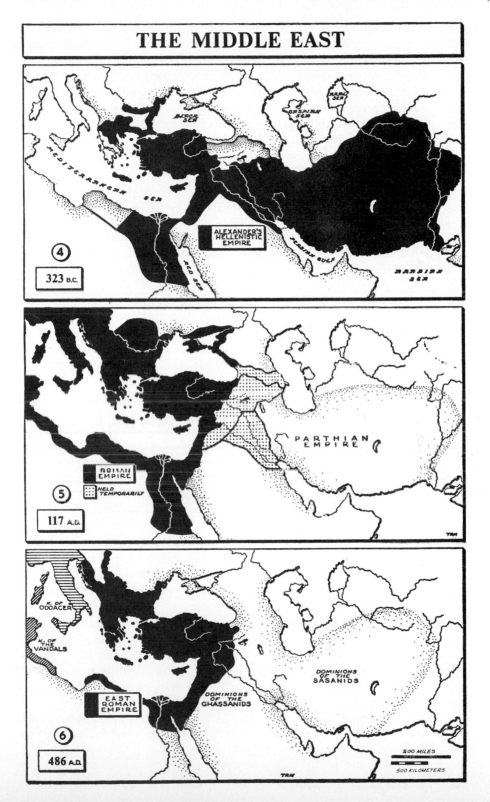

THE MIDDLE EAST

(4) 323 B.C. — ALEXANDER'S HELLENISTIC EMPIRE

(5) 117 A.D. — ROMAN EMPIRE / HELD TEMPORARILY / PARTHIAN EMPIRE

(6) 486 A.D. — EAST ROMAN EMPIRE / K. OF ODOACER / K. OF THE VANDALS / DOMINIONS OF THE GHASSANIDS / DOMINIONS OF THE SASANIDS

500 MILES / 500 KILOMETERS

speculation and investment. (There is little evidence of local industry in Mecca or the Hijaz. There were orchards and cereal production at al-Taif, and dates grew at the oasis of Medina; but Mecca was set in the midst of barren land.)

Nomads—Bedouins, or desert Arabs—dwelt with their herds in the neighborhood of Mecca. Moving about in search of pasturage, they enjoyed a free, open, precarious existence; yet they were exceedingly jealous of their rights in the desert where they roamed. Brigandage to them was perfectly legitimate, whether upon oases or caravans. The Bedouins were good fighters, and when the advent of the North Arabian saddle greatly enhanced their raiding abilities, merchants, cities, and agriculturists often bought protection in the form of tribute. Between city and nomad an interdependence developed, and the welfare and station of the nomad in the Hijaz improved with the growing prosperity and population of Mecca.

In Muhammad's time the Quraysh tribe of Arabs dominated life in Mecca. The Quraysh were north Arabians who had controlled affairs in Mecca for more than a century, although families from the older inhabitants still lived in the city. The tribe had split into a dozen or more clans, which were grouped into two federations. Muhammad's clan was the Hashim, so named for his great-grandfather. Other notable clans were Makhzum, Abd Shams, al-Muttalib, Taym, and Adi. The last three belonged to the same federation as the Hashim. The other two were the most powerful clans of Mecca in Muhammad's day.

Membership in a clan was based on kinship through the male line. Security of person and property was a clan responsibility; violation of either was a cause for reprisal by the clan. An irresponsible member was usually disowned by the clan and consequently became a kind of social, political, and economic outcast.

Manly virtues were still largely those related to desert nomadism—"bravery in battle, patience in misfortune, persistence in revenge, protection of the weak, defiance of the strong." Other admirable qualities which were expressed in poetry were generosity, hospitality, loyalty, and fidelity. The man with honor and moral excellence was the man who exhibited the possession of these characteristics and who, with judgment, demonstrated his capacity to govern his life by them.

Government in Mecca was simple, direct, unorganized, and exceedingly democratic. An assembly of chiefs and leading men of the clans met as a council, but each clan was independent and could go its own way. Individuals within a clan might differ with the majority and act accordingly, but they were sure to find such action difficult and the results uncomfortable. Unanimity of clan action had to be achieved by personal negotiation among the leaders who commanded respect because of wealth, wisdom, and strength of character. A few offices possessed privileges, sometimes with opportunities for profit, such as control over the water of the sacred well or supplying sustenance to pilgrims.

Political affairs in the foreign field taxed the skill and ingenuity of the Meccan leaders, for the Arabs were buffeted by the contest between the Byzantine and Sasanid empires. Eastern Arabs were satellites of Iran, and such Arabs as the Ghassanids east of the Jordan were on the Byzantine side. Upon the development of an Iranian-sponsored rule in Yemen, Meccan commerce from south Arabia northward to Byzantine Syria became a touchy enterprise. But Meccan neutrality and diplomatic and economic shrewdness consolidated the caravan trade from the south into the hands of the Makhzum and Abd Shams clans.

Previously, the Hashim clan had operated caravans north to Syria, but in Muhammad's time it began to lose that monopoly. Hashim, Muhammad's great-grandfather, had obtained from the Byzantine ruler protection for Meccan merchants and their goods in Syria. To complement this arrangement, Hashim organized what some have labeled the "Commonwealth of Mecca." He and his successors secured a novel partnership with hitherto hostile Bedouin tribes in the northern area of Arabia whereby, through a sharing of the profits between Meccan merchants and leaders of the tribes, as well as the hiring of the tribes to escort the caravans, Meccan commerce prospered. Other factors in strengthening the Meccan trade position were the innovations of joining poor members of Meccan families to their rich brethren and of including some Bedouin goods in merchandise marketed in Mecca and in Syria. Furthermore, many Meccan leaders married daughters of prominent Bedouin leaders. Thus, beginning with Hashim many groups developed a common interest in the Meccan trade enterprise.

Society in Mecca was reeling from the strains of this swift transition. Not only had the emphasis among the Quraysh shifted from tribe to clan membership, with intense rivalry developing among clans, but individualism within a clan was growing at a quickening tempo. Business partnerships were being formed across clan lines. And the leaders and powerful men of Mecca were successful businessmen and merchants, who did not always live by the long-accepted Arab standards of manliness and honor. Common material interests seemed to be replacing common blood in the determination of kinship in the new Mecca. Social maladjustment resulted from the failure of the new economic life to accommodate itself to the old moral values of Arab life.

Pagan Mecca had numerous gods and goddesses, most of whom possessed abstract characteristics. Stones, trees, and other objects were venerated as places in which these deities were thought to reside. Magic and superstition were inextricably interwoven in this paganism, but belief in the gods had begun to fade in Muhammad's time.

A more forceful religion was one that was bound up with the belief in the immortality of the tribe and clan. Honor, bravery, generosity, and the other manly virtues were possessions that ensured the survival of the tribe. Fate was believed to govern life in only a few ways, determining, for instance, one's provisions, the length of life, sex, and happiness. Otherwise individuals controlled their own destiny. It was not quite the same for the desert Arab, however, for life in the desert was so precarious that it seemed to be governed by some unfathomable law or whim of a force beyond one's control or responsibility. As everything in one's life was considered transient, the fate of the individual was unimportant. There was no belief in personal immortality; immortality rested with the tribe.

Finally, in Mecca a conception of monotheism was evolving. The Arab word *Allah* was derived from the words *al-ilah,* meaning "the god." Allah, then, was The God, The Supreme God; and Muhammad in using this word did not have to give his audiences any explanation. The idea, evidently, was in the air at Mecca, though undoubtedly the understanding of monotheism was vague and ill-defined in Meccan minds. The source of monotheism in Mecca and surrounding Arabia is an interesting question for speculation and has been debated by scholars at great length. Judaism and Christianity have had their champions, and certainly the Meccans had had ample opportunities to become acquainted with each of these religions.

It is important to note that Muhammad and Meccan society were not entirely unfamiliar with monotheistic concepts. Obviously from the events that followed, they were ready to have these thoughts organized and marshaled into a systematic religion—a religion that was distinctly Arab in character. That was the great work and accomplishment of Muhammad.

REFERENCES

Bowersock, G. W. *Roman Arabia.* Cambridge, Mass.: Harvard University Press, 1983. Particularly useful for early Arab-Roman contacts.

Bulliet, Richard W. *The Camel and the Wheel.* Cambridge, Mass.: Harvard University Press, 1975. Discusses the domestication of the camel, and how it displaced the wheel in transportation in the Middle East.

Crone, Patricia. *Meccan Trade and the Rise of Islam.* Princeton, N.J.: Princeton University Press, 1987. A controversial revision of earlier works on Mecca before Islam; asserts trade was local and regional, and that there was little social upheaval in Mecca at this time.

Hallo, William W., and William Kelly Simpson. *The Ancient Near East: A History.* New York: Harcourt Brace Jovanovich, 1971. Concentrates on Mesopotamia and Egypt, and is the best introductory account of their histories in antiquity.

Lewis, Naphtali. *Life in Egypt Under Roman Rule.* Oxford: Oxford University Press, 1983. A witty and careful look at social history and the life of those outside the ruling circles.

Mellaart, James. *Earliest Civilizations of the Near East.* London: Thames and Hudson, 1965. An important survey.

Moscati, Sabatino. *The Face of the Ancient Orient.* New York: Anchor, 1962.

Nock, Arthur Darby. *Early Gentile Christianity and Its Hellenistic Background.* New York: Harper, 1964. Although somewhat outdated, still thought-provoking.

O'Leary, DeLacy. *Arabia Before Muhammad.* London: Kegan-Paul, 1927. The standard work on the Arabs and Arabia before the birth of Islam.

Ostrogorsky, George. *History of the Byzantine State.* New Brunswick, N.J.: Rutgers University Press, 1969. The standard political history of the Byzantine Empire.

Peters, Frank E. *The Harvest of Hellenism.* New York: Simon and Schuster, 1971. A broad view of late antiquity, concentrating on intellectual and philosophical approaches and issues.

Shahid, Irfan. "Pre-Islamic Arabia," in P. M. Holt *et al.,* eds., *The Cambridge History of Islam.* Vol. 1A. *The Central Islamic Lands from Pre-Islamic Times to the First World War.* Cambridge: Cambridge University Press, 1970. A broad survey of the subject.

Wilson, John A. *The Culture of Ancient Egypt.* Chicago: University of Chicago Press, 1951. The standard account of the topic.

Yarshater, Ehsan, ed. *The Cambridge History of Iran. Vol. 3. The Seleucid, Parthian and Sasanian Periods.* Cambridge: Cambridge University Press, 1983. Scholarly essays on political, social, religious, and cultural aspects of Iranian history before the rise of Islam.

Part One

The Rise and Spread of Islam

3

Muhammad: His Life and Leadership

"*T*here is no god but God, and Muhammad is the messenger of God." The acceptance of this statement as the fundamental truth of life identifies all who follow the teachings of Muhammad. Allah is the God worshiped by Jews and Christians. But who was this man Muhammad?

It has been said that Muhammad was the only great prophet born in the full light of history. However, the first biography of Muhammad was not written until he had been dead for one hundred years; at least four others were compiled during the second century after his passing. It is from these sources that the traditional accounts of Muhammad's life have come, and recent investigations have shown that these early biographies were somewhat fictionalized. Nevertheless, modern students have been able to sift out some of the stories and have established many points. By analyzing words and phrases of various early accounts of his life and the lives of his contemporaries and by studying social, economic, political, religious, and anthropologic aspects of the society in which he moved, they have been able to reconstruct most of Muhammad's life so as to make it reasonable and understandable.

Muhammad was a mortal human being; he never professed otherwise and always emphasized this point to his followers, indicating that he would die like any other man. Nevertheless, as the founder of a great religion, he was revered as a most holy man even within his own lifetime. It is not strange, then, to find his biographies, written five or six generations later, full of fabricated and supernatural incidents to show his spirituality and his virtues. Perhaps this traditional figure has been more important than the real one in fashioning the culture and civilization of the Middle East from his day to our own.

MUHAMMAD'S EARLY LIFE

In the year A.D. 570 or 571, or perhaps as late as 580, a male child was born in Mecca to the Hashim family of the Quraysh tribe. He was given the name Muhammad, meaning "highly praised." His family was not one of the wealthier or more powerful of the city nor was it of the poorest or lowliest class. His father, Abd Allah, died before he was born; and his mother died when Muhammad was about six years old. First, as a fatherless boy, and then as an orphan, his lot was not easy. His paternal grandfather, Abd al-Muttalib, cared for and protected him. Upon his grandfather's death Muhammad became the ward of his uncle Abu Talib.

From many of Muhammad's statements it is apparent that his uncle was not a prosperous man and that they lived in modest circumstances. Evidently there was no opportunity for Muhammad in any of the businesses of his uncles; and without any capital from his father, a job had to be found for him outside the family circle. Such a post was located with the rich widow, Khadijah, of a distantly related family. She had been married twice and had children from each marriage.

Khadijah was older than Muhammad, some say as much as fifteen years; and certainly her social position in Mecca was far superior to his. She was an astute businesswoman and continued her husbands' commercial activities. At what age Muhammad began working for her, exactly what he did, and how old he was when she asked him to marry her are uncertainties. The story of her proposal is probably factual. In Mecca it was not the usual custom for a woman to propose; but in this instance, on account of her wealth, her better social class, and her position as employer, it would not have been unlikely. This step altered Muhammad's life greatly and at this point he becomes a clearer historical personage.

Muhammad had already gained recognition as a successful trader and skilled administrator and this marriage reinforced his reputation. He and Khadijah had four daughters who grew to maturity and several sons, all of whom died in infancy. Khadijah died about A.D. 619, but as long as she lived, Muhammad had no other wife. Since he continued to act as Khadijah's commercial agent after their marriage, giving him a security heretofore lacking, Muhammad now had means and a definite position in the society of Mecca.

HIS CALL

In the Middle East, from time immemorial, it has been the custom for men who have some means and who are troubled intellectually and emotionally by the cares and ills of society to retreat to a lonely spot to think and to find answers for problems of the day. Muhammad, after his marriage, began to follow this practice.

One day in the year 610, Muhammad must have had a sudden and unusual experience in the form of thoughts flooding upon him and arranging themselves in a clear and definite order. In the language and understanding of his time it was a revelation, and he readily accepted it as such. (This day is celebrated each year by the faithful as The Night of Power.) Probably occurring in a cave on one of the hillsides outside Mecca, the message commanded Muhammad to preach the Truth to his fellow Meccans. This was his call.

Beginning with this first revelation, Muhammad on frequent occasions heard voices. Certainly he fully believed in the verses that seemed to come to him. He was his first convert. The voices only spoke ideas that he had heard others repeat

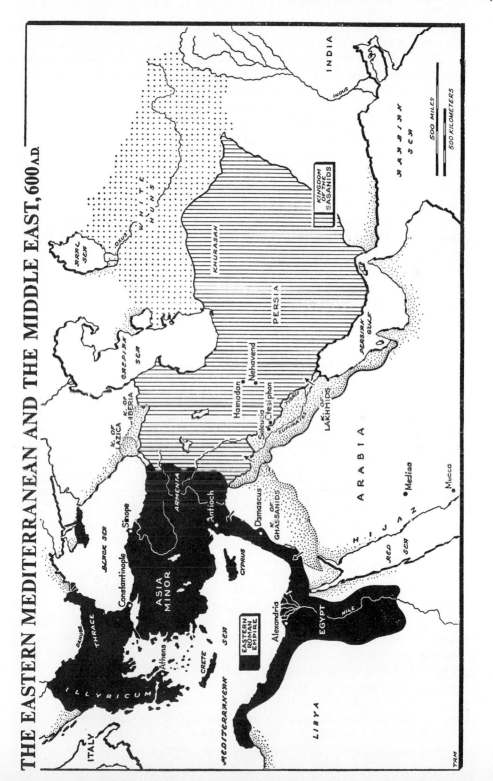

THE EASTERN MEDITERRANEAN AND THE MIDDLE EAST, 600 A.D.

KINGDOM OF THE SASANIDS

INDIA

ARABIAN SEA

500 MILES

500 KILOMETERS

WHITE HUNS

ARAL SEA

OXUS

KHURASAN

PERSIA

PERSIAN GULF

CASPIAN SEA

K. OF LAZICA

K. OF IBERIA

ARMENIA

Hamadan

Nehavend

Seleucia

Ctesiphon

EUPHRATES

TIGRIS

K. OF LAKHMIDS

ARABIA

Medina

Mecca

Antioch

Damascus

K. OF GHASSANIDS

HIJAZ

RED SEA

CYPRUS

Constantinople

Sinope

BLACK SEA

THRACE

DANUBE

ASIA MINOR

Athens

CRETE

MEDITERRANEAN SEA

EASTERN ROMAN EMPIRE

Alexandria

EGYPT

NILE

LIBYA

ILLYRICUM

ITALY

TRM

or that he had contemplated in more objective moods. There can be no real doubt of his own sincerity and conviction.

With respect to religion, Muhammad had grown up in the pagan society of Mecca. One of his sons, Abd Manaf, bore a pagan name. Mecca was a holy place, famed for the Kaaba, the earthly abode of many gods. And the Quraysh had a special relationship and certain responsibilities to this abode.

Mecca and the Hijaz, however, were experiencing at this time a gradual trend toward a more intellectual religion. (Muhammad was not the only prophet to appear in Arabia or the Hijaz in that century. One of Khadijah's cousins already had been preaching, and some of his ideas were not much different from those later espoused by Muhammad.) Moreover, the ideas and teachings of Judaism and Christianity had spread and become known in Mecca through slaves, pilgrims, and traders as the city grew more prosperous and its life more settled. Repeatedly, Muhammad referred to Judaism and Christianity, and to demonstrate the truth of the revelations he claimed agreement with those older faiths. Although Muhammad never showed the ability to read anything other than the most simple writing, he was familiar with many of the ideas and perhaps some of the ecclesiastical tracts of the Monophysite sect of Christians in Syria.

PREACHING AND CONVERTS

The first revelations presented quite a simple religion. God was represented as all-powerful, good, and loving. Created existence was transitory; the Creator was permanent. But God in creating humans implanted in them moral responsibility for themselves and, particularly, for their fellows. There would be a final judgment on the Day of Resurrection. Pure individuals were those who were grateful to God, worshiped Him, appealed to Him for the forgiveness of sin, offered prayers frequently, helped their fellows, avoided all forms of cheating, led chaste lives, and had cleansed themselves from love of wealth. Such persons, then, would recognize the goodness and power of God and their dependence upon God. This was Islam—the surrender to God—and the pious who thus purified themselves became Muslims.

At first, Muhammad was reluctant to tell many people about the revelations. However, the heavenly truths had been revealed to him and duty compelled him to remind the Arabs of Mecca of these truths in order to save them from divine wrath on the approaching Day of Judgment. And in the beginning his preaching brought no firm opposition. His first converts were in his own household: his wife Khadijah, his cousin Ali, and Zayd, a former slave. The most important of the others were Abu Bakr, Umar, al-Zubayr, Talhah, and Uthman. Some of the early converts were younger sons of influential men of the leading families and clans of Mecca. The father of one was the most prominent financier in Mecca; another's father had been a religious leader prior to Muhammad's time; and two were nephews of the head of the Makhzum clan, the wealthiest and dominant family among the Quraysh. The majority, however, were young men of no great social standing.

Some had neither family nor clan ties, and the families of others had ceased for one reason or another to afford them protection.

To characterize this group, the terms "young men" and "weak people" are the most appropriate. Early Islam was a movement of young people, mostly well under forty years old and from the middle class of Mecca. They were individuals who felt their positions to be inferior when they compared their wealth and influence with the fortunes and power of those at the top.

Such a generalization certainly implies that economic, social, and political conditions in Mecca had a hand in fostering the development and growth of Islam. At least for several decades before Muhammad's call, life in Mecca had been changing. The rapid growth of commerce and a money economy had widened the gap between rich and poor and between the influential and their dependents. Wealth and the life of a merchant promoted individualism as contrasted to family and clan solidarity. Kinship of money was supplanting that of blood, a substitution that did not satisfy the less "successful." Nomadic manly virtues were hardly those to be esteemed in a mercantile society. Old ideals of generosity, honor, the moral responsibilities of family and clan, and the group's accountability for trespasses of its members were seriously challenged in the evolving individualistic society. Seemingly, anything could be obtained through money and power.

Muhammad and his early converts, however, were not consciously frustrated men seeking solace in religion. In these first days, they were conservatives preaching against the abandonment of the old virtues. Nevertheless, Islam did recognize individualism as a permanent aspect of society. The Last Judgment concerned individuals; for it was said that on the Day of the Last Judgment "one shall have no influence on behalf of another." Salvation came from taking care of poor relatives, making sure of the well-being of orphans, and being generous to the poor. For the rich it meant sacrificing and cooperating with the poor.

PERSECUTION

Muhammad and Islam in 615 entered a new period of development. Monotheism was plainly recognized, and opposition and persecution began. Muslims were subjected to tongue-lashing and all manner of verbal insults. Garbage was dumped at their doors. Unprotected individuals were beaten, as were Quraysh Muslims by their fellow clansmen. Economic pressure was exerted by refusal to pay debts and by a severe boycott that greatly reduced the fortunes of many, including Muhammad's closest friend, Abu Bakr.

Abu Jahl, the head of the Makhzum clan, declared economic war upon the Muslims and asserted that every one of them would be ruined financially. He coaxed and threatened Abu Talib, Muhammad's uncle and the leader of the Hashim clan, to abandon Muhammad. Failure in this approach led to the formation of an alliance of all the Quraysh clans to pursue an economic boycott of the Hashim clan and its closest ally, the al-Muttalib clan. There were to be no business dealings and no intermarriage with any member of either clan.

This open economic break had long been brewing, and the controversy over

Muhammad offered the excuse. Apparently during this break the Hashim maintained their own caravans to Syria and withstood the pressure. After two years the grand alliance was dissolved and the economic sanctions lapsed, since they had proved unsuccessful in destroying Muhammad. In fact, they had tended to increase the financial and economic hegemony of the Makhzum clan over the others.

More significant was the verbal assault, which indicated the opinions held by those in opposition. They scoffed at the idea of the Day of Last Judgment and ridiculed Muhammad's preaching of the resurrection of the body after it had moldered in the grave. They kept asking scornfully: "When is the Hour?" Muhammad's conviction that God was One and only One and that all idolatry was evil disturbed Meccan society because, to a considerable degree, this meant forsaking the religion of the forefathers. Muhammad tried to counter this with the contention that he was following in the footsteps of the religion of Abraham and the prophets of old, and thus, that Muslims were only regaining the old Arab religion.

The opposition jeered at Muhammad's claim to prophethood, calling him a magician, a soothsayer, a poet possessed by spirits, and even a madman. If God had desired to reveal the Truth, they asserted sarcastically, He would have selected someone more important than Muhammad for this role. And why was not the full revelation made all at one time? How else could Muhammad explain the driblets of revelation except that he and some assistants were busy making up the verses!

Traditionally, the opposition to Muhammad by the leaders of Mecca centered around his preaching of the unity of God and his rejection of the use of idols. More likely, they objected to his cardinal message that the rich, meaning Meccan and Bedouin leaders, should help the poor among them, fearing that the adoption and practice of these beliefs would alienate the Bedouin tribes and ruin Mecca as a flourishing commercial center. Abu Jahl, the most ambitious financier of Mecca, recognized the threat of Islam and its philosophy to his way of life and realized that widespread acceptance would give the leadership of the city to Muhammad. He felt that it would destroy the "Commonwealth of Mecca," whereas Muhammad believed that only this course would save and preserve it. Other leaders, whose positions seemed beyond jeopardy, regarded Muhammad as an innovator who was disrupting the political and social development of Mecca. Because of the rapid social evolution of Mecca many were cognizant of the disintegration of the old political, social, economic, and intellectual values. Muhammad sought to preserve and adjust these values through religion.

The ending of the economic boycott in 619 possibly was interpreted as the harbinger of acceptance and success. But one incident after another quickly dashed such optimism and brought Muhammad close to the breaking point. Khadijah died, and then his uncle and protector, Abu Talib, followed her. Abu Lahab, another uncle, who now became the leader of the Hashim, refused to continue protection. Several years had elapsed since any important person had accepted Islam. Signs indicate that Muhammad began to suffer from a kind of mental depression and fatigue. There was no Muslim in Mecca with sufficient stature to offer him protection. How easily Islam could have perished! The only alternative was to leave the city.

FLIGHT TO MEDINA

Muhammad first visited the neighboring town of al-Taif to explore the possibilities of establishing residence and the headquarters of Islam there. He was met with a quick rebuff and upon leaving was stoned. Several of the nomadic tribes around Mecca were approached but without success.

Some 200 miles (about 320 km.) to the north and east lay the town of Yathrib—later called Medina (*the* city, i.e., the city of the prophet) by the Muslims. Yathrib comprised an area of twenty square miles of date oases, fertile lands, and scattered settlements. Numerous tribes occupied quarters of the town and had been engaged in bloody and exhausting civil war, in part over the limited cultivated lands of Yathrib. The most important clans were Aws, Khazraj, Nadir, Qurayzah, and Qaynuqa, of which the last three adhered to Judaism.

During the pilgrimage of 620 and following the rebuff at al-Taif, Muhammad discussed Islam with several pilgrims of the Khazraj tribe of Yathrib and raised the question of asylum. The following year additional people from Yathrib participated in the pilgrimage and more discussions occurred. One of Muhammad's trusted supporters returned with them, and converts were obtained from every important family except one. In the pilgrimage of 622, seventy-five Muslims from Yathrib came to Mecca and there made the famous Pledge of al-Aqabah to protect Muhammad and to recognize him as a prophet to whom disputes were to be referred. Furthermore, there was some agreement concerning the migration of the Muslims, including Muhammad, from Mecca to Yathrib and the establishment of an alliance between Muslims and the people of Yathrib. Later additions to the pledge in the so-called Constitution of Medina granted Muhammad sufficient authority to form the Commonwealth of Medina. (Why these pagan Arabs from Yathrib so readily accepted Muhammad and the others has aroused much speculation. One probable reason was that Islam offered the possibility of a united community of people free of political rivalry and of the continual feuding of the many clans. Moreover, in addition to Muhammed, whose business acumen was well established, Yathrib would be acquiring some seventy Meccans who were also experts in trade.)

As soon as agreement had been reached, Muhammad urged all Muslims to go to Yathrib. Over a period of weeks they left secretly in small groups until only Muhammad, Abu Bakr, Ali, and a handful of Muslims remained in Mecca. After all who planned to migrate had gone, Muhammad and Abu Bakr slipped away at night, hid in a nearby cave for a couple of days until the search for them had relaxed, and then proceeded to Yathrib. On September 24, 622, they were joyously greeted at the outskirts of the city.

This migration, or *Hijrah* (Hegira), was a dangerous move on the part of the Muslims, for they were abandoning the protection of their families and their city for the untested protection of strangers. Almost overnight their position was so changed that the Hijrah came to mark the new era. The Muslim calendar A.H. 1 begins on July 16, 622, the first day of the year in which the Hijrah occurred. In Mecca, Muhammad and the preaching of Islam had failed to alter society or to break down either the growing individualism or the family ties. In Medina,

Muhammad immediately became the acknowledged political and social leader as well as the religious head of a compact community.

Residence in Medina placed new demands on Muhammad's diplomatic and executive talents. He could count definitely on the full support of the *Muhajirun*—the "emigrants" from Mecca—and the converts of Medina, called *Ansar,* or "helpers." For protection and sustenance, Muhammad created a new kind of brotherhood between every two emigrants. Also, each emigrant was assigned one Medinese as a special brother and protector. The problems and the affairs of the Muslim community were to be brought before God and Muhammad, whose judgments had to be obeyed. Herein lay the basis for the establishment of Muslim theocracy. God was Muhammad's Guide and Protector and the disobedient would suffer the agonies of hell. The revelations received in Medina turned more to social and political matters and stressed, to a much lesser degree, forms of worship and religious ideas that had been revealed in the Meccan prophecies.

Feuds among the disparate groups in Medina, however, could be rekindled quickly. The Jews soon began to quiz and mock Muhammad because of their knowledge of the Torah. He had expected that they would testify to the validity of his message, but they could not accept an Arab as the Messiah, even though Islam accepted Abrahim and Moses as prophets. New religious concepts were molded with the old, and Islam gained a distinct Arab cultural flavor. This aspect came to be emphasized with the beginning of Muhammad's Medinese residence.

In the first days following the Hijrah the Muslims had adopted several of the Jewish rites. They prayed facing Jerusalem; they observed midday prayers and Jewish fast days; and Friday, market day as well as the Jewish day of preparation for the Sabbath, became the Muslim day of public prayer. Later, when relations with the Medinese Jews became tense, Muslims, in accordance with new revelations, turned away from some of the Jewish forms. In worship the faithful now faced the sanctuary in Mecca; an annual pilgrimage to Mecca was prescribed for Muslims—*Hajj*—and a period of fasting—the month of Ramadan—was ordered.

CONFLICT WITH MECCA

During the winter of the first year in Medina, Muhammad and his followers were busy establishing their new homes. When spring and summer came and the rich caravans began to pass northward toward Syria, armed Muslim bands from Medina menaced the Meccan merchants. No booty was taken, and the caravans were so well protected that these incidents served only as reconnaissance missions. However, the need to provide a livelihood for the expatriates of Mecca forced Muhammad to direct attacks upon the passing caravans. It was a normal expediency in Arabia.

Late in 623 a handful of Muslims under orders from Muhammad surprised a small Meccan caravan on the road between Mecca and al-Taif. One Meccan was killed, two were held for ransom, and much booty was captured. Nevertheless, sentiment in Medina was divided. The Medinese had promised the emigrants from Mecca protection from attack but had not agreed to let their city serve as a base of operations against Mecca. The success of the venture, however, invited other and larger expeditions.

Muhammad decided to ambush the main caravan of the Quraysh upon its return from Syria. Muhammad himself led the band of 305 to waylay the caravan under Abu Sufyan, the head of the powerful Umayyad family. At Badr, twenty miles (32 km.) southwest of Medina, Muhammad was challenged by a force of some 800 or 900 armed Meccans. The fighting was fierce and bloody, but the smaller force of Muslims was victorious. As a battle it was hardly more than a minor fracas. Muhammad lost 14 men; the Meccans had 50 killed and 50 captured. The Muslim booty consisted of 14 horses, 115 camels, some coats-of-mail, and other pieces of military equipment. But the significance of the Battle of Badr was such that some have called it one of the decisive battles of history. To the Muslims it was a miracle, positive proof that God was supreme.

Henceforth Muhammad was a marked man, for the news of this victory traveled quickly to every tribe and tent of Arabia. Moreover, the battle set the stage and the pattern of the future: a fifth of all booty was assigned to Muhammad to be allotted to the needy or used by the state. The Commonwealth of Medina now became a real possibility. From the moment of victory there could be no peace until the supremacy between pagan and Muslims was decided. Within two decades Muslims came to appreciate the importance of this battle; those who had participated in it were the "nobility of Islam"; and a cloak that had been worn at the Battle of Badr was a most distinguished robe of honor.

This victory by no means guaranteed to Muhammad a straight and easy path to his now clearly recognizable goal: control over Mecca and the incorporation of all its inhabitants into his Muslim community. Indeed, although the battle showed the Muslims that such a goal was attainable, it also goaded the leaders of Mecca into a real effort to annihilate the Muslim community.

Muhammad, taking advantage of his success, moved to consolidate his position. Alliances were made with a number of neighboring Bedouin tribes, the first steps toward the new commonwealth. The Qaynuqa tribe, the weakest of those adhering to the Jewish faith, was driven from Medina. In 625, however, Abu Sufyan, the new leader of Mecca since the death of Abu Jahl on the battlefield of Badr, set forth with an army of 3,000 for revenge. Electing to meet the enemy outside the city at the foot of the hill of Uhud, the Muslims appeared at first to be winning but were subsequently overrun in the flank and rear by the Meccan cavalry. In the melee Muhammad was wounded but managed to establish a position on the slopes of Uhud. Torn with dissension as usual, the Meccan army neither pursued the Muslims nor pressed on to Medina. Two years later, Abu Sufyan returned again with an even larger army. Forewarned, Muhammad ordered a wide ditch dug in front of the less protected sides of Medina. After a fortnight's siege, the withdrawal of the Meccans was prompted by bad weather, persistent quarrels, and the disaffection of some of the nomad allies. In addition, the Meccans claimed that the Muslim trench was a dishonorable artifice to which no Arab would resort. The Battle of the Ditch joined with Badr and Uhud to make the three battles where lines were drawn between the pagans and Muslims. The battles were in some measure part of a civil war. Participants on each side were well known to each other. Old slights and grudges were remembered, and emotions and the spirit of vengeance ran high.

Following each of these failures by pagan Mecca, Muhammad moved quickly to solidify the Medina community. When the Medinese Jews failed to hide their delight over the Uhud misadventure, the Muslims attacked the Jewish Nadir clan and drove them from Medina to Khaybar. After the third battle the men in the last Jewish tribe, the Qurayzah, were killed, and the women and children were sold as slaves, because the Muslims felt the Qurayzah had betrayed them. Citizens of Medina who, until now, had neither accepted Islam nor recognized Muhammad as their leader joined the Muslim band. This meant that by the end of 627 Muhammad had established Medina as a united community with one religion as its cohesive force.

The next spring Muhammad was advised that some of the men of Mecca wished to arrange peace with the Muslims. With this information Muhammad called for an advance upon Mecca during the month of a minor pilgrimage. His Bedouin allies would not join him, and Mecca sent forth an armed force to contest his entry. A compromise was reached stipulating that the Muslims might participate freely in the lesser pilgrimage the following year, and marking Muhammad's first success in his peaceful conquest of Mecca. Later that year, the Muslims captured the fertile oasis of Khaybar, largely inhabited by Jews. This acquisition made the Muslims wealthy, since the lands were most productive. The inhabitants were not exiled but remained on their lands, paying yearly taxes to the conquerors and establishing a precedent for the years and centuries to come.

VICTORY

In March 629 Muhammad led more than a thousand of his men into Mecca to perform the rites of the lesser pilgrimage as agreed upon the previous year. A number of Meccans joined him, recognizing in Muhammad the coming leader. Two of the most redoubtable military figures of Islam were among those who joined: Amr ibn al-As and Khalid ibn al-Walid. Even Abu Sufyan in secret negotiations tried to adjust to the inevitable.

As more Bedouin tribes joined the Muslims, Muhammad began to insist that they accept Islam and become an integral part of the community rather than serve merely as political allies. However, the sense of completeness and fulfillment of the Muslim community was lacking so long as Mecca did not recognize Muhammad as the leader and refused to accept Islam. Mecca was the site of the Kaaba, the religious sanctuary and holy shrine designated by Muhammad. It had also been the home of the leaders of the Muslim community.

An insignificant incident brought Muhammad and the Muslims to Mecca to do battle in 630. Hardly anyone in Mecca was disposed to fight, however. Abu Sufyan came out from the city to pay homage to Muhammad and received amnesty for all who would submit. Upon entering the city Muhammad gave gifts to everyone and demanded the destruction of all idols in Mecca. He had merged his commonwealth with that of Mecca.

Muhammad's astuteness in politics and diplomacy was revealed by his decision not to settle again in Mecca but to return to his adopted city of Medina. The

Quraysh were a proud people and it had not been easy for them to acknowledge Muhammad as the leader. He did not tarry to remind them too plainly of their new position. Moreover, the rapid spread of Islam and the increasing numbers of Muslims were presenting a multitude of problems. A rather unsuccessful campaign occurred in Transjordan, and missions went as far as Bahrayn and Oman. There were small Muslim groups to be found in all parts of Arabia, but many still denied that Muhammad was God's messenger. (In all areas where Muslim political authority had penetrated, Christians, Jews, and Zoroastrians were tolerated on condition that they concede political rule to the Muslims.)

Muhammad could now see that Arabia was rapidly becoming one great united religious community—a community where religion rather than blood, language, customs, or economics held the people together and a community where there were no distinctions among the believers except that of the degree of piety. He understood that many professed Islam, not because they submitted to the will of God, but because they feared not being a Muslim or because they wanted the political, social, and economic advantages of being one.

Although Mecca acknowledged Muhammad as its leader, many in the host of visitors to the Kaaba in the month of the great pilgrimage were still pagan Arabs. Perhaps because of a possibility of dishonor, Muhammad declined to go on the great pilgrimage in 631 and sent Abu Bakr at the head of 300 Muslims. Ali, Muhammad's cousin and son-in-law, was deputized to announce that after four months no pagan would be permitted to participate in a pilgrimage to Mecca and that all political alliances between Muslims and Arab tribes would be revoked if Islam were not accepted. Muhammad's authority and Muslim power were such that no trouble arose from these pronouncements, although later developments indicated that compliance was hardly voluntary.

Thus, the stage was set for Muhammad to lead the initial reformed pilgrimage in March 632. Only Muslims would be present, and the veneration for the one God would be complete. Since Muhammad died soon after this pilgrimage, it has been called the Farewell Pilgrimage; and the events of the occasion are steeped in tradition. Muhammad eliminated many of the purely pagan aspects from the ceremonious rites that had been performed at the Meccan sanctuary. His every move and act have been described and followed by devout pilgrims. He knew the significance of this first solidly Muslim pilgrimage; and in his address, as leader, he must have said something like, "Today I have perfected your religion and completed my favors for you and chosen Islam as a religion for you."

Three days later, he departed for Medina and in less than three months (June 8, 632) he died from fever. He had no sons still living, and no provision had been made for a successor as leader of the Muslim community-state. Genuine bewilderment reigned in Medina. For a whole day his body lay disregarded. It was finally buried under the floor of the hut of Aishah, one of his wives.

The personality and private life of Muhammad remain to be considered. In general his tastes were quite simple. There is no evidence that his standard of living changed greatly upon the successes and the growth of the Muslim community. Perhaps the only significant change was his views regarding marriage. After Khadijah died, Muhammad married several times. At one time he had nine wives. Without question, his favorite was the daughter of Abu Bakr, Aishah, whom he married soon after the Hijrah while she was still a child. His disposition to all was kindly and gentle, and he made no distinction in his treatment of people. The frailties of human nature were well appreciated, and Muhammad never expected too much from his converts. When he found wrongdoing, he upbraided the culprits for their actions but he was lenient and cautious in his interdicts.

Most outstanding, however, were Muhammad's personality and character. The loyalty and compliance rendered naturally and generously to Muhammad by his companions in Mecca and Medina stemmed from the charisma of his being. His display of a sense of justice and his revelation of religious truth centered the attention of the citizens of Medina upon him. His converts, from first to last, testified to something special and irresistible in his nature. Lacking this quality, Muhammad's stand as a prophet of God would surely have been ignored by the worldly citizens of Mecca.

REFERENCES

Cook, Michael. *Muhammad.* Oxford: Oxford University Press, 1983. A short and simply written account of the life of Muhammad which includes new views that are critical of the sources often used.

Haykal, Muhammad Husayn. *The Life of Muhammad.* Translated by Ismail al Faruqi. Philadelphia: North American Trust Publications, 1976. The first Arabic edition of the book appeared in 1935; it is perhaps the most influential of the modern biographies of the Prophet written by a Muslim.

Hodgson, Marshall G. S. *The Venture of Islam: Conscience and History in a World Civilization.* Vol. 1. *The Classical Age of Islam.* Chicago: University of Chicago Press, 1974. Written in a difficult style, this, the first of three volumes, covers pre-Islamic and early Islamic history, with an emphasis on religious thought, philosophy, and literary developments.

ibn Ishaq, Muhammad. *The Life of Muhammad.* Edited by Abd al-Malik ibn Hisham. Translated by Alfred Guillaume. New York: Oxford University Press, 1955. Ibn Ishaq was born about 705 and died in 767 in Baghdad. His work is the earliest known biography of the Prophet. The original is lost but remains in the edited version by ibn Hisham, who died in 833. This is the source of most traditional accounts of Muhammad's life.

Rodinson, Maxime. *Mohammed.* Translated by Anne Carter. New York: Pantheon, 1971. The author uses a psychological approach in analyzing stories and events to explain and interpret the Prophet's life.

Schimmel, Annemarie. *And Muhammad Is His Messenger: The Veneration of the Prophet in Islamic Piety.* Chapel Hill: University of North Carolina Press, 1985. The views of later generations of Muslims in regard to Muhammad are shown through developments in philosophy, poetry, and theology.

Shaban, M. A. *Islamic History, A.D. 600–750 (A.H. 132): A New Interpretation.* Cambridge: Cambridge University Press, 1971. This is a most significant volume giving many ideas about developments during this formative period in the Middle East.

Watt, W. Montgomery. *Muhammad: Prophet and Statesman.* London: Oxford University Press, 1961. A thorough and scholarly study of the life of the Prophet and his social setting.

4

The Establishment of the Muslim State

THE CALIPHATE

Muhammad's position as a prophet of God precluded the nomination of a successor, even though his other roles as head of state, chief judge, and commander in chief of the armed forces did warrant some provisions for his replacement. Muhammad had sought counsel and taken advice from his companions as situations demanded. After his death, his three most frequent and trusted counselors agreed that Abu Bakr should be the leader of the Muslims. Muhammad's closest friend, Abu Bakr had led the prayers in the mosque and presided over the gatherings of Muslims in the last days when the Prophet had been too ill to perform these functions of leadership. When news of his death spread through the city, the native Medinese nominated one of their own as head of the community; but the Meccan Quraysh prevailed upon all to accept Abu Bakr as their commander. The following day in the mosque, even before Muhammad was laid to rest, the assembled citizens swore allegiance to Abu Bakr as the successor of Muhammad.

This outcome was neither unusual nor startling. Chiefs in Mecca and Medina, as well as in Arab tribes, were chosen by the heads of families meeting more or less openly. Leadership often passed to another within the same family, but without any idea of inheritance or of legal claim; the power and prestige of a family prejudiced the decision in its favor. In this instance Abu Bakr commanded the support of the Muslims who had emigrated to Medina, and that fact won the election for Abu Bakr. Other aspirants would have been from the Makhzum or Umayyad families of Mecca, from a prominent family of Medina, or perhaps from Muhammad's immediate family; but the election of one of these would not have been based on religious considerations. Authority passing into the hands of Abu Bakr, one of Muhammad's close companions, meant the survival of the Muslim community.

Khalifa Rasul Allah (Successor of the messenger of God) was the name frequently used to describe Abu Bakr and his position. Abu Bakr probably used it himself, although not as a title. From this appellation came the title *khalifa* ("caliph"), used for centuries in the Muslim world. It implied the assumption of all the duties and prerogatives exercised by Muhammad except those connected with his role as prophet. The caliph was head of the state, supreme judge, leader in public worship, and commander in chief of the army. If he did not actually occupy the pulpit in the mosque, the sermon was delivered in his name and he issued authoritative rulings on law. His name appeared on coins. And it was he whom Muslims revered.

ABU BAKR

Abu Bakr, about three years younger than Muhammad, had probably been the first convert outside the immediate family. A prosperous merchant from one of the lesser Quraysh families and totally devoted to Muhammad and Islam, Abu Bakr maintained his position of great respect because of a gentle and genial personality coupled with a clear head in matters of judgment and advice. It was a fortunate election in that Abu Bakr pursued Muhammad's ways and thoughts. No innovator, he succeeded in holding together the remarkable and talented men who had risen to prominence in this new society.

The first significant task facing the new leadership was to maintain the degree of centralization in Arabia already established by Muhammad. Except for Medina, Mecca, and a few other nearby places thoroughly controlled by the Muslims of Medina, most Arabs questioned the political and fiscal authority of Medina. Some even denounced Islam, seizing the end of personal allegiance to Muhammad as an opportunity to cast off the yoke of submission.

Abu Bakr met the challenge with the vigor and fire of the Prophet. Khalid ibn al-Walid, a general and a fortunate choice, subdued the tribes of central Arabia, many of which had not given their allegiance to Muhammad. Encouraged, other Muslim generals suppressed revolts and more thoroughly established Islam throughout Arabia, including Bahrayn, Oman, Yemen, and Hadhramaut. Treating the vanquished and renegade with mercy, Abu Bakr in less than a year had subjugated most of Arabia.

Indirectly, the complete Islamization of the Hijaz and the domination of the Arabian peninsula by the Muslims led, in the year 633, to military expeditions into Syria and Iraq. Although fighting among Muslims was contrary to the principles of the new society, raiding was an economic necessity in Arabia as well as the natural activity of most Arab tribes; thus, ventures into adjacent lands were inevitable. Muslims also wished to fight in the *jihad,* or holy war. With little cognizance on the part of Medina, Khalid finished the conquest of northeastern Arabia and then, joining some loyal Muslim tribes, spilled over into the Sasanid lands in Iraq, taking Hirah, a city west of the Euphrates and almost on a line with modern Baghdad.

For the men of Mecca and Medina, Syria was far more important than Iraq. Their caravans went there; it was more accessible; and to them it was a land flowing with milk and honey. The Syrian expedition was thus a calculated raiding campaign. Three forces of 3,000 men each, led by Amr ibn al-As and Yazid ibn Abu Sufyan, defeated the Byzantine governor of Palestine near the Dead Sea and destroyed his fleeing troops near Gaza early in 634. To oppose the fresh Byzantine levies Abu Bakr ordered Khalid to cross the desert from Iraq to Syria. Appearing almost miraculously, Khalid, as the supreme commander of the united Arab forces, defeated the Byzantine army in July 634, in the historic battle at Ajnadayn, thus opening all of Palestine to the Muslims.

The news of this victory reached Medina after the death of Abu Bakr. His passing, however, hardly caused a ripple across Arabia, for Umar immediately assumed the power of leadership that he had been exercising behind the scenes. Recognition and fealty were given to Umar publicly and voluntarily by all. But the two-year caliphate of Abu Bakr must not be considered as a brief empty interlude between two glorious periods nor should Abu Bakr be seen as a shallow, colorless figure. He made the important distinction between state property and the privy purse of the ruler, even though this action irreconcilably alienated Muhammad's daughter Fatimah. Perhaps most important, when war booty was first coming to Medina from outside of Arabia, Abu Bakr held fast to Muhammad's dictum on the spoils of war—all true believers, whether at the front or at home in Arabia, had equal rights.

UMAR

Umar's accession to the caliphate marked the opening of a ten-year administration of an energetic and brilliant man, then only forty-three years old, whom Muslims consider the second founder of Islam. An early convert, Umar, like Abu Bakr, belonged to one of the less important families of Mecca. Leadership in the hands of Umar signified that Muslim aspects of the community continued.

The affairs most pressing upon Umar at his accession were the military adventures in Iraq and Syria. At that very moment the brilliant Bedouin general al Muthanna, commander of the Muslim armies in Iraq, was in Medina pleading for reinforcements, even though he had just defeated the Sasanid army. He begged that troops be raised among the Arab tribes guilty of opposing the Muslim state upon Muhammad's death, rightly judging that, however moribund Sasanid society and government might be, surrender to the Arabs would not be without a struggle.

Although the lifting of the ban against apostates brought streams of warriors into Iraq, superb Iranian generalship, the use of elephants, the size of the armies, and the wealth available to the Sasanid kings more than matched the ardor and gallantry of al-Muthanna's tribesmen. Ravaging far and wide, even to the gates of Ctesiphon, the Arab forces acquired vast herds and immense stores of grain; yet they had to retire from Iraq into the western desert when faced by an organized Iranian army under royal leadership.

Umar soon recognized that to hold Iraq and secure its borders it would be necessary to destroy the main Iranian army and reduce the capital at Ctesiphon. A major force was gathered, and in a decisive four-day battle at Qadisiyyah in 637 the Iranian army was routed. Ctesiphon capitulated, and other battles consolidated the lands bordering on the Tigris and Euphrates rivers as far north as Mosul. These years saw the permanent conquest and occupation of Mesopotamia.

The booty that fell to the Arabs suddenly showered great wealth and unknown luxuries upon the simple nomad, altering immeasurably his standards of

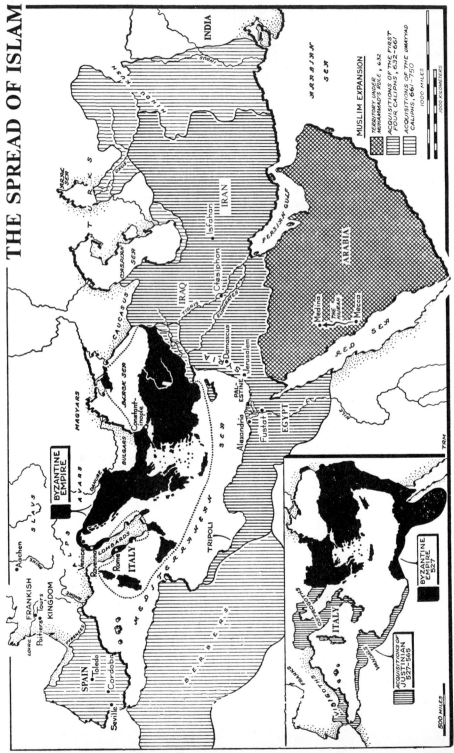

THE SPREAD OF ISLAM

living. After the Battle of Qadisiyyah each soldier received 6,000 pieces of silver. At the fall of Ctesiphon each of the 60,000 soldiers received 12,000 pieces. Gold became as common as silver; and fabulous objects, such as a life-size silver camel with rider of gold or a golden horse with trappings of gold, emeralds for teeth, and its neck set with rubies, became the prizes of the day. One Bedouin who sold a beauteous maiden for 1,000 pieces of silver was chided by another for having sold her for so little. The excuse offered was that he had not known any sum larger than ten hundred. From the palace of Ctesiphon the army sent to Umar the royal banquet carpet, measuring 105 by 90 feet (32 by 27 meters) and portraying a landscape. The ground was represented by gold and the paths were silver; meadows were made of emeralds; streams were cascades of pearls; trees, flowers, and fruits were depicted by diamonds, rubies, and other precious stones. Some suggested that the carpet be kept as a trophy; but when many pointed out that earthly goods were but passing things, the carpet was cut into pieces.

Over the next several years Muslim parties raided Khuzistan and advanced toward Isfahan. Iranian forces rallied at Hamadan; but with the removal of Umar's ban on advances into Iran, Muslims overran that land from one end to the other. In the ten years of Umar's caliphate Muslim armies had in an almost unbelievable sweep conquered Mesopotamia and Iran. They repeatedly crushed armies that only a few years previously had been able to stand up against Byzantium. This success was even more remarkable considering that other Arab armies at the same time were engaged in conquering Syria, Mesopotamia, and Egypt.

Umar's accession to the caliphate did not change Muslim activities in Palestine or Syria. Several Arab forces converged on Damascus in 635, and after a siege of more than six months the city surrendered on terms to Khalid. The emperor Heraclius, not willing to cede Syria to the invader, gathered a large army; but it, too, succumbed to Khalid, in the summer of 637 at the decisive Battle of Yarmuk. Upon receiving the news of this disaster Heraclius left Syria and Palestine to the Muslims; north Syria fell from 637 to 647 and Jerusalem surrendered in 638. In the next two years Arab tribes entered the Jazirah between the Euphrates and the Tigris in the north and ruled that vast and fertile area.

Conclusively, in only four years, the Muslims had occupied these provinces of the Byzantine Empire. Mountains to the north discouraged further advance into Byzantine lands or the vigorous pursuit of the emperor's armies. Arab generals and many tribes, however, finding repose galling, looked for new adventures. Amr ibn al-As, who had traded in Egypt in earlier days, decided upon an expedition in that direction. Although Alexandria, the second city of the Byzantines and an important naval base, was strongly tied to Constantinople by sea routes, the loss of Syria and Palestine cut off Egypt from the empire. Egypt, the chief granary of Constantinople and one of the richest and most populous areas of the Middle East, was very inviting to an ambitious general like Amr. Umar gave his assent to the campaign, but reluctantly. Amazed at the extent of the territory already occupied by his armies, he was fearful lest they be spread too thinly.

Leaving Palestine by the historic route along the coast, Amr with 4,000 men entered Egypt late in 639 and captured Pelusium, not far from the modern Port Said. Amr then moved toward the apex of the Nile delta, taking Heliopolis and, after a lengthy siege, Babylon (near modern Cairo). Joined by a larger Arab contingent under one of the Companions of the Prophet ("those who knew Muhammad"), Amr moved on Alexandria and forced its surrender in 642. It was a great and rich metropolis, whose public buildings, harbor facilities, and defense walls and towers were a cause of wonder to the desert and urban Arabs.

To protect his position Amr pushed on westward into Cyrenaica and even received tribute from Berber tribes around Tripoli. Egypt, from Alexandria up the Nile to a point well beyond modern Cairo, was now a Muslim possession, thus completing the circle of conquests under Umar. During his caliphate, Iran, Iraq, Syria, Palestine, and Egypt became parts of the Muslim world. They, together with Arabia, are still today the heartland of Islam.

PROBLEMS OF ADMINISTRATION

These conquests alone would have assured Umar the position of second founder of Islam. But Umar's orders regarding the occupation and administration of the new territories were equally important in setting the Muslim pattern that has persisted to the present. Except in some parts of Syria and a few other places, the people of the conquered provinces continued to work and live as they had for centuries, generally with the advantage of paying less in tribute than the former rulers had taxed them. Armies were destroyed and administrators either departed or were employed in similar capacities by the Muslims, but most inhabitants were hardly touched.

Indeed, in some instances, Arab domination was not only tolerable but welcome. In Syria and Palestine urbanites had acquired a Hellenistic affectation and many of them, especially in Syria, left with the defeated Byzantine armies; but the rural peoples had retained contact with the desert Arab, thus easing the transition to Arab rule. In Iraq, Sasanid rule had been a foreign rule, and native tribes rejoiced in the Sasanid defeats. In Iran, however, the Arab was never wholly accepted and the rapidity of the Muslim conquest can be attributed to the collapse of the Sasanid dynasty and royal government and the momentary inability of the Iranian people to organize a resistance.

In Syria, Palestine, and Egypt, heavy imperial taxes and the arrogant, highhanded attitude of officials from Constantinople embittered the provinces. More aggravating and more emotional were the religious persecutions inflicted upon local Christians. The orthodox Council of Chalcedon in the year 451 condemned the Monophysite doctrine of Egypt and Syria according to which divinity and humanity make one compound nature in Christ. This Monophysite heresy was persecuted savagely by many emperors without success, until Heraclius, under whose rule these provinces were lost to Islam. Heraclius tried to effect a compromise by supporting the Monothelite doctrine that Christ had two natures in one person with one will. In Syria and Egypt, the churches were ardently Monophysite; in Egypt that faith assumed a patriotic coloration which persists today in the Coptic church. Thus, when it became apparent that Muslim rule meant religious freedom as well as lower taxes, the Arabs had little difficulty in obtaining cooperation from the local peoples. Since at this time Muslims paid no taxes, this toleration of tax-paying Christians and Jews is the origin of the often repeated but little understood Muslim formula of the three-way choice—Islam, taxes, or death—offered to conquered peoples.

Except in Iran the armies of occupation were held aloof from the established urban centers as much as possible. Umar, distressed at the soft appearance and paleness of some of the troops occupying Iraq and quartered in old Ctesiphon, ordered that camps be placed in the open near the desert. Later, camp cities were established in each of the newly won provinces—Basrah in lower Iraq, Kufah in central Iraq, Jabiyah in Syria, Ramlah in Palestine, and Fustat (Babylon) in Egypt.

In Syria, Muslim soldiers and local Arabs took over partially deserted towns and some lands whose owners, being Byzantine supporters, had departed. Some 20,000 of the Muslims moved into Hims and Damascus, but the Byzantine Christians were more numerous. Jealousy and strife arose over available houses and lands, so much so that Umar visited Syria and made an even-handed redistribution among everyone.

In all the conquered territories governors were appointed to collect taxes and maintain order. Only a handful of administrators accompanied the governors, and, in general, bureaus of government were manned by previous officials. Non-Muslims could not bear arms and were subject to their own laws, a practice that established Islamic society as one of the most tolerant of all ages and developed into the famous Millet (or self-administered religious community) system of the Ottoman Empire. Arabs from Arabia were eventually not permitted to own agricultural lands in conquered territory. Later, this injunction evolved into a system of land ownership and rights of tenancy which still prevails in the Middle East. Considering all aspects of life, the conquered peoples of the Middle East were disturbed very little by Muslim occupation.

Many other developments occurred during Umar's caliphate. Arabia was declared a holy land, and all non-Muslims were forced to leave, although by this time few remained who did not profess Islam. Even today this decree obtains in Mecca and Medina. With wealth from victories pouring in, the character of these two cities began to change. There was great building activity, particularly in Medina, where apartments were needed for retired soldiers, administrators, and others who flocked to the capital city as well as for the old inhabitants whose wealth had now greatly increased.

Umar enunciated again Muhammad's policy that although prisoners and movable property belonged to the soldiers who won them, land and taxes from conquest belonged to the whole Muslim community, and one-fifth of all income from conquered territory was to be forwarded to Medina. To facilitate distribution among the Muslims, Umar had a census taken in Arabia and a register (*diwan*) made of the sum each was to receive each year from the public treasury. The list included Muslims of all ranks, from Aishah and the Prophet's family down to the lowliest women and children of non-Arab warriors. Aishah received 12,000 dirhams (a silver coin); Companions of the Prophet, 5,000; and a child of the lowliest, 200.

Perhaps Umar's regulation of the calendar best showed the belief that a new state and society had been born. Numbering the new era with the Prophet's emigration to Medina, Umar decreed that Muslim dating should be counted as so many years after the Hijrah and that he had become caliph in the year A.H. 13.

As the years went by and wealth and opportunity grew, Umar had more and more difficulty with his provincial governors and their administrations. Since he had no power to enforce his will, the governors were nearly independent. Consequently, the required income from conquered lands was not always forthcoming; Syria, in fact, never sent any. Among the leaders of Islam, Umar was only first among equals. This was especially true in the camp cities of Kufah and Basrah, inhabited by many nomad warriors who were proud, hardy, political Muslims, resentful of Quraysh rule. Al-Mughirah, Umar's governor of Basrah, was a brilliant, tough, scheming, licentious native of al-Taif, just the sort of rough-and-ready genius that a new city would require. But when caught in adultery, the protests from Basrah were so vociferous that he was recalled to Medina for trial. Although he escaped punishment by slipping through a legal loophole, Umar relieved him of his post. Later al-Mughirah was able to wangle the appointment to Kufah. He retained this appointment for many years, augmenting its power and scope until he became one of the most powerful men in the Muslim world.

In 644, at the very height of Umar's power and prestige, he was assassinated at worship in the mosque of Medina by an Iranian Christian slave who had a personal grudge to settle. On his deathbed Umar selected six leading notables of Medina, all ex-Meccans, to choose his successor and directed his own son to wait upon them. Shortly after he had been buried beside Muhammad and Abu Bakr, the notables, probably on the basis of seniority and a pledge to follow the policies and practices of Umar, selected Uthman ibn Affan, who ruled as caliph from 644 to 656. Another leading candidate popular with the older Medinese families was Muhammad's cousin, Ali, who was passed by because he would not promise to follow in Umar's footsteps.

UTHMAN

Uthman was a member of the very prominent and powerful Umayyad family of the Quraysh. Noted for his mild manner and piety, his only distinction as a Muslim leader was having been a respected Companion of the Prophet. His three predecessors had belonged to lesser Quraysh families, as had most of the emigrants to Medina. Perhaps it was because of this that they had ignored the traditional Arab policy of nepotism and regarded all Muslims as members of one community and one brotherhood. This new social philosophy was one of the revolutionary aspects of Islam.

Although Uthman was seventy when he became caliph and not particularly energetic, he nevertheless sought greater control over the provinces. He was fortunate to have at his command within his own clan a number of vigorous governors and generals to carry forward the banners of Islam. His brother Abd Allah was appointed governor of Egypt with financial and civil control, while the conquering Amr was left as commander of the Muslim army. Outraged, Amr immediately repaired to Medina and refused to serve, with the acid remark: "To be over the army and not over the revenue was like holding the cow's horns while another milked her." Abd Allah carried on campaigns for booty to the west and south. His armies held Benghazi and Tripoli, ravaged Tunisia, and raided Nubia for slaves. But Abd Allah's great contribution was the development of a Muslim fleet, which in 652 repulsed a Byzantine armada before it could attack Alexandria.

In Syria, Uthman had as governor his shrewd and aggressive cousin Muawiyah ibn Abu Sufyan, one of the greatest administrators in Muslim history. Umar had appointed him governor of Damascus; and as other governorships in Syria fell vacant they were added to Muawiyah's territory until under Uthman he became the powerful ruler of all of Syria. He rebuffed a large Byzantine army in 647 and in subsequent years sent raiding parties into Asia Minor. He, too, built a fleet, took Cyprus in 649, ravaged the island of Rhodes, and in 655 in conjunction with Abd Allah's ships destroyed a large part of the Byzantine navy.

Other cousins of Uthman were appointed as governors of Kufah and Basrah and they led Arab armies during these years in Iran, continuing to fan out eastward. Fars was fully subdued by 650; Khurasan was taken in 651; inroads were made into Armenia in 652; and before the end of Uthman's caliphate, raiding expeditions reached Balkh, Kabul, and Ghazna.

Even though the caliph might not be personally aggressive, the valor, might, and leadership of the Muslim army and navy were no longer questioned in the Middle East. The growing problem was the impact of the new empire upon the Muslim community which had so recently emerged from Arab society. Most of the original emigrants who still lived were now notables and exceedingly wealthy. One, reputedly, had 1,000 slaves and a palace in each of the great cities; another left a fortune of 400,000 dinars; and many had villas in Mecca and Medina or in the hills nearby.

A second and new generation was coming to full manhood. The amusements and luxuries of Alexandria, Damascus, Ctesiphon, and the camp cities of Basrah, Kufah, and Fustat were tempting. Wine, women, and gambling were the undoing of many. Gone were days when, as Aishah easily recalled, Muhammad considered wheat bread a rare treat and usually made a meal of dates or milk but never had the luxury of both at the same time. Sumptuous living, however, was neither the sole difficulty nor the root of the other evils. Personal politics, power, and prestige began to eat at the vitals of Muslim society, and certainly Uthman was not strong enough to stem the process. Probably no one could have halted it.

MUSLIM POLITICAL PARTIES

Three political parties were developing in the Islamic world. The first considered itself the party of Muhammad. Led by members of the less important families of Mecca, it was composed of those who had established the Muslim community. Abu Bakr and Umar had been members of this party; and in most circles Ali, as the husband of Muhammad's daughter Fatimah, was looked upon as the leader. The strength of the party, sometimes called legitimists, lay in Egypt and Iraq.

Leaders of the second party were members of the Umayyad family and their associates among the Quraysh. It had been one of the two wealthiest and leading Meccan families in the pre-Islamic period—a family that had bitterly attacked Muhammad and had led the campaigns against the Muslims in Medina. Uthman was an Umayyad, as were Muawiyah, Abd Allah in Egypt, and Marwan, who served as Uthman's executive secretary in Medina. Though latecomers to Islam, they possessed great managerial talent and were rapidly surging to the fore in administering the empire. Umar had used them and controlled them; but the legitimists contended that the Umayyads controlled Uthman through their great power and wealth in Syria.

The third party was composed of Arab soldiers who had joined the Muslims just before or after Muhammad's death. They outnumbered the other two parties, but they were unorganized and their leaders did not have the prestige of the Quraysh. Yet, it was their swords that had been the instruments responsible for the rapid expansion of the domain of Islam, and since Islam acknowledged no distinctions among peoples or individuals, they resented the inferior political position forced upon them. The third party had followers everywhere, but their forces were concentrated in Arabia and the two great military cities in Iraq.

Having lost the election that followed Umar's death, the legitimists carped at Uthman for his policies and caviled at his inaction. He was censured for enlarging the square around the Kaaba in Mecca and for rebuilding and embellishing the mosque in Medina. Even his standardization of the Koran (Qur'an; still the canonical text today) was attacked, many feeling that he had no superior religious insight or authority for such an undertaking. But the most severe criticism was leveled at him for appointing so many members of the Umayyad family to high office, and for distributing unjustly the spoils of war. His political opponents claimed that he was reverting to the old order of Arab society where blood ties had ruled. Muhammad had preached earnestly to create a unitary Muslim community wherein all members would be brothers and where social, economic, and political equality would prevail; yet after a dozen years the traditional predilection for the family reasserted its consuming role.

Malcontents across the empire fed on the stories and rumors regarding the sale of positions and the power and wealth of favorites. Supporters of Ali in Kufah first raised the banners of revolt. When a band of tribesmen from Egypt arrived in Medina and surrounded Uthman's residence, the caliph would not permit an army to be raised in his defense and commanded Muawiyah not to come to his rescue. After a siege of several months in 656 the rebels stormed the palace and murdered Uthman, the first dagger being struck by Abu Bakr's son. Anarchy reigned for a week in Medina until a group of notables, under pressure from the rebels from Egypt, elected Ali to the caliphate and restored order.

ALI

Ali, Muhammad's cousin, adopted son, and son-in-law, was a pious and esteemed Muslim, who as an individual soldier in his younger days had shone as one of the great heroes of Muslim battles. He had already been disappointed three times in not being elected caliph, and he may have known of the move to kill Uthman. Generally throughout the Muslim world he was recognized as the caliph; and the new governors appointed by him were accepted everywhere except in Syria, where Muawiyah refused to resign. There were, however, many individuals who did not acknowledge Ali as caliph, largely because of jealousy or shock over the murder of Uthman.

Disgruntled elements among the legitimists aided by Aishah, who bitterly hated Ali, hatched a rebellion in Mecca on the pretext that Ali had implicated himself by not punishing the regicides. Ali led his army from Medina, which from that day to the present ceased to be the residence of any caliph, and defeated the insurgents near Basrah in the renowned Battle of the Camel (so-called because the fighting swirled around Aishah on her camel). In this first battle of Muslim against Muslim neither booty nor reprisal against the vanquished was taken. Many illustrious Companions of the Prophet were killed. Aishah was captured but was permitted to return to Medina, where she lived on for twenty-two years in her apartment, which was the place where, beneath the floor, Muhammad, Abu Bakr, and Umar had been buried.

Denouncing Ali as the contrere of the murderers of the caliph, Muawiyah withheld his fealty and met Ali's forces at Siffin on the banks of the Euphrates in northern Syria in 657. In the midst of battle, fighting between Muslims was dramatically halted upon agreement that the contest would be decided by referring to the Koran. Arbitration was unsuccessful; Muawiyah refused to accept Ali as caliph until Ali punished the murderers of Uthman, and Ali could not kill his supporters nor would he abdicate. Each force, however, retired from the field, and a stalemate ensued.

Following the Battle of the Camel, Ali had made his capital at Kufah. His episode with Muawiyah was, in part, a revival of the persistent rivalry between Syria and Iraq for dominance in the Middle East. It was also a struggle between the Umayyad Quraysh and the Arab settled tribesmen of Iraq and the Hijaz.

At the Battle of the Camel so many of the legitimist party perished that it disappeared from the annals of Islam, leaving Ali, in Kufah, at the mercy of the dominant local and religious groups. In fact, some members took the name Kharijites ("Seceders") and revolted against Ali in protest against his willingness to arbitrate. Ali destroyed their force in 659, but was assassinated in 661 by a Kharijite in Kufah on the way to prayer. Hasan, Ali's eldest son, was declared caliph in Kufah; but Muawiyah was recognized as caliph in Damascus. A few months later Hasan reached an agreement with Muawiyah and retired on a royal pension to the pleasures of his palace in Medina. Muawiyah, thenceforth, was accepted throughout the Muslim Empire as the sole caliph, and the center of the state shifted to Damascus.

Thus ended the so-called republican and democratic era of the caliphate wherein the rulers were elected or chosen for reasons other than birth or military might. Throughout most of this period Medina still served as the capital of the Muslim world, and the leaders of society had known the Prophet personally. It was an Arab state; the conquered provinces had not yet conquered their rulers. With the transfer of the seat of authority to Damascus and the caliphate to Muawiyah of the Umayyad family, a new era was born.

REFERENCES

References at the end of Chapters 1–3 relate to this chapter as well.

Arnold, Thomas W. *The Caliphate.* Oxford: Clarendon Press, 1924. A careful discussion of the formation and history of the rule of the Muslim state.

Donner, Fred McGraw. *The Early Islamic Conquests.* Princeton, N.J.: Princeton University Press, 1981. The standard account of the Muslim conquests of Syria and Iraq, this work also contains a valuable analysis of the relations between nomadic tribesmen and the Medina government.

Frye, R. N., ed. *The Cambridge History of Iran.* Vol. 4. *The Period from the Arab Invasion to the Saljuqs.* London: Cambridge University Press, 1975. Seven scholarly chapters on the history of Iran during this period, followed by excellent chapters on social, cultural, religious, and intellectual history.

Kennedy, Hugh. *The Prophet and the Age of the Caliphates: The Islamic Near East from the Sixth to the Eleventh Century.* London: Longman, 1986. This detailed political history incorporates recent scholarly research as well as the original sources; the author considers, but ultimately rejects, revisionist historians who have attacked the reliability of the primary sources.

Lewis, Bernard. *The Arabs in History.* London: Hutchison's University Library, 1950. A concise account of the rise of the Arabs, emphasizing the broad economic movements through the ages and correlating these developments with historical processes among the Arabs.

Shoufani, Elias. *Al-Riddah and the Muslim Conquest of Arabia.* Toronto: University of Toronto Press, 1973. A study of the wars in Arabia upon the death of Muhammad, showing that Arabia was far from united at the time of the Prophet's death.

Vaglieri, L. Vecchia. "Ali ibn Abi Talib." *Encyclopaedia of Islam.* New ed. Vol. 1, pp. 381–386. Leiden: Brill, 1960. This article, like the one cited below by W. Montgomery Watt, shows the high standards and thorough scholarship of the authors in the *Encyclopaedia of Islam,* a basic reference tool for all who are concerned with the Islamic Middle East.

Watt, W. Montgomery. "Abu Bakr." *Encyclopaedia of Islam.* New ed. Vol. 1, pp. 109–111. Leiden: Brill, 1960.

5

Islam

*T*he accession of Muawiyah inaugurated a period of Umayyad and Syrian domination of Islam during which the Hellenistic philosophy and theology of Egypt and Syria rapidly effected a revolution within Islamic thought and practice. Almost immediately the new concepts and dogmas within Islam gave birth to numerous Muslim sects; and under the Umayyads the unity of theology, as well as politics, was forever lost in the Muslim world.

After 660 the various Muslim schools of law, theologies, customs, and practices deviated and multiplied until the simple straightforward conceptualism of Islam vanished and the masses found the exact nature of their religion difficult to determine. Furthermore, rapidity of expansion and multifold conversions admitted to Muslim society many whose knowledge of Islam was limited to a few phrases. Throughout all these divergencies and vicissitudes there remained, nevertheless, considerable similarity. The central belief of all variants retained the simple monotheistic religion preached by Muhammad.

Acceptance of monotheism was the most important facet of religion to Muhammad. To be a Muslim it was sufficient to profess the unity of God and to admit Muhammad as His messenger. God had ninety-nine names, each with a related attribute. The mere recitation of some of these indicates Islam's conception of God: omniscient, omnipotent, the Judge, the Mighty, the Creator, merciful, compassionate, self-subsistent, forgiving, magnificent, everlasting, most generous, and most high

Of the infinite qualities of God, Islam constantly stressed everlastingness. God was the Creator of creation and existed through all eternity. All people were His creatures and He "misleads whom He will and guides whom He will." Fear of God and the Day of Judgment was particularly emphasized in Muhammad's early days to impress materialistic Meccan society; but God was also visualized as a loving, bountiful, and forgiving Protector, "closer to a man than his own jugular vein." A third important attribute of God was mystical in nature: He was termed the Light of the Heavens and of the Earth. In later centuries theologians developed this quality into various organized mysticisms which served as powerful forces in the spread and influence of Islam.

THE KORAN

The basis for Muhammad's views of God and religion and for the central belief of Muslims of every sect rested upon the Koran ("lecture" or "recitation"), the collection of revelations. Consisting of 114 chapters, called *surahs,* made up of 6,236 verses (77,934 words), the earliest versions were assembled soon after Muhammad's death. Most of the revelations had been written down in his later years by his secretaries; other revelations were only remembered word for word by his companions. Tradition has it that after a battle in which many reciters of the Koran perished, Abu Bakr ordered the full Koran to be committed to parchment so that it would not be lost. Later, Uthman established the copy held in Medina as the true Koran. In the tenth century the text, as it now stands, was adopted from different readings which evolved because of the lack of vowels and diacritical marks in the Arabic script.

Except for the first, which is a short prayer, the chapters were arranged according to length, so that the later but longer Medinese chapters are located at the beginning. The Koran is about two-thirds the length of an Arabic version of the New Testament.

Muslims regard the Koran as the word of God, transmitted to Muhammad by the angel Gabriel; and for many centuries they considered that the Koran contained all knowledge of any value. It furnished the basis for law in the Islamic world for all Muslims; like a modern constitution, it was the skeleton of the legal and judicial systems. It also prescribed a pattern of daily individual and community living which distinguished Islamic culture from all others. Since no official translation was made until modern times, Koranic Arabic served as a common language and a bond for all Muslims from one end of the world to the other. The Koran was the schoolbook, and committing it to memory was standard practice for children everywhere. The very sound of the Arabic words stirs the emotions of Muslims; read silently, the Koran loses much of its power.

The major part of the Koran is concerned with God: His attributes are cited, His powers proclaimed, and the individual's relations to Him defined. Associated with a vivid explanation of the Day of Judgment are portrayals of the resurrection, paradise and hell, and angels and devils. Religious and ethical paths to follow in life are sometimes presented directly, almost as codes and commandments; but for the most part they are contained in parables and stories, many of which are similar to those in the Old and New Testaments and their associated literature. Adam, Noah, Abraham, Joseph, Moses, David, Solomon, Elijah, Job, Zachariah, John the Baptist, Mary, and Jesus are all set forth, not in any special historical sense but to verify that God rewards the righteous and punishes the wicked.

A perusal of the Torah, the Bible, and the Koran discloses a number of very similar passages. Surah 21, verse 105, is identical to Psalm 37, verse 9: "For evil doers shall be cut off; but those that wait upon the Lord, they shall inherit the earth." The Christians of Constantinople and the West branded Islam as a Christian heresy—a castigation which led to the abhorrence of Muslims and an exaggeration of the differences between Christianity and Islam. In reality, Judaism, Christianity, and Islam have a great deal in common. The dissimilitude is more in language, style, and form than in substance. Through each of these three religions runs a strong message of personal salvation for righteous individuals. This message of hope gives to the individual a sense of significance and equality that is not ordinarily available in cultures where other religions prevail.

TRADITIONS

Following the Prophet's death it became obvious that revelations did not provide an answer to every problem that arises in daily life. Muhammad had recognized, at least after he became the ruler of Medina, that decisions he made personally were obeyed in the same measure that the revelations of God's will were obeyed. Muhammad always distinguished carefully between his own individual thoughts and divine revelation. God's word was law; Muhammad's words were only guides to lead to a wise and holy life.

As the years slipped by, leaving fewer and fewer Muslims who knew from their own memories what Muhammad had said and done, collections of his comments and deeds were considered vital for following his precedents. Traditions (*hadith*) by the hundreds of thousands appeared; these have been used to establish the bases for the *sunnah,* the custom, usual procedure, or behavior of the Prophet. Each of the different sects and parties that developed in Islam accepted certain hadith and rejected others as forgeries to prove the correctness of the party's views, no matter whether the contention affected militarism or pacifism, predestination or free will, mysticism or realism, asceticism or worldliness.

By the second or third century after the Hijrah, hadith had become very intricate in response to the philosophical and theological demands of the scholars of the time. In the early days of Islam, hadith had comprised the simple, unvarnished ideas and stories that Muhammad had voiced or that his friends had repeated word for word. They are of varied topics, for Muhammad had definite opinions on all types of subjects. On one occasion he said: "God curse the woman who wears false hair and the woman who ties it on." When Aishah acquired a pictured cushion, Muhammad exploded: "Verily, the makers of these pictures will be severely punished on the Day of Resurrection." On slavery he remonstrated: "A slave must not be given a task which he is unable to perform." Muhammad sometimes perceived the difference between legality and righteousness, as when he observed: "Of the things which are lawful the most hateful to God is divorce." In a similar vein he declared: "There is no man who receives a bodily injury and forgives the offender but God will exalt his rank and diminish his sin." Having been an orphan, Muhammad was always concerned with such unfortunates and proclaimed: "The best house amidst the Muslim community is that which contains an orphan who is well treated, and the worst is that wherein an orphan is wronged." Perhaps best known is the attitude Muhammad held toward usury and moneylenders. In commenting on persons paying or charging usurious rates of interest, he proclaimed, "They are equally culpable." Among Muslims one of his oft-quoted commands indicated Muhammad's view that sexual activity and piety could coexist: "No monkery in Islam!"

DOGMAS

Muhammad was not a systematic theologian. But after his death Muslim theologians and philosophers classified the faith into three fundamentals: religious beliefs (*iman*), religious duties (*ibadat*), and good works (*ihsan*).

First and foremost, of course, is the belief that God is One and has all of the attributes ascribed to Him. It has never been clear, however, how the attribute of omnipotence ought to be interpreted, and this problem has engendered controversy among Muslims from the days of the first caliphs to the present. In the early unaffected period, God's omnipotence simply meant that the individual is completely subordinate to God and can do nothing unless God permits it. Yet, all persons are responsible for what they do and will be rewarded or punished accordingly. Muhammad preached incessantly on this point and declared that people would fall into evil ways if they did not believe in God.

Muhammad and the first Muslims referred so frequently to the Day of Judgment and the Resurrection that belief in these two has become one of the significant aspects of Islam. When the cataclysmic day comes, each individual's faith and deeds will be weighed, one's body will rise, and either enter paradise or be cast into hell. Martyrs for the faith do not wait for the Judgment Day but immediately enter paradise. Paradise is clearly described as a beautiful garden by a flowing river where the blessed rest on silken couches, partake of heavenly food and drink, enjoy spiritual joys, associate with their families, and are entertained by dark-eyed maidens and wives of perfect purity. The terrors of hell are beyond description. Waters are boiling; sinners' bellies are filled with molten brass. Into this fiery hell go the unbelieving, the covetous, and those who worship other gods.

Another basic point in the religious belief of Muslims is the role played by angels and *jinn*. Heaven and earth are populated by these invisible spirits who serve as God's messengers and record one's deeds. Gabriel is recognized as the leading angel and the spirit who brought the Koran to Muhammad. Rebellious jinn are devils, and like humans will be cast into hell on the Last Day. The leading devil is an angel who at the time of creation did not worship Adam and who continues to seduce people into evil ways until the Resurrection.

Muslims believe that God has sent many human messengers to teach the world His ways and that the last and greatest was Muhammad. The Koran specifically mentions twenty-eight prophets: four are Arabs; one is Greek (Alexander the Great); three (Zachariah, John the Baptist, and Jesus) come from the New Testament; and the remainder come from the Old Testament. The most important of all the prophets are Adam, Noah, Abraham, Moses, and Jesus. The last is Muhammad, whom God sent as the "Seal" of all. Prophets did not perform miracles except on special occasions when God gave them these powers. Divine revelation was granted to Moses in the Jewish Torah, to David in the Psalms, to Jesus in the Gospels, and to Muhammad in the Koran, which was his only miracle. All of them preached salvation through the recognition that God is One.

Muslims are to accept and believe all of these scriptures, for they are the word of God and they corroborate each other. The final word of God, the Koran, attests the revelations in the other scriptures, clarifies all previous uncertainties, and brings perfect Truth. The Koran is believed to be eternal and uncreated; its earthly reproduction is identical in language and spelling to the heavenly original, every word and letter of which is sacred and divine.

DUTIES

The second essential in Islam as taught by Muhammad comprised religious duties. These are actions less obligatory than those of faith; but their performance required and constituted the individual's recognition of the omnipotence of God. These duties have usually been termed the "five pillars" or acts of worship of Islam; they are the easiest to observe and, unfortunately for many uninformed non-Muslims and even for some Muslims, these five pillars have been mistaken for the true religious substance of Islam.

The first and foremost pillar is the open profession of faith. Often reduced to the Koranic formula "No god but God and Muhammad is the messenger of God," this declaration is used throughout a Muslim's life and suffices to ensure one's acceptance as a nominal Muslim.

Muhammad emphasized prayer as the second obligation for Muslims. The Koran mentions directly no set ritual for prayer, but bids the faithful to pray frequently. Before Muhammad's death it had become customary for Muslims to pray formally five times daily: daybreak, noon, midafternoon, sunset, and nightfall. A Muslim prays at these times wherever he may be, but it is preferable to pray in unison with others and in a mosque if possible, with one acting as leader and the others standing in rows behind, all facing Mecca. Each prayer is composed of a certain number of bows: two at daybreak, three at sunset, and four at the other times. Each bow consists of seven distinct acts. (1) placing the open hands at each side of the head and repeating, "God is most great"; (2) standing upright and repeating the opening prayer of the Koran and at least one other Koranic passage; (3) bending from the hips and touching the knees with the hands; (4) straightening up, saying, "God listens to the one who praises Him"; (5) falling to the knees and prostrating oneself with the forehead touching the ground; (6) sitting on the haunches; and (7) a second prostration. Most Muslim prayers are concerned with God and His attributes, and devout Muslims pray frequently at other times during the day and night. Certain events such as burials, eclipses, serious decisions, and religious celebrations demand specially prescribed prayers. The Friday noon prayer is the great congregational prayer wherein a sermon (*Khutbah*) is usually delivered. At first, the sermon was delivered by Muhammad, then by the caliph or his representative, and now by a learned Muslim, who also offers a prayer on behalf of the ruling head of the state.

At the time of prayer one must be in a state of spiritual and physical purity, which is determined in various ways. Usually before prayers, simple purity, as defined in the Koran, is achieved by washing the hands and arms to the elbows, the face, and the feet up to the ankles. In the absence of water, sand may be used.

Of all the features of Islam, prayer in its public form has been the most constant democratizing force. Side by side at prayer are common soldier and general, prince and pauper, merchant and holy man. No distinction is made and the proudest individual falls to his knees and humbly and reverently prostrates himself in complete obeisance in the presence of the omnipotent and omniscient God.

The third pillar of Islam is almsgiving. Muhammad at first regarded giving to the poor and needy as a personal atonement and a means of salvation. Sometime in the Medinese period of his prophecy almsgiving was regularized to become a 2.5 percent voluntary tax on all produce and revenue of each Muslim above a certain minimum of goods. Termed *zakat,* the proceeds were used to support the poor, to erect religious buildings, and to help defray government expenses. In later years when states were much weaker, it was not possible to collect alms on any such basis and it became solely a free-will offering. Alms are also to be given generously for various religious and human charities such as mosques, hospitals, poorhouses, and schools. Likewise, beggars and the destitute are never turned away from the door empty-handed. On the Day of Judgment in a Muslim's book of deeds will be recorded the alms given.

Fasting, the fourth pillar of Islam, was enjoined upon all Muslims during Ramadan (the ninth lunar month), a month of fasting. From the very first flush of dawn to nightfall, food, drink, and smoke are not to pass the lips; bleeding, application of leeches, and sexual intercourse are also forbidden. At various times and places in history Muslims who have failed to observe Ramadan have been beaten. Fasting is considered the best means of expiating one's sins of the year.

The fifth pillar of Islam, that of the yearly pilgrimage to Mecca (*hajj*), stands as the symbol of Muslim unity. It was a maxim that each Muslim, man and woman, should participate in the pilgrimage each year if possible. Later, as the Muslim world grew, it became too arduous for many to go from Iraq, Syria, and Egypt; and when Islam had spread to India and Spain, the pilgrimage became obligatory only once in a lifetime and only for those who could afford it. Occurring in the twelfth month (*Dhu al-Hijjah*), the pilgrimage ritual is celebrated on certain days by elaborate and involved rites at the Kaaba in Mecca and at other sacred spots in the neighborhood. Since Muhammad's Farewell Pilgrimage in 632, non-Muslims have not been permitted to be present in Mecca during the pilgrimage; and in general they are forbidden entry into the city at all times.

Throughout the entire course of Muslim history the pilgrimage has been a most valuable unifying force within Islamic civilization. Pilgrims have come to Mecca from the four corners of the Muslim world. There, on the way, and in returning the interchange of philosophical and theological dogmas, the gaining of geographical and economic knowledge, the exchange of seeds and agricultural products, and the interplay of political forces and ideas have been factors in maintaining a common Muslim culture among the diverse peoples embracing Islam.

To some Muslims a sixth pillar of Islam has been added: that of holy war and striving for the faith (*jihad*). Many consider that every Muslim bears the duty to expand the frontiers of Islam, by force if necessary, until the entire world has been won.

VIRTUES

It might well be thought that after professing the religious beliefs of Islam and performing the various duties of a Muslim, the circle of religion had been completed. In addition, however, the Koran imposes upon all a course of righteous living, thus giving a religious character to private and public morality. From the virtues extolled, Islam emerges as moralistic and puritanical. The Koran limits the number of wives to four, and then adds: "But if you fear that you will act unjustly among them, then marry only one." There are many other commandments that raised the status of women in Arabian society. Settlements are required to be made upon a woman if she is divorced; a widow can marry whomever she wishes; and the burying alive of daughters is prohibited.

Murderers are promised burning in hell; and earthly penalties are imposed for homicide, stealing, fraud, perjury, and libel. Injunctions are delivered against gambling, usury, and monopolistic practices. The use of wine and the eating of pork are forbidden. Idolatry is most sinful, and the making of images is only one step removed from worshiping other gods. Most of these declarations of right living are injunctions against practices that were common in the pagan and hedonistic society of Mecca.

In view of the comprehensive scope of Islam with respect to religious beliefs, religious duties, and virtues, Muhammad must be regarded as a very successful prophet and reformer. Muhammad found Mecca, as one writer has well expressed it, a "materialistic commercial" city "where lust of gain and usury reigned supreme, where women, wine, and gambling filled up the leisure time, where might was right, and widows, orphans, and the feeble were treated as superfluous ballast." Muhammad, practically a nobody in the social order of Mecca, brought to his people and to Meccans a knowledge of God and a way of salvation that changed the life and philosophy of all Arabia. Since Islam required individual belief and morality, the tribal and family morality of pre-Islamic Arabia was replaced by the personal responsibilities of the individual Muslim as a member of the universal Muslim community.

REFERENCES

Ali, Abdullah Yusuf. *The Holy Qur'an: Text, Translation and Commentary.* Washington, D.C.: The Islamic Center, 1978. One of the best translations, with comments and analysis, and the English and Arabic texts facing each other.

Arberry, Arthur J. *The Koran Interpreted.* New York: Macmillan, 1955. The translation catches much of the majesty and beauty of the original; it should be used in conjunction with Watt's *Companion to the Qur'an,* cited below.

Ayoub, Mahmoud. *The Qur'an and Its Interpreters.* Vol. 1. Albany: State University of New York Press, 1984. This presentation and general elucidation of the first two chapters of the Koran shows the ways Muslims have analyzed the text.

Burton, John. *The Collection of the Qur'an.* Cambridge: Cambridge University Press, 1977. A radical interpretation of the history of the text of the Koran that maintains that Muhammad himself was involved in its compilation and editing.

Denny, Frederick Mathewson. *An Introduction to Islam.* New York: Macmillan, 1985. This general survey of Islam, now the best available for the beginning student of the religion, deals with all aspects of the subject, with an emphasis on mysticism and personal faith as well as the historical development from pre-Islamic days to the present.

Gibb, H. A. R. *Mohammedanism: An Historical Survey.* London: Oxford University Press, 1961. Although somewhat dated, this remains the most influential short account and discussion of Islam by a non-Muslim. The style is simple and direct, the language is readily understood, and the scholarship is beyond reproach.

Martin, Richard C. *Islam: A Cultural Approach.* Englewood Cliffs, N.J.: Prentice-Hall, 1982. A broad and easily understood survey of most aspects of Islam.

al-Said, Labib. *The Recited Koran.* Translated by Bernard Weiss *et al.* Princeton, N.J.: Darwin Press, 1975. The history of the Koran is discussed in the first part of this book, while the making of the first complete recording of the Koran is examined in the second part.

Tritton, A. S. *Muslim Theology.* London: Luzac, 1947. The basic principles are well presented in this volume and the variants are explained.

Watt, W. Montgomery. *Companion to the Qur'an: Based on the Arberry Translation.* London: George Allen and Unwin, 1967. Certain sections of the Koran are explained or put in context.

————. *What Is Islam?* New York: Praeger, 1968. A survey of the background of Islam, the historical perspective, the work of religious intellectuals, and the Islamic world view.

Welch, A. T. "Al-Kur'an." *Encyclopaedia of Islam.* New ed. Vol. V, pp. 400–429. Leiden: Brill, 1981. A complete account of the various controversies, the arrangement of the text, the meaning of different sections, the final compilation, and the importance of the Koran for Muslims.

6

The Spread and Organization of the Muslim Empire Under the Umayyads

*T*he death of Ali left no serious rival to Muawiyah and his leadership over all Muslims. Proclaimed caliph at Jerusalem in 661 while in his fifties, Muawiyah established Damascus as his chief residence and seat of government. Until his death nineteen years later, he managed the provinces through energetic, capable, and forceful governors, who tried to maintain a strong discipline over the proud and turbulent Arab soldiery. In Iraq, however, the crowded garrison cities and determined leaders declared their autonomy so vigorously that Muawiyah wisely acquiesced and challenged them only when feasible. Muslim soldiers held the province and the Sasanid governmental lands as theirs by right of conquest and rarely sent any part of the income to Damascus.

At home Muawiyah ruled confidently and nobly as the first among equals. He discussed policies of state with the notables about him, frequently explaining the course of government publicly from the pulpit of the mosque. In truth, his power rested upon the personal loyalty of the Syrian army, which was the strongest and best organized of any in the state. More and more he built an administration in the Romano-Byzantine tradition; less and less was he the tribal Arab shaykh governing purely on a personal basis. He was the first Muslim ruler to execute a fellow Muslim for political reasons.

Five years before his death, Muawiyah induced the leaders of the empire to recognize his son Yazid as his successor. Thereupon, Yazid was taken to Medina and Mecca to have those holy cities accept him as the next caliph. This procedure was definitely a dynastic custom, and the Muslim aristocracy of Medina, declaring the step to be a sinful innovation, refused to render the requested homage. Essentially, this method of succession made the position of caliph a hereditary one, or at least a family prerogative, and overtly established the Umayyad Empire, which lasted until 750. Twice during the period there was a question who the next caliph would be; and only once a serious contender arose outside of the Umayyad family.

In general and by comparison with other ruling families, the Umayyads produced talented, competent caliphs. They were much maligned by later Muslim historians, especially the pious religious scholars, who wrote under the patronage of the succeeding dynasty and who depicted the Umayyads as hard-riding, wine-bibbing, luxury-loving, worldly-minded usurpers of the caliphate. But the Umayyads organized the Muslim state into a more centralized force that once again carried forward the banners of Islam into distant places. They were hard-hitting realists who, in order to meet existing and evolving situations, could not always follow the principles of government and law being formulated by theologians and jurists in the holy city of Medina.

CAMPAIGNS AGAINST BYZANTIUM

The nearest and greatest rival power of the Umayyad state was the Byzantine Empire; the nearest and richest land for the Muslims to raid was Asia Minor. Battles with Byzantine forces were not novel experiences for Muawiyah. As governor of Syria, he had driven Byzantine armies from north Syria, twice defeated Byzantine fleets, and occupied Cyprus. Muawiyah's army exploited the weakness of the rule from Constantinople by annual summer excursions through the passes into Asia Minor as far north as Caesarea (Kayseri). After he became caliph, Muawiyah's forces roamed far and wide over Anatolia; one Muslim general wintered in 668 across the Bosphorus

Umayyah

| Abu al-As | | | Harb |

al-Hakam — Affan — Abu Sufyan

Marwan (683–685) — Uthman (644–656) — Muawiyah (661–680)

Muhammad — Abd al-Malik (685–705) — Abd al-Aziz — Yazid (680–683)

Marwan II (744–750) — Umar II (717–720) — Muawiyah II (683)

al-Walid (705–715) — Sulayman (715–717) — Yazid II (720–724) — Hisham (724–743)

Yazid III (744) — Ibrahim (744) — al-Walid II (743–744)

The Umayyad Caliphs

from Constantinople. From 674 to 680 the Muslim fleet and land forces attacked Constantinople, but the land and sea walls of the city proved too great a barrier for the Arabs. From this campaign has come the legendary hero Abu Ayyub (Eyub), who died and was buried near the walls of Constantinople. The standard-bearer of the Prophet, the then aged Abu Ayyub had accompanied the soldiers to stimulate their enthusiasm. His remains, discovered in 1453 when the Turks were storming the walls, have been entombed in a mosque-mausoleum near the Golden Horn, where the Ottoman sultans were girded with the sword of their authority.

The raising of the siege of Constantinople upon Muawiyah's death did not presage the relaxation of Muslim pressure on the Byzantine Empire. Another assault upon Constantinople was launched by the caliph Sulayman, who subscribed to the legend that Constantinople would be taken by the bearer of a prophet's name. His brother Maslamah, supported by land and sea forces, occupied both shores of the Bosphorus and held a tight siege of Constantinople for fourteen months. In 717, however, he was foiled by Greek fire and the brilliant defenses of the new emperor, Leo the Isaurian (a Syrian from Marash) and by the ravages of disease, hunger, and an unusually severe winter. At the same time the new caliph, Umar II, strongly opposed to all expansionist policies, ordered the siege lifted and the Muslim forces withdrawn. Several generations elapsed before the Muslims appeared again before the walls of Constantinople, which always proved too thick and too strong for the Arabs to penetrate without the aid of gunpowder.

NORTH AFRICA AND SPAIN

The records do not disclose any planned pincers movement on Europe by the Umayyads, although simultaneously with their last attacks upon Constantinople the greatest westward movement of Islam was being executed. Amr, governor of Egypt, sent a Muslim force westward into North Africa and took Tripoli around 644. Following the accession of the Umayyads, conquests were resumed. A camp city built in 670 at Qayrawan in Tunisia served as headquarters to subdue Berber tribes and the coastal cities dependent upon Constantinople. Toward the end of the century Byzantine rule over the coast was ended by a cooperative army-fleet maneuver which drove the Greeks from Carthage. Appointed governor of Northwest Africa sometime between 698 and 705, Musa ibn Nusayr consolidated the region, conquered Morocco, and added greatly to his military force by recruiting from among the Berber tribesmen. Most of Morocco, however, subsequently remained beyond the effective control of the Umayyad governors for decades.

One of Musa's Berber lieutenants led a small reconnoitering band across the Strait of Gibraltar in 710 and returned easily with such valuable booty that Tarik crossed on his celebrated raid in the early summer of 711 with several thousand men, mostly Berbers, and established a base on the strong height which still is called Tarik's mountain—*Jabal Tarik,* or Gibraltar. Crushing the Visigothic forces of Spain, Tarik fanned out northward at will. Málaga, Cordoba, and Toledo fell; and by winter Tarik found himself master of half of Spain with an almost unlimited amount of booty at his disposal.

Scolding Tarik for acting independently, Musa joined his heroic henchman in 712. Within two years nearly all of Spain had been overrun by Muslim forces. From Galicia, Musa looked down upon the waters of the Atlantic and the Bay of Biscay. At this time, a messenger ordered Musa to appear before the caliph in Damascus. Accompanied by Tarik, Musa made the long trek overland and presented to the court his trophies and many Visigothic nobles and maidens. Shortly thereafter a new caliph stripped Musa of his wealth and degraded him, perhaps because of fear or jealousy of Musa's great popularity. Musa died in poverty a few years later in the Hijaz, a strange fate for one who had opened Europe to the Muslims.

Within six or seven years the conquest of Spain was completed. The Arabs called the province al-Andalusia ("Land of the Vandals") and it, or some part of it, remained a Muslim land for almost eight centuries. The Arab-Berber-Muslim (Moorish) culture left its indelible mark on Spain, which in turn had a profound influence on Islamic society. The speed and ease with which Spain was conquered indicated that it was in a state of near anarchy, waiting for a positive force to enter the vacuum. The Visigoths, ruling in a most oppressive and tyrannical fashion and attempting to convert all Jews to Christianity by force, had been at odds with the Romano-Spanish peoples, who looked upon their Teutonic masters as barbarians.

As in Syria, Iraq, and Egypt, the Muslims fought not against the native inhabitants but only against the armies of the rulers. Spain was taken so quickly that in many towns and cities no Arab or Berber forces could be spared for garrison duty; and since Muslim administrators were usually not available, native Jews were left in charge.

In 720 Arab-Berber invaders seized Narbonne on the Mediterranean and established an arsenal and base for operations north of the Pyrenees. Predatory columns rode out of Narbonne every year, terrorizing the countryside and carrying off rich booty, especially from the treasures of churches and convents. The greatest of these expeditions was the renowned foray of 732 led by the governor of Spain, Abd al-Rahman, who burned churches in Bordeaux and outside of Poitiers. The raiders turned back from their northward course only after the loss of their leader in the determined and bloody resistance put up by Charles Martel in the celebrated but indecisive Battle of Tours. Never again did an organized expedition of Muslims approach so near to Paris, but Muslim forces did succeed in taking Avignon in 734 and several years later sacked Lyons.

Although Narbonne was not abandoned until 759, the Arab-Berbers of Spain never fashioned a real hold upon southern France because of their lack of manpower, the distance from Damascus, and a running feud between Berber and Arab which led to violent insurrection in North Africa and Spain. Conversions to Islam among the Berbers were so extensive as to compromise the relationship between conquerors and vanquished in North Africa. Arabs looked down on the Berbers, who upon becoming Muslims anticipated equality with the proud Arab. When the expected treatment was not forthcoming, rebellion burst out everywhere. From 739 to 742 North Africa was in flames from one end to the other. Berbers claimed that they were given semiarid plateau lands in Spain while the Arabs acquired all of the fertile areas.

In addition, factional strife among the Arabs existed at every turn. Political, religious, and family quarrels were at this moment rocking the Islamic world from the Pyrenees to the Indus, making incursions beyond well-established frontiers wholly ineffective. Furthermore, rivalry developed between Arabs from Arabia and the Syrian army sent to subdue Berber uprisings; their bickerings with the Arab governors and lords of Toledo and Cordoba were interminable. From the time of the Battle of Tours to the landing of the Umayyad prince in Spain in 755, the term of the governorship of Spain averaged twelve months. With such turmoil, uncertainty, and anarchy permanent conquests in France were impossible.

EXPANSION IN ASIA

While the Umayyads were extending Islam westward into North Africa and Spain, a similar expansion carried Muslim rule to the Indus River and the frontiers of China. Often territory was surrendered by treaty rather than conquered. Becoming viceroy of the eastern lands of the caliphate in 695, al-Hajjaj, a schoolmaster of al-Taif, gave his governor of Khurasan several thousand Arab troops to establish a strong base at Merv (Mary). These were added to the 50,000 Arabs from Kufah and Basrah that Muawiyah had sent to settle in the oases around Merv to relieve the population pressures of those cities. From there he crossed the Amu Darya River (known then as the Oxus) and in a series of brilliant campaigns brought Transoxiana under Muslim domination. Balkh, Bukhara, and Samarkand in Turkestan and Khiva were subdued between 705 and 712 and soon became Islamic strongholds; Buddhist temples and monasteries were destroyed. Native Turkish and Persian rulers were left in charge of civil affairs, although Muslim tax collectors and military inspectors represented the imperial authority. A generation later another caliph sent an Arab general to Transoxiana as far as Kashgar to reconquer the area and bring the Turkish rulers, some of whom had accepted Islam, again under caliphal authority.

Further south, al-Hajjaj's son-in-law was authorized to lead a column toward India. Taking Makran, he occupied Baluchistan and subdued Sind. Muslim control along the Indus was permanent. Steady conversion to Islam soon made this northwestern corner of India an important part of the Muslim world and laid the foundations for the Islamic state known today as Pakistan.

FISCAL DEVELOPMENTS

This second wave of Muslim expansion under the Umayyads brought to a head certain economic and fiscal problems which had been developing at an accelerated pace. From the time of the Hijrah, Muslims were subject to a small tax to support their poor and unfortunate brethren, but there was no general taxation. Toward the end of the seventh century, with Arabs scattered over the face of the earth and conversions among conquered non-Arab peoples growing by leaps and bounds, questions of state annuities to worthy Muslims, land ownership, and taxation arose to vex one caliph after another and ignited serious disturbances in Muslim society.

Besides the state's share of booty, which in the Umayyad era was very sizable, the principal source of revenue came in taxes from land and subject peoples. Each free non-Muslim was required to pay for his protection a poll tax (*jizyah*) of four, two, or one dinar, according to his wealth and position. Land taxes were far more complex. In the days of the earliest conquests Muslims (Arabs) were forbidden to possess land outside of Arabia proper. Domain lands of ousted Byzantine and Sasanid governments and vacant lands fell to the caliph as agent for the Muslim community, and the income went into provincial coffers, with all surplus supposedly being forwarded to Damascus. As the Umayyad rulers established irrigation and agricultural development projects, the ensuing revenues from the provinces proved a valuable supplement to taxation. Ownership of other land was not changed, and in most cases the taxes (*kharaj*) remained the same and were collected by the same agents. As Arab Muslims acquired properties in Syria, Iraq, and other provinces outside Arabia, freedom from land taxes usually prevailed. The state leased domain land to Muslim Arabs, who bought and sold the rights so that the land had the appearance of private property. Consequently, Arab laws governing land ownership and tenure adhered generally to Byzantine, Persian, and more ancient practices and customs, thereby assuring to tillers of the soil throughout the Middle East a continuity which changed only imperceptibly.

As the number of non-Arab Muslims increased through conversion, many deserted the land for the city in the expectation of living on state annuities as Arabs did. They paid no taxes on the land left behind in the village and ceased to pay the poll tax. This disastrously affected the treasuries, especially in North Africa, Iraq, and Khurasan.

Furthermore, in order to eliminate increasing resentment of non-Arab Muslims and to prevent incipient revolutions in several of the provinces, Umar II decided to free Muslims, irrespective of origin or state, from paying poll and land taxes. The result was a lowering of revenues that upset the fiscal system of the government beyond the point of toleration. Caliph Hisham withdrew the order and instituted the policy, generally permanent in Muslim lands ever since, that although poll taxes "fell off" upon conversion to Islam, land taxes did not. At that time in the provinces these tax measures were considered by non-Arab Muslims, the principal landowners, to be very inequitable. Great disaffection led to civil war in North Africa and proved to be a major factor in the overthrow of the Umayyad regime by the troops from Iraq and Khurasan.

SOCIAL ORGANIZATION

As the Arabs and the native inhabitants of the conquered territories began to coalesce, there arose four social classes: Muslim Arabs; Muslim non-Arabs; non-Muslim free persons (Christians, Jews, Zoroastrians); and slaves.

The Arab was the aristocrat of the Muslim world, and the Quraysh claimed to be the noblest. Wherever Islam spread, Arabs regarded themselves as the rightful leaders of society, and at first only they could live in the new garrison cities such as Qayrawan, Cairo, and Kufah. Although Islam taught the equality of all believers and disavowed family connections in favor of religious ties, Muslim Arabs everywhere retained pride in their lineage: clan and tribe feelings ran high, and marriage between an Arab woman and a non-Arab man was considered a serious misalliance. In the Umayyad period all Arabs were enrolled in the imperial registry, each receiving regular payments from the state treasury on the theory that the receipts of the Muslim community were divided among all its members. In practice the Arabs acted as if it were decreed that the Arab minority would rule the non-Arab majority, Muslims as well as non-Muslims.

By the beginning of the eighth century, non-Arab Muslims, often called clients (*mawali*), outnumbered the Arab Muslims in all parts of the Umayyad Empire except Arabia. Moreover, the masses in lower Iraq, Syria, and Khurasan had been converted so rapidly that revenues in those provinces had dropped very conspicuously. Rarely were these converts accepted as equals by the Arabs and usually they attached themselves to a member of an Arab tribe or family (thus the nomenclature "clients"). Yet the converts were in many instances trained and educated individuals with skills not possessed by many Arabs. Several generations later, because of the universality of the Arabic language and considerable intermarriage, the pure Arab of Arabia who had migrated to conquered territory had been lost in the welter of peoples, all of whom participated in the common culture and practices of that particular section of the Middle East. In Syria and Iraq, where most of the Arabs settled, non-Arab Muslims were absorbed quickly, and the new culture became Arab. In more distant lands such as Iran, India, and Spain, the few ruling Arabs dominated society only temporarily. The non-Arab Muslims soon engulfed their rulers, and Iranian, Indian, and Berber characteristics triumphed.

Non-Muslims—Jews, Christians, Zoroastrians, pagan Berbers, and a few scattered others—were called *dhimmis* and were recognized legally as second-class subjects. They were judged almost entirely in their own courts in accordance with their own laws and were permitted to worship in their own way and to live their personal lives as they wished. They were, nevertheless, greatly circumscribed in matters of civil rights and community affairs. Non-Muslims could not bear arms; instead, they paid taxes. They were subject to many distinctive regulations concerning dress, styles of coiffures, types of saddles, and manner of riding. Finally, the *dhimmis* could neither hold public office nor give evidence in court against a Muslim.

At the bottom of the social ladder were the slaves. Slavery in the Middle East was as old as time itself. Although Muhammad openly condemned it, saying that freeing the slaves was pleasing in the sight of God, he declared slavery legal. In Islamic society, no Muslim could be enslaved legally; acceptance of Islam, however, did not give a slave freedom. Children of a slave woman remained slaves unless the owner of the slave accepted them as his children. Marriage between master and slave was not permissible, although concubinage was. A concubine who presented her master with children could not be sold, was accorded special recognition as the mother of his children, and gained her freedom upon his death.

Slave trading was a very active and profitable business in the Middle East under the Umayyads. Most slaves were acquired as booty in victorious campaigns and successful raiding expeditions, but many were purchased through regular slave channels. Greeks, Armenians, Turks, Kurds, Spaniards, Goths, Iranians, black Africans, and Berbers predominated; but slaves were of every color and description. Prices rose and fell with the supply. Most Arab Muslims possessed several slaves, and the wealthy frequently counted theirs in the thousands.

POLITICAL ADMINISTRATION

When Muawiyah became caliph, his first task was to effect a systematic administration for the empire. Obviously following the example and practices of the East Roman Empire current in Syria and even using much of its personnel, Muawiyah organized his government along three main functional or departmental lines: political and military affairs; tax collection; and religious administration, including courts and endowments.

The caliphs governed Syria, Palestine, and upper Iraq directly. The rest of the empire was divided by the Umayyads into three great provinces, each with a viceroy appointed by the caliph: (1) Kufah, and (2) Basrah, which were often governed by one viceroy, who in turn controlled the Muslim lands farther east; and (3) Egypt, which administered Africa, running from Cyrenaica to the Atlantic and the Pyrenees. The provinces were often subdivided, merged, and reorganized.

The religious officials, tribal army leaders, and the civil administrators in each lesser province acted upon the authority of a governor, and all were directed by and responsible to the viceroy. Local expenses were defrayed from taxes collected in the provinces, only the tax balances being forwarded to Damascus. Toward the end of the Umayyad regime when administration began to weaken, viceroys and provincial governors built up great personal fortunes by neglecting to forward the full balance to the caliph. Viceroys even remained in Damascus, hiring agents to go to the provinces to perform irksome functions. Frequently, special officers were sent directly by the caliph to collect taxes and to be responsible solely to him rather than to the viceroy, who always resented the implied lack of confidence. (It was this action that aroused the enmity of Amr in Egypt toward the caliph Uthman.)

As the empire expanded, problems of trained and loyal personnel, of communications, and of money came to the fore. The number of qualified Arabs was too small to fill the positions required to keep the government functioning. In Syria, Iraq, and Egypt, Muawiyah retained the services of most of the government employees he found there upon the conquest. These employees used Greek, Persian, and Coptic to keep their records. Not until the time of Abd al-Malik was the process of supplanting these civil servants with Arabic-speaking officers begun. By the end of the Umayyad era, however, government affairs were recorded in Arabic, and clerks were Arabic-speaking and usually Muslim in faith.

At the time of their conquest, the Byzantine and Sasanid empires were largely on a money economy with gold, silver, and copper coins in wide circulation. The Muslims took these over as media of exchange, sometimes with a phrase from the Koran stamped on. True Muslim-Arabic coins, first minted at Damascus in the reign of Abd al-Malik, were similar in value to coins already in circulation. The gold ones were called dinars after the Roman denarius; the silver, dirhams, from the Greek drachma.

Muslim judges (*qadis*) for the various cities of the empire were usually chosen by the provincial governors and were responsible to them. Since these judges were concerned only with the Muslims, there was little occasion for judges in the villages at this time. Caliphs, viceroys, and governors also held court and handed out justice personally.

As long as Muawiyah lived, his firm hand checked the factious spirit of the Arabs. However, the two great tribal parties of the Arabs, which existed certainly for a century or two before the advent of Islam, persisted even though submerged throughout the period of the first caliphs. Muhammad refused to recognize the differences and Umar was most intolerant of any display of partisanship. Under the Umayyads with the rule of Abd al-Malik and his ruthless viceroy, al-Hajjaj, party strife reached a high point and influenced every aspect of political life in all parts of the empire.

Reminiscent of the famous Blues and Greens of the Byzantine Empire, the rivalry of the Arab parties became keen and often bitter. These party rivalries were frequently family affairs, and each group went by a variety of names depending on what particular family was dominant at any given time and place. One main division was called the South Arabian party. Its members argued that the disintegration of economic and political life in the region of Yemen—perhaps capped by the breaking of the Marib Dam—had forced them to migrate northward and settle on the confines of the desert east of the Jordan River and the Dead Sea. Claiming common descent from Qahtan (Joktan of the Book of Genesis), they affected a culture superior to others. The other party, North Arabians, had been nomadic in character and believed that its families came from the central and northern areas of Arabia. Calling their common ancestor Adnan, the North Arabians were clearly the Ishmaelites of the Bible.

Between the two parties any differences of language, culture, and physiognomy had long since disappeared; only legend and rivalry remained to perpetuate the factions. Nevertheless, the feuding between the two was very real, as is attested by the oft-repeated incident of the two-year war in Damascus that was touched off because a member of one party stole a watermelon from a garden belonging to a member of the other party.

Beginning with Abd al-Malik until the downfall of the Umayyads, differences between the two parties became fixed upon two central issues, one political and one social. The first was the question of military campaigns of expansion. The South Arabians, or Yemenis as they were then termed, were opposed to these campaigns, and when Sulayman, a Yemeni sympathizer, became caliph in 715, he tolerated only expeditions that would consolidate frontiers. His attack on Constantinople was necessitated by Byzantine problems on the northern frontier; his withdrawal in the east and his humbling of Musa were examples more indicative of his policy. Umar II, a staunch supporter of this nonexpansionist view, stopped every campaign in 717 when he became caliph. His successors, however, were all expansionist North Arabians, or Qaysites as they called themselves, and al-Hajjaj lieutenants were reappointed to high positions. They believed that the social and economic ills of the empire, such as pres-

sures for equality, taxation, fiscal policies of stipends for all Arabs, and civil disturbances caused by some Arabs' refusing to go on campaigns, could be met by expansion on the frontiers, which would occupy the soldiers and avert civil wars, at the
same time bringing in booty for soldier and imperial treasury alike.

The social problem was over assimilation—the granting of full civil rights to
non-Arab Muslims. Yemenis believed that Islam recognized equality between Arab,
Iranian, Berber, Egyptian, and all Muslims, and that the caliph should lead the state
and society to this end. The Qaysite view, on the other hand, held that Arabs
formed a special elite. In general, Yemenis, as exemplified by Sulayman and Umar
II, felt that successful rule could be effected only by the consent and cooperation
of those ruled. Qaysites relied on authority, force, and favoritism to maintain order
and peace. (In spite of their views concerning equal rights, the Yemenis excluded
non-Arabs from their leadership, as did, of course, the Qaysites. For example, Abd
al-Malik raised thirteen sons, but only the six born of Arab mothers could be considered as possible successors; even the capable Maslamah was ineligible because
his mother was non-Arab.)

Under Muawiyah, rebellious forces among Muslims never had an opportunity
to show their colors. However, upon the death of Ali's son Hasan, who had relinquished his caliphate in Kufah to make way for Muawiyah, Hasan's brother Husayn
became the head of the house of Ali. He remained at peace with the Umayyads
until Muawiyah's death; then, refusing to recognize Yazid as successor and caliph,
he and others from the families of Muhammad's early Companions rebelled
openly. Husayn set out for Kufah with a meager force and at Karbala in Iraq was
surrounded and cut down by Umayyad supporters on the tenth of Muharram, A.H.
61 (October 10, 680). Although at the time it caused hardly a ripple across the
Muslim body politic, his death was later observed by the Shiite sect of Muslims,
who came to regard Husayn and his brother Hasan as martyrs for the faith. Karbala
has become a most holy spot, and frequently a kind of passion play is enacted on
the tenth of Muharram.

Husayn's martyrdom left the opposition to the Umayyads in a very weakened position. When Medina, the center of remaining opposition, surrendered to Yazid's
army, the rebels sought the protection of the supposed inviolability of Mecca but were
pursued by the Syrian forces. In the midst of siege operations, which shattered the
Kaaba and broke the mysterious Black Stone, news of Yazid's death led the Syrian
army to withdraw. The North Arabian party in Mecca thereupon openly supported
Abd Allah ibn al-Zubayr, who was recognized as caliph throughout Arabia, Iraq, Egypt,
Iran, al-Jazirah, and even in parts of Syria. Had he been willing to transfer his residence to Damascus, it is possible that all Muslims would have accepted his rule. Instead, Ibn al-Zubayr's followers were defeated by the South Arabians on the field of
Marj Rahit in Syria and Marwan, Muawiyah's cousin and formerly executive secretary
to Caliph Uthman, took power. Nine months later Marwan was dead, and the task of
reuniting the state fell to his son Abd al-Malik. In 692, eight years later, a Syrian army
led by al-Hajjaj defeated Ibn al-Zubayr after a six-month siege of Mecca and thus ended
the second Muslim civil war.

This violent struggle of the Umayyads with Husayn and Ibn al-Zubayr was
more than a personal or dynastic struggle; it was even more than a bitter outbreak

of political party rivalry. In the first instance, the lesser families and clans of the Quraysh of Mecca still resented and begrudged the power and dominance that the Umayyad clan had possessed in the decades just prior to the Hijrah. Added to this jealousy was indignation over the fact that Umayyads had opposed Muhammad almost to the very end; in fact, Muawiyah's father had driven Muhammad and the Muslims from Mecca. That Abu Sufyan's sons and family should inherit Muhammad's mantle was more than the Prophet's Companions could stomach.

More serious in the long run was the moving of the center of the state to Syria. It was inevitable that the wealth and worldliness of that Roman province would effect a marked transformation of the simple Arab life. Visitors from Arabia and religious scholars from Kufah were shocked at the elegance and pomp of the Damascus court and were scandalized by the flow of wine, the singing girls, and the devotion to the chase exhibited there. All these seemed far removed from the teachings of Muhammad. As the wealth and power of the ruling society increased, idleness, pleasure seeking, and disregard for Muslim virtues multiplied. It was often told, for example, that Caliph Yazid drank wine daily and had a pet monkey which would become drunk along with him. Caliph al-Walid drank only every other day, whereas Hisham drank wine only on Fridays. The prize went to al Walid II who enjoyed swimming in a pool of wine, drinking as he swam.

Such antics and the increasing centralization alienated the provinces. The regime in Damascus, starting with the reign of Abd al-Malik, introduced greater centralization in government, reliance on members of the Umayyad family in administration, an army reorganization, and more Arabization in the operations of the bureaucracy. These policies and the neglect of strict Muslim precepts fanned the propaganda fires of all malcontents of Islam. Shiite and Kharijite parties flourished in Iraq, Iran, and Khurasan. Iraq took umbrage over Syrian rule. In a sense it revived the old enmity between East and West exemplified in the wars of the Sasanid and Byzantine empires. Shiites, who held the view that the mantle of the Prophet rightfully belonged to the family of Muhammad and Ali and objected to the idea that might makes right, formed the nucleus of the opposition. At this time they were joined by the Kharijites, centered near Basrah, Fars, and the Arabian peninsula. They were religious democrats who proposed that piety be the criterion used for selecting the leader of the Muslim community; they objected to designation or inheritance, as claimed by the Umayyads and the Shiites. Instead, the consensus of the faithful should determine the leader.

The third subversive party was that of the Abbasids, led first by Muhammad, a great-grandson of al-Abbas, who in turn was an uncle of the Prophet. This Muhammad circulated the story that one of Ali's grandsons on his deathbed had transferred the rights of the Alids (followers of Ali) to the Abbasid family. Beginning about the year 740, Abbasids posed as the leaders of the House of Hashim—Alid as well as Abbasid—and from their headquarters south of the Dead Sea gathered under their standard all anti-Umayyads of Islam. The Umayyads should have seen the handwriting on the wall when many Arabs in Syria, finding life too comfortable, refused to answer the call to arms, forcing Marwan II to depend upon Qaysite forces from al-Jazirah.

The most valuable support to Alids and Abbasids came from Arab and non-Arab Muslims of Iran and Khurasan, who objected to an inferior position, demanded the equality preached in Islam, and rebelled against Marwanid policies of expansion and authoritarian rule. The organizational structure of the Umayyad Empire was decaying rapidly. An atmosphere of petty, vicious, and sometimes murderous rivalry surrounded the court; and in every corner of the empire there was strife between the two Arab parties. Such violent partisanship, coupled with the Sybarite life of many Arab leaders, invited rebellion everywhere and played into the hands of non-Arab Muslims. The Abbasids utilized these factors to the full in their propaganda in the east and gathered Iranians, Khurasanians, Shiites, Alids, and all the malcontents around their banner, for which they chose the Prophet's color of black. The Umayyads' and Alids' banners were white; that of the Kharijites, red.

In June 747, Abu al-Abbas, a great-great-grandson of al-Abbas, raised the standard of revolt, and under his Iranian agent a band of Iranians, Khurasanians, and South Arabians took the city of Merv. Iraq fell in 749, and Abu al-Abbas was recognized in Kufah as caliph. Marwan II met the rival force early in 750 on the bank of the Zab, a tributary of the Tigris. The great Abbasid victory there opened all Syria, and Damascus surrendered in April 750. At an infamous banquet near Jaffa some eighty Umayyads were murdered; other members of the family were hunted from one end of the empire to the other in an Abbasid attempt to extirpate the entire Umayyad family. Among the few who escaped was Hisham's grandson, Abd al-Rahman, who made his way to Spain and established the great Umayyad caliphate of Cordoba.

Abu al-Abbas moved the capital of Islam from Damascus to Kufah, establishing Iraq as the center of the Abbasid empire. The East had been triumphant over the West.

REFERENCES

Volumes cited at the end of Chapter 4 are pertinent to this chapter.

Crone, Patricia, and Martin Hinds. *God's Caliph: Religious Authority in the First Centuries of Islam.* Cambridge: Cambridge University Press, 1986. A detailed examination of the use of the title "caliph," and a revisionist interpretation of the role of the Umayyads as religious leaders.

Dennett, D. C. *Conversion and the Poll Tax in Early Islam.* Cambridge: Harvard University Press, 1950. This volume deals with one of the most vexatious problems of the Umayyads.

Fahmy, Aly Mohamed. *Muslim Naval Organization in the Eastern Mediterranean from the Seventh to the Tenth Century A.D.* 2d ed. Cairo: National Publication and Printing House, 1966. A detailed study of naval centers with a chapter on shipbuilding materials.

Glubb, John B. *The Great Arab Conquests.* Englewood Cliffs, N.J.: Prentice-Hall, 1964. A military history by an English general with long experience in the Middle East.

Hawting, G. R. *The First Dynasty of Islam: The Umayyad Caliphate, AD 661–750.* Carbondale: Southern Illinois University Press, 1987. This is a careful and balanced political and military history with especially important information on tribal relations with the Umayyads.

Morony, Michael G. *Iraq After the Muslim Conquest.* Princeton, N.J.: Princeton University Press, 1984. The continuity of Sasanid with Islamic Iraq is examined in the areas of administration, taxes, and ethnic and religious groups.

Shaban, M. A. *The Abbasid Revolution.* Cambridge: Cambridge University Press, 1970. The volume is a detailed account of the Arab conquest of Iran and Khurasan and highlights the importance of assimilation between Arabs and Iranians up to the Abbasid victory.

Sharon, Moshe. *Black Banners from the East: The Establishment of the Abbasid State—Incubation of a Revolt.* Jerusalem: Magnes Press, 1983. The tangled early history of the Abbasids and their use of propaganda to gain victory over the Umayyads are thoroughly traced.

al-Tabari, Muhammad ibn Jarir. *The History of al-Tabari.* Vol. 18. *Between Civil Wars: The Caliphate of Muawiyah.* Translated by Michael G. Morony. Albany: State University of New York Press, 1987. This monumental and vitally important chronicle is being published in 38 volumes, translated and annotated by various authors. They are essential original sources on which most subsequent historians have based their own work.

Watt, W. Montgomery. *A History of Islamic Spain.* Edinburgh: Edinburgh University Press, 1965. Concise coverage of all aspects of the Muslims in Spain.

7

The Flowering of the Muslim World Under the Abbasids

*T*he destruction of the Umayyads marked the opening of a new era in Muslim development. With the establishment of the Abbasid family in the caliphate, the political center of Islam shifted eastward to the Tigris-Euphrates valley. Since Arabia proper had become less significant in power and wealth, Damascus with its interior lines of communication and transport no longer held an advantage as the capital of such an empire, and Syria would become a home to pro-Umayyad rebellions as late as 842. Iraq was more productive than Syria or Egypt and profited from extensive trade with India, China, the Indies, and central Asia, whereas commerce languished in the Mediterranean and Europe. The markets of India and China were fabulous and their industry was varied; the decaying economy of the West, except for Spain and Constantinople, was yielding rapidly to the demands of a self-subsistent agricultural life.

As has been pointed out, the Abbasids had shrewdly capitalized on the many grievances that various factions held against the Umayyads and, in an adroit propaganda campaign throughout Islam, posed as the champions of each disgruntled group. However, hardly was Abu al-Abbas, the first of the line, seated on the throne than he openly showed the insincerity of Abbasid promises. Though he surrounded himself with theologians and pretended to take their advice, positions of authority and power were filled by Abbasids or by trusted family agents. The chief executioner, who was a new governmental official, always stood near the caliph's throne. Alids were honored but powerless; Kharijites, who had generally opposed the Umayyads, received little consideration; viceroys, generals, and ministers who became too wealthy or too popular were executed. Abbasid rulers governed more imperiously than their predecessors, and beheadings were the order of the day. Indeed, many governors and leaders who had engineered the Abbasid revolution were liquidated in the first years of the new regime by Abu al-Abbas, who assumed the name of al-Saffah ("the bloodletter").

It was at the end of Abu al-Abbas's reign, however, that the true installation of the new empire occurred with the ascension to the caliphate in 754 of Abu al-

Abbas's brother, Abu Jafar. This ancestor of the next thirty-five caliphs took the so-briquet al-Mansur (meaning "rendered victorious").

Like many of the Abbasids who followed, al-Mansur pursued and destroyed rivals from the Alid, or Shiite, party. On one occasion, when his troops had gone to Medina to disperse disloyal Shiites, al-Mansur discovered that his personal safety was in question, especially since his residence lay so close to hostile Kufah. The danger led him to build in 762–766 a new capital at Baghdad only 30 kilometers north of Ctesiphon, where a personal bodyguard of several thousand was on hand at all times. This new circular fortress-palace of al-Mansur grew within a few decades into the fabled luxury-filled city of Baghdad, which has thrilled the imagination of peoples from the Atlantic to the Pacific.

Again like many of the Abbasids who followed, al-Mansur had to face a struggle that eventually sapped the strength and effectiveness of the Abbasid government: the question of succession to the throne. This was an issue that increasingly served as a vehicle by which social and governmental groups could strive for power. To obtain the recognition for his son al-Mahdi, al-Mansur gave prodigious bribes to his cousin, who had been named to the line of succession by al-Saffah. Nonetheless, al-Mahdi's elder son and designated heir, Musa al-Hadi, was almost passed over by the generals and court ministers in favor of his more popular younger brother, Harun al-Rashid. The court intrigues involving the accession of later caliphs grew more direct and perfidious as time passed. By the close of the ninth century, the question of succession overshadowed every act of the caliph and dominated the thoughts of the court. By the tenth century caliphs were removed, blinded, and turned out into the streets to beg.

Succession to the caliphate and the rivalry between the Abbasids and the Alids were not, of course, the only internal struggles of the Abbasid government. Simultaneously, issues concerning theology and jurisprudence (which will be examined in the following chapter) added fuel to the political fires, while differences in governmental philosophy complicated the political jockeying at the Abbasid court almost from the beginning until the rule of al-Mamun and his immediate successors. The religious scholars preached that the life of state and society should be based on the Koran and the normal practice of traditional Arab society; whereas the other main contestants for the caliph's ear, the civil secretaries and governing officials, looked for a political structure tending toward absolutism so that their decisions would be enforced. The latter group desired the "guidance of an inspired or charismatic leader"; the former sought security in the "collective wisdom of a charismatic community." Caliph al-Mamun looked in vain for a compromise between these two factions.

THE GLORY OF BAGHDAD

During the great first century of the Abbasid caliphs Baghdad was the hub of the Middle East. Officially named Madinat al-Salam (the "City of Peace"), Baghdad was a circular garrison fortress, situated on the west bank of the Tigris near a canal connecting with the Euphrates. The central area had a mosque and a green-domed palace with an audience hall 130 feet (40 meters) in height and was surrounded by a wall, a deep moat, and two thick outer brick walls. Numerous other luxurious palaces for princes and ministers of state were erected, and beyond these rose the busy metropolis of the Muslim world.

The setting of the Abbasids in the lavish fortress capital of Baghdad ensured that their rule would follow the pattern of the Persian and Oriental monarchies of earlier days. In comparison to the unabashed prodigality of royal life in Baghdad and to the difficulty an ordinary Arab had in approaching the caliph, the rule of the Umayyads seemed the essence of frugality and simplicity.

The wealth and magnificence of the court of al-Rashid were renowned in his own day, and through the tales of *The Arabian Nights* the splendors of his court and life in Baghdad have captured popular fancy in all ages, although, in fact, he often resided elsewhere. The center of display was, of course, the palace of the caliph, where Zubaydah, al-Rashid's favorite wife, held sway. She insisted that all dishes be made of gold and the tapestries be studded with precious gems. She outfitted several hundred of her most attractive maidservants as pageboys (a fashion that was soon all the rage in Baghdad), largely to amuse her son and to divert his affections from a favorite eunuch. At a festival celebrating the marriage of a prince, a thousand matched pearls were showered upon the couple as they sat upon a jewel-encrusted mat of gold.

In Baghdad, the wheel of fortune turned easily. This aspect of Abbasid rule was exemplified in the life of Khayzuran, al-Rashid's mother. Given as a slave to al-Mahdi, she became his favorite; and her sons were recognized at an early age as the heirs to the throne. Khayzuran had her family brought to court (perhaps from Yemen); her father was given a prominent position; and her sister married a prince whose daughter was the famous Zubaydah. Before Khayzuran died she held vast properties bringing in an annual income of more than 160 million dirhams. Her power at court was inestimable, and the preference of the generals and courtiers for al-Rashid over al-Hadi was stimulated considerably by her acknowledged favor for the former. (Although Khayzuran's fortunes seemed to have steadily improved, wealth, position, and favor in Baghdad were always precarious, as the sudden fall of many favorites and advisers attested.)

At the court any word or act of flattery, a song or poem that pleased, or a deed well done was rewarded handsomely: 60,000 dinars tossed to the singer of a pleasant tune with complimentary lines; 100,000 dirhams to a poet who beguiled at the right moment; a landed estate to an entertainer or a dancer! For a sonnet extolling al-Rashid on a trivial occasion a poet was given 5,000 gold pieces, a robe of honor, ten Greek slave girls, and a horse from the imperial stables.

From the four corners of the known world came royal embassies bearing gifts and seeking the caliph's favor. Most publicized of these, at least in the West, was the mission sent by Charlemagne in 797 to secure greater safety for Frankish pilgrims to the Holy Land. No mention of this embassy has been found in Eastern sources, and there is little evidence that it ever accomplished any of its aims. Still, the trophies brought back from the journey, the most fantastic being an elephant, so magnified the incident for the West that Baghdad and Arabia became romantic,

Hashim
|
Abd al-Muttalib

Abd Allah	Abu Talib		Abbas
MUHAMMAD	ALI		Abd Allah
			Ali
	HASAN	HUSAYN	Muhammad

al-Saffah (749–754)　　　　　al-Mansur (754–775)
|
al-Mahdi (775–785)
|
al-Hadi (785–786)　　　　　al-Rashid (786–809)

al-Amin (809–813)　　　al-Mamun (813–833)　　　al-Mutasim (833–842)

Muhammad　　al-Wathiq　　　　　al-Mutawakkil (847–861)
|　　　　　(842–847)
al-Mustain　　al-Muhtadi　　al-Muwaffaq　　al-Muntasir　　al-Mutazz　　al-Mutamid
(862–866)　　(869–870)　　　　　　　　　(861–862)　　(866–869)　　(870–892)
　　　　　　　　　　　　al-Mutadid
　　　　　　　　　　　　(892–902)

al-Muktafi　　　　　al-Muqtadir (908–932)　　　al-Qahir (932–934)
(902–908)
|
al-Mustakfi
(944 946)　　al-Radi (934–940)　　al-Muttaqi (940–944)　　al-Muti (946–974)
　　　　　　　　　　　al-Qadir (991 1031)　　al-Tai (974–991)
　　　　　　　　　　　al-Qaim (1031 1075)
　　　　　　　　　　　Muhammad
　　　　　　　　　　　al-Muqtadi (1075–1094)
　　　　　　　　　　　al-Mustazhir (1095–1118)

al-Mustarshid (1118–1135)　　　　　al-Muqtafi (1136–1160)
|
al-Rashid (1135–1136)　　　　　　al-Mustanjid (1160–1170)
　　　　　　　　　　　　　　　al-Mustadi (1170–1180)
　　　　　　　　　　　　　　　al-Nasir (1180–1225)
　　　　　　　　　　　　　　　al-Zahir (1225–1226)
　　　　　　　　　　　　　　　al-Mustansir (1226–1242)
　　　　　　　　　　　　　　　al-Mustasim (1242–1258)

The Abbasid Caliphs

incredible, and fabulous places and Harun al-Rashid a person in some far-off never-never land.

Intellectual interests of the Abbasids, hand in hand with imperial munificence, produced a great cultural flowering. The learning of the Greco-Romans, the Iranians, and the Hindus was translated into Arabic and assimilated into Muslim culture. Arabic became the common language not only for theology and jurisprudence but for philosophy, science, and the humanities. History, political treatises, literature, poetry, and etiquette came largely from Iran; astronomy and mathematics, from India; philosophy, medicine, and science, from Greece. By the middle of the ninth century the main works of Aristotle, Plato, Euclid, Ptolemy, Hippocrates, and Galen had been translated into Arabic and were well known the length and breadth of the Islamic world. Royal patronage set the stage for translations and the expansion and dissemination of knowledge. Every prince, governor, and high official followed the same course and became, on a lesser scale, a patron of scholars.

ADMINISTRATIVE ORGANIZATION

The Khurasani soldiery was the power that had raised the Abbasids to the caliphate; and for several generations a Khurasan bodyguard maintained imperial authority in Baghdad and elsewhere. Eastern, or Iranian, influences grew apace at the court. After the building of Baghdad, Iranian dress, manners, and techniques spread quickly throughout the empire, especially in fashionable society, although Arabic remained the language of administration and court culture.

The Umayyads had advisers and ministers heading various departments of the government. Under the Abbasids, however, there arose the office of chief minister, the vizir, who became the alter ego of the caliph. The vizir's power was almost unlimited and the office was frequently handed down from father to son. The first family of vizirs was the famous Barmakids of the second half of the eighth century. Khalid ibn Barmak, son of a Buddhist chief priest of Balkh, held the confidence of al-Saffah and al-Mansur. Khalid served as minister of finance and then as governor, became a general, and acted as guardian of al-Rashid. Khalid amassed a great fortune; on one occasion he was forced to pay 3 million dirhams of taxes which as governor he had not forwarded to Baghdad. His son, Yahya, served al-Mahdi as vizir but fell into disfavor and was imprisoned by al-Hadi.

The apogee of Barmakid fortunes was reached under al-Rashid. Yahya became the first true grand vizir, issuing orders and managing the empire with great skill and profit. He favored a policy of strict centralization, both in provincial government and taxation. He became alienated from the military, who generally preferred decentralization, which advanced their interests in the provincial garrisons. Yahya's sons al-Fadl and Jafar also exercised unlimited power. The son al-Fadl followed in his father's footsteps as governor and vizir, while Jafar became al-Rashid's boon companion and confidant. The Barmakids lived in a sumptuous manner, and their generosity to their own favorites and clients became proverbial throughout the Islamic world. Yahya, however, was distressed by Jafar's personal and intimate relationship with al-Rashid, fearing that it would bring disaster. The family could not hope for social, political, or religious equality with the Abbasids. In 803, without warning, Jafar was beheaded because of policy differences in regard to Khurasan and because he had used al-Rashid's friendship to impinge too far upon royal prerogatives; Yahya, al-Fadl, and two others were imprisoned; and the Barmakid fortune—palaces, lands, and some 30 million dinars in cash—was confiscated.

Other families of vizirs rose and fell, and with them rival generals and armies. Under the Abbasids, generals were always a significant force in obtaining the throne. Following al-Rashid's reign, intense rivalry arose between two of his offspring, the voluptuary al-Amin, son of the famed Zubaydah, and the more serious and steady al-Mamun, son of an Iranian slave girl. The latter had the better generals, and with the full support of the Khurasani army, he attacked Baghdad and beheaded his caliph brother. Al-Mamun's rule of twenty years was marred by insurrections that were overcome only very slowly. Egypt was brought to obedience by 827; the Aghlabids in Tunis paid tribute, but most of North Africa was lost to the empire. On the other hand, mountainous Azerbayjan and the Caspian shores were conquered.

By 861, the succession to the throne was to be decided for a time by the leaders of the army. The rulers al-Mamun and al-Mutasim had brought Turks and Persians, some slave and some free, to Baghdad and Samarra (al-Mutasim's capital) in such numbers that they were dominent in the imperial bodyguard, which in turn controlled the caliph.

After the beginning of the tenth century, the Abbasid caliphs rapidly receded into the background as puppet rulers. Diverse groups from the geographic margins of the empire now ran its center. The old elites, including the Arab tribal leaders, the descendants of the Khurasanians long settled in Iraq, and the Abbasid family, declined in importance. Powerful captains in the eastern and western provinces seized authority and established autonomous Muslim states. The political unity of Islam, which had already been cracked in the 750s by the establishment of the Umayyad state in Spain, was gradually shattered with the advent of the military groups who controlled the Abbasid caliphate.

ECONOMIC AND SOCIAL LIFE

The bases of Abbasid wealth rested on agriculture and a century of relatively capable, honest, and stable administration of the provinces. Caliph al-Mansur established such a vigilant and judicious system of government throughout the empire and enforced such thrift that it took more than a century of profligate largesse to dislocate the economy of the state. In Iraq the ancient canal system initially was operated so efficiently and extended to such a degree that productivity rose. In that same century imperial revenues from Egypt, Syria, and Iran showered great wealth upon the ruling circles and the inhabitants of the capital cities.

As a natural corollary to this organized agriculture and governmental stability, a flourishing commerce and, for that age, an advanced technical industry arose. The great preponderance of commerce was in the nature of "domestic" trade. Caravans plied the trade routes from the Indus to the Pyrenees, distributing the wares of each province throughout the empire and exchanging manufactures of Iran for those of Egypt, carpets of Tabaristan for paper of Baghdad. Handsome profits were realized, but great fortunes were as easily lost.

The bulk of "foreign" trade was with the Far East. From Baghdad and Basrah, Muslim merchants carried their goods by sea to China, India, and the Archipelago, but the main route to China lay overland through Samarkand. A flourishing trade across the Sahara subsequently developed between the North African Muslims and the populations of the Senegal River region. Trade with Italy, France, and Germany, or with Constantinople, Russia, and Scandinavia, was undoubtedly profitable. It seemed so trivial, however, that Muslim traders left it for the most part to Christian and Jewish itinerants. Goods from the Middle East were too expensive and too refined for barbarous Western tastes, and the West had little to offer in exchange.

Concurrent with the rich agriculture and brisk commerce of the Abbasid empire there developed an active industry in every province. Artisan traditions of the ancient Middle East had never perished, and under a relatively secure political system these industries revived and expanded. Textiles of linen, cotton, silk, and wool were the most important. Although each area produced high-quality fabrics of many types, every city or province excelled in some particular pattern or technique; carpets from Bukhara, silk kerchiefs from Kufah, linens from Egypt, damask from Damascus, and brocades from Shiraz gained world renown. Special skills were often localized, and families guarded trade secrets, which were passed on as prized possessions from father to son through the centuries.

The science of paper making was acquired from China, and by the tenth century, paper mills existed in Iran, Iraq, and Egypt; in the twelfth century one was built in Spain. Paper made from flax facilitated the production of books on an enormous scale. Private and public libraries spread widely; paper was even made that was light enough to be transported by carrier pigeon. Fine glass was produced in Egypt, and the glass industry flourished in Syria. The ceramic industry in the Middle East reached back into the most distant past, and the Abbasid era created some of the finest potteries and glazed tile; tin glazing and luster painting were used to create painted ornamentation. Samarkand, Rayy, Baghdad, and Damascus won fame for their decorated porcelains and their fine blues, greens, and turquoise shades. Middle Eastern artisans were equally skilled in the shaping, working, and hammering of metals: iron, steel, copper, brass, silver, and gold. Other industries of great note manufactured dyes, perfume, jewelry, leather, inlaid and decorated wood, and enamelwork on wood and metal. Soap manufacture in Syria produced hand soaps and colored perfumed toilet soaps.

The Middle East in the eighth and ninth centuries utilized many of the arts and techniques of handicraft of China, India, Iran, and the East Roman Empire, and those of the early civilizations of Greece, Egypt, and Mesopotamia. The synthesis of these gave great life to Muslim industry, which was regarded in Europe as the marvel of the ages. The slow movement of Middle Eastern knowhow across the Mediterranean and over the Pyrenees gave rise to the development of similar handicrafts in Europe.

The Abbasid championing of non-Arab people within the Muslim Empire promoted a rapid Arabization of the empire. Iranians, Berbers, Syrian Christians, Copts, and others began to speak Arabic in their daily lives. Science, philosophy, literature, and books of knowledge from other cultures and tongues were rendered into Arabic. And an Arab civilization evolved in which poets, scholars, musicians, merchants, soldiers, viziers, and concubines were considered cultural Arabs; little heed was given to parentage or birthplace.

Although Arab civilization prevailed in the Abbasid era from the borders of China to the Pyrenees, there was never more than a fleeting political unity. The followers of Ali and his descendants were never completely mollified, and more and more religious sects arose to battle against authority. As more of the subject population became Muslim the cohesion of the Muslim ruling elite and its mutual loyalty declined; instead, local attachments and loyalties grew, while allegiance to the central government and the caliphate relatively declined. Social and economic ills disturbed the empire periodically. Ambitious and not too loyal soldiers sought to carve out their own principalities whose armed forces increasingly were based on professional cavalry, often recruited from Turks or Berbers. Centered upon a land area, communications and transportation over most of the Abbasid empire were costly, slow, and tedious. Distant provinces were difficult to control; and, as caliphs grew less and less concerned with the grueling task of governing, even nearer provinces flaunted the wishes of the Abbasid rulers. Revenues declined by about one-half from 788 to 915. The increasing salinity of the soil in central Iraq sharply reduced agriculture and the taxes derived from it, resources located at the center of the empire and formerly very important. The canals in Iraq were not properly maintained; taxes were raised and collected in a harsh manner, often through a system of tax farming; and the insurgencies of the late ninth century created widespread havoc. When Abbasid caliphs degenerated into mere puppets in the hands of bureaucrats in Baghdad and then were dominated by generals, governors and soldiers in the provinces opted for local autonomy.

Local rulers, however, followed the common patterns of Abbasid government and administration, and Muslim civilization continued to prevail. Political loyalties might differ as more often than not religious doctrines did; but artists, men of letters, scientists, merchants, and travelers were as much at home in Cordoba as in Cairo, Baghdad, or Samarkand. Provincial governors, even those who still paid tribute to Baghdad, imitated as sumptuously as they could the court at Baghdad. From India to Spain palaces and mosques were built where petty princes lived in the grand manner among poets, scholars, artists, soldiers, dancing slaves, and fawning courtiers.

SPAIN AND NORTH AFRICA

Abd al-Rahman, grandson of the Umayyad caliph Hisham, escaped from Abbasid vengeance, and, making his way in disguise through Syria, Egypt, and North Africa, reestablished the Umayyad dynasty in Spain in 756. First as amirs and then in the tenth century as caliphs, the rulers maintained at Cordoba a court that enjoyed an eminence that rivaled its contemporary in Baghdad. Many distinguished scholars, scientists, and literati of the Muslim world flourished under their patronage. At its zenith in the tenth century, Cordoba had 500,000 inhabitants, 700 mosques, 300 public baths, and a royal palace comprising 400 rooms which ranked second only in size and splendor to those at Baghdad and Constantinople.

Umayyad power, however, began to deteriorate toward the middle of the tenth century. The palace chamberlains seized control; and Muslim Spain disintegrated into smaller states (Seville, Málaga, Toledo, Saragossa, and Granada) under the leadership of various families. In the eleventh century, resurgent Christian Spain began a drive that ended in 1492 with the capitulation of the ruler of Granada, the last Muslim prince in Spain. Though Muslim law and government were terminated, the deportation of the Spanish Muslims (Moriscos) was not enforced until a special edict was issued in 1609 by Philip III.

In 788 Idris, a descendant of Ali, established an independent Sunnite regime in Morocco. From their capital at Fez the Idrisids ruled most of Morocco for two centuries, firmly implanting Islam in that corner of Africa and establishing a flourishing trade with sub-Saharan Africa. Arabic became the dominant language in the towns, while Berber was used widely in the countryside. The Idrisids succumbed to the Umayyads of Cordoba. In the middle of the eleventh century a reformist and fundamentalist religious-military-tribal group, the Murabit dynasty (Almoravides) conquered western Algeria, Morocco, and southern Spain and established Marrakesh and Seville as their capitals. The Murabits governed with the support of the men of religion and the military backing of the tribes. When Christians began to take districts in Spain from the Murabits, their legitimacy declined while their dogmatism offended many Muslims. The luxuries, vices, and complexities of civilization also prepared the way for the submission of the Murabits in the twelfth century to the Muwahhids (Almohades), a band of Muslim Berber reformers originating in the Atlas region of Morocco. The founder of the Muwahhids claimed to be the Mahdi, or the expected deliverer, and he reinforced this religious claim with tribal military alliances. His successor, Abd al-Mumin (reigned 1130–1163), destroyed the Murabits and conquered part of Spain. Responding to the Norman expansion from Sicily into North Africa, he gained control of Algeria and Tunisia, and took Tripoli. He then established the principle of succession to power through dynastic inheritance within his family, and thereby transformed the nature of the state. The Muwahhids became patrons of philosophers. They economically united most of Northwestern Africa, providing economic prosperity. Rebellions in Tunisia, the inevitable gap between religious ideals and political reality, tribal disaffections, deportation from Spain, and the rise of new and vigorous alternative leadership led to the disintegration of the Muwahhids in the middle of the thirteenth century.

Harun al-Rashid appointed Ibrahim ibn al-Aghlab governor of Africa (roughly, modern Algeria and Tunisia) in 800. For a century the Aghlabids ruled as free amirs from Qayrawan in Tunisia. Their fleets ravaged the coasts of Italy and France, seizing Malta, Sicily, and Sardinia. The great mosque of Qayrawan was built by the

Aghlabids and soon became for western Muslims a venerated shrine, next in importance and holiness to Mecca, Medina, and Jerusalem. But in 909 the Aghlabids were engulfed by a Shiite uprising which placed on the throne a ruler who claimed to be a descendant of Fatimah, the Prophet's daughter.

Meanwhile, beginning with the middle of the ninth century, a succession of clever governors and two short-lived Turkish dynasties, Tulunids and Ikhshidids, ruled Egypt in the name of the Abbasids, who received some revenues from that distant province, but who exercized no real power there. Conversion to Islam had been slow, and the Muslims remained largely an urban-based minority group. Foreign slave and mercenary armies were recruited by the new dynasties.

In the second half of the tenth century Egypt was conquered by the Fatimids of North Africa, whose claim of descent from Ali and Fatimah (Fatimids) persuaded many to accept them as the valid leaders of the Muslim state. With the help of North African Berber troops, the dynasty which had overcome the Aghlabids and various Sunnite and Kharijite forces built a navy and recruited slaves for an expanded army. Upon their conquest of Egypt, the Fatimids took the title of caliph and transferred their capital from Tunisia to the new city of Cairo, which they planned and built.

Under the Tulunids and Ikhshidids and to a great extent under the Fatimids, the Egyptian court and its society experienced a prosperity and a great burst of accomplishment in commerce, art, letters, and learning. No longer did even a part of the produce or taxes of Egypt flow to Baghdad. Fatimid prosperity came from the peace and security given to the peasants of Egypt, and from imports of gold from Nubia, a sound coinage, textile manufacturing, and a flourishing international trade. The majority of the population remained Sunnite. Fatimid Egypt participated greatly in the artistic and intellectual endeavors of the Muslim world; many great works of early medieval Muslim art and architecture still extant in Egypt date from the Tulunid and Fatimid periods.

The Tulunids had added Syria to their realm and established a naval base at Acre in Palestine, and the Ikhshidids had acquired the Hijaz and Yemen. With difficulty, these areas were regained by the Fatimids, who ultimately defeated the Qarmatians in Syria and various nomadic and Turkish groups. Thus, at their height, about the year 1000, the Fatimids ruled most of the western Muslim world except Spain and northern Syria (which was under Byzantine control): the Fatimid caliph's name was mentioned in the Friday prayers from Tunisia to the Euphrates. However, because of eccentric and idle rulers, quarrels among the various ethnic units in the armies, and the inability to convince the masses of the central Middle East that Fatimid Shiism was the true version of Islam, the Fatimid empire began to break up early in the eleventh century. Vizirs then dominated the caliphs, and these ministers became heads of both the military and civil branches of government. To a considerable degree it was this disintegration that permitted first the continuation of Byzantine power in northern Syria, and, second, the incursions of the handfuls of Western knights called Crusaders, who penetrated, captured, and held the Christian Holy Land, Palestine, and the Syrian littoral in the twelfth and thirteenth centuries.

THE EASTERN PROVINCES

East and south of Baghdad the Abbasid empire was likewise succumbing to the laxity of the caliph's rule and falling into the hands of aggressive soldiers and politicians who founded ephemeral dynasties (which usually acknowledged the nominal overlordship of the Abbasids). The greatest dangers were closest to hand: the rebellions of the Zanj and the Qarmatians.

Since early Islamic times the marshlands of southern Iraq, a perfect area for guerrilla warfare, had been the scene of large-scale agricultural slavery; the slaves, who were harshly treated, were mostly of East African origins. Under the leadership of Ali ibn Muhammad, an Arab from Iran, and with the help of Arab tribal allies, they rose against their owners in 869, took Basrah, and were a major threat to the Abbasid political and social order. In 883, the caliph finally conquered the Zanj in southern Iraq, but the prosperity of that region was ruined. The Qarmatians were Ismaili Shiites (like the Fatimids in Egypt) who, starting in the ninth century, steadily attempted to overthrow Abbasid power, basing their forces in Kufah, among the nomadic tribes of Syria, and in Bahrayn and eastern Arabia generally. In 923, they conquered Basrah, and in 930 the Qarmatians raided Mecca and carried off the sacred Black Stone from the Kaaba. Internal disputes stopped their expansion, the Black Stone was returned to Mecca, and the Qarmatians became a local force enjoying peace and prosperity until the late tenth century. Although their enemies accused them of practices contrary to Islamic morality, they were most noteworthy for the existence of an advisory council whose opinions the ruler was obliged to consider.

To the east, in the ninth century the Tahirids extended their sway from Merv to the frontiers of India. They were a family of local governors who sent extensive taxes to the Abbasid caliphs, and they played a major role in the internal political life of Baghdad. The Saffarid dynasty in the ninth century spread from Sistan, destroyed the Tahirids, invaded Afghanistan, and ruled with the investiture of the caliphs but in uneasy rivalry with them. Also in the ninth century the truly independent Persian Sunni Samanid dynasty was acknowledged by the caliphs as local governors; by the tenth century, they seized all of Khurasan, but settled in Transoxiana, establishing Bukhara as their capital and Samarkand as the leading city of the state. Culture continued to flourish under Samanid rule, and the new forces were quickly assimilated, as illustrated by the Samanid ruler who invited the young Ibn Sina (Avicenna) to Bukhara and gave him free run of the state library. Under the Samanids, Firdawsi wrote his first poetry, marking the rebirth of Persian literature. From the Muslim conquest to the Samanid period, Arabic had been the language used everywhere by scholars and men of letters; this new era signaled the advent of the brilliant works of Muslim Iran, written in Persian, not Arabic.

The Turkish leader of the bodyguard of the Samanids, Alptigin, rose through the ranks to struggle for power. Forced to flee from the Samanid domain, he captured Ghaznah and established the famed Persianate Sunni Ghaznavid empire of Afghanistan and the Punjab. The most eminent of the family was Alptigin's grandson Mahmud, who led nearly a score of expeditions into India and in the eleventh century laid the foundations of the permanent

Islamization of north and northwest India. Loot from Hindu temples gave him the material strength to destroy the Samanids and extend his state to include most of the eastern provinces of the Muslim world. Although a vestige of the Ghaznavid empire remained at Lahore until 1186, decline followed rapidly on the death of Mahmud in 1030. Muslim independent states in India broke away, and Buwayhid Iranians and Seljuk Turks appeared in western areas of the Ghaznavid empire.

In Baghdad itself, the authority of the Abbasid caliph vanished almost completely. Only the appellation remained. Turkish captains of the bodyguard deposed caliphs at will; at one time three blind ex-caliphs were beggars on the streets of Baghdad. Taking the title *amir al-umara* (literally, "commander of commanders," but better, "prince of princes"), the de facto ruler imprinted his name on coins and insisted that his name be coupled with the puppet caliph in the Friday prayers.

Toward the middle of the tenth century a Shiite Iranian, Ahmad ibn Buwayh, entered Baghdad with a strong army and was recognized by the caliph as the commander of commanders. Making and unmaking caliphs openly, the Buwayhid federation of rulers was usually led by the member of the dynasty residing in Shiraz, who took various titles such as "king" or "king of kings." The Buwayhids beautified Shiraz and brought to it many learned men. For a century Shiraz rivaled Baghdad, Ghaznah, Bukhara, Cairo, and Cordoba in culture and splendor, while massive irrigation projects improved agriculture in the countryside. The Buwayhids assigned government revenues to specific employees of the state, usually for a short time, so as to pay for services. This system was subsequently adopted with modifications by other dynasties and became a hallmark of decentralized administration. In the middle of the eleventh century Buwayhid fought against Buwayhid for the position of king and this, along with the internal disagreements of their troops and the diversion of international trade to the north and south of the Buwayhid lands, made them easy prey for the Turks riding in from the east.

THE TURKS

Turkish nomads from the Kirghiz steppes of Turkestan wandered into the Transoxiana region and became partially settled there toward the end of the tenth century. Unlike earlier Turks who had served individually as professional soldiers, the new arrivals came as tribal groups, preserving their identity, and seeking permanent control of grazing lands for their animals. One of their chieftains, or khans, under the Samanids was Seljuk. For three centuries his dynasty played such an outstanding role in the Muslim world from Syria eastward and so dominated the Turkish elements of society that even today Muslim Turks of that time bear the name of Seljuk Turks.

The true founder of the dynasty, Seljuk's grandson Tughril, ascended to power rapidly in Khurasan. Defeating the Ghaznavids and ejecting the Buwayhids from Iran, Tughril entered Baghdad with an army in 1055; he was recognized King of the East and the West and *al-Sultan* (the holder of power). Henceforth, these Seljuk Sunnite rulers adopted "sultan" as their official title.

Tughril's nephew Alparslan followed as sultan and succeeded in gathering within his domain the vast lands of the Muslim world from the frontiers of China to the Mediterranean. Having expanded into Armenia and taken the Byzantine emperor prisoner in the decisive Battle of Manzikert in 1071, Alparslan opened Syria and Asia Minor to his Turkish and Kurdish nomads. His horsemen camped on the shores of the Sea of Marmara and lay astride the commercial and pilgrim routes of Asia Minor. His son, Malikshah, pushed westward and southward, taking Damascus, Jerusalem, and parts of Arabia, and threatening Fatimid Egypt, while making Isfahan his capital.

As the Seljuks became strong, they encountered the Kurdish tribal states that had reappeared in the Zagros Mountains, the mountains of northern Syria and southeastern Anatolia, and in Azerbayjan, subsequent to the decline of the Abbasids between 950 and 1050. The Kurds, who had their own language and culture, established their rule based on nomadic groups, and brought a good deal of economic prosperity to the diverse regions they controlled. They were in deadly competition with the nomadic Turkish tribes for pasturage—a competition won by the Seljuks, in part because of their superior political organization.

The political genius through the reigns of Alparslan and Malikshah was Nizam al-Mulk, their principal vizir. A cultured and versatile Iranian, Nizam al-Mulk founded the renowned Nizamiyah, an academy in Baghdad, and wrote the *Siyasatnamah,* a scholarly monograph on the science of government. Nizam also revised the calendar and is perhaps best known in the Western world as the patron of the Persian astronomer-poet Umar Khayyam.

Any semblance of unity among the Seljuks vanished in 1092 on the death of Malikshah and the assassination of Nizam al-Mulk. In prior years, there had been numerous civil wars among members of the family; upon the demise of these two leaders what little central control over the various petty Seljuk states that had existed was gradually lost. One son succeeded to the sultanate in Baghdad. A brother held Damascus and Aleppo, although these cities were soon seized by different sons. A cousin ruled Asia Minor from Konya; others possessed Jerusalem, Edessa, Mosul, Diyarbakir, and Amasya. Soon afterward, the appearance of the Crusaders from the West disrupted Seljuk rule in Syria even further, though the main branch of the dynasty maintained its hold upon Baghdad until 1194.

The death of Malikshah and the collapse of the Seljuk state definitely heralded for medieval times the end of a Muslim political entity strong enough and sufficiently organized to dominate the central Middle East. Under the rule of Malikshah, a merchant could travel alone unmolested with his goods from Samarkand to Aleppo. But within a few years intraregional political anarchy and its disastrous military chaos lured the Crusaders eastward and the Mongols westward. However, the bewildering series of successor states to the Abbasids were sometimes more successful in providing a government suitable to local conditions than had been the all-encompassing empires of the Umayyads and the Abbasids. These latter dynasties lost their power basically because the territories they controlled were too large to be ruled centrally, given the technology of the age, and because they could not find a means of gaining the support of the Muslim community. An enormous gap developed between the Islamic ideals of political life and the reality of government, a gap that neither Sunnite nor Shiite ruler could easily close. Power fell into the hands of regional dynasties who were often drawn from or based upon foreign military groups, converts to Islam, and aliens to the vast majority of the people whose lives they controlled. As the general population withdrew from public life, the new Islamic civilization flourished despite political diversity bordering on chaos. Not until the appearance of the Ottoman Turks and the Safavids in the sixteenth century did the Middle East again experience large and centralized Muslim empires that reunited political, military, and cultural accomplishments on the scale of the Umayyads and Abbasids.

REFERENCES

Titles mentioned at the end of Chapters 4 and 6 contain material pertinent to this chapter.

Abbott, Nabia. *Two Queens of Baghdad: Mother and Wife of Harun ul-Rashid.* Chicago: University of Chicago Press, 1946. Not only does this volume detail the lives of Khayzuran and Zubaydah, but it is full of the color and life of Baghdad in the eighth and ninth centuries.

Abun-Nasr, Jamil M. *A History of the Maghrib in the Islamic Period.* Cambridge: Cambridge University Press, 1987. An excellent survey.

Bacharach, Jere L. "African Military Slaves in the Medieval Middle East." *International Journal of Middle East Studies* 13 (1981): 471–495. A careful look at a controversial subject that involves questions of race as well as slavery and the military.

Canard, M. "Fatimids." *Encyclopaedia of Islam.* New ed. Vol. 2, pp. 850–862. Leiden. Brill, 1965.

Daniel, Elton L. *The Political and Social History of Khurasan Under Abbasid Rule, 747–820.* Minneapolis, Minn.: Bibliotheca Islamica, 1979. This detailed book follows the victory of small landowners in a key province and their subsequent fate, with attention to tax policy and regional particularism, as well as rural unrest.

Hodgson, Marshall G. S. *The Venture of Islam: Conscience and History in a World Civilization.* Vol. 2. *The Expansion of Islam in the Middle Periods.* Chicago: University of Chicago Press, 1974. The author discusses the establishment of the international Islamic civilization.

Lassner, Jacob. *The Shaping of Abbasid Rule.* Princeton, N.J.: Princeton University Press, 1980. Separate essays cover the topics of crises over the succession to the throne, the clients of the Abbasids, the army, the city of Baghdad, and the royal palace.

Le Strange, Guy. *Baghdad During the Abbasid Caliphate.* London: Oxford University Press, 1924. An interesting description of the great city at its height.

Mottahedeh, Roy P. *Loyalty and Leadership in an Early Islamic Society.* Princeton, N.J.: Princeton University Press, 1980. This fascinating exploration of the values prevalent in Buwayhid society examines oaths of allegiance, patron-client relationships, membership in social categories, and the role of the king as arbiter of society.

Pipes, Daniel. *Slave Soldiers and Islam: The Genesis of a Military System.* New Haven, Conn.: Yale University Press, 1981. In a broad essay, the author examines the evolution of Muslim military history.

Salibi, Kamal S. *Syria Under Islam.* Vol. 1. *Empire on Trial, 634–1097.* Delmar, N.Y.: Caravan Books, 1977. The complicated history of the tribes of Syria is carefully presented and analyzed, along with a general discussion of Syrian history during this period.

Shaban, M. A. *Islamic History: A New Interpretation.* Vol. 2. *A.D. 750–1055 (A.H. 132–448).* Cambridge: Cambridge University Press, 1976. This valuable and occasionally polemical book centers on the themes of trade, taxes, and regions as bases for interpreting the history of the Abbasids and their successors.

Waines, David. "The Third Century Internal Crisis of the Abbasids." *Journal of the Economic and Social History of the Orient* 20 (1977): 282–306. In the ninth century an internal economic and political crisis gripped the Abbasids; this crisis is ably analyzed and shown to be as important as the external threats to the empire's central authority.

8

Muslim Theology and Law

THEOLOGY

The uncomplicated, direct, and ethical religion preached by Muhammad appealed to the untutored Arab of Mecca and Medina and to the unlettered nomad of the desert. In general, it easily adjusted to the needs of the theocratic state under Muhammad and the Companions who immediately followed him at Medina.

Upon the spread of Islam and Muslim rule beyond Arabia and the establishment of regimes based on military power, Muhammad's theocracy faced unforeseen conditions. Succeeding generations of Muslims were exposed to the intellectualized philosophies current in the acquired provinces and developed a finely drawn Islamic theology.

Though the political capital of Islam was transferred to Damascus and then to Baghdad, Medina maintained its ascendancy as a center of Muslim theology for several centuries. Opinions not subscribed to by the thinkers of Medina were declared to be in serious error. Divergent views led to the formation of groups branded as heretical by the Medinan theologians.

At the time of the dispute between Ali and Muawiyah, the Kharijites broke away, rejecting the concept of compromise that Ali proposed. They believed that might does not make right and that only God can judge among people. A Muslim who committed great sins was no longer a Muslim. They nevertheless professed their way of life to be the right way, and when they quoted the Koran, "be patient until God judges between us," they meant that the fight should be continued until God granted them victory. The Kharijites were against both Ali and Muawiyah and opposed the growing organized structure of society in which they were being enveloped. Coming from a nomadic background, they found settled life in large groups alien to their spirits. Shortly thereafter, the Kharijites hardened into a sect that held that good works are the measure of faith and the only path to salvation. They also insisted on pursuing openly and literally egalitarianism and the commandment to preach to all persons a righteous life and to restrain them, by the sword if necessary, from doing evil.

Laxity of life in Damascus induced others to uphold belief in the adequacy of inherent faith in attaining personal salvation. In essence, these Murjites, as they were termed, were opposites of Kharijites, for they readily accepted rulers whose conduct was sinful. They held that as long as persons profess God's unity, they should not be judged because of their sins (unless they worship idols), but should be accepted as believers. In the first two centuries of Islam, the Murjites' concern was to preserve the unity of the Muslim community. Rebuked by Medina, they eased their ethics to political accommodation under the Umayyads and found their redemption in the doctrine of predestination. When the Abbasid revolution approached, Murjites supported the Umayyad claim to the caliphate, but once the Abbasids had won, they found no reason to oppose them.

In the formative period of Muslim theology Mutazilites held a view between these two extremes. By the time of Harun al-Rashid, Mutazilites, accepting the doctrine of free will, were entangled in Aristotelian and Hellenistic Christian philosophies and engaged in adjusting Islam to Greek logic. Adhering to rationalism, free will, and philosophical theology in the ninth century, they lost much of their following when Muslim theology was pronounced in the tenth century by al-Ashari of Baghdad and fixed in the early twelfth century by al-Ghazali (Algazel) of Khurasan.

A myriad of theological questions appeared, several arising over and over again. Foremost was the question of God's omnipotence in relation to human responsibility or, as it devolved to the religious plane, the problem of predestination and free will. The second great problem related to the nature of the Koran: Was it uncreated and eternal or was it created? The third troublesome subject centered upon the nature of God and His attributes. If God could hear, see, and speak, was not His unity in doubt?

Mutazilites held that if God rendered punishment for deeds that had been predetermined, He would be an unjust God, and that therefore the human being does have free will. They professed that the Koran had been created in time by God and that between God and His creation, the human being, there is no resemblance. On other points Mutazilites believed that God does not forgive the grave sinner except after repentance, and being just, He punishes all persons equally. They stood between Kharijites and Murjites with regard to the Umayyads and their sins, saying that judgment should not be rendered. On the question of one's duty to judge others, they asserted that one should command one's fellows to follow the right path. Wrongful actions should be forbidden—which meant that armed revolt against an unjust ruler was justified when there was a chance of success.

According to al-Ashari, the apparent contradiction embodied in the concepts of predestination and free will was explained by the doctrine that human beings are responsible for their actions but only because God has willed it. For al-Ashari and others, including the theologian ibn Hanbal, the Koran was preexistent and eternal; the words or expressions were created and revealed by the angels to the Prophet only as guides to the eternal Word. The apparent contradiction between the unity of God and His other, more human attributes referred to in the Koran was explained by the dogma that God is One and Eternal, but that His existence is not the same as existence in the world, and therefore one should not speak of God in human terms. Thus, these attributes are real but divested of all anthropomorphism.

Many other points in theology were established by al-Ashari, including the dogma that right and wrong are what they are because God declared them to be so, and that God could inflict pain in this world or in the next without being unjust.

Even al-Ashari, however, was cursed by the religious men of Medina, because they considered his theology too rationalistic and too far removed from the Islam of Muhammad. Asharite scholastics remained unpopular in Baghdad until the advent of al-Ghazali, whose writing and teaching united the modified Greek logic and philosophy of al-Ashari with Muhammad's religion to create a faith that has remained the basis of the mainstream of Islam to the present day.

THE SCIENCE OF TRADITION

When the word of the Koran did not appear to give the answer to some specific problem, the divines of Medina and the pious throughout Islam looked for guidance in the words and actions of Muhammad or in those which he had allowed. Arab tribes were devoted to traditions and normal practice, and custom (*sunnah*) was a powerful force in their lives. In the new community established by Muhammad and severed from many tribal customs, the life of Muhammad served as the touchstone for proper Muslim thought and conduct.

Early in Muslim history great collections of the statements and deeds of Muhammad were made. Aishah was the source of hundreds; and the city of Medina, where a great many Companions resided, became a center of the compilations. Each saying was called a *hadith,* or a tradition; and the whole body of these traditions was known as the hadith. Each hadith had an introduction giving its full pedigree of transmission. Scholars developed a science with respect to these traditions to establish which were authentic and which spurious. Many traditions were fabricated, particularly in Iraq, starting in the eighth century, and the task of selecting which ones were sound and which were forged became a difficult one. Each sect of Islam, each lawyer, and each theologian chose the most suitable traditions on which to base some contentions or press a point.

The first written collections were instigated for judicial ends, and each city had its own. By the ninth century the literature on the subject had grown so voluminous that it brought about the evolution of the science of hadith. The author al-Bukhari, who died in 870, published his collection under the title *al-Sahih* ("The Genuine"). Containing over 7,000 hadiths, it was generally pronounced the most authoritative source of tradition. One of the largest collections was that of Ahmad ibn Hanbal, who assembled nearly 30,000 to form a corpus of tradition that served as the basis of his legal and theological systems. Each major Muslim city or province eventually adopted as standard practice the collected traditions of one of the noted theologians.

Acceptance of a body of traditions in time established for Islam the Sunnah, a new customary, or common, law. Attachment to these traditions by any Muslims and a willingness to abide by the consensus of the community and its religious scholars identified them as following the Islamic Sunnah and thus gave them the name of Sunnites.

Muslim Law

Early Muslims, pious and devout, perceived hardly any difference between law and religion. Only God knew the perfect law, and coexisting with Him was natural law, comprising right and justice. Islam, then, was the ideal system, and its law pointed the "right path"(*shariah*) to an individual's salvation; divine law recognized good and evil. Law preceded the state, which existed only to enforce the law. If the state failed to enforce the law, the state's validity ceased. The caliph as head of the state was charged principally with the enforcement of law. Divine law was inexorable and unchanging, allowing no consideration for time or place. Muslims living beyond the pale of Islam still were bound by the law. Law upheld the common good of the community and served individual interests only when these conformed to those of the Muslim community as a whole. Islamic law had to be observed in good faith and sincerity; duplicity and dissimulation were repudiated.

Muslim systems of law, both Sunnite and Shiite, grew largely from two roots: the Koran and the traditions. However, caliphs and their judges, even in Medina, discovered early that the Koran and the traditions were not explicit with respect to many situations with which they had to deal. In the absence of a definite statement, judges and lawyers resorted to the use of analogy to some instance in the Koran or the traditions in deciding a case brought before them. Although the strictest judges did not practice analogy, on the grounds that it left too much to human judgment, it was, nevertheless, adopted widely in the eighth century as a legal aid, and from precedent to precedent became an integral part of the shariah. In the same century Malik ibn Anas, a jurist-theologian of Medina, compiled a book of traditions that incorporated many of the local juridical customs and practices. This procedure introduced the institution of consensus (*ijma*), which at first was reserved to Medina.

In the next generation al-Shafii drew together these several elements and expanded consensus to include the Muslim community at large. In thus establishing Sunni Islam, al-Shafii was instrumental in advancing the idea in law of following the "idealized practice as recognized by representative scholars." Questions of law were to be resolved ultimately through the four fundamental principles: the Koran; the traditions, as communicating the Sunnah; analogy; and consensus. Al-Shafii's general doctrine became widely accepted, with the modification of restricting consensus to that of scholars rather than to the whole community. The inclusion of consensus in the principles of the shariah established the classical Sunni theory of the roots of jurisprudence and enabled Islam through the centuries to adapt its institutions to a changing world.

Another additional source of Muslim law has been private opinion (*ray.*) Private opinion was never quite accepted as a fifth principle of the shariah, but it was widely practiced. Early caliphs employed it extensively until bitter complaints that human legislation corrupted divine law forced its abandonment. Nevertheless, most caliphs and later rulers were compelled by administrative necessity to issue laws and decrees that were sanctioned almost wholly by opinion. Such laws and regulations were later termed *Kanuns,* from the Greek and Latin word. Thus, Muslim canon law meant civil and secular law, whereas Islamic divine law was the equivalent of Western canon law. In addition to the theoretical and theological bases of the law, and the decrees of the rulers, Islamic law in the Middle East was also influenced in practice by the preexisting Roman, Sasanid, and Greek laws of the provinces conquered by the Muslim armies.

FOUR SUNNI SCHOOLS

The Sunni jurists accepted the five roots of the shariah but differed as to which traditions were genuine and the weight that ought to be allowed to analogy, consensus, and opinion in establishing a viable Muslim code of law. At the time of al-Mansur, it was suggested that he codify and enforce the diverse laws in the empire. Local particularism, however, won the day, and numerous systems prevailed among the Muslims. Since the eleventh century four principal schools of legal practice have been recognized as permissible by the Sunnites, and law schools such as al-Azhar in Cairo have carried instruction in all four rites.

In point of development the earliest school was the Hanafite. Abu Hanifah, legal scholar of Kufah and Baghdad, who died in 767, held a tolerant view on the use of analogy and consensus and particularly emphasized the value and necessity of private opinion and judgment by those administering the law. By the eleventh century, however, a strong conservative movement closed the door on further innovations in the matter of juridical opinions. Henceforth, judges could allow only opinions previously rendered and were required to adhere closely to the Hanafite teachings. The Hanafite rite was the established procedure followed in the Ottoman Empire, parts of India, and central Asia.

Historically, the second orthodox school was the Malikite. Malik ibn Anas of Medina, who died in 795, codified the traditions of Islam and acknowledged the authority of the consensus of the Medina community. Malikite jurists, however, never equivocated in their stand against general consensus, private opinion, and the broad use of analogy. The Malikite school was accepted in Spain, and still prevails in North Africa, Upper Egypt, and eastern Arabia.

Next to the Hanafite school in general acceptance has been that of the Shafiite. The jurist al-Shafii studied under Malik in Medina and taught in Baghdad and Fustat (Cairo), where he died in 820. The Shafiite rites permitted wider use of consensus than those of the Malikites, and al-Shafii asserted that consensus was the safest and highest legislative authority in Islam. The Shafiite school dominates legal practice in Palestine, Lower Egypt, eastern Africa, western and southern Arabia, parts of India, and Indonesia.

The Hanbalite school was the fourth and smallest among the orthodox schools. Its founder, Ahmad ibn Hanbal, a student of al-Shafii, rebelled against the teachings of his master. The Hanbalites accepted neither private opinion nor analogy and scorned the use of consensus. They maintained that the only valid basis of Muslim law, besides the Koran, was the traditions. For his refusal to disavow his views Ibn Hanbal was beaten and persecuted by al-Mamun and al-Mutasim. Despite Ibn Hanbal's apparent personal appeal, as suggested by the 500,000 who attended his funeral in Baghdad in 855, Hanbalism outside Baghdad was too rigid to be popular or practical over the centuries and had only scattered followers in Syria, Egypt, and Iraq. After the Ottoman conquest the doctrine perished, to be revived in the eighteenth century by the Wahhabis in central Arabia, where the Hanbalite rites are still observed.

In addition to the four principal codes of law, another body of law evolved from a court practice of submitting the summary of involved and important cases to a learned jurist, as a consultant, for an opinion known as a *fatwa,* while the opinion giver was called a *mufti.* Fatwas, which presented the legal issues and indicated the proper decision, were later collected and used as guides to the courts in rendering judgments. Until the advent of the Ottoman Empire, muftis more or less remained free from control or restraint by the government.

RATIONALISM

In essence, all of these jurist-theologians were attempting to fashion a system of law by a synthesis of Islamic truths and the highly refined and developed rationalism of the Greek philosophers. In the Umayyad period, those favoring the introduction of Hellenistic logic into Muslim theology were called Mutazilites. The arguments regarding the nature of God and the Koran rocked the empire. The debates lasted for several centuries, and the particular views of the reigning caliph determined which opinion flourished at any given time. Hisham put to death several who preached the doctrines of the created Koran and of free will. Caliph al-Mamun persecuted all but Mutazilites and ruthlessly suppressed all who did not support free thought. Caliph al-Mutawakkil ousted the Mutazilites. Eventually, theologians under al-Ashari and the learned founders of the schools of religious law brought the controversy to rest, and established theology, tradition, and law as separate from, and occasionally antagonistic toward, the caliphate and the state apparatus it controlled.

The great philosophic efforts, however, had the effect of taking Islam away from the people and ran the danger of destroying it as a practical religion. People desired a living experience of God, not a metaphysical or conceptual discussion of religion. To the simple Muslim, God was a personage always near at hand. One could talk to God, as a Bedouin's prayer in a time of drought attested: "O God of the devotees, what is the matter with us and You? You used to give us water—What has possessed You? Do send rain down on us. Exert Yourself!"

ASCETICISM AND MYSTICISM

In the first years after Muhammad, piety in Islam sometimes took the form of asceticism. In a manner similar to the practices of holy men in Christian Syria and Mesopotamia, pious Muslims seeking knowledge of God and salvation for themselves adopted and preached asceticism. Study of the traditions of the Prophet, prayer, fasting, solitary meditations, and prolonged vigils would lead the soul to God. Poverty, humility, patience, repentance, and silence in this world would save believers seeking godliness from eternal chastisement and permit them to come into the presence of God by means of the annihilation of the self, to taste the unalloyed and unabated joys of paradise, and to abide therein to eternity.

In spite of a waning of ascetic tendencies in the Abbasid period, the traits and virtues of asceticism remained strong forces among both male and female Muslims across the centuries. Sultans, generals, rich merchants, judges, and scholars might not adopt ascetic practices themselves, but they usually paid open deference, sometimes approaching veneration, to those who did.

Toward the end of the eighth century, mysticism entered into Islam with a great force. Theology and philosophy had not greatly affected the masses, and after the first half of the ninth century the majority of the literate community found little of interest in the hair splitting of the scholastics. For religious experience the masses turned to mysticism. Knowledge of God was to be achieved by the inner light of the individual soul, not by the intellectual methods of the philosopher.

Muhammad the Prophet came to be seen as the perfect or ideal human being, without sin, and popular piety viewed him as a model for what human life should be. The major roots of Islamic mysticism were the Koran and the traditions of Muhammad; to them were added the quietism and occult practices and beliefs of Buddhist stories, Hindu monism, Zoroastrian dualism, Gnostic ideas from Iraq, and miracles from the Gospels. The second coming of Christ became the doctrine of the coming of the Mahdi, the rightly-guided one, who would bring complete victory to Islam.

The essence of mysticism was love, an ecstatic communion with the divine, and final absorption into the godhead. Nothing existed but God. To know and love God and to be united with Him, without any thought of reward or salvation, was an emotional means of purifying the soul. God was eternal beauty and the path leading to Him was love. The mystic sought to lose the self in life with God and he felt a sense of union with the godhead that offended nonmystical Muslims. The process of comingling self with God could best be achieved by love and thought of God and a unifying of the senses which might be exercised as one. A mystic poet has expressed the thought in these lines:

My eye conversed whilst my tongue gazed;
My ear spoke and my hand listened;
And whilst my ear was an eye to behold everything visible,
My eye was an ear listening to song.

Until the twelfth century, popular preachers who based much of their message on mysticism and won their wide appeal through mysticism and miracles were despised by philosophers and theologians and were frequently adjudged guilty of heresy. Then, as al-Ashari had made rationalism and Islamic theology compatible, so al-Ghazali led the learned and pious doctors and jurists to accept mysticism.

Appointed professor at the Nizamiyah at Baghdad in 1091, the Persian legal scholar Abu Hamid al-Ghazali had the court and the scholars at his feet, and for four or five years his fame spread far and wide. Apparently secure for life, some sort of personal admonition flashed through him; he abandoned everything to become a mendicant mystic. After about a decade of wandering, contemplation, and writing, he returned to society and taught at the Nizamiyah at Nishapur, and died in his home-town of Tus in 1111. His great contribution, largely through his writings, vitalized Islam by making personal experience and emotion a part of religion. Islam began to live again for the ordinary man, both through law and mysticism.

FRATERNAL ORDERS

At the time of the appearance of mysticism a holy man was called a *sufi,* meaning "one garbed in wool." Sufis preached to the masses, and as pious men, mystics, and often occultists, they lived a life of example for their admirers. (It was evidently as a Sufi that al-Ghazali spent his years of abdication.) Without question the conversion to Islam of the Berber tribesmen of North Africa, the peasants of Egypt, and the masses in many of the Muslim lands of today was the accomplishment of the Sufis.

For several centuries Sufism was an unorganized movement throughout Islam, an entirely individual pursuit. Certain Sufis obtained a devoted following, but partisanship was usually personal. Before the end of the tenth century, however, groups of Sufis formed compact brotherhoods. The master Sufi (a *shaykh, baba,* or *pir*) was the teacher and initiated disciples into the order. The members, by study, ritual, and piety, proceeded up the ladder of the order until they were ready to leave to establish a branch center.

A master's residence was called a *ribat, khanqah,* or *tekkeh.* By the thirteenth century, thousands of such lodges dotted the Muslim landscape from Morocco to India. Each order had its own peculiar ritual and liturgy (*dhikr*). Some were elaborate and others simple; but all were mystical efforts to reach God. Most fraternities had hundreds, sometimes thousands, of lay members, who went about their normal occupations in city or town. At stated times they met at the lodge to observe their ceremonies. A few of the orders increased the mystical stimulus by an accompaniment of music or by dancing or whirling.

It was not possible to know how many different orders existed at any one time; new splinter fraternities were springing into being and others disappearing at regular intervals. One of the strongest and best known was the Qadiriya, founded by the Hanbalite Abd al-Qadir al-Jilani in the twelfth century, which had its center in Baghdad and spread throughout Islam. More conservative than most, its members have been noted for their philanthropy and humility. Another order, the Rifaiya, was famed for glass-eating, fire-walking, and self-mortification. In Turkey, the two best-known orders were the Bektashi, to which most of the Ottoman janissaries belonged, and the Mevlevis, whose members were popularly called "whirling dervishes" because of certain aspects in their ritual. In the central and eastern parts of the Middle East, India, China, and Malaysia there was the Naqshbandiya order.

As a great social and religious development, the significance of the fraternal orders lay in the members' extensive participation in the spread and popularization of Islam, resulting in the majority of the people in North Africa, Sudan, Asia Minor, central Asia, certain parts of India, and Indonesia becoming converted to Islam. In this process, much to the horror and disapproval of Muslim theologians, local beliefs and religious customs were grafted upon the original doctrines to form a popular Islam. In most instances, therefore, popular Islam in different parts of the world became exceedingly diverse in form and practice and was far removed from the teachings of either Muhammad or Muslim theologians. Only the barest fundamentals and the simplest of externals were retained.

SHIISM

Differences of opinion and belief have usually been accepted in Islam. Variations in practice and doctrine among the four main Sunni legal systems, the many conflicting interpretations of tradition in vogue throughout the Muslim world, and the confusing welter of exotic ideas rampant in popular Islam have made a definitive imputation of heresy difficult to verify on purely theological grounds.

Until comparatively recently, rulers throughout the world usually persecuted subjects whose religion was at marked variance with theirs. Nonetheless, Islam was exceedingly tolerant, as the treatment of Christians and Jews testifies, and the caliphs permitted many types of religious deviation. In general, deviation became a serious matter only when religious doctrines denied to the caliph the right of his position and his power. Therein lay the true seeds of accusations of heresy.

Following the death of Ali and the ascension of the Umayyads, die-hard Alids contended that caliphs were usurpers and that the imamate, as they called the leadership position for the Muslim community, should be lodged in the house of the Prophet Muhammad, through Ali and Fatimah. Within that family, succession to the imamate could be decided according to one or more different criteria: strictly hereditary succession from Ali's son Husayn; designation by the previous imam, which would be given to a member of the family but not necessarily the eldest son; self-designation through action against the enemies of the family, as Alid pretenders rose against the Umayyad and Abbasid caliphs. For more than two centuries, intermittent political and military attempts were made by the Shiites (the partisans, or sect, of Ali) to unseat the caliph. Constant opposition to established authority made the Shiites into a general umbrella movement that attracted numerous social and economic groups antagonistic to caliphal policies and the existing order. Although successful in reaching political power in some places at certain times, the Shiites usually were ruled by Sunnites, and the Shiites developed an intricate theology, heavily influenced as of the eleventh century by Mutazilite thought, which engendered some dogmas repugnant to Sunni Islam.

The Shiites held that Ali had been the legitimate *imam* ("leader") and that the imamate was rightfully transmitted to his descendants. Ali had been given an esoteric power to interpret the Koran, a knowledge that was handed in turn on to his sons and grandsons. (Later, some extremists even professed that God's revelations had been intended for Ali but that the angel Gabriel had mistakenly given them to Muhammad.) Ali's descendants, therefore, ruled by a divine right that was handed down to them from Adam; they were infallible, impeccable, and certainly beyond human censure, and therefore not subject to the consensus of the Muslim community.

To substantiate their theological and political claims, the Shiites offered their own interpretation of the early history of Islam. They rejected the legitimacy of the first three caliphs—Abu Bakr, Umar, and Uthman—and claimed that Muhammad had announced in 632, before his death, that Ali (who they said had been the first or second convert to Islam) was his rightful successor. Muawiyah and the Umayyads in general were particularly castigated by the Shiites because they had overthrown Ali, and they were responsible for the murder of Ali's son, Husayn, in 680, as he led an unsuccessful rebellion against the caliph Yazid. The tragic martyrdom of Husayn became the most fervently celebrated event in the Shiite religious calendar and the chief emotional impetus for the spread of the faith.

The Shiites have been divided into numerous sects since the eighth century. The majority, the Twelvers, adhered to the belief that there was a succession by

1. Ali   d. 661

2. Hasan   d. 669

3. Husayn   d. 680

4. Ali Zayn al-Abidin   d. 712

Zayd

5. Muhammad al-Baqir   d. 731

6. Jafar al-Sadiq   d. 765

Ismail   d. 760

7. Musa al-Kazim   d. 799

8. Ali al-Rida   d. 818

9. Muhammad al-Jawad   d. 835

10. Ali al-Hadi   d. 868

11. Hasan al-Askari   d. 874

12. Muhammad al-Muntazar

The Twelve Imams

prior designation of twelve imams to Muhammad al-Muntazar ("The Expected"), who in 873 disappeared in a cave and who will return as the savior (*Mahdi*) of humanity. In his absence the law and the creed were interpreted originally by four agents who acted for him, but upon the death of the last of these in 940 the "great occultation" or concealment began, and no definitive interpretation of the will of the imam was possible. This meant that historical precedent and the faith could not be interpreted in an absolutely binding way after 940, and intellectual speculation and judicial ingenuity could be exercised by Shiite scholars and jurists. Thus, in law, the Twelver Shiites accepted only the Koran, the sunnah of the Prophet Muhammad, those traditions of Muhammad narrated by a recognized imam and the imam's own views on law and theology as compiled in the tenth and eleventh centuries, and a scholar's or judge's personal opinion when it could be upheld by tradition or precedent established by an imam. Justice was strongly emphasized, and oppression and tyranny were considered to be great evils. Analogy and consensus among the learned scholars were restricted in application and their use was not widely accepted until a much later time.

Aside from petty ritualistic differences, the chief peculiarities of these Shiites were the allowance of temporary marriage and the practice of dissimulation. The latter permitted Shiites to deny their faith to avoid persecution when caliphs and Sunnites attacked them for disavowing caliphal authority.

The Twelver Shiites held political power only occasionally before the sixteenth century, as in the Buwayhid dynasty that controlled the Sunnite Abbasid caliphate in Baghdad, and several Syrian and Iraqi tribal dynasties. However, other types of Shiites established themselves in various parts of the Middle East in the ninth and tenth centuries, and in the late twentieth century the majority of Muslims in Iran and Iraq are Shiites of the Twelver persuasion.

The most conservative of the Shiites are found in Morocco and Yemen. In political organization Morocco became Shiite; yet her theology and law were strictly Sunnite. In parts of northern Yemen the Zaydi sect, which arrived there in the ninth century at about the same time the sect was also flourishing in northern Iran, recognized a series of imams who were descended from Zayd, a son of the fourth imam. The Zaydis allow for little supernaturalism in their theology; succession to the imamate was by ability, among the descendants of Ali and Fatimah, and not by designation by the incumbent imam.

More extreme Shiite groups included a score or more of divergent heterodoxies. Of these the sect of the Ismailis, or Seveners, has had the greatest following. They regarded Ismail as the rightful seventh imam. At first, Jafar al-Sadiq named Ismail, his eldest son, as successor; but because Ismail imbibed wine freely, Jafar designated another son, Musa, as successor. The Seveners rejected this substitution, arguing that the imam was incapable of erring and that drinking wine did not therefore affect him or the succession. Seven became a sacred and mystical number as in the Pythagorean system. The essence of the universe came in seven steps: God, universal mind, universal soul, matter, space, time, and earth and the human being.

The Ismailis were masters of organization and tactics. Sent out by the true founder, Abd Allah ibn Maymun, from Salamiyah in Syria, missionaries traveled through the Muslim world preaching that the language of the Koran was an occult veil covering an inner and true meaning which could be revealed only to the adept. Initiation of the novice proceeded in seven graded degrees, wherein was divulged secret knowledge such as transmigration of souls, the divinity of Ismail, and the coming of the Mahdi. One part of the Ismaili sect established its rule in North Africa early in the tenth century. The Fatimids, who claimed universal dominion as their goal, ruled much of the western portion of the Muslim world, while the Qarmatians, who were also Ismailis, ruled much of eastern Arabia, although the majority of the Muslims of the Middle East remained Sunnites.

Another Ismaili sect was the notorious Assassins, founded in Iran by Hasan ibn al-Sabbah, who studied Ismaili rites and doctrine in Fatimid Egypt and then returned to his home as a missionary. In 1090 near Qazvin in the Elburz Mountains, he seized the fort of Alamut, which became the residence of the grand master of the order. Below him were priors and propagandists; at the lowest rank stood the *fidais*, who risked death for the faith. Their familiar name, Assassins, was derived from the Arabic word for hashish, which they were said to use in their fearless raids from mountain fortresses. Adopting values based vaguely on Ismaili theology, the Assassins freed themselves from the law of Islam and were encouraged to "believe nothing and dare all." Exact information is lacking, however, because many of their records and books were destroyed in 1256 when the Mongols razed Alamut.

Spreading westward, the Assassins in the twelfth century held numerous castles in north Syria. The assassination of the famous vizir Nizam al-Mulk in 1092 was the first in a series of assassinations of prominent individuals that struck terror through Islam. The western branch of the order was eliminated by the Mamluks in 1272.

Other Ismaili sects were the Nusayris, or Alawites, of northern Syria and the Druzes of Lebanon, Syria, and Jordan. The Nusayris were devotees of the eleventh imam but nevertheless adhered to the main tenets of the Seveners. They looked upon Ali as the incarnation of God and possessed a liturgy with many Christian borrowings. The Druze sect was an eleventh-century splinter group from Fatimid Egypt. Its members settled in Syria and the Lebanon mountain region, where they developed an elaborate ritual and a pattern of life distinctive even in minor detail. Both the Druze and the Nusayri maintained strict secrecy with respect to their faith and practices; even today mystery shrouds their beliefs and ceremonies.

Probably the best-known Ismaili in the twentieth century was the incomparable Agha Khan III of Bombay, London, Paris, and the Riviera, who traced his descent through the last grand master of the Assassins at Alamut to the seventh imam. Regarded as infallible and impeccable by his followers in Syria, India, Pakistan, and Zanzibar, he received a tenth of their revenues.

In addition to the sects and divisions of these branches of Islam already described, there have been many more. Perhaps the most different are the Yazidis of Syria, who follow much of the theology of the Ismailis but assign the divine attributes to the Umayyad caliphs Yazid and Marwan.

Thus, the plain unvarnished revelations of the Prophet Muhammad and the simple direct philosophy of his preaching passed through the fires of Greek logic,

Hellenistic Christianity, and Persian dualism to evolve a finely drawn legalistic and intellectual theology, a highly charged supernatural recondite religion, and a semiascetic mysticism. The apocryphal words of Muhammad have apparently been fulfilled: When told that there were seventy-two varieties of Christianity, the Prophet was supposed to have said that Islam would have seventy-three!

REFERENCES

References for Chapters 3 and 5 relate to the subject matter of this chapter.

Abu-Izzeddin, Nejla M. *The Druzes: A New Study of Their History, Faith and Society*. Leiden: Brill, 1984. The origins of the Druzes are discussed up to about 1840.

Arberry, A. J. *Sufism: An Account of the Mystics of Islam*. New York: Harper and Row, 1970. This succinct book by an expert in the field looks at the Koran, Muhammad, ascetics, mystics, the Sufi orders, and Persian mystical poets.

Azami, Muhammad Mustafa. *Studies in Hadith Methodology and Literature*. Indianapolis, Ind.: American Trust Publishers, 1977. Hadith criticism and the chief compilers of hadith are examined in a traditional manner.

Crone, Patricia. *Roman, Provincial and Islamic Law: The Origins of the Islamic Patronate*. Cambridge: Cambridge University Press, 1987. An analysis of clientage, traditions, and the bases of law showing the influence of preexisting provincial law.

Jafri, Husain M. *Origins and Early Development of Shi'a Islam*. London: Longman, 1979. The author follows events from the days of Muhammad to Jafar al-Sadiq from the point of view of Shiite Islam.

Juynboll, G. H. A. *Muslim Tradition: Studies in Chronology, Provenance and Authorship of Early Hadith*. Cambridge: Cambridge University Press, 1983.

Khalidi, Tarif. *Classical Arab Islam: The Culture and Heritage of the Golden Age*. Princeton, N.J.: Darwin Press, 1985. Thoughtful essays on a broad range of subjects include mysticism, reason, nature, and the Prophet Muhammad.

Lambton, Ann K. S. *State and Government in Medieval Islam*. Oxford: Oxford University Press, 1981. A recognized authority looks at religion, politics, law, community, philosophy, Shiites, and the individual and the state.

Lewis, Bernard. *The Assassins: A Radical Sect in Islam*. New York: Weidenfeld & Nicolson, 1967. Well researched, well written, and authoritative.

Liebesny, Herbert J. *The Law of the Near and Middle East: Readings, Cases and Materials*. Albany: State University of New York Press, 1974. A systematic treatment of the subject from early to modern times.

Massignon, Louis. *The Passion of al-Hallaj: Mystical Martyr of Islam*. Vol. 1. *Life*. Translated by H. Mason. Princeton, N.J.: Princeton University Press, 1982. The moving account of the life of one of the most extreme and famous of the mystics.

Momen, Moojan. *An Introduction to Shi'i Islam: The History and Doctrines of Twelver Shi'ism*. New Haven, Conn.: Yale University Press, 1985. Shiism as a political, religious, and intellectual movement is thoroughly examined in a detailed manner.

Petrushevsky, I. P. *Islam in Iran*. Albany: State University of New York Press, 1985. Despite the title, the book covers the whole geographical range of Islam, and its political and religious history, from the point of view of a Soviet scholar.

Schacht, Joseph. *An Introduction to Islamic Law*. New York: Oxford University Press, 1964. The best book in the field and more than an introduction, as the author sheds light on the importance of al-Shafii.

Schimmel, Annemarie. *Mystical Dimensions of Islam*. Chapel Hill: University of North Carolina Press, 1975. This is a synthesis of Sufi theory and practice, its history, psychological and social significance, and literary output.

Trimingham, J. Spencer. *The Sufi Orders of Islam*. Oxford: Clarendon Press, 1971. A comprehensive treatment of mystical movements.

Watt, W. Montgomery. *Muslim Intellectual: A Study of al-Ghazali*. Edinburgh: Edinburgh University Press, 1963. A full study of this great theological philosopher.

————. *The Formative Period of Islamic Thought*. Edinburgh: Edinburgh University Press, 1973. A detailed study of Islamic ideas from 632 to 945. This important work closely relates the effect of the development of ideas and beliefs upon political events.

Williams, John Alden, ed. *Islam*. New York: George Braziller, 1962. A good sourcebook for excerpts from documents and books including the Koran, traditions, law, mysticism, theology, Kharijites, and Shiites.

————. *Themes of Islamic Civilization*. Berkeley: University of California Press, 1971. Readings in chronological order drawn from original sources, with informative introductions, on the topics of the community, the perfect ruler, the will of God, the Mahdi, holy war, and mysticism.

9

Muslim Culture

*T*he Arabs burst from the cities of the Hijaz and the deserts of Arabia into the complex Greco-Roman civilizations of Syria and Egypt, into the cultured valleys of India, and into the refined society of Mesopotamia and Iran. Everywhere they demonstrated a remarkable genius for assimilating various attributes of these native cultures and blending them with their own to form a new and varied Muslim culture. Belief in the oneness of God, acceptance of Muhammad as His prophet, and the Arabic language became the significant distinguishing characteristics of Islamic culture. For the first few centuries following the death of Muhammad in 632, Arabic remained the universal language; non-Arab Muslims and non-Muslims alike, if they learned the Arabic language, could and did participate in most aspects of Muslim culture. Jews, Christians, and others made substantial contributions to the development of the new civilization that often transcended religious as well as political and geographic differences.

PHILOSOPHY

The emergence of the Mutazilites indicated that Greek logic was studied during the Umayyad era. Not until the reign of the Abbasid al-Mamun, however, was the bulk of Hellenistic thought and science translated into Arabic. Beginning with a majority of the works of Aristotle and Plato, translators soon rendered almost the whole of Hellenic and Hellenistic philosophies into Arabic. It was upon this base and religious disputation that Muslim philosophy was erected.

The earliest of the prominent Arab philosophers was al-Kindi (Alkindius), born in Kufah in the first half of the ninth century. He excelled in the study of optics, chemistry, medicine, and music; but above all he was a philosopher. A Neoplatonist of the school of Plotinus and Porphyry, al-Kindi also studied the ideas of Aristotle and Plato. He intermingled philosophy and theology, holding that the world of intelligence is supreme. Immortality results from having the correct knowledge of God and the universe. A century later, al-Farabi (Alpharabius), a Turk from Transoxiana, blended Aristotelian, Platonic, and Sufi thought. He presented his philosophy in a political treatise by describing a model city where the ruler was a moral and intellectual being and the happiness of all was the governing force. Al-Farabi's classification of the sciences influenced Muslim scholars for centuries to come. However, he shocked Muslims by claiming that the world was not created and had no beginning.

Muslim philosophers better known to the Western world were Ibn Sina (Avicenna) and Ibn Rushd (Averroes). The former, called by the Muslims "the shaykh and the prince of the learned," was born in 980 in a village near Bukhara. An Ismaili Iranian, Ibn Sina lived as a young man at the Samanid library of Bukhara, where he acquired an encyclopedic knowledge of medicine, mathematics, astronomy, and philosophy. Since he was able to write concisely, yet in a popular style, Ibn Sina's numerous works on these diverse subjects had a wide vogue among Muslims and greatly influenced the advancement of philosophic thought in medieval Europe. Pursuing Aristotelian philosophy, Ibn Sina developed and passed on to the Western schoolmen the notion that there are two intelligibles—the concept of an object such as a chair, and the pursuant or logical concept of a chair in relation to its abstract universal concept. He taught that the idea of a chair existed before the chair was created, that in each chair existed the idea of chair, and that from many chairs came the idea of chair.

Ibn Rushd, the Malikite Muslim judge and philosopher, lived in Cordoba, Seville, and Marrakesh during the Muwahhid regime, and he died in 1198. He wrote in the fields of philosophy, medicine, mathematics, law, and theology. As the last of the classical Muslim philosophers of Spain, he built on the systems of al-Farabi, Ibn Sina, and his fellow countrymen. He declared that active human reason and possible reason or knowledge are one and present in everyone. Ibn Rushd's commentaries on Aristotle were more popular and influential in Christian Europe than they were in the Muslim world.

From Aristotle, Plato, and other Greek philosophers the Muslim scholars, writing in Arabic, created a school of philosophy that had a profound and recognized influence on Christian philosophers of medieval Europe. More significant to the Middle East, however, was their permanent popularity throughout the Muslim world. Summaries, treatises, and commentaries on these philosophers and scores of others less well known were widely read and discussed; public and private libraries bulged with books on metaphysics, cosmology, and philosophy. Scientific method itself became a field of controversy where philosophers, theologians, and the practitioners of the individual sciences fiercely debated theories of knowledge and investigation.

MEDICINE

Muhammad supposedly declared that there exist two sciences: the science of God and the science of the human—theology and medicine. Consequently, throughout the period of medieval Islam most Muslim philosophers and scientists were students of medicine; frequently they were also practicing physicians. Muslims first became aware of medical knowledge at the Damascus court of the Umayyads, through their Greek, Syrian, and Iranian physicians, whose skills were based almost exclusively on works of Greek scientists. A few Greek or Syriac treatises were translated into Arabic, and the Alexandrine medical school was transferred, part to Antioch and part to Harran in Iraq.

Great strides in medicine were made under Abbasid rule in Baghdad. Greek, Persian, Indian, and Syrian influences were felt, but the medical works of Galen, Hippocrates, and the materia medica of Dioscorides were especially important when translated into Arabic. Seven of Galen's books, lost in the original Greek, were preserved in Arabic. Galen was highly influential in forming medical theory. Several schools of medicine developed, and a physician took state examinations to obtain a license to practice his profession. In the year 931, there were 860 physicians registered in Baghdad; they swore to work for the benefit of humanity and for the relief and cure of the sick and not to give deadly medicines. Traveling clinics for the poor were supported by the state and hospitals were introduced into the Muslim world by the caliph Harun al-Rashid. Most physicians were general practitioners, but there was some specialization in ophthalmology and surgery. The Seljuk Turkish sultan Malikshah had with him on most of his campaigns a mobile hospital, carried on forty camels. Pharmacists were also examined and licensed, and schools of pharmacy and drugstores were established. In 776, Jabir ibn Hayyan compiled the first Arabic pharmacopoeia.

In 765 the Nestorian Jurjis ibn Bukhtishu, dean of the academy of medicine of Jundishapur (Shahabad in southwestern Iran), came to the court of al-Mansur to cure the caliph's stomach ailment. Fortunes were made by court physicians, who passed on their professional skills and practices as valued possessions from father to son for generations. Ibn Bukhtishu's grandson understood psychiatry; he cured, through a form of hypnosis, one of al-Rashid's slave girls of hysterical paralysis by pretending to disrobe her publicly. Descendants of Ibn Bukhtishu served the Abbasid court for nearly three centuries.

The arrival of physicians from Jundishapur opened the way for medical investigations beyond the works of the ancient Greeks, and the ninth century in Baghdad was a period of many advances in medical knowledge. The compendium by Thabit ibn Qurra of Harran (died in 901) discussed general hygiene. It stated causes, symptoms, and treatment for diseases of the skin and every part of the body from head to foot. Infectious diseases were classified; fractures and dislocations were described; and the importance of climate, food, diet, and sex was explained.

The most ingenious Muslim physician was the Persian al-Razi (Rhazes), chief of the Baghdad hospital during the first quarter of the tenth century. Considered the best original mind and clinician of the Middle Ages, he developed the use of seton in surgery, treated bladder and kidney stones, and presented the first clinical report on smallpox. He had some fifty-six monographs on medicine and surgery to his credit. His comprehensive medical encyclopedia was based on clinical observations and experimentation.

The most famous Muslim medical work was *al-Qanun,* written in the eleventh century by Ibn Sina (Avicenna) of Bukhara. Encyclopedic in character, it showed the advances of Muslim knowledge and the originality of Ibn Sina in this field. Among other things, it explained the contagious nature of tuberculosis, showed that disease could be spread through water, recognized pleurisy, diagnosed bilharziasis, and described 760 different drugs. *Al-Qanun,* along with the works of Galen and Hippocrates, was among the chief medical books of the Middle East and western Europe from the twelfth to the seventeenth century. It ran through sixteen printed editions in Latin before the end of the fifteenth century.

Muslim Spain possessed superior physicians and surgeons. The ablest surgeon was Abu al-Qasim (Abulcasis) of Cordoba. He practiced the art of crushing bladder stones, cauterized wounds, and advocated dissection, even though Muslims generally did not engage in dissection. His surgical writings were translated and became the surgical manual at the medical schools of European centers. In Seville, Ibn Zuhr (Avenzoar), vizir and court physician to the Muwahhid rulers, carried on the family profession and found time to write six medical works, of which the most valuable is on therapeutics and diet. At the time of the Black Death in the middle of the fourteenth century, the Muslim physicians of Granada, Ibn al-Khatib and Ibn Khatima, recognized its contagious character; and in their treatises they noted that a patient's symptoms were identical to those of the person from whom he had been infected. Although religious law denied contagion, Ibn al-Khatib held that "experience, investigation, the evidence of the senses and trustworthy reports" established without a doubt the reality of infection from the afflicted.

Building on Greek and Persian sources, the galaxy of Muslim physicians pushed the frontiers of medicine forward. Their practice, monographs, and compendiums demonstrated originality and ingenuity. The diversity and number of their works, translated into Latin and eventually printed, further established the place of Muslim physicians in the history of medical science. Evidence of their actual skill was attested by the eagerness with which the Crusaders sought the services of Muslim doctors. Part of the progress originated in the popularity and fashionable reputation enjoyed by medical knowledge. Since the chief avocation of countless leading Muslims was medicine and the study of its lore, every medical practitioner was encouraged to reach the pinnacle of his ability and capacity.

MATHEMATICS

Muslim scholars also found mathematics an attractive and useful science, especially in company with astronomy and astrology. By far the greatest achievement of the Arab mathematicians was the adoption and wide use of "Arabic numerals." It is not known whether they were brought from India or developed locally. In any case, the use of these numerals, including the use of zero and the placing of the digit in a series to denote units, tens, hundreds, and so on, made "everyday arithmetic" possible and simplified calculations, enabling Arabs to take the square and cube roots of numbers with ease. The word "cipher," meaning zero, was taken directly from the Arabic *sifr,* meaning "empty."

Building on Indian and Greek works, Middle Eastern scholars advanced mathematical knowledge considerably. In the ninth century al-Khwarizmi of Khurasan did a study on numerals which later circulated in the West. Through his name came the word "algorism." He wrote on the solution of quadratic equations; and from part of the title of one of his books was derived the word "algebra" (*al-jabr*—"integration").

In the same century, the geometrician Thabit ibn Qurra developed new propositions and studied irrationals. The Iranian al-Battani (Albategnius) was the first to present ideas on trigonometric ratios. Toward the end of the tenth century another Iranian, Abu al-Wafa of Baghdad, established the formula in trigonometry for the addition of angles. Through a simple geometric process al-Karaji was able to determine the sum of successive numbers raised to the third power $(1^3 + 2^3 + 3^3 + \cdots + n^3)$. By using the intersection of a hyperbola and a circle, Sijzi gave the solution to the problem of the trisection of an angle.

One of the most distinguished mathematicians was the Iranian poet Umar Khayyam. He advanced far beyond al-Khwarizmi, establishing procedures for the solution of cubic and quadrinomial equations and developing analytical geometry in numerous ways to the same level achieved much later by Descartes. The last great medieval mathematician of the Middle East was the Iranian Nasir al-Din al-Tusi, who assembled his laboratory in northwestern Iran under the patronage of the Mongols. Here he wrote his famous *Treatise on the Quadrilateral* and carried on his brilliant studies in the field of spherical trigonometry.

Thus, besides assimilating and transmitting to posterity the mathematics of the ancients, Middle Eastern savants made many original contributions in the practical and theoretical branches of the subject. The widespread use of numerals gave arithmetic an everyday value. Algebra became an exact science, and solid foundations were laid in the fields of analytical geometry and plane and spherical trigonometry. Through Spain and Sicily most of these ideas passed at an early date to the Western world, where they contributed to the scientific advancement of Europe.

ASTRONOMY

Mathematics and astronomy were closely related, especially since in the construction of any mosque it was always necessary to fix the *kibla* (the direction of Mecca) in order to build the *mihrab* (the prayer niche), and accurate time keeping was important to determine the occasions for prayers. Furthermore, since astrology and horoscopy were much pursued and the latitude and longitude of one's birthplace entered into one's horoscope, the movement of the stars was significant. Muslim astronomy started from Iranian, Greek, and Indian contributions.

When the Abbasid caliph al-Mansur decided to build his new palace in Baghdad, the Iranian astronomer Naubakht was employed to draw the plans. Many palaces in Baghdad had private astronomical observatories. The main professional observatories were at Jundishapur and Baghdad. It was from the latter that scientists at the time of al-Mamun went to the plain of Sinjar to determine the length of a degree of latitude. Walking north and south until the pole star rose or sank a degree (thus assuming the earth to be round), they took the mean distance for one degree. From this they calculated the diameter of the earth to be about 6,500 miles (10,461 km.) and the circumference roughly 20,400 miles (32,831 km.); in both cases they still were rather far from the actual distances. This made the Mediterranean 52° in length, as compared to Ptolemy's 62°. Rather exact astronomical tables and calendars with a compendium were prepared by al-Farghani (Alfraganus) of Transoxiana in the ninth century, and were translated into Latin in the twelfth century.

Thabit ibn Qurra determined the altitude of the sun and computed the length of the solar year; Muhammad al-Battani (Albategnius) recorded his observations on the appearance of the new moon, the inclination of the ecliptic, the length of the tropic and sideral year, and eclipses of the sun. The astronomer and geographer al-Biruni at Ghaznah in Afghanistan proposed the idea that the earth rotates on its axis and reckoned quite accurately latitudes and longitudes for every important city in the Middle East, as well as writing excellent cultural geographies. Umar Khayyam, who was a better astronomer than poet, arranged for Sultan Malikshah a calendar with an error of only one day in 5,000 years.

In the West al-Zarkali (Arzachel) of Toledo invented a refined version of the astrolabe, on which he wrote a treatise later used by Copernicus. Near Cordoba a century later lived the great astronomer al-Bitruji (Alpetragius), who computed the length of the Mediterranean and found it to be 42° of longitude, a nearly correct measurement. He advanced the idea of diurnal movements of the earth and explained the movement of the stars by the turning of the earth on its axis as well as by its circling about the sun.

One of the finest observatories was established by the Mongols at Maraghah, where the scientist Nasir al-Din al-Tusi developed the most precise instruments of medieval times. Because of his excellent equipment his *Ilkhanian Tables* were long regarded as the most exact of astronomical tables.

The Arabic names of many stars and constellations and the Arabic origin of such words as "azimuth," "nadir," and "zenith" vouch for the brilliance of the Middle Eastern astronomers and the acceptance of their contributions by the West. One can only wonder if Columbus would have had the courage to set sail westward for India and China had he known the size of the earth as determined by al-Bitruji.

SCIENCES

In addition to medicine, mathematics, and astronomy, the medieval Middle Easterners investigated and frequently brought about fundamental redefinitions in the basic and natural sciences. It is not possible here to detail the various advances made in each science. Works on botany existed, chiefly in connection with drugs for the pharmacist and physician. Zoological studies were made, some for use by veterinarians. Al-Masudi, who died about 957 in Cairo, discussed earthquakes, described windmills, and advanced a theory of evolution. In his book on geology, Ibn Sina suggested several postulates about earthquakes, winds, climate, and geologic sedimentation.

However, the greatest strides in the sciences were taken in chemistry and physics. Chemistry was studied mostly in connection with alchemy, although some famous scientists, such as Ibn Sina and al-Kindi, did not believe in the transmutation of metals. Even its name affirms the Arabic origins of the science of chemistry; the Arabic term is *al-kimya,* which was probably derived from an ancient Egyptian word. Alchemy was founded on the belief that all metals contain the same essences and that it is possible to transmute one to another. Further, it was believed that gold is the purest form of metal and that some substance exists that can transform baser metals into gold. Throughout the Muslim world countless individuals engaged in the search for this substance and the technique of its use. Celebrated philosophers and physicians gave their time and genius to the quest. One of these men, al-Razi, distinguished volatile and nonvolatile bodies and classified all matter as vegetable, animal, or mineral. Others in their research determined the specific weights of stones and metals.

The greatest chemist, or alchemist, was Jabir ibn Hayyan (Geber), who lived in Kufah toward the end of the eighth century. Jabir advocated experimentation and recognized the importance of confirming by careful observation theories that are based only on previous writings and hypotheses. He was able to prepare arsenious oxide, lead acetate, sulphide of mercury, and sal ammoniac, the last of which had been unknown to the Greeks. Jabir presented new and improved methods of evaporation, filtration, sublimation, melting, crystallization, and distillation. Jabir's works, translated into Latin in the twelfth century, proved to be the foundation of Western alchemy and chemistry. The Arabic origin of such words as "alkali," "alcohol," "antimony," and "alembic" and "aludel" (parts of the older typical apparatus for distilling) attests to Western dependence upon Middle Eastern discoveries in this branch of science.

In physics the widest interest lay in theoretical and applied mechanics as related to problems of irrigation and the flow of water. Water wheels and clocks were built in many cities of the Middle East, some of the water clocks being exceedingly ingenious in design. (Clock design was one of the very few areas of science and technology where European innovations were brought into the Islamic world; generally, the flow of knowledge went the other way.) In the twelfth century, al-Khazini observed the greater density of water when it was nearer the center of the earth, and he displayed a strong preference for experimentation rather than theorizing.

The most significant developments in physics, however, were in the field of optics. Many prominent scientists of the age investigated the subject. The most outstanding was Abu Ali ibn al-Haytham (Alhazen), who flourished in Cairo at the time of the Fatimids, and who also extensively studied momentum and gravity. In his book *On Optics,* he refused to accept Euclid's and Ptolemy's theory that the eye emits visual rays; instead he advanced the theory that vision is due to the impact of light rays. Experimenting with reflection and optic illusions, he studied refraction through spherical segments filled with water. In another work, *On Light,* he proposed that light is fire reflected at the spheric limit of the atmosphere; and from observing phenomena at twilight he reckoned the atmosphere to be about ten miles (16 km.) high. In what was probably the first recorded observation of the camera obscura, he noticed during eclipses the semilunar shape of the sun's image on a wall opposite a fine hole in a window shutter. Ibn al-Haytham's studies greatly influenced, through translation, the works of Roger Bacon, Kepler, and Leonardo da Vinci.

GEOGRAPHY

The religious precept of a pilgrimage to Mecca once in a lifetime undoubtedly reinforced a persistent urge among many in medieval Islamic lands to travel and see the world. Because geographic data were needed by these travelers as well as by traders and administrators, travelers wrote detailed books on where they had been and what they had seen. Geography became one of the most popular pursuits of the Middle Ages.

Before the end of the ninth century, Ptolemy's *Geography* had been translated into Arabic, and Muslim geographers always had difficulty in freeing themselves from some of the Greek, Persian, and Indian concepts of the world. The scientist al-Khwarizmi, at the caliph al-Mamun's command, prepared a great map of the earth and a companion text which was used by geographers until the fourteenth century. Largely following Ptolemy, al-Khwarizmi pictured the world encircled by a continuous ocean from which the Sea of Rum (Mediterranean) and the Sea of Fars (Indian Ocean) branched to separate the land of the earth, which was divided into seven climate zones. The western prime meridian of longitude ran through the Canary Islands, and all east and west directions came from the "world cupola" located in India.

Fortunately, the conservative and classical geographers, whose views upheld the Koran, were ignored by travelers and sailors who recognized irregular coasts strewn with gulfs and peninsulas and stated that the Indian Ocean, in certain directions, has no limit. The tales of these voyagers came down through the ages as the stories of Sindbad the Sailor. They described China in the ninth century and Russia in the tenth. Their road books were a mine of historical topography and economic and political geography. The tenth-century scholar was frequently on the move. The greatest globe-trotter was al-Masudi, who visited most of the countries of Asia, Zanzibar, and most of North Africa. His thirty-volume work became one of the two recognized geographical encyclopedias of the medieval period. Other travelers and geographers left numerous works, many with special merit for their colored maps of separate countries and areas. One of the last discerning voyagers was Ibn Battutah of Morocco. Living in the fourteenth century, he was on the move for nearly three decades. He made four pilgrimages to Mecca and visited China, Ceylon, Constantinople, and central Africa.

The most noted geographer of the Muslim world was al-Idrisi (Edrisi), born in Ceuta in 1100 and for many years the chief geographer for King Roger II of Sicily. In his writings and discourses (in Arabic), he summed up the ideas and contributions of Ptolemy, al-Khwarizmi, and al-Masudi. Using silver, al-Idrisi constructed for his patron a celestial sphere and a disklike map of the earth. It is interesting that the latter distinctly showed the source of the Nile to be a lake in central Africa.

The last eminent medieval Muslim geographer was Yakut ibn Abdallah al-Hamawi, a Greek slave from Asia Minor who was educated and given his freedom.

Before his death in 1229 Yakut compiled his famous *Mujam al-Buldan,* a vast encyclopedia of geographical information. Arranged alphabetically, it summed up the whole fund of knowledge available to him in this field and thus became an invaluable source book for all scholars.

AGRICULTURE

Most of the first Muslims in the Hijaz were not farmers; however, intensive and irrigated agriculture was widespread in parts of Yemen and Oman, areas that contributed many soldiers to the Muslim armies and settlers in the newly conquered empire. In the rich agricultural lands of Iraq, Syria, and Egypt, the Muslims quickly came to appreciate the methods needed to efficiently cultivate the soil. As the native populations of these provinces and other fertile areas (such as Spain and Sogdiana) were converted to Islam, Muslims were engaged directly in agriculture. Accordingly, the governing classes, the landowners, and the actual farmers all were concerned with agricultural progress.

In the Middle East in Islamic times, the prime factor in agriculture has been water; the need for irrigation increased as new crops were introduced that required water in the summer when little rain fell. Problems of irrigation and canal building were not private affairs, and everywhere rulers were asked to pay strict attention to digging, reopening, and repairing water channels. Under Muslim governments gardens flourished, with many different plants, vegetables, and fruit trees being propagated, and they were celebrated in poetry. Rulers often sought to acquire new plants, and Arab manuals on farming and botany were written. The Arabs had known numerous varieties of dates, and families treasured their own species with favored qualities of flavor, sweetness, and moisture. The same interest and care was given to other produce of the land as Islam spread into new areas and new crops were grown, mainly fruit trees, grains, and vegetables, as well as flowers and ornamentals. Middle Easterners usually took keen pride in their gardens and land.

Agricultural productivity rose with higher-yielding crops and more specialized land use, including greater development in rotation of crops, labor-intensive methods, and a summer growing season. The agricultural surplus became so great it could support much larger cities.

Cultivators were interested in improving the quality and variety of their crops, and they took specimens wherever they went. Many crops were introduced from India through sailors and merchants from Oman and Yemen who carried knowledge of irrigation technology as well as seeds and cuttings from South Asia to the Middle East. On pilgrimages to Mecca, and on other travels, people exchanged information on agriculture. Thus, the best varieties of plants were distributed far and wide. The cultivation of cotton, sugar cane, apricots, peaches, and rice was introduced into Spain on the distant edge of the Islamic world. Spanish authors produced many treatises on agriculture; one of the best-known and most beautiful gardens of the world was near the Alhambra. The technique of controlled pollenization was known and frequently practiced with special and prized varieties of the date palm and fruit trees. The Crusaders learned to value Middle Eastern agriculture and acquired a taste for many of its products. Yet, it was largely through Sicily, Spain, and Cyprus that agricultural knowledge and skills slowly passed to Christian Europe.

POETRY

In pre-Islamic Arabia poetry was a favorite vehicle of expression. Epic and lyric poetry was popular. A talented poet was highly esteemed, and the cultured person was one who appreciated fine poetry and could recite an endless quantity of verse. Muhammad found much of this poetry distasteful, since the way of life extolled was not the way of Islam.

The advent of the Umayyad regime set the stage for the return of poetry to its pre-Islamic popularity. The poet Umar wrote with charming grace of free and erotic love, and his directness and simplicity influenced generations of Arab poets. Singers and entertainers found his style well suited to their ballads. Lyric poetry reached its height in the Majnun-Layla romance. The author-hero became mad *(majnun)* because of his burning passion for a lady whose father compelled her to marry another. The deranged lover roamed the world seeking his beloved. Ever after, Majnun was the typical hero of unrequited-love poems throughout the Middle East.

In addition, there reappeared in the Umayyad period many writers of eulogistic and epic poetry of the pre-Islamic style. Noted for their dissolute language and political invective, these panegyrists pleased their patrons; but their poetry was more revealing of the life and morals of the age than deserving of a niche in world literature. Many Umayyad caliphs were themselves poets.

With the coming of the Abbasids, the court moved to Baghdad and the poets followed. Persian influence and rich caliphal patronage introduced an elegance and a licentiousness unknown in Umayyad poetry. One of the first poets in this period was Bashshar ibn Burd, whose paeans of love were so popular and so apt for singing that al-Mahdi had him executed in 783 for endangering public morals. The boon companion of Harun al-Rashid was the sparkling and lusty Abu Nuwas, whose libidinous poetry is typified by his verse:

> *Ho! a cup, and fill it up, and tell me it is wine.*
> *For I will never drink in shade if I can drink in shine!*
> *Curst and poor is every hour that sober I must go,*
> *But rich am I whene'er well drunk I stagger to and fro.*
> *Speak, for shame, the loved one's name, let vain disguise alone:*
> *No good there is in pleasures o'er which a veil is thrown.*

Poetry, however, was not all wine, women, and song. Abu al-Alahiyah raised his voice against the lascivious and frivolous verses of his contemporaries and sang the praises of a moral and ascetic life. Unmindful of the reproaches, al-Rashid pensioned him generously.

At the court and in wealthy society poetry was on the lips of all, and every elegant household had its poet. The immediate material rewards were great, as was, consequently, the quantity of verse, much of it ephemeral doggerel or limerick eulogizing the patron or adorning the moment. Since the golden days of Baghdad the poetry of that classical age has retained its favored position among educated Arabic-speaking Middle Eastern peoples.

In the West the best-known poet was Ali ibn Hazm of eleventh-century Cordoba, whose platonic love verses, collected in an anthology called *Tawq al-Hamamah* ("The Dove's Necklace"), have been much translated. Much more significant was the indigenous development of the *zajal* and the *muwashshah* (the ballad and folk song) of Muslim Spain, which were popularized and spread by wandering minstrels. The epoch of the troubadour in northern Spain, Italy, and France was largely dependent upon this Spanish development; the idealization of the lady and love found in the troubadour songs was a Christian characterization of themes prevalent in Arabic lyrics of the Muslim world.

At the other end of the Muslim world in the province of Fars and especially in Shiraz, there arose the school of Persian poets. As an outgrowth of national feeling Firdawsi, who died in 1020, presented his *Shahnamah,* or great national epic, to Mahmud of Ghaznah. No poetry has ever stirred the soul of the Iranian people as has Firdawsi's *Shahnamah;* even today illiterates recite national legends and history from Firdawsi's poetry with great emotion.

The Persian poet best known outside of Iran is, of course, Umar Khayyam, and his *Rubaiyat.* FitzGerald's unrivaled rendering into English, a translation often far from the original texts, has come in the West to be regarded as the very epitome of Middle Eastern poetry. Khayyam's quatrains expressed the cultured sophistry of twelfth-century Nishapur and were merely the product of the idle moments of this illustrious mathematician.

Besides Firdawsi, the other poets regarded as truly gifted by Iranians were Nizami (died in 1209), whose romantic *Five Treasuries* was exceptionally popular and whose rendition of the Majnun-Layla theme was depicted in countless miniatures; Jalal al-Din Rumi, the mystic poet who founded the Mawlawi (Mevlevi) dervish order and died at Konya in Asia Minor in 1273; Sadi of Shiraz, another mystic whose *Gulistan* ("Rose Garden") and *Bustan* ("Orchard") were among the most favorite poems of Iran; and the fourteenth-century Hafiz, the master of Persian lyricists, a materialist yet a mystic, whose love for the shady gardens, wine and women, and the laughter-loving people of Shiraz was shown in his *Diwan,* or *Collection of Odes.*

LITERATURE

Umayyad literature featured epistles addressed to the caliphs and others, often written by the newly Arabized bureaucrats and secretaries in Damascus. Another style was represented by the ninth-century essayist, humorist, and litterateur, al-Jahiz of Basrah—a notable and witty example of the cultivated writer who set high standards for subsequent authors.

For the most part, the later classical literature of the medieval Middle East consisted of the writings of famous philosophers, theologians, bureaucrats, geographers, historians, travelers, and men of like interests, writing under the patronage of rulers and officials. Belles-lettres, prose fiction, wisdom literature, and drama were not so highly regarded among the Arabs; not until the tenth century did Persian contacts influence the general taste to produce Arabic literature of this type. Rhymed prose emphasized elegant form over substance, which sounded affected and ornate to the Westerner and was embellished with philological curiosities. In Muslim Spain a type of anecdote, frequently introducing a moral lesson through the adventure of some dashing hero, became the prototype of the Spanish picaresque novel. In his rhetorical tales al-Hariri of Basrah (1054–1122) criticized rather subtly the existing social order.

Superb, however, were a number of delightful anthologies—each one partly a treasury of poetry, literature, and history and partly the original work of the compiler. Today they serve as invaluable sources for the study of Muslim civilization. Two outstanding examples are the twenty-volume *Kitab al-Aghani (Book of Songs)* gathered by Abu al-Faraj al-Isfahani, who died in 967, and *al-Iqd al-Farid (The Unique Necklace)* by Ibn Abd Rabbih, who died in 940.

Of all the literature of the Middle East the most colorful, fanciful, and noteworthy through many centuries has been *The Arabian Nights.* Taking the core of the stories and names of leading characters from an old Persian collection, al-Jahshiyari in the first half of the tenth century in Iraq blended local color and current episodes and romances of the courts of al-Rashid, al-Mamun, and the other spirited caliphs to produce the great *Alf Laylah wa Laylah (One Thousand and One Nights).* Its present form was achieved in the fourteenth century in Mamluk Egypt. In the nineteenth century, excellent English translations were made by Edward W. Lane, John Payne, and Sir Richard F. Burton.

HISTORY

Middle Eastern peoples have been mindful of their own history, the Muslims not excepted. Shiites were especially active in writing history, as reference to the early history of Islam was crucial to their political and theological positions.

The epic poetry of pre-Islamic days related the history and genealogy of the tribes of Arabia and their battles, and the collecting and arranging of the hadith helped preserve a great deal of historical material.

Umayyad historians were largely suppressed by the succeeding Abbasid dynasty. By the middle of the eighth century, historical works, especially biography and genealogy, attracted the attention of Muslim scholars. The first known biography of the Prophet Muhammad was composed by Ibn Ishaq, who died in 767. In the ninth century, accounts of the early battles of Islam, tales of the astonishing Arab expansion, and biographical dictionaries of historical figures appeared. The two best were those of Ibn Abd al-Hakam (an Egyptian), the story of the conquest of Egypt, North Africa, and Spain, and of al-Baladhuri (an Iranian), a carefully compiled and balanced narrative of Muslim expansion.

The lengthy and more formal histories of the Middle East produced in the Abbasid era were numerous and varied. Every century and court had professional chroniclers. One of the more noted was al-Tabari (838–923), who traveled widely and studied at many important Muslim centers. A most prolific writer for more than forty years, al-Tabari left a monumental historical chronicle incorporating data sifted from innumerable monographs. His contemporary from Baghdad, the Twelver Shiite al-Masudi, dealt with the same material but treated the unfolding of civilizations topically instead of chronologically as al-Tabari had done. Written after years of travel, al-Masudi's work ran to thirty volumes.

Probably the best known of Muslim historians is the Tunisian Ibn Khaldun (1332–1406). A citizen of the Muslim world, he studied and held important political positions in Fez, Granada, Algeria, and Cairo. His history of the Muslim states and peoples was a significant contribution to knowledge, especially the sections about North Africa. But Ibn Khaldun's fame rested on his history's first volume, entitled *Muqaddimah (Prolegomena),* in which he presented his philosophy of the cyclical development of civilization, social solidarity, and the relationship of nomadic and settled groups, and explained how the historian should record and study the interrelated forces of society. Since he considered the factors of climate, geography, economics, and culture as the basic causes of major events, so as to provide lessons and rules about the patterns of history, Ibn Khaldun can be called the first modern historian.

EDUCATION

In the early days of the Muslim Empire the ruling Arabs held that a man was educated if he learned to read and write, to use the bow and arrow, and to swim. A man should be taught courage, endurance, justice, hospitality, honesty, manliness, generosity, and respect for women. Among the conquered peoples schools of various types and grades existed, and in general they attained high proficiency in their intellectual skills. By the opening of the eighth century most leading Muslims employed tutors or owned slaves to teach their children. The only education available for the masses was that obtained from Koran readers in the mosques.

In the Abbasid period, the number of elementary schools increased, so that many children were taught to read and write. The curriculum centered on the Koran and allied religious texts, and memory achievement was the goal. Children of wealthy and prominent families continued to get rigorous and comprehensive private instruction. It was still not easy to acquire an advanced education, although to make one's way about the Muslim world in quest of the great teacher was less arduous than in earlier days. Various academies and mosques where one could study existed, some with charitable endowments; but they were unorganized and did not furnish any systematic education.

The first collegiate institution to be established under Islam was at Cordoba, founded by the Umayyad Abd al-Rahman III in the middle of the tenth century. Expanded and placed upon a more solid financial basis by al-Hakam, Cordoba gathered professors and attracted students from every Muslim land. Professorial chairs were endowed, and fellowships were granted to advanced students. One of the most famous of the Islamic institutions for advanced study was al-Azhar in Cairo, founded by the Fatimids in the latter part of the tenth century. Through the centuries al-Azhar maintained a reputation for scholarship and a high quality of education, especially in the fields of theology and law, which it still has to this day. Separate from the schools where law was the basic curriculum were the Sufi monasteries, where mystics studied traditions, their own approach to law, and the mystical path to knowledge. A bureau for translation, a library, and an observatory in al-Mamun's House of Wisdom in Baghdad served as a kind of collegiate institution.

Libraries were widespread. The honor of creating one of the first centers of learning in the east fell to Nizam al-Mulk, the ingenious eleventh-century vizir. His Nizamiyah in Baghdad, intended as a private institution to teach Shafiites religion, was followed within a few years throughout the Muslim world by construction of other madrasahs (schools). In the leading cities of Islam each of the larger mosques included a privately organized and funded madrasah, where religious and legal subjects predominated. Philosophy, mathematics, medicine, and the natural sciences were taught in the homes of scholars, in hospitals, or in the madrasahs as auxiliary to religious subjects.

Rote learning predominated as in most educational establishments in all civilizations throughout the ages; but the need to acquire dialectical skills in deriving legal opinions encouraged analysis and synthesis for some thinkers. The obligation to show the relation between the ideas they imparted and the ethical and social requirements of society was recognized by noted Muslim teachers.

ARCHITECTURE

One notable architectural feature of Muslim civilization is the mosque and its accompanying minaret. The house of the urban Arab in Muhammad's time was almost invariably a simple enclosure, usually square, with a few huts placed in a rather haphazard way along the edge. The first mosque was none other than the house of Muhammad. Before he died it assumed a public character, for here the followers congregated to pray with Muhammad and to hear his revelations, sermons, and instructions. Along one side palm trunks were set up and covered with palm leaves as a protection from the sun. Muhammad first used to lean against a trunk when he spoke; later he stood on a piece of a palm trunk. Some pointer indicated the direction of Mecca so that prayers could be made facing that holy city. Bilal, an early follower of Muhammad, stood on some roof top to call the Muslims to prayer or to a community meeting. Thus were established the essentials of a mosque.

As the Arabs and Muslims expanded into other lands, they employed local masons, carpenters, stonecutters, and other craftsmen in the building of mosques. Consequently, skills, techniques, and materials differed from place to place. But the fundamentals of a congregational mosque remained unchanged. A large part of the mosque area was an open courtyard, usually with a fountain where ablutions could be performed and sometimes with a narrow covered arcade on three sides.

On the fourth side was the mosque proper. In most mosques in Syria, Egypt, North Africa, Spain, and Iraq, the mosque proper consisted of a system of arches supported by piers or columns arranged in series of parallel aisles and upholding domes, vaults, and either a flat or a gabled wooden roof. Where the dome covered a square chamber or area, the transition from the arch was made by the use of squinches or spherical triangular pendentives. Stilted and horseshoe arches appeared early in the development of Islamic architecture, largely because the available cut columns taken from older structures were not long enough to hold the roof at the desired height. At Cordoba this problem was met by a series of columns and arches superimposed upon another series.

At one or more of the corners of the enclosure there stood a minaret. First appearing at the mosque in Damascus, it was a square towerlike structure from which the call to prayer was given. Round or pencil-shaped minarets did not develop until late in the medieval period, although circular ziggurat-type minarets are known to have existed in ninth-century Iraq and Iran.

In the wall of the mosque on the side toward Mecca the mihrab, or niche, was usually constructed to indicate the exact direction of the Holy City. This was particularly helpful in converted churches, since they were often not correctly oriented. A wooden or marble pulpit *(minbar)* was a necessary piece of furniture of a congregational mosque, enabling the imam who delivered the Friday sermon to be seen and heard by all. The façade encasing the main portal of the mosque enclosure as well as the inner façade around the doorway to the mosque itself in time was elaborately decorated, taking on the appearance of an external mihrab. Semidomes, vaults, arcatures, stalactite corbeling, marble paneling, and molding surrounded these entrances and made peerless approaches for the mosques. In Iran and the east some mosques had lofty and imposing portals showing an unmistakable influence of ancient structures of Persepolis and Ctesiphon upon Muslim architecture. The prevalence of the distinctive stalactite or honeycomb vault occurred in the late eleventh century.

The exterior and interior decoration of the mosques was based upon matched and quartered panels of marble, porphyry, and other types of stone, different-colored stones being used in alternate courses in the walls or in alternate voussoirs in the arches. Capitals, spandrils, and other spaces were often covered with finely carved geometric and floral patterns; and in many instances the walls were given color, warmth, and depth by the use of plain or figured tiles. One of the most frequent and pleasing patterns employed in stone, wood, or ceramics was that composed of highly stylized Arabic letters, almost invariably a verse from the Koran. Human and animal figures rarely appeared in a mosque.

Some of the imposing mosques of the Middle East that date from the early medieval period are the Umayyad mosque of Damascus, begun in 705; the Mosque of Ibn Tulun in Cairo, finished in 879; the Great Mosque of Qayrawan, built about 836; the Great Mosque of Cordoba, begun in 785 (now the cathedral); the Friday Mosque of Isfahan, built about 760; and the Mosque of Sultan Ala al-Din of Konya, built in 1220.

In the east the Ghaznavids and the Seljuks used mud brick or baked brick to rapidly build monumental structures, usually decorated with stucco or stone, including mosques with a courtyard surrounded by four vaulted niches framing a portal. The dramatic height of the portals and niches contrasted with the smaller proportions of the courtyard at ground level. Mausoleums were usually square chambers covered by domes, and also came in the form of tomb towers, cylindrical or polygonal towers with conical roofs.

Although mosques and great mausoleums have been the most permanent of Middle Eastern edifices of the medieval period, various books contain descriptions of numerous libraries, hospitals, bazaars, palaces, forts, shrines, and palatial public baths in Baghdad and other cities. Probably the most widely known sacred building in the Muslim Middle East is the revered Dome of the Rock in Jerusalem. An annular structure, it was begun in 685 by Caliph Abd al-Malik to cover and enshrine the spot from where, according to legend, Muhammad made his nocturnal journey to heaven. Termed the oldest extant Muslim place of worship except for the Kaaba in Mecca, it comprises an octagon surmounted by a dome which rests upon an interior circle of piers and columns. The space between the inner circle and the octagonal wall was too wide to be spanned by beams, necessitating an intermediate octagon of arches borne by piers and columns. Thus were formed two rings which were used for ceremonial circumambulation. Originally the upper part of the exterior was covered with marble and gold mosaics, but these were replaced with the decorated tiles that are now there. The style of the building was a composite of Syrian, Roman, and Byzantine traditions and contained a number of novel adaptations. The style, however, was followed in later Muslim architecture only in technical and decorative details and not as a general model for other structures.

THE MINOR ARTS

In the whole field of the so-called minor arts Muslims in the medieval period carried on the skills and techniques of antiquity in a notable fashion. Far ahead of western Europe in each of the minor arts, at least until the High Renaissance of the fifteenth century, the Middle East produced outstanding rugs, silk and cotton textiles, leatherwork, fine glass, highly glazed ceramics of many types, shapes, and varieties, and exquisite pieces in gold, silver, copper, brass, and bronze, many of the pieces heavily inlaid with other metals or encrusted with precious gems. The illumination of manuscripts and the painting of miniature pictures developed into a fine and precise art. Skilled penmanship produced a calligraphy so graceful and so pleasing that later Western artists frequently employed strips of Arabic script in their own decorations. The expertise of the Middle Eastern artist in the medium of enamel inlay upon metal was manifest to the Crusaders, so much so that many terms used in describing color (enamelwork) in armorial bearings and in heraldry were derived from Arabic words.

Between the seventh and thirteenth centuries, proof of the real unity of the Muslim world was the ease and extent of exchange of knowledge and movement of individuals. Such a circulation dictated a considerable universality of Muslim civilization, and the minor arts are an excellent example. From Marrakesh and Toledo on the west to Samarkand in the east, each of the great cities boasted reputable craftsmen and artists in all of the arts.

THE ROLES OF WOMEN IN PUBLIC LIFE

By the tenth century the role of wealthy, middle-class, and urban women in the family and in society had undergone a marked change. The veil, seclusion, and segregation of the sexes were practiced by Muslims and by many non-Muslims in the Middle East. Their origins and the reasons for their introduction are not certain, but the best indications point to Byzantine civilization as the main influence. With the general and wide acceptance of concubinage, the rank of the actual wife was greatly elevated. Slave girls might sing, dance, and entertain quite openly and freely for the guests of their masters, but never the wives. Thus, the veil and seclusion grew as a protection and a mark of distinction. However, the freedom and the public life of women such as enjoyed by Aishah, the wife of Muhammad, and in Abbasid times by Khayzuran and Zubaydah lessened. The social segregation of the sexes encouraged the widespread expression of homosexuality, which was often celebrated in verse, even though condemned by theologians.

Women's roles in society were affected by the practice of birth control, through both contraception and abortion. Scientific, legal, and popular literature was written on the subject, and the authors assumed a free wife could choose to avoid contraception so as to have children, if she wished, while the rights of a slave wife were somewhat limited, and those of a concubine in this area were nil. Although men were legally dominant in marriage, women retained the marriage settlement as their own property in the event of divorce, which could be instituted by the husband or, rarely, by the wife. Marriages were arranged and contracted between individuals or families of roughly equal status; the marriage of a Muslim woman to a non-Muslim man was uniformly opposed by the legal scholars.

Some women became prominent despite the difficulties placed in their way. The eighth-century celibate mystic Rabiah al-Adawiyyah of Basrah was one of the most influential of the early mystics and ascetics, and other mystics in later times were women. Several female poets gained some renown, especially the eleventh-century Spanish Umayyad princess Wallada.

RECREATION

The great mass of people in the medieval Middle East, as in all other regions and in other periods except for the present, had little time or energy for recreation and entertainment. People of moderate means as well as the wealthy and the leaders of society in the Middle East enjoyed poetry and music. Although Muhammad had castigated music as one of the devil's handmaidens, song and music from various instruments were exceedingly popular. Accomplished musicians were praised, highly rewarded, and accepted as companions in high society. Slaves with musical talent and training commanded high prices. The elite themselves sometimes performed, and the Abbasid caliph al-Rashid's brother Ibrahim was regarded as a truly accomplished musician.

Upper-class men (and, separately, women) relaxed at home or at a public bath which served as their club, open for the sexes on alternating days. Baghdad in its heyday boasted several thousand such establishments. After soaking and steaming and a vigorous massage the patron might sip cool sherbet, listen to music, and engage in a game of dice, backgammon, or chess. Chess was an ancient Indian game which came to Christian Europe by way of Iran and the Muslims. The word "chess" is a corruption of the Persian *shah;* "rook" is the Persian *rukh,* or the dreaded roc described by Sindbad the Sailor. The caliphs al-Rashid and al-Mamun were enthusiastic chess players.

Outdoor sports were many; favorites were archery, javelin-throwing, fencing, polo, and a ball game that may have been the ancestor of tennis. Hunting with its allied sports of hawking and falconry was much in vogue in the Umayyad and Abbasid eras. Caliphs and generals organized great hunts in which thousands participated in driving the game into confined quarters where the hunters could shoot the quarry without much effort. However, certain wild game at close range frequently provided a dangerous and exciting sport, sometimes depicted in painting and ceramic decoration. The art of falconry was greatly refined, and there were numerous books on the subject.

The most royal of all sports in the Middle East was horse racing. In ancient Iran, in Greece, and in Roman and Byzantine times, racing was the sport of kings and the favorite of the masses. The Arabs loved and prized horses; and the Muslim rulers quickly took to racing their horses in Syria, Iraq, and Egypt, as the Byzantine and Sasanid governors had done when the Arabs appeared on the scene. Caliphs had their own stables, and al-Rashid apparently took great pleasure in seeing his horses win their races. Betting accompanied horse racing, as it did all sports, and made the races and games more exciting. Pedigrees and an interest in the breeding of horses advanced to the point where Arabian horses were recognized and valued everywhere.

From the foregoing survey of the many aspects of Muslim culture and its development in the medieval period, it can be seen that Muslim culture was formed by the Umayyad and Abbasid empires. The Muslims appropriated and adapted from other civilizations and societies valuable ideas, experiences, and skills to create the new Muslim civilization. Few civilizations have been able to endure for long or to pursue any dynamic course when isolated either geographically or intellectually. Progress has been accelerated by the exchange of knowledge among people and cultures; the greater the exchange, the faster the acceleration. Although the Muslim empires were politically unstable, investigation of Muslim society reveals a continuing progress until the havoc and chaos that followed in the wake of the Mongol invasions of the thirteenth century, which brought upon much of the Middle East a penury and a despair shed only in the sixteenth century.

REFERENCES

Among the volumes already cited, those of particular value for this chapter are in Chapters 5 and 8.

Ahmad, S. Maqbul. "Djughrafiya." *Encyclopaedia of Islam.* New ed. Vol. 2, pp. 575–587. Leiden: Brill, 1965. A useful survey of geography.

Ahsan, Muhammad Manazir. *Social Life Under the Abbasids, 170–289 AH 786–902 AD*. London: Longman, 1979. The author examines costume, food, housing, hunting, games, and festivals, and gives many specific examples.

Ardalan, Nader, and Laleh Bakhtiar. *The Sense of Unity: The Sufi Tradition in Persian Architecture*. Chicago: University of Chicago Press, 1973. A beautiful book showing the place and effect of Sufi thought in Iranian architecture.

Beeston, A. F. L., *et al. The Cambridge History of Arabic Literature: Arabic Literature to the End of the Umayyad Period*. Cambridge: Cambridge University Press, 1983. A thorough study of the subject written by several authors.

Browne, E. G. *A Literary History of Persia.* 4 vols. Cambridge: Cambridge University Press, 1928. Still an important work, and one that relates to political and social developments.

Creswell, K. A. C. *A Short Account of Early Muslim Architecture*. Baltimore, Md.: Penguin, 1958. A brief survey of Creswell's earlier works, covering Umayyad, Abbasid, and Tulunid periods.

Dodge, Bayard, ed. and trans. *The Fihrist of al-Nadim: A Tenth-Century Survey of Muslim Culture*. 2 vols. New York: Columbia University Press, 1970. A translation of a compendium of all knowledge written in the tenth century.

———. *Muslim Education in Medieval Times*. Washington, D.C.: The Middle East Institute, 1962. An unusual and scholarly work.

Dunlop, D. M. *Arab Civilization to A.D. 1500*. New York: Praeger, 1971. Covers literature, history, geography, philosophy, science, and famous women.

Duri, Abd al-Aziz. *The Rise of Historical Writing Among the Arabs*. Edited and translated by Lawrence I. Conrad. Princeton, N.J.: Princeton University Press, 1983. Especially valuable for developments in Medina and Iraq during the seventh, eighth, and ninth centuries.

Fakhry, Majid. *A History of Islamic Philosophy*. New York: Columbia University Press, 1983. 2d ed. A substantial and comprehensive history of Islamic theoretical philosophy, theology, and mysticism.

Gibb, H. A. R. *Arabic Literature: An Introduction*. 2d ed. Oxford: Clarendon Press, 1963.

Grabar, Oleg. *The Formation of Islamic Art*. Rev. ed. New Haven, Conn.: Yale University Press, 1987. The author's treatment is very sensitive, his insights are thought-provoking, and his expression superb. He defines the originality and uniqueness of Islamic art. A most important work.

Grube, Ernst J. *The World of Islam*. New York: McGraw-Hill, 1966. Landmarks of Islamic art.

Grunebaum, Gustave von. *Islam: Essays in the Nature and Growth of a Cultural Tradition*. New York: Barnes & Noble, 1961. Important in linking Islam and culture.

Hassan, Ahmad Y. al-, and Donald R. Hill. *Islamic Technology: An Illustrated History*. Cambridge: Cambridge University Press, 1986. One of the very few works on this subject; although written by specialists it is accessible to beginners in the field.

Hill, Derek. *Islamic Architecture and Its Decoration: A Photographic Survey*. London: Faber & Faber, 1964. Excellent pictures and interpretive descriptions and analysis.

Hoag, John D. *Islamic Architecture.* New York: Harry Abrams, 1977.

Humphreys, R. Stephen. *Islamic History: A Framework for Inquiry.* Minneapolis, Minn.: Bibliotheca Islamica, 1988. A sophisticated introduction to the sources and problems of Middle Eastern history from 600 to 1500.

Kraemer, Joel L. *Humanism in the Renaissance of Islam: The Cultural Revival During the Buyid Age.* Leiden: Brill, 1986. Buwayhid political history is related to religious and cultural life.

Kritzeck, James. *Anthology of Islamic Literature from the Rise of Islam to Modern Times.* New York: Holt, Rinehart and Winston, 1964. Discusses all forms of literature from the Koran and early commentaries to political theory, history, stories, and Ottoman puppet plays.

Leaman, Oliver. *An Introduction to Medieval Islamic Philosophy.* Cambridge: Cambridge University Press, 1985. Al-Farabi, Ibn Sina, al-Ghazali, Ibn Rushd, and Maimonides on the creation of the world, immortality, God's knowledge of particulars, ethics, and happiness.

Leiser, Gary. "Medical Education in Islamic Lands from the Seventh to the Fourteenth Century." *Journal of the History of Medicine and Allied Sciences* 38 (1983): 48–75. Valuable for its connection of education and medicine, especially in Egypt.

Levey, Martin. *Early Arabic Pharmacology: An Introduction Based on Ancient and Medieval Sources.* Leiden: Brill, 1973. Focuses on materia medica and therapeutics, beginning with pre-Islamic pharmacology.

Levy, Reuben. *The Social Structure of Islam.* Cambridge: Cambridge University Press, 1957. A thorough study and analysis of all aspects of society in the Islamic world from the earliest times.

Lewis, Bernard, and P. M. Holt, eds. *Historians of the Middle East.* New York: Oxford University Press, 1962. A most important work.

McNeill, William H., and Marilyn Waldman, eds. *The Islamic World.* New York: Oxford University Press, 1973. A wide variety of original sources in translation, dealing with poetry, history, literature, philosophy, etc.

Makdisi, George. *The Rise of Colleges: Institutions of Learning in Islam and the West.* Edinburgh: Edinburgh University Press, 1981. This, the best study now available on the subject, includes the role of religion, curricula, students, the position of professors, and a variety of other aspects of the topic.

Morrison, George, Julian Baldick, and Shafii Kadkani. *History of Persian Literature from the Beginning of the Islamic Period to the Present Day.* Leiden: Brill, 1981.

Musallam, B. F. *Sex and Society in Islam: Birth Control Before the Nineteenth Century.* Cambridge: Cambridge University Press, 1983. A valuable and unusual study of a subject often neglected.

Nashat, Guity, and Judith Tucker. *Restoring Women to History: Middle East.* Bloomington, Ind.: Organization of American Historians, 1988. An excellent survey from antiquity to the present; issued as part of a series on various parts of the world.

Nasr, Seyyed Hossein. *Science and Civilization in Islam.* Cambridge: Harvard University

Press, 1968. A discussion of the development of science, technology, and scientific methodology in medieval Islam.

————. *Islamic Science: An Illustrated Study*. London: World of Islam Festival Publishing Company, 1976. Beautiful illustrations of various scientific inventions and charts; also links together science, including agriculture, to broader questions of the meaning of the universe and creation.

Peters, F. E. *Aristotle and the Arabs: The Aristotelian Tradition in Islam*. New York: New York University Press, 1968. A study of the synthesis of Hellenism and Islam.

Pope, Arthur Upham. *An Introduction to Persian Art Since the Seventh Century A.D.* New York: Scribners, 1931. Well written and amply illustrated by an authority for the beginner, but interesting also to the specialist in the field of Middle Eastern studies.

Ullmann, Manfred. *Islamic Medicine*. Edinburgh: Edinburgh University Press, 1978. A brief review of translations of medical works, and of physiology, anatomy, pathology, disease transmission, dietetics, and the occult.

Watson, Andrew M. *Agricultural Innovation in the Early Islamic World: The Diffusion of Crops and Farming Techniques, 700–1100*. Cambridge: Cambridge University Press, 1983. A significant breakthrough in research on Islamic agriculture, this work is crucial reading.

10

The End of Medieval Islam

THE CRUSADES

In preaching the Crusade in 1095 at Clermont, France, Pope Urban II was unquestionably governed by religious spirit and motivation. Pilgrims returning from the East brought tales of the woe that recent Seljuk conquests had inflicted upon them in Asia Minor and Syria. They also reported that disunity and internecine warfare among the petty Muslim states of Syria and their leaders would make possible a victorious assault by Christian knights of Europe. Furthermore, the desperate appeal sent by Alexius Comnenus, emperor of Constantinople, promised the cooperation of the Byzantine army and fleet.

Western feudal Christendom had developed economically, socially, politically, and psychologically to a degree that it could outfit and send a temporary expeditionary force overseas. The success this force might have stemmed from the power vacuum and political chaos that descended upon the Middle East after the death of the Seljuk sultan Malikshah.

Gathering at Constantinople as an advance base, the Crusaders, almost always called Franks by Middle Easterners, departed for the Holy Land in the spring of 1097. Taking by force Iznik (Nicaea) in June and Eskishehir in July, the Crusaders were welcomed with enthusiasm by the Armenians in Edessa. The main Frankish army won Antakya (Antioch) after many heroic and emotional encounters and a nine-month siege. By an inland route the Crusaders began the siege of Jerusalem on June 7, 1099, and successfully stormed the walls on July 15. After the conquest, Muslims and Jews were barred from living in the city. Later that year, the first victory on the coast was scored at Ascalon, and in the ensuing decade one after another of the coastal cities of the Levant fell to the merchant fleets of Pisa, Venice, and Genoa.

Shortly after the conquest of the Holy City, Godfrey of Bouillon became the Defender of the Holy Sepulchre and the titular head of the kingdom of Jerusalem. Other prominent Crusaders scattered along the coast to become the count of Edessa, prince of Antioch, and count of Tripoli, these newly created principalities being held as fiefs of Jerusalem. Merely extensions of feudal Europe, these four little Crusader states along the Mediterranean littoral were the so-called Latin king-doms of the East. Most of the Crusaders returned home as soon as the first victo-ries were won, and those who stayed on were continuously hard-pressed to retain their possessions. In fact, they were a minority of the total population and would have been lost at an early date had not an uninterrupted stream of knights ap-peared from the West and had not the merchant cities of the western Mediterranean maintained fleets in the Levant.

Eventually the kingdom of Jerusalem was extended eastward across the Dead Sea and southward in a narrow tongue of land to touch the Gulf of Aqaba. In the north the county of Edessa reached eastward to the headwaters of the Tigris. Else-where, the Franks clung close to the coast, in some places holding a strip barely ten to fifteen miles wide. They never gained possession of such cities as Aleppo, Homs, or Damascus.

The great majority of Western successes sprang from the complete disunity of the Muslim rulers. The amirs of Syria were delighted by the Crusaders' defeat of the Seljuks in Asia Minor; and during the siege of Antioch emissaries from Egypt proposed an alliance of the Crusaders and the Fatimids against the Turks. Alliances by Muslim princes with Latins against fellow Muslims, or by Franks with Muslim amirs against fellow Crusader feudal lords, were commonplace.

Before a decade had passed only a newly arrived naïve Crusader carried the religious spirit and fervor that had launched the First Crusade. In the Middle East the Latin knight reverted to the search for fiefs and the constant fighting that he had known in the West. That he could do this and feel at home in Syria and Palestine in the twelfth century was a result of the political chaos already present at his arrival. Nevertheless, the more advanced civilization of the Middle East be-gan to influence the barbarous Westerners. Latin nobles emulated the ways and adopted the higher standard of living of Middle Eastern ruling classes, thus open-ing the way for some of the knowledge of the East to find its way to western Europe and hasten the coming of the Renaissance.

Baghdad and the eastern Seljuk sultans were hardly perturbed by the inroads of the Crusaders, especially since the latter succumbed within a few years to the general preexisting political pattern of the Middle East. Resistance to the West awaited the appearance of a vigorous leader capable of creating an extensive Muslim state that might serve as a base for an attack upon the Franks.

Such a man was the blue-eyed Zangi, Turkish lord of Mosul. Consolidating the northern arc of the Fertile Crescent from Mosul to Aleppo into one Muslim state, Imad al-Din Zangi stormed and took Edessa in 1144, an act that touched off the so-called Second Crusade. Although such notables as Louis VII of France and Conrad III of Germany participated, the chief effect of this expedition was to bring fresh recruits to ward off other blows and hold the line.

The Zangid principality subsequently augmented its power as the Seljuk rule in Baghdad and the Fatimid power in Cairo waned. Zangi's son, Nur al-Din, added Damascus to his state, conquered all of the county of Edessa, and wrested territory from Antioch and Tripoli. Bypassing the Franks in Jerusalem, his armies forced the Fatimid caliph of Egypt to surrender control of that fair Muslim province to a Zangid lieutenant, Salah al-Din Yusuf ibn Ayyub (Saladin).

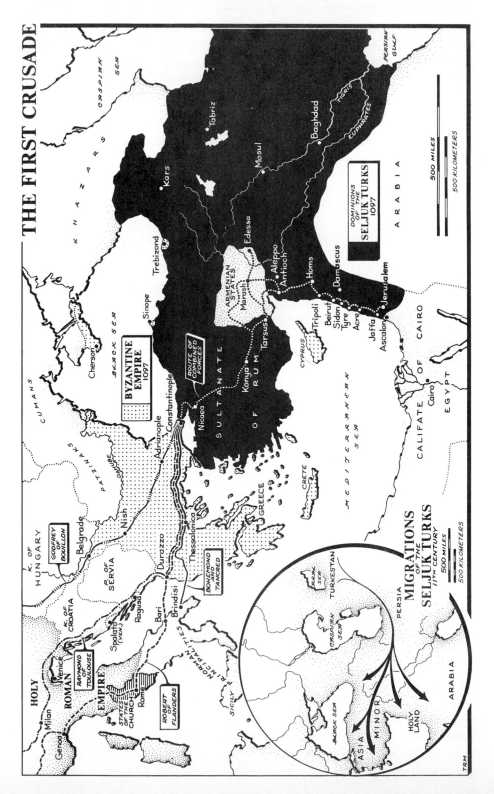

THE FIRST CRUSADE

DOMINIONS
OF THE
SELJUK TURKS
1097

BYZANTINE
EMPIRE
1097

ROUTE
OF
COMBINED
FORCES

500 MILES
500 KILOMETERS

GODFREY
OF
BOUILLON

RAYMOND
OF
TOULOUSE

ROBERT
OF
FLANDERS

BOHEMOND
AND
TANCRED

HOLY
ROMAN
EMPIRE

STATES
OF THE
CHURCH

K. OF
HUNGARY

K. OF
CROATIA

P. OF
SERVIA

MIGRATIONS
OF THE
SELJUK TURKS
11TH CENTURY

500 MILES
500 KILOMETERS

TRM

Of Kurdish stock, Salah al-Din sought to unify Islam and destroy the Crusaders. In 1171, he refused to recognize the Fatimid Shiite caliph and restored Egypt to the Sunnite creed, and the Abbasid caliph's name was once again mentioned in public prayers. Upon the death of the Zangid Nur al-Din, Salah al-Din used his Kurdish, Turkish, and Arab Bedouin army to seize Syria, went on to take Mosul, and eventually was accepted as the sultan in the Hijaz and Yemen as well. Long-distance trade flourished and the spices of the East were a major source of wealth. Salah al-Din and the Zangids before him encouraged education and the construction of schools and other buildings in the cities of Syria, while Salah al-Din's citadel above Cairo dominated that city.

Turning upon the Franks, Salah al-Din wiped out the cream of the knights' armies at the Battle of Hattin on July 4, 1187. This victory enabled him to retake Jerusalem and all the principal cities except Antioch, Tripoli, and Tyre.

Jerusalem's fall initiated the Third Crusade, which gave rise to more romantic episodes in the history and literature of Islam and Christendom alike than any of the other Crusades. Philip Augustus, Frederick Barbarossa, and Richard the Lion-Hearted could not recapture Jerusalem; but after a siege of two years, Acre (Akka), which became the new Crusader capital city, fell to Richard. When the demanded ransom was not forthcoming, Richard decreed the execution of the garrison of 2,700. This was in sharp contrast to Salah al-Din's clemency following the fall of Jerusalem, when all who were not ransomed were set free.

Pursuant to the victory at Acre, Richard suggested the marriage of his sister and Salah al-Din's brother. Jerusalem was to be a wedding gift, and general peace was to be arranged between Frank and Muslim. The marriage did not occur, but an armistice was concluded, leaving a narrow coastal area in possession of the Latins.

Salah al-Din died the next spring (1193), and upon his passing the usual political dismemberment developed, and his Ayyubid dynasty lasted only about fifty more years. One son held Damascus; others governed at Cairo and Aleppo. A brother ruled Jordan and conquered Syria and Egypt. Upon his death division and anarchy again ruled the Ayyubids' principalities until their own slaves destroyed them.

The recurring Muslim turmoil played into the Westerners' hands, enabling them to retake Beirut, Ascalon, and Jerusalem (1229). However, disputes over succession to the throne, and quarrels of Venetian against Genoese, Templar against Hospitaler, and baron against baron prevented lasting achievements. Salah al-Din's nephew forced the Latins to abandon Damietta in Egypt, where they had landed hoping to seize Egypt and the Red Sea and their commerce with India and the East. Nevertheless, he made friendly treaties with the Italian city-states, entertained and discussed theology with St. Francis of Assisi, and gave Jerusalem to Frederick II, the Holy Roman Emperor.

Jerusalem was taken in 1244 by a band of Turks; Louis IX's crusade to Egypt fell victim to the plague in 1249; and in that same year the Ayyubid family in Egypt was supplanted by Turkish generals from its slave army. A new era in Muslim history was emerging—the Mamluk (slave) period. Baybars, the fourth Mamluk sultan, captured much of Palestine and moved northward along an inland route to take Antioch. His successor continued the drive against the Latin state, and in 1291 another Mamluk took Acre. This was the signal for the remaining Crusader towns of Beirut, Sidon, and Tyre to surrender. An episode in the history of the Middle East had ended.

As significant events influencing the development of civilizations and the destiny of humanity, the Crusades have been greatly overrated. Nineteenth-century romanticists dramatized them and enlarged their role far beyond the actual facts. Most of the Crusaders remained in the Middle East such a short time and were so poorly prepared psychologically and educationally that they profited little from the experience. Of the few who resided in the Middle East for any length of time only the rare knight was willing to exchange the rich and interesting life in his new abode for the dull monotony on his former estate in the West.

Trade between East and West in the Mediterranean did, however, increase markedly. Jewish merchants in Cairo were part of a network of traders who flourished throughout the Mediterranean. Italian merchants now had for the first time a paying eastbound cargo: Crusaders. This reduced the cost of Eastern goods in Western markets. Furthermore, returning Crusaders created an expanded Western market for Eastern goods, since even those who remained in the Middle East only a brief time did acquire a taste for Oriental foods and a preference for its superior manufactured goods such as textiles, cutlery, metal wares, and leather goods. However, the main channels of Muslim influence upon western Europe were Sicily and Spain. Perhaps the flow through these areas was accelerated as a result of the Crusades and the returning Crusaders' awakened consciousness, if not appreciation, of a foreign civilization obviously richer than their own.

The effects upon the Middle East were much less significant. Its people became convinced that the Westerner was a ruthless soldier, semibarbarous in nature, ignorant, and uncivilized. Even today Syrian mothers frighten their children when they misbehave by threatening them with "Richard the Lion-Hearted will get you." For centuries, Crusaders' castles dotted the landscape, but these never altered in any measurable degree the architecture of the Levant. Indigenous Christians were the object of suspicion by their Muslim rulers, and their position in society declined after the departure of the Crusaders. The Middle East was politically disunited when the Crusaders arrived; it was still in fragments when they departed. In the interim, to be sure, the Ayyubids and then the Mamluks united the Muslims from the Nile to the Tigris. But this had no relationship to the Crusades; it was only an example of the recurring pattern of centralizing and decentralizing political forces continually at work in the area. In general, it can be said that the Crusaders were more destructive than constructive, and that the Middle East was poorer because of the experience.

THE MONGOL INVASIONS

In the thirteenth century as the Crusades were waning, devastation rode in upon the Muslim world from the east. Born about 1160 in the neighborhood of Lake Baikal, Genghiz Khan, ruler over Mongol nomads and the self-styled Scourge of God, consolidated in his hands the military might of the tireless Mongol warriors.

Shortly after the opening of the thirteenth century, Genghiz and his hordes moved westward to Iran, conquering all lands in their path. Bukhara, Samarkand, Merv, Nishapur, Hamadan, Maraghah, and many other centers of civilization were stormed and sacked. Inhabitants were slain by the hundreds of thousands, perhaps millions.

Iraq, Syria, and provinces in the west were spared by Genghiz's death in 1227 and by the subsequent division of the empire among his sons. But his sons and grandsons and other Mongol khans maintained the great empire. Pressure continued upon the Middle East. The Seljuk Turks in Asia Minor were defeated in a ruinous battle in 1243, and the Mongols levied tribute upon them. Under Mangu, the third successor to the position of supreme khan, a great expedition moved westward under the direction of Mangu's younger brother Hulagu. Starting in 1252 to rid the world of the Assassins and to destroy the Abbasid caliphate, Hulagu Khan razed Alamut, the Assassin headquarters.

The Abbasid caliph al-Nasir, who reigned from 1180 to 1225, had managed to restore some real political power to the caliphate in Iraq. But now in 1258 Baghdad and the Abbasids were to come into the hands of the non-Muslim Mongols. Following a siege of several months, the city fell and was given over completely to the troops for a week. Destruction continued for a month. The Mongol armies, including local auxiliaries from the Middle East, then proceeded westward as far as Damascus, but were halted by Baybars, the Mamluk sultan of Egypt, in a historic battle in 1260 at Ayn Jalut, near Nazareth. Egypt was spared Mongol violence; and Baybars pressed his victory, freeing Syria from Mongol control.

The Mongols in their conquests helped themselves to whatever they wanted and destroyed the rest, not knowing what to do with it. They could not garrison the cities adequately; they were pagans; and the first generations neither understood nor appreciated the cultures and civilizations of the peoples they conquered. The effects of the devastation wrought by the Mongols are only now in the twentieth century being mended. Millions of people perished; cities vanished; canals silted and irrigation decreased; lands became barren and deserted; government disintegrated; civilization foundered; and life returned to the bare essentials. Taxes were sharply increased and land grants to fiefholders became hereditary. Through the previous ages conquering armies and peoples had come and gone— Medes, Persians, Sasanids, Greeks, Romans, Byzantines, and Arabs—and customs, religions, knowledge, and culture had been modified, developed, and altered. But through all this time the Middle East had never suffered such a cataclysmic and paralytic shock as it received from the Mongol invasions.

MAMLUK RULE IN EGYPT

Untouched by the Mongol devastation, Egypt suddenly became the great stronghold of Muslim civilization, even though she herself had just entered into the strangest epoch of her long history.

Upon the death of the Ayyubid sultan in 1249, one of his widows seized power with the support of a Turkish slave general whom she married. When she later had him murdered in his bath, she was beaten to death by his slave soldiers. The rule of Egypt then passed briefly to his son and then to other slave generals, one after another until 1517 when Egypt was conquered by the Ottomans. This long period of two and a half centuries of Egyptian history was termed the Mamluk ("slave") era. Until 1382 the Mamluks were mostly Turkish and Mongol in origin, and they went by the name of Bahri ("river") Mamluks. Between 1382 and 1517, they were generally Circassians and were known as the Burji ("citadel") Mamluks.

Begun by the later Ayyubids as a slave army and bodyguard of foreign origin, the Mamluks evolved into a Turkish-speaking self-perpetuating urban slave military oligarchy. The recruit was purchased, usually in an eastern slave market, by the agent of a slave general or officer and rigorously trained in the arts of war, especially cavalry, within a household where he would form a sense of common identity with his fellow Mamluks. As he developed and progressed toward the top, he in turn made new purchases of slaves. (The sons of the Mamluks might become part of the army, but they usually lacked the prestige and special position of their fathers; they were not Mamluks themselves.) A score of generals or amirs at the summit intrigued and battled for supremacy and held the chief posts of government, though nominally electing the successor to the late Mamluk sultan. Many never bothered to learn Arabic and were Sunnite Muslims in name only. Aloof from the native Egyptians, whom they despised, the Mamluks usually showed toleration for religious minorities; conversion to Islam was widespread. The Mamluks supervised the pilgrimage to Mecca, and many went to the Holy City.

Although frequently illiterate, the Mamluk sultans were usually crafty, and some of them were capable organizers and redoubtable generals. Nevertheless, their lives were fearfully uncertain, the average reign of the forty-seven Mamluk sultans being less than six years. The most resourceful, and one of the most enduring, Sultan Baybars (1260–1277), not only turned back the Mongols in Palestine but also cracked the strength of the Crusaders in Syria. Understanding diplomacy and statecraft, he established friendly relations with Sicily, Aragon, and Seville, sent envoys to the Byzantine emperor, and made an alliance with the Kipchak Turks of the Volga River basin (his own birthplace) against the Mongols of Iran and Iraq. Bringing from Damascus a refugee scion of the Abbasid family, Baybars originated the practice of having an Abbasid in Cairo as titular caliph without actual power. Such caliphs resided there up to the time of the Ottoman conquest, and their presence gave to Mamluk rulers a mark of legal recognition.

Under the Mamluks (and earlier), a type of feudalism spread in Egypt and elsewhere in their domains. Since late Roman rule in the Middle East certain practices of feudalism had been present, and many of these were accepted by the Muslim conquerors. But in the tenth and eleventh centuries, as the power of the Abbasid government declined, army generals, captains, and cavalrymen were assigned provinces and estates from which they collected taxes for their own support. For these privileges and benefits they were expected to serve the caliph or sultan, usually in a military capacity. Land grants were frequently changed under the Mamluks, especially after a cadastral survey, and peasants came to be treated in some respects as serfs. Gradually most of the revenue from the lands of Egypt was granted to Mamluk officers who had to support, equip, and ensure the service of a number of soldiers, the number depending upon their rank and the size of the grant. However, after 1315, about one-half of the revenues from these grants was assigned to the sultan himself, for the same purposes.

DESTRUCTION OF THE MEDIEVAL MUSLIM WORLD

Simultaneously with the development of Middle Eastern "feudalism" came the spread of a more self-subsistent economy. As the uncertainties of government mounted and the difficulties of transportation and communication increased, industry and commerce were depressed and the money economy was greatly weakened. Political anarchy and civil wars destroyed the controls over the nomads within the Middle East and the perpetual battle between the Desert and the Sown was resumed as agricultural production in most parts of the Middle East decreased. A number of factors contributed to this: the overuse of resources; an inability or unwillingness to overcome technical barriers so as to deal with past farming problems, such as increased salinity; a rigid social conservatism that opposed most forms of innovation; and widespread disease, as in the case of the Black Death in the middle of the fourteenth century, and subsequent plagues that killed millions. The Middle Eastern lands entered into this new era piecemeal over a long period of time.

The major portion of the central Middle East was under the Mongol Empire. This region was split into a variety of provinces. Government and wealth moved eastward. From time to time in the century following the conquests of Hulagu, peace among Genghiz Khan's descendants allowed for passage of traders and travelers such as Marco Polo and Ibn Battutah. But the persistent military violence, direct or threatened, stunted the growth of middle-class merchants and tradesmen.

Initially, the Il-Khans, or Mongol rulers of Iran and Iraq, with their capitals at Tabriz and Maraghah, remained non-Muslims, and were tolerant protectors of the Christian and other minorities of the region. With the accession to the throne of Ghazan in 1295 the dynasty became Muslim, and Turkish began to replace Mongol as the language of the elite. Some cultural accomplishments took place under Mongol rule: the Persian historian and statesmen Rashid al-Din (1247–1318) wrote a famous world history; the study of astronomy flourished; and great literary figures such as Sadi and Hafiz produced beautiful literature. Patronage of the arts nearly came to an end with Abu Said, who was the last of the Mongols to rule over a united Iran and Iraq. Civil war and puppet rulers followed each other after his death in 1335, and small and ephemeral dynasties came to rule where the Mongols had once dominated. Moreover, in 1368, the founder of the Ming dynasty in China conquered the Mongols and closed the overland trade routes from central Asia into China, diverting all commerce with the Mediterranean to the sea route through the Indian Ocean, the Red Sea, and Egypt.

The final blows to the highly developed Muslim culture and civilization of the medieval period in Iraq, central and eastern Asia Minor, and parts of Iran were administered by the Mongolian Turks. For a quarter of a century, 1380–1405, the east was in turmoil because of the eruption of the Mongolian Turks led by the

Sunnite Muslim Timur Leng ("Timur the Lame," or Tamerlane). Son of a Turkish chieftain, Timur first won control of Transoxiana, which served as a base for expansion, both eastward and westward. He called himself by the title amir, while retaining the fiction of Mongol overlordship. In 1380, his hordes began the conquest of Afghanistan, Iran, and Kurdistan. In rapid succession he captured Baghdad, Isfahan, Delhi, Aleppo, Damascus (where he interviewed at length the historian Ibn Khaldun), Ankara, and Izmir—but not Egypt. Timur's death in 1405 and the subsequent anarchy among his heirs brought relief to the Middle East; but the majority of the middle class had disappeared, and much of the desolation wrought at his hands was never repaired. His most notorious custom was the construction of pyramids of human heads after the sacking of cities; at Isfahan 40,000 heads were built into such markers. Schools, libraries, and mosques were destroyed, and only the walls of the famed Umayyad mosque in Damascus were left. Skilled artisans and their families were deported to Samarkand, where they erected magnificent buildings; many ancient skills that had survived through the ages were now lost forever in the central Middle East.

In the wake of this barbarian tide three major states remained in the Middle East: a fragmentized Iran; a broken and reduced Ottoman state; and the wealthy if tumultuous Mamluk state of Egypt. Fifteenth-century affairs in the Middle East revolved around the economic, political, and international problems and interrelationships of these three powers.

THE OTTOMAN TURKS

The fortunes of the Ottoman state are considered in more detail elsewhere in this volume. Here it is sufficient to point out that the Ottoman state was reunited by Sultan Mehmed I within fifteen years after the debacle of his father at the Battle of Ankara in 1402, when Timur captured the Ottoman sultan. The process of building an empire by adding provinces in the Balkans and Asia Minor was resumed, with Constantinople falling to Sultan Mehmed II in 1453. Following that renowned event, the Ottomans in their expansion southward and eastward came into conflict with Iranians and Mamluks. Mehmed II in 1473 turned back Uzun Hasan of Iran, and Selim I soundly trounced Shah Ismail, clearing Anatolia of most of the Iranian sympathizers and fellow Shiites. Under Mehmed II border disputes flared between Turkey and Syria and between the satellites of the Mamluks and the Ottomans. In the 1490s Bayezid II was engaged in seven campaigns against the Mamluks. The latter won technical decisions in each case; but twenty years later (1517) Selim I and his army marched victoriously into Cairo, reducing the Mamluk state to an Ottoman province and carrying off the last puppet Abbasid caliph to Istanbul.

IRAN

Iran in 1409 came under the rule of Timur's son Shah Rukh, who attempted to rebuild Herat and Merv and to establish a peaceful and prosperous regime. The succeeding Timurids until 1506 were able to rule most of eastern Iran and

Afghanistan, where they were great patrons of the sciences and arts (and particularly miniature painting, which reached a brilliant stage of accomplishment in Herat). Trigonometry and astronomy were extensively studied. Sufi themes in poetry were frequent, as in the works of the biographer and poet Jami (d. 1492). The later Timurids, however, battled among themselves to such an extent that they were unable to control the Turkish nomadic tribes of the area. Despite some attempts by Timurid rulers to restore the damage done by the Mongols and by Timur himself, the general economic situation was bleak. New groups and families arose to divide Iran and to render her impotent in the struggle for power in the Middle East. Raids by Uzbeg tribes in Transoxiana and the absence of trade to the East led the center of population and importance to shift westward.

In the Caucasus and the highlands of eastern Anatolia, Turkish tribes under the leadership of the Shiite Qara Quyunlu (Black Sheep Turkomans) seized control of Armenia and Azerbayjan. For a time in the fifteenth century after the death of Timur, the Qara Quyunlu ruled Baghdad and established Tabriz as their capital, building the famous "Blue Mosque" there. Other Turkish tribes in a Sunnite Aq Quyunlu (White Sheep Turkomans) federation were established in Armenia and northern Iraq with Diyarbakir as their capital. The pinnacle of Aq Quyunlu power came under Uzun Hasan, who ruled Iraq, much of eastern Anatolia, and nearly all of Iran from about 1467 until his death in 1478. Married to a daughter of the Greek emperor of Trebizond, Uzun Hasan through his in-laws was approached by Venice to fight battles against the Ottomans. However, he found the Ottoman sultan Mehmed II a formidable foe, especially since Venice made no move to engage the Ottomans in another quarter.

After the death of Uzun Hasan the Aq Quyunlu state disintegrated, preparing the ground for the rise of the more native Safavid dynasty under Shah Ismail.

EGYPT

The trade of the Far East and India passed to Europe through the Red Sea and to the Mediterranean either by way of Egypt or by the historic caravan routes in the Hijaz to Jordan, Damascus, Aleppo, and Alexandretta. The Mamluk Empire, therefore, possessed a strong, almost monopolistic, control over East-West trade. The steady growth of this trade in the fourteenth century together with the natural productivity of the Nile valley and the skilled artisan manufactures of Egypt gave to the Mamluk-Arab society a brilliance unrivaled in any other Arab land. What cultural life and quest for knowledge remained in the Arab world found refuge and patronage in Cairo, which drew scholars and ambitious students from all parts of the Middle East. Mamluk Egypt and Syria in the fourteenth century excelled in the production of beautiful enameled and gilded glass, especially mosque lamps, and book illumination, calligraphy, and binding flourished. Inlaid metalwork, as in brass candlesticks, was also noteworthy, while decorated silk textiles were a valued export to Europe. Although originality had largely passed, science and literature were cultivated by students and supported by the court and the wealthy.

The greatest activity was in the construction of madrasahs and mausoleum-mosques. Of these the most outstanding was that of Sultan Qaitbay, who died in 1495. Noted for its alternate red and white stone courses, the mosque-tomb-school has a stately high dome over the tomb chamber. The exterior of the dome is covered by an elaborate geometric pattern interspaced with intricate floral designs. The minaret, in several stories, is one of the most handsome in Cairo. The arched gallery of the second floor of the school reminds one of the arched loggias of Venice.

Yet, despite all the trade and wealth and the escape from invasion and devastation, society and civilization in Egypt were decadent. Government was uncertain. Mamluk sultans succeeded each other with frequency and violence. In the fifteenth century, there were twenty-two changes of sultan; on one occasion there were three sultans in a single year. The system of training Mamluk officers and soldiers broke down, and the quality of new slaves deteriorated as the difficulty of purchasing slaves in the Volga and the Black Sea areas increased. Law became the whim of the ruler, and the ruling class was beyond the law. Graft, corruption, and inefficiency within the Mamluk order mushroomed. As land revenues declined, government officials grew more venal.

The death of the sultan al-Nasir in 1340 signaled the end of a period of clear economic growth and of the tight control of government by the sultan, and began a time of internal strife. The Circassian Mamluks' regime after 1382 brought even more factionalism. Bedouin unrest, increased taxation, state monopolies that reduced business flexibility, outbreaks of disease and subsequent depopulation (especially among the Mamluks themselves), inflation of prices, neglect of irrigation by the government, and famine all contributed to a decline of Mamluk Egypt.

Between native Arab-Egyptian and Mamluk the chasm widened; the community of interests decreased. Personal insult was added to exploitation and civil degradation until the Mamluk, although a coreligionist, was loathed by the native Egyptian. Nevertheless, rich merchants flourished in Cairo, and the presence of such wealth gave the city an aura of prosperous strength that misled most European visitors.

The Mamluk Empire included the Hijaz and Syria as well as Egypt, the outlying provinces being held through semiautonomous amirs. These satellites to the north were tied to Cairo loosely when the sultan was weak; and frequently at such moments the amirs played the dangerous game of flirting with the reviving Ottoman state or with whatever prince ruled in Iran. Border disputes were inevitable, and in 1485 when a war broke out between rivals for the throne of Dhu al-Qadr (Dulgadir), Ottoman sultan Bayezid II backed one contender while Mamluk sultan Qaitbay supported the other. Six campaigns followed. At one time the Ottomans occupied Aleppo; at other times Mamluk generals penetrated Anatolia. The Mamluks won the battles but could not achieve victory, and in 1491 peace was arranged.

Within a decade after this successful defense of the distant frontiers of the state, Mamluk good fortune was irretrievably lost. The Mamluk households' loyalty to their leaders declined and was replaced by insubordination and mutiny. Training for the Mamluk cavalry was of poor quality and the Mamluks were reluctant to use cannons and handguns on the battlefield. Repeated attacks of disease also devastated Egypt and Syria. Then the Portuguese rounded Africa and strongly established themselves in the Indian trade, since they could afford to pay higher prices for goods than the Mamluks. In 1502, the Portuguese attempted to block the Gulf of Aden to prevent ships from entering the Red Sea. Portuguese ships threatened the port of Jidda on the Red Sea, and in 1506 the Portuguese occupied and fortified the Island of Socotra near the entrance to the Gulf of Aden. The small Mamluk fleet was damaged in 1509 by the Portuguese, but with Ottoman help the Red Sea was defended against further incursions.

When the Ottoman sultan, Selim I, arrived in Syria, conditions in the Mamluk Empire were in disarray. The Mamluk sultan brought his army to Aleppo to threaten the rear and flank of Selim, who was engaged with Shah Ismail of Iran. Selim turned quickly, crossed the Taurus mountains, and routed the Mamluks at Marj Dabiq in August 1516. Previously, the Mamluk army was well paid and well equipped, but the force before the Ottomans here was a sullen, dispirited, and unpaid mob using obsolete armament, whereas the Ottoman armies had powerful and mobile cannons. Selim proceeded southward taking all of Syria with ease; cities such as Damascus, Tripoli, and Beirut surrendered peacefully.

Cairo was taken by assault in January 1517, and the last Mamluk sultan, Tumanbay, was seized and hanged. Egypt became an Ottoman province, and the Abbasid puppet caliph, al-Mutawakkil, was taken to Istanbul. With Selim I's departure from Egypt the center of the Middle East politically, economically, and culturally shifted to Istanbul and the Ottoman Empire. An age had wearily come to an end. Although Turkish sultans, Turkish generals, and Turkish slaves had been ruling in many Arab countries for several centuries, clearly the future now belonged to an Ottoman rule that identified itself as Turkish.

REFERENCES

Many volumes already cited bear upon this chapter, including several in Chapters 4, 7, and 9.

Ashtor, E. *A Social and Economic History of the Near East in the Middle Ages.* Berkeley: University of California Press, 1976. An extremely important synthesis of earlier work, with discussions of agriculture, feudalism, city life, Iraq and the Mediterranean areas, and the Mamluks.

Atil, Esin. *Renaissance of Islam: Art of the Mamluks.* Washington, D.C.: Smithsonian Institution Press, 1981. Sumptuously illustrated, with chapters on manuscripts, metalwork, glass, ceramics, and textiles.

Ayalon, David. *Gunpowder and Firearms in the Mamluk Kingdom.* London: Valentine, Mitchell, 1956. A valuable work, referring to the Ottoman and Safavid armies as well.

Boyle, J. A., ed. *The Cambridge History of Iran.* Vol. 5. *The Saljuq and Mongol Periods.* Cambridge: Cambridge University Press, 1968. Beginning with the political and dynastic history of Iran from 1000 to 1217, the volume describes the internal structure of the Seljuk empire and its religion. It continues with a discussion of the Il-Khans, the Ismaili state, and the Mongols. Chapters on poetry and prose, the arts, and sciences are most useful.

Dols, Michael W. *The Black Death in the Middle East.* Princeton, N.J.: Princeton University Press, 1977. An excellent discussion of the subject.

Ehrenkreutz, Andrew S. *Saladin.* Albany: State University of New York Press, 1972. Still an extremely interesting study of Salah al-Din, this work examines his liquidation of the Fatimid dynasty in Egypt, the establishment of his house as a princely family, and the unification of Egypt and Syria; it indicates that the Crusades were a small side issue.

Glubb, John Bagot. *Soldiers of Fortune: The Story of the Mamluks.* London: Hodder and Stoughton, 1973. A detailed account of the rivalry for power among the cliques and various military contingents and the utter ruthlessness of the process.

Goitein, S. D. *A Mediterranean Society: The Jewish Communities of the Arab World in the Documents of the Cairo Geniza.* 4 vols. Berkeley: University of California Press, 1967–84. Monumental works of scholarship that study the life of Jews in the Arab world during the Middle Ages.

Holt, Peter M. *The Age of the Crusaders: The Near East from the Eleventh Century to 1517.* London: Longman, 1985. Holt is the leading historian of the period for political history, and this broad and detailed work examines all aspects of the subject. It is especially valuable in discussing the Mamluks.

Humphreys, R. Stephen. *From Saladin to the Mongols: The Ayyubids of Damascus, 1193–1260.* Albany: State University of New York Press, 1977. This author explains the Ayyubid confederation of principalities.

Irwin, Robert. *The Middle East in the Middle Ages: The Early Mamluk Sultanate, 1250–1382.* Carbondale: Southern Illinois University Press, 1986.

Jackson, Peter, and Laurence Lockhart, eds. *The Cambridge History of Iran.* Vol. 6. *The Timurid and Safavid Periods.* Cambridge: Cambridge University Press, 1986. A detailed examination of the political history of the age in various chapters is followed by discussions of administration, European contacts, trade, social affairs, sciences, religion, art and architecture, and literature. Invaluable for all serious readers.

Lapidus, Ira Marvin. *Muslim Cities in the Later Middle Ages.* Cambridge, Mass.: Harvard University Press, 1967. Centered on Cairo and Damascus, this book is extremely important for Mamluk social history.

Little, Donald P. "Religion Under the Mamluks." *The Muslim World* 73 (1983): 165–181.

Petry, Carl F. *The Civilian Elite of Cairo in the Later Middle Ages.* Princeton, N.J.: Princeton University Press, 1981. The quantitative methodology employed here for fifteenth-century Cairo represents one of the relatively few attempts to use these analytical tools in the study of the medieval Middle East.

Runciman, Steven. *A History of the Crusades.* 3 vols. Cambridge: Cambridge University Press, 1951–58. Thorough and readable. Largely from the Western point of view.

Sourdel, Dominique. *Medieval Islam.* Translated by J. Montgomery Watt. London: Routledge and Kegan Paul, 1983. The author provides a sophisticated discussion of a number of disputed interpretations.

Spuler, Bertold. *The Mongols in History.* Translated by Geoffrey Wheeler. London: Pall Mall Press, 1971.

Wolff, Robert Lee, and Harry W. Hazard, eds. *A History of the Crusades*. Vol. 2. *The Later Crusades (1189–1311)*. Philadelphia: University of Pennsylvania Press, 1962.

Woods, John E. *The Aqquyunlu Clan, Confederation, Empire: A Study in 15th/9th Century Turko-Iranian Politics*. Minneapolis, Minn.: Bibliotheca Islamica, 1976.

Zacour, Norman, and Harry W. Hazard, eds. *A History of the Crusades*. Vol. 5. *The Impact of the Crusades on the Near East*. Madison: University of Wisconsin Press, 1985.

Part Two

The Ottoman and Safavid Empires

11

The Byzantine Empire

ESTABLISHMENT OF THE STATE

A prominent student of Byzantine history has defined the Byzantine Empire as "the Roman Empire in its Christian form." If this is true, then its history must begin with the era of the emperor Constantine and his building of the city of Constantinople on the site of ancient Byzantium.

Except for a period in the thirteenth century when Western European knights of the Fourth Crusade occupied it, Constantinople was the hub of the Eastern Roman Empire until its fall to the Turks in 1453. Thus, the Roman Empire under Christianity endured for more than eleven centuries—centuries that witnessed, especially in Constantinople, the preservation and propagation of the Christian faith and its theology; the knowledge of the Hellenistic and Roman ages; the art and architecture of the ancient world; the artisan skills of Greece, Rome, and the Orient; and many techniques of government discovered through centuries of Roman rule.

In establishing a new capital for the empire Constantine placed his chief residence close to the populous part of the empire and in a situation for the defense of the Balkan provinces. Moreover, he was able to break more completely with obsolete paraphernalia of government in Rome. His reforms, and those of Diocletian before him, were easier to sustain in a new location.

In Constantinople, the emperor was the accepted absolute monarch with power strictly centralized in his hands. Except in a very few provinces, civil and military powers were separated, and a regular civil service system for the various bureaus of government was expanded on a basis of merit and seniority.

Finally, but perhaps first in significance, was Constantine's recognition of Christianity, his participation in Christian affairs to the extent of calling the first general council of the Christian Church at Nicaea in 325, and his use of the emperor's power to try to achieve uniformity in Christian doctrine. Constantine's action resulted in the union of Church and state and the interdependence of emperor and patriarch that is known as the Caesaro-papism of the Byzantine Empire.

From the first days, therefore, the Byzantine state embodied imperial tradition, Christian orthodoxy, and Hellenistic culture—forces that gave direction to government, religion, and literature in Constantinople for a thousand years.

POLITICAL HISTORY

Following Constantine, more than seventy emperors or empresses graced the imperial throne of Constantinople before its fall in 1204 to Fourth Crusaders. A relatively large number of these rulers were capable leaders; many were outstanding. Theodosius I (r. 379–395) made Christianity the official and sole religion of the empire. Theodosius II (r. 408–450) published the code of Roman law bearing his name and constructed the storied land walls of Constantinople, which stretch from the Sea of Marmara five miles to the Golden Horn. Without a doubt this formidable barrier on countless occasions saved the imperial city, and therefore the empire, from northern barbarians and the Arabs.

Justinian I (r. 527–565) has enjoyed fame through the ages. Many of his structures still stand in Istanbul (the former Constantinople), the noblest of which are the incomparable Church of Hagia Sophia and the majestic aqueducts north of the city. Equally celebrated were the Justinian codes of laws, compiled and digested by a commission of leading jurists and law professors. These codes remained the foundation of law through the years in the Byzantine Empire; they appeared in Italy in the twelfth century and served as the basis for the reintroduction of Roman law in the West. Probably the main reason for publication of the laws was Justinian's need for rigorous control of the empire and efficient collection of taxes to provide funds for his military campaigns in North Africa, Italy, and Spain.

The next gifted emperor, Heraclius (r. 610–641), an Armenian, was the reviver of the medieval Byzantine period. It was under him that Greek became the official language of the empire. Upon his accession he found the empire in a disturbed and debilitated condition, with Slavs and Sasanids threatening its existence. By reuniting Church and state, by revitalizing the army and navy, and by reinstituting strict economy, Heraclius defeated the Iranians in a series of brilliant campaigns and freed Syria and Egypt from Sasanid control. However, the financial strain of these wars and the cost in manpower left him unable to meet the Muslim Arabs in a favorable posture, and the recovered provinces were lost to Islam in Heraclius' last days.

During the remainder of the seventh century the frontiers contracted, and North Africa was lost, to be followed by the Byzantine portions of Italy in the next century, and the economy of the state materially weakened. Muslim armies ravaged Asia Minor, camped on the shores of the Sea of Marmara, and took to the sea in the eastern Mediterranean. But the empire was preserved by the accession of Leo III (r. 717–740), from Marash in the region of the Taurus Mountains. Besides shielding the empire from Eastern onslaughts, he favored legal and religious reforms, and advanced Heraclius' administrative system of *themes,* which were provinces where the military general was also governor. Thus, they were military districts, although judges and other civil officials did submit their accounts directly to the central administration. At first only a few were organized in this manner, but by the time of the Fourth Crusade thirty-eight provinces had been transformed into themes, the most important of which were in Asia Minor facing the Muslims.

A contemporary of the Abbasid caliph Harun al-Rashid, the empress Irene (r. 797–802) captured the imagination of many ages. The Greek wife of Leo's grandson and the power behind the throne of her son for twenty years, Irene blinded her son and ruled alone as *emperor* until overthrown by a revolution. She paid tribute to Harun al-Rashid, and gave her support to factions in the capital that opposed iconoclastic policy. The first action was indicative of the decline of Byzantine power. The latter disclosed the deep-seated religious division that persisted in the empire. Many with Monophysite tendencies, especially those from eastern reaches of the empire, objected to icons, images, pictures, and in particular representations of the Virgin Mary in church services and decorations. Leo III, over the protests of many bishops and monastics in Constantinople, forbade the use of icons, an act pleasing to the soldiery of his eastern themes. Irene made a political alliance with orthodox churchmen, and for their favor in her struggle for imperial position and power she pursued orthodox doctrines of anti-iconoclasm.

Evil days again fell upon the Byzantine Empire until the ascent of Basil the Macedonian (r. 867–886). Maintaining its supremacy until 1056, the Macedonian dynasty led the empire during one of the more brilliant periods of its long life. Basil, of humble origin, rose from the imperial stables, where his superb physique and feats of prowess attracted the attention of the emperor. Soon co ruler, Basil I took the next step and had his patron murdered. Nevertheless, he and his successors, particularly Basil II (r. 976–1025), were capable emperors, republishing old codes of laws, restoring harmony in the Church, sponsoring a classical cultural re vival, and pursuing a vigorous expansion of the state against Arabs, Armenians, and Bulgarians.

From the death of Basil II until the fall of Constantinople to the Fourth Crusaders in 1204, a series of calamities befell the Byzantine state, reducing its effective power to an alarming degree. Beginning in the tenth century, transformation of the rural society and economy proceeded relentlessly and sometimes rapidly. The free peasant and the free landholding soldier, especially in Asia Minor, were disappearing as a result of the expansion of great estates held by the landed military aristocracy and the Church. Heavy taxes, bad weather, famine, and insecurity caused the peasants to lose their lands to powerful lords. The stronger the magnates became, the more certain they were to obtain privileges, reduced taxes, and many other concessions from the central authorities. In turn, these events weakened the Byzantine fiscal position, lowered the available supply of loyal soldiers, and created a powerful class in the provinces able and eager to threaten or overthrow an unwary or uncooperative emperor. By the middle of the tenth century, emperors began to issue decrees to halt this process of aggrandizement, but to no avail.

When the strong hand of Basil II was removed, intense rivalry between the landed military aristocrats of the provinces and the powerful capital bureaucrats flared openly for competition for the throne. The capital bureaucrats controlled the central administration, the imperial navy, the troops around the emperor, and the finances of the empire. In their party were included a number of aristocratic families, many senators, most of the cultured segments of society, and almost all the important administrators. From 1025 until 1057, the civilian government thwarted some thirty rebellions and exiled, executed, or blinded a long list of generals who had mounted these insurrections. But the bureaucracy, looking for compliant emperors, found for the most part those "ill, old, or dominated by women and the eunuchs, and concerned only with enjoying the pleasures of their office."

Since the main strength of the great Anatolian families lay in their control of the armies stationed in their midst, the bureaucrats had set out to dismantle these local troops by withholding financial support from them, dismissing competent generals, and terminating obligations of various groups that owed military service. This was done at a time when Seljuk Turks were pressing on the frontiers in the east, the Normans of southern Italy were expanding, and others were invading the Balkans. The result was an increasing use of foreign mercenary troops. The difficulty with such forces was their lack of loyalty. In addition to the ease with which they changed sides, these mercenaries (their number included Kurds, Turks, Armenians, Arabs, English, Germans, Iranians) frequently ravaged the Anatolian countryside, held towns for ransom, and invariably reduced the flow of taxes to the imperial treasury. The economy of the empire sagged and the power of the state ebbed as the rival parties for political power, in spite of all consequences and at all costs, vied for supremacy.

With the accession of Alexius I Comnenus to the throne in 1081 the generals began a reign that lasted until the fall of Constantinople in 1204. During that time two dynasties—the Comneni and the Angeli—ruled the empire. Of these, the Comneni (1081–1185) was the more illustrious, perhaps because it held the throne throughout most of the period of the Crusades.

Civil wars continued unabated with generals and leading families feuding among themselves and seeking to establish semi-independent fiefdoms. Not least among these rivals were former mercenary leaders, many of them Normans and Turks. Alexius I found himself between Turk on the east and Catholic Frank on the west, hardly knowing which to fear more. His daughter, Anna Comnena, left a most interesting account of the arrival of the First Crusade at Constantinople; the contrast in culture and civilization of the two Christian societies of her day was sharply drawn. In 1054, the western Christian Church, led by the bishop of Rome, had officially declared the eastern Church, headed by the patriarch of Constantinople, to be schismatic. The division between the two parts of Europe was even more emphatic in light of the flourishing of Byzantine culture, especially in the areas of rhetoric, history writing, theology, and the making of icons and other forms of art.

Unfortunately for the Comneni, during their last days there was a large influx of western Catholics into Constantinople. Many influential government positions were given to them, much to the displeasure of the local bureaucracy. A French noblewoman, Mary of Antioch, served as regent for her son Alexius II (1180–1183) and became so much the target of public hatred that a pleasing scoundrel, Andronicus I, stirred up the capital to murder Latins quite indiscriminately and to sell others into captivity. As one author says, "the seed of the fanatic enmity between West and East, if not planted, was watered." Two decades later, Constantinople finally fell to Venetians and Fourth Crusaders, an act that ended the true Byzantine Empire. What later passed for that empire proved to be only a shell of its former power, grandeur, and significance.

THE CHURCH

Before discussing this later phase of the empire, it may be well to study a few institutions of society as they were at the height of Byzantine glory, for their forms persevered into the weak last days and even beyond into the Ottoman period. The strongest and most vital arm of the emperor was the Christian Church. After the demise of paganism in the fourth century, Constantinople, the Balkans, Greece, and Asia Minor were devoted in their support and loyalty to the Church. The Church's tight organization, with the patriarch at its hierarchical apex, gave powerful support or presented determined opposition to the emperor and government. Consequently, the emperor always tried to control the selection of the patriarch and reckoned with his views.

Monastic orders were socially, economically, and religiously important, and the monks were often popular heroes. Frequently, the government found it necessary to follow doctrines espoused by the populace, even though other dogmas were preferable for reasons of imperial policies. Whenever an emperor compromised with heresy to mollify a distant province or the army in some Asian theme or entered into an understanding with the papacy regarding the universal Christian Church, the orthodox voice of Constantinople was heard.

In a way, the Church resembled an administrative department of the government, and the patriarch acted as a minister of state in charge of religion. Charity to the poor was largely supplied by the churches and monasteries. A dynamic emperor chose, appointed, and dismissed patriarchs; an energetic patriarch bent weak emperors to his will—yet at most times, the emperor was supreme and the Church was subordinate to the state. It was this interrelationship that has been called Caesaro-papism.

AGRICULTURE AND INDUSTRY

After the loss of Egypt to the Arabs, Constantinople and cities of the empire were supplied with necessary sustenance by Asia Minor, Thrace, and the Balkans. The lot of the peasant was hard, and few envied him his life. Yet he seldom lacked food, clothing, or shelter, and famines were rare. Land was fundamental to the economy, and livestock such as oxen greatly increased productivity of the land and peasant. Monasteries in the capital and elsewhere possessed numerous estates which provided monks with their living. One bought and held land for the money income that it produced.

Although agriculture was the mainstay of the empire, industry and commerce gave it wealth and luxury. In the great cities of the empire compact populations were engaged to a considerable degree in manufacturing articles of everyday use. Many, too, produced luxury goods of great value which were used in rituals and services of thousands of churches and monasteries and which were vital to the pageantry of the imperial court. Sumptuous living was much enjoyed; and the wealth of silk fabrics, gold brocades, jewelry, reliquaries, enameled wares, fine glassware, and all the precious and refined luxury of the medieval age dazzled visitors. Crafts and skills of Hellenistic artisans prevailed for a thousand years in the Byzantine world, making it almost as much an industrial society as it was agricultural.

TRADE

The most active commercial city of the Byzantine Empire, Constantinople was filled with warehouses, depots, caravansarais, banks, moneychangers, and all aids and agents for promotion of foreign and domestic commerce. Trade from the Black Sea area and most of Russia centered upon Constantinople. Goods from the Far East and western Asia passed down the Bosphorus to quays on the Golden Horn. Surplus produce—manufactures and raw materials—of the empire gravitated to the capital for exchange and transshipment. Ships plied regularly between Constantinople and Cherson, Trebizond, Salonica, Venice, Amalfi, and Genoa. A standard tax of 10 percent, levied on all imports and exports, brought to the imperial government a large part of its revenue. Italian cities, however, found it possible to obtain tariff concessions from the emperors which allowed them to dominate long-distance trade. Industry and commerce were strictly regulated by the government. Controls were exercised over prices, quality, and quantity of goods produced or imported, profits, locations of business, labor conditions, and movement of workers.

GUILDS

Implementation of these controls was effected by individual guilds—industrial, commercial, and financial—which were highly organized and fully developed before A.D. 900. Most guilds were granted special privileges and certain monopolies, making membership in the respective guild a great advantage in any business or trade. To some extent guilds were restrictive in character. At times they were repressive, and they were always conservative. Yet they prevented speculation and collusion, protected rights of individuals in local and distant markets, and performed many social and legal functions for members. The state appointed the heads of the guilds, and by minutely regulating their activities, it controlled the economy of the state.

Through the ages and up to the present, writers have maligned the Byzantine Empire, its civilization, and particularly its rulers. Intrigue, court politics and so-called palace revolutions, the sharp business acumen of the merchants, and the mercenary character of some aspects of its life all led historians to use the word "byzantine" in a malicious and derogatory manner. Nevertheless, a close study of Byzantine records reveals a fully civilized society that possessed an efficient government and excellent public services, managed and directed by an educated and sophisticated bureaucracy, and protected by an army of high tactical ability. At a time when western Europe was semibarbaric, some inhabitants of the Byzantine Empire were enjoying literature, philosophy, urban social culture, and a much higher standard of living.

THE CRUSADES

In 1071 when Emperor Romanus IV Diogenes was defeated by the Seljuk Alparslan at the Battle of Manzikert near Lake Van in eastern Asia Minor, the rout was so complete that central Asia Minor was overrun with Turkish bands. Food supplies and raw materials, revenues, commerce, trade routes, and manpower supplies were lost; this further contraction of the empire spelled its doom.

However shocking this major defeat in 1071 may have been, it had been in the making for the half century since the death of Basil II. For more than a decade prior to Manzikert the armed battles to control Constantinople had denuded the Anatolian provinces of their military might, opening the way for Turkish invaders. When Romanus IV Diogenes marched out to meet Alparslan, not only was his military equipment woefully inferior but half of his soldiers were merely untrained city youths and the other half were unreliable mercenaries. On his way to battle he had to subdue his own unruly Germans; he also attacked Armenians at Sivas because they had been so merciless toward the Greeks there. In the heat of the battle Andronicus Ducas, leader of the contingent of bureaucrats in the emperor's army, spread the word that Romanus was being defeated and withdrew his men. Turkish forces, witnessing the anarchy, attacked the Byzantine army in flight and captured the emperor. It had been more than 250 years since an emperor had been taken prisoner in battle!

The humiliation of the Battle of Manzikert accelerated the fragmentation of society. When the Turks set Romanus IV free, war erupted between him and Michael VII Ducas, cousin of the treacherous Andronicus, further destroying military power in Anatolia and creating a power vacuum. Petty independent states sprang up everywhere: Normans in Bithynia; Seljuk Turks at Nicaea; Armenians in the southeast; and Turkoman tribes everywhere. Before the able general Alexius I Comnenus seized the imperial throne in 1081, several contenders had relied on Turkish armies in their battles against each other. These actions and the encouragement of Alparslan to Turkoman tribes to invade Anatolia brought Turkish sieges of many walled towns and the general ravaging of the countryside in every corner of Anatolia.

At last Alexius I Comnenus sent out a desperate call to Western Christendom for aid. The Crusades were the response; but they did more harm than good. Italian merchants traveled in the Crusaders' vanguard and, as soon as the Latin states were founded, they arranged to carry their Oriental trade through Syria, frequently bypassing Constantinople. The West expended little sentiment over the Byzantine Empire, as the Fourth Crusade demonstrated. The fall of Constantinople to Venetian merchants and soldiers in 1204 terminated abruptly the Byzantine Empire, and its society and civilization collapsed. The Orthodox Church was Latinized; monasteries disappeared; wealth of the churches was carried off; learning and literature vanished; books and libraries were lost; and works of art were destroyed.

The flight of the Byzantine court and ruling classes from Constantinople in 1204 had the immediate effect of producing several independent Greek principalities in the Byzantine provinces. Shortly, the fragmentation was reduced to three: Trebizond on the Black Sea coast in eastern Asia Minor; Nicaea in Bithynia in northwestern Asia Minor; and Arta and Salonica in Epirus and Thrace. At Nicaea, Theodore Lascaris gathered many of the old aristocracy and had the patriarch crown him emperor, thereby gaining a prestige never enjoyed by his two rivals. Meanwhile, the Latin empire of Constantinople hardly had a chance. Fraught with internal feuding and largely deserted by the West, the Crusaders were hemmed in by the Bulgarian kingdom and the Greeks of Epirus and

Nicaea. Finally in 1261, Michael Palaeologus, a general who usurped the Lascaris throne, overthrew the Latins and reestablished the Byzantine state in Constantinople under Palaeologi rule.

THE END OF BYZANTINE RULE

From 1261 to 1453 Byzantine rule held in Constantinople; but it cannot justly be regarded as a restoration of the Byzantine Empire. It was never more than a Greek kingdom, and for the final half century nothing more than the capital city itself. The old empire was broken beyond repair. Furthermore, the Mongol invasions first weakened and then began to replace the Seljuks of Anatolia, who in the absence of Byzantine authority had come to control much of Asia Minor. Thus, this sector of the Middle East was groping for new leadership, and adjustment of the balance of power to new conditions became inevitable. Upon the ruins of these two empires a new Ottoman state arose.

The Palaeologi tried to maintain a style of imperial government unjustified by the extent of their actual domain. Only a small part of northwestern Asia Minor remained in their hands, and most of the Balkans were held by Bulgarian and Serbian rulers. Land revenue was extremely low, as fiscal, judicial, and administrative affairs increasingly fell into the hands of the Church, towns, and local landlords. Grants of revenue became hereditary and the services owed by the grant holders were frequently ignored. The peasants in the fourteenth century were becoming even poorer and the central government lost power and authority. Indeed, with so much trade passing to western Europe through Mamluk Egypt the imperial crown jewels had to be pawned in Venice.

One mediocre ruler succeeded another; palace poverty and intrigue spawned civil wars and revolutions. Toward the middle of the fourteenth century the poor rose in Constantinople and massacred the aristocracy and the rich, while in 1347 bubonic plague devastated Byzantine cities. Interminable strife also marked the history of the Church. The Palaeologi, in their desperation for aid, repeatedly made and accepted bids to subordinate the Orthodox Church to the pope of Rome and his authority. Monks, churchmen, and the people always objected, and religious unity with the West was continually being postponed or abandoned.

In foreign affairs, the Greek state of Constantinople, in addition to negotiating with the papacy over church matters, was confronted with the dynamic Ottoman Turks in Asia Minor and the Bulgars and Serbs in the Balkans. Foreign and transit trade of Constantinople fell into the hands of Venetians and Genoese. From their docks and counting houses of Galata, a suburb across the Golden Horn from Constantinople, the Venetians and Genoese yearly grew more powerful and more insolent in their dealings with the Palaeologi. Since the Genoese possessed numerous ports and stations on the shores of the Black Sea and the Sea of Azov, many old Greek trading families of Constantinople found themselves excluded from their traditional haunts.

The most spectacular group of foreigners that came to the Byzantine state was the mercenary Catalan Grand Company of soldiers, who were hired in 1302 to combat the mounting aggression of the Turks. The emperor, however, was soon more terrified of the Catalans than he was of the Turks. No longer could the state afford a regular standing army; only when a crisis arose or a threat appeared could an army be supported.

In the century and a half preceding the fall of Constantinople international politics in the Byzantine area consisted almost entirely of constantly shifting alliances and realignments among the Byzantine successor states, of which the Greek state was only one. However, when Venetians and Serbs banded together to seize Constantinople, Orhan, the Ottoman ruler, was given the hand of Theodora, the daughter of John VI Cantacuzenus, as partial inducement to bring his forces across the Dardanelles into Europe to defend Thrace from that combination. A rival emperor in alliance with the Genoese drove the Ottomans back to Asia and sent his predecessor to a monastery, where he spent the rest of his days writing his brilliant memoirs. Deposed by his own son and the Genoese, the new emperor called for Ottoman support, which returned him victoriously to Constantinople in 1379.

From that time on Ottoman sultans were deeply involved in Byzantine affairs. Emperors frequently recognized sultans as their suzerains, sent their sons as hostages to the Ottoman court, and sometimes led the Turkish fleet on adventures into the Black Sea. Sultans plotted palace revolutions in Constantinople, and emperors sponsored rivals to the sultan's throne and intrigued with Turkish principalities against the Ottomans. Manuel II and Mehmed I personally discussed affairs from their respective galleys on the European shores of the Bosphorus and then crossed to the Asiatic side for a picnic, although the emperor did not descend from his galley. When an emperor died childless in 1448, Murad II approved the selection of Constantine XI, whose niece married Mehmed II.

Genoese, Venetians, Serbs, Bulgars, Greeks, and Ottomans were the active groups in the Straits area of the Middle East in that epoch, their religious and linguistic differences proving not to be significant barriers to political or economic partnerships. A blending of social patterns and institutional structures was proceeding so naturally that contemporary observers who were familiar with the situation showed no burning concern over the thought that the Ottomans might take Constantinople and the Straits. Little fear was evidenced that an Ottoman society and government on the Golden Horn would be very different from the Greek state. Life, trade, government, and religion would go on much the same. The Ottomans showed every indication of being as much European as they were Asian.

From a Byzantine point of view the debacle in Asia Minor following the Mongol invasions nurtured a new Turkish principality under the leader Osman. Within a few decades the northwestern section of Asia Minor came under Ottoman control. ("Ottoman" was an Italian corruption of "Uthman," just as "Osman" was a Turkish corruption of "Uthman.") And for the remainder of the century Ottoman activity was centered in Europe. At first the Ottomans were invited and hired by Byzantine emperors to fight in battles against Serbs, Bulgars, and Italians or for one faction of Palaeologi against another. Later they settled in Europe, and before the close of the fourteenth century they had become masters of Thrace, Macedonia, Bulgaria, and parts of Serbia. Constantinople was isolated but obtained a fifty-year reprieve from Timur's crushing defeat of the Ottomans at the Battle of Ankara in 1402.

For fifty years Constantinople was all that remained of the Byzantine Empire. That it did not fall to the Ottomans after their state was re-created under Mehmed I can be credited almost wholly to its superb defensive position. With water on three sides and the marvelous Theodosian Wall between the Golden Horn and the Sea of Marmara making the fourth side, the inhabitants of Constantinople felt secure. Any attacker had seemingly insurmountable obstacles to overcome.

By building the famous castles on the European shore of the Bosphorus in 1452 Mehmed II was able to blockade Constantinople by sea. Control of the Balkans gave him complete freedom to mass an army equipped with heavy artillery before the land walls in the spring of 1453. The plight of the city was obvious to all. When the walls were breached and his navy transported from the Bosphorus over the hills of Pera to the Golden Horn, the fate of Constantinople was sealed. Constantine XI died on the walls; Muslim prayers were recited in Hagia Sophia; and bells tolled in Europe. The once great and vigorous Byzantine Empire finally succumbed of old age after a long and painful illness. The young Ottoman Empire ushered in a new day for the great imperial site on the Bosphorus.

REFERENCES

Volumes cited at the end of Chapters 2 and 10 are also important for this chapter.

Barker, Ernest, ed. *Social and Political Thought in Byzantium, from Justinian I to the Last Palaeologus.* New York: Oxford University Press, 1957.

Browning, Robert. *The Byzantine Empire.* New York: Scribners, 1980. A profusely illustrated general introduction.

Diehl, Charles. *Byzantium: Greatness and Decline.* Translated by Naomi Walford. New Brunswick, N.J.: Rutgers University Press, 1957. An English translation of the French classic. It also contains a fine bibliographical essay by Peter Charanis.

————. *History of the Byzantine Empire.* Translated by George B. Ives. Princeton, N.J.: Princeton University Press, 1925. An important work.

Laiou-Thomadakis, Angeliki E. *Peasant Society in the Late Byzantine Empire: A Social and Demographic Study.* Princeton, N.J.: Princeton University Press, 1977. Expert analysis of the sad situation of fourteenth-century peasant life, with discussions of the Church as landlord and the nature of Byzantine feudalism.

Mango, Cyril. *Byzantium: The Empire of New Rome.* London: Weidenfeld and Nicolson, 1980. Social history is related with care, as the author discusses cities, heresies, the economy, monasticism, education, and intellectual life and self-image.

Nicol, Donald M. *Church and Society in the Last Centuries of Byzantium.* Cambridge: Cambridge University Press, 1979.

Obolensky, Dimitri. *The Byzantine Commonwealth: Eastern Europe, 500–1453.* New York: Praeger, 1971. An excellent study of the Balkan and eastern European relations to Constantinople under the Byzantine emperors.

Underwood, Paul A. *The Kariye Djami.* 4 vols. New York: Pantheon Books, 1966–75. A historical introduction and description of a beautiful Byzantine church of the late empire.

Vasiliev, A. A. *History of the Byzantine Empire, 324–1453.* Madison: University of Wisconsin Press, 1952. The standard history of the Byzantine Empire, especially regarding political and military matters.

Vryonis, Speros, Jr. *Byzantium and Europe.* London: Thames and Hudson, 1967. A concise survey of Byzantine history by a leading scholar, with great insight into the complete life of the empire.

———. *The Decline of Medieval Hellenism in Asia Minor and the Process of Islamization from the Eleventh Through the Fifteenth Century.* Berkeley: University of California Press, 1971; paperback reprint, 1986. Without question this work is a great landmark in scholarship and has altered the concepts of developments in later Byzantine times and the Turkish rule in Asia Minor.

Whitting, Philip, ed. *Byzantium: An Introduction.* New York: New York University Press, 1971. Seven chapters by different authors who are leading experts in the field.

12

Early Turkish States of Asia Minor

TURKISH PENETRATION OF ASIA MINOR

The Battle of Manzikert in 1071, wherein Alparslan completely routed the Byzantine army, ranks as a decisive historical event: it opened Asia Minor to Turkish settlement. Suleiman, one of Alparslan's distant cousins, was assigned responsibility for the Seljuk frontier facing the Byzantine Empire. Within ten years Turkish forces fanned out over Asia Minor and established themselves so solidly that Suleiman could choose Nicaea, a western city, as his capital.

The ease with which the Turks conquered Asia Minor suggests that a vacuum existed and that some Turks were conditioned already to exploit the opportunity. Emperors had taxed the Anatolian provinces heavily and withdrew financial support and governmental privileges from frontier districts. March warriors (*akritoi*) and Armenian areas were disaffected, and gave the emperors little aid. After the humiliation of Manzikert these groups deserted the empire. When Suleiman entered Asia Minor, he found numerous Armenian principalities asserting their independence. To the serfs he gave freedom from all dues. Many *akritoi* had already joined their arms with those of Turkish frontier warriors (*ghazis*) in overrunning Asia Minor—in effect opening Anatolia for the entry of Suleiman, his Seljuk cohorts, other Turkish princely dynasties, and independent Turkomans by the tens of thousands.

Alparslan never expected to conquer Asia Minor; his victory at Manzikert was a maneuver to guarantee his right flank while he subdued Syria. Suleiman, whose father had been guilty of treason, was sent partially as an exile; but he looked upon the post as a fortuitous opportunity to gather a loyal army and following with which he might return victorious to the main Seljuk state. However, Suleiman and his Seljuk organization did not conquer Anatolia; many Turkish tribes and bands infiltrated the provinces and settled upon the land. The Seljuk family only systematized the conquest but never controlled all of it.

Since the seventh-century era of great victories and Muslim expansion the Taurus Mountains and Armenian highlands of eastern Asia Minor had served as an effective boundary between Christendom and Islam. Their armies raided and penetrated across each others' frontiers, but no extensive change in the line occurred. On each border semiautonomous provinces arose to attract adventurers, outcasts, heretics, fanatics, and the unemployed from each society. Muslims called them *ghazis,* "warriors of the faith"; to the Byzantines they were *akritoi.* Together they comprised a typical body of freethinkers and freebooters, forming one society with one culture, even though nominally part were Christian and part were Muslim.

Prior to the Battle of Manzikert, Turkish bands plundered Asia Minor, even such cities as Sivas, Kayseri, and Konya. Afterward, most of Anatolia was opened to the ghazis, who for more than a century had been chiefly Turkish in origin and language. As they scattered over the land, great numbers of Turkish nomadic tribes found the roads and passes inviting. These peoples, traditionally called Turkomans, were identical in blood, and nearly so in dialect, to Seljuks and their Turkish adherents or to Turkish ghazis. In fact, nomadic Turks were staunch allies of organized Turkish forces. One day a Turkoman would be peacefully tending his flocks or threshing his grain, and the next he might be lending his sword to Seljuk or ghazi in furthering the conquest of Asia Minor.

SELJUK TURKS OF RUM

The First Crusade infused Byzantine forces with a new strength to stem the Turkish tide. Nicaea was retaken, and western sections of Asia Minor were restored to Byzantine control. Central and eastern Anatolia remained Turkish. Ruling in Baghdad, Syria, and Iran, the Seljuk family took cognizance of this new province of Islam and sent Suleiman to reign over that land. Since little power accompanied him and no prestige, his authority in Asia Minor was only nominal. As long as he and his heirs confined their dreams of power and favor only to the older Muslim world, the local Turks tolerated them. Turkish ghazi, Turkoman, and Seljuk Turk united against Byzantines and Crusaders. Kilij Arslan II, Suleiman's great-grandson, recognized that his opportunity lay only in Asia Minor and thus emphasized a pol-icy of creating an empire centered upon Konya. With this new intention began the Seljuk kingdom of Rum (Asia Minor).

Turkish ghazi bands were sensitive to every change and immediately chal-lenged the new Seljuk ambition. Chief among these was the Danishmend ghazi family, long the recognized ghazi leader of Anatolia, who made Sivas their head-quarters and held sway from the Taurus Mountains to the Black Sea. The Danishmends, like other ghazi states, never developed much governmental appa-ratus and lived mainly from booty taken on raids beyond the frontier. When Byzantine forces under the Comneni organized their frontiers, ghazi raids became less profitable, and Turkish bands began to attack each other.

At this crucial point in Anatolian development Kilij Arslan II became lord and master of the Turks of Rum. The true founder of the Seljuk dynasty in Asia Minor, he ruled from 1155 to 1192, subduing Danishmend ghazis, fighting against Zangids over the frontier between Syria and Anatolia, and obtaining from Emperor Manuel Comnenus recognition as the commanding and responsible Turkish lord of Asia

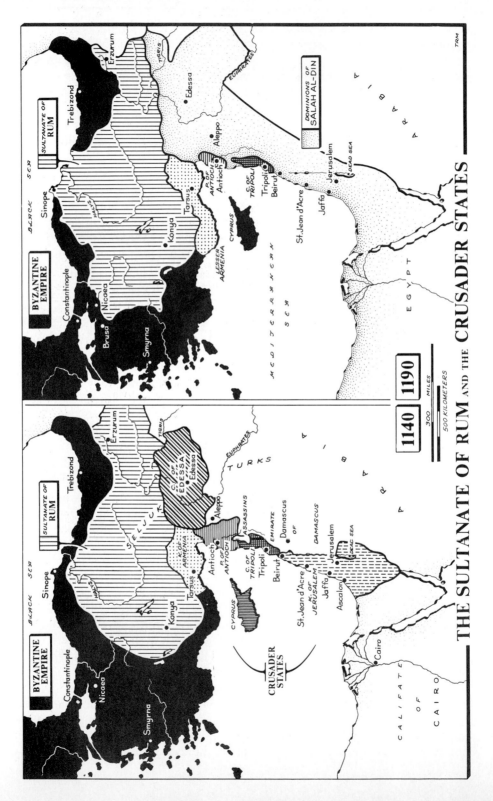

THE SULTANATE OF RUM AND THE **CRUSADER STATES**

Minor. Because of the great prestige of the Seljuk name, Konya attracted learned Muslim divines to teach in its schools; mystics, dervishes, and poets frequented its court. The Seljuks established Muslim financial administration throughout their state and built mosques, mausoleums, schools, palaces, and caravansarais in the high Muslim style, imposing remains of which may still be seen in and near Konya, Sivas, Kayseri, and other cities of Anatolia.

Yet the Seljuk state displayed a mixed and varied culture, and centralization of government was a goal not attained. As Seljuk authority was extended, Kilij Arslan II assigned governorships to his twelve sons, who declared their independence in their father's declining years.

Ghazi independence in Anatolia was never crushed by the Seljuks; its spirit and viewpoint remained a political and social force with which Seljuk sultans continually had to reckon. Seljuks made peace with Byzantine emperors; and on one occasion Kilij Arslan was welcomed and entertained royally by Emperor Manuel I in Constantinople, much to the consternation of the ghazi element. To receive Christian renegades at the court in Konya and give them responsible positions or to possess Christian women in the harem and have a Christian mother were understandable, but to fraternize with Christian potentates was unthinkable. Christian churches and monasteries remained in many urban centers, even owing their allegiance to the patriarch in Constantinople. The mixed culture prevailed in rural areas, in former ghazi districts, and definitely at the frontiers toward the Byzantine Empire.

```
                              Arslan
                                |
                              Kuthmish
                                |
                              Suleiman I
                                |
                              Kilij Arslan I (d. 1107)
                                |
                              Masud I (d. 1155)                    Malikshah
                                |
                              Kilij Arslan II (d. 1192)
                                |
Kaikhusraw I (d. 1210)    Malikshah (1188–1191)         Suleiman II (d. 1204)
        |                         |                              |
Kaikaus I (d. 1219)       Kaikobad I (d. 1237)          Kilij Arslan III (d. 1204)
                                  |
                          Kaikhusraw II (d. 1245)
                                  |
Kaikobad II (d. 1257)     Kilij Arslan IV (d. 1266)     Kaikaus II (d. 1280)
                                  |                              |
                          Kaikhusraw III (d. 1283)       Masud II (d. 1302)
                                  |
                          Kaikobad III (d. 1302)
```

Seljuk Dynasty of Rum

Neither Kilij Arslan nor, in fact, any Seljuk or Danishmend prince could control Turkomans in Anatolia, and they penetrated every corner of the land, constantly raiding Byzantine lands even to the point of capturing and leveling towns. The process of Turkification and Islamization of the population was proceeding. Some Greeks fled westward; others were killed or enslaved; many became Muslims and gradually learned to speak Turkish. Manuel I Comnenus conducted campaigns in various parts of western Anatolia, killing Turkomans by the thousands. In turn, Turkoman bands entered Byzantine territories to the north, carrying off as many inhabitants and selling them on slave markets in Mamluk Syria and Egypt. Manuel then set out to destroy the Seljuk state. In 1176 in a mountain pass at Myriocephalon, west of Konya, he met Kilij Arslan's forces. Already crippled by the constant raiding of his immense baggage train and harassed by Turkomans, "numerous as the locusts," who realized the emperor had come to drive them from their valley and upland pasturages, the emperor's army was destroyed. Though the sultan offered a generous peace which the emperor accepted, the significance of this battle, almost equal to that of Manzikert, was obvious. Manuel and his successors gave up any idea of reconquering Asia Minor, and the Seljuk sultans henceforth felt secure from any serious attack from Constantinople. After Myriocephalon, the Seljuks, other Turkish rulers, ghazi bands, and Turkomans controlled Asia Minor except for a small district around Trebizond on the Black Sea coast and the area between Brusa, Nicaea, and Constantinople.

Thus, through most of the century from 1150 to 1250 the Seljuk sultanate of Konya, or Rum, shone brightly. Muslim and Christian traders frequented its markets, and a considerable share of Far Eastern trade passed through the area to enrich various treasuries. Schools were crowded and the arts flourished. Armenian stonecutters, Iranian tile decorators, Persian poets, and Arab calligraphers practiced their crafts and were much appreciated. Ghazis settled down, Turks became villagers, communities were established, and life and people in central and eastern Asia Minor in the course of 150 years grew increasingly homogeneous in every aspect.

Nevertheless, frontier marches were never fully consolidated within the culture of the central provinces of the Seljuk state. Brothers, cousins, and nephews of sultans were in continual rebellion and usually found support or refuge among frontier warriors, from whom the Seljuk sultans never commanded complete obedience. Unreformed ghazis could not comprehend Seljuk peace treaties with Christian emperors and did not accept the idea of coexistence in any part of Asia Minor.

Peace and more settled life quickly produced many effects of population pressures. Another blow to ghazi life and economy fell when Seljuk sultans ceased sending out raiding parties. More and more, warfare in Anatolia was only among contestants for the sultanate of Konya. Then, early in the thirteenth century, Turks, nomadic families and tribes, soldiers, princes, bureaucrats, dervishes, artisans, and scholars began drifting into Anatolia in swelling numbers. Mongols, under the leadership of Genghiz Khan and his heirs, drove them westward, and Seljuks encouraged these displaced persons to settle on the frontiers.

A complicating factor of significant proportions for the Seljuks and the frontier marches resulted from the fall of Constantinople to the Fourth Crusade. With their capital moved to Nicaea, Byzantine emperors gave full attention to Anatolia and its defenses. Ghazi aggressions suddenly met sterner resistance; frontier lines became rigid; and the growing Turkish population was ready to burst its bounds.

That the land was in a state of ferment was demonstrated by a movement in 1240 against Kaikhusraw II led by Baba Ishaq, a holy man and mystic who protested against the luxurious life of the sultan and his court. To a considerable degree it was a revolt of seminomadic Turkomans and warriors against the sedentary Seljuk townsmen. The sultan suppressed this socioreligious outbreak unmercifully, but in so doing forever alienated the allegiance of ghazi Turks and Turkomans of Anatolia. Martyrdom of the holy Baba at the hands of Christian and Norman mercenaries ensured the wide and permanent acceptance of his doctrines throughout Asia Minor.

MONGOL INVASION

No sooner was Baba Ishaq's resistance movement driven underground than Kaikhusraw II was confronted by Mongol invasions. Erzurum was taken, and at the fateful Battle of Kozadagh in 1243 the Seljuk armies were crushed. Upon the sultan's sudden death two years later, Seljuk independence was extinguished. Kilij Arslan IV journeyed eastward to Karakorum, where his position as Seljuk sultan of Rum was confirmed.

All Seljuk rulers, thenceforth, were only puppets or vassals of the Mongols. At the time of Kilij Arslan IV's appointment, the amount of yearly tribute was set, and from its size the fiscal extortion by the Mongols became apparent. Later the Mongol Hulagu divided Muslim Anatolia in two. The Seljuks and Turkomans unsuccessfully revolted against the Mongols in 1277, but as this jihad (religious warfare) was suppressed new tribes were brought into Anatolia from the east, and the losing Turkomans fled westward against the Byzantines.

In the face of such actions and because of obvious weakness, all respect for Seljuk rulers by other Turks of Anatolia vanished. Since Mongol rulers never had the time or interest to establish their authority firmly in Asia Minor, their invasion politically fragmentized Turkish Anatolia. Each Turkish prince in western Anatolia was suddenly on his own, and every Turkoman followed his own whim. Almost simultaneously the Byzantine emperors regained Constantinople and became involved immediately in Balkan affairs. Their Asian provinces were neglected. Turkish ghazis and Turkoman tribes discovered not only that the restraining hand of the Seljuk sultan could be ignored but also that Byzantine frontiers could be easily penetrated.

TURKIFICATION OF ASIA MINOR

Within a few years, Asia Minor was overrun by Turkish tribes except for a small northwestern corner. The eastern half of the Seljuk state remained for many decades under Mongol authority and continued to render tribute to the great khan in central Asia. In the western half, however, and in the newly acquired more westerly areas, Turkish independence was openly declared and easily maintained.

The greatest strides in the transformation of Asia Minor from a Greek and Armenian Christian society to a Turkish Muslim land were made in this epoch. Throughout the twelfth and thirteenth centuries and on into the fourteenth, constant pressure was exerted on every aspect of Christian life and society. Decisive victories for Muslim armies, continual battles and marches across the land by hungry soldiers and rapacious mercenaries, sacking of cities, and scorched-earth policies generated massacres, flight, enslavement, plague, and famine. The majority who remained were filled with insecurity and a sense of helplessness.

As the various areas fell into Turkish hands, certain factors made it fairly easy to assume the customs and manners of the victors. In the first place, non-Muslims were discriminated against in many ways with regard to dress and life and unquestionably they were second-class subjects. Converts, on the other hand, escaped discrimination—as well as many taxes. Furthermore, Christian communities became leaderless at a time of great psychological and economic crisis. Consequently, whole villages turned Muslim overnight.

The Seljuk state tolerated Christians and the Church. But Muslims were favored, and Islamic institutions were supported generously. Within a few decades Asia Minor was blanketed with mosques, madrasahs (advanced schools), hospitals, rest homes, caravansarais, and even halfway houses for converts to Islam. Most of these were endowed by leading Turks or by the state from confiscated Christian church and monastic estates, usually the income from Christian villages. Christian communities cut off from support and communication with bishops and the patriarch found penury and isolation too difficult to face for long. Christianity had been defeated; victorious, affluent Islam was nearly irresistible. Moreover, Anatolia was saturated by Sufis and dervishes who preached a mystical popular Islam that reached the people. They pressed conversion to Islam and presented a kind of religious syncretism that equated Islamic practices and holy men to those of the Christians. The twelve apostles became the twelve imams and the Trinity came to consist of God, Muhammad, and Ali. This phenomenon of cultural change continued in Asia Minor until the mid-fifteenth century when the Ottoman Turks captured Constantinople, recognizing the patriarch as subject to the sultan, and in essence institutionalizing and protecting the Church as a part of the state. As a consequence, Christian communities could look to the patriarch and bishops without fear of reprisal and the Church hierarchy felt responsible for its flock throughout the Ottoman domain.

TURKISH STATES

Turkoman tribal groups from Malatya to Antalya on the Mediterranean formed principalities which, with the passing of time, assumed the way of life of ghazi states. The leaders, for whom the states were named, however, seldom adopted the title "ghazi." One of the more important of these states was Dhu al-Qadr at Diyarbakir, Malatya, and Elbistan.

From the ghazi states arose the political and social patterns that dominated Asia Minor and Turkish life for several centuries. Countless new leaders created independent baronies in the wake of the Mongol demolition of the Seljuk state. Gradually, energetic leaders consolidated numerous petty holdings into sizable ghazi principalities, or amirates. At the time, the amirate founded by Osman near Eskishehir was quite insignificant. In the 1260s, a principality of considerable importance in connection with the development of the Ottoman state was that of Germiyan at Kutahya. Never calling themselves ghazis, Germiyan rulers were more typical of the Seljuk rulers, but they were allied with the ghazi states around them. Eventually the state founded by Osman conquered or annexed all the others.

Karamania, situated in the foothills of the Taurus Mountains southwest of Konya and originally a ghazi state, offered the most persistent opposition to the Ottomans. Arising among the partisans of Baba Ishaq, Karaman was the son of a Sufi mystic. The demise of the Seljuk state encouraged the Karamans to assume Turkish leadership and to move to Konya as the Seljuk heirs. In so doing they lost many ghazi characteristics and acquired qualities of older Muslim governments. These qualities gave greater stability and permanence to the organization of the state, and enabled the Karamans to maintain their independence from the Ottoman Empire until the beginning of the sixteenth century.

Other ghazi amirates of Anatolia were similar to these three, and that established by Osman at Sögüt had few attributes different from usual ghazi traditions upheld in these principalities. Ibn Battutah, the fourteenth-century Moroccan globe-trotter, visited Asia Minor and left a record of his impressions of these amirates. Entertained at the courts of many, he reserved no special tribute for Orhan, Osman's son, and in no way singled out the Ottomans for the fame they would achieve.

GHAZI SOCIETY

What were ghazi traditions and attributes? Foremost, a ghazi state possessed as the reason for its existence a duty to battle against the infidel. It consisted of a band of dedicated warriors, whose leaders, mostly of tribal origin, rode out on raids beyond the frontiers of Islam, bringing back rich plunder (including slaves) that in most instances gave economic viability to the group. Although ghazis held fiefs of land, the state collapsed when raids were unsuccessful. Ghazis were equal socially and politically; aristocracy was derived from actions and leadership rather than from blood. It was a typical frontier society. To become a ghazi, however, was not an automatic step. One had to prove his worth by deeds and by strength of character. In a ghazi state, society was organized into several classes or corporations, the ghazi group being the highest.

Another feature of ghazi life was recognition and acceptance of the *futuwwa,* a set of rules by which the virtuous should live. In fact, ghazi brotherhoods were organized on this moral and ethical base. Mutual fidelity among the membership was particularly emphasized. Likewise, almost every ghazi brotherhood recognized a spiritual leader; in most cases this leader was a Sufi, so ghazis usually adhered to some dervish order. Frequently a badge or special headgear would be worn to distinguish ghazis from other individuals.

A ghazi, then, was one who had a sense of belonging to a separate and distinct group of individuals whose main occupation was military conquest. In a world of confusion and a period of political disintegration the ghazi movement flourished. But ghazi states found that raids eventually ceased, whereupon the states withered because life was not devised on a solid internal economy. To make the transition required more administrative apparatus than ghazis possessed. This problem confronted the Ottomans constantly in their meteoric path across Anatolia and the Balkans. The success with which they solved this continuing problem determined, in considerable measure, the permanent or ephemeral character of Ottoman conquests. This theme is more or less central in the understanding and explanation of the rise and spread of the Ottoman state.

REFERENCES

Material can be found in Chapters 7, 9, 10, and 11.

Cahen, Claude. *Pre-Ottoman Turkey: A General Survey of the Material and Spiritual Culture and History, c. 1071–1330.* Translated from the French by J. Jones-Williams. London: Sidgwick & Jackson, 1968. A very important work by an outstanding scholar. Dealing with the coming of the Seljuks, it contains a full description of society and the institutions developed in Asia Minor. This is followed by a section of thirteen chapters covering the Mongol period.

Gibbons, Herbert A. *The Foundation of the Ottoman Empire.* Oxford: Clarendon Press, 1916. The first book to tackle the problem; still useful.

Kissling, E. J., F. R. C. Bagley, N. Barbour, J. S. Trimingham, H. Braun, and H. Hartel. *The Muslim World: A Historical Survey.* Pt. 3. *The Last Great Muslim Empires.* Translation and adaptations by F. R. C. Bagley. Leiden: Brill, 1969. A good text that spans the end of the Mongol period to the nineteenth century.

Rice, Tamara Talbot. *The Seljuks in Asia Minor.* New York: Praeger, 1961. An architectural history.

Sümer, Faruk, Ahmet E. Uysal, and Warren S. Walker, trans. and eds. *The Book of Dede Korkut: A Turkish Epic.* Austin: University of Texas Press, 1972. A fine translation of the great tenth-century epic Turkish tale and song from medieval Turkish courts. Called by some the greatest monument of Turkish literature.

Ünsal, Behçet. *Turkish Islamic Architecture in Seljuk and Ottoman Times, 1071–1923.* London: Tiranti, 1959. The author discusses geographical, historical, physical, and cultural conditions affecting Turkish architecture. Describes mosques, inns, markets, palaces, illustrating different kinds of materials and types of construction and comparing Turkish architects.

Vryonis, Speros. "Seljuk Gulams and Ottoman Devshirmes." *Der Islam* 41 (October 1965): 224–252. This is a very basic article showing how the system developed and operated, what the slaves became, and whence they had come.

13

Ottoman Origins and Early Institutions

OTTOMAN ORIGINS

Osman, founder of the Ottoman state, was the son of Ertogrul, a Turkish frontier warrior who possessed the land of Sögüt as a fief, given by one of the later Seljuk sultans. An insignificant place and an extreme outpost on the frontier, Sögüt was not particularly desirable. Nothing of certainty is known about Ertogrul's ancestry or background, but he must not have been very outstanding or he would have commanded a more important assignment. Probably he was one of the countless seminomadic Turkomans looking for a place in Anatolia.

Like any other frontier warrior, Ertogrul led raiding excursions into Byzantine territory, but he bequeathed to his son Osman little more than the original fief of Sögüt. Moreover, the conquest and absorption of neighboring villages and fortified places began only in the 1280s. This was presumably after Osman had married the daughter of Shaykh Edebali, who adhered to one of the mystical or Sufi sects common to those frontiers. It was probably he who introduced Osman to the ghazi group and gave him the moral and ethical ideas of the *futuwwa*.

In any case, Osman as a leader of tribesmen began to acquire by capture or alliance a number of small towns. Between 1300 and 1320 Osman seized the countryside west of the Sakarya River as far south as the Germiyan amirate, and west and north to the Sea of Marmara. Yet he was not strong enough or sufficiently well equipped to take the walled towns of Brusa, Nicaea, and Nicomedia. Not until Osman was on his deathbed in 1326 did his followers under the leadership of his son Orhan take Brusa, which surrendered without a struggle after several years of siege.

The fall of Brusa was the signal for Byzantine collapse in that corner of Asia Minor. Orhan occupied Nicaea in 1331 and Nicomedia in 1337. Later, he dispossessed the quarreling sons of the amir of Karasi and placed Ottoman rulers over Bergama (Pergamum) and other towns of that amirate. Thus, by 1345, the Ottoman state included the entire northwestern corner of Asia Minor from the Aegean to the Black Sea.

Several factors prepared the way and assisted in this accelerating growth of the Ottoman state. No doubt the personality and spirit of Osman counted heavily.

Certainly his men and his lieutenants were loyal and devoted to him. At first, Osman was placed in an exposed position between and near fortified areas within one day's sail from Constantinople. Even though emperors were weak and were consumed with constant intrigues, they possessed sufficient determination to resist Turkish attacks until the fourteenth century. Thereafter, Byzantine force weakened rapidly, and such towns as Brusa and Nicaea were summarily abandoned to their fate.

A most important element in the growth of Ottoman forces was the policy of welcoming any and all fighting men. Köse Mikhal, a Greek who became a Muslim, was one of Osman's favorite comrades. His descendants (the Mikhaloglu) held prominent positions through centuries of Ottoman history. In 1305, some of the Catalan Company joined the Ottoman camp; defeated Mongol raiders, given clemency, fell in with the men under Orhan. Many disillusioned Greek soldiers defending Brusa became Muslims and fought as Ottomans after that city capitulated. Fighting men from various tribal, ghazi, and Byzantine backgrounds flocked to the Ottoman infantry and cavalry as their successes multiplied. Some Christians worked as bureaucrats for the Ottomans in the early fourteenth century.

In the first half century under Osman and Orhan, Ottoman expansion was gradual enough to permit the organization of some governmental administration. Moreover, the Muslim world was in such disorder that Muslim artisans, merchants, bureaucrats, theologians, jurists, fiscal experts, teachers, and scribes were attracted by opportunities in this new frontier Muslim state. Schools of theology were built in Bursa and Iznik (Turkish names for Brusa and Nicaea) soon after their capture, and Bursa remained the center of learning and philosophical discussion for the Ottomans. It was these new Ottomans who emphasized the ghazi nature of the state.

Furthermore, the immigrant artisans and merchants formed corporations known as *akhis*. Somewhat like European guilds, these akhis were closely knit bodies subscribing to specific *futuwwa* very similar to the ghazi code of honor. A close alliance and understanding between ghazi and akhi gave to Ottoman society an economic strength lacking in other ghazi states. The early arrival of Muslim judges, theologians, and scholars (*ulema*) expanded the social structure beyond the ruling ghazi and Turkoman family circles. Orhan also accepted the Muslim practice of allowing Christians and Jews to live in a Muslim land by paying taxes and special tribute. Thus, at an early date social and economic disturbances in towns passing into Ottoman hands were largely minimized. Life went on in much the same way with considerable intermingling of people. Orhan himself married Nilufer, a daughter of the Greek lord of a captured town.

By the middle of the fourteenth century Orhan had become amir of a sizable state facing the historic Straits and Europe beyond. Silver coins were minted, and a lively trade developed in such prosperous towns as Bursa, Iznik, Izmid (Nicomedia), and Bergama. The Ottoman state assumed a place as an important powerful component in the political, diplomatic, and military turbulence concomitant with the decline of an obsolete Byzantine Empire.

Ghazis were long accustomed to raiding parties in Thrace and Macedonia. Orhan and his men became allies of Emperor John VI Cantacuzenus in 1345 to fight against his rival Emperor John V Palaeologus. Part of Orhan's bargain was the privilege of plundering; another part was the hand in marriage of

Theodora, Cantacuzenus' daughter. Six thousand Ottomans ravaged the hinterland of Constantinople and the Black Sea coast and were instrumental in taking Adrianople. Similarly, every year thereafter Ottoman soldiers practiced their profession in Thrace and the Lower Balkans, amassing fortunes in booty.

OTTOMANS IN EUROPE

In these same years two natural disasters softened Byzantine resistance to Ottoman expansion. The Black Death reached Constantinople first in 1347 and spread in following years through the Balkans and on to the rest of Europe, leaving dislocations and terror everywhere. It ended all talk of a crusade to crush the Ottomans or to regain Constantinople again for the Franks. The Black Death made victories for the Ottomans much easier in Europe. In 1354, a severe earthquake demolished the walls of Gallipoli on the European shore of the Dardanelles. Ottoman forces in Europe rushed into Gallipoli, asserting that God had given it to them. Orhan refused to return it to his father-in-law and sent Ottomans there to colonize the city, much of whose population had been carried off by the Black Death.

From this bridgehead in Europe, Ottomans stormed over eastern Thrace, seizing all areas between the Aegean and the Black seas except, of course, the imperial city of Constantinople. Adrianople opened its gates in 1361 to Murad, third in the Ottoman line of rulers, and for nearly a century that city (which the Turks call Edirne) stood as the Ottoman European capital.

Murad I, the younger son of Orhan and Nilufer, followed in his father's footsteps, vigorously pushing one campaign after another northward and westward into the Balkans. Rival emperors of Constantinople, Serbian and Bulgarian tsars, independent princes of Greece, the city-states of Venice and Genoa, popes, and Crusaders kept the Balkans in such a constant turmoil and confusion that Murad in his expeditions never had to worry about facing a consolidated offensive and usually had several Christian allies in his camp.

Under Murad's leadership (r. 1360–1389), Ottoman armies and raiders succeeded in conquering most of Bulgaria, Macedonia, and parts of Serbia to Lake Ochrida, including Sofia and Nish. During the crushing defeat of the Serbs in the Battle of Kossovo in 1389, Murad lost his own life but sealed the doom of independence for any Christian Balkan state and securely established the Ottoman position in southern Europe.

Likewise, Murad made extensive advances in Asia. He took Ankara and by a combination of prestige, power, money, and diplomacy nearly doubled his Anatolian possessions. Marriage of his son Bayezid to the daughter of the Germiyan amir brought the town of Kutahya as a dowry. Murad forced the amir of Hamid to "sell" most of his domain and will the balance to the Ottomans. Campaigns were launched against Karamania, but with little success, because ghazis were unwilling to fight against those whom they considered to be "warriors of the faith." In these Anatolian campaigns Murad's most loyal supporters were contingents of his Slavic allies and mercenaries.

When Bayezid I succeeded to the Ottoman sultanship on the field of Kossovo, he inherited a state that in the brief span of two generations had grown from a petty principality to a dominant power stretching from the Danube to the Taurus Mountains.

Osman (1281–1324)
|
Orhan (1324–1360)
|
Murad I (1360–1389)
|
Bayezid I (1389–1402)
|
Mehmed I (1403–1421)
|
Murad II (1421–1444; 1446–1451)
|
Mehmed II (1444–1446; 1451–1481)
|
Bayezid II (1481–1512)
|
Selim I (1512–1520)
|
Suleiman I (1520–1566)

Ottoman Rulers, 1281–1566

The Black Death, political anarchy in Europe and Asia, religious fervor, and a search for booty by the ghazis may have accounted for some of the rapidity of the development. Credit, however, should also be given to the dynamic personalities, the administrative talents, the lengthy reigns, and the driving genius of Orhan and Murad.

OTTOMAN ARMY

Among the Ottomans, the army, its organization, and its recruitment were matters of prime importance. Under Osman, criers went through the villages announcing that anyone who wished to participate in a raid should meet at a given place at a specific time. Orhan, however, organized the army. Traditionally, he did this on the counsel of a maternal relative, Kara Khalil Chandarli, who was probably of akhi membership and has usually been considered to have had some formal education. Moreover, in the wars of Orhan and Murad closer contacts with the Byzantine military provided examples from which the Ottoman army obtained useful suggestions.

The army was organized on a basis of units of 10, 100, and 1,000 men, with a responsible officer over each group. This was as true of irregular infantry (*azab*) and volunteer horsemen and cavalry scouts (*akinji*) as it was of regular feudal cavalry (*sipahi*) and the newly formed janissaries (*yeni cheri*). Officers of the immediate family and entourage of the Ottoman ruler were placed in overall charge of the armies. Evrenos Bey, a Greek from Karasi, became chief of the European frontier and always led the feudal sipahi, while Köse Mikhal was responsible for the scouts. Suleiman Pasha, Orhan's eldest son, was the first to be commander in chief (*beylerbey*) of the troops in Europe.

The institution of the janissaries held a special place in Ottoman annals. The origin of this corps has been much debated. Their role in innumerable Ottoman victories through several centuries was so prominent that many authors have sought for some special beginning or at least for the name of their brilliant innovator. In a Muslim state, beginning in the time of the Prophet, the ruler as the embodiment of the state usually received one-fifth of the booty of war. Since human beings had long been valuable prizes of successful campaigns and since their lot was invariably one of slavery, Ottomans under Orhan and Murad found more slaves on their hands than they knew how to employ in customary tasks. Moreover, the market for slaves in surrounding areas was slack. The answer was to turn them into soldiers to fight for their captors.

Caliphs and sultans in the past had slave bodyguards, and in contemporary Egypt the ruling Mamluks were slaves. Seljuk rulers had slaves (*gulams*) by the thousands who were trained as soldiers, led their armies, and rose to become high officials. Most of them were Greek youths of Anatolia taken as prisoners or levied as a tribute from the Greek subjects. Youths captured in battle were kept as slaves by the Ottoman sultans as well. Nominally converted to Islam, they were banded together and trained as special corps in the army about the sultan. Their name, *yeni cheri* ("new soldier"), was corrupted to "janissary" by Europeans, who learned to fear these soldiers and stand in awe of their discipline, their esprit de corps, and their prowess with arms. Many younger captives were "farmed out" for a number of years to Ottoman feudal officers as apprentices. During these years they learned some Turkish, which became the Ottoman lingua franca, and they grew, were toughened, and became adept in the skills of fighting. To assimilate the janissaries into the Ottoman ranks as soldiers and as people was not difficult. Most of these captives were Greek Orthodox, Armenians, Serbs, and Bulgars, and were hardly different, socially or culturally, from many of those free renegades who voluntarily became ghazis and Ottomans.

In the days of Murad I the janissaries probably did not exceed 3,000 in number. They were paid a small daily wage and did not marry while active as soldiers. Living together in barracks, drilling, training, and being garbed alike gave the janissaries the status of a standing army more than a century before standing armies became the European practice. Some were cavalry; most were infantrymen; others were members of a specially honored left-handed guard. Many rose through the ranks and became high officers and trusted civil officials; a few were beheaded for dishonesty or disobedience. Before a century passed, only those who became regular infantrymen were known as janissaries. Other ranks and other corps had their own special designations.

Another important factor contributing to Ottoman successes was the development of sipahis, who answered the need for regular cavalry, for colonization of newly won lands, and for local provincial administration. Adapting Seljuk, Arab, and Byzantine feudal practices, Ottoman rulers rewarded ghazis and fighting men with grants of land from which they derived their living. Actual dispensation of land was made by the commander on the field. Greater valor resulted in larger fiefs.

Each year when a campaign was announced, sipahis left their estates and appeared equipped to fight under the immediate leadership of a local officer whom they elected. This feudal cavalry not only was the main force of the Ottoman armies but also was engaged almost continually in raids beyond the frontier. Sons went along on campaigns with their fathers and learned the profession of arms. They were eligible to inherit their fathers' trade and were usually awarded at least a part of the family fief. By settling and rearing families on the land, the feudal cavalry served as the first Ottoman colonizers and administrators of new territories.

Running strongly through the ranks of the Ottoman feudal cavalry until the end of the sixteenth century was the ghazi spirit and ideology. In certain areas where the frontier was long a battleground, as in Bosnia, northern Epirus, the Albanian mountains, Macedonia, and Thrace, a ghazi society emerged similar to those of earlier ghazi frontier areas in Anatolia. A thorough admixture of Ottoman warriors with local populations occurred, giving rise in the Balkans to Greek-, Serb-, and Albanian-speaking Muslims.

BAYEZID I

Seizing the reins of government on the field of Kossovo in 1389, Bayezid I avenged his father's death with victory over the Serbians. His only brother, Yakub, was assassinated by the supporters of Bayezid, leaving him the only male alive in the Ottoman family. Having the example of bitter and destructive rivalries of the Byzantine imperial family before him, Bayezid judged that executing his brother was for the best. Practices of this kind became standard procedure for a new sultan upon accession to the throne and prevailed in the Ottoman family for more than 200 years.

With the rise of modern nationalism, Kossovo was to become the symbol among the Serbs for lost national identity and for subjection, but in 1389 no great ill-feeling seemed to be generated. The Serbian royal princess Despina was married to the victorious Bayezid, who became devoted to her; and Serb levies and contingents remained extremely loyal to Bayezid throughout his reign. In succeeding years Ottoman forces raided Bosnia and Hungary, even crossing the Danube, and Bayezid brought greater numbers of Ottomans into Europe, especially into Thrace.

Indeed, beginning in 1391, all of Thrace was occupied up to the very walls of Constantinople: the city was virtually blockaded from the land side. A full investiture of Constantinople was outlined and a full blockade planned. On the Asian side of the Bosphorus at Anadolu Hisar, fortifications were constructed in 1393. Bayezid attempted to close the Bosphorus and the Dardanelles to ships destined for the imperial city. But attacks, first in Europe and later in Asia, saved Constantinople for half a century.

Sigismund, then king of Hungary, but later Holy Roman Emperor, was concerned over successful Ottoman aggressions. He therefore invaded Bulgaria in 1392 and captured the fortress of Nicopolis, only to withdraw within a few months before a large Ottoman force. The following year, Bayezid judged it necessary to eject his Bulgarian vassal, whose capital, Tirnovo, fell before the onslaughts of Bayezid's son Suleiman. These actions, in addition to the creation of an Ottoman navy which began depredations in the Adriatic, led Europe to heed Sigismund's loud cries for a crusade.

The romantic and fateful crusade of Nicopolis of 1396 was the result. Nobles from England, France, and Germany, laden with wine and women, joined as if on a picnic. Leadership went to Jean de Nevers, grandson of the king of France, who appeared with Sigismund and Hungarian and Wallachian armies before Nicopolis. They foolishly charged the center of the Ottoman forces, commanded personally by Bayezid, who had left the siege of Constantinople to meet the knights of Europe. Utterly outmaneuvered, the flower of Western nobility fell on the battlefield of Nicopolis, and thousands were captured. Those under twenty years of age were taken for the janissary corps or the sultan's court. Many, like Jean de Nevers, were held for ransom, and others were impressed to row in the galleys as ordinary slaves. This first serious encounter between Europeans and Ottomans had brought disaster to the Crusaders and vetoed for several decades any thought of another crusade on their part.

A follow-up campaign deep into Europe was feared by Venice, but Bayezid turned his attention instead to Greece. Ottoman armies overran Thessaly, penetrated the Peloponnesus, and captured towns and smaller cities. Ottomans were settled in the northeastern corner of the Peloponnesus, then called Morea, and fiefs were handed out in northern Greece. But fortified cities that could still be supplied from the sea were, like Constantinople, beyond Ottoman reach.

Bayezid's involvements in Europe and the investment of Constantinople did not deter him from campaigns in Asia Minor. Without question, one of his burning ambitions was to unite under his rule all Muslim lands of Asia Minor and perhaps of the entire Middle East. Although this idea paralleled naturally the common phenomena of expansion and unification attendant upon the rise and growth of a new state, Bayezid's haughty manner and ruthless tactics spelled his ruin.

In rapid succession between 1390 and 1397 Ottoman forces, frequently led by Bayezid in person, captured and annexed old ghazi and Turkoman amirates such as Karaman, and seized the areas of Kayseri, Sivas, Samsun, and Sinop. The dispossessed princes, instead of being commissioned with Ottoman responsibilities to weld them into the Ottoman people, fled with revenge in their hearts to the court of Timur Leng (Tamerlane).

In 1390, the first Ottoman navy was formed. Ships harried the coasts of Greece and descended upon various islands of the Aegean. With Bayezid engaged in subduing Bulgaria and in besieging Constantinople, the Karaman leaders judged that a revolt might be successful. However, Bayezid transferred his troops to Asia with amazing speed and destroyed the Karamans in front of Bursa. He did this so completely and so quickly that his soldiers dubbed him Yildirim ("Lightning").

Except for a few walled towns like Constantinople and Athens, Bayezid was now lord and master of the land from the Adriatic and the plains of Hungary to the Euphrates. In barely a decade he had doubled his Asian possessions and gained recognition as lord of the Balkans. In 1395 Serbian princes and Byzantine emperors rendered homage. The uncomplicated Ottoman state of Osman and Orhan had vanished, and the rulers were no longer humble and unaffected.

TRADE

The extension of the Mongol Empire into Asia Minor in the thirteenth century had established profitable trade routes, especially for Chinese and Persian silks, through Tabriz to Erzurum and Sivas and then branching off to Konya or Constantinople. At the same time, Arab merchants brought spices, sugar, and Indian fabrics to Aleppo or by sea to Antalya. From these entrepôts the goods were carried to Konya and thence to the principal markets of Anatolia and to Constantinople. In the fourteenth century, with the disintegration of the Mongol state and the rise of the Ottomans, more and more of this trade found its way to Bursa, which by the year 1400 had become the most important trading city in Anatolia. As Bayezid extended his rule in Asia Minor, merchants could travel safely from Tabriz and Aleppo to Bursa where merchants from Venice, Genoa, Florence, Pisa, and Lucca (the center of European silk industry) bought their supplies.

The Ottomans were always interested in commerce and industry and the akhi groups were influential members of their society. Ibn Battutah noted in 1333 that Orhan, because he held Bursa, was the richest Turkish ruler in Anatolia. And as early as 1340 Orhan had built a bazaar and an enclosed market in Bursa where valuable goods could be safely stored and sold. Again, even before the Ottomans took Adrianople, they had concluded commercial treaties with the Genoese to facilitate their merchant trade in Bursa. Such interests had greatly aided the Ottoman successes.

POLITICAL AND SOCIAL DEVELOPMENT

In the time of Murad I the government began to grow; under Bayezid I expansion was rapid and very noticeable. The first cadastral registers, designed to record land revenue assignments, were compiled. Government organization by religious leaders and graduates of the schools of Bursa and Iznik introduced more efficiency and rigidity in administration. At the same time evolution of the post of grand vizir in the hands of Kara Khalil Chandarli aroused considerable opposition and much unhappiness among most Ottoman soldiers, accustomed for generations to great freedom.

Dismay also stemmed from Bayezid's dreams of empire. In 1394 he sent an embassy to the Abbasid caliph in Egypt requesting to be invested with the title sultan of Rum. Even Bayezid's grandfather had used that title, and evidently it was commonly applied to Bayezid. Yet he wished recognition from the older Muslim world. Numerous Turkoman amirates of Asia Minor that he engulfed looked upon him as a tyrant and spread treasonable ideas at every turn. Few true ghazis participated in his Asian campaigns; Bayezid learned that in operations against fellow Muslims he could be sure only of his janissaries and contingents sent by his European Christian vassals. Many Muslims in Asia could hardly escape questioning Bayezid's own faith when he led Christian soldiers against Muslim soldiers.

There were other ways in which Bayezid's actions alienated his subjects. The cultural background of Ottoman leaders left them open for many innovations, and with a medley of individuals appearing among them, eclecticism developed. Discussions among religious leaders of various sects within the Ottoman state led to proposals for a common religion from a composite of Islam, Judaism, and Christianity. Undoubtedly this trend can be seen in the names of Bayezid's younger sons—Musa (Moses), Isa (Jesus), and Mehmed (Muhammad). Other sons were Ertogrul (Turkish name), Mustafa (Muslim mysticism), Kasimir (Balkan Christian), and Suleiman (Solomon).

Even more objectionable were Bayezid's personal habits. Increasingly, he took on the ways of Balkan and Byzantine rulers and nobles. Manners and dress changed; court ceremony became more elaborate. Many still remembered the ease with which they could approach Orhan and contrasted the simplicity of Orhan's establishment to the complexity of Bayezid's. Bayezid, though brilliant and energetic at first, fell under the spell of grandeur and sumptuous living. He became addicted to wine and sodomy, both of which scandalized the Ottomans. His harem was large and he began to follow in the footsteps of the caliphs of old. Even the increase in the number of his sons (Osman had only two, Orhan three, and Murad three) would indicate a devotion to his harem, an institution not mentioned in connection with either Osman or Orhan.

DEFEAT AT ANKARA

This dissatisfaction and unrest among Bayezid's subjects, especially the Muslims, and the presence of many Anatolian émigré amirs in the entourage of Timur induced the latter to lead an incursion into Anatolia. In addition, Bayezid had invaded territory beyond the Euphrates to the Tigris and given indications of ambitions in Syria, thereby threatening Timur's vassals. After Bayezid ignored letters from Timur advising him to mend his ways, Timur marched into Asia Minor.

Surprisingly overconfident, Bayezid moved leisurely to meet the threat. In the face of so great a danger he organized a huge hunting party, wasting valuable time and tiring his men. The contest came in 1402 at Ankara, where only the janissaries and the Christian vassals of the Balkans stood fast. Bayezid, a prisoner, was brought before Timur, who honored him until his haughtiness became insufferable. Within a few weeks he died, and his body was returned to Bursa, the chief Ottoman burial site.

Following his great victory, Timur marched across Anatolia to Izmir on the Aegean. He showed little desire to hold Anatolia directly, however. Ottoman conquests in Europe and the early holdings of Osman and Orhan in Asia were divided among Bayezid's remaining sons: Suleiman, Musa, Isa, and Mehmed. Anatolian amirates taken by Murad and Bayezid were restored to their previous hereditary families.

Bayezid had a dream of empire, but it was shattered at Ankara. The Ottoman family was left in possession of those holdings which were considered legitimate. Bayezid's sons and all other amirs of Anatolia swore allegiance to Timur and became his vassals. Three years later when Timur died, the amirs of western Asia Minor renounced all dependence upon the Timurids, and Anatolia was left as it had been before the invasion except for the breakup of the Ottoman domain among Bayezid's four heirs. If there was to be an Ottoman Empire, it was yet to be fashioned.

REFERENCES

Volumes cited at the end of Chapters 11 and 12 are important for this chapter.

Alderson, A. D. *The Structure of the Ottoman Dynasty.* Oxford: Clarendon Press, 1956. An important volume on the Ottoman family and the lives of the individual sultans.

Cook, M. A., ed. *A History of the Ottoman Empire to 1730.* Cambridge: Cambridge University Press, 1976. Seven chapters by different authors; the essays are drawn from the *Cambridge History of Islam* and the *New Cambridge Modern History.*

Davison, Roderic H. *Turkey.* Englewood Cliffs, N.J.: Prentice-Hall, 1968. A fine volume by an outstanding scholar on the early Turks down to the time of publication.

Inalcik, Halil. *The Ottoman Empire: The Classical Age, 1300–1600.* 2d ed. New Rochelle, N.Y.: Caratzas, 1987. A new chapter on rural society has been added to this thorough history by the outstanding Ottoman scholar. In addition to political matters, the author discusses in a most enlightened way law, economic and social life, and culture.

Itzkowitz, Norman. *Ottoman Empire and Islamic Tradition.* New York: Knopf, 1973. This is an excellent introduction to the Ottoman Empire by a well-known scholar. Deals with the early history leading to the formation of the empire.

Kinross, Lord (Patrick Balfour). *The Ottoman Centuries: The Rise and Fall of the Turkish Empire.* New York: Morrow, 1977. A well-written, popular account of the history of the Ottomans.

Lindner, Rudi Paul. *Nomads and Ottomans in Medieval Anatolia.* Bloomington, Ind.: Research Institute for Inner Asian Studies, 1983. The author discounts the ghazi and emphasizes the tribal identity of the early Ottomans. There is also an excellent account of the treatment of Anatolian nomads by the Ottomans in the middle period of the empire's long history.

Pitcher, Donald Edgar. *An Historical Geography of the Ottoman Empire: From the Earliest Times to the End of the Sixteenth Century, with Detailed Maps to Illustrate the Expansion of the Sultanate.* Leiden: Brill, 1972. Emphasis is on political geography with thirty-six colored maps and an extensive index of names and their equivalents in different languages.

Shaw, Stanford. *History of the Ottoman Empire and Modern Turkey.* Vol. 1. *Empire of the Gazis: The Rise and Decline of the Ottoman Empire, 1280–1808.* Cambridge: Cambridge University Press, 1976. This is an outstanding contribution by a leading scholar in the field. He analyzes the many forces in Asia Minor that produced the Ottoman Empire and relates the factors that led to its decline.

Shinder, Joel. "Early Ottoman Administration in the Wilderness." *International Journal of Middle East Studies* 9 (1978): 497–517. This review of earlier theories of Ottoman administration acknowledges the influence of the Il-Khans, but also points to Ottoman innovations.

Sugar, Peter F. *Southeastern Europe Under Ottoman Rule, 1354–1804*. Seattle: University of Washington Press, 1977.

Wittek, Paul. *The Rise of the Ottoman Empire*. London: Royal Asiatic Society, 1938. A masterful work that is still the basis of discussion in the field.

14

The Winning of the Ottoman Empire

MEHMED I REUNITES THE STATE

The capture of Sultan Bayezid I at the Battle of Ankara in 1402 left the remaining Ottoman provinces to be apportioned among his sons. Timur recognized Mehmed, probably the youngest, as governor of Amasya, his residence under his father. Isa was designated as lord of Bursa. Suleiman, the eldest and formerly governor at Manisa, went to Edirne and ruled the Ottoman possessions in Europe. Musa, taken prisoner by Timur, was placed on parole to the Germiyan family at Kutahya. Shortly afterward, he was authorized to take his father's body to Bursa for burial and was then sent to the court of his brother Mehmed.

The transitory character of Timur's conquest permitted the four sons to quarrel among themselves over their patrimony. At first Mehmed and Musa teamed up against Suleiman and Isa, striking their first blows in Asia. With Mehmed's compliance Musa drove Isa from Bursa. Fleeing to Constantinople, Isa was encouraged by Suleiman, himself under pressure from Musa, to make a bid to regain his city. He was, however, beaten by Mehmed and vanished from the scene.

Meanwhile, having escaped from the Ankara disaster with Ali Pasha Chandarli and the leader of the janissaries, Suleiman arrived at Edirne, European headquarters for the Ottoman family. With the richest part of the state in his hands and supported by his father's chief ministers, Suleiman in 1403 claimed to be ruler of the Ottomans. But Mehmed and Musa refused to acknowledge his supremacy.

Rivalry among the three brothers endured for a decade. Its genesis was the killing of Bayezid I's own brother. But competition among Suleiman, Musa, and Mehmed also arose from the factionalism in Ottoman politics that emerged from their father's attempts to consolidate and centralize the state.

The imperial clique found its candidate in Suleiman. Supported by the Chandarli and Evrenos families, by the governmental machinery in Edirne, and by the janissaries who survived the rout at Ankara, Suleiman reigned until 1411. Treaties with the Venetian doge and the Byzantine emperor recognized him as Ottoman ruler and facilitated trade and commerce in Europe, affairs in which the

Chandarli family was personally interested. Suleiman failed, however, in his campaigns to dislodge Musa and Mehmed from Bursa.

With the aid of discontented Serbs and Wallachians, Musa carried the struggle against Suleiman to Europe in 1410, engaging him in battle between Edirne and Constantinople. Unsuccessful in the first attempt, Musa caught Suleiman the next year in a surprise raid upon Edirne and killed him as he was fleeing to Constantinople. Ibrahim Chandarli, the Evrenos family, and the court immediately transferred their loyalty to Musa, who was now recognized as lord of Europe. Mehmed remained supreme in Asia Minor.

Besides Balkan vassals and Ottoman European officialdom, Musa was supported by a freethinking religious coterie pursuing a theological eclecticism popular at that time. As chief judge in Ottoman European territories, he appointed one of its leaders, Shaykh Badr al-Din Simavni, who held views leading toward an egalitarian society and a union of Judaism, Christianity, and Islam. Some years later Shaykh Badr al-Din led an unsuccessful rebellion against the state, and in the mid-sixteenth century his views were still being preached by one of his descendants.

Musa was an energetic individual and sent out raiding parties into Greece and as far into Europe as Carinthia. The siege of Constantinople that had been lifted upon the coming of Timur into Anatolia was resumed. Strangely, Mehmed aided the emperor against his brother. Musa's revolutionary tendencies and his open favoring of the common people drove many of his supporters such as Ibrahim Chandarli over to Mehmed, who carried on an active campaign for allies among high-placed Ottoman feudal lords in Europe. Most of these went over to Mehmed; and in 1413 Edirne fell to Mehmed, who caught up with Musa near Sofia. Musa perished, and his body was returned with honor to Bursa to be buried beside Sultan Murad I.

Mehmed now reigned alone and all Ottomans paid him homage. Having first governed in Amasya, heartland of the old ghazi district, Mehmed professed the ghazi way of life and throughout remained its champion. With the favor of this powerful faction, essentially the military foundation of the state, propaganda for him among frontier raiders and Ottoman colonists in Europe took root easily, while the slave troops and officials were lowered in position and rank. Mehmed represented the "good old days" of Osman and Orhan.

In looking for factors in the success of Mehmed, the role of his tutor (*lala*) cannot be disregarded. As was customary, Mehmed was sent as a boy to govern a province and learn the art of ruling. A high state dignitary accompanied the prince "to advise" in all matters. In this instance, the tutor was Bayezid Pasha, an Albanian by birth and a war captive retained by Murad and raised at court. Bayezid Pasha proved to be an outstanding general and a devoted slave to Mehmed, winning battles, organizing campaigns, and above all leading Mehmed to the task of reuniting the Ottoman state. Bayezid Pasha was one of the very first of a new type of high Ottoman official who in his attachment to his masters, the Ottoman family, showed his proclivity for a strongly centralized state.

Most important, in strongly identifying himself with Anatolia and the old ghazi way of life, Mehmed avoided the mistakes of his father and his brother Suleiman in their European and Balkan manners. He chose for his wife a daughter of the amir of Dhu al-Qadr, a Turkoman amirate of the Syrian frontier. Mehmed grew to be revered by the Ottomans for his gentleness, integrity, and modesty.

EXPANSION IN ASIA

There were in Asia Minor many Turks, however, who were not considered Ottomans and who did not accept the idea of one united state or acquiesce in its rule. Although forces from Karaman and Dhu al-Qadr fought with Mehmed when he ousted his brother Isa from Bursa, the Karaman prince, always the prime Ottoman rival in Anatolia, besieged Bursa when Mehmed was destroying Musa in Rumeli. (The European part of the Ottoman state was always referred to as Rumeli—the land of the Romans, i.e., Byzantines.) The Karamans were defeated in 1414, but their state was not conquered.

Except for the states of Karaman, Dhu al-Qadr, and Isfendiyar, Turkish families recognized the dominant position of the Ottomans in central and western Anatolia. The disruption of society resulting from Timur's invasion and continued by the civil wars of Bayezid's sons generated many religious and mystical sects in Asia Minor. A number of dervish orders founded by holy men from Iran date their origin from this period. Social unrest, too, was common. In 1416, Bayezid Pasha had to raise levies from most of Anatolia to quell a socioreligious revolutionary movement in the peninsula north of Izmir (and in Europe)—a movement led by the mystic Badr al-Din, one-time European army judge under Musa.

As a genuine ghazi, Mehmed could not ignore Europe and the great conquests there. Furthermore, Rumeli produced far greater revenue for the Ottoman government than did Anatolia. Any slackening of the sultan's activity in Europe always brought on financial repercussions. Mehmed intervened in Wallachia, built fortresses north of the Danube, and encouraged ghazi raids in Hungary, Bosnia, and Styria. Mehmed refused to resume the attack that his father and brothers had begun upon Constantinople.

Unquestionably, Mehmed reestablished Ottoman unity approximately to the extent that it had existed in his father's time. But an Ottoman Empire was not yet created, and it could not be created without Constantinople, geographic and economic center of the area. Mehmed made no attempt to conquer it. Friendly relations with the emperor in times of distress prevented him from entertaining any designs on the city. Nonetheless, his early death from a stroke in 1421 may have saved the city from attack.

MURAD II

The idea of the continuity of the state and the sultan's relationship to governmental power had so grown that Mehmed's closest advisers, of whom Bayezid Pasha was one, concealed his death for forty days until his son and successor Murad II arrived in Edirne from Amasya to take charge. Nearly eighteen years old, Murad had resided with his advisers and tutors at Manisa before being moved to Amasya. At the time of his father's death, Murad had one surviving brother, Mustafa, who was thirteen years old. Afraid that Murad would kill him as Bayezid had strangled Yakub, Mustafa fled from his Anatolian governorship with his tutors to the protection of the Karaman family in Konya.

Murad surrounded himself with representatives of old Ottoman families such as Chandarli, Evrenos, Timurtash, and Mikhaloglu and with leaders of the new courtiers like Bayezid Pasha, although this latter group was less numerous. At the very outset of Murad's reign the Byzantine emperor freed the old pretender Mustafa, supposed son of Bayezid I, who circulated in Rumeli gathering supporters. Mustafa and his supporters defeated and killed Bayezid Pasha, seized Gallipoli with the emperor's aid, and invaded Anatolia. Murad rallied and drove them back to Europe. In 1422 Genoese cooperation in transporting his troops across the Straits permitted him to catch and kill the pretender Mustafa and the rebels in Edirne.

Murad raged at the emperor for his duplicity and ordered resumption of the siege of Constantinople. With prodigious effort, much enthusiasm, and the use of breaching cannon for the first time in Ottoman history, Murad and his soldiers stormed the walls. After two months of failure Murad lifted the siege to meet a new threat in Asia Minor: Byzantine diplomacy with the Karamans had brought Murad's brother Mustafa from his refuge in Konya to an unsuccessful attack upon Bursa.

Though Mustafa was caught and hanged, Murad never resumed the attack upon Constantinople. The emperor agreed to pay the Ottomans a yearly tribute of 30,000 ducats and surrender all territory outside the walls, except for areas that fed the aqueducts of the city. In Anatolia, Murad judiciously alternated between diplomacy and force. A slight engagement with the amir of Isfendiyar ended when Murad married the amir's daughter and obtained possession of the copper mines in that region. The Karaman amir sued for peace. Peace with Karaman, however, was never sure; and whenever Murad became deeply engrossed or embarrassed in Europe, war with the princes of Konya became imminent and sometimes necessary.

Murad's greatest efforts were expended in Europe, and there lay his greater gains. In 1430 Salonica was taken after a long struggle. Upon the accession to the throne of Hungary of Ladislaus, king of Lithuania and Poland, dissident elements banded their arms together and invaded Ottoman territory. In 1443, the invaders won numerous strongholds, were victorious at Nish and Sofia, and brought Murad to the edge of ruin.

Nevertheless, Murad and King Ladislaus concluded an honorable peace in 1444, each promising not to invade the other's territory for ten years. Murad had defeated the Karamans, and Hunyadi realized that the Ottoman army, with Murad at its head and the janissaries included, would be quite a different body from the feudal army that he had met the previous year. Murad gave up suzerainty over Wallachia and Serbia and ransomed his son-in-law for 60,000 ducats.

OTTOMAN SOCIETY AND CULTURE

Evidently Murad felt that he had made peace with the world in Europe and Asia and that the time was propitious for retirement from an active rule. He was forty years old

and had been sultan for twenty-three years. His two older sons having died, Murad abdicated in favor of his fifteen-year-old third son, Mehmed, who went to Edirne with
Khalil Pasha Chandarli as grand vizir. Murad himself withdrew to his favorite residence in Manisa, where he intended to live in ease and peace with poets, mystics,
theologians, and men of letters. He wished to pursue the *futuwwa,* the ideal life, mod-
estly studying and writing in quiet contemplation.

It was the time of an incipient Turkish renaissance. The Turkish language, as
spoken at the Ottoman court and in western Anatolia, became a medium of cultured expression. Konya, Kutahya, and Bursa in Asia Minor and Edirne in Europe
were its centers; its patrons were the Karaman, Germiyan, and Ottoman families
and their courts. Heretofore, Persian and Arabic were the languages of poetry,
records, and education. But Turkish was growing more popular. Many Persian and
Arabic works were translated into Ottoman Turkish, and poets were held in high
esteem. Sufis, mystics, and holy men were numerous and earnestly venerated.

Ottoman history was first cultivated under Murad, when a "romantic" movement arose. Until this time, Ottoman chronicles were sagas of ghazis and their
great deeds. Under Murad, there developed a new and formal Ottoman history,
which included illustrious ancestors going back to the most noble of Turkish
tribes—the Oghuz tribe. Beautiful tales were written of Osman's ancestors riding
with 400 horsemen into Asia Minor from Turkestan and plunging into a battle they
witnessed. Naturally bringing victory to the side they aided, they were richly rewarded with fiefs. In this manner the Ottomans received their start! It must be remembered that at the time of Murad's retirement 150 years had passed since
Osman's first conquests, and that in a new and rapidly evolving society not many
men could relate the exploits of their great-great-great-grandfathers.

Murad's intellectual and cultural concerns were reflected in the education of his
children. He employed as teachers for the princes the most enlightened and distinguished scholars of the state. Many had important army or administrative positions.
Included with the princes in the palace school were other boys, some of whom were
captives of war or sons of distinguished vassals of the sultan. Murad desired not only
to educate his own sons to their responsibilities but also to train other youths in discipline, integrity, and moral values that might serve state and sultan intelligently and
faithfully. Proof of the value and thoroughness of this school was first demonstrated in
the education and ability of Murad's son, Mehmed.

MILITARY DEVELOPMENTS

For a few months all went well in the Ottoman state. Murad had retired to Manisa,
and the boy Mehmed II was surrounded by advisers and teachers at Edirne. But
the Hungarians broke the peace in the autumn of 1444, perhaps thinking that the
treaty with Murad was invalidated by his retirement and that victory would be possible against a boy ruler. Murad was recalled from his retirement and crushed the
invaders near Varna. King Ladislaus, who had insisted upon breaking the treaty
against Hunyadi's admonitions, lost his life, and his army was defeated and dispersed.

Ottomans now easily overran Serbia and Bosnia. Since Ottomans were tolerant of all forms of Christianity whereas Hungarians in their brief sway had begun to impose Latin rites upon Serbian and Bosnian churches, many fortresses opened their gates to Murad.

With this affair apparently settled, Murad abdicated a second time in 1445 and returned to Manisa. It was not long, however, before an open demonstration of rebellion against Mehmed II by the janissaries brought Murad back to active rule in Edirne. The ringleaders were executed, imprisoned, or exiled from the capital, and the sultan's authority was fully restored.

This episode was a harbinger of future grave difficulties that Ottoman sultans would experience with janissary and other imperial troops, who were becoming hardened ruthless professional soldiers. Simply educated, reared and trained exclusively for warfare, and not too well paid because of the expectation that they would be richly rewarded from plunder won on campaigns, the janissaries felt their power and importance and were easily induced to demand favors of many kinds. Between them and older Ottomans—feudal cavalry and old family administrators like those closest to Murad—rivalry was keen and often bitter.

For this reason, in about 1430 Murad reinstituted for the janissary corps a draft (*devshirmeh*) procedure. Every few years army officers toured the Anatolian and Balkan rural districts, conscripting Christian boys between the ages of ten and fifteen. These youths were brought to Edirne. As slaves of the sultan they were parceled out among court officers, the feudatory, and the sultan himself. The draftees from the Balkans were sent to Asia Minor and vice versa. After a few years of growth, toughening, Islamization, and Turkification in language and customs they were returned to Edirne, where they received military training and were assigned to a janissary barracks. The more favored were attached to the palace; the very best attended the princes' school, whereupon any position in the state was open to them. At first employed to augment the ranks of the janissaries when wars and raids failed to yield sufficient captives, the draft was justified as another form of taxation for the subject communities, analogous to poll taxes except they paid taxes in boys! More significant was the fact that the most vigorous and capable youths were being removed from their villages and raised as Ottomans. Some observers remarked that this policy helped to keep the Christian population in subjection by drawing away future leaders. Some families turned to Islam rather than lose their sons.

It was also the custom for vassal Christian princes to send a son or two as hostages to the sultan's court. Various defeated Balkan leaders were permitted to retain their lands, but sent their sons to be reared as Ottomans. One such hostage was George Kastriota, who was sent to Murad II. He was educated in the princes' school, served in various responsible posts under Murad, but deserted in 1443. Skanderbeg, as he was now called, returned to his native Albania; and there for twenty-five years he led resistance movements and guerrilla warfare against Murad and Mehmed II.

After the janissary revolt of 1445 was put down, Murad did not again retire but engaged in campaigns in Europe. Twice he entered Albania in pursuit of Skanderbeg. Bulgaria was fully absorbed into the Ottoman system of direct rule. In 1448, he drove Hunyadi out of Serbia, defeating him on the plains of Kossovo.

Early in 1451, the aged warrior (about fifty years old) died in Edirne. The young Mehmed, now grown to manhood, when apprised in Manisa of his father's death, supposedly leaped on his horse and raced to Edirne to take charge.

MEHMED II

In some ways Mehmed II's character was an extension of his father's. Since he had the benefits of the princes' school, his mind was well trained. He knew literary Turkish, Arabic, Persian, and Greek, and was able to converse in ordinary Serbian and Italian. He enjoyed poetry and was familiar with the classical poetry of Iran, Greece, and Rome. Mehmed was an accomplished poet himself and gathered about him poets from the four corners of the Muslim world. As a student he read philosophy and was much taken with writings of the Stoics and the Peripatetics. He loved history, particularly biographies of Alexander the Great and the Caesars. The study of war and of everything associated with war, such as strategy, supplies, munitions, and topography, aroused his interest greatly. Every Ottoman, even of the royal family, had a trade—perhaps because of the akhi heritage—and Mehmed was an accomplished gardener. Later, between campaigns and for relaxation, he worked in the gardens of the royal palace.

With regard to administration, however, Mehmed was quite unlike his father. Thoroughness and efficiency combined with great energy and promptness became the order of the day whenever Mehmed was present. Delay and procrastination were foreign to his nature, but he was known for his furious temper. He showed remarkable toleration in religious matters.

In many respects Murad had not been very businesslike in his administration, and Mehmed spent the first year of his reign reorganizing the government. The treasury, in particular, was tightened up; many tax officials were forced to straighten their accounts, whereupon they were dismissed. Tax rates were raised, monopolies established, and pious foundations (Arabic, waqf/awqaf; Turkish, vakif/evkaf) were confiscated to the benefit of the imperial treasury. The entire administration of the royal palace was surveyed, registers of the troops scrutinized, and soldiers' pay increased. Some provincial governors were removed, others were promoted. Mehmed's criteria for determining an individual's fitness for holding a position were his knowledge and his sense of diplomacy and justice. One unhappy episode was his order that his only brother, an infant, be drowned in his bath, thus perpetuating the custom begun by Bayezid I of eliminating rival heirs. Years later, Mehmed decreed that whoever of his sons seized the throne should execute his brothers.

CAPTURE OF CONSTANTINOPLE

With the coming of 1452 Mehmed began his plans for taking Constantinople. Munitions were gathered: armor, bows, arrows, mortars, cannon, balls, gunpowder, timbers, and war articles of every sort. At Gallipoli a fleet was assembled and new ships built. Mehmed and his officers studied every inch of the terrain along the land walls of Constantinople and for miles around in every direction. To control the Bosphorus he ordered the construction of a fortress on its European shore opposite the fortifications built on the Asian side half a century earlier by his great-grandfather. Erected just above the narrowest point of the Bosphorus, these three formidable towers (called Rumeli Hisar) were connected with heavy walls and formed a castle harboring cannon whose range controlled the passage of the Bosphorus.

The true attack upon Constantinople (or Stambul, as the citizens called their city) began in April 1453. More than 50,000 of the best soldiers that Mehmed could muster were assembled for the assault. The fleet numbered between 300 and 400 ships, but even these were unable to control the Straits completely. For fifty-four days cannon balls pounded the land walls of the city. The sea walls were bombarded by the fleet, but the walls along the Golden Horn could not be reached. Mortars from the shores of the Bosphorus did sink some Greek ships on the Golden Horn, but a heavy chain from Galata to Constantinople effectively closed the Horn to Mehmed's ships. Not to be thwarted, Mehmed constructed a greased wooden runway from the shore of the Bosphorus up the hill of Beyoglu (Pera) and down the slope to the Golden Horn. Sixty-seven ships of the Ottoman fleet were hauled up over the incline and slid down to the Golden Horn, from where they threw their stone cannon balls on the city walls.

Cut off completely and bombarded from every side, the defenders of Constantinople resisted the attacks valiantly. The Genoese and other Italians in Galata and Pera gave no assistance, and most of the 50,000 inhabitants of the once great city acted supremely indifferent to their fate, perhaps because Emperor Constantine in desperation called for aid from the West and announced submission to the pope in exchange for promises of soldiers. A few came, but help was entirely inadequate. The citizenry preferred Ottoman rule to Latin rule and Muslim tolerance to Roman intolerance.

A stupendous assault was launched on May 29, 1453; cannon fire breached the walls, and the city was taken. Following the universal custom of that age, the conquering troops had complete license in the city, except that no public buildings could be touched. Mehmed entered the city, and the plundering ceased. He went to Hagia Sophia, where prayers were said. He then quickly turned to the problem of the city that the Ottomans have always called Istanbul. A governor was appointed; inhabitants were encouraged to remain by exempting them from taxes and by giving them back their houses; the sultan ransomed many on condition that they would stay; the army was disbanded; and Mehmed returned to Edirne, his capital.

The economic, military, and cultural effects of the capture of Constantinople have usually been exaggerated. Later centuries developed a myth that the fall of Constantinople blocked the trade routes to the Far East, thereby forcing the Age of Discoveries and the voyages of Columbus. According to another legend, the fall of Constantinople resulted in the migration of Greek monks and manuscripts to Italy, thus initiating the Renaissance. Another story has related that the fall of Constantinople removed the Balkan bastion, at once enabling the Ottoman Turks to conquer the whole peninsula of southeast Europe. All three of these myths have been exploded by careful examination of historical development. Yet even today these tales are repeated and found in modern books.

Nevertheless, the emotional impact of the fall of Constantinople on the people of the fifteenth century should not be minimized. To Christian Europe, and

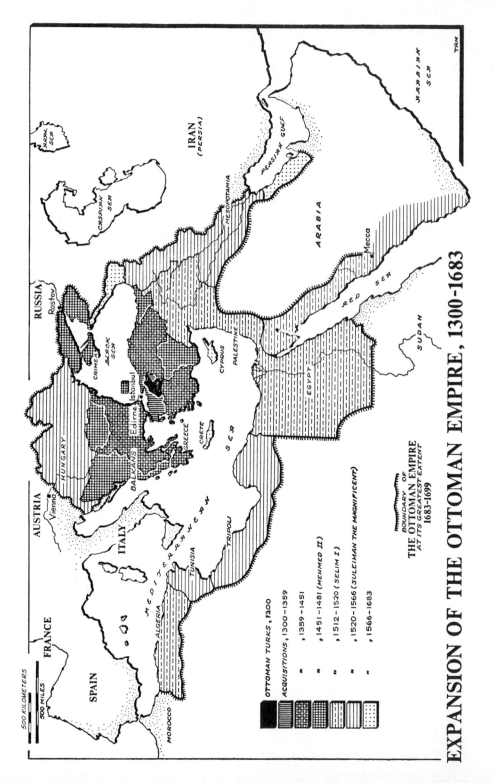

EXPANSION OF THE OTTOMAN EMPIRE, 1300-1683

BOUNDARY OF
THE OTTOMAN EMPIRE
AT ITS GREATEST EXTENT
1683-1699

OTTOMAN TURKS, 1300

ACQUISITIONS, 1300-1359

" , 1359-1451

" , 1451-1481 (MEHMED II)

" , 1512-1520 (SELIM I)

" , 1520-1566 (SULEIMAN THE MAGNIFICENT)

" , 1566-1683

500 KILOMETERS

500 MILES

especially to the West, the great imperial city had fallen. In a sense the Roman Empire had come to an end. Heretofore the Turks had been raiding "unknown and uncertain" areas, but Constantinople was a real place in Western thinking. Everywhere there was talk of a crusade; but of course, it was only talk.

To Muslims, the fall of Constantinople was a great and glorious achievement. Islamic rulers and armies had attempted it many times in the past. To them, Constantinople was the majestic city of imperial tradition whose conquest had always been a goal of the great caliphs. Now a new Muslim state had accomplished the impossible, and consequently Mehmed II received great acclaim and respect throughout the East.

To the Ottomans, it was the conquest of the natural capital and center of their state. Since the time of Bayezid I its incorporation in the state had been a logical and necessary step, but it had been long in coming. Its acquisition served as the keystone in creating the Ottoman Empire.

REFERENCES

References in Chapters 11, 12, and 13 are important for this chapter.

Babinger, Franz. *Mehmed the Conqueror and His Time*. Edited by William C. Hickman and translated by Ralph Manheim. Princeton, N.J.: Princeton University Press, 1978. This excellently annotated classic biography emphasizes diplomacy, military, and political history.

Cook, M. A., ed. *Studies in the Economic History of the Middle East from the Rise of Islam to the Present Day*. London: Oxford University Press, 1970. All the articles are by major authors and many explore new ideas.

Inalcik, Halil. *The Ottoman Empire: Conquest, Organization and Economy*. London: Variorum, 1978. A collection of sixteen articles dealing with Ottoman conquests and organization, the economy, and decline and reform.

Kritovoulos. *History of Mehmed the Conqueror*. Translated by Charles T. Riggs. Princeton, N.J.: Princeton University Press, 1954. A contemporary account by a Greek in the service of the Ottomans.

Kuran, Aptullah. *The Mosque in Early Ottoman Architecture*. Chicago: University of Chicago Press, 1968. Develops the idea that the basic unit in early Ottoman architecture was the domed square. Scholarly and authoritative.

Runciman, Steven. *The Fall of Constantinople, 1453*. Cambridge: Cambridge University Press, 1969. A paperback edition of a first-rate book published in 1965. The author, a recognized scholar, has scoured the sources and presented in great detail and with much understanding a very readable and reliable account of the taking of the city.

Tursun Beg. *The History of Mehmed the Conqueror*. Translated by Halil Inalcik and Rhoads Murphy. Minneapolis, Minn.: Bibliotheca Islamica, 1978. In addition to a facsimile text of a manuscript of the work by Tursun Beg in the original Turkish, the translators have provided a summary translation and a discussion of the author.

15

Building the Ottoman and Safavid Empires

CONSOLIDATION OF THE EMPIRE

Beyond taking Constantinople, Mehmed II, always called Fatih ("The Conqueror") by his subjects, extended the periphery of his empire substantially. Campaigns and wars were scheduled almost every year. Operations were conducted in the Balkans and Asia Minor and from Venice and southern Italy to Iran and the Crimea. Affairs of any one area always involved those of others; and Mehmed never was able to isolate his many international and domestic problems to deal with one at a time. Moreover, Venetian envoys were plotting at every court to swell the number of his enemies and bring his downfall.

Ottoman campaigns, colonization, and government had been proceeding in the Balkans for a century. Nonetheless, Ottoman rule was still not effective in several regions, and many provinces that were tied to the Ottomans by a kind of vassalage or alliance were not integrated units of the state. Byzantine practices persisted in local administration, and especially on the extensive church and monastery lands. Conversion to Islam was slow and gradual; the languages of the conquered peoples persisted even when Ottoman judicial, fiscal, and feudal structures were introduced. A land reform in the entire empire was conducted and the ownership of most of the land was centralized in the hands of the state, and it was assigned as fiefs.

Pressure on the Balkans, however, was maintained continuously. In the next decade, Serbia and Bosnia were subjected to Ottoman rule and organized as regular imperial provinces. Wallachia and Moldavia were forced to become allies. Skanderbeg was checked in Albania, and after his death in 1478 Albania and Herzegovina became provinces of the empire. Greece and the Peloponnesus, except for a few Venetian ports of call such as Coron and Modon, were conquered, and some of the lands were parceled out as fiefs.

Mehmed also pursued a vigorous policy in Asia Minor. The most resistant foe had always been the Karaman dynasty; in 1466 Karaman opposition was broken. Later Cilicia was acquired; and as his reign closed, Mehmed became involved in family quarrels of the Dhu al-Qadr of Diyarbakir. The entire Mediterranean coast of Asia Minor was now in Ottoman hands.

Since Istanbul and the Straits were now Ottoman, Mehmed moved eastward, hoping to control the Black Sea shores. That same year (1461), with the cooperation of the navy from Gallipoli, Mehmed forced the surrender of the Greek emperor of Trebizond, thus obliterating the last remnant of the Byzantine Empire.

These activities led the Ottomans into conflict with the Aq Quyunlu, who dominated Iran, Armenia, and eastern Asia Minor. Venetian ambassadors traveled to the court of Uzun Hasan at Tabriz and encouraged war against Mehmed. Although Venice was concerned with Eastern trade, the main consideration was to lessen Ottoman pressure upon Venice and her European territory. Mehmed collected a mighty army including his two sons, Mustafa and Bayezid, his grand vizir, and Gedik Ahmed Pasha, a burly general who had risen from the ranks of the ordinary janissaries. He defeated Uzun Hasan in 1473 near Erzinjan in eastern Asia Minor. Next the Crimea, which was ruled by Turkish khans, came under Ottoman aegis. Except for the coast between the Crimea and the Danube, the Black Sea was now an Ottoman lake.

Although Venetian envoys professed friendship for Mehmed, conflict between Venice and the Ottoman Empire was almost inevitable. To ensure control of the Aegean coast of Anatolia and safeguard Ottoman ventures into the Morea, it was necessary to incorporate into the empire the Aegean Islands. This was particularly important because Venetians and pirates used these islands and their numerous harbors as bases to harry the Ottoman coast and hold up trade. Mehmed's fleet, therefore, captured these islands along with Cephalonia in the Ionian Islands; and for fifteen years (1463–1478) he was at war sporadically with Venice. Pressure on Venetian outposts along the Dalmatian coast was constant, and ghazis from Albania and Bosnia kept alarms sounding on St. Mark's Square. In 1477 Ottoman raiders descended to the Italian plain north of Venice. At night Venetian senators from the roof of St. Mark's could see Ottoman camp fires and burning villages. When autumn came the Ottomans returned home laden with booty. Venice concluded peace with Mehmed and recognized his island acquisitions.

In 1480 an Ottoman army under Gedik Ahmed Pasha crossed the Adriatic and took Otranto in the heel of the Italian peninsula, thus establishing a bridgehead for the conquest of Italy. Gedik Ahmed wintered there, but upon Mehmed's sudden death in May 1481 the expedition to Otranto was withdrawn, never to be launched again. Simultaneously (1480) there was an unsuccessful attack upon the Knights of St. John on the island of Rhodes.

The conqueror was dead. Secrecy was maintained in the Ottoman Empire until a successor could ascend the throne. Bells pealed in Europe when the news arrived. There was no doubt anywhere that a great man had died.

SETTLEMENT OF ISTANBUL

Never recovering from the devastation wrought by the Fourth Crusade, and gradually strangling economically after the first Ottoman crossing to Europe, Constantinople when it fell in 1453 was only a half-populated city, and had been depressed and dying slowly for more than two centuries. Many buildings were empty and in various stages of decay. From the outset Mehmed was concerned about repopulating the city. He viewed this task as even a mightier one than the actual conquest of the city. For twenty days he tarried in Istanbul, freeing many prisoners allocated to him, encouraging others to remain, and exempting many from taxation. The Christian population, as in most Ottoman cities, was never subjected to the *devshirmeh*. In almost every conquest in later years inhabitants of other towns were ordered to move to Istanbul, a policy also followed in regard to the cities of Salonica and Trabzon (Trebizond).

When Mehmed "Fatih" entered Istanbul, he learned that the patriarch was dead. Appreciating the need for the election of a new patriarch and understanding the stability that such a move would give the Greek community of Istanbul as well as the entire empire, Mehmed indicated confidence in the teacher and philosopher George Scholarius, who had long been popular with the Greeks of the city and in disfavor with the last Byzantine emperor because he headed the anti-Roman faction. Duly elected, Scholarius took the name Gennadius. Mehmed feted him, recognized him as patriarch and leader of the Christians in Istanbul, and ordered the vizir and officers to accord him proper respect. Gennadius was charged with responsibility for the obedience, conduct, and life of the Greek people and their relationship to the Ottoman government. Thus, in many ways Orthodox Christians were encouraged to reside in Istanbul and allowed to live according to their own ways and laws as long as they did not infringe upon or come into conflict with the administration of the government and the lives of Muslim subjects. In like manner, Mehmed II recognized a head of the Armenian Christian community in Istanbul, as well as other Armenian religious leaders for other regions. The chief Jewish rabbi of Istanbul was treated as preeminent among the rabbis of the empire, while the heads of local Jewish communities in other cities were acknowledged as local leaders.

Public buildings were reserved for the state, and many churches were converted into mosques. The outstanding example was Justinian's great church Hagia Sophia which became the Muslim Aya Sofya. Since the decline in population had left many empty churches and chapels, the conversion of the churches created little hardship for the Greek inhabitants.

Fatih chose as his residence the Monastery of the Pantocrator in the old Forum of Theodosius, the most populous part of the city and today the site of the University of Istanbul. Various additions were made to the monastery, which he occupied for about twelve years whenever in Istanbul. In 1459 he chose a new spot for his quarters, and here in 1465 a new palace was completed which remained the chief domicile of sultans until the nineteenth century. The new palace, Yeni Saray, was erected on the site of the fortress of ancient Byzantium on the point of land between the Golden Horn and the Sea of Marmara. Facing the entrance to the Bosphorus, it was the most natural and beautiful spot in the city for an imperial residence. It was soon called popularly Topkapi Saray ("Cannon Gate Palace") because of the heavily fortified gate at the tip of the point of land. The whole area enclosed by walls was soon known everywhere by its Italian name, Seraglio; it was famed for its many splendid buildings and large number of inhabitants. Yet Fatih passed winters, summers, and many seasons at the palace in Edirne or at family lodges in Bursa, Demotika, and other cities of the empire. Edirne remained the favorite summer headquarters of sultans until the eighteenth century.

THE PALACE SCHOOL

In the years of Mehmed's reign full integration of the empire with governors for all provinces appointed by the sultan, along with expansion of the state, its growing complexity, and diversity of population, augmented the need for trained personnel to operate the government. Murad II had faced a similar problem and had resolved it by placing the most promising of his young slaves in the school beside his own sons. Mehmed met the crisis by creating the Palace School of Istanbul. It was first established at the old palace, but was later transferred to the Seraglio, where it maintained continuous operation until the twentieth century. Students, called pages, were selected after a very careful screening from the boys between ten and fourteen years old among war captives and those drafted from Christian provinces. At the Palace School, they received a thorough education in languages, literature, music, law and theology, military science, mathematics, philosophy, governmental administration, taxation, finance, physical training, personal conduct, sports, and manual training. Only the very best lasted through the ten to twelve rigorous years of the course; those unable to continue drew governmental positions commensurate to their abilities.

Graduates were appointed to administrative posts in various departments of the government. The instructional staff was drawn from the finest teachers in mosque schools of Bursa, Edirne, and Istanbul and from high administrative offices of the government. It was thought fitting that each should learn a trade in case he should some day have to earn a living as a craftsman. All in all, a tremendous spirit was induced into the students; graduates of the Palace School formed a firmly knit group that stood apart in conduct and loyalty to the sultanship. Trained by one sultan, they often served his son or held the government together until a successor was determined. These "courtiers," as Western observers and envoys termed them, were reported to be more cultured, more faultless in their courtesy, more devoted to their master, and more skilled in their operation of the government than the courtiers and advisers of any Western king or emperor. At the time of the great success, efficiency, and strength of the Ottoman government, the entire system was based on merit. Merit alone brought appointment to government office and subsequent promotions and favors. When factors other than merit began to have weight, the government stagnated.

BAYEZID AND JEM

Mehmed II left two sons. Bayezid, aged thirty-three, was governor of Amasya, the old ghazi center. Jem, aged twenty-one, was governor of Konya, the former Seljuk capital. Since Amasya was eight days' ride from Istanbul whereas Konya was only four, the younger son had an advantage in obtaining control of the central administration. But the janissaries, the pages of the palace, and the government officials who were slaves of the sultan and graduates of the Palace School preferred Bayezid. Mehmed's last grand vizir, however, belonged by birth to the old Muslim aristocracy of Anatolia and was partial to Jem. He tried to conceal Fatih's death, secretly dispatched couriers to Jem, and moved to isolate Istanbul until Jem's arrival. However, Mehmed's death became known, whereupon the slave officials and the janissaries seized control, murdered the grand vizir, impaled his messengers to Jem, and awaited Bayezid's appearance. They chose the latter because they considered his residence of twenty-five years or more at Amasya as wedding him to the ghazi tradition, of which they were fast becoming the heirs. Moreover, recognizing the so-called law of fratricide, Bayezid cleverly attached through marriages and political friendship several potent figures of the government hierarchy to his candidacy. Jem was supported by the conservative Muslim community of Asia Minor. His chief difficulty was his comparative youth; Bayezid for years had been gathering his party for the eventual day, and Bayezid's eldest son was already, with his preceptors, governor of Manisa.

To break through the cordon of officers blocking the gate to the palace, Bayezid pledged a handsome gift of money to every janissary, declared an amnesty for all plundering and crimes committed in the period of interregnum, and, most significant, agreed to appoint to the vizirship only men from the soldier-palace-slave group.

Jem with forces from Karaman and Konya occupied Bursa and challenged Bayezid for the throne. Gedik Ahmed was recalled from Otranto and with the army that Mehmed had gathered defeated Jem, who fled to Egypt whence he made the holy pilgrimage to Mecca. Bayezid offered him a princely income if he would live peacefully in Jerusalem, but Jem returned in 1482 and made a second vain attempt at the throne. Escaping to the protection of the Knights of St. John of the island of Rhodes, he was held in custody by them and used to obtain a favorable treaty of peace with the Ottomans. Bayezid agreed to pay 40,000 ducats a year as long as Jem remained in captivity. The knights subsequently moved him to their castles in France, where he fell into the hands of Charles VIII. Later, Jem was presented to the pope, then was borrowed by Charles in 1494, from Pope Alexander VI, ostensibly to participate in a crusade against the Ottomans. Jem, however, died of a fever in Naples early the next year. His body was finally obtained by Bayezid and interred at Bursa.

WARS OF BAYEZID II

Between 1482 and 1495, Bayezid's fear of his brother's return somewhat restricted him in foreign activities. Yet the organization of the Ottoman state was conditioned to aggressive expansion. When campaigns were not in progress, feudal sipahi, janissaries, and the court became uneasy. During these years, therefore, a number of expeditions along the Dalmatian coast and into Hungary, Styria, and Carinthia were undertaken and a large navy was built. Although these raids were usually indecisive, they were rewarding in plunder. Akkerman, on the Black Sea at the mouth of the Dniester River, was taken, and Wallachia and Moldavia were subdued.

In this early period of Bayezid's reign, war broke out with the Mamluk sultans of Egypt. Dynastic difficulties among the Dhu al-Qadr involved Egyptians and Ottomans in a border dispute. In 1484, after aid and asylum had been given to Jem, open war broke out. The peace concluded in 1491 left Egypt in possession of the disputed border areas; but no difficulties appeared for two decades.

Following Jem's death, Bayezid pursued a more aggressive policy in the West. The tempo of Ottoman raids along the Dalmatian coast increased; ports rang with the noise of carpenters, coopers, and caulkers constructing war galleys and ships of all kinds. When war broke out with Venice in 1499, Ottomans took Modon and Coron in the Peloponnesus and defeated the Venetian fleet in a great sea engagement at Navarino. Peace was not concluded until 1503. The war further eclipsed Venetian power in Greece and the eastern Mediterranean, and Ottoman sea power became strongly established. Thereafter in Bayezid's reign, contingents of the Ottoman navy raided every Mediterranean shore, and Ottoman admirals and captains followed the pattern of the old ghazi corsairs.

The end of the war with Venice marked the rise of a new figure on the Ottoman frontier, Shah Ismail of Iran, who kindled a religious enthusiasm in the peoples of Iran and eastern Asia Minor. Claiming descent from the Prophet Muhammad, Ali, and the seventh imam and from Aq Quyunlu Turks and Byzantine emperors, Ismail united Iranians, Turks, and Shiites in devotion to his mystical being. Ismail (often called the Great Sufi) became shah in 1503 and pronounced Twelver Shiism as the official doctrine of his realm. Political agents—Sufis and shaykhs—permeated Asia Minor, concentrating in mountainous areas of the east, south, and southwest. Ismail's followers were called *kizilbash* ("red head") because of the red hats they wore.

Muslims of the Ottoman Empire had been eclectic and tolerant; Bayezid was a philosopher by nature and enough of a mystic that one of his nicknames was Sufi; and the janissaries as well as Bayezid and many court officers belonged to the Bektashi dervish order. Despite or perhaps because of these facts, the Ottomans could not permit the subversive ideas of a foreign monarch free rein within their state.

Shah Ismail's doctrines proved popular and open revolt among the Turkoman tribes developed in 1511. The rebels besieged and took Konya, seized Kutahya (Ottoman Anatolian army headquarters), and impaled the Ottoman commander in chief. However, they were defeated in a battle against an army that included 4,000 janissaries under the grand vizir and three Ottoman princes.

SELIM'S SUCCESSION

After the end of the Venetian war Bayezid suffered poor health and was often carried on a stretcher so that the troops might see him. With each illness his sons and grandsons became exceedingly nervous about the future. Of his eight sons, only three remained in 1511: Korkud at Manisa; Ahmed at Amasya; and Selim, the youngest, at Trabzon. Each was jockeying for advantages and seeking favors and strategic appointments for friends and sons. The janissaries and the soldiers preferred Selim, since he was the most energetic and devoted to warfare. Bayezid and the high officials advanced Ahmed as the solid administrator. The poets, philosophers, and theologians supported Korkud, for he was one of them.

Selim moved his forces to Edirne, and when Bayezid and his close advisers began granting vast authority and prodigious sums of money to Ahmed, Selim seized Edirne. To gain friends in Anatolia, Ahmed had donned the red hat of the *kizilbash*. Upon this development the staunchly Sunnite Bayezid called Selim to

Istanbul in 1512 and abdicated in his favor. A month later Bayezid died while en route to retirement in the palace at Demotika, where he had been born.

For thirty-one years Bayezid, a peace-loving, scholarly, and contemplative philosopher, had governed the Ottoman Empire. Never attacking a neighboring state without provocation, he spent years in organizing the administration of the government for the well-being of the state, and its inhabitants. He took great interest in the Palace School, often quizzing the students himself. Trade flourished, with merchants from Venice, Genoa, Florence, and Ragusa thronging to Istanbul and merchants from the East and the Arab lands coming to Bursa. Bayezid was exceedingly tolerant of other religions, and more than 100,000 Jews came to Istanbul, Izmir, Edirne, and Salonica when they were driven from Spain in 1492. Yet he was strict with Muslims. His father's unorthodox ways disturbed him, and one of Bayezid's first acts as sultan was to clear from the palace the pictures of his father and court officials painted by Gentile Bellini. He sold them in the bazaar.

Selim I (nicknamed Yavuz, meaning "stern" or "inflexible") gave a munificent bonus to each soldier, as had become the custom in securing the throne. But he entered the palace by a side gate in order not to bow openly to their demands. The facts were that he held only Rumeli with Istanbul, Ahmed controlling most of Anatolia from Amasya. Upon Selim's enthronement, Ahmed sent his son to take Bursa. Selim instantly crossed to Asia and carried the attack against Ahmed, who resisted with political guile and force until the following spring, when he was defeated and strangled. Meanwhile, five of Selim's nephews and his brother Korkud were similarly disposed of. Because Ahmed had obtained considerable support from the *kizilbash* of Anatolia, Selim decided to curb the growth of the sect, particularly since it was popular in the difficult mountainous and frontier areas of Karaman and Diyarbakir. Late in 1513, Selim stationed troops and agents in all parts of the empire, and at a given notice about 40,000 were cut down. By transporting others to Europe, Selim hoped that he had eradicated religious dissent in Asia Minor.

WAR AGAINST IRAN

In this ferocious act Selim recognized the role of Shah Ismail in Asia Minor, who was supported by *kizilbash* and regarded by many in Anatolia as a holy saint. Following Ismail's interference in the affairs of Dhu al-Qadr and the Ottoman succession, and Iranian intervention along Ottoman frontiers, Selim sent the fleet with his commissariat to Trabzon. With several thousand janissaries, the grand vizir, and feudal troops of Rumeli and Anatolia, supported by batteries of cannon, he marched eastward. Shah Ismail scorched the earth as he retreated; Selim's soldiers complained as they were driven on. But Selim would not turn back. In August 1514 at Chaldiran, northeast of Lake Van and not far from the foot of Mount Ararat, Selim's cannon and his army's superior numbers turned the tide against the Iranian cavalry. Ismail fled, leaving even his harem to be captured.

Although the victory at Chaldiran momentarily settled Selim's problems on his eastern frontier, in no way did it destroy the new state arising in Iran or eliminate the Safavid dynasty and its spreading of Shiite Islam.

ESTABLISHMENT OF THE SAFAVIDS IN IRAN

As the Mongol state declined in the late thirteenth and fourteenth centuries, many Turkoman tribes became autonomous, each constituting a virtual state within a state; and at the same time numerous Sufi orders appeared, each quite independent from the other. Some of the Turkoman tribes and the Sufi orders converted to Shiism; Sufi leadership became hereditary and powerful not only as religious leaders but as commanders of the warriors of the faith.

When the Mongols had raided northwestern Iran in 1220, the city of Ardabil was destroyed; it subsequently revived, but only as a small provincial town. A Sufi order in Ardabil was called Safavid after its first leader, Safi al-Din, a Sunnite, who died in 1334. (As mentioned, their name *kizilbash,* or "red head," was derived from the hat they adopted as a distinctive mark—a scarlet cone-shaped affair with twelve scallops, or gores, one for each of the twelve imams.)

The tomb of the Safavid leader became a shrine, and the complex of buildings around it served as a place of pilgrimage for the devotees of the order who flocked to Ardabil. Political chaos and change in rulers disturbed the town and northwestern Iran as a whole, so the Safavid family maintained their own local freedom of action. They became Shiites at some time after 1392; by the 1450s they were seeking political power as allies first of the Qara Quyunlu and then the Aq Quyunlu Turkomans. Raids against Byzantine Trabzon and Christian Georgia in the Caucasus earned the appellation ghazi for the Safavid leaders. Following the death in battle of the Safavid Haydar in 1488, his eldest son took the title padishah (king or emperor), and in the late fifteenth century the charismatic Safavids claimed to be the Hidden Imam of the Twelver Shiites, who came to that position as a result of inheritance and not by designation of a predecessor.

In time, powerful Turkoman tribes of western Iran and eastern Asia Minor, accepting Shiism, supported this Safavid order and became instrumental in its rise to power. The young Ismail, son of Haydar, became the leader of the Safavid dynasty. With the indispensable aid of Turkish-speaking *kizilbash* tribes and a small group of advisers, Ismail defeated the prince of Shirvan and the Aq Quyunlu, took Armenia and Azerbayjan in 1501, and, at the age of fourteen, was proclaimed shah in Tabriz.

Ismail then gained central and southern Iran in 1503, Baghdad and southwest Iran in 1508, and Khurasan in 1510. He seized most of the Tigris-Euphrates basin including Diyarbakir in 1504, and reached Dhu al-Qadr and the frontiers of the Ottomans.

As leader of the Safavid religious order, Ismail regarded himself in his poetry—and was accepted—as a divine reincarnation. He was worshiped during his lifetime as a saint who possessed supernatural attributes and who, consequently,

Ismail (1501–1524)
|
Tahmasp (1524–1576)
|

| Ismail II (1576–1578) | Muhammad Khudabanda (1578–1588) |
| | | |

Muhammad Khudabanda (1578–1588)
|
Abbas (1588–1629)
|
Safi Mirza
|
Safi (1629–1642)
|
Abbas II (1642–1666)
|
Suleiman (Safi II) (1666–1694)
|
Husayn (1694–1722)
|
Tahmasp II (1722–1732)

The Safavids

was invincible; his subjects prostrated themselves before him as before God. His state, from the very first, was based on the principles of Shiism and his task in Iran was to spread that sect. Wherever his edict reached, the choice was fixed: conversion to Shiism or death. Though most Iranians had been Sunni Muslims, Ismail's cruelty, coupled with his policy of confiscating properties of Sunnites, expropriating endowments of Sunni Sufi orders, executing or exiling Sunni religious leaders, bringing into Iran Shiite scholars from the Arab world (especially from southern Lebanon), and the already existing Shiite sentiment in Qumm and Khurasan and among guilds, all changed Iran into a Shiite state by the time of his death in 1524. His power was based on the support of the Turkish tribal leaders, held by a mystical allegiance and tied to urban populations who were devotees of the Safavids. The tribal and Sufi leaders together could be called a kind of religious fraternity. With economic interests shifting into the hands of the Shiites, a permanent attachment to the Safavid dynasty occurred and peace and prosperity were sought. In return for soldiers and revenue, each *kizilbash* chief was given a province as a fief, with the power of life and death over its populace and the obligation to convert all to Shiism.

Claiming descent from Ali, Sasanid, Byzantine, and Turkoman princes, Ismail established a theocratic state in western Iran with his principal strength in the north. Expanding eastward, he successfully waged war against the Uzbegs of central Asia, killing their chieftain in 1510. Herat now became the second most important city in the state, and the residence of the heir to the throne, despite the temporary resurgence of the Uzbegs in 1512.

Having controversies with Bayezid II over Shiite *kizilbash* followers in southern Anatolia, Cilicia, and especially in the Taurus mountain area, Ismail had the Uzbeg chieftain's skin stuffed with straw and sent to Bayezid II as a warning. (In an even more typically macabre gesture Ismail had that same victim's skull rimmed with gold and set with jewels, using it as his favorite drinking cup.)

In order to establish the true faith, Ismail felt it necessary to maintain well-organized political power. To this end a governing apparatus of three main divisions was formed: military, religious, and bureaucratic. At first, no sharp distinction in the ruling establishment existed between military and civilian officers: all were members of the monarch's household. (The only real distinction was that most of the military were Turkish and most of the civilian force Iranian.) As political centralization gained momentum, the reins of government were gathered into the hands of Ismail's associates and officials. At the top of the hierarchy stood the viceroy (*vakil*), who exercised both temporal and spiritual authority. He took a leading role in political affairs, acted as a military commander, and influenced the selecting of other officials. The viceroys were Iranian, a fact deeply resented by the *kizilbash* Turkish leaders. In the midst of a battle against the Uzbegs in 1512, the *kizilbash* forces deserted, guaranteeing the defeat and death of the viceroy. After another viceroy was killed in the battle of Chaldiran in 1514, the position was limited to supervision of the bureaucracy and the temporal administration. Next in line stood the commander in chief (*amir al-umara*), a post that was originally held by the viceroy and that, in addition to controlling the military, had considerable influence in administrative and political matters. In 1509, Ismail chose an obscure officer for this post in an obvious move to weaken the power of the Turkoman leaders. Iranians also held the posts of supervisor (*sadr*) of the ulema, or men of religion, and vizir. Naturally there developed among these officials a great deal of rivalry for power and for Ismail's favor, and the strains between the Turkish forces and the Iranian elements were constantly felt.

When Selim seized the Ottoman throne in Istanbul in 1512, he became involved in the raging quarrel in Anatolia over the *kizilbash* tribes. Finding the possible disloyalty of his subjects intolerable, Selim set out to destroy Ismail. At Chaldiran the superiority of janissary discipline, muskets, and Ottoman artillery over swords, spears, and bows and arrows was demonstrated. (The Safavids had used cannons in sieges, but they were reluctant to use cannons and handguns, since they regarded them as cowardly weapons; the Ottomans did not share this attitude, and consequently adapted their warfare to the new technology.) Most of the outstanding Turkoman *kizilbash* leaders and many high Iranian officials were killed. The Ottomans temporarily occupied the Safavid capital of Tabriz, but the long lines of transportation back to Anatolia, the opposition of the soldiers to such a distant campaign, and the bitter cold of some parts of the area induced Selim to retreat. The Ottomans did, however, gain and keep Diyarbakir.

Ismail's spirit was crushed; it is said that he never smiled again. And he began to drink excessively. Henceforth the Turkoman leaders no longer accepted Ismail's claim of supernatural powers. But with Selim seizing Kurdistan, Diyarbakir, and Marash, and wiping out *kizilbash* rebellion in Anatolia, Turkoman ties with those regions were severed; they had no choice but to remain and give lip service to Ismail. Ismail never again led troops into battle and he virtually withdrew from conduct of state affairs. He tried to put civilians into positions of trust and power in order to break the might of the *kizilbash* leaders but he could not control all the provinces, especially Khurasan. Only after his death in 1524 at the age of thirty-six did the full extent of the decline of the ruling institution become apparent.

Because Ismail's son, Tahmasp, was a boy of only ten years, Turkoman leaders were able to regain their power. But after a decade Tahmasp established his personal authority, civilian rule as set by Ismail became dominant, and the Safavid state survived. Though it appeared to be a theocracy, the Sufi organization was unsuccessful in penetrating or subverting the administrative system of the Safavid government. During this period in Iran the main lines of monarchy were worked out, the capital was fixed in the north and west of the state, and Shiism became the established official religion. In a sense, the Safavid state was almost an adequate heir to the Sasanid Empire in its absolutist administrative and cultural ideals.

THE CONQUEST OF EGYPT

With Shah Ismail's defeat, Selim began to use the title shah and sometimes *shahinshah* ("king of kings"), or *padishah* ("father of kings"). More important, the balance of power among the three eastern Muslim states—Iran, Egypt, and the Ottomans—was fully upset in favor of the last. Ismail wrote to the Mamluk sultan for aid against Selim. In 1516 the Mamluks, feigning peace, marched into Syria in full force. Having been kept well informed by Ottoman agents, Selim as usual took the offensive, crushing the Mamluk army at Marj Dabiq, north of Aleppo. Again it was a victory of artillery, and muskets, in the hands of a well-disciplined, well-paid, and well-supplied army over an undisciplined, unpaid, and disloyal motley force. Aleppo, Damascus, Beirut, and other cities opened their gates to the Ottomans. Ottoman governors were appointed everywhere, but little else was changed. Taxes continued to be farmed; the amirs of the Lebanon Mountains became only nominal vassals; and Jews and Christians were treated well.

By January 1517, Selim and his army were on the outskirts of Cairo, which they stormed and took after several days of fighting. Selim was now sultan from the Danube to the cataracts of the Nile. Shah Ismail hastened to congratulate him on his new territories, and from every side of the Middle East the Ottoman Empire was recognized as the dominant power.

A quarter of a century earlier, the Mamluk power had defeated the Ottomans in several campaigns over successive years. Now Selim took their measure with little difficulty and captured the Mamluk Empire in one campaign. By extension, he became sovereign of Mecca and Medina, the principal holy cities of Islam. The Mamluk government had become impoverished and could no longer meet its commitments or protect the state. Evidence of this condition began to appear late in the reign of Bayezid II and progressed rapidly in the years before the conquest.

Back in Istanbul, by midsummer 1518 after an absence of two years, Selim faced the question of the meaning of the extensive conquests. At Aleppo the puppet Abbasid caliph al-Mutawakkil, whom the Mamluks brought along on the expedition, fell into Selim's possession. Selim took the caliph to Istanbul, where he was confined to the state prison. Much later, in 1543, he was permitted to return to Cairo where he died. The Ottoman royal family had used the title of "caliph" since Murad I, a title that was now nearly meaningless. With the new dominions, they added to their titles "servant of the two holy sanctuaries" of Mecca and Medina, and saw themselves as protectors of Islam and the pilgrimage to the Hijaz, and as the most powerful of the Muslim rulers, in accordance with the will of God.

In Selim's long absence his only son, Suleiman, wielded power in Edirne; Piri Pasha, the great admiral, managed Istanbul; and Bursa was governed by Hersekoglu Ahmed Pasha, several times grand vizir and cavalry officer under Mehmed II and Bayezid II. Even under such able guidance the affairs of state suffered and the treasury was depleted. Selim remained in Edirne and Istanbul, straightening out accounts, collecting back taxes, and preparing a navy adequate for an attack upon Rhodes. However, cancer struck him in the spring of 1520 and he died that autumn.

SELIM I

Selim Yavuz was a controversial figure. *Yavuz* means "good," "just," "stern," "inflexible," "ferocious"; and he was all of those. He massacred 40,000 *kizilbash* in his land. Vizirs and generals lost their heads at seemingly the slightest failure. A standard curse came to be, "May you become Selim's vizir!" He was an excellent general, a brilliant poet, and a skillful administrator. His court supported philosophers, historians, theologians, and literary figures of many kinds. His tastes were simple; he read widely, slept little, and was uninterested in his harem. Some attributed his moods to an addiction to opium, but there is no evidence that he used the drug before cancer troubled him.

In Selim's brief reign of eight years Ottoman territory increased greatly—almost exclusively in Asia at the expense of other Muslim states. Dominating the Middle East, the Ottoman Empire became the outstanding Muslim Empire of the area, heir of the medieval Umayyad and Abbasid empires and ruler of the Muslim holy lands. These acquisitions were a determining factor in the process of orientalizing the Ottoman Empire. Selim's sole male heir, Suleiman, reigned over the Ottomans for forty-six years. Longer than any among his forefathers, Suleiman's rule brought the Ottoman Empire and the life of its people to the pinnacle of power and luster. The fabric of society and the sources of power and wealth, however, were well fixed by the time of Selim's death. The eminence of Suleiman's period rested on the firm building of his ancestors.

REFERENCES

Works mentioned at the end of Chapters 10, 12, 13, and 14 relate to this chapter.

Arjomand, Said Amir. *The Shadow of God and the Hidden Imam: Religion, Political Order, and Societal Change in Shi'ite Iran from the Beginning to 1890.* Chicago:

University of Chicago Press, 1984. A review of religion and politics from a social scientist's viewpoint.

Aslanapa, Oktay. *Turkish Art and Architecture*. New York: Praeger, 1971. Full of fine illustrations and a complete bibliography, including many articles. This is a first-rate book in every detail.

Bryer, Anthony, and Heath Lowry, eds. *Continuity and Change in Late Byzantine and Early Ottoman Society*. Birmingham, Eng., and Washington, D.C.: University of Birmingham Centre for Byzantine Studies/Dumbarton Oaks Research Library and Collection, 1986. Twelve chapters by eight authors on local changes in various regions from late Byzantine to early Ottoman times. Highly detailed and very valuable.

Davis, Fanny. *The Palace of Topkapi in Istanbul*. New York: Scribners, 1970. A detailed study which shows all the latest materials on the palace and is well-illustrated. Scholarly and popular.

Fisher, Sydney Nettleton. *The Foreign Relations of Turkey, 1481–1512*. Urbana: University of Illinois Press, 1948. Deals with the period of the reign of Bayezid II.

Goodwin, Godfrey. *A History of Ottoman Architecture, with 4 Colour Plates and 521 Illustrations, Including 81 Plans*. Baltimore, Md.: Johns Hopkins Press, 1971. One of the outstanding works of its kind, covering Bursa, Edirne, Istanbul including Sinan's works, baroque, and with an excellent chapter on the Ottoman house.

Hess, A. C. "The Ottoman Conquest of Egypt (1517) and the Beginning of the Sixteenth-Century World War." *International Journal of Middle East Studies* 4 (1973): 55–76. A valuable sketch of the interrelationships of Europe, the Ottomans, Mamluks, and Safavids.

Hodgson, Marshall G. S. *The Venture of Islam: Conscience and History in a World Civilization*. Vol. 3. *The Gunpowder Empires and Modern Times*. Chicago: University of Chicago Press, 1974. This volume emphasizes the period from about 1500 to the time of Napoleon.

Lewis, Bernard. *Istanbul and the Civilization of the Ottoman Empire*. Norman: University of Oklahoma Press, 1963. A brilliant survey of the city at its heyday.

Mihailović, Konstantin. *Memoirs of a Janissary*. Translated by Benjamin Stolz, with historical commentary and notes by Svat Soucek. Ann Arbor: University of Michigan Press, 1975. This volume contains the Czech original along with the translation. Very interesting and illuminating.

Miller, Barnette. *Beyond the Sublime Porte: The Grand Seraglio of Stambul*. New Haven, Conn.: Yale University Press, 1931. An authoritative account of this great, historic monument.

———. *The Palace School of Muhammed the Conqueror*. Cambridge, Mass.: Harvard University Press, 1941. A thorough and well-written exposition of this important institution of the Ottomans.

Runciman, Steven. *The Great Church in Captivity: A Study of the Patriarchate of Constantinople from the Eve of the Turkish Conquest to the Greek War of Independence*. Cambridge: Cambridge University Press, 1968. The author contends that under the sultans the patriarch became a lay ruler of a state within a state and that the church endured as a great spiritual force.

Savory, Roger. *Iran Under the Safavids.* Cambridge: Cambridge University Press, 1980. In addition to political events, there is full discussion of foreign policy, the arts, the city of Isfahan, social and economic history, and intellectual life. A brilliant and impressive work, crucial for the era.

16

Institutions of the Ottoman Empire

THE SULTAN

At the head of the Ottoman Empire and at the pinnacle of the various social strata stood the sultan. In the West his government was called the Sublime Porte, presumably because edicts and decisions emanated from the principal gate of the palace, called the Gate of Felicity. The sultan's authority was derived from the military power that he controlled, from the allegiance and obedience that his subjects gave him, and from his religious legitimacy for Sunnite Muslims.

All military power was under his command. Whether slaves, feudal cavalry, irregular infantry, vassals, or sailors of the fleet, all were supposed to obey his orders. Not that they always did, of course. Feudal cavalry groups frequently went on unauthorized raids into Christian lands, often to the embarrassment of the sultan. On numerous occasions the army insisted on abandoning long and arduous campaigns which took them from the pleasures of Edirne and Istanbul during winter months or from their homes in the provinces. And the janissaries came to demand bonuses and concessions from the sultan upon his accession to the throne.

Nevertheless, the armed services were generally loyal, and certainly they were more obedient than similar forces in western Europe were to their kings and emperors. Upholding the sultan was the long ghazi tradition of his leadership; no other family possessed the prestige of the Ottoman dynasty. Moreover, the slave status of most of the commanding officers and the nature of their rearing gave the sultan such a hold over their lives that deviation from his wishes was risky.

The sultan was head of the Islamic state, defender of the faith, protector of the pilgrimage, and executor of sacred law. Sunnite Muslims rendered obedience to him. Indirectly, Christians and Jews did likewise, since the sultan appointed some of the leaders of their faiths and ordered officials and laymen to consult them.

In general, Ottomans followed the law and jurisprudence of Sunnite Islam as developed formerly by earlier Muslims. Four distinct bodies or sources of law existed. Foremost and supreme over the other three stood sacred law (*shariah*). (The Ottoman interpretation of sacred law followed that of the Hanafite school.) Sultan and judges were bound by sacred law, and to ignore it invited disaster. Sec-

ond stood *kanuns,* or published decrees of sultans, which either were administrative in character or were said to be supplementary to sacred law. Kanuns, for
example, dealt with intricate ceremonial law of the Ottoman government and with
feudal, military, financial, criminal, and police law. Last in the strata of law were
adet and *urf.* Adet was customary law as observed by Turks from time immemorial, by Ottomans, and by peoples conquered by them. Thus, adet in Bosnia might
be different from adet in the Morea, and both might be different from adet in
Ankara. Urf was the sovereignty or will of the ruling sultan and might contravene
adet. Kanuns could change adet and urf and could annul or amend other kanuns.
Shariah, or sacred law, was thought of as inviolable.

The great institutions of the state, established either by sacred law or kanuns,
were accepted as emanating from God or from the sultan's supreme will; in no
sense were they considered to flow from the desires of the people. In examining
governmental institutions of the Ottoman Empire it becomes apparent that over
the 600 years of the empire's existence the structure and procedures of government were not necessarily identical from one century to the next. Ceremonial
forms may have often remained the same, but the power, realities, relationships,
and even the character of the personnel varied from period to period. All the personnel and their families can be said to have belonged to the "ruling class."

At the time of the accession of Suleiman in 1520 there were four principal
divisions of government: the palace services; the military-governing administration; the scribal-financial bureaucracy; and the religious-judicial establishment. In
theory and in practice the sultan supervised all of these and the officials in each
were directly or indirectly answerable to him. In common parlance the officials
belonged to the military (*askeri*) class, and many went on campaigns with the sultan, even if they were not trained to fight. This terminology was used to differentiate them from the *rayah* (*reaya*) class—those Turks, Muslims, and non-Muslims
who did not belong to the Ottoman service and system. The leaders and upper
echelons in these four branches of government were, certainly, the elite of state
and society. Furthermore, most members of these branches, except those of the
religious establishment, were slaves of the sultan, though many were not.

THE PALACE SERVICES

Since the sultan was the supreme head of the government with absolute power,
the center of the government was wherever he happened to be. Thus his household, the palace, gained a special significance and power through the influence
that could be exercised upon him. Technically, individuals of the "ruling class"
with the exception of the feudatory enjoyed membership in the sultan's court and
were expected to be a part of his retinue on ceremonial occasions and sometimes
in camp. More specifically, the court consisted of the harem, the Inside Service,
and the Outside Service.

Until about 1540 there were relatively few in the harem, which was quartered
in the Old Palace in Istanbul or in the palaces in Edirne and Demotika. It formed
a palace within a palace and included consorts of the sultan, female servants of the

court, and girls in training, who upon reaching the age of twenty-five were married to court officers unless they had moved up the well-defined hierarchy in the harem. The greatest lady of the harem was the sultan's mother (*valide sultan*); after her came the mother of the sultan's first-born son, and then mothers of other sons. Numbering about 200 and guarded by 40 black eunuchs, the harem was transferred to the Great Palace in 1540; the Old Palace still housed elderly and retired women of the harem.

Functionaries who took care of the sultan's personal affairs comprised the Inside Service. Chief of the entire Inside Service was the general of the gate, a white eunuch. He was invariably a high state dignitary, who served also as grand master of ceremonies for the palace, director in chief of the Palace School, and confidential agent of the sultan.

Aside from the white eunuchs, members of the halls were called pages and were young men usually chosen from the elite of the captives and tribute children. Those who did not obtain advancements joined the sultan's cavalry at various levels or received other suitable appointments. The pages remained as officials in the Inside Service or were appointed as provincial governors, high officers in the janissary corps or cavalry, or as officials in the Outside Service or another principal branch of government.

Whereas the Inside Service controlled the relations of the sultan's life within the palace, the Outside Service coordinated his relations with life in the world outside. In the Outside Service the most important official for the military-governing administration was the grand vizir; others were the remaining vizirs; commanders of the janissaries and the sultan's cavalry divisions; generals of the armies when not on campaigns; officers responsible for the palace security, discipline, and protocol; the kitchen service; gardeners; tent-pitchers; masters of the hunt; equerries; officers of supply; the treasurer; record keepers; the personal bodyguard; learned associates of the sultan; and all other top officials who made the government function. The learned associates of the sultan were members of the religious-judicial establishment, constituted by the sultan's religious teacher and adviser, preachers, muezzins, chanters, readers, astrologers, physicians, and surgeons. The bodyguard was drawn from sons of high officials, choice graduates from the Inside Service, and veteran janissaries—in all about 400 men. Many palace guards were responsible officials, and to that group belonged ambassadors and executioners. The treasurer and record keepers were members of the scribal-financial bureaucracy, which was just beginning to form at this time. Others tended the palace gardens or rowed the sultan's caïques on Bosphorus excursions.

At the time of Suleiman I the sultan's court with its three services numbered in the neighborhood of 10,000 persons. Earlier Ottoman sultans lived more simply; several accounts of public ceremonies in mosques and other places report that it was difficult to distinguish the sultan from his attendants. Probably in the court of Murad II and certainly in that of Mehmed II, magnificence in ceremony appeared. After the conquest of Constantinople, Mehmed II introduced into his bodyguard a company of 100 halberdiers, copied in arms, costumes, and manners from the Byzantine emperor's bodyguard. By the middle of the sixteenth century, rituals and functions of each section of the services became so elaborate and rigid

that a law of ceremonies was drawn, and observance of details involving procedure equaled in importance the fulfilling of duties.

Until the reign of Suleiman I the court and its personnel seldom trespassed
upon the direct field of government and administration. The court served the personal needs of sultan and palace. Insofar as court officers and chamberlains had
direct access to the sultan, they could be influential persons whose favor was eagerly sought. To have a friend highly placed at court was a precious asset.

THE MILITARY-GOVERNING ADMINISTRATION

The administrators in the sixteenth century who ran the government and the army
were usually products of the Inside Service of the palace. From the end of
Mehmed II's reign through most of the following century, the great majority were
chiefly recruited, though not entirely so, from the tribute and captive children. At
the top was the vizir, or chief minister; later, when four ministers had the title of
vizir, one was designated first vizir, or under Suleiman I, grand vizir. The sultan
delegated his political and executive authority only to his vizirs. When they were in
the provinces or on campaign they could even impose the death penalty. The
grand vizir by the law of Mehmed II had power greater than all other men and was
in all matters the sultan's absolute deputy. In ceremonies and meetings he took his
place before all others. He was also entrusted with the sultan's personal seal (the
taking away of which signaled dismissal from office). Murad I had appointed the
first such vizir from one of the prominent Ottoman families. Murad II chose vizirs
from the religious-judicial establishment and from the army. Mehmed II picked
them from the graduates of the Palace School and from Ottoman families of
Anatolia, but from the accession of Bayezid II until late in the sixteenth century all
were from some part of the palace service.

The vizirs, under the chairmanship of the grand vizir, made up a council, or
divan, with whom the sultan conferred on matters of state. Other members of the
divan, also often called vizirs, were the head of the janissaries; two chief judges—
one for Anatolia and one for Rumeli; two *defterdars,* or treasurers, again one each
for Anatolia and Rumeli; the chief secretary of state; and the chief admiral of the
navy. (Since judges were members of the religious-judicial establishment, their responsibilities will be described later.)

The divan met with the sultan for several hours every Saturday, Sunday,
Monday, and Tuesday to decide all matters of government. Analogous to a modern
cabinet meeting but also bearing some resemblance to a supreme court, the divan
meeting served as a kind of union and capstone to the several branches of the
Ottoman government. However, by the time of Mehmed II the sultan, rather than
attending divan meetings himself, would after each session receive the divan members in the room behind the Sublime Porte to listen to and consider their decisions.

It was a rule that no one, not even the other vizirs, could be privy to the grand
vizir's dealings with the sultan and to their secret decisions. Yet there were many
checks on the authority of the grand vizir, for he was obliged before making any

important decision to consult with the other members of the divan. Failure to abide by this procedure was an important factor in the dismissal and execution of the grand vizir Ibrahim in 1536. In addition, the heads of the janissaries, the treasury, and the judiciary also dealt directly with the sultan. (As stated by Mehmed II, not a single penny would enter or leave the treasury unless the head of the treasury ordered it.) One other item of note was the custom, even the compulsion, of vizirs and other officials to maintain a household similar to that of the sultan, with the number of slaves, pages, and aides usually dictated by the position. Rustem Pasha, one of Suleiman's grand vizirs, had 1,700 slaves at the time of his death.

By the middle of the sixteenth century the core of the Ottoman army was the janissary corps, numbering over 10,000. They were commanded by an *aga* (general) who was directly responsible to the sultan. Usually this aga was an officer trained in the palace, although sometimes he rose from the ranks like other janissary officers. In addition to the ordinary janissaries there were a number of specialized units.

The regular cavalry, generally called *sipahi* of the Porte to distinguish it from the feudal cavalry, or *sipahi,* was drawn principally from the ordinary janissaries and the pages of the palace. A few of the feudal cavalry, however, were rewarded with admission to the regular cavalry. One special battalion was a kind of Foreign Legion, consisting of non-Ottoman Turks, Kurds, Arabs, Christian renegades, and horsemen from sources outside the sultan's court.

The Ottomans gave special attention to the technical services; and all European observers at that time marveled at the equipment, food, transport, and roads provided for Ottoman armies. Most important were the artillery corps and ordnance services which cast cannon and manufactured gunpowder. These branches more than any other brought victory after victory to Ottoman armies.

Beginning with Murad II, the navy became an effective division of the armed services. Development of sea power advanced reign by reign until under Selim I and Suleiman I the navy applied its force everywhere in the Mediterranean. Ships were built at many different ports from the Black Sea to the Adriatic. Venetian master shipbuilders along with Greek and Turkish builders, frequently working by flares at night, kept the navy in fighting trim. Commanded by the Kapudan Pasha, who ranked with the vizirs, the navy was manned by experienced seafaring men from North African coasts and the eastern Mediterranean area.

Fleets of 300 to 400 ships, as large and as well armed as those of Spain, France, or Venice, were maintained at all times. In peaceful years Ottoman sea captains, many of them Greek or Italian renegades, sailed on their own responsibility and often turned to piracy against Christian Europe in much the same fashion as ghazis on land raided Carinthia and Styria.

One of the superior segments of the Ottoman army came from the provinces and from fiefholders. Whenever a campaign was announced, the governor of each province assembled the feudal cavalry, which until the end of the sixteenth century matched any cavalry of western Europe. Each soldier came with a predetermined number of warriors in his entourage. They elected their own immediate leaders, although their provincial commander (*sanjakbey*) was an appointee of the sultan (after the time of Murad II, frequently a graduate of the Palace School). Prior to the period of Suleiman I supreme command of the feudal cavalry rested on the shoulders of two generals—the beylerbey of Anatolia and the beylerbey of Rumeli. (At a later time additional beylerbeys were designated for areas such as Syria, Hungary, and Baghdad.) These two generals acted as viziers, attended meetings of the divan when convenient, and commanded the wings of the army in battle. They rewarded the brave directly with fiefs and meted out punishment to laggards.

Other branches of the armed forces were the *akinjis* and the *azabs*. The former were irregular, unpaid, volunteer cavalrymen who answered the call to arms in hopes of booty or the gift of a fief for valor. *Azabs* were similar to *akinjis* except that they were foot soldiers. Usually in any battle *akinjis* and *azabs* were used as front-line troops to absorb the first shocks of contact with the enemy.

THE SCRIBAL-FINANCIAL BUREAUCRACY

Every official of the government had his private secretary, a corps of scribes, and personal bureaucrats commensurate with the tasks involved. Most of the private secretaries became indispensable and influential with their superiors, drafting laws, and advising on matters of state. On a broader base, however, three main branches of the bureaucracy evolved into the executive office of the divan, the chancery, and the treasury. In the early days, individuals manning these offices had usually come from the palace, but by the middle of the sixteenth century most were recruited from the families of Ottoman officials and their clients and from sons and relatives of members of the bureaucracy. Clerks entered the bureaus as apprentices and learned on the job, often simultaneously taking courses to enhance their knowledge of law and religious sciences. Promotions in the bureaus came at regular intervals, and diligent and intelligent clerks could work their way to the top. Changing from one bureau to another was possible but unlikely except when one had reached a fairly high position.

The divan had a secretarial staff, and as time passed, a regular bureau under a bureau head was formalized to draw up and execute the approved orders to governors and officials of the state. The head of this bureau, in turn, became the first secretary of the grand vizier, and in later centuries became a minister of state and foreign minister. The chancellor, who was a member of the divan, checked on all appointments to office (including the assignment of benefices in land), had responsibility for the land surveys, kept records of salaries, and recorded all ordinances and commands of the sultan, the divan, the viziers, and other officials, affixing the seal of authority and the sultan's signature to official documents. The chancellor had personal access to the sultan, was responsible only to him, and in his public capacity could be judged only by him. The treasurer (*defterdar*) collected state income, ascertained its sources, and was charged with accounting for all receipts and expenditures of the central government. Until the time of Mehmed II, collection of taxes was generally administered directly by the treasury, chiefly through the fiefholders; but difficulties and leakages in collections later led to a system of tax farming. The Ottoman Empire was greatly decentralized financially; provincial governments collected and spent their own funds; and the religious establishment was supported by revenues from properties granted as endowments and not always funneled through the treasury. Total revenue for the central government in the 1520s has been estimated at from 6 to 8 million ducats, a sum that compared quite favorably with incomes of contemporary governments of western Europe. The treasurer, like the chancellor, was a member of the divan and responsible only to the sultan.

In addition to these main departments of government, there were a number of others, including the mint, the customs bureaus, commissionerships, governors in the provinces, courts, and endowments that developed bureaucracies of their own. Consequently, there were thousands of secretaries and scribes in the Ottoman Empire in the sixteenth century—as evidenced by the tons of records in the archives in Istanbul and elsewhere.

THE RELIGIOUS-JUDICIAL ESTABLISHMENT

Parallel with the three main branches of government already described stood the purely Muslim branch. In many ways it was quite separate from the others but never fully independent of them. Since Islam was the religion of the government (with the sultan responsible for the enforcement of Islamic law) and all officials by this time were Muslims, every aspect of government was touched by the religious-judicial establishment. Government personnel at the top levels often moved to other branches of government, particularly from the religious-judicial group into the others. Functionally, this establishment had three main divisions: religion, education, and law.

Since Islam has no priesthood, no clergy, and no monks, it has always been difficult to describe Muslim religious personnel in Western terms. Teachers in all schools and others who had passed through schools beyond the primary grades were classified as the learned (*ulema*). Other purely religious members of the Muslim group were preachers, mosque caretakers, muezzins, professional leaders of prayers in mosques, Sufi dervishes, and sharifs and sayyids. Mosque endowments provided for regular attendants and leaders in mosque activities on a full-time basis. Dervishes were for Islam what monks, hermits, and begging friars were for Christianity; they preached holy wars, spread the faith, and inspired emotional public demonstrations. Sharifs and sayyids traced their descent from Hasan and Husayn, grandsons of the Prophet, wore green turbans, and had numerous personal prerogatives. One was always the sultan's standard-bearer and ranked above all officers of the army.

Every mosque, large and small, had a primary, or reading, school, where pupils studied reading, writing, Arabic, and the Koran. Schools of higher learning called *madrasahs* (*medreses* in Turkish) taught grammar, logic, metaphysics, geometry; and advanced madrasahs gave courses in law and theology. Students were partially supported by religious endowments; those in law were completely subsidized. Madrasahs were numerous throughout the empire, and in Istanbul every sizable mosque had one or more attached to it. Fatih's mosque had eight, Suleiman's five, the former being the most prestigious in the empire until

Suleiman's more advanced madrasahs were founded. Each stage of education was rigidly graded; those who completed the courses belonged to the learned class. A graduate received a degree and became qualified to teach in a primary school. Further study raised the holder to higher ratings which permitted him to be a professor, jurist, or judge.

The learned who completed law courses, especially those given in Istanbul, usually received appointments as teachers, then as a judge (*qadi* in Arabic, *kadi* in Turkish) or as a legal counselor (*mufti*), or as an assistant in the office of one of these. In every city and large town the sultan appointed a judge who exercised juridical control over the surrounding territory. Slaves of the sultan, sharifs, and sayyids had their own judges and courts. Except in cases that involved Muslims, foreigners and non-Muslims were subject to their own laws. Sanjakbeys, beylerbeys, and vizirs also administered justice in their courts except in cases involving sacred law. The hierarchy of judges was based on carefully classified grades, and advancement usually proceeded from one grade to another.

At the top of the system of judges were two judges—one for Europe and one for Asia—who nominated all the other judges of the empire. Appeals progressed from court to court, and sentences were executed by the civil authorities.

Associated with the judge of many cities was a mufti who was assigned to interpret sacred law for the judge and government officials. Appointed for life, the muftis remained private citizens; in legal matters they had no initiative of action. When a judge, or even a private citizen, was faced with a legal problem, he submitted the question in point to the mufti for legal opinion. The mufti examined the law and gave his answer. In Istanbul the mufti, who was usually selected from the ranks of the judges and teachers rather than other muftis, ranked above the judge; and since the sultan and vizirs might pose important questions vital to the life of the whole empire, he became a significant official. Mehmed II added to the mufti's dignity by conferring upon him the title *shaykh al-Islam* (*Şeyhülislam* in Turkish), "Leader of Islam," and in ceremonies he took precedence over the grand vizir.

The Muslim establishment within the Ottoman Empire, from the Shaykh al-Islam to the lowliest teacher in a mosque primary school, welded the empire together under one type of education and one body of law. Any male Muslim child, if he studied hard and passed the various examinations, might rise in the ranks, just as fighting men and the sultan's slaves advanced on merit in their branches of government.

Poverty was no barrier to advancement, but important friends or relatives did help. Perhaps one-third of the land of the empire was set aside as endowment for various religious activities. In Anatolia and Europe cash endowments were also established, despite the opposition of some men of religion. The money that constituted the basis of the foundation was lent to peasants and townspeople, leading to their increasing indebtedness. Both sorts of endowments, in land and in cash, could be given by sultans and private individuals, and were, at least theoretically, intended for the support of some specific mosque, library, school, almshouse, hospital, bridge, inn, or fountain. The imperial treasury actually handled the funds established by the sultan, and an official was designated as trustee. Private donors often stipulated in the deed of transfer that their own descendants should be administrators of the endowment, and thus, much of the revenue from the endowment could be diverted for private and personal gain. Slaves of the sultan found this method a convenience in providing perpetual and inalienable income for their descendants. However, in many cases the property and wealth of men of the state were confiscated by the sultan upon their deaths.

NON-MUSLIM SUBJECTS

Following the arrival of Muslim ulema in the Ottoman state at the time of Sultan Orhan, Ottomans grew tolerant of non-Muslims in the fashion of the older Muslim world. Christian and Jewish groups were given their religious and cultural freedom; many Balkan communities preferred such autonomy under the Ottomans to the religious and cultural restrictions and persecutions suffered under Hungarian and Hapsburg rule. In the first centuries of the empire's existence, some non-Muslims served as fiefholders and warriors; by the late sixteenth century this practice seems to have stopped.

When the settlement of Istanbul was made in 1453, Mehmed II, in recognizing the election of Gennadius as patriarch of the Orthodox Church, pursued the custom of Byzantine emperors in confirming the election of patriarchs. (The patriarchs were obliged to pay an annual tax to the sultan, and their terms of office were precarious.) The sultan also acknowledged the practice, already well established in the Ottoman state, of permitting Christians to retain the independence of their religious community. Likewise, Mehmed II recognized Jewish and Armenian Gregorian communities, although separate organizations in the provinces were maintained for these faiths.

The various religious groups were termed communities (and, much later, *millets*), which meant a group of people with a particular religion within the Ottoman Empire. Each millet had the legal right to use its own language, develop its own institutions, collect taxes and render them to the imperial treasury, and maintain courts for trying members in all cases except those involving public security and crime. Each millet had a leader or leaders who were responsible to the sultan for the payments of taxes and for the good behavior and loyalty of members of the community. Resident non-Ottoman Muslims and non-Muslims who were subjects of other Muslim states were both taxed and treated in the same way as Ottoman Muslims. However, Iranians began to be treated as a somewhat separate category in at least some of the Ottoman provinces in a later time.

FOREIGNERS

Further paralleling these millets as part of the empire were groups of foreigners, chiefly merchants residing in Istanbul, such as the Genoese residents in Galata across the Golden Horn. Each group lived under provisions of a formal treaty drawn up between the sultan and the foreign authority; the agreements were periodically renewed.

The general tenor of these treaties was exemplified in the Treaty of 1503 between Bayezid II and Venice. Among other things, the sultan agreed that a Venetian consul might come to Istanbul with his family and reside there for three years. Although Venetians could live in certain designated cities of the empire for one year and although the sultan agreed to be reasonable in extending their residence, they could travel about only with the consul's permission. The consul should settle all cases and disputes among Venetians; and Venetian testimony was recognized as valid in courts of Christian and Jewish Ottoman subjects. In criminal cases Venetians were guaranteed justice in regular Ottoman courts.

These treaties recognizing certain rights and obligations for European residents in the Ottoman Empire were based on the assumption that since Christians could not avail themselves of Muslim sacred law, they would have to live by their own Christian laws. However, in later years when the balance of power between western Europe and the Ottoman Empire shifted in favor of Europe, such arrangements evolved into the famous capitulatory treaties, which gave nationals of other governments an apparent privileged position in the Ottoman Empire and frequently allowed foreign governments untold influence over vital policies of the Sublime Porte.

REFERENCES

In addition to general studies on Middle Eastern history and Muslim institutions, references in Chapters 12, 13, 14, and 15 are of particular importance.

Birge, John Kingsley. *The Bektashi Order of Dervishes*. Hartford, Conn.: Hartford Seminary Press, 1937. A significant work by a careful scholar on the origin and development of this order and its relationship to the leaders and various strata of Ottoman society.

Braude, Benjamin, and Bernard Lewis, eds. *Christians and Jews in the Ottoman Empire: The Functioning of a Plural Society.* 2 vols. New York: Holmes and Meier, 1982. This excellent collection of twenty-nine articles features an emphasis on the late Ottoman period, and deals extensively with the Arab lands as well as the central government.

De Busbecq, Ogier G. *Turkish Letters*. Translated by Edward S. Forster. Oxford: Clarendon Press, 1927. De Busbecq was imperial ambassador to the Porte for many years; his observations were singularly objective and discerning.

Gibb, H. A. R., and Harold Bowen. *Islamic Society and the West: A Study of the Impact of Western Civilization on Moslem Culture in the Near East*. Vol. 1 (in two parts). *Islamic Society in the Eighteenth Century*. London: Oxford University Press, 1950 and 1957. A detailed and penetrating study of Ottoman institutions as they existed in the eighteenth century and as they had evolved from earlier forms since the fourteenth century.

Itzkowitz, Norman. "Eighteenth Century Ottoman Realities." *Studia Islamica* 41 (1962): 73–94. A very important article examining the structure and institutions of the government of the Ottoman Empire from the sixteenth to the nineteenth century, opening new ideas.

Knolles, Richard. *The Generall Historie of the Turkes, from the First Beginning of That Nation to the Rising of the Othoman Familie: With all the Notable Expeditions of the Christian Princes Against Them. Together with the Lives and Conquests of the Othoman Kings and Emperours*...London, 1603. This is still the most extensive and longest Ottoman history in the English language, written by an Englishman, long a resident in Turkey. There are many later editions.

Lewis, Bernard. *The Jews of Islam.* Princeton, N.J.: Princeton University Press, 1984. A thorough and well-written treatment of the subject.

Mandaville, Jon E. "Usurious Piety: The Cash Waqf Controversy in the Ottoman Empire." *International Journal of Middle East Studies* 10 (1979): 289–308. An interesting examination of the flexibility of Ottoman legal thinking.

Masters, Bruce. "Trading Diasporas and 'Nations': The Genesis of National Identities in Ottoman Aleppo." *The International History Review* 9 (1987): 345–367.

Mitler, Louis. "The Genoese in Galata: 1453–1682." *International Journal of Middle East Studies* 10 (1979): 71–91.

Pixley, Michael M. "The Development and Role of the Şeyhülislam in Early Ottoman History." *Journal of the American Oriental Society* 96 (1976): 89–96. The author concludes that this office was not of much significance until the middle of the sixteenth century.

Repp, Richard C. *The Müfti of Istanbul: A Study in the Development of the Ottoman Learned Hierarchy.* London: Ithaca Press, 1986. Traces in an extremely careful and detailed way career patterns and lives of individuals who held the post.

Simsar, Muhammed Ahmed. *The Waqfiyah of Ahmed Paša.* Philadelphia: University of Pennsylvania Press, 1940. A fine translation with notes on a perpetual trust established in 1511 by Ahmed Hersekoglu Pasha, who was the son of the last duke of Herzegovina and who became an Ottoman vizir.

17

The Ottoman Empire as a World Power

SULEIMAN I

The government of the Ottoman Empire was so well organized, regulated, and staffed under Mehmed II, Bayezid II, and Selim I and the number of intelligent, trained, and disciplined officers, pages, and students in the palace was so great that the government could function well without much direction from the sultan. And since Selim I left only one son, the transfer of authority in 1520 generated no stress and no factious activities at the Porte. His son, Suleiman, moreover, was born in the year A.H. 900, the opening year of the tenth century of Islam, and was the tenth of his dynasty. Because of these portentous beginnings his subjects believed that he was destined to rule over a great part of the world.

In this favorable setting the youthful Suleiman appeared as a magnificent sovereign, certainly the match of his equally youthful contemporaries Charles V of the Holy Roman Empire, Francis I of France, and Henry VIII of England. Suleiman reigned for forty-six years. During those years the Ottoman Empire, built on solid foundations by his predecessors, reached its height in power, wealth, and brilliance. Accordingly, Suleiman, called "The Magnificent" by Europeans and "Kanuni" ("The Lawgiver") by his own people, has been regarded as a majestic figure among the galaxy of distinguished rulers of all ages.

During the latter years of Bayezid II's reign Suleiman, then a lad of fifteen or so, was assigned as governor of Bolu. But after strong protests by his uncle Ahmed, he was transferred to Kaffa in the Crimea, where his mother, daughter of a Tartar khan, had been reared. After his father seized the throne, Suleiman was called to govern Istanbul, while Selim fought against brothers and nephews in Asia Minor. Suleiman governed Edirne again during his father's long wars in Iran and Egypt. Only upon Selim's return to Istanbul in 1517 was Suleiman sent to rule the province around Manisa in western Anatolia. Thus Suleiman attended the pages' school in Istanbul and resided for more than five years at the palaces of Istanbul and Edirne. In addition, he had nearly six years of experience as provincial governor, surrounded by teachers, advisers, and graduates of the famous Palace School. No prince of his time had better training or more practical preparation for the responsibility of ruling a great empire.

BELGRAD AND RHODES

Suleiman passed the first winter of his reign becoming acquainted with his elevated position. When spring came, Suleiman met the demand for action by choosing Belgrad for the campaign of 1521. At Sofia, he gathered his army and supplies, including 3,000 camels carrying ammunition and 30,000 laden with grain. At least 10,000 wagonloads of grain were requisitioned locally, and 300 cannon were brought up the Danube from Istanbul.

As expected, there was little opposition from Europe. Charles V was busily engaged preparing for war against Francis I and also deeply involved with Luther and imperial problems. Belgrad held out for three weeks, as Ottoman cannon, implanted on an island in the Danube, demolished a part of the inner fortress and ended all resistance. Many Serbs were transplanted to the outskirts of Istanbul, where the Belgrad Forest still remains as testimony to this important victory which opened the Hungarian plains and the upper Danube basin to the Ottomans.

The following year, Suleiman assembled his forces in Asia for the heralded attack on the island of Rhodes. Rhodes lay six miles off the coast of Asia Minor astride the sea route from Istanbul to Alexandria, and since the conquest of Egypt the Knights of St. John had continually harassed Ottoman trade. Frequently, Ottoman prisoners were slaughtered, contrary to the provisions of the treaty concluded with Bayezid II, who regarded the knights as professional pirates and cutthroats.

Rhodes was a highly fortified port, and large contingents of knights from many European commanderies of the order arrived to defend the citadel. Venice sent her fleet, but to protect Cyprus! Massing 300 ships and 100,000 men, Suleiman led the attack. It lasted from July until December. Thousands of stone cannon balls of prodigious size bombarded the walls, and a few rudimentary explosive shells were hurled into the town. Effective attacks were launched in conjunction with sapping and mining operations against the walls, but the cost in men on each side was beyond reason. The knights surrendered on Christmas Day 1522. They were allowed to depart with all mercenary soldiers and townsmen who desired to leave. Those who remained were unmolested and freed from taxation for five years.

SULEIMAN'S COURT

For the following three summers Suleiman remained in Edirne, Istanbul, or their environs enjoying peace. He loved the gardens of the palace, and one of his greatest pleasures was boating on the Bosphorus and the Sea of Marmara. Frequently he would be rowed across to the Asian shore to walk in his gardens there.

It was also during these years that a Russian slave girl named Khurrem caught his fancy. Known generally to posterity as Roxelana, meaning "the Russian," she soon captivated Suleiman completely, became his legal wife, and dominated him until her death in 1558. Suleiman's mother ruled his harem until her death in 1533; after that date Roxelana forced her way into political affairs. Her chief rival, Gulbahar, a Montenegrin slave girl and mother of Suleiman's oldest living son, Mustafa, departed to Manisa in 1534 in the company of her son when he was established there as governor. Roxelana bore Suleiman three children: Selim, Bayezid, and a daughter, Mihrimah. Suleiman had two other sons who grew to manhood: Mehmed, who was older than Selim; and Jihangir, a hunchback. Competition in the harem for Suleiman's affections and intense rivalry among the mothers for the advancement and protection of their sons brought dismay and affliction upon Suleiman and the government in later days.

At this same time the grand vizir retired on a handsome pension, and Suleiman advanced to the grand vizirate his favorite and boon companion, Ibrahim. The son of a Greek sailor, Ibrahim had been captured by pirates and sold to a lady of Manisa, who gave her slave an excellent education. As a prince in Manisa, Suleiman recognized Ibrahim's talents, enjoyed his violin playing, and brought him to Istanbul as chief falconer and head of the pages of the inner chamber (royal bedchamber). Instead of advancing the second vizir, who fully expected the promotion because of his meritorious conduct during the siege of Rhodes, Suleiman appointed the youthful Ibrahim to the post vacated by Piri Pasha, and also to the office of beylerbey of Rumeli. For the following thirteen years Ibrahim governed the empire, year by year relieving Suleiman of more of the tiresome duties of ruling. He even took the title of Seriasker-Sultan ("commander in chief of the armies" with the power of sultan). He dined with Suleiman, was with him at all hours, and even slept in the sultan's apartments. Between 1523 and 1536 no policy of state was reached without Ibrahim's consideration and approval.

Unfortunately, Ibrahim's rapid advancement to chief of the royal bedchamber and then to grand vizir ran counter to the system of promotions based on merit and service. There could be no question that Ibrahim was a brilliant and successful administrator and adviser. Still, others who had proved their abilities through service were passed over by the sultan's personal favorite. Thus, early in Suleiman's reign the personalities of Roxelana and Ibrahim and their roles at the palace sowed the seeds of harem influence and personal favoritism that proved so disastrous in succeeding centuries.

The first demonstration of Ibrahim's genius came in Egypt. The second vizir in 1523 had asked for and received as a consolation the governorship of Egypt. Within months after his arrival in Cairo he was deeply involved in treason and was murdered in his bath by loyal Ottomans. Other revolts by Arab tribes and Mamluks led Suleiman to commission Ibrahim to go to Egypt for six months to inaugurate a more stable regime. Finances, administration, law, and trade procedures were thoroughly overhauled. The Ottoman pasha was also given more responsibility.

THE SIEGE OF VIENNA

But the janissaries and palace troops grew restless under the long inactivity and the paucity of booty that Suleiman's repose enforced upon them. In April 1526,

Suleiman, Ibrahim, and other vizirs set out from Istanbul with 100,000 men and several hundred cannon. Early in August the Ottomans crossed the Drava and moved toward Mohacs, where a crushing victory opened all of Hungary. Early in September, Buda surrendered to Suleiman, and two weeks later Pest on the east bank of the Danube was burned. The following day Suleiman and his army began the long trek homeward, reaching Istanbul in the middle of November.

But the expedition into Hungary, even with its exciting battles, ended only as a magnified raid. Suleiman did not possess adequate manpower to garrison such distant cities as Budapest and Mohacs. No lands were handed out as fiefs to Ottoman officers; and Hungary remained a political vacuum.

Subsequently, John Zapolya, duke of Transylvania, occupied Budapest and was crowned king of Hungary. Then Ferdinand of Hapsburg, archduke of Austria, defeated Zapolya in 1527 and claimed to be Hungarian king. In desperation, Zapolya turned to the Ottomans. Suleiman moved in 1529 to oust the Austrians from Hungary. Not until the middle of May did the army leave Istanbul, and continuous drenching rains impeded its march. The larger cannon had to be abandoned along the way. Mohacs was reached only in mid-August; Budapest, a month later. Soon afterward *akinjis* penetrated into Austria like swarms of locusts, and the attack upon Vienna opened on September 29. Although Ferdinand had all summer to meet the threat, forces to defend Vienna assembled less than a week before the siege began.

Mining operations, assaults, countermining, and sorties raged day after day. On October 12, 1529, mines seriously damaged the walls, and infantry attacks almost succeeded. Both sides grew weary, however, and on the fifteenth the Ottomans retired. To the defenders of Vienna it seemed miraculous, for they were on the point of surrender. In truth, the retreat was forced by the grumbling of the janissaries, indicating that they wished to reach Edirne and Istanbul before winter. Ferdinand recognized Suleiman's hold upon Hungary in a peace treaty in 1533.

Vienna had not been taken by Suleiman because his communications were so extended that his forces could not be effective. Incessant rains in the Balkans and in Austria made the long marches arduous and the hauling of the heavy cannon that took Belgrad almost impossible. The army left Istanbul only after the mud dried late in April and insisted upon returning before the winter rains began in December. Neither the janissaries nor the feudal cavalry would campaign in the winter. Vienna was thus beyond Ottoman reach, although Christendom failed to appreciate the full facts of the sultan's limitations.

NAVAL ACTIVITIES

While Suleiman was engaged in Hungary combating the Hapsburgs, the French looked to him as a useful ally in their struggle against the Holy Roman Emperor, Charles V. Relations with the French and Hapsburgs inevitably led the Ottomans to extend their interests to the entire Mediterranean. Ottoman navies had existed before the fall of Constantinople and had grown in competence. Mehmed II was able in 1480 to support an expedition across the Adriatic to the heel of Italy. Under

Bayezid II, Ottoman sea power came of age, controlled the eastern Mediterranean, and repeatedly plundered the shores of Spain. Under Suleiman the navy occupied and added much of North Africa to the empire.

While Selim I was conquering Egypt, Aruj Barbarossa and his more famous brother Khair al-Din appeared in Tunis to lead the fleets against Christian Europe. Their father was an Ottoman fiefholder from Rumeli who had settled on the island of Mytilene following its conquest by Mehmed II, and they followed the sea-ghazi tradition prevalent along that coast for more than two centuries. After retaking Algiers, Aruj lost his life in an assault upon Tlemcen. Thereupon Khair al-Din, who inherited his brother's sobriquet Barbarossa, sent word that he would consent to Selim's overlordship in exchange for aid and official position. Appointed beylerbey of Algiers and North Africa with absolute authority to rule those provinces and to raise and organize a janissary army, Barbarossa exercised Ottoman power in the Mediterranean until his death in 1546. His ships raked the coasts of Spain and maintained unceasing pressure upon Charles V. Barbarossa's men were of all nationalities, thus truly Ottoman; but his personal bodyguard was composed exclusively of Spanish renegades.

In 1533, Suleiman summoned Khair al-Din to Istanbul, where with much fanfare he was reappointed beylerbey of Algiers and given a fleet of eighty-four ships, many of which were built under his supervision. He regarded himself as a veritable sea ghazi, and on this occasion visited the tomb of Jelal al-Din Rumi in Konya to obtain the blessings of this patron saint of all ghazis. After ravaging the coast of southern Italy in a manner long remembered, Barbarossa descended upon Bizerta and became master of Tunis.

Such a victory could not be left unchallenged. The following year Charles V and Admiral Andrea Doria, employing a large fleet and a powerful army, dislodged the Ottomans from Tunis. But Barbarossa escaped with a score of his ships to Algiers to pillage Minorca and the coast of Valencia. Thence he proceeded with his loot to Istanbul—where Suleiman appointed him Kapudan Pasha and made him responsible for all naval activities.

No important naval conquests graced the remainder of Suleiman's reign. After the treaty with France in 1536, French ships frequently cooperated with Ottoman fleets in the western Mediterranean. In the winter of 1543, the harbor and town of Toulon were given over entirely to Barbarossa, his ships, and men; the inhabitants gladly moved out to avoid unpleasant incidents. After Khair al-Din died in 1546, his role was admirably filled by Turgut (Dragut), Piale Pasha, and Khair al-Din's son Hasan. Tripoli was stormed and became the headquarters of Turgut, who was named its beylerbey. The strategic island of Jerba off the eastern coast of Tunisia fell to Piale Pasha, and the Ottomans now ruled nearly all of North Africa, except for Morocco, which never came under their control.

In 1565, Suleiman sent Piale with 200 ships and a landing force of nearly 30,000 men to take the island of Malta from the Knights of St. John, whom he had driven from Rhodes more than forty years earlier. After several months of costly and fruitless assaults upon the island fortresses, the Ottomans withdrew. Curiously, the Christian forces made no attempt to follow up this failure. Ottoman supremacy upon the Mediterranean continued for many years after Suleiman's death.

EASTERN CAMPAIGNS

On several occasions in the early years of Suleiman's reign, there were difficulties with the Safavid shah of Iran. The Ottoman court, being Sunnite, looked with contempt upon the Shiites of the East. They also feared any successes of the Shiite Safavid devotees who lived in various parts of the Ottoman Empire. Although Selim I had beaten Shah Ismail and killed thousands of his followers in Anatolia, border chieftains in eastern Asia Minor vacillated in their loyalty from Tabriz to Istanbul and back to Tabriz again as advantages shifted from one to the other. Such changing allegiance brought conflict between the two great empires and perpetuated minor border engagements.

The first Eastern campaign conducted personally by Suleiman was in 1534. Ibrahim led the advance contingents into Tabriz, Suleiman reaching the Iranian capital weeks later. Not being able to come to grips with Shah Tahmasp, they moved southward and captured Baghdad. There Suleiman passed the winter, arranging the administration of this new addition to his empire. Suleiman then sacked and fired Tabriz. He returned to Istanbul early in 1536, having been gone for eighteen months.

A decade later Shah Tahmasp's brother appeared at the Porte, seeking help in a bid for the Iranian throne. Suleiman left Istanbul in 1548, recaptured Tabriz, wintered in Aleppo, and spent all of 1549 pillaging cities and pursuing the elusive Tahmasp, who never dared risk a battle.

Again in 1553, perhaps believing that the Ottomans were fully engaged in Europe, Tahmasp adopted an aggressive policy toward the Porte and seized Erzurum. Rustem Pasha, the grand vizir, headed a large army to halt the Iranians. However, the sipahis in the army disliked the domination of the state by the devshirmeh converts and other "slaves" of the Porte. Dissidents began to mutter that if Suleiman were too old to lead them his eldest living son, Prince Mustafa, should. Egged on by Roxelana, who was plotting for the favored position for one of her sons, Suleiman took the field, then summoned Mustafa to Eregli, where he had three mutes strangle his son. Suleiman again wintered at Aleppo and spent 1554 subjugating the lands east of the Euphrates. Then, recognizing the futility of trying to hold these Eastern conquests, the Porte arranged a peace that allowed the Ottomans to retain Iraq, including Baghdad, and a port on the Persian Gulf, as well as most of Kurdistan and western Armenia.

Suleiman also took an interest in developments in the Red Sea area and along the shores of the Arabian Sea. In 1538, an Ottoman admiral sailed from Suez, installed loyal governors in Aden and Yemen, and then passed on to the Malabar coast of India, where he landed and unsuccessfully besieged Diu. Suleiman also found that the Portuguese blocked the exit from the Persian Gulf, in part nullifying his capture of Baghdad and Basrah. When the famous geographer-sea captain Piri Pasha failed to oust the Portuguese from the Straits of Hormuz, he was beheaded for cowardice. His successors were likewise unsuccessful in driving them from Hormuz. Nonetheless, the Ottomans retained control over the Persian Gulf, Aden, Yemen, and the Red Sea, including the coastal areas of the Sudan and portions of Ethiopia, as the spice trade to Egypt through the Red Sea then revived.

HUNGARY AGAIN

Suleiman, like other rulers of his time, had too many irons in the fire to press his Eastern campaigns vigorously. In the latter half of his reign he became involved again in Hungary, occupying Budapest in 1541 and for the first time merging central Hungary directly into his empire. Some twenty-five provinces were formed, each with a governor under the beylerbey of Budapest.

Ferdinand of Austria tried to retaliate, but his siege of Budapest failed. Peace treaties were signed in 1547; each party retained the lands in his possession, and Austria paid a tribute of 30,000 ducats a year to the Porte. The Hapsburgs, however, violated the peace; and in 1552 Suleiman's second vizir captured fortress after fortress and incorporated the Banat of Temesvar into the empire. Only a minor fortress of Sziget in Hungary remained.

Maximilian II succeeded his father, Ferdinand, in 1564. He, too, refused to pay the tribute and attacked Ottoman territory. When governors clamored for support in 1566, Suleiman set forth on his seventh campaign into Hungary. He was over seventy years of age, and being no longer able to ride a horse, he traveled in a carriage. Pointing for Erlau, the troops were deflected to reduce the fortress at Sziget, where a Croatian count had killed one of Suleiman's favorite officers. Situated on lowlands near the Danube, Sziget was surrounded by marshes and lakes. Dry weather prevailed, however, and Sziget fell on the evening of September 5 with the explosion of a huge mine under the walls. That same night—the eve of the consolidation of Hungary, the fulfillment of the conquest that had begun with the fall of Belgrad in his first year of campaigning—Suleiman died.

SULEIMAN'S FAMILY AND FRIENDS

Mehmed Sokolli, the grand vizir, kept Suleiman's death a secret for over three weeks, while a messenger went to Kutahya to summon Selim to the succession. Suleiman had had eight sons, but only one outlived him. Three died as small children in the first years of his reign. Mehmed, who was Suleiman's favorite, died in 1543 at the age of twenty-one. The fate of Mustafa, the son of Roxelana's chief harem rival, has already been narrated; and his brother, Jihangir the hunchback, committed suicide upon learning of Mustafa's death. The remaining two, Selim and Bayezid, were Roxelana's sons. Selim, the elder, drank to excess and was given to intrigue. The soldiers preferred Bayezid, who resembled Suleiman and who was probably the choice of Suleiman and Roxelana.

Each brother had a following at court, and rivalry between the two was intense. Selim and his friends employed every means to advance his power, even daring to risk forging and intercepting letters between Bayezid and his father. Especially after Roxelana's death in 1558, Selim's fortunes were watched over by the grand vizir Rustem Pasha. The latter was the husband of Roxelana's daughter Mihrimah, who had as much power over her father as her mother did. Civil war between the brothers broke out in 1559. Suleiman ordered the provincial governors in Asia Minor to give active support to Selim, who was then victorious in a battle near Konya. Bayezid wrote to Suleiman asking to be forgiven, but the letter never reached his father. Fleeing to the court of Shah Tahmasp, Bayezid became the source of much diplomatic correspondence. Eventually on the payment of 400,000 ducats he and his four sons were turned over to Suleiman's agent, who executed all of them. Thus, when Suleiman died, there remained of his sons only Selim the Drunkard—a fat, fun-loving, and debauched person.

Another unhappy personal incident of Suleiman's reign involved his companion and grand vizir Ibrahim. Presumably, Suleiman came to feel that Ibrahim was amassing too much power. One evening in 1536 Ibrahim dined as usual with Suleiman and retired for the night to his customary place in Suleiman's apartments. The next morning his strangled body was found outside the palace. No explanation was ever given. His immense wealth reverted to the crown, since he was Suleiman's slave. In later years Suleiman tried to avoid promoting officers too rapidly or elevating them too obviously over the heads of their seniors.

IMPERIAL PROBLEMS

The relationship between Suleiman and Ibrahim and its calamitous end were symptomatic of the rapidly changing scene in and about the government. The expansion into eastern Asia Minor, Syria, and Egypt by Selim I was followed without much breathing space by Suleiman's conquests in Serbia, Hungary, North Africa, and Iraq. The result was that in two decades the empire experienced an astonishing increment not only of power and wealth but also of responsibilities.

More and more provinces were created with a proportionate increase in the number of governors, judges, tax collectors, and clerks. The janissary corps was doubled in size. Wealth poured into Istanbul; and high officers of the court adopted a life of sumptuous pomp and splendor. (To celebrate the circumcision of Mustafa, Mehmed, and Selim in the summer of 1530, high dignitaries gathered in Istanbul for festivities that lasted three weeks.) Each vizir had a magnificent court of his own, modeled after that of his master. Each had his own slaves, whom he trained and employed for his own interests. Ibrahim even established a school. Mehmed Sokolli, the grand vizir at the time of Suleiman's death, had become Suleiman's slave when Iskender Chelebi, the chief treasurer, was executed and his property confiscated in 1534. Ayas Pasha, Ibrahim's successor as grand vizir and a slave of Albanian origin, lived in the grand manner. At his death from the plague, it was cryptically noted that there were 40 cradles at one time at his palace and that he left 120 children!

As governmental administration became vaster and more complex, favoritism, corruption, and intrigue multiplied. The situation was abetted by the haphazard growth of Ottoman law and legal procedures. Suleiman, therefore, reissued and modified numerous laws dating from his predecessors' reigns, and codified old laws, particularly those affecting the provinces, in an attempt to regularize his administration. (It is on the basis of this legal activity that he has been known in Ottoman history as Suleiman Kanuni—"The Lawgiver.") Many laws related to matters of inheritance, salary, rank, and ceremony for officers of the court. Market and guild regulations were modified and one of the greatest collections of laws was that fashioned for the feudal class in 1530. It eliminated confusion and was designed to end the growing corruption by changing the granting of all fiefs from the hands of the beylerbey to those of the sultan. A sipahi or a prospective sipahi received a note from the beylerbey, but had to appear at the Porte to obtain his confirmation.

A social problem also emerged in connection with the relatively new drink, coffee, which had come into general use in the fifteenth century. Opposition to it first emerged among some governmental and religious circles in Mecca and Cairo, despite the economic advantages created by the trade in coffee during the sixteenth century. Popular coffeehouses were viewed with suspicion by the central Ottoman government officials as likely to lead to sloth and sedition, but despite condemnations, they spread ever more widely and increased the male public's opportunities for social interaction.

Suleiman's revenues were greater than those of any of the contemporary monarchs in Europe. Income was derived from many sources. Since the Ottomans usually followed the customs that were practiced in a province before its conquest, the sources varied from province to province. Tithes on land, poll taxes, special taxes on lands of non-Muslims, trade, animals, produce, markets, mines, confiscations, escheat, and booty annually brought Suleiman about 12 million ducats. Even so, Suleiman, like each of the European monarchs, was often hard-pressed for funds; and in his later years he forced gifts from his officers upon their appointment to a higher position, a practice that unfortunately opened the door to venality.

SELIM II

Throughout his reign of eight years Selim II retained his father's last grand vizir, Mehmed Sokolli, who administered the government and might well be called the actual ruler. Virtually afraid of his grand vizir, Selim generally deferred to him and to other high officials of proven abilities, though at times he embarrassed Sokolli by acting on the advice of an old tutor. Selim was highly emotional and sensitive, and a truly gifted poet. But he was also self-centered. He was unaware of how the court and the soldiers felt toward him and lived in the company of, and was easily influenced by, fawning courtiers and unscrupulous adventurers.

Since Sokolli continued as grand vizir throughout Selim's reign and on into that of his successor, there was no break in governmental procedure or policy, although there was some difficulty at the onset. Selim and his personal friends erred in not comprehending the power and fearlessness of the janissaries; and at first they declined to give the customary accession donations to the soldiers. Complaints, demands, and a show of force followed until Selim promised the money.

Otherwise, the course of events proceeded as it had under Suleiman. Piale Pasha took the island of Chios from the Genoese; peace was signed with Austria and Poland; and more of Yemen was subjected. An ambitious project was undertaken in 1569: forces were sent to conquer Astrakhan at the mouth of the Volga River; meanwhile, engineers and excavators started digging a canal to connect the Don and the Volga at a point where they are only about thirty miles apart. The purpose was to enable ships and military supplies to be sent to the Caspian Sea and to support attacks upon Iran. The garrison at Astrakhan withstood the storm, however, and an army under Prince Serebinoff drove away the workmen on the canal. The enterprise was abandoned and peace between Muscovy and the Porte was reestablished.

Sokolli had a similar dream of cutting a waterway across Suez, but affairs in Yemen and Arabia and then Selim's insistence upon war against Venice for the conquest of Cyprus postponed the work. Lala Mustafa, Selim's tutor who had intrigued and plotted so successfully to destroy Bayezid, obtained command of the war against Venice. The whole island of Cyprus was subdued at heavy cost by midsummer of 1571. Cyprus became a unified part of the empire (and Selim could now command the entire output of Cypriote wine of which he was so fond).

The attack on Cyprus and the extraordinary naval preparations of the Ottomans not only alarmed Venice but instigated the formation of a redoubtable naval league which included Spain, Venice, Savoy, the pope, and the Knights of Malta. Commanded by Don Juan of Austria, the Christian fleet met the Ottomans at the Gulf of Lepanto in October 1571. A furious battle ensued with the Ottomans losing over 200 ships and many men. The allied fleets suffered less, and victory was theirs. To the Ottomans and the East the Battle of Lepanto was a severe loss in a long series of naval engagements. However, a new fleet was built that winter in the naval yards of Gallipoli and Istanbul; and by the spring of 1572 the Ottoman naval position was largely repaired. To the Christians, however, it had seemed a notable victory; it gave them courage and proved that the Ottomans were not invincible upon the sea. Nevertheless, they failed to follow up the victory. Tunis later joined Algiers and Tripoli as Ottoman strongholds on the north shore of Africa and remained an Ottoman possession until the nineteenth century.

Whether the decay and weakening of the Ottoman Empire would have become noticeable under Selim had he lived longer is difficult to determine. In any case, late in 1574 Selim was inspecting a new bath at the palace; and to protect himself from any dampness of the fresh plaster, he drained an entire bottle of Cypriote wine. Being slightly unsteady, he fell on the damp floor, and died a few days later from a brain concussion. His death, followed a year later by the assassination of Mehmed Sokolli, terminated an era in Middle Eastern history. The powerful and dynamic Ottoman Empire soon turned into stagnation and decline, and gradually gave way to the weak and corrupt state that the rising centralized monarchies and nation-states of Europe found so tempting.

*O*TTOMAN ARCHITECTURE AND ART

In this illustrious period of Ottoman history the most viable and lasting evidence of its greatness and magnificence was the galaxy of majestic mosques that still silhouette the skyline of Istanbul from every quarter. Sultans, grand viziers, kapudan pashas, princes and princesses, and ladies of the harem—all built impressive pavilions, tombs, mosques, and mosque complexes (the latter centered around the mosque, but including madrasahs, hospitals, etc.) to memorialize themselves. Most of the prominent mosques of the empire, and of Istanbul in particular, date from the sixteenth century, beginning with the mosque of Sultan Bayezid II (completed about 1500), and ending with the Blue Mosque of Sultan Ahmed I (1617). They surpassed the already high standard of imperial architecture established at Bursa and Edirne.

The simplest style and form, exemplified in the mosque of Sultan Selim I in Istanbul, consisted of a plain square building carrying one large dome. The transition between square and circle was accomplished by flat and spherical triangular pendentives.

The second type of imperial mosque was evolved in the mosques of Bayezid II and Suleiman I. These mosques showed that Ottoman architects studied Hagia Sophia, saw its grandeur, and appreciated its solution of the problem of building a domed open square or rectangular structure suitable for congregational worship. In these two mosques, the great rectangle was roofed by a large dome on spherical pendentives which effected the transition from the dome to the four broad pointed arches resting upon four piers. The dome was abutted longitudinally by semidomes fitted to their rectangles by pendentives or small semidomes, which in Suleimaniye were anchored to their corners by stalactite pendentives. The pendentives confused the eye and thereby hid the awkwardness, thus serving much the same function as the colored mosaics of the Byzantines. The strong buttresses in the lateral walls were admirably concealed by external porches. In some details the influences of Italian Renaissance architecture were also evident.

The architect Sinan was the master of the age and he contended that his early Shahzade mosque in memory of Suleiman's son Mehmed was the work of an apprentice; his later mosque of Suleiman was the work of a journeyman; and Sultan Selim II's mosque in Edirne, completed in 1574, was the work of a master. In Shahzade, Sinan presented a new style aimed at opening the entire edifice into one congregational hall so that every worshiper could see the mihrab. The great mosque of Sultan Ahmed I followed the same principle and achieved its goal by replacing the small domes of the lateral aisle by one large semidome. The central dome at Ahmed was supported by large circular piers. Upon entering Ahmed, one noticed immediately that the whole area was unified and that the central space was vaster than in Hagia Sophia.

At the mosque of Sultan Selim II in Edirne, Sinan developed another type of imperial mosque. The dome, thirty-one meters across, was supported by an octagon of arches, pendentives of stalactite corbels, and eight sturdy paneled piers which Sinan called "elephant feet." Again, as in Suleimaniye, the buttresses were hidden by external porches.

The internal centers of the domes were usually decorated with flowered and calligraphic frescoes, and the walls were embellished by panels of colored and veined marble or colored ceramic tiles. The Ottomans were more conscious of esthetic external lines and composition than Byzantine builders, and this accounts for the architectural evolution that gave to the Istanbul horizon its splendor of domes and slender minarets.

The mosques and palaces were furnished with the richly colored and geometrically patterned carpets and rugs for which the Ottoman Empire became so famous, and also with pottery, whose style was initially influenced by Chinese porcelain models. By the middle of the sixteenth century, Ottoman pottery and tiles, especially those produced at Iznik and Damascus, developed a variety of beautiful colors and motifs which dazzled as they pleased. Calligraphy was an art form favored by the sultans; and so was miniature painting, influenced by Safavid artists in the early and middle sixteenth century, and later developing a more independent style. The "minor" arts also flourished; Sultan Suleiman was himself a goldsmith and a patron of art on an enormous scale. Ottoman silk weavings were much sought after in Europe. All the various forms of art were largely produced in workshops organized by the imperial government, which consumed most of their production. Officials of the state, grandees living in the provinces, and the wealthier members of the protected religious minorities also patronized similar artists and artisans.

OTTOMAN LITERATURE

The sixteenth century led in architectural achievement; but it was also a brilliant period of Ottoman literary activity. Suleiman had a strong historical feeling; he emphasized the parallelism of Mehmed II and Constantine and equated himself with Justinian. Like Justinian, Suleiman was lawgiver and law codifier, builder of remarkable religious edifices and aqueducts, leader of armies, and generous patron of scholars and men of letters.

A quarter of the eminent Ottoman poets and writers belonged to the period of Suleiman and Selim II. Poetry and history were the outstanding forms of literary effort. Lyric poetry often had a Sufi content and was expressed in forms heavily influenced by Sufi mysticism. Many themes remained persistent for centuries—the garden; the lover/beloved; an urban orientation, especially toward Istanbul; and images of roses, nightingales, and wine. Jem, son of Mehmed II, wrote poetry reflective of his life and its melancholy circumstances. The Turkish-Iraqi poet Mehmet Fuzuli (d. 1556) wrote a panegyric on Suleiman's conquest of Baghdad, and became famous for his romantic poems. Sufi poets and wandering minstrels recited poetry for the masses in the countryside, poetry that strikingly differed from that of the palace and the capital city. Both Suleiman and Selim were accomplished poets, Suleiman writing in Persian and Turkish under the nom de plume Muhibbi (one who loves). The shining lyric poet of that age and perhaps of the Turkish language of all ages was Abd al-Baki, whose elegy for Sultan Suleiman was his greatest public work.

Historians flourished. Their works were sometimes general in scope and sometimes specific, describing only one phase or incident of the period, and were often sumptuously illustrated with miniature paintings. Early histories had been straightforward and written in a popular style, but Sultan Bayezid II commissioned a more ornate comprehensive history of the Ottomans. The ornate style involved first works written in Persian and Arabic, and later, an infusion of words and grammatical units from those languages into Turkish. Cultural intermingling, amalgamation, and synthesis were reflected in language, but the gains in literary elegance were counterbalanced by the increasing gap between the style of the imperial court and the literati on the one hand, and the great mass of Turkish speakers on the other. The latter could often not understand the new high-flown rhetoric of the imperial style.

Among the historians, Ramazan wrote of the capture of Rhodes; Kemalpashazade, whose career included service as a sipahi, and much later, as shaykh al-Islam, narrated the victorious campaign of Mohacs, and wrote a general history of the dynasty. One of the most revered of Ottoman historians appeared late in the sixteenth century in the person of Sad al-Din. Tutor of Suleiman's grandson Murad III, he wrote and compiled *The Crown of Histories,* which covered in numerous volumes, and in an analytical manner, the gamut of Ottoman history. Continued by Sad al-Din's son, for several centuries it dominated concepts of Ottoman development from the earliest times to his own day. The prolific bureaucrat, poet, and historian Mustafa Ali of Gallipoli (d. 1600) wrote an important book of counsel for sultans and a history of the world and the Ottoman Empire, begun in the year 1100 after the Hijrah (1591–1592 A.D.). For such writers, historical chronicles were literary accomplishments, reflecting the increasingly complex and rich nature of Ottoman Turkish, as well as following the format of chronologically arranged annals.

The history of the Ottoman Empire in the sixteenth century and the nature of its rulers were typical of the range of experience found in other Mediterranean and European countries. Selim I was a harsh, brilliant, demanding, energetic tyrant, who set the governmental machinery in motion toward momentous conquest. Suleiman was a dignified, orderly, just, conscientious, and artistic soldier and gentleman, who gave the Ottoman Empire a sense of distinction and cultural urbanity. Selim II was a talented, irresponsible, emotional, dissolute drunkard, who hastened the decay of the state.

REFERENCES

Most titles already cited for the chapters discussing the Ottoman Empire are relevant to this chapter. Especially noteworthy are those in Chapters 12, 13, 14, 15, and 16.

Andrews, Walter G. *Poetry's Voice, Society's Song: Ottoman Lyric Poetry.* Seattle: University of Washington Press, 1985. This excellent study places Ottoman lyrical poetry in the context of modern literary analysis and examines the meaning of poetry.

Atil, Esin. *The Age of Sultan Süleyman the Magnificent.* New York: Harry N. Abrams, 1987. The text and pictures illustrate all aspects of the art of the age.

———. *Süleymanname: The Illustrated History of Süleyman the Magnificent.* New York: Harry N. Abrams, 1986. Lavish display of miniatures from a history of the sultan.

Carswell, John, and C. J. F. Dowsett. *Kutahya Tiles and Pottery from the Armenian Cathedral of St. James, Jerusalem.* 2 vols. London: Oxford University Press, 1972.

Faroqhi, Suraiya. *Peasants, Dervishes and Traders in the Ottoman Empire.* London: Variorum, 1986.

Fleischer, Cornell H. *Bureaucrat and Intellectual in the Ottoman Empire: The Historian Mustafa Ali (1541–1600).* Princeton, N.J.: Princeton University Press, 1986. A sophisticated analysis not only of the life of this particular historian, but of historiography for the entire period.

Gibb, E. J. W. *A History of Ottoman Poetry.* 6 vols. London: Luzac, 1900–1909. This is the standard work.

Guilmartin, John Francis, Jr. *Gunpowder and Galleys: Changing Technology and Mediterranean Warfare at Sea in the Sixteenth Century.* London: Cambridge University Press, 1974. A masterful study on ships, provisions, sea battles, and their influence on the politics and economies of the Ottoman Empire, Venice, and other Italian states.

Hattox, Ralph S. *Coffee and Coffeehouses: The Origins of a Social Beverage in the Medieval Near East.* Seattle: University of Washington Press, 1985. A charming and convincing account dealing with social history.

Kortepeter, Carl Max. *Ottoman Imperialism During the Reformation: Europe and the Caucasus.* New York: New York University Press, 1972. A study of relationships of political units in the great span between Europe and the Caucasus and Ottoman relationships to them all.

Levey, Michael. *The World of Ottoman Art.* London: Thames and Hudson, 1975.

Menemencioglu, Nermin, and Fahir Iz, eds. *The Penguin Book of Turkish Verse.* Harmondsworth, Eng.: Penguin Books, 1978. Translations and commentaries on a wide range of Ottoman poets and modern Turkish poets as well.

Merriman, R. B. *Suleiman the Magnificent, 1520–1566.* Cambridge, Mass.: Harvard University Press, 1944. An adequate summary of the life of the great sultan.

Petsopoulis, Yanni, ed. *Tulips, Arabesques and Turbans: Decorative Art from the Ottoman Empire.* New York: Abbeville Press, 1982. Informative chapters by a number of authors on many aspects of Ottoman art.

Rogers, J. M. *Islamic Art and Design, 1500–1700.* London: British Museum, 1983. Treats Ottomans, Safavids, and Moguls of India comparatively.

Stoye, John. *Siege of Vienna.* New York: Holt, 1965. A detailed account.

Stratton, Arthur. *Sinan.* New York: Scribners, 1972. A narrative biography that depicts the court society of the time more than it does the life of the great architect Sinan.

18

The Flowering and Decay of Safavid Iran, and a Century of Stagnation in the Ottoman Empire

SHAH TAHMASP I OF SAFAVID IRAN

When the despondent Ismail died in 1524, he was succeeded by his eldest son, Tahmasp, a lad of ten years. Though Ismail had been trying for more than fifteen years to elevate Iranian elements in the state and subordinate domineering *kizilbash* Turkoman tribal leaders, the kizilbash gained power after his death and held it for a decade. However, civil war among the Turkoman tribes kept the state in turmoil until Tahmasp subdued the rebellions and ended the strife by establishing an Iranian viceroy in 1533. Despite this political turmoil, textiles, ceramics, and miniature painting flourished during Tahmasp's reign. The shah himself was a noted poet, calligrapher, and painter. Illustrations for Firdawsi's *Shahnamah* commissioned by Ismail and Tahmasp were especially splendid. In religious matters, Tahmasp did not regard himself as being semidivine; instead, he designated a leading cleric as the deputy of the Hidden Imam (a position later called the mujtahid of the age).

When the Ottoman sultan Suleiman threatened Iran over her support of various Turkoman chiefs, Tahmasp in vain sent envoys to Hungary and Charles V for aid. In 1534 the Ottomans, led by Suleiman, invaded, sacking Tabriz and Gilan, and capturing Baghdad. (Central Iraq remained in Ottoman hands for ninety years.) Another campaign occurred in 1548 when Tahmasp's brother induced the Ottomans to send an invading army that seized Azerbayjan. Peace was arranged in 1555, but the shah did not retain Tabriz or Baghdad because his forces were inadequate to defeat the main Ottoman army. Nevertheless, although the lack of artillery and muskets was a critical disadvantage to Tahmasp, his scorched-earth strategy, distances from Istanbul, difficult terrain, problems in the Danube basin and the Mediterranean, and the psychology of Ottoman fighting men made it equally unlikely for Ottoman forces to reach Tahmasp and impose a settlement. Thus, Tahmasp was able to enforce his rule from the Tigris to Transoxiana and from the Persian Gulf to both sides of the Caspian Sea. Border provinces lost their autonomy and were directly incorporated into the state.

Within the Safavid state great strife raged over the competition between kizilbash Turkomans and non-Turkish Iranian populace. Shah Tahmasp attempted, as his father had before him, to find an alternative to the power of unreliable Sufis and kizilbash. Nearly every province was held as a fief by one of their leaders, and their incomes and retainers gave an independence difficult to offset. Between 1540 and 1544 Tahmasp sent four expeditions to Georgia, bringing back 30,000 prisoners, most of whom were boys to be trained as *ghulams* or slaves to serve in his army or to be trained as governing administrators. The girls served as concubines whose sons also entered the shah's service. This policy of creating a Georgian and Circassian counterweight to the kizilbash in the end proved disastrous, as civil war broke out between them in 1572 when Tahmasp grew old and feeble. His many sons and their mothers began to intrigue for the succession. Two leading candidates were Prince Suleiman, whose mother was a Circassian, and Prince Haydar, whose mother was Georgian. In the end the kizilbash declared they would support sons of Turkish mothers only.

In 1576, Tahmasp was poisoned and the kizilbash had the power to put Ismail, his fourth son, on the throne. Having been incarcerated for years by his father, he was half mad and given to drink and drugs. He killed all the royal princes except Prince Muhammad Khudabanda, who was nearly blind and not considered a threat. Ismail executed many kizilbash and Sufi leaders who had supported his brothers and finally gave orders to have his sole remaining brother executed. Before the deed could be committed, however, poison was mixed one night in 1577 with Ismail's usual juice of opium poppy and Indian hemp, and he was found dead in the morning. After placing Muhammad on the throne (since he had a Turkoman mother), the kizilbash were thwarted for eighteen months by the new shah's ambitious Iranian wife until she was assassinated.

Shah Muhammad Khudabanda ruled as a kind of puppet in Turkoman hands for ten years until 1587, when he was overthrown and killed by Turkoman leaders who had seized Qazvin, the capital, and put his seven-year-old son, Abbas, on the throne. Ruling for forty-one years, Abbas ushered in a new age in Iranian history. By 1587, religious zeal for the Safavid rule had been frittered away, and over the century the shah's position as the head of a secular state dominated. There had been a gradual change and evolution under Tahmasp with acceptance of the idea of a central government. He strengthened the government by moving the capital from Tabriz to Qazvin, which was safer from Ottoman assault. Moreover, Shiite doctrinal unity had been achieved to a great extent, making religion much less of an emotional issue. One could now recognize the consolidation of Safavid Iran into a state of considerable permanence.

SHAH ABBAS THE GREAT OF ISFAHAN

After the kizilbash chieftains left Herat for Qazvin in 1587 to install Abbas on the Safavid throne, the Sunnite Uzbeg tribes invaded and captured Herat. Shah Abbas met them at Meshhed, but crucial rebellions of local princes in his western provinces demanded his immediate return. With the combined forces of local kizilbash tribes and an army improvised from Georgian prisoners and held together by his personal leadership, Abbas was able to put down a very serious uprising in Shiraz and soon had central Iran pacified. The Ottoman attack in the west could not be thwarted, however; and by the peace of 1590 with Murad III, Tabriz, some Caspian ports, and surrounding areas were ceded.

During the following seven years Abbas consolidated his position and power, his initial step being the destruction of kizilbash forces. Their leaders were killed and their provinces and lands confiscated. With the income from these holdings plus the funds of the royal household, Abbas formed a standing army of 10,000 horsemen and 20,000 foot soldiers from prisoners and slaves from Armenia and Georgia. In addition to this strengthening of manpower, Abbas significantly improved his firepower. In 1597, Sir Anthony, Sir Robert, and Sir Thomas Sherley, along with twenty-six other Englishmen, arrived in Isfahan, the new capital, to discuss trade and an alliance against the Turks and the Dutch. They helped Abbas train musketeers and taught his men how to cast cannon. Within a few years, Abbas had a force of 12,000 artillery men equipped with 500 brass and bronze cannon with which he effectively challenged the Ottoman armies as well as dissidents within his own state. A new corps of 12,000 mounted musketeers was raised from the peasantry and another 10,000 Georgian prisoners were added to the army. Throughout his reign Abbas continued the policy of turning prisoners of war into soldiers: on one occasion 20,000 Armenians were taken from the region of Erzurum and pressed into service; on another, an expedition into Georgia in 1617, 130,000 prisoners were taken and moved into his state in various areas and capacities.

In 1597, Abbas began to clear the frontiers of challengers. He drove the Uzbegs from Meshhed, Herat, and Khurasan and moved eastward to Balkh. Abbas attempted to stamp out Sunnism in eastern Iran. To defend Khurasan he transported thousands of Kurdish horsemen and their families to the frontier, establishing them so securely that many of their descendants still reside in that area. War against the Ottomans erupted in 1601, and Tabriz, Erivan, and Kars were recaptured. With the decline of the Ottomans, Abbas took Kurdistan and Shirvan from Ahmed I and in 1623 recaptured Baghdad, Mosul, and Diyarbakir, restoring to Iran the territories held at the time of Shah Ismail. On other fronts, Abbas defeated the Moguls, taking Kandahar; seized the island of Bahrayn in the Persian Gulf; and with British aid drove the Portuguese from Hormuz in 1622, founding the important trading post of Bandar Abbas. When Shah Abbas died in 1629, his land was at peace and prospering. In contrast, the Ottoman Empire was declining, Russia was recovering from her Time of Troubles, and the Moguls in India were losing hold of that country.

ADMINISTRATION AND TRADE UNDER ABBAS

By the year 1600, Shah Abbas had established his authoritarian rule over most of the provinces of Iran. Warfare was relegated to the frontiers and was fought by professional soldiers. The administration of the provinces was overseen by royal governors, all of whom were subservient to the royal will. Like Allahvardi Khan, governor of Fars and one of Abbas's first appointees, many of these officials were slaves. In due course, more than a fifth of the central government came from the ghulam ranks. Each city had its mayor, responsible for taxes and civil order. The numerous craft guilds were strictly regulated, their chief masters meeting with the mayor once a month to debate taxes and matters of general concern; on occasion they protested government restrictions and officials' oppressions.

The shah created numerous religious endowments as symbols of his commitment to Twelver Shiism, and the post of *sadr*, an administrative official and head of the religious and judicial hierarchy, gained in power by becoming charged with the administration of many religious endowments. Madrasahs, courts, and mosques were flourishing, but they were never as organized and as subservient to imperial authority as in the Ottoman Empire. Shiite ulema were brought to Iran from the Arab theological centers of southern Lebanon and Bahrayn, and the shah persecuted the Shiite Sufi orders. The great philosopher and metaphysician Mullah Sadra Shirazi (d. 1640), writing in Arabic, espoused Gnostic views. As a result, he was strongly attacked by the Shiite ulema; the shah ordered the compilation of a legal treatise that became the basis of law for the century.

Abbas had a special concern for commerce, domestic and foreign. To connect all major cities throughout the land, Abbas provided a network of roads that every twenty miles or so had a secure caravansarai where several caravans could spend the night safe from marauders. With regard to the silk trade, which was important and highly profitable, Abbas showed similar initiative. Since Armenian communities were basic in the silk trade, with one of their centers at Julfa on the Aras River in Azerbayjan, Abbas imported 3,000 Armenian families and created New Julfa for them on the outskirts of Isfahan, exempting them from various taxes, and permitting them to elect their own mayor. A monopoly over the silk trade was established and the Armenians ran it for the shah. They prospered so greatly that some Armenian merchants lived in the style of the Safavid imperial court. Armenian religious manuscript illumination reached new heights, as well as the printing of secular works in 1608.

To exploit European enthusiasm for fine porcelain from China, Abbas brought 300 Chinese potters to Isfahan to create pottery in the Chinese style. Not only was an additional export developed but an important tradition was established, for the most skillful and resourceful potters since the seventeenth century have been in Isfahan.

It was not long before Iranian goods were highly esteemed and their quality and artistry became legendary. Among the more important were silk and wool carpets and textiles of all types, porcelains, miniature paintings, enamelwork, glassware, dyes, jewelry, lacquered and inlaid woods, bookbindings, leather goods, gold and silver plates, vases, and fine steel swords. Since many of these items were the product of court workshops, they were of a design and workmanship that were nearly always superb and could be afforded only by the most wealthy. However, as commercial relations with Europe increased, especially in the seventeenth century, export goods declined somewhat in quality and were increasingly influenced by foreign motifs.

Undoubtedly the best-known articles have been the Persian carpets. The finest of these carpets were made in court workshops for the court and the wealthiest patrons, few if any being exported. In their manufacture, only materials of the highest quality were employed. Sheep were specially bred for their delicate wool and were tended like children so that their wool would never be soiled or roughened. Even the water for washing the wool was important. Court painters designed the carpets, generally employing refined stylized motifs that incorporated gardens, animals, and pools. Great carpet factories were located at the time of Abbas at Kerman, Herat, Hamadan, Tabriz, and Karabagh, but most cities and provinces produced fine carpets which were much in demand, especially in Europe. Rugs manufactured for export, though of a lesser quality, were nevertheless rich in color, design, and fabrication, most coming from workshops closely allied to the court. However, even the carpet weaving of nomads and villagers followed the highest traditions.

Skills in other manufactures and arts were also highly developed. Velvets, brocades, and embroideries were produced with the greatest care and exquisite design, and the finest pieces of these materials were, of course, very costly. Painting and the decorative arts were of a highly intricate style that displayed a keen sense of blending floral and geometric patterns to create a pleasing whole. The pierced and repoussé work of goldsmiths and silversmiths has hardly been surpassed. Potters learned how to decorate their wares in many colors, often firing seven or more colors at once on large tiles.

The splendor of isfahan

The internal stability established by Shah Abbas the Great encouraged a vast increase in trade, raised levels of production, opened wider avenues of opportunity for many, and ensured a great prosperity for all. At the court in Isfahan the resulting wealth transformed the style of life to a scale of lavishness seldom seen. European visitors gave nearly incredible descriptions of the dazzling opulence: Abbas on his throne surrounded by several hundred courtiers clothed in gold and silver with an array of gray, scarlet, yellow, green, plum, blue, and maroon silks embroidered with the rarest of jewels. What Abbas lacked in terms of the size of his palaces he made up for in number—over 100 in Isfahan alone. Each of these palaces was a masterpiece of design and decoration, as can be seen from Ali Kapu and Chihil Sutun, which still stand.

In the center of the new, planned district of Isfahan, Abbas surrounded a great open square, 560 yards (512 meters) by 174 yards (159 meters), with magnificent buildings; the square was used for polo—the popular sport of the courtiers at that time—horse races, fireworks displays, and other spectacles. On one side of the square was the main entrance to the palace, Ali Kapu, featuring a lovely pavilion in which Abbas liked to lounge with his courtiers and watch the festivities of the square. On another side was the imperial mosque, Masjid-i-Shah, masterpiece of Safavid architecture. An impressive pointed archway more than eighty feet (24 meters) high led to an inner courtyard surrounded by a graceful two-storied arcade. Opposite the entrance was another portal leading to the mosque proper, whose walls carried a large dome, the exterior of which was covered by exquisite enameled bricks with arabesque patterns in dark blue and green on a sky-blue background. On another side of the area was a great covered bazaar with a monumental arched entrance. The dome of the imperial mosque served as a landmark of the center of the heavily walled city, which had 600,000 inhabitants and boasted 1,802 caravansarais, 162 mosques, 273 public baths, and 48 colleges and academies. Isfahan with its rich verdure, pools, bridges, and watercourses was a flower-lover's paradise, its gardens displaying roses, jasmine, stocks, lilies, irises, poppies, and many other flowers in every variety and shade. Abbas himself laid out the gardens, planned the buildings, and even gave detailed instructions to the workmen.

DECLINE AND END OF SAFAVID RULE

For more than a hundred years following his death, Abbas the Great's Safavid heirs succeeded to the throne, and most of their reigns were odious. The provinces were increasingly governed by civilians, and the power of the central government over the distant regions steadily weakened. Had it not been for the strength of the administration, the quality of many of the officials, the vitality of commerce, the general peace, and the weakness of the forces beyond the frontiers, the dynasty and the state might well have disappeared.

Despite the decline in the effective power of the central government, some cultural and artistic successes were achieved. In ceramics, armor, miniature paintings, drawings, and textiles works of considerable beauty were still being created. However, literature and poetry were generally in decay, in part because of the attractions offered Persian writers by the rulers of India and the Ottoman Empire, who enticed many prominent thinkers and artists to join them. The sciences in Iran were stagnant, except for limited advances in medicine and in the production of astrolabes.

The seeds of the political decline might be said to have been sown by Abbas himself. Because he could brook no rival and feared the popularity of his own sons, he had his eldest executed and the other two blinded, making them ineligible to rule. In addition, he instituted the insidious practice of keeping the royal princes as indulged prisoners within the palace, in the company of women and servants who satisfied their every sensual whim. Catapulted to the throne after years of sheltered pampering, their incompetence and incorrigibility were compounded by the influence of scheming, ignorant women and fawning, unscrupulous slave officials. Often naïve and upright when ascending the throne, a young shah would be intentionally corrupted with drink and perverted by court attendants to enable them to rule without his interference.

Consequently, upon his death in 1629, Abbas was succeeded by his young grandson, Shah Safi, whose debauchery was thoroughgoing. He murdered his mother, a sister, his favorite wife, army generals, provincial governors, and many of the court officials. Nevertheless, the government under Safi did have the strength and will to repel Uzbeg incursions into Khurasan and suppress rebellions in Gilan, although the Moguls repossessed Kandahar and the Ottomans retook Baghdad in 1638. There ensued a peace treaty that ended the incessant Safavid-Ottoman wars.

Safi was followed by his nine-year-old son, Abbas II, who started with real promise and at the age of sixteen showed vigor and flashes of his great-grandfather's character by leading an army in the recapture of Kandahar and by conciliating the Uzbeg chiefs. Abbas II usually chose peace with his neighbors, and during his reign an intellectual form of Sufism and gnosticism reached a high level. He appointed slaves to high posts in the provincial governments. Abbas II's rule was marred when he turned to drink and sensualities, murdering many around him.

Upon his death, probably caused by syphilis, at the age of thirty-three in 1666, Abbas was succeeded by his seventeen-year-old son who first took the title Safi II but because of illness was recrowned the following year as Shah Suleiman. He reigned (it could not be said that he ruled) for twenty-eight long years, dying in 1694. A drunkard and a voluptuary, he loved peace and thought little about the state: once, when told that the Turks were about to attack, he replied that it made no difference to him, as long as he could keep Isfahan. He built the famous palace called "eight paradises" in 1669, known for its pavilions and tile work. The shah had many of the generals and government officials executed, leaving more of the administration to his palace cronies, who were only too happy to step into the vacuum he was creating. When he died in 1694, he had already executed his eldest son and left the choice between his other sons to the eunuchs and courtiers of the palace. They chose Husayn. Having been shut up in the harem of the palace for twenty-six years, Husayn was ignorant, superstitious, extremely credulous, and easily influenced—just the kind of shah the courtiers desired.

Subject to excessive piety, Husayn inaugurated his reign by prohibiting the use of wine: he had all the wine jars in the palace broken and would not permit the Armenians who controlled the wine trade to sell in Isfahan. As a youth he had become a partisan of religious teachers and leaders, or *mullahs,* so much so that many jokingly called him Mullah Husayn. Through all, Husayn's piousness was never lost. In 1706, he organized a pilgrimage to the holy shrine at Qum, the site of the family tombs. Over 60,000 accompanied him on this outing, the tents and pavilions of his retinue stretching out for more than six miles along the country road. This venture proved so enjoyable that he went with an equal number of retainers on the 600-mile pilgrimage to Meshhed, remaining there a whole year. The extravagance of this expedition not only emptied the treasury but ruined all the provinces through which it passed.

Thanks to an aunt who prevailed upon him to permit her to drink in the palace, Husayn did not remain abstemious for long. Soon wine flowed freely everywhere. Husayn became licentious, and his agents were constantly on the lookout for attractive faces to kidnap for his harem. Unable to curb his lavish habits and faced with the mounting cost of maintaining a standing army with cannon and muskets, Husayn's ministers had to find additional income. The most convenient means was to squeeze more revenue from the provinces. Under Safi I and Abbas II many provinces had been transferred to the royal household and their governorships sold to court favorites, who reimbursed themselves by gouging the inhabitants.

The economy was in decline as the value of exports fell, foreign competition increased, and insecurity on the trade routes grew. At the same time, Shiism became ever more widespread among the peoples of Iran, and many of the Sufi orders were repressed by the state.

Upon the raiding of Kandahar by Baluchis, Shah Husayn sent a Georgian general as the new governor in 1703. He turned out to be exceedingly harsh and rapacious, very energetic and clever, and adopted such severe measures against the Sunnite Ghalzai Afghan inhabitants that they rose in revolt under Mir Vays in 1709. Husayn sent an army from Isfahan in 1711 to destroy Mir Vays, but being ill-paid and divided by jealousies among three different components, it was routed in front of the walls of Kandahar. Mir Vays thus became an independent ruler, calling himself regent of Kandahar.

In 1715 Mir Vays was succeeded by his sixteen-year-old son Mahmud, an ambitious youth who took the offense and began to attack the shah's kingdom, advancing to a point only nine miles from Isfahan. The battle for Isfahan was joined in March 1722, with Mahmud occupying the Armenian suburb of New Julfa and investing the city. After a six-month siege which saw 60,000 inhabitants killed by starvation or epidemics, and 20,000 killed in fighting, Husayn surrendered. In a humiliating ceremony Husayn went out to Mahmud's headquarters and there, with his own hands, took from his turban the imperial plume of heron's feathers set with jewels   the sign of sovereignty—placed it on Mahmud's head, and bade him rule in peace.

During the siege Tahmasp, one of Husayn's older sons, escaped from Isfahan and made his way to Qazvin, where he was recognized as Shah Tahmasp II. Affairs were not favorable, however. The Ottomans seized Tiflis, Tabriz, and Hamadan; Peter the Great of Russia, outfitting a fleet on the Caspian, took Shirvan and Gilan, and compelled Tahmasp II to sign a treaty in July 1722, ceding to Russia Darband, Baku, Gilan, Astarabad, and Mazandaran in exchange for Peter's commitment to drive the Afghans from Isfahan. When Mahmud learned of the proposed Russian incursion to place Tahmasp II back on the throne in Isfahan, he had all the members of the Safavid family assembled in the palace courtyard; he and two of his friends then hacked them to death, except for Husayn and two small children whom Husayn shielded with his own body. Mahmud was rapidly growing insane and died in 1725, being succeeded by his cousin Ashraf. The Ottoman armies meanwhile pressed forward into Iran, asserting that they planned to restore the Safavids to their rightful possessions. Ashraf thereupon had Husayn executed and sent his head to the Ottoman commander to forestall his need to attack Isfahan.

Meanwhile, Tahmasp II gathered an army in Mazandaran in 1727, being supported by Fath Ali Khan, the chief of the Qajar tribe, and Nadir Kuli Khan of the Afshar tribe, each bringing several thousand experienced soldiers. They marched into Khurasan and recaptured Meshhed and Herat from the Abdali Afghans in 1729; along the way Nadir Khan murdered his rival, Fath Ali, and thus became the sole commander of the royal army. Nadir routed the Afghans under Ashraf, expelling them from Isfahan and Shiraz. Tahmasp II returned as shah to Isfahan but gave powers of taxation and independent control to Nadir. In 1732 Nadir dethroned him and sent him as a prisoner to Khurasan, where he was later killed. Nadir put Tahmasp's infant son on the throne as Abbas III, but the child died in 1736 and Nadir assumed the title shah, the powers of which he had been holding for several years. Safavid rule had ended.

OTTOMAN DECENTRALIZATION, INDOLENCE, AND CORRUPTION

The death of Selim II in 1574 ushered in a century and a quarter of stagnation in Ottoman history. A dozen sultans ruled during the period. Four were under sixteen years of age when they succeeded to the throne, and most of the rest were undisciplined young men. The wealth, splendor, and ease of the court sapped their energy and morals. The Ottoman political system, which had developed with an absolute sultan as the keystone of the arch of power, changed as the military, administrative, and religious establishments lost power to the palace and scribal services.

The causes of this obvious change are difficult to pinpoint. The character of Selim II or the influence of Ibrahim and Roxelana has frequently been described as a cancerous development that brought the downfall. Others have ascribed the collapse to an evolving process discernible for a number of years. Certainly, seeds of decay were nurtured for several decades and the causes of the decline were varied and profound. From its earliest days, the Ottoman state supported itself in considerable part from raids and conquest. As frontiers in Europe were extended, the enemy increased in number, and campaign costs became staggering. The booty obtained hardly met expenses, and little was left for palace extravagances which continued nevertheless.

The gradual shift in world trade from the Mediterranean to the Atlantic in the end brought a marked decline in Ottoman revenues from international trade. Simultaneously, Europe and the Mediterranean world were experiencing a continuing monetary inflation. Government income never quite met expenditures, and most contemporary monarchs were plagued with unbalanced budgets.

In the last two decades of Suleiman's life and in the reigns of Selim II and his successors finances were always straitened. Without loot from beyond the frontiers coming into Istanbul it was difficult to maintain the magnificence to which all had grown accustomed. To make up for this loss of revenue officials were obliged to

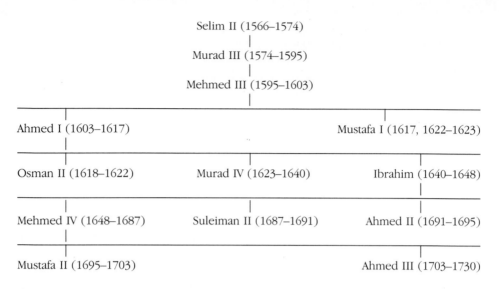

Selim II (1566–1574)

Murad III (1574–1595)

Mehmed III (1595–1603)

Ahmed I (1603–1617)   Mustafa I (1617, 1622–1623)

Osman II (1618–1622)   Murad IV (1623–1640)   Ibrahim (1640–1648)

Mehmed IV (1648–1687)   Suleiman II (1687–1691)   Ahmed II (1691–1695)

Mustafa II (1695–1703)   Ahmed III (1703–1730)

Ottoman Rulers, 1566–1730

give liberal sums to the sultan upon promotions. With the reign of Murad III the sultan obtained bribes for appointments, and by the time of Sultan Ibrahim there was open trafficking in offices at the Porte. Such corruption quickly filtered down to the lowliest official.

As a result of the conquests of Selim I and Suleiman I and the doubling of the size of the empire, administrative problems became more and more difficult. As the work of governing increased to overwhelming proportions, the sultan left more affairs of state to the grand vizir. Suleiman threw over most of the work to Ibrahim and began to defer to him in policy decisions. Later sultans frequently were unwilling to perform any onerous duties as head of the state and gave themselves up to a life of total voluptuousness and frivolity. Meanwhile, vizirs, beylerbeys, and leading officers drew unprecedented power into their hands. Beginning with Selim II's son Murad III, the sultans gave high office and substantial authority to their favorites, who were usually ill-fitted for the jobs to be done. As long as Mehmed Sokolli lived, he tried unsuccessfully to prevent this trend, but after his assassination in 1579 the palace favorites held full sway.

Equally damaging to affairs of state were the influence and even the actual formulation of policies by women of the palace. Murad III was controlled by his mother and by his harem favorite, Sultana Safiye Baffo, who actually ruled the empire while her son Mehmed III occupied the throne. Daughter of the Venetian governor of Corfu and from the noble Baffo family, Safiye had been captured by corsairs and presented to Suleiman, who in turn gave her to his grandson. For a time Murad was so faithful to Safiye that his mother and sister, the wife of Sokolli, fretted over her undue power and made presents of pretty and clever slaves to distract Murad's attention. In at least one respect they were obviously successful: Murad fathered over 100 children, of whom 20 sons and 27 daughters survived him.

Another enervating and corrupting practice developed upon the accession of Ahmed I in 1603. Unlike his father, who had had his own nineteen brothers strangled, Ahmed allowed his insane brother, Mustafa, to live closeted in the palace. Henceforth, the usual practice was to immure brothers and sons in the palace, the eldest male of the dynasty succeeding upon the death or abdication of the sultan. Ibrahim, for example, was so frightened when the vizirs came to announce his accession that he barricaded the doors and refused to let them enter until they brought the dead body of his brother.

The sultans were surrounded by fawning officials and courtiers, truckling women and slaves, jugglers, wrestlers, musicians, buffoons, dwarfs, eunuchs, soothsayers, astrologers, and servile literati. They usually found it impossible to differentiate the important from the petty and frequently were of a mentality that bordered upon derangement. Mustafa I was, in fact, quite mad, and Ibrahim's reign of eight years was one long series of wild caprices. Among many other things, the latter disrupted divan meetings, on one occasion calling out the grand vizir to purchase some carts of firewood for the harem kitchens. Ibrahim had a great passion for furs and commanded that the floors and walls of his apartments be carpeted and covered with sable.

In such an atmosphere intrigue flourished. Personal spies and agents, forgeries, intercepted letters, perjury, and malicious gossip became acknowledged techniques of government. Apparently, the executions of Suleiman's sons, Mustafa and Bayezid, resulted from machinations in the palace. Another evil of Ottoman society sprang from the slave system in the army and government. Separated from family and country at an early age, soldiers and officials of the court were trained to be loyal to the sultan and to serve him. Wealth, high office, and the sultan's favor were the rewards; the irresolute found the emoluments irresistible and were governed by mercenary motives. Earlier, Venetian envoys had remarked on the eagerness of Bayezid II's vizirs for rich presents and pouches of ducats. When the sultans could no longer command true respect from their slaves, officers, and bureaucrats, venality ruled, the power and services of the state degenerating rapidly.

The degradation of sultans, high officers of the state, and the military invited insubordination and rebellion from the rank and file of the armed forces. By the time of Mehmed II the janissaries and sipahis of the palace were already headstrong groups that had to be placated by monetary donations at festivals and, especially, at accessions of new sultans. The janissaries ordered the retirement of Bayezid II and frequently dictated policies in Suleiman's time. Beginning with the reign of Murad III, soldiers often stormed the palace to demand the head of a particular official, usually one who was obnoxious or corrupt and whose rapacity or incompetence inflicted hardship and injury upon them. Once this type of action proved successful, ambitious officials through clever propaganda instigated movements among the troops to remove rivals.

Equally debilitating were civil wars between different branches of the services and open revolts of garrisons or local forces in the provinces. Bad blood developed between the janissaries and the sipahi of the court. In the reign of Murad III warfare broke out in the streets of Istanbul. Under Mehmed III the janissaries, at the bidding of Safiye Baffo, broke the insubordination of the sipahi. Wishing to weaken the power of the janissaries, Osman II entered into war against Poland with the purpose of thinning the janissaries' ranks; he then intended to set out for

Anatolia to gather an army of Kurds and Turkomans to fight the janissaries, a project that led to his dethronement and murder.

The saddest chapter in seventeenth-century Ottoman history was the sixteen-year period embracing the reign of Ibrahim and the minority of Mehmed IV. Ibrahim, a voluptuary of the lowest type, commissioned a trusted woman of the harem to make the rounds of Istanbul baths to seek out special beauties and de-scribe their charms. Her master then contrived to install the more comely in his harem. No person and no property were secure against Ibrahim; he even seduced the daughter of the shaykh al-Islam. In 1648 the janissaries and ulema, led by the shaykh al-Islam, deposed Ibrahim as unfit to rule and placed his seven-year-old son on the throne. Ten days later when the sipahi rioted in his favor, the execu-tioners were sent to his cell. For eight years the Ottoman Empire was the scene of "court intrigue, military insubordination and violence, judicial venality, local op-pression and provincial revolt." Ibrahim's mother was murdered, and chaos de-scended upon Istanbul. Sultana Turhan, Mehmed IV's mother, saved the day for her son by appointing an old, experienced, and honest official (Mehmed Köprülü) as grand vizir with absolute power and authority.

With all the evil developments appearing in the Ottoman Empire there persisted evidence of a remarkable devotion to the government and a substantial body of capa-ble, trained, and right-minded officials. Even before the advent of Köprülü there were flashes of old Ottoman vigor. Murad IV was cast in the same mold as his ancestor Selim I, the conqueror of Egypt. At Murad's accession the treasury was empty, the coinage debased, and the soldiery of Istanbul unruly and lawless. His mother had tal-ent and energy and preserved the sultan's authority for several years until he became of age. In 1632 the sipahi rose in revolt, camped for three days in the hippodrome, and called for the heads of seventeen high officials, including the shaykh al-Islam and the grand vizir. The sipahi were appeased, but more heads were demanded. For two months terror reigned at the Porte. Murad perceived that his own turn might easily come unless he acted swiftly. Gathering a few faithful officers and obtaining the full support of the janissaries and the judges, he seized and executed the leaders of the rebellious sipahis and through vigorous measures restored a semblance of order and government to Istanbul and the provinces.

Twice Murad personally led expeditions eastward in Asia Minor. The second time, in 1638, he reconquered Baghdad from the Iranians, personally performing prodigious feats with his sword; but in the same year Yemen was lost to the Zaydi Shiite imams. As the years passed, however, he grew hardened to the presence of the executioner. Frequently through mere caprice he removed someone's head, perhaps just for crossing the road in front of him. Furthermore, he took to exces-sive drinking bouts which undermined his rugged physique and carried him to the grave at the age of twenty-eight.

THE FUNDAMENTALS OF DECLINE

The foregoing account of the hedonism and corruption that pervaded the upper reaches of the state might well lead one to explain the decline of the empire in terms of a Turkish proverb current at the time: "The fish stinks from the head." However, sultanic rot was not the entire story.

Until about the 1580s, life and society in the Ottoman Empire, especially in Istanbul and the central provinces, seemed to be stable and secure. Incomes were ensured, and prices were constant; food and goods were abundant; and optimism reigned. With this confidence and well-being, the population had increased over the century—40 percent in villages, 80 percent or more in towns and cities. Population pressure on the available land began to be felt, and deforestation ensued in much of Anatolia and the eastern Mediterranean area. The influx of people into cities was altering their character to the extent that rootless and volatile elements stood ready to respond to emotional situations, introducing a demoralizing instability and doubt.

Likewise, a smugness and an opposition to all innovation arose among so many of the ulema that education faltered and there developed an antipathy to inquiring theology and intellectual sciences. Those supporting innovation in thought or belief were anathematized by popular preachers from Istanbul pulpits. Song, coffee, tobacco, and intellectual sciences were attacked in the same breath with luxury, lax morals, and injustice, all as factors undermining religious faith. An uprising led by these preachers was quelled by Mehmed Köprülü, who exiled them. Murad III built an observatory in Galata in 1577 for astrological purposes but, with instruments as fine as any in Europe, the scientists used it for astronomy. Shortly thereafter an outbreak of the plague was attributed to God's vengeance against those who had penetrated His secrets. The shaykh al-Islam petitioned the sultan to have the observatory dismantled and without waiting, the janissaries leveled it to the ground. Fanaticism and stagnation triumphed along with anti-intellectualism.

The cultural and artistic life of the imperial court had continued at the high standards of the mid-sixteenth century for some decades, but decline became noticeable in a number of areas by the late seventeenth century. Originality of design and fineness of execution in Iznik pottery and tiles deteriorated, and some art forms stagnated, as in the case of miniature paintings. However, creative genius still remained. The great calligrapher Hafiz Osman (d. 1698) created a style that served as a basis of imitation for later generations; he influenced the imperial court directly, serving as a teacher for Mustafa II and Ahmed III. History writing for the sultans became institutionalized as the post of court chronicler was officially established.

Fireworks, public festivities, processions, and sumptuous luxury were on display to the public in Istanbul and Edirne, especially for the circumcision ceremonies of the royal princes. The widow of Sultan Ibrahim ordered the construction of a large mosque complex beside the Golden Horn, and Murad IV added impressive new buildings to the Topkapi Palace. Society was much affected by the use of tobacco, a new product brought to the Middle East by the English; it soon spread, and smoking was associated with the flourishing coffeehouses, despite the objections by the men of religion, many of whom despised it.

Despite some cultural accomplishments, military affairs were in fundamental decline as conquests ceased. For centuries the Ottomans had expanded on schedule, with the body politic living sumptuously on the conquests. But now Austria, Russia, Iran, the western Mediterranean, and North Africa were proving too removed, and campaigns in those areas too costly, to be pressed fully. When the conquests ended, not only did the elite find new incomes not forthcoming but the central government discovered many of the distant provinces a continuing expense. Treasury reports showed that empire was not a paying proposition.

Compounding this problem was the increased military sophistication of European forces, which created a growing need for improved Ottoman manpower and weaponry. Between Suleiman's accession to the throne and the end of the century, the janissaries increased from 8,000 to 38,000 and the sipahis of the Porte from 5,000 to 21,000. By 1600, the total of the sultan's household troops had grown to around 85,000, and they had to be paid in cash. Under Suleiman many native-born Turks entered these corps, and janissaries were allowed to marry so that by 1600 their grandsons were in the service. Spirit and merit were less significant. Moreover, the central and provincial governments formed new troops in Anatolia called *sekbans,* who had to be trained in the use of firearms. Money had to be found to pay the salaries of the larger armies, at a time when income was declining. When payless days arrived the sekbans ravaged the countryside. Joined by landless vagrant peasants, they, under the name of *jelalis,* menaced Anatolia from one end to the other for many years, beginning in 1595. These rampages left many dead and large areas deserted as people fled to Iraq, Iran, and Syria. Government troops finally gained control and inaugurated the policy of stationing salaried and privileged janissary contingents in the provinces. Almost immediately the janissaries joined the merchants, the guild masters, and the ulema in the upper class. They amassed great fortunes by tax-farming extortions, acquiring vast tracts of land and forcing villagers to become sharecroppers. From this janissary infusion came many of the local dynastic families that dominated the provinces in the eighteenth century, weakening the central government still more.

If not the root causes of all these changes of fortune, as some economic historians contend, at least major complicating factors were the massive influx of gold and silver into Europe from Africa and America, the ensuing monetary and price inflation, and the failure of the Porte to adopt a mercantile economy. The biggest impact of these changes came in the 1580s, producing tremors felt throughout the next century. Silver began to flood the market. In 1510, 1 gold coin equaled 54 silver ones, in 1580, still only 60; but by 1590 it took 120 silver coins to buy 1 gold coin, and by 1640, 250. Within twenty years wheat and meat tripled in price. People on fixed incomes—government officeholders, judges, janissaries, sipahi, endowment holders—were ruined unless they turned to bribery and corruption. For the central government it was fully as disastrous. In 1534 the treasury had an income of 5 million gold ducats, but by 1591 it was only half that, for taxes were levied in silver. To counteract this, new taxes were levied, tax farming was tried, and local communities were asked to make lump sum tax payments. Many of these measures had the effect of increasing the decentralization of the empire, and thereby exacerbating the fiscal crisis.

Domestically, the government tried to hold down prices in the face of tremendous increases in Europe. The resulting price differentials stimulated the smuggling of significant quantities of wheat, copper, wool, silk, and other raw and basic materials from the empire, producing local shortages and even greater inflation. Because of the enormous profits to be had, large farms conveniently located for this trade began to be oriented to an agrarian regime better suited to this massive commercialization. (However, small peasant possessors of land, not large landlords, continued to be predominant in the seventeenth century, especially in Anatolia and the Arab provinces.) Local industries were underfunded as capital for investment did not accumulate, even though credit was often available at rates of 10 to 20 percent; a higher rate of annual interest was labeled by the courts as usury and was condemned. The balance of trade was probably negative; precious metals flowed to India and Persia.

Against new Western mercantilist policies the Porte clung to an international free market, concerned only with providing the home market with an abundance of necessities. It encouraged imports and discouraged exports, prohibiting the export of certain commodities for fear of domestic shortages. It saw no danger in extending capitulations to foreigners to the point that by the eighteenth century Europeans controlled much of the carrying trade, even between Mediterranean ports of the empire. Muslims dominated most aspects of trade by land, and guild artisanal production was not yet substantially disrupted by European competition.

Social patterns and the relationships between the sexes apparently remained intact without major change. In seventeenth-century Egypt, Anatolia, and Syria, as presumably throughout the empire, women took part in court cases; frequently were owners and administrators of real property, mostly in the cities but occasionally including village farm land; inherited estates; and lent money. Women engaged in cottage industry, but seldom belonged to guilds, and males maintained their legal and political superiority.

The Ottomans saw little reason to change their society. In cultural, political, religious, social, and economic matters they were still convinced of their own superiority.

CHANGES IN THE PROVINCES

The political situation in the provinces varied tremendously from one region to another. As the central Ottoman government in Istanbul lost much of its power, local elites in many of the provinces gained more autonomy. They welcomed the "decline" of the dynasty and administration because it often resulted in an effective transfer of authority to themselves, as leaders of the great cities or tribes, and as provincial tax farmers or officeholders.

Local leaders remained within the Ottoman system: they acknowledged the overlordship of the sultans, used their names in the Friday noon prayers, remitted some revenues to Istanbul, provided troops for the imperial armies when called upon, and made no attempt to establish an independent foreign policy or to mint coins in their own names. The provinces closest to Istanbul, which were crucial to the provisioning of the capital and to providing money to the treasury, were especially closely supervised. They were more fully integrated into the Ottoman political and military structures than were the more distant lands. Some leaders did not follow this pattern, and a prominent example was Ali Janbulad (Jumblat), who led a rebellion in northern Syria aiming at real independence, suppressed only with the greatest difficulty in 1607. The Manid amir of southern Lebanon, Fakhr al-Din, similarly sought so much freedom of action in running his local administration as to provoke an Ottoman invasion and his ouster in 1633. Southern Iraq was autonomous for the first half of the seventeenth century, as tribes and local notables directed affairs; but it was brought more closely under Ottoman control after 1668.

Egypt was reorganized in the 1520s after a revolt. The viceroy of Egypt was appointed by the sultan as was the chief judge, while the revenues of local districts, especially those along the upper Nile, were farmed out to tax collectors. The sipahi and timar feudal system was not established in Egypt, and Ottoman military contingents in Egypt were soon rivaled by a revival of the old Mamluk military system. Ensuing competition for power among these groups turned the Ottoman governors into figureheads; real authority resided with the military contingents. Occasionally, when the local forces grew too anarchic or were perceived in Istanbul to be too strong, the central government would directly intervene. Following the insurrection of 1711, Ottoman power decreased, and the local forces dominated the country. However, justice was enforced in Ottoman Egypt in the seventeenth century with remarkable fairness; both holy law and secular decrees provided the bases for social legitimacy. The population of the larger Arab-Ottoman cities, in Egypt and elsewhere, increased from the sixteenth through the eighteenth centuries, despite political uncertainties and rivalries.

The vassal states of Moldavia and Wallachia in the northern Balkans were tributary to the Ottoman Empire. They acknowledged Ottoman overlordship, and in return the Ottomans granted them the right to elect their own rulers as long as they paid tribute, supplied food to Istanbul, and permitted some Ottoman garrisons on their territories. The local princes and nobles otherwise controlled their own affairs. Ottoman power in Transylvania was even lighter, as the amount of tribute demanded was small.

EXTERNAL AFFAIRS: EUROPE, THE MEDITERRANEAN, AND THE EAST

Even though there were occasional upsurges of reform and governmental strength and even though Europe was convulsed by bitter struggles such as the Thirty Years' War, external affairs of the empire fell moribund. For leaders at the Porte, however, it was campaigning as usual. The great victory of Ottoman arms in 1596 at Mezőkeresztes kept the Hapsburgs at bay. With each side worn out, peace was signed in 1606 on the basis of the status quo. This was the first time an Ottoman peace treaty had been negotiated outside the empire; and it was the first time the Hapsburg ruler was recognized as a fellow emperor who did not have to pay tribute. He did, however, make a single cash contribution of 200,000 Dutch guldens. Fortunately for the Ottomans, whose depleted treasury would have made further military engagements precarious, the Thirty Years' War soon engulfed the Hapsburgs.

The question of the security of the eastern Mediterranean was important and perennial. Wheat, barley, rice, sugar, and other vital supplies came from Egypt, as did an annual surplus revenue, sometimes amounting to half a million ducats. With Venice threatening the routes from Egypt because of her use of the new broadsided tall ships, one of which was the match of ten Ottoman ships, the Porte sought to capture Crete from Venice, and war began in 1643. In June 1656, one in a series of inept admirals, Kenan Pasha, whose only qualification was his position as son-in-law of the sultan's mother, led the fleet out of the Dardanelles to total destruction. Venice blockaded the Straits, failing to land on the Gallipoli peninsula only because of the fortuitous presence of an Ottoman force about to leave for the north. Istanbul was in panic: prices of foodstuffs soared, and property values slumped as many fled for Anatolia.

Ottoman weakness showed in other quarters as well. English and Dutch pirates had begun to operate in the Red Sea in 1613 and Ottoman forces in the Persian Gulf and Indian Ocean became ineffective. Cossacks in the north raided at will on the Black Sea. Meanwhile the sultans increasingly lost their hold on North Africa, which came to grant hardly more than the nominal gesture toward the caliph.

From 1578 to 1639, the Ottomans had repeated military adventures in the East. Aid from the Crimean khan kept them at Darband on the Caspian, and Kars was converted into a fortress and Eastern base in 1579. Baghdad, Mosul, and all of Iraq were formally annexed in 1586, and a favorable treaty in 1590 with Iran left Tabriz in Ottoman hands. But by 1603, Shah Abbas I had reorganized his army and had added cannon cast in Iran by the English Sherley brothers. Taking the offensive while the Ottomans were still engaged in Hungary, the shah captured Tabriz, much of the Caucasus, and Kars. In 1623 another Ottoman army was crushed and Abbas took Baghdad and the rest of Iraq. By the middle of the next decade, however, Murad IV had sufficiently revitalized the Ottoman army to take Erivan and to recapture Baghdad in 1638. The peace that was arranged in 1639 settled Eastern affairs for many years, leaving Iraq and Kars to the sultan and Azerbayjan to the shah.

Resurgence under the Köprülüs

The problems of state seemed beyond solution. But Mehmed Köprülü assumed office in 1656 with a ruthless determination to cleanse the government. In 1658, he repressed the rebel Anatolian governors who had defied the power of Istanbul and the janissaries since the 1620s. In five years of his grand vizirate some 30,000 officers, officials, judges, and theologians were executed for acts contrary to the interests of the sultan. His son Ahmed Köprülü succeeded to the post and remained grand vizir until his death in 1676. Restoration of law and order under these two vizirs revealed that the strength of the state had not been sapped beyond repair.

Although Mehmed IV gave himself up completely to hunting and to the harem, he remained steadfast in his support of the Köprülüs. In 1663 Mehmed placed the battle standard in the hands of Ahmed Köprülü, who then led the largest force assembled since the campaigns of Suleiman I to Belgrad and beyond. However, Ahmed Köprülü was repulsed at the renowned Battle of St. Gotthard in Austria.

Ahmed Köprülü then turned his attention to the island of Crete. In 1645 Ibrahim had ordered its conquest because Maltese pirates seized several Ottoman ships and took them to Crete under the shelter of the Venetian rulers. But Candia, the ancient Knossos, resisted sporadic Ottoman assaults for twenty years; to the Porte it became like a running sore. Köprülü conducted a three-year siege of Candia until it fell in 1669; and Crete, in Venetian hands since the Fourth Crusade, became an Ottoman possession.

Next, the scene shifted to Galicia, Podolia, and the Ukraine. Cossacks of the Dneiper and the Bug threw off their Polish yoke; joining the Tartars of the Crimea, they sought the protection of the Porte. When the cossack leader came to Istanbul in 1672, he received a two-horsetail standard from Köprülü and was named sanjakbey of the Ukraine. Poland protested; and the grand vizir led an army that forced Poland to surrender Podolia and the Ukraine and to pay an annual tribute of 220,000 ducats. Several more campaigns followed, and a treaty in 1676 incorporated Podolia and the Ukraine into the empire.

Three days after the signing of this treaty Ahmed Köprülü died. Unfortunately, Mehmed IV filled his place with his court favorite, Kara Mustafa. In 1683 he organized the last attack upon Vienna. Early in the spring the ambitious Kara Mustafa gathered as many as 200,000 men and marched north through Belgrad, reaching Vienna in the middle of July. For two months the army mined and bombarded the walls of Vienna, which were defended by a force of only 11,000 men. As September approached, the weakness of Vienna and the depletion of its garrison were obvious. The janissaries felt confident that Vienna would fall and fretted that the grand vizir did not order a full assault upon the walls. But Kara Mustafa held back, hoping that the city would surrender: if it did, its wealth would be his, whereas if the soldiers took the city by storm, it would be theirs to loot. He meanwhile ignored the information that King John Sobieski of Poland was approaching with an army of 70,000 to relieve the city. When Sobieski encamped on the heights outside Vienna, Kara Mustafa virtually dismissed his presence as a threat. The debacle occurred on September 12, 1683, with only a small portion of the Ottomans escaping. Kara Mustafa was subsequently executed by the sultan for incompetence.

RETREAT FROM VIENNA

In the next four years one calamity after another descended upon the empire. Venetians captured the Morea, Corinth, and Athens. In the siege of Athens the Ottoman defenders made their last stand on the Acropolis, which the Venetians shelled, exploding the Parthenon which was serving as a powder magazine. The Austrian forces pursued the victory at Vienna, took Budapest, and seized Hungary. In 1687 the loss of Mohacs so infuriated the Ottoman soldiers that they forced Mehmed's deposition and placed his next younger brother on the throne as Suleiman II. The new sultan, who had been incarcerated in the palace for forty-five years and had passed his time in study, did not know how to cope with the situation. Janissaries and sipahis rioted in Istanbul, partially sacked the city, and completely dislocated the administration; a sort of civil war broke out between sekbans and janissaries and Belgrad fell in 1688, Vidin and Nish, in 1689.

Previously when Ottomans had suffered reverses, they recouped their losses quickly and returned to fight in strength. This was notably true before Vienna in 1529 and at Lepanto in 1571. But the calamities of the seventeenth century left their mark upon the finances and institutions of Ottoman society, especially upon the military. Governorships were given to court favorites and estates were left vacant so that the income would devolve upon the governor. Governorships were sold to new courtiers every two or three years, and a succession of rulers seeking the money payments needed by Istanbul often led to overtaxation. The elaborate households of the provincial governors were an added expense.

When the call for a campaign was sounded, the feudal sipahis hid on their estates or bribed the commanding officer to excuse them. Only the poorest and weakest appeared for duty. At one time a census was ordered, compelling all sipahis in Europe to register in order to expose unfit and fraudulent fiefholders. Unfortunately, the inspectors were so incompetent that they could not distinguish a soldier from a pastry cook, and no one was caught. However, the number and quality of the sipahis were no longer as important as they had been, since few were equipped with up-to-date firearms and they lacked the new skills needed in warfare. Instead, many timars were sold or rented by the imperial government so as to gain the money to pay the sekban musketeers. By the eighteenth century there were only about 25,000 sipahis, and they were relegated to digging trenches and hauling cannons.

The degeneration of the janissaries, the sipahi of the court, and palace soldiers was no less deplorable. Captive boys and renegades diminished in numbers as the seventeenth century progressed; and the drafting of Christian boys ceased entirely during the reign of Murad IV. In his attempt to restore the vigor of the state, Ahmed Köprülü reinstituted the program and collected 3,000 boys in 1675, but the policy was dropped after his death. Free local Muslims, sons and grandsons of janissaries, and court officials joined the ranks; even jugglers, acrobats, and other unsuited persons were rewarded by membership in the privileged bands. Worst of all was the ignoring of merit in questions of promotion, for it meant that officers were not necessarily skilled in military affairs. Many janissaries had other occupations and were members of the corps only on payday. European commanders in the seventeenth century observed the mediocre leadership of Ottoman armies and outmaneuvered them time and time again. By the beginning of the eighteenth century the janissaries had become an ill-disciplined, oddly equipped, turbulent gang, more dangerous at the palace and on the streets of Istanbul and Edirne than against aggressors at the frontiers.

After the loss of Nish in 1689 Suleiman II recognized the desperate plight of his empire and appointed as grand vizir Mustafa Köprülü, brother of the late Ahmed Köprülü. The genius of the Köprülü family ran strong in the new grand vizir. He instituted financial measures that made it possible to assemble an army and regain Nish, Semendra, and Belgrad. Köprülü attempted again the following summer to drive the Austrians further back but lost his life in battle.

The energy of Mustafa II, an opponent of the Köprülü faction, brought a series of minor Balkan victories; but when faced by Prince Eugene of Savoy in 1697 at Zenta, the Ottoman companies were crushed, and Hungary and the lands north of Belgrad were lost forever. Meanwhile, the city of Azov surrendered to Peter the Great of Russia after repeated attacks.

TREATY OF KARLOWITZ

In the face of these reverses Mustafa called to the vizirate Husayn Köprülü. After much preliminary correspondence, negotiators met at Karlowitz north of Belgrad in modern Yugoslavia. Under the chairmanship of the English ambassador the Ottomans and representatives of the Netherlands, Austria, Venice, Poland, and Russia agreed on a general principle that each power should retain what it possessed. Peace was signed in 1699. In addition, the sultan reiterated that he would give his Christian subjects consideration and protection, as he always had. Venice gave up Athens, but retained the Morea and Dalmatia. Austria obtained Transylvania and Hungary with the exception of the Banat of Temesvar. Poland received the provinces of Kamenets and Podolia. As for Russia, only a two-year truce was signed; England wished to keep the Porte occupied with Russia to prevent Ottoman arms from supporting the French in the forthcoming struggle over Spain. Russian envoys, however, came to the Porte and agreed to the treaty of Istanbul in 1700, drawn up on the basis of their Karlowitz armistice.

Karlowitz domestically helped underline the weakness of the sultanate, and encouraged the rebels of 1703 in Istanbul to depose Mustafa I. Karlowitz marks a definite period in Middle Eastern history, especially in the relations of the Porte and Europe. First, it was a treaty with European states arranged by and participated in by one or more nonbelligerent powers, thereby acknowledging that all European states were rightfully concerned with questions of the Middle East. It recognized the interest and importance of the Russian tsars with respect to the Ottoman Empire and the Middle East. The treaty and the negotiations preceding it indicated the entrance of the sultan's Christian subjects into the diplomatic pouches of European foreign offices.

At the peace conference of Karlowitz, European emissaries carried on their negotiations largely through the Ottoman-Greek interpreter and assistant, Alexander Mavrocordatos, and carried away the erroneous impression that he was chief of the delegation. But his presence and evident role signified the change that was transpiring in the Ottoman government and its civil service. For a century the great majority of Ottoman officials had been Turks at least of the second and third generations. Many were not educated in the palace and their schooling was less secular than in previous generations. To be sure, they called themselves Ottomans, were proud of that distinction, and had a background and training quite different from most Turks living in Asia Minor. Yet more and more they became dependent upon Christian subjects, chiefly Greeks residing in Istanbul, for secretaries, interpreters, and counselors.

As for Europe, Karlowitz ended the fear of an Ottoman invasion of central Europe and opened an avenue for further European expansion toward Istanbul and the Straits. When Europe was engaged in its own internal struggles, Ottoman forces were able to win victories, but from the beginning of the eighteenth century, Ottoman armies and navies were no match for first-rate European soldiers. No longer was the Ottoman Empire a grave military question. As one writer aptly put it, her importance became diplomatic.

REFERENCES

Works relevant to this chapter are listed in Chapters 10, 13, 14, 15, 16, and 17.

Abu-Husayn, Abdul-Rahim. *Provincial Leaderships in Syria, 1575–1650.* Beirut: American University of Beirut Press, 1985. Traces the tangled web and diversity of Ottoman Syria, with attention to political history.

Bayerle, Gustav. *Ottoman Diplomacy in Hungary.* Bloomington: Indiana University Press, 1972. Presents documents written by pashas of Buda to Austrian officials and the emperor around 1590.

Cook, M. A. *Population Pressure in Rural Anatolia, 1450–1600.* London: Oxford University Press, 1972. A thorough examination of population trends of the period and their effects. Penetrating.

El-Nahal, Galal H. *The Judicial Administration of Ottoman Egypt in the Seventeenth Century.* Minneapolis, Minn.: Bibliotheca Islamica, 1979. This is a well-balanced and judicious examination of Ottoman provincial institutions.

Faroqhi, Suraiya. *Men of Modest Substance: House Owners and House Property in Seventeenth-Century Ankara and Kayseri.* Cambridge: Cambridge University Press, 1987.

Gerber, Haim. "Social and Economic Position of Women in an Ottoman City, Bursa, 1600–1700." *International Journal of Middle East Studies* 12 (1980): 231–244. A trailblazing study based on legal documents.

———. *The Social Origins of the Modern Middle East.* Boulder: Lynne Rienner, 1987. Traces the impact of landholding patterns in the Ottoman Empire from early days up through the twentieth-century Middle East. Important.

Griswold, William J. *The Great Anatolian Rebellion 1000–1020/1591–1611.* Berlin: Klaus Schwarz, 1983. A wide-ranging and convincing study of this question, including discussions of Syria and Ottoman policy toward the Safavids.

Heyd, Uriel. *Ottoman Documents on Palestine, 1552–1615.* London: Oxford University Press, 1960. Valuable source material.

Holt, Peter. *Egypt and the Fertile Crescent, 1516–1922.* Ithaca, N.Y.: Cornell University Press, 1966. Authoritative on Ottoman-Arab relations.

Inalcik, Halil. *Studies in Ottoman Social and Economic History.* London: Variorum Reprints, 1985.

Jennings, Ronald C. "Urban Population in Anatolia in the Sixteenth Century: A Study of Kayseri, Karaman, Amasya, Trabzon, and Erzurum." *International Journal of Middle*

East Studies 7 (1976): 21–57. An illuminating and comparative study, including discussions of minorities and neighborhoods.

Keyvani, Mehdi. *Artisans and Guild Life in the Later Safavid Period: Contributions to the Social-Economic History of Persia.* Berlin: Klaus Schwarz, 1982.

Kunt, I. Metin. *The Sultan's Servants: The Transformation of Ottoman Provincial Government, 1550–1650.* New York: Columbia University Press, 1983. An outstanding study of Ottoman administration.

Lockhart, Laurence. *The Fall of the Safavi Dynasty and the Afghan Occupation of Persia.* New York: Cambridge University Press, 1958. Deals largely with the eighteenth century. Excellent.

McChesney, Robert D. "Waqf and Public Policy: The Waqfs of Shah 'Abbas, 1011–1023/1602–1614." *Asian and African Studies* 15 (1981): 165–190.

Matuz, Josef. "The Nature and Stages of Ottoman Feudalism." *Asian and African Studies* 16 (1982): 281–292. An analytical approach to the subject, especially for the Balkans and Anatolia.

Monshi, Eskandar Beg. *History of Shah 'Abbas the Great.* 2 vols. Translated by Roger M. Savory. Boulder, Colo.: Westview, 1978. A monumental "insider's" look at Safavid court history.

Raymond, André. *The Great Arab Cities in the 16th–18th Centuries: An Introduction.* New York: New York University Press, 1984. A refreshingly written and informative survey that shows Ottoman-Arab cities to have had a variety of experiences hitherto not widely appreciated.

Rycaut, Paul. *History of the Turkish Empire, 1623–1677.* 2 vols. in one. London: Clabell and Roper, 1680. A detailed account by an eyewitness.

———. *The Present State of the Ottoman Empire.* London: Clabell and Roper, 1686. Really a third volume to the reference cited above.

Shaw, Stanford J. *The Financial and Administrative Organization and Development of Ottoman Egypt, 1517–1798.* Princeton, N.J.: Princeton University Press, 1962. Basically this is a study of Egyptian revenues and their relationship to the Ottoman treasury.

Tietze, Andreas, trans. and ed. *Mustafa 'Ali's Counsel for Sultans of 1581.* Pt. I. Vienna: Austrian Academy of Sciences, 1979. An Ottoman self-view of the causes of decline and corruption.

Welch, Stuart Cary. *A King's Book of Kings: The Shah-Nameh of Shah Tahmasp.* New York: Metropolitan Museum of Art, 1976. Sumptuous and beautiful.

Zilfi, Madeline C. *The Politics of Piety: The Ottoman Ulema in the Postclassical Age (1600–1800).* Minneapolis, Minn.: Bibliotheca Islamica, 1988. Discusses Sufism and puritanical movements as well as the careers of the ulema.

19

The Decline and Retreat of the Ottoman Empire

WEAK SULTANS

Most of the sultans of the eighteenth century were weak figures, unequal to the vicissitudes facing the empire. To cope with the corruption, inefficiency, incompetence, harem intrigue, vested interests, and indolence of the court, will power was required; to comprehend the policies of state, training and education were necessary. Each of the sultans, however, came to the throne after decades of confinement; none had opportunity to learn the art of statecraft or to develop an effective personality. Usually, his mother or the harem favorite dominated the government; and though clever and forceful, these women lacked the experience to conduct the business of government.

The training of about one-half of new officials took place in the households of major officeholders. The household factions formed by these associations dominated the key posts of government. Increasingly, the grand vizir and sultan called special councils, composed of prominent officials and leaders, to debate the severe problems facing the empire. By this means, some of the responsibility for different decisions could be spread among a wide number of people. Sultans also changed their grand vizirs so frequently (their terms averaged around seventeen months) that few of them were able to carry out any long-range projects. Ability within the religious establishment declined, and posts of high authority went to unqualified favorites of the ruler.

Many of the rulers were frivolous; Ahmed III was interested in birds and his tulip gardens, and was a patron of poets. Fortunes were spent on festivals and illuminations for the women of the court. Ahmed also had a more serious side—by balancing off his enemies against each other he regained a good deal of power for himself. He then embarked upon a naval reorganization and he expanded the feudal and standing armies.

Sultan Mahmud I loved literature and surrounded himself with second-rate poets and men of letters. The rest of his energy was devoted to building mosques, palaces, kiosks, and structures of questionable utility. Osman III, Mustafa III, and Abdul Hamid I were well along in years when they ascended the throne; and they proved to be mild, ineffectual rulers. The last may at least be commended for the freer life he permitted his nephew Selim, the heir apparent; for with Selim's accession in 1789 began more vigorous attempts at reform that marked the nineteenth century.

WARS WITH RUSSIA AND AUSTRIA

Austria and Venice contested the power of the Ottomans in the seventeenth century; and Russia replaced Venice in this role in the eighteenth century. Although Karlowitz ceded Azov and about eighty miles of hinterland, Tsar Peter was not satisfied. The Black Sea, the Straits—an outlet to the Mediterranean which would mean freer commerce with the West—and, most important, Tsargrad (Constantinople) all beckoned the Russians on against the Ottomans. When Peter led his army across the Pruth in 1711, he fell into an Ottoman trap. To escape, he accepted the famous surrender of the Pruth, which returned Azov to the sultan, razed all fortresses in the neighborhood, and relinquished the right to have Russian ships in the Black Sea. Ahmed III dismissed the grand vizir for agreeing to such easy terms when the Ottoman army might have destroyed Peter and crushed the Russians for decades.

Peace with Russia and Austria freed the Ottomans to regain their possessions lost to Venice at Karlowitz. The grand vizir swept Venice from the Peleponnesus in 1715 and proceeded to attack Venetian towns along the Adriatic. These victories enticed Austria to break with the Porte. Prince Eugene won several smashing engagements, capturing Temesvar and Belgrad. Britain, as eager as ever to mediate peace, arranged the treaty of Passarowitz of 1718, which ceded to Austria all the conquered territory but permitted the Ottomans to retain the lands taken from Venice.

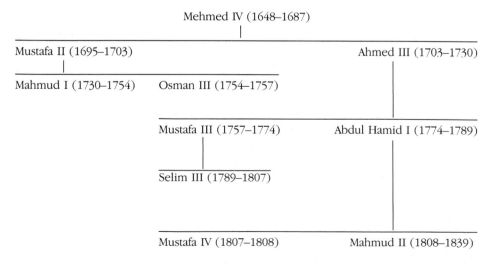

Ottoman Rulers, 1730–1839

Peace between Russia, Austria, and the Ottomans allowed the fun-loving sultan to begin a period known for its luxury, its love of flowers (especially tulips), its imitation of European styles, and its translations of works from Persian and Arabic as well as European languages into Turkish. Cultural innovations of all types flourished. A printing press began to issue books in Istanbul. Rococo decoration modeled on that of Europe abounded in the capital, just as Ottoman styles influenced Western European art and architecture. The new grand imperial mosques, fountains, and kiosks that were built reflected the elegance, grace, and lightheartedness of the rococo style as modified by earlier Ottoman traditions. Later, the famous poetess Fitnat (d. 1780), a member of a distinguished ulema family, wrote sonnets that celebrated such classic themes as tulips, roses, and the season of spring.

Cadastral surveys for land and fiscal demarcation were reinstituted after a lapse of a century. This and other measures raised the money needed for the imperial court, but they also caused mounting opposition to the sultan and his policies. Ahmed III was overthrown in 1730 after suffering a defeat by Iran, and his changes temporarily were suspended.

Further aggression against the Ottoman Empire resumed when Austria and Russia formed an alliance. Russia overran the Crimea and demanded the sultan's lands from the Danube to the Caucasus. The Porte refused, and Austria entered the fray. When an Ottoman resurgence in 1739 pushed the fighting back to the walls of Belgrad, the French ambassador skillfully engineered the amazing treaty of Belgrad, which returned that city to the Ottoman Empire. Even though Russia won great victories, she gained little: an unfortified Azov and permission to trade in the Black Sea area. For thirty-five years after the treaty there was peace in Europe for the sultans, although they fought several wars against Iran. The growing weakness of the Ottomans compared to European states remained unrevealed. In fact, by "depriving" the Ottomans of military experience and the necessity for new arms for a full generation, the treaty of Belgrad accelerated the decline. Internally, the Ottoman soldiers rejected the use of new weapons, such as the bayonet, because they would necessitate a military reorganization that would hurt the vested interests of the officers.

TREATY OF CAPITULATIONS

As trade with Europe increased substantially in the eighteenth century, it was governed by a series of agreements known as capitulations. France and England, and to a lesser extent the Netherlands, had valuable commercial interests in the Middle East. Ottoman wars with Venice, Austria, and Russia disturbed their trade, a factor that animated English, French, and Dutch mediation.

The trading privileges that the French enjoyed under the Mamluk sultans in Egypt since the treaty obtained in 1251 by Saint Louis were reconfirmed by Suleiman in 1528; and a regular treaty with France was concluded, though never formally ratified, in 1536, a treaty similar to those made with Venice, Florence, Naples, and Hungary, by Mehmed II and Bayezid II. The French treaty was reaffirmed in 1740. The significant points of the treaty of 1740, to which almost all similar treaties of later dates with foreign states refer, granted Frenchmen the right to travel and trade in any part of the Ottoman Empire. Frenchmen and their goods were exempt from all forms of taxation except ad valorem import and export duties, which were set at 3 percent. The French ambassador and consuls were recognized as having full jurisdiction over Frenchmen in the Ottoman Empire, and no Frenchman could be arrested by an Ottoman officer except in the presence of a French consular official. The French were allowed to possess and erect churches of their own and worship freely, special considerations being made for French pilgrims and monks in the Holy Land. The property of Frenchmen in the Ottoman Empire fell upon death to the French consul, who administered the estate of the deceased according to French law. Moreover, heirs were permitted to acquire and remove their inheritance.

Most important was the article that gave France the privilege of enrolling under her flag and her protection Portuguese, Sicilians, and others who had no ambassador or consul at the Porte. All Roman Catholics were considered and treated as Frenchmen, giving them a very special consideration among Christians in the Ottoman Empire. Furthermore, France and other nations which had such an article in their treaties (England, Austria, the Netherlands, and later Russia) could sell *berats* to Ottoman subjects—usually Greeks, Armenians, Jews, and Balkan Christians—extending trading privileges to holders of such documents. As a result of these provisions a large portion of the exterior trade of the Ottoman Empire was exempt from all control by the Porte.

TREATY OF KUCHUK KAINARJI

Upon the termination of the Seven Years' War in 1763 the powers of Europe were free to turn their attentions to Poland and the Ottoman Empire. They were, however, compelled to weave these ambitions into the general European diplomatic fabric. Louis XV sent Vergennes as ambassador and Baron de Tott as military adviser to strengthen the Porte's position against Russian pressure. Upon the advice of Vergennes, Mustafa III unwisely rushed headlong into war against Russia in 1768, when his demands with respect to Poland were not met. Since the Turkish armies were quite unprepared, the Russians occupied Jassy and Bucharest and within two years held all of Moldavia and Wallachia.

Meanwhile, a Russian fleet sailed unmolested from the Baltic to the Aegean where it proceeded to win a victory at Chios and to destroy the Ottoman fleet. Nonetheless, Baron de Tott had repaired the fortifications sufficiently to thwart the Russians, who sailed off to Egypt to threaten the Porte from that direction.

Russian successes in the Danubian provinces caused the Austrians in 1771 to sign a secret treaty of assistance with the Porte, pledging military support if the Russians crossed the Danube. Informed of this maneuver by the English ambassador, Berlin prevented war between Austria and Russia by speeding the partition of Poland among the three neighbors and simultaneously inducing Catherine II of Russia to relinquish her conquests on the Pruth and the Danube. Partition of the

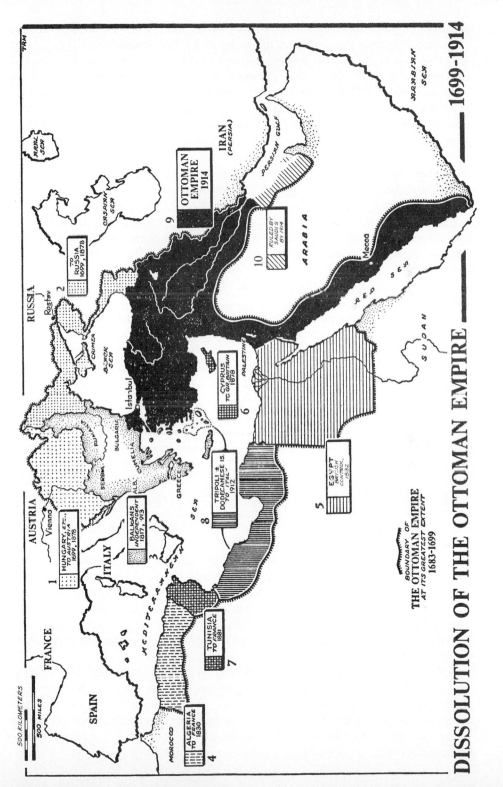

1699-1914

DISSOLUTION OF THE OTTOMAN EMPIRE

BOUNDARY OF
THE OTTOMAN EMPIRE
AT ITS GREATEST EXTENT
1683-1699

1 — HUNGARY, ETC.
TO AUSTRIA
1699, 1878

2 — TO RUSSIA
1699, 1878

3 — BALKANS
INDEPENDENT
1817, 1913

4 — ALGERIA
TO FRANCE
1830

5 — EGYPT
BRITISH
CONTROL
1882

6 — CYPRUS
TO GREAT BRITAIN
1878

7 — TUNISIA
TO FRANCE
1881

8 — TRIPOLI #
DODECANESE IS.
TO ITALY
1912

9 — OTTOMAN
EMPIRE
1914

10 — RULED BY
SAUDIS
BY 1914

Ottoman Empire was saved by the sacrifice of Poland! Desultory fighting came to a halt in 1774 upon the signing of the treaty of Kuchuk Kainarji.

This famous treaty was a landmark in Russo-Ottoman relations for nearly a century and a half. The sultan regained possession of Bessarabia, Moldavia, Wallachia, and the Greek islands, and Catherine's hold on Azov and the political but not the religious independence of the Crimean Tartars were confirmed. Navigation on the Danube was freed, and the Black Sea was opened to Russian shipping; but an Ottoman fort controlled the entrances of the Bug and the Dnieper on the Black Sea. A permanent Russian ambassador was accepted at the Porte; and Russian consuls could be stationed wherever the tsar thought necessary. The right of Russian pilgrimages to holy places was admitted.

Of particular significance for the future were two articles which stated in vague terms that the sultan promised to protect the Christian religion in his empire. More important, Russia as a "neighboring and sincerely friendly Power" could offer the sultan representations in behalf of his Christian subjects and could speak in favor of Bessarabia and the Danubian provinces. These two articles served Russia in the nineteenth century as useful wedges in her ambitions in the Balkans and the Straits.

The Ottomans reacted to the new military situation with a naval construction campaign, the building of a more modern artillery corps, changes in military education, and a purge of the janissaries so as to eliminate those who were soldiers in name only. French advisers provided new approaches to warfare, and traditional reforms were also undertaken.

PEACE OF JASSY

The actions and diplomacy of Austria were pursued to prevent Russia from gaining an advantageous position over the Ottoman Empire. As soon as the sultan agreed to the terms of Kuchuk Kainarji, Austria delivered her demand for the province of Bukovina as a reward for nonbelligerency during the Russian war. When Vienna ordered the occupation, the Porte recognized its helplessness and ceded Bukovina to the Hapsburgs.

For a decade and a half the sultan was left in peace, while Russia and Austria discussed the problems and possibilities of further Ottoman disintegration. By the treaties of Ainali Kavak in 1779 and 1784, Russia's role in selecting the khan of the Crimea for the "independent" Tartars was conceded, and the fate of the Crimea was established by annexation in 1783. Yet the "Greek project" of Catherine II and Emperor Joseph of Austria in 1782 marked the first specific design for partitioning the Ottoman Empire.

War broke in 1787. Austria and Russia won initial victories; but international complications in Europe and serious internal disorders in the Hapsburg realm enabled the Porte to obtain the peace of Sistova with Austria (1791) and the peace of Jassy with Russia (1792). The former returned the frontier to the status quo ante, but the latter allowed Russia to advance her frontier to the Dniester River.

The second (1793) and third (1795) partitions of Poland, the death of Catherine II (1796), and the outbreak of the French Revolution gave Selim III (1789–1807) a relief from European aggression. Napoleon's rise naturally implicated the Ottoman Empire in the wars and diplomacy of that era. Incidents and circumstances of those affairs, however, fall more into the pattern of nineteenth-century European imperialism in the Middle East. The radical upsetting of the balance of power in the world by Europe after 1815 was reflected in European intrigue and activities at the Porte. Meanwhile, significant changes transpired in the Ottoman Empire to weaken the state still further and to drive the entire Middle East to the brink of complete disintegration into petty political units.

DOMESTIC CHANGES

In the seventeenth and eighteenth centuries some feudal soldiers and managers of pious endowments hired tax farmers to manage the collection of revenues for them. Also, as the power of the central government's bureaucracy decreased, many tax farms were converted to positions whose incumbents held them for life. This further weakened the Istanbul administration, since it reduced the flexibility of making appointments.

Another change took place among the protected religious minorities as they began to come increasingly into contact with their coreligionists outside the empire. The Roman Catholic Church secured the allegiance of many Ottoman Christians; the new small Unitate churches, while linked with Rome, also preserved their own liturgies and customs as they learned more about the international ramifications of their faith. Among some of the Muslim men of religion, especially those in Mecca and Medina, there was a similar broadening of interest in reform of the faith. This found expression in a renewed study of hadith and a strengthening of Sufi brotherhoods.

One of the more baneful developments in Istanbul was the rise of the so-called Phanariotes. In the seventeenth century the residence of the Orthodox patriarch was established in a district bordering the Golden Horn, taking its name Phanar from the Greek word meaning "lighthouse." Earlier, most Greeks who served the sultan had become Muslims, but by the end of the seventeenth century it was no longer necessary for Greeks to adopt Islam to hold office. Out of this circumstance grew the term *Phanariot,* used to designate a Greek or Hellenized Christian in Ottoman service. (Most Orthodox Ottoman Christians were thoroughly under the control of the Greeks, even though such peoples as Bulgarians, Arabs, and Rumanians were not Greek-speaking.)

The ascendancy of the Phanariotes took place gradually in the last half of the seventeenth century. From the Phanariotes and their associates came patriarchs, bishops, bankers, dragomans of the Porte, ambassadors, and governors of Moldavia and Wallachia from 1714 to 1821. Of these posts, the most lucrative and therefore the most expensive to purchase were the usually short-term governorships of Moldavia and Wallachia. Consequently, Phanariot governors found it necessary to sell every office and favor, ruling over their subjects in a fashion more extortionate than that of the sultan in Istanbul. The local armies were abolished, intellectual contacts with central Europe decreased, and nobles completed the enserfment of the peasants. By the end of Phanariot rule the peasants had fallen to an estate lowlier than any in the Balkans. Certainly, the tone of society in Bucharest and Jassy was more corrupt and cynical than in Belgrad, Sofia, or Athens.

Yet the Danubian principalities remained the larder of Istanbul. Wheat, butter, cheese, honey, wax, lumber, horses, and livestock of every sort were sent to Istanbul. More than 500,000 head of sheep moved every year. As the production of Anatolia became less available, the Danubian provinces assumed greater importance as an imperial granary, especially after the loss of the Crimea. Certain portions were requisitioned by the palace; and much trade remained in the hands of Armenians, Jews, and Greeks. The frequent wars of the eighteenth century fought on Danubian soil and four Russian occupations increased the misery of the peasants by their wholesale requisitioning, by their spread of epidemics, and by the plundering and havoc of their ill-disciplined troops.

The Danubian principalities were much freer from the political and financial control of the Porte than most provinces of the empire. However, by the middle of the eighteenth century the process of disintegration had reached a point where any energetic and ambitious governor could build up his own independent military, political, and economic power and defy the commands of the sultan. Throughout the empire, the local wealthy urban elite families gained power as the central government's writ was progressively weakened, and the nomads moved into cultivated areas, thereby decreasing the number of villages and the taxes paid by them.

REBELLIOUS PROVINCES

To describe each one of the petty provincial lords and to relate the incidents of his rise to power and his local government would be monotonous and superfluous. In Europe the best-known were Ali Pasha of Janina, who ruled Epirus from 1788 to 1822, and Osman Pasvanoglu of Vidin, who terrorized the lower Danube from Belgrad to the sea. Both recognized the Porte's suzerainty and occasionally sent tribute to the sultan; yet, unlike the seventeenth-century local elites, each also regularly defied the central government and entered into diplomatic relations with European powers. They established order in their own areas, and their rule, though harsh, was at least less so than the circumstances created by the near anarchy that prevailed where robber bands and ex-janissaries held sway.

The most famous of the quasi-independent lords in other parts of the empire were the beys and deys (rulers) of the Barbary states of North Africa. Even in the sixteenth century, at the heyday of the sultan's power, the authority of the Porte in Algiers, Tunis, and Tripoli was never very imposing. In the eighteenth century, North African corsairs recognized the sultan's overlordship only to the extent of sending him an annual token gift.

With respect to the weakening of central government and the Porte's loss of revenue, the more significant developments of the eighteenth century occurred in

Egypt, Syria, Iraq, and Anatolia. The Mamluk system was never fully eradicated, and once the reins from Istanbul were loosened, it flourished again from 1711 to 1798. Ali Bey, the Mamluk leader of Egypt, secured total military and fiscal power, centralized the civil administration in his own hands, expanded contacts with Europe, and directed Egypt on an independent course, as when the Russians made overtures to him following the Russian fiasco in the Greek islands. In 1786 the Ottoman central government conquered Egypt again, but was unable to directly govern such a distant province, so it reverted to Mamluk control and ensuing economic decline. From 1704 to 1831 Baghdad was in the hands of a Mamluk dynasty, and Mosul was held for more than a century by the Jalili family. The al-Azm family ruled strongly on behalf of the central government in Damascus and adjacent areas, and they created there private homes of great splendor as well as some degree of administrative continuity and public order for the populace. Other families held Jerusalem; and Aleppo was so torn with strife and civil wars that between 1765 and 1785 hundreds of villages disappeared.

The most adventurous career was that of Ahmed Jezzar (Ahmed the "Butcher"). Of Bosnian origin, he obtained his nickname from his ruthless tactics when he was employed by Ali Bey of Egypt. Gaining the favor of Istanbul, he became pasha of Sidon and Acre (1785–1805), augmenting his territory later to include Damascus. Ahmed Jezzar Pasha maintained a private army of Albanians, Moroccans, and fellow Bosnians, built a fleet, suppressed the nomads, drastically increased taxes on the peasants, established monopolies, made commercial agreements with Western merchants, and created an efficient governmental organization. All this was done in the name of the sultan, and his policies gained Ahmed the approval of Istanbul.

Even in Anatolia an identical situation existed in the eighteenth century. *Derebeys* ("valley lords"), who were leaders of local families, seized power; and the central government was compelled to appease their whims in order to obtain any recognition of authority or any compliance with respect to law, taxes, and military support.

SEARCH FOR REFORM

Beset by foreign powers and enfeebled by internal political dissolution, the empire somehow persisted. In Istanbul and other cities the many trade and craft guilds served as a powerful bonding agent, giving individuals a sense of security and a definite place in society. (There were even guilds for prostitutes and pickpockets!) Guild members found their lives regulated by their guild, experienced their social life in the guild, and had their contacts with government almost exclusively through guild leadership. In the countryside, landowners avoided political association as much as possible, and peasants were concerned only with their landlords. Simple village life was the chief aim of the peasants.

Nevertheless, many Ottomans perceived that the state was stagnating and predicted that the future of the empire was surely doomed unless reforms were undertaken. Ex-officials of the government wrote treatises deploring practices that inevitably led to corruption and inefficiency. Notable essays on these points appeared in 1616, 1630, 1657, 1725, and 1777; each of them condemned most emphatically the practice of selling offices and recounted specific abuses by every official from the sultan down to the lowliest scribe. In a book written in 1725, a former imperial treasurer prescribed as a remedy a return to the higher ethical and moral values that had prevailed two centuries earlier in the reign of Suleiman.

No reforms could be initiated with any hope of success unless supported by the sultan. In fact, it was necessary that reforms should come from the hands of the sultan himself! Many sultans of the eighteenth century desired reforms but did not know how to inaugurate them. Selim III, who succeeded to the throne in 1789, introduced many innovations and hoped to change the course of affairs from further decay to progress and growth. But a reorientation of the government demanded the labors of many dedicated souls who understood Ottoman conditions in relation to the developments and advances unfolding in Europe. Also, the money needed for the changes was in short supply as the revenues available to Istanbul declined while the needs of the state grew.

ANARCHY IN IRAN

The weak Safavid shah Tahmasp II suffered several reversals at the hands of the Ottoman armies in 1731 and ceded Tiflis, Erivan, and Daghestan to the Porte. The real power in the land, Nadir, removed Tahmasp from the throne. After some further losses to the Ottomans, Nadir managed to revitalize his forces and effect the recovery of Tiflis and Erivan. Following the death of Peter the Great, the Russians evacuated Gilan, Baku, and Darband. Nadir was crowned shah in 1736 and he placed his capital at Meshhed, not far from where he had been a poor shepherd boy of the Afshar tribe.

Nadir owed his position to the strength of his army and his ability to lead. For several decades the state's economy had been worsening. Taxes on the peasants had doubled, excise taxes had greatly increased, and internal trade had been impaired by the anarchy within the upper echelons of government. A standing army with artillery and muskets had become so expensive that the only way Nadir could keep his regime in funds was through expansion and conquest. First he successfully pressed the Bakhtiyari chieftains in the southwest to accept his rule, many of them enrolling their armies under his banner. In 1738 he took Kandahar after having laid siege to it for over a year with an army of 80,000 men.

Nadir proceeded to Kabul, and through the Khyber Pass to India. Here he began to find rich stores of money with which to support his army. In 1738 he took Peshawar and moved on to meet the Mogul emperor at the Battle of Karnal, sixty miles from Delhi. Victory allowed him to proceed triumphantly into Delhi where the emperor handed over his immense wealth, most of which Nadir carried off to his treasure house near Meshhed. (The most famous trophy in this loot was the peacock throne, built of gold and covered with priceless pearls and jewels, which became the throne for the ruler of Iran. Another well-known prize was the Kuh-i-Nur diamond, later stolen by an Afghan general after Nadir's death and now adorning the British crown.)

On his return he occupied Herat, and in 1740 invaded the lands of the Uzbegs, taking Bukhara and Khiva. In 1744 he subdued the districts of Shirvan, Shiraz, and Astarabad with severity; and in 1745 his forces defeated an Ottoman army advancing from Kars, with its artillery and military stores falling to Nadir, who then concluded peace with Mahmud I. Nadir began to build a navy in the Persian Gulf, but this attempt was ultimately without result. The state that Nadir had begun to fashion was crumbling. A military adventurer, Nadir never appreciated the relationship between military means and political ends. He administered the state poorly, and coordination between military and civilian forms of power was nonexistent. His experiment in the restoration of Sunnite Islam was a failure. By the time of his assassination in 1747, he had become a bloody tyrant who marked his triumphs by having his victims' skulls stacked into high pyramids.

Immediately upon Nadir's murder, his army broke up into segments under various tribal groupings and leaders. For the better part of the following half century, Iran suffered under a frightful anarchy among contenders for the throne. The land was rife with massacres and wholesale blindings. When Kerman fell to Aga Muhammad, for instance, he ordered that 20,000 pairs of eyes be presented to him! Under the rule of Karim Khan Zand, who maintained his capital at Shiraz, there was a hiatus to this savagery. Karim had a sense of humor, was kind, upheld justice, and gave Iran two decades of calm and internal peace. He temporarily extended Iran's control over Basrah in southern Iraq and unsuccessfully tried to assert Iranian power in Oman, while all the time continuing his modest fiction of simply being the deputy of a puppet Safavid prince. But upon Karim's death in 1779 absolute confusion again engulfed Iran, with cities falling to one attacking force after another, in many cases suffering devastation that was felt up to the twentieth century. In 1794, Aqa Muhammad, the leader of the Qajar tribe which had been one of the *kizilbash* tribes to support Shah Ismail in 1500, won out over all rivals, and his chief residence of Tehran became the capital of Iran. This shah, who had been castrated at the age of five by Nadir's nephew, nevertheless established a Qajar rule that held sway in Iran until 1921.

REFERENCES

Important for this chapter are books cited in Chapters 13, 15, 16, 17, and 18.

Abou-El-Haj, Rifaat Ali. *The 1703 Rebellion and the Structure of Ottoman Politics.* Istanbul: Netherlands Historical-Archaeological Institute, 1984. In addition to a detailed account of the rebellion, this valuable work contains an analysis of the Ottoman Empire in the seventeenth century.

Anderson, M. S. *The Eastern Question, 1774–1923: A Study in International Relations.* London: Macmillan, 1966. A detailed study of European diplomacy as it related to the Ottoman Empire.

Barbir, Karl. *Ottoman Rule in Damascus, 1708–1758.* Princeton, N.J.: Princeton University Press, 1980. An excellent study showing the subtlety of Ottoman-provincial relations.

Cohen, Amnon. *Palestine in the 18th Century: Patterns of Government and Administration.* Jerusalem: Magnes Press, 1973. An authoritative study.

Crecilius, Daniel. *The Roots of Modern Egypt: A Study of the Regimes of Ali Bey al-Kabir and Muhammad Bey Abu al-Dhahab, 1760–1775.* Minneapolis, Minn.: Bibliotheca Islamica, 1981.

Fisher, Alan W. *The Russian Annexation of the Crimea, 1772–1783.* Cambridge: Cambridge University Press, 1970. Based on Russian and Ottoman archival materials, this work shows that the idea of Russian liberation of the Crimea was a myth.

Hurewitz, J. C. *The Middle East and North Africa in World Politics: A Documentary Record.* Vol. 1. *European Expansion, 1535–1914.* New Haven, Conn.: Yale University Press, 1975. The first volume of the three-volume revision and expansion of his earlier work. Indispensable for scholars working in the field of Middle East and North African studies.

Itzkowitz, Norman, and Max Mote, trans. and annot. *Mubadele: An Ottoman-Russian Exchange of Ambassadors.* Chicago: University of Chicago Press, 1970. The reports and diaries of the two ambassadors going to Istanbul and Moscow, 1775–1776. Very interesting, illuminating in regard to court life and problems of travel.

Jelavich, Barbara. *History of the Balkans.* Vol. 1. *Eighteenth and Nineteenth Centuries.* Cambridge: Cambridge University Press, 1983.

Levy, Avigdor. "Military Reform and the Problem of Centralization in the Ottoman Empire in the Eighteenth Century." *Middle Eastern Studies* 18 (1982): 227–249.

Naff, Thomas, and Roger Owen, eds. *Studies in Eighteenth Century Islamic History.* Carbondale: Southern Illinois University Press, 1977. Sixteen chapters by various experts on government, economy, and culture, mostly in the Ottoman Empire.

Pallis, Alexander. *In the Days of the Janissaries.* London: Hutchinson, 1951. A good account of the janissaries in their later days.

Perry, John R. *Karim Khan Zand. A History of Iran, 1747–1779.* Chicago: University of Chicago Press, 1979. Outstanding discussion of political, military, provincial, economic, and external events as they affected Iran in the second half of the eighteenth century.

Rafeq, Abdul-Karim. *The Province of Damascus, 1723–1783.* Beirut: Khayats, 1966. A detailed work that emphasizes the decline of the Ottoman regime.

Salibi, K. S. *The Modern History of Lebanon.* New York: Praeger, 1965. From the seventeenth century to recent days, the author covers the period of the eighteenth and nineteenth centuries in considerable detail.

Seton-Watson, R. W. *A History of the Roumanians from Roman Times to the Completion of Unity.* Cambridge: Cambridge University Press, 1934. A good summary of the history of the Danubian provinces under the Phanariotes.

Sumner, B. H. *Peter the Great and the Ottoman Empire.* Oxford: Blackwell's, 1949.

Thomas, Lewis V. *A Study of Naima.* Edited by Norman Itzkowitz. New York: New York University Press, 1972. A perceptive study of the life, ideas, and contributions of the great Ottoman historian and chronicler of the late seventeenth and early eighteenth centuries.

Voll, John O. "Hadith Scholars and Tariqahs: An Ulama Group in the 18th Century Haramayn and Their Impact in the Islamic World." *Journal of Asian and African Studies* 15 (1980): 264–273.

Part Three

European Imperialism in the Modern Middle East

20

The Era of the French Revolution and Napoleon

SELIM'S REFORMS

In the month preceding the convening of the Estates General at Versailles which ushered in the French Revolution, Selim III was girt with the sword of Osman, and a new era in Ottoman history opened. Selim took his position seriously and desired to restore the power of court and governmental authority. That he thought of himself as a reformer in a modern sense or regarded the changes that he sought in terms of progress is doubtful. But he did understand that techniques pursued in Russia and the West had unquestionably placed great power in the hands of the ruler and his government.

In 1789, Selim was about twenty-seven years old and had studied more widely than most of his immediate predecessors. At first, wars with Austria and Russia tied his hands. The French Revolution, however, dissipated the attention of the European powers, gave the Ottoman Empire a few years of respite from Western imperialism, and offered Selim an unexpected opportunity to show his true character.

In the central government Selim sought to curb the powers and intrigues of the grand vizir by reorganizing the imperial divan to consist of twelve ministers and by commanding that it be consulted on all important measures. Specialized commissions and advisory councils, each for a particular matter, were formed, and the divan ministers were ordered to consider their recommendations. One of the greatest difficulties in administering any reform was the lack of officials who thought of their position as anything but an opportunity for personal profit at the expense of the state and the people.

In the provinces Selim found that his word received little heed and foresaw that reforms would prove ineffectual unless a thorough transformation could be carried out in the army. The janissaries and standing cavalry had degenerated into virtual worthlessness; the training and weapons of all were hopelessly obsolete.

Following the peace of Jassy, Selim recruited a corps of 600 men, who were outfitted in the current European military garb and trained in European tactics. When Selim suggested to the divan that the janissaries adopt similar uniforms and be drilled in the same manner, he was able to appease mutineers only by withdrawing the request.

Selim instituted similar reforms in the old army units by reorganizing the financing of the army and giving the administrative and financial duties of the commanders to other officers, thus allowing the agas to concentrate on military aspects of their leadership. Fortunately, French revolutionary governments sent several of the latest pieces of artillery, munitions, artillerymen, and army engineers to advise in the use and manufacture of the new pieces and drill sergeants from French regiments to organize and train a new Ottoman army.

A new force, called Nizam-i Jedid (Army of the New Order), came into being about 1792, almost accidentally, and grew slowly, first hardly more than a toy for Selim's amusement. By 1801 there were over 9,000 men and 27 officers in the new army; in 1807 there were 23,000 men and 1,600 officers. But because of the rapidity of this expansion, training and discipline were superficial, and many of the troops were idle much of the time. Since a majority of the recruits came from villages, they were unaccustomed to a regulated and confining life; they became unruly and took to plundering Istanbul suburbs. The janissaries refused to adopt any "Christian" devices and objected to serving alongside the Nizam-i Jedid. Thus these troops played only a token role in the 1806 and 1807 campaigns against the Serbs and Russians, leaving the main fighting to the ineffective janissaries and sipahis.

Selim encouraged the founding of schools, especially engineering academies, which he felt were necessary adjuncts to any military reform. The Imperial Naval Engineering School included courses in naval architecture at the insistence of the French naval architect Le Brun. The arsenal was improved, and by 1798, forty-five naval vessels had been launched, including three large ships of the line. In all, there were twenty ships of the line and twenty-five frigates with 40,000 sailors. The navy could compete with European fleets whereas the army could not. At Tophane a cannon foundry was built and a new gunpowder plant set up north of Istanbul where supplies of good quality were manufactured. Other scattered technical improvements included the founding of the naval school of medicine and the reintroduction of printing establishments which made possible the printing of mathematical and technical books, some translated from Western sources.

There is no evidence, however, that Selim felt a need for innovative social, economic, and political reforms to support these military and technical changes. To improve foreign and economic policy, permanent Ottoman embassies were sent to London, Paris, Vienna, and Berlin, and commercial consuls were named to many Western cities. The published reports of many of the Ottoman ambassadors contributed to the limited, but growing, Ottoman knowledge about conditions in Christian Europe. Ottoman artists also came to follow European conventions and methods in some fields, as seen in book illustrations, landscape painting, and architectural decoration, but not in such cultural areas as music and literature.

Selim sought greater government efficiency and therefore issued orders to reduce the number of officials, doing away with the positions of many who did no work. He increased taxes, debased the coinage, seized private property, and melted down all gold and silver utensils, sending the bullion to the mint. But these measures were merely palliative, leading to inflation, hunger, and, ultimately, economic disaster. In Istanbul laws to regulate costumes of persons according to creed, profession, trade, and position were openly flouted. To reduce violence and disorder on the streets, Selim demanded that laws be enforced, including those regarding sumptuary rules for clothing according to personal status, and even went out in disguise to catch offenders himself. Another attempt to bring law and order to the capital and to reduce its burgeoning population was an edict to cut down on the number of taverns and coffeehouses, to forbid the building of any new hotels or lodging houses, and to send idlers back to their villages. When grain became scarce, Selim controlled the supply and the trade: bakers had to buy their grain and sell their bread at fixed prices. Many of the reforms failed because of the sultan's personal weakness and lack of determination; the reforms lapsed entirely when General Napoleon Bonaparte invaded Egypt.

NAPOLEON INVADES EGYPT

The sultan's authority in Egypt had been only nominal for nearly a century. As the power of Istanbul waned, Mamluks grew wealthy and independent.

Ostensibly, Bonaparte invaded Egypt to destroy the Mamluks, who were proving so troublesome to his ally Sultan Selim III. However, Bonaparte's real objectives are shrouded in mystery even today. Claims have been put forward that the French looked upon the campaign as an attack upon Britain and the route to India, which the French had so recently surrendered to England, and believed that the possession of Egypt would widen the French sphere in the Mediterranean and offset the loss of India. In view of Napoleon's known regard for the importance of Istanbul, perhaps he intended to take Egypt and thence move upon Istanbul, the Balkans, and Austria.

In any case, Bonaparte, accompanied by engineers, historians, archaeologists, architects, mathematicians, chemists, and Egyptologists, set sail in May 1798 to take Malta and Egypt. He landed on July 1, took Alexandria on July 2, and defeated the Mamluks at the famous Battle of the Pyramids outside Cairo on July 21. His fleet, however, was destroyed by the British at Aboukir Bay; his line of supply was thus cut and his freedom of action impeded.

Since Egypt was a province of the Ottoman Empire, the attack brought a declaration of war from the Porte, which joined with England and Russia in a coalition against France—an alliance whose terms scandalized the ulema, who considered the treaty as too subservient to the infidels and contrary to the Holy Law. Selim gave Ahmed Jezzar command of the army in Syria, and a fleet and army were collected at Rhodes for the relief of Egypt. Napoleon marched on Syria in 1799 in the hope that discontented Muslim Arabs, Druzes in Lebanon, and Christians in Syria would rise against the Turks. He took Gaza and Jaffa, where in cold blood he murdered 2,000 Turkish prisoners. But Jezzar, with reinforcements landed by an English squadron, held off Napoleon's attack at Acre. Repulsed there, Napoleon hurried to Egypt to meet a landing of Ottoman infantry and cavalry at Aboukir Bay. These he drove into the sea, regaining mastery of Egypt. He then deserted his troops and sailed for France, where he executed his famous coup d'état.

The French forces remaining in Egypt were not conquered or evacuated until 1801. Several Ottoman expeditions, in collaboration with an English army and naval squadron, forced the surrender of the French and gave them a guarantee of safe-conduct home. British forces held Egypt and prevented the several local competing factions from open warfare until the peace of Amiens in 1802 required the departure of the British. At that point Muhammad Ali, leader of one of the Ottoman factions, took advantage of the prevailing political and military anarchy and set the course of his meteoric ascent. His rise was of great significance for the Middle East, but it separated to a very marked degree the affairs of the Nile from those of Istanbul.

At the time that the peace of Amiens was concluded, agreement was reached between Selim III and Napoleon. Selim was also at peace with England, Russia, and Austria. Trade revived in Ottoman ports, and shipping was brisk on the Black Sea and the Bosphorus. The Russians and British, however, used every device to offset French influence and to gain the Porte as an ally for their European policies.

UPRISING IN SERBIA

Upon the general establishment of peace in Europe, Selim expected to proceed with his reforms, but calamity befell him in Serbia. The treaty of Sistova had provided for the return of Belgrad and its environs to the sultan; but it also stipulated that the janissaries, who previously ruled the area in a most ferocious manner, would not be permitted to return. Selim's new governor gave Serbia the most peaceful, prosperous, and enlightened rule she had known for nearly a century. However, to appease Pasvanoglu Pasha of Vidin, Selim agreed to the return of the janissaries to Belgrad in 1799. Murdering the enlightened governor, four janissary leaders defied Selim's authority and divided Serbia among themselves. Outrage upon Christians and Muslims followed outrage, until there occurred the famous uprising of 1804 against janissary rule.

Aided by Austrian arms and led by Kara George, Serbian insurgents were successful in destroying the janissaries. Selim sought to reestablish Ottoman rule in Belgrad, but the Serb leaders insisted that the terms of settlement be supervised by an Austrian commissioner. Selim declared he could not consent to foreign interference in domestic affairs, and Austria refused to break the treaty of Sistova. When the Serbs then turned to Russia for recognition, the Porte sent troops against the rebels. Victorious, the Serbs organized a provisional autonomous regime and again defeated the Ottomans. In 1806 the outbreak of war between the Ottoman Empire and Russia enabled Serbia to clear Ottoman arms from the entire province. Thereupon Serbian affairs became a part of the European tangle of international diplomacy and power politics.

When Selim removed the two pro-Russian governors of Wallachia and Moldavia, replacing them with pro-French officials, Russia invaded the Danubian provinces in 1806, and the Ottomans declared war and closed the Straits to Russian ships. Britain cooperated with Russia by assembling a squadron near the mouth of the Dardanelles and sending it into the Sea of Marmara to lie near Istanbul. With Russian troops invading Moldavia, the Porte considered a peremptory rebuff of the British unwise. While the sultan's ministers spun out the negotiations, military engineers hurriedly repaired the defenses of the Straits, and before escape became impossible the British retired from their foolhardy venture.

OVERTHROW OF SELIM

A change of equipment for the garrisons on the Bosphorus incited the janissaries to demand the dismissal of the divan. And since payments due them were in arrears, the janissaries overturned their soup kettles, the traditional sign of revolt. The ensuing uprising by unruly and idle janissary trainees precipitated Selim's deposition and the elevation of his cousin Mustafa IV in May 1807. Formal charges against Selim were that he incited revolution by military innovations and that he had fathered no children after more than seventeen years of rule.

As has been indicated, Selim did not possess the resolute will and ruthlessness necessary to cope with the turbulence of the age. Surrounded by self-seeking, dishonest, insubordinate, and often traitorous officials, his every act was thwarted; he realized that his only hope was to play one faction against another. Each suggested innovation jeopardized some vested interest, the most perceptibly threatened group being the janissaries whose distress brought his downfall. The masses were agitated over prices and by fears of uprisings in many of the provinces. French and Russian promises and threats kept everyone on edge, and the presence of a growing number of Europeans in influential positions introduced a pervasive leaven that disturbed the political elite. Selim's removal from office was nearly inevitable.

Mustafa IV was a mild and ineffectual person, the puppet of those who had overthrown Selim. Although the French officers and technicians were dismissed, the new sultan sent Napoleon a present of ten fine horses to indicate friendship for France—an amity that led to a truce between Russia and Turkey. The truce, however, was disastrous for Mustafa and the rebellious janissaries, since it freed the Ottoman armies on the Danube. An Ottoman army of Bosnians and Albanians, commanded by Bayraktar, governor of Ruschuk, marched on Istanbul and camped near the capital. Bayraktar called many leaders to his camp and in July 1808 moved upon the city and the palace. Before Bayraktar's men could force the gates, Mustafa executed Selim and gave orders for the strangling of his own brother Mahmud. The insurgents, however, imprisoned Mustafa and placed on the throne Mahmud II, who had been hidden in an empty furnace of the palace.

MAHMUD II AND THE NAPOLEONIC WARS

Mahmud II gave the office of grand vizir to Bayraktar, and the movement for reform proceeded along the lines drawn by Selim. After the organization of a new Europeanized army Bayraktar permitted his Bosnians and Albanians to return home. Thereupon the janissaries rose up and destroyed Bayraktar. Civil war raged in the streets of Istanbul for a week, with serious fires, explosions, and chaos, during which Mustafa was executed. Mahmud, now the sole surviving male of the Ottoman dynasty, was fairly safe; but friends of the janissaries controlled the government, and military reforms were out of the question.

The French and Russians were furious as Mahmud seemed to favor Britain; and the tsar sent his troops to the Danube, taking Silistria, Ruschuk, Nicopolis, and Sistova. These victories were valueless, however, because in 1811 the break with Napoleon was foreseen and operations in the Balkans came to a halt. Luckily for Russia, the treaty of Bucharest was signed a month before the French attack on Russia was launched. If this had not been the case, the Porte might have obtained better terms. Mahmud II dismissed the grand vizir and executed the negotiators for giving Bessarabia to the tsar.

The treaty abandoned the Serbs to the sultan, who pledged that Serbs could manage their own internal affairs. The Russian regiment left Belgrad, and the Turks attempted to rule the province. Although Kara George departed, a new leader, Milosh Obrenovitch, continued the Serbian revolt. The Congress of Vienna in 1815 allowed the Serbs to retain their arms and gave them a voice in the management of their own government through an elected parliament. The sultan's suzerainty over Serbia was hardly more than a legal fiction, as most of the taxes that the Serbs collected remained in Serbia. Despite this, the Ottoman Empire in 1815 successfully weathered the wars and cataclysms of the French Revolution and Napoleon. Bessarabia was lost; a semiautonomous regime was legalized in Belgrad; and two sultans were slain by military revolts. But little change resulted in the internal organization of the empire. Nonetheless, the seeds of nationalism and reform were sown by wide movements of men and ideas, and a growth in commerce raised incentives to a new high.

The Ottoman Empire was on the threshold of a new century and a new life.

THE QAJAR DYNASTY IN IRAN

The Shiite Qajar tribe of northern Iran was a major player in the chaotic struggle for power in eighteenth-century Iran. Aqa Muhammad Shah of the Qajars, who won out in 1794 over other rivals for the throne of Iran following the demise of Karim Khan Zand in 1779, had as a child been captured and castrated. Subsequently freed, he had gained ascendancy in the leading Qajar clan as a young man and then passed many years as a political hostage at the court of Karim Khan. In the commotion over Karim's death Aqa Muhammad made his way to Tehran, where he organized a force, drove the Russians from Ashraf in 1781, and had so strengthened his position that by the fall of Kerman in 1794 major resistance to Qajar rule was eliminated in the central Iranian lands.

Aqa Muhammad, attacking the Georgians and their Russian allies, took Tiflis and Erivan. When the Russians in 1796 occupied Baku and Darband, his position would have been quite hopeless had not Catherine the Great's death that year brought about a Russian withdrawal. He managed to pacify Kurdistan and subdued parts of Khurasan and fortified it against Uzbeg forays.

Aqa Muhammad was generally recognized to have had four passions: power, avarice, revenge, and hunting, the greatest being power. He has been described as a "conniving, vindictive, cruel, and stingy misanthrope." Widely cursed in Iran by his own people, he was murdered by his personal servants in 1797.

Aqa Muhammad had chosen as his successor his nephew Fath Ali. Governor at Shiraz at the time of his uncle's assassination, Fath Ali hastened to Tehran by forced marches while a Qajar general held the throne for him. Scions of the Afshar and Zand tribes made bids for the throne, but Fath Ali had an army and the throne which gave him sufficient edge to overwhelm them. Whenever a Qajar shah died, and even prior to the Qajars, several contenders, within and outside the royal family, always battled for the imperial turban and plunged the state into disorder. Two centuries earlier the central government's acquisition of artillery and muskets gave the opposition little chance, but at the outset of the nineteenth century many forces and contingents in Iran possessed these weapons and could seriously question any designated heir. Eventually, however, the throne passed more peacefully, even though the government's army, largely consisting of cavalry, was weak. British and Russian contingents more or less guaranteed a regular succession, since they preferred the status quo.

The monarchy was the dominant feature of Iranian politics, and the shah's word was law, final at the court and within the central government. If he made prudent decisions, the state prospered; if he made unfortunate ones, all suffered. But Iran was not truly unified: there was no social cohesion, and the absolutism of the shah was a myth. Within the royal family and among the elite there remained almost complete self-interest and self-indulgence, with little sense of nation and even less concern for the welfare of Iran. In addition, the cleft between Turk and Tajik (old Iranian stock) reached such proportions that some even predicted dismemberment of the state. Each faction was inordinately proud and each despised the other.

The shah had power over the central government and some authority over taxation but his capricious actions were made tolerable throughout Iran by corruption, distance, and inefficiency. There were almost no railroads in Iran until after World War I. Between the urban centers of the central provinces there were vast stretches of hostile or barren countryside controlled by nomadic and seminomadic tribes, which the central government in Iran found impossible to bridle until the advent of the airplane after World War I. Inefficiency was everywhere, and outside of Tehran the government did little beyond collect revenue.

The general population in Iran in the nineteenth century disliked the Qajars and on the whole looked to their religious leaders for inspiration and guidance. The ulema held considerable power for several reasons. Shiite theology allowed more leeway for the ulema and religious judges to interpret the Koran and the traditions, and gave rulings by religious jurists on legal and political matters a force often greater than those made by Qajar officials. The ulema frequently mediated confrontations arising between cities and provinces, since the central government could not manage such an arduous task. Even Fath Ali Shah, an avowed tyrant, maintained a close and lasting association with many of the ulema and welcomed, at times, their participation in governmental matters. He knew that an appearance of piety was useful and sometimes necessary. He built mosques and commissioned theological works. To the great pleasure of the ulema, he also suppressed the Sufi orders, which never subsequently became real rivals for religious leadership of the masses. The ulema also possessed great wealth, as well as undisputed religious leadership. The wealth was derived from the taxes that all Shiites were obligated to pay directly to them as well as from rich endowments scattered across the land. Another factor in the power wielded by the ulema was that the recognized center of Shiite thought and jurisdiction lay in centers in Ottoman Iraq outside of Iran and beyond the reach of Qajar power.

Diplomacy in Iran

For Fath Ali and his ministers Russian power and aggression engendered apprehension throughout his entire reign. During the French Revolution and the Napoleonic Wars in Europe, French, British, and Russian envoys and military missions journeyed to Tehran vying for Iranian favors and alliances. The French were looking for aid against the British in India, and the British were cajoling Iran to stand firm against France. The Russians sometimes were allies of the French and usually opposed the influence of the British. After Napoleon had been defeated, the British had a greater interest in Iranian policies, since to a certain degree India's northwest frontier was more peaceful when Iran blocked Russia and held the Afghans in check.

Until 1805, British missions to Tehran and Fath Ali's to Bombay discussed relations with the Afghans. French approaches in 1805 proposed that Fath Ali sever his undertakings with the British and invade India with French support. At the same time an alliance against Russia was suggested with the idea of French aid in regaining Georgia from Russia. Sent to France to undertake negotiations, Prince Reza caught up with Napoleon at Tilsit and signed the treaty of Finkenstein in May 1807. By its terms, Iran pledged to declare war on Great Britain, to incite the Afghans to attack India, and to grant French troops right of passage across Iran; the French meanwhile recognized Iran's right to Georgia, agreeing "to compel Russia to relinquish Georgia," and committed a military mission to Tehran. General Claude Gardane and seventy officers and technicians soon arrived to train the Iranian army in European warfare. This was a monumental task, compounded by the poor pay of the soldiers, the absence of any heavy artillery, and the tribal composition of the fighting units.

Sorely disappointed by the treaty of Tilsit because it contained no mention of Iran, Fath Ali did not declare war against Great Britain. In 1809 the British envoy presented the shah with an exceptionally large diamond and signed a treaty that promised an annual subsidy to Iran as long as Great Britain was at war with Russia and pledged a mission of British officers to train the Iranian army. General

Gardane was given his passport to leave and the British sent a fine contingent of officers. One in particular, Captain Henry Lindsay Bethune, an artillery officer who was six feet eight inches tall, so captivated the Iranians that he remained there for many years and became commander in chief of the Iranian army. The shah sent one of the princes to London to learn how the substantial subsidy was to be paid and from these negotiations the treaty of Tehran of 1814 was signed. According to this treaty all alliances between Iran and European powers hostile to Great Britain were null and void; Iran agreed to induce the rulers of Bukhara and other places to prohibit armies from marching against India; frontiers between Iran and Russia were to be determined by Iran, Russia, and Great Britain; and a large subsidy was to be given each year to Iran by the British minister resident in Tehran. Frequently called the Definitive Treaty, this arrangement was the basis of relations between the two countries for many years.

The previous year the treaty of Gulistan, signed with the Russians, ended the war of 1804–1813 that had been declared a jihad by the ulema, and ceded Georgia, Baku, Shirvan, Armenia, and other areas in the Caucasus, with the stipulation that Iran would have no navy on the Caspian Sea. It also committed Russia to support Prince Abbas, son of Fath Ali Shah, for succession to the throne. Vagueness in the treaty of Gulistan led to border warfare and in 1827 the Russians captured Erivan and Tabriz. The important treaty of Turkumanchai of 1828 signaled the definitive loss of the Caucasus to Russia, provided certain indemnities to Russia, and most significant, gave Russians capitulatory rights in Iran, rights that soon were extended to other Europeans.

REFORM IN IRAN

Even before the Gardane mission arrived in Iran, Prince Abbas as governor of Azerbayjan had been reorganizing the Iranian army along European lines. Russian officers were employed to train the soldiers of this "new army," the Nizam-i Jadid, who were recruited on a permanent basis with fixed pay, disciplined and dressed as European troops, and equipped with modern weapons. They were similar to the New Army of Selim III in Istanbul, and the ulema in Iran, who were gaining in power and self-confidence, objected to them just as those in the Ottoman Empire had. (Prince Abbas drilled with the new soldiers but had to do so in private so that his religious faith would not be questioned.) French officers replaced the Russians in 1808, only to be replaced in turn by the British, who continued in the role of military advisers for several decades. Prince Abbas began many other reforms in Tabriz and was most energetic in improving the systems of taxation and justice. He also encouraged the production of local cloth. These changes represented the first elements of westernization and modernization in the social structure of Iran. Small groups of students were sent to Europe. However, Abbas fell ill and died suddenly in 1833, to be followed the next year by his father, Fath Ali Shah. Thus, in 1834, Prince Abbas's son Prince Muhammad, who had been residing at Isfahan, was urged by the British and Russian ambassadors to proceed to Tehran and take the throne. Supported by troops from both countries and a large financial grant from Great Britain, he ascended as Muhammad Shah. The new shah's grandfather, Fath Ali Shah, at his death had left 53 sons, 46 daughters, and 784 grandchildren. The number of his progeny and the length of his white beard were his claims to fame; his summer palaces near Tehran at least provided some degree of beauty for the few permitted to enjoy them. With such a large royal family, Muhammad Shah would have had difficulty in surviving the bitter rivalry for the throne had it not been for the aid of the British and the staunch support of General Sir Henry Lindsay Bethune.

REFERENCES

Among volumes already cited, those of particular value for this chapter are in Chapters 13, 16, and 19.

Atkin, Muriel. *Russia and Iran, 1780–1828.* Minneapolis: University of Minnesota Press, 1980.

Bier, Carol, ed. *Woven from the Soul, Spun from the Heart: Textile Arts of Safavid and Qajar Iran, 16th–19th Centuries.* Washington, D.C.: The Textile Museum, 1987. This beautiful book helps put the textiles of Iran in their social and historical settings.

Eton, William. *A Survey of the Turkish Empire.* London: Cadell & Davies, 1799. An interesting and useful contemporary account.

Fasa'i, Hasan-e. *History of Persia Under Qajar Rule.* A translation by Heribert Busse of *Farsnama-ye Naseri.* New York: Columbia University Press, 1972. This is a detailed native account of the Qajar dynasty and rule to 1882. Factual, anecdotal, and illuminating.

Findley, Carter V. *Bureaucratic Reform in the Ottoman Empire: The Sublime Porte, 1789–1922.* Princeton, N.J.: Princeton University Press, 1980. An able analysis of the transformation of the scribal service into a civil bureaucracy; also discusses with great insight the general political transformation of the Ottoman Empire.

Kelly, J. B. *Britain and the Persian Gulf, 1795–1880.* Oxford: Clarendon Press, 1968. A monumental work of the first order dealing with the British interest and activities on all sides of the Persian Gulf during this period.

Landen, Robert G. *The Emergence of the Modern Middle East: Selected Readings.* New York: Van Nostrand Reinhold, 1970. Very useful readings of original documents in translation; concentrates on the Ottomans and Arabs.

Lewis, Bernard. *The Muslim Discovery of Europe.* New York: W. W. Norton, 1982. A fascinating account of Muslim views of Europe as seen in language, media, scholarship, religion, culture, and on a personal level.

Puryear, Vernon J. *Napoleon and the Dardanelles.* Berkeley: University of California Press, 1951. A comprehensive work on the diplomacy of the Middle East during the period of the French Revolution and Napoleon.

Shaw, Stanford J. *Between the Old and New: The Ottoman Empire Under Sultan Selim III, 1789–1807.* Cambridge, Mass.: Harvard University Press, 1971. A comprehensive description by a leading authority.

Temperley, Harold W. V. *England and the Near East.* Vol. 1. *The Crimea.* London: Longmans, Green, 1936. An indispensable work covering the years from 1808 to 1854.

21

Mahmud II: Nationalism and Reform

THE GREEK REVOLUTION

One of the exciting legacies of the French Revolution to the Middle East was the rise of the Greek nation. Eighteenth-century liberal Europeans wished to emulate ancient Greek society and culture; they particularly admired Greek political ideas. Therefore, when Greeks came into contact with Europeans at the turn of the century, they were impressed with their own heritage and fostered an intellectual and literary renaissance of significant proportions in all Greek communities, from Odessa to Marseilles. Before 1820, over 3,000 different books had been published in modern Greek. These included not only translations of the important works of Voltaire, Goethe, and Montesquieu but also renditions of the ancient Greek classics into a form which modern Greeks could read and understand.

Outstanding Greek intellectual patriots roused their countrymen to arms and formed a society to raise money and munitions to cast off the Ottoman rule. They glorified the heroic deeds of ancient Greeks and advanced the reconstruction of modern Greek by condemning foreign words and abandoning colloquialisms and barbarisms that had crept into the ancient tongue. The labors of such patriots would have been fruitless had it not been for the Greek Orthodox Church, which preserved the identity of the Greek community, and for Greek schools, everywhere present to train churchmen and incidentally to teach many to read and write Greek. As Greeks became prosperous, they founded more schools, and many pursued advanced studies in Italy and France. After the fall of Venice in 1797, the Greek cultural center moved to Vienna, where a Greek press published books and newspapers that circulated wherever Greeks went.

The decay of the Ottoman government gave rise to many outlaw bands in the mountains of Greece. They fired the Greek spirit and created a nucleus of Greeks familiar with the handling of weapons. Also, as in antiquity, many Greeks were drawn to the sea and foreign commerce; and their knowledge of the ways and languages of the Middle East proved extremely beneficial in trade between Ottoman and Mediterranean ports. During the Napoleonic Wars they reaped enormous profits.

In 1814, a group of Greeks in Odessa founded a secret band named Philike Hetaeria ("Friendly Society") to organize a rising against the Turks. Similar to contemporary European secret societies, the Philike Hetaeria grew rapidly with the commercial depression after 1815. Its members could not be restrained; and in 1821 Alexander Ypsilantis, a distinguished Phanariot Greek and a general in the Russian army, unfurled the banner of revolt.

He crossed the Pruth River from Russian Bessarabia into Moldavia. This was not the most propitious spot to launch a Greek revolution, since the native Rumanians hated Phanariot Greeks as much as Turks, and local Rumanian notables had gained a good deal of autonomy from the Ottomans. Turks in Galatz and Jassy were impaled, and the leader of a simultaneous Rumanian peasant revolt was killed by Ypsilantis. Bankers were blackmailed. The Great Powers induced Russia to strike Ypsilantis's name from Russian army rolls and disown the adventure. When an Ottoman army drove him from Bucharest he deserted his followers and fled to Hungary.

Within a few weeks of the crossing of the Pruth, the revolution was in full swing in the Peloponnesus. From Kalamata to Patras to Corinth, Turks were massacred and the population of surrendered towns put to the sword. When Tripolitsa, the Ottoman capital, fell, over 8,000 Turks were butchered. Athens, except for the Acropolis, fell, as did Mesolonghi and other towns on the northern shore of the Gulf of Corinth. Immediately the Turks fought back; on Crete and some of the Aegean Islands reprisals and counterreprisals were common.

The rebellions in the Danubian provinces and the Peloponnesus led Mahmud II to take action against suspected Hetaeriaists in Istanbul. A number of leading Phanariotes were executed, and on Easter Sunday the Greek patriarch was hanged from the gate of his residence by janissaries despite his denunciation of the rebels. Of all the Aegean islands, Chios with its famous mastic gardens was the most wealthy, and its inhabitants showed no interest in the uprisings on the mainland. Early in 1822, however, Greek adventurers took over the island against the wishes of the Chiotes. Thereupon, an Ottoman admiral landed. Greek sailors counterattacked in vain. The Turks leveled villages, put Chios to the torch, and massacred nearly 25,000 Greeks, scattering the rest to all parts of the world. Shortly thereafter, Turks surrendered the Acropolis in Athens on the pledge that their lives would be spared. The promise was not kept.

One of the factors that had led to these uprisings was Sultan Mahmud's decision to settle some scores with Ali, the rebellious pasha of Janina. Indeed because Ottoman forces were weak and dispersed, Mahmud's withdrawal of the best of his soldiers to subdue Ali virtually ensured Greek success. A strange mixture of eighteenth-century European enlightenment, Oriental splendor, and devotion to ancient Greek literature, Ali had ruled as a benevolent tyrant for thirty years, corresponding with Napoleon and negotiating with British governors of the Ionian Islands. In 1820, Mahmud sent an army to Epirus to bring in his head. During this campaign the Ottoman garrisons in Athens, Tripolitsa, and other Greek towns were reduced to the barest minimum, leaving the towns defenseless against a popular uprising. When, however, Ali Pasha's head and those of his sons and grandsons were exhibited on a silver platter outside the sultan's palace in Istanbul in 1822, Mahmud's forces intimidated the Greeks. The sultan's forces were considerably spent, but the Greeks were torn already with dissension.

INTERVENTION BY EGYPT AND THE POWERS

The European Great Powers looked upon the Greek activities with uncertainty and considerable misgivings, but philhellenic committees in England and France compelled their governments to take an interest in Greek affairs. Furthermore, the Greek provisional government obtained in 1824 the first of a series of loans from British bankers, a move that guaranteed a continuing interest from London. Considerable romantic publicity accompanied the enlistment of veteran European soldiers, especially philhellenes. The most famous of these was Lord Byron, whose death in 1824 at Mesolonghi created more sentiment for the Greek revolution than any other single event in the long struggle.

In 1824, Mahmud commissioned his powerful vassal of Egypt, Muhammad Ali, to aid in suppressing the insurrection. His son Ibrahim was appointed governor of the Peloponnesus and set out to subjugate his new charge. He proceeded to establish his authority by fire and sword. Meanwhile, an Ottoman army subdued western Greece and recaptured Athens. Greek independence seemed very doubtful.

The victories of Mahmud's lieutenants hastened the intervention of the Powers. Various preliminary discussions suggesting local Greek autonomy led to the treaty of London, signed in 1827 by England, Russia, and France. In this treaty the three demanded an armistice from Turkey and the Greeks and the mediation of any differences. Since Mahmud refused to declare an armistice, Admiral Codrington was ordered to intercept, with cannon balls if necessary, all supplies and reinforcements destined for Ibrahim. The Battle of Navarino on October 20, 1827, completely shattered Egyptian and Ottoman naval forces, and a French army compelled Ibrahim to withdraw.

Russian interests in Greece were tied to the affairs of Serbia and the Danubian provinces. Even before Russia agreed to the London treaty, an ultimatum had been delivered to the Porte demanding cession of Kars and other eastern provinces; evacuation of Moldavia and Wallachia, whose governors would be elected for seven-year terms by the native aristocracy and could be removed only upon Russian consent; and immediate autonomy for Serbia. On the last day of grace Mahmud accepted the terms, which were incorporated in the convention of Akkerman of 1826.

After the destruction of the Ottoman navy at Navarino, Russia could not resist taking advantage of Ottoman weakness. A peculiar kind of war was declared in 1828: Russia became a belligerent in the Balkans and the Black Sea but remained a neutral in the Mediterranean. One army advanced in the Caucasus with considerable success, taking Ardahan, Bayezid, and Erzurum; another took Varna and Burgas on the Black Sea, crossed the Balkans, and entered Edirne.

TREATY OF ADRIANOPLE

Upon the advice of Prussian and British envoys Mahmud sought peace. The treaty of Adrianople (Edirne) of 1829 reestablished the frontiers much as they had been before the war, and compelled the Ottomans to pay a heavy indemnity to Russia. The Straits were open again to Russian trade. The Danubian provinces no longer had to supply corn, wood, and mutton to the sultan's government; only the annual tribute to the Porte was continued. Governors held their posts for life and ruled in consultation with native assemblies. The ties with the Ottomans were reduced to a minimum, and Russia moved into the vacuum.

Other provisions of the treaty stipulated that the articles of the convention of Akkerman should be put into immediate effect. Another article declared that the Ottomans adhered to a second treaty of London which England, France, and Russia had concluded earlier in 1829 and which established an independent Greek kingdom. In consequence of its inclusiveness the treaty of Adrianople was an important landmark in Balkan development as well as in the relationship of the Ottoman Empire to the great European states.

DESTRUCTION OF THE JANISSARIES

An event of vaster proportions and ramifications, however, preceded the treaty of Adrianople and was in part responsible for it. In 1826, Mahmud destroyed the janissaries. For more than 300 years sultans found the janissary corps unruly; and since the beginning of the seventeenth century these soldiers frequently vetoed policies of state, and grand viziers were beheaded at their behest. Through the eighteenth century several of the sultans contrived to modernize the army and equip the janissaries with more efficient weapons, but each scheme was successfully rebuffed. Since the sultan's authority in the provinces was continually snubbed by recalcitrant governors, a reliable standing army had to be created before he could reassert his power. The modernization of the army became even more urgent as Ottoman units met with Austrian and Russian regiments, to which they compared adversely.

Selim lost his life in the attempt to modernize the army. Mahmud plotted more warily. Although Ali Pasha of Janina and Muhammad Ali of Egypt possessed competent standing armies, the sultan depended upon janissaries and feudal levies.

Ottoman artillery was carefully improved, and more than 14,000 artillerymen were gathered in Istanbul. When the blow was readied, Mahmud had the loyalty of the artillerymen, the grand vizir, the shaykh al-Islam, the chief of the janissaries, and a sizable force of Anatolian levies stationed across the Bosphorus.

In 1826, Mahmud forced the divan to order some janissaries to drill in European fashion. The revolution broke, as was expected. The artillery mowed down the janissaries as they charged the palace and then shelled their barracks into a mass of ruins, burying 4,000 beneath the rubble. Victory was followed up in the provinces, where many janissaries were hunted down and either exterminated or completely scattered. New troops were ordered to be assembled, and Mahmud planned to organize and train an army of 40,000. Although the Russian attacks in

1828 and 1829 were launched before the new troops were trained and weakened them permanently as the Russians had hoped, Mahmud rid his state of an anachronism that had considerably retarded the process of change in the empire. It was a first step in destroying the power of the governors in outlying provinces and in rebuilding the centralized control that had proved so effective in the fifteenth and sixteenth centuries. Other reforms could now occur.

MUHAMMAD ALI AND MAHMUD II

But there was hardly any time for sound reform. Peace was no more than established when Mahmud faced rebellion and serious attack by Muhammad Ali, his vassal in Egypt. The actions of this dynamic newcomer affected Mahmud's empire profoundly, particularly in its relationship to the Powers.

For lending aid to the sultan, Muhammad Ali had been given an outright promise of Crete and of the governorship of the Peloponnesus for his son Ibrahim. The latter promise did not endure, however, because the Powers established the kingdom of Greece; and Crete by itself was inadequate, so he diverted his attention to Syria, which he requested for Ibrahim in lieu of the Peloponnesus. Since some reward in Syria was originally offered for the Greek adventure, this request seemed appropriate. When Mahmud refused, Muhammad Ali invaded Syria on the pretext that such action would coerce Abd Allah of Acre to subserve the sultan and would chastise him for harboring Egyptian conscript dodgers and practicing the arts of extortion upon Egyptian merchants.

Ibrahim meanwhile waged a combined land and sea attack upon Acre, which finally fell in 1832 after a prolonged siege and several bloody assaults. Mahmud hardly lifted a finger to aid Abd Allah; Ibrahim easily routed an Ottoman army collected near Homs; and in rapid succession Damascus, Aleppo, Adana, and Konya were occupied by the Egyptian army. Up to this point the Powers were unconcerned; France even looked with favor upon the expansion of Muhammad Ali's territory. When Ibrahim defeated the main Ottoman army near Konya and pushed on to Kutahya, however, Mahmud grew frantic and begged the Powers to rescue him. Only Russia responded. Early in 1833 a Russian fleet anchored in the Bosphorus, and 14,000 Russian marines landed to protect Mahmud from his vassal and to guarantee the concessions and treaties the Russians had obtained from the Porte since 1774.

Meanwhile Russian and Ottoman envoys in Cairo were discussing peace terms, while French diplomatic and consular agents were pressing Mahmud to accept some of the Egyptian demands. Compromises were effected. Syria, including Damascus and Aleppo, was assigned to Muhammad Ali on condition that he pay an annual tribute; he was also to retain Adana, which would give him easy access to the Taurus passes and Anatolia. Ibrahim's troops were recalled from Anatolia. The Russian fleet and troops, however, postponed their departure from the Bosphorus. Two days before they reembarked from the Bosphorus village of Hunkiar Iskelesi, where they had encamped, a treaty was signed that shocked the other European powers and achieved for Russia a long-sought goal. The treaty of Hunkiar Iskelesi of 1833 was a straightforward alliance between Russia and the Ottoman Empire, providing for perpetual friendship, peace, and mutual assistance. The provocation lay in a secret article, which did not remain unknown very long, stating that upon Russian request the sultan would close the Straits to the extent of "not allowing any foreign vessel of war to enter therein, under any pretext whatsoever." Although diplomats questioned the significance of the secret article, the value of Hunkiar Iskelesi to Russia, and the objection of the Powers, rested on the right of Russia to interfere in Ottoman affairs "to the exclusion of the alliance and intervention of the Powers."

MAHMUD'S REFORMS

Whereas England and France recognized immediately the advantage won by Russia and initiated action to recoup their losses, Mahmud used the peace he had so dearly purchased to carry forward the reform of his government. Destruction of the janissaries and the formation of new troops, termed Muslim Soldiers, were only publicized aspects of his military innovations. The abolition of feudalism ruined the cavalry and levies upon which sultans had greatly depended and which had proved valuable for Mahmud. Income from fiefs now went directly to the treasury, and officers of the sultan enlisted recruits from these areas. The best sipahis were enrolled in four new squadrons of cavalry and the rest were pensioned. A group of Prussians participated in training Ottoman officers; other Ottomans studied at Woolwich in England. Military and medical colleges were opened in 1830; and a national militia was organized in 1834 to give rudimentary training in the provinces. Connected with these colleges and previously established engineering schools were primary and secondary schools where a secular education was given to prepare students for advanced training. Mahmud in 1824 declared a primary education compulsory for all, but means for carrying out this decree never materialized. The best primary-secondary school was the one attached to the medical college at Galatasaray. With instruction given in Turkish and French, it became the precursor of one of the more influential forces for the education of leaders of the country in the latter part of the nineteenth century. Another important preparatory school with instruction in Turkish and French was connected with a newly established school of military sciences. Medicine, mathematics, and physics were now seen, understood, and taught as in western Europe; old concepts in these fields gradually faded away.

Since the ulema had opposed previous attempts at reform, Mahmud attempted to silence them. In 1826 he gave an office building to the shaykh al-Islam and created it as a regular department of government; courts for Muslim subjects came under its authority. However, the appointment of teachers and the control of schools passed to the new Ministry of Education and the selection of judges and the administration of law went to a Ministry of Justice. Even more damaging to the ulema, and to the chief officers of the state who also had their own pious endowments, was the creation of a Ministry of Pious Foundations to which was given the income of most religious and charitable endowments. This ministry collected the funds and paid out what was needed to the various foundations, placing the remainder in the treasury. Sufi orders' financial independence was attacked. Bektashi Sufi leaders were exiled and the order's buildings confiscated, supposedly because of the order's heretical views, but actually as part of the suppression of the janissaries. However, Sufi houses remained in the possession of Bektashis in parts of the empire, even in Istanbul, until the twentieth century. The fez was adopted as the headgear for government officials. The frock coat was also adopted. And within a few years the fez, the frock coat, trousers, and black leather boots became the standard dress in urban centers. When the shaykh al-Islam objected, Mahmud removed him, giving public notice of his earnestness in these matters.

Changes in the military were the means to strengthen and reorganize the government. The independent local lords in Anatolia were checked, Iraq was subdued in 1831, and other governors began to feel and respect the sultan's authority. To a certain extent the war with Egypt resulted from Mahmud's desire to project his power into every corner of the realm. As a further curb on local rulers, governors were forbidden to execute anyone without referring the case to Istanbul. This removal of the death sentence from a governor's whim gave people throughout the empire a deeper sense of security.

In addition to ministries already cited, two bureaus within the office of the grand vizir were cut off and formed into ministries: Foreign Affairs, and Civil Affairs. This development took away the power of the grand vizir as a supreme and all-powerful deputy of the sultan and made him a prime minister, for a number of years holding this title instead of that of grand vizir. Even when the latter title was restored, the grand vizir remained merely chairman of the Council of Ministers. One of the more important innovations came after the Greek revolution when Greek Phanariotes were no longer trusted to serve as translators and interpreters for Foreign Affairs. Within a few years a translation bureau was attached to the Ministry of Foreign Affairs, and officials in this bureau became significant members of the government, many later in the century rising to be grand vizirs. Every department of government was staffed by some better-trained civil servants. Better salaries lessened bribery, and more attention was given to promotion on merit. Many sinecures were abolished and much governmental red tape was eliminated.

To a significant degree the changes that were instituted came as a result of closer contact with the West. The first steamship arrived in the Golden Horn in 1828, and within a few years regular schedules were established between Istanbul and western Mediterranean ports. The time of a trip from France was cut from a month to twelve days. Thus, the 1830s saw an influx of Western visitors, merchants, and missionaries joining Istanbul and other Ottoman coastal cities to the West as nothing previously had ever done. As a result, European techniques of government were studied and employed in many ways.

The end of the wars with Russia and Egypt left the empire almost bankrupt. Foreign observers commented on the great wealth and bountiful produce of the country but inefficiency in the collection of taxes reduced the sultan to penury. Under new procedures the central government tried to assume direct responsibility and sent out its own agents or tax farmers, thereby reducing the number of hands through which the taxes passed. New roads improved trade, and Muslims were encouraged to enter business by the abolition of the Court of Confiscations in which the government seized the property of an exiled or condemned individual. Creditors henceforth felt less personal danger in pressing the government and its high officials for the payment of debts. In general, these measures were effective. By the end of Mahmud's reign, European consular officials were reporting that the empire had progressed remarkably in the preceding twenty years, despite numerous outbreaks of epidemic diseases and some recurrent famines.

Mahmud also recognized the stimulus to reform that a general circulation of books and newspapers would generate. Presses were established in Istanbul and Izmir, publishing with those of Muhammad Ali in Egypt several thousand books in Turkish and Arabic between 1830 and 1840. The military and medical colleges introduced many young Ottomans to French and German literature of the eighteenth and nineteenth centuries. Newspapers in French were founded in Izmir in the 1820s; and in 1832 the first Turkish newspaper appeared in Istanbul with official support from Mahmud.

The Ottoman Empire found in Mahmud a sultan whose high ability in the craft of ruling broke the conservative and reactionary grip held by special interest groups upon the government and society. In later decades of the nineteenth century the progress of reform might seem slow and uncertain. Yet after Mahmud's changes a return to the old order was impossible, and a liberalizing movement prevailed.

REFERENCES

Works containing material pertinent to this chapter are cited in Chapters 13, 18, 19, and 20.

Barnes, John Robert. *An Introduction to Religious Foundations in the Ottoman Empire.* Leiden: Brill, 1986. An excellent discussion of the origins of pious foundations, the Ottoman land system, and the actual administration of the foundations.

Clogg, Richard. *A Short History of Modern Greece.* 2d ed. Cambridge: Cambridge University Press, 1986.

Cunningham, Allan. "The Sick Man and the British Physician." *Middle Eastern Studies* 17 (1981): 147–173. Europeans who visited or commented upon the Ottoman Empire are thoroughly discussed.

Keddie, Nikki, ed. *Sufis, Scholars and Saints: Muslim Religious Institutions Since 1500.* Berkeley: University of California Press, 1972. A fine collection of articles dealing with the learned and popular aspects of Islam in various parts of the Muslim world.

Lewis, Bernard. *The Emergence of Modern Turkey.* London: Oxford University Press, 1961. An account of the development of Turkey in the nineteenth century that is first-rate.

Lewis, Geoffrey. *Turkey.* New York: Praeger, 1960. A standard work that is very reliable.

Puryear, Vernon John. *France and the Levant from the Bourbon Restoration to the Peace of Kutiah.* Berkeley: University of California Press, 1941. A history of diplomacy in the Middle East for the period.

Shaw, Stanford J., and Ezel Kural Shaw. *History of the Ottoman Empire and Modern Turkey.* Vol. 2. *Reform, Revolution, and Republic: The Rise of Modern Turkey, 1808–1975.* Cambridge: Cambridge University Press, 1977. This very substantial volume touches upon every aspect of change and growth in the Ottoman Empire and Turkey over these years. It is especially strong in explaining the governmental structure that developed in the nineteenth century and in relating it to the events of the times.

22

Muhammad Ali and the Development of Modern Egypt

RISE OF MUHAMMAD ALI

Nineteenth-century Egypt was largely the creation of Muhammad Ali, who must be recognized as one of the great rulers of his age. In 1798 when Selim III raised an army to send to Egypt against Napoleon, the governor of Kavalla in Thrace supplied 300 men, the second in command being Muhammad Ali, an Ottoman probably of Albanian descent and then about twenty-nine years old. (His name as spelled here follows the form used in Egypt and the Arab world. In Turkish he was called Mehmed Ali, as he referred to himself.)

He had been engaged in the tobacco trade, but his latent political talent was soon manifested in Egypt. The peace of Amiens in 1802 and the British evacuation of the Nile found Muhammad Ali responsible for several thousand Albanian and Bosnian troops. At that time three major powers existed in Egypt: the Ottoman pasha, who ruled in the name of the sultan; the Mamluks, who held landed estates and were hopelessly split in jealous factions; and the Albanians. The people of Cairo constituted a weak fourth.

Muhammad Ali played his cards extremely well. When the British left Egypt in 1803, he sided with the Mamluks and drove the Turkish governor from Cairo. Muhammad Ali then turned one Mamluk faction against another. Finally, with the aid of the Cairo populace, he chased the Mamluks into the desert and deposed the new governor who had just arrived from Istanbul, becoming himself recognized as governor by the citizens of Cairo. In 1805 Muhammad Ali asserted his submission to Sultan Selim, who appointed him governor of Egypt.

Affairs in Europe in 1807 pushed the Ottomans into the French camp; since Muhammad Ali persisted in his loyalty to the Porte, a British expeditionary force was landed at Alexandria. In league with Mamluk remnants, the British occupied Alexandria, but were defeated and withdrew. After the treaty of Tilsit, which threw England and Turkey into each other's arms, Britain re-

274

nounced all designs upon Egypt. Muhammad Ali was now the actual as well as the titular ruler of Egypt.

Finances cramped him severely. On several occasions Muhammad Ali's own Albanians, their pay considerably in arrears, shot at him as he passed in the streets of Cairo. War and the successive passage of troops in Lower Egypt reduced the delta to barrenness. In previous administrations taxes and levies supported an Egyptian army, but Muhammad Ali found little to levy upon, and taxes proved quite insufficient. Consequently, he ordered a cadastral survey of all landholdings and confiscated properties with irregular titles. Later he seized land grants upon which payments to the state were in arrears, modified the ancient system of land tenure, and expropriated the remaining fiefs (*iltizams*). Even exemptions for lands belonging to religious institutions were rescinded and their lands were surveyed to be sure none escaped.

As land taxes increased, Muhammad Ali turned his attention to commerce and established a government monopoly on the export of grain. In several of these years the Nile valley possessed the only exportable surplus available to the British. Demand was brisk, and profits in the grain trade often reached 500 percent.

Muhammad Ali's power and the loyalty of his troops rose in direct proportion to his improved finances. One longstanding score remained to be settled, not only for himself but for the authority of his suzerain, the Ottoman sultan. The Mamluks, particularly those holding fiefs in Upper Egypt, had never been fully subjected, defying one Ottoman governor after another. For several years Muhammad Ali threatened, cajoled, and attacked them. His entreaties induced many to settle at Giza across from Cairo; and at the ceremonies of the investiture of his son as governor of Jidda in 1811 they were tricked into entering the citadel of Cairo, where the Albanian soldiers slaughtered them. A year later another thousand were executed in Upper Egypt.

ARABIA AND THE SUDAN

Organization of the finances of Egypt and destruction of the Mamluk power enabled Muhammad Ali to consider widening his rule. For many decades the Porte

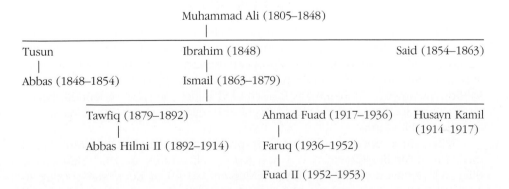

Dynasty of Muhammad Ali

was troubled by attacks and depredations of the Wahhabis of Arabia. In the middle of the eighteenth century Muhammad ibn Saud became converted to the teachings of Muhammad ibn Abd al-Wahhab, a native of Nejd who had studied in Damascus and Baghdad. Returning home, the latter grew convinced of the necessity of eliminating from Muslim practices the pagan superstitions that had become prevalent among the desert Arab tribesmen. He also felt compelled to destroy the philosophic subtleties and the worldly deviations that had crept into Islam over the ages and to restore Islam to the pure, original, and simple form as pronounced by the Prophet, and as set forth in the Hanbali doctrines, one of the four Sunni Muslim law schools.

Muhammad ibn Saud and his descendants, armed with the Wahhabi faith, spread their rule over many tribes in Arabia, pillaging Shiite and Sunnite shrines. Their seizure of the Hijaz during the Napoleonic Wars disrupted Meccan pilgrimages, and the Porte entreated Muhammad Ali to drive them from Medina and Mecca. In 1811 his son Tusun headed an expedition to subdue and annex the Hijaz. Not until 1818, however, under the firm and courageous leadership of Muhammad Ali's able son Ibrahim, did the superior equipment and discipline of the Egyptian troops turn the scales against the Saudi-Wahhabi forces. The Saudi capital was taken and razed to the ground, and the Saudi prince was conveyed to Istanbul, where he was executed. Ibrahim became governor of the Hijaz and Ethiopia, the latter consisting then of a few Red Sea ports which served as outlets for the Sudan.

Muhammad Ali looked upon the Sudan as a boundless area full of gold, precious stones, and slaves. He also believed that he could develop a fine army from black slaves from the Sudan, thereby securing independence from his unruly Albanians. An expedition went southward in 1820 under Ismail, another of his sons. The Sudan was politically divided and had become the refuge for some Mamluks who had fled Egypt. The sedentary tribes along the Nile capitulated after little resistance, and the Funj sultanate was conquered, but gold proved to be relatively scarce. Khartoum became the capital of Egyptian administration.

GREEK EXPEDITION

The experiment with an army of Sudanese slaves proved a failure. Disease and fatalities among the Sudanese constrained Muhammad Ali to build an army around Egyptian soldiers and Turkish and European officers. Over 30,000 Egyptian peasants were sent to Aswan, where in a short time they were drilled into effective soldiers. Meanwhile, Muhammad Ali assembled a fleet. One ship mounting sixteen guns was built at Suez; others were bought in Bombay, Genoa, Venice, Marseilles, and the Greek islands.

While these developments were in process, the Greek revolution turned the eastern Mediterranean into a nest for Greek pirates. In 1822 Mahmud II offered the governorship of Crete to Muhammad Ali, if he would subdue it. After Muhammad Ali had taken Crete, Mahmud bestowed upon Ibrahim the overlordship of the Peloponnesus on like terms. Under Ibrahim's command

16,000 men and a navy of 63 ships left Alexandria in 1824 to clear the Aegean of the Greek pirate-nationalist navy. Various islands were attacked and plundered, Muhammad Ali replacing his losses with new ships from France and Italy; he even bought some from Greek shipbuilders. Ibrahim and Suleiman Pasha landed in Greece in 1825; but that adventure was extremely costly for Muhammad Ali: his fleet was ruined, and his trained and disciplined army returned to Egypt starved and crippled.

CONQUEST OF SYRIA

But Muhammad Ali was not a ruler to be discouraged easily. From his ready income provided by the changed tax base he rapidly reconstituted an army. And by 1829 the new self-sufficient naval arsenal at Alexandria had begun to turn out frigates, corvettes, and other men-of-war.

Syria was inviting, especially since its four districts were pledged to Muhammad Ali as payment for his undertaking in Greece. Using a variety of excuses, Muhammad Ali sent Ibrahim against Acre, which fell in May 1832. He then turned upon Turkish forces, speedily entered the Beylan pass south of Alexandretta, and marched northward to the outskirts of Konya. Ibrahim's devastating victory at Konya carried him on to Kutahya, where peace between Mahmud and his rebellious viceroy was concluded in 1833. Crete, Egypt, Syria, Adana, and Tarsus were assigned to Muhammad Ali, for which he agreed to pay a tribute to Istanbul.

Ibrahim governed Syria for eight years. Taxes were regularized, justice was more secure for members of the religious minorities, commerce was encouraged, privileges for foreigners were less abused, education was stimulated, law and order were more prevalent. The resolute rule that Muhammad Ali created in Egypt was also attempted in Syria. Had it been given a longer period of trial, it might have succeeded. Conscription, however, was resisted; the new taxes were hated; and rebellion faced Ibrahim on several occasions. A strong army was an absolute necessity for Muhammad Ali and Ibrahim; and Mahmud was rebuilding an army while European officers were training new Ottoman regiments. Since the governorships of Egypt, Syria, and Crete were granted for only one year at a time, and since there were constant disputes over tribute, Muhammad Ali considered maintenance of an ever-ready army a prime requisite for his own safety. When, therefore, European governments urged abandonment of conscription in Syria, reduction of his armaments by half, and withdrawal of his troops from Syria, Muhammad Ali gladly agreed, but on condition that Mahmud grant him hereditary title to his territories and that the Powers guarantee him against aggression.

Ottoman forces invaded Syria and were destroyed at Nazib by Ibrahim in June 1839. Five days later Mahmud II died, and before July was out the Ottoman fleet deserted to join the Egyptians at Alexandria. Muhammad Ali was now master of the situation, and the Porte prepared to surrender to his demands of hereditary vassalage for all territories then in his possession. However, a joint note from Austria, England, France, Prussia, and Russia informed the sultan that they were concerned with developments within the Middle East and recommended that no action be taken on Muhammad Ali's claims without their approval. The British feared that Russia would call into operation provisions of the hated treaty of Hunkiar Iskelesi or that France through Muhammad Ali would dominate Syria and Egypt and control all routes from the Mediterranean to India. The British, therefore, preferred a united action to Russian or French unilateral steps. Fortified with this backing, the Porte informed Muhammad Ali of European concern and awaited the decision of the Powers. In the end Lord Palmerston prevailed upon Russia, Prussia, and Austria to sign the treaty of London in 1840. This treaty was a diplomatic defeat in the Levant for France. It allowed Muhammad Ali the hereditary governorship of Egypt if he agreed to the settlement within twenty days, and a lifetime rule over south Syria if he agreed in ten days. Otherwise, the four powers would blockade Egypt and defend the integrity of the Ottoman Empire.

Since Muhammad Ali refused to budge, the only recourse was force. British agents in Lebanon and Syria helped raise a rebellion against Ibrahim, while a combined British-Austrian fleet landed troops at Beirut and captured Acre. Muhammad Ali was forced to recall Ibrahim from Syria and accept British terms. He also withdrew from central and western Arabia, allowing the Wahhabis and Saudis to return to power in the central regions, and the Ottomans to regain Mecca. Egypt was left as a hereditary province to Muhammad Ali and his heirs, but the size of his army was limited to no more than 18,000 men. Since communications were slow, it was not until July 1841 that the Porte confirmed him in the hereditary position in Egypt and granted him authority to make military appointments below the rank of general. France agreed to the terms and returned to the concert of European powers in their concern with affairs of the Middle East.

ORGANIZATION OF EGYPT

The defeats of 1840 and the diplomatic negotiations of 1841 gave Muhammad Ali full political power in Egypt but left him an old and broken man. He lapsed into senility in 1847 and died two years later.

For forty years Muhammad Ali had ruled Egypt, and every phase of life and society had interested him at one time or another. He had created a new government and developed a cabinet with ministers of war, navy, finance, commerce and foreign affairs, education, and security. Real power, however, had never slipped from the hands of the Pasha, as Muhammad Ali was always known. Most of the top officials were related to him or were personally associated with his household. In the 1830s councils of notables were appointed to discuss governmental affairs. Western travelers were greatly impressed. But the Pasha never intended that his rule be other than that of a benevolent despot.

Exports were reoriented away from the rest of the Ottoman Empire and instead were now directed toward Europe. The trade monopoly for grain was extended to include cotton, tobacco, and indigo, although the British terminated the monopoly system after the 1838 new commercial treaty for the entire Ottoman Empire was eventually forced upon Egypt. Muhammad Ali revised the tax laws and instituted harsher methods of collection, confiscated Mamluk holdings, and attacked religious endowments. He also extended the corvée or forced labor of the peasants, which, along with various acquisitions of land, brought the state—that is, Muhammad Ali—control by 1840 of more than half the cultivable land in Egypt. This meant that many of the peasants were deprived of their land. Though he had given vast tracts to various members of his extended family by the time of his death, the ruling family fully controlled the domestic market. (Some called Egypt "Muhammad Ali's farm.") Through the various state enterprises, the import trade was strongly affected by his policics, and for more than a decade he enjoyed a monopoly over imports as well as exports. By the treaties of 1840 and 1841 Muhammad Ali was forced to recognize the Ottoman sultan as his suzerain and to agree to abide by the sultan's laws, especially the capitulations held by the Great Powers. Since taxes were paid in kind, the Pasha's government continued to be the principal participant in the export trade; and most foreign merchants in Alexandria did not object after Muhammad Ali agreed to offer his goods at public auction to export houses. Corn and rice were introduced. In many areas steam pumps and better canals allowed summer irrigation, enabling the fellaheen, or peasants, to double the yield by growing two crops a year. Great attention was given to the science of irrigation. Swamp lands were drained, old canals opened, and new ones built. North of Cairo a great barrage was constructed to raise canal levels, especially in years of scanty floods. However, since the engineering work was not too sound, it proved ineffective until rebuilt in the 1880s.

The age of Muhammad Ali in Egypt coincided with the first industrial surge in western Europe, and the Pasha became convinced of the value of such a program for his land. He imported textile plants and built sugar factories. But technical knowledge, capital, suitable labor, power-driven machines, and supplies of coal and iron were lacking, while European pressure restricted Egyptian opportunities. Even before Muhammad Ali died, the failure to industrialize Egypt was apparent.

Muhammad Ali's successful endeavors were sanitation and education. Great plagues raged every year; and annual deaths from cholera and bubonic plague sometimes rose to 10 percent or more of the population. A more effective quarantine was organized, and the foreign consuls in Alexandria were appointed to a board of sanitation, which was given ample funds and absolute authority. After 1840 visitations of these diseases were restricted and health conditions in general were improved. The marked increase in the population was largely attributed to advances in public security, agriculture, and the absence of epidemics.

The first new government schools established were for the military—infantry, cavalry, engineers, navy, and artillery. Most of the instructors in these schools were French; and boys were sent to study in France, Italy, and England. In 1833, however, the Polytechnic School was founded with a staff comprised almost entirely of Egyptian teachers. Soon preparatory schools to feed the Polytechnic were organized in Cairo and Alexandria. In connection with the schools a government press was set up at Bulaq near Cairo; most of its publications were translations of European technical works. Newspapers printed in both Arabic and French not only gave urban society access to Western ideas but also made Egypt a leader in the new intellectual life of the Arab world.

A neoclassical cultural revival along indigenous intellectual lines also took place in the early years of Muhammad Ali's reign. The notable historian and religious scholar Abd al-Rahman al-Jabarti, who was antagonistic toward the ruler, compiled a massive and sophisticated history of the era.

Muhammad Ali was impatient and tried to change society rapidly without a sufficient number of sympathetic officials. Many of his innovations were too hurried and too shallow to endure, but Alexandria was transformed into a Mediterranean city resembling Marseilles, Genoa, or Naples. Construction of the great Mahmudiyah Canal brought all Nile trade and traffic from Cairo to Alexandria and turned the latter into a boom town. Its population increased from 15,000 in 1805 to 150,000 in 1847. Since many of its inhabitants were Europeans, Alexandria became one of the most cosmopolitan cities of the world. During his reign, Muhammad Ali had given Egypt the first constructive leadership in centuries and sown the seeds for the establishment of a separate state. Incredibly, this was done without incurring any debts.

Unfortunately, much of Muhammad Ali's work was undone by his successor, his grandson Abbas Pasha. A conservative, traditional Ottoman gentleman who had headed an army in Syria under Ibrahim, Abbas Pasha disliked Europeans and resented the presence of the large number of them in Egypt; but he also realized that his interests paralleled those of the British. He shunned Frenchmen and permitted many of his grandfather's innovations to lapse. Uneconomic factories were abandoned, and schools were closed. Aggressive policies were curtailed, and the army was halved. Although a British firm constructed the first railway between Alexandria and Cairo, French agents seeking to build the Suez Canal were unable to receive a hearing. Upon Abbas Pasha's murder in 1854, authority passed to his uncle Said, Muhammad Ali's favorite son, who surrounded himself with Frenchmen.

THE SUEZ CANAL

In Said's youth he had formed a friendship with Ferdinand de Lesseps, son of the French political agent in Egypt, and within four months after his accession Said granted his friend a broad concession to construct the Suez Canal. Officially promulgated in 1855, the news touched off a long diplomatic imbroglio. The British government opposed the scheme, believing that it would impair British commercial advantages with the Orient and that it would inevitably create an Egyptian question for European diplomacy. Because it was involved at the moment in the Crimean War, the Porte could ill afford to antagonize England and thus did not accord the project the necessary ratification.

In 1856 an international commission of engineers surveyed the land and reported on the proposal, setting an estimate of £6 million as a maximum cost. Some stock in the Suez Canal Company went to Said for granting the concession and for furnishing the labor required to dig the canal. Other shares were held by the organizers or were given without cost to influential personages, while ordinary shares sold for 500 francs each.

Until 1858 Napoleon III seemed unconcerned, but when the subscription lists were opened for the ordinary shares, his views changed. It is believed that de Lesseps gave a substantial number of founder shares to influential members of Napoleon's court, if not to the emperor and empress themselves. Although Said warned that construction of the canal should not begin until approved in Istanbul, digging started in April 1859. The British protested vigorously over the use of forced labor and were able to keep the sultan from ratifying the concession. Little work had been accomplished when Said died in 1863 and Ismail, Ibrahim's oldest living son, became governor.

Ismail was thirty-three years old. He had been educated in Paris at the École d'État-Major and had gone for Said on missions to Turkey, France, and the Vatican. At his accession Ismail accepted the commitments concerning the canal, and by 1866 the British no longer opposed it. Under pressure from Napoleon III the Porte gave its authorization. Ismail paid an indemnity for not supplying forced labor, and the construction proceeded rapidly. When it was finished in 1869, Ismail spent £1 million on the opening ceremonies. Empress Eugénie was the guest of honor among 6,000 guests, including the emperor of Austria and the crown prince of Prussia. Verdi's *Aida,* composed for this event, was later performed in Cairo at the opera house built for the occasion.

For the first several years the canal operated at a loss, and the company was perilously close to bankruptcy. However, traffic increased, the canal showing profits continuously after 1875. Ismail and Egypt, nevertheless, did not benefit from it. The cost of the canal to Said and Ismail was estimated at £11.5 million, for which Egypt received no return. To a considerable extent this was because Ismail was impractical and a spendthrift.

The Suez Canal concession also stipulated that the canal would be open, without any preferential treatment, to merchant vessels of every flag. During the Egyptian crisis of 1881 and 1882 the British closed the canal for four days, and navigation by warships was debated. A conference in Istanbul in 1888 attended by Austria, France, Germany, Great Britain, Italy, the Netherlands, Russia, Spain, and the Ottoman Empire agreed to an earlier convention, which declared that the canal should "always be free and open, in the time of war as in time of peace, to every vessel of commerce or of war, without distinction of flag." Britain signed this agreement with reservations which she did not relinquish until 1904.

ISMAIL'S RULE

From the moment of Ismail's accession in 1863 until his deposition in 1879, life at the court in Egypt was sumptuous: money flowed like the waters of the Nile. Ismail showered munificent gifts upon all, and his trips to Europe and Istanbul were lavish in every detail. Presents to the sultan on the order of £1 million and a diamond-encrusted solid-gold dinner service were not unusual. Ismail possessed a charismatic personality which dispelled all opposition; and his use of flattery and urbane suavity earned him the acclaim of Europe. Shortly after Ismail's accession, Sultan Abd al-Aziz visited him in Egypt, being the first Ottoman sultan to come to Cairo since its capture in 1517. (It should be pointed out that these two rulers, who resembled each other in many ways, were cousins, their mothers being sisters.) In 1866–1867 Ismail visited Istanbul, where through princely gifts he won the title khedive and recognition of the succession to the Egyptian throne by the law of primogeniture. At the same time, for the doubling of his tribute he was allowed to strengthen his army, coin money, and bestow decorations and titles on his own. In 1869 he was received, entertained, and decorated by the crowned heads of Europe. However, Ismail was rapidly falling into the clutches of unscrupulous moneylenders and European bankers.

At Ismail's accession Egypt had a foreign debt of £3 million and a domestic debt of £4 million. Thirteen years later it had a foreign debt of £68 million and a domestic debt of £30 million. Of this, nearly 35 percent was incurred in the form of discounts and commissions, putting the rates on the "verge of fraudulence." Interest charges mounted to £5 million per annum, more than half the total annual revenue of the government. Ismail flogged the fellaheen to increase taxes and sought new sources of income. In 1874 he sold his 176,602 ordinary shares of Canal stock to the British government for nearly £4 million. But this only delayed the day of reckoning, which came in 1876 when Ismail ceased payment on his bills and debts.

Before detailing Ismail's bankruptcy his reign should be examined to provide a balance against his financial profligacy by acknowledging his imagination and leadership. Egypt in 1880, the end of Ismail's rule, was a far cry, indeed, from the Egypt of 1863.

Perhaps the most apparent change during Ismail's reign was the Europeanization of urban Egypt. The social and cultural gap between the cities and the countryside widened greatly, as by 1880 more than 100,000 Europeans were living in Cairo and Alexandria. The leading citizens of Egypt meanwhile were sending most of their sons to Europe to be educated. Ismail's fondness for saying that Egypt was a part of Europe was not without foundation. And, in fact, it was the Europeanized elite, participating in government, education, and general culture, who maintained his drive and aims and sustained and improved upon most of his works.

In government Ismail inaugurated in 1866 the Assembly of Delegates, made up of seventy-five members elected for three-year terms. Though only a quasi-parliamentary body, the assembly, most of whose members came from a new class of wealthy and influential headmen, served Ismail as a kind of constitutional shield to offset the Turkish elite that was evolving from the privileged army-officer and government-official classes. It also served as a potential means of impressing French and British bankers. Until 1875 the assembly meetings were superficial and under Ismail's thumb, but then the financial crisis emboldened the members to criticize foreign financial powers and to demand ministerial responsibility for the assembly. In a session in 1876 it requested an explanation of government operations and suggested that the assembly supervise government expenditures. The assembly's increasing assertiveness in 1878 brought foreign pressure on Ismail, and in 1879 he dissolved the assembly. The delegates, continuing to meet unofficially in various members' homes, formed a nucleus of leaders who showed the way to a nationalist cause in years to come.

Long-staple cotton had been introduced in 1821 from the Ethiopian-Sudanese border, and Muhammad Ali had eagerly spread its cultivation. By 1850, 35 million pounds (about 16 million kilograms) were being grown annually, as Egypt became integrated into the world market dominated by Europe. During the American Civil War production soared to 250 million pounds (113 million kilograms) per year, and the price increased by 400 percent to a total of over £25 million. At all levels everyone hastened to profit from this bonanza, but with the end of the war, prices tumbled, and peasants were thrown into a miserable condition of mortgage foreclosures and usurious indebtedness. Village headmen improved their influence and prosperity throughout these times by lending to their bankrupt neighbors. Their dominance in the assembly, formed at a time of peasant hardship and depression, was not just a coincidence. Since cotton was a cash crop, it tended to destroy the old communal economy of the village; and in steps under Said and Ismail, family proprietorship with an individualistic economy began to prevail. The state monopoly over agricultural products was terminated, and in 1871 Ismail gave full right of ownership to villages. Still, with heavy taxes a peasant flight from the land persisted. Big estates flourished and were subject to taxation only after 1854, though at a lower rate. Village headmen, however, remained important in the political, economic, and social life of the country, and their sons, no longer exempt from conscription under Said, began to improve the quality of the rank and file in the army and even to change its character as some higher ranks were opened to them. Large estates, swollen by abandoned lands, were owned by the khedivial family and the elite of the Turkish officials. Yet there was a certain fluidity in ownership caused by personal mismanagement and indebtedness and the fractioning of landholdings under Muslim laws of inheritance. Undoubtedly all Ismail's policies and actions, including the building of roads, railroads, and the Ibrahimiyya Canal from the Nile at Asyut northward and the bringing of over a million acres (400,000 hectares) of new land under cultivation, were efforts to increase his income; nevertheless, they did benefit the whole nation, as the population growth during his sixteen years of rule testified.

In the sphere of international affairs, Ismail had certain autonomous rights granted by several decrees from the Porte. In addition to the ability to contract loans, Ismail could negotiate with foreign governments, but only through consuls, never ambassadors. As a part of the Ottoman Empire, Egypt was subject to the capitulatory treaties with other states, chiefly European. Abused by traders and all foreigners, the treaties practically ensured that law cases were settled by diplomatic pressure rather than on a basis of merit or justice. The variety of foreign nationals residing in Egypt and their number (100,000 in 1875) made cases of one foreigner against another difficult to adjudicate. In 1867 Ismail's foreign minister, Nubar Pasha, proposed a mixed court staffed by Egyptians and foreign judges which would administer codes of law to be drawn up by an international commission on the basis of French law. It would deal with civil and criminal cases, with jurisdiction reserved by the consuls only over their own nationals. Eventually a conference in Istanbul in 1873 authorized the Mixed

Courts and the six law codes that they would apply. France finally agreed the next year, and the courts began in 1875 with a majority of foreign judges and the French language used in all proceedings. Judges, Egyptian and foreign, were appointed by the khedive, although foreigners were nominated by participating governments which agreed to recognize judgments of these courts. Establishment of the Mixed Courts, however, weakened the government and frequently frustrated its operation. They did not end the capitulations but modified them in an important way.

Ismail's boldest venture was the extension of Egyptian rule into the Sudan. Muhammad Ali had conquered parts of the region, and in 1842 the sultan had recognized him as governor-general of the Sudan. During the middle of the century under Abbas and Said, interest lapsed. Ismail set up a new southern province with Fashoda on the White Nile as its capital. Ismail was Europeanized to the extent of considering Egypt as a participant in the partitioning of Africa, and he devised ambitious schemes of expanding Egypt to the equator and including all of the basin of the White Nile. In 1869, he declared that steps were being taken to end the slave trade in the Sudan and sent the British explorer Sir Samuel Baker to govern equatorial Sudan. Under Ismail's aegis Sir Samuel led expeditions to the equatorial lakes district that resulted in the attachment of Bahr al-Ghazal to the Sudan. His successor, General Charles George Gordon, led two unsuccessful forays against Ethiopia in 1875 and 1876 but had more luck curtailing the slave trade. In fact, he was so successful in the latter endeavor as to disturb the local economy and dislocate the principal preoccupation of local leaders. Gordon departed with many of his European assistants in 1877, and upon Ismail's deposition in 1879 the Sudan was left in a state of near anarchy. Taxes throughout the period of Egyptian rule were high, and the depopulation of many areas and the disruption of much of the economy ensued. Without financial resources from Cairo, the mild Egyptian replacement was no match for the uprising led by Muhammad Ahmad of Dongola, who declared himself Mahdi in 1881.

Ismail in his European travels partook of the social and cultural life and insisted on creating a similar society in Egypt. Hardly any facet escaped his attention. His improvements in the cities and towns brought residential quarters, squares, and parks along with water service, gas supplies, and street lighting. Societies were organized for archaeology, music, and poetry, for the construction of libraries (the Khedivial Library in 1870) and museums (the Egyptian Museum in 1863) for the advancement of Egyptology, and in 1875 the Khedivial Geographical Society for African exploration. In 1868 Ismail opened a comedy theater in Cairo and brought European companies to perform theatricals such as he had seen in Paris. The next year the Cairo Opera House was opened with a performance of Verdi's *Rigoletto* followed by the première of *Aïda* in December 1869. Newspapers were encouraged and the famous daily *Al-Ahram* was born in 1876.

As neighborhoods, guilds, and religious groups began to be affected by change, the role of men in society remained predominant. However, many midwives were professionally trained, and some women participated in the new education or worked in factories. Women were active in the court system, and they took part in the general economy—buying, selling, inheriting, loaning and borrowing, and pursuing debtors. As conscription and forced labor for the state increased in the country, family life was often disrupted. A frequent, though unintended, consequence of the reforms was to decrease the freedom of social action of many women.

Above all else, Ismail believed firmly that education would Westernize his state. Western influences and culture had been weakened under Abbas, who banished some educators to Khartoum. Although they returned during Said's rule, education did not come into its own until the advent of Ismail. A ministry of education was established, separate from the military, and headed at times by Ali Pasha Mubarak, a great scholar and vigorous administrator. A law of 1868 created a state system of education, which set up the first school for girls five years later. Specialized schools were started for lawyers, engineers, and administrators; Teachers College was founded in 1872; and the renowned School of Languages was reopened under the direction of Rifaa al-Tahtawi, a scholar and author who was to inspire many of the leaders of Egyptian public life for the following half century.

There is no question that Ismail was exceedingly extravagant. He had little understanding of the value of money: it was merely a ready commodity for obtaining what he wanted. For years European bankers had been anxious to lend him funds for his many whims and projects. But the capitulations practically condemned Egypt to the penurious role of an agriculturally based economy which in the period following the Crimean War and the American Civil War reduced it to a level of relative inferiority. Universal hard times in the mid-1870s found Ismail bankrupt; further loans were impossible to obtain at any price, and state revenues were inadequate.

To extricate himself from bankruptcy Ismail conducted a losing battle against European bondholders, "unofficial" government officials, commissions of inquiry, and consuls general. Despite substantial increases in revenues, Ismail suspended all payments on loans, whereupon British and French creditors appointed representatives to negotiate for new arrangements with Ismail. In 1876 the entire debt was unified, and Ismail agreed to set up the Caisse de la Dette Publique with four members representing the British, French, Italian, and Austrian creditors. These fund directors (the British member was Major Evelyn Baring of the Baring banking family and later Lord Cromer) supervised all revenues and expenditures in Egypt, channeling 60 percent of the revenues to pay off the debt and enabling the servicing of the debt to be met fully in 1877. But Ismail had been forced in 1876 to appoint dual controllers: Major Baring for the British and M. de Blignières for the French. The controllers could attend cabinet meetings, demand information, give advice, and report to their diplomatic representatives in the event advice was ignored. They became the real rulers of Egypt. On the findings of an international commission of inquiry a law was enacted squeezing the debt down to £85 million and reserving £4.5 million of the annual government income for the budget. All excess income, then estimated at £4 million, was to be employed to retire the debt. Unfortunately for the future development of Egypt, expanding revenues resulting from increased productivity and hard work or from inflation would not benefit Egyptians or improve services of the government. Since the controllers were duty-bound to guard the revenue and pay off the debt, they could hardly fail to be unpopular with the Egyptians, to whom their regime appeared unduly oppressive.

The commission of inquiry demanded that Ismail accept a civil list for himself and his family and the idea of ministerial responsibility. Moreover, an international cabinet was installed with Nubar Pasha as prime minister, Mr. Rivers Wilson (a member of the commission) as finance minister, and M. de Blignières as minister of public works, and with many Europeans serving in the various offices at generous salaries. Times were hard everywhere; government expenditures were greatly curtailed; and the Nile flooding of 1877–1878 was exceedingly low, drastically reducing crop yields. The crisis encouraged independent activity of the Assembly of Delegates, military conspiracies, press agitation, and the formation of national secret societies, some of which were probably encouraged by Ismail.

In 1879 Nubar Pasha and Rivers Wilson were mobbed in Cairo by a group of army officers whose pay had just been cut in half, and they were saved only by Ismail's personal intervention. Ismail then dismissed Nubar Pasha and the international ministry, eventually appointing in its place an all-Egyptian cabinet. With a great deal of constitutional enthusiasm arising, Ismail defied Europe. He summoned the consuls general to confront them with the discontent of the Assembly of Delegates, the disaffection of the army, and the disquiet of the public. A draft constitution of forty-nine articles was submitted to the assembly, giving among other things full control of finances to the assembly. There was great jubilation all around when the assembly accepted the constitution. The British and the French, however, were determined that Ismail be deposed. The European powers persuaded the sultan in Istanbul to send a telegram on June 26, 1879, addressed to the "former" Khedive Ismail informing him that rule had passed to his son Tawfiq. Ismail left for Italy, where he died in 1895.

EUROPEAN INTERVENTION

Soon after Ismail's deposition a crisis developed over the question of Egyptian autonomy under laws decreed by the Porte as against subservience to the European powers as represented by French and British officials. Authority passed to the revived dual controllers, who naturally cut expenditures to the bone. The size of the army was reduced; many officers were retired; civil budgets and personnel were pared. Yet a sizable number of foreign administrators came in at inordinate salaries. Opposition quickly formed in Egypt. The evolution of society under Ismail had brought four parties to the fore: a weak reactionary party; a vigorous Islamic modernist party developed by Muhammad Abduh; a constitutional party of wealthy Europeanized Egyptian landowners organized by Sharif Pasha from membership in the assembly and from other groups; and an army group composed of Egyptians in the lower-officer echelons and inspired by Colonel Ahmad Urabi. Only the first party acquiesced in the foreign dual control, preferring it to any of the Egyptian groups. The army was the most violent in its opposition, because high-ranking officers were Turks or Circassians and the dual control did not remove these officers to the extent that it curbed the rise of native Egyptians.

When in January 1882 England and France presented a joint note to the khedive protesting the formation of a constitutional government, the army partly gained control of the cabinet. The army's leaders sought reforms within the context of Egypt's continued local autonomy inside the Ottoman Empire. England and France had to occupy the country or give up the dual control. Riots in Alexandria served as the pretext. A change in the French government, however, altered French policy; and England alone intervened. The British occupied Egypt in July 1882 to overthrow Colonel Urabi and reestablish European control. Alexandria was shelled; the British navy occupied the Canal cities; and in September, British troops won the Battle of Tel al-Kebir, and took Cairo. At this point resistance to European control in Egypt collapsed.

REFERENCES

Readings for this chapter are also found in Chapters 19, 20, and 21.

Abu-Lughod, Ibrahim. *Arab Rediscovery of Europe: A Study in Cultural Encounters.* Princeton, N.J.: Princeton University Press, 1963. A study of Arab travelers and students in Europe in the century after Napoleon. Also discusses the impact of books printed in Arabic about their life and travels in Europe.

Arkell, A. J. *A History of the Sudan to 1821.* London: Athlone Press, 1961.

Baer, Gabriel. *Egyptian Guilds in Modern Times.* Jerusalem: The Israel Oriental Society, 1964. An important contribution.

————. *A History of Landownership in Modern Egypt, 1800–1950.* New York: Oxford University Press, 1962. A most important work.

Blunt, Wilfrid S. *Secret History of the English Occupation of Egypt.* London: Unwin, 1907. Written by a long-time resident of Egypt who was a friend of many of the leading Egyptian nationalists.

Crabbs, Jack A., Jr. *The Writing of History in Nineteenth-Century Egypt.* Detroit, Mich.: Wayne State University Press, 1984. A very useful contribution to the historiography of the Middle East.

Deeb, Marius. "The Socioeconomic Role of the Local Foreign Minorities in Modern Egypt, 1805–1961." *International Journal of Middle East Studies* 9 (1978): 11–22.

De Jong, F. *Turuq and Turuq-Linked Institutions in Nineteenth Century Egypt: A Historical Study in Organizational Dimensions of Islamic Mysticism.* Leiden: Brill, 1978.

Farnie, D. A. *East and West of Suez: The Suez Canal in History, 1854–1956.* Oxford: Clarendon Press, 1969. A monumental work, derived from a vast range of Western-language sources.

Goldschmidt, Arthur, Jr. *Modern Egypt: The Formation of a Nation-State.* Boulder, Colo.: Westview Press, 1988. The bibliography is especially valuable in this clear, concise, and thoughtful analysis of Egypt from Muhammad Ali to Mubarak.

Gran, Peter. *Islamic Roots of Capitalism: Egypt, 1760–1840.* Austin: University of Texas Press, 1979. Stimulating discussion of Egyptian economic conditions and intellectual life.

Hunter, F. Robert. *Egypt Under the Khedives, 1805–1879: From Household Government to Modern Bureaucracy.* Pittsburgh, Pa.: University of Pittsburgh Press, 1984. A detailed study of the growth and changes in government and administration.

Landau, Jacob M. *Jews in Nineteenth-Century Egypt.* New York: New York University Press, 1969. A study of the internal organization and external relationships of the Jewish community and its extensive growth in the nineteenth century.

Landes, David S. *Bankers and Pashas: International Finance and Economic Imperialism in Egypt.* Cambridge, Mass.: Harvard University Press, 1958. A highly significant case study of private banking in Egypt in the 1860s.

Lane, E. W. *Manners and Customs of the Modern Egyptians.* New York: Dutton, 1923. Still the most valuable work for the social history of nineteenth-century urban Egypt, this book is full of fascinating observations on life in Cairo.

McCarthy, Justin. "Nineteenth-Century Egyptian Population." *Middle Eastern Studies* 12 (1976): 1–40. A sophisticated analysis of a complicated issue, showing that substantial population growth was largely caused by civil order and political stability.

Marlowe, John. *A History of Modern Egypt and Anglo-Egyptian Relations, 1800–1956.* Hamden, Conn.: Archon, 1965. A useful survey.

———. *World Ditch: The Making of the Suez Canal.* New York: Macmillan, 1964. A careful study of the building of the canal.

Marsot, Afaf Lutfi al-Sayyid. *Egypt in the Reign of Muhammad Ali.* Cambridge: Cambridge University Press, 1984. A valuable political biography which analyzes most aspects of Egyptian history of the period.

———. *A Short History of Modern Egypt.* Cambridge: Cambridge University Press, 1985. An excellent introduction to the subject.

Morsy, Magali. *North Africa 1800–1900: A Survey from the Nile Valley to the Atlantic.* London: Longman, 1984. Especially useful for discussions of the Sudan and the role of the Sahara in the history of North Africa.

Owen, E. R. J. *Cotton and the Egyptian Economy, 1820–1914: A Study in Trade and Development.* Oxford: Clarendon Press, 1969. A stimulating and scholarly analysis of the Egyptian economy.

Rivlin, Helen Anne B. *The Agricultural Policy of Muhammad Ali in Egypt.* Cambridge, Mass.: Harvard University Press, 1961. An outstanding work which considers the entire economy of Egypt.

Schölch, Alexander. *Egypt for the Egyptians! The Socio-Political Crisis in Egypt, 1878–1882.* London: Ithaca Press, 1981. The best study of the fall of Ismail and the rise of Urabi and the Egyptian army.

Tucker, Judith E. *Women in Nineteenth-Century Egypt.* Cambridge: Cambridge University Press, 1985. A path-breaking work of great value for the urban history of Egypt and the role of women in Egyptian society.

Vatikiotis, P. J. *The History of Egypt: From Muhammad Ali to Mubarak.* 3rd ed. Baltimore, Md.: Johns Hopkins University Press, 1986. A fine detailed book on nineteenth- and twentieth-century Egypt. Strong on social and intellectual movements in the rise of Egyptian nationalism.

Wakefield, Gordon. *Egypt.* New York: Walker, 1967.

23

European Ambitions and Diplomacy in the Middle East

EUROPEAN INTERESTS

Throughout the nineteenth century, Russia, England, Austria, and France maintained a continuing interest in the affairs of the Ottoman Empire. Toward the end of the century Germany became the fifth major European power involved in imperialism in the Middle East.

Dynastic aggrandizement at the expense of the Ottomans motivated Austrian and Russian conquests in the eighteenth century. The Hapsburgs desired Hungary, Transylvania, Dalmatia, and Serbia; and at the turn of the century they would have pushed southward in the Balkans had not the Napoleonic Wars absorbed their full strength. Austria was apprehensive lest Russia gain advantages in the Balkans, control Istanbul and the Straits, and flank Austria dangerously from the south.

France thought of the Ottoman Empire in terms of commerce, imperial geopolitical strategy, diplomacy, military and naval alliances, culture, and tradition. The merchants of Marseilles, who were engrossed in trade in every port of the Levant, were most instrumental in obtaining the great treaty of capitulations from the Porte in 1740. France was interested in empire and commerce in India and farther in Asia in addition to her interests in North Africa and the Mediterranean. The land mass of the Middle East lay astride the routes to the Orient. Since England rivaled France in the East, whichever power gained secure access to Middle Eastern routes could threaten and block the communications of the other. For this reason Muhammad Ali of Egypt appeared to be an excellent ally, and the French cultivated him and his successors assiduously.

British interest in the Middle East began during the reign of Elizabeth I, but remained almost exclusively commercial until the Napoleonic era. In the nineteenth century, especially after the treaty of Adrianople (Edirne), a changing emphasis in trade and a shifting European balance of power won over Britain to the maintenance of the Ottoman Empire as a means of blocking Russian egress into the Mediterranean.

This policy impelled England to oppose partition of the Ottoman Empire and to pursue a positive course to strengthen the sultan's government.

Russia proved the most consistent and persistent enemy of the Ottoman Empire in the eighteenth and nineteenth centuries. The tsars and tsarinas dreamed of gaining Istanbul and reestablishing a Christian empire in the city of Constantine. Joined to this ambition was the belief that control of navigation through the Straits for commerce and war was an absolute necessity to complete the full sovereignty of Russia. Means to these ends, but eventually ends in themselves, were interests in the Holy Land; concern over the welfare, security, and friendship of all Christians in the Ottoman Empire; and creation of friendly Christian satellite states in the Balkans and the Caucasus.

Although war and peace recurred intermittently between Russia and the Ottoman Empire, the first notable landmark of their relationship in the nineteenth century was fixed by the famous treaty of Kuchuk Kainarji of 1774. A number of subsequent treaties concluded between the two states confirmed the concessions granted by the Porte but without greatly augmenting them. The treaty of Adrianople, however, altered the status quo. It gave Russia an increased role in the Balkans. Nicholas therefore accepted in 1833 the invitation to protect the Ottoman Empire against attack by Muhammad Ali and sent a fleet and marines to the Bosphorus to defend the helpless Mahmud. After thwarting Muhammad Ali but before the armed forces departed the Russians obtained the treaty of Hunkiar Iskelesi, which proclaimed a defensive alliance between the two states and promised aid to each other in case of need. In particular, the Ottoman Empire declared anew the closing of the Straits to all warships. The chief importance of the treaty, however, lay in its affirmation of friendship, which indicated the direction in which Ottoman diplomacy had turned.

COMMERCE AND TRADE

In 1838, the signing of the important and advantageous commercial convention of Balta Liman dealt a significant blow to Russian favoritism. British traders were permitted to import goods upon payment of an ad valorem duty of 5 percent; upon the export of Ottoman goods a duty of 12 percent was charged. Furthermore, monopolistic practices were abolished on goods exported from the empire. This provision specifically included Egypt. The most important result of the arrangement was the ability, henceforth, of British merchants to carry on foreign trade at the same rates as applied to Ottoman nationals. Since British firms had a wider organization and were not subject to Ottoman taxation, the convention soon proved to be a blow to Ottoman traders. Articles of the Balta Liman convention did not in themselves bestow upon Great Britain any marked position in the Middle East. France, the Netherlands, and other nations were accorded identical treatment before the year was out.

The European powers agreed in 1840 that any occupation within the Straits by foreign armed forces to protect the sultan from Muhammad Ali had to be only temporary. The following year the convention among Great Britain, Austria, France, Prussia, Russia, and the Ottoman Empire reaffirmed the earlier practice, mentioning the Bosphorus as well as the Dardanelles. Each European signatory was thus committed to defend the sultan's sovereignty over the Straits and to prohibit warships from entering those waters while the sultan was at peace. With the expiration of Hunkiar Iskelesi that autumn no European state had any special privilege that others did not possess. Europe recognized that the treaties of Kuchuk Kainarji, Akkerman, and Adrianople were still valid and that Russia enjoyed specified rights in the Balkans and among certain Christian groups throughout the empire. But in the Straits and at the Porte no nation had a treaty advantage or position of favor over another.

The convention of Balta Liman marked a definite upsurge in commerce between the Ottoman Empire and western Europe. Port cities such as Beirut and Izmir grew rapidly in population and wealth. After 1846, the grain trade with the Ottoman Empire and especially with the Danubian provinces rose to unprecedented heights. Within a few years Britain was obtaining as much grain from the Ottomans as she was from Russia (a development that should not be ignored in considering the factors leading to the Crimean War). In 1827 British exports to the Ottoman Empire were about £500,000; in 1849 they were more than £2,400,000. Britain's imports from the Middle East in this period were nearly as great as her exports and were expanding no less rapidly.

The trade of France, the Netherlands, Prussia, and Austria in the Middle East also developed, though not as markedly as that of Britain. Marseilles remained an important trading city for the Levant, and Austrian trade with the Balkan provinces improved as transport developed along the Danube. Growing industrial areas in western Europe found in the Middle East a source of foodstuffs and raw materials that could be obtained in exchange for the products of the new machines of the West. The trade, however, gradually affected handicraft industries in the Middle East, largely substituting machine-made textiles of western Europe for local homespun cloth.

Great Britain forced the Ottoman Empire, Egypt, and Iran to stop almost entirely commerce in slaves. In the 1840s and 1850s the British secured some measures to stop the importation of black slaves by sea and the public sale of slaves. By the 1880s the slave trade was officially banned and only small numbers of slaves were being smuggled into the Ottoman Empire. (Abolition of slavery, however, had to wait until the next century.)

Use of machines and new types of power made it possible for the West to forge far ahead of the Middle East in matters of material welfare and wealth; and the imbalance of power and prestige of Western industrialized states over the agricultural Middle Eastern areas became more preponderant with each decade. The central government of the Ottoman Empire and the coastal regions of that state (and their immediate hinterlands) speedily developed into economic colonies of western Europe. The privileges known as capitulations hastened the process and fastened the bonds more securely.

THE CAPITULATIONS

Originally given to foreign merchants in the fifteenth century in order to encourage commerce with Christian states, the capitulations indicated procedures, laws, regulations, and responsibilities of nationals of a state residing and trading in the Ottoman Empire. With great increases in trade in the nineteenth century and shifting power relationships, the capitulations became exceedingly onerous for the Ottoman Empire. With the support of their governments foreigners took advantage of every loosely worded phrase, and all significant external trade within the Ottoman Empire devolved into foreign hands. Any Turkish subject who wished to enter the field sought means by which he could become a foreigner in his own country. This step was done by securing from a consul or ambassador of a foreign country—for a consideration—a document called a *berat,* which conferred upon the holder the rights of a national of that country as expressed in the capitulatory treaty, and outright sale of citizenship and passports was practiced openly by the unscrupulous. Consequently, in Ottoman ports Greeks, Jews, Armenians, and Levantines were often nationals of some European state even though neither they nor any of their ancestors had ever set foot on their "native land." Furthermore, their children and their children's descendants, though born within the Ottoman Empire, retained foreign citizenship.

Three facets of the capitulations were particularly important: law, taxes, and tariffs. Foreigners had the right to be tried in their own consular courts, where laws of their own country prevailed. Since Ottoman government officials frequently relied upon the advice of powerful European ambassadors, consuls could usually have criminal cases against their nationals dropped. No foreigner could be arrested or held by Ottoman police, unless an official from his consulate was present. This regulation meant that most misdemeanors by foreigners were ignored or glossed over by the Ottoman authorities to avoid difficulties, arguments, and awkward situations.

Foreigners were exempt from local taxes and were thus able to conduct local business with less interference from the government and at a lower cost than Ottoman subjects. The sultan found it impractical to increase many business taxes, since the result was only deleterious to Ottoman nationals.

Important export tariffs were established by the capitulations and could not be changed except by consent of each party in a specific treaty. Since each treaty also contained a "most favored nation" clause, it was necessary to change all treaties in concert to make any successful change at all: to get all to agree was virtually impossible. Because the Ottoman Empire was not strong enough to defy all the Great Powers at once and denounce all treaties simultaneously, tariffs in the nineteenth century moved only in the direction of free trade. Such a situation made possible the commercial exploitation of the weak Middle East by the powerful Western nations. No relief could be expected until the capitulations were abrogated; and to this the Powers would not give their consent because of the benefits their nationals derived with respect to residence, law, and taxes, as well as to trade.

RELIGIOUS ISSUES

Into this picture of the capitulations was injected an additional feature: religion. Oddly enough, the reasons for many of the so-called capitulatory articles were religious. Mehmed II, after conquering Constantinople, recognized the native Orthodox Greek religious community and soon thereafter the Armenian and Jewish communities as special legal entities, later called *Millets*. In a parallel way, various foreign national communities such as Venetians, Florentines, Genoese, and French, each under a designated representative, were recognized by the capitulations as "national Millets." Frequently a treaty, like the French treaty of 1740, permitted a foreign community to adopt other nationals whose governments possessed no treaty with the Porte.

The most extraordinary extension came with assertions in the French treaty of 1740 and the treaty of Kuchuk Kainarji in 1774 that Roman Catholics were under the protection of the French and Orthodox Christians under the aegis of the tsar. In subsequent negotiations, the Porte pressed for its understanding that only the respective clergy were included, but France and Russia held that the entire communities were embraced. The extension of foreign interest, therefore, had a widening concern in Ottoman domestic affairs; and, coupled with the ancient Millet system, it led to an identification of creed with nationality, helping to make nationalism synonymous with religion.

Prior to the treaty of Adrianople and the recognition of Greek independence, there were still only three Millets in the Ottoman Empire. But by 1914 there were seventeen, and almost all enjoyed the sponsorship of a foreign government. Not entirely responsible for this movement but certainly encouraging it were the foreign missionaries and Bible societies. Christian missionaries from Europe had labored in the Middle East for centuries; and Roman Catholic churches, convents, hospices, and missions were well established in the Levant before the nineteenth century. The great drive in the Middle East, however, began during the Napoleonic Wars and has carried through to the present. Russian, Austrian, German, French, Italian, British, American, and other mission groups of many denominations established schools, churches, hospitals, printing presses, orphanages, and a variety of other service groups to carry the Christian message and Western concepts of society to Middle Eastern peoples. Completely unsuccessful in converting Muslims, they concentrated their efforts upon the indigenous Christian groups. With respect to the Muslims they philosophized that they might Christianize them by first Westernizing them.

In 1860, with the founding of the Alliance Israélite Universelle and later other groups, Jews in Europe began to organize to better the welfare of Jews in other parts of the world, especially those in the Middle East. Most Jews in the Middle East did not have the diplomatic protection granted Christians by European governments and as a result, they suffered less from the rising antagonism directed by some elements of the Muslim population against minorities who depended on foreigners for advancement and security.

The Christian European governments often subsidized Christian Ottoman groups for ulterior aims and gave direction to their work for political ends. Russia and England, for instance, competed for the Armenians, and neither wished to see American missionaries enter the field. Missionaries were regarded as an advance guard in the process of imperialism—political and economic—and the *Millet* system lent itself wonderfully to the business of expanding a national influence.

The European powers quarreled and competed for the minds and souls of the Christian population of the Middle East and the expected advantages of religious and missionary patronage. Through the efforts of Sir Stratford Canning, later Viscount de Redcliffe, the famous British ambassador, Protestants in the Ottoman Empire were recognized as a *Millet* in 1850. This move was certainly warranted; yet it could hardly do other than favor British interests, since the French had the Roman Catholics and Russia the Orthodox.

The greatest rivalry occurred in the Holy Land between the Russians and the French. Since medieval times Latin monks and clerics had attended the shrines and Holy Places in Bethlehem, Jerusalem, and Nazareth. The capitulatory treaty of 1740 confirmed the right of the French government to protect these churchmen and accorded them certain privileges, one of which was possession of the key to the main door of the Church of the Nativity in Bethlehem. Since almost every treaty or convention signed by the Porte with any European state contained equal recognition, the true legal situation was entirely confused by the middle of the nineteenth century.

Orthodox churchmen dated their rights to control and protect the Holy Sepulchre from the seventeenth century. They protested against the French rights, claiming that they were false and had been wrung from the sultan when Orthodox support had been weak. Whatever the rights may have been, few Latin pilgrims visited the Holy Land in the eighteenth and nineteenth centuries, whereas crowds of Orthodox traveled thousands of miles to pray at the Holy Sepulchre or the Grotto of the Holy Manger in Bethlehem. Latin privileges, therefore, lapsed through neglect and default. In 1808 the Church of the Holy Sepulchre was ruined by fire. The Orthodox, under the direction of the patriarch of Istanbul, rebuilt it, levying a tax on all Orthodox Christians in the Ottoman Empire for the purpose.

Beginning about 1840 there was a rising crescendo in France over the Holy Land and the position of the Latin Church therein. In 1842, when the cupola of the Church of the Holy Sepulchre needed repair, a great commotion arose over which sect should enjoy the privilege. Actual fighting broke out in 1847, and at Christmastime in Bethlehem, Latin and Greek monks attacked each other with candlesticks and crosses at the Church of the Nativity. The Ottoman governor of Jerusalem posted sixty soldiers inside the Church of the Holy Sepulchre to prevent disorder and bloodshed.

THE CRIMEAN WAR

With the election of Louis Napoleon as president of France followed by his coup d'état in 1852, rivalry between Russia and France at the Golden Horn and in the Holy Land became acute. Each insisted upon historic rights over the Holy Places. The Porte confounded the issue by sending a note to the French acceding to their demands for changes, at the same time issuing a royal decree to the patriarch in Istanbul assuring that no changes would be made. The matter now stood as one of national honor and a question of religion upon which compromise was difficult. Since the royal decree was never publicly read and thus was never fully legal, the

Russians felt that they had been duped by the sultan and the French. Consequently, it was the tsar who took the initial overt action.

Prince Menshikov arrived at the Porte in 1853 with Russia's demands for full restoration and public recognition of Orthodox privileges in the Holy Land; Russian right to repair the cupola of the Church of the Holy Sepulchre; special treaty or convention with Russia again guaranteeing privileges for all Orthodox Christians in the empire; and conclusion of a secret defensive alliance with Russia.

Settlement was reached on two items: both Orthodox and Latins would receive concessions at the Holy Places, and the sultan would repair the Church of the Holy Sepulchre, following the plans of its original construction. But Menshikov's ultimatums and Russian mobilization along the Pruth did not intimidate the sultan's government, which refused to accede to the demands regarding protection of Orthodox Christians. To do so was in the view of the imperial divan tantamount to giving Russia the right to govern between 10 million and 12 million inhabitants of the Ottoman Empire.

Tsar Nicholas ordered the crossing of the Pruth and occupation of the Danubian provinces. The British and French sent their Mediterranean squadrons to Besika Bay, just outside the Dardanelles. Still there were no declarations and no intention of war. The Porte sent a note to European diplomats convening at Vienna, stressing the sultan's peaceful sentiments, and also forwarded copies of recent decrees granting anew in perpetuity the ancient privileges to Orthodox Christians. Ottoman feelings now ran high; and this note was regarded as the final appeasement. At Vienna, however, the Powers substituted their own version of a settlement, which stated that France and Russia would guarantee the status quo regarding Christians in the Ottoman Empire. Bolstered and excited by the recent arrival of a large Egyptian fleet at the Golden Horn, the Ottomans rejected the Vienna note, and declared war. Omar Pasha attacked the Russians on the Danube. Inconsequential Ottoman successes were obtained there and in the Caucasus; but real victory was won by the Russians when the Ottoman navy was destroyed in the Black Sea. Then the British and French governments sent their combined fleets into the Black Sea to bring about the withdrawal of all Russian ships to the harbor at Sevastopol, which Russia rejected.

No European power was prepared to participate in, much less to allow, the partition of the Ottoman Empire. Russia and England had had an entente to that effect ever since Tsar Nicholas's verbal agreement with the British in 1844. Russia, however, blundered into a difficult position over the religious controversy. Russia followed her time-honored procedure of occupying the Danubian provinces, a step that sent the British and French fleets to the Bosphorus to ensure the security of the Ottomans. In the spring of 1854 Austria and Prussia joined in the concert against Russia by requesting assurances of the integrity of the Ottoman Empire. When Austria mobilized her forces, the tsar's army retired behind the Pruth; Nicholas was not prepared to face all Europe, and war should have terminated then. Disturbances in Serbia were quelled, and British and French troops occupied Athens to force the Greeks to abandon their attack upon Turkey. But sentiment in England and France, on the streets and in the governments, was for further war.

Since a treaty of alliance had already been consummated by Britain, France, and the Ottoman Empire, the sultan followed suit. There is no need to relate the episodes of the Crimean War here, since it was a European rather than a Middle Eastern war. About 7,000 Ottoman soldiers, nearly 10 percent of the allied army, fought before Sevastopol. Ottoman monetary debts to English and French bankers mounted as costs mushroomed. Cholera weakened the armies more than did battles, but the will to fight persisted. Nicholas died in February 1855; peace overtures failed; and war continued until the fall of Sevastopol to the allies in September and the fall of Kars in Anatolia to the Russians in November. Austria suggested peace, which was speedily concluded at Paris in March 1856 after less than five weeks of discussion.

RESULTS OF THE WAR

The treaty of Paris with two additional conventions solemnly declared that the Ottoman Empire was a European power. In a separate treaty England, France, and Austria agreed to respect, defend, and guarantee its independence and integrity. Special vassalage status was conferred upon Wallachia and Moldavia; and navigation upon the Danube and Black Sea was made free and unrestricted under the administration of a commission composed of the signatories. The Black Sea was neutralized and demilitarized; except for small, defined coastal police vessels for Russia and the Ottomans, warships were banned. Equally important was European acceptance of a new reform edict already promulgated by Abdul Mejid, guaranteeing many reforms for Christians.

The war brought the Middle East to the attention of a great many Europeans, for the battles and incidents of the Crimean War were discussed in the newspapers more vividly than those of any previous war. For the first time Europe became fully conscious of the Near East, as it was then called; and events there were regarded by the general public as of prime importance.

The modern state of Rumania was born at Paris in 1856. The victors decided that a stronger and more independent rule for the Danubian principalities would serve as a better buffer between the Ottoman Empire and Russia. Eventually the desire of the two peoples for union was permitted, and in 1866 Rumanian leaders chose young Prince Charles of Hohenzollern as their Prince Carol. Rumania had taken a further step toward independence, and thereafter her development touched the course of Middle East affairs only indirectly.

THE LEBANON

While issues on the Danube were testing the friendship of the recent allies of the Crimean War, a series of bloody events in Syria and Lebanon furnished another pretext for forging the pattern of European intervention in internal problems of the Middle East. After the ejection of Ibrahim from Syria, a political vacuum arose in Lebanon, or the Mountain as it was usually called. Since the time of Napoleon, Amir Bashir Shihab, the leader of a local dynasty which had been paramount in the area since 1697, had ruled Mount Lebanon with ruthless calculation. His staunch loyalty to Ibrahim compelled the Porte to replace him in 1840 with an incompetent nephew. Maronites and Druzes soon fell to fighting. European pressure elicited a pacification from the sultan in 1843: the northern regions of the Mountain were governed by a Maronite, supported by the French; the southern portion was left to the Druzes, who were favored by the British.

An uneasy peace and prosperity reigned for a decade in Mount Lebanon. However, a new and weak governor in the Maronite district, installed in 1854, permitted feudal lords to abuse villagers; and population pressures were felt keenly. In 1858 a kind of social upheaval broke out; and in 1860 in the Druze district, where many of the peasants were Maronites, and in the city of Damascus, massacres of Christians took place. The Powers permitted Napoleon III of France to send a force of 6,000 to restore order there. The Ottomans, however, had the situation under control before the French arrived; and a European commission drew up a statute at Beirut for autonomous rule in Lebanon. Signed by Sultan Abdul Mejid in 1861, it provided for an Ottoman Christian governor appointed with consent of the Powers. He was to have full executive power and was to be assisted by a central administrative council composed of members of all important sectarian communal groups. Feudal law was to be ended, and a separate police force and judiciary were created. The first governor, Daud Pasha, an Armenian Catholic, proved exceptionally able as a diplomat and administrator; and the rule under the statute, redrawn in 1864, remained in effect with a great degree of success until the Ottomans assumed direct rule during World War I.

OTTOMAN FINANCES

While better government was being established in the Mountain of Lebanon, the same could not be said for the central government on the Golden Horn. One of its most unfortunate developments, which concerned the Powers and which they condoned and abetted, was the contracting of foreign loans. Beginning with the Crimean War, the Ottoman government contracted loans to meet extraordinary expenses of the army and navy. As has been pointed out, the financial structure and tax system of the empire were antiquated even before the war; and for years the sultan had borrowed locally to satisfy current expenses. Tax anticipations were, therefore, hopelessly inadequate for a loan of the size needed in 1854. Guaranteed by the Egyptian tribute, a £3 million loan was handled in London.

Once the habit was fixed, loans were contracted almost every year, with Istanbul customs duties, tobacco and salt taxes, sheep taxes, and various revenues pledged as security. By 1875 Ottoman foreign debts had risen to £200 million bearing annual charges of £12 million. The total revenue of the government stood at £22 million. Either bankruptcy or government reorganization was in order, but European moneylenders could not bring themselves to terminate such a golden bonanza. Even in 1874 there was a loan of £40 million issued at 43.5!

Although these loans were made chiefly in London and Paris, no idea of annexing the Ottoman Empire to the British or French empire was entertained. Money was seeking investment, and issue prices ran interest rates well over 10 percent. As long as confidence could be maintained, bankers had little difficulty in floating bonds, and profits were enormous. When one grand vizir balked at taking a loan, Palmer, a British banker, used his influence to replace him for a more willing borrower. Bankers in Galata, the commercial district of Istanbul, made current loans to the government or discounted its bills at ruinous rates.

The theory of the right of European governments to intervene in Ottoman affairs grew with the series of loans. Commissioners were appointed to investigate spending of funds and the financial feasibility of the loans and to supervise the collection of the moneys designated as security for the loans. But there is ample evidence that intervention remained only theoretical. On October 6, 1875, the Ottoman government announced, in face of a large budget deficit, that only half the amounts due on foreign bonds would be paid in cash. The balance was to be met by five-year bonds bearing 5 percent interest. The end had come.

The growing financial crisis affected every part of the empire. The burden of the foreign debt left the treasury a diminishing sum to meet expenses of government. Officials who went unpaid resorted to corrupt practices, while the government adopted harsher methods of taxation. Peasants everywhere were squeezed, and provinces stirred with an uneasy patience. The most serious rebellion burst in Bosnia.

BALKAN PROBLEMS

From their mountain retreats descendants of Muslim Slavic ghazis of earlier days resisted innovations of a new age. In 1831 they fought Mahmud's reforms. European disturbances in 1848 and unrest among the Serbs again provoked the Bosnians to rebel. This time they were subdued in 1850. Financial difficulties called for rigid collection of taxes in Bosnia in 1875, even though there had been a scanty harvest the previous year. Revolt throughout Herzegovina and other Balkan areas erupted over the stringent measures. Montenegrins and Serbs sympathetically transformed the revolt into an open declaration of war in July 1876.

Before formal hostilities began, the insurgents had tasted considerable success—and pan-Slavs in Russia, Serbia, and Austria were jubilant. Britain's Prime Minister Disraeli, however, was still the enigma, and the presence of the British fleet at Besika Bay added to the uncertainty about his intentions. At this juncture news of Bulgarian massacres jolted Europeans. The Balkan revolt was spreading to Bulgarian districts, despite the economic prosperity of the past years. An irregular Ottoman militia perpetrated a horrible massacre upon the villagers of Batak, who were preparing to join in the uprising. Perhaps 5,000 individuals out of 7,000 in Batak were killed. Reports from correspondents, describing many shocking incidents, appeared in London papers.

Because of the high emotion aroused in British politics by the Bulgarian atrocities, Russia and Austria considered the moment propitious for a change in the Balkan status quo. The Porte still declined the proffered armistice; and Ottoman armies defeated the Serbs, especially when the latter were led by Russians. Annihilation of Serbia was imminent. Serbia asked the Powers to intervene, and Russia gave the Porte forty-eight hours to arrange an armistice. When this was granted, a conference of the Powers met to discuss peace between Serbia and the Porte and to review the future of European Turkey. A distinguished assemblage of statesmen convened at Istanbul two days before Christmas 1876.

The Constantinople conference, as Europe termed it, was shocked on its opening day by the sultan's proclamation of a full-drawn constitution for his empire, providing for a bicameral legislature, a cabinet, freedom of the press, compulsory education, and a reformed judiciary. Midhat Pasha, the reforming grand vizir, and the British had been discussing the constitution for more than a year, and this moment was regarded as most appropriate for its announcement. With a constitution in hand and the friendship of the British, the Porte refused to accede to the Powers, and the conference broke up in January 1877. Peace was signed directly between Serbia and Turkey in February upon the basis of the status quo.

RUSSO-TURKISH WAR

Russia had several hundred thousand men mobilized along the Pruth, and declared war on April 24, 1877. Russia believed she had squared herself with Austria and Germany and reasoned that Britain would protest only if the Straits were threatened. No one expected the war to last very long, because neither contestant had any ready cash, and loans did not materialize. The Ottoman navy dominated the Black Sea. But Rumania deserted the Ottomans, declared full independence, and aided Russia. Crossing Rumania, the Russians passed the Danube and appeared to be on their way to Edirne and Istanbul. Then Osman Pasha dug in near Plevna in Bulgaria, resisting the Russian siege from July until December. The Ottomans mobilized armies totaling about 250,000 men on the European and Caucasian fronts. Meanwhile, Ottoman forces were defeated at Kars by a Russian general, in Herzegovina by the Montenegrins, and at Nish by the Serbs. The Ottomans threw themselves upon the mercy of the European concert. Russia, Rumania, Serbia, and Montenegro, however, continued the war, occupying Edirne on January 20, 1878. Muslims fled before the advancing armies, since cossacks and Balkan armies were as brutal in their atrocities as Ottoman irregulars had been at Batak.

The Russian lines approached Istanbul, and Grand Duke Nicholas placed his headquarters at the village of Yeşilköy (San Stefano), only ten miles from the Ottoman capital. Part of the British fleet was ordered up from Besika Bay to Istanbul. Excitement ran high, and London music halls rang with the song

We don't want to fight:
But, by jingo, if we do,
We've got the men, we've got the ships,
And, we've got the money too.

Sultan Abdul Hamid begged the British to withdraw to Besika Bay, since the Russians threatened to counter by an entry into Istanbul. After the fleet left, the treaty of San Stefano was signed on March 3, 1878, recognizing the independence of Montenegro, Serbia, and Rumania, each of which received considerable territory at Ottoman expense. Bosnia and Herzegovina obtained autonomous rule; and Russia acquired Batum, Kars, and eastern Anatolia up to Trabzon and Erzurum. Bulgaria was created as a large self-governing Christian principality from the Aegean to the Black Sea and westward to Albania, including Edirne but not Salonika. As a final blow 300 million rubles (roughly £30 million) was set as an indemnity for the Ottoman Empire to pay to Russia.

THE CONGRESS OF BERLIN

Almost before the ink dried, objections arose. Rumania and Serbia felt slighted, Austria was ignored, and the creation of "Big Bulgaria" produced a storm. Greece, Serbia, Rumania, and Montenegro protested, and representatives of Albanian groups petitioned to be heard. British and Austrian opposition demanded a settlement of the Eastern question by the concert of Europe. At Berlin there gathered on June 13, 1878, a galaxy of statesmen, foreign ministers, and diplomatic stars. The Anglo-Turkish convention of June 4, 1878, ceding the administration of Cyprus to Britain, was announced.

The treaty of Berlin reduced the "Big Bulgaria" of the treaty of San Stefano to a small autonomous principality, where the prince would be chosen by an assembly of Bulgarian notables and confirmed by the Porte. A province of Eastern Rumelia was constructed, where the governor-general was appointed by the sultan with consent of the Powers. Although the Ottoman Empire could maintain troops and erect fortresses there, the police force was to be drawn from the native population. Commissions and constitutions were to be enacted for the remaining Ottoman provinces in Europe. Rumania, Montenegro, and Serbia became independent kingdoms; and Austria-Hungary occupied and administered Bosnia and Herzegovina. Navigation of the Danube was to be supervised by a commission. Ardahan, Kars, and Batum were given to Russia, and the provisions of the treaty of Paris of 1856 regarding the Black Sea and the Straits were preserved. Finally, the Ottomans pledged religious liberty and civil equality for the sultan's subjects in Europe and Asia alike. The dignitaries rejoiced when they signed the treaty, because a troublesome question had been handled without a major war.

Because of recrimination and jealous rivalry generated among the Powers as an aftermath, a number of the clauses of the treaty were not carefully followed by the Porte. Nevertheless, European ambitions and diplomacy with respect to the Near and Middle East were momentarily less rampant. Soon, however, an epoch opened when a new and modern European imperialism discovered with consternation the rising nationalism of many Middle Eastern peoples—Arabs, Armenians, Iranians, and Turks, each with many variants.

REFERENCES

Many of the references in the preceding chapter relate to this chapter. In addition to these, others cited in Chapters 16, 19, and 20 are pertinent.

Blaisdell, Donald C. *European Financial Control in the Ottoman Empire: A Study of the Establishment, Activities and Significance of the Ottoman Public Debt.* New York: Columbia University Press, 1929. The most complete picture of this extraordinary episode of Ottoman history.

Fawaz, Leila Tarazi. *Merchants and Migrants in Nineteenth-Century Beirut.* Cambridge, Mass.: Harvard University Press, 1983. Traces the growth of the city and the changes in its social and economic composition.

Finnie, David H. *Pioneers East: The Early American Experience in the Middle East.* Cambridge, Mass.: Harvard University Press, 1967. Stops with 1950 and is concerned with all American interests, from diplomats to navy men, shipbuilders, scholars, and missionaries.

Grabill, Joseph L. *Protestant Diplomacy and the Near East: Missionary Influence in American Policy, 1810 1927.* Minneapolis: University of Minnesota Press, 1971. The great bulk of this outstanding book deals with the period around World War I.

Harik, Iliya. *Politics and Change: Lebanon, 1711–1845.* Princeton, N.J.: Princeton University Press, 1968. This study explains the peculiar political base of modern Lebanon.

Jelavich, Charles, and Barbara Jelavich. *The Establishment of the Balkan National States, 1804 1920.* Seattle: University of Washington Press, 1977. An excellent survey of the various Balkan countries.

Khalaf, Samir. *Persistence and Change in 19th Century Lebanon: A Sociological Essay.* Beirut: American University of Beirut Press, 1979.

Kuneralp, Sınan, ed. *Studies on Ottoman Diplomatic History I.* Istanbul: Isis Press, 1987. The first of a series, with each volume to include diverse essays based on Ottoman and European sources.

Ma'oz, Moshe. *Ottoman Reform in Syria and Palestine, 1840–1861.* London: Oxford University Press, 1968. A well-balanced description of political, social, and religious conditions from the end of Egyptian occupation to the death of Abd al-Aziz. Excludes Mount Lebanon. Excellent.

Pamuk, Şevket. *The Ottoman Empire and European Capitalism, 1820–1913: Trade, Investment and Production.* Cambridge: Cambridge University Press, 1987. A sophisticated analysis, based on the "dependency school" approach, which sees the Ottoman Empire as part of Europe's periphery.

Polk, William R. *The Opening of South Lebanon, 1788–1840.* Cambridge, Mass.: Harvard University Press, 1963. A detailed and comprehensive study.

Raccagni, Michelle. "The French Economic Interests in the Ottoman Empire." *International Journal of Middle East Studies* 11 (1980): 339–376.

Seton-Watson, R. W. *Disraeli, Gladstone, and the Eastern Question: A Study in Diplomacy and Party Politics.* London: Macmillan, 1935.

Sousa, N. *The Capitulatory Regime of Turkey: Its History, Origin, and Nature.* Baltimore, Md.: Johns Hopkins Press, 1933. A survey from 1535 to 1923.

Spagnolo, John P. *France and Ottoman Lebanon 1861–1914.* London: Ithaca Press, 1977. A superb discussion of all aspects of this subject.

Tibawi, A. L. *American Interests in Syria, 1800–1901: A Study of Educational, Literary, and Religious Works.* London: Oxford University Press, 1966. Deals with greater Syria and compares the work of Americans with that of other foreign groups.

———. *British Interests in Palestine, 1800–1901.* London: Oxford University Press, 1961. The relations of the British consulate with British missionaries.

Toledano, Ehud R. *The Ottoman Slave Trade and Its Suppression, 1840–1890.* Princeton, N.J.: Princeton University Press, 1982. Based on Ottoman and European sources, this is a thorough treatment of a difficult topic.

24

The Ottoman Empire: from Tanzimat to the Constitution

HATT-I SHARIF

The reforms of Mahmud II were conceived to strengthen and widen the authority of the central regime. Destruction of the janissaries had been the primary requirement, and upon their abolition a more effective and responsive army was developed, and other changes introduced. Disobedient and unmanageable provincial governors succumbed one after another to the force of Mahmud. From his desire to enforce the subservience of Muhammad Ali, however, issued the disastrous defeats of 1832–1833 and 1839. In the latter struggle Mahmud's reconstituted army and navy were lost. Mahmud died on July 1, 1839, leaving his sixteen-year-old son, Abdul Mejid, to face military defeat and to be saved by the Powers.

The new sultan had only a scanty, informal education. Since his view of the world, his own country, and human society hardly extended beyond the palace walls, his understanding of the problems of his empire and their solution was extremely rudimentary. His misconceptions, uncertainties, and personal whims led to constant shifts of grand viziers and other ministers, frequently at the instigation of powerful ambassadors at the Porte.

Four months after his accession Abdul Mejid declared the Hatt-i Sharif ("Illustrious Rescript"), ushering in a new political era for the Ottoman Empire. It abolished capital punishment without a trial; guaranteed justice to all with respect to life, honor, and property; and supported the establishment of the Supreme Council of Judicial Ordinances to frame laws as well as a new penal code against which no infringements would be tolerated because of personal rank or influence. Mixed tribunals, composed of Muslims and non-Muslims, were formed to handle commercial cases involving foreigners. Most significant, testimony by a Christian against a Muslim was made admissible in the courts.

The second reform measure of the Hatt-i Sharif was designed to end the system of tax farming and institute the collection of taxes by government officials. (In reality, some forms of tax farms and feudal holdings persisted until at least 1908.) Finally, methods of army recruitment and length of service were to be reviewed by the imperial military council, and new procedures were promised to ensure regularity and impartiality for all parts of the state. It was also embodied in the decree that its provisions pertained to all subjects, irrespective of religion or sect.

One of the more lasting effects of the Hatt-i Sharif was its call for the development of the Supreme Council of Judicial Ordinances, which Mahmud II had instituted the year before as a substitute for a legislative body. The members of the Supreme Council were high officials of the government and were well paid to ensure their devotion to the position and their independence. However, although these members were appointed by the sultan, the positions were usually reserved for favorites of the grand vizir and his disciples. As a legislative body the council was thus fully controlled by the executive.

The Hatt-i Sharif was the Porte's demonstration to Europe that the Ottoman Empire was capable of self-preservation and reorganization to withstand pressures from non-Turkish groups for independence or autonomous rule. Its issuance made enactment of the London treaties of 1840 and 1841 concerning the Straits and the integrity of the Ottoman Empire appear more reasonable and just, thus easing British adherence to the settlement. The foreign minister, Mustafa Reshid, had served as ambassador for four years in London and Paris, and recognized the value and appeal that statements in the Hatt-i Sharif would generate in European capitals. Whether he brought them forth as a brilliant diplomatic coup or whether he had drunk deeply of the liberal political philosophies current in Paris has been much debated. In any case, Reshid in this act committed himself to a more liberal regime. Though sometimes weak in holding to a course and often personally corruptible, he became the advocate of reform and was thoroughly pro-British in his leanings.

Though the Hatt-i Sharif was endorsed by the grand vizir, the shaykh al-Islam, and the sultan, the new spirit was soon curbed. As soon as the Powers decided to drive Muhammad Ali back to Egypt, reaction set in. Reshid had introduced a new penal code, based somewhat on French models, but after he fell from office in 1841 over discussions of the new commercial code, which eventually was decreed in 1850, the course of reform took a different direction. Under Riza Pasha, a conservative court favorite and commander in chief of the army, a more rigorous conscription among Muslims was effected and some foreign officers were hired. (Christians were excluded from the conscription.) The regular army and the reserve were increased to 400,000; in practice the Ottomans could only raise a force of 300,000, and many of those were tied down in police operations. The currency situation was greatly improved by withdrawing most of the paper money in circulation and introducing a silver coinage. Government officials who went out to collect taxes proved so incompetent that peasants—Muslims and Christians alike—clamored for a return to tax farmers as the lesser of two evils.

TANZIMAT

Reshid returned to office as foreign minister in 1845 and became grand vizir the following year. Immediately, he set about to reestablish the forward movement of the Hatt-i Sharif by initiating *Tanzimat,* a movement for reorganization. His friends and supporters, Ali and Fuad, strove to organize education on a more formal and widespread basis. The Ottoman Imperial University was created in 1846 to coordinate the various colleges launched earlier, but many delays and difficulties postponed its effective organization. A special council appointed to study the needs of secondary education recommended universal, compulsory, and free education, with free textbooks. Six schools providing such education were operating by 1851, but the drive collapsed because of lack of funds and the return to power of reactionary leaders.

The Tanzimat period resulted primarily not from foreign intervention but from internal pressures and growth. With the great increases in British commerce in the Middle East occurring in the 1840s, Reshid, who was friendly with the West and who pushed changes at the Porte favorable to England and France, naturally found an eager ally in the British ambassador.

The Tanzimat spirit was manifested in the growing number of Ottomans who were educated in the West or in a Western manner and who thus became more secular in their outlook. The best evidence of this growth was the plethora of newspapers, journals, and books that appeared in the decade preceding the Crimean War. Politics, history, biography, and philosophy were popular subjects; and new ideas awakened the younger generation. Everywhere in Europe revolts against conservatism and the old order were stirring; and Turkey, on the edge of Europe, felt some of this movement. Ever-growing nationalist sentiment among Greeks, Armenians, Bulgarians, and others could not fail to arouse some Ottoman patriotism, too.

Some of Reshid's reforms were extended beyond the capital and appeared in measures regarding equal justice, withdrawal of capital punishment from the hands of local governors, an increase in the size of the bureaucracy, and creation of local assemblies elected to advise the governor and give their consent before he could take action. Since assemblies were usually composed of wealthy, influential notables and conservatives, they prevented changes from being adopted and were frequently in collusion with the governor. They did, however, check the prevalence of arbitrary local government. In addition to provincial assemblies, the grand vizir checked on actions of the governor by sending out commissioners to inspect a province and receive petitions from local groups.

In 1840, Europeans who had not been in Istanbul for twenty years commented that the changes that had transpired during those two decades were so momentous as to alter beyond restoration the physical, social, political, economic, and intellectual situation. By 1850 the Tanzimat spirit had rooted itself permanently in Istanbul society. No longer was the government or the state solely an instrument for the sovereign to collect revenue, raise armies, and administer justice. Matters of education, public works, and economic development were of some concern to the rulers. This "reordering" spirit was also manifest in the modernization of law, diplomacy, government administration, and education. A secular attitude was injecting new ideas of law and education into the Muslim as well as into the non-Muslim communities: the individual was coming to be regarded as having rights outside of the group. Although many Muslims still rebelled at the idea, Ottomanism, promising equality for all subjects, was beginning to have a sizable following. The spirit of Ottomanism could be seen in the appointment of Ottoman Christians and Jews to the reform councils and institutions.

No law or ordinance could become effective until it had been discussed by the Tanzimat Council and approved by the Council of Ministers. It was very active in legislative matters and it enacted new legislation for various councils, ministries, departments, schools, and state organizations. In 1868 a Council of State was organized with Midhat Pasha as its first president and a Judicial Council headed by Jevdet Pasha. The latter had fourteen members, including two Armenians, a Greek, a Bulgarian, and Muslims from various areas of the empire. This council served as a court of appeals for cases arising from new, Westernized civil laws, but not from religious laws, as these were handled by Millet courts. Under Midhat's leadership many innovations were introduced, including the standardization of weights and measures under the metric system, regulations on mining, a new nationality law, a lending bank for small businesses, and a reorganization of public instruction. Unfortunately, Midhat and Alı Pasha, the grand vizir, quarreled continuously; their conflict ended only when Midhat was appointed governor of Baghdad.

HATT-I HUMAYUN

The process of change was accelerated greatly by the Crimean War. The presence in Istanbul of large numbers of British, French, and Italian soldiers, government officials, merchants, journalists, and tourists had marked social repercussions upon the Ottomans. Contacts between East and West had not been so widespread in many generations, and the quantities of money expended by the Crimean War Allies gave to many the opportunity of satisfying their desire for European travel, study, books, and ideas. A European education became the fashion; every young man of a good or ambitious family was sent to Paris, Geneva, London, or some other center to assimilate as much Western culture as possible. The movement eventually transformed the Ottoman Empire, but the results were not immediately evident.

England, France, and Sardinia were allied to the Ottoman Empire during the Crimean War and were ostensibly fighting for the empire's preservation. Before the Treaty of Paris could be completed and the public in western Europe satisfied that the Ottoman state was worth saving, a new reform document had to be issued. This was the Hatt-i Humayun ("Imperial Rescript") of February 18, 1856, which reendorsed the Hatt-i Sharif and the Tanzimat. But it was far more specific in its details and certainly more extensive in scope than previous reform measures.

The imperial decree was in the main concerned with the Christian population of the empire; it granted them the rights and privileges that the Muslim community possessed or, at least, imagined that it enjoyed. Patriarchs and heads of communities (Millets) were appointed for life, and through self-chosen assemblies each community was to control its own temporal administration. Freedom of worship was declared, and no one could be compelled to change religion. Religion or nationality could not be a hindrance to holding public office, employment by the state, entry into a school, or service in the army.

In matters of justice and court procedures, commercial and criminal cases between Muslims and non-Muslims and among non-Muslims of different sects were referred to mixed tribunals whose proceedings were open to the public. Equality of taxes and army service among the various religious groups were pronounced, and a full new law regarding military service was promised "with as little delay as possible." Foreigners were henceforth permitted to own, purchase, and dispose of real property in the sultan's realm.

A budget for the state would be drawn up each year; banks and other financial institutions formed; and concrete steps taken to reform the monetary and financial systems of the empire. Roads and canals were envisaged. Commerce and agriculture were to be encouraged. Schools for every community were authorized. And every means was to be sought for the empire "to profit by the science, the art, and the funds of Europe."

On paper the Hatt-i Humayun contained the essentials necessary for a strong revival. The Ottomans sought to show this strength by extending their power over such areas as Yemen that had for long been independent of Istanbul. In 1849 they landed there, and in 1872 they took Sana in the interior. But in many of the more distant provinces, such as the Hijaz in Arabia, the Tanzimat reforms were unpopular and were not, for the most part, put into effect.

To make the reforms work both in the central government and in the provinces required the backing and valiant service of more people than were available. Moreover, the Hatt-i Humayun ignored the rising tide of nationalism among non-Muslims and failed to appreciate the effect of foreign residents upon the Millet system. Through their schools and literature the nationalists accepted the dictum that people could only enjoy the greatest happiness when governing themselves. The capitulations in the Ottoman Empire, including Egypt, gave political, social, and economic privileges to foreign nationals, individuals, and groups. Thus the Hatt-i Humayun, in spite of the efforts of such men as Fuad, Ali, and Midhat Pashas, was doomed to failure almost from the beginning. Too many others were opposed to it. The wars in Europe from 1859 to 1871 that accompanied the unification of Italy and Germany and the reforms that occupied Alexander II of Russia allowed the Ottoman Empire to follow her own political course. This meant preserving the basic status quo.

Bankruptcy

Since there were not enough Ottomans sincerely and deeply dedicated to a new order, the last days of Abdul Mejid and the entire reign of his brother, Abdul Aziz (1861–1876) were marked by disappointment. The few who preached modernization were sometimes silenced by those who wished to maintain the political stagnation of the realm. In 1867 Abdul Aziz visited Paris and London in the company of his nephews, Murad and Abdul Hamid, and his foreign minister, Fuad Pasha. He returned home full of the desire for reform.

Instead of reform, the Ottoman Empire rushed precipitously into bankruptcy. Between 1854 and 1875 one billion dollars was borrowed from Western Europe; at the end of that period almost nothing remained to show for such a vast sum— except debts. The tax system was still antiquated; the increasing national income augmented tax income but not to the degree needed to keep up with the costs of government. To meet the rising cost of military supplies purchased abroad, more loans were contracted and bonds floated in the money markets of the West. At the same time the Ottomans had a yearly excess of imports over exports. The great bulk of imports were consumer goods, and loans did not bring in the capital goods which in the end might have expanded Ottoman productivity and facilitated repayment of the loans.

Obviously the process could not continue indefinitely. The severe famines that took place in central Anatolia and a financial crisis in Europe helped bring on an Ottoman partial suspension of payments. In October 1875, the grand vizir announced the Ottoman Empire's insolvency by declaring that obligations could not be honored in full. This statement opened the door to a new era of wide European control of the Ottoman Empire to be ushered in a few years later. The approaching bankruptcy served to tighten the tax screws upon the provinces and brought open revolt in Bosnia and Herzegovina. The general repercussions and consequences in Europe of these disturbances were discussed in the preceding chapter.

SOCIAL REFORM AND POLITICAL REFORMERS

The widening influence of Western European books and ideas upon political affairs was more and more noticeable in Ottoman circles after the Crimean War. Ottomans, including especially members of the religious minorities, imitated French poetry, art, philosophy, and social forms; nationalism was discussed instead of religion; European-style plays were performed; and Persian elegance of phrasing became outmoded. French manners, liberalism, urbanity, and sophistication were now the fashion. The effect, however, that this innovative group had upon Ottoman society and the state as a whole was small. Its day came a generation later.

More immediately, European style was increasingly influential in the design of enormous new imperial palaces built along the Bosphorus. Ponderous, opulent, and Westernized in interior decoration, these palaces marked the end of Ottoman imperial artistic traditions. Many parts of Istanbul were changed, as streets were widened and straightened, transportation was improved, and urban services were increased.

A conservative influence came from the millions of Muslim immigrants who came to the Ottoman Empire from the provinces that had been lost to Russian and Balkan state expansionism. Resettlement of the refugees from the Caucasus, the Crimea, and the various Balkan regions was a costly and laborious process, but one that the Ottoman government welcomed. The refugees were viewed as a source of additional agricultural labor to put to work on productive land that had been vacant. One consequence of the refugee settlements was that the proportion of the Ottoman Empire's Muslim population substantially increased.

The Ottoman Land Law of 1858 enabled the new immigrants and others already settled on the land to register their rights and obtain deeds. Land ownership in most parts of the Ottoman Empire probably remained in the hands of small holders. Some large estates were created by tribal leaders who registered as their own property enormous amounts of land that was collectively utilized by their tribes. The central government also sold unutilized land in public auctions and large sections could be accumulated by absentee investers, especially in regions newly brought under the effective control of the state. Protection from raids by the nomads enabled the peasants to extend their planting of crops into outlying regions, such as in Syria and Jordan. Some of the Tanzimat changes affected the role of peasant women and those living in cities. Those who were wealthy urbanites were especially affected. Mode of dress became similar to that in western Europe. The central government began to train small numbers of midwives, and thousands of girls attended the new public and private schools by the end of the century. A women's teachers training school was established in 1872. Female education was supported by political leaders and reformers such as Midhat Pasha and Namik Kemal.

Until Reshid Pasha died early in 1858, he had been for twenty years the most commanding figure in the Ottoman government, having held all the high offices at one time or another. As was the custom, he found young, talented men in the government service, "protected" them, and advanced them to higher positions if their views dovetailed with his. Two, Mehmed Emin Ali Pasha and Kechejizade Mehmed Fuad Pasha, came to be regarded as Reshid's disciples and his successors. Both were "liberals," reformers, and Freemasons, and together they dominated the Ottoman government for fifteen years following the Hatt-i Humayun. Both were born in 1815, and for the decade from 1861 to 1871 one was always foreign minister while the other was usually grand vizir.

Ali Pasha, the son of an Istanbul shopkeeper, entered government service as a clerk at the age of fifteen, moved into the famed translation bureau in 1833, went to Vienna where he improved his French as secretary in the embassy in 1836, became ambassador to London in 1841, foreign minister in 1846, and grand vizir in 1852 at the age of thirty-seven. By that time he had already been governor of two provinces and, in 1854, had been named the first president of the newly created Tanzimat Council. During the Crimean War he served as foreign minister, and then in 1855 as grand vizir. In 1856 he attended the Paris Peace Conference as the Turkish plenipotentiary. When Reshid Pasha died in 1858, Ali was named grand vizir again. He was to be, variously, and sometimes simultaneously, grand vizir, foreign minister, and minister of the interior for the next sixteen years.

A small, frail person who spoke hardly above a whisper, Ali Pasha knew when to be silent and possessed complete self-control; he could hear the most startling news without a "flicker in his expression." He was a hard worker and honest, although it was supposed that he received a sizable "gift" from Khedive Ismail in 1866. Ali, as an Ottoman leader, endeavored to uphold order in the state, to ensure prosperity for all, and to initiate required and gradual changes in government and society. A moderate and cautious liberal, he proposed—to no avail—the opening of all public offices to all subjects. He believed in mixed schools where Muslims and Christians could study together, and hoped for the development of a citizenry of fully equal Ottomans. He was, however, opposed to the introduction of an elected constitutional government, arguing that the people were not sufficiently educated for that.

The only rival permitted in Ali Pasha's circle was his fellow moderate liberal, Fuad Pasha, who teamed so well with Ali yet differed from him in so many ways. Fuad, who belonged to a well-known Istanbul family, was the son of a famous poet and literary innovator. He was graduated from Galatasaray medical school, where instruction was in French, and then served in the army medical corps. His fluency in French was such that his witticisms in that language became famous throughout Europe. Entering the translation bureau in 1837, he soon became its highest officer. In 1840 he began a three-year stint as secretary to the embassy in London. Fuad conducted special negotiations for the Porte in Spain, Russia, and Egypt, and then in 1852 assumed the office of foreign minister, a post he was to hold on five separate occasions. He served terms as grand vizir, the first in 1861.

Fuad was tall, handsome, loquacious, forgiving, enterprising, and much more Westernized in his habits and manners than was Ali. Nevertheless, Fuad was devoted to the service of the Ottoman state and felt that its preservation was his first and most important duty. Though somewhat of a dilettante in most branches of knowledge and often quite superficial in world affairs, he strongly believed that to survive the Ottoman Empire would have to change her political and civil institutions to keep pace with progress in Europe. Noting that Islam was out of date in some respects, he argued that it was not a closed system and could accept new truths no matter whence they came. He recognized and moved to dampen the growing nationalisms in the Balkans by calling for an Ottoman identity and equality, with liberties for all non-Muslims. To overcome the weakness and irresponsibility of Abdul Aziz, Fuad urged that the grand vizir and the council of ministers be free from interference from the sultan and his coterie at the palace.

Fuad, Ali, and Reshid were the guiding hands of the Tanzimat period. Though others might carp at them for pushing for changes too slowly or sometimes not at all, they recognized that politics is the "art of the possible" and that their ideas and hopes were being suffocated by the overwhelming ignorance and inertia about them. Under the leadership of these three statesmen, many changes were introduced into the Ottoman system. They never did resolve how these changes could be debated or legislated; they frequently aired ideas for parliaments, elected or appointed, but generally feared to realize them.

YOUNG OTTOMANS

The reorderings of the Ottoman state discussed above were only part of the total efforts and changes introduced by Ali and Fuad Pashas. Conservative, staunchly Islamic sectors of society opposed anything that even resembled Westernism. On some occasions Abdul Aziz and the palace sympathized with the supporters of the status quo, so that Ali and Fuad had to be on their guard at every turn. There were, as well, those who chafed at the slow progress exhibited by the leaders. By the mid-1860s quite a number of young Turks and many non-Muslims had studied in Europe, where the political turmoil and revolutions of 1848 and the unification movements in Italy and Germany had stirred European students and, in turn, those from the Ottoman Empire. Young army officers, medical students, junior govern-ment officials, sons of wealthy pashas, and many others took to the newspapers to criticize the shortcomings of the government's ministers. Following the terminol-ogy of such groups in Italy, France, and elsewhere, Europeans labeled them all Young Turks or Young Ottomans.

Foremost among them was Namik Kemal, whose father was court astronomer (astrologer). Namik Kemal was a clerk for a time in the translation bureau but left this job for journalism, writing for a number of different papers and editing a jour-nal. A poet and an Ottoman patriot, he made the words "freedom" and "fa-therland" popular in Istanbul. Later, in 1873, his play *Vatan* (Fatherland) created such a fervent stir that it was shut down by the government and Kemal was exiled. He was an idealist immersed in the ideas of Western Liberalism, in the abstractions of many nineteenth-century political image makers, yet he wrote as an Ottomanist with such emotion as to keep his Ottoman audiences spellbound.

Uprisings in Crete and appeasement of the Cretans by Istanbul infuriated the Young Ottomans, who lashed out at the "duumvirate" as being shallow, blind, and traitorous. Abdulhamid Ziya joined Namik Kemal and the others in the onslaught, turning his pen and influence against Ali, with whom he had a personal quarrel. An admirer of Western science and Persian poetry, Ziya was an Ottoman patriot who veered toward agnosticism. In the spring of 1867 he was exiled to Cyprus. Ali Suavi was another who loved Ottoman and Turkish society. He was a man of hum-ble origins who had attended traditional schools and had taught in secondary schools in Bursa and in the Bulgarian province. Patronized by prominent officials, Suavi assailed the government by delivering nationalist harangues in Istanbul's mosques. Early in 1867 he started a newspaper in which he praised Turkish racial qualities. He excited the capital when rumors circulated that Suavi was engaged in a plot to kill Ali Pasha. Thereupon, Suavi was told to remain at Kastamonu.

Many of the Young Ottomans went into exile in Europe where they agitated for far-reaching reforms in their homeland. Their lack of internal cohesiveness made it easy for the central government in the late 1860s and early 1870s to secure their services and separate them one from another.

MIDHAT PASHA AND THE CONSTITUTION

Another group of men did find in their study of the West political institutions and practices that, in their eyes, would greatly benefit the Ottoman Empire. Their leader was Ahmed Midhat Pasha (1822–1884), a first rate administrator in provin-cial government, devoted to reform, and an open enemy of corruption. After his success in quelling two different outbreaks of brigandage in the Balkans, he was appointed governor of Nish. Conditions became relatively so salutary in Nish that

Midhat was recalled in 1864 to Istanbul, where with Fuad and Ali Pashas he drew up a new law of the provinces. The law reorganized the empire into twenty-eight large provinces *(vilayets)* and provided for mixed tribunals for cases involving Christians and Muslims and for assemblies of notables to counsel the governor. Yet, since final authority and the power of appointing the governor rested in the hands of the sultan or his advisers, the quality and type of administration enjoyed by a province depended almost wholly upon the governor's personality.

The energetic Midhat returned to Bulgaria where for a few years he served as governor of the new Province of the Danube. He built roads, bridges, railroads, orphanages, schools, hospitals, banks, agricultural cooperatives, and stagecoach routes. Even more important was his establishment of law and order and his just treatment of the Christian population. On the other hand, Midhat Pasha refused to condone revolutionary action and ruthlessly suppressed several outbursts of nationalism aimed at self-government and independence.

In rapid succession following the Bulgarian assignment Midhat served on the imperial council of state, governed the province of Iraq, became grand vizir for three months in 1871, held the governorship of Salonika, and then retired to private life in Istanbul. The government of the Ottoman Empire had been disintegrating since the death, in 1869, of Fuad Pasha and, in 1871, of Ali Pasha. The moderating influence of the French had almost disappeared with France's defeat in the Franco-Prussian War in 1871. The whims and vacillations of Abdul Aziz could not fill the political vacuum. The financial collapse under Grand Vizir Mahmud Nedim and violent uprisings in the Balkans, with their corollary of European intervention, heartened Midhat Pasha to engineer the deposition of the incompetent Abdul Aziz and install his nephew, Murad V, on May 30, 1876. In August Murad had a nervous breakdown and was replaced by his brother Abdul Hamid II.

Nine years before, Abdul Hamid had accompanied his uncle and the liberal Fuad Pasha on their European tour. It was generally believed from the impressions he made and from the knowledge he supposedly acquired that his accession to the throne augured well for a liberal progressive regime. Midhat Pasha's designation as grand vizir was also interpreted throughout the Ottoman Empire and in Europe as an indication of the new governmental steps to be taken.

Midhat Pasha disappointed very few, for on December 23, 1876, Abdul Hamid proclaimed the constitution that Midhat and others had been formulating since the deposition of Abdul Aziz. Accepted with great rejoicing among the liberals of Istanbul, the constitution provided for a cabinet and an elected parliament. It reaffirmed that all subjects of the sultan were equal, regardless of race or creed. Freedom of religion, education, and the press and equality of taxation were guaranteed.

Parliament held two sessions in a chamber in the Ministry of Justice. But the outbreak of war with Russia enabled Abdul Hamid in February 1878 to prorogue parliament and quietly ignore the constitution. By the end of the war and the settlement at the Congress of Berlin, Abdul Hamid and his entourage had the government well in hand. In 1884 Midhat was strangled in the dungeons of al-Taif, near Mecca. Modernization through political action died quietly while the Ottoman Empire tried technological Europeanization.

REFERENCES

Almost all volumes concerned with the Ottoman Middle East in the nineteenth century relate to subjects discussed in this chapter. Of special significance are those found in Chapters 18, 19, 20, 21, and 23.

Çelik, Zeynep. *The Remaking of Istanbul: Portrait of an Ottoman City in the Nineteenth Century.* Seattle: University of Washington Press, 1986. An excellent study of urban change.

Davis, Fanny. *The Ottoman Lady: A Social History from 1718 to 1918.* New York: Greenwood, 1986. Along with charming anecdotes of upper-class life for Ottoman women, there are numerous bits of information on economic, cultural, and political activities of women in Ottoman cities, especially Istanbul.

Davison, Roderic H. *Reform in the Ottoman Empire, 1856–1876.* Princeton, N.J.: Princeton University Press, 1963. First-rate study of ideas and forces in the Ottoman Empire.

Devereux, Robert. *The First Ottoman Constitutional Period: A Study of the Midhat Constitution and Parliament.* Baltimore, Md.: Johns Hopkins Press, 1963. This work, with those by Davison and Mardin, makes a fine trilogy.

Hershlag, Z. Y. *Introduction to the Modern Economic History of the Middle East.* Leiden: Brill, 1980.

Heyd, Uriel. *The Foundations of Turkish Nationalism.* London: Harwell Press, 1950.

Issawi, Charles. *An Economic History of the Middle East and North Africa.* New York: Columbia University Press, 1982. An outstanding volume that concentrates on the nineteenth century.

———. *The Economic History of Turkey, 1800–1914.* Chicago: University of Chicago Press, 1980. A wide variety of readings drawn from foreign and Ottoman sources that illustrate economic history.

Karpat, Kemal H. *Ottoman Population, 1830–1914: Demographic and Social Characteristics.* Madison: University of Wisconsin Press, 1985. Very useful statistical information and fine analysis.

Lane-Poole, Stanley. *The Life of the Right Honorable Stratford Canning, Viscount Stratford de Redcliffe.* 2 vols. London: Longmans, Green, 1888. In any study of the Middle East of the nineteenth century the life of this great ambassador cannot be disregarded.

Lewis, Norman N. *Nomads and Settlers in Syria and Jordan, 1800–1980.* Cambridge: Cambridge University Press, 1987. A stimulating study of nomadic tribes and their interactions with Ottomans and the national states of the twentieth century.

Mardin, Şerif. *The Genesis of Young Ottoman Thought: A Study in the Modernization of Turkish Political Ideas.* Princeton, N.J.: Princeton University Press, 1962. The best study of early Turkish nationalism.

Midhat, Ali Haydar. *The Life of Midhat Pasha.* London: J. Murray, 1903. A fine biography of the great Ottoman statesman, written by his son.

Ochsenwald, William. *Religion, Society and the State in Arabia: The Hijaz Under Ottoman Control, 1840–1908.* Columbus: Ohio State University Press, 1984.

Owen, Roger. *The Middle East in the World Economy, 1800–1914.* London: Methuen, 1981. An excellent study.

Pears, Edwin. *Forty Years in Constantinople, 1873–1915.* New York: Appleton, 1916. Sir Edwin was a British lawyer in Constantinople and corresponded with several London newspapers. He was a keen observer and often knew inside details of events.

Polk, William R., and Richard L. Chambers, eds. *Beginnings of Modernization in the Middle East: The Nineteenth Century.* Chicago: University of Chicago Press, 1968. Twenty papers by distinguished scholars on the many facets of change in the nineteenth-century Middle East.

Rosenthal, Steven T. *The Politics of Dependency: Urban Reform in Istanbul.* Westport, Conn.: Greenwood Press, 1980. Traces the European-supported reform in municipal government in parts of Istanbul during the Tanzimat.

25

Abdul Hamid II and Despotism

BULGARIA

The strange events of the summer of 1876, which brought the deposition first of Abdul Aziz and then of his nephew Murad V, and resulted in the accession of Abdul Hamid II, were symptomatic of the general unrest pervading the entire empire. Nowhere was this uneasy state of affairs more evident than in Bulgaria. So thoroughly had the Bulgarian area been dominated by the Ottoman government, feudal lords, and Greek clergy that many travelers passing through that region were not even aware that a Bulgarian people existed. By the 1830s, however, the basic causes of nationalism took effect; and Bulgarian schools, history, language, folklore, and national consciousness began to develop rapidly. Not least in importance in this growth were the opening of the area commercially, the marketing of wheat, flour, lumber, and attar of roses in western Europe, and the migration of Bulgarians to Odessa, Istanbul, Moscow, and the West.

In discussing Bulgarian nationalism, recognition must be given to the important advancements and indirect encouragement resulting from Midhat Pasha's benevolent rule. Education, economic prosperity, and personal security improved markedly in the 1860s, culminating in 1870 in the creation of the Bulgarian Exarchate, which included most of the Province of the Danube. Headed by an autonomous Exarch, the Bulgarian Church stimulated the nationalist movement and turned Macedonia, still a part of the Ottoman Empire, into a battleground between Bulgars and Greeks. While the Ottomans stood over the two parties and tried to preserve peace and order, Bulgarian political nationalists organized revolutionary societies in Bucharest and brought agents and literature into the province to maintain the nationalist spirit at fever pitch. Further unrest and agitation arose in the Bulgarian province by the settlement in the 1860s of 10,000 Crimean Tartars and many more Circassians from Russia. The latter, in particular, terrorized peasants and kept villages in a state of perpetual siege.

The situation in Bulgaria became tragic in 1876. Discontent in Bosnia and Herzegovina burst into a revolution, and Russian volunteers streamed across the Balkans to join the rebels. In the autumn of 1875 the Porte announced interest payments on its bonds could not be met in full. Apparently pressed to the wall, the Ottoman government reacted desperately against the Bulgarian uprising by sending wild Circassians and an ill-disciplined militia to pacify the area. Massacres followed; villages were destroyed; and British newspapers informed the world of what was happening.

International events set in motion by these disturbances have been discussed: the Constantinople Conference of Ambassadors, the Russo-Turkish War, the Treaty of San Stefano, and the Congress of Berlin. Equally important for Europe and far more significant for the Middle East were domestic events in the Ottoman Empire. In May 1876 theological students (*softas*) demonstrated against Abdul Aziz on the streets of Istanbul, obtaining, as had been done so frequently in preceding centuries, the dismissal of the grand vizir and the shaykh al-Islam.

ACCESSION OF ABDUL HAMID II

Two political groups were in formation. One was distinctly liberal and Western in its desire for constitutional government, fiscal reforms, and economic progress looking toward industrial and commercial development. The other was conservative. The liberals were now led by Midhat Pasha and Husayn Avni Pasha; the conservatives soon fell under the sway of Damad Mahmud Jelal al-Din and Redif Pasha.

The populace of Istanbul awoke on the morning of May 31, 1876, to find a new sultan on the throne. Midhat and Husayn Avni, with a handful of followers and the cooperation of the fleet and a few soldiers, had deposed the extravagant Abdul Aziz and enthroned Murad V. The liberal ministers were retained, and two immensely popular liberal journalists, Ziya and Namik Kemal, became the sultan's private secretaries. The reactionary party held its fire as Midhat proceeded to draft a constitution that would introduce responsible parliamentary and cabinet government to the Ottoman Empire.

Murad proved mentally unstable. The suddenness and circumstances of his accession quite unnerved him, as any hitch in the plot on that fateful night or a subsequent reversal of the coup would have meant his execution. A few days later Abdul Aziz committed suicide. Ten days later a crazed officer broke into a cabinet meeting and assassinated four officials, including two ministers. These incidents tipped the balance and Murad became incapable of governing. Affairs of state stood still, until in August Midhat deposed Murad in favor of Abdul Hamid II.

The latter promised to support the liberal party and to retain Ziya and Namik Kemal as his private secretaries. Abdul Hamid, however, had much more sympathy for the party of Damad Mahmud Jelal al-Din. Although Abdul Hamid never appointed the liberals as his secretaries, he did make Midhat grand vizir and promulgated the constitution. As soon as the conference of Powers adjourned from Istanbul, however, Midhat was called to the palace, placed aboard the sultan's yacht, and carried away to Italy and exile. Parliament met in March 1877, but Abdul Hamid obtained its adjournment after a few weeks and, in

February 1878, prorogued it and completely shelved the constitution. Until 1908 the constitution was printed each year in the official register, but remained ignored in every respect. The war with Russia served as the excuse for its suppression and became the pretext for Abdul Hamid to rule as the complete autocrat.

OTTOMAN PUBLIC DEBT ADMINISTRATION

The suspension of the payment of half of the interest due on Ottoman bonds in 1875 was a potent factor in producing the accession and removal of Murad in 1876. It is not clear whether bankruptcy was the cause or only a symptom of the failure of the Ottoman government to keep pace with the changing society of the Middle East. But in any case, bankruptcy, followed so closely by defeat in the war with Russia, compelled Abdul Hamid and his ministers to resort to measures not consonant with complete sovereignty.

On December 20, 1881, Abdul Hamid issued an imperial decree legalizing an arrangement with bondholders' groups whereby about £191 million of the external debt of the empire was consolidated and reduced to £106 million. The Council of Administration of the Ottoman Public Debt was devised as an authorized body to collect and disburse revenues and taxes on behalf of the bondholders. The Council consisted of seven members. five represented foreign bondholders; one was nominated by the Ottoman Bank, which was foreign-controlled; and one was appointed by the sultan. Largely the work of the British ambassador, this Decree of Muharram regularized Ottoman finances and reestablished the sultan's credit, while large sums were transferred abroad. By the late 1880s about one-fifth of all revenues were paid as interest on the external debt.

Within a few years after its inception the Ottoman Public Debt Administration became more than merely a collecting and banking agency. Slowly, debts began to be liquidated and, even more important, Ottoman credit was rehabilitated so that railways could be built and many Western innovations installed. In almost every case in which Ottoman credit or public operation was involved, an agreement provided that the Ottoman Public Debt Administration should act for the government. Thus, by 1900 many railways in Turkey were supervised by the Public Debt Administration, and railway bonds became the administration's obligations. It was so successful and in such good repute that the government itself used the organization to collect various unassigned taxes.

Sometimes the Ottoman Public Debt Administration served as an instrument of economic imperialism and, by its strength, sometimes as a political force. By and large, however, it was characterized by its restraint. It recognized that the interests of the bondholders would be best served by an improved economy. That its existence impinged upon Ottoman sovereignty there could be no doubt, and Turkish nationalists found it particularly offensive. But even the Young Turks in their revolt in 1908 were not strong enough to force its demise. The Kemalists, however, although they never denied the validity of the Ottoman debts, refused categorically to entertain even the idea of foreign intervention as indirectly implied in the Debt Administration. The Ottoman Public Debt Administration died quietly in 1923, when the Treaty of Lausanne omitted all reference to it.

SUPPRESSION OF THE CONSTITUTION

Abdul Hamid II eliminated the opposition. Some were bought, but Midhat Pasha was strangled in the dungeons of Arabia and illustrious Ottomans died in exile or in the inhospitable spots to which they were consigned. Surrounded by adventurers and sycophants, Abdul Hamid lived constantly in mortal terror of his subjects. He took refuge at Yildiz, which he enhanced and rebuilt and then protected by a double encircling wall. Cunning and suspicious, he had spies everywhere. He employed General von der Goltz of Germany to train the army. England was engaged to organize a police force for the empire. Fine new ships for the navy were ordered in England, France, and the United States.

Changes and improvements in government and society did proceed, and Abdul Hamid was not categorically opposed to reform. In 1879, after he suspended parliament, he appointed the minister of justice, "Kuchuk" Mehmed Said Pasha, as grand vizir, with the idea and hope that Said would meet the pressing problems of the empire in a more traditional fashion. As minister of justice Said had reorganized that ministry and had tightened and improved legal procedures in all the nonreligious courts. He had also attempted to exercise some control over the mixed courts in which cases between foreigners and Ottoman subjects were tried. Foreign governments objected so successfully, however, that the latter attempt was dropped.

While minister of justice, Said Pasha had written a memorandum to Abdul Hamid proposing financial reforms to strengthen the state and improve the army; administrative reforms to end the drift toward local autonomy; and educational reforms to achieve greater allegiance to Abdul Hamid from his Muslim subjects. By this initiative Said Pasha became grand vizir, a post he held eight different times, six under Abdul Hamid, two under the Young Turks.

In 1880, Said, in a more lengthy memorandum, stressed the importance of an improved and greatly extended educational system as the key to better administration of the empire, to the just application of laws, to a more efficient army, and to increased state revenues from a more beneficent economy. Throughout the provinces the number of elementary and secondary schools was greatly increased and teacher training schools were established, and in 1883 a special education tax was introduced to support these schools. Said opened a school for training civil servants for the government; it had a modernized curriculum and boarding facilities for students from the provinces. Eighteen new professional schools or faculties were founded in Istanbul, teaching law, finance, fine arts, commerce, civil engineering, veterinary medicine, police work, and tariffs. Finally, the Imperial University in Istanbul opened in 1900.

Said Pasha also understood the need to adjust the Ottoman system to the realities of Europe, which were pressing upon the empire. The decimal system of measurement was adopted in 1881, and in 1882 the Istanbul Chamber of Commerce was created to aid Ottoman merchants in meeting the impact of Western business practices and policies. After 1885, however, Said Pasha had difficulty in overcoming Abdul Hamid's suspicion of innovation; Said's power waned, and his later terms as grand vizir were of short duration.

EFFECTS ON THE PRESS

In such an uncertain atmosphere the press had a difficult time. In the 1860s several Turkish newspapers were launched, most of which were liberal in their attitudes toward government. Ziya, Namik Kemal, and Ali Suavi were the most noteworthy and capable editors and writers. But newspaper work meant "patriotic martyr-dom," since editors and popular authors were almost invariably exiled and news-papers were suspended frequently. Ziya died a broken man in 1880 in Adana; Namik Kemal followed in 1887; and Ali Suavi was executed for his part in a plot against Abdul Hamid in 1878. Many writers lived and published their works abroad and sent them into the Ottoman Empire through the protection of the various for-eign post offices established by the states of Europe under the capitulations.

Yet the work of the press went indefatigably on, educating the literate popu-lation to developments and thoughts in the outside world. Many books appeared as single publications. Over three hundred were published in 1890, many of them exciting French novels that introduced Ottomans to a very different world. Abdul Hamid controlled the press and suspended opposition papers as they appeared. But he did not have enough spies to police the entire empire; consequently, the verbal and printed attacks upon him could not be wholly suppressed.

Two other authors, Tevfik Fikret and Ahmed Midhat, left their marks during those decades of Abdul Hamid's stultifying influence. Fikret, whose writings flow-ered later under the Young Turks, was editor from 1895 to 1901 of the *Servet-i Fünun* (Treasury of Science), which at first was an illustrated scientific and literary supplement to an Istanbul evening newspaper and then an independent periodi-cal. A pictorial news magazine on the model of the French *L'Illustration,* it was directed to the educated elite and contained articles on biography, art, science, and literature. Because of censorship and the strict prohibition even of indirect political comment, Fikret and other authors attacked social ills through fictional writing and introduced Turkish readers to European cultural and intellectual life.

The most prolific author of the period was Ahmed Midhat, the son of a hum-ble cloth merchant of Istanbul. Educated by his elder brother in a simple elemen-tary school, Ahmed Midhat entered government in the civil service, which he left in 1871 at the age of twenty-seven to be a printer and a writer. He fell in with the New Ottomans and found himself deported to Rhodes for four years, returning with most of the exiles upon the deposition of Abdul Aziz. In 1877 he published a book vindicating Abdul Hamid's accession and title to the throne, an act that won for him the directorship of the state printing press and, subsequently, numerous official positions. For the next thirty-one years this acquiescent mediocrity made a great contribution to the development of Ottoman society.

Ahmed Midhat edited a daily newspaper, *Interpreter of Truth,* that had a weekly supplement distributed to the students of the nation's elementary schools.

Most of the stories, serials, articles, and features were written or translated by Ahmed Midhat, who at the same time was writing books, more than 150 in all, on history, ethics, religion, philosophy, and science, as well as producing many works of fiction modeled after contemporary European authors. He also wrote, in fourteen volumes, separate histories of European countries and a three-volume world history. These were the first serious efforts to give the ordinary Turkish reader a view of history beyond the Islamic world. Because Ahmed Midhat did not possess outstanding style or distinction and had little originality, men of literary talent were contemptuous of his work and deprecated the volume of his output. Yet his prodigious outpouring of books, periodicals, and newspapers—particularly those for schoolchildren—probably did more to change the outlook of the Ottomans, preparing them for a more secular and European world, than did the work of any other author.

The spreading of Western thought in Ottoman schools swelled the ranks of the discontented, most of whom fled as exiles to western Europe. Strangely enough, Abdul Hamid continued to found many schools and even supplied the students with pocket money in hopes they would remain loyal to their patron. Such, of course, was not the case; thrown together from every class of society, they became militant and dissatisfied. Perhaps because the teachers in the medical and military schools had had European experience, their students were the most unsettled of all. In pursuing their studies many were exposed to French or German, which immediately opened to them the ideas of nineteenth-century Europe. As a result, army officers and medical men from 1900 until recent times held positions of political leadership in Turkey all out of proportion to their numbers in society.

THE ARMENIAN QUESTION

Abdul Hamid became odious to many Europeans and his non-Turkish subjects, in large measure because of his treatment of the Armenians. As national aspirations stirred Serbs, Greeks, Rumanians, and Bulgars, so Armenians were moved in the latter half of the nineteenth century.

Muslim Turks and Kurds, Greeks, and Armenians in Anatolia were relatively prosperous between 1878 and 1911, as the peninsula's population increased by about one-half. Of the seventeen million or so people living in it in 1911–1912, about one and a half million were Armenians, and about the same number were Greeks, while a large majority, about fourteen and a half million, were Muslims. Of the latter, most were Turks, but in the eastern provinces there were many Kurds as well.

Encouraged by the Russian government and stimulated by European and American missionaries, the three Armenian religious communities—Gregorian, Catholic, and Protestant—and their respective educational institutions worked to develop national consciousness. Perhaps because confidential representations regarding Armenian cultural autonomy within the Ottoman Empire were allowed at the Congress of Berlin, political societies flourished. Visions of an independent

Armenia also were encouraged by revolutionary committees in Russia and the United States.

Abdul Hamid became frightened of the Armenian situation. He feared that six or more eastern provinces forming the Armenian highlands, where most of the Armenians were concentrated, and Little Armenia, or Cilicia, might become separated from the empire. To subdue the people, break their spirit, and forestall the possibility of an Armenian state, from 1894 to 1897 violent attacks upon the villages and shocking massacres were perpetrated especially by Kurdish irregular Ottoman forces. Outrages occurred in Yozgat, Erzinjan, Harput, Sivas, Marash, Urfa, and many other places, even in Istanbul. In all, perhaps one hundred thousand or more Armenians lost their lives.

These atrocities had a very deep effect upon Turkey. The few revolutionary societies were wiped out; Armenians were entirely cowed; and most thoughtful Ottomans were genuinely depressed by their government's action. Charitable foreign aid societies provided some relief, but emigration appeared to be the only solution. Economic life in many areas was disrupted. The British, French, Italian, and American governments protested in vain. Newspapers, magazines, churches, and lecture halls told and echoed to stories of the "Terrible Turks." As a result, for several decades Western governmental and diplomatic actions in the Ottoman Empire were guided to a considerable degree by unfriendly public opinion in the West.

CRETE

The regime's despotic nature affected Crete also. The quality of government on Crete varied greatly, since the distance of the island from Istanbul and the remoteness of certain parts of it left governors considerable autonomy. A small uprising occurred in 1841, and demands by local assemblies for reforms multiplied after the Hatt-i Humayun was issued. In the 1860s the better educated subscribed to Greek nationalism, the first outburst for union with Greece taking place in 1866. Desultory fighting and Ottoman countermeasures persisted until 1870.

In 1885, upon the union of Eastern Rumelia and Bulgaria, the concentration of European naval units at Suda Bay in Crete placed a damper on Greek preparations for war against the Ottomans and discouraged Cretan enthusiasts for union with Greece. Nonetheless, disorders of various origins and intensities continued to maintain the tension. In 1896 and 1897, after bloody battles on the streets of Canea between Greeks and Turks brought matters to a head, Prince George of Greece cut off Ottoman reinforcements and the Powers occupied Canea. Boiling national sentiment in Athens compelled the king to initiate a war against the Ottoman Empire. Although the king hoped the Powers would prevent it, they held off. The "Thirty Days' War," better known as the Greco-Turkish War of 1897, was a series of Greek disasters. Only the intervention of the Powers saved Athens from a Turkish occupation. The Peace of Istanbul, which restored the boundaries, placed a heavy indemnity upon Greece. Not until the end of 1898 did Europe effect a settlement in Crete by recognizing Prince George as high commissioner under the suzerainty of the sultan. The Turkish minority emigrated from Crete gradually; by 1908, when union with Greece was finally achieved, less than 10 percent of the population was Muslim.

MACEDONIA

Armenia and Crete were enough to keep the Porte embroiled with the European powers and to stampede Abdul Hamid into innumerable unwise and bloody decisions. It was the complex affairs of Macedonia, however, that sealed his fate and substantiated the charge that the Balkans were the powder keg of Europe. Populated by Turks, Bulgars, Greeks, Serbs, Albanians, Rumanians, and many other groups, Macedonia became the focus of the chauvinistic nationalisms rampant in the Balkans for several decades prior to World War I. A proviso of the Bulgarian Exarchate, permitting churches in Macedonia a choice between Greek and Bulgarian affiliation, touched off the explosion. Balkan nationalism erupted. Nationalistic schools, scholarships, newspapers, and books, as well as raids, village burning, kidnapping, and assassination, were among the tactics employed to achieve nationalist ends.

A Macedonian committee purporting to advance a movement of "Macedonia for the Macedonians" was formed in Sofia. It suggested the organization of an autonomous Macedonia with its own government at Salonika. The obvious intention was a repetition of the Eastern Rumelia episode and the union within five years of Macedonia and Bulgaria. The proposition was rejected by all except the Bulgarians, and Macedonia was consigned to disorder and chaos. Ottoman police forces and the imposition of martial law were unable to cope with the situation. In 1903 the Mürzsteg Program, suggested by the Powers, went into effect. Accordingly, the British, French, Italians, Austrians, and Russians each policed an area. Although some regions were excluded from the agreement, European control was sufficiently successful to induce the Powers in 1908 to extend the Mürzsteg Program for another six years.

BERLIN TO BAGHDAD RAILWAY

Direct foreign investment in the Ottoman Empire tripled between 1890 and 1914, and France and Germany were the leaders in the development of the Ottoman infrastructure that ensued. It should be noted that Germany did not participate in the pacification of Macedonia. Until this era German imperial interests in the Ottoman Empire were negligible. Bismarck regarded the area as worthless to Germany, and his exertions were designed only to keep Russia and Austria from fighting each other. But with the accession of Wilhelm II, Germany's role changed. General von der Goltz began to advise the Ottoman army in 1883, and the army was equipped with good Mauser rifles. In 1888 Baron Hirsch's Oriental Railway was completed through to Istanbul, while a newly formed German syndicate, the Anatolian Railway Company, was granted a concession to construct a railroad from the Bosphorus to Ankara; it was in operation by 1893.

The German penetration of Anatolia increased. In 1889 and again in 1898, Wilhelm II paid official visits to Istanbul; on the latter trip he went to Jerusalem and Damascus where he uttered the famous speech promising Muslims that the German emperor would be their friend. But above all else, German interests focused upon railroad concessions, which blossomed into the much-publicized Berlin-to-Baghdad venture.

Abdul Hamid, the Porte, army leaders, and officials of the Ottoman Public Debt Administration favored building railroads to all parts of the empire. They fancied that railroads would unify the empire and bring the central government more effective power and authority over outlying regions. More of the untold resources of Anatolia and Arabia would be developed, guaranteeing a burgeoning prosperity. The military posture of the state would be improved and independence protected. Although railroads were costly enterprises, it was believed that the advantageous results would amply repay the effort and monies expended.

In the case of the Hijaz Railroad, which linked Syria to Ottoman western Arabia, the Ottoman government itself financed, built, and operated the railway. Another favorite project of the sultan was building a railroad from the Bosphorus to the Persian Gulf. British and French companies already had built and were operating several lines connecting Izmir with the Anatolian hinterland, when the Anatolian Railway Company took over the British railroad from Haydar Pasha on the Bosphorus to Izmit and extended it to Ankara.

These railroad concessions usually called for a government subsidy to the construction firm, a guarantee of a minimum annual revenue, or both. For extending the line to Ankara, the sultan assured the Anatolian Railway Company at least 15,000 francs per kilometer annual revenue. This money was to come from the taxes of several provinces, the collection of these taxes being assigned to the Debt Administration. In 1896, when the German line reached Konya, other railroads in Asiatic districts were the Izmir-Aydin, the Izmir-Kassaba-Afyon-Karahisar, the Mersin-Adana, the Jaffa-Jerusalem, and the Beirut-Damascus-Aleppo lines. The government naturally desired to link these together and push on to Iraq and the Persian Gulf.

Abdul Hamid insisted that the railroad should not approach the Mediterranean, where gunfire from enemy fleets could interrupt traffic. The Germans, therefore, proposed to proceed from Konya to Adana, then through the Amanus range eastward to the valley of the Tigris near Mosul, and down the river to the Persian Gulf. This plan was more expensive than others, but was militarily more secure. Actually, British and French capitalists accepted the idea that the concession would be awarded to the Germans, and their governments were fully satisfied. Agreements were reached among the three groups in 1899. In that year Lord Curzon arranged for Britain to conduct all foreign relations for the shaykh of Kuwayt; this permitted England to block the railroad's best terminus on the Persian Gulf.

The Ottoman Empire paid 275,000 francs per kilometer for building the rail road, guaranteed 4,500 francs per kilometer annual gross operating receipts, granted mineral rights twenty kilometers on each side of the right of way, exempted from taxation all construction material imported, and gave numerous minor benefits to the company. The necessary bonds were floated and construction began. In October 1904, the first section was opened. The terrain crossed was not difficult; building cost less than was expected and profits were high. In 1906 the Porte arranged with the Powers for a slight increase in tariffs to pay for further extensions. New loans were provided in 1908, but because of the Young Turk Revolution, it was not until 1909 that a construction company was organized to undertake the second leg across the Taurus and Amanus ranges. Certain bridges and tunnels in the Taurus Mountains were still not finished at the outbreak of war in 1914. Thus, a through route to northern Iraq or Syria was not opened to traffic until the post-World War I period.

The railways to Ankara and to points beyond Konya brought an agricultural revolution to Anatolia. In districts penetrated by these roads new settlements were formed, produce marketed, and new lands cultivated. The companies initiated irrigation projects and agricultural training centers to stimulate traffic on their railroads; in these details the Germans were the most efficient and thorough. By 1910 mileage guarantees for annual receipts were no longer necessary and railroads were paying profits into the Ottoman treasury. Simultaneously, German business and banking penetration between 1899 and 1908 was facilitated and encouraged by railroad interests.

By opening up vast areas to world commerce, the railroads improved local economic conditions and gave many Middle Eastern districts their first touch with world economy. There was a distinct possibility that these developments might effect a real recuperation for the "sick man" of Europe. The railroads also brought German imperialism, which the Middle East actually found to be a relief from British and French colonialism. Usually Germans were more tactful and considerate of Ottoman feelings. But German inroads into the Middle East frightened the British, who after 1904 and 1907 convinced the French and Russian governments to cooperate with them in trying to block German aspirations.

REFERENCES

Many readings touch upon this chapter. Those cited in Chapters 19, 20, 23, and 24 are of particular value.

And, Metin. *A History of Theatre and Popular Entertainment in Turkey.* Ankara: Forum Yayinlari, 1964. An important paperback on a little-known subject.

Berkes, Niyazi. *The Development of Secularism in Turkey.* Montreal: McGill University Press, 1964. The most profound and stimulating book on this subject to appear.

Chapman, Maybelle K. *Great Britain and the Bagdad Railway, 1881–1914.* Northampton, Mass.: Smith College Press, 1948. A late reappraisal of the diplomatic rivalries and the complications in the Middle East with special reference to the railroad.

Earle, Edward Mead. *Turkey, the Great Powers and the Baghdad Railway: A Study in Imperialism.* New York: Macmillan, 1923. A classic.

Edib, Halidé. *Memoirs.* New York: Century, 1926. The life of a Western-educated Turkish woman.

Eliot, Charles N. E. *Turkey in Europe.* London: E. Arnold, 1908. Particularly strong on the Balkans and Macedonia.

Haddad, William, and William Ochsenwald, eds. *Nationalism in a Non-National State: The Dissolution of the Ottoman Empire.* Columbus: Ohio State University Press, 1977. This volume contains a series of essays on the development of nationalism in the nineteenth and twentieth centuries in the Balkan and Arab provinces of the empire.

McCarthy, Justin. *Muslims and Minorities: The Population of Ottoman Anatolia and the End of the Empire.* New York: New York University Press, 1983. An excellent study of this controversial subject; relies on census data from the Ottoman archives.

Mears, Eliot Grinnell, ed. *Modern Turkey, A Politico-Economic Interpretation, 1908–1923, Inclusive, with Selected Chapters by Representative Authorities.* New York: Macmillan, 1924. A collection of essays written by excellent observers of Turkey. One entitled "Levantine Concession-Hunting," by Mears, is most revealing of this type of financial imperialism.

Ochsenwald, William. *The Hijaz Railroad.* Charlottesville: University Press of Virginia, 1980.

Pears, Edwin. *Life of Abdul Hamid.* London: Constable, 1917. A good biography by an English barrister who was a resident in Istanbul throughout the reign of Abdul Hamid II.

Quataert, Donald. *Social Disintegration and Popular Resistance in the Ottoman Empire, 1881–1908: Reactions to European Economic Penetration.* New York: New York University Press, 1983. Excellent essays on various aspects of European economic investments in Anatolia and European Turkey. Especially valuable on the Anatolian railroads.

Ramsaur, Ernest E., Jr. *The Young Turks.* Princeton, N.J.: Princeton University Press, 1957. The best volume in English on this topic, especially on the period before 1908. Based on many letters and communications from leading Young Turks.

26

The Young Turks

SECRET SOCIETIES

The Young Turk Revolution of 1908 was a natural reaction to oppression, absolutism, and corruption in the regime of Abdul Hamid II. Added to this was the growing Westernization of certain portions of the empire and the consequent effect of contemporary European ideas upon Ottoman youth. At various times in the nineteenth century dissident Ottomans lived in exile in Europe and dreamed of governmental reform at home. Many saw a temporary fruition of these hopes in the ousting of Abdul Aziz and in Midhat's constitution of 1876. When Abdul Hamid's true nature became evident, some Ottomans plotted revolution.

In 1889, at the Istanbul Imperial Military Medical College, a group of students led by an Albanian, Ibrahim Temo, organized a secret society, the Committee of Progress and Union. Membership spread to the Military Academy, the Naval Academy, the Artillery and Engineering School, the Veterinary School, and the Civil College. Similar to the Carbonari societies in Italy, Progress and Union subscribed to nationalist ideas and reforms.

Abdul Hamid heard of the committee through his secret agents and took reprisals against the students and school officials. Nonetheless, the committee flourished, gathering new recruits from each succeeding class at the various schools. By 1896 more important elements of Ottoman society dominated the committee, and it attracted members who had belonged to such earlier groups of rebellious spirits as the Young Ottomans and Young Turks.

Committee members who escaped to Europe joined with other Ottoman malcontents. The best known of these was Ahmed Riza, whose newspaper, *Meshveret* (Deliberation) became the committee's official publication. At the same time, Murad Bey, a history teacher at the Civil College who had once been an employee of the Ottoman Public Debt Administration, fled to Paris and published a more popular newspaper, *Mizan* (Balance). These two papers, which obtained easy entrance into the empire through foreign post offices, gathered a considerable following.

Membership in Progress and Union became widespread, but rumor exaggerated its number to the point at which Abdul Hamid took fright and even the members themselves believed a coup d'état might be possible, although the committee's program denounced violence or any thought of overthrowing the reigning family; it preached reform, rejected slavish Westernization, advocated Ottoman nationalism, and opposed the intervention of European powers as a substitute for Ottoman authority. But a series of arrests nipped in the bud the society's coup planned for August 1896. Abdul Hamid, curiously enough, only sent the leaders to remote parts of the empire, whence they slipped away to Paris and Geneva. The program was reduced to the simple formula that all evils stemmed from Abdul Hamid. Remove him, restore the constitution, and all would be well. But the wily sultan, promising a general amnesty and agreeing to listen to arguments for reform, enticed Murad Bey to Istanbul and in 1897 shattered the Committee of Progress and Union.

Nevertheless, every class at the Military Academy was infected with the virus of revolution, and at the General Staff Academy in 1905 Mustafa Kemal was arrested as a revolutionary agitator on the very day he was commissioned. Later, when released and stationed in Damascus, he helped organize *Vatan* (Fatherland), a secret revolutionary society, among officers of the Fifth Army Corps in Syria. Because Macedonia and its cosmopolitan center of Salonika were susceptible to revolutionary propaganda, Kemal journeyed there surreptitiously to organize branches of Fatherland among officers of the Third Army Corps. In Salonika the society came to be called Fatherland and Liberty, and it merged with another group before Kemal arranged his transfer there in 1907.

The other group in Salonika, the Ottoman Society of Liberty, included in its earliest membership Talat Bey, Fethi Bey, and Colonel Jemal Bey. Absorbing Fatherland and Liberty, it spread rapidly throughout European Turkey. Pledged to overthrow Abdul Hamid and establish a just government, the Ottoman Society of Liberty drew to its ranks liberal and freethinking Turks, especially Bektashis, Melamis, and Freemasons. When army officers fraternized with their European colleagues stationed in Macedonia, pursuant to the Mürzsteg Program of 1903, they compared their own unfavorable lot and arrears in pay with the pleasant life of European officers.

In 1907 fugitives from Salonika won over Ahmed Riza in Paris to the possibility of armed revolution. Abdul Hamid's enemies joined them in a second congress of Ottoman Liberals, at which even an Armenian revolutionary society was represented. After this meeting the Paris and Macedonia groups merged under the name Society of Union and Progress and set up a permanent committee to implement the program adopted by the congress—opposition to the Ottoman government in every way possible.

THE REVOLUTION

The real revolution began in the Middle East, not in Paris. Army mutinies became frequent in 1906, largely because of miserable conditions and arrears in pay. When rebellions were seen to bring immediate improvements, many more occurred in 1907, with civilians joining to protest against corrupt officials in Erzurum, Bitlis, Izmir, and even in Istanbul. In 1907 and 1908, there were crop failures in wide areas of the empire; the prices of grain and meat rose very sharply. Real income fell. Beginning in June 1908, mutinies broke out in Macedonia; an officer whom Abdul Hamid had sent to investigate was shot and wounded on June 11 at Salonika, the same day that Nicholas II of Russia and Edward VII of England met at Reval to arrive at some method of reform in Macedonia that might end the anarchy. Both events hastened the action. Majors Enver and Niyazi and other officers of the Third Army Corps took to the hills and officers and agents of the sultan were assassinated. Many units of the society and the Third Army Corps in Macedonia demanded the restoration of the constitution. Messages from scores of cities and towns poured into Istanbul and meetings of soldiers and civilians proclaimed the constitution. On July 23 came the fateful telegram announcing that the Third Army Corps would march on Istanbul to enforce the reproclamation of the constitution.

The army threat was the telling blow. On that evening, July 23, 1908, Abdul Hamid restored the constitution and ordered elections for members of the Chamber of Deputies. Abdul Hamid bowed to the force of the demands and rode with the popular tide. But he did not surrender.

The summer of 1908 was spent in preparing for the elections and readjusting government ministries in accordance with the wishes of the committee of the Society of Union and Progress. The committee's program called for the sultan's deposition. The society, however, had never cultivated the masses, and the popular cries in the capital were: "Long Live the Constitution," "Long Live the Sultan," and "Down with the Spies." Abdul Hamid went to Aya Sofya mosque for his public prayers on the first Friday after the revolution and received much adulation from the throngs that gathered. He was fostering the view that he was happy over the turn of events! The committee was not fooled, but recognized that it did not have the force or following to depose him. In fact, no member of the committee or prominent member of the society even became a cabinet minister. It was believed then that a certain skill, mystique, and rearing were required for conducting a minister's office, qualifications that none of the committee members possessed. Abdul Hamid, following their wishes, appointed Kiamil Pasha grand vizir on August 6.

The committee publicly declared its support of Kiamil and his cabinet. Now the government and the committee controlled state affairs; the palace was isolated. Social unrest ensued as the Anatolian Railway Company workers went on strike.

On December 17, 1908, in the chambers near Aya Sofya where Midhat's parliament had met thirty-one years earlier, Abdul Hamid opened parliament and gave a speech from the throne. Major religious and national groups of the empire were represented and various political views were in evidence. Attending were 147 Turks, 60 Arabs, 27 Albanians, 26 Greeks, 14 Armenians, 4 Jews, 5 Bulgars, 4 Serbs, and 1 Vlach. The best-organized group was the Macedonia-Salonika branch of Union and Progress, but it was far from having complete control of the situation. Ahmed Riza, their distinguished publicist from Paris, was chosen president of the Chamber of Deputies and served as a valuable figurehead for the anonymous members of the committee of the society.

Members of parliament coalesced into three political groups. In addition to Union and Progress, there were the Liberal Unionists, who believed the solution to the ills of the empire could be found in creating a loosely federated state of locally autonomous nationalist provinces. The third group was the Muslim Association, which supported pan-Islamism and firm adherence to religious law. Union and Progress, however, showed its power in February 1909 by causing the downfall of the grand vizir on a motion of no confidence when he appointed, without consultation with the committee, his friends as minister of war and minister of marine.

FAILURE OF THE COUNTERREVOLUTION

The counterrevolution struck on April 13, 1909, and leading members of Union and Progress went into hiding. Developing spontaneously among soldiers of the First Army Corps in Istanbul, the cries were: "Down with the Constitution," "Down with the Committee," and "Long Live the Sacred Law." Abdul Hamid gave his blessing to the counterrevolution, and a new grand vizir took office. The Young Turks of the Revolution, as they were called, were inexperienced in government and few in number. Moreover, they harbored the illusion that the proclamation of the constitution and the announcement of just, efficient, honest, and rational government would erase all evils and that all good people would rise up and usher in the promised day. But it did not happen. Soldiers' pay was no better, and general conditions remained about the same. The people of the Ottoman Empire were not prepared to abandon the mental attitudes of the Millet system or to tolerate equality among Turk, Greek, Armenian, Bulgar, Jew, Arab, Albanian, and the other people of the empire. "Under the same blue sky we are all equal; we glory in being Ottomans." These oft-quoted words of Enver, one of the committee members who later rose to fame, stirred emotions but were not accepted as fact.

The committee of Union and Progress, however, acted decisively. Mahmud Shevket Pasha, commander of the Third Army Corps in Macedonia, was invited to march on Istanbul to defend the constitution. When he arrived at Yeşilköy on April 23, he proposed to parliament, which was holding a rump session there, the declaration of martial law, punishment for mutineers, and full obedience to him. His terms were accepted; on April 25, Istanbul was occupied, and order was restored in five hours. In an executive session on April 27, parliament deposed Abdul Hamid, having obtained a favorable *fetva* (religious law decision) from the shaykh al-Islam. The new sultan, Mehmed V, a mild gentleman born in 1844, declared he had not read a newspaper in the last twenty years. He had been completely surrounded by his brother's spies and minions—even the ladies of his harem—and had lost all initiative. He was the perfect constitutional monarch for the Young Turks.

ITALIAN WAR

The task before the Young Turks would have staggered the most experienced administrators. Internal problems commanded the highest priority as many bureaucrats sympathetic to the old order were purged, but foreign affairs and war rose to occupy the minds of the committee and consumed the meager funds available. Europe feared that the Young Turk regime would restore vigor to the empire. Contemplated acts of aggression should be made at once. On October 5, 1908,

Prince Ferdinand of Bulgaria cut all ties with the sultan and took the title of tsar. On October 6 Austria-Hungary announced annexation of Bosnia and Herzegovina. That same day Crete revolted and declared union with Greece. None of these acts was surprising or momentous for the Ottoman government; these territorial losses had been all but written off several years previously. Politically, however, they were hard blows against the prestige of the Young Turks and were factors in the counterrevolution of April 1909.

A far greater shock was delivered by the Italian ultimatum of September 28, 1911, demanding that the Ottoman Empire not object to an Italian military expedition to Libya. The Ottomans declared war on Italy immediately. Although the Ottomans were driven from the coastal towns of Tripoli and Benghazi, guerrilla warfare continued in the interior. Italy then occupied Rhodes and the Dodecanese Islands and shelled the Dardanelles. Sentiment ran high in the empire. Enver Bey and Fethi Bey, both prominent members of Union and Progress and military attachés in Berlin and Paris respectively, along with other officers of later distinction like Mustafa Kemal, made their way with difficulty to Libya, where they organized and for a time led a resistance movement.

An Ottoman victory was hopeless; and when it appeared that the Balkan states were plotting a common war against the Ottoman Empire, the Ottomans hastily signed the Treaty of Ouchy on October 18, 1912. Under the terms of the treaty the Ottoman Empire withdrew from Libya; Italy, from the Aegean Islands. Italy agreed to assume a share of the Ottoman debt and the authority of the caliph was recognized in Libya. Italy, however, refused to evacuate her island conquests, claiming the empire continued to incite Arab warfare in Libya.

THE COMMITTEE OF UNION AND PROGRESS

Shortly after the deposition of Abdul Hamid in 1909, the Society of Union and Progress held a party congress in Salonika and established a central executive committee that remained active until the party was dissolved at the end of World War I. From its headquarters in Salonika it ruled the party and, when the party was in power, the government and the ministers. After 1912, when the Balkan wars broke out, the central executive committee sat in Istanbul and there dictated to the membership.

The many activities of the Union and Progress party began to tell on its popularity. Even before the defeat by the Italians, the party's control of parliament weakened, and to forestall a defeat in the Chamber of Deputies the Young Turks had Mehmed V dissolve the chamber and call for a new election. The new chamber was also closed in August 1912, when radical young leaders of Union and Progress attacked a cabinet composed of men of more experience and prestige. Two ministries largely representing the Liberal Unionist party followed. The latter, however, succumbed to a coup d'état by the Union and Progress party in January 1913, when extremists rebelled at surrendering Edirne to the Balkan states. From that moment until the end of World War I leaders of Union and Progress maintained firm control over the government.

The desires of the Young Turks flowed out in every direction. Their intention was to examine all the institutions of their society, changing any that had become outdated. The Finance Ministry was reorganized and tax farming was abolished. General Liman von Sanders headed a German mission to transform the army under the direction of Enver Pasha. Secular law was gaining as the ulema were brought under the control of the state. The Committee of Union and Progress changed the legal rights of women, and magazines and newspapers increasingly published essays dealing with the status of women. During World War I reformers achieved basic changes in marriage laws, which now came under the aegis of the Ministry of Justice. The writer and educator Halidé Edib (Adivar) and other women founded several women's organizations while in 1916 the University in Istanbul admitted women students. In education and social services reformers took the helm: Ziya Gökalp, Tevfik Fikret, Fuad Köprülü, and many others devoted their energies and talents to improving education.

These Young Turks sought to improve the well-being of the great mass of Ottoman subjects. They deplored their poor quality of life and wished to give pride, dignity, and an energetic determination to the nation. They recognized that the empire remained an exporter of foodstuffs and raw materials, and an importer of manufactured goods. They wanted to create a national consciousness. They were, after all, nationalists. In the Middle East, however, society lacked ethnic and national homogeneity. There were religions by the score. Languages and dialects were so diverse that young British consular officers coming to Istanbul had to take lessons in Turkish, Greek, Persian, Arabic, Armenian, and Russian! And rural and urban cultures and manners were so foreign to each other that no common grouping appeared to be possible.

NATIONALISM

The sociologist and essayist Ziya Gökalp (1876–1924) and his friends debated these problems of their budding nationalism and at various times emphasized one factor over another. Because of the complexities three main types of nationalism developed: Ottomanism, pan-Islamism, and pan-Turanism. Ottomanism possessed the greatest attraction in the earlier days of the revolution. It was recognized that origins were mixed, and as good nineteenth-century European liberals and radicals they minimized and scoffed at religion. Language was less of a barrier as Turkish had long been the *lingua franca* of the Ottoman Empire. It was easy to note that genteel Turks had manners similar to well-bred Greeks and Armenians and that peasants and artisans were alike in many respects. Ottomanism was fashionable; thus, the bold rejoicing of all groups and nations when the revolution came in 1908.

But fundamental views and historic feelings soon triumphed. Usually most non-Turks in the Chamber of Deputies voted as a bloc in opposition to the Turks. So-called programs for Ottomanization were branded as attempts to Turkify all others. Such moves eventually provoked a revolt in Albania, where the tribes and nationalists resisted fiercely. Equality in the army, holding government posts, and paying taxes went against the customs and views of too many groups in the empire to be accepted voluntarily very long. As soon as Ottomanism was advocated and practiced overtly, differences were highlighted and proved insurmountable.

The next move was toward religion and pan-Islamism. Throughout the nineteenth century there were drives to seek rapport among Muslim states and peoples and to strengthen the position of the empire by building wider support for the caliph. Missions were sent to Kabul, and Abdul Hamid subsidized Jamal al-Din al-Afghani in his work in Egypt of preaching for reform in Islam. Many Young Turks in their nationalist enthusiasm found great satisfaction in pan-Islamic dreams. Unfortunately, these reveries, when translated into reality, encouraged all manner of harshness, discrimination, and persecution for non-Muslims and freethinkers. Full responsibility for the atrocious massacres of Armenians in Cilicia in 1909 was never ascertained, but some blame should probably be shouldered by both the Young Turks and the reactionary elements, each of whom had strong pan-Islamic tendencies. The stringent and reactionary measures of a pan-Islamic nature adopted by the Union and Progress party from April 1909 to July 1912 led, at least in part, to its downfall.

The third form of nationalism appeared in pan-Turanism, which espoused the union or federation of all Turkish peoples as far eastward as central Asia and recognized kinship to Finns, Hungarians, Tartars, and many Turkish tribes in Russia. The main efforts of the pan-Turanists were devoted to the policy of Turkification of all non-Turks and to the task of instilling a national, historical, and linguistic common feeling among all classes of Turks within the Ottoman Empire, especially in Istanbul and Anatolia. In literature, music, and cultural matters generally, Turkish nationalists espoused reforms and "purification" that would emphasize what they saw as the Turkish core of Ottoman identity. To accomplish this the Committee of Union and Progress created an institution called *Türk Ojak* (Turkish Hearth), which sponsored lectures on diverse subjects in a program of adult education aimed at developing a national consciousness.

ALBANIA AND THE BALKAN WARS

The non-Turkish communities bitterly resisted the young Turks' Turkification drives. In several districts in Asia Minor trouble arose with Greeks and Armenians, whose boycotts and attacks caused serious dislocations of commerce. Some Arabs became disillusioned. Revolts broke out in Yemen and Asir, and Arab nationalist societies were formed in Baghdad, Damascus, and Beirut. In part these Arab societies were made up of Arab members of Union and Progress, Fatherland, and other Young Turk revolutionary societies.

The most violent storm broke in Albania, when in the process of Turkification the government took steps to enforce a decree forbidding the possession of arms. Albanians also objected to a census, taxes, and the drafting of young men to serve in Yemen (which was called the graveyard of Ottoman armies). The Albanian rebellion was quelled early in 1911 after diplomatic intervention by Montenegro and a grant of considerable local autonomy.

Concessions to the Albanians, however, aroused hopes among other nationalities; the Macedonians particularly hoped for the establishment of a regime similar to the one in Eastern Rumelia. These concessions also excited the ambitions and jealousies of officials in Greece, Bulgaria, Serbia, and Montenegro. The Young Turks, nevertheless, pushed their policies of centralization of government, thus keeping the provinces at the boiling point. Although the Liberal Unionists achieved ascendancy in Istanbul during the last half of 1912, their proposals of decentralization came too late. The Balkan states declared war on the Ottoman Empire in October.

The Powers, sensing that a Balkan league was being formed, had previously notified the Balkan governments that no aggrandizements won as a result of aggression would be countenanced. Ignoring the warning, Bulgaria, Greece, Serbia, and Montenegro agreed on the division of Macedonia; within a month after the start of the war these allies, who possessed a decided numerical advantage over the Ottoman armies, overran all of European Turkey north of the Chatalja lines protecting Istanbul, except for Edirne, Skodra, and Janina. The effects of the reorganization of the Balkan armies in the preceding decade surprised the Great Powers, which accepted the fact that the status quo could not be enforced. Many Muslims left the territories that came under the control of the European Christian states and fled to Ottoman land.

In December an armistice was signed and the five belligerents met in London to negotiate peace. The Balkan allies demanded the cession of Edirne as their price. When it became apparent that Kiamil Pasha, the grand vizir, and the Liberal Unionists were willing to pay the price, Enver Bey and about two hundred members of Union and Progress staged a successful coup d'état. They assassinated the minister of war, Nazim Bey, and returned the radical party to power. In February 1913 war was resumed. In rapid succession Janina, Edirne, and Skodra fell to Greek, Bulgarian, and Montenegrin forces. Meanwhile, the Greek navy defeated the Ottoman forces outside the Dardanelles and occupied a number of the Aegean Islands.

In April a second armistice was arranged, and a peace treaty was signed in London on May 30, 1913. The Ottoman Empire ceded to the victors all her European possessions north of a line from Enos on the Aegean to Midia on the Black Sea and consigned to the Powers financial, judicial, commercial, and nationalist questions arising from the transfer of territory and the division of the loot among the Balkan states. The establishment of Albania upon the insistence of the Great Powers goaded Greece and Serbia to demand a revision of their previous understandings with Bulgaria. Failure to reach agreement brought war between Bulgaria and Serbia on June 30, 1913. Greece, Montenegro, and then Rumania entered the war against Bulgaria. On July 15, 1913, the Ottomans invaded Thrace and Enver Bey reoccupied Edirne. The Treaty of Bucharest ended this Second Balkan War in August, although a separate settlement in Istanbul between Turkey and Bulgaria, which restored Edirne to the Ottoman Empire, was not drawn up until September.

THE TRIUMVIRATE

The Balkan wars were over and the Young Turks had lost almost all Ottoman possessions in Europe. From a long-range point of view this was probably a happy development, as it removed a heavy drain upon Ottoman resources. At the moment, though, it gave power to the radical wing of the Young Turks. Following their coup d'état in January 1913, Mahmud Shevket Pasha became grand vizir. But his assassination in June and the succeeding grand vizirate of Said Halim Pasha, a mild and weak Egyptian prince, permitted the reins of government to fall into the hands of a triumvirate of Young Turks: Talat, Enver, and Jemal.

Talat Bey was born of a poor family near Edirne and began work as a telegraph operator in the government office at Salonika. Possessing a brilliant mind, he was one of the organizers of the revolutionary movement in Macedonia and served as minister of interior in several cabinets of the Young Turks. He was a dedicated man who stayed poor and remained modest in character and habits throughout his career. Ruthless in his tactics, he made a distinction between personal and national morality, believing that many acts that would be entirely immoral and cruel if perpetrated by and for an individual were perfectly moral if performed in the interests of the state. Polite and exceedingly considerate, he never forgot his humble origins.

Enver Bey came from a lower-middle-class family and received a military education. Catapulted to public attention by his defiance of Abdul Hamid and his flight to the Macedonian hills in the first stage of the revolution in 1908, Enver loved the heroics of Turkish nationalism and won fame in the war in Libya against Italy. He was a man of action and quick decisions. As an attaché in Berlin, Enver fell under the spell of Prussian militarism and thoroughly believed in the superiority and invincibility of the German military machine. He, more than any other, brought Turkey into World War I as a German ally. As he rose to power, he became vain and more distant—a development that many of his former friends and admirers deplored. As one remarked: "Enver Pasha has destroyed Enver Bey." An advocate of pan-Turanism, Enver died in 1922 pursuing this policy in Turkestan.

Jemal Pasha, who became minister of the navy, was an early member of the Society of Union and Progress. He came from an old Ottoman family and had been a pan-Islamist, but in the days of the triumvirate he became an ardent Turkish nationalist. The weakest of the three, Jemal served as a kind of policeman for the Young Turks, maintaining discipline and holding the faltering in line.

To the day of the entry of the Ottoman Empire into World War I, the triumvirate ruled with a strong hand. Disobedient party members were punished, opponents were eliminated, and uncertainty and terror returned to government circles. Thus, even before the carnage of World War I, the internal violence and external wars of the period from 1908 to 1914 created an atmosphere seemingly so threatening to the existence of the state as to justify extreme repression and radical reform.

REFERENCES

Many references mentioned in the three preceding chapters are important for this chapter; in addition, those of particular note are in Chapters 13, 19, and 20.

Ahmad, Feroz. *The Young Turks: The Committee of Union and Progress in Turkish Politics, 1908–1914.* Oxford: The Clarendon Press, 1969. The most thorough work in English on the politics of the Young Turk Revolution from 1908 to 1914. The committee, it points out, did not hold absolute power during this period and was able to adapt to altering circumstances.

Berkes, Niyazi, trans. and ed. *Turkish Nationalism and Western Civilization: Selected Essays of Ziya Gökalp.* New York: Columbia University Press, 1959. An important source for the thoughts of the founder of Turkish nationalism.

Gawrych, George. "The Culture and Politics of Violence in Turkish Society, 1903–14." *Middle Eastern Studies* 22 (1986): 307–330. An enlightening essay on the political and military problems of the time, including a discussion of the psychological atmosphere and literary developments that reflected the violence of the period.

————. "Tolerant Dimensions of Cultural Pluralism in the Ottoman Empire: The Albanian Community, 1800–1912." *International Journal of Middle East Studies* 15 (1983): 519–536.

Helmreich, E. C. *The Diplomacy of the Balkan Wars, 1912–1913.* Cambridge, Mass.: Harvard University Press, 1938. Basic for this topic.

Kushner, David. *The Rise of Turkish Nationalism, 1876–1908.* London: Frank Cass, 1977. This is a brief study of the intellectual origins of Turkish nationalism as it grew in the last decades of the nineteenth century.

Parla, Taha. *The Social and Political Thought of Ziya Gökalp, 1876–1924.* Leiden: Brill, 1985. Also discusses his life, political career, and contemporary relevance.

Zürcher, Erik Jan. *The Unionist Factor: The Role of the Committee of Union and Progress in the Turkish National Movement, 1905–1926.* Leiden: Brill, 1984. A revisionist interpretation that stresses the continuity between the Union and Progress period with that of the Turkish Republic. Stimulating.

27

British Occupation of Egypt and the Sudan

LORD CROMER IN EGYPT

The British army occupied Cairo and took control of Egypt in September 1882. The British administration presumed that its occupation would be of short duration, hoping to put the khedive in a powerful position and then to withdraw. But the British cabinet recognized that certain aspects of Egyptian society needed to be stabilized before evacuation was possible. To this end Lord Dufferin, British ambassador to the Porte, was sent to Egypt in November to advise the khedive in reestablishing his authority and in arranging for "the well-being of all classes of the population." Dufferin found Egypt in chaos. The cabinet had fallen and Khedive Tawfiq, frightened and vindictive, had asked Sharif Pasha to form a new government. Almost immediately this new government was humiliated by the British. Colonel Urabi, the national hero, who had surrendered to the British at the Battle of Tel al-Kebir, had been turned over to the khedive for trial. Urabi was found guilty of treason and sentenced to be executed, but the British intervened and insisted instead that he be exiled to Ceylon.

Lord Dufferin spent seven months forcing the changes in the Egyptian government that the British needed in order to withdraw. First the army and the police were reorganized in order to guarantee freedom of passage through the Suez Canal. A new Egyptian army, provisionally set at 6,000, was created under General Sir Evelyn Wood as *Sirdar* (commander in chief), with a number of British officers serving in various high posts. The British army of occupation was cut from 12,000 to 9,500, the intention being to withdraw it entirely as soon as the new Egyptian forces could be trained. In the cities a police force was formed, commanded by Europeans.

The British believed that financial reforms were the second step to ensure stability and tranquility. The Dual Control, terminated by the occupation, was replaced with a single British financial adviser, who in reality became fiscal master of Egypt. Also Dufferin placed a British adviser in those key ministries whose recommendations had the force of commands and suggested cutting the staffs and reducing the proportion of highly paid Europeans. In the provinces he revived the

Commission for the Reform of Native Tribunals and civil and criminal codes, based on Napoleonic codes, were adopted, and in 1883 a system of lower courts and courts of appeal was decreed with forty Belgian and Dutch judges installed in conjunction with a British general prosecutor. The system was extended to Upper Egypt in 1889. However, then and for a long time thereafter, the courts and the justice dispensed by them were poorly understood by most Egyptians, who continued to regard them as unjust and foreign.

Lord Dufferin was also instructed to see to "the establishment of institutions favourable to the prudent development of liberty," a fond hope of many English liberals. On May 1, 1883, two days before Lord Dufferin's departure, the khedive decreed that there should be a four-to-eight member advisory council elected in each province and convoked by each governor; a twenty-six member Legislative Council (ten members appointed by the khedive, the remainder elected by the provincial councils) that could examine and debate proposed legislation but could only make suggestions to the government; and a General Assembly, consisting of eighty members (eight ministers, the Legislative Council, and forty-six delegates from the provinces), whose chief function was to approve or disapprove new tax levies.

One of Lord Dufferin's more lasting reforms was the bringing in of engineers as irrigation advisers to the Ministry of Public Works in 1883. They set to work to rehabilitate the old Nile Barrage built by Muhammad Ali at the apex of the delta. In 1884, after the barrage was restored, the cotton yield was 30,000 tons greater than in the previous year. With cotton at £35 per ton this increased Egypt's cotton income by over £1 million; the cost of the renovation had been only £26,000. Cromer recognized the significance of such operations and in 1885 asked the London Conference for £1 million for irrigation projects, making perennial irrigation and two or three crops a year standard agricultural practice in many parts of Egypt. The British also paid the workers on these projects and abolished forced labor under the lash of the *kurbash* (rhinoceros-hide bullwhip).

Between 1896 and 1903 Sir William Willcocks supervised the building of a dam at Aswan which by 1905 made perennial cropping possible for over a quarter of a million acres in Middle and Upper Egypt, guaranteed water for summer irrigation, and ensured a high cotton yield. However, in the long run, perennial cropping posed a serious health and ecological hazard to the farm workers and to the soil itself. The water-borne disease bilharzia came to affect as many as one-half of the peasants of Lower Egypt.

Greatly increased revenues from these changes were largely responsible for the public and private profits that made the British occupation of Egypt acceptable to the Great Powers and their bondholders and tolerable to the Egyptian landlords. Ownership of much of the agricultural land was concentrated in the hands of this elite: some 12,000 people owned about 40 percent of the cultivated area. And foreigners, who strongly welcomed British control, dominated Egyptian finance, banking, and the export trade (including cotton). Egypt became a net importer of food as cotton was by far the greatest crop grown in the country.

With the framework for a new regime in place, Lord Dufferin returned to his post in Istanbul. In September 1883, Sir Evelyn Baring returned to Egypt as the

British agent and consul general. Elevated to the peerage as Lord Cromer in 1892, he ruled Egypt autocratically until his retirement in 1907.

Britain's position in regard to the khedive, the Ottoman suzerain, and the other Powers was never clearly defined. No formal machinery for control was established. The capitulations remained, as did the mixed courts, the Public Debt Fund, and the Law of Liquidation. Khedive Tawfiq continued as ruler, the cabinet and the ministries functioned, local administration governed the cities and provinces, and the courts and judiciary performed their duties. The ultimate power of decision, however, resided in the British agent, who usually exercised it through a British adviser to a specific minister or through a British general or controlling officer. This indirect rule was facilitated by an unspoken alliance fashioned early between Lord Cromer and Tawfiq, in which Egyptian ministers and governors either followed the advice of the British agent or forfeited their posts. Lord Cromer and his British advisers and officials determined and administered trade policies, agriculture, communications, irrigation, health, and foreign affairs in addition to Egypt's army and finances. Education failed to fit into any program. The illiteracy of the masses was hardly touched; and the number receiving a secondary education with any technical or proficient skill was very limited. Sufi brotherhoods were brought more closely under the control of the Egyptian state; religion was one of the few areas which both continued to flourish and yet remained largely outside the sphere of the British.

Several prime ministers served under Cromer. Mustafa Pasha Fahmi served the longest continuous period and was so subservient to the British that he caused promising Egyptians to join societies and political parties whose first principle was nationalistic and anti-British.

The British occupation only worsened the financial chaos. Until 1885 the situation was desperate. The French, embittered by Britain's unilateral occupation and the abolition of the Dual Control, used every device possible to embarrass the British and to prevent any amelioration of Egypt's financial prostration. Revenues such as railway and telegraph receipts, customs duties, port fees at Alexandria, and proceeds from khedivial estates, allotted by the Law of Liquidation to the Fund for debt payments, continued to be collected, but funds for the administration of government and payment of tribute to the Porte were insufficient. By the end of 1883 government workers' salaries were in arrears and the floating current debt of £4 million had doubled. British proposals to reduce interest payments on the debt, lower the rate of amortization, and transfer some funds to pay for administration were vetoed by the French through the Fund.

Finally, at a London conference in 1885 agreement was reached to float an internationally guaranteed loan to pay off the current debt, to reduce interest payments and debt amortization, and to provide for Egyptian irrigation needs. Any surplus funds annually accruing to the Fund were to be divided equally between the administration and debt funding. By 1889 the Egyptian treasury began to show surpluses.

With Egypt's finances seemingly adjusted the British turned to the thorny problem of withdrawal from the country. Badgered from every side—and especially by France—to set a definite date and equally encouraged by Cromer to be vague on this issue, England sent Sir Henry Drummond-Wolff to Cairo and Istanbul in 1885 to conclude a withdrawal agreement in concert with the sultan and with the approval of the Powers. The French and Russians protested so strenuously against British proposals that Abdul Hamid failed to ratify a convention. As a result, the British position in Egypt remained anomalous until 1914.

Meanwhile, British imperial strategy shifted its focus to Cairo and Suez from Istanbul and the Straits where German influence was mounting. British withdrawal from Egypt was now pushed to some nebulous future. However, the Powers and the trading nations of Europe needed an understanding of the status of the Suez Canal. Consequently, a meeting was called in Istanbul in 1888 at which the Constantinople Convention, as previously outlined, was signed. Though Lord Cromer secretly railed at the many disabilities suffered by Egyptians, the international position of Egypt under the suzerainty of the Ottoman Empire and the control of Great Britain remained virtually unchanged until World War I.

KHEDIVE ABBAS HILMI II VS. LORD CROMER

Mustafa Pasha Fahmi became prime minister in 1891. An elegant Turk, weak in resolve, gentlemanly, honest, hardworking, an ally of Ismail, a friend of Urabi, and devoted to Tawfiq, Fahmi continued as prime minister until Cromer's retirement in 1907. Affairs moved so smoothly during Fahmi's stewardship that Cromer allowed that he was almost bored. With imports and exports on the rise, treasury surpluses building up, and the cabinet and khedive docile, the British occupation appeared to be succeeding. Then, in January 1892, Tawfiq fell ill and died. His son and successor, Abbas Hilmi II, not quite eighteen years old, was studying at the Princes' Academy in Vienna and was an untested and unknown figure. Cromer realized that the "alliance" had been broken; he would have to start afresh to educate the new khedive to reality.

From his French tutor Rouiller, Abbas had gained French ideas: liberalism, free political discussion, and Anglophobic proclivities. Coming to Cairo as the khedive's European secretary, Rouiller encouraged Abbas to show independence of Cromer and evidently suggested that France would aid the new khedive to get rid of the British. Thereafter, Abbas was friendly toward the French and showed a strong dislike for the British. The firman of his authorization from the Porte busied the new khedive in the first few months of his rule, as Abdul Hamid had neglected to include the Sinai peninsula in Abbas's territory. Cromer was intensely disturbed over his omission, jeopardizing the Suez Canal as it did, and fully supported Abbas in the final drafting in favor of Egypt.

A few months later, however, Cromer was calling Abbas a foolish youth, for Abbas had decided to replace the seriously ill Fahmi with a prime minister of his own choosing. Abbas dismissed the kowtowing Fahmi and appointed in his place Fakhri Pasha, a former minister of justice who had crossed Cromer on more than one occasion. Cromer was angry because Fakhri had been appointed without consultation with the British. London cabled Abbas that England could not "sanction the proposed nomination." Cromer forced Abbas to declare that he "would always most willingly adopt British advice."

Suddenly Abbas became a hero to many of the budding Egyptian nationalists, who saw in him a young and vigorous voice for "Egypt for the Egyptians." Abbas now had the sympathies of the Egyptian people and especially of the Egyptian army, but timidity and caution kept him in subjugation. Moreover, in 1894 he discovered that the rather small army might hail him at one moment but abandon him in a contest of will with the British. Abbas, with Mahir Pasha, undersecretary of state for war, and Kitchener, who had now become Sirdar of the Egyptian army, were making a tour of inspection in Upper Egypt. At Wadi Halfa, on the frontier, Abbas remarked disparagingly to Kitchener on the performance of the troops. Kitchener took offense, accused Abbas of criticizing British officers, and demanded a public apology. Sensing this as a suitable opportunity to put Abbas in his place, Cromer supported Kitchener's stand. Abbas was forced to publish a retraction of his remarks and had to fire Mahir Pasha after Cromer hinted that British public opinion would likely insist on deposing the khedive. The Egyptian army would not, and could not, in view of all the British officers in dominant positions, act to support Abbas against British rule.

ABBAS HILMI II AND EGYPTIAN NATIONALISM

For support in his opposition to British occupation, Abbas then turned to the Egyptian nationalists, who had been increasing in number and influence. Cromer, never worried very much about Egypt's educated minority, had permitted a free press to exist. Now, a number of teachers and writers, most of whom had studied or lived in Europe, were espousing Egyptian territorial patriotism, but not yet Arab nationalism.

Egyptian nationalists began to appear early in the nineteenth century. One of the first advocates was Rifaa Rafi al-Tahtawi, who had studied at Cairo's al-Azhar University and then in 1826 was sent by Muhammad Ali to Paris as the religious guardian of a group of Egyptian students. He remained there for five years, learning precise French and reading widely. From 1831 until his death forty years later, al-Tahtawi taught two generations of Egyptian students and wrote and translated many significant books, among them, *Guiding Truths for Girls and Youths* and *The Paths of Egyptian Hearts in the Joys of the Contemporary Arts.* These works championed the love of Egypt but pointed out that Egypt's destiny could not be attained until the ulema were modernized and the schools offered a more secular education.

Many other writers contributed to the intellectual and ideological ferment in Egypt in the time of Said and Ismail. One was Jamal al-Din al-Afghani, who lived, taught, and conspired in Cairo from 1871 to 1879. A Shiite from Iran, he posed as a Sunnite from Afghanistan (in Afghanistan he claimed to be a Turk). He had studied in Iraq and lived in Afghanistan and Istanbul before coming to Cairo. Jamal al-Din's life can be summed up in a phrase recently used as the title of a book about him, *An Islamic Response to Imperialism.* In Egypt he found a coterie of devotees who were swept up by his compelling personality, his lucid and persuasive presentation of ideas, and the innovation and dedication of his beliefs. He argued that when the Muslim community returned to the truth of Islam, society would cease to be weak; only then would there be a regeneration. Jamal al-Din believed that the essence of Islam was identical to that of modern rationalism and that the outward trappings of Islamic scholasticism had shackled Muslim philosophers. He held that Islam came from God and was exalted above the universe. He believed also in reason, that one should use one's mind freely to know and test all. Furthermore, every mind was capable of providing the individual with self-respect and a sense of equality. Lastly, Jamal al-Din was convinced that Islam was an active way of life; it was not a passive resignation to whatever might come but a responsible activity in doing the will of God.

These preachings, which were debated privately in closed circles, were heady stuff. They were aimed against Christian imperialistic attacks upon Islamic societies and against Westernizing influences and materialism. Jamal al-Din al-Afghani was a pan-Islamist who wanted to reform Islam by means of education and to adapt Islam to the conditions of modern life. He did not see how this could be done without revolution, the political unity of the Muslim world, and freedom from foreign domination. Wherever he went, whether in Egypt, Turkey, or Iran, he vigorously stirred the minds and imaginations of Muslims to react in defense of an embattled Islamic society and against its debasement by Christian Europe. He became so influential in Egypt that the government asked him to leave. The remainder of his life was spent in Iran, France, England, and the Ottoman Empire. Some of his most effective writing was done in Paris. He died in 1897.

Jamal al-Din's most illustrious pupil was Muhammad Abduh, a peasant from Lower Egypt who had a distinguished career as a mystic, journalist, judge, and teacher. Differing from his mentor, Muhammad Abduh deplored the use of violence and believed that true reforms came only by a gradual process. He advocated a reform of Islam that would return it to its earliest, purest dogma, permitting a more flexible interpretation of its precepts than was allowed in the al Azhar University of his day. Muhammad Abduh, like Urabi Pasha, wished to free the people of Egypt from despotic rule and to institute a more democratic society. He also worked for the development of Arabic into a more unified language, attempting to draw newspaper Arabic and the spoken vernacular together and bring both nearer to classical Koranic Arabic.

Abduh supported the Urabi movement, was an active member of the Nationalist party, and was exiled along with Urabi. He found his way to Paris to join al-Afghani; together they edited a short-lived but influential pan-Islamic journal. At Cromer's urging, Abduh was allowed by Tawfiq to return to Egypt in 1888. He was appointed a judge in a local court and in 1899 became Grand Mufti of Egypt, a post he retained until his death in 1905. In France, Abduh had concluded that Egypt's poverty-stricken traditional society could neither mount a successful revolution nor drive out the British. Henceforth he taught that reason and the pragmatic accommodation of Islam to the modern world must supersede customary practice and belief; one should adopt what is reasonable and just for society.

Abduh and Cromer respected each other and met frequently. Abduh recognized Egypt's need for a benevolent despot and probably would have supported Cromer had he been an Egyptian. Cromer backed Abduh against the vindictiveness of Tawfiq and Abbas, which made them dislike and distrust Abduh. Abbas even went so far as to accuse him of having sold out to the British. Abbas circulated such rumors about Abduh that only after Abduh's death was he fully accorded his rightful honors as a patriot, scholar, teacher, judge, and reformer.

Another prominent nationalist, a contemporary and sometimes rival of Muhammad Abduh, was Ali Yusuf. As a teacher at al-Azhar University he preached reform in much the same vein as did Abduh, but without the philosophical and intellectual substance. In 1889, Ali Yusuf founded *al-Muayyad* (The Supporter), a newspaper financed by the anti-English element, which within a few years became the leading pro-Egyptian journal. Ali Yusuf was a good journalist and his articles were always Muslim-oriented and even pro-Ottoman. When Abbas II became khedive he befriended Ali Yusuf, subsidized the newspaper, and often took him on his travels. Naturally, *al-Muayyad* supported Abbas in his attempts to become independent of Cromer. In 1907 Ali Yusuf formed, under Abbas's patronage, the nationalist Party of Constitutional Reform, which died in 1911 with Ali Yusuf. Ali Yusuf was a conservative, orthodox nationalist who wanted Egypt governed by Egyptians. However, he doomed his movement by tying it to Abbas, for Abbas's surrender to Cromer had turned most Egyptian nationalists against him by 1905.

No nationalist was more fiery than Mustafa Kamil. Coming from the new educated class, he entered the School of Law in 1891 at the age of seventeen, then attended the newly opened French School of Law, and went on to France where he was graduated in law in 1894. He had been introduced to many prominent Egyptian leaders at the home of Ali Pasha Mubarak, and in Paris, supplied with funds from Abbas, he became acquainted with leading French literary figures who displayed this genuine Egyptian nationalist in order to disprove British claims that their occupation was fully approved by the Egyptians. Returning to Egypt in 1896, he spent the remaining twelve years of his life agitating for Egyptian national independence. A spellbinding orator who fired audiences with his ideals and ideas, Mustafa Kamil pleaded with all Egyptians of whatever origin or religion to unite into one nationalistic force to eliminate ignorance and to support the khedive as a rallying point against the occupation. His slogans, such as, "Had I not been born an Egyptian, I would have wished to become one," instilled in his followers a love of Egypt and a pride in her past glories. Kamil worked to erase the defeatism and the sense of inferiority that the capitulations and the occupation had generated. In 1900 he founded the radical newspaper, *al-Liwa* (The Standard), and gathered nationalists about him informally, calling them *al-Hizb al-Watani,* the Nationalist party, which did not become an organized party until 1907. Something of a pan-Islamist, whose goal was to achieve Islamic liberation of Egypt from alien rule and autonomy within the Ottoman Empire under the caliph, he accused the British of impairing the authority of the khedive, destroying Arabic as the language of the educated, depriving Egypt of the Sudan, exploiting Egyptian agriculture, excluding Egyptians from top government positions, and stultifying Islam to secure the British position in India. Cromer called him a fanatic.

THE ANGLO-EGYPTIAN SUDAN

Throughout the nineteenth century the governing forces in Egypt maintained a lively interest in the Sudan. Muhammad Ali sent an expedition into that area in 1820, and in 1842 the Ottoman sultan recognized him as governor-general of the Sudan. During the middle of the century the chief activities with regard to the Sudan consisted of conflicts with Ethiopia over Red Sea ports, such as Massawa. A regular commerce in ivory and slaves developed, despite vigorous measures taken later by the khedive Ismail against the slave trade. Ismail extended Egyptian control up the Nile, to the east and west of the great river, and toward Ethiopia. Many of his appointees in the Sudan were European Christians who did not know Arabic and who were greeted with great hostility by the Sudanese. At the time of Ismail's ouster from office and the crisis over Urabi and the finances of Egypt, affairs in the Sudan were beginning to be difficult to manage.

In 1881 Muhammad Ahmad (ca. 1841–1885) of Dongola, an ascetic Sufi leader, proclaimed himself to be the Mahdi, the religious leader sent to complete the work of the prophet Muhammad and to signal the last days of the world. He gained support among the northern tribes and the western nomads, and he preached a message filled with appeals to revolutionary justice and Sunnite fundamentalism. He claimed to be recreating the exact circumstances of the early Islamic community in Mecca and Medina. He said Egypt and the "corrupt" Islam practiced there were the enemy, while the harsh rule of the Sudan by Muhammad Ali and his successors provided a powerful sense of resentment that fueled the Mahdist movement among the Sudanese. When revolt broke out south of Khartoum in the province of Kordofan, affairs in Egypt were so chaotic and finances so desperate that the Sudan was left to herself. However, in 1883 Khedive Tawfiq sent an Egyptian army to the Sudan. It was cut to pieces by the forces of the Mahdi, and Sir Evelyn Baring upon his arrival in Egypt insisted upon complete withdrawal from the Sudan, largely for financial reasons. Charles George Gordon was then sent in 1884 to arrange for the evacuation of Khartoum, but he delayed the operation and a relief expedition from Cairo arrived too late. In 1885 Khartoum fell to the Mahdi, and Gordon and his men were slain.

For the following decade the Sudan was an independent theocratic state under the Mahdi and his successors. Wadi Halfa became the frontier post of Egypt. The Mahdi established a judicial system based on his own unique position as the recipient of communications from the prophet Muhammad. Sufi fraternities were outlawed and the pilgrimage to Mecca was forbidden, because Mecca was under the control of the Ottoman Empire. The Mahdi minted coins, collected the Koranic taxes, and permitted slavery and the slave trade once again to flourish. Following his death in 1885, the caliph Abd Allah of the western tribes overcame a series of revolts, bad harvests, and the outbreak of disease. He sought to conquer Ethiopia and Egypt, but was disastrously defeated by the Anglo-Egyptians in 1889. Taxes were increased, and the major government positions were assigned to members of Abd Allah's tribe as the state authority came to resemble personal rule exercised through a bureaucracy rather than the charismatic appeal of the Mahdi.

In the 1890s, the Italian war in Eritrea and French pressure upon Ethiopia led the British to consider the reconquest of the Sudan. Kitchener took Dongola in 1896. Two years later, with the support of Indian and English troops, he moved up the Nile, taking Omdurman and Khartoum and completely routing Caliph Abd Allah's forces.

In 1899, the Sudan Convention was consummated in Cairo, establishing what soon came to be known as the Anglo-Egyptian Sudan. Theoretically, it was a condominium or joint rule, but the Egyptian voice in ruling the Sudan remained only nominal. Military and civil power was vested in a governor-general chosen by the British. Egyptian law was not valid in the Sudan, nor were the mixed tribunals extended there. Import duties were not levied on goods coming from Egypt, and the slave trade was prohibited. Consular agents of other powers could be accredited in the Sudan only upon the consent of the British government.

By World War I, the borders of the Sudan with its neighbors were determined. But within the country, British control was limited by vast spaces, the heterogeneous population, and inadequate funding. Egypt paid for the armed forces and provided a subsidy until the Sudanese budget was finally balanced in 1913. British officers in the Egyptian army and Egyptian civilians were the main sources of government employees. Personal law came from the Islamic holy law; tribal law dominated the nomadic tribal countryside; and secular law began to prevail in criminal matters. The southern Sudan was treated differently than the rest of the country: the English language was encouraged, missionaries were supported, and Islam, the Arabic language, and Arab customs were opposed. The Condominium built railroads to Khartoum from Egypt and to the Red Sea from Khartoum, and by the beginning of World War I the British were planning for massive irrigation projects that would enable a dramatic increase in the growing of cotton. Although the British and Egyptian flags were flown side by side over all public buildings, no one ever doubted which power ruled the Sudan.

TABA AND DINSHWAI

Though nationalist attacks in the press made life more difficult for Cromer, he expected that greatly improved economic conditions would blunt the campaigns of the educated few who mounted the opposition and would allay the antagonisms of the Egyptian masses. Events seemed to be working in his favor and dashing the hopes of Abbas, Kamil, Ali Yusuf, Abduh, and others. Kitchener had secured the Anglo-Egyptian condominium over the Sudan. Meanwhile, there had been an inconclusive showdown between Kitchener and French officers at Fashoda. The Anglo-French Agreement of 1904, part of the Entente Cordiale, stated quite frankly that the French accepted the indefinite postponement of British evacuation and would not object to freeing Egypt from most of the financial restrictions imposed on her by the Fund. Two years later, however, three inflammatory incidents rekindled the nationalist fires, setting the stage for Cromer's retirement.

In January 1906, Ottoman forces landed at Taba, a desert spot near the head of the Gulf of Aqaba, and established a post there. The British protested that Taba was in the territory of Egypt but the Porte disagreed, arguing that Taba was in the Sinai peninsula and that it was a part of Syria. Mustafa Kamil, pan-Islamist Ali Yusuf, and other Egyptian editors came out strongly in support of the sultan and bitterly attacked Cromer and the British for trying to humiliate the caliph and Islam. Cromer considered the pro-Ottoman clamor only another anti-British outcry. Istanbul succumbed to a British ultimatum to delimit the frontier in Egypt's favor.

Almost before the Taba affair was concluded the students at the School of Law, ardent followers of Kamil, went out on strike, the first demonstration of its kind in Egypt. In the end Cromer had to arbitrate the matter. By 1908 student strikes and disturbances became ordinary occurrences.

Then, in May 1906, the Dinshwai Affair altered irrevocably the course of political life in Egypt. A group of British officers went to Dinshwai, a village near Tanta, to shoot pigeons, a favorite sport of theirs. Without securing permission from the village headman, they greatly antagonized the villagers, who regarded the pigeons as their domesticated birds. A fire broke out, a fracas developed, a gun went off, a village woman was shot, British officers were mauled and one died from heat exhaustion, and a peasant was beaten to death before order was restored. The British judged that stern measures were needed and set up at Cromer's insistence a special tribunal to try the Dinshwai villagers on charges of murder. Composed of Butros Pasha Ghali, the minister of justice, the British judicial adviser, the British vice president of the courts, the Egyptian president of the native courts, and a British army judge, the special tribunal handed down the verdict: thirty-one villagers were found not guilty and released; two were sentenced to life imprisonment; one was given fifteen years; six received seven years; three were given one year and fifty lashes; five received fifty lashes; and four were condemned to death by hanging. Punishments were carried out immediately, in public view, in the village. The severity of the judgment stunned Egypt and shocked Europe. Kamil wrote an article for *Le Figaro* in Paris and George Bernard Shaw wrote the play *John Bull's Other Island.* For many Egyptians this naked display of power was the birth of nationalism. It led to the formation of political parties. Mustafa Kamil set up the Nationalist party; Ali Yusuf founded the Party of Constitutional Reform; and followers of Muhammad Abduh organized the Party of the Nation, *Hizb al-Umma.* All these parties urged the institution of representative government in Egypt, replacement of European officials by Egyptians, and transfer of criminal jurisdiction over foreigners from consular courts to the mixed courts. None of the parties demanded immediate British departure. Though Cromer secured the appointment of Saad Zaghlul, a leading member of *al-Umma,* as minister of education, Cromer's style of governing Egypt now was outmoded and he resigned on March 28, 1907. Kamil, on the occasion, wrote in his paper that Cromer had negated the khedive's authority, had seized the Sudan with Egyptian men and money and then stripped Egypt of any influence there, had denied Egyptians any power at home, had insulted Islam, had forced Egyptians to be governed by Englishmen, had impugned Egyptian nationalism, and had converted Egypt into a British colony. Kamil's condemnation was widely accepted not only in Egypt but in England and throughout the world.

SIR ELDON GORST AND LORD KITCHENER

Even in 1906, the year of crises, and during the 1907 financial crisis, no threat of a nationalist uprising surfaced. To be sure, the newspapers sharpened their attacks. The alliance of nationalists and the palace against the British raised more fears in London than in Cairo, for many educated Egyptians, especially among the Coptic Christians, supported the Party of the Nation, *al-Umma,* a moderate group under the leadership of the scholar and lawyer Ahmad Lutfi al-Sayyid. The leaders of *al-Umma,* although desirous of a British departure, recognized that Cromer had found chaos, financial ruin, and general frustration upon his arrival and within a decade had established financial equilibrium, organized an orderly and a tolerably efficient government, and instituted considerable justice in the administration and the courts. For this they were thankful. Life was not bad enough to warrant a revolt.

To replace Cromer, London sent Sir Eldon Gorst, who had been in Egyptian government service from 1886 to 1904. Gorst had instructions to win over Abbas, with whom he had once been friendly, and thus break the alliance between the palace and the nationalists. He had been assigned to Egypt with the recognition that a more liberal policy was needed and that he should prepare Egypt for self-rule.

Gorst began by opening up more administrative positions for Egyptians and by trying to share the formulation of policy with them. Most English officials in Egypt resented the change; Gorst got rid of the more unsympathetic ones. He extended the power of the provincial councils by giving them control over local education, trade schools, public markets, and some police, but would not consider the nationalists' call for true legislative institutions and a constitution, even though the Ottomans got a constitution in 1908. Gorst did alienate the nationalists from Abbas by deferring to the khedive on almost all minor matters. But the new alliance between the palace and the British Agency cost Gorst the support of the moderate nationalists and *al-Umma,* for they considered the unbridled authority of Abbas to be as dangerous as that of the British.

In 1908, Mustafa Pasha Fahmi bowed to pressure on all sides and resigned as prime minister. Gorst had found him difficult; the nationalists considered him a British straw man; and *al-Umma* and Fahmi's son-in-law Saad Zaghlul encouraged him to desert the British. In his place Gorst installed Butros Pasha Ghali, a government minister and a leader of the reformist group inside the Coptic Christian community. For the nationalists a worse choice could not have been found. As a minister Butros had signed the Anglo-Egyptian condominium over the Sudan and as a judge he had sat at the Dinshwai trial. Also, in 1909, the Suez Canal Company, whose concession ran until 1969, offered to pay the Egyptian government a million pounds a year to extend the concession an additional forty years. Many thought this to be an attractive proposition and, urged on by *al-Umma* leaders and by Gorst, Butros requested the Legislative Council's approval. The debate over the extension was most vehement; Butros was accused of selling Egyptian property and perpetrating a dishonorable arrangement. In February 1910, before it was rejected, a young fanatic assassinated Butros.

These events broke Gorst's spirit; overcome by ill health he returned to England, where he died in 1911. He was replaced by Lord Kitchener, who had served with distinction in Egypt in various capacities from 1883 to 1899. Kitchener has been characterized as "an extremely able and ambitious soldier, overbearing, tactless, very much aware of his own importance, and without very much sense of humor."

Kitchener's appointment presaged the end of Gorst's liberalizing experiment. International tensions mounted rapidly with the Italian invasion of Tripoli, Balkan wars, other war scares and naval rivalries, and diplomatic maneuvers between the Triple Entente (Britain, France, and Russia) and the Triple Alliance (Germany, Austria, and Italy). London therefore wanted serenity and security in Egypt. Kitchener had no faith in Abbas's loyalty, dealt with him harshly, and wanted to depose him. But Kitchener's instructions, though stressing a return to order, enjoined him not to reverse Gorst's policies leading to more self-rule. He approached many leaders and worked with them in creating in 1913 a new Legislative Assembly that joined together the old Legislative Council and General Assembly. Sixty-six of the new legislature's members were elected publicly; its effective head was an elected vice president; most of the members were prosperous landowners; no seats were reserved for religious minorities; and the Party of the Nation, *al-Umma,* held a majority.

In 1912 Kitchener, who disliked Saad Zaghlul, managed a petty quarrel that provoked Zaghlul into resigning from the cabinet. After a few months a minor post that Zaghlul wanted became vacant—the leadership of a student mission in Europe—but Kitchener refused to appoint him. Instead, Zaghlul ran for a seat in the Legislative Assembly, with a program for attaining justice in the courts, spreading public education, and increasing freedom of the press. He was the most popular figure in the campaign and had the backing of the bar association, the Party of the Nation, the Nationalist party, and the khedive, the last being noteworthy, for up to that time Abbas had refused Zaghlul any appointment.

In the elections in 1913 Zaghlul won handsomely and was popularly designated as the natural leader of the opposition. By an overwhelming vote the Assembly elected him its vice president (the president was appointed by the government). Within three months Zaghlul's popularity and his leadership in the Assembly made the prime minister's position untenable. Abbas and Kitchener then agreed that Mustafa Pasha Fahmi, Zaghlul's father-in-law, should be the new prime minister. When Kitchener questioned Fahmi it came to light that he intended within a matter of months to sweep from office all the ministers of the cabinet who "had been most loyal" to the British and to "install men devoted to Saad Zaghlul." Consequently, Fahmi was ruled out and Husayn Rushdi was named to form a cabinet, which remained in office until the end of World War I. Kitchener's adviser in the ministry of the interior noted at the time that cabinet ministers were not supported by the khedive and were timid in opposing the Assembly for fear of being branded unpatriotic. The adviser warned Kitchener that in the future "the success and even the existence of Egyptian Cabinets" depended upon the will of the Legislative Assembly. The Assembly adjourned on June 7, 1914; it was scheduled to meet again on November 1.

Zaghlul, Abduh, Lutfi al-Sayyid, and most of the modern middle-class nationalists agreed on the emancipation of women. They favored more education for women, abolishing the veil (although rather few Egyptian women wore it in any case), and making polygamy more difficult. Qasim Amin's book of 1899, *The Emancipation of Women,* was especially influential, as it presented the argument that European political and scientific superiority was, in part, based on the relatively better educated condition of women in Europe. Women's ignorance also created a harmful intellectual gap between wives and husbands. Despite these and other arguments, very few women were enrolled in either public or private schools by World War I. Men continued to completely dominate public life, including elections.

During the summer of 1914, Kitchener became minister of war in London; Abbas Hilmi, who was in Istanbul, was not permitted to return to Cairo; and martial law was invoked in Egypt. In December Great Britain declared a protectorate over Egypt and the Sudan. Kitchener's mission as British agent had failed. By 1914 the efficiency of British officials in Egypt could be legitimately questioned, for their effectiveness had long ago been dissipated by the fact that they were not Egyptians. The problems the British were to experience in the post-World War I period were coming rapidly to the fore even before 1914. The population was growing very rapidly, and social changes, such as the emergence of the new professionals or the disappearance of the guilds, placed even more pressure on the existing political structure. Only the outbreak of war and subsequent strong military occupation prevented Egyptian nationalists from openly attacking the British position. Such action was reserved for the time following the war.

REFERENCES

Works cited at the end of Chapters 19, 22, and 24 are valuable for this chapter.

Abbas, Mekki. *The Sudan Question: The Dispute over the Anglo-Egyptian Condominium, 1884–1951.* London: Faber, 1952. Written by a Sudanese, it is neither pro-British nor pro-Egyptian.

Ahmed, Jamal Mohammed. *The Intellectual Origins of Egyptian Nationalism.* London: Oxford University Press, 1960. A fine account of the intellectual ferment preceding the British occupation and a commentary on Abduh's views on the value of religion.

Amin, Osman. *Muhammad Abduh.* Translated by Charles Wendell. Washington, D.C.: American Council of Learned Societies, 1953.

Baer, Gabriel. *Studies in the Social History of Modern Egypt.* Chicago: University of Chicago Press, 1969. A study of the social background that helps mold political events.

Berque, Jacques. *Egypt: Imperialism and Revolution.* Translated by Jean Stewart. New York: Praeger, 1972. A description of the rise and decline of British power in Egypt, or the interrelated processes of colonization and decolonization, 1882–1952.

Cole, Juan Ricardo. "Feminism, Class, and Islam in Turn-of-the-Century Egypt." *International Journal of Middle East Studies* 13 (1981): 387–407. A discussion of the subtle factors that link economic and social values.

Cromer, Evelyn Baring. *Modern Egypt.* 2 vols. London: Macmillan, 1908. Cromer's account of his rule in Egypt.

Holt, P. M. *The Mahdist State in the Sudan, 1881–1898: A Study of Its Origins, Development and Overthrow.* 2d ed. Oxford: Clarendon Press, 1970.

————, and M. W. Daly. *A History of the Sudan from the Coming of Islam to the Present Day.* 4th ed. London: Longman, 1988. A classic discussion of the subject by two authorities on the Sudan.

Keddie, Nikki R. *An Islamic Response to Imperialism: Political and Religious Writings of Sayyid Jamal ad-Din "Al-Afghani."* Berkeley: University of California Press, 1968. A short biography and analysis of al-Afghani followed by translations of his important works.

————. *Sayyid Jamal ad-Din "Al-Afghani": A Political Biography.* Berkeley: University of California Press, 1972. A definitive biography of the almost legendary political activist and publicist.

Lloyd, George Ambrose L. *Egypt Since Cromer.* 2 vols. London: Macmillan, 1933–1934. Lord Lloyd was an official in Egypt.

Marlowe, John. *Cromer in Egypt.* New York: Praeger, 1970. Based on British documentary sources. Covers Egyptian finances and British negotiations with other European powers as well as the details of Cromer's administration.

Richards, Alan. *Egypt's Agricultural Development, 1800–1980: Technical and Social Change.* Boulder, Colo.: Westview Press, 1981. Excellent treatment of the social impact of agricultural and technical changes; emphasizes importance of drainage and shows the damage caused by its neglect.

al-Sayyid, Afaf Lutfi. *Egypt and Cromer: A Study in Anglo-Egyptian Relations.* New York: Praeger, 1968. The nationalist movement and the British reaction to it. The author had access to many private papers of nationalist leaders.

Seikaly, Samir. "Coptic Communal Reform, 1860–1914." *Middle Eastern Studies* 6 (1970): 247–275. An excellent study of a neglected subject, this article shows that the Christian Copts of Egypt went through many of the same changes as the religious Millets in the other parts of the Ottoman Empire in the late nineteenth century.

Tignor, Robert L. *Modernization and British Colonial Rule in Egypt, 1882–1914.* Princeton, N.J.: Princeton University Press, 1966. A balanced and fair evaluation written in a clear and orderly fashion; invaluable for the period.

Voll, John. "The Sudanese Mahdi: Frontier Fundamentalist." *International Journal of Middle East Studies* 10 (1979): 145–166. Valuable for putting the Mahdi into a broad analytical framework and discussing the importance of his life for today's world.

Zayid, Mahmud Y. *Egypt's Struggle for Independence.* Beirut: Khayats, 1965. Contains two fine chapters on the history of Egypt in the nineteenth century, going as far as 1914, and material on the 1920s and 1930s. The author taught history at the American University of Beirut.

28

Arab Nationalism

THE ROLE OF EDUCATION

At the opening of the twentieth century the twin questions of an Arab nationalism separate and distinct from Ottomanism or Egyptian patriotism and the formation of an independent Arab nationalist state were in the minds of only a very few. But the nationalist movement and feelings surrounding it were already reaching a degree of development that could burst at any moment into the full light of world attention.

In Syria, the leading role in revitalizing Arab intellectualism was first played by Western educators. Although Jesuits had arrived in the seventeenth century to teach in Maronite and Catholic communities, little rejuvenation of Arab thought occurred until 1820, when American Presbyterian missionaries landed in Beirut. The latter organized schools almost immediately. The Catholics now increased their energies to compete with the American Protestants, and Ibrahim, the son of Muhammad Ali, furthered the educational drive by establishing many elementary schools for boys on the model of those in Egypt. Girls' schools were also opened. In 1866, the Syrian Protestant College of Beirut opened its doors. Later, as the American University, it played an important role in training young people (Muslim and Christian alike) from every corner of the Arab world. Almost simultaneously, Catholic missionaries, largely from France, settled in Syria in great numbers, and schools spread from Beirut to Damascus, Aleppo, and many other towns. In 1875 the University of St. Joseph in Beirut opened; it would educate many outstanding leaders of Syrian national and cultural life. Later, Ottoman and Egyptian state schools played an even more important role than the missionary institutions in spreading secular and patriotic concepts.

Numerous writers, thinkers, and teachers influenced the growth of Arab nationalism. Three of them were Christian Arabs from Lebanon. Nasif al-Yaziji taught Arabic near Beirut until his death in 1871. His masterly writings in Arabic pioneered a style, manner, and vocabulary suitable for expressing the life and ideas of the modern world and paved the way for an Arabic renaissance.

Butrus al-Bustani, a Maronite, as was al-Yaziji, assisted American Protestant missionaries in translating the Bible into Arabic. His dictionary, encyclopedia, and the many Arabic-language periodicals he wrote and published helped to create a modern Arabic prose that could present the concepts of contemporary thought in language simple enough for use in newspapers; he is the father of so-called news-paper Arabic. Butrus also founded the National School, where studies were secular and based on national rather than religious principles. He was at the same time both a Syrian Arab patriot and an Ottoman loyalist, and seemingly saw no contradiction between these two positions.

The third Lebanese Christian was Jurji Zaydan, whose historical novels, modeled on those of Sir Walter Scott, built the modern romantic Arab image of the Arab past.

In Egypt, an educational and literary renaissance, explained in the previous chapter, was under way. The famous Bulaq Press, started in Cairo in 1822, printed over 300 books in Arabic, Turkish, and Persian before 1850. It gave to Cairo the distinction of being a literary center and drew there many intellectuals from every part of the Arab world. Without the printing press Arab nationalism and the regeneration of the Arab people would have progressed very slowly. Books were published in ever-growing numbers, and newspapers sprang up in the leading cities. An incomplete tally in 1913 showed 118 Arabic-language newspapers in the Ottoman Empire, excluding Egypt.

In the last half of the nineteenth century, Arabic presses in several cities were publishing original works and many translations of European books, and these were circulating readily in all parts of the Arab world. From French North Africa to British India, ideas of patriotism, nationalism, Islamic reform, and modernization were being developed in a unifying pattern to free Arab minds from concepts stemming from and contingent upon Western Christian imperialism. Intellectuals and publicists were traveling back and forth to Istanbul, Beirut, Damascus, Baghdad, Cairo, Tunis, and Algiers, gathering converts to new viewpoints. Every event had an impact everywhere, two of the greatest being the Dinshwai Affair and the Young Turk Revolution.

With the accession of Abdul Hamid as Ottoman sultan, clandestine societies multiplied in the Arab provinces. In Egypt, however, local autonomy freed nationalism from the sultan's surveillance. Cairo and Alexandria became centers for national exhortation; Egypt, along with France and Switzerland, became a haven for exiled Arab nationalists.

One of these exiles was Abd al-Rahman Kawakibi of Aleppo, who wrote *Umm al-Qura,* a humorous yet penetrating anthology on the future of Islamic society, and *The Attributes of Tyranny,* published anonymously in Cairo. Together they analyzed the decrepit world of Arab society. Kawakibi attacked the ignorance of the masses and the obscurantism of the theologians who dominated the educational field. He was also one of the first to separate Arab national revival from pan-Islamism.

THE BIRTH OF ARAB NATIONALISM

For centuries leaders and intellectuals in the Middle East had felt the East to be superior to the West. After the Napoleonic Wars economic, cultural, and social contacts between the Middle East and western Europe expanded greatly and the wealth and power of Europe became evident. Middle Easterners were shaken by the new perception they had of the West. Nineteenth-century nationalists such as Nasif al-Yaziji and Butrus al-Bustani put their faith in an educational revival as a means of catching up. Differences between Arabs and Turks were barely considered. The Middle Eastern culture and Islam, its central theme, were regarded as the valid bases of the society that had produced the wondrous ages of the past. Accepting the fact that Arabic was the language of religion and Turkish the language of government and politics, the early nationalist thinkers supported both Islam and the Ottoman way of life as being fundamentally sound and superior to that of the West. Conservative Ottomanists, such as Tanzimat reformers Rifaa Rafi al-Tahtawi, the Egyptian patriot, wrote that it would be necessary only to borrow certain things from the West, such as the natural and physical sciences, and the gap would close.

As the years passed and the obvious gap between the strength and development of the East and the West widened, questions began to be raised about various aspects of Middle Eastern life and culture. New polemicists such as al-Afghani and his pupil Muhammad Abduh asserted that Islam was in a deplorable condition because over the centuries society had corrupted true primitive Islam, and as a consequence Muslims had been unable to continue their remarkable progress. They believed that primitive Islam had demanded that Muslims exercise reason and examine the bases of faith. Aware of Guizot's dictum that Europe began to progress with the advent of Protestantism, they drew an analogy and insisted that the Middle East must return to primitive Islam in order to become truly modern. Among these modernist Ottomans were Muhammad Rashid Rida, whose periodical, *al-Manar,* advanced these theories to the full. None of these reformers was prepared to overturn the Ottoman caliph-sultan.

Political changes led the way for conservative Ottomanism to become modernist Ottomanism, which in turn was transformed into Arabism. Rida, Kawakibi, and other Arab nationalists met the Islamists by proclaiming that Islam was only one of the infinite glories of the Arab nation. They cried out against bigotry and fanaticism and called for ejecting foreigners and alien influences from the Arab scene. After the Turkish revolution of 1908 it became more apparent that Ottomanism and pan-Islamism were no substitutes for Arab nationalism, though most Arab leaders clung to these ideologies until the end of World War I.

THE YOUNG TURKS AND ARAB NATIONALISM

The program of the Young Turks before the counterrevolution in 1909 appealed to many Arab leaders, who saw in it the destruction of Abdul Hamid's tyranny. They fully subscribed to the Ottoman program of the Committee of Union and Progress because they translated it to mean decentralization of the empire and equality of Arab with Turk. Abdul Hamid had exiled many Young Turks to Damascus, Jerusalem, and Baghdad. Along with many unhappy Turkish army officers languishing in these remote parts, the rising Arab nationalists looked upon the Turkish liberal struggle as their fight, too.

In the early days of the Revolution there was much cooperation between the Young Turks and the Arabs. The Young Turks insisted that Abdul Hamid designate Sharif Husayn of the Hashimite family Prince of Mecca. Although Husayn had resided quietly for fifteen years in Istanbul as a kind of hostage, Abdul Hamid astutely judged the man to have ambitions to rule an autonomous Arab state and warned the Young Turks of the folly of their recommendation. In September 1908, however, Abdul Hamid acquiesced and appointed Husayn to the post.

After the counterrevolution of 1909, centralization of government, Turkification, secularism, and disallowance of all local customs and tradition contrary to Turkish practice became veiled objectives of the Young Turks. As non-Turkish political societies were suppressed, the Arabs, among others, went underground. Here, then, was the birth of passionate Arabism among the new professionals who were teachers, journalists, civil servants, military officers, lawyers, and local notables.

In Palestine, another source of Arab nationalism appeared in addition to the ethnic, cultural, intellectual, and political factors outlined above. Jewish nationalism or Zionism created a strong local backlash as the Arab majority in Ottoman Palestine felt increasingly threatened by Jewish settlers and their foreign supporters. Palestinian Arab representatives in the Ottoman parliament after 1908 joined the Arabic press in harsh criticism of what they felt might be the Zionist aspiration for independent statehood and unilateral control of the land. Since the Ottoman authorities usually shared the views of the Arab nationalists on this question, many barriers were placed in the way of Zionism in Palestine before World War I—barriers that were often evaded with the help of the European powers.

ARAB SOCIETIES

As usual, a welter of societies and parties sprang into being not only among the Arabs in Istanbul, but also among those in Damascus, Beirut, Baghdad, Aleppo, and other Arab cities. An important one in Istanbul was the Literary Club, which disavowed political activities; it posed as a meeting place, library, and clubhouse for Arabs living at the capital, and as a center for Arab travelers. But it was impossible, of course, to prevent Arabs, sitting relaxed in the clubhouse, from discussing political philosophy as it pertained to the Arab situation. Within a short time the club's membership reached the thousands, and branches were located throughout Syria and Iraq, a testimony to growing Arab consciousness.

The second important open group was the Ottoman Decentralization party, established in Cairo in 1912 by experienced Arab public figures. Its objectives were to mobilize Arab public opinion and impress upon the Young Turks the need to organize the new Ottoman Empire on a more federal basis. The group's headquarters remained safely in Cairo, although branches calling themselves reform societies were located in Iraq and Syria and maintained close contact with the Literary Club in Istanbul. The Decentralization party stressed party machinery and enjoyed partial success during the last half of 1912 when the Union and Progress party was out of power.

One interesting secret society was called *al-Qahtaniya.* (Qahtan was a legendary ancestor of the Arabs.) It advocated the creation of a dual Turko-Arab empire, much like the Austro-Hungarian Empire, in which "unity" of the two peoples could be attained by "separation." As the Turkish leaders of Union and Progress showed their hands and guided affairs definitely along paths of Turkification, aspirations for a Turko-Arab accommodation died. With these hopes went *al-Qahtaniya.*

Suppression by the Turks drove many Arabs abroad. As did the Turks a decade earlier, they flocked to Paris. Already Arabs were active there. In 1904 Najib Azuri had founded the League of the Arab Fatherland, and in 1907 he had set up his newspaper, *Arab Independence.* In 1911 the Arab refugees formed the Young Arab Society, better known as *al-Fatat* (Youth). A secret society, *al-Fatat* rejected the idea of any integration within the empire and worked for full Arab freedom and independence. It became the most widespread and effective force among Arabs, moving its headquarters to Damascus in 1914.

In view of these activities and the Arab enthusiasm they evinced, the Young Turks adopted more stringent measures to combat them. A committee of reform, which gathered in Beirut in 1913, publicly announced a program for Arab home rule and won such wide acclaim that the Young Turks suppressed it. After shops and offices in Beirut closed, and newspapers went into mourning, the committee's leaders were arrested. Under the leadership of *al-Fatat* a congress of Arabs was held in Paris. Attended by twenty-four delegates representing many Arab parties, the congress adopted the platforms of the Decentralization party and the committee of reform. The results of the congress were ostensibly accepted by the Young Turks; an imperial decree in 1913 incorporated the declarations as stated policy in the Arab provinces. However, the reforms remained unenforced, and the Arabs believed they had been duped.

Partially in reply, an Arab, Major Aziz Ali al-Misri of the Ottoman general staff, initiated a new society called *al-Ahd* (The Covenant). Aziz Ali had been a member of Union and Progress in Salonika before 1908 and had won honors in the march on Istanbul in 1909, in a military mission to Yemen in 1910, and in the war against Italy in Libya. The Covenant was comprised exclusively of army officers and became for the military what the Young Arab Society was for civilians. It had members in Beirut, Damascus, and Baghdad. In 1914, the Young Turks arrested Aziz Ali without warning. Charged with treason in Libya, he was tried, found guilty, and condemned to death. Public opinion became so indignant, especially in Egypt, that the British protested to the Porte. Aziz Ali was pardoned and sailed for Egypt as a public hero, to lead The Covenant from Cairo. Any hope that the Young Turk leaders had for Arab nationalist cooperation and participation was now completely dispelled. Ottomanism and pan-Islamism for Arab leaders disintegrated in the face of an obvious and understandable drift to Turkish nationalism shown in the actions of the radical Young Turks.

THE ARAB PRINCES

Not only did the Ottoman Turks have difficulty with Arab nationalists and their many patriotic societies but they also discovered that Arab semiautonomous rulers employed every means to resist centralization. Unsuccessful expeditions were sent to bring the inner sections of Yemen, then under the rule of Imam Yahya, and Asir, ruled by Muhammad al-Idrisi, to heel. Tiring of the continual drain on resources, the Young Turks reached an accord with the two, granting them many local powers. In central Arabia the Young Turks found their support of the Rashid family unavailing against Abd al-Aziz ibn Saud of the Wahhabis, who drove the Ottomans from the rich province of al-Hasa in eastern Arabia in 1913.

Had it not been for the Hijaz Railway, which connected Syria with Medina, the Ottoman authority over Sharif Husayn in Mecca would have been even weaker. However, the Hijaz was too dependent upon religion and the pilgrimage to welcome secular Arab nationalism. Husayn did find substantial local help in his opposition to Turkification, centralization of power, the attempted introduction of conscription, the extension of the Hijaz Railway to Mecca, and the Europeanization espoused by the Committee of Union and Progress. An Ottoman garrison stationed at Mecca rendered overt revolution foolhardy without considerable strength and careful planning. Early in 1914, Prince Abd Allah, Husayn's second son, an Arab member of the Ottoman parliament, hinted vaguely to the British as he passed through Cairo that his father would be open to suggestions and assistance from them for rebellion against the Ottomans. These overtures, very discreet in nature, indicated that Husayn was considering a treaty similar to that which the British had with Arab princes and shaykhs in the Persian Gulf area. Such treaties provided for British recognition of the Arab ruler's independence, protection, and a pension in exchange for British conduct of all foreign relations, friendship, and permission for a British resident minister to live at the local court.

Suspicion that Husayn was harboring these intentions drifted back to Istanbul, where the Young Turks acted to limit his authority. They planned to build the Hijaz Railway south of Medina toward Mecca, and a new governor was assigned to the Hijaz with instructions to destroy Husayn. In the spring of 1914, the Ottomans came to understand that Husayn had consolidated his position with the townspeople and tribes of the Hijaz, and to forestall a violent insurrection the new governor was ordered to make peace and the railway extension was stopped.

It was very unlikely that any substantial connection could exist between the actions of the various Arab princes in the Arabian peninsula on the one hand and the revolutionary societies of the Ottoman Arab world on the other. They were too different in beliefs and circumstances to make joint action possible. However, some foreign governments were friendly to the secret societies; British and French officials in Beirut and Egypt gave encouragement to them. British and French consuls general received delegations of Arab nationalists. A delegation from Damascus, visiting Lord Kitchener in Egypt, suggested that Britain annex Syria to Egypt, giving it a separate administration.

When World War I began in 1914 the Young Turk triumvirate realized that defection in Arab provinces was likely and that the loyalty of Arab officers was highly questionable. Yet Enver, Talat, and Jemal hoped that the natural Arab proclivity for dissension and a strong commitment to Islam would save the day. Their hope was justified. The secret societies of officers and nationalists in the urban centers were opposed to the autocratic rule of kings and suspected them of princely ambitions. Most Arabs remained loyal to the Ottoman Empire, either because they felt an emotional loyalty to it or because they feared its destruction would lead to the dissolution of the only remaining barrier against European imperialism. Equally apprehensive were the various princes, each of the other. With such diverse fears and hopes prevalent, united action from all groups and factions was unlikely. The Ottoman Empire was saved for the moment. But it was only a question of time before Arab nationalism would flare into the open. World War I and the disturbances, confusion, and promises it brought hastened the day of Arab revolt.

REFERENCES

Works cited at the end of Chapter 27 are valuable for this chapter.

Abu-Manneh, Butrus. "The Christians Between Ottomanism and Syrian Nationalism: The Ideas of Butrus al-Bustani." *International Journal of Middle East Studies* 11 (1980): 287–304.

Antonius, George. *The Arab Awakening: The Story of the Arab National Movement.* New York: Hamilton, 1938. This is the fundamental work on this topic, but its conclusions and data have been subjected to serious revision by more recent scholarship, especially the book of Professor Dawn, cited below.

Cleveland, William L. *The Making of an Arab Nationalist: Ottomanism and Arabism in the Life and Thought of Sati' al-Husri.* Princeton, N.J.: Princeton University Press, 1971. The life of an Ottoman Arab who chose to be an Arab nationalist after World War I.

Dawn, C. Ernest. *From Ottomanism to Arabism: Essays on the Origins of Arab Nationalism.* Urbana: University of Illinois Press, 1973. Shows the most subtle aspects of the Arab revolt and its relationship to Arab nationalism, bringing out many of the misconceptions about it.

Duri, A. A. *The Historical Formation of the Arab Nation: A Study in Identity and Consciousness.* Translated by Lawrence I. Conrad. London: Croom Helm, 1987. Traces the emergence of Arabic, Arab-Islamic culture, and Arab patriotism.

Hourani, Albert H. *Arabic Thought in the Liberal Age, 1798–1939.* New York: Oxford University Press, 1962. Brilliant, authoritative treatment of Arabic thought and Arab nationalism.

————. *Syria and Lebanon, a Political Essay.* London: Oxford University Press, 1946. The earlier chapters give a clear picture of the rise of Arab nationalism; the later chapters still provide an important view of the French Mandate period.

al-Husry, Khaldun S. *Three Reformers: A Study in Modern Arab Political Thought.* Beirut: Khayats, 1966. An account of the ideas of al-Tahtawi, Khair al-Din al-Tunisi, and al-Kawakibi.

Khalidi, Rashid, *et al.*, eds. *Early Arab Nationalism.* New York: Columbia University Press, forthcoming. Extensive treatment of all aspects of the topic, concentrating on Syria, Iraq, and the Hijaz.

Khoury, Philip S. *Urban Notables and Arab Nationalism: The Politics of Damascus, 1860–1920.* Cambridge: Cambridge University Press, 1983. An analysis of the governing elite and who among them came to be Arab nationalists and why.

Mandel, Neville J. *The Arabs and Zionism Before World War I.* Berkeley: University of California Press, 1976. An excellent study of a very complex relationship that also involved the Ottoman government.

Öke, Mim Kemal. "The Ottoman Empire, Zionism, and the Question of Palestine (1880–1908)." *International Journal of Middle East Studies* 14 (1982): 329–341.

Sharabi, Hisham. *Arab Intellectuals and the West: The Formative Years, 1875–1914.* Baltimore, Md.: Johns Hopkins Press, 1970. Explains the intellectual and ideological background of modernization and transformation in the Arab world.

Zeine, Zeine N. *The Emergence of Arab Nationalism.* 2d ed. Delmar: Caravan Books, 1973.

29

Unrest in Iran and the Revolution of 1907 and 1908

MUHAMMAD SHAH

Upon the death of Fath Ali Shah Qajar in 1834, the throne passed to his twenty-eight-year-old grandson, Muhammad. Two of Muhammad's uncles refused to recognize him and moved to contest the throne. However, the British and Russian ministers in Iran cooperated to fund Muhammad's armed supporters and General Sir Henry Lindsay Bethune led a force that assured Muhammad the throne.

The new shah appointed his tutor, Hajji Mirza Aqasi, as chief minister, a post he held throughout Muhammad's rule. Hajji Mirza had studied under the famous Sufis of the time and, before coming to Tabriz to tutor Prince Abbas's sons, had been a wandering dervish. One English observer called him lewd, ignorant, fanatic, and avaricious, noting that "his words and actions are strongly tinctured with real or affected insanity." The shah believed that he could perform miracles and had "direct and frequent communications with the divinity."

Throughout his reign the shah and his minister favored Sufis and Sufism against the established, conservative ulema, a natural preference, considering the fact that many of the ulema treated the Qajars as usurpers. The shah's subjects found themselves caught between the realities of monarchical power and the doctrinal conceptions of the religious authority of the ulema, a conflict that was never resolved.

By enhancing Sufism Muhammad Shah strengthened the state and the central government. He proceeded to remove many types of cases from religious courts, subjected provincial governors to closer scrutiny from Tehran, continued military reforms, banned torture as a means of punishment and a device for obtaining information, and abolished the slave trade. An abstainer, he prohibited the sale of alcohol as well.

```
                           Muhammad Hasan Khan
                                   |
 _____
|                                                                |
Aqa Muhammad (1779–1797)                        Husayn Quli Khan
                                                      |
                                                Fath Ali (1797–1834)
                                                      |
                                                Abbas
                                                      |
                                                Muhammad (1834–1848)
                                                      |
                                                Nasir al-Din (1848–1896)
                                                      |
                                                Muzaffar al-Din (1896–1907)
                                                      |
                                                Muhammad Ali (1907–1909)
                                                      |
                                                Ahmad (1909–1924)
```

The Qajars

The Qajars considered Herat to be the capital of Khurasan and thus a rightful part of their realm, and in 1836 Muhammad Shah set out with an army to regain it from Afghanistan. The British tried to dissuade him from the campaign as they felt it would open Afghanistan and the approaches to India to Russian interference. The British minister accompanied the shah on the expedition and attempted to mediate the differences; the Russians egged Muhammad on to battle. An English artillery officer successfully contrived Herat's defense even though such interven tion was contrary to the Definitive Treaty of 1814 and the British occupied portions of Iran along the Persian Gulf. The shah was so enraged that after peace was arranged in 1838 he dismissed all British officers in Iran. In the 1830s and 1840s, there were also frequent incidents along the long and indeterminate Ottoman-Persian border. The British, Russian, Persian, and Ottoman agreement at Erzurum in 1847 recognized Suleimaniyah as Ottoman and the east bank of the Shatt al-Arab as Iranian.

Trade and conditions in general were improving when Muhammad Shah died in 1848. Had it not been for the rise of a new, somewhat revolutionary religious movement that was attracting numerous adherents, the shah would have ended his days in peace.

BABISM

Babism began in Shiraz with the preaching and teaching of Sayyid Ali Muhammad, a twenty-five-year-old native of that city who had spent his youth in religious study. In 1844, one thousand lunar years after the disappearance of the Twelfth Imam of the Shiites, his followers hailed him as the *Bab,* or Gate, between the world of the flesh and that of the spirit. Only through him, the Bab, was the Twelfth Imam in touch with the world. He assumed the role of point of manifestation of the divine essence of the world and called for universal peace, improvement of the life of women, destruction of many class distinctions, and a society that followed the spirit rather than the letter of religion.

Iran was witnessing considerable spiritual, social, and intellectual unrest at the time. For more than a generation numerous religious leaders had been preaching about the return of the Twelfth Imam and the coming regeneration of the world. Outbreaks of cholera, military losses to Russia and Britain, the Ottoman "reconquest" of the Shiite Holy City of Karbala in Iraq, and the brutality and inefficacy of Qajar rule all contributed to create an environment where a new religion could flourish. Also, as Shiite theology became more restricted and narrowly defined, theologians with new interpretations and views found it difficult to gain acceptance among the mainstream ulema. Many people hoped the Bab would lead Iran on a spiritual plane to combat the guns, ships, and materialism of the world outside.

At the time of Muhammad Shah's death the Bab was imprisoned in Tabriz and had been interrogated by the crown prince. He now claimed to be the Mahdi-Imam, and he was accused also of being addicted to hashish. That year, the Bab and his followers seceded from Islam.

In 1850 Nasir al-Din Shah, experiencing serious insurrections by devotees of the Bab, ordered that he be put to death. Sanctions for the execution were first obtained from three Muslim religious leaders, to counter any popular demonstrations.

Two years after the Bab had been executed, a member of the sect attempted to assassinate the shah. As a consequence, many Babists were massacred throughout Iran. Some leaders of the new religion escaped from Iran to establish two branches of the faith: one became headquartered in European Turkey but died out by the end of the century; the other was centered in Acre and Haifa in Ottoman Palestine. It later spread widely in Europe and the United States under the name of the Baha'i faith and thrives to this day. It renounced the use of force, even when persecuted, as in Iran during the nineteenth century and some parts of the twentieth century.

FIRST YEARS OF NASIR AL-DIN SHAH

When Muhammad Shah died in 1848, the customary disturbances and family rivalries were held in check by British and Russian officers. The British legation in Tehran induced a local council of notables to form a regency council for the sixteen-year-old Prince Nasir al-Din while he made his way from Tabriz. Nasir al-Din Shah appointed his tutor Mirza Taqi Khan Amir-i Kabir as first minister. Taqi was the son of the cook of a high government official, who had given him a fine education. Prior to his elevation to his high post, Taqi had been in Erzurum, where he had learned about the Tanzimat. He had also participated in a mission to St.

Petersburg, where he saw quite a different world. Taqi became known as a man of stern integrity who possessed great zeal for reform. Naturally, the palace courtiers and the queen mother, who dominated the harem, disliked him. With an empty treasury and a serious revolt in Khurasan, Taqi faced a difficult situation.

Though Taqi's predecessor was superstitious and even irrational at times, he was aware of the economic and agricultural changes creeping across the land. Hajji Mirza recognized that cotton, opium, silk, dried fruits, and nuts had become cash crops in foreign markets, tempting the landlords to press their peasants severely in order to garner huge profits from Russian and British merchants. Land now produced wealth in addition to the high social status it had previously conferred. Taqi extended this policy and became the merchants' friend. He built the great bazaar in Tehran and encouraged the growth of a mercantile class.

In these years three politically active classes arose beneath the royal court. There was the old elite, landed aristocratic nobles who, though generally ignorant, relied for their power on inherited privileges, extortion, and intrigue. The second class was the clergy, who controlled the courts, justice, morals, education, religion, and even the very level and nature of thought in Iran. They had accumulated wealth and vast landholdings. The third class was the new merchants, many of whom had traveled to Istanbul, Odessa, Cairo, Bombay, Calcutta, and Canton, and brought home not only wealth but ideas of a wider world. They relied on money to attain influence.

In suppressing the rebellion in Khurasan, Taqi formed an army of soldiers whose pay was not in arrears. Believing that the clergy should not participate in politics, he sent the army to Tabriz in 1850 and carried off the chief religious figure. But Taqi had gone too far, and in 1851 Nasir al-Din was induced by the clergy, the court, and his mother to dismiss the chief minister and to acquiesce in his murder shortly thereafter.

Taqi was replaced by Mirza Aqa Khan Nuri, a vindictive mediocrity who was wily in managing diplomacy and public affairs for his own advantage. Nasir al Din was never happy with him. Filled with remorse for having executed "the wisest man" in the state, the shah retired to his harem. His rule became based on fear rather than consent, and the shrewd divines and crafty self-seeking elite allied against him.

With the Crimean War weakening the Russian position, Aqa Khan forced the recall of the Russian minister and manipulated affairs so that the British minister offended him and had to leave. Aqa Khan could now follow independent policies, attacking and occupying Herat. The British in India declared war and sent a naval force, cavalry, and artillery into the Persian Gulf, taking Bushire, Khorramshahr, and the island of Kharg. In 1857, at the conclusion of the Crimean War, Nasir al-Din's envoy in Paris negotiated a settlement with the British. By the terms of the treaty Iran withdrew from Herat and recognized it as a part of Afghanistan and the British evacuated the Iranian territories they had occupied in the Persian Gulf. The treaty also assigned special commercial privileges to the British and gave standard capitulatory rights to British nationals in Iran. The following year Nasir al-Din dismissed Aqa Khan and refused to appoint anyone to that post, declaring that he himself would govern.

THE AGE OF CONCESSIONS

The government in Tehran might not have persisted through the century, were it not that the British and the Russians in Iran competed against each other for the favors of Nasir al-Din and his ministers. Incompetent administrators remained in high office for lengthy periods, transportation was primitive, distances were great between principal cities, the great famine of 1869–1872 killed many thousands, and several parts of the country were nearly autonomous. The clergy opposed the shah's government in Tehran and in every province; the strife between the religious community and the state was constant. Every innovation was resisted, and preachers easily inflamed the populace against those who ruled.

With Iran at peace Nasir al-Din made a trip in 1870 to the Shiite holy places in Ottoman Iraq. He was escorted about by Prince Husayn Khan, the Iranian ambassador in Istanbul, and met Midhat Pasha, then governor of Baghdad, with whom he discussed programs being introduced to modernize the Ottoman state. Husayn accompanied the shah back to Tehran, where he became first minister and dominated much of the government for the next ten years. The journey to Iraq was so pleasant that Nasir al-Din subsequently made three visits to Europe, nearly bankrupting the Iranian treasury. The shah was impressed with the display of vast wealth in Europe, which he believed was a kind of money tree from which power and great comfort were derived. He returned home convinced that more money in Iran would turn the country into a prosperous modern state similar to those he saw in Europe.

The building of telegraph lines across Iran, in the main to connect London to India, played an important role in opening Iran to the modern world. The first line was merely a toy to impress the shah, but within a few years Tehran was connected with several parts of the state. The rights to the international lines were sold to English companies beginning in 1862, and a local line, alongside the international ones, carried Iranian messages. No longer was Iran isolated.

The shah and the ministers, always short of funds, soon learned that Europeans would pay handsome sums in ready cash and give enormous bribes for one privilege, right, concession, or opportunity after another. In 1872, the shah granted to Baron Julius de Reuter a seventy-year economic concession for the development of Iran's economy and industry. So much clamor against this monopolistic concession was raised in all sectors of society in Iran and in Russia as well that obstacles were placed in de Reuter's way to prevent his compliance with the contracts. The money guarantees accrued to the shah, the bribes were kept, and Russia and the populace were satisfied by the concession's termination and appeased by the dismissal of Prince Husayn Khan as first minister. But concession hunting continued.

In 1888, Sir Henry Drummond-Wolff arrived in Tehran as the new British minister. He intended to open the Karun River to international steamer traffic to meet Russian railroad competition in the north. Sir Henry gave the shah a written guarantee that England would "prevent any infringement of the integrity" of Iran by any other power and would "make earnest representations" against any foreign attack upon the shah. With this guarantee against Russian actions, the shah issued a decree opening the Karun River to commercial steamers of all nations. Following this coup, Wolff helped his friend de Reuter salvage from his old concession the right to establish the Imperial Bank of Persia, which for sixty years would have the right to issue notes of legal tender in Iran and to engage in any operations on its own account or for others in the fields of finance, commerce, and industry.

Russian influence, however, was not completely negated. On the shah's second trip to Europe he saw the crowds of Russian soldiers not yet demobilized after the Congress of Berlin and was frequently escorted by smart looking Russian cossacks. He requested the tsar to send some Russian military instructors to Iran to reform and improve the army. Colonel Domantovich arrived in Tehran early in 1879 and before the summer was out he presented to the shah a brilliantly dressed and trained cossack brigade. For a number of years its leadership was rather desultory but in 1894 it became again a disciplined and effective instrument of Russian pressure in Iran, lasting until 1921. It was the only effective unit in the Persian army, the balance of which consisted for the most part of irregular tribal cavalry and the provincial armed forces under the command of local governors (Iran had no navy at all until 1885, and thereafter only a very small one.) Russia also had a letter from Nasir al-Din in 1887 engaging Iran not to give any concession for building a railroad or a waterway without consulting Russia. Trade between the two countries sharply increased.

Pressure for railroad building in Iran became so intense that in 1890 Ali Asghar Khan agreed to the Russian minister's demand that no railroad would be built on Iranian territory for the next ten years. British complaints soon subsided; in 1900 the convention was renewed and practically no railways were built in Iran prior to World War I.

Nasir al-Din Shah did accomplish some centralizing and modernizing reforms. Government operations were reorganized several times, and various ministries and high advisory councils were created. The shah consolidated in the capital the minting of coins. An official newspaper was published; an establishment of higher education, the Dar al-Funun, was founded; a translation bureau was created; and about 160 books were printed in the country during the century. A modern Persian journalistic style of writing came into use. The shah set up a European-style police force in Tehran.

Some factories were built by the government in the 1850s and 1860s but they were failures economically. The shah, largely in response to pressure from the British, took measures against the importation of slaves and the slave trade. The first modern government hospital was opened in Tehran in 1869; the hospital was managed by Germans. The shah also sent students to Europe to study at government expense.

Culturally, Nasir al-Din Shah's long reign saw the decay of Iranian art in such fields as metalwork and royal portraiture, but new art forms, especially photography, were supported by the royal court. Old architectural traditions were perpetuated in building palaces, although they were somewhat modified by European influences, and the shah sponsored the building of some new religious structures. Persian writers, including the shah himself, adopted a more comprehensible literary style; the flowery and elaborate forms of earlier days were gradually simplified and clarified.

Many announced reforms were only partially implemented or, after the fall of their sponsors from government office, were abandoned. Nasir al-Din was unable to push through major innovations in government and the military, and the number of reform-minded government leaders was too small to allow them to assume control of the process. Powerful vested interests, including foreign powers, saw the reforms as a threat to their positions, while most Iranians perceived the reforms and the reformers to be too Europeanized. The population of Iran remained roughly stable as economic, agricultural, and health factors were unfavorable to growth. And many provinces remained in the hands of semihereditary rulers; provincial revenues were kept largely in the provinces and not sent on to Tehran. Provincial officials resisted the shah's centralizing, as in the case of attempted judicial reforms.

THE TOBACCO CONCESSION AND ITS AFTERMATH

Prices for agricultural products and raw materials fell dramatically throughout the world after the mid-1870s, producing financial crises in many countries. Iran suffered too. The amount of wheat exported in 1894 was eight times what it had been a quarter of a century before, but the price had decreased so that the total receipts for the wheat exports remained the same.

It was different for some exported commodities, such as opium, cotton, and rice, whose production and value rose sharply in the 1870s. Agriculture became more diversified and more oriented toward exporting cash crops. In response to demand from Europe, knotted pile carpet production became a major industry, although European imports nearly destroyed the cotton- and wool-weaving textile industries in southern and central Iran. With the opening up of the country to world trade, imports and exports doubled and tripled and their prices increased markedly. Despite some limited increases in agriculture, year by year the government, the shah, public officials, wealthy merchants, and the clergy found it more difficult to make ends meet. Aside from the element of greed, fundamentally the idea behind the granting of most of the concessions to Europeans was to try to consolidate and centralize the economy and to entice foreign capital and expertise to develop the resources of the state. The hope of attracting foreign capital was one motive for the shah's trips to Europe. Unfortunately, the entire process was riddled with corrupt practices and managed by unscrupulous adventurers. Iran was being sold bit by bit to foreigners.

In England in the summer of 1889, Wolff had introduced the shah to Major Talbot, who asked for the monopoly to buy, sell, and manufacture tobacco in Iran for fifty years. Generous bribes were handed to the shah, to Ali Asghar Khan, and to others, and Talbot pursued the shah back to Tehran, where the concession was given in March 1890. The company to be formed would pay the Iranian treasury £15,000 and 25 percent of its net profits annually; in return the company would control the entire traffic in tobacco—even members of the tobacco sellers' guilds would have to obtain permits from the company to engage in local trade. For many this would mean selling their tobacco to the company and then buying it back.

The Imperial Tobacco Corporation of Persia bought the concession from Talbot and set out to implement the monopoly. By 1891 a campaign was organized against the government and concentrated on the tobacco issue, for of all the concessions granted to foreign capital this one touched the most people directly. Jamal al-Din al-Afghani, who had returned to Iran in 1889 upon the shah's invitation, was one of the leaders. Jamal al-Din so aroused the shah's ire by preaching openly against the government and the shah that he had to take sanctuary in the shrine of Shah Abd al-Azim outside Tehran. From there he continued his attack, scattering leaflets throughout the capital, until Nasir al-Din ordered him removed from the shrine, thus violating sanctuary. He was deposited across the Ottoman frontier.

But the eviction did not end the crisis. Revolt was threatened in Shiraz, Tabriz, Isfahan, Meshhed, and other cities, and some property was damaged. Merchants rebelled; warnings of violence against those who used tobacco spread across the land; and some merchants burned their entire stock rather than sell it to the company. Religious leaders petitioned the shah against the monopoly, stating that the Koran prohibited infidels to have control over Muslims, and accused the shah of selling Muslims like slaves to the Christians. When the British manager of the monopoly arrived in Shiraz word was spread that this newly arrived infidel was responsible for Jamal al-Din's expulsion. Soldiers had to dispel the crowds of protesters in several cities, and some people were killed. Women participated significantly in the protests. A religious decree, promulgated by Hasan Shirazi, the leading Shiite divine at the holy places in Iraq, calling upon all Muslims to abstain from smoking, was, to everyone's amazement, observed everywhere in Iran. Even the shah's wives refused to smoke! On December 25 there were rumors of a holy war to be declared if the concession was not withdrawn in two days. Three days later the shah canceled the concession. This popular victory over the government and the shah by the religious and city leaders made further movements of this nature possible. Moreover, a massive loan to the government to pay indemnities arising from the cancellation of the tobacco concession opened the door to many more such loans in the following decade, leading Iran closer to the brink of bankruptcy and dissolution.

In the midst of the tobacco crisis Russian nationals obtained concessions for insurance companies, lumbering, and other endeavors. One of the more important privileges granted Russia was permission to open the Discount and Loan Bank of Persia, which, in fact, was a branch of the Russian ministry of finance and part of the Central Bank of Russia. Without real stockholders or a need to show a profit, the bank made loans on easy terms to princes, officials, divines, and merchants; by 1900 it was said that Russia had nearly bought off the ruling elite.

For the next few years there was a standoff between England and Russia in their diplomatic and economic maneuvers in Iran. Each was afraid of the other. Russian activity centered in the north while the British dominated the south. Pessimism was the paramount mood even in high circles in Iran, and as the shah's energy and interest waned, "graft, bribery, theft reached incredible proportions." Prince Masud repeatedly stated that after the shah died he would take the southern half of the state and Crown Prince Muzaffar al-Din would take the northern half. The shah's brother suggested that Iran was like "a lump of sugar in a glass of water" gradually melting away. Apparently there were no trustworthy courts of justice, no stable currency, and since the shah's third son as commander in chief neglected and robbed the troops the army was a mere rabble. It seemed hopeless as the shah continued "selling appointments and marrying new wives after his wont." In desperation the first minister, Ali Asghar Khan, even suggested to the British minister that England bribe the shah to reform! What the outcome might have been remains uncertain, for on May 1, 1896, Nasir al-Din was assassinated by Jamal al-Din al-Afghani's servant and follower at the Shah Abd al-Azim shrine, where his master's sanctuary had been violated.

MUZAFFAR AL-DIN SHAH AND THE CONSTITUTION

That same day the Russians and the British recognized Muzaffar al-Din as the new shah and made arrangements to escort him to Tehran. He ordered Ali Asghar Khan to remain as prime minister, and the new shah's brothers pledged their loyalty and obedience to Muzaffar. The transfer of power was the most peaceful in Iran in more than a century.

Muzaffar al-Din was a sickly, uneducated, good-natured forty-three-year-old prince who was bored and baffled by governmental affairs and preferred the company of his wives, astrologers, and chance favorites. His first thought after his enthronement was a trip to Europe, supposedly for his health.

Ali Asghar Khan Amin al-Sultan, prime minister for more than a decade of hard times, had collected so many enemies that they were able to prevail upon the weak shah to dismiss him. His replacement lasted nine months, and after a year under yet another, the shah begged Ali Asghar Khan to return to his post. The difficulty was money—without it the shah could not travel in Europe. Payments to the troops and the salaries of most officials were at least six months in arrears, and the new ministers were unskilled in the ways of Iranian administration. It was said the minister of taxation "took no bribes, which was thought foolish, and he gave none, which was thought wicked." Only Ali Asghar Khan was considered able to end the chaos. Back in office his first act was to reorganize the customs posts and offices in Tabriz and Kermanshah with Belgian officials in charge, and to take a loan from Russia. After paying Iran's debts Muzaffar al-Din and his retinue set out for Europe, visiting several health spas for his kidney ailment. By the time he arrived back in Tehran the treasury was again empty. The natural recourse was another loan.

To many, the financial and economic conditions in Iran in the autumn of 1902 seemed intolerable, worse than ever before. With troubles brewing at home and in the Far East with Japan, Russia was unwilling to make further loans and the Discount and Loan Bank was tightening the screws on merchants and others. Joseph Naus, a Belgian, Iran's director of customs, worked out a new commercial agreement with Russia, lowering the tariff on many imports from Russia and giving

Russia a powerful grip on Iran's finances. All tariffs on cotton cloth were removed, thereby ruining most Iranian cloth manufacturers. The court was in a turmoil with rumors that the shah would be overthrown and that Ali Asghar Khan's influence had vanished. After the shah ordered a pension of £3,000 a year plus a big lump sum payment for the court astrologer because he had saved the shah's life when the shah dreamed he was drowning, Ali Asghar Khan lost his temper and said he had "raised large sums to pay for the Shah's tours and toys, but must protest paying for his dreams." In September a new prime minister was named: the cruel Prince Abd al-Majid, Muzaffar al-Din's son-in-law and grandson of Fath Ali Shah. Ali Asghar Khan went on a world tour.

A change in prime ministers was not a cure for the ills of Iran. Agitation by the clergy and popular preachers against the ministers and the arrogant efficiency of the Belgian customs officials was easily blunted by Abd al-Majid, for the central government was much stronger in 1903 than it had been in 1890 at the time of the tobacco affair.

A bad harvest, cholera, the Russo-Japanese War, the high cost of food, and unemployment in the cities helped bring about the Revolution of 1905–1906. The direct cause occurred in 1905 when several bazaar merchants in Tehran were publicly flogged by the authorities for raising the price of sugar. Immediately, the merchants closed the bazaar and went on strike. The government ordered them to open the shops or have all their goods confiscated. Thereupon, about 2,000 merchants, joined by preachers and religious leaders, took sanctuary at the Imperial Mosque, the traditional form of protest in Iran, then fled to the shrine of Shah Abd al-Azim. Supported by Ali Asghar Khan and the crown prince, they insisted upon the removal of Abd al-Majid and other ministers, the ousting of the governor of Tehran, the dismissal of Joseph Naus and the Belgians from the customs offices, and the convening of a "House of Justice," to be composed of merchants, land owners, and clergy. In January 1906 the shah acceded to their demands and they returned to Tehran.

In the spring, amid further turmoil, the shah had a stroke. Authority was weakened and responsibility diffused. Recognizing that sanctuary in mosques and shrines was no longer being respected, merchants, guild members, and divines took sanctuary at the British legation on July 19, 1906. Within a fortnight some 14,000 protesters were camping in the legation garden. Giant cauldrons were brought in to prepare food. Russia did not protest, and the British tolerated the invasion. Abd al-Majid was dismissed, and the shah, after being nudged by the British, on August 5 called for a representative assembly. On September 17, 1906, the shah signed the imperial decree calling for parliamentary elections. It appeared that Iran had taken a step toward democracy, pushed not by an armed intervention or a revolution but by passive resistance.

Elections were held early in October. Not waiting for the representatives from the provinces, the successful candidates from Tehran met on October 7, 1906, to write a constitution and enact basic laws for a legislative body. Tehran was dramatically overrepresented in the parliament, as compared to the more distant provinces. The shah had, by this time, recovered sufficiently to return to the capital to open the assembly (*Majlis*), although a minister had to read his speech from the throne. A new prime minister, Prince Nasrullah Khan, found the treasury empty, tax returns at a low ebb, salaries unpaid for six months, and sentiment in the majlis utterly opposed to any loan. Inexperienced and at his wit's end, he even wrote a letter to the disgraced former prime minister Ali Asghar Khan asking for suggestions on solving the dilemma. In the end the majlis voted unanimously to float a loan internally.

On December 30, 1906, the constitution was signed by Muzaffar al-Din, Prime Minister Nasrullah, and Crown Prince Muhammad Ali, who had come to the capital two weeks before, since all knew that the shah was dying. The constitution, in fifty-one articles, provided for an elected majlis of sixty representatives from Tehran, including four from the court and four divines, and one hundred to one hundred forty representatives from the provinces, all to serve two-year terms, and a senate of sixty members, half to be elected and half appointed by the shah. The majlis was the dominant body and would control finances and foreign affairs. Equality before the law was guaranteed for all subjects, irrespective of religion. (A supplementary fundamental law was added to the constitution in October 1907.)

The British applauded the formation of the constitution; the Russians found it distasteful. The crown prince, an open Russophile who even spoke Russian, frankly loathed it. Muzaffar al-Din Shah died January 8, 1907, and Muhammad was crowned as shah on January 19. With an enemy on the throne the constitution's future was in jeopardy.

MUHAMMAD ALI SHAH AND THE COUNTERREVOLUTION

Had the majlis been well organized by skillful leaders with a modicum of political experience, a representative government under a constitution might have succeeded in managing Iranian affairs and found a way to avoid bankruptcy and constant turbulence. As the members elected in the provinces joined the majlis, however, it became less and less coherent. The members from all parts of the country came from various strata of society: guilds, merchants, ulema, bureaucrats, landowners, and professionals. Few of them thought of defending any aspect of the old government, and rival leaders quarreled over old antagonisms. A member of a prominent Tehran family was elected president of the majlis and gathered friends and hangers-on around him. His personal enemy led the opposition. Most of the members from Tabriz were radical in their views as they had been affected by revolutionaries fleeing from Russia. Political cliques or societies (*anjumans*) formed in every locality to influence events; some felt that the majlis was the largest anjuman of all. Within a few months even local anjumans split—in Tabriz between senior and junior clergy and in Meshhed between merchants and shrine officials. The majlis sitting in Tehran could not enforce authority in the provinces, but it prevented local governors from doing so. Local anjumans defied the majlis, the central government, and the local administration. Land taxes went unpaid and no one collected road tolls. Smuggling prevailed. One force remaining in the provincial cities was the divines, who had been opposed to all governments for centuries. They claimed they represented justice since they dispensed holy law while the government with its laws symbolized injustice, an idea that played a decisive role in the thinking of the anjumans; some of the ulema opposed the constitution, while many favored it, at least initially.

Bankruptcy was never admitted, and the Belgian customs regime continued to operate under a new head, frequently turning over revenues to ministers rather than to the banks that had made loans. When the finance minister made his report to the majlis, itemizing necessary expenditures, the majlis authorized him to borrow the required funds from the National Bank, which, however, did not exist. It was generally recognized that no government could function without cooperating with the majlis, but it became apparent that the majlis had difficulty functioning at all.

In March 1907, when bankruptcy was near, all agreed that Ali Asghar Khan, the ingenious, detested negotiator of the two Russian loans, should be invited back from his repose in Switzerland. He nearly had arranged a loan with Russian, French, German, and British backing when on August 31, 1907, he was assassinated by a radical anjuman member from Tabriz. This blow eventually led to the demise of the majlis.

The constitutionalists suffered a second fatal injury the very same day with the signing of the Anglo-Russian Convention in St. Petersburg. In part, the document set aside the northern portion of Iran, including Tabriz, Tehran, and Meshhed, as a sphere of influence for Russia, and a small, southeastern portion from the Afghanistan border to the Persian Gulf near Bandar Abbas as a British zone; neither power would be paramount in the land between the two zones. London was more concerned with the security of India than with any interests in Iran. Russia obtained a free hand, which the constitutionalists in Tehran considered deplorable and dishonorable. Prince Abd al-Qasim Khan, who soon succeeded Ali Asghar Khan, could not comprehend how his British friends could abandon efforts for political regeneration in Iran after all their encouraging words. From that day British ministers and officials in Tehran were treated rudely by the Russians and their messages and suggestions ignored.

With a "palsied tranquility" circulating in Tehran, Hartwig, the Russian minister, set about to strengthen the power of the shah. Muhammad Ali, though he swore three times to uphold the constitution, never intended to tolerate it for long. Late in the spring a new financial adviser from France advocated a tax on tea and sugar to meet the budget deficit. The British and Russians vetoed it, but it stirred such a commotion the shah suggested that Russian forces be called in to prevent riots. Prince Masud, long a friend of the British, led a split of the Qajars against this move and allied himself with many members of the majlis. At this juncture a delegation from Tehran asked the shah to remove from his court all those opposed to the constitution. The shah left the capital, gathered his forces, and with Russian approval moved on Tehran on June 23, 1908, where a cossack brigade bombarded the Majlis building, arrested many leaders, and executed three of them. As a score or more fled to the British legation for sanctuary, Hartwig ordered the cossacks to surround the legation; to the humiliation of the British many majlis members seeking sanctuary were kept back. Muhammad Ali Shah, hand in hand with the Russians, was now the absolute ruler of Iran.

MUHAMMAD ALI SHAH ABDICATES

The shah's victory gave him control of the government in Tehran but it also handed him full responsibility for the country's dire problems. His close friends took over the various ministries and filled their pockets as rapidly as possible to pay personal debts incurred over the years when they had not been in control. Pressed to find a loan, the government received the same message from the Russians and British as before—reform the finances first.

Throughout Iran it was anarchy that reigned, rather than Muhammad Ali. The shah did not have much control or influence outside of Tehran. Religious leaders dominated the local anjumans and city councils. In Tabriz the anjumans and constitutionalists revolted and gradually ruled the entire city. The shah, with the support of the Russians, besieged Tabriz for nine months without much success until Russian troops surrounded and invaded the city in April 1909. Rebellious forces by this time held Meshhed, Isfahan, and Rasht, and the entire south had slipped away. In Isfahan, power had been seized by Najaf Quli Khan, chief of the Bakhtiyari tribes, whom the shah had tried to remove. In league with the anjumans, Najaf Quli Khan revived the constitutional drive and set out with his forces for Tehran.

The shah's party in Tehran, along with British and Russian diplomats, failed to grasp the magnitude or the temper of the opposition. The Bakhtiyari from the south joined forces from the north to encircle Tehran, which fell on July 15, 1909. The constitution was restored; Muhammad Ali abdicated and took sanctuary in the Russian legation. Granted a pension, he left Tehran in September with four children, a harem of ten, and a party of forty and settled in Odessa, where the Russian government found him an ample villa. Eventually, six of his staunchest henchmen were tried and executed.

CONSTITUTIONAL GOVERNMENT, 1909–1911

A few days after Muhammad Ali abdicated, his twelve-year-old son took the throne as Ahmad Shah. Prince Ali Reza Khan, the aged and trusted head of the Qajar family, was named regent. Weeping when taken from his parents, Ahmad promised that he would be a good shah. In Tehran the leaders designated a directory to serve until constitutional government could be reestablished.

Elections for the second majlis were held August 17, 1909, but it did not convene until mid-November. Officially opened by the young shah in the presence of the regent, cabinet, diplomatic corps, clergy, princes, notables, and merchants, it contained sixty-five delegates; others joined as they arrived in Tehran. In September a general amnesty was declared and new British and Russian ministers presented their credentials. Constitutionalism (*mashrutiyat*) was supported by nationalists of all hues and at first even by most of the clergy who had been opposed to rule by any shah and who wanted government to follow Muslim law (*mashruiyat*), which they equated with *mashrutiyat*. As weeks passed the two groups separated and the majlis divided into Social Moderates and Social Democrats. The latter believed in the separation of temporal and religious power, compulsory conscription, universal education, and land reform; the former, the majority, were more evolutionary in their ideas and supported the clergy, the nobility, and the landowners who had opposed Shah Muhammad Ali.

Russian troops never withdrew from the northern provinces; in 1910 there were still several thousand stationed from Tabriz to Khurasan. The leaders of the cabinet repeatedly complained to the British minister, who explained that his hands were tied and that they should make their peace with the Russians. Russian demands were greater than any Iranian minister could meet. When word went out that Iran needed a sizable loan, representatives of various European bankers appeared in Tehran to negotiate, suggesting reasonable terms. Whenever a loan neared consummation, however, Russia appealed to the British, who easily negated it. Russia evidently intended to thwart any independence on the part of Tehran until Iran's leaders recognized the overriding position of Russia in every aspect of their affairs.

In July 1910, a new cabinet under Prince Hasan Khan, with a more radical composition of Social Democrats, was sworn in. However, its activities were hampered by even more radical nationalists who began to assassinate moderate leaders. With Russian approval these extreme anjumans were attacked, dispersed, and driven from Tehran.

The regent died in September 1910, and after considerable tension between Democrats and Moderates, the latter's candidate, Abd al-Qasim Khan, was elected regent, though he would not return from Europe until the following March. A new cabinet in which Moderates prevailed was formed, with Muhammad Vali Khan again as prime minister.

On November 5, 1910, Germany and Russia signed the Potsdam Agreement, wherein Germany acknowledged the Russian sphere of influence in Iran. Russia, with thousands of troops in northern Iran, enjoyed an even freer hand now. The Iranian leaders in Tehran who looked for aid against their overpowering neighbor to the north grew more discouraged.

In 1911 W. Morgan Shuster, an American who had had financial experience in the Philippines, was hired to be financial adviser to the government. Neither Russia nor England was ever pleased with Shuster's presence in Tehran, and they acted to make his position untenable. Shuster took the view that the Iranian government had employed him to organize and reform the finances and the treasury and he tried to be loyal and faithful to his charge. He believed that the majlis and the cabinet were important and virtuous forces in Iran and that the foreign influences were iniquitous. Favoring the Democrats and disappointing the Bakhtiyari, Shuster pressed the majlis to adopt a law establishing the Office of Treasurer-General to collect and disburse all revenues, and to appoint him Treasurer-General. Russia foresaw the possibility of Iranian emancipation through these financial reforms and fought against them. Finding loans impossible to arrange, as the British and Russians openly warned any banker who showed signs of giving one, Shuster began to collect taxes from notables in Tehran who had not paid their taxes in years. Many of these now sided with the cabinet members and foreign legations against the American.

During the summer of 1911 Iran was torn asunder. In the middle of July ex-shah Muhammad Ali, with Russian aid and British acquiescence, crossed the

Caspian Sea. Met by Turkoman supporters, they seized control of the province of Mazandaran. As word spread through the country of the landing many provinces revolted against Tehran and declared for Muhammad Ali. Before the end of July the cabinet of Muhammad Vali fell and a new one under Najaf Quli Khan, dominated by the Bakhtiyari forces, took office. Loyal government troops defeated the ex-shah in October; Muhammad Ali remained in a small village in the north until he returned to Russia in March 1912. The government's army, which the cabinet and the majlis had put in the field, was financed in part by funds collected and transmitted to it by Shuster. That autumn, on a slight pretext, the Russians invaded Iran. A Russian ultimatum on November 29, 1911, demanded the dismissal of Shuster and stipulated that the Tehran government could not hire foreigners without Russian approval. The Russians also wanted Iran to pay the cost of the Russian invasion. Najaf Quli Khan was ready to comply, but the majlis voted to reject the ultimatum. The cabinet fell. Twelve thousand Russian troops captured Tabriz and prepared to take Tehran. The ousted cabinet, however, expelled the majlis from its building on December 24, 1911. The majlis did not meet again until January 1915. Shuster was fired the next day.

THE STRANGLING OF PERSIA

When Shuster returned to America in 1912, he wrote a book about his experiences in Iran, entitled *The Strangling of Persia*. This phrase was accepted widely, and the term has been given to the period extending from Shuster's dismissal to the outbreak of World War I. Shuster's departure was a blow to the Democrats from which they never recovered. Bakhtiyari leaders controlled the government, and their chieftain ruled from behind the scenes. Over the next three years a series of prime ministers proceeded through that office. Many Bakhtiyari khans received lucrative provincial governorships and ministries. The state disintegrated rapidly; local authority soon superseded central rule. Roads were unsafe, and the company that had the concession on the Karun River and overland traffic to Shiraz had to pay local brigands for protection. Trade came to a standstill in many provinces. Leading officials preyed on the government treasury.

In March 1912 the Russian government gave up on Muhammad Ali and attempted to disburse his sympathizers gathered at Meshhed. The city was bombarded and the sacred shrine there was looted and shattered, sending a traumatic wave across Iran and destroying any possibility of an understanding or genuine cooperation with Russian officials.

In May 1912 Abd al-Qasim, the regent, left for Switzerland and found excuses for not returning. According to the constitution his appointment as regent could only be terminated by the majlis and only he could convene it. The Russians and British brought many pressures on the ministers in 1913 and 1914 to grant major concessions for building railways across Iran, but no concession was valid unless approved by the majlis. Abd al-Qasim refused to come home to call it; the two powers were quietly frustrated by a classic Iranian stratagem.

The British discovery of oil in southwestern Iran increased their willingness to grant the Russians a free hand in the north. Among the constant stream of concessions granted at the turn of the century, one signed on May 29, 1901, gave to William Knox D'Arcy the exclusive rights to search for, obtain, exploit, develop, refine, transport, and sell natural gas, petroleum, and asphalt in all of Iran except the five northern provinces for sixty years. French archaeologists in southwestern Iran had first reported the existence of oil there in 1892. A gusher was brought in at Masjid Sulayman in May 1908, and the Anglo-Persian Oil Company was organized the next year. The British bought one square mile of land on Abadan Island in the Shatt al-Arab to build a refinery and obtained rights of way for pipelines. All these negotiations with the local shaykh were carried on without the advice or participation of any official from Tehran. In this area the British were as independent as the Russians were in the north and had fewer obstacles and greater success. Britain was deeply concerned about oil and access to it; the British admiralty purchased a majority interest in the company in 1914 as the navy was turning from coal to oil.

Ahmad Shah was crowned on July 21, 1914, in the presence of many national and international dignitaries. Ten days later Europe was engulfed in war, and on November 1, 1914, the shah issued an imperial decree declaring strict neutrality for Iran. As Russia warred with the Ottoman Empire, Turkey said she wished to respect Iranian neutrality but could not as long as Russian troops remained in Azerbayjan, where attacks on Turkey could be easily mounted. Prince Hasan Khan, Iran's prime minister, requested a Russian withdrawal to obviate a Turkish invasion. Russia demanded promises from Turkey that no attack would be made should Russian troops be withdrawn. Such guarantees were not forthcoming. Kurds from Turkey invaded Iran in the vicinity of Lake Urumiyah and Russian troops poured into northern Iran. The third majlis opened on January 4, 1915, but Iran was no longer in control of her own affairs. A constitutional regime would have to await the end of the war.

REFERENCES

Works cited at the end of Chapters 20 and 27 are especially important for this chapter.

Abrahamian, Ervand. "The Causes of the Constitutional Revolution in Iran." *International Journal of Middle East Studies* 10 (1979): 381–414. Examines the social causes of the Revolution.

Algar, Hamid. *Religion and State in Iran, 1785–1906.* Berkeley: University of California Press, 1970. Explains the relationships between spiritual and temporal powers within the sociopolitical system of Iran. A significant work.

Avery, Peter. *Modern Iran.* New York: Praeger, 1970. A very substantial, detailed work that begins with the mid-nineteenth century.

Bakhash, Shaul. *Iran: Monarchy, Bureaucracy and Reform Under the Qajars: 1858–1896.* London: Ithaca, 1978. A comprehensive treatment of all aspects of the subject.

Bayat, Mangol. *Mysticism and Dissent: Socioreligious Thought in Qajar Iran.* Syracuse, N.Y.: Syracuse University Press, 1982.

Bosworth, Edmund, and Carole Hillenbrand, eds. *Qajar Iran: Political, Social and Cultural Change, 1800–1925.* Edinburgh: Edinburgh University Press, 1983. Twenty-one essays dealing with a wide variety of subjects.

Browne, Edward G. *The Persian Revolution of 1905–1909.* New York: Barnes and Noble, 1966. A new impression of the 1910 edition. A full account of the revolution with eyewitness reports by a keen student of Iranian society.

Busch, Briton Cooper. *Britain and the Persian Gulf, 1894–1914.* Berkeley: University of California Press, 1967. A study of the formation and execution of British policy toward the whole area. Makes extensive use of primary sources.

Farmayan, Hafez. "Portrait of a Nineteenth-Century Iranian Statesman: The Life and Times of Grand Vizier Amin ud-Dawlah, 1844–1904." *International Journal of Middle East Studies* 15 (1983): 337–351. A revealing study of the chief rival of Ali Asghar Khan in the 1890s.

Ferrier, R. W. *The History of the British Petroleum Company.* Vol. 1. *The Developing Years, 1901–1932.* Cambridge: Cambridge University Press, 1982. This official history is based in part upon the company's own archives.

Gilbar, Gad. "Demographic Developments in Late Qajar Persia, 1870–1906." *Asian and African Studies* 11 (1976): 125–156. One of a series of thoughtful and judicious analyses of Iran's economy.

———. "Persian Agriculture in the Late Qajar Period, 1860–1906: Some Economic and Social Aspects." *Asian and African Studies* 12 (1978): 312–365.

———. "The Persian Economy in the Mid-19th Century." *Die Welt des Islams* 19 (1979): 177–211.

Issawi, Charles, ed. *The Economic History of Iran, 1800–1914.* Chicago: University of Chicago Press, 1971. Here is some of the documentary material needed for writing a coherent history of the Iranian economy.

Kazemzadeh, Firuz. *Russia and Britain in Persia, 1864–1914: A Study in Imperialism.* New Haven, Conn.: Yale University Press, 1968. A detailed chronicle and interpretation of diplomatic history, using primary sources.

Keddie, Nikki R. *Religion and Rebellion in Iran: The Iranian Tobacco Protest of 1891–1892.* New York: Humanities Press, 1966. An important work on mass movements against foreign concessions and the weakening of the authority of the shah prior to the constitutional movement of 1906.

———. *Roots of Revolution: An Interpretive History of Modern Iran.* New Haven, Conn.: Yale University Press, 1981. A brilliant summary and analysis of Iranian history.

McDaniel, Robert A. *The Shuster Mission and the Persian Constitutional Revolution.* Minneapolis, Minn.: Bibliotheca Islamica, 1974. A thorough study of the revolution in Iran in 1906 and the failure of the Shuster mission in 1911.

McLean, David. *Britain and Her Buffer State: The Collapse of the Persian Empire, 1890–1914.* London: Royal Historical Society, 1979. Valuable for its discussion of Russian-British relations and the relationship between diplomacy and economic factors.

Momen, Moojan. "The Social Basis of the Babi Upheavals in Iran (1848–53): A Preliminary Analysis." *International Journal of Middle East Studies* 15 (1983): 157–183.

Nashat, Guity. *The Origins of Modern Reform in Iran, 1870–80.* Urbana: University of Illinois Press, 1982. A thorough discussion of the reforms of Prince Husayn Khan and his experiences.

Ramazani, Rouhollah K. *The Foreign Policy of Iran, 1500–1941: A Developing Nation in World Affairs.* Charlottesville: University Press of Virginia, 1966. The author's analysis is lucid and his interpretations are sound and perceptive. The period before 1800 is dealt with very briefly.

Said, Kurban. *Ali and Nino.* Translated by Jenia Graman. New York: Pocket Books, 1972. An exciting novel set in Baku and Tehran ca. 1900–1920 which gives a personal view of the impacts of modernization.

Smith, Peter. *The Babi and Baha'i Religions: From Messianic Shi'ism to a World Religion.* Cambridge: Cambridge University Press, 1987. Traces origins and growth in Iran and later; sympathetic to the Baha'i point of view.

Volodarsky, Mikhail. "Persia's Foreign Policy Between the Two Herat Crises, 1831–56." *Middle Eastern Studies* 21 (1985): 111–151. A very useful study based in part on the Russian archives.

———. "Persia and the Great Powers, 1856–1869." *Middle Eastern Studies* 19 (1983): 75–92.

Wright, Denis. *The English Amongst the Persians During the Qajar Period, 1787–1921.* London: Heinemann, 1977. Colorful and full of anecdotes that illustrate the personal side of the relations of the two peoples.

Part Four

The Contemporary Middle East

30

Impact of World War I Upon the Middle East

TURKEY ENTERS THE WAR

The shot at Sarajevo that killed Franz Ferdinand of Austria ricocheted around the world. It proved fatal as well to the Ottoman Empire. Sentiments in the empire were mixed regarding the war. The great majority of influential people desired neutrality and believed that therein lay the best interests of the state, already torn, defeated, and impoverished by the Balkan wars, revolutions, and mediocre governments. Some leaders, trained in the liberal traditions of French and British political and university circles, inclined toward the Entente, although the inclusion of Russia, the traditional Ottoman enemy, disturbed them considerably.

A hard core of army officers, however, dominant in the Committee of Union and Progress, had come under the spell of German military genius in their schooling by soldiers such as von der Goltz Pasha. Guided by Minister of War Enver Pasha who was confident that superior German arms ensured victory, and spirited by Baron von Wangenheim, the German ambassador, the triumvirate of the Ottoman cabinet signed with Germany on August 2, 1914, a secret alliance directed against Russia, the perpetual enemy of the Ottomans. Russia's desire for possession of the Ottoman capital of Istanbul was a spur to the Ottomans to enter the war allied with Germany, as was the desire of some pan-Turkish leaders who wanted to annex Russian central Asia and the Turkish peoples living there.

Known to only five people in the empire, the alliance was reinforced a week later by the entry into the Straits and "purchase" of two German cruisers. The Ottomans used the entry as a lever to obtain additional points in the alliance agreement, the most significant being "assistance in the abolition of the capitulations." Purportedly, the purchase was made to replace two Ottoman ships built and ready for delivery in England but sequestered by Britain on the outbreak of war. Renamed the *Sultan Selim Yavuz* and *Midilli,* but still manned by their German officers and crews, these warships played an important role in relations between the two powers.

During the following eleven weeks military and diplomatic events in Europe and in Istanbul moved rapidly. Ottoman conversations with the Entente for an alliance raised questions about terminating the capitulations, Ottoman mobilization on her eastern borders, and German concessions in Anatolia, Thrace, and the Aegean Islands. The Ottoman price was too high. The Allies—Russia, England, and France—held the military strength of the Ottomans in low esteem and believed that a push through would be comparatively easy. They, therefore, decided that it would be more convenient to let the Ottomans join the Central Powers and to partition her after her defeat. How else would Russia ever obtain her coveted Constantinople and the Straits?

Extremists and adventurers in high Ottoman circles prevailed, even though they were a small minority. The executive committee of Union and Progress was closely divided between interventionists such as Enver and those who preferred neutrality. Berlin kept pressing Turkey to come into the war. Even Enver hung back, however, asking for more from Germany while protesting that Ottoman mobilization was incomplete. On October 11, 1914, Enver, Talat, Jemal, and Speaker of the Assembly Halil met with von Wangenheim at the German embassy and indicated the Ottoman Empire was nearly ready to join if Germany would shoulder a major share of the burden of war materials, transport, general supplies, and financing. As part of the bargain, Enver demanded a loan of £5 million in gold and promised to attack Russia in the Black Sea as soon as £2 million in gold coin had been deposited to the Ottoman government's account in Istanbul. The next day £1 million was shipped from Berlin; it arrived on October 16; the second shipment reached Istanbul on October 21.

Enver was determined to have war so that he could also liberate Egypt. The government-subsidized press was in readiness; von Wangenheim had even bought one newspaper outright. The Ottoman Empire closed the Dardanelles on September 26; "Ottoman" Admiral Souchon with the *Yavuz, Midilli,* and the fleet steamed up the Bosphorus into the Black Sea and on October 29 shelled Sevastopol and Odessa, mined sea lanes, and destroyed a number of Russian ships. Russia formally declared war on November 4; England and France followed the next day. The sultan pronounced a jihad or "holy war" on November 14. In the estimation of many leaders, the Ottoman Empire had begun to dig its own grave.

The great mass of Turks—Anatolian villagers—would fight for and support the sultan and his government with or without a "holy war" declaration. But perhaps calling for a holy war might induce Muslims under the French in North Africa, under the British in Egypt, the Sudan, and India, and under Russia in central Asia to rebel. Moreover, the war party of the Committee of Union and Progress held illusions of recapturing Egypt and Libya and recognized the need for active Arab cooperation in the venture. But the call fell upon unreceptive ears. Revolts of even the slightest significance did not materialize. Furthermore, since the caliph was allied with the Christian powers of Germany and Austria-Hungary, the cynicism involved in the declaration of a holy war against the infidels escaped no one.

The immediate Arab reaction was threefold. One group looked upon the outbreak of a war involving the Ottoman Empire and the imperialistic European states as a God-given opportunity to obtain a united and independent Arab national state. A second group, consisting largely of some princely Arab families and their clients, regarded the war as a time to rebel against the Ottoman sultan and establish independent Arab kingdoms—each for himself and heaven protect the others. Another more numerous group viewed the Ottoman state as the only protection against European imperialism and the preserver of Islamic independence, and thus continued to support the empire.

With the formal entry of the Ottoman Empire into the war Germany dominated actions and affairs. General von Sanders directed the army, and Admiral Souchon, the navy. Though transportation, food supplies, finance, and many other highly important wartime problems were frequently left in Ottoman hands, German officials regularly acted as they pleased. The Ottoman Empire swarmed with Germans.

GALLIPOLI CAMPAIGN

In January 1915, the British War Cabinet acquiesced to the views of Winston Churchill and agreed to send a force to break through the Straits, take the Ottomans out of the war, and open a first-rate munitions supply route to Russia. The British army command, however, sabotaged the venture and greatly lessened its chances of success. After unsuccessful attacks in February and March by naval forces, an Anglo-French army began landing operations on the Gallipoli peninsula in April 1915. The attackers met withering fire and stubborn defense by Ottoman forces led by Mustafa Kemal and some German officers under the command of General von Sanders. Suffering huge losses, the British Imperial and French forces, joined by the Italians in August, clung on, and twice nearly succeeded in a breakthrough. Lack of cooperation by the Russians at the Bosphorus end of the Straits, skillful tactics on the part of the Germans and Ottomans, and faulty intelligence work by the offensive forces led first to a stalemate and then to Allied withdrawal from the Straits in January 1916.

WAR OPERATIONS

The Russians were perturbed over the Dardanelles campaign for fear the British and French would take the Straits, capture Istanbul, and fail to relinquish them to the Russians. Nonetheless, they made the first overtures for some kind of a campaign to relieve the Ottoman pressure in the Caucasus. The overall Ottoman war plan called for an attack upon the Russians in the east and an expedition to drive the British from Egypt. In the last months of 1914 Ottoman forces moved east to take Kars and Batum, but the strategy was poorly conceived by Enver. After a few initial successes the Ottomans fell back—nearly 90 percent of the Third Army had been lost to frostbite, hunger, disease, and enemy action. Enver relinquished his command and returned to Istanbul. All news of the disaster was censored.

In the campaigns of 1915–1916, with the aid of Armenian revolutionaries and irregular forces, the Russians captured Erzurum, Van, Trabzon, Erzinjan, and other lesser cities in the east. In 1916 Mustafa Kemal Pasha, in command of the Second Army, joined the Third Army on the Caucasus front, but little was accomplished. Transportation was next to impossible; ammunition and supplies of every kind were scarce; and disease was rampant. In February 1917, forty-two Ottoman army surgeons died of spotted typhus alone, and thousands of soldiers died of starvation and general debility. The dreadful casualties of Enver's first campaign and the considerable depopulation of the eastern areas as a result of the Armenian massacres and deportations in 1915 created such a weakness on the front facing Russia that it would have been fatal had not Russia been so hard-pressed in the European war theaters from 1915 to 1917.

The revolutions in Russia in 1917, especially the Bolshevik Revolution in the autumn, affected the Caucasus front very markedly. All the Russian troops except for the Armenian and Georgian divisions melted away. The Ottomans advanced rapidly to occupy Kars, Ardahan, and Batum, which the Treaty of Brest-Litovsk gave to the Ottomans. Georgian and German forces, however, retook Batum. Later, a Bolshevik-Armenian coup in Baku and the massacre of 10,000 Ottomans produced a concerted drive that led to the capture of the city in September 1918 and the killing of many Armenians. Germany deplored the Ottoman inroads into the Caucasus and even went so far as to conclude a Bolshevik-German agreement, according to which German forces would protect the Caucasus and in particular Baku from attacks by a third party. However, at the end of war in 1918 the Caucasus area became an Allied problem.

The second ambition of Enver was the conquest of Egypt. In August 1914, Britain took precautionary measures there, and after Ottoman entry into the war Britain established a protectorate in Egypt on December 18, 1914. Khedive Abbas Hilmi was deposed and Husayn, his uncle, was appointed sultan of Egypt. Jemal Pasha, minister of marine and one of the triumvirate, took command of the Fourth Ottoman Army and assumed responsibility for Syria, including Palestine. In February 1915, his forces made a surprise attack upon the Suez Canal, but possessing inadequate strength to hold the eastern bank, they retired. Throughout 1915 small flying columns raided points on the Suez Canal. These raids compelled the British to maintain a large force there, but the morale of the Ottoman armies was low because they inevitably had to retreat.

A massive assault against the Canal was ordered for February 1916, but poor transport delayed the attack until the least opportune weather of midsummer. The assault proved a dismal failure, and from that moment until the end of the war Turko-German armies were on the defensive in this theater of operations. Furthermore, the repressive and harsh policies of Jemal Pasha in Syria turned many Arabs hostile. In March and April 1917 at the famous battles of Gaza, Ottoman arms withstood heavy British fire and drove the enemy back to a line in Sinai. Later in that year a German-ordered-and-directed operation commanded by General von Falkenhayn attempted to gain a favorable decision in Palestine. Again, failure of transport, sabotage of supplies en route, continuing harassment by Arab desert bands, and a buildup of British forces under General Allenby brought disaster.

The fourth area of major hostilities in the Middle East was Iraq. British contingents from India seized Basrah even before the Ottoman entry into the war and proceeded northward to the confluence of the Tigris and Euphrates. A sizable force under General Townshend captured Kut al-Amara in 1915, but it was defeated just south of Baghdad and fell back to Kut al-Amara, where the Ottomans forced a surrender in 1916. However, Halil Pasha, Enver's uncle, failed to pursue his victory and permitted the British and Indian divisions to reestablish their hold on southern Iraq. A railroad was built and superior concentrations of men, artillery, and supplies enabled the British to retake Kut al-Amara and capture Baghdad in 1917. Before the year was out the British were halfway between Mosul and Baghdad, but they had not yet reached the former at the time of the armistice in 1918.

THE ARMENIANS

While World War I was unfolding in the Middle East and shattering the Ottoman Empire, some members of two national groups within the state, the Arabs and the Armenians, openly aided the enemy. Wealthy Armenians insisted that their people support the Ottoman government and the war, but some Armenians claimed that the Russian tsar was the protector of all Armenians. Thus, in Istanbul and the western cities of the empire Armenians complied with war orders, while in eastern Asia Minor some of the Armenian population, often following Westernized Armenian radicals, aided Russia by rebelling, and in the region of Van and Erzurum, by open warfare. In April 1915, an Armenian government was proclaimed in Van. In some districts, part of the Muslim population was killed.

These incidents touched off the unfortunate Armenian deportations ordered in June 1915, which led to the massacres of 1915 and 1916. An estimated 1,500,000 Armenians had lived in Turkey at the outbreak of the war. The great preponderance were in the eastern regions. The transfer of all non-Muslims away from points of military concentration and from lines of communication was authorized and all non-Muslims in the military forces were relegated to rear service units without arms. Many of the latter were murdered. Thousands of civilian Armenians also had already died.

During the deportation, disease and inadequate provisions in the Syrian deserts, the general destination, led to the death of tens of thousands from exposure, illness, exhaustion, and starvation. Many were marched off into the desert to die. Everyone suffered. The prosecution of the war on the Caucasus front was hampered from 1915 to 1917 because of the absence of the services normally provided by the Armenian inhabitants of eastern Anatolia. Many Armenians were set upon by marauding bands of Kurds and Turks, who perpetrated numerous atrocities. Representatives of neutral governments protested to Istanbul, and German officials privately lamented the action. Talat, Enver, and the Ottoman government, however, were deaf to all pleas, since influential individuals in the government were actually bent on exterminating the Armenian population in eastern Turkey. Perhaps 600,000 or more Armenians (about 40 percent of the Ottoman Armenian population) perished, while hundreds of thousands fled elsewhere. Almost no Armenians were left in their ancient homeland in eastern Anatolia. No doubt certain deportations were required, but the total action was entirely inconsonant with the need. Many Turks did shield and protect Armenian individuals from the authorities; the severity of the Armenian deportations and massacres was a blot on the record of the Ottoman Empire.

ARAB MOVEMENTS

The other pressing national problem confronting the leaders of the Ottoman government was the loyalty and aspirations of the Arabs. No open break occurred until June 1916, when Sharif Husayn of Mecca proclaimed his personal rule in the Hijaz. Prior to that move, Jemal Pasha as an Ottoman viceroy and commander of the Fourth Army maintained discipline and surface calm in Syria. Jemal supported pan-Islamism and sought to obtain the active support of the Arabs in the war. However, documents implicating numerous Muslim and Christian leaders in treasonable activities fell into his hands. Arrests were made, and in 1915 eleven persons were hanged in the main square of Beirut. When Enver called upon Jemal for troops for the Gallipoli campaign, an Arab division, including many leaders of *al-Ahd,* was sent in order that the more reliable troops might remain in Beirut and Damascus. In April 1916, about two hundred Arabs, including many well-known and influential men from the most prominent families in Beirut and Damascus, were arrested, tried, and sentenced; twenty-two were hanged.

Before examining the moves for independence made by the western Arabs in Syria and the Hijaz, Arab-British relations should be placed in their proper setting. Arab states existed along the western shore of the Persian Gulf and the southern coasts of Arabia. Almost every one had a treaty of friendship with Great Britain in which the latter exercised power over Arab foreign relations. In effect, protectorates were created. A British minister resident or an agent resided in the shaykhdom or the sultanate, advised on all governmental matters, and doled out gold sovereigns or Maria Theresa silver dollars to keep everybody happy.

When war became imminent, Captain Shakespear of the British Royal Navy, then attached to the India Office, visited Abd al-Aziz ibn Saud of the Nejd and entered into a standard Arab-British agreement: Ibn Saud placed his foreign affairs in British hands and accepted a generous subsidy. In regard to the Arabs as a whole and the question of a unified Arab nation, no reference was made and none was implied. Ibn Saud controlled an important segment of the interior of Arabia, and the India Office was merely ensuring his neutrality, at least in the struggle between Britons and the Ottomans in Iraq and the Persian Gulf area.

A more significant Arab development involved Husayn, who was the Ottoman prince of Mecca, and a lineal descendant of the prophet Muhammad. Early in 1914 Husayn's second son, Abd Allah, in passing through Cairo had sounded out the British on the subject of their aid to Husayn, who desired to break with the Ottoman Empire. After the advent of war, the British raised the question of an alliance with Husayn and a declaration against the Ottomans.

Thus began the celebrated correspondence between Sharif Husayn and the British in Egypt. Husayn found himself in a delicate situation. His third son, Faysal, did not trust the British or French and felt that it would be better policy to cooperate with the Ottomans and win their gratitude. Abd Allah, however, favored independence from the Ottomans and proposed, in cooperation with Arab secret societies in Damascus and Beirut, to take advantage of the world struggle in order to obtain British aid. Husayn postponed the decision until June 1916. Meanwhile, an exchange of letters between Husayn and Sir Henry McMahon, high commissioner for Egypt and the Sudan, brought to a head the issue of Arab independence and an Arab state. Britain promised, upon the successful conclusion of the war, to agree to the creation of an Arab state. The area of the state was to be bounded on the north by a line drawn eastward from Alexandretta to the Iranian frontier and thence southward to the Persian Gulf and was to include much of the western Arabian peninsula. Excepted from this were the districts of Syria west of Damascus, Homs, Hama, and Aleppo. The British refused to pledge the latter without the consent of France.

Husayn, however, was not a free agent in dealing with the British. His son Faysal had conferred clandestinely in Damascus with leaders of the Arab movement, and in 1915 he presented the secret Damascus Protocol to his father. This document defined the Arab state's frontiers as Husayn later insisted upon them with McMahon, and it demanded abolition of the capitulations in return for economic preference to Great Britain. Its authors invited Husayn to forward their terms to the British as the basis on which the Arabs would revolt against the Ottoman Empire. Thus, the Husayn-McMahon correspondence should be regarded not as a negotiation entirely between two individuals but as a negotiation in part between representatives of two principals the British government and the Arab nationalists of Syria.

THE SECRET TREATIES

While these negotiations with Husayn were in process, the Allies were engaged in formulating their secret treaties, dividing among themselves both Turkish and Arab parts of the Ottoman Empire. As soon as war broke out in 1914 Russia pressed England and France for Istanbul as well as the Straits and considerable hinterland on each side. After many diplomatic exchanges Russia was reluctantly promised the object of her age-old quest. In exchange, British and French rights in Asiatic Turkey would be defined by special agreement and the neutral zone in Iran would be included in the British sphere of influence.

Later the Pact of London was signed to bring Italy into the war. This pact promised Italy sovereignty over the Dodecanese Islands and the elimination of all rights of the Ottoman caliph yet remaining in Libya. Italian interests in Antalya were conceded and that area promised to her; in case Turkey was not dismembered Italy would be given recompense elsewhere.

The most far-reaching of the secret treaties—the Sykes-Picot Agreement of May 16, 1916—allotted to Russia the already promised Straits area, the vilayets of Erzurum, Trabzon, Van, and Bitlis, and Kurdistan. France was granted the coastal strip of Syria northward from Tyre, the vilayet of Adana including Mersin, and a vague area of Cilicia which comprised a triangle of Anatolia marked off by Adana, Sivas, and Mardin. Britain obtained an enclave about Haifa and Acre on the

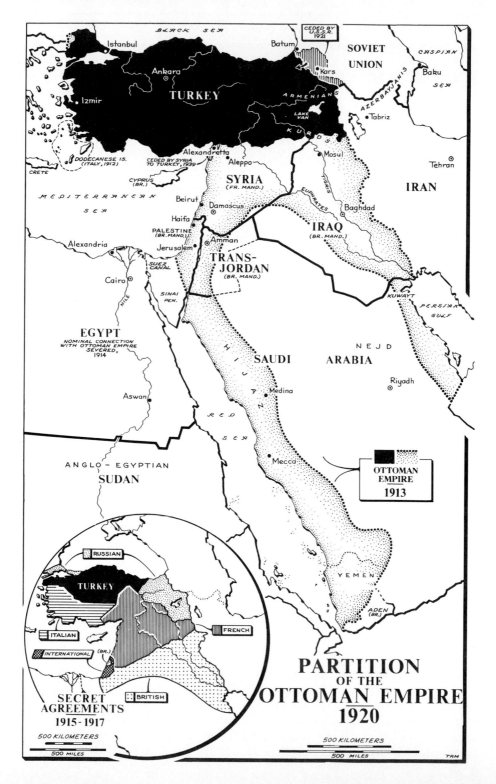

PARTITION
OF THE
OTTOMAN EMPIRE
1920

Mediterranean, and part of Iraq from Baghdad to the Persian Gulf. Palestine west of the Jordan River and from Gaza to Tyre was, upon the insistence of Russia, cut from French Syria and promised an international administration because of the Holy Places and numerous Russian Orthodox establishments. The area of Syria from Damascus and Aleppo eastward through Mosul to the Iranian frontier was consigned to French protection, while the region from Kirkuk to Aqaba became a British sphere. Alexandretta was designated a free port.

The secret Sykes-Picot Agreement was signed only a few months after agreements embodied in the Husayn-McMahon correspondence were concluded. Husayn did not learn of the perfidy until late in 1917, when the Bolsheviks published the secret agreements found in the imperial archives. Husayn requested an explanation. In January 1918 he received an official British statement virtually denying the existence of the Sykes-Picot Agreement and adding a cryptic remark about the consent of the populations concerned. Husayn trusted the British until after the war ended.

The Italians, however, learning of the Sykes-Picot arrangements, insisted upon a further delimitation of their ambitions. Thus, in 1917 the prime ministers of England, France, and Italy agreed that Italy should have the districts of Izmir, Antalya, and Konya, and all of southwestern Anatolia. A district north of Izmir also became an Italian prize. At the same time that Italy secured Izmir, Greece was promised Cyprus and the territory of western Asia Minor including Izmir as an inducement to join the war on the Allied side. Pledges and counterpledges with regard to the future of the Middle East were beginning to mount.

THE BALFOUR DECLARATION

Zionism had yet to be heard. Zionism was a sociopolitical and nationalistic movement that developed among European Jews in the last quarter of the nineteenth century. Pogroms in Russia and anti-Jewish sentiment in the nationalistic states of Europe fostered political Zionism and provoked Theodor Herzl to establish the World Zionist Organization in Basle in 1897. Concessions were repeatedly sought from the Porte for a Jewish settlement company in Palestine, but the sultan refused, believing this would increase his already diffuse problems of nationalism. The Zionist Congress had declined a British offer in 1903 of a settlement in Uganda, for Zionism without Zion would be a paradox. At the outbreak of war in 1914, Zionist activities were centered in Germany. Upon the division of Europe into two camps, however, another center arose in London, led by Dr. Chaim Weizmann.

The Zionists wanted an Allied commitment to create a Jewish commonwealth in Palestine upon the demise of the Ottoman Empire. Political pressure to this end was exerted, generally in the public press, and individually upon public and political figures. Slowly an influential group came to favor such a state, especially when the Zionists pledged that the new creation, so strategically placed with respect to Suez, would be in the British sphere of influence. Success came on November 2, 1917, when Lord Balfour wrote to Lord Rothschild:

His Majesty's Government view with favour the establishment in Palestine of a national home for the Jewish people and will use their best endeavours to facilitate the achievement of this object, it being clearly understood that nothing shall be done which may prejudice the civil and religious rights of existing non-Jewish communities in Palestine or the rights and political status enjoyed by Jews in any other country.

This letter, the famous Balfour Declaration, had the approval of the British Cabinet as well as that of President Wilson, who insisted upon adding the modifying clauses. Later, France and Italy accepted the declaration, and Wilson publicly acknowledged it in October 1918. The exact meaning of the declaration has been much debated in the last decades, but at the time of its writing there was no doubt of its intent. Also it was definitely contrary both to the Sykes-Picot Agreement and to the Husayn-McMahon correspondence. Reasons for its issuance have been advanced by those responsible. It was alleged that its pronouncement was required to gain support for the Allies from Jewish circles in Germany and Austria. There may be some basis to this, for in 1918 Germany and the Ottomans also offered the Zionists a charter for a Jewish settlement company in Palestine. It was constant political pressure and the winning of important men to their cause, for whatever reason, that brought success to the Zionists. They were disappointed, however, that the declaration did not read "recognizing Palestine as the national home for the Jewish people." Husayn was dismayed when the news of the Balfour Declaration reached him.

THE FOURTEEN POINTS

One other Allied promise was made during the war. When Baghdad and Jerusalem fell to British forces, the victorious generals announced that any future settlement would be made with the consent of local populations. These utterances foreshadowed the broad concepts of Wilson's Fourteen Points, presented to the American Congress on January 8, 1918. In particular they foreshadowed Wilson's twelfth point, which stated that the Turkish parts of the Ottoman Empire should have a "secure sovereignty" and that other nationalities should be given "an undoubted security of life and an absolute unmolested opportunity of development." Greeks, Armenians, and Arabs felt that this point alluded to them and they built their hopes upon it. Arabs believed that Wilson's declaration recognized their aspirations as proposed by Husayn, and that the Fourteen Points nullified the Balfour Declaration and all secret treaties, agreements, commitments, understandings, and promises made under the duress of total war.

ALLIED VICTORY

Failure of the German-Turkish campaign in the summer of 1917 opened the way for the British in Egypt to move into Palestine. Jerusalem fell to General Allenby in December 1917. British forces, accompanied by French detachments, then proceeded northward along the coast, taking Tyre, Sidon, Beirut, and Tripoli. The Turks' interior lines of communication were continuously harassed by the Arabs under Faysal. The Arab revolution of June 1916 shattered the Ottoman regime in the Hijaz, and Arabs under Faysal east of the Jordan paralleled the actions of Allenby. Under the stimulus and encouragement of such British liaison officers as Colonel T. E. Lawrence, and receiving British equipment and gold, the Arabs captured Aqaba and Maan and entered Damascus in October 1918, at about the same time as the British Imperial forces. The Seventh Ottoman Army under Mustafa Kemal held the Allies before Aleppo, as the armistice signed at Mudros between the Allies and the Ottomans ended all hostilities.

German failures on the Western Front in the summer of 1918 and the imminent collapse of Germany spelled the end of warfare in the Middle East. Without German matériel and general assistance the Ottoman Empire could not maintain effective resistance. Admiral Gough-Calthorpe, commander of the British Mediterranean Fleet, received representatives of the new Ottoman government aboard the *Agamemnon* off Mudros on the island of Lemnos and on October 30, 1918, signed an armistice ending the war. It was not an unconditional surrender, but Ottoman forces were to be demobilized, and the Allies were to have free access and control of the Straits. Opening the door to total Allied control was Article VII which stated: "The Allies have the right to occupy any strategic points in the event of any situation arising which threatens the security of the Allies." Under such an article any action was allowable.

The war, four years almost to the day, brought many changes to Turkish society, which disintegrated so fully under the terrible conditions of the war that the British leader Asquith declared "the Sick Man had really died this time." To describe the miserable conditions in Turkey to those who did not experience them would require many pages. Suffice it to say that the larger cities were disturbed more than the villages, and Istanbul most of all. Shortages of every kind developed; war profiteers appeared; physical suffering among the masses became widespread; disease and famine were everywhere; and the general low standard of living deteriorated rapidly, as inflation lifted the prices of everything without much change in wages. About 2,500,000 Ottoman Muslims died in Anatolia from 1914 to 1922; this was about 18 percent of the total Ottoman Muslim population. Hundreds of thousands of the minorities also died. Most commodities were scarce. Foreign goods could not be imported, and domestic produce was largely requisitioned by the government. Worse still, the government proved entirely incapable of governing. Inefficiency, mismanagement, and malfeasance dominated every government office. The capitulations were abolished; the Ottoman Public Debt Administration was terminated; and the war-burdened government assumed control over many unaccustomed activities. The end of the Ottoman state seemed obvious, and Asquith completed his declaration on the Sick Man with the pronouncement that "his resurrection was impossible."

The war generated many new and positive forces in society. As the power of the Ottoman government waned, Arabs, Greeks, Armenians, and all subject nationalities of the empire gave more open expression to their nationalism. For the Armenians, it led to destruction. To the Greeks, it brought a temporary fulfillment of cherished dreams. And among the Arabs, it created revolt and new Arab states. For the Turks the rapid decay gave to many liberals and democrats, such as Halidé

Edib and Ahmed Emin, and to uncompromising nationalists, such as Mustafa Kemal, an opportunity to be heard and to have some heed paid to their demands for governmental leadership that would place the welfare of the nation above self-interest.

Of the other effects of the war, one of the more salutary for the Middle East was the presence of many British, French, Italian, and German soldiers, and their equipment. Thousands of Middle Easterners saw Westerners and their manner of living for the first time. Their machines opened a new world to Arabs and Turks. The impact of the West upon the Middle East in every facet of its living, from transportation to religion, was more profound and penetrating in these four war years than it had been in several centuries of contact through religious, commercial, and intellectual missions from the West. A new age for the Middle East was born.

REFERENCES

Volumes cited in Chapters 23, 25, 26, and 28 are pertinent to this chapter.

Busch, Briton Cooper. *Britain, India and the Arabs, 1914–1921.* Berkeley: University of California Press, 1971. A detailed account of World War I in the Middle East from the viewpoint of the British in India, using Indian archives.

DeNovo, John A. *American Interests and Policies in the Middle East, 1900–1939.* Minneapolis: The University of Minnesota Press, 1963. A thorough work that includes all aspects of American interests.

Djemal Pasha, Ahmed. *Memories of a Turkish Statesman, 1913–1919.* New York: Doran, 1922. The autobiography of one of the Ottoman triumvirate during the war.

Dyer, Gwynne. "Turkish 'Falsifiers' and Armenian 'Deceivers': Historiography and the Armenian Massacres." *Middle Eastern Studies* 12 (1976): 99–107. An excellent sketch of some books on the Armenian massacres; shows the highly partisan nature of much written on both sides of the issue.

Emin, Ahmed. *Turkey in the World War.* New Haven, Conn.: Yale University Press, 1930. A basic and thorough study of the political, economic, and social forces in the Ottoman Empire during the war years.

Evans, Laurence. *United States Policy and the Partition of Turkey, 1914–1924.* Baltimore, Md.: Johns Hopkins Press, 1965.

Gunter, Michael M. *"Pursuing the Just Cause of Their People": A Study of Contemporary Armenian Terrorism.* New York: Greenwood Press, 1986. This work contains a valuable chapter on the historical origins of Armenian violence as well as a discussion of more recent happenings.

Hovannisian, Richard G. "The Historical Dimensions of the Armenian Question, 1878–1923." In Richard G. Hovannisian, ed. *The Armenian Genocide in Perspective.* New Brunswick, N.J.: Transaction Books, 1986, pp. 19–41. A very able summary of evidence supporting Armenian claims of Ottoman guilt in the massacres as well as a general discussion of Ottoman-Armenian relations.

Howard, Harry N. *The Partition of Turkey; A Diplomatic History, 1913–1923*. Norman: Oklahoma University Press, 1931. The most definitive work on the political, diplomatic, and international aspects of World War I in the Middle East.

Hurewitz, J. C., compiler, trans., ed. *The Middle East and North Africa in World Politics: A Documentary Record*. Vol. 2. *British-French Supremacy, 1914–1945*. 2d ed. New Haven, Conn.: Yale University Press, 1979. This volume contains the significant documents for the area in this crucial period.

Kedourie, Elie. *In the Anglo-Arab Labyrinth: The McMahon-Husayn Correspondence and Its Interpretations, 1914–1939*. Cambridge: Cambridge University Press, 1976. A thorough examination of the correspondence and the conversations, followed by a full analysis of the various interpretations and historical reports of them.

Lawrence, T. E. *Seven Pillars of Wisdom*. London: Jonathan Cape, 1935. The full account of Lawrence of Arabia's activities among the Arabs during the war; a literary masterpiece whose historical accuracy has been subject to much debate.

Macfie, A. L. "The Straits Question in the First World War, 1914–18." *Middle Eastern Studies* 19 (1983): 43–74. Especially good on relationships between Britain, France, and Russia.

Moorehead, Alan. *Gallipoli*. New York: Harper, 1956. The story of the famous campaign.

Mousa, Suleiman. *T. E. Lawrence: An Arab View*. London: Oxford University Press, 1966. A careful revisionist study of the real actions and importance of Lawrence during the war.

Nevakivi, Jukka. *Britain, France and the Arab Middle East, 1914–1920*. New York: Oxford University Press, 1969. A new study making use of British archives for the period. Scholarly and sound.

Sachar, Howard M. *The Emergence of the Middle East: 1914–1924*. New York: Knopf, 1969. A well-documented account of the area in those years from a European rather than a Middle Eastern view

von Sanders, Liman. *Five Years in Turkey*. Baltimore, Md.: Williams & Wilkins, 1928. The record of the German commanding general stationed in Turkey during the war.

Stein, Leonard. *The Balfour Declaration*. New York: Simon and Schuster, 1961. First good complete history.

Storrs, Ronald. *Orientations*. London: Nicholson & Watson, 1937. Storrs was the Oriental secretary to the British high commissioner in Egypt during the war.

Townshend, Charles V. *My Campaign in Mesopotamia*. London: T. Butterworth, 1920. By the commanding general of the British forces.

Trumpener, Ulrich. *Germany and the Ottoman Empire, 1914–1918*. Princeton, N.J.: Princeton University Press, 1968. A detailed account largely from German sources. Discusses the alliance of 1914, the conduct of the war, financing, Armenian persecutions, German economic efforts, and political evolution of the alliance. An outstanding work, with many new interpretations.

Wilson, Arnold T. *Loyalties: Mesopotamia, 1914–1917*. London: Oxford University Press, 1930. A detailed record of the military occupation of Iraq by a British participant long active in that part of the world.

31

The Middle East at the Paris Peace Conference

ALLIED CLAIMS AND PROMISES

Less than two weeks after the Mudros armistice halted World War I in the Middle East, Germany signed the armistice with the Allies and war officially ceased. The fate of the Middle East devolved then upon the several armies of occupation and, perhaps even more importantly, upon "the smoke-filled rooms" of Paris, where politicians, diplomats, statesmen, generals, journalists, and representatives of every special interest gathered to make peace. The Middle East, however, was only a small part of the total settlement. Problems with respect to Germany took precedence over all others, and decisions affecting France, Germany, and central Europe frequently compromised the verdict on the Middle East.

The prime conflict concerning the Middle East appeared in the frightful disparity contained in the assorted secret treaties, agreements, and letters exchanged among the Allies—such as the London Pact of 1915, the Sykes-Picot Agreement, the Balfour Declaration, the Husayn-McMahon correspondence, the Fourteen Points, the liberation statements at Baghdad and Jerusalem, and the "make the world safe for democracy" slogan—to say nothing of contradictions in numerous pious, platitudinous, and public pronouncements by Allied leaders during the war. Thus, the hopes of the many who traveled to Paris were high.

The British prime minister David Lloyd George went to the conference professing friendliness and good will for the peoples of the Middle East and clamoring for their welfare and aspirations. But he had every intention of advancing the interest, power, and possessions of the British Empire. Egypt, Iraq, Arabia, Palestine, Iran, Cyprus, and the Caucasus were considered British prizes. Lloyd George regarded the entire Middle East, with the possible exception of Syria and parts of Anatolia, as an economic adjunct of the British Empire. The French leader Georges Clemenceau, on the other hand, stood for a French hold upon Syria and southern Anatolia, hoped to acquire or at least dominate the Straits, and dreamed of having a French adviser at the elbow of the sultan of Turkey who would exercise a role similar to that of the British adviser in Egypt. President Wilson, on his trip across the Atlantic aboard the *George Washington,* met daily with his advisers and sincerely discussed plans for peace in the Middle East that would fulfill the pledge made in his Fourteen Points. Since Allied governments concurred in that declaration, he believed it wiped away all previous "sins."

The Big Three held major decisions in their hands; hosts of others, however, had greater personal or national interests in the Middle East. Prince Faysal came to Paris to represent the Arabs, his father, and the Kingdom of the Hijaz, which had been a belligerent since June 1916. Faysal expected England to abide by her pledges given to the Arabs for their national state. Three groups of Armenians presented conflicting claims for their nation, and President Wilson sent out the Harbord Mission to ascertain the facts. Venizelos, the prime minister of Greece, used all of his charm and diplomatic blandishments to obtain Allied promises with respect to the Greek "Great Idea," that is, restoration of the Greek empire to include western Asia Minor, Constantinople, and the Straits. Prime Minister Orlando of Italy intended to receive the Dodecanese Islands, southwestern Asia Minor around Antalya, and an area in and about Izmir.

Bankers, oil men, exporters, bondholders, missionaries, churchmen, shippers, and humanitarians of sundry types also converged at Paris to lobby for their respective interests. Amid receptions, lively dinner dances, and weekends at rented chateaux within easy motoring distance of Paris, the future of the Middle East was being debated. Everyone was there except the Ottomans. They did, however, have unofficial agents in Geneva, and Damad Ferid Pasha, the grand vizir, was permitted on one occasion to deliver a statement before the supreme council of the conference.

Zionists shepherded the Balfour Declaration through the negotiations to assure its incorporation in all final settlements for the Middle East. Opposing these ardent Zionists stood a few Jews who felt that Zionism endangered the slow process of assimilation of Jews occurring in Europe and America. Nevertheless, a coterie of active Zionists won the support of Lloyd George, as well as the sympathy of President Wilson. The policy of self-determination, however, seemed to be blocking Zionist aims. At the time, Jews constituted not more than 15 percent of the population of Palestine, and a policy of counting heads would have favored Palestine's inclusion in an Arab state as pledged to Sharif Husayn. Lloyd George was unimpressed by Zionist pleas, but he wanted Palestine as a stronghold to protect Suez and other British interests in the Middle East. The Zionists reinforced this hope by declaring openly that Jews would opt for a British mandate and by talking of eventual home rule for a Jewish Palestine within the British Commonwealth of Nations. The Zionists' dreams were achieved as a paraphrase of the Balfour Declaration was included in the peace treaties and accepted by the League of Nations.

Out of the welter of claims and counterclaims for the Middle East was born the King-Crane commission. Wilson proposed to the supreme council that a commission of inquiry composed of American, British, French, and Italian representatives go to Syria, Palestine, Iraq, and Armenia to obtain the information needed to implement the program of supervised self-determination. At first the French, British, and Italians agreed, but later they refused to cooperate. Therefore, President Henry C. King of Oberlin College and businessman Charles R. Crane, the American appointees, proceeded alone in the spring of 1919 with a staff of experts.

They visited Palestine, Syria, and Turkey, receiving petitions and local deputations. Having faith in Western democratic principles, the Arabs rejoiced in the coming of the commission. The King-Crane report was submitted in the autumn of 1919 but was suppressed as it ran counter to arrangements already dictated between England and France. Wilson's illness caused the issue to be shelved.

SAN REMO AGREEMENT

No permanent decisions regarding the Middle East could be reached in Paris in 1919, and the signing of a peace treaty for the area seemed more uncertain than ever. Wilson became gravely ill. The American Senate and people were not favorably disposed to accept a mandate for any territory. Russia was out of the picture. Germany and Austria were broken. And Italy was suffering from internal dissension and disillusionment. Questions of the Middle East, therefore, lay squarely between England and France. Meanwhile, armies of occupation governed the Middle East and the peoples grew restless waiting for peace.

British forces under Allenby controlled Egypt, Palestine, and Lebanon; Faysal and the Arabs held sway over the Hijaz and Syria, including Damascus; and Britain was again master in Iraq with an army from Mosul to the Persian Gulf. Official British policy was set to retain as much of the occupied area as possible and to make the Middle East a definite part of the British Empire.

But policy was not the chief concern of the soldiers in the armies of occupation. The British army in 1919 was still the civilian army created during the war, and the aim of the great majority of men was to be demobilized as quickly as possible. As officers in the Middle East pulled every string to get out, the turnover in personnel grew serious. Added to the confusion was the fact that there was little planning or thought for military government or occupation.

In the last months of 1919 British contingents in Beirut and along the Lebanese coast were replaced by French units, and under arrangements concluded in Paris, General Gouraud became Allied administrator in Syria. These moves gave advance notice to the Arabs that settlement of the war in the Middle East would follow lines drawn in the hated Sykes Picot Agreement. Anti-Jewish riots in Jerusalem and Jaffa, the election of Faysal as king of Syria and of Abd Allah as king of Iraq by the Arab National Congress in Damascus, growing tenseness in Baghdad, insurrection in Egypt and the dispatch of the Milner Mission to Cairo drove Britain to realize that a treaty for the Middle East was imperative.

One of the sensitive questions in the settlement between England and France revolved around the division of Mosul oil. The Turkish Petroleum Company, about 50 percent British and 25 percent German, had obtained in 1914 a concession to exploit the oil of Mosul. The Sykes-Picot Agreement, however, assigned Mosul to France. As early as December 1918, therefore, Britain began pressing the French to allow Mosul to be attached to the rest of Iraq. In Paris in May 1919, after much haggling, the Long-Bérenger Agreement was initialed: Britain and France would split equally all oil rights obtained in Russia, Rumania, and Galicia; France would be able to purchase 34 percent of all disposable oil in the British crown colonies and Britain to purchase 34 percent in the French colonies; France would receive 25 percent of the Turkish Petroleum Company; and England was given the right to build two pipelines across French-mandated areas from Mosul to the Mediterranean. Lloyd George stormily vetoed the arrangement when he learned of it, on the basis that political settlements would have to be agreed upon first. In February 1920, the Greenwood-Bérenger Agreement, containing similar terms, was approved. Added were provisions that France could buy 25 percent of the crude oil from all Iraqi fields. With this in hand the Allied negotiators journeyed to San Remo on the Italian Riviera, where on April 24, 1920, they reached an agreement on oil, pipelines, mandates, and united action with respect to the Turks and Arabs.

THE TREATY OF SÈVRES

The San Remo Agreement prepared the way for a peace settlement with the Ottoman Empire, and the Treaty of Sèvres was signed on August 10, 1920. By this treaty the Ottoman sultan recognized the separation of Syria, Iraq, Arabia, and Egypt from his empire. A British protectorate over Egypt was allowed and the independence of the Arab rulers and their states, subject to treaties of friendship with Britain, was accepted. Provisional independence for Syria and Iraq under the tutelage of a mandatory power was acknowledged. Syria, already assigned to France, included the cities of Alexandretta, Aleppo, Damascus, and Beirut. The vilayet of Mosul was attached to Baghdad and Basrah to form the state of Iraq under British supervision. Palestine, including the lands on each side of the Jordan and extending to the Gulf of Aqaba, was given as a mandate to Britain, with the Balfour Declaration written into the authorization. In addition to the oil understandings, France was given a free hand to deal with Faysal and the Arab Syrian kingdom with force—to crush them if necessary.

The Treaty of Sèvres was obsolete before it was drawn, and because of various exigencies within Turkish portions of the Ottoman Empire it was never fully ratified. Theoretically, then, final arrangements in the Middle East awaited the Treaty of Lausanne in 1923; yet divisions, boundaries, and the disposal of non-Turkish parts of the Ottoman Empire in that final treaty varied only slightly from the transfer of legal authority that was proposed at San Remo and Sèvres. Provisional mandates bargained for at San Remo dictated Arab political and economic life for the next twenty years, and Britain and France immediately took action in their respective spheres.

There was one additional settlement in this era of treaties and engagements. In March 1921, Winston Churchill, who was then colonial secretary, held a lengthy conference in Cairo with most of the British Middle Eastern experts, including Sir Herbert Samuel and Sir Percy Cox, high commissioners for Palestine and Iraq, respectively. They hatched a scheme that put Faysal, ousted by the French from Damascus, on the throne of Iraq and carved from the part of Palestine east of the Jordan the state of Transjordan for Prince Abd Allah, who originally had been promised Iraq. Since the British did not wish to be under any obligation to the

French in getting oil out through Syria, a section of the Syrian desert was claimed for Transjordan. This created a British-controlled route from Mosul to the Mediterranean.

ALLIED OCCUPATION OF TURKEY

The Allies were not faring too well in the Turkish parts of the Ottoman Empire. On November 13, 1918, a combined Allied fleet traversed the Bosphorus and dropped anchor in the Golden Horn. Ten days later an Allied army under a French general entered Istanbul. Soon thereafter, British, French, Italian, and American high commissioners arrived to assume responsibility for the four zones established in the city. In this fashion the capital of the six-hundred-year-old Ottoman state, under Muslim control since 1453, fell into the hands of foreign Christians.

Istanbul immediately attracted Western commercial interest, and imports to satisfy the lack of goods in the war years gave the city many characteristics of a boom town. Greeks and Armenians in Turkey welcomed the Allies as liberators. The Allies rolled back time to 1914; the capitulations were restored; the Ottoman Public Debt Administration functioned again; and concession hunting became once more the sport of the day.

At first the Turks were relieved that the fighting had ended, as they were genuinely weary of war; there had been more than the usual share of orphans, refugees, invalids, and general victims. As the occupation proceeded, however, thoughtful Turks grew dismayed at the Allies' lack of justice, understanding, and political wisdom. It soon became apparent that Sultan Mehmed VI and his ministers were only convenient Allied puppets. It also became clear that Anatolia would be carved up, if the Allies could agree on a partition without fighting among themselves.

Britain moved northward from Mosul; France claimed Cilicia as an extension of Syria; and Italian forces landed at Antalya to assure that promises would be fulfilled. One of the tragedies of the time was initiated, when under cover of an Allied fleet Greek troops landed at Izmir to take possession of what the Greeks had been awarded in Paris. Supported by Britain and France, Venizelos had won Wilson over to the Greek occupation, which began on May 15, 1919. Small incidents of organized Turkish resistance occurred almost immediately, and a few atrocities committed by the Greeks, especially at the village of Menemen near Izmir, made Turkish acceptance of Greek rule in Asia Minor impossible.

TURKISH NATIONALISTS

The day following the Greek landing at Izmir, Mustafa Kemal Pasha, appointed as inspector general of the Third Army by the Allied high commissioners and the sultan, sailed for Samsun on the Black Sea coast with orders to commence demobilization and restore law and peace to Anatolia. Before the summer was over Kemal resigned his commission and convened rebellious national congresses at Erzurum and Sivas, calling for all patriotic Turks to join the Association for the Defense of Rights in Europe and Anatolia.

The Greek landing at Izmir produced extensive street demonstrations in Istanbul; resentment toward the Allies swelled. As the strength of the nationalists grew in Istanbul, many members of the Ottoman parliament in Istanbul openly supported the movement. In January 1920 they drew up a six-point program as the basis for a lasting peace. It proposed self-determination for the Arabs, western Thrace, and the eastern provinces of Kars, Ardahan, and Batum; complete political and economic unity and independence of Turkish areas; international protection of minorities; and internationalization of the Straits, if Istanbul were guaranteed as a secure residence for the sultan-caliph. The increasing popularity of the nationalists in Istanbul and the active collaboration of many leaders with them spurred the British in March 1920 to occupy the city of Istanbul with a strong military force. Nationalist leaders and prominent Turks who were unable to hide or flee to Anatolia to Mustafa Kemal were seized and sent to Malta.

Heretofore, the occupation had been nominal. With the British in full control, patriotic Turks flocked to Kemal and the nationalists. Many former leaders of the Committee of Union and Progress and other nationalists had already formed local Turkish resistance organizations in various regions. Then, in April 1920, a Grand National Assembly met at Ankara, adopted the six-point program, and elected Kemal as its president. The Turkish resistance was now fully committed to fight for independence.

The Allies never imagined that the "sick man" of Europe, after the punishment he had taken during World War I, could ever rise from his coma. The San Remo Conference blithely beckoned the Powers to the Treaty of Sèvres and its unreality. Greece was given western and eastern Thrace, including Edirne and territory up to a line twenty miles from Istanbul. The district and city of Izmir would be administered by Greece for five years, after which a plebiscite would determine its future. Armenia was established as an independent state, whose frontier with Turkey would be arbitrated by President Wilson. Kurdistan, east of the Euphrates River, obtained local autonomy, which might be transferred to independence upon the consent of the League of Nations. Although Istanbul remained under Turkish sovereignty, the Straits area was to be controlled by an international commission. Turkey would maintain an army of 50,000 men, all armaments being under Allied supervision. Minority rights were to be respected. New, humiliating articles were added to the reestablished capitulations. And the Ottoman Public Debt Administration under British, French, and Italian direction was given almost absolute control over economic, financial, and budgetary matters. Equally galling to the Turks was the announcement of the Tripartite Agreement among England, France, and Italy, dividing what remained of Turkey into three spheres of influence almost exactly along the line marked by wartime secret treaties. The Treaty of Sèvres left Turkey prostrate, and no self-respecting Turk could countenance it.

It was little wonder that Mustafa Kemal and the nationalists in Ankara were alternately termed bandits and futile wild men. They faced the British in Istanbul and the Straits, the Greeks at Izmir, the Italians at Antalya, the French at Adana and in Cilicia, the British in Kurdistan, and the Armenianss in the northeastern vilayets. Fortunately for Kemal, the enemy never presented a concerted attack, and he was able to meet them one by one.

MUSTAFA KEMAL

Modern Turkish nationalism, conceived in the latter part of the nineteenth century and nourished by the poems and polemics of the Young Turk period, was born in 1919 and 1920. It first saw the light of day on the plateaus of central Anatolia, and its birth pangs were a series of wars for independence against the several enemies cited above. Mustafa Kemal, its military and political midwife, was born in Salonika in 1881. He belonged to the lower middle class and attended military schools in Monastir and Istanbul, where he distinguished himself in mathematics and oratory. As an officer he served in Damascus and Monastir and took an active part in the various revolutionary societies that honeycombed the army in the days prior to and after the Young Turk Revolution of 1908. He served in Libya in the war against Italy and participated briefly in the Balkan wars. The outbreak of war in 1914 found him military attaché to Sofia, but he soon effected his transfer and became a hero as one of General Liman von Sanders' most valued Turkish officers in the Gallipoli campaign. By 1918 he had commanded armies on every Turkish front.

Mustafa Kemal possessed a brilliant, razor-edged mind. He demanded first-rate performance from himself and from those about and beneath him. An early teacher had given him the sobriquet *Kemal* (Perfection), a name he eventually came to use almost exclusively. Kemal was contemptuous of pomp and hollow ceremony, and sometimes gave the appearance of being vicious. Although a devoted nationalist with energy, an indomitable will, and an incorruptibility that was frightening to many, he was wild and licentious in his private life.

At Ankara in 1920, this tough and uncompromising leader stood as a Turkish nationalist defying the victors of World War I. He commanded the scanty resources of a dozen poor upland provinces of central Asia Minor, bedraggled veterans of several scattered armies, and an enthusiastic band of patriots trailing in from Istanbul. However, the crack, undefeated Turkish Ninth Army, which had operated in the Caucasus and marched to the Caspian Sea, served as his nucleus, and Kemal organized a force about them. In the spring of 1920 he drove the French back to Aleppo and signed an armistice removing them from the combat. Then the Turks under Kazim Karabekir captured Kars, Ardahan, and Mount Ararat from the Armenian republic; the Russian Bolsheviks then gained control over the Armenian state and it was incorporated ultimately into the Union of Soviet Socialist Republics. In the Treaty of Gümrü in December 1920 Turkey ceded Batum to Russia in exchange for Russian acknowledgment of Turkish control over the provinces of Kars and Ardahan. A few months later the Treaty of Moscow confirmed this new frontier and pledged Russian aid against the imperialists' aims in Turkey. In March 1921 Kemal reached an agreement whereby the Italians, for certain well-defined economic concessions, evacuated Antalya and Scala Nuova, south of Izmir. Consequently, by the opening of the summer of 1921 Kemal faced only the Greek army and some weak British occupational contingents on the Straits.

TURKISH-GREEK WAR

Since June 1920 the Allies, through British insistence, had assigned to the Greeks the task of protecting the Allied position in Turkey, "liberating" the country from the Kemalists, and enforcing the peace terms upon the Turks. Immediately, Greek armies advanced in Thrace and Anatolia. Over the following fourteen months they had remarkable success, taking Edirne in Europe and Afyon-Karahisar, Kutahya, Eskishehir, and Izmit in Asia Minor. The only victories Kemal could show were the two tactical battles of Inönü, where Colonel Ismet won lasting fame in 1921.

Time, however, was on Kemal's side. Britain and France quarreled over German reparations, the question of the Rhineland, and a host of other problems. These quarrels finally caused a break over Turkish policies. A secret treaty of peace and friendship between France and the nationalist government was concluded in October 1921. France hoped to get in on the ground floor in an economic reorganization that would include the development of the rich resources of Asia Minor.

King Alexander of Greece died from the bite of his pet monkey in October 1920. He was succeeded by his father, Constantine, who was recalled from exile. The British distrusted Constantine, and when the Greeks refused to heed British advice against the Anatolian venture, the British decided to let them manage it on their own. King Constantine called for an advance upon Ankara. After French and Italian reconciliations with Kemal, the Allies officially declared their neutrality. Lloyd George could promise the Greeks only his political assistance. Although arms were denied the Greeks, the Turkish nationalists were obtaining war matériel from France, Italy, and Russia.

The Greek advance was checked by the three-week Battle of Sakarya, which ended in September 1921. Stubborn and heroic Turkish resistance and extended Greek lines of communication decided the issue, although the Kemalists needed a whole year to regroup their forces for the victorious rush upon Izmir. After the Turkish victory on the Sakarya lines on August 26, 1922, the rout became general: Mustafa Kemal entered Izmir on September 11, and by September 19 all Greek forces were cleared from Anatolia. The war with Greece had been won, but intense bitterness remained. The Greek army in retreat pursued a scorched-earth policy and committed atrocities against defenseless Turkish villagers in its path. Shortly after the occupation of Izmir fire broke out and destroyed nearly half of the city. Who started the fire has never been determined, but once under way explosions of hidden Greek bombs and ammunition supplies rendered it uncontrollable.

From Izmir the nationalists turned to the Straits. Lloyd George called in vain upon the British Dominions for reinforcements as the fleet stood by. General Harrington, in command of the Straits, recognized the hopelessness of his position without more troops. He arranged an armistice between the Allies and the government of the Grand National Assembly, which was signed at Mudanya on October 11, 1922. Eastern Thrace with Edirne was ceded to the Turks, and the proposition for a conference to negotiate peace was accepted. Kemal had won; the British postwar policy for Turkey collapsed, taking Lloyd George with it.

LAUSANNE CONFERENCE

Invitations to meet at Lausanne were issued on October 27, 1922. Kemal accepted on October 31. A similar invitation to the sultan's government compelled the Grand National Assembly to pass a law on November 1 deposing Mehmed VI and voiding all laws of his government. The nationalists took over control of Istanbul on November 5, and Mehmed VI fled aboard a British cruiser for Malta. On November 18 the Grand National Assembly chose Mehmed's cousin, Abdul Mejid, as caliph. The Ottoman sultanate had come to its end.

Convening on November 20, 1922, the Lausanne Conference had a stormy course and one adjournment before the final acts were signed on July 24, 1923. England, France, Italy, Russia, Japan, Bulgaria, Rumania, Yugoslavia, Greece, and Turkey participated in the deliberations and signed one or more of the several documents drawn up. The United States sent only unofficial observers, who did, however, from time to time take an active part in discussions. Lord Curzon, the British foreign minister, dominated the conference until it broke up; his imperious six-foot-four-inch figure was a sharp contrast to that of the Turkish delegate, Ismet Pasha, who was only five feet four inches tall. Few people had ever seen or heard of Ismet until this conference, and all predicted he could hardly be a match for the foreign minister of Great Britain. But Ismet proved to be a stubborn, inflexible, and skillful negotiator. After all, the Turkish people were willing to fight again to obtain independence, whereas the British had just sacked their prime minister rather than run the risk of further war. Frequently, when Lord Curzon would arrogantly deliver some advice and admonition, he would become infuriated almost to the breaking point when Ismet, who was a trifle deaf, would cup his bad ear and ask him to repeat what he said: "Répétez-vous, s'il vous plaît?"

At the conference eastern Thrace with Edirne went with full sovereignty to Turkey. Of the Aegean Islands, Tenedos and Imbros went to Turkey, the Dodecanese to Italy, and the remainder to Greece. The settlement with regard to the Straits, in which the Russian delegate Chicherin participated, gave Turkey full sovereignty over the area. It was, however, stipulated that each shore be demilitarized to a depth of fifteen kilometers and that navigation of the Straits be regulated according to terms of a special international convention enacted concurrently with the Treaty of Lausanne. The Mosul frontier was left to be negotiated at a later date directly between Turkey and Britain, the latter acting for the kingdom of Iraq. In regard to the Armenian and Greek minorities Turkey accepted articles similar to minority clauses inserted in treaties with Austria, Hungary, and Bulgaria, and the Greeks agreed to a compulsory exchange of populations, excluding the Greeks of Istanbul and the Turks of western Thrace. The capitulations and the privileges of foreigners in Turkey were abolished entirely. Financial questions were settled by terminating the Ottoman Public Debt Administration in all of its manifestations and by a proportionate assumption of Ottoman debts by all successor states. Finally, the Allies accepted the cancellation of all prewar concessions and contracts, and Turkey agreed not to alter her tariff for five years after the Treaty of Lausanne came into force.

The conference broke temporarily in February 1923 over the last three points. Before the conference reconvened in April, the Grand National Assembly rejected any compromise on Ismet's stand, Lord Curzon was replaced, and the Turks threw a real scare into the Allies by granting a concession for the development of oil, railroads, and other resources to an American group headed by retired Admiral Chester. The United States government protested that it was not actively supporting the Chester group, but when the conference reopened, the new American listener let it be known that the United States expected to share in any development of oil resources in Turkey and the Middle East. Such a declaration provided a salutary rein upon British and French ambitions and paved the way for a relaxation of demands upon the Turks. Ismet went home to Ankara in the summer with the knowledge that Turkey was recognized as an independent free nation, except for the demilitarization of the Straits and the undefined border with Iraq.

The exchange of populations between Turkey and Greece, begun in the summer of 1923 under the aegis of the League of Nations, proceeded over many months. One million Greeks and half a million Turks were moved, at considerable hardship to the individuals involved. The impact upon Greece was most serious. Turkey lost a valuable merchant and commercial class, but Ismet argued at Lausanne that such a loss would be more than offset by the advantages of a homogeneous and united Turkish nation.

The Treaty of Lausanne and its various conventions were ratified during the summer of 1923. On October 29, 1923, just nine years after the Ottoman Empire entered World War I, the Grand National Assembly in Ankara declared Turkey a republic and elected Ghazi Mustafa Kemal Pasha president.

REFERENCES

Works important to this chapter are cited in Chapters 13, 23, 25, 26, 28, and 30.

Busch, Briton Cooper. *Mudros to Lausanne: Britain's Frontier in West Asia, 1918–1923*. Albany: State University of New York Press, 1976. A study of British policy in the area between the Straits and central Asia after the breakup of the Ottoman and Russian empires and the emergence of a new balance of power.

Cummings, H. H. *Franco-British Rivalry in the Post-War Near East*. London: Oxford University Press, 1938. Discusses the decline of French influence after World War I.

Edib (Adivar), Halidé. *The Turkish Ordeal*. New York: Century, 1928. Written by a Western-educated Turkish woman who participated in the Turkish struggle for independence.

Edmonds, C. J. *Kurds, Turks and Arabs: Politics, Travel, and Research in North-Eastern Iraq, 1919–1925.* London: Oxford University Press, 1957. A detailed record in the first person of the problems and settlement of the Mosul border region.

Helmreich, Paul C. *From Paris to Sèvres: The Partition of the Ottoman Empire at the Peace Conference of 1919–1920.* Columbus: Ohio State University Press, 1974. A thorough examination of most of the sources for the war period, including the British archives. Objective and very well-organized topically and chronologically.

Howard, Harry N. *The King-Crane Commission: An American Inquiry in the Middle East.* Beirut: Khayats, 1963. A definitive work by the leading authority on the subject, based on an examination and critical study of all the sources available.

Kent, Marian, ed. *The Great Powers and the End of the Ottoman Empire.* London: George Allen and Unwin, 1984. Seven authors evaluate the diplomatic history of the Ottoman Empire, Austria, Italy, Russia, Germany, France, and Great Britain from around 1900 to 1923.

Klieman, Aaron S. *Foundations of British Policy in the Arab World: The Cairo Conference of 1921.* Baltimore, Md.: Johns Hopkins University Press, 1970. A first-rate account of this historic and prestigious meeting, drawn from official sources.

Macfie, A. L. "The Straits Question: The Conference of Lausanne (November 1922–July 1923)." *Middle Eastern Studies* 15 (1979): 211–238. A detailed and able study of the British role at Lausanne.

Monroe, Elizabeth. *Britain's Moment in the Middle East, 1914–1971.* 2d ed. Baltimore, Md.: Johns Hopkins Press, 1981. A comprehensive and objective survey.

Sonyel, Salahi Ramsdan. *Turkish Diplomacy, 1918–1923: Mustafa Kemal and the Turkish National Movement.* London: Sage Publications, 1975. A very clear and sober study of the international diplomacy of the period centering around the diplomacy of the nationalists. Based on archival and primary sources in Turkish and Western languages.

Stivers, William. *Supremacy and Oil: Iraq, Turkey, and the Anglo-American World Order, 1918–1930.* Ithaca, N.Y.: Cornell University Press, 1982.

Temperley, H. W. V. *A History of the Peace Conference of Paris.* Vol. 6. London: Henry Frowde & Hodder & Stoughton, 1924. By one of the British experts and historians at the conference.

Toynbee, Arnold J. *Survey of International Affairs, 1925.* Vol. 1. *The Islamic World Since the Peace Settlement.* London: Oxford University Press, 1927. By the renowned historian who wrote world historical studies, as well as works dealing with the Middle East.

———. *The Western Question in Greece and Turkey.* London: Constable, 1922. An account of the events in Turkey after 1918.

———, and K. P. Kirkwood. *Turkey.* London: Ernest Benn, 1926.

Volkan, Vamik D., and Norman Itzkowitz. *The Immortal Atatürk: A Psychobiography.* Chicago: University of Chicago Press, 1984. An attempt to explain the major events of Atatürk's life on the basis of his personal character.

32

The Turkish Republic Under Atatürk

ESTABLISHMENT OF THE REPUBLIC

Between September 1911 and September 1922, there were five wars and only 22 months of peace for the Ottoman Empire and Turkey. About 20 percent of the population of Anatolia died, and there were millions of refugees in the country. Overcoming those problems posed major difficulties for the new Turkish Republic as it sought basic structural reforms in society.

On October 29, 1923, the Grand National Assembly voted approval of a declaration asserting that "the form of government of the Turkish State is a Republic." That same day it elected Ghazi Mustafa Kemal Pasha president of the republic. The idea of a republic, however, was not entirely novel, and its declaration only revealed an evolution proceeding naturally since the autumn of 1919.

The shift of power and representation of the Turkish nation from the sultan's government to Kemal's occurred in October 1919, when the nationalists proved strong enough to prompt the sultan and his supporters to dismiss the Ferid Pasha cabinet, call for the election of a new parliament, and induce the new cabinet of Ali Riza Pasha to seek an accord with them. Although Kemal failed to persuade the newly elected parliament to sit at Ankara, it adopted so much of his program that the British fully occupied Istanbul "to protect" the sultan. Kemal then called for the convening of an extraordinary Grand National Assembly. It met on April 23, 1920, at Ankara, recognized the prisoner-like status of the sultan, and declared that there was "no power superior to the Grand National Assembly." Kemal became its president and a council of state was elected to serve as the executive arm of the Ankara government, as it was called.

The Grand National Assembly, however, continued to debate whether it was a permanent or provisional government until January 30, 1921, when it passed ten fundamental articles of government as amendments to the Ottoman constitution of 1876. These articles established the assembly as a permanent institution, to be elected every two years. They also served as the basis of government until April 20, 1924, when a new constitution was adopted. Meanwhile, a second assembly was elected in April 1923, giving Kemal and his cohorts at the reopening of the

Lausanne Conference a strong mandate in their uncompromising stand for full financial, economic, and administrative independence. It was this second assembly in Ankara—something akin to a rump parliament—that proclaimed the republic and later adopted the constitution.

Meanwhile, Kemal's Association for the Defense of Rights in Europe and Anatolia changed into the People's party (*Halk Firkasi*) in 1922 and then in 1923 to the Republican People's party (*Cumhuriyet Halk Firkasi*). Kemal as president of the People's party used frequent party caucuses for debate and formulation of policy; at these meetings, often continuing through the night, actual government policy decisions were made. While the Greek war was in progress goals were easy to determine, but after the Mudanya armistice Kemal used every wile and force at his command to carry through his points. When Ismet found Lord Curzon intractable at Lausanne, many Anatolian leaders of the party counseled direct military action against the British in Istanbul as the best solution. This step, which would have been highly successful initially, was skillfully countered by Kemal, who understood how the Allies would eventually react.

Before the constitution was adopted, a fundamental change had been made in the religio-political structure of the state. When Mehmed VI left Istanbul for Malta in 1922, the Grand National Assembly declared the caliphate vacant and elected to that office Abdul Mejid, who had never masked his sympathy for the nationalist cause. Certainly, Kemal and his associates did not want to shock the conservative majority of Turks by destroying the caliphate precipitously. However, the anomaly of a caliph without temporal power was not clearly understood; Kemal proposed that the caliphate be abolished and in March 1924 the Assembly did so. In addition, the Ottoman family was banished from Turkey, and the Sacred Law courts were abolished. The functions of the ministries governing pious foundations were transferred to a newly created presidency of religious affairs.

Until the spring of 1924, the Turkish government followed the provisions of the Ottoman constitution of 1876 except where it had been modified. The widely anticipated Constitution of the Republic was promulgated on April 20, 1924. Drawn up without too much controversy, it stated that sovereignty resided in the Turkish nation, whose representative was the Grand National Assembly. It declared all Turks equal before the law and forbade special privileges for groups or individuals. A Turk was defined as anyone who is a citizen of the Turkish Republic, without distinction as to ethnicity or creed. Freedom of speech, thought, press, and travel were guaranteed. The religion of the state was declared to be Islam; the language, Turkish; and the seat of government, Ankara.

The government established by the constitution was in form a democracy but was in fact, at that time and for twenty years to follow, a one-party government controlled by Kemal and his close political associates. The Grand National Assembly was elected for a four-year term by universal male suffrage. (Women received the vote in 1934.) The president of the republic was elected by the Assembly from its membership for a similar term. The president appointed the prime minister, who selected his cabinet from the deputies with the approval of the president and consent of the Assembly. Until 1945, the machinery of government was almost entirely in the hands of the Republican People's party. Candidates for election as deputies from the various districts to the Grand National Assembly were nominated by that party, and only one slate of names was presented to voters. Party caucuses determined who ran for which office and from which province. Debates in the Grand National Assembly were largely perfunctory. Kemal made the final decisions.

Mustafa Kemal was correctly labeled a dictator: he determined high policy, selected high officials of state, and forced his will upon the party and nation. But in most matters affecting the nation and the public at large, he was careful to prepare the people by skillfully organized speeches before action was taken. Kemal was convinced that he knew what was best for the Turkish people and also knew the best way to obtain it. His abiding ambition was for the Turkish people, not for himself. In this way he was a benevolent dictator and extremely popular.

Reforms touched every aspect of life and society in Turkey in the 1920s and 1930s. In the earlier period change was rapid and followed no clear pattern of planned or coordinated development. Perhaps sensing the difficulty of keeping in mind the sequence of these reforms, Kemal terminated the uncoordinated and rather haphazard course of modernization in 1931. Terming the entire program "Kemalism," he defined his reforms along six broad classifications. These six became the party's campaign platform for the elections of 1935 and were adopted as the basic principles of the new Turkish nation when they were incorporated into the constitution by amendment in 1937. They were: republicanism, secularism, populism, nationalism, statism, and reformism.

Article 1 of the constitution reads: *The Turkish State is a Republic.* Kemal could have made himself king or sultan. He insisted upon a republic, though, because it was more Western and more democratic and because he believed it suited Turkey. But conservative elements, clients of the Ottoman family, the religious hierarchy, and the devout clung to the old order.

Abolishing the caliphate and closing the Shariah courts did not change the basis of law in Turkey. Law reforms in the nineteenth century had Westernized the commercial and criminal laws, but civil law and legal procedures were still tied to Sacred Law. In the autumn of 1925, a new law school opened in Ankara to instruct lawyers and judges in the fundamentals of Western laws. Then, early in 1926, the Grand National Assembly adopted the new Civil Code and Debts Law, based on Swiss law; the new Penal Code, taken from Italian law; and the new Commercial Code, which was a modification of the German Code. With new codes of a Western and secular nature thoroughly installed, the old regime became such an outmoded way of life that any departure from the republic was unthinkable.

SECULARIZATION

The second most important reform movement was the secularization of the state and society. Islam pervaded all aspects of life in Turkey, and Kemal and many leaders subscribed to the theory, learned from their contacts with the West, that Islam's hold upon society retarded development and created the difference between West and East. Friday, the Muslim holy day, was made a compulsory day of rest throughout the land in 1924, in part to give the day another emphasis. In 1925 Sufi orders were forbidden, and their tekkes, holy shrines, and mausoleums were closed. Most startling of all in that year was the law forbidding men to wear the fez and ordering all headgear to have a brim or a visor. Earlier, Kemal was photographed in a straw Panama, and the armed services were outfitted in Western-style military caps. The fez was considered a Muslim symbol, although it came from Europe at the time of Mahmud II. The veil was never outlawed, but its use was discouraged in every possible way.

The Muslim calendar for legal, official, and everyday use was abandoned and replaced by the Western Gregorian calendar. Everywhere the Muslim year of 1342 became 1926, although the Muslim calendar was still employed in calculating Ramadan, the month of fasting, and all other religious holidays.

A far-reaching effect of Western law was the official end of polygamy and the new status of women. Since not many men had been able to afford more than one wife, the prohibition against polygamy was not very drastic. More important were equal rights of divorce, joint custody of children, and equality in inheritance and in courtroom testimony. However, the husband was still considered the head of the family in law, and many of the legal changes were ignored or opposed, especially in the countryside, while they began to take effect at first primarily in the cities.

Progress in secularization went so far that in 1928 the constitution was amended, removing the statement that Turkey is an Islamic state and providing that government officials, on being inducted into office, would swear on their honor rather than before God to fulfill their duties. Later, in 1935, the day of rest was changed to Sunday, and the *vikend* (weekend) was established by law from Saturday at 1:00 P.M. to Sunday midnight.

Kemal probably was an atheist, but many about him were sincerely religious. Yet, all deemphasized the place of religion in national life. Fewer individuals observed religious days; in Istanbul and Ankara many persons paid no attention to Ramadan and many children were not taught their prayers. Religious instruction was gradually removed from public and private schools. The faculty of theology at the University of Istanbul enrolled so few that it was consolidated in 1933 with the department of literature. By 1939 Turkey was a secular state, as typical in this respect as France, Germany, or the United States.

POPULISM

In the Ottoman Empire the capitulations and the Millet system gave special privileges to foreigners and to many religious minorities. In the republic, however, Article 69 of the constitution stated that all Turks are equal before the law and that all "privileges of whatever description claimed by groups, classes, families, and individuals are abolished and forbidden." It was this idea that Kemal incorporated in the word "populism."

Early Turkish society was democratic in character; certain aspects of ghazi and akhi life were almost communal. Peasant villages in Anatolia still retained many of these traits. The new, free republic of Turkey was won by these peasants, and to them the new Turkish society was dedicated. Tax burdens upon them had always been inordinately heavy, so Kemal in an early speech promised them relief on this score in payment for their efforts in the national struggle. The Grand National Assembly in 1925 abolished the tithe upon their lands, and taxes upon agriculture were lightened in order to stimulate greater production.

In the 1930s world prices for Turkish exports decreased as the Great Depression also hurt Turkish commerce. Taxes on peasants effectively rose once again, as unemployment in the cities increased. Life expectancy rose, and land was still available for new agricultural expansion.

Primary education in government-supervised schools became obligatory, as free and universal education was established as another expression of populism. In conformity with the constitutional law for universal education, schools were built by the thousands during this era of Turkish history. Emphasis at first was placed upon teacher training schools, since a lack of teachers handicapped the program's success. Each village was required to have a primary school of five grades. Secondary schools were constructed in the towns to prepare students for various vocations and for entrance to *lycées*, which were the equivalent of American senior high schools and junior colleges. Beyond the *lycée* was the University of Istanbul and, later, Ankara University and specialized schools.

With the illiteracy rate at an estimated 80 percent or more, the ability to read became a privilege that Kemal desired for all. The Arabic script was never satisfactory for the Turkish language, in which vowels not present in Arabic play an important part in word formation. Writing and spelling were arduous exercises, and sometimes to read a specific passage was difficult unless one had some idea of what had been written. In 1928, the Grand National Assembly adopted a new, strictly phonetic Turkish alphabet based on Latin characters; it became compulsory January 1, 1929, and after that date all public signs, newspapers, books, etc., were in the new script. The work involved in the changeover was staggering. New textbooks had to be printed for every subject; in the autumn of 1928 schools opened several weeks late because books were unavailable. The literate had to learn to read and write all over again, and the heritage of the past, written using the old alphabet, gradually became unavailable to the young, who knew only the Latin letters. Kemal and members of the Grand National Assembly traveled about the country giving public reading lessons in the Latin characters. Changing headgear was relatively easy in comparison to the alphabet transition. But the campaign was effective. Millions learned to read within the next decade, as the illiteracy rate was slowly reduced. Newspapers multiplied, typewriters became less complex, and a modern national life embracing a majority of the population was born.

NATIONALISM

The fourth point in the Kemalist program was the development of nationalism. The growth of nationalism in the nineteenth century was affected in the Ottoman Empire in diverse ways. Greeks, Serbs, Bulgarians, Armenians, and others were stirred toward independence. Nationalist wars of liberation followed, bringing massacres, atrocities, and devastation to Turks as well as to others. Turkish Ottomans, when they were touched by nationalism, often were waylaid by pan-Islamism, pan-Turanism, or a synthetic Ottoman nationalism. Kemal was a fiery Turkish patriot, proud of being a Turk. He set out in his program to make all Turks proud of their heritage.

Although all the reforms of the Kemalist regime were tinged with nationalism, none was more pointed than the new histories in the Latin alphabet for elementary and secondary schools. Though the books minimized the history of the Ottoman Turks, in order to forget the centuries after Suleiman I, they set out for the Turks a glorious and significant past. Sumerians and Hittites became Turks. Most non-Semites of Middle Eastern antiquity were claimed as Turks; indeed, all peoples who came from central Asia were classified as Turks. Since the Turkish word for man is *adam* and since Adam traditionally was the first man, it was popularly said that Adam was Turkish and, therefore, that all peoples are Turkish. Individuals who viewed these theories critically were berated, so most skeptics remained silent. Many Turks found genuine satisfaction in these theories, and they helped in generating a more dynamic Turkish national feeling.

For half a century Turkish literature and even newspaper Turkish had been filled with a heavy burden of words taken from Arabic. Since these words were not used in conversational Turkish, they made written Turkish unintelligible to the great majority. After the adoption of the new alphabet, the drive to free Turkish from an Arabic vocabulary and even to resurrect Turkish words from obsolescence made great headway. For a period of several years in the mid-1930s the government published every few weeks a list of new Turkish words and their old equivalents. Since all government publications used the new words and since communications to the government containing old words were often ignored, business concerns and foreign organizations frequently employed someone to keep up with the rapid language changes. As a result, Turkish perhaps lost the richness and variety of the Arabic language, but an immeasurable gain came in giving Turks a written language closely resembling their vernacular.

One of the more dramatic and publicized events in Kemal's program of Turkish nationalism was the forced adoption and use of family names. Only a few of the old Turkish families had names, and many did not use them. The Grand National Assembly gave to Kemal the name of *Atatürk* (Father of the Turks); Inönü, to Ismet in honor of his two victories there; and other appropriate names to party leaders. The head of each family went to precinct police headquarters and selected the family name from a list of approved Turkish words and names, or a combination of these. No one else in that district could take that name. Most names had a meaning, such as Biyiklioğlu (son of the man with a mustache), Üstündağ (mountaintop), and Kirkağaçlioğlu (son of the man with forty trees).

At times nationalism seemed to engulf the Turks, and certainly it made them extremely sensitive even to objective and friendly criticism. Whether Atatürk believed in all the theories he supported is debatable, but he certainly believed in the necessity of not tolerating public debate about them. In any case they were efficacious, and Atatürk's slogan, "Turkey for the Turks and the Turks for Turkey," was proudly accepted by the nation.

STATISM

At Lausanne the most bitter wrangling had been over the capitulations and implications of economic and judicial imperialism. Turkish victory in these presaged the law reforms and the establishment of better court procedures. Economic independence was compromised by the promise not to tamper with the tariff for five years. Kemal's advisers desired to develop the economic resources of Turkey and to inaugurate industrialization without too much foreign influence or participation. The unfortunate experience that the Ottoman Empire had suffered from foreign loans, capital, and concessions conditioned Kemal against any repetition for the republic. His idea was that Turkey would develop her own resources and industrialize behind a strong protective tariff that could become effective in 1929. Within a short time the Turks discovered that imports and exports could be more easily regulated through exchange control than by tariffs and quotas and that a managed economy could be introduced.

With the depression, Turkey's exports dropped; in consequence there was a tightening on import permits. When, therefore, Nazi Germany proposed an attractive compensation trade agreement, the Turks readily accepted. Trade with Germany boomed, and in 1936 over 50 percent of Turkey's exports went to Germany. When World War II broke out, Turkey had clearing agreements with twenty countries and had just entered into a reciprocal trade agreement with the United States.

Kemal understood that agriculture was the principal occupation and resource of his nation and he strove to increase the output. He established a model farm near Ankara, where the latest techniques, modern machinery, and implements were demonstrated for all to see. Activities of the Bank of Agriculture, founded by the Ottomans in 1889, were greatly expanded; its loan service to small farmers was increased, and credit cooperatives were authorized in 1929. Agricultural prices began to be supported by the government in 1932, and in 1933 the Higher Agricultural School was opened in Ankara, later to become a part of Ankara University. With all these aids Turkish farmers improved their national position greatly under the Kemalists, even in the face of a worldwide depression in agricultural prices. When World War II broke out, they were relatively prosperous.

Kemal felt that advances in industry moved too slowly, in contrast to the progress in agriculture. Too few people had any industrial know-how, and those with capital tended to follow the traditional practice of investing in buildings or land. Private industry lagged. On the other hand, government monopolies in matches, tobacco and cigarettes, alcohol, and salt and the government acquisition and operation of railroads, harbor facilities, electric utilities, and coastwise steamers were highly successful. Expansion programs were effective, and railroad lines were extended in several areas. From state monopolies and public works Kemal turned to state enterprises; thus, in 1933 the government inaugurated a Five-Year Plan for the development of industry, and the Sümer (Sumerian) Bank was created to own and operate such enterprises. A score of factories were built to produce textiles, paper, glass, sugar, and steel.

In Turkey this policy of state enterprises, created and managed by the government, was called "statism" and gave rise to some debate. Some branded the course as a step toward communism, while others claimed it was a kind of autarchy as preached by Hitler and Mussolini and thus linked Atatürk with the two dictators. Still a third group supported it strongly, asserting that it was a type of state capitalism that would develop the nation without creating individuals of great power and wealth such as Rockefeller, Carnegie, Morgan, and Ford. Different views were held even in high places in the Republican People's party. And in 1937 when Ismet Inönü resigned as prime minister and was replaced by Celal Bayar, the minister of economy, a rumor circulated that Atatürk had brought in the latter because he was a more enthusiastic believer in statism.

CONTINUING REFORM

The sixth and final arrow on the shield of Kemalism stood for reformism. By this Atatürk meant opposition to blind conservatism and a rigid adherence to the status quo. He did not believe in change for change's sake, but he knew all too well how reformers grow old and conservative, especially when they hold responsible government posts. Kemal wanted his revolution to evolve and expand, as a continuing process. The program with respect to women fell into this category. He wished more than just a change in their legal status and costume. He compelled wives of cabinet ministers to learn to dance; he encouraged girls to become actresses and airplane pilots; and he opened the way for women to become lawyers, doctors, bankers, and public officials. Of 399 members elected to the Grand National Assembly in 1935, 18 were women. About one-third of all students were female.

In cultural matters, the Ottoman past was to be superseded by European styles and usages. Traditional art music was opposed, and in 1936 in Ankara a new conservatory for actors, ballet dancers, opera singers, and musicians was opened. Both Turkish folk music and Western classical and popular music were encouraged—including the tango and Charleston! Atatürk secured the services of refugees from central Europe who were experts in such fields as medicine and archaeology. Novels and poetry became extremely diverse in style and substance; many writers discussed political themes and the new reforms of the republic. Atatürk personally encouraged touring theatrical groups whose plays were intended to spread new values and ideas, and he dictated changes to some of the plays. The old religious opposition to sculpture was abandoned, and idealized and heroic monuments were erected.

Turkish architects initially continued a revival of Ottoman styles, but in the 1930s the government employed foreign, especially German, architects whose buildings were of the new, stark, international Bauhaus style. Young Turkish architects soon adopted this new approach.

Another important change was in regard to sports. Early Ottomans were keen sports enthusiasts and had competitions in archery, polo, horse racing, wrestling, and many other sports. In the eighteenth century there was a complete reversal; physical exertion was looked upon as degrading and sports participation as undignified. Before Atatürk died in 1938 every city had several sports clubs. Turkey sent entries to the Olympics and to the Balkan Games. And soccer (*futbol*) became the new national sport, which boys and girls everywhere played with great enthusiasm.

The old Ottoman government was very corrupt. Bribes and tips were widespread, and everyone knew that often the magnitude of the service or permission governed the size of the bribe. Kemal was ruthless in his treatment of this custom; and although it did not disappear entirely, anyone in the government found guilty of it was speedily dismissed and prosecuted. When it was intimated that one of Kemal's secretaries of long service accepted a silver cigarette case for some service rendered, he was suddenly appointed ambassador to a foreign capital and soon thereafter recalled and dismissed.

One of the most fruitful reforms had to do with the idea of the role of destiny in human affairs. If some unpleasant circumstance developed or an unfortunate event occurred, the natural reaction was to shrug the shoulders and blame it on God and fate. Through persistent education and practical demonstrations in sanitation, orderly government, and mental attitudes, people's attitudes changed so that they accepted responsibility for their destiny, and did not blame supernatural forces.

TURKISH POLITICS

Even though there was only one political party under Kemal through most of this period, and all politicians supported the six points of Kemalism, it should not be assumed that there was no politics in Turkey. The Progressive party was organized by members of the nationalist movement in opposition to Kemal. Some were ultraconservatives who wished to restore the sultan-caliph; some were personally ambitious; and others were genuine liberal democrats who looked askance upon Kemal's forceful and dictatorial methods and hoped for true democratic procedures.

Ismet Pasha, the prime minister, pushed through a law for the maintenance of order under which a Tribunal of Independence was set up. The Progressive party was disbanded. Some opponents of the reforms and of Atatürk, many of whom were also former leaders of the Committee of Union and Progress, were tried as enemies of the state and executed. Others were exiled. Newspapers were closed, and editors such as the illustrious Ahmet Emin were exiled for varying lengths of time. The liberal Halidé Edib and her husband, Dr. Adnan Adivar, left Turkey and lived in various places in Europe until the exile laws were repealed and political amnesty was declared in 1938 to all, even to Ottoman royalty. A revolt among Kurds and religious conservatives was suppressed in 1925.

At a congress of the Republic People's party in 1927 Kemal made a historic six-day speech, reviewing in detail the events of 1918 to 1927. Feeling more secure, Kemalists withdrew the laws for the maintenance of order in 1929; the following spring Kemal invited Fethi Bey, then ambassador to France, to return and form an opposition party. The Liberal party, as it was called, drew to its support many disgruntled persons from Istanbul and Izmir, where the worldwide depression and new tariffs were affecting commerce adversely. The Liberals called for more free enterprise and less statism, claiming that the Republicans were too slow in improving the national economy. They were successful enough to frighten the Republicans, and when a few political rallies ended in disorderly fights, Kemal judged that the time had not yet arrived when Turkey might have more than one party. Fethi's party was disbanded in 1930. The quadrennial elections, held in 1931, reaffirmed the Republican party's hold on the nation, as Kemal was elected to a third term.

In October 1937 Ismet Inönü resigned again as prime minister, to be replaced by Celal Bayar. Although Kemal and Ismet had worked together for seventeen years, basically they were of very different temperaments. Their mutual belief in party discipline, strong public authority, and central control kept them together. But differences in foreign affairs relating to Italy in the Mediterranean and France in Syria led to the break.

Atatürk died November 10, 1938. Excessive drinking and a profligate personal life eventually undermined his iron constitution. His death was a shock to the nation, and the emotional wave it unleashed demonstrated the love and devotion that he had won from the Turkish people. Inönü was elected president the following day, and the Republican People's party carried on with only a slight break. Bayar soon stepped down from the prime ministership, and more conservative steps were taken in government practices and directions. A new Grand National Assembly was elected in 1939, and Inönü became president again for a full four-year term. Europe and the world were entering into the stages preparatory to World War II. Inönü was faced with this as well as with additional problems of Turkish development.

INTERNATIONAL AFFAIRS

The remarkable internal progress of Turkey was paralleled by success and peace in the foreign field. The Treaty of Lausanne left the undetermined frontier with Iraq to be settled directly with Great Britain as trustee for Iraq. Negotiations dragged on and reached a highly flammable point in 1925. Kemal became convinced, with considerable justification, that Britain was fomenting Kurdish revolts in the southeast. To stir the Kurdish tribes was not difficult; the Mosul province, the area in dispute, had a large Kurdish population whose leaders wanted an independent Kurdistan. Moreover, Kurds within Turkey resisted the centralization process and secularization program of the nationalists. On several occasions war over Mosul was debated in party caucuses in Ankara, but peace prevailed. In 1926, a treaty was signed and ratified by England and Turkey, giving Mosul to Iraq. The treaty did, however, give Turkey 10 percent of all oil royalties paid by the concessionaire to Iraq for the following twenty-five years. Turkey promptly settled for a cash payment of £500,000 from Iraq.

Relations with Greece after the exchange of populations improved rapidly. Venizelos made a state visit to Turkey and was received with much fanfare in Istanbul and Ankara. In 1934 the Balkan Pact or Entente was signed, guaranteeing all frontiers and pledging collective security for the Balkans. However, Bulgaria and Albania refused to adhere, because other members declined to discuss minority questions or territorial revision.

In 1932 Turkey was admitted to membership in the League of Nations, and in 1934 was elected to a seat on the Council. For a small nation Turkey took an active part in League affairs. She cooperated with League efforts to control illicit traffic in narcotics and maintain collective security.

Almost immediately after Italy's attack upon Ethiopia Turkey entered into diplomatic action for changing the demilitarized status of the Straits. The Lausanne signatories met at Montreux, where on July 20, 1936, Bulgaria, France, Great Britain, Japan, Rumania, Turkey, and the U.S.S.R. signed a convention governing the Straits. Because of Turkey's actions at the League regarding sanctions against Italy in her Ethiopian adventure, Italy refused to sign the convention until 1938.

Britain went to the conference with the intention of giving Turkey the right to fortify the Straits and administer the Straits regime. It was also the British intention, however, to keep the Straits relatively open to warships when Turkey was a nonbelligerent, thus maintaining an open channel for British naval forces to press upon Russia. The U.S.S.R. attended the conference to give Turkey full sovereignty over the Straits with a proviso limiting very markedly the entry of foreign warships into the Black Sea. Through the centuries Russia had desired the Straits open when she felt strong and closed when she felt weak; in 1936 she felt weak. At first the Turkish negotiators at Montreux followed the Soviet line, with every intention of swinging more toward British views at the propitious moment as a necessary compromise. In this way Turkey might come out victorious without offending any power too greatly. That Turkish policy succeeded cannot be doubted, as Turkey gained the right to erect fortifications and full sovereignty over the Straits. When he received news of the agreement at Montreux, Atatürk in full dress attire was seen on the sands in front of his villa near the Sea of Marmara doing handsprings and cartwheels in full celebration of his triumph. Turkey thus gained a heightened sense of international security in a period of growing distrust of collective security and nonaggression pacts.

Two other notable achievements in international affairs followed. In 1937 Turkey entered into the Saadabad Pact with Iran, Iraq, and Afghanistan in much the same fashion as she had in the earlier Balkan Pact. It was Turkey's attempt to bridge the gap between Asia and Europe and maintain friendly relations with her neighbors on both continents.

Turkey's most troublesome frontier was to the south with Syria. In obtaining the mandate for Syria, France promised to give Alexandretta, where more than 90,000 Turks resided, a separate administration. When in 1936 France was apparently preparing to give Syria independence, Turkey was concerned about the future of Turks in Alexandretta. In July 1938, a Turko-French condominium for Alexandretta was established, and later that year the population gave pro-Turks 22 seats out of 40 in the provincial assembly. Voting themselves autonomy, the deputies proclaimed the Republic of Hatay and immediately sought a union with Turkey. France, not without bitter protests from the Arabs of Syria, acquiesced in this action; Hatay was annexed to Turkey in June 1939. This territorial acquisition was the only exception to a general Turkish policy of preserving the status quo and peace with its neighbors.

In 1939, as maneuvering among the powers in the diplomatic prelude to World War II became more tense, Turkey's international position grew in importance. Hitler sent Franz von Papen as ambassador to Ankara to cement German relations. Britain and France, however, secured a military alliance and nonaggression pact. After the Mosul agreement relations with England improved, and when Edward VIII and Mrs. Simpson were cruising in the Mediterranean on the king's yacht in the summer of 1936, a rapprochement between Atatürk and England was consummated in the bar of the Park Hotel in Istanbul. In May 1939 a "declaration of mutual guarantee" was made that was generally recognized as a veiled alliance. At the same time military items and heavy industrial goods were validated for purchase through credit agreements. Meanwhile, in connection with the annexation of Hatay, Turkey signed a nonaggression pact with France and obtained an arms credit. Thus, in World War II Turkish leaders found themselves in a neutral position between Germany and the West, yet more committed and more friendly to England and France.

REFERENCES

Volumes already cited and valuable for this chapter are found in Chapters 25, 26, 30, and 31.

Abadan-Unat, Nermin, ed. *Women in Turkish Society.* Leiden: Brill, 1981.

Allen, Henry E. *The Turkish Transformation: A Study in Social and Religious Development.* Chicago: University of Chicago Press, 1935.

Armstrong, Harold C. *Grey Wolf, Mustafa Kemal: An Intimate Study of a Dictator.* London: Barker, 1932. Not always flattering, yet sympathetic.

Beck, Peter J. "'A Tedious and Perilous Controversy': Britain and the Settlement of the Mosul Dispute, 1918–1926." *Middle Eastern Studies* 17 (1981): 256–276. Valuable for British diplomacy.

Bisbee, Eleanor. *The New Turks: Pioneers of the Republic, 1920–1950.* Philadelphia: University of Pennsylvania Press, 1951. A spirited study of the many changes in Turkey in the latter part of the 1930s and during the 1940s.

Edib (Adivar), Halidé. *Conflict of East and West in Turkey.* 2d ed. Lahore: M. Ashraf, 1935. A personal account of the Revolution.

————. *Turkey Faces West; A Turkish View of Recent Changes and Their Origin.* New Haven, Conn.: Yale University Press, 1930. An interesting essay on why Turkey turned toward the West rather than toward Russia.

Hale, William. *The Political and Economic Development of Modern Turkey.* London: Croom Helm, 1981. A useful analysis, concentrating on the period since 1960.

Heper, Metin. *The State Tradition in Turkey.* North Humberside, Eng.: Eothen Press, 1985. An essay on state ideology and political thought.

Holod, Renata, and Ahmet Evin, eds. *Modern Turkish Architecture.* Philadelphia: University of Pennsylvania Press, 1984. Excellent chapters by various authors on twentieth-century Turkish architecture.

Kazancıgıl, Ali, and Ergun Özbüdün, eds. *Atatürk: Founder of a Modern State*. London: C. Hurst and Co., 1981. One of several works published on the occasion of the centenary of Atatürk's birth, this book is especially notable for comparisons by authors coming from numerous countries.

Keyder, Çağlar. *The Definition of a Peripheral Economy: Turkey, 1923–1929*. Cambridge: Cambridge University Press, 1981. An important example of the new light that can be cast on Turkish history by the "dependency school" scholars who are becoming increasingly widespread in Turkey.

Kinross, Lord (Patrick Balfour). *Ataturk: A Biography of Mustafa Kemal, Father of Modern Turkey*. New York: Morrow, 1965. Full and well-documented from Turkish sources; a lengthy and excellent biography.

Landau, Jacob M., ed. *Atatürk and the Modernization of Turkey*. Boulder, Colo.: Westview, 1984. Seventeen chapters by various authors; the discussions of culture are particularly important.

McCarthy, Justin. "Foundations of the Turkish Republic: Social and Economic Change." *Middle Eastern Studies* 19 (1983): 139–151. This study shows in a brilliant way the changes among the populace that permitted acceptance of radical change.

Renda, Günsel, and C. Max Kortepeter, eds. *The Transformation of Turkish Culture: The Atatürk Legacy*. Princeton, N.J.: Kingston Press, 1986. Discusses the arts and culture during and after Atatürk's days.

Smith, Elaine Diana. *Turkey: Origins of the Kemalist Movement and the Government of the Grand National Assembly (1919–1923)*. Washington, D.C.: The author, 1959. The best account of this period.

Thomas, Lewis V., and Richard N. Frye. *The United States and Turkey and Iran*. Cambridge, Mass.: Harvard University Press, 1951. A concise and accurate analysis of American interests in these two countries.

Trask, Roger R. *The United States Response to Turkish Nationalism and Reform, 1914–1939*. Minneapolis: University of Minnesota Press, 1971. Shows the evolution of United States attitudes from misinformed hostility to benevolent toleration to warm understanding.

Webster, Donald Everett. *The Turkey of Atatürk: Social Process in the Turkish Reformation*. Philadelphia, Pa.: American Academy of Political & Social Science, 1939. A detailed study of political and sociological developments in Turkey to 1938.

Weiker, Walter F. *Political Tutelage and Democracy in Turkey: The Free Party and Its Aftermath*. Leiden: Brill, 1973. The period of "tutelage" was from 1923 to 1946, when there was but a single political party responsible for both modernization and democracy.

Yalman, Ahmed Emin. *Turkey in My Time*. Norman: University of Oklahoma Press, 1956. The autobiography of Turkey's outstanding newspaper editor.

33

The Fertile Crescent Under the Mandate System: Lebanon, Syria, and Iraq

FRENCH OCCUPATION OF LEBANON AND SYRIA

When Prince Faysal galloped at the head of his cavalry into Damascus on October 3, 1918, aspirations for a new Arab nation seemed assured of fulfillment. Some political and intellectual leaders were deeply stirred by the thought of a modern state in which Arab peoples might work and achieve the regeneration of their culture and society in a modern independent setting. From the sincere-sounding promises and public statements made by Allied officials Arabs anticipated the creation of an Arab national state. On the horizon, to be sure, were the Balfour Declaration and the Sykes-Picot Agreement that seemed to indicate imperialist plans by the British and the French.

Faysal and his supporters advanced northward pressing upon Aleppo, while the British proceeded along the coast to Alexandretta. During 1919 the British controlled the coastal regions of Syria, and Arabs held the interior. Since the Arabs inhabited that area they found it rather incongruous that they were supposedly occupying enemy territory.

Throughout 1919 little headway toward a settlement satisfactory to Arab nationalists developed. The Syrian economy was in a state of near collapse, although the British subsidy to Faysal's government did keep it afloat financially. The Anglo-French agreement in September was a crushing blow, as it cut off Palestine and provided for a French military occupation of Syria. By December, General Gouraud and French troops replaced the British in Beirut and along the Syrian littoral. Faysal's Arabs held the interior. The General Syrian Congress, composed of members elected and appointed from all parts of Syria, including Palestine, met in

Damascus in July and after considerable discussion passed resolutions that requested independence for Syria, including Palestine, with Faysal as king, independence for Iraq with Abd Allah as king, repudiation of the Sykes-Picot Agreement and the Balfour Declaration, and rejection of the mandate idea. Another resolution called for rejection of assistance from France in any form. In many ways actions of the Syrian congress resembled and paralleled those of the Kemalist nationalists, who at that moment were meeting in Ankara.

Obtaining no redress, the General Syrian Congress declared on March 8, 1920, the independence of Syria, including Palestine and Lebanon, as a constitutional monarchy under Faysal. The French declined to recognize the announcement; the meeting of the Allied supreme council at San Remo answered the Syrian action by acknowledging, informally yet firmly, a French mandate over Syria and Lebanon and separation of Palestine under the British. Many members of the old Syrian political elite now viewed Faysal and the Arab nationalists as incompetent newcomers.

Faysal, whose government was nearly bankrupt, was caught between the superior force of the Allies and the unrealistic national patriotism of the new Arab political elite. Gouraud sent Faysal an ultimatum (July 14, 1920), demanding within four days unqualified acceptance of the French mandate. In the face of a French army advancing from Beirut to occupy Damascus, Faysal telegraphed his agreement. Obviously, the French did not foresee that the ultimatum would be accepted, as new conditions were added and the march proceeded. Faysal ordered the disbanding of the Arab army, but isolated groups opened fire on the French. A bloody engagement occurred at Maysalun Pass, and accompanied by airplanes, tanks, and the rattle of machine-gun fire General Gouraud captured Damascus on July 25. Faysal left within a few days, and the French occupied the whole province of Syria in rapid order.

Although full legal title to the mandate did not materialize until the Treaty of Lausanne in 1923, the actions of 1920 confirmed French possession. Detailed French administration began at once. General Gouraud, as high commissioner, issued a decree (September 1, 1920) dividing the mandate for Syria and Lebanon into four separate districts: greater Lebanon; Aleppo, including Alexandretta; Latakia; and Damascus. The latter comprised the Jabal Druze area in the south and all remaining interior regions. The plan seemed to be: divide and rule.

MANDATE FOR LEBANON

The day before the mandate was splintered General Gouraud issued a decree that added the city of Beirut, coastal regions to the north and south including Tripoli, Sidon, and Tyre, and the Biqa Valley to the old sanjak of Lebanon to form a new greater Lebanon. Since 1861 the sanjak had had an autonomous political existence under an elected central administrative assembly selected according to religious community. By extending the area of Lebanon in response to pleas from many Lebanese Maronite Christians, the French increased the economic viability of the country but also reduced the preponderance of the Maronite sect by changing population proportions, increasing Sunnite Muslims so that the Christians held only a slight overall majority.

In the new regime for a larger Lebanon, above the governor of Lebanon stood the high commissioner, who had a government of his own to assist him. Separated into departments such as security, education, and public works, this administration was manned by Frenchmen and French colonials who served as the authority to which the Lebanese government looked. A most important group under the high commissioner was that of the information officers, who served in every district of Lebanon, reported developments to the high commissioner, exercised unlimited influence over local affairs, and stood as "tutors" to prepare the country and its people for full independence.

Certain functions of government such as customs, posts, telegraph, railways, public utilities, currency, and local troop levies were not divided locally by the four Syrian and Lebanese administrative units. And the high commissioner reserved for his own government full supervision of these "common interests." Income from the central operations paid common expenses, and the balance was apportioned among the four state units, always with bickering and dissatisfaction.

The mandate system in theory allowed for two parallel governments, one held by the mandatory power and one local, where the French would instruct the Lebanese. In actual practice this system allowed for a fully determined colonialism to operate more or less unmolested behind a semblance of local self-government.

FRENCH IMPERIALISM IN LEBANON

French imperialism manifested itself in Lebanon in many ways. In a number of districts martial law was established, and throughout the mandate period the French were quick to decree its use. The press was muzzled effectively; numerous papers accepted French subsidies and published accounts of all events in a version favorable to French interests. French investors largely owned and operated the railways, public utilities, and banks of Lebanon; the entire fiscal and economic policy was initiated by the French. New concessions and general contracts granted by the Lebanese government went to French concerns or to Lebanese firms with strong French connections. The new Lebanese currency was tied to the French franc, which had the disadvantage of fluctuating with depreciating French currency—the fall of the franc played an important role in uprisings in Syria and Lebanon in 1925.

French imperialists spoke of their "civilizing mission," a phrase that expressed the view that an area, region, or people would be permanently and indissolubly linked to France if French language and culture flourished in their midst. The chief work was accomplished through education and the use of French as a second language. French schools of primary, secondary, and *lycée* rank were opened in many communities, and these always obtained more funds and aid than schools in which Arabic or some other language prevailed. All schools taught French, and textbooks for history, social sciences, literature, and the humanities had a French coloration on every page. French newspapers were encouraged, and

French was an official language in the courts, government offices, contracts, and every walk of life.

There were, however, many favorable aspects of French rule, a concrete indication of which was the higher standard of living and growth of the population. Schools improved and increased in number; food and clothing became more plentiful; roads were built; motorcars and transport became available; doctors were trained; disease was controlled; and sanitation and health standards were greatly raised. Striking changes came in the city of Beirut, but developments were widespread across the state. Emigration declined, as life in Lebanon grew more attractive.

LOCAL LEBANESE GOVERNMENT

In Lebanon, as conditions of life flourished, the desire for independence and true self-government spread. In 1922 a representative council was elected and began meeting. General Weygand, the second high commissioner, instituted a Lebanese council of state and won Lebanese confidence and affection by his intelligent and judicious decisions. His sudden replacement in January 1925 by General Sarrail altered the peaceful developments almost immediately. Sarrail's arrogant manners, unwise tactics, anticlericalism, and inopportune appointments fomented quarrels with the Maronite Church, the Druzes, and many Lebanese leaders. One example was his appointing an unpopular Frenchman as governor of Lebanon after first stating he intended to name a native Lebanese.

When the general uprisings of 1925, provoked by General Sarrail, refused to burn themselves out, the general was recalled and replaced by Henri de Jouvenel. He called upon the representative council to draft a constitution that would recognize the mandate and French responsibility for Lebanon's foreign affairs and give the high commissioner veto power and the right to dismiss the executive head of the state and to dissolve the legislature. Beyond those restrictions de Jouvenel readily surrendered to the Lebanese authority over their own affairs. On May 23, 1926, the Lebanese Republic was proclaimed. Charles Dabbas, an Orthodox Christian, was chosen president by the assembly, which consisted of the old representative council and a new senate of twelve appointed by the high commissioner in accordance with the constitution.

No major political problem arose until the acute world economic crisis and its repercussions on trade, unemployment, and finance in Beirut caused the suspension of the constitution in 1932. A new constitution in 1934 called for the power of the assembly to be restricted, and the sectarian basis of election and membership in previous assemblies was ignored. Political life in Lebanon maintained an uneasy calm, until disturbances in 1936 in Syria forced France to examine her position in her mandates and negotiate a treaty with Syria.

The sheer weight of French military forces kept political agitation under wraps. Moreover, the French encouraged Maronite and other Christian leaders in Lebanon to feel that their security against a Muslim majority required full trust in

France and cooperation with French rule. However, British concessions to nationalism in Iraq and Egypt incited Syrian uprisings.

Syrian-French negotiations for a treaty forced similar actions in Lebanon. France could hardly be less generous to a more friendly Lebanon than she was to a recalcitrant Syria. Inhabitants in the Muslim parts of Lebanon, which the French had added to Lebanon in 1920, were divided in their sentiments and wishes in 1936. Many agitated for union with Syria. Others preferred the more stable political life and higher standard of living in Lebanon. The latter began openly to fraternize with Christian groups. Christians reciprocated by emphasizing their common interests, language, and general culture and by making much of the tacit arrangement by which the president of Lebanon was always a Christian and the prime minister always a Muslim. The Maronites wished to avoid the chances of greater Lebanon being dissolved, for they assumed that the old mountain Lebanon was too small to survive in the twentieth century.

Negotiations for the treaty were opened in October 1936 in Beirut; a twenty-five year Franco-Lebanese Treaty of Friendship and Alliance was signed November 13. The independence of Lebanon was recognized. Lebanon agreed to respect French interests and nationals and to maintain the established parity of the two currencies. French troops were permitted in Lebanon without restriction. In Beirut the Christians rejoiced, but many Muslims did not, as they hoped to reunite Lebanon with Syria. Despite some bloody fighting in the streets, the Lebanese assembly ratified the treaty in four days and independence seemed assured. In January 1937, the constitution of 1926 was restored, but difficulties loomed ahead. First, negotiations with Syria over economic matters and a settlement of "common interest" affairs dictated by the treaties with France hit a snag. Then, the Blum government fell in Paris; the insecure international position frightened French conservatives into refusing the treaties, which the conservatives believed would weaken France still further. Badly disappointed, the Lebanese marked time while World War II was brewing. Local political parties continued their maneuvers, the conflict centering upon local matters and more often than not on local personalities.

MANDATE FOR SYRIA

All other divisions of Syria created by the 1920 decree had a life during this period even more variegated than Lebanon's. When the decree was issued, native governments were ordered for Latakia, Aleppo, Damascus, and the Jabal Druze. With Alexandretta attached to Aleppo as a special province, Damascene Syrians felt that France was deliberately blocking them from the sea and never admitted the legality of the fragmentation. In June 1922, the independence of the Jabal Druze was proclaimed; the remaining states were grouped into a federation. In 1924, just before quitting Beirut, General Weygand laid the foundations for a treaty settlement with the mandate similar to that which the British gave Iraq. At the same time he terminated the federation by recognizing a separate government for the Alawis and amalgamating Aleppo into the state of Damascus, which then became Syria. Alexandretta, though a part of Syria, had its own administration.

Every action taken by General Sarrail seemed to be ill-conceived. In the Jabal Druze, an area already beginning to be densely populated, he touched off a bloody uprising by inviting the Druze leaders who opposed the local French administration to Damascus, where they were arrested. Revolt flared rapidly across the entire mandate, and severe fighting occurred in the Jabal Druze. In October 1925, Druze columns appeared at Damascus, and the French bombardment of that city caused damages estimated at several millions of dollars and considerable loss of life.

This tragedy brought Sarrail's immediate recall, and his successor called for elections in Latakia and Syria. The presidency was offered to Taj al-Din al-Hasani, chief judge of Damascus, but since his program was unacceptable to the French, he refused the post. Every succeeding Syrian request over the following two decades was based on Taj al-Din's platform. He demanded that Latakia and Jabal Druze be joined to Syria; that areas within Lebanon be allowed to choose between Syria and Lebanon; that Syria join the League of Nations; that French troops be evacuated; that a currency reform be enacted; and that Syria be entirely independent in her domestic affairs. Guerrilla warfare continued, and in May 1926 Damascus was again shelled. This time fighting was even more destructive and more savage than in the previous October. Both France and the Syrian nationalists began to realize that some compromise was necessary. The latter asked France to forget the past, and the French announced that a constituent assembly would be elected, a constitution drafted by Syrians, a Syrian government inaugurated, and a treaty of alliance with France concluded, in that order.

LOCAL SYRIAN GOVERNMENT

In 1928, France appointed Taj al-Din president of a Syrian council of ministers to form a provisional government and hold elections. This was done in April, the constituent assembly meeting in June. Most of the members were Sunnite Muslims, and urban-based landowners and merchants were an important part of the membership. (The same groups dominated local Syrian governments throughout the mandate.) A secular nationalist bloc under the leadership of Jamil Mardam, Hashim al-Atasi, and Faris al-Khuri began to take shape, while a more radical independence wing was led by Shukri al-Kuwatli and Riyad al-Sulh. The constituent assembly entered into the task of drafting a constitution, which was presented to the assembly in August. It established a Western-type republic with a president, prime minister, cabinet, unicameral legislature, and high court. Syria was pronounced to include Lebanon and Palestine; the official religion was to be Islam; and no mention was made of France as a mandatory power. Since several articles violated French international commitments and were contrary to League of Nations stipulations, France found the constitution unacceptable.

In 1929 the assembly was prorogued, but debate over the constitution continued. In a surprise move in 1930 France unilaterally promulgated new governments for Alexandretta, Latakia, and the Jabal Druze, simultaneously establishing in

Syria a constitution. Elections were not decreed, however, until the spring of 1932. A middle-of-the-road candidate was elected president of the republic, while nationalists soon took the lead in parliament and pressed for conclusion of a treaty of independence with France. When the treaty was presented by the French to the parliament it raised such a howl that the high commissioner suggested its withdrawal. Parliament was dissolved, with the president governing by decrees. In 1934 Taj al-Din became prime minister and held on to that post for nearly two years.

From January 20 to March 1, 1936, Damascus and most of the towns of Syria became the scene of an organized strike against the French regime. In the midst of the strike Taj al-Din resigned as prime minister and was replaced by Ata al-Ayyubi, a moderate. Negotiations for a treaty were resumed in Paris on the basis of Alexandretta being a part of Syria and Lebanon being recognized as a separate state. The long discussions ended only after the French agreed that the Jabal Druze and Latakia be incorporated into Syria. Rejoicing, Syria elected the nationalists to power in November 1936. Hashim al-Atasi became president of the republic and Mardam headed the cabinet. The Syrians ratified the treaty, but, as with the similar Lebanese treaty discussed above, the French government never did ratify it.

In 1939 the cabinet and president resigned, and the high commissioner suspended the chamber of deputies. The Alawite Latakia area and Jabal Druze were once again separated from Syria until their final unity inside Syria was achieved in 1942. Syria was back where she was in 1920 when the mandate began. At the outbreak of World War II, Syria was governed by an appointed council under the immediate control of the French high commissioner.

French economic policy in Syria had assisted the Bedouin shaykhs in acquiring unsettled lands. The shaykhs and urban-based large landlords dominated agriculture in the Hamah, Latakia, and northeastern areas, but small landowners and peasant owners played a substantial role in other parts of the country. The French conducted a cadastral survey of part of the land and revised the agricultural taxes applicable there. About two-thirds of the Syrian population was rural and agricultural during the mandate, and the peasants lived in thousands of villages. Annual variations in rainfall created large fluctuations in grain production. Industry was slow to develop, but textile factories replaced many hand looms. Unemployment and inflation were grave problems.

By 1938 there were about 100,000 schoolchildren, and only one small university, located in Damascus. Expenditures for education grew substantially in the 1930s. The Homs military academy trained young Syrians, especially those from rural areas and from the religious minorities, such as the Alawites, to become officers in the small army that France permitted to exist. Noncommissioned officers were also generally recruited from the same social groups. Two-thirds of the total population was Sunnite Muslim, and of the remainder one-half were Christians and one-half Shiites and Druzes of various types. There were also several thousand Jews.

The bitterest "foreign policy" event for the Syrians to swallow during the mandate years was the gift of Alexandretta to Turkey. In 1920 the French had declared a special administration for Alexandretta in view of the large Turkish population residing there. At first, it was attached to Aleppo but under separate rule. When Aleppo was joined to Damascus to form Syria, Alexandretta retained its own semiautonomous regime as part of Syria but was responsive directly to the will of the French high commissioner in Beirut. When questions over its status were raised by the Turks in 1936 and conversations initiated, the Syrians objected. As discussions proceeded to Franco-Turkish responsibility, to an independent Hatay, and to outright annexation to Turkey in 1939, Syrian nationalists protested every step of the way. With considerable justification and legality they declared that the terms of the mandate forbade France from any such action.

For two decades France tried to govern Syria but failed ingloriously. Policies dictated by Paris were high-handed, unwise, and based on an almost complete misunderstanding or disregard of the situation. To cap these mistakes French administrative personnel delegated to Syria were generally either pompous incompetents or officials transferred from North Africa, where at the time they were able to look upon the inhabitants as "natives" without starting a revolt. The Syrians did not want French rule or even French advisers in the first instance, and the French did little to endear themselves to the Syrians.

BRITISH OCCUPATION OF IRAQ

Eastward, the British were having their troubles in Iraq. At the end of World War I the British were occupying Basrah, Baghdad, and Mosul and controlling much of the land in between and on the far sides of both the Tigris and the Euphrates. Many British administrators coming in at the end of hostilities brought their families, evidently understanding that this territory was not a temporary acquisition. Sir Arnold Wilson, acting high commissioner, made a virtue of efficient government, irrespective of sentiment, prestige, or local desires. Arab unrest grew from the uncertainties over an Arab state of Iraq. When the news from San Remo arrived, the rebellion burst. From June to August 1920 a real war, reportedly costing the British nearly £40 million, raged in Iraq, with resistance forces dominating the Euphrates region and its tribes, as well as areas north and east of Baghdad. The cities and the Kurdish areas were unaffected by the fighting.

Hurriedly, Sir Percy Z. Cox was recalled from the ambassadorship in Tehran and sent to Iraq as high commissioner. The affection and esteem in which he was held by Iraqis was attested to by the welcome showered upon him at his arrival on October 1, 1920, and by the rebellion's termination. Having been British political agent for the Persian Gulf for a number of years and civil commissioner in Iraq during the war years and immediately thereafter, Sir Percy gathered about him a star-studded galaxy of advisers and assistants such as Gertrude Bell, his Oriental secretary, and H. St. J. B. Philby. Quickly he organized a provisional council of state in which Sayyid Abd al-Rahman al-Kaylani, Baghdad's *naqib* (official head of the Sunni Arab community), became prime minister. Other portfolios were distributed among influential families and religious sects from different parts of the state. Each minister had a British adviser, and in reality the council was supervised by these advisers. All were under the direction of the high commissioner; few Iraqis held any illusion that they had a true national government.

THE KINGDOM OF IRAQ

The British selected Faysal as king of Iraq in 1920. There were other candidates, but the return of several hundred Arab officers who had served with the Hashimites in the Hijaz and Syria gave the necessary weight to the acceptance of Faysal. His brother Abd Allah withdrew his own name, and Faysal arrived in Baghdad at the end of June 1921. The council of state invited him to become king; after a referendum was held, Faysal was enthroned on August 23, 1921. Sir Percy Cox and his associates managed affairs wonderfully.

Faysal served until his death twelve years later. His charm, tact, and broad tolerance made him an admirable choice, as his knowledge and experience made him acceptable to desert shaykhs, landowners, and the townsmen of Iraq. At the same time, Faysal recognized fully the British position of control and appreciated the fact that without British support he would never have become king. Through the winter and spring of 1922, a treaty was drafted by the British in conjunction with Faysal and al-Kaylani. At the last stages the council of state was brought in, and after a serious crisis the treaty was ratified in October. It defined the special position of Great Britain in Iraq, actually giving the British military and economic control and, in a veiled manner, granting English nationals many immunities and privileges in the country. British advisers were accepted in all offices. The treaty's many articles justified the objections by the nationalists that it was only a sugar-coated mandate which, however translated, meant "subjection and colonization."

ANGLO-IRAQI AFFAIRS

Much uncertainty and agitation accompanied the elections for a constituent assembly in 1924. King Faysal in his speech from the throne urged the assembly to ratify the treaty with Great Britain, pass upon the constitution, and enact an electoral law for a parliament—all of which was done in 1924.

Six years later, the highly unpopular and extremely important Anglo-Iraqi Treaty of 1930, which became the prototype of the Anglo-Egyptian Treaty of 1936

Husayn (1916–1924, Hijaz)

Ali (1924–1925, Hijaz)	Abd Allah (1921–1951, Jordan)	Faysal (1919–1920, Syria; 1921–1933, Iraq)
Abd al-Ilah	Talal (1951–1952)	Ghazi (1933–1939, Iraq)
	Husayn (1952–)	Faysal II (1939–1958)

The Hashimites

and the treaties of France with Syria and Lebanon in the same year, established a twenty-five-year alliance between Iraq and Great Britain. The two countries agreed to follow a foreign policy not inconsistent with the treaty, which meant that Iraq assented to "full and frank consultation in all matters" of foreign affairs. Iraq concurred to the presence of British troops in Mosul and other districts for five years and gave a lease on several air bases. In return, Britain contracted to defend Iraq in case of war. Attached to the treaty were annexes giving England considerable power in matters of finance, business, and education, and indicating that British advisers were to be employed rather than advisers of other nations. The signing of this treaty cleared the way for Iraq's membership in the League of Nations, which voted admission unanimously on October 3, 1932. The high commissioner became British ambassador; the mandate was terminated; and Iraq stood ostensibly as an independent state.

THE GOVERNMENT OF IRAQ

The constitution placed executive administrative power in the hands of a cabinet headed by a prime minister. The cabinet was jointly responsible to the chamber of deputies, which could force the cabinet to resign upon a vote of no confidence. The king, however, could dissolve the chamber. Parliament was bicameral. The chamber of deputies, elected indirectly by universal manhood suffrage, had one representative for every 20,000 male inhabitants, with a special provision that four Christians and four Jews were to be elected. (There were eighty-eight in the first chamber.) The first chamber was elected in 1925 and elections in 1939 were held for the ninth. The senate was appointed by the king and had a membership of not more than one-fourth that of the chamber. Only the chamber could initiate legislation; in appearance the chamber, as representative of the people, held the dominant position in the government.

In practical application, however, the cabinet was the powerful body, and no cabinet ever fell from a vote of no confidence. The cabinet controlled elections and obtained the dismissal of the chamber when necessary. Yet, there were twenty cabinets from 1925, when the constitution came into force, until the outbreak of World War II in 1939. A cabinet would promise to obtain full independence from Great Britain, and when it failed, it invited the opposition to try its hand. Ministers moved about from post to post in succeeding cabinets. Nuri al-Said Pasha, four times prime minister in that period, appropriately quipped: "With a small pack of cards, you must shuffle them often."

Perhaps the political and ministerial ferris wheel would not have been so pronounced had King Faysal lived longer. In 1933 Faysal became worn with fatigue. His health broke, and he died in Switzerland, where he had gone for rest and medical care. He was succeeded immediately by his twenty-one-year-old son Ghazi. Young and inexperienced, the new king followed a constitutional policy in the Western tradition. However, Iraq might have been spared some of her political confusion of those years had Ghazi been more mature. Addicted to fast motor cars, he was killed in an accident in 1939. He was succeeded by his four-year-old son, who became the boy-king Faysal II under the regency of Prince Abd al-Ilah, the king's maternal uncle and son of Prince Ali, King Faysal I's oldest brother.

MINORITY PROBLEMS IN IRAQ

Iraq's problems were far from solved by the adoption of constitutional government, technical independence from Great Britain, and admission to the League of Nations. In the northern part of the state Kurdish tribes were preponderant, and with their fellow tribesmen in Turkey and Iran they hoped for a peace settlement that would bring forth a Kurdistan. The Kurdish tribes were seminomadic and roamed the mountains and valleys of the eastern highlands, moving freely from country to country and resisting outside authorities. They had no desire to be taxed or organized. The Iraqi government took punitive measures repeatedly against uprisings in the neighborhood of Mosul and Suleimaniyah in the 1920s and early 1930s. Kurds were elected to parliament and served in Baghdad, but real power in the government was in the hands of Sunnite Arabic-speaking nationalists.

During World War I a group of Assyrians (Nestorians living along the upper Euphrates) had joined with the British and fought against the Ottomans. Leaving Turkey at the end of the conflict and finding themselves a homeless minority in Iraq, many had accepted service in the British army stationed there. In 1933, after Iraq was free and a member of the League, incidents between Assyrians (who demanded full local autonomy) and Arabs led to bloody engagements, massacres in Assyrian villages, and looting and suppression of the Assyrians by Kurdish tribesmen as well as by Iraqi army forces commanded by General Bakr Sidqi. Britain helped Iraq obtain a generous whitewash of the affair before the League in order not to jeopardize her position in Iraq.

The most serious political problem in Iraq arose from the fragmentation of Iraqi society along both ethnic and religious lines. In addition to the ethnic Sunnite Kurds and such religious minorities as the Assyrians, there was the lasting schism between Sunnite and Shiite Arabs. The latter held a population majority; the former dominated the government and society.

Until Shiites could be brought into the national identity, the elite of Iraq consisted of a small and precarious group of Sunnite notables. The Ministry of Education attempted with some success to create and make grow a secular nationalist school system which aimed at unifying the next generation in its values and pan-Arab national identity. This was done especially through teaching history that glorified the early period of the Arab empires. Still, such occurrences as the Shiite tribal rebellions in 1935–1936 that were suppressed by Bakr Sidqi showed the deep-rooted opposition to Sunnite dominance of politics.

SOCIAL PROBLEMS

In addition to minorities there was a grave social and economic cleavage between the townspeople and the settled and nomadic tribes. The government of Iraq was definitely in the hands of the townspeople; yet the tribes, and particularly their shaykhs, were powerful forces in the Iraqi nation. At least 70 percent of the population won their livelihood from the land, much of which was irrigated. But the science of irrigation had so degenerated over the centuries in Iraq that soils became salty and channels silted rapidly, compelling peasants to move frequently to new land. In the middle Euphrates area the tribes also engaged in stock raising, moving their herds from sparse pasturage as the cover was grazed. Thus the tribes had a constant tie with desert Bedouins. The tribal shaykhs were recognized by the British in their occupation of Iraq as the responsible heads of the districts, thereby obtaining a quasi-title of ownership of the land, and the land law of 1932 reinforced their power and that of the ex-Ottoman military officers around the king. Many peasants were treated as serfs. Enormous estates owned by only a small number of families controlled vast amounts of the land. The cropped area increased fivefold from 1913 to 1943, thanks largely to the introduction of mechanical irrigation pumps, but salinity and drainage problems continued.

Every assembly and parliament in Iraq had a goodly number of the tribal shaykhs as members. They were invariably conservative and friendly to the British, in whom they saw a protection from town-dwelling Iraqi politicians. The tribes of the middle Euphrates were a force with which to contend until the Iraqi army was equipped with the strength and mobility of more mechanized weapons. General Bakr Sidqi won his spurs of acclaim again in 1935 by leading an armed expedition to quell a rising of the tribes of the middle Euphrates.

IRAQI OIL

One of the jarring factors in Iraqi politics, domestic and international, has been the oil resources of the country and their exploitation. Before the war oil rights were granted by the Ottoman government to two German concerns. When the D'Arcy Exploration Company became interested in the Mosul fields, the Turkish Petroleum Company was formed in 1912 with German, Dutch, and British ownership. The San Remo Conference turned over the German interests to the French. And during the Lausanne Conference the British agreed very reluctantly that half of their holdings, which by this time were owned by the Anglo-Persian Oil Company, would be made available for purchase by America's Standard Oil Company of New Jersey and its associates.

The Mosul controversy between England and Turkey was partly over oil; when in 1925 it appeared likely that Mosul would be awarded to Iraq, that government gave a seventy-five-year concession to the Turkish Petroleum Company. Development, however, moved very slowly. Whereas the oil production by 1930 in Iran had increased to nearly 46,000,000 barrels, in Iraq it was only 909,000 barrels. Iraqi leaders charged that Western oil concerns were holding back in Iraq and exploiting their wells in other parts of the world. Although this might be good business for the companies, to Iraq it seemed entirely negligent, for she was losing revenue when it was sorely needed.

A gigantic gusher was struck near Kirkuk in 1927. By 1929 the company had not taken up all the concession, but the government refused to extend the time.

After consideration by the League and much negotiating a new concession was made in 1931 to the Iraq Petroleum Company, the company's name having been changed in 1929. The 1931 agreement gave an outright concession to lands in the Baghdad and Mosul provinces east of the Tigris, except for a few districts where the Anglo-Persian Company had historic rights. Furthermore, the company pledged to build before 1936 a pipeline system to Haifa and the Syrian coast and to begin annual payments of £400,000 against future royalties. Half of this sum would be nonrecoverable. Royalties were fixed at four gold shillings a ton for a period of twenty years. The pipeline was built from Kirkuk across the Tigris and the Euphrates. There it divided, one branch going to Haifa and one to Tripoli. Both branches began delivering oil in 1934.

By the time Iraq attained her formal independence she was fast becoming independent economically. However, the Iraq Petroleum Company through further concessions in 1938 held the oil production of all of Iraq in its hands.

While oil brought Iraq in touch with the great powers, border raids by nomads on the deserts and in the mountains led to interminable negotiations and difficulties with the states upon her frontiers. Boundary settlements with varying degrees of permanence were made with Kuwayt, Saudi Arabia, Transjordan, Syria, Turkey, and Iran. As a further step in regulating the frontiers and relations with Turkey and Iran, the Saadabad Pact was signed by the foreign ministers of Iraq, Iran, Turkey, and Afghanistan at the shah's palace near Tehran on July 8, 1937.

POLITICS IN IRAQ

Domestic politics from the very beginning in Iraq were heavily charged with personalities. Each dynamic figure gathered about him a clientele, published a newspaper, and organized a political party. Eagerness for personal power, prestige, and position, however, was in some cases sublimated in the struggle for independence. Parties emerged, flourished, and died quickly; members went from one to another with considerable ease. In the 1920s the most important parties were the National and the People's parties. Each pledged to throw off the treaty-mandate subterfuge and obtain real independence. The People's party was headed by Yasin al-Hashimi, who in the 1930s led his followers into a collective party known as the National Brotherhood. Prime minister twice, he was active in politics and held various portfolios in a number of ministries until a coup d'état in 1936 forced him into exile. Jafar Abu al-Timman, a Shiite merchant who participated in different ministries, organized the National party. Disillusioned by the acts of his political associates, he moved toward the left. In 1933 he joined the Reform party and took an active part in the 1936 coup.

Nuri al-Said Pasha, who had concluded the 1930 Anglo-Iraqi Treaty of Alliance, was an Iraqi who had also served in the Ottoman army and then joined the Arab revolt. Returning to Baghdad, he worked for the kingship of Faysal and held office in many cabinets as foreign minister. Prime minister four times before the outbreak of World War II, he was a strong stabilizing force and pro-British.

Nuri's opponents in 1930 joined together under al-Hashimi and Rashid Ali al-Kaylani to form the National Brotherhood party. This party dominated the government and the cabinets from 1932, when Iraq was admitted to the League of Nations, until it was overthrown by the 1936 coup. Meanwhile, a Reform party (*Ahali*) resulted from the meetings and discussions of younger Western-educated men who were liberal in their views and desirous of a more democratic and socialistic government. They were disgusted with the shuffling corruption of the conservative governments conducted by their elders. For a few years they gained wide influence through their party newspaper, but they soon succumbed to experienced politicians.

Realizing that the power of the National Brotherhood government could not be broken and that the cabinet of al-Hashimi and Ali al-Kaylani could not be removed without active assistance from the army, Hikmat Sulayman brought about a coalescence of the *Ahali* group with disgruntled army officers who felt that Iraq was not yet ready for full-blown Western democracy and its inefficiencies. The army "hero" proved to be Bakr Sidqi.

The plot ripened, and in the autumn of 1936 Sidqi moved on Baghdad. Rashid Ali al-Kaylani, Nuri al-Said, and al-Hashimi escaped into exile; al-Askari Pasha, perennial minister of defense, was assassinated; and Hikmat Sulayman became the new prime minister. This was the first of the cases when an Arab army seized power in the period of independence; it was the precursor of many other such seizures of power in other Arab states as well as in Iraq.

Parliament was dissolved and new elections were rigged so as to seat a great number of deputies who had never served in any previous chamber. Spending on the military increased, and the size and strength of the army grew. (Conscription had already been introduced in 1934.) The socialist predilections of the Ahali group led to quarrels with Sidqi and his army officers. Other officers became jealous of Sidqi, and in August 1937 he was assassinated. Since the army officer corps was dominated by urban Sunnite Arabs—Shiites, Kurds, Christians, and Jews were very few—the same religious and ethnic groups continued to control Iraq, as they had done under the preceding civilian regimes.

Another army coup d'état soon ended the first, and until 1941 one army coup followed another most methodically, while politics descended to personal vilification and vulgar invective. Iraq was deeply immersed in this pattern when World War II began.

REFERENCES

Important works for this chapter are in Chapters 23, 28, 30, and 31.

Batatu, Hanna. *The Old Social Classes and the Revolutionary Movements of Iraq*. Princeton, N.J.: Princeton University Press, 1978. A massive and outstanding study of Iraq, centering around the Communist movement, but also illuminating many other aspects of the political and economic life of the country.

Be'eri, Eliezer. *Army Officers in Arab Politics and Society*. New York: Praeger, 1970. A thorough survey of the Arab officers and armies from the Baghdad coup of 1936 to the 1967 Arab-Israeli War.

Cleveland, William L. *Islam Against the West: Shakib Arslan and the Campaign for Islamic Nationalism.* Austin: University of Texas Press, 1985. The ably-told story of a Druze writer and leader who became a prominent spokesman for Arab and Muslim independence and Islamic reform.

Davis, Helen Miller. *Constitutions, Electoral Laws, Treaties of States in the Near and Middle East.* Durham, N.C.: Duke University Press, 1947.

Dawn, C. Ernest. "The Formation of Pan-Arab Ideology in the Interwar Years." *International Journal of Middle East Studies* 20 (1988): 67–91. An excellent account by a leading scholar.

Devlin, John F. *Syria: Modern State in an Ancient Land.* Boulder, Colo.: Westview Press, 1983. An outstanding general survey of the topic.

Farouk-Sluglett, Marion, and Peter Sluglett. "The Transformation of Land Tenure and Rural Social Structure in Central and Southern Iraq, c. 1870–1958." *International Journal of Middle East Studies* 15 (1983): 491–505. A perceptive and careful study.

Hurewitz, J. C. *Middle East Politics: The Military Dimension.* New York: Praeger, 1968. An analysis of the way military and political functions interact.

Ireland, Philip Willard. *Iraq: A Study in Political Development.* London: Jonathan Cape, 1935. Especially good for the war years and the peace settlement.

Khadduri, Majid. *Independent Iraq: A Study in Iraqi Politics, 1932–1958.* 2d ed. London: Oxford University Press, 1960. An excellent work on this subject.

Khoury, Philip S. *Syria and the French Mandate: The Politics of Arab Nationalism, 1920–1945.* Princeton, N.J.: Princeton University Press, 1987. Outstanding.

Longrigg, Stephen Hemsley. *Four Centuries of Modern Iraq.* Oxford: Clarendon Press, 1925. A very substantial work giving an excellent background.

———. *Iraq, 1900–1950.* London: Oxford University Press, 1953. A fine continuation of his earlier work.

———. *Syria and Lebanon Under the French Mandate.* New York: Oxford University Press, 1958. Covers the period from the end of World War I to the aftermath of World War II. A fair and judicious account with sound conclusions.

Marr, Phebe. *The Modern History of Iraq.* Boulder, Colo.: Westview Press, 1985. Another fine general survey in a series that deals with various Middle Eastern countries.

Russell, Malcolm B. *The First Modern Arab State: Syria Under Faysal, 1918–1920.* Minneapolis, Minn.: Bibliotheca Islamica, 1985. The best work in English on the topic; full of insights not only for this period, but for succeeding periods in Syrian and Iraqi history.

Seton-Williams, M. N. *Britain and the Arab States: A Survey of Anglo-Arab Relations, 1920–1948.* London: Luzac, 1948. Pro-British.

Silverfarb, Daniel. *Britain's Informal Empire in the Middle East: A Case Study of Iraq, 1929–1941.* New York: Oxford University Press, 1986. A good book based on British sources.

Simon, Reeva S. *Iraq Between the Two World Wars: The Creation and Implementation of a Nationalist Ideology.* New York: Columbia University Press, 1986. Especially valuable for a discussion of education and the use of history in shaping nationalism.

Sluglett, Peter. *Britain in Iraq, 1914–1932.* London: Ithaca Press, 1976.

Suleiman, Michael W. *Political Parties in Lebanon: The Challenge of a Fragmented Political Culture.* Ithaca, N.Y.: Cornell University Press, 1967. An informative work describing in detail the Lebanese political parties. Most useful.

Tarbush, Mohammad A. *The Role of the Military in Politics: A Case Study of Iraq to 1941.* London: Kegan Paul, 1982. A thorough analysis.

Tibawi, A. L. *A Modern History of Syria Including Lebanon and Palestine.* New York: St. Martin's Press, 1969. A history of geographical Syria from the closing decades of the eighteenth century to 1921; thereafter, the history of Lebanon and Palestine is not included.

United Nations, International Bank for Reconstruction and Development. *The Economic Development of Syria.* Baltimore, Md.: Johns Hopkins University Press, 1955. A complete study of the economic situation in Syria.

Warriner, Doreen. *Land Reform and Development in the Middle East.* New York: Oxford University Press, 1957. Excellent chapters on Syria and Iraq.

Zamir, Meir. *The Formation of Modern Lebanon.* London: Croom Helm, 1985. Concentrates on the 1920s and the role of the Maronites and the French.

Ziadeh, Nicola A. *Syria and Lebanon.* New York: Praeger, 1957. A study of the complex political patterns in these states.

34

Palestine and Transjordan

ZIONISTS, ARABS, AND THE BRITISH

The British under General Allenby captured Palestine, including the Ottoman district of Jerusalem, in 1917. From then until July 1, 1920, it was occupied and administered by the British army. The future of Palestine remained up in the air until the San Remo Conference in April 1920, when it was awarded to England. Till then, uncertainty nurtured every rumor and fear, and those who lived in Palestine experienced a restlessness that later events never did resolve.

At the close of World War I the population comprised about 550,000 Muslims, 70,000 Christians, and 50,000 Jews. The Muslims and most Christians were Arabic-speaking natives. Some Jews were cultural Arabs, having lived there for many centuries. Some had resided there a generation or two, having immigrated to live and work in Jewish agricultural community projects typical of mid-nineteenth-century socialistic utopian societies. The great majority of Jews, however, were newcomers. They belonged to *Haluka* (distribution) communities living on charity from world Jewry, and included elderly Jews of various nationalities who had emigrated to the Jewish Holy Land to pray and to spend their last days there. During the war immigration ceased, some Jews left Palestine, others were expelled by the Turks, and the Jewish population dropped to an estimated 20,000. Moreover, a normal percentage of the *Haluka* died without the usual influx of others who wished to die in Palestine.

The Balfour Declaration stated that Great Britain "viewed with favour the establishment in Palestine of a national home for the Jewish people." But Zionists had hoped for "Palestine as the national home of the Jewish people, and the right of the Jewish people to build up its national life in Palestine." Active Zionists were confident that with work and time a Jewish national state having all the rights and appurtenances of a typical European national state would be created. They worked toward that goal; many acclaimed it openly.

The Arabs of Palestine considered their land to be a part of Syria and placed their faith in promises made to Sharif Husayn with regard to an Arab state, in Wilson's Fourteen Points, and in the Anglo-French Declaration. Since the Arabs enjoyed a majority of 85 to 90 percent of the population, they hoped to become an integral part of the eventual Arab national state. The arrival of the King-Crane commission encouraged them to believe that the Arab view would prevail. The Zionist commission, however, disturbed them; and the return of Jews who had fled during the war, accompanied by the immediate postwar agitation for Jewish immigration to Palestine, raised a multitude of fears in their hearts.

The British wanted to incorporate Palestine into their empire because of its proximity to Suez, its suitability as an outlet for Mosul oil, and its strategic position with respect to Arabia. The British army was occupying Palestine, and there seemed to be no good reason for leaving. A Zionist alliance might serve Britain's imperial interests and prevent the French from holding the entire Levantine coast and from approaching close to Suez.

Obviously, had these British views been clearly focused by the cabinet, the military administration in Palestine would never have been slighted to the extent of having a succession of three chief administrators in 1919. Procrastination, intrigue, war weariness, faction, and strife plagued the British military administration and intensified public unrest throughout Palestine.

BRITISH MANDATE

Reprisals and bloodshed first occurred in April 1920, when many Arab villagers flocked to Jerusalem to the Nabi Musa celebrations. Rumors turned into riots; Arabs who inflamed the villagers and Zionists with caches of arms were seized and sentenced by British military courts to penal servitude. That same month the Powers, meeting at San Remo, affirmed the British mandate over Palestine; on July 1, 1920, Sir Herbert Samuel, the first high commissioner for Palestine, including Transjordan, relieved the military authorities of their burden.

During the five years of Sir Herbert's civil administration four separate, yet parallel, governments were formed. Most important was the British executive government, composed of various administrative departments over each of which the high commissioner appointed a British director or secretary. Departments were established for public works, education, immigration, customs, excise and trade, antiquities, treasury, revenue, attorney general, police, health, agriculture and forests, posts and telegraphs, lands, and audit. An elective legislative council was projected, but it never came into existence because of disagreement over the ratio of representation between Arabs and Jews.

The Jewish community inaugurated the second government. In the fall of 1920 a Jewish national assembly was elected. It, in turn, appointed a Jewish national council (*Vaad Leumi*), which the high commissioner recognized as representative of the Jewish community in Palestine. The national council governed the Jews of Palestine in personal, communal, and religious affairs and recommended actions to British authorities concerning matters affecting the Jewish community. Certain Jews of prewar Palestinian residence, however, clung to a theocratic concept of Jewish life and refused to be governed by the national council. Supported by *Agudath Israel,* they disclaimed all connections with political and nationalistic

Zionism, but they proved too small a minority for the British Palestine administration to recognize in any formal way.

The third government was the international Zionist organization, with headquarters in London. It represented the more than thirty Zionist groups in many parts of the world that had sponsored the drive to obtain the Balfour Declaration. A number of its executives who lived and worked in Palestine between 1921 and 1929 were known as the Palestine Zionist executive. Each member was responsible for some department of work: political, immigration, education, industry, health, and public works. Sometimes referred to as a quasi-government, the Zionist executive followed the policies established by the Zionist organization in London and augmented the administration of the mandatory administration in Palestine. Frequently when the high commissioner's government and the Zionist executive were at odds, the Zionist organization proved more effective in persuading the British cabinet and House of Commons to follow the Zionist course than the foreign or colonial secretary was in obtaining support for the policies of the high commissioner.

These three "governments" represented imperialism, Jewish settlers, and world Jewry, respectively. The fourth government tried to represent the great majority of the people of Palestine—Muslim and Christian Arabs. Arab notables—of which the two most prominent families were the al-Husaynis and the Nashashibis—at first voiced the opinion that Arab Palestine was and should continue to be a part of Syria. But they had no love for the French and, therefore, dropped that contention after Faysal's defeat at Damascus. Following a large Arab congress at Haifa in December 1920, the Arab executive was born. Musa Kazim al-Husayni, former mayor of Jerusalem, was its chairman until his death in 1934. Although the Arab executive attempted to parallel the activities of the Zionist executive, it never had the latter's extensive resources or personnel at its call. The Arab community was also internally divided and often quarrelsome. Without any effective political muscle or singleness of purpose, this fourth force could in no way compete with any of the other three.

In addition to the Arab executive the British created the supreme Muslim council in 1921 to deal with Muslim religious affairs, especially custody of religious endowments and administration of Muslim courts. Fines, fees, and patronage gave the supreme Muslim council considerable power; and its president, Hajj Amin al-Husayni, became the leading political Muslim figure in Palestine in the 1930s. Commonly known as the Mufti, Hajj Amin was chosen, with Sir Herbert Samuel's connivance, for that office in 1921. A position held for life, the mufti of Jerusalem, like muftis in other cities, gave legal opinions on Sacred Law for citizens and the courts.

With four governments in Palestine, each with several parties or groups, and with the eyes of the world upon the Holy Land of three religions, Sir Herbert found the task of governing the mandate a challenge to human ingenuity. He had to remember Britain's imperial concern for Palestine and the entire Middle East. He had to govern the mandate economically and peacefully. He had to fulfill the mission of the mandatory power in instructing the people, 85 percent of whom were Arabs, and in preparing the way for self-government and independence. And he had to follow the instructions of the cabinet in London, which was persistently dogged by political pressure to honor not only the letter of the Balfour Declaration but also its spirit as interpreted by the Zionists who were already building the foundations for a national state of Israel. The dilemmas posed kept the political scene in Palestine shifting, with first one faction and then another playing the leading role.

IMMIGRATION POLICIES

No problem weighed more heavily upon Palestine than that of immigration and population. Zionist leaders, who wished to obtain a Jewish majority as quickly as possible, encouraged mass immigration. When a majority was achieved, Great Britain would be asked to relinquish her mandate, and Palestine would become an independent Jewish national state.

Upon assuming office in 1920, Sir Herbert Samuel announced that Jewish immigrants would be permitted to enter Palestine at the rate of 1,000 per month; later that same year an annual quota of 16,500 was set. Under this program nearly 10,000 Jewish immigrants entered Palestine up to May 4, 1921, when immigration was suspended because of serious Arab riots in Jaffa. A month later immigration was permitted to continue; Winston Churchill, then colonial secretary, announced in a famous memorandum of July 1922, in answer to Samuel's demand for a policy statement, that Britain intended to honor the Balfour Declaration and to fulfill the pledge of allowing the Jewish community to increase its numbers through immigration. The pledge with respect to immigration, however, would be interpreted and regulated so that the volume of immigration should not exceed the economic capacity of Palestine to absorb new arrivals.

In actual practice middle-class families or anyone who had $2,500 could obtain an entry permit, and a skilled workman needed only half that sum. In addition the Zionist organization, through various funds collected in Europe and America, provided the necessary funds for immigrants. Immigration increased rapidly, and nearly 35,000 Jews entered in the year of 1925. From 1927 until 1933 the number arriving in Palestine did not always offset those leaving. Beginning in 1933 entries rose sharply and in several years reached 40,000. Moreover, many Jewish visitors remained in Palestine illegally so that the precise number "ingathered" between 1920 and 1939 was unknown, but it was well over 300,000. The total Jewish population rose to 445,000 in 1939, not quite 30 percent of the total population.

Arab influx and natural growth were high, but did not keep pace with the Jews. There were 620,000 Arabs in 1918, and in 1939 the estimate tallied some 1,044,000. The high Arab birth rate accounted for natural growth of about 20,000 a year. The Jews, with 6,000 births a year, had to find 14,000 immigrants annually to keep pace in their desperate population race.

Whenever immigration reached high figures, riots between Arabs and Jews resulted. The gates would be barred for a few months. Then, political pressure in London resulted in the order being rescinded. Principles of economic absorptive capacity were constantly discussed, but how to apply them and by what standard they could be judged were never determined. To the Zionist organization any limitation upon "ingathering" smacked of heresy and appeared fatal to the whole nationalist movement.

LAND POLICIES

A large majority of Jews settling in Palestine came from urban centers in Europe. Yet one of the underlying philosophies of Zionism called for an agricultural society in Palestine, and workers on the land enjoyed an honored position in Zionist society. Zionists pledged that Arab tenant farmers would not be driven from lands purchased by their Jewish National Fund, but this guarantee proved impossible to fulfill. Some of the very best lands in Palestine were purchased at inflated prices from Arab absentee landlords living in Damascus and Beirut. Arab peasants were very adversely affected by poor harvests and falling prices for their products in the 1930s. They also had to deal with locusts, cattle plagues, indebtedness, droughts, and a rising population that put great pressure on the available land.

Land bought by the National Fund became the inalienable property of the Jewish community with express provisos that only Jews might work the land or be employed upon it. Some tenant farmers who had lived in villages and tilled the land about them were evicted, sometimes summarily. Since rumors are rampant in the Middle East, each tenant farmer feared he would be the next and reacted vigorously against any Jewish immigration.

Land was expensive in Palestine, because the population was relatively dense already and in order to expand the cultivable area a considerable outlay of funds was required for irrigation, fertilizers, draining, flushing to counteract salinity, removal of stones, and so on. In the 1930s farm land cost on an average about four times what it did in the United States, and the wages of farm labor were so high that general agriculture on a commercial basis was not feasible. Very few private individual farms were set up. The Jewish National Fund purchased most of the farm land and rented it at nominal fees to farmers, who would live in a private village or colony (*moshavah*), a cooperative village (*moshav ovdim*), or a collective village (*kibbutz*). Cultivation of citrus fruits was encouraged, and in the years before 1939 annual exports reached 10,000,000 cases. These exports provided Palestine with almost all of her earned foreign exchange.

The improved agricultural development had a marked effect upon the Arab rural community. In 1936 at least half of the citrus production came from Arab lands. Hill-country land that could not be farmed by mechanized equipment and would not easily submit to intensified cultivation was shunned by the Zionist organization and left to Arab peasants. It was marginal farming at best, but the tax structure of the administration bore heavily upon the peasants who worked these lands, and their poverty was sharply depicted against the higher Jewish standard of living.

INDUSTRIAL PROGRESS

The majority of Jews settled in urban communities, the greatest of which became Tel Aviv. Other centers were Jaffa, Haifa, and Jerusalem. The overall Jewish urban population amounted to 75 percent of the Jewish community. At the end of World War I Tel Aviv was a small dingy town of 2,000 inhabitants on the outskirts of Jaffa; in 1939 it contained over 150,000 inhabitants and was called "the only purely Jewish city in the world." Much of the industry was located there, and it became the center of artistic and cultural life in Jewish Palestine. The Zionist organization had continual difficulties in persuading immigrants from European cities to settle in rural agricultural villages after they had been sheltered in Tel Aviv.

A relatively large amount of industry developed in Palestine, but up to 1939 it was directed to supplying the local market. Exports from Dead Sea potash and chemical industries were just beginning to show in the trade statistics. In 1935 the pipeline from Iraq began to discharge oil at its terminus in Haifa, but only a negligible amount was refined locally. Palestinians had visions of supplying the industrial needs of a wide area in the Middle East, but at that time they could not meet local requirements.

The industrial and labor picture in Palestine was dominated by the General Federation of Jewish Labor (*Histadrut*), founded in 1920. Owning and operating a number of industries, the Histadrut represented about three-fourths of the Jewish workers, whose wages were higher than those of nonmembers. Most Arab laborers were unorganized; and the obvious wage disparity and discrimination in favor of Jewish workers incited bitter feelings. Yet unemployment figures were low, and many regulations against hiring Arabs were ignored. For example, by 1935 only 28 percent of the labor on Jewish orange plantations was Jewish. Wages for Arab workmen were higher in Palestine than in neighboring states, but the higher cost of living held any increase in real wages to a minimum.

SOCIAL DEVELOPMENTS

On social and cultural endeavors, the Zionist organization and many individuals and groups, such as the Histadrut and *Hadassah* (the American Zionist women's organization), expended much time, effort, and money. From the outset, education was deemed most important. The cornerstone of Hebrew University in British-occupied Jerusalem on Mt. Scopus was laid July 24, 1918, even before the end of the war. Schools of every description—primary, secondary, teacher training, vocational, agricultural—came into existence, and before 1939 every Jewish child received at least a primary education. Hospitals, clinics, maternity and infant care, medical-research laboratories, and public-health campaigns also received much attention. Contributions from abroad, particularly America, enabled the Jewish community to maintain a level of public services comparable to those of Western society.

The revival of the Hebrew language, a major accomplishment of the Jewish settlers in Palestine, was celebrated in newspapers published by the Zionists. Fine arts, theater, and writers, such as S. Y. Agnon and Martin Buber, flourished. While many Jews already knew or learned Arabic, only a very few Arabs learned Hebrew. The Palestine Orchestra—some of whose concerts were conducted by the Italian maestro Arturo Toscanini—and a state radio broadcasting service both began in 1936. Palestine participated in the New York World's Fair in 1939.

Arab writers often emphasized Arab nationalism and anti-Zionism, and they used primarily such media as newspaper essays and pamphlets, poetry, short stories, and histories. Arif al-Arif of Jerusalem epitomized many such Arab intellectuals: he founded a newspaper, was briefly a secretary to Amir Abd Allah of Transjordan, served in the Palestine civil service, and wrote many histories of towns and cities in that country, including a history of Jerusalem.

Public funds from the Palestine government for social services to help the Arab majority of the population were insignificant, so many of their needs went unfulfilled.

FINANCES

The activities of the Zionist organization in purchasing land, supporting new immigrants, building schools and hospitals, starting industries, and financing its myriad of projects were made possible by contributions from world Jewry. Estimates show that about $400 million was the cost of the Zionist development in Palestine between 1919 and 1939. Annual exports in the last years before World War II reached $4 million, most of which were receipts from the citrus industry. Annual imports rose to about $18 million. Other expenses came from the outlay for new land and its rehabilitation—$55 million in 1935—building materials, machinery, and arms and ammunition. A significant number of settlers brought capital with them in the form of foreign exchange, enabling Palestine to make purchases of machinery, capital goods of all sorts, and consumption goods necessary to maintain life.

Without the steady flow of money and resources into Palestine the Zionist achievement could not have been recorded. At no time in that period did Palestine ever approach a self-supporting status, and the bountiful gifts stabilized the society at a standard of living far above what any reasonable expectation of the exploitation of the country's resources could produce. To that degree the entire economy of Palestine was not self-sufficient. After the end of the first great surge of immigration, which came to 33,000 in 1925, the fall in the value of Polish currency, slackening of interest in the West, and then worldwide depression brought emigration from Palestine and severe economic crisis. Only the advent of Hitler and the accompanying sympathy toward the Jews saved the Zionist program for Palestine.

BRITISH ADMINISTRATION

Sir Herbert Samuel served as high commissioner for five years. Only one serious outbreak of violence (1921) between Jews and Arabs occurred during his term, and perhaps a recurrence of the riots was averted by Churchill's White Paper of 1922 which promised the Arab community that nothing would be done to jeopardize Arab rights. Outward peace reigned, and prosperity and activity dominated the Palestine scene. The Hebrew University in Jerusalem opened its doors; commerce and agriculture advanced; and political passions seemed to have cooled.

After considerable political controversy, and following the Churchill White Paper, the League of Nations on July 24, 1922, approved the mandate for Palestine. In entrusting the state to Great Britain, the League incorporated the Balfour Declaration in the preamble and recognized the historic association of the Jewish people with Palestine. The terms of conveyance instructed Great Britain to recognize the Zionist organization and in cooperation with it to facilitate Jewish immigration and "close settlement by Jews on the land" without prejudicing the "rights and position of other sections of the population." The mandatory instrument gave Great Britain authority with regard to all Holy Places and Muslim Foundations with the express injunction that they be administered according to religious law, existing rights, and public order. Free access to Holy Places and free exercise of worship were guaranteed. English, Arabic, and Hebrew were designated as official languages. Article 25 of the mandate exempted all the land of Palestine east of the Jordan River from the execution of such provisions of the mandate as Great Britain deemed inapplicable to that area.

To say the least, the terms of the mandate were not easy to fulfill. Every high commissioner from 1920 to 1939 tried to comply with the instructions. But each one discovered how difficult—almost impossible—it was to follow the dictates of the colonial office in London, to "cooperate" with the Zionists, and to maintain the Arab rights and position. Sir Herbert attempted to have a constitution adopted and a legislature elected and convened, but found Arab leaders unwilling to cooperate. Through political boycott and threats to riot the Arabs hoped to obtain British recognition that their preponderant majority entitled them to control the institutions of self-government.

Field Marshal Lord Plumer, who came as high commissioner in July 1925, had been the administrator of Malta and a distinguished soldier in World War I. He pursued the instructions of the mandate, resisting pressure and threats from any and all sources. His three years were peaceful ones, and British armed forces were reduced as an unnecessary financial burden.

THE JEWISH AGENCY

In 1929 the sixteenth Zionist congress voted to create a Jewish Agency in Palestine. The precarious world economic situation made it imperative for Zionists to win support from whatever source, and the announced objectives of the new Jewish Agency were cultural as well as political. Dr. Weizmann, who was the president of the Zionist organization, served automatically as the president of the Jewish Agency, becoming its first president. Some Zionists were hesitant about uniting with non-Zionists for fear that the program would be diluted and compromised. In actual practice the Jewish Agency drew in more and more Jews to support its ambitions, finally committing most Jews to the full program.

In addition to the non-Zionist Jews of the Western world who desired full integration into Western society in Western nation-states, two groups were opposed to the policies of the Jewish Agency. The more numerous was composed of the rigidly orthodox in Palestine and elsewhere, who felt that the Zionist program, being nationalistic, destroyed the religious basis of Judaism. The other group, led by Vladimir Jabotinsky, rebelled against the acquiescence of the Zionist organization to the Churchill White Paper of 1922. Calling themselves the revisionists, they demanded immediate fulfillment by the Palestinian government of the national home on both sides of the Jordan River, appealed especially to middle-class Jews, and condemned the inclusion of non-Zionists, whom they regarded as traitors.

THE PASSFIELD WHITE PAPER

The vocal outbursts of these revisionists, along with disturbances in 1928 near the Western Wall, frightened the Arabs and actuated them to be more concerned with Muslim rights along the Wall, which was part of the enclosure around the area surrounding the Dome of the Rock. (The Wall is all that remains of the Second Temple after its destruction by the Romans.) Muslim Arabs, agitated by many wild rumors, irritated worshippers and aroused Jewish ire by disturbing prayers and religious services. Custom and precedent have always been powerful claims in religious law in the Middle East, and Arab acts, which to Jews and Westerners seemed intentional aggravations, were efforts to maintain legal rights and prohibit new rights from developing.

Hostilities broke out in August 1929. A group of young Zionists from Tel Aviv, in open defiance of orders from the acting high commissioner, sang the Zionist anthem and raised their flag at the Western Wall. The next day a Muslim ceremony took place at the same spot, with minor disturbances occurring. In Jerusalem a Jewish boy kicked his football into an Arab tomato patch, and a fight ensued in which the boy was stabbed. British police arrested the Arab, but were then mobbed by a Jewish throng. Rioting continued for several days, with a dozen assaults upon Arabs and seven on Jews. On August 23 Muslims attacked Jews in Jerusalem, and serious incidents followed in Hebron and Safed. Troops were called from Egypt and Transjordan. On August 26 Jews invaded a mosque in Jerusalem, killing the imam. Later the same day a Muslim shrine was damaged and the tombs of the prophets desecrated.

Sir John Chancellor, the high commissioner since 1928, condemned the Arab leadership for the outrages. Over 130 Jews were killed and 339 wounded; 116 Arabs were killed and an unknown number wounded. Trials were held for over 1,000 persons—90 percent Arabs, 10 percent Jews—and 25 Arabs and 1 Jew were condemned to death.

Meanwhile, Whitehall sent out Sir Walter Shaw as head of a commission "to inquire into the immediate causes which led to the recent outbreak in Palestine and to make recommendations as to the steps necessary to avoid recurrence." The League of Nations also sent its own commission to find some "solution of the problems relating to the question of the Holy Places of Palestine." Furthermore, the British government sent Sir John Hope Simpson to study and report on land settlement, immigration, and development in Palestine. Certainly information would not be lacking!

All the reports were submitted. In October 1930 Lord Passfield (Sidney Webb), the colonial secretary, issued his famous White Paper outlining British policy on Palestine. The Passfield White Paper repeated the same general view presented in 1922 by the Churchill White Paper and emphasized the equal responsibility of the Palestine government to the Jewish and non-Jewish populations. Attention was drawn to the "economic absorptive capacity" of Palestine, and also the statement differentiated between a Jewish national home and a Jewish nationalist state.

In a constructive vein, Lord Passfield indicated that additional armed forces would be stationed in Palestine to add greater security, especially for the more exposed Jewish settlements. He condemned the Arabs for noncooperation in establishing a legislative council and promised that steps would be taken to give some self-government to Palestine with or without the help of any particular group in Palestine. The White Paper stressed the poor condition of Arab peasants and pointed out the need for Arab land development. It stated that the immediate task of the Palestine administration would be to assist agricultural progress of the Arabs and to close Jewish immigration if it prevented any Arab from obtaining employment.

The storm of protest which arose from the Zionist camp was serious. The tone and interpretation of British intentions expressed in the Passfield White Paper crushed the leaders of the Jewish Agency. Pressure upon the British government moved Prime Minister MacDonald to announce misgivings over the White Paper and to write a public letter in February 1931 to Dr. Weizmann, emasculating the White Paper on almost every position it had taken. Then the Arabs were up in arms, and the Palestine Arab executive denounced MacDonald's letter as a breach of faith. British indecision and wavering invited many leaders of the Middle East to reason that the Passfield White Paper resulted from the Arab outbreak of August 1929 and that the MacDonald letter stemmed from Jewish agitation against the White Paper. British prestige suffered; the rewards of violence and threats appeared consequential. Under such conditions a peaceful future for Palestine looked rather bleak.

Economic advances

Although the political situation remained unsettled through the next several years, and British attempts at inducing some form of self-government proved as fruitless as the first overtures of Sir Herbert Samuel, the economic boom into which Palestine entered gave optimists an opportunity to assert that all was well. Lieutenant-General Sir Arthur Wauchope became high commissioner in November 1931, just when the boom was first accelerating. Jewish immigration picked up; agricultural and industrial production jumped; government revenue trebled and quadrupled; citrus cultivation spread; and new capital investments gave greater opportunities for labor, which in turn kept wages at a high level. After 1932 the arrival of German artisans and capitalists in flight from Hitler provided greater stimulus to the boom.

Legal and illegal immigration swelled. Meanwhile, the revisionist Zionists continued to inveigh against the mild course of the Jewish Agency and its collaboration with the British, and they left the World Zionist Organization, the Histadrut, and the Haganah to form their own institutions.

The amazing growth of the Jewish community in the years between 1933 and 1936 affected even remote Arab villages in the hill country of Palestine. The great influx encouraged the leaders of the Jewish Agency to predict publicly that at the current rate of "ingathering" Jews would comprise a majority of the population by 1947. Arab political efforts and leadership coalesced into one united group, which called itself the Arab Higher Committee.

PEEL REPORT

The Arabs in November 1935 petitioned the high commissioner to establish, among other things, "democratic government in accordance with the Covenant of the League of Nations and Article 2 of the Palestine Mandate." A month later, Sir Arthur Wauchope presented details of a legislative council to be composed of 11 Muslims, 7 Jews, 3 Christians, 2 business representatives, and 5 British officials. Accompanying the announcement was the statement that the high commissioner would proceed with the establishment of the council whether or not any community refused to participate in the elections. The Arabs announced they would cooperate; the Jews declared they would not. Outnumbered, they feared they would lose on the immigration issue. Far better to delay self-government for a few years more until a Jewish majority was achieved. The Zionist cause was supported by the English House of Commons. In April 1936 the high commissioner acknowledged that plans for self-government were postponed. At a time when Arab strikes and disorders in Iraq, Syria, Lebanon, and Egypt forced England and France to grant self-government, peaceful persuasion in Palestine failed to bring similar concessions.

Violence in Palestine came first from the Arab peasant population; only later was it directed by the Arab Higher Committee. Rioting began and continued in a sporadic way for many months. Strikes ensued; many groups refused to pay taxes; and before the end of April 1936, a general Arab strike spread to all Palestine. The Arab Higher Committee declared the strike would continue until the British agreed to grant self-government, halt Jewish immigration, and prohibit transfer of Arab lands to Jews. Arab rebels, joined by volunteers from Arab states, fought in the hills, and by the end of 1936 there was a full-scale revolt. Bombings and property destruction were frequent, and there were as many attacks directed against the British as against the Zionists.

In May, Great Britain sought to pacify Palestine by sending Earl Peel as head of a commission of inquiry. But an impasse developed: the Peel Commission would not leave England until the strike ended; the Arab Higher Committee would not end the strike until Jewish immigration was suspended; and the British refused to cancel the immigration schedules. Palestine had grown important to the British Empire with regard to air routes to Asia and Africa, sea lanes through Suez and the

Mediterranean, and oil deliveries from Iraq. The security of these interests was presented to the British public as dependent upon the success of Zionism in Palestine. British difficulties and embarrassment mounted. Sentiment and pronouncements in Turkey, Iraq, Egypt, and India sided with the Arabs; Poland and the United States, each with large Jewish groups, pressed England to favor the Zionists.

In October 1936, upon pleas from the kings of Iraq and Saudi Arabia—both of whom were at that time subservient to Britain and British pressure—the Higher Committee called off the strike without obtaining its demands. Zionism and Britain won, but only by giving neighboring Arab governments an active hand in Palestinian Arab affairs (undoubtedly at British invitation). In November, Lord Peel and his colleagues arrived in Palestine, made their survey, and in July 1937 published their report. Without too much difficulty the Peel Report concluded that an "irrepressible conflict" had arisen over the question: "Who, ultimately, would rule the country?" The report recommended the division of Palestine and proceeded to suggest frontiers and conditions of partition. Simultaneously, a White Paper was issued by the cabinet supporting the Peel Report as official policy.

The partition scheme was bitterly assailed by Zionists, non-Zionists, and Arabs. Non-Zionists ruled out a national state of any kind, and the partition plan established one. Zionists, while not shutting the door on the idea of partition, argued that partition had already been enacted when Transjordan was cut off and that further decrease of the national home was contrary to the letter and the spirit of the mandate. The Arab Higher Committee and even the Nashashibi-controlled and usually more accommodating Arab National Defense party denounced the principle of partition. With unlimited immigration the Jewish state would become overpopulated and demand more space from the Arabs, who would be subject "to perpetual encroachments, political and economic." To Arabs any partition was unreasonable and in violation of the mandate and the Covenant of the League of Nations.

Pursuing the suggestions given in the Peel Report and White Paper, the Palestine administration took more positive action. Jewish immigration was curtailed and a firmer hand was directed against the Arabs. In September 1937, after the murder of a British official, Hajj Amin al-Husayni was removed from the presidency of the supreme Muslim council and five of the Higher Committee were deported to the Seychelles Islands. (Hajj Amin escaped to Lebanon.) These acts accelerated the Arab rebellion and guerrilla warfare against the British, although numerous attacks upon the Jewish community also occurred. To defend themselves the Jews, with the approval of the authorities, greatly expanded their illegal force, the *Haganah,* which totaled over 10,000 men, well-trained and well-armed by the Jewish Agency.

Into this maelstrom was sent the Woodhead Commission in April 1938 to report on detailed frontiers for the two states. Published in October 1938, the Woodhead Report outlined three different possibilities. Plan A was the Peel Partition. Plan B left much of Galilee to the British permanent mandate and reduced the Jewish enclave south of Jaffa. Plan C suggested only small Jewish and Arab states, retaining most of Palestine in a mandated territory.

CIVIL WAR

But the plans fell on deaf ears. Palestine was in open revolt. Bands of Arab rebels attacked police stations, driving officials from town to town; by October 1938 even the Old City of Jerusalem was occupied by the rebels. The *Irgun,* an illegal and secret national military organization set up by the revisionists, perpetrated many attacks upon the Arabs, and the *Haganah* increased its membership and obtained many "opportunities for broader experience." Palestine was on the verge of civil war and rebellion.

The open revolt in Palestine coincided with the pressure of Hitler upon Czechoslovakia, the Munich accord, and the nadir of British prestige. Germany and Italy showered propaganda and courtesies upon the Arabs of Palestine, and England quickly realized how vulnerable her position with the Arab states had become. The new colonial secretary declared that plans for partition were being dropped and invited Arabs and Jews to a conference in London.

Representatives of Egypt, Iraq, Transjordan, Saudi Arabia, Yemen, and Palestine Arabs—Husaynis and Nashashibis—came from the Arab side. Representatives of the Jewish Agency and Zionist and non-Zionist Jewish groups from Great Britain, the United States, France, Germany, Belgium, Poland, eastern Europe, and South Africa filled out the roster. The conference opened on February 7, 1939. In essence the British proposed (first to the Arabs and then to the Jews, since the two groups would not sit down with each other) a considerable reduction in Jewish immigration and land purchases and the establishment of a single self-governing Palestine after ten years. The Jews refused to discuss the question further and left, since the terms ruled that Arabs would comprise two-thirds of the population and Jews would forever be a minority in Palestine. Although definitely more favorably disposed, the Arabs declined to accept the proposals because they did not go far enough toward curbing the Zionist presence.

Rebuffed on both sides and with time running out in Europe, Great Britain issued a White Paper on May 17, 1939, declaring her unilateral solution of the Palestine impasse. Proposals followed the earlier scheme. About 75,000 Jewish immigrants would be allowed to enter over the next five years, after which the doors would be open only upon Arab consent. Land sales from Arabs to Jews would be strictly regulated. After ten years self-rule would be established on lines similar to those already prevailing in Iraq.

The Arab Higher Committee rejected this solution, asking for independence at the beginning rather than the end of the ten-year period. Remembering distinctly how the Churchill and Passfield White Papers were quickly disowned by British governments when Jewish pressure was applied, the Arabs could not believe that this White Paper would have a different ending. Jews in Palestine and Zionists throughout the world denounced the White Paper as a treacherous document. David Ben-Gurion, who had taken over from Weizmann as chairman of the Jewish Agency executive, at the Zionist congress in August 1939 urged that Jews defy Britain and act in Palestine as though the Jewish Agency were the state.

To what extent Great Britain would have moved to implement the White Paper of 1939 cannot be judged. In the summer of that year she was too weak and the crisis in central Europe too serious for any action to be initiated. When World War II broke out Zionists and Arabs alike recognized that the ultimate outcome of the struggle among the great powers would probably be the determining factor in the future of Palestine. The decision might be made on the battlefields of Europe.

The history of Palestine in the two decades between the World Wars had three component parts. The Zionist society worked hard with great faith, courage, and determination to build the Jewish national home in Palestine. Any compromise from that goal was dishonorable. The diligence, the improvement of agriculture and land, and the spirit of society were laudable. The Zionists were blind, however, to the fact that they were viewed as intruders in another people's home and insensitive to the distrust and fear they generated in Arab hearts. Arab society believed that an Arab independent state had been promised and that any infringement of that pledge was dishonorable. The lesser-organized Arabs in Saudi Arabia, Kuwayt, Yemen, Iraq, and Transjordan became independent or were in the process of gaining their independence, and the more developed Arabs of Egypt, Syria, and Lebanon had representative legislatures and considerable independence. Was it not strange that they, the Arabs of Palestine, did not have similar freedom? No peoples from distant places gave them hundreds of millions of dollars to develop their country. They felt the indictment that they did not utilize their land was disproved by the facts that their citrus groves were as productive as those of the Zionists and that they were better grain farmers than the Jews. The Arabs, however, suffered from benighted leadership, which erroneously judged that violence would intimidate Jew and Briton into giving the Arabs independence. The third component, the British, acted administratively as though Palestine were a colony but economically as though the land belonged to someone else. British businessmen saw little profit in investing or settling in Palestine when its permanence within the empire was doubtful. Through those years Great Britain tried, usually unsuccessfully, to balance her budget; consequently, the idea of spending sums to raise standards of living in Palestine or increase productivity of the land for the benefit of native inhabitants had few supporters. Thus, England just muddled along, gaining enmity on all sides.

TRANSJORDAN

East of the Jordan River, however, British policy fell more into traditional patterns of imperial behavior. Since the area east of the river was promised to the Arabs and Sharif Husayn, the British found it good policy as well as convenient to grant the administration of that land to Prince Abd Allah as a reward for not attacking the French in Damascus. Accordingly, Transjordan was given to Abd Allah in 1921. In 1922 the League council exempted it from many provisions of the mandate for Palestine, particularly those referring to Holy Places and implementation of the Balfour Declaration. The following year in Amman, capital of Transjordan, Sir Herbert Samuel announced the independence of Transjordan, which was also proclaimed simultaneously by Abd Allah. England, nevertheless, remained in control until an understanding was concluded between the two governments. In actual practice, from 1921 onward Britain gave financial grants to Abd Allah, and his administration was assisted by British officials.

In 1926, Abd Allah convened a group of Arab notables to prepare the way for an elective legislative assembly. In 1927, petitions were submitted to him demanding a national representative council and freedom from British rule. To meet this pressure on Abd Allah, a treaty was concluded in February 1928 at Jerusalem between Great Britain and Transjordan, placing their relations upon a firm basis. Legislation and administration in Transjordan was exercised by the prince under authority of the British high commissioner through the British resident stationed in Amman. The British were to control the budget, finances, army, economic development, and foreign affairs. Shortly thereafter, Abd Allah issued a constitution providing for a legislative council, which first met in 1929. Seats in the council were reserved for the Christian minority and for the nomadic tribes.

Great Britain continued to dominate Transjordan between World War I and World War II, largely through annual financial support to Abd Allah, support that increased from about $500,000 a year in the 1920s to $1 million in 1939. Britain had two military forces in Transjordan. First, there was the Arab Legion, organized in 1921 by Captain Peake. It was planned as a police force, but it defended the frontiers from foreign Bedouin infiltration. Originally, it had no desert section and no airplanes, but after 1930 it expanded and blossomed into one of the most significant military forces in the Middle East. Although under the command of the prince of Transjordan, it received five-sixths of its financial requirements direct from the British treasury. In the treaty of 1928, provision was made for formation of the Transjordan Frontier Force under the direct control of the high commissioner, since he was responsible for Transjordanian foreign affairs and the protection of her frontiers.

Both armies were instruments of the British government in the Middle East. They served to protect the frontiers of Palestine, Transjordan, and Iraq from raids by Abd al-Aziz (ibn Saud) of Arabia and to maintain and police the corridor between Iraq and Transjordan through which ran the oil pipeline from Kirkuk to Haifa. The nomadic raids stopped, and Transjordan's borders were accepted by the Saudis. After the droughts of the 1920s ended, with more security and new transportation methods, agriculture expanded and many nomads turned to raising sheep rather than camels. A government cadastral survey gave the peasants and many newly settled nomads surety of land ownership.

Transjordan not only was an anchor for the British position in the Middle East but also stood as an important link in her empire. Prince Abd Allah performed well for the British and they sustained him in a dignified manner, while his policies consolidated the state and aided the people.

REFERENCES

Almost every volume discussing affairs of the Middle East in modern times bears some relationship to the events and movements presented in this chapter. Of special note, however, are those found in Chapters 28, 30, 31, and 33.

Abu-Ghazaleh, Adnan Mohammed. *Arab Cultural Nationalism in Palestine During the British Mandate.* Beirut: Institute for Palestine Studies, 1973. One of the very few sources for this topic.

Abu-Lugod, Ibrahim, ed. *The Transformation of Palestine: Essays on the Origin and Development of the Arab-Israel Conflict.* Evanston, Ill.: Northwestern University Press, 1971. Sixteen scholars discuss the resistance to Zionism among the Arabs from the time of the mandate. Generally sympathetic to the Arabs.

Aruri, Naseer H. *Jordan: A Study in Political Development (1921–1965).* The Hague: Nijhoff, 1972. Offers insight into the interdependence of domestic and international politics.

Bentwich, Norman. *England in Palestine.* London: Kegan Paul, Trench, Trubner, 1932. Written by the mildly Zionist British official who served as head of the Department of Justice in Palestine until 1930.

Bowle, John. *Viscount Samuel: A Biography.* London: Gollancz, 1957. An objective study of the life of the first high commissioner.

Cohen, Israel. *Theodor Herzl, Founder of Political Zionism.* New York: Thomas Yoseloff, 1959. A fine biography of the founder of Zionism.

Cohen, Michael J. *The Origins and Evolution of the Arab-Zionist Conflict.* Berkeley: University of California Press, 1987. A concise and well written study especially valuable in regard to British policy up to 1948.

Dann, Uriel. *Studies in the History of Transjordan, 1920–1949: The Making of a State.* Boulder, Colo.: Westview, 1984. Collected essays on diverse aspects of Transjordanian history.

Elon, Amos. *The Israelis: Founders and Sons.* New York: Holt, Rinehart and Winston, 1971. Well-written, stimulating, and provocative. Shows the personalities, ideology, and feelings behind the early and contemporary Zionist movement.

Esco Foundation for Palestine. *Palestine: A Study of Jewish, Arab, and British Policies.* 2 vols. New Haven, Conn.: Yale University Press, 1947. A vast work that includes important information on the period of the mandate. Almost a source book.

Furlonge, Sir Geoffrey. *Palestine Is My Country: The Story of Musa Alami.* New York: Praeger, 1969. A study of Musa Alami's life and the work of his school.

Glubb, John Bagot. *The Story of the Arab Legion.* London: Hodder & Stoughton, 1948. Glubb was the commanding officer as well as historian.

Goldmann, Nahum. *The Autobiography of Nahum Goldmann: Sixty Years of Jewish Life.* New York: Holt, Rinehart and Winston, 1969. A leader of the World Zionist Organization and the World Jewish Congress for many years. Clashed with and lost out to Ben-Gurion.

Graves, Philip P., ed. *Memoirs of King Abdullah of Transjordan.* New York: Philosophical Library, 1950. Covers the important events of the king's earlier life.

Halpern, Ben. *The Idea of the Jewish State.* Cambridge, Mass.: Harvard University Press, 1961. A profound book on this subject.

Hurewitz, J. C. *The Struggle for Palestine.* New York: Norton, 1950. A first-rate book by a careful scholar.

Jewish Museum (New York). *Artists of Israel, 1920–1980.* Detroit, Mich.: Wayne State University Press, 1981. Presents useful general essays and looks at individual artists.

Katz, Samuel. *Days of Fire.* Garden City, N.Y.: Doubleday, 1968. An account of underground work in Palestine before 1948, written by a founder of the Irgun. Contemptuous of those Zionists who compromised with the British and the Arabs.

Kayyali, A. W. *Palestine: A Modern History.* London: Croom Helm, 1978. A political history ending basically in 1939 written from the point of view of the Palestinian Arabs. Shows the emergence of new leaders for that community in the 1930s.

Kazziha, Walid. "The Political Evolution of Transjordan." *Middle Eastern Studies* 15 (1979): 239–257. Covers the years 1918–1923 and is critical of the Amir Abd Allah; valuable for relations between Abd Allah and the British.

Khalidi, Walid. *Before Their Diaspora: A Photographic History of the Palestinians, 1876–1948.* Washington, D.C.: Institute for Palestine Studies, 1984. Excellent commentary as well as photographs.

———, ed. *From Haven to Conquest: Readings in Zionism and the Palestine Problem Until 1948.* Beirut: Institute for Palestine Studies, 1971. Eighty articles and documents by leading political figures.

Laqueur, Walter. *A History of Zionism.* New York: Holt, Rinehart and Winston, 1972. This is a sympathetic but not uncritical account of the pre-state period.

———, and Barry Rubin, eds. *The Israel-Arab Reader: A Documentary History of the Middle East Conflict.* 4th rev. ed. New York: Penguin Books, 1987. Valuable documents from the 1880s to the 1980s; highly useful.

Lesch, Ann Mosely. *Arab Politics in Palestine, 1917–1939: The Frustration of a Nationalist Movement.* Ithaca, N.Y.: Cornell University Press, 1979. The best discussion of the subject; outstanding.

McTague, John J. "The British Military Administration in Palestine, 1917–1920." *Journal of Palestine Studies* 7:3 (1978): 55–76.

Marlowe, John. *The Seat of Pilate: An Account of the Palestine Mandate.* London: Cresset Press, 1959. A British view.

Mattar, Philip. "The Mufti of Jerusalem and the Politics of Palestine." *Middle East Journal* 42 (1988): 227–240. The best account so far of the life of this very controversial figure.

Miller, Ylana N. *Government and Society in Rural Palestine, 1920–1948.* Austin: University of Texas Press, 1985. Coverage of village education is quite important.

Moore, John Norton, ed. *The Arab-Israeli Conflict.* Princeton, N.J.: Princeton University Press, 1974. A massive three-volume work which contains documents, government publications, a bibliography, and many readings.

Porath, Y. *The Emergence of the Palestinian-Arab National Movement, 1918–1929.* London: Cass, 1974. A brilliant monograph on the foundations of the Palestinian cause; this work is completed by the volume cited below.

———. *The Palestinian Arab National Movement, 1929–1939: From Riots to Rebellion.* London: Cass, 1978.

Sachar, Howard M. *A History of Israel from the Rise of Zionism to Our Time.* New York: Knopf, 1979. An excellent general study.

Smith, Charles D. *Palestine and the Arab-Israeli Conflict.* New York: St. Martin's Press, 1988. Another outstanding survey of the subject.

Stein, Kenneth W. *The Land Question in Palestine, 1917–1939.* Chapel Hill: University of North Carolina Press, 1984. A meticulous work of scholarship; shows the actual procedures of land sales and their political ramifications.

Taylor, Alan R. *Prelude to Israel: An Analysis of Jewish Diplomacy, 1897–1947.* New York: Philosophical Library, 1959.

Vatikiotis, P. J. *Politics and the Military in Jordan: A Study of the Arab Legion, 1921–1957.* New York: Praeger, 1967. A detailed study of civil-military relationships.

Weissbrod, Lilly. "Economic Factors and Political Strategies: The Defeat of the Revisionists in Mandatory Palestine." *Middle Eastern Studies* 19 (1983): 326–344. An insightful examination of the causes for the weakness of the revisionist Zionists in the 1930s.

Weizmann, Chaim. *Trial and Error: The Autobiography of Chaim Weizmann.* New York: Harper, 1949. The life of the leader of Zionism during the mandate period.

35

Egypt and the Sudan

THE BRITISH PROTECTORATE

On December 18, 1914, Great Britain unilaterally declared the establishment of a protectorate over Egypt, thus ending Egypt's tenuous association with the Ottoman Empire. Although the announcement carried a pledge of ultimate self-government, a protectorate was humiliating to Egyptians. Its Arabic translation was the word used to refer to dependence of certain Christian minorities on European powers. The Egyptian ministry of foreign affairs was abolished, its functions appropriated by the British agent and consul general, who under the protectorate became high commissioner. Khedive Abbas Hilmi II, pro-Ottoman and violently anti-British, had not returned from his summer palace on the Bosphorus when hostilities broke. He was deposed; his uncle, Prince Husayn Kamil, was proclaimed sultan of Egypt.

For nearly four years Egypt served as a military base for British and Allied forces. Troops requisitioned supplies, taking camels and donkeys from peasants. Egyptians were drafted into an army which fought alongside the British, although Britain had promised to recognize Egyptian neutrality. Inflation was rampant, and fortunes were made by corrupt and illegal practices. The price of cotton more than trebled, and wheat became scarce and high-priced.

The personnel of the British civil service deteriorated in quality and the British military ignored Egyptian sensibilities. The public blamed the British for every ill that befell Egypt in the war years. Apparently British officials were out of touch with sentiment in Egypt. Their reports to London did not enlighten the Foreign Office with a true description of trends, but followed the traditional imperialistic philosophy of Lord Curzon, the foreign secretary. The presence of so many Westerners in Egypt, public declarations from Allied politicians, and the coming of age of a new generation hurried Egyptian nationalism forward with great strides in the years between 1914 and 1918.

EGYPTIAN NATIONALISM AND THE WAFD

Two days after the end of the war in Europe, Saad Zaghlul Pasha, an ardent nationalist who had been minister of education, presented the high commissioner with a list of demands. If allowed, these demands would have given Egypt independence. Informed that London would reply, Zaghlul asked permission to proceed with his delegation (*Wafd*) to London to discuss his independence program. British officials in Cairo urged London to grant the wish, but the Foreign Office refused, because Zaghlul had no organized party and in no sense represented the government of Egypt. Upon the approval of Sultan Fuad, Prime Minister Rushdi sought an invitation immediately to go to London to discuss the future status of Egypt. (Sultan Husayn died in 1917 and was succeeded by his brother Fuad.) Downing Street, busy with preparations for the Paris conference, declined, and thus encouraged the deterioration of political conditions in Egypt.

Zaghlul and his delegation avidly organized committees throughout the country and stimulated vigorous nationalistic feeling against the British. Rushdi resigned after his rebuff. Zaghlul threatened dire consequences should the sultan appoint a successor. At this juncture (March 8, 1919), Zaghlul and three other leading Wafd party members were arrested by the British military with Foreign Office approval (Egypt being under martial law) and deported to Malta. Egyptian reaction was spontaneous: Insurrection and violence spread to all districts within ten days, and included Muslims and Christians, workers and capitalists, urbanites and peasants, men and women. The patriotic revolutionaries sought independence for Egypt, an independence they felt was justified by the long history of the country and by the right of national self-determination. British military forces rushed to Egypt and crushed the revolt by the end of the month.

The British suddenly awoke to the fact that something needed to be done. General Allenby was appointed high commissioner. Lord Milner was designated head of a commission of inquiry to investigate the situation and report on the nature of a constitution that would be best for Egypt under the protectorate. Zaghlul and his fellow internees in Malta were freed to lay their demands before the peace conference, but their demands were ignored.

A memorandum containing the principles on which a treaty of alliance between Egypt and England might be drawn was composed in August 1920. It recognized Egypt as a sovereign independent constitutional monarchy with representative institutions. Britain would undertake to defend Egypt, and Egypt would offer all assistance within her borders to England. Egypt would have diplomatic representation abroad, but would coordinate her policies with those of Britain. Egypt would appoint British judicial and financial advisers and would permit Britain to maintain a military force in Egypt. The capitulations would be abolished but England would have the right to prevent the adoption of laws inconsistent with legislation enacted under the previous regime. The final point pledged Egypt to call a constituent assembly to ratify the treaty and to adopt a constitution.

Lord Milner signed the document as the basis for a treaty that he would be willing to recommend to the cabinet. But Zaghlul temporized, asserting that the memorandum would have to be approved by the people of Egypt before he could go ahead. Several of his party returned to Egypt, where the memorandum was published and Egyptian sentiment tested. The response was lukewarm, largely because Zaghlul gave out public declarations quite noncommittal in tone. At this point, he informed Lord Milner that the memorandum was not clear on several points. The British, however, would bargain no further, and conversations were broken off completely.

EGYPTIAN INDEPENDENCE

In December 1921, Sarwat, acting prime minister, formed a new cabinet on the premise that Great Britain would immediately recognize Egypt as an independent sovereign state. Zaghlul's activities were redoubled. Allenby, appreciating that no treaty that Britain would be prepared to sign would be acceptable to Zaghlul, deported him to the Seychelles. Still the British cabinet did not agree to recognize Egyptian independence; it took a personal trip to London by Allenby to impress upon England the necessity of accepting the quasi-commitments made in the Milner-Zaghlul memorandum and to Sarwat. On February 28, 1922, the day of Allenby's return to Egypt, he gave out the unilateral British declaration ending the protectorate and elevating Egypt to the rank of an independent sovereign state. Martial law, proclaimed on November 2, 1914, was to be terminated as soon as the sultan's government passed an act of indemnity. Until Egypt and England could conclude an agreement England reserved to herself the security of communications, defense, the protection of foreign interests and minorities, and the affairs of the Sudan. Egyptian nationalists were annoyed that their country's independence was declared by another state. Yet, England had assumed the protectorate by unilateral action and might relinquish it in like manner.

THE CONSTITUTION OF 1923

Sultan Fuad became king of Egypt, and a succession of men passed through the chambers of the prime minister. Politics became a three-way embroilment among nationalists, the king, and the residency (as the British high commissioner's office was termed).

The residency pressed Fuad to appoint a prime minister who would present a constitution for the new sovereign state. The king insisted upon an article naming him king of Egypt and the Sudan, thus taking a stand that he knew the British would not tolerate. Finally, a constitution was drawn up and promulgated on April 21, 1923; martial law was withdrawn in July and elections for a parliament were held in September.

The constitution gave to the king considerable powers. He could dissolve or adjourn parliament. He called parliament, and he could veto acts of parliament. (A two-thirds majority of the membership of each house could, however, override his veto.) The king appointed and dismissed ministers, and could issue decrees in the absence of parliament. The king was commander in chief of the armed forces. In reality, a determined king could be chief executive of the state. Ministers were responsible to parliament; but since they held office at the pleasure of the king, they found it difficult to serve two masters. Two-fifths of the senators were appointed by the king; three-fifths were elected. Nowhere in the constitution was Great Britain mentioned. But with British troops and many British advisers in Egypt and with an Englishman as commander in chief of the Egyptian army, Egyptians were fully justified in doubting that independence had been attained.

EGYPTIAN POLITICS

Zaghlul was released from detention in March 1923, and, together with other Wafd leaders who had also been freed, he returned to Egypt in September in time for elections. The Wafd gained 188 seats out of 215 in the chamber of deputies. When parliament convened the next January, Zaghlul promptly accepted Fuad's invitation to form a ministry upon the condition that as prime minister he would not compromise the program of the Wafd, of which he remained president. His Wafd program had not been completed: British troops and advisers must go; the Sudan must be "returned" to Egypt; and any British claim to share in protecting the Suez Canal must be abandoned. These goals called for the continuation of intimidation by demonstrations against the British and veiled invitations to violence. Similar stirrings, to which the British reacted strongly, were "encouraged" in the Sudan. The situation was anomalous. As prime minister, Zaghlul was responsible for the maintenance of law and order in Egypt; as head of the Wafd, he was in open defiance of law and order.

In the summer of 1924, Zaghlul went to London, ostensibly to negotiate a treaty of alliance. What he did was to present his entire program as unequivocal demands. No treaty was signed, yet Zaghlul returned triumphantly to Cairo. Four days later, on November 19, 1924, Sir Lee Stack, governor-general of the Sudan and commander in chief of the Egyptian army, was assassinated on the streets of Cairo. Zaghlul immediately pledged swift and thorough action to bring the culprits to trial. Nevertheless, the deed was the logical and indirect result of open invitations to violence instigated by Zaghlul and the Wafd. Subsequent judicial proceedings demonstrated that leading Wafdists, including two members of Zaghlul's cabinet, were implicated.

On the afternoon of November 22, escorted by a regiment of British cavalry, Lord Allenby called at the offices of the council of ministers, read in English two communications to Zaghlul, handed him copies in French, and departed. Allenby was angry, and he took every opportunity to display force and humiliate Zaghlul. The note placed blame for Sir Lee Stack's murder upon Zaghlul's "campaign of hostility to British rights and British subjects in Egypt and the Sudan" and asserted that the Egyptian government was held in contempt by all civilized peoples. Egypt was given about thirty hours to meet the following demands: apologize for the crime; punish the criminals; forbid and suppress public political demonstrations; pay a fine of £500,000; recall all Egyptian officers and army units from the Sudan; notify the competent departments that the Sudan would increase irrigated areas to an unlimited figure; and withdraw all opposition to British wishes in regard to the protection of foreign interests in Egypt.

The demands were stiff. Zaghlul discussed them with the cabinet and King Fuad and laid them before the chamber of deputies that evening in secret session. Compliance was voted for the first four demands. Upon refusal of the last three, Allenby notified the Sudan government to take all necessary actions and ordered the British army to occupy the Alexandrian customs offices. Zaghlul resigned; Fuad appointed Ahmad Ziwar Pasha, who speedily came to terms with the British concerning the role of British advisers in the Egyptian government.

Parliament was dissolved in December and new elections were held. The Liberal party, led by intellectuals and elder politicians who were descended from Ottoman Turkish families long resident in Egypt, and a new Unionist party, made up of the king's friends, combined with numerous independents from the provinces to defeat the Wafd. Nevertheless, the chamber of deputies elected Zaghlul its president in March 1925. This act led the king to dismiss parliament immediately. He was now determined to crush Zaghlul, who seemed to be growing more prominent than the king.

New elections were not held until May 1926. In the meantime Fuad appointed several new ministers from among his friends. Allenby retired, and Lord Lloyd, formerly governor of Bombay, became high commissioner. He made common cause with the Wafd to force the king to call for elections, in which the Wafd again obtained a sweeping victory. Despite the victory Adli Pasha of the Liberal party headed a ministry of three Liberals, six Wafdists, and one Independent.

In August 1927, Zaghlul died and was succeeded as Wafd leader by Mustafa al-Nahhas Pasha, who at that time was hardly more than a figurehead. Fuad forced Nahhas to resign by exposing a political scandal. The next prime minister, Muhammad Mahmud, an original Wafdist exiled to Malta with Zaghlul but in 1928 supported by residency and palace, dissolved parliament and suspended the constitution for three years, thereafter governing as a mild dictator with bitter opposition from the Wafd. Mahmud reached agreement with the British over the Nile waters, the old Ottoman debt, and other financial matters. But desire for a treaty with Great Britain remained paramount, and in 1929 while on a holiday in England Mahmud judged the right moment had arrived.

In June 1929 negotiations began, and the Labour cabinet made sweeping concessions with respect to Egyptian national feelings. British troops would remain only around the Canal, the capitulations would be abolished, England would relinquish her right to protect foreigners, and the Sudan question would be considered a subject for further negotiations. However, England would only recognize a treaty ratified by a freely elected Egyptian parliament. The draft treaty was a great victory for Mahmud, but upon his return to Egypt his position became untenable. Since the Wafd refused to accept his treaty and since the British insisted upon elections, Mahmud resigned.

Elections returned the Wafdists to power, and Nahhas Pasha again became prime minister. But his position was impossible. He had denounced the draft treaty obtained by Mahmud, and the British declared that they had reached the "high-water mark" of concessions. Treaty negotiations were dropped temporarily. King Fuad, fearing the apparent alliance of the Wafd and the residency, engineered the resignation of Nahhas and appointed Ismail Sidqi Pasha as prime minister.

THE CONSTITUTION OF 1930

Parliament was prorogued; Nahhas incited riots; the British sent warships. Sidqi, protesting against foreign intervention, restored order. In this coup d'état of June 1930 Sidqi appeared as the strong man. The constitution of 1923 was abrogated and a new constitution with a new electoral law rigged to keep Wafdists out of office was quickly adopted. Sidqi organized a new political party, the People's party. In coalition with the Unionists and Independents, the People's party defeated a Wafdist-Liberal united front, which boycotted the election. Sidqi was able to establish his dictatorship only through the ineptitude of the British government, which maneuvered both Liberals and Wafdists into indefensible positions. Sidqi sent the students back to their studies; politicians muttered rather meekly; and the wealthy landowners gladly supported the new rule, for they were surfeited with the petty quibbling, jealous vindictiveness, and political arrogance of the nationalistic Wafd lawyers whom they had largely created. No treaty with England was attempted; prime ministers who tried always fell from office, and both Sidqi and Fuad preferred British troops in Egypt to the Wafd. Furthermore, Sidqi must have understood that the British government would not interfere in Egyptian domestic politics as long as British imperial interests were not directly jeopardized.

Fuad again did not intend to permit a potential rival to remain in office very long. Sidqi fell from power in September 1933 on the issue of a minor scandal, although a paralytic stroke had reduced his command of affairs several months earlier. A procession of ineffectual prime ministers followed. Power rapidly gravitated to the king, who was also amassing a great fortune.

THE ANGLO-EGYPTIAN TREATY OF 1936

In November 1934, the 1930 constitution was abrogated in favor of the 1923 constitution. The latter was not reissued, however, because the British secretly vetoed it. At this juncture a crisis of an entirely different order appeared—the Italian adventure in Ethiopia. Britain increased her military establishment in Egypt and announced that British naval headquarters in the Mediterranean would be transferred from Malta to Alexandria. The British foreign secretary heaped more coals on the fire by publicly stating that the Egyptian constitutions of 1923 and 1930 were ill-adapted documents, and government-inspired London editorials advised the Egyptians not to manipulate the Ethiopian crisis by blackmailing England into promises.

The constitution of 1923 was then reissued, elections were set for late spring, and the return to more responsible parliamentary government was envisaged. In April 1936 King Fuad died. His only son, the young Faruq, ascended the throne. In new elections the Wafd party won 166 seats out of 232 in the chamber of deputies and obtained a majority in the senate. With such a solid backing Nahhas became prime minister with a Wafd cabinet. Since he named the regency, the power of the Wafd was, for once, supreme. For several months already he had been chairman of the all-party delegation negotiating the treaty with England. Without fear of recrimination, Nahhas consummated the Anglo-Egyptian treaty on August 26, 1936. A landmark had been achieved.

Beyond the malice of internal Egyptian politics the chief stumbling blocks to such a treaty had been: the Sudan, British armed forces, and the capitulations. In 1930 negotiations foundered on the Sudan question; in 1936 all predicted failure when Britain announced that disposition of her forces in Egypt needed reconsideration. Between 1930 and 1936, however, changes in the international military situation became obvious to politician and public alike. When, therefore, the British asked for a wider area in the Canal Zone and more military facilities on land, sea, and air, Egyptian objection was only nominal. The occupation was changed to a twenty-year military alliance. Britain was to help Egypt gain admission to the League of Nations. The Sudan settlement again permitted unlimited Egyptian immigration to the Sudan and the use of Egyptian troops in the Sudan. The end of the capitulations, actually arranged by the Montreux convention of 1937, proved of the utmost consequence to Egypt. The abolition of mixed tribunals and curtailment of consular courts were not abrupt, but the end was set for 1949. Henceforth, foreigners and foreign companies would be subject to Egyptian laws, especially taxation and financial legislation. Increased taxation from this and other sources allowed the army's budget to be doubled in the late 1930s.

The 1936 treaty was immensely popular in Egypt. Parliament ratified it and the unprecedented happened when British troops were cheered on the streets of Cairo. But Nahhas Pasha's popularity waned when King Faruq reached his majority in 1937 and the palace again became a political force. Even the treaty was no longer popular, probably because the Italian conquest in East Africa was legitimized and the threat of war in the Mediterranean subsided. Nahhas resigned at the end of 1937. A new election, arranged in 1938, defeated the Wafdists, and the palace gained ascendancy. Just before World War II broke out Ali Mahir, the Saadist party leader, became prime minister of a cabinet from which both Liberals and Wafdists were excluded. The wheel turned; Faruq and his palace officials won full power.

SOCIAL AND ECONOMIC PROBLEMS

Internal politics and the problem of getting rid of the British consumed the energies and attention of Egyptian leaders between World War I and World War II, and these were the topics eternally discussed in Egypt. However, other problems, certainly basic and significant for the Egyptian nation and perhaps even more difficult to solve, did exist. Foremost was the increasing population pressure. The population increased from 12,718,000 in 1917 to 15,721,000 in 1937, although the cultivated area remained constant. Increased agricultural yields, improved irrigation techniques, and intensive cultivation—three crops per year instead of two—met the situation in part, but there was a general lowering of the standard of living among Egyptian peasantry. Sanitation and health conditions were poor, and were made worse by perennial irrigation which helped spread the intestinal disease bilharzia to most of the rural population. The death rate was very high. Yet, the birth rate was higher. These factors, coupled with a lack of coal and industrial development, gave the waters of the Nile an importance that other national societies found difficult to appreciate. This dependence on the Nile explained the critical blow to Egypt intended by Allenby's ultimatum to Zaghlul regarding unlimited irrigation in the Sudan. Although heightening the Aswan Dam and the construction of dams in the Sudan and Uganda augmented water supplies in Egypt, such developments barely kept pace with the growing population.

Tied to this pressure of population were many economic, financial, and commercial problems. Cotton was king, and the government and landowners subverted the entire economy for the benefit of cotton culture. Agricultural experimentation, types of irrigation, industrialization, trade practices, tenant farm policies, and land reform—all were considered in the light of their relationship to the production of cotton. Taxation in general rested lightly on agriculture and landowners and bore heavily upon imports, industry, and commerce. The protective tariff of 1930 helped Egyptian industry compete against foreign goods. Ownership of land was extremely inequitable. Many peasants were landless or were poor sharecroppers, while about 21,000 rich persons owned one-half of the land. About 70 percent of the labor force was engaged in agriculture.

Abolition of the capitulations following the Anglo-Egyptian treaty of 1936 and the Montreux convention in 1937 began to alter the commercial world of Cairo and Alexandria. A general exemption from taxation had given foreigners advantages that enabled them to dominate Egyptian finance and commerce. After 1936 the situation was partly reversed. Foreigners suddenly found it advantageous to have Egyptians as partners. Some resident foreigners became Egyptian citizens. The Bank Misr group of industries tried to lead the way in Egyptian industrialization in the 1920s and 1930s, but it ultimately came to cooperate with foreign capital.

EDUCATION AND INTELLECTUAL LIFE

A big development in the period between the two wars was in education. In 1914, with a budget of slightly more than half a million pounds, the ministry of education had 15,000 students in all of Egypt. By 1939 the budget rose to four and a half million and the number of students to 232,000. But there was still much to do. Illiteracy was high, and the size of the task ahead was staggering. The stress was upon literature, languages, and the humanities. The needs of Egypt at the lower levels of sciences, shop work, and vocational training as well as at the higher levels of engineers, scientists, and industrial managers were ignored.

Elementary schools to teach the four R's—reading, writing, arithmetic, and religion—were organized in many villages. By 1939 nearly 1 million children were enrolled in these schools. Unfortunately, after children had finished a village school they were not prepared to enter a vocational or secondary school. Elementary schools attempted only to stamp out illiteracy. The Egyptian (subsequently Fuad I, then Cairo) University, a private school opened in 1908, was put under government control in 1925 and joined to schools of law, medicine, and science. European faculty members played a key role in the 1920s and 1930s until Egyptians who had achieved European doctorates and who had largely acquired the methodology of their teachers became dominant. The educational system was slowly creating a national consciousness among the various strata of Egyptian society.

The first Egyptian women to be admitted as students at the university were enrolled in 1928. Organizations of upper-class women, who were increasingly not wearing veils, now played a larger role in public life. They banded together to establish social services. They set up hospitals, dispensaries, clinics, orphanages, and schools for girls. For males, relatively new social organizations included sports clubs active in such areas as soccer, boxing, and weightlifting.

Egyptian intellectuals debated the basic nature of Egypt and most concluded that its long history and geographic territory had determined the national character. Many Egyptians sought to find the roots of their national existence in the Pharaonic period of antiquity, when Egypt was strong and powerful. By doing so, they deemphasized an Arab or pan Islamic identity in favor of putting more weight on a territorial nationalism. On the other hand, Arabism gained ground in the 1930s, especially in connection with increased Egyptian interest in events in the British mandate of Palestine.

Intellectuals such as Taha Husayn tested public limits on freedom of expression by publishing books critical of accepted beliefs. When the ulema reacted with violent criticism such works were either withdrawn or modified. Liberal and secularly minded humanists advocated controversial ideas such as Darwinian theories of human evolution, socialism, and rationalism. But a change took place in the 1930s as many of these same writers started to produce books about the glories of early Islam and the heroic age of the Muslim conquests.

Literature in the 1920s was still heavily influenced by the neoclassical Ahmad Shawqi (1868–1932), court poet of Abbas II, who was proclaimed by Arabs from throughout the Middle East to be "the prince of poets." However, novelists, short-story writers, essayists, and poets more attuned to new genres, styles, and influences gradually gained ground. Free verse and a romantic and personal approach became popular among the poets of the 1930s. Many novelists participated in a nationalistic and realistic approach to their depictions of life. The novelist and playwright Tawfiq al-Hakim wrote in the 1930s and 1940s works that captured the essence of Egyptian life. Their popularity had the effect of directing attention to such social problems as the gap between peasants, the middle class, and the new legal system. Similar results were achieved by Najib Mahfuz, whose historical novels and later works set in Cairo were to be among the greatest modern Arab literature.

National rebirth and a lively interest in the day-to-day life of the average Egyptian were also seen in the sculpture of Mahmud Mukhtar, as in his "Rebirth of Egypt" of 1928 and two monumental statues of Saad Zaghlul. Even in music Egyptian nationalists called for changes that would help raise national consciousness. They rejected the traditional Arab tonal system and urged composers to draw their themes from Egyptian life. Nationalism thus dominated Egyptian culture as well as political activities.

THE ANGLO-EGYPTIAN SUDAN

Whenever Egyptians considered severing British ties, the enormous area of the Sudan loomed impressively in their thinking. In the nineteenth century the Sudan had been important to Egypt because of the border warfare and slave raids that so frequently disturbed their relationship. In the twentieth century fitting solutions to controversies over Nile water, dams, barrages, irrigation projects, and immigration became vital for Egypt and her burgeoning population.

During World War I the British relaxed their restrictions on Abd al-Rahman, the son of the Mahdi; with his help and that of the Sufi brotherhoods, and because of the increasing prosperity of the country, the Sudan remained quiet during the war. The British also sought in the years following 1918 to gain additional support by extending more authority to tribal shaykhs, but nationalist sentiment was steadily although slowly growing among the Sudanese military and government officials. So as to reduce contacts with Egyptian nationalism, Egyptian troops were forced to withdraw in 1924, after anti-British strikes, demonstrations, and army mutinies among the Sudanese were crushed.

The new Sudan Defense Force consisted solely of Sudanese but this small military group was still financed in part by Egypt. Spending on education in the 1920s, already quite low, was further cut so as to decrease the emergence of Sudanese nationalism. Abd al-Rahman al-Mahdi built up a following among the tribes and the young intelligentsia and gained great influence through his religious status, wealth, and perspicacity.

The British tried to increase the separate cultural identity of the southern districts. English was encouraged and the Arabic language was opposed, and the region was closed to northern, Arabic-speaking, Muslim Sudanese. However, the Arabs of the central Sudan did benefit from a change in British policy starting in 1934. Schools of engineering, agriculture, law, and veterinary medicine were set up and were ultimately merged into a new Gordon Memorial College in 1945 (subsequently the University of Khartoum). Tribalism was now less encouraged by the British administration. Sudanese living on the geographical peripheries of the country saw little social change and economic development; for many of them government remained simply a tax-collecting agency conducted by and for strangers.

Throughout the interwar years educated Sudanese debated at length, but with no clear resolution, the nature of the relationship that ought to exist between their country and Egypt. Shortly after the close of World War I the interrelationship of the Sudan and Egypt had come to the fore again with the setting up of the Gezira project, the operation of which began in 1925. The scheme went back to at least 1900 and Lord Kitchener, who envisaged the irrigation of the triangular stretch of land south of Khartoum between the Blue and White Niles. Much preliminary work was done, but World War I delayed the building of the Sennar Dam on the Blue Nile, and its completion did not come until 1925. Under Allenby's direction the Gezira commission put management in the hands of the Sudan Plantations Syndicate, a British organization. Land tenancies were established at 40 acres (16 hectares) each, and tenants had to follow directions from the Syndicate as to what crops to plant. One-quarter of the land had to be planted in cotton, of which the tenant, the Syndicate, and the Sudan government received 40 percent, 25 percent, and 35 percent, respectively.

The Gezira scheme was highly successful. Since, however, the cotton crop was exported to Great Britain and since Sudan cotton gave the British textile industry a greater independence from Egyptian supply, Egypt grew sensitive to any expansion of irrigated tracts in the Gezira. Also, when the worldwide depression of the 1930s caused the price of cotton to fall, Sudan's economy suffered greatly. Many Sudanese, however, were still engaged in subsistence agriculture or nomadic activities, so the fate of the cash crops did not unduly disturb them.

Egyptian leaders never abandoned their claim that Sudan and Egypt were indissoluble, chiefly because of the water and the expectation that the undeveloped Sudan would serve as an escape valve for growing population pressures in Egypt. Fears and tensions, however, diminished with the treaty arranged in 1929 to allocate the water of the Nile. The Sudan was allotted nearly one billion cubic meters of water by the agreement. The Nile projects commission estimated that this Nile water agreement would leave for Egypt a guaranteed annual irrigation water supply of about twenty-two billion cubic meters. After 1929, Egypt seemed assured of all the water she could use, and at least for the moment, control of the Sudan ceased to be a major political matter. Many Sudanese objected strenuously to the water agreement and to the 1936 treaty because the Sudan and its interests were not directly consulted in these arrangements.

In the months and years immediately preceding 1939 many Egyptians (although not many Sudanese) could look with pride upon the accomplishments of the previous two decades. The Anglo-Egyptian treaty of 1936 gave Egypt political freedom and sovereignty; the constitution, if it were applied, assured political democracy and responsible government; the Montreux convention of 1937 removed the bonds of economic servitude and set the stage for industrial, commercial, and financial independence; and the Nile water agreement of 1929 allayed the fears of the Egyptians that a foreign power would be able to force a thirsty Egypt into submission. Poor Egyptians shared in the nationalist successes, but their plight was not being seriously addressed. All Egyptians hoped that since they now controlled their own lives and destinies for the first time in over 3,000 years, great days lay ahead.

REFERENCES

Numerous volumes already cited contain material of value to this chapter, especially those in Chapters 22, 27, 28, and 31.

Abdel Kader, Soha. *Egyptian Women in a Changing Society, 1899–1987.* Boulder, Colo.: Lynne Rienner, 1987. Examines feminism from the intellectual, nationalist, social, and contemporary political perspectives.

Abdel Rahim, Muddathir. *Imperialism & Nationalism in the Sudan: A Study in Constitutional & Political Development, 1899–1956.* London: Khartoum University Press, 1986. A reprint of the 1969 edition, this constitutional study of the peculiar relationships of the Sudan with Egypt and Britain is comprehensive.

Beshir, Mohamed Omer. *The Southern Sudan: Background to Conflict.* New York: Praeger, 1968. An explanation of the natural and ethnic character of the southern Sudan. Traces its political, social, and economic history.

Brugman, J. *An Introduction to the History of Modern Arabic Literature in Egypt.* Leiden: Brill, 1984. A massive and thorough study, including analysis of the growth of literary criticism, with a discussion of nearly every major literary figure up to about 1950.

Carter, B. L. *The Copts in Egyptian Politics.* London: Croom Helm, 1986. Discusses internal aspects of Coptic Church history as well as the relations of the Copts with nationalists and the British; ends with the revolution of 1952.

Daly, M. W. *Empire on the Nile: The Anglo-Egyptian Sudan, 1898–1934.* Cambridge: Cambridge University Press, 1986. An excellent study that includes discussions of education, economics, health, politics, the British, etc.

Davis, Eric. *Challenging Colonialism: Bank Misr and Egyptian Industrialization, 1920–1941.* Princeton, N.J.: Princeton University Press, 1983.

Deeb, Marius. "Labour and Politics in Egypt, 1919–1939." *International Journal of Middle East Studies* 10 (1979): 187–203. Shows the domination of the Wafd.

Gershoni, Israel, and James P. Jankowski. *Egypt, Islam, and the Arabs: The Search for Egyptian Nationhood, 1900–1930.* New York: Oxford University Press, 1986. A thorough examination of Egyptian thought about territorial nationalism.

Landau, Jacob M. *Parliaments and Parties in Egypt.* Tel Aviv: Israel Oriental Society, 1953. The author is strong in discussing the developments of the 1920s.

Mitchell, Richard P. *The Society of the Muslim Brothers.* London: Oxford University Press, 1968. The most exhaustively researched treatment of the subject.

Niblock, Tim. *Class and Power in Sudan: The Dynamics of Sudanese Politics, 1898–1985.* Albany: State University of New York Press, 1987. Particularly valuable for its treatment of regions, social groups, religion, the economy, as well as political happenings.

Reid, Donald M. "Cairo University and the Orientalists." *International Journal of Middle East Studies* 19 (1987): 51–76. One of an excellent series of articles by the author on aspects of Egyptian academic life.

Richards, Alan. "Agricultural Technology and Rural Social Classes in Egypt, 1920–1939." *Middle Eastern Studies* 16 (1980): 56–83. Shows how technical changes and population increase lowered the standard of living of the peasants.

Royal Institute of International Affairs. *Great Britain and Egypt, 1914–1951.* London: Oxford University Press, 1952.

Sanderson, Lilian Passmore, and Neville Sanderson. *Education, Religion, and Politics in Southern Sudan, 1899–1964.* London: Ithaca Press, 1981.

al-Sayyid-Marsot, Afaf Lutfi. *Egypt's Liberal Experiment: 1922–1936.* Berkeley: University of California Press, 1977. Outlines the social and economic bases as well as the politics of the period. Excellent.

Smith, Charles D. *Islam and the Search for Social Order in Modern Egypt: A Biography of Muhammad Husayn Haykal.* Albany: State University of New York Press, 1983. The intellectual and political life of a prominent Egyptian thinker.

Terry, Janice J. *Cornerstone of Egyptian Political Power: The Wafd, 1919–1952.* London: Third World Centre, 1982.

Tignor, Robert L. *State, Private Enterprise, and Economic Change in Egypt, 1918–1952.* Princeton, N.J.: Princeton University Press, 1984. A thorough and systematic treatment of the Egyptian middle class and the role of foreign companies operating in Egypt.

Woodward, Peter. *Condominium and Sudanese Nationalism.* London: Rex Collings, 1979. Concentrates on the 1942–1956 period.

Ziadeh, Farhat J. *Lawyers, the Rule of Law, and Liberalism in Modern Egypt.* Stanford: Hoover Institution, 1968. Traces the role of liberal tradition, national independence, and constitutionalism in the work of lawyers in Egypt.

36

Reza Shah's Iran

IMPERIALISM IN IRAN

When World War I burst upon the Middle East, Iran was experiencing chaotic problems involving internal political and constitutional developments, financial and economic turmoil, and intense imperial rivalry among Russia, Great Britain, and Germany. After 1911, democratic nationalists believed that Germany offered the only hope of avoiding an impending partition of Iran by British and Russian imperialists. In the few years prior to 1914, German activities in Iran had been fruitful, and during the first months of the war Germany concluded a secret treaty with the Iranian government promising arms, ammunition, money, and independence in return for cooperation.

Britain and Russia, aware of these agreements, acted swiftly to hold Iran in their power. Russian troops moved from Qazvin, which they had been occupying for several years, to the outskirts of Tehran. Supporters of the Central Powers then fled to Kermanshah, where an anti-Allied Iranian government was formed. Ahmad Shah remained in his capital with his cabinet, and technically Iran maintained her neutrality, as the shah received subventions from Britain. The German consul, Wassmuss, stirred the Qashqai and Bakhtiyari tribes in southern Iran and threatened British oil operations. To counter this danger and protect the wells, whose production had greatly increased during the war, the British eventually sent Sir Percy Sykes to organize the South Persian Rifles. In 1917, in cooperation with Russian cossacks from the north, they occupied Kerman, Isfahan, Shiraz, and most of Fars. Russia's collapse, however, left the northern provinces open; for a time German and Ottoman troops held Azerbayjan, but they were recalled at the end of the war and the British remained dominant in Iran. A famine further devastated northern Iran and the country experienced great difficulties.

POSTWAR PROBLEMS

Lord Curzon had dreams of a British Empire from the Mediterranean to Singapore. With Iraq and Palestine already pledged, Iran was the missing link. Sir Percy Cox was sent from Baghdad to Tehran to escort Iran into the British Empire. An Iranian delegation went to Paris, but being anti-British, it was not permitted to attend the peace conference or to state Iran's case, though Iran did secure an invitation to join the League of Nations and did so. A less hostile delegation negotiated and signed on August 9, 1919, an Anglo-Iranian treaty. Though the words were friendly, it virtually transformed Iran into a dependency of the British Empire, and public opinion throughout the world rightly judged it in that light. Iranian government departments, finances, public services, and the army would be in British hands. Iran already received a monthly subsidy and would now gain a loan of £2 million; in return, her tariffs would be adjusted and customs controlled by the British as collateral against the loan.

The Iranian Assembly (*Majlis*) refused to ratify the treaty; and general world-wide British military retrenchment effected a withdrawal of British forces and the demobilization of the South Persian Rifles. Bolshevik Russia pursued a more be-guiling course by denouncing the capitulations and tsarist treaties with Iran. In pursuing tsarist General Denikin, Soviet forces landed troops in 1920, occupied Iranian territory north of the Elburz Mountains, and refused to depart until all British military were evacuated. A Soviet Republic of Gilan was established at Resht under the leadership of Kuchuk Khan, over whom, Moscow alleged, she had no authority.

Iran protested to the League of Nations. There she was given quantities of sympathy but informed that better results could be obtained by direct negotiations with the Bolsheviks. Taking these words to heart, she concluded a treaty of friend-ship at Moscow on February 26, 1921. The frontiers and independence of each were to be respected; Iranian debts to Russia were canceled; all concessions were relinquished, except the Caspian Sea fisheries, since even Communists had to have caviar; neither would harbor enemies of the other; and if a third power menaced or occupied any part of Iran, Russia might send troops to Iran. Also, Iran promised not to cede to any other power or national thereof any privilege or concession being relinquished by Russia. Shortly thereafter, Russia withdrew her troops and her support of the Soviet Republic of Gilan, which promptly succumbed to inter-nal disputes and an Iranian military expedition.

Thus, rejection by the majlis of the Anglo-Iranian treaty of 1919, the with-drawal of British troops, and the Soviet-Iranian treaty of 1921 confirmed the inde-pendence of Iran. However, she did not possess sufficient leadership or experi-ence for political democracy and was torn with strife and economic disorder. Disease, poverty, corruption, and debased public morality prevailed everywhere throughout the land. The areas encompassing the installations of the Anglo-Persian Oil Company were the only flourishing districts of the country, and they were fully under the thumb of the British government. World War I left Iran in a seemingly hopeless state with little outside interest willing to lend a helping hand.

REZA KHAN

Five days before the signing of the Russo-Iranian treaty in Moscow, Reza Khan, an officer of the Iranian cossacks, led his men into Tehran and with a coup d'état took over the reins of government. A self-educated trooper with a keen nationalist feel-ing, Reza rose from the ranks of the Russian-officered Iranian cossacks and became one of their leaders when the Russian officers were ousted in 1920. On his march on Tehran in 1921, he was advised in part by British officers; consequently, opponents charged, though quite incorrectly, that Reza was a pawn in British imperialistic ambitions.

For two decades Reza Khan and his army controlled the Iranian government, although following the coup d'état a fiery crusading journalist, Sayyid Ziya al-Din Tabatabai, became prime minister. Several others succeeded to that post, until Reza, who had also taken command of the gendarmerie, assumed office in 1923 and invited Ahmad Shah to take "an extended and prolonged tour" of Europe. Republican sentiment was astir as Reza looked westward to pattern his state after Turkey. But in 1924, when the stage was set for a republican declaration, the Turkish assembly abolished the caliphate and advanced along its secular path. Frightened Iranian ulema raised such a storm that Reza met with a group of religious leaders at Qum. Thereafter, public mention of a republic was forbidden. In 1925, Reza Khan Pahlevi, with the support of the parliament and the ulema, became shah, and the throne was vested in male members of the Pahlevi family born of Iranian mothers. One of the few members of parliament to vote against Reza as shah was the young Mohammad Mosaddeq, a liberal lawyer related to the Qajars, who was subsequently barred from politics by the new shah.

The problems facing Reza Shah in Iran were similar to those before Kemal in Turkey, only far more difficult. The two most pressing were reestablishment of a recognized central governmental authority and reform of national finances. The former was largely a matter for Reza and the army to resolve; the latter remained the work of an American, Dr. Arthur C. Millspaugh, formerly economic adviser to the secretary of state. Employed by the Iranian government in 1922 as administrator-general of finances, he held the power and authority of a cabinet minister. With vast powers and the staunch support of Reza's military force Dr. Millspaugh balanced the budget by reorganizing the tax structure and enforcing the collection of taxes. State enterprises were inaugurated and economic conditions improved gradually. However, Dr. Millspaugh was frequently tactless and too rigid in his manners for a proud and sensitive people in whom, through centuries of personal government, pliability had become deeply ingrained. In 1927 he and his American staff departed after he refused to renew his contract except on the same terms of power and authority as before.

One stipulation between Reza and Dr. Millspaugh provided that the budget of the ministry of war would always be met, for Reza understood the source of his power. By 1926, when Reza crowned himself shah, he had personally led his army to end rebellions in Azerbayjan and Khurasan and had partially defeated the nomadic tribes. He went on to forcibly settle, conscript, and disarm the nomadic tribes; he deprived them of their livelihood and earned their bitter hatred, as expressed in such events as the unsuccessful rebellions of the Qashqai confederation in 1929 and 1932. Reza's greatest success along these lines was achieved in ending the independent rule of Shaykh Khazal of Mohammerah, with whom the British had a "working agreement" with respect to the operations of the Anglo-Persian Oil Company. The imposition of Reza's authority over the distant provinces, peoples, and governors of Iran upped state revenues and made Dr. Millspaugh's policies more effective and widespread. This in turn assured a more certain execution of royal government.

According to the constitution of 1906, which was still in force, the power of the nation was vested in the shah, the senate, and the assembly, which by 1926 was filled with Reza's supporters. The senate was appointive, but Reza never called it and never made any appointments to it. The assembly nominated a prime minister who was appointed by the shah. Reza Shah's greatest work, perhaps, was the instilling of an enthusiastic attitude toward work among the personnel of the ministries. Sometimes he would appear at a government office early in the morning to see if the officials were on duty and on time.

REFORMS

Public veneration given to religious leaders had proved a stumbling block to many Iranian governments. Reza, therefore, attempted to relegate religion, its institutions, and its leaders to a less influential position in national life, particularly after the Shiite divines raised such an effective furor over republicanism in 1924. Sufis were forbidden to appear on the streets or along the roads of the countryside. Public parades and presentations of the passion play in memory of the death of Husayn were prohibited. Other overt acts showed the supremacy of Reza over the clergy. In 1928, when a religious leader in the mosque at Qum digressed from his sermon to admonish the queen for unveiling her face, Reza hurried there with two armored cars, entered the mosque without removing his boots, and publicly whipped the offending preacher. Veils were outlawed in 1936; at the same time the shah and other officials took to removing their hats and caps in public buildings. All citizens were required to use family last names.

Equally significant and more pointed was the confiscation of many religious properties and endowments, the income from which went to the support of schools, hospitals, state industries, and other state enterprises. No longer were religious leaders and teachers *mullahs*) completely independent, and some of their schools were closed. However, the theological schools at Qum were rebuilt and renovated, and they attracted the leading religious authorities among the Shiites to that city southwest of Tehran. Much of the ulema's livelihood henceforth came from the state, and their hold over the population was diminished. Furthermore, secularization of the law was speeded up. A mixture of shariah and French judicial principles was enacted into the new law codes of 1925–1928. Men retained a legal superiority over women, but religious law was limited in scope and in authority. By 1931, religious courts exercised jurisdiction only over domestic relations, personal status, and notarial acts. In 1928 the capitulations, which granted rights to foreigners concerning courts, trials, and legal privileges, were abolished. Theological students were subjected to military conscription, and education became a public responsibility under the supervision and regulation of the central government.

By 1940, about 10 percent of the population was receiving an elementary school education, and Tehran University, founded in 1935, was expanding. It admitted women students in 1937; the first government primary school for girls was opened in 1918. Intellectual life had begun to change during World War I, when poets, novelists, and journalists emphasized Iranian nationalism and morality by alluding to the glories of the pre-Islamic empires of Iran, such as that of the Sasanid dynasty. Some writers later began to experiment with new forms of expression, including the use of colloquial idioms, while others dealt with new themes such as the emancipation of women. Often such authors were heavily influenced by European schools of expression. Strict censorship and repression of opposition by the government of Reza Shah led many authors either to go into exile or to limit the circulation of their publications to a small circle of friends. Neoclassicists favored old forms with new content; they often backed mild reform measures and enjoyed the support of the political authorities. The shah did everything possible to spread the Persian language and to lessen the use of other languages, such as Turkish and Arabic, that were spoken in various regions of Iran.

One of Reza Shah's permanent contributions stemmed from his need for better communications to bring the more distant parts of his realm within his power. There may have been 2,000 miles (3,200 kilometers) of roads in Iran on the day of his coup d'état; by the outbreak of World War II the road system had been extended to about 17,000 miles (27,000 kilometers). In view of Iran's role in the supply line to Russia in World War II, perhaps Reza's most far-reaching achievement was the construction of the Trans-Iranian railway from Bandarshapur on the Persian Gulf to Bandarshah on the Caspian Sea, a distance of 865 miles (1,392 kilometers). Completed in 1938, it was an engineering marvel, consisting of 224 tunnels and passing from sea level to an altitude of nearly 9,000 feet (2,700 meters) and then down to below sea level. The railway was entirely financed by Iran. Its route pleased neither Russia nor Britain; from their points of view it began nowhere, passed through Tehran, and again ended nowhere, since it had no links to the frontiers of Russia, Iraq, India, and Turkey. But as the Iranians saw it, the railroad connected the northern fertile provinces with the south and by passing through nomad country facilitated the movement of the shah's military strength.

The Iranian army increased in size and strength, especially following the enactment of conscription in 1925. In 1921 when Reza seized Tehran, the Cossack Brigade had about 4,000 men; but in the 1930s the number of troops in the imperial army had risen to about 100,000. Initially, officer candidates were largely trained abroad, especially in France. Later, training schools were also opened in Tehran. Between 25 percent to 40 percent of government expenditures were for the military. Military trucks used the newly built highways, and aircraft, tanks, and a small navy were also acquired. Increased security allowed a freer circulation of people and goods and thus helped economic growth.

Like Mustafa Kemal Atatürk in Turkey, Reza felt the need of industrialization and economic development. Iran had an agricultural economy, and most of the labor force was engaged in farming. Thoroughgoing reforms should have been undertaken in that direction. Improved irrigation was proposed, and better agricultural methods were studied. Some beneficial results were obtained. Yet, progress fell far short of the envisaged goals, largely because two-thirds of the arable land was held by absentee landlords who were satisfied with the old techniques and who demanded an immediate high return on their investment. Reza did not change the basic system of land ownership. Also, one of the new reforms actually hurt the peasants—registration of land ownership claims implicity favored the rich landowners. In general, economic development aided the cities at the expense of the countryside.

In 1928, when Iran was fully able to set its own tariffs, duties were increased so as to raise more revenue and protect industry. New factories were built for refining sugar and for spinning and weaving cotton, silk, and wool. Most of these were state enterprises and varied widely in efficiency and capacity. Prices for the goods produced were high, but a state monopoly over most frontier trade rendered competition with imported goods negligible. Nonetheless, since Iranian industry suffered from a shortage of technicians and plant managers, industrial development under Reza proved unsatisfactory.

The world economic depression of the 1930s made the value of Iran's primary exports sink, while the cost of imports increased. Reza created a state trading mechanism under which much of the foreign trade was managed by the government. Various other monopolies were instituted for special purposes; monopolies on sugar and tea, for instance, helped finance the building of the Trans-Iranian railway.

Oil developments

By far the most important industrial enterprise in Iran during the period of Reza Shah's rule was the Anglo-Persian Oil Company, which by agreement paid Iran 16 percent of the profits. During World War I the company property, installations, and pipelines had been protected by a light infantry force organized by the British. After the war the question of what profits to include while calculating the Iranian government's 16 percent was bitterly debated.

The difficulty originated from the fact that Iran had no control over the quantity of oil produced and no guaranteed annual income from the concession. With the complexity of oil operations and the multiplicity of companies, Iran lost confidence in the integrity of the company's bookkeeping practices. Fluctuations in the amounts received by Iran—£411,000 in 1923; £1,400,000 in 1926; £502,000 in 1927; £1,437,000 in 1929; and £307,000 in 1931—left the finances and the budget of the government completely at the mercy of the company, which could shut off the oil wells in Iran at will and obtain the necessary crude oil for its markets in other fields. Furthermore, in 1931 Great Britain went off the gold standard, and Iran's sterling balances were depreciated. In that same year, the Iranian government received only about one-half of the amount the British government was obtaining from the company. Finally, a new concession was negotiated in 1931 by the Iraq Petroleum Company giving more favorable terms to Iraq. Since the Anglo-Persian Oil Company was one of the principal owners in Iraq, the Iranian government felt it should have treatment equally favorable.

After bitter wrangling, sharp notes, and the dispatch of British warships to the Persian Gulf, England took the case to the League council and tried to submit it to the Permanent Court of International Justice at The Hague. Neither body took action; Iran protested that neither had jurisdiction, the case being between a private company and the Iranian government. Iran did, however, inform the company that she was agreeable to the granting of a new concession, provided that its terms were more favorable to Iran than those in the previous concession.

The new concession, which was signed in Tehran in April 1933, included the following provisions: The area covered was immediately reduced by half, to be selected by the company. The company relinquished its exclusive right to build and operate pipelines in Iran. Iran would receive four shillings per ton on all oil sold in Iran or exported. Iran would be paid 20 percent of all dividends over £671,250, and the company guaranteed that total annual payments to Iran would never be under £750,000. Iran would be secured against any depreciation of sterling. The company was exempt from taxation, but in lieu of such charges the company agreed to pay the government nine pence per ton on the first 6 million tons exported and six pence per ton above that, the minimum annual payment to be £225,000. The Iranian government oil commissioner had the right to examine the books and attend directors' meetings.

Undoubtedly, the winning of this agreement by Reza Shah was his finest economic and diplomatic victory. Some observers at the time believed that Iran, by this stroke, obtained her independence. Certainly her oil income was placed on a more sustaining basis, even though it seemed clear that the British admiralty was still able to purchase Iranian oil more cheaply than the Iranian government.

INTERNATIONAL AFFAIRS

Reza Shah in his foreign affairs maintained friendly relations with his neighbors. Visits were exchanged, and in 1934 he was entertained in Ankara. The crowning achievement was the signing of the Saadabad pact in 1937 with Turkey, Iraq, and Afghanistan at Reza's Garden Palace in the mountains near Tehran. The pact provided for mutual cooperation, consultations, and nonaggression.

In addition to the concession of the Anglo-Persian Oil Company, which became the Anglo-Iranian Oil Company in 1935, when Reza insisted on use of the word "Iran" to denote his country, the Anglo-Iranian treaty of 1928 helped to settle affairs with England. Imperial Airways was allowed to fly planes over Iran; Britain recognized the end of the capitulations; British support for Shaykh Khazal of Mohammerah was terminated and Reza took over the shaykh's role in protecting the oil pipelines; British consuls and agents were still permitted to deal directly with tribes such as the Lurs, Bakhtiyaris, and the Qashqais; and Iran recognized British rule in Iraq. Except for Iran's claim to the Bahrayn Islands, all outstanding matters were considered, and anti-British feelings in Iran became quiescent temporarily. Such feelings could, however, easily be brought to the surface, for twisting the British lion's tail was a sporting event for all Iranian nationalists.

Reza Shah's relations with Soviet Russia were more complicated, especially since Iran and Russia had a long common frontier. Iran was traversed by Soviet agents of all kinds, and rebellions occurred in Azerbayjan and Khurasan. When the rebellions were suppressed, all Communist activities went underground. In the Russo-Iranian treaty of 1921 Russia had formally renounced all concessions and

Iran was forbidden to grant these concessions to other foreigners. Thus, in the 1920s and again in the 1930s, Russia protested vehemently when Iran granted oil concessions in her northern provinces. Since northern Iran's export market was almost exclusively Russian, Russia could and frequently did exert great pressure on Iran by closing her frontiers to Iranian goods. This weapon was invoked in 1926 to obtain a fishing agreement for the Caspian Sea. For political ends Russia dumped goods on Iran and by 1931 had all but ruined Iranian exporters. Sensing the inability of private traders in Iran to challenge the Soviet state trading companies, Reza placed all foreign trade in Iran under state monopoly and control. This device and Germany's return to the Iranian scene with the advent of Hitler gave Iran some freedom from economic domination by the colossus to the north.

Caught between the British in the south and the Soviets in the north, Iran turned to Germany as a counterpoise. German technicians were invited in great numbers, advising various ministries. When compensation and bank-clearing agreements were concluded in 1935, the volume of trade between the two countries jumped. In 1939 over 40 percent of Iran's foreign trade was with Germany. Iranian schools hired German professors and numerous Iranians took advanced degrees in German universities. Modern Iranian architecture showed strong German influences.

REZA SHAH EVALUATED

Reza Shah Pahlevi was an uneducated soldier who had a soldier's respect for authority and expected his will to be followed implicitly. The subterfuges of traditional Iranian officialdom frustrated him into direct and ruthless conduct. Discovering that the minutiae of governing frequently were not accomplished when his back was turned, he consumed too much of his time with the details. There was a vast amount of work that needed to be done in Iran and too few to do it, and Reza became immersed in a welter of programs too numerous for him to carry through alone. Taking so much responsibility on his own shoulders discouraged initiative in those about him; in consequence the promising projects for agricultural reform, educational and secular development, and state industrial enterprise fell far short of their goals. Reza's lack of education did, however, make it possible for him to discard many traditions of Iranian society that a man trained in the niceties and subtleties of Iranian culture and its long history would have been incapable of ignoring. Westernization in Iran had a stout ally in Reza Shah. He was opposed by the ulema, some of the large landowners, political liberals, and the tribes.

In the end Reza became interested in acquiring a great personal fortune in estates and funds in foreign accounts. He grew tired, his temper rose, his sensitivity to criticism mounted, and his power became more absolute, as he purged the government of his closest advisers and associates in the early 1930s. On the other hand, chaos had been replaced by order, the nation was stronger in 1939 than it had been in 1919, and a beginning had been made in economic development. Modernization from above was underway when World War II violently changed the political situation in Iran.

REFERENCES

See works already cited in Chapters 29 and 31.

Abrahamian, Ervand. *Iran Between Two Revolutions.* Princeton, N.J.: Princeton University Press, 1982. A detailed political and economic history, with an emphasis on the Tudeh Party's development.

Amirsadeghi, Hossein, ed. *Twentieth Century Iran.* New York: Holmes and Meier, 1977. Valuable essays on political history, oil, the economy, social change, and foreign policy.

Amuzegar, Jahangir, and M. Ali Fekrat. *Iran: Economic Development Under Dualistic Conditions.* Chicago: University of Chicago Press, 1971. A fine analysis of the reasons for slow economic growth prior to 1950 and of the conditions that led to rapid development after 1954.

Banani, Amin. *The Modernization of Iran, 1921–1941.* Stanford: Stanford University Press, 1961. This study, based largely on Iranian sources, gives a detailed survey of the impact of Reza Shah on his country.

Beck, Lois. *The Qashqa'i of Iran.* New Haven, Conn.: Yale University Press, 1986. An excellent study that includes the nineteenth and twentieth centuries.

Binder, Leonard. *Iran: Political Development in a Changing Society.* Berkeley: University of California Press, 1962. One of the most important studies of recent Iran.

Cottam, Richard W. *Nationalism in Iran.* 2d ed. Pittsburgh, Pa.: University of Pittsburgh Press, 1979. A comprehensive, systematic, and stimulating study emphasizing the interrelated themes of liberal nationalism and the policy of the United States toward Iran.

Diba, Farhad. *Mohammad Mossadegh. A Political Biography.* London. Croom Helm, 1986. A work very favorable to its subject.

Faghfoory, Mohammad H. "The Ulama-State Relations in Iran: 1921–1941." *International Journal of Middle East Studies* 19 (1987): 413–432.

Fatemi, Nasrollah S. *Diplomatic History of Persia, 1917–1923: Anglo-Russian Power Politics in Iran.* New York: R. F. Moore, 1952.

Kamshad, Hassan. *Modern Persian Prose Literature.* Cambridge: The University Press, 1966. Accounts of the authors' lives, summaries of important works, and many translated excerpts.

Lambton, A. K. S. *Landlord and Peasant in Persia.* London: Oxford University Press, 1953.

Lenczowski, George, ed. *Iran Under the Pahlavis.* Stanford: Hoover Institution, 1978. A very favorable view of Reza Shah's dynasty and its accomplishments in social change, the economy, oil policy, land reform, education, culture, and other topics.

————. *Russia and the West in Iran, 1918–1948, A Study in Big Power Rivalry.* Ithaca, N.Y.: Cornell University Press, 1949. A first-rate study.

Millspaugh, Arthur C. *The American Task in Persia.* New York: Century, 1925. An account of the author's first tour of duty in Iran.

————. *Americans in Persia.* Washington, D.C.: The Brookings Institution, 1946. A personal account by the American adviser to the shah.

Olson, William J. *Anglo-Iranian Relations During World War I.* London: Frank Cass, 1984. An excellent treatment of British policy and Iranian governments during World War I and up to 1920.

Rezun, Miron. "Reza Shah's Court Minister: Teymourtash." *International Journal of Middle East Studies* 12 (1980): 119–137. One of the very few studies of a prominent member of Reza Shah's entourage; especially valuable for a discussion of relations with the Soviet Union.

Ricks, Thomas, ed. *Critical Perspectives on Modern Persian Literature.* Washington, D.C.: Three Continents Press, 1984. A multitude of critical essays on individual authors and general trends which show the relationship of political and social changes with literature.

Sykes, Christopher. *Wassmuss, "the German Lawrence."* London: Longmans, Green, 1936. The fascinating story of the German agent in Iran during World War I.

Wilber, Donald N. *Iran: Past and Present.* 9th ed. Princeton, N.J.: Princeton University Press, 1981. A classic summary of Iran's history, largely since 1921.

———. *Riza Shah Pahlavi: The Resurrection and Reconstruction of Iran, 1878–1944.* New York: Exposition Press, 1975. An account of the shah's life almost week by week, blow by blow.

Yarshater, Ehsan, ed. *Persian Literature.* Albany: State University of New York Press, 1987.

37

World War II and the Middle East

TURKISH NEUTRALITY

Upon the outbreak of World War II, Turkey declared her neutrality. Yet, her position was not clear-cut. In the fifteen months before the actual rupture of peace and even as early as 1936, Turkish foreign policy had been veering toward Britain and France. In September 1939, Turkey was joined to England and France by several pacts regarding credits, chrome ore, and nonaggression. On the other hand, almost 50 percent of her trade was with Germany. Furthermore, the Nazi-Soviet pact of August 1939 gave Turkish leadership every reason for caution, since Russian power and objectives in the Black Sea area and eastern Asia Minor were difficult to assess.

On October 19, Turkey signed a formal fifteen-year treaty of alliance with France and the United Kingdom. Its terms held that in the event of an act of aggression upon Turkey her allies would come to her assistance, that Turkey on her part would enter the war should it come to the Mediterranean, but that under no circumstances would Turkey be drawn into a conflict against the U.S.S.R. At the same time loans and credits were made to Turkey to bolster her financial position and speed the flow of arms. Britain also had an all-important agreement, which ran until January 1, 1943, whereby she could, if she so desired, purchase and export the entire output of Turkish chrome ore.

Upon the fall of France, the entry of Italy into the war, and the loss of British armor at Dunkirk, the Turkish government quickly reassessed its international position. It was suspected that Russia, surely having been awarded Istanbul and the Straits by Hitler, might soon move to seize the prize, as she was already doing in Finland, the Baltic, and Bessarabia. Turkey had bravely cast her lot with Britain and France, but the likelihood of a German defeat was far removed in the summer of 1940 and the winter of 1940–1941. War came to the Mediterranean upon Italy's declaration, but Turkey maintained her neutrality and continued in that course through the Italian campaign against Greece, the German conquest of Yugoslavia and Greece, and the occupation of Bulgaria.

British naval and air personnel in civilian garb were numerous in Turkey, and the British urged Turkish entry into the war at the time of the debacle in Greece.

Steadfastly, the Turkish leaders refused. They pointed out that Britain was no more prepared to give planes and heavy armor to Turkey than to Greece and that recklessness on Turkey's part would invite German retaliation. Also, if Turkey could maintain a neutral role, she would serve as a land barrier to Syria, Suez, and the Persian Gulf. Furthermore, the leaders could see no purely Turkish reason for joining in the war.

Hitler's invasion of Russia acutely disturbed the orientation of Turkish neutrality. The Turks clearly foresaw that a German defeat would leave Soviet Russia the dominant continental power of Europe. Since the British had promised Russia the Straits in World War I and since the appeasers had been so free with other nations' territories, England might easily concede the Straits to Russia to seal the sudden new alliance between them. Moreover the Straits might be safe from German aggression as long as German arms were engaged deeply in Russia. As American lend-lease began to rebuild British strength, it became possible for the Turks to envisage a negotiated peace without victory that might eventually safeguard Turkish frontiers and leave the Straits in their hands.

The might of Germany from the middle of 1941 to the spring of 1943 awed Turkish leaders. Turkey signed a ten-year nonaggression pact with Germany in June 1941, although the Turks insisted on a statement that this pact did not contravene any previous Turkish commitments. In October a trade agreement was concluded, providing for the shipment of various raw materials to Germany, among which would be chrome ore. After January 1, 1943, when the chrome agreement with Great Britain would expire, Germany would be enabled to purchase 90,000 tons of ore in exchange for war equipment, most of which would have to be delivered to Turkey before the chrome ore could be exported. Although it was a hollow German victory, the Turkish press played it up as a concrete evidence of Turkish neutrality. One reason for President Inönü's reluctance to ally Turkey fully with Britain was his doubts about the future good will of Stalin with regard to the Straits.

Throughout 1943 the discussions among the United States, the Soviet Union, and Great Britain centered on opening a second front and the possibility of Turkish cooperation and open participation. The topic was raised early in 1942 in a general way; in 1943 it was again considered and debated. Churchill repeatedly pressed the case for Turkish entry and for a concerted attack upon Germany through the Balkans as the best way to defeat Germany and save central Europe and the Balkans from the Bolsheviks. Russia, on the other hand, believed that Turkey should declare her position against the Axis and shoulder some of the real burdens of the war. But Turkey steadfastly refused to abandon her neutrality, recognizing that German bombers from bases in Bulgaria, only twenty minutes from Istanbul, could pulverize that fair city almost at will. The decisive veto on Churchill's plan was exercised by U.S. General George C. Marshall. No arms would be spared from the cross-channel attack upon Europe, for the Americans at that moment were demanding a frontal attack upon Germany. Without aid, Turkey would not enter the war. She did, however, permit British and American officers to circulate quite freely "incognito."

In April 1944, chrome shipments to Germany were halted; in August, following British and American promises that they would take adequate measures to prevent the collapse of the Turkish economy, Turkey severed diplomatic and economic relations with Germany. Finally, in February 1945, in order to become a charter member of the United Nations and attend the San Francisco conference, Turkey declared war upon Germany. But for all practical purposes the war was over, and Turkey entered the tense postwar period.

During the war years the Turkish economy was subjected to constant pressure from all sides. At times more than 1 million men were under arms, and the Turkish budget called for vast military expenditures. Deficit financing brought inflation, price controls being either absent or ineffective. Moreover, large sums were thrown about by agents, spics, and "tourists" from the belligerent powers. Extensive German purchases of mohair, olive oil, hazelnuts, chrome ore, tanning materials, and tobacco, in addition to tobacco and chrome exported to England and the United States, gave Turkey great purchasing power at a time when the importation of consumer articles and capital goods was exceedingly difficult.

Another cause of inflation was the policy of preclusive or preemptive buying pursued by England and the United States in Turkey. Several hundred million dollars' worth of low-grade chrome ore, mohair, hazelnuts, olive oil, and valonia were bought and stored in Turkey for the sole purpose of keeping these goods from Germany. An active market in these commodities forced prices up and increased production. The end of the war found Turkey with a sizable fund of foreign exchange acquired from exports and sales that were never balanced by imports.

The general shipping shortage of the Allies and the difficulty of importing goods into Turkey through the Mediterranean created many other abnormalities in Turkish trade. Furthermore, since Turkey was a neutral power, all exports from the United States and the British Empire were carefully screened to make sure that goods would not be reexported to the Axis.

Inflation and mounting deficits induced Inönü in 1942 to experiment with a capital levy tax in hopes of lowering prices, balancing the budget, and absorbing some of the abundance of money. A law (*Varlik Vergisi*) authorized the creation of a special committee in each province to levy a tax on all persons according to their capital and in varying percentages on the assumption they were evading their proper income taxes. Particularly in Istanbul, gross inequalities developed. Greeks, Armenians, Jews, and foreigners were hard-pressed, some being assessed sums nearly equal to their total capital. Those who did not pay were sentenced to hard labor on railroads in eastern Anatolia. Representatives of the Allied governments protested to Inönü, but the situation with regard to Turkish neutrality was so delicate that all news of the capital tax was censored in Western presses until the spring of 1943. Upon official pressure at the highest levels in wartime conferences in 1943, the tax was abolished and those who had not paid were released. The experience, however, left an unpleasant residue of insecurity on the part of non-Muslim citizens, who regarded the tax as an expression of unbridled nationalism.

When Turkey broke with Germany in August 1944, it was feared that a sudden termination of preclusive buying and the cessation of German purchases of strategic raw materials along with comestibles such as figs, raisins, and fish would be a ruinous shock to the Turkish economy. However, no crash occurred. Shipping became more plentiful, Turkish ports were opened, and Turkish products found a ready market in a world apparently short of almost everything.

For Turkey the period of the war from September 1, 1939, to February 23, 1945, had marked a difficult course of neutrality. Turkey wished to live in peace with the victorious powers, but during the course of the war it was not always clear who would win. Furthermore, at first Russia and Germany were opposed to England and France; then, at one stroke, in 1941 Russia and England were combined to crush Germany. Those five and one-half years seemed endless to President Inönü and the leaders of Turkey.

EGYPT AND THE WAR

In other areas of the Middle East World War II brought armies, shortages, inflation, political strain, economic opportunities, and a variety of social and intellectual upheavals. At the very outset Egypt held a pivotal position. Ali Mahir, the prime minister and a person with a great influence over King Faruq, induced the government to sever diplomatic relations with Germany as soon as Britain declared war. In accordance with the 1936 Anglo-Egyptian treaty, martial law was declared; ports were placed under the authority of the British navy; and censorship of posts and telegraph was established. When parliament convened in November the speech from the throne indicated that Egypt would give active and willing cooperation to England in defense of Egypt. Some concern arose over the price and market for cotton, particularly since nearly 20 percent of Egyptian cotton exports had gone in the previous year to Germany and countries under her control. Demand, however, was brisk, and open-market prices climbed higher than those guaranteed by the government. When Mussolini entered the war, Egypt broke off relations with Italy, but notified him that war would not be declared unless Italy attacked Egypt. As a result of British pressure, Ali Mahir, now recognized as anti-British, was replaced by Hasan Sabri, an independent, who formed a broad government.

The Italian declaration brought the war to Egypt's doorstep. In September 1940, Italian forces advanced some fifty miles into Egypt toward Alexandria, resting at Sidi Barrani until December, when the British drove them west of Benghazi. Then, in April 1941, after contributing heavily to the support of Greece, British forces reeled toward the Egyptian frontier, although the fortress of Tobruk held. From then until May 1942, Germany's General Rommel and his Afrika Korps fought a see-saw battle against the British, pushing the front to al-Alamayn, only seventy miles west of Alexandria. In October 1942, a two-week battle at al-Alamayn broke the German army, which continued to fall back, as the British Eighth Army followed in full pursuit. British and American forces, which landed in Morocco and Algeria on November 8, 1942, under the command of General Dwight D.

Eisenhower, met the British in Tunisia at the end of March 1943, and the war in North Africa came to its end.

As war raged in the western desert, life in Egypt changed rapidly. Although a few British continued their afternoon cricket matches at the famed Gezira Sporting Club, most found the tensions of war pressing upon them. When the Mediterranean was virtually closed to shipping, a glut of cotton loomed ominously, but Britain solved the problem by agreeing to buy the entire crop at a price Egyptians admitted was generous.

Shortages of cereals, inadequate price regulations, inflation, a decline in fertilizer imports, and the lack of import and export controls created hardships for the population. These developments furthered political disintegration and made the anti-British intrigues of King Faruq and the palace clique more effective. The British took steps to suppress dissent; Hasan al-Banna, leader of the fundamentalist Muslim Brotherhood, was confined to a residence in a rural area.

Husayn Sirri, a nonparty engineer, resigned as prime minister on February 2, 1942. The following day the British ambassador, in an audience with the king, complained that Sirri's cooperation with the British had been thwarted at every step, urged that a new government commanding the support of a majority of the country be formed without delay, and suggested that Nahhas Pasha and the Wafd be called to head the government. On February 4 an ultimatum by the British demanded that King Faruq make the appointment or accept the consequences. Faruq refused. That evening the British ambassador, accompanied by a tank force, called on the king at Abdin Palace and offered him the alternative of abdicating. The king chose to appoint Nahhas and a Wafdist government rather than board a British warship at Suez and spend the remainder of the war period in exile. Egypt thus remained under the control of Britain.

Corruption and inefficiency increased; patronage to "deserving" Wafdists became rife; but the Allies no longer had a troublesome, uncooperative Egyptian government with which to cope. Nahhas held office until October 1944, and the hatred between Nahhas and Faruq became notorious. Nahhas further weakened his position and his party by succumbing to unabated nepotism, especially with regard to his wife's family. He quarreled with prominent supporters, many of whom left the Wafd and formed a new party. His dismissal was a foregone conclusion. As soon as the theaters of the war were removed to a distance far from Egypt, British insistence upon retaining the Nahhas government could no longer be valid. Pledging cooperation with Britain against Germany and Japan, the Saadist Ahmad Mahir formed a government composed of Saadists, Liberals, and others. On February 24, 1945, he informed the chamber of deputies of his intention to declare war upon Germany in order that Egypt might become a charter member of the United Nations. As he left, he was assassinated by a young Egyptian fascist. Mahmud al-Nuqrashi, the second in command of the Saadist party, assumed the prime ministership, and a formal declaration of a defensive war against Germany and Japan was issued on February 26. Strangely enough, Egypt entered the postwar world with both the leading nationalist party—the Wafd—and the king discredited. The Wafd was seen as too willing to accept power from the British and Faruq had cravenly accepted the British ultimatum.

INDEPENDENCE OF LEBANON AND SYRIA

The probability of war stiffened the French government's attitude toward Syria and Lebanon, and the high commissioner's delegate in Damascus took over control of the police from the minister of the interior. In July 1939, Hashim al-Atasi, president of Syria, resigned in protest over the gift of Alexandretta to Turkey. The French thereupon dissolved the chamber of deputies, suspended the constitution, placed foreign affairs and defense directly in French hands, established a council of five to govern Syria, and again formed separate regimes for Jabal Druze and Latakia.

Upon the outbreak of war General Weygand was sent from France as commander in chief of French forces in the Levant. The appointment cheered the Syrians and Lebanese, since Weygand had been exceedingly popular as high commissioner. In September the Lebanese constitution was suspended and the powers of the cabinet transferred to a Lebanese secretary of state, assisted by French advisers. However, the fall of France to Nazi Germany left the situation uncertain.

Many French officers slipped away to Palestine, where they proceeded to join the Free French forces of General Charles de Gaulle. Others were arrested and imprisoned in Syria and Lebanon. When the French general Henri Dentz appeared in November as high commissioner, collaboration with the pro-German French government at Vichy and with the Axis became even more open. From the Hotel Metropole in Beirut, German agents who flocked into the French mandate began to prepare the states for German control. Economic difficulties and the collapse of the French franc, to which Syrian and Lebanese currencies were tied, led to strikes and political demonstrations. General Dentz attempted to soothe local feelings by establishing new governments under Khalid al-Azm in Syria and Alfred Naccache in Lebanon.

The new arrangements only partially settled the atmosphere, because the leaders of Syria and Lebanon were planning to acquire complete independence at this moment of French embarrassment and did not relish the thought of falling into the orbit of Germany or Italy. In the spring of 1941, infiltration by German "tourists" and the use of Syrian airfields for German aid to Iraq posed a serious threat to the British position in the Middle East. Lebanon and Syria were blockaded, and England declared that the use of Syria or Lebanon as a base by any hostile power would not be tolerated. British and Free French forces then entered the French mandate from Palestine and Transjordan in June. Resistance by General Dentz was unexpectedly strong, and the Allied forces battled their way into Beirut and Damascus. An armistice was signed in July at Acre. Those French who wished to be repatriated were permitted to leave, but many remained at their posts, since French cultural institutions were respected and their work was unimpaired.

On the first day of the invasion of the French Levant, General de Gaulle designated General Catroux delegate general and plenipotentiary of Free France in the Levant. He appointed Alfred Naccache president of Lebanon and Taj al-Din al-Hasani president of Syria, and recognized these two states as independent and free republics. Meanwhile, Britain sent General Sir Edward Spears as head of a British mission to the Levant, incorporated the "republics" into the sterling bloc, and brought the supplying of their requirements under the machinery of the Middle East Supply Center in Cairo.

These provisions did not satisfy the nationalists, who complained that the people had no hand in them. Under such pressures the suspended constitutions were reestablished in 1943 and elections were held for legislative bodies. In Syria the leader of the National Bloc, Shukri al-Kuwatli, became president of the republic. In Lebanon Bishara al-Khuri was chosen president and Riyad al-Sulh prime minister; the newly elected Chamber had thirty Christian and twenty-five Muslim members. The French, however, found it extremely difficult to relinquish prerogatives such as issuing decrees and maintaining special troops and agents in the states. Lebanese and Syrians objected to the continuation of these forms of colonialism and adopted resolutions dropping all references to France from their constitutions. When al-Khuri and the Lebanese cabinet were arrested, a general strike and spontaneous anti-French riots forced the French to give in. When the National Bloc in Syria also demanded the withdrawal of French controls, General Catroux agreed (December 1943). In 1944, the U.S.S.R. and the United States gave full diplomatic recognition of the independence of the two states, which declared war upon the Axis on February 27, 1945, thereby becoming charter members of the United Nations. The actions of the Russians and Americans compelled the weakened French to accept Syrian and Lebanese delegates at the San Francisco conference and to respect the free position of these two republics of the Levant.

UNREST IN IRAQ

World War II found Iraq weak economically and in a highly charged political atmosphere. In 1939 Britain lent Iraq nearly £4 million for armaments and railroads, and the Iraq Petroleum Company advanced £3 million to cover ordinary governmental expenses. Nuri al-Said, the prime minister, broke relations with Germany, took over German property, and interned all Germans who remained in Iraq. Although the government declared it would live up to its treaty obligations with Britain, most leaders quietly rejoiced over the embarrassment of England and France and expected that their fellow Arabs in Palestine, Syria, and Lebanon would secure independence during the struggle. Hajj Amin al-Husayni, the Jerusalem mufti, took up residence in Baghdad in October 1939 and from there continued his campaign to obtain an Arab state in Palestine.

Early in 1940, because of local politics, Nuri al-Said resigned his office in favor of the lawyer, judge, and cabinet member Rashid Ali al-Kaylani, who was a "hard worker, a persuasive speaker, a passionate nationalist, ambitious and reckless." Unfortunately Rashid Ali had little knowledge of the world outside of Iraq and thus judged the results of his actions in a narrow local perspective. In July 1940 he offered to join the war openly on the side of Great Britain if Palestine would be established as a state immediately. At that time an Arab state would have resulted, since Jews comprised only one-third of its population. Churchill's refusal split the Iraqi government right down the middle. Nuri led the moderates; Rashid Ali championed the uncompromising nationalists, who succumbed easily to Axis flattery and thought to use German and Italian arms and money to achieve their nationalist goals.

In November the British ambassador suggested to the regent that a more amicable prime minister be found, an overture which prompted Rashid Ali to look to the Axis for material aid. In December, after refusing the regent's request to resign, he publicly stated that Iraq's foreign affairs were being strengthened with "friendly states" other than Britain. As clandestine relations with the Axis developed, Nuri and other ministers resigned. When a parliamentary vote of no confidence loomed before Rashid Ali, his plea for the dissolution of parliament was denied by the regent, who then left Baghdad to be free from pressures. In the face of such opposition Rashid Ali resigned, and the regent appointed Taha al-Hashimi upon the insistence of Rashid Ali's middle-class, pan-Arab nationalist army friends who were known as the Golden Square.

Taking office February 3, 1941, Taha al-Hashimi failed to curb the power of the Golden Square. Rashid Ali grew desperate and worked incessantly to return to power. On the night of April 1, 1941, supported by the army, Rashid Ali returned to power in a kind of coup d'état. The regent was smuggled out of the country by the American minister. The British, fearing the worst, landed an Indian army brigade at Basrah to protect an important air assembling base. Discussions between Rashid Ali and the British ambassador did not improve matters. The extreme nationalists rejected the wise advice of Saudi King Abd al-Aziz, who suggested that the well-fed lion (Britain) was a safer companion than the hungry vulture (Germany)!

When more British forces were landed at Basrah, the Iraqi army threatened the meager British units stationed at the air base at Habbaniyah in the vicinity of Baghdad, who in turn attacked the Iraqis. Bombings and artillery attacks by the Iraqis lasted from May 2 until May 30, when the British and the Arab Legion from Transjordan relieved Habbaniyah, destroyed most of the Iraqi air force, and occupied Baghdad. Rashid Ali and his allies fled to Iran and Turkey; German planes, which had just arrived, flew off to Syria; the regent returned with Nuri al-Said and the British; and Nuri eventually became prime minister at the head of a new government.

For the remainder of World War II relative political peace reigned in Iraq, as the British indirectly controlled the economy, the army, the bureaucracy, and education. Many of the nationalists of the Rashid Ali government were executed and the army officer corps was purged. Nuri al-Said devoted time and energy to building the Arab League and promoting Arab unity. Iraq declared war on the Axis in January 1943, signed the United Nations Declaration the same month, and was the first Middle Eastern state to qualify for membership in the United Nations. Iraqi oil was of great assistance to Britain and its allies in winning the war.

Iraq became greatly involved in the process of supplying goods to the U.S.S.R., and vast numbers of British and American troops were stationed there. In 1942, Iraq was made eligible to receive lend-lease aid, and quantities of military and necessary civilian goods were dispatched. Inflation disrupted her economy in many ways, as British and American expenditures introduced great purchasing power over a wide segment of the population without a concomitant importation or production of consumers' goods. Iraq's economic requirements were screened by the Middle East Supply Center in Cairo. Since Iraq was a member of the sterling bloc, Britain also had an effective instrument for controlling and channeling Iraq's foreign trade to British Empire sources, often to the great discomfiture of American and Iraqi business interests. As World War II came to an end Iraq attempted to break the economic domination that London had effectively maintained since the end of World War I.

OCCUPATION OF IRAN

At the outbreak of World War II, Iran under Reza Shah was deeply involved economically with Germany. Although Iran declared her neutrality, official Iranian attitudes were mixed and occasionally pro-German until the Nazi invasion of Russia in 1941. Reza Shah was decidedly anti-Russian and anti-British, largely because of the imperialism of those powers in Iran's recent history. However, until 1941, Reza feared the Soviets more, and he was willing to view the British as a possible makeweight against Russian intervention backed by its then ally, Germany.

Iran also swarmed with Axis officials and agents of every sort, but Hitler's invasion of Russia in June 1941 changed the situation in Iran almost overnight. On June 26, the Soviets informed Reza Shah that the Germans planned a coup d'état in Iran and that the U.S.S.R. could not ignore the unfriendly activities of Germans there. In July, after the Anglo-Soviet agreement for mutual assistance, the two governments initiated joint pressure on Iran to force the unusually large number of Germans in Iran to depart. Reza was furious at such requests, and no action was taken.

Arrangements were rapidly developing whereby Russia would be supplied with military equipment from Britain and the United States through Iran. Great Britain also wished to secure the safety of the Iranian oil fields as well as those of neighboring Iraq. Of necessity, Iran could not be permitted to become a tool of Germany. British and Soviet troops, therefore, began their occupation of Iran on August 25, 1941. Token Iranian resistance was offered for two days, until a new government ordered submission and British-Soviet contacts were made at two points northwest of Tehran. Since Reza was still defiant, Allied forces approached Tehran with the intention of occupying the capital. Instead, the shah abdicated on September 17 because of "failing health" and his twenty-one-year-old son, Muhammad Reza, was proclaimed shah. Reza was eventually taken to South Africa, where he died in 1944. A roundup of Axis agents and friends bagged several hundred, but the mufti of Jerusalem and some German agents escaped the net. (The Mufti Amin al-Husayni wound up in Germany, where he hoped to secure support for Arab independence.)

For the remainder of the war Iran cooperated with the Allies. At the famous Tehran conference of 1943, the Big Three, at President Franklin D. Roosevelt's suggestion, complimented Iran on her service in the supplying of Russia. The quantities of goods that passed to the Soviet Union over the Trans-

Iranian railway and by motor truck through Iran were so vast the figures of tonnage are incomprehensible. The operations influenced life in the country markedly. In time, more than 30,000 American troops were stationed there along with many British and Russians. Their expenditures brought quantities of foreign exchange. But the Iranians found little to purchase with these sums, as imports were held to a minimum by the Middle East Supply Center, which controlled Iranian foreign trade. Inflation, which had already become a major problem in the period 1936–1941, now was very serious with prices for scarce items soaring to such an extent that truck tires sold for £450 each, and bread was so expensive there were bread riots. Before the end of the war the general price level had increased nearly 1,000 percent over 1936, and the dislocation of the Iranian economy became general.

As was frequently the case, the Allied ousting of Reza also removed the strong hand at the helm of internal governmental affairs. For the next thirteen years Iran was politically volatile, as the various elements in Iranian society that Reza had ruthlessly controlled immediately appeared and played havoc with the centralizing processes that Reza had engendered. Nomads secured rifles and local autonomy; Shiite divines returned to do battle against a secular state and regained control of many pious foundations; wealthy landowners ignored taxation; liberals and leftists were released from jails. Iranian censorship was relaxed, but the occupying authorities established their own censors. Somewhat free elections for parliament were held, and the new parties represented a wide variety of interest groups, classes, and programs. In the provinces, linguistic and ethnic minorities tried to gain power over their own affairs at the expense of the central government.

The American, Dr. Millspaugh, was invited again to administer Iran's finances. Another American reorganized the police, and an American military mission advised the army, which the new shah kept under his personal control. German undercover activities continued for many months after the forced reversal of Iranian policy. The German military penetration of Russia and the British retreat in North Africa to al-Alamayn encouraged a restlessness among Iranian leaders. General Fazl Allah Zahedi joined a nationalist and pro-German movement and aided in the revolt of the Kurds and the southern tribes. All these activities faded quickly, however, when the Germans faltered at Stalingrad.

In 1942 a tripartite treaty of alliance was signed by Iran, Great Britain, and the U.S.S.R. Iran recognized the foreign troops as in no sense an occupying force, while the other two parties to the treaty acknowledged the independence of Iran and agreed to a withdrawal of their forces not later than six months after the end of the war with the Axis. The supply route to Russia was the major concern. Russia, nevertheless, utilized this golden opportunity to further her imperialistic and communistic interests in Iran. She aided the Masses (*Tudeh*) party, protected their rallies with Soviet tanks, published Communist newspapers, intrigued with Armenians and Kurds, and finally in 1944 demanded an oil concession. Britain tried to counter such moves with her own propaganda, but she was only partially successful. Iran declared war on Germany in September 1943, thus qualifying at an early date for membership in the United Nations.

THE MIDDLE EAST SUPPLY CENTER

World War II brought many innovations and organizational devices to the Middle East. None was more encompassing than the Middle East Supply Center. As the volume of supplies for the British poured in, tonnage for civilian use did not abate. Ports and docks were so choked with goods, many of them luxuries, that at times it seemed certain the war would be lost for want of anchorage and unloading space. Out of this chaos was born, in April 1941, an executive agency that grew and spread its effective control everywhere in the Middle East except Turkey. It allocated available shipping for the several areas; it ascertained the types and quantity of goods to be imported and it passed upon import permits; it determined from which country imported goods should come; it guaranteed the Middle East at least minimum requirements of scarce and rationed articles and commodities; and it maintained in the Middle East common stocks of wheat and other bulk items for emergency use.

In the beginning the Middle East Supply Center was operated entirely by the British. But in 1942, when lend-lease goods went to the Middle East and more and more shipments originated in the United States, American officials participated in the direction of policy at the Cairo headquarters, and an operational office was established in Washington. However, representatives of Middle Eastern governments did not sit on any of the boards or have any voice in determining policy. Officers of the Middle East Supply Center grew to regard their work and the functions being performed not only as an indispensable contribution to the war effort but also as a benevolent tutelage in techniques of economic planning, area coordination, and development of resources. Middle Easterners questioned the advantages and benefits of the Middle East Supply Center, and as the war drew to a close its original justification disappeared.

As early as 1944 it became manifest that Britain, through control of imports, use of the sterling area pool, and the denial of dollar exchange, was employing the center as a restraint of trade and as an instrument for maintaining the economic colonialism of the British Empire. Since such acts were contrary to American foreign trade policies, the United States withdrew from the operations in 1945 and the center wound up its affairs. Undoubtedly many of its regional activities would have been advantageous to perpetuate, but nothing had been done to bring in Middle Eastern governments or train local personnel to maintain the work. Thus, when the center was abandoned, its possible peacetime usefulness did not materialize, and the Middle East returned to divisive and national economic policies. For many states of the Middle East the demise of the Middle East Supply Center more accurately announced the termination of World War II than did armistices, treaties, or the birth of the United Nations.

World War II so exhausted the political, military, and economic strength of Britain and France that they were eventually forced to withdraw from their imperial control of most parts of the Middle East. The two new superpowers, the United States and the Soviet Union, then extended their influence throughout the Middle East region as the Western European countries declined. The preeminent role of the United States gradually became clear to the peoples of the Middle East following 1945. Competition, hostility, and rivalry between the U.S.S.R. and the United States became the chief external factors influencing the nationalists of the Middle East in the years after World War II as the new world created by the defeat of Germany, Italy, and Japan emerged.

REFERENCES

Reference items in Chapters 22, 33, 35, and 36 are useful for this chapter.

Deringil, Selim. "The Preservation of Turkey's Neutrality During the Second World War: 1940." *Middle Eastern Studies* 18 (1982): 30–52. A thorough analysis, based on British, German, and Turkish sources, for a crucial year.

Eagleton, William, Jr. *The Kurdish Republic of 1946.* New York: Oxford University Press, 1963. The story of the Soviet attempt to penetrate this area in World War II.

Eshraghi, F. "Anglo-Soviet Occupation of Iran in August 1941." *Middle Eastern Studies* 20 (1984): 27–52. Valuable for a study of British motives.

———. "The Immediate Aftermath of Anglo-Soviet Occupation of Iran in August 1941." *Middle Eastern Studies* 20 (1984): 324–351.

Gaunson, A. B. *The Anglo-French Clash in Lebanon and Syria, 1940–45.* New York: St. Martin's Press, 1987. Anglo-French relations.

Hirschfeld, Yair. "British Achievements in Iran, 1 September 1939–25 August 1941." *Asian and African Studies* 14 (1980): 211–240. A revisionist interpretation that shows Reza was at times friendly to Britain and not uniformly pro-German.

Hirszowicz, Lukasz. *The Third Reich and the Arab East.* London: Routledge & Kegan Paul, 1966. A study of the relations of Germany with Arab movements and nations.

Howard, Harry N. *Turkey, the Straits and U.S. Policy.* Baltimore, Md.: Johns Hopkins University Press, 1974. Covers the years from 1830 to the 1970s. Is especially good on the August 1946 crisis.

Kirk, George. *The Middle East in the War, Survey of International Affairs, 1939–1946.* Vol. 2. London: Oxford University Press, 1953. A standard work by an outstanding author. Thorough, inclusive, and objective.

———. *The Middle East, 1945–1950. Survey of International Affairs, 1939–1946.* London: Oxford University Press, 1954.

———. "Turkey," in *The War and the Neutrals. Survey of International Affairs, 1939–1946.* Edited by Arnold Toynbee and Veronica M. Toynbee. London: Oxford University Press, 1956.

Kuniholm, Bruce Robellet. *The Origins of the Cold War in the Near East: Great Power Conflict and Diplomacy in Iran, Turkey, and Greece.* Princeton, N.J.: Princeton University Press, 1980. An excellent study.

Lytle, Mark Hamilton. *The Origins of the Iranian-American Alliance, 1941–1953.* New York: Holmes and Meier, 1987.

Mahfouz, Neguib. *Midaq Alley.* Translated by Trevor Le Gassick. London: Heinemann, 1975.

An excellent novel set in Cairo during World War II; shows the impact of the war upon poor, urban Egyptians.

Ökte, Faik. *The Tragedy of the Turkish Capital Tax.* Translated by Geoffrey Cox. London: Croom Helm, 1987. A frank account of the discriminatory tax by the director of finance of Istanbul during its implementation.

Paiforce. *The Official Story of the Persia and Iraq Command, 1941–1946.* London: H. M. Stationery Office, 1948. A detailed report.

Rubin, Barry. *The Great Powers in the Middle East, 1941–1947: The Road to the Cold War.* London: Frank Cass, 1980. Concentrates on Anglo-American as well as Soviet relations and includes the Arab countries.

Sachar, Howard M. *Europe Leaves the Middle East, 1936–1954.* New York: Knopf, 1972. The last five chapters deal with the Palestine problem.

Smith, Charles D. "4 February 1942: Its Causes and Its Influence on Egyptian Politics and on the Future of Anglo-Egyptian Relations, 1937–1945." *International Journal of Middle East Studies* 10 (1979): 453–479.

von Papen, Franz. "Postscript," in L. C. Moyzisch, *Operation Cicero.* Translated by Constantine Fitzgibbon and Heinrich Fraenkel. New York: Bantam, 1952. The famous story of the German spy in Ankara during the war.

Weisband, Edward. *Turkish Foreign Policy, 1943–1945. Small-State Diplomacy and Great Power Politics.* Princeton, N.J.: Princeton University Press, 1973. A pointed account of Turkey's responses to the war and the policy-making process in Ankara.

Wilmington, Martin W. *The Middle East Supply Center.* Albany: State University of New York Press, 1971. An amazing story of British and American cooperation at a difficult and sensitive time.

Young, Desmond. *Rommel, the Desert Fox.* New York: Harper, 1950. An interesting study of the Nazi general who led the German drive in North Africa.

38

Turkey Becomes a Democracy

THE DEMOCRAT PARTY

The Turkish constitution stated that Turkey is a democracy, and references to this were made frequently in speeches and in schoolbooks. However, only one political party existed, and various electoral and press laws were adopted that could hardly be classed as democratic in principle or in practice. In 1945, in discussing the charter of the United Nations, a number of deputies in the Grand National Assembly pointed out that by subscribing to the charter and joining the United Nations, Turkey would be obligated to practice "genuine democracy." A motion to modify all laws of a dictatorial and unconstitutional nature failed to pass, and violent discussion ensued.

President Inönü in opening the Grand National Assembly in 1945 recommended a change in the electoral law to provide for direct election of deputies. Articles in the press appeared immediately criticizing the government on many issues. Leaders of a new group, the Democrat party, began to formulate a program and to organize. The four principal advocates were: Celal Bayar, the last prime minister under Atatürk; Adnan Menderes, Republican deputy for Aydin; Refik Koraltan, deputy and one-time governor of Artvin; and Fuad Köprülü, scion of the famous family of seventeenth-century Ottoman grand viziers, deputy, internationally known historian, and professor at the University of Istanbul.

The Democrat party subscribed to the six points of the Republican party—after all they were incorporated into the constitution. But the war years had brought many economic dislocations producing inflation, shortages, wealth for a few, hardship for many, and corruption. The Democrats capitalized on these and attracted to their banner all who had any grievance with the government. They asserted that the Republicans sacrificed private enterprise in the interest of government ownership and promised that they, if elected, would undertake to turn state industries over to private ownership and would operate the government more efficiently.

Elections for the Grand National Assembly in July 1946 gave the Republicans 391 seats and the Democrats 65. The Democrats questioned the election of 300 Republicans, claiming stuffing of ballot boxes, faulty counting of ballots or no counting at all, and all manner of irregularities. Nevertheless, the election stood as announced and the Democrats began to plan for 1950.

After 1946 several other parties were formed by disgruntled deputies, and the Democrats proclaimed they would not participate in another election until concrete election reforms were introduced. Election booths were adopted, and regulations for nonpartisan election boards were passed. Democrat leaders toured the country and gathered into their party young, energetic men and women from the provincial towns and cities. In the elections in May 1950 the Democrat party won a resounding victory. Totals in the new Grand National Assembly were: Democrats 408 and Republicans 69. Almost 90 percent of the electorate went to the polls; in popular balloting, the Democrats obtained 53 percent against 40 percent for the Republicans. On May 22, Celal Bayar was elected president of the republic to succeed Ismet Inönü, who gracefully relinquished the office and power he had held for nearly twelve years. Adnan Menderes assumed the office of prime minister and formed a new cabinet. The triumph was complete. Of the former leading Republicans, only Inönü and the last prime minister won election to the Grand National Assembly.

During the following four years the first effects of American aid programs were felt in Turkey, and the Turkish economy surged forward. The Democrat party reaped the benefits of that prosperity. Although there were numerous cabinet shifts, Adnan Menderes retained his position of prime minister under Bayar's presidency. In the elections of May 1954 more than 80 percent of the registered electorate returned 503 Democrats and 31 Republicans, with 58 percent of the popular vote going to the Democrats and 35 percent to the Republicans.

Almost immediately, however, weaknesses in the Turkish economy put the Democrats in a bad light. The Democrat leadership reacted vigorously against criticism caused by the economic situation. Radio stations were not allowed to broadcast criticisms of government policies and newspaper editors were imprisoned for "inciting" public opinion or for "insulting" the prime minister. In 1955, the Republican party refused to take part in local elections, charging that the Democrats would not allow free elections.

Restrictive press laws were passed; at one time in 1955 five of the leading newspapers of Istanbul were suspended by government order. Even some Democrat deputies of the Grand National Assembly were expelled from the party for criticizing the new press laws. A number of deputies resigned from the party to form a new Freedom party, which in 1956 gathered greater strength and some illustrious names, such as that of the son of Fuad Köprülü, the Democrat foreign minister. The popularity of the Democrat party in Turkish cities sank in 1956 to a low point, and Republican leaders began to take heart that victory might be won in 1958, if they could gain greater support in rural areas. Suddenly Menderes moved up the date of the elections, and in October 1957 the Democrats won 424 seats in the Grand National Assembly to 178 for the Republicans. Victory gave Menderes a new lease on the prime ministership.

MILITARY COUP OF MAY 1960

Droughts, beginning in the middle of the 1950s, turned wheat surpluses into shortages, further upset the balance of payments, and undermined the entire economy. Debts mounted, and though Menderes still refused to adhere to any planning, he vigorously and heedlessly pursued developments in every sector of the economy. With returns from most of these investments many years away, inflation and its attendant ills were aggravated and went unchecked. Efforts to curtail luxury imports, black-market activities, and rising prices proved futile. In the summer of 1958, in order to obtain a new loan from the International Monetary Fund and the United States, Menderes agreed to a stabilization program, which included devaluation, rigorous import controls, investment regulations, an end of deficit financing, and the curtailment of domestic credit. The shock to the urban economy was intense. By the spring of 1959, unemployment, business failures, and shortages had developed everywhere, but still there was no planning. Vocal opposition to the Democrat regime became commonplace among the educated and articulate urban classes who were most affected by the economic dislocation.

General carping at governmental ineptitude turned to outright criticism. In those years politics between the Democrat and Republican People's parties was passionate and angry. Legal actions for libel were almost unknown, and the party in power usually exercised control over the press and radio to suppress opposition. In the spring of 1959, while on a speaking tour in southwestern Turkey, Inönü was set upon by a rough pro-Democrat crowd and fell to the ground when hit in the head by a stone. Furious accusations were hurled about the National Assembly in Ankara.

Menderes was indifferent to the attitudes of the urban elite as long as he retained the support of the villagers, who comprised 70 percent of the electorate. In 1959, on an airplane trip to London to sign the Cyprus treaties he had quite miraculously walked away unscathed from a crash that killed most of the passengers. From that moment, Menderes' followers loudly proclaimed that he had been saved by an Act of God in order to lead his country, and many Republicans began to despair of ever defeating him. Early in 1960 several sessions of the National Assembly ended in fistfights. Menderes and Inönü continued to make speeches throughout the country, and political tension mounted.

In April, Inönü and some of his party deputies were on their way to Kayseri to participate in a political meeting when their train was stopped by the army acting on orders from the government. Inönü refused to give way, claiming that the constitution guaranteed freedom of travel to Turkish citizens and that the penal code prohibited interference with a deputy carrying out his duties. He was allowed to proceed to Kayseri. The uproar from this action and the involvement of the army in politics had not abated when the National Assembly voted to establish the extralegal Committee of Fifteen to Investigate the Activities of the Republican People's Party and a Section of the Press. References to the committee were banned in the press, and Inönü was expelled from the Assembly for the next twelve sessions.

Within a few days, on April 28 and 29, university students marched in the streets until they were suppressed by military action and gunfire. Demands for Menderes' resignation were shouted at him whenever he appeared. Then, on May 27, 1960, at 4 A.M. the army struck. President Bayar, Prime Minister Menderes, the entire cabinet, and Democrat deputies of the National Assembly were arrested, government offices were seized, and within four hours a bloodless revolution had been accomplished. The military curfew was lifted that afternoon and joyously wild celebrations occurred in Ankara and Istanbul.

THE NATIONAL UNITY COMMITTEE

The day of the coup, the army flew General Cemal Gürsel to Ankara where he was installed as head of the provisional government. A father figure at the age of sixty-six, he was a necessary link between the senior officers, the older politicians, and the public on the one hand, and the colonels, majors, and captains who had insti-gated the coup. The military body formed to govern the nation was known as the National Unity Committee.

Who were these officers? Five held the rank of general, six were captains, and the rest were colonels and majors; most of them at the time of the coup held key posts. Twenty-two were born after the end of World War I and all but a few had been educated in the 1920s and 1930s during the heyday of Kemalism. None came from a prominent family. In various public interviews each one declared that he had participated in the revolution to restore the reforms of Atatürk.

The day after the coup NUC appointed a cabinet, most of whom had not been identified with any political party; only four army officers were included. In June, a provisional constitution was promulgated providing for a head of state, commander in chief, and cabinet. Laws were proposed by the cabinet, approved by NUC, and de-creed by the head of state within ten days. In July, NUC announced the government's program to balance the budget and end inflation, to free imports and exports of all controls, to devise a constitution on a democratic basis following the United Nations Charter, to reorganize state enterprises and gain entry into the European Common Market, to improve education and health, to undertake land reform, to restrict public works to need only, and to establish a nonpartisan administrative force in govern-ment. There was something for everyone in this program.

To reorient the government was a large order, but to reform the armed ser-vices was a task more manageable. In August, 235 generals and admirals were re-tired; the next day nearly 5,000 colonels and majors were retired with two years' severance pay and full pension.

Within the NUC a division arose with one group under the leadership of Colo-nel Alparslan Türkeş, who advocated pushing through the entire program of the revolution forcefully and quickly. Elections and the return to civilian rule were to be postponed indefinitely, thus raising the specter of dictatorship. On November 13, fourteen members of the NUC received messages of their dismissal and were ordered not to leave their homes. In a few days all were sent abroad; Türkeş was sent to New Delhi.

A broadly based Constituent Assembly dominated by members of the Repub-lican People's party was convened in January 1961. The resulting constitution was approved in July 1961 in a national referendum.

From the autumn of 1960 until the end of the summer of 1961, the attention of the nation was in large part focused on Yassi Island in the Sea of Marmara where Bayar, Menderes, the cabinet, governors, police officers, and Democrat members of the Grand National Assembly, 592 defendants in all, were being tried.

Prosecutors strove to show violations of law and the constitution, personal use of state funds, acts bordering on treason, and a great variety of peccadilloes, in an attempt to obtain convictions or at least to destroy these politicians in the eyes of the nation. Many came to believe the tale that each night Menderes mounted his white horse and rode over the water to pray at a famous mosque on the Golden Horn! Most of those who had voted Democrat in the past were unconvinced by these trials, regarded the charges as trumped up, and the evidence as fraudulent. The trials closed in September 1961 with 15 receiving the death sentence, 31 getting life imprisonment, and 133 acquitted. Prime Minister Menderes, Foreign Minister Zorlu, and Finance Minister Polatkan were hanged. President Bayar's death sentence, because of his age and poor health, was commuted to life imprisonment.

About a month after the hangings, the electorate went to the polls to choose 150 senators and 450 members of the Assembly. The constitution provided for a two-house parliament—in addition to the elected senators, the president of the republic could appoint fifteen and the remaining twenty-two (one refused) members of NUC were given life membership. The two houses meeting together as the Grand National Assembly would elect a president for a seven-year term. Upon the successful referendum on the constitution political parties expanded their activities. Ismet Inönü, as the respected leader of the Republican People's party, expected to win a majority in each house and thus to become the new prime minister. Since the Democrat party had been outlawed, two new parties were formed with the hope of attracting former Bayar-Menderes followers. The Justice party selected its name to signify the need to assure justice to the former national political leaders; it openly asked for Democrat votes. The New Turkey party pitched its campaign to attract intellectuals who had been Democrats in 1950 but who had withdrawn from the party after the election of 1954.

Over 81 percent of the electorate voted. In the popular vote, the Republican People's party won about the same number of votes it had in the elections of 1950, 1954, and 1957, and no one could deny that the Justice party had inherited most of Menderes' votes. No party held a majority in either house so that there was no question over the election of Cemal Gürsel as president on October 26, 1961, by the Grand National Assembly. He promptly resigned from the army and was sworn in as fourth president of the Turkish Republic.

THE SECOND TURKISH REPUBLIC

President Gürsel's first obligation was to appoint the prime minister, but a corollary to this task was to find someone who could form a cabinet that would obtain the support of the House of Representatives (Assembly). The election showed that a coalition was the only choice. Gürsel picked Inönü as the most likely to succeed as prime minister under such conditions. Inönü induced the Justice party to join with his Republican People's in forming a coalition cabinet in which each party held eleven posts, although the major ones were occupied by his party. In the Justice party program one of the major attractions was an implied pledge to obtain amnesty and the release of

Democrat political figures held since the day of the coup. Inönü discovered that an amnesty for Bayar and all of the others was a daily plea of Justice leaders, who later withdrew from the coalition, but Inönü was able to form a new cabinet with the support of the New Turkey and Republican Peasants' Nation parties.

Early in 1963, a law was approved granting amnesty to many Democrats, and Bayar was freed for six months for medical treatments. Massive demonstrations against his release occurred, and Justice leaders accused the Republicans of having fomented these protests; the tension touched off another attempted army coup. These incidents, coupled with a general economic stagnation, brought a reaction favorable to the Justice party, which then won 65 percent of the popular vote in local elections. Consequently, Inönü was deserted by his allies and resigned. But, when the Justice leaders were unable to find a majority, Inönü put together a third cabinet by obtaining the support of the independents in the Assembly. Massive foreign loans created an improvement in Turkish economic conditions, and fine harvests of wheat, cotton, and tobacco gave Inönü a base on which to hope for a successful administration.

Whatever chances Inönü had to maintain the Republican People's party in office were ruined by affairs in Cyprus in 1964. The grievances of the Turkish Cypriot minority incensed the Turkish nation; many Turks felt that their government had the right to intervene openly and blamed Inönü for being too subservient to American exactions. On February 13, 1965, the budget bill was defeated, the cabinet resigned, and President Gürsel invited an independent to serve as the head of a caretaker cabinet. However, Süleyman Demirel, the Justice leader, was appointed his deputy and ten Justice men were in the cabinet. Demirel declared that the Justice party wanted to prove to the military and to the voters that it could govern peacefully and successfully. He pledged support of the 1960 coup and its program. Cleverly, he adopted a gray horse as the party symbol, plainly bidding for those still loyal to Menderes and his "white horse."

Inönü, the Republican People's leader, now eighty-one years old, appealed to those in governmental circles, the older established families, dedicated Kemalists, army officers, and many intellectuals to return his party to office. As the campaign progressed, he turned more toward the U.S.S.R. and asserted that his party was neither an American stooge nor a capitalistic pawn and was, in fact, somewhat left of center.

In spite of acute differences, the election was held in an orderly manner. Only 60 percent of the electorate exercised their rights, and it was apparent that a million of Inönü's party had remained at home rather than vote left of center. The Justice party won 240 seats and a clear majority; the Republican People's garnered 134; and the new leftist Labor party won only 15. President Gürsel invited Demirel to form a new government; within a few days an entire Justice cabinet was announced and was given a vote of confidence by the Assembly.

THE JUSTICE PARTY

The dire predictions concerning the advent to power of the Justice party were unfounded. Prime Minister Demirel steered a middle course between East and West.

Soviet Premier Kosygin visited Turkey in 1966, and his call for the withdrawal of all foreign troops from Cyprus was well received. Demirel initiated the construction of the massive Keban Dam on the Euphrates River. A Family Planning Law passed in 1965 legalized contraceptives, although abortions remained illegal.

In March 1966, President Gürsel, who was ill, was declared incapable of carrying out his duties. In his place, General Cevdet Sunay was elected to be the fifth president of Turkey.

The Republican People's party elected as its new leader Bülent Ecevit, a vigorous young member of the Assembly who had been minister of labor from 1961 to 1964. Since both Ecevit and Demirel were American-educated, the vocal anti-American forces gravitated to the other parties. Many of the old Democrat party leaders were pardoned. A euphoria seemed to engulf the nation as tensions lessened and the economy moved forward with yearly increases in the gross national product, expanding markets in Europe, many Turkish workers sending back income from jobs in Germany, and the widening development of industry at home.

In the nationwide Assembly election of 1969, Justice indicated its popularity among the electorate by garnering 252 seats to 143 for the Republican People's party.

But the world malaise of the years between 1968 and 1972 affected Turkey as well. There were vast numbers of unemployed; galloping inflation and devaluation; miserable shanty towns in Istanbul, Ankara, Izmir, and smaller cities; student disturbances; labor unrest; and many unsatisfied wants in education and land distribution. In February 1970, when Demirel's budget was defeated in the Assembly because many Justice members voted against it, he resigned, formed a new cabinet, and expelled twenty-five Assembly members from the party, leaving him with a margin of two. With disorders mounting, martial law was established in Istanbul in June.

Opposition became more open, however. In the first months of 1971 students rioted repeatedly. Terrorist activities by the extreme left and right grew apace, including bank robberies, bombings, and kidnappings. Demonstrators called for withdrawal from NATO and CENTO. Anti-Americanism appeared everywhere. On March 12, 1971, the four leaders of the military forces, extremely fearful of the trend of events, issued a statement that they would take over governmental authority if the situation did not improve immediately.

COUP BY COMMUNIQUÉ

The memorandum blamed parliament and the government for driving the country into "anarchy, fratricidal strife, and social and economic unrest," leading the public "to lose all hope" of rising to the levels set as goals by Atatürk, and failing "to realize the reforms stipulated by the Constitution." It called for an end to politics and for the forming of a "strong and credible government" to halt the "anarchical situation" and to implement "reformist laws." Demirel resigned immediately; President Sunay viewed the military demand as a constitutional requirement; editorial writers and leaders of the other political parties were dubious about ending anarchy quickly and bringing unity. They were not even in agreement on what Atatürk's principles were.

President Sunay invited Nihat Erim, a senator, professor of law, and a former member of the Republican People's party, to form a nonparty government and stabilize the nation. Erim presented a program for land reform, more education at every level, and improved government services in agriculture and finance. Martial law was imposed in eleven critical provinces; in June, 2,000 persons were arrested, accused of terrorism and of being members of the self-styled People's Liberation Army. To alter the mood throughout the land was a herculean task, not one for a weak caretaker, nonpolitical administration. As one Turkish political analyst noted, unless the holders of the levers of political and economic power in a community change hands, nothing changes.

For thirty-four months the three successive caretaker prime ministers and cabinets who tried to govern barely held affairs together. Erim put through a constitutional amendment restricting the autonomy of universities and the freedom of the press and radio. In May 1972, former Defense Minister Ferit Melen formed a cabinet composed of eight Justice party members, five from the Republican People's party, two Reliance party members, and nine technocrats. This was a mix to satisfy the military and the politicians. In November, when the Republican People's party moved further to the left, its five cabinet officers resigned their positions. İnönü lost control to Bülent Ecevit and left the party, taking twenty-five parliament members with him. The military leaders again cautioned that they would not tolerate another descent into political chaos. In March 1973, President Sunay's term expired and the military pressed to have the constitution changed to allow him two more years. When this was refused, voting for several candidates went on and on, ballot after ballot, in the Grand National Assembly. The military warned Demirel, and on the fifteenth ballot a compromise resulted in the election to the presidency of Fahri Korutürk, a former admiral and one-time ambassador to the U.S.S.R.

Under Ecevit the Republican People's party waged a vigorous campaign, urging state control of the economy, amnesty for political prisoners, reduced interest rates and better credits for small industries and farmers, real land reform, revision of agreements with the European Economic Community, and greater interest in Eastern-bloc nations and the Third World. Ecevit stressed that his party was no longer the party of the elite, and that Demirel and the Justice party represented the rich and stood for stagnation. Other legal parties included the National Salvation party, which went along generally with Ecevit's program except that it also stood for a return to rigid Islamic practices. When the vote was in, the Republican People's party had won 185 seats, the Justice party 149, National Salvation 48, and others 68. None achieved a majority. President Korutürk asked Ecevit and then Demirel, but neither was able to form a cabinet.

How long could such a stalemate continue? Another general election did not seem to be the answer. At the end of January 1974, Ecevit formed a weak coalition government with the Islamic fundamentalist National Salvation party. Progress, or even political movement, proved difficult until the July coup on Cyprus, after which Ecevit directed the Turkish military landings and occupation of the northern 40 percent of the island. In the face of Greek and American opposition and condemnation,

Turkish success redounded to the favor of Ecevit, whose popularity soared at home. In September, at the peak of his triumph, he stepped down, stating that his domestic program had not been achieved; in fact, he resigned to get rid of the National Salvation party, force a new general election, and ride (he expected) to a solid majority on his Cyprus and foreign policies. To call for general elections required a positive vote in the Assembly and this he could not obtain. Demirel and the other leaders, recognizing that Ecevit might win a smashing victory were elections held immediately, decided to put them off until the regular date in 1977.

Ecevit had overplayed his hand. For two months he and Demirel unsuccessfully attempted to put together a coalition. Then, President Korutürk tried in vain to form a nonpolitical government. Finally, Demirel threatened the small right-wing parties, saying he would form a coalition with Ecevit unless they joined with him to stave off the elections until a time when Ecevit's popularity had waned.

On April 12, 1975, the new Justice–right-wing coalition was put to the test in the Assembly and won 222 to 218, with two abstentions and four absentees. There was actual fighting on the floor of the Assembly, and the Republican People's party accused Justice leaders of locking the four absentees in their hotel rooms so they could not vote!

Throughout 1976 there were strikes, machine-gun battles between rival student political groups, kidnappings, airplane hijackings, and many demonstrations. Calls for law and order were heard amidst much unemployment, poverty, and inflation. In September a strike by the Revolutionary Trade Unions Confederation, in alliance with municipality and petroleum industry workers, was ended by the arrest of seven leaders, but the methods of breaking it only heightened the tension. Shortages of various commodities were daily occurrences, largely because the balance of payments deficit had emptied the treasury. Finally, Demirel proposed that elections for the assembly be moved up from October to June 1977.

Campaigning was vigorous. Ecevit pledged to stop extremist violence, to reconcile social justice, democracy, and development, and to maintain high economic growth without inflation. When the final returns were tabulated the Republican People's party under Ecevit had won in the bigger cities and had gained a plurality with 213 seats. Justice won 189, Erbakan's National Salvation party 24, and others 24. By law President Korutürk had to invite Ecevit to form a government, but he lost his first vote of confidence in fifteen days. Demirel and Erbakan put together a short-lived coalition, but Ecevit ultimately formed a weak government that lasted until late 1979, when Demirel once again became prime minister.

Through 1980 inflation continued, and the economy was on the verge of collapse. Disorders were not curbed and pessimism prevailed as martial law was declared in various provinces.

THE MILITARY TAKES POWER AGAIN

In December 1978, Shiite-Sunnite conflict left over one hundred people dead. By 1980 an average of about twenty people per day were being killed in political assassinations and brawls, inflation was around 100 percent, unemployment was high, and the gross national product, which had been nearly stagnant in 1978 and

1979, now actually declined. The Demirel government in January 1980 embarked upon a severe and far-reaching economic stabilization, liberalization, and reform program led by Turgut Özal, as the country sought relief from foreign economic obligations; but it was unable to bring about a cessation of partisan political bickering, which blocked the election of a new president as well as action against violence in the streets.

These immediate crises were made even more tense by a long-range challenge to the political system posed by formerly suppressed groups that now emerged into the political light of day. They had demands and desires that strained the hitherto-existing political consensus. The six million or so Kurds, the Shiite Alevis, urban workers, displaced villagers who had migrated to the cities, Islamic fundamentalists, and leftist and rightist ideologues expressed ideas or desired the state to adopt policies which were contrary to the consensus Atatürk and Inönü had earlier created. Since the two major political groups—the Republican People's party and the Justice party—were increasingly polarized and would not or could not cooperate with each other, no political remedy for the long-term or more immediate problems of Turkey seemed to be at hand.

Now the pendulum of Turkish politics has swung back and forth several times between liberal parliamentary democracy and authoritarian military rule. The conflicts of the late 1970s and especially the political crises caused by weak and ineffective governments that could not address the economic and social problems of the country caused renewed military intervention on September 12, 1980, as the leaders of the armed forces seized power. Parliament was dismissed, a cabinet of technocrats was appointed, and tens of thousands of people were arrested.

Once power in Ankara was consolidated, the military clamped down on possible opposition and on groups believed to have caused the chaos that had led to the seizure of power. The old political parties were banned. Universities were deprived of their autonomy, many faculty members were dismissed, and the regime tried to depoliticize both students and faculty. Bureaucrats were purged. Ecevit and Demirel, who continued to criticize the new regime, were periodically put under house arrest. Violations of human rights of political prisoners, including the (officially unsanctioned) use of torture, were widespread; this and the censorship of the press and intimidation of leftists and rightists gave rise to widespread criticism in Europe of the military government.

Inflation was somewhat reduced in the early 1980s, while exports increased, the trade gap narrowed, and the Turkish currency was devalued. The Özal government of the middle 1980s privatized some sectors of the economy and presided over a generally healthy and growing society, but could not overcome persistent inflation that was usually in the 40 percent to 50 percent per year range.

A new constitution that expressed the military's point of view was adopted by national referendum on November 6, 1982. The constitution upheld the political authority of the state, potentially limited civil liberties in times of emergency, curbed the political activities of trade unions, and gave considerably more power to the presidency. Proportional representation in parliamentary elections was retained, but parties that received less than 10 percent of the votes were not to gain seats in the new one-chamber Assembly. General Kenan Evren officially became president of the republic for a seven-year term upon the ratification of the constitution. Politicians who had been active up to 1980 were banned from running for office for ten years, and political parties were barred from having the paramilitary formations that had been seen in the 1970s. The chief principles of Atatürk and his major legislation were incorporated into the new constitution, thus reaffirming the basic continuity of Turkish politics.

For the parliamentary elections of November 1983, the generals limited participation to three political parties, including the Motherland party led by Turgut Özal, an engineer and economist who had presided over economic reforms in 1980–1982. Despite the clear preference of the military for the other parties, the Motherland party won an absolute majority, 212 of 400 seats, with 45 percent of the popular vote. Its delegation in the Assembly was dominated by businessmen, administrators, engineers, and public servants. The Motherland party espoused social policies that attracted many of the former supporters of the Republican People's party, while its economic statements suggested a decreased role for state enterprises, which brought it votes from the former backers of the Justice party. Politically, the Motherland party supported the new system and constitution, but since it did not receive the backing of the military, it attracted many voters who wished to oppose the coup and its results. The two other parties that had contested the 1983 elections subsequently dissolved, and new, more appealing opposition parties appeared in the middle 1980s. These included the moderately leftist Social Democracy party, modeled on similarly named parties in western Europe, and led by Erdal Inönü, son of Ismet Inönü, which merged with the Populist party in late 1985. Another "new" party was the True Path group led by Süleyman Demirel, whose reappearance in politics (along with other banned politicians) was authorized by a small majority vote in a national constitutional referendum in 1987. Political participation was widespread, but only twelve women were elected to parliament in 1983, a low number that indicated that political participation did not necessarily lead to empowerment.

General parliamentary elections had been expected to take place in 1988, but they were moved up to November 29, 1987. Prime Minister Özal's Motherland party won 292 seats in the 450-member Assembly, but it received only 36 percent of the vote. The Social Democrats were second with 99 seats and 25 percent of the vote, and Demirel's True Path party had 59 seats and 19 percent among the electors. The other parties with 20 percent of the total vote had no representation at all since none of them individually had reached the 10 percent minimum vote cutoff.

Despite some clashes with Kurdish nationalists in the southeastern provinces, Özal decided in July 1987 to lift martial law from many of the provinces where it had still remained in effect. Thus, by the late 1980s the whole country was beginning to approach a greater degree of internal political stability, liberty, and freedom.

FOREIGN RELATIONS: THE UNITED STATES AND THE SOVIET UNION

In 1938, when Kemal Atatürk died, his prime minister and negotiator of the Lausanne Treaty, Ismet Inönü, was elected president by the Grand National Assembly. At the same time he acquired the leadership of the Republican party, the one legal political party in Turkey. Almost immediately, Turkey was caught in the mael-strom of World War II. Though Inönü preserved the neutrality of his country until 1945, Turkey found an independent policy exceedingly difficult and at times of doubtful value.

In the winter of 1939–1940, Russia tried in vain to gain an advantage in east-ern Anatolia and at the Straits, and throughout the war she repeatedly indicated dissatisfaction with Turkey's inactive role. In March 1945, Russia terminated, as ob-solete, the Turkish-Soviet treaty of neutrality and nonaggression. In June, with the war in Europe ended and the United States still facing Japan, with the expected prospect of bitter and large-scale engagements in the Far East for another eighteen months, Russia demanded the cession of Kars and Ardahan and the granting of Soviet bases on the Straits. Courageously the Turks replied with a categorical "No."

At Potsdam the Americans, Soviets, and British agreed that the Montreux con-vention of 1936 governing the Straits should be revised and that each should dis-cuss the question directly with Turkey. In August 1946, Russia called for a regime for the Straits controlled only by Turkey and the other Black Sea powers, and in-vited Turkey to organize with Russia a joint defense of the Straits to prevent their use by other countries having aims hostile to the Black Sea powers. Turkey replied that Russia's points were "not compatible with the inalienable rights of sovereignty of Turkey" and could not be considered. The subject was dropped, and no revi-sion or alteration of the Straits regime was effected.

In the 1970s and 1980s, with the development of a Soviet presence in the Mediterranean, Soviet warships passed through the Straits in great numbers. Small- and medium-sized aircraft carriers, guided-missile submarines, and destroy-ers of various types were permitted passage, as ships of these classes were either not mentioned or not prohibited in the Montreux convention.

The Soviets maintained strong pressure on Turkey by deploying sizable army groups in areas from which attacks upon Turkey could be launched. Turkey, in turn, considered it expedient to keep under arms nearly 1 million men, even though such a force could only delay by a few weeks a Russian conquest. Contin-ued Soviet pressure on Turkey in the immediate postwar period had an adverse effect on the Turkish economy. Government leaders understood Russia could maintain the pressure almost indefinitely and sought a way out of their dilemma. The solution was found in the Truman Doctrine, proclaimed to the American Con-gress in March 1947; $100 million was requested, along with $300 million for Greece, to bolster Turkey to be more self-sustaining in her long-range resistance to Russia.

The plan was conceived and worked out by Turkish and American military, economic, and political leaders. It entailed two primary objectives. The first was to mechanize and modernize the Turkish army, so that the effectiveness and fire-power of each unit would be doubled; this would allow a proportionate cut in the size of the army without a reduction in strength. The other objective called for an improvement in the systems of communication and transportation, to give the army greater maneuverability. A large portion of the first grant to Turkey appeared in the form of military equipment, but a significant $5 million was set aside for a public road-building program.

From 1947 until the United States Congress cut off military aid to Turkey in 1975, between $6 and $7 billion had been expended by the United States on the program for Turkey. The army was reorganized from top to bottom; tanks, trucks, new artillery, and sophisticated equipment of every description were brought into Turkey accompanied by teacher-technicians. A new air force was created, and a steady flow of the latest planes kept the Turkish air force an important modern power. American military missions were everywhere, especially along the northern coast where the most modern eavesdropping and electronic stations were located. By 1970 some 23,000 American military personnel were based in Turkey. The navy was enlarged and warships of most classes were added. Ports were updated, and hard-surface all-weather roads connecting major cities were built. With new harbor facilities, Iskenderun (Alexandretta) became a major terminus in the south, from which new roads extending northward and eastward toward the Russian frontier were constructed. A major airfield was built near Adana and others in eastern Anatolia were laid. Hydroelectric projects were undertaken; irrigation was advanced and dams were built; and internal national strength grew by leaps and bounds.

When war broke out in Korea in June 1950, Turkey sent a brigade of 5,000 men to support the United Nations position. In the ensuing battles the Turkish forces distinguished themselves. Simultaneously, Turkey applied for membership in the North Atlantic Treaty Organization and in 1952 was admitted along with Greece. In 1975, when the American Congress voted an arms embargo against Turkey because of the action in Cyprus, the status of some American bases was changed and Turkish forces occupied them. Later, there was an easing of the embargo and some bases were reopened to American personnel though overall Turkish authority was not relinquished.

After an estimate in 1970 that nearly 80 percent of the heroin illegally sold in the United States was manufactured from Turkish opium, the Turkish government banned the growing of poppies in many of twenty-one producing provinces and the United States agreed to aid the farmers switch to other crops. As some 300,000 farmers were involved in opium cultivation and enjoyed a profitable market in edible poppy seeds and oil, the elimination of their crop wrought hardships.

GREECE AND CYPRUS

The most serious foreign policy problem for Turkey developed on the island of Cyprus where some Greek governments worked in conjunction with Greek Cypriots to effect the union of Cyprus with Greece. Since 20 percent of the population was Turkish and since Cyprus is close to the southern Turkish shore, the Turkish government took a firm stand in opposition to the proposed union. Turkey argued that the Ottomans gave the island to England to administer in 1878, and that if Britain relinquished control the island should be returned to Turkey as the heir to the Ottoman Empire. Believing that Cyprus held strong strategic importance for the Turkish ports of Antalya, Mersin, and Iskenderun, Turkish spokesmen threatened that Turks would fight to prevent

Cyprus from joining Greece. The British in 1957 broached partition as the only possible peaceful solution to the growing civil war and struggle for independence; Ankara accepted this course reluctantly, but Athens rejected the proposal. Greece and Turkey thus became mutually suspicious, thereby weakening the eastern section of NATO.

In 1959, as the only apparent recourse, the three involved powers, Greece, Turkey, and Britain, signed three treaties in London establishing and guaranteeing a Republic of Cyprus. Coming into being in August 1960, Cyprus joined the United Nations. Archbishop Makarios, head of the Greek Orthodox Church in Cyprus and leader of the Greek Cypriot community, and Dr. Fazil Küçük, leader of the Turkish Cypriot community, accepted this settlement. According to the constitution, partition or union (*enosis*) with Greece was barred, and the nation was to have two official languages, Greek and Turkish. The Greek Cypriots would elect the president and the Turkish Cypriots the vice president, and both officials would have to sign acts to make them law. There was provision for a council of ministers and a house of representatives, with membership set at a 70 to 30 ratio of Greeks to Turks. In addition, separate Turkish and Greek Cypriot communal chambers were set up to control education, religion, social welfare, and personal affairs, almost like the Millets of the Ottoman Empire. This ratio was also to hold in the civil service and police, whereas in the army a ratio of 60 to 40 was to prevail. In the ensuing elections in 1960, Archbishop Makarios became president, and Dr. Küçük was elected vice president. Britain retained two large bases and other posts including an airfield and radar stations. Greece was allowed a military force of 950 and Turkey one of 650 on the island with the right of periodic rotation of personnel. (No unified Cypriot army was formed because of the ethnic divisions between the two communities.) An independent, unified Cyprus was inherently difficult to achieve because of the ethnic, linguistic, religious, cultural, and economic differences that separated Greek and Turkish Cypriots.

In 1963, Archbishop-President Makarios touched off a new crisis by decreeing the end of separate Turkish and Greek municipalities in the cities and proposing thirteen constitutional changes, one of which would terminate the requirement that the vice president approve all legislation. This meant the end of any Turkish veto power. Makarios asserted that the present constitution was unworkable, but his opponents declared he had never intended that it succeed.

Bloodshed occurred between the communities in December 1963, with Greece and Turkey supporting their respective nationality groups on Cyprus. Violence erupted and the issue went to the United Nations, where a mediator was appointed and the Security Council sent a peacekeeping force. Greece and Turkey privately arrived at various compromise solutions, but Makarios vetoed them as well as the settlement formulated by the United Nations. Prime Ministers Inönü of Turkey and George Papandreou of Greece restrained the hotheads from leading their countries into war. At one time when it appeared Turkey would intervene militarily, President Lyndon Johnson sent a stiff note to Inönü warning him of the dire consequences of such an act. Turkish resentment at the note ended automatic cooperation with the United States, and it alerted many Turks to the desirability of a somewhat more flexible foreign policy.

By 1964 the situation in the eastern Mediterranean was grave. Greek security forces on the island jumped from 20,000 to 40,000, with volunteers coming from Greece. Supplies came from the U.S.S.R., which looked with favor on Makarios' stand for independence immediately and union with Greece, or enosis, later. Greek Cypriot forces attacked ports on the north side of the island where supplies were being landed from Turkey. The Turkish air force strafed Greek Cypriot positions, and Turkey threatened to invade the island. Apparently the Greek government decided there was too much flirting with Moscow and too much independence of action. General George Grivas, the hero of the Cypriot struggle in the 1950s and an advocate of instant enosis, was returned to Cyprus to control the irregulars.

Fighting erupted again in Cyprus in November 1967, and both the new military government of Greece and Turkey ordered partial mobilization, but with foreign help the crisis was defused. In 1968 President Makarios was reelected, progress for peace seemed to be a reality, and signs of economic improvement appeared. However, in July 1974 Makarios wrote a sharp letter to the military junta in Athens demanding the recall of 650 Greek officers in Cyprus. In quick reaction the Greek Cypriot National Guard, with the approval of the junta in Athens, overthrew Makarios, appointing the violent Nikos Sampson as the new president. Makarios escaped with the aid of the British to plead his case at the U.N.

On July 20 Turkey, to prevent enosis, landed 40,000 troops on the northern coast of Cyprus and seized Kyrenia and a strip of territory to Nicosia. The Greek government mobilized but, recognizing the overwhelming superiority of the Turkish forces, agreed to a cease-fire on July 22. The following day the Athens junta handed over power to a civilian government under former Prime Minister Constantine Caramanlis. That same day Sampson was removed and Glafkos Clerides became acting president of Cyprus. Talks soon took place in Geneva among the British, Greeks, and Turks, but no solution could be found. A second Turkish drive on August 14 ended with nearly 40 percent of the island in Turkish hands. Some 200,000 Greeks and more than 20,000 Turks became homeless refugees. Both Turkey and Greece denounced the United States for not being impartial, and the U.S. imposed a complete arms embargo on deliveries to Turkey in February 1975. Turkey closed U.S. installations, and in September the United States modified its arms delivery policy so as to lessen the embargo. (Arms deliveries were completely resumed in September 1978.) Makarios returned to Cyprus in December, granting amnesty to those who overthrew him but declaring partition unacceptable.

Prime Minister Ecevit gained immense popularity throughout Turkey for his bold actions in Cyprus. He resigned in September, expecting to force a general election in which the Republican People's party would gain a working majority in the National Assembly. An election did not materialize and timid caretaker ministers held office until April 1975, when Demirel formed a weak coalition government, calling for a bizonal federal solution in Cyprus. After more talks, Rauf Denktas, vice president of Cyprus since the 1973 elections, called in February 1975 for an autonomous Turkish state in northern Cyprus. Approved in Ankara by Demirel, the idea led to a constitutional vote in June by Turkish Cypriots and discussions between Clerides and Denktaş, both moderates, who secretly agreed to the bizonal federation under a weak central government. This interim understanding was a signal for all parties to make concessions, but since none felt sufficiently secure for such a deviation, the Cypriot impasse remained.

With no solution in sight, Denktaş organized a National Unity party and fostered the idea of separate and autonomous Greek and Turkish Cypriot states linked together in a federal union. Elections in June 1976 in the Turkish area gave Denktaş the title of President of the Turkish Federated State of Cyprus, and his National Unity party won 30 of 40 seats in the state assembly. In April 1977, President Makarios suffered a heart attack and died on August 3, 1977. Spyros Kyprianou, leader of the assembly, became president until 1988, and promises of a settlement between the Turkish and Greek factions had to be postponed.

In addition to the tension over Cyprus, Turkey and Greece found themselves in a controversy over oil. Foreign companies had been prospecting for oil for the Turkish government in Thrace and offshore since 1970. In 1974, Turkey and Greece disputed the location of the continental shelf in the Aegean, and Greece withdrew from military participation in NATO until 1980. With so many Greek-held islands in the Aegean in shallow water close to the Turkish coast, the rights and claims of the two countries overlapped everywhere. In the summer of 1976, Turkey sent an oil-exploring ship on several missions into the Aegean, an act that Greece declared illegal. Greece took the matter to the United Nations, but it soon became clear that only negotiations and compromise between the two countries could resolve the issue.

Andreas Papandreou, the new prime minister of Greece after 1981, exacerbated tensions with Turkey over the Aegean oil issue and a similar dispute over control of the air over the Aegean, as well as over Cyprus, the level of U.S. aid to the two countries, and participation of Greece and Turkey in NATO. However, in 1988 the Turkish and Greek prime ministers met in Switzerland and then in Athens and agreed on a set of confidence-building measures including annual summit meetings, a direct telephone link between the two leaders, and the establishment of joint Turkish-Greek committees to negotiate on their mutual disputes.

Cyprus had again become a crucial factor in Turkey's foreign policy with the declaration of independence on November 15, 1983, by the Turkish Cypriot Legislative Assembly. The new Turkish Republic of Northern Cyprus was recognized diplomatically only by Turkey. Many members of the U.S. Congress attempted to reduce U.S. aid to Turkey because of Turkish support of the new state and Turkey's apparent unwillingness to seriously negotiate with the Greek-dominated Cypriot Republic. Nevertheless, Turkey continued to be a major recipient of U.S. assistance, second only to Israel and Egypt, and mediation directed by the United Nations led to a resumption of talks in 1985 between Turkish and Greek Cypriots about a compromise to their disputes. After a hiatus, talks began again in September 1988.

THE MIDDLE EAST

In February 1955, Turkey and Iraq joined in a five-year pact to consult in all matters of defense. In an exchange of letters the countries agreed to cooperate "in resisting any aggression directed against either of them." The Baghdad pact provided that other nations of the Arab League and any other nation concerned with the Middle East might join. The United Kingdom, and later Pakistan and Iran, became the third, fourth, and fifth members. The Turks believed that these treaties bolstered their flanks and enabled them to play an important role in the Middle East as a link to NATO and the West.

The Iraqi revolution and withdrawal from the Baghdad pact in 1958 led the members to reorganize it as the Central Treaty Organization (CENTO), and to enhance Turkey's position in it. Airfields at Adana facilitated the airlift of American troops and supplies in their occupation of Lebanon, thereby committing Turkey more overtly to the power struggles in the Middle East. In April 1963, however, Turkey announced the abandoning of her Jupiter missile bases and the return of all the NATO-based nuclear warheads to the United States. This played a part in the United States-Soviet maneuvering in the Cuban missile crisis.

In general, Turkey maintained friendly relations with the Arab states. Turkey and Syria began negotiations for a treaty covering cultural exchanges, transit and tourism arrangements, and questions of land dispute. Beginning in 1974, the most vexatious issue was that of the water flow in the Euphrates River. The great Keban Dam, 205 meters high, was started in 1966; now completed, it has produced enormous amounts of hydroelectric power. When the cost of imported oil jumped suddenly in 1973, Turkey decided to store sufficient water by July 1974 to begin producing more of her own energy. Because 60 percent of Turkey's energy came from petroleum, two-thirds of which was imported from the Arab states, Ecevit felt compelled to act. In the spring of 1974, when Turkey reduced the Euphrates' flow below previously agreed levels, Syria complained bitterly and wanted the flow doubled, because the level was so low that dams in Syria were reducing the flow into Iraq to a mere trickle. Turkey remained steadfast and did not increase the flow until midsummer, when Saudi Arabia mediated the quarrel between Iraq and Syria.

A 975-kilometer oil pipeline from Kirkuk in Iraq to Iskenderun in Turkey, with an annual capacity of 35,000,000 tons, was completed in 1977. Each country paid for the costs within her borders (for Turkey about $350 million). And in August 1987, a second Iraqi-Turkish oil pipeline was opened.

Support from the Arab states over Cyprus greatly strengthened Arab-Turkish ties. Turkey extended diplomatic recognition to the Palestine Liberation Organization in 1979, while at the same time maintaining diplomatic relations with Israel.

The outbreak of war in 1980 between Iraq and Iran, both neighbors of Turkey, threatened to drag it into that long and bitter struggle. Turkey went to great lengths to ensure its neutrality and concluded economic agreements with both sides. Traffic has steadily flowed over highways linking Turkey with Iran and Iraq. In 1983 and 1984 Turkey, acting with the permission of Iraq, attacked Kurdish and Armenian revolutionary bases in northern Iraq. These attacks were made partly to curtail the activities of Armenians who had assassinated Turkish officials abroad and partly to preclude Kurdish separatism from expanding further in eastern Anatolia. Another result of cooperation with Iran and Iraq was the increased trade: trade with the Middle East as a whole surpassed Turkish trade with Europe by

1981, as relations with Libya, Saudi Arabia, and the Islamic Conference countries also improved.

THE COMMON MARKET

Turkish association with the European Economic Community or Common Market symbolized political, military, and emotional as well as economic ties between the Turkish Republic and the democratic nations of western and southern Europe. Most Turks saw their country as part of Europe; from the days of the great Ottoman reforms in the middle of the nineteenth century to the radical transformations of Atatürk, Turkish elites had been moving the country toward a European identity. When the chief non-Communist countries of Europe planned for eventual economic and political union through the Treaty of Rome in 1957, Turkish political and economic leaders wished to join the new community, but they recognized that a long transition period would be needed.

A Treaty of Association between Turkey and the Common Market was signed on September 12, 1963. For nine years the Community gave economic aid and preferential tariffs to Turkey. An Additional Protocol in 1970 organized the gradual elimination of mutual tariffs and trade barriers for most industrial and agricultural goods. Some Turks on both the left and right ends of the political spectrum feared these agreements would lead to the increased economic subordination of Turkey to Europe and to the loss of effective national independence in economic matters, but the major problems in connection with the Common Market in the late 1970s were continuing mutual trade barriers and the chaotic condition of the Turkish economy.

Greece became a full member of the European Economic Community in 1981 and thus gained a potential veto over any future Turkish application for full membership. The Common Market froze relations with Turkey because of the military intervention of 1980 and only reopened talks in 1984, following the restoration of competing political parties. Serious debate within Turkey and among the member states of the European Economic Community about the desirability of Turkish membership persisted, as Turkey formally applied for full membership in April 1987. The future identity and character of the Turkish state and people will be greatly influenced by the outcome of that debate.

ECONOMIC PROGRESS

In 1944, Turkey severed economic relations with Germany, on the understanding that the Western Allies would not permit her economy to founder. She based her fears of economic collapse on the knowledge that she would no longer be able to sell quantities of goods to Germany and that the Allies would cease their preclusive buying programs. However, no decline was apparent, and inflation forced prices upward. The continued unbalanced budget over the next years maintained economic activity at a high level. With vast American aid beginning to flow in 1947, the economic development of Turkey progressed rapidly.

In the years after 1946, Turkish industry grew by leaps and bounds. The purchasing power of the peasants, who constituted the great majority of Turks, was sustained at a high level by the government, and suddenly the wants of the peasant burgeoned to an unprecedented degree. New industries, often founded by foreign capital in partnership with Turkish capital, were sprouting in all regions of the country. Yet, the expansion was not entirely healthy. Many accused Menderes of wasteful activities and found fault with his rapid rebuilding of parts of Istanbul; in fact when a building was summarily torn down, it was said to have been "Menderized." Still he forged ahead. His energies and ambition were indefatigable.

On the other hand, the Democrat party did not find it easy to dispose of state-owned enterprises, and long-range planning did not take into account many short-range problems. By the beginning of Bayar's second term as president the Turkish economy was in serious jeopardy. Foreign exchange was scarce, commercial payments abroad were months in arrears, and business obligations were mounting. In 1958 grants and loans were obtained from the United States and western Europe to prevent a collapse. As already indicated, however, the shock of the stabilization program was so severe that it was an important factor in bringing on the coup of 1960. Menderes had found an increasing majority clamoring for an ever-larger share of the national product for immediate consumption; after he was gone the leaders of the Second Republic experienced the same pressures.

When NUC took over, the Menderes regime was branded as economically incompetent and dishonest. It was revealed that the total public debt was over $1 billion and the nation's foreign debt stood at $965 million, a sum so vast that it crushed any hope for solvency and posed an intolerable burden on future foreign exchange earnings. These findings led many business people, even those who had profited from and strongly supported Democrat policies, to acquiesce in NUC restrictions and to appreciate the attempts of Inönü and Demirel to proceed with economic plans and an orderly development.

Nevertheless, the foreign debt continued to grow and by 1966 stood at approximately $2.4 billion, taking about 40 percent of Turkey's foreign earnings to service the debt. The gross national product, however, increased markedly during these years, from $6 billion at the time of the coup to over $9 billion by 1967 and more than four times that figure a decade later. Government budgets jumped 10 to 30 percent yearly, with sums for capital investment often amounting to a quarter of the total. The momentum to develop the economy, set in the Menderes years, was irresistible, and though Inönü, Demirel, Ecevit, and others might deplore its effects on inflation, deficits, interest rates, and social unrest, they did not halt it. Many contended that the extraordinary economic activities and innovations of the controversial 1950s were only now bearing fruit. In spite of inflation and devaluations of Turkish and world currencies, the Turkish economy grew 8 to 10 percent a year.

By the end of 1962 all needs for refined petroleum were being met by local refineries, but in succeeding years oil production did not keep pace with energy demands. Despite the building of new dams and a constant increase in domestic oil production, 60 percent of local petroleum needs still were being met by imports in 1976. The cost was draining Turkey's economy. And in 1985 Turkey still spent nearly one-half of its total export revenues for oil imports.

Exports were needed to earn foreign exchange to pay the bills. Turkey began earnestly in 1964 to seek European tourists to visit her beaches, to explore her cities and countryside, and to view her antiquities. To attract these tourists, roads, hotels, transportation, and numerous other facilities had to be furnished; along the way the Turkish economy and social fabric began to be transformed.

Similarly, in the 1960s more and more Turkish workers found jobs in western Europe, principally in West Germany. In 1965 there were about 200,000 remitting about $100 million back home, and in 1973, a peak year, over 1 million workers returned over $900 million. In 1974, with 2 million Turks unemployed, the European recession closed the door on further emigration, and European labor forces demanded that Turkish workers be sent home. With population in Turkey increasing at a rate of 2.5 percent a year, unemployment and the lack of capital investment to create jobs bred political and social instability. In the 1980s, between 1.5 and 2 million Turks were still working in Europe, and hundreds of thousands were also working in various parts of the Middle East, especially in the oil-rich countries. Remittances sent home by these workers continued as a vital part of the Turkish economy, and were estimated at close to $2 billion.

One major advance was the completion in 1973 of the great suspension bridge across the Bosphorus. Situated north of the center of Istanbul, and de-signed to carry 21,000 vehicles per day, it had exceeded that target by 10 percent in its second year of operation and by 1977 revenue from tolls had paid for it. Connecting with another heavy-duty bridge over the upper reaches of the Golden Horn, it became the final link in an outer-belt superhighway that bypasses some of the traffic congestion of Istanbul and makes practical the trucking of produce from the garden areas of Anatolia to the metropolitan centers of western and northern Europe. Prior to the building of the bridge, unrefrigerated trucks laden with to-matoes had been known to stand in line for three or four days waiting for the ferry to cross from Asia to Europe. Another bridge across the Bosphorus was opened in 1988.

In the later 1970s and 1980s, economic change has persisted and accelerated. Population grew rapidly, from about 34 million in 1968, to 45 million in 1981, and 52 million in 1988. About one-half of the population was under 20 years of age. Industry surpassed agriculture in the gross national product by the early 1980s, and nearly one-half of the citizenry was living in cities. National prosperity and a marked increase in the standard of living were tempered by persistently high rates of inflation, substantial inequities in the distribution of wealth (by geographic re-gion as well as by economic class), peasants' pressure on the land leading to mas-sive migration to the cities, and the resulting strain on urban services, especially in Ankara and Istanbul. The balance of payments was often negative, and the external debt grew to more than $11 billion in 1979 and $19 billion in 1984. On the other hand, exports increased in the early 1980s, the currency was realistically devalued, inflation fell somewhat, and many uneconomic state enterprises were reformed. The new settlers in the cities often found jobs that provided them with higher in-comes than were possible in the villages from which they had come, and their hastily built housing and urban amenities, although lower in quality than those for more long-term residents, were often finer than similar facilities in rural areas.

AGRICULTURE

Starting in the days of Atatürk the government patronized the peasants and did not impose direct taxes on farm income. Unbalanced budgets and, to some degree, the ills of the economy resulted from the lack of such taxes. The government established a soil office, which bought grain, tobacco, and other farm produce at established prices, frequently above world prices. Production was stimulated, and after the road-building program opened up many new areas in Anatolia and greatly reduced the costs of transportation, the quantities of wheat delivered to the soil office soared. This program, coupled with bountiful rains and the importation of tractors, plows, and harvesters, led in 1952 to an exportable surplus of 1.5 million tons of wheat. Unfortunately, droughts in 1956 and 1957 changed the wheat surpluses into deficits.

Part of the earlier surge in agricultural production may have resulted from land-distribution programs, which were approved after bitter debate in 1945 and slowly implemented. Almost 5 million acres of land were slated to be distributed among 200,000 peasant families. After 1950 the Democrat party reduced but continued the program. The large, wealthy landowners remained powerful allies of Menderes and his commercial and industrial friends.

The well-being of the farmers in Anatolia and their staunch support of the Democrat party were significant factors in the strength of Menderes after 1954. The government provided credit to the farmers, and crops were purchased at high prices—higher than the world market. Peasants and large landowners used the ensuing profits to buy tractors and begin to mechanize agriculture. Although crises in foreign trade and in finance shook the faith of the inhabitants of the larger cities in Menderes' leadership, his following in rural provinces enabled him to enact restrictive press laws silencing his urban critics without offending his wealthy agricultural friends, who reelected him in 1954 and again in 1957.

As would be expected, the leaders of the coup in 1960 treated the agricultural sector of the economy most carefully. Agricultural investments continued to hold a high priority, especially under Justice party rule. In 1961 an income tax was levied on agricultural incomes for the first time. This touched the wealthier farmers and the largest producers, whose tax-free incomes under Menderes had been under attack by economists and merchants.

Improved conditions lifted annual exports of cotton and tobacco to $100 million each in 1965, as agriculture accounted for 85 percent of Turkey's exports and about 40 percent of the gross national product. New dams and irrigation systems and the expanded use of fertilizers and farm machinery continued to increase the total output.

A continuous question in Turkey ever since the eighteenth century has been who owns and controls agricultural lands. At times vacant tillable lands were assigned by the government to nomads and Turkish peasants returning to Anatolia from the frontiers of the shrinking empire. When there were no more vacant lands, the only solution was to take land from large holdings and parcel it out to those who had none, and various reformers over the years have sought to do this. Later, a prize-winning Turkish novelist adopted as his theme the life of landless peasants.

The Justice party, supported by large landholders, followed the policies of Menderes and moved slowly. Republican People's party leaders advocated a vigorous program as part of an overall solution to the disorders of 1971. Demirel was opposed to such a sweeping change, whereas Ecevit urged its rapid implementation in hopes of solving unemployment, slowing the drift of villagers to the city, and lessening the need to export workers. He asserted that it was social injustice to have 4 percent of the farmers tilling 34 percent of the land, leaving 96 percent to work the remaining 66 percent.

In the election campaign of 1973, Ecevit proposed that the holdings of all absentee landlords be nationalized and that the owners be compensated; that maximum acreage holdings be set by the Assembly; that no partnerships be established to circumvent the intent of redistribution; and that recipients of land be required to participate in farm cooperatives. His inability to meet these promises when he became prime minister was cited as a reason for his resignation in September 1974.

In the late 1970s agricultural productivity increased because of the greater use of tractors, seed drills, and combine harvesters. Government measures helped irrigation, the production of new crops, and credit. In 1977, however, land reform was stopped when the Constitutional Court annulled the enabling law.

RELIGION, EDUCATION, AND CULTURE

One of the greatest changes in Turkey brought about by the advent of democracy was in religion and education. The rural population never really subscribed to Atatürk's program of deemphasizing Islam. As soon as the peasants had a voice in affairs, they insisted that religion be restored to some of its former position in society, although they did not insist that the separation of state and religion be undone. Many serious-minded leaders concluded that much would be gained by reinstating the spiritual and ethical values of Islam, and lay teachers were permitted to give religious instruction in the schools. In 1949 the College of Theology, which had been closed at the University of Istanbul by Atatürk, was reopened as a part of Ankara University, and a new Institute of Islamic Studies was founded at the University of Istanbul. Study of the old script became possible; the mausoleums of holy men and the sultans were once again open to the public; a few new mosques were built; religious days of fasting and feasting were more widely observed, and the muezzin's call to prayer was again sounded in the traditional Arabic. Radio Ankara programed readings from the Koran, and attendance at mosques increased.

Traditional Islam entered politics when İnönü permitted a multiparty system in 1946. The Democrat party of Bayar and Menderes, including in its program strong attractions for the conservative and simple Islam of the Anatolian villagers, was successful to a degree never possible for the heirs of Atatürk. The Republican People's party was never able to erase from the villagers' minds the incessant Kemalist line that "they were primitive and nasty and superstitious" and that to participate in modern Turkey they would have to abandon their ancestral ways and become "civilized." The Democrats, by contrast, built 15,000 mosques in ten years and subsidized Koran reciters for mosques in every village. On the other hand, of the 60,000 "men of religion" in the country barely 8 percent had as much as a primary school education (five grades).

Educated and Westernized Turks, especially Republicans, deplored what they called an abuse of religion in order to win votes, and officers of NUC cited this tactic as one of the most significant in moving them to revolt. They were particularly infuriated by, and at the same time ashamed of, the Democrats' use of Menderes' escape from the airplane crash in England in 1959. Every radio in the land blared forth the view that God had saved him to lead his country, and henceforth a vote against Menderes was a vote against God. Moreover, when he returned to Istanbul over 100,000 loyal followers were at the airport to greet him. As Menderes stepped from the craft a score of sheep had their throats cut to satiate the evil force that had sought his blood; this ceremony was repeated twice before he reached his hotel, and reports and pictures of the demonstrations and rites were circulated to every village, to the dismay of secularized Turks. Against this kind of religio-political campaigning, opponents felt helpless.

Although leaders of the Republican People's party and NUC delivered scathing rebukes to Menderes for pursuing this policy, they too were following a like practice within a short time—6,000 mosques were built between 1960 and 1964, and NUC gave sizable sums to religious training schools. In the 1965 elections many villagers voted for Justice party candidates, recognizing in them the heirs of the Democrats. When Inönü moved his party left of center, Justice campaigners equated this with atheistic Russian communism. Turkish peasants have hated Russians for generations; to this was added the word *communist,* which replaced *infidel* as the common insult to hurl at opponents.

Religion was still a strong political force, as the new National Salvation party demonstrated in the election of 1973. Winning slightly over 10 percent of the seats in the Assembly, it was the party of revivalist Islam in regard to education, culture, and religious practices, while supporting leftish approaches to many socioeconomic problems. Islam pervades Turkish society and is a political force demanding to be recognized as a valid component of Turkish thought and culture.

In the schools, a real awakening in the study of Ottoman history occurred. Atatürk, to strengthen Turkish nationalism and to forget the unhappy seventeenth- and eighteenth-century Ottoman experiences, hurdled all of Ottoman history and found glory for the Turks in earlier epochs. After World War II the writings on early Ottoman history were rediscovered, and a more systematic and scholarly investigation into the origins of Ottoman institutions and the foundations of Turkish life in Asia Minor began. Higher education was advanced by the opening of Atatürk University in 1958 at Erzurum and by the founding of the Middle East Technical University in Ankara.

Following the 1960 coup education at all levels received heavy emphasis. By the end of the decade Middle East Technical University had a faculty of more than 600 and a student body of over 6,000. Hacettepe University in Ankara, begun in 1958, had grown to have full faculties in the social sciences, medicine, and hygiene. New universities were founded, Seljuk University and Ege University, among them, in widely separated districts of Anatolia. Part of Robert College, an American school, was given to the government in 1971 and renamed Boğaziçi (Bosphorus) University.

In the election campaign of 1973 both Demirel and Ecevit promised to establish universities throughout the land to enable attendance by every student who wished to enroll. At the elementary level there were nearly 5 million children in 30,000 schools, 200,000 students in 900 vocational schools, and 100,000 in the universities.

The literacy rate increased, especially for women, so that by 1975 about one-half were literate, while three-fourths of the men were able to read and write. By the 1980s there were over 350,000 students at 18 universities, and 6 million children were enrolled in primary schools. A number of educational institutions used a foreign language, often English, as the language of instruction or taught several foreign languages to their students. Turkey has entered into the modern world of universal education. The flood of articles and monographs from the pens of Turkish scholars in almost every field has indicated a flourishing intellectual development. Professional journals publishing articles in these disciplines attested to the arrival of Turkish learning upon the world scene.

On the other hand, this major development did not produce a more stable and balanced society. There were still wide gaps between the economic and social levels of Turkish life, and university circles were painfully aware of the chasms. Beginning with the several years preceding Menderes' fall, demonstrations, riots, and disorders were common events. A law passed in 1973 gave the government the right to take full control of a university during student disorders, but the government soon discovered its only recourse was to close the university in question. Disruptions of every kind continued and accelerated in the late 1970s as student disturbances were widespread. Violent outbreaks between leftist and rightist students helped bring about the military coup of 1980. The new regime purged the universities, suppressed student political groups, and attempted to depoliticize education.

The cultural life of the country and its education were greatly affected by urbanization. Between 1950 and 1960 over 2 million people moved to urban areas. This led to a direct confrontation of rural, and usually conservative, manners, habits, and values with their urban and usually more cosmopolitan counterparts.

National and municipal governments sponsored high culture modeled upon the accomplishments and heritage of Europe. In most aspects of culture and the arts the makers of the new forms and artistic products were initially Europeans or Americans, but gradually Turks replaced them. In the 1950s, a state opera and ballet were established in Ankara and Istanbul, and by the 1970s and 1980s they were increasingly performing compositions by Turks and with Turkish themes. Turks had been producing films at a rate of less than two per year between 1916 and 1944, but starting in the 1950s the number and quality of films increased dramatically. In the 1960s more than 200 per year were made; however, their directors in the 1970s had to deal with competition from television. Regular television broadcasts began in 1968. In the 1970s more than half of broadcasting time was filled with foreign material; in the 1980s more locally produced shows were broadcast even though foreign-made programs remained popular. By 1984 there were more than 6 million television sets in the nation!

In the fine arts a similar pattern of Turkish artists initially following the examples of the international artistic environment and then developing more indigenous and individual modifications has been followed. Sculptors and composers of serious music participated in the modernism, abstract, and experimental movements of Europe. Painters became extremely diverse in approach as schools, art galleries, journals, and the public supported different styles. Figural painting is still predominant but many other methods and techniques are also followed. Poetry flourished in the period after the 1960 revolution, as many young poets were heavily influenced by socialist criticism of society. Novelists, playwrights, and short-story writers expressed a realistic criticism of the existing order. This trend was seen especially in the popular novels of Yaşar Kemal (b. 1922), whose stormy career and deep commitment to a political approach to literature epitomized the post-1950 generations.

The international style dominated Turkish architecture and replaced the Turkish National Movement in the 1950s and 1960s. Architects designed buildings for industry and business as well as for government, and with the growth in the numbers of people engaged in the profession, architecture became more diverse and responsive to popular taste. In the 1970s and 1980s some smaller buildings that incorporated earlier, Ottoman architectural features have been built. Architecture in general remains predominantly influenced by the international style.

Most modernized Turks have looked upon their country as a bridge between the West and the Middle East, a concept discussed by Prime Minister Özal in a speech to parliament in 1983. They have frequently objected to the inclusion of Turkey in the concept of the "Middle East." Turkish leaders in 1953, at the time of the celebrations of the five-hundredth anniversary of the Turkish capture of Constantinople, presented the thesis that the Ottoman occupation of the Balkans, at a time when the peoples of western Europe were weak, had preserved Europe from destruction by the barbarians of the East. In the minds of Turkish leaders NATO and the European Economic Community were the logical continuations of this age-old role of the western Turks.

In more recent times Turkey has tried to maintain a balanced approach, keeping open its economic and cultural links with the Middle East. As Turkey and Europe draw nearer to a time when a definitive decision on Turkish full membership in the Common Market must be made, Turkey's rich historical heritage from Ottoman days and from Atatürk's republic will play a great role in determining its future identity.

REFERENCES

Additional references for this chapter are found in Chapters 32 and 37.

Ahmad, Feroz. *The Turkish Experiment in Democracy, 1950–1975.* London: C. Hurst & Co., 1977. The most thorough study of Turkish politics from the end of World War II to 1975 to have appeared.

Barchard, David. *Turkey and the West.* London: Routledge and Kegan Paul, 1985. A short but excellent work that discusses economic as well as diplomatic relations between Turkey and the West. Concentrates on the 1980s.

Berberoglu, Berch. *Turkey in Crisis: From State Capitalism to Neo-Colonialism.* London: Zed Press, 1982. A short and strongly leftist critique of the political economy of Turkey from the 1920s through the 1970s.

Dodd, C. H. *The Crisis of Turkish Democracy.* North Humberside, Eng.: Eothen Press, 1983. An excellent essay on recent developments; includes excerpts of the new constitution.

———. *Democracy and Development in Turkey.* North Humberside, Eng.: Eothen Press, 1979.

Frey, Frederick W. *The Turkish Political Elite.* Cambridge, Mass.: MIT Press, 1965. A survey of Turkish rulers and their social backgrounds.

Harris, George S. *Turkey: Coping with Crisis.* Boulder, Colo.: Westview Press, 1985. Another outstanding discussion of recent developments.

Karpat, Kemal H. *Turkey's Politics, the Transition to a Multi-Party System.* Princeton, N.J.: Princeton University Press, 1959. A penetrating work by an outstanding scholar on modern Turkish politics.

———. "Turkish Democracy at Impasse: Ideology, Party Politics and the Third Military Intervention." *International Journal of Turkish Studies* 2 (1981): 1–43. A careful examination of the 1980 coup and its causes.

Landau, Jacob M. *Radical Politics in Modern Turkey.* Leiden: Brill, 1974. A study of radical parties of the right and left.

Makal, Mahmut. *A Village in Anatolia.* London: Valentine, Mitchell, 1954. An important insight into village life in Asia Minor.

Mayes, Stanley. *Makarios: A Biography.* New York: St. Martin's Press, 1981. A thorough biography of a crucial figure.

McFadden, John H. "Civil-Military Relations in the Third Turkish Republic." *Middle East Journal* 39 (1985): 69–85. Sound analysis of the topic in the 1980s.

Oberling, Pierre. *The Road to Bellapais: The Turkish Cypriot Exodus to Northern Cyprus.* New York: Columbia University Press, 1982. Wider in scope than the title indicates, this book examines carefully developments in the crucial 1960s and 1970s.

Okyar, Osman. "Development Background of the Turkish Economy, 1923–1973." *International Journal of Middle East Studies* 10 (1979): 325–344. A broad survey by a thoughtful observer of Turkish economics and society.

Robinson, Richard D. *The First Turkish Republic: A Case Study in National Development.* Cambridge, Mass.: Harvard University Press, 1963. A judicious apologia for the Menderes regime.

Rustow, Dankwart A. *Turkey: America's Forgotten Ally.* New York: Council on Foreign Relations, 1987. Examines domestic as well as foreign policy.

Singer, Morris. "The Economic Performance of the Turkish Republic." *Middle Eastern Studies* 20 (1984): 155–165.

Tachau, Frank. *Turkey: The Politics of Authority, Democracy, and Development.* New York: Praeger, 1984. An excellent survey with an emphasis on the period of the 1950s and after.

Tamkoç, Metin. *The Warrior Diplomats: Guardians of the National Security and Modernization of Turkey.* Salt Lake City: University of Utah Press, 1976. A study that reveals the interplay between foreign and domestic policy and the determining role of the political elite.

Weiker, Walter F. *The Turkish Revolution, 1960–1961: Aspects of Military Politics.* Washington, D.C.: The Brookings Institution, 1963. A detailed account of the military government.

39

Iran: Nationalism Versus Imperialism Versus Islam

U.S.S.R. AND AZERBAYJAN

The treaty of alliance signed on January 29, 1942, by Great Britain, the U.S.S.R., and Iran provided that Allied forces would be withdrawn from Iran within six months after an armistice with Germany and Japan. At the Tehran conference in 1943 Roosevelt, Stalin, and Churchill signed a statement that their governments desired to maintain "the independence, sovereignty, and territorial integrity of Iran."

After the armistice with Japan on September 2, 1945, Iranian nationalists looked forward to March 1946, when all foreign troops would be evacuated. Their high hopes were soon dashed; in December the Soviets engineered and supported a revolution in Tabriz. Although the Tudeh party had been dissolved in Azerbayjan, a new Democrat party under the leadership of the Communist Jafar Pishevari had established the autonomous Republic of Azerbayjan. During World War II this province was under complete Russian control, and officials of the Iranian government from Tehran were even denied entry there. Taxes could not be collected, and local officials usually discovered that orders from Tudeh party leaders carried more authority than their own. A Kurdish autonomous republic was also established.

Almost immediately government troops were sent from Tehran to quell the rebellion, but Soviet troops blocked the roads. Open interference by the U.S.S.R. was charged by Iran, and in January 1946 an appeal was made to the United Nations. Russia pursued delaying tactics there, evidently hoping to bring additional troops into Iran and in the end present the West with an accomplished deed. A week later, when the Iranian parliament by a margin of only one vote chose Ahmad Qavam as the new prime minister, the Western press assumed that Iran was on her way behind the Iron Curtain, since Qavam had befriended the Tudeh party.

March 2, 1946, passed without any sign of the withdrawal of Soviet troops. The American troops had gone before January 1 and the British left in February. But additional Russians entered Iran in March, and the cold war began.

Qavam's first task was to cajole the Russians into removing their troops. He delayed until parliament legally ended its term. This allowed Qavam to rule by decree until a new parliament would be elected. He closed down anti-Soviet newspapers and arrested rightist political and army leaders. Meanwhile, Iran laid a complaint before the Security Council of the United Nations and pursued a vigorous policy to secure Soviet withdrawal.

In the face of strong British and American statements in support of Iran, and the worldwide publicity flowing from the United Nations' first large problem, Stalin decided not to use force in Iran. On March 24 Russia announced that the evacuation of Soviet troops would begin immediately and would be completed in five or six weeks. As a part of the bargain, Qavam agreed to allow an autonomous regime in Azerbayjan and to form a Soviet-Iranian Oil Company, 51 percent Soviet-owned, to exploit oil in northern Iran. Cleverly, Qavam obtained an admission from Russia that Azerbayjan was an internal Iranian problem with which the Tehran government would deal "benevolently." Qavam received Azerbayjani Communist leaders in Tehran and appointed one who had been educated in Russia as Iranian governor-general in Tabriz.

Russian troops departed on May 6, 1946. Qavam played his cards well. The Tudeh party and Azerbayjan Democrats held huge demonstrations in Tehran, and a vociferous attack was launched against the Anglo-Iranian Oil Company. Three Tudeh members and a fellow-traveler were included in a new Qavam coalition cabinet.

However, Qavam may have been cautiously leading the Russians into a trap. He pledged his loyalty to the shah and promised to fire the three Tudeh members of the cabinet, liquidate the autonomous Azerbayjan province, and organize a real party to face Tudeh. Parades and demonstrations of Qavam's Iran Democrats suddenly outshone those of the Tudeh party, and Qavam won the shah's support. He also won a majority for his party in the parliamentary elections that winter. Since Qavam declared that elections in all provinces, including Fars and Azerbayjan, would be held under the supervision of government forces, the Soviets were presented with a difficult choice. Only if Qavam's Iran Democrats won the election could the new parliament be expected to vote an oil concession to the Soviet-controlled company. Only if an election were held could an oil concession be submitted to an Iranian parliament. But no national elections could be held so long as the Soviet-supported autonomous province of Azerbayjan existed. Tehran troops entered Azerbayjan in November, and fighting developed. Since the Soviet Union did not wish to send in troops, she stood by and witnessed the collapse of the autonomous Kurdish and Azerbayjani regimes. The Tudeh party in Tehran refused to participate in parliamentary elections.

Elections were held in a leisurely fashion throughout the country during the winter months. Qavam's coalition won handily and the shah opened the new parliament in July 1947; a few weeks later it gave to Qavam a vote of confidence. Almost immediately the Soviets pressed for ratification of the oil concession to the Soviet-Iranian Oil Company that Qavam had initialed in the spring of 1946. Qavam, at this juncture, informed the Soviet ambassador that the oil agreement was unsatisfactory. Russian reaction was sharp, and Qavam was accused of treacherously violating his agreement and returning to the policy of hostility and discrimination practiced by Reza Shah and previous reactionary governments.

The Iranian government took heart from the decisive stand and support of the United States. Qavam's new cabinet included three graduates of the American College of Tehran, and the United States extended a military credit to Iran.

As it became more apparent that the Iranian parliament would rebuff the Soviets, the British became fearful that a categorical refusal might lead also to the nationalization of the Anglo-Iranian Oil Company. The English ambassador advised Qavam not to slam the door in the face of the Russians but to leave it somewhat ajar. Sentiment in parliament was inflamed, however, and Mohammad Mosaddeq (a politician, lawyer, and landowner) reminded Qavam of the law of 1944, sponsored by that fiery nationalist, forbidding an Iranian government from granting or even negotiating an oil concession with a foreign state without parliament's consent. With an agreement by the United States to send a military mission to raise the efficiency of the Iranian army, parliament on October 22, 1947, voted 102 to 2 to void Qavam's agreement with the U.S.S.R., to exempt Qavam from penalties under the 1944 law, and to authorize the government to enter into negotiations to regain Iran's rights with respect to oil in areas where the British held concessions.

The U.S.S.R. fumed, hurled charges at Qavam, and stated that Russia would consider Iran a bitter enemy. But the crisis passed. Iranian leaders breathed easier; Iranian politics returned to normal. At the same time Qavam's coalition evaporated. In December he failed on a vote of confidence, and within two weeks his parliamentary opponents accused him of embezzlement, ordering improper arrests, and governing by decree without parliamentary approval. He was arrested and allowed to go to Paris for "his health."

IRAN LOOKS TO THE UNITED STATES

When the United States had supported Iran in her stand against the Soviets, its prestige had soared and Iranian leaders had anticipated all manner of benefits and assistance. American help in providing capital and technical know-how was acceptable to the Iranians, because the United States seemed less imperialistic than other powers and was not associated with Iran's past struggles against Russia and Britain.

Although American leaders were sympathetic to Iranian needs, they believed that Iranian politics were unstable and that funds would be largely wasted and lost. Cabinets came and went in Tehran. Between Qavam's ousting and the appointment of Mohammad Mosaddeq on April 29, 1951, Iran had six prime ministers, some for only a month or two. The outbreak of the Korean War ended any prospect of obtaining American aid, and a member of parliament asked the government to explain why Iran should "bother" anymore with the United States!

The shah announced that a program of land reform was being inaugurated by splitting up his royal estates into small farms that would be sold to peasants on long-term installment payments. But the program moved slowly because of administrative lethargy, and other landowners failed to follow suit.

Iran's economy floundered seriously. The end of World War II and the evacuation of foreign troops had halted a sizable influx of foreign exchange, and a general decline in world trade in 1948 and 1949 depressed the economy still further. Receipts from oil payments slumped under the administration of the British Labour party because of its general restrictions on dividend payments. Although the deterioration threatened a collapse of the government and a likely victory for a resurgent Tudeh force, the upper class appeared supremely indifferent. Corruption continued unabated; land reform was quietly opposed; the wealthy and influential ignored their income taxes; and prestige politics remained the sport of the great landowners. Pressures developed to reconsider the concessions held by the Anglo-Iranian Oil Company as commanded by parliament in 1947.

OIL PROBLEMS

Ever since 1940, voices had been raised over the question of oil concessions and in particular with respect to royalties. In 1944 Mosaddeq, almost single-handedly, pushed through parliament a law forbidding further oil concessions or even their discussion with foreigners. Following the resolution of 1947, cabinet leaders reconsidered the position of the Anglo-Iranian Oil Company and the income from oil. The income was never enough and did not compare favorably with receipts of Latin American countries. As finances grew desperate and American aid did not materialize, eyes turned more and more toward the prospering Anglo-Iranian Oil Company, which had every appearance of possessing greater wealth and income than the Iranian government.

For the public the oil crisis began on June 1, 1948, when the company announced that payments would remain the same as in 1947, even though the company's net profit after taxation jumped from $26.9 million in 1947 to $52.1 million in 1948. In 1947, the Iranian government received $20 million in royalties and taxation, whereas the British government received $56 million directly in dividends and taxation. When these figures were presented to the Iranian public, the outcry was sharp. Then the announcement followed that the British government was limiting dividends, which according to the royalty formula would keep payments at the 1947 level. In addition, the Iranian public believed that substantial profits were concealed by the selling of petroleum products cheaply to affiliated concerns. In this way higher profits would flow to stockholders, but would not be reflected in higher royalties to Iran.

In view of the dissatisfaction in Iran, officials of the Anglo-Iranian Oil Company visited Tehran in the summer of 1948 and received a memorandum asking for an agreement similar to that which Venezuela had with American companies. In particular, this meant 50 percent of the company's profits. Moreover, the prime minister informed the company negotiators that a 50-50 sharing of profits was being discussed at that moment in Saudi Arabia by the Arabian-American Oil Company.

After considerable delay a supplementary agreement was signed in 1949 by the company and the Iranian government. Payments would double those stipulated in the old 1933 schedules. However, for prosperous years payments fell short of 50 percent. In lean years, as the company pointed out, they might be better than that. Just at that time, the company's 1948 report was published, showing that Britain received $79 million in taxes and Iran $37.8 million in royalties. The uproar was deafening but parliament took no action on the agreement. When the new parliament met in 1950 the question of the agreement fell to a newly created oil committee, headed by Mosaddeq. The prime minister was unable to induce the company to consider a 50-50 split.

The United States warned Great Britain that some appeasement would be necessary. Since the company refused to take any action until the government brought the agreement to parliament, debates were held and the oil committee rejected the agreement. Almost immediately the company urged the prime minister to reopen negotiations to seek a 50-50 split of the profits. But it was now too late. Mosaddeq had presented a resolution demanding nationalization of the oil industry and calling upon the prime minister to find out whether such a step was feasible. After consultation, the prime minister reported publicly on March 3, 1951, that nationalization was impractical; he was assassinated four days later.

Nationalization of Oil

Within a week parliament passed a bill nationalizing the oil industry, although it was not signed by the shah until May. Britain objected, and the new prime minister rejected the protest. Riots, strikes, and wild demonstrations affected the area of the oil installations. British cruisers appeared in the Persian Gulf, and refineries at Abadan shut down. When the prime minister did not move to take over the properties of the Anglo Iranian Oil Company, parliament forced his resignation, and Mohammad Mosaddeq, hero and chairman of the oil committee, became prime minister on April 29, 1951. The following day a law was passed to evict the company, and Mosaddeq ousted it on October 1.

In May, as soon as the Mosaddeq government took steps to implement the nationalization law, the company and the British government proposed arbitration applying to the International Court of Justice at The Hague for a decision. Mosaddeq declared the Court had no jurisdiction over the case, which was a dispute between a private company and the sovereign state of Iran. When the British complained that the Iranian government had not responded to requests for negotiation, and admitted that they were prepared to consider a settlement that would involve some form of nationalization, Mosaddeq supposed that the main battle had been won. He was now ready to begin negotiations with the company.

But negotiations proved arduous. Each side believed it possessed the stronger bargaining weapons to back up its legal position. In addition, each had to be mindful of powerful psychological, political, and economic forces in its own nation. Finally, each side either ignored or was misinformed about the views, intentions, and strength of its opponent.

The company asserted that only it could operate the intricate industry and the Abadan refinery. The tottering Iranian economy could not withstand the added shock of a loss of royalties, and political leaders who had benefited from the oil income would quickly force Mosaddeq to come to terms. Also, the company held that the action of the Iranian government was illegal, since it contravened the 1933 agreement.

On the other hand, the company and the British government failed to read the signs of the times in Tehran or to comprehend that nationalization of the Anglo-Iranian Oil Company united the various divergent classes in Iran as nothing had done since the Tobacco Concession two generations earlier. Nationalization suddenly meant independence, and Mosaddeq not only had twisted the British lion's tail—something all Iranians had been longing to do for a long time—but had pitted the Iranian lion against the British lion and had won. A recent prime minister had faltered on that point and was murdered. Mosaddeq always understood that a like fate could be his.

Mosaddeq encouraged the Iranian populace to assume that income from the oil industry would enable them to live in ease and comfort. But he did not realize the complexities of the international oil industry or the difficulties involved in selling Iranian oil without world cooperation. Furthermore, he did not take into account that neighboring countries such as Iraq, Kuwait, and Saudi Arabia might object if oil companies restricted production in their fields to provide a market for Iranian oil.

Mosaddeq believed that Britain and western Europe required Iranian oil for the continuance of their economies and thus would be forced to come to terms. He also expected that the United States would support Iran in her struggle with the company, because American ambassadors were friendly and had warned Britain of the serious consequences of the loss of Iranian oil. Moreover, he fully anticipated that the United States would give aid to Iran for fear that Iran would drift behind the Iron Curtain if her economic position became more chaotic than it was already.

Iranians perhaps misjudged British tempers. Iran's leaders had studied the legality of the nationalization of industry in Great Britain; they assumed that England would recognize the legality of the same process in Iran. Moreover, they failed to perceive that Britain's acceptance would invite nationalization in Iraq, Saudi Arabia, Bahrayn, and Kuwayt—a thought that gave nightmares to oil officials the world over.

In the ensuing debate between the company and Iran the position of Prime Minister Mosaddeq was exceedingly strong. Although his National Front party had a delegation of only 8 out of 136 in parliament when he became leader of the government, his following and influence were widespread. One of his staunchest supporters was a leader of the Shiite divines, Ayatollah Sayyid Abd al-Qasim Kashani. He hated the British, who had interned him as a German agent during World War II. In 1949, after an unsuccessful attempt upon the life of the shah, Kashani was suspected of inciting the Devotees of Islam to commit such assassinations and was exiled. Elected to parliament in 1950, he returned to take his seat and was no doubt implicated in the death of the preceding prime minister. As long as Mosaddeq was uncompromising with the British, Kashani worked with the government and used his position to excite popular religious fervor in support of Mosaddeq.

OIL STALEMATE

From the moment of Mosaddeq's entry into office and the beginning of the drive to eject the Anglo-Iranian Oil Company, until August 1953, the drama of the nationalization of oil in Iran had many scenes, a large cast of players, and a constant shift of location. There were five proposals made by the British, the United States, or international groups to effect a settlement; all failed. In June 1951, the company agreed to the principle of nationalization and proposed the formation of a new company with British and Iranian directors to handle the production and distribution of petroleum products for Iran. Mosaddeq refused, on the basis that some understanding on compensation should first be reached.

By the end of the summer of 1951 the oil industry in Iran was shut down; the tanks were full, and no oil was being loaded. When the Security Council of the United Nations considered the question at the request of Great Britain, Mosaddeq came to New York to state again that this was not a subject for United Nations concern since the Charter forbade acts that impair the sovereignty of any member. While in the United States Mosaddeq discussed the question with high American officials, but no meeting of minds occurred. Production was hurriedly upped in other Persian Gulf oil-producing states, since the situation appeared to be critical.

After these failures the issue was reduced to the amount of compensation. In August 1952, Truman and Churchill sent a joint proposal that the question be submitted to the International Court. In October, Iran severed diplomatic relations with Great Britain, while Mosaddeq said that he would agree to an International Court adjudication of compensation if the bases used were those employed by the British government when it nationalized properties in the United Kingdom.

Each time exchanges were made tempers became worse, and charges and countercharges, repeated in all of the presses of the world, grew bitter and exaggerated. Mosaddeq asserted that the British were asking compensation for future expected profits now to be lost and that he would, therefore, demand payment by the company of all royalties that Iran should have, but had not, received in the past.

As the controversy dragged on, Britain and the West adjusted to the loss of Iranian oil. By the spring of 1953, there was a glut of oil on the world market, and many oil companies were actually worrying about what they would do with Iranian oil and where they could market it if it suddenly became available again.

GOVERNMENTAL CRISIS

In Iran, affairs were descending rapidly to a state of chaos. The loss of royalties was beginning to pinch. Thousands of Iranian oil workers were transferred to the public payroll. And scarcity of foreign exchange and the absence of any great earning power destroyed Iran's foreign credit. Since the great mass of Iranians, however, were not dependent upon or affected by royalty payments or foreign exchange, life did go on. Nevertheless, Mosaddeq was not nearing any solution. The nationalists were becoming frustrated; the army was being purged by Mosaddeq; and the wealthy landowners who governed the country soon discovered that the loss of the royalty revenues on which their corrupt governmental practices battened was forcing them to change their ways.

A crisis developed in July 1952 upon the opening of the newly elected seventeenth parliament. Before Mosaddeq would accept the prime ministership, he demanded absolute power for six months to inaugurate governmental, economic, and social reforms. Many members of his own party objected. So did the shah, when he was asked to allow Mosaddeq to become minister of war as well as prime minister. Thereupon Mosaddeq resigned, and the shah appointed Qavam to form a cabinet. Qavam publicly branded Mosaddeq a demagogue and Kashani a hypocrite, and stated that he would settle with the British. Quite understandably, he was forced to resign. But first there were four days of bloody rioting led in Tehran by Mosaddeq, Kashani, and a resurgent Tudeh party.

To avoid civil war the shah sent for Mosaddeq, whereupon Kashani through his influence halted the violence in Tehran. Kashani was elected speaker of parliament. In August, Mosaddeq became minister of war and was granted unlimited powers. He had reached the pinnacle of his career; soon the cracks in his structure began to appear. Quarrels within his own party arose over appointments, and in January 1953, when he obtained a continuation of his personal rule for another year, Kashani deserted him. In July, General Fazl Allah Zahedi, his former backer, a retired popular strong man in the army, started plotting Mosaddeq's overthrow, and he soon secured the help of the Bakhtiyari tribe.

When Mosaddeq announced that a popular referendum would be held on the question of the dissolution of parliament, the storm began to break. Only the shah could dissolve the parliament. Kashani placed a religious boycott on the referendum, but voting proceeded. Mosaddeq won with 99.93 percent of the vote. On August 12, 1953, he announced his intention to dissolve parliament.

MOSADDEQ'S FALL

By this time the government of Mosaddeq had lost the support of many political and social groups in Iran, although he remained enormously popular with many of the people of the country. Mosaddeq had tried for too long to make political capital from his nationalization of oil, without adding any new funds to this original backing or capital, and now he faced political bankruptcy. He did not understand the world ramifications of the oil industry. He did not have the real courage or the personality to become a dictator. His toying with the Communists failed to gain any support from the United States. Lacking any solid support from the Iranian army, landowners, religious groups, or the shah, Mosaddeq lost out completely.

Many Iranians had believed that Mosaddeq would be able to obtain aid from the United States. However, in 1953 the United States was secretly engaged in funding groups who opposed Mosaddeq and who split his National Front. Secretary of State Dulles said that aid would be withheld from Iran because Mosaddeq openly countenanced and apparently cooperated with the illegal Tudeh party.

On August 13, after Mosaddeq decided to dissolve parliament, the shah dismissed Mosaddeq. The shah appointed General Zahedi as prime minister. Mosaddeq refused to be dismissed and remained in office. On August 16, Muhammad Reza fled by plane to Baghdad and Rome, and Zahedi escaped to the provinces. But on August 19, crowds in the streets of Tehran began to shout: "Long live the Shah!" Zahedi's men, the police, and the military attacked Mosaddeq. This opposition to Mosaddeq was coordinated and funded by the U.S. Central Intelligence Agency; the U.S. was convinced Iran was drifting toward the Soviet camp.

A minor battle decided the issue in favor of Zahedi, who appeared before nightfall. The shah returned on August 22; Mosaddeq was caught and arrested; a new cabinet under Zahedi was approved; and on September 5, President Eisenhower granted $45 million to Iran on an emergency basis. The new government arrested Communists and all opponents. Mosaddeq was found guilty of attempted rebellion and sentenced to three years' imprisonment; he subsequently died in 1967. Mosaddeq came to be seen by many as a martyr to the shah's dictatorship and the struggle against American imperialism. The shah told Kermit Roosevelt of the Central Intelligence Agency, "I owe my throne to God, my people, my army—and to you."

THE OIL SETTLEMENT

The grant from the United States was made on the condition that the oil dispute be terminated. A consortium of eight major oil-producing companies was formed: U.S. firms had 40 percent and British Petroleum (the old Anglo-Iranian Oil Company) held the same percentage of the new consortium. Key decisions on production and sales were to be made by the consortium and not by Iran.

On August 5, 1954, Iran signed an agreement whereby the consortium would extract, refine, and market petroleum for the National Iranian Oil Company (NIOC). The Iranian company would receive half of the profits and pay $70 million a year for ten years as compensation for nationalization. Parliament ratified the agreement, and oil began to gush immediately. The pivotal problem was solved. After that date the world demand for oil products expanded rapidly, enabling the sale of Iran's oil without market dislocations, and yearly payments to Iran rose sharply to approximate $300 million by 1960.

Exploration for other oil fields continued apace. The island of Kharg in the Persian Gulf was chosen as a convenient base for oil operations, including those of the consortium, and pipelines were laid between Kharg and the mainland in 1960. NIOC acquired tankers and began to find markets for its oil.

Schemes for the piping and utilization of the seemingly limitless quantities of natural gas in the oil fields, burned off and wasted for decades, turned into a reality in 1965 with the founding of the National Iranian Gas Corporation (NIGC). A mill was shipped from the United States to roll pipe for the line, Great Britain agreed to help finance it, and the U.S.S.R. signed an arrangement to aid in the engineering and construction of the line to the Caspian Sea area in the U.S.S.R., completed in 1970, and to receive payment in natural gas deliveries.

In 1950, the last year of normal oil activities before nationalization, the average daily production had been about 660,000 barrels. Not until late in 1956 was this rate achieved again; after 1956 increases reached over 13 percent annually. Oil and gas income to the government soared, and in 1970 it stood at $1.1 billion. The shah, complaining regularly to the consortium that it was not upping production fast enough, kept pressing for larger payments. In 1969 the energetic Manuchehr Eqbal was appointed to head NIOC. He applied new pressures to the consortium and all concessionaires to expand production and increase payments to the state. In 1970 the consortium agreed to a small increase in the posted price of crude oil from Iranian wells and to raise the Iranian share of the profits to 55 percent. Iran also gained a greater voice in production and pricing. This action signaled the entry of a new age in the production and pricing of petroleum, not only for Iran but for the entire world.

IRAN AND OPEC

In 1960, at a meeting in Baghdad, representatives of Iran, Iraq, Kuwayt, Saudi Arabia, and Venezuela formed the Organization of Petroleum Exporting Countries (OPEC) to try to coordinate oil policies regarding levels of production, export prices, percentages of profits to be paid in taxes and royalties, and concession policies in the hiring and training of nationals of the host countries. Over the ensuing decade meetings of OPEC were held regularly without much world impact. As other oil-producing states—United Arab Emirates, Algeria, Ecuador, Gabon, Indonesia, Libya, Nigeria, and Qatar—joined OPEC, more and more of the petroleum needs of the world were being met from OPEC resources.

In Tehran in February 1971, during an OPEC meeting, representatives of some twenty-two of the world oil companies agreed that 55 percent of the profits would accrue to the producing countries. The companies also agreed to a sizable increase in the posted price of crude oil (the base from which profits are calculated), and to a set formula for changing the posted price in accordance with fluctuations in the value of the dollar. OPEC, with Iran playing a significant role, by this action established its leverage over petroleum markets. By the end of 1972 crude oil was selling for $3 per barrel, almost double the price in early 1970.

World demand for oil appeared insatiable. In 1973 world consumption jumped more than 4 million barrels per day, most of the increase coming from expanded output in the Persian Gulf area. OPEC raised the price of oil twice in 1973; by the end of the year the posted price was set at $11.65 per barrel, and Persian Gulf oil was frequently bringing $18 per barrel at auction. Iran did not join the Arab states in their embargo or reduction of output during the 1973 Arab-Israeli War, and its average daily production topped 6 million barrels. Budget revenues jumped far beyond estimates, since oil income provided nearly 90 percent of Iran's annual budget. Revenues for 1973–1974, originally set for $7 billion, were increased to $11.7 billion. Budget revenues for 1974–1975 moved up to $30.8 billion. For 1977–1978 they were estimated at $49 billion.

It was widely estimated that Iran's oil resources would be diminished very significantly within twenty years unless new discoveries were made at an accelerated pace, and that they might be nearly depleted by the end of the century. The shah, therefore, was greatly concerned that the oil income be used to generate a balanced economy and to develop other mineral resources and a self-sustaining industry. His first goal was to boost non-oil revenues so that they would equal oil revenues by 1985. His hope was to industrialize Iran and make his empire the equal of any Western European country. He spoke of Iran as another Japan.

ECONOMIC DEVELOPMENT

At the end of World War II it was anticipated that the other natural resources of Iran, in addition to oil and gas, could be developed. As soon as the oil crisis was settled Zahedi announced the inauguration of a second five-year development plan to be financed by oil revenues. The plan, beginning with the budget year 1954–1955, concentrated on building dams, hydroelectric power plants, irrigation systems in arid regions, and draining of land in swampy areas. Recognizing that the vast majority of Iranians were peasants and that the well-being of the nation would be served best by improving their productivity, the government made loans to finance agricultural transportation, industries, social services, and electric power development.

Iran's oil production in 1966 was almost three times what it had been ten years earlier. Prices had not risen greatly and income, therefore, went up nearly 300 percent. Annual budgets and the gross national product reflected these riches.

The shah laid grandiose plans for an atomic reactor center at Tehran University. In 1967 a pipe-rolling mill was opened at Ahwaz, most of the initial production of which would go into the trans-Iranian gas pipelines. When high grade ore was discovered, government officials talked of Iran becoming one of the world's major copper producers.

The fourth economic development plan, covering 1968 to 1973, reflected undue optimism. Industrial production would be doubled, agricultural output increased by 25 percent, and 1 million new jobs created to eradicate unemployment, a troublesome urban problem.

Simultaneous with this new five-year plan the Iranian economy took off. The budget for 1968–1969 was established at $3.6 billion, a staggering 270 percent rise over the previous year. In each of the following four years the budget leaped 20 percent or more to reach $7.3 billion in 1972–1973. Allocations for defense and development were doubled year after year, and the annual gross national product topped $12 billion in 1972.

Wherever one turned new projects appeared. No wonder the shah had the courage to invite the world's leaders to Persepolis in 1971 to celebrate the rebirth of the Persian Empire; he believed he was propelling his people from the sixteenth to the twenty-first century, when Iran once again would be one of the world's powers!

A second economic transformation began to overtake Iran in 1973 with the quadrupling of oil prices. The budget for 1974–1975 rose to $30.8 billion by the year's end. The budget for 1976–1977 soared to $45 billion. Expenditures, however, quickly were extended beyond revenues, and Iran returned to the borrowing patterns of previous years.

The shah vowed in a speech that development would progress so rapidly and Iran's vast resources would be so thoroughly exploited that non-oil revenues would reach 50 percent of oil revenues by 1985. However, the quadrupling of oil prices had brought on a world economic recession, which greatly affected affairs in Iran. The demand for petroleum products slumped badly, bringing on a $4 billion trade deficit in 1975. Despite this, West Germans started construction on the first of four nuclear power generating units after Iran accepted international nuclear inspection. From 1963 to the late 1970s per capita gross national product increased five times, even after allowing for inflation. With ever-increasing amounts of factories, sophisticated equipment, and accompanying technicians, the modernization of Iran and its economy seemed to be rapidly underway. Perhaps the predictions of the shah were attainable.

AFFAIRS OF GOVERNMENT

The second compelling situation after Mosaddeq's downfall was the restoration of stable government. In December 1953, the shah dismissed parliament and called for elections to begin that month. Zahedi's followers and the shah's friends won in the elections and dominated the new parliament. In April 1955, Zahedi retired as prime minister and the shah appointed Husayn Ala to the post. Husayn Ala had been prime minister, foreign minister, minister of the court, and ambassador in Washington and was recognized as friendly to the West. Elections were held again in 1956. This time the lists of candidates and the manner of the elections insured a victory for conservatives, landowners, and friends of the shah. Former members of the National Front party protested the injustice and mockery of the election.

Beginning in 1961, Muhammad Reza Shah exercised his influence and power for what came to be termed the "White Revolution," or "Revolution from the Throne." He appointed an independent, Dr. Ali Amini, prime minister, who formed a completely independent cabinet. Income from oil was on the increase but the state coffers were empty. Dr. Amini was a sensitive, well-educated, and honest aristocrat with a keen feeling for social responsibility and the welfare of the masses. Within a few days parliament was dismissed and for the next two and one-half years the shah and the cabinet ruled by decree. The cabinet issued a land law decree requiring all landowners to sell to the government all landholdings in excess of one village and stating that the government would sell such land to villagers. In March 1962, the shah presided at such a distribution in Azerbayjan.

In July 1962, Dr. Amini tried to reduce the army's budget and this was rejected by the shah. Amini then resigned. The shah appointed Asad Allah Alam, the leader of the People's party, who pledged to continue the reforms.

The shah presented a six-point program for his White Revolution: (1) the breakup of large estates held by religious foundations and individuals and the distribution of these to peasants; (2) the nationalization of forest areas; (3) the sale of some 200 government industries to privately owned companies to obtain funds to compensate the landlords; (4) the compulsory payment of 20 percent of industrial and business profits to the employees; (5) the forming of a literacy corps from those in military service to go into the villages to teach the illiterate; and (6) the enacting of new electoral laws to eliminate corruption in the elections and to allow women's suffrage. Political liberals and Shiite religious leaders, including Ruh Allah Khomeini (b. 1902), protested vehemently, but their censure was suppressed. Khomeini was arrested and eventually exiled because of his strong speeches against the shah and his reforms, and the country's subservience to the U.S. and to Israel that Khomeini detested. Other opponents of the regime were coopted; they received comfortable government jobs and, in return, they abandoned their critical attitudes. Still other opponents, such as the tribal leaders, were gradually crushed by the regime.

The promised elections came in September 1963, not only for the majlis but for the thirty elective seats of the Senate; the old parties were not permitted to present candidates. The New Iran party was organized by Ali Mansur particularly to support the shah's six-point program. Mansur's party handily controlled the majlis, which was now dominated by agrarian reformers and city dwellers, and not as in the past by the great landowners. The shah appointed thirty new members of the Senate, including two women. Six women had been elected to the majlis. For the first time in Iranian history women's votes were counted, and in the cities women went to the polls in great numbers.

The shah appointed the former finance minister, Amir Abbas Hoveyda, a New Iran member, as prime minister in 1965. The land reform measures did not progress as rapidly as many had hoped, but eventually about one-half of village families acquired some land ownership. However, most peasants did not gain much from the land redistribution plans; while their expectations were raised, their real economic positions gradually fell. The power of the absentee landlord was now often transferred to the hands of the government.

With Prime Minister Hoveyda working closely with him, the shah believed he had attained political stability. Amid a gathering of national leaders and international figures at Gulistan Palace in Tehran, he celebrated his forty-eighth birthday on October 26, 1967, by placing the crowns of the empire upon his head and that of Queen Farah. Parliamentary elections followed one after the other, and the shah and Hoveyda managed them handily.

To enhance the international stature of the shah and the state, the "Feast of the Last Twenty-Five Centuries" was celebrated for four days in October 1971. At Persepolis, surrounded by all the pomp and circumstance that $100 million can generate, royalty, religious dignitaries, and governmental figures from more than 100 states gathered to mark the alleged 2,500th anniversary of the Persian Empire. Many criticized the great cost, in view of the poverty suffered by most Iranians.

The pageantry failed to impress various elements in Iranian society who viewed the shah's worldwide travels and self-acclaim and Hoveyda's political structure as idle theatricals. With society and the economy evolving rapidly, Iran's cultural patterns of individuality, religious idealism, and contempt for government, of family privilege, and of tribal and provincial loyalties plus new ideologies produced many incidents of unrest. Communists, socialists, democratic intellectuals, religious dissidents, tribal leaders, republican sympathizers, disaffected army personnel, and alienated students found open opposition to the government difficult and any united action impossible. Some turned to terrorism. Attempts were made on the life of the shah and his family, and a number of lesser leaders were assassinated. SAVAK, the secret police, founded in 1957, energetically suppressed and intimidated violent and peaceful opponents of the regime.

The political parties did not appear to possess any allure or dynamism. In 1975 the shah dissolved them and one political party was formed—the Iranian People's Resurgence party, with Prime Minister Hoveyda as its secretary-general. The government weeded out unwanted candidates, and then the people were given a choice among individuals sympathetic to the shah. Political participation under such circumstances appeared futile to many Iranians.

CULTURE AND EDUCATION

Public education expanded rapidly in the 1960s and 1970s, as new universities were founded and old schools were renovated. Elementary schools were built all over the country, and the literacy rate slowly began to increase. By the mid-1970s, there were about 7 million primary and secondary school pupils in Iran, and about one-half of them were girls.

The shah set up a parallel educational, financial, and clerical network to rival those features provided by the Shiite ulema. Anti-shah clergy and interested laymen began to formulate the intellectual basis for a renovation of Shiite Islamic theology and practices so as to counter the government's secularization. The ulema also objected strongly to the "Westoxification" or widespread infatuation with the West among young people as well as the growing autocracy of the shah.

Such criticism of the regime was also present in literature. The major themes of most twentieth-century Persian prose were social protest against government tyranny and corruption, and attacks on opportunism in all classes of society, including the clergy. Another widespread theme has been the problem of readjustment of foreign-educated Iranians upon their return home. Many novels, short stories, and plays concentrated on the lives of ordinary people, while a celebrated Iranian film was set in a village; earlier, village life had often been ignored. During the 1940s and early 1950s a large number of thinkers and artists had been attracted to the Tudeh party; following its suppression, they turned to village studies, folk art, and the difficulties of the urban poor to find subject matter which would still express their commitment to social and economic reform. Such writers and artists were equally opposed to the shah's rule and to Islamic fundamentalism. Not only was there new content, but also radically new modernist forms emerged in Persian poetry. And theater finally began to provide plays that were popular and successfully depicted Iranian life.

While engagé thinkers were important in elite circles, popular culture was dominated by political conservatives. Television shows initially featured American programing although eventually Iranian shows began to predominate. By the middle 1970s there were about 4 million radios and 1.7 million television sets in Iran, and government control of the media was a significant asset in maintaining control over society. Film-making flourished: from 1967 to 1977 about 480 feature films were produced in Iran.

Changes in relations between men and women accelerated in the period following World War II, particularly in the cities. A Family Protection Law passed in 1967 and revised in 1975 changed marriage, divorce, and family law so as to decrease men's control over women and give women more extensive rights. The literacy rate of women, especially those living in the countryside, remained, however, very low. Iran's birth rates were remarkably high; in the middle 1970s the population was growing at over 3 percent per year. Millions of people moved from the countryside to the cities. In 1956 about one-third of the total population lived in cities; by 1975 this proportion had risen to nearly one-half. The amenities available to the new migrants, particularly those who were poor, were extremely inadequate. Two-thirds of the population was under the age of thirty! Given these circumstances, there was a strong pressure for change in society.

THE SOVIET UNION AND IRAN AFTER MOSADDEQ

Soon after Zahedi assumed power, relations improved with the U.S.S.R. A trade agreement doubling the amount of goods previously exchanged was signed, and the Soviets indicated a desire to settle outstanding boundary and financial controversies. In 1954, a new commercial protocol was concluded with the U.S.S.R., whereby Iranian imports of machinery were permitted, and Russia agreed to return to Iran eleven tons of gold and $8 million in goods held for safekeeping in Russia since the early days of World War II. However, Iran had joined the pro-Western Baghdad pact on October 11, 1955. This move brought protests from the U.S.S.R., declaring that adherence to the pact violated Iran's treaty obligations. These notes were viewed as thinly veiled threats to implement clauses in other treaties giving Russia the right to intervene or enter the northern provinces of Iran if the latter's independence were threatened. After the revolution in Iraq in 1958, Iran suddenly seemed to take on greater strategic value for the United States, and in 1959 Iran and the United States signed a bilateral agreement whereby the United States would render aid in case of any aggression upon Iran.

Soviet aid projects therefore moved slowly but a number came to be fulfilled in 1966 when the U.S.S.R. agreed to help build a natural gas pipeline from the oil fields of southern Iran to a Soviet port on the Caspian Sea, and to take natural gas as payment.

When the United States declared that its aid programs would terminate in 1968, on the grounds that the Iranian economy had reached the level at which it could progress on its own, the shah began to look elsewhere for trade and arms. Although military assistance from the United States continued, the shah announced the purchase of $110 million in Soviet arms to be paid by the delivery of natural gas and other commodities. The shah returned to Moscow in 1972 to sign an agreement augmenting trade by 1,000 percent within five years.

In 1970, the natural gas pipeline from Qum to Baku was opened. As funds began to flow to Iran from higher oil prices, foreign loans tapered off, but in 1975 when money became tight again a $3 billion trade agreement was concluded with the U.S.S.R.

RELATIONS WITH THE UNITED STATES AND THE WEST

Friendly relations with the United States were pursued by Zahedi and the prime ministers who followed. An American military mission was established to train the Iranian army, and sizable quantities of military equipment were received under mutual defense arrangements until 1966, when the United States declared that the Iranian economy had become strong enough to support its army. In addition to equipment $30 million was expended annually to subsidize the army; in the two decades from 1946 to 1966 over $700 million in military aid and matériel had been given by the United States. By 1966 nonmilitary aid—grants for technical aid, loans from the World Bank, and outright gifts from the United States—totaled over $550 million.

Beginning in the late 1960s, the shah, who always loved to travel abroad in the manner of his nineteenth-century predecessors, led missions to many Western capitals to negotiate diplomatic, military, financial, and economic development matters. He visited Washington almost yearly beginning in 1968. In 1975 Muhammad Reza Shah obtained promises of nuclear reactors and very large quantities of military items.

After 1970 Iran's expenditures for new armaments skyrocketed; it is estimated that from 1973 to 1976 Iran bought or contracted for $12 billion in ships, tanks, planes, guns, and support equipment from the United States alone. Iran was the United States' single largest buyer of armaments in the world. Thousands of American technicians accompanied such weapons to train Iranians in their use. Vast amounts were also spent in western Europe for military goods. Iran now had the fifth largest military in the world!

ARAB-IRANIAN FOREIGN RELATIONS

Throughout the first half of the twentieth century, relations between Iran and the Arab states were not particularly warm. The age-old antagonisms between the Arab and Persian cultures and peoples were exacerbated by the running controversies between Sunnite and Shiite Islam, with non-Arab Iran being primarily Shiite and most of the Arab countries' population being Sunnite.

After World War II the international oil companies played off the Arab oil producers against Iran and drove the wedge still deeper. In 1965, increasing friction with Iraq over respective rights in the Shatt al-Arab waterway and Iranian rebels harbored at Karbala led to the severing of diplomatic relations. Affairs with republican and pan-Arab Egypt and Syria were strained; during the June 1967 Arab-Israeli War, Iran adopted a very mild pro-Arab stance at the United Nations and continued to supply oil to Israel.

In 1969, when Britain's intention to withdraw her military presence from the Persian Gulf area became known, the shah proclaimed an increased role for Iran there. When in 1970 Bahrayn sought to become an independent state, Iran relinquished her claim on Bahrayn. However, the shah announced that Iran would prevent Abu Musa and the two Tunb Islands from falling into "hostile" hands. Iran declared that these islands had been seized from her eighty years ago, when she had been weak, and now that she was strong she would protect them. These islands occupy a strategic position just inside the Strait of Hormuz, and any unfriendly power holding them could deny passage to tankers laden with Iranian oil. On November 30, 1971, one day before the British abandoned them, the shah occupied the islands. The shah proposed to the amir of Sharjah that the latter fly his flag over Abu Musa and retain sovereignty over the 800 inhabitants, and that any oil found there should be divided evenly between the two states. The amir of Ras al-Khaymah, however, objected to the Iranian landing on Greater and Lesser Tunbs, and five persons were killed in the fighting that ensued.

Iran's feud with Iraq was aggravated by the fact that both states front on the Shatt al-Arab. Abadan and Khorramshahr, two of Iran's vital ports, are located there, and Ahwaz is on the Karun River only a short distance upstream from the Shatt al-Arab. When Iraq began to erect significant fortifications at the entrance to the Gulf, the shah protested. Iraq bitterly condemned Iran's occupation of Abu Musa and the Tunbs in 1971 and severed diplomatic relations, deporting 60,000 Iranians from the Shiite holy cities of Karbala and Najaf. The shah, in turn, extended military aid to the Kurds, who were in rebellion in northern Iraq, and gave sanctuary to 70,000 fleeing Kurds. At the outset of the Arab-Israeli War of October 1973, Iraq became uneasy and offered to resume diplomatic relations with Iran. The shah welcomed the request, and stated that Iraq need not worry about her frontier with Iran. Early in 1975 a detente between the two was reached and Iranian support for the Kurds suddenly ended, leaving many of them in very precarious positions. Through the good offices of Algeria a treaty was signed by Iran and Iraq in June 1975, which included a comprehensive delineation of the border based on the 1913 Constantinople Protocol. Iran gained control of part of the Shatt al-Arab and an understanding to allow 12,000 Iranians per year to visit their holy shrines in Iraq.

Beginning with the Tehran OPEC meeting in 1971, relations with the Arab states were ameliorated by common oil interests. After the massive oil price increases in 1973, the shah's concern for the Arab states grew perceptibly.

Above all, the shah was striving for a "Pax Irana" in the Persian Gulf and Gulf of Oman. In 1973, at the request of Sultan Qabus of Oman the shah sent a military force to Oman to assist in defeating a rebellion aided by leftist agents from South Yemen. Some 2,000 Iranian troops were in Oman by the end of 1974. By 1976 most of the rebellion had been quelled; the troops were withdrawn only in 1979 by a new and very different Iranian government.

THE ISLAMIC REVOLUTION

A multitude of long-term and shorter-range causes led to the surprising and dramatic Iranian revolution of 1978–1979, which in turn led to the creation of the Islamic Republic and a radically new situation in Iran. The structural political causes of the Islamic Revolution included the increasingly centralized nature of decision making in the royal government; the inability or unwillingness of the shah to adjust to new political circumstances; the suppression, destruction, or radicalization of moderate opponents of the regime; and the resultant strengthening of the only remaining alternative group, the ulema. With the abrupt creation of a one-party state in 1975, the shah made very clear his own direct control of the political process. He therefore bore responsibility for any errors and misfortunes that might befall the nation. Iran's seeming economic success, her large role in OPEC, the armaments being purchased so extravagantly, and the close friendship with the United States—all these factors reinforced Muhammad Reza Shah's belief in his own intuition and ability. He surrounded himself with "yes men" who told him what he wanted to hear, and he became increasingly unrealistic in his aspirations. Corruption and bribe taking were widespread. New ideas, political programs, and leaders could not easily emerge because of their repression by the secret police. Moderates who simply wanted to implement the constitution were hounded by the regime almost to the same degree as were the "reds and the blacks," that is, the extreme leftists and clerical opponents of change, whom the shah blamed for any failings his government might suffer. Yet, despite the all-encompassing nature of the regime, which extended its power in the 1960s and 1970s even to the villagers and the nomad tribesmen, many Iranians remained skeptical about the legitimacy of the shah's personal rule and about the whole system of government.

The shah's right to rule was based ultimately on the army, on being a nationalist, and on his success in administering the government and leading the nation. While the armed forces officers were mostly loyal to him, many Iranians doubted the nationalistic claims of the regime. Muhammad Reza had reigned since 1941, when he was installed by his father, the British, and the Russians; he had ruled since the 1953 overthrow of Mosaddeq, which was engineered, in part, by the United States and Britain. American influence in oil, the army and police, and the pro-American orientation of Iranian foreign policy all seemed to prove to many Iranian nationalists that the shah was subservient to the United States. No matter what successes might be achieved in the economy or foreign policy, from the point of view of the ulema the Westernized and secularly oriented shah had to be considered a moral failure. The clergy felt that secularism was destroying the soul of Iran, while at the same time the shah was selling the country to the United States and Israel. Materialism, Christianity, and Judaism were felt to be corrupting Islam and the people—according to the ulema. Only a revolution could overthrow such a regime.

Many Iranians disagreed with such judgments because they had benefited from the shah's programs. Yet their support was weak and wavering. The reason for this was that despite the shah's successes, especially in the economy, the political system was so tightly centralized that the new middle classes and the wealthier peasants could not find a way of expressing their new-found status in politics. Iran demonstrated the difficulty of having economic development without political development.

The economic wealth of Iran resulting from oil and development was very unequally distributed. Income inequalities increased with the oil bonanza. Urban areas, the armed forces, some industrial workers, and especially the top government officials were much better off. Ethnic-linguistic minorities, rural regions, the unemployed and semi-employed, and most peasants were either worse off or only marginally in a better situation. Since the government fixed prices at a low rate for basic food products, peasants and nomadic sheepherders received low returns for their goods. Industrial and energy policy ignored small producers and favored splashy large projects, many of which were unrealistic or not truly competitive on the world market. Those persons engaged in commercial distribution through the traditional bazaars resented government favoritism for foreigners and large enterprises. Urban amenities were sadly lacking. Many people in Tehran wondered how Iran could be part of the "Great Civilization" the shah talked about when the most elementary services, such as a workable sewerage system, were lacking!

The cultural Westernization favored by the shah offended Iranian nationalists, the merchants, and the ulema. Western styles of clothing and music, Western views on sex and gender relationships, Western habits in regard to alcohol and gambling offended devout Muslims who saw the cultural Westernization of their country as part of political and military imperialism. Repression of writers, censorship of the media, and refusal to recognize the cultural and linguistic diversity of the country also offended many intellectuals.

More immediate causes of the revolution centered around economic, personal, and political issues. Inflation was rampant in the middle 1970s. The government was trying to do too much, and bottlenecks appeared in transportation and distribution. A new prime minister in 1977 replaced the veteran Hoveyda, who had been in office since 1965, and a deflationary program which led to unemployment was launched. Since most people had rising expectations for better times, the new economic situation made them unhappy. The shah knew he was suffering from cancer, so he began to relax slightly his hold on the government. At this time, the new U.S. president, James Earl Carter, pushed for furtherance of human rights (especially regarding the use of torture) and a strengthening of civil liberty in Iran. Intellectuals and students, inside Iran and abroad, publicly demonstrated and protested against the shah, while small guerrilla groups assassinated officials.

A government-inspired newspaper attack against Ruh Allah Khomeini in January 1978 caused a large demonstration of theological students in Qum. As the government suppressed the demonstrators security forces killed at least seventy persons. Massive memorial demonstrations were organized forty days later to commemorate the victims; these occasions again saw new deaths which led to a new forty-day cycle that was repeated. For Shiite Muslims martyrdom at the hands of oppressors had a strong appeal based on the circumstances surrounding the death of Husayn, the prophet Muhammad's grandson. The Ayatollah Khomeini in exile pictured the shah as being like the Umayyads and the people of Iran as like the martyrs at Karbala in the year 680. New martyrs meant still more and larger demonstrations that eventually spread to cities and towns throughout Iran and involved millions of persons.

Banks, shops, and cinemas were attacked by the crowds which included all sorts of people. The revolutionary movement came to include the ulema, liberals, leftists of various types, trade unionists, bazaaris, the unemployed, many women, the oil workers, and many other groups.

The shah attempted to meet the demands of the crowds by appointing reformist prime ministers or, alternately, by using the army to repress the demonstrations. Fortunately for the regime, most peasants remained uninvolved until late 1978, but at that time villages close to cities became active and favored the Khomeini-led revolution. In the cities, hundreds of people were shot but the crowds were too large, and the loyalty of the troops too suspect, so the shah decided against a bloodbath of the scale needed against such enormous numbers of demonstrators. Strikes paralyzed the economy and the government in late summer of 1978. Production of oil fell by 80 percent. Perhaps as many as a million people demonstrated in Tehran on December 11, the anniversary of the death of Husayn. Despite this, the United States continued to support the shah's rule, and the Soviet Union warned the U.S. against military intervention.

The pressure finally became too intense, and Muhammad Reza hoped that if he went into exile the monarchy and army could be preserved under a regency for the crown prince. A nationalistic and moderate prime minister, Shahpur Bakhtiyar, was appointed. But the revolutionary movement was so widespread, and its leadership in France under the direction of Khomeini was so adamantly anti-monarchical, that this policy failed. The shah left Iran on January 16, 1979. Khomeini returned to Iran on February 1. Short but intense fighting between the revolutionaries and royalists ended with the transition of power to Khomeini on February 11. All of the shah's enormous stockpile of weapons, the attention given to the officer corps, and his nationalistic aspirations for glory and grandeur went for naught. Amid great popular rejoicing, the old system of government was ended and a new, chaotic experiment began. As in the constitutional revolution of the 1900s, Iranians had determined their own fate, irrespective of the wishes of the great powers.

GOVERNING THE ISLAMIC REPUBLIC

The new regime was initially the beneficiary of the good wishes of nearly all Iranians and it retained much of its base of support for many years to come, but some segments of the revolutionary movement almost immediately became disillusioned with the course of events. Khomeini and his associates had a far more permanent purpose in mind than just ousting the shah and the monarchy; instead, they aimed at a basic transformation of government and society in all its aspects. The basic goal of the clerical revolutionaries was the establishment of a Godly social order to be founded on fundamentalist Shiite Islam. Others who held a different set of priorities were soon ousted and the ulema legitimized their own theocratic rule in an uncompromising and heavy-handed fashion. The pace of political-religious change was extremely rapid, but economic and social reformation was slowed by a series of foreign policy crises and especially by the 1980 war with Iraq.

The establishment of a new order was given second place to the purging of the old regime and most of its adherents. Revolutionary courts quickly "tried," convicted, and executed hundreds of political and administrative leaders. Torture was once again widely employed, and a new version of the shah's SAVAK secret police was created. The armed forces were purged of those associated with the shah, and the government favored the civilian Revolutionary Guards at the expense of the army. Censorship and suppression of public dissent soon crushed the media. Within a few years the last vestige of independent and free expression of opinion had disappeared. Minority groups of all sorts were persecuted by the new regime so as to force their acquiescence to its rule. Kurds, Baluchis, Turkomans, Sunnites, Jews, tribal nomads, and others were repressed. Bahais were forbidden government jobs or attendance in public schools because they were said to be apostates from Islam.

Prime Minister Mehdi Bazargan soon discovered that while he and his cabinet of technocrats and reformers were supposedly encharged by Khomeini with the responsibility for governing Iran, real power was located elsewhere. In the chaotic atmosphere of the revolution, local neighborhood committees of religious leaders, youths, and radicals soon exercised local control. They were armed, and they served as distribution networks for scarce goods. They also policed their districts and arrested counterrevolutionaries. At the national level, prominent clergymen and various organizations that enjoyed Khomeini's backing could and did act independently from the official government. Agreements on how to share power were soon broken as new crises emerged. On November 6, 1979, Khomeini assigned power to the Revolutionary Council, which was composed of ulema and laymen, while a new constitution was drafted beginning in August. The constitution was approved in a national referendum in December.

This constitution recognized the guardianship of the chief Shiite theologian (at that time, Khomeini) on behalf of the Hidden Imam, who had disappeared in 878. Pending the Hidden Imam's expected return, legitimate political power could only be held by the ulema and among them, by the best as qualified by reason of insight, wisdom, and piety. (This nearly unheard-of idea was derided by those Iranians who believed in popular sovereignty, and was also opposed on theological grounds by some Shiite ulema.) The constitution also set up a formal government of a unicameral legislature, judiciary, and executive. But the president, prime minister, and all other officials were subservient to the theological leader and to the ulema's Council of Guardians, who scrutinized new laws to see if they were in accordance with Islam. Pan-Islam and not Iranian nationalism became the official ideology of the state.

The first presidential election in early 1980 resulted in the victory, by 11 million of 14 million votes cast, of Abu al-Hasan Bani Sadr, a Western-educated social scientist and backer of Khomeini. Bani Sadr was placed in charge of the war effort; his lack of success in repelling Iraq was a signal of his subsequent downfall. In

1980–1981 the Islamic Republican party (I.R.P.) gradually took control of most branches of government including parliament, the courts, and the provinces. This party was dominated by the ulema, many of whom had been students of Khomeini at Qum, and it was led by Ayatollah Muhammad Beheshti. Its street gangs, known as the "party of God" (*Hizb Allah*), intimidated political opponents, while its contacts with guilds and the bazaaris gave it extra strength.

Bani Sadr and other moderates were driven into exile or ousted by the Islamic Republican party and the Revolutionary Guards. The president of the republic fled in June 1981 just before he would have been arrested. In subsequent days, I.R.P. candidates were elected as president: first Ali Raja'i, who was soon assassinated, and then Ali Khamene'i, for the first time in October 1981 and then for a second four-year term in August 1985. Despite the I.R.P.'s complete control of government, under the ultimate aegis of Khomeini, the parliament retained some freedom of action in criticizing the party and the government. Disputes centered over the degree of government control of industry and business, and over land reform.

Government ministries, the foreign service, universities, radio and television, neighborhood organizations, factories, banks, the police, and provincial administration were purged, renovated, and revolutionized by the Islamic Republican party and the ulema. Vigilantes were in charge of justice, the universities were closed, Friday prayer leaders ran the chief provincial cities, and all concerned sought to create a new structure for public life.

Opposition to this system soon emerged, but it was rapidly decimated. Leftist-religious guerrillas were able to assassinate many of the top leaders of the regime, including Beheshti himself in 1981, but they in turn were arrested, tortured, and executed. The Tudeh party leaders were arrested and the party was disbanded in 1983.

Kurds and other ethnic and tribal groups presented a more profound problem. In 1979, Kurdish leaders demanded that the constitution provide local autonomy, recognition of Kurdish as an official language, a Kurdish university, and freedom of the press. These demands were opposed by Khomeini, who used the army against the Kurds. According to Khomeini, ethnic regionalism was equivalent to treason, while loyalty to Islam should be the first "political" value. By 1984 the central government had once again gained control of most of Iranian Kurdistan. The Qashqai tribe maintained local control for nearly three years after the revolution, but it was also eventually overcome by the central government.

To lessen urban middle-class unhappiness with the regime, some of the more flagrant abuses of the judicial system were ended in 1982–1983. The war with Iraq and economic problems caused some strikes and demonstrations in the middle 1980s.

Ayatollah Husayn Ali Montazeri, the designated heir to Khomeini, engaged in a struggle for influence against the speaker of the parliament, Hojjat al-Islam Hashemi Rafsanjani, beginning in 1985. Montazeri seemed to favor expansion of the revolution outside Iran, a continuation of the war with Iraq, and a relaxation of the regime's harsh rule inside the country. Rafsanjani favored the opposite policies. When his involvement in the "Iran-Contra" arms for hostages negotiations became known in 1986, he suffered a temporary setback. Rafsanjani's role in the Islamic Republican party seemed at risk, despite his help in securing its resounding victory in the parliamentary elections of 1984. Khomeini intervened on June 2, 1987, to abolish the I.R.P. so as to avoid discord among his followers. Despite the official dissolution of the party, its adherents completely dominated the 1988 parliamentary election and retained total control of parliament. In March 1989 Khomeini dismissed Montazeri as his heir in the leadership of Iran, thereby making Rafsanjani the dominant political figure.

Economic and Social Changes

The economy received little attention from Khomeini. Few basic changes in the distribution of wealth have been made except for the displacement of the shah and his supporters. Initially, the revolutionaries tried to establish coherent policies on land distribution, workers' participation in factory management, and conservation of oil resources, but the internal struggle for power and the ensuing war with Iraq sidetracked economic policy. The flight of middle- and upper-class opponents of the new regime deprived Iran of a multitude of educated professionals. Capital also left the country as those who feared the political and economic insecurity of the times sent money abroad. Some of the shah's expensive showpiece projects were canceled. Revolutionary turmoil, the war with Iraq, and the relatively low price of exported oil in the middle 1980s have caused economic austerity, rationing, very high unemployment rates, foreign exchange controls, inflation, a flourishing black market, government budget deficits, and the spending of foreign reserves to cover deficits. A million refugees from the war zones have had to be clothed, housed, and fed.

Conflicting and vague land reform laws passed in 1980–1983 caused chaos, confusion, and turmoil in many parts of the country. Persistent budget deficits led to increases in the money supply; finally in 1984–1985 measures were taken to reduce the money in circulation and curb the economy.

Oil production gradually rose in the early 1980s. By 1981, Iran earned $8.6 billion from its sale. Within OPEC Iran pushed steadily for higher prices and found itself in this respect, as in most other oil policy matters, opposed to Saudi Arabia. Because of the Iran-Iraq War, the Iranians wished to produce more than their 1982 production quota of 2.4 million barrels of oil per day, and they charged less than the official OPEC price, so as to secure foreign sales despite the risks of Iraqi attacks on tankers. Iraq repeatedly attempted to destroy Iran's ability to export oil. Despite this, oil revenues in 1983 reached an estimated $20 to $26 billion! But as the world price of oil fell, so did Iran's income from it; by 1985 it was only $13 billion and in 1987 about $10 billion. One compensation for Iran was that the same factors adversely affected her enemy, Iraq, and Iraq's Arab backers.

Despite all these negative factors and a general fall in the standard of living, minimum Iranian needs have been met, and the rural and poorer urban sectors of society have been perhaps slightly better off materially than they were under the shah.

An Islamic banking system has been instituted. Private banks and insurance companies were nationalized, while many other small private enterprises were taken over by the government. Housing has been a particular problem because of the war refugees and the million Afghans in Iran who have fled their own chaotic war-torn land. Most larger industries have been nationalized, while subsidies for fertilizer, higher prices for agricultural goods, and imports of agricultural machinery have helped some peasants.

Social changes have included substantial modifications in law and in the role of women. New criminal, civil, and commercial law codes have been put in place. Koranic punishments, including executions for such crimes as adultery and homosexuality, were publicly enforced. And secularly trained judges gradually have been dismissed in favor of those educated in religious seminaries. The government has created Sunnite courts in areas that were inhabited primarily by Sunnites. Many women had participated in the revolution, often while wearing black chadors—a head and body covering, so as to show their opposition to the shah's Westernization. In following years, they saw a major emphasis placed on tradition, on the extended family, and on the domestic responsibility of women working in the home. The legal age for women to marry was lowered to thirteen; the Family Protection Law of 1967 was annulled, thereby changing once again the legal status of divorce and allowing polygamy; government birth control efforts were abandoned. Primary school children were now segregated by gender. Women were still eligible to run for election to parliament and two were selected in 1980, but they could not serve as judges. "Modesty," as interpreted by the ulema, was enforced in women's clothing. These and other changes were reinforced by the shrinking economy which no longer needed the employment of women outside the home to the same degree as before 1978.

Cultural life has been radically changed as many of Iran's leading pre-Revolutionary writers and artists fled the country. New school textbooks, especially those for literature and history, have been written. They emphasized Islamic values, the teaching of Arabic, and attacked medieval poets who were viewed as toadying to kings. Universities were closed and faculty members who were accused of being secularists or leftists were fired. When universities reopened in 1982–1983 there were far fewer students; women comprised only about 10 percent of the total number of students. The new government sponsored the making of films that promoted its values. In educational and cultural institutions, as in many other fields, the Islamic Republic instituted loyalty tests, used Islamic and ideological criteria to determine employment, and purged those accused of disloyalty or immorality.

THE IRAN-IRAQ WAR, 1980–1988

The Iran-Iraq War that began in 1980 has strongly influenced nearly all aspects of the history of the Islamic Republic. The causes of the war were several: the long rivalry between Iran and Iraq over border questions; the competition of each for regional leadership; ideological, national, political, and religious differences; and mutual interference in each other's affairs. President Saddam Husayn of Iraq also chose to attack because of more immediate concerns. He saw an opportunity to fill a regional power vacuum. In addition, Iraq's leadership hoped to secure border alignments favorable to itself and thereby to reverse the humiliating deal made between the two countries in 1975. There was also a personal rivalry between Saddam and Khomeini, going back to the forced 1978 expulsion of the latter from Iraq. Socialist, secularist, Arab nationalist Iraq was an obvious target for the export of the Islamic Republic's revolution. Tehran backed Iraqi Shiites in attempts to overthrow Saddam. The two countries broke diplomatic relations in June 1980.

On September 17, Iraq abrogated the 1975 border agreement, and five days later it invaded Iran. Initially, Iraqi expectations of a rapid victory over a demoralized and weak foe were substantiated. Iraq seized much of southwestern Iran, and then moved into Kurdistan, while Saddam appealed to memories of the Arab Muslim conquest of Iran in the seventh century. Iran spent months mobilizing, training, and organizing its armed forces, including the Revolutionary Guards. By March 1981, Iraq reached its maximum advance into Iran, but Iran assumed the offensive, first in air attacks and then, despite internal political turmoil, on the ground.

Iraq was weakened when Syria closed Iraq's oil pipeline to the Mediterranean in 1982, and Iran eliminated Iraqi export of oil through the Persian Gulf at the beginning of the war. The Soviet Union was slow to supply arms to Iraq, which turned to France and Egypt for additional sources of weapons. Arabic-speaking Iranians did not support Iraq in the war; instead, they remained loyal to the Islamic Republic, just as Iraqi Shiites remained loyal to Iraq. In general, the Iraqi invasion had the unintended result of uniting many Iranians behind their leaders. Subsequent Iraqi attacks on Iranian cities, starting in 1983, seemed to have the same effect.

Iran had great difficulty in securing new military aircraft and spare parts for its older, U.S.-built planes. As a result, its troops often fought without air support and underwent heavy losses, while the air force was occupied in defensive roles. However, in the major Iranian offensives in 1982, when Iran first took sizable Iraqi territories, and in the Iranian push into Kurdistan in 1983–1984, which ultimately led to Iranian occupation of parts of Iraqi Kurdish areas, the Iranian armed forces coordinated their actions. (Khorramshahr was retaken by Iran in May 1982.)

Iraq was now nearly bankrupt and was borrowing heavily from the French and the Gulf Arab oil states. Iranian revenues from oil sales were sufficient to maintain its war effort although financial reserves were consumed. Iraq was ready to accept foreign mediation to end the war, as seen in the United Nations Security Council resolution of November 1983, but Iran rejected this and similar later attempts. Iran's position was that Iraq had started the war and its ruling group must pay a severe price for doing so. While Iran's position on peace changed slightly over the years, basically Khomeini demanded the payment of reparations, and the punishment and/or overthrow of Saddam Husayn and his regime. The Islamic Republic of Iran hoped to see a similar government created in Baghdad.

In early 1984, Iran launched major attacks on south-central Iraq, expecting to isolate Basrah, and the Iranian troops did succeed in taking the oil-rich Majnun

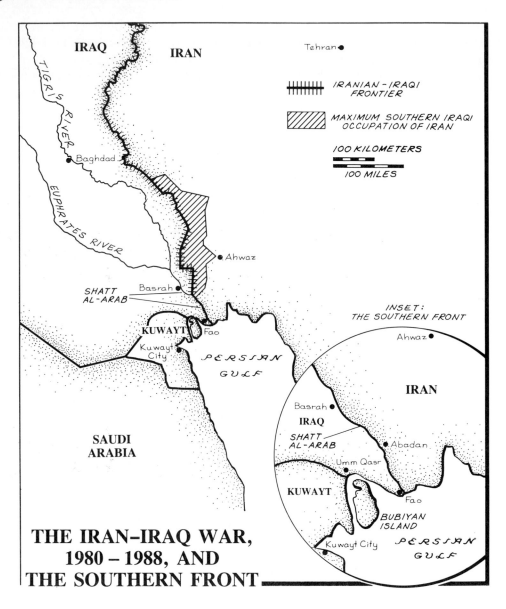

IRAQ

IRAN

Tehran

|||||| IRANIAN - IRAQI
FRONTIER

///// MAXIMUM SOUTHERN IRAQI
OCCUPATION OF IRAN

100 KILOMETERS

100 MILES

TIGRIS RIVER

Baghdad

EUPHRATES RIVER

Ahwaz

SHATT
AL-ARAB

Basrah

KUWAYT

Fao

Kuwayt
City

PERSIAN
GULF

SAUDI
ARABIA

INSET:
THE SOUTHERN FRONT

Ahwaz

IRAN

Basrah

IRAQ

SHATT
AL-ARAB

Abadan

Umm Qasr

KUWAYT

Fao

BUBIYAN
ISLAND

Kuwayt City

PERSIAN
GULF

THE IRAN–IRAQ WAR, 1980 – 1988, AND THE SOUTHERN FRONT

islands located in a marshy area. Nearly 500,000 men fought each other in this difficult terrain, and casualties were heavy, especially for Iran. Iraq's use of poison gas, its aerial superiority, and the relative lack of offensive heavy equipment on the Iranian side led to Iran's greater casualties. But since the Iranian population was about three times larger than that of Iraq, and since many of the Iranian fighters believed that death would make them religious martyrs entitled to go to paradise, Iran accepted very heavy casualties. Massed "human waves" of Iranians attacked entrenched Iraqi positions. By early 1984 perhaps 170,000 Iranian combatants had been killed, versus 80,000 Iraqis. Many hundreds of thousands on both sides had been wounded, and millions of civilians had become refugees.

Iraq in 1984 intensified its efforts to stop Iranian exports of oil. Attacks on Iranian oil facilities, especially those at Kharg Island, increased. Iraq had already attacked some 60 oil tankers in the Persian Gulf; now it attacked many more, but these efforts failed. Iranian exports of oil by 1986 had reached about 1.5 to 2 million barrels per day. In response to Iraqi attacks, Iran searched vessels in the Gulf en route to Arab nations that were sympathetic to Iraq.

In the spring of 1985 Iran began a major offensive across the Shatt al-Arab River and Iraq responded with the so-called war of the cities, which lasted intermittently for years. Iraq heavily bombed Tehran, Isfahan, and other cities, while Iran responded with missile attacks against Baghdad. In a surprise attack, Iran in February 1986 took the Iraqi Fao peninsula close to Kuwayt. Casualties mounted steadily; more than 250,000 Iranians had died and perhaps twice that number had been injured, and 100,000 Iraqis had died and 500,000 were injured.

From 1980, and particularly in 1985–1988, Iraqi Kurdish rebels backed by Iran fought against the Baghdad government with some considerable local success. Iraq ultimately crushed them, in part through the use of poison gas attacks. Iraq tried to aid Iranian Kurdish rebels against Tehran but to little effect.

Iran came within 10 kilometers of Basrah as a result of very large-scale campaigns in early 1987, but that nearly deserted and heavily damaged city remained in Iraqi hands. Iraq then assumed the offensive and took back the Fao peninsula in April and the Majnun islands in June 1988.

Iraq was advancing in most sections of the front lines when suddenly the morale of the Iranian armed forces collapsed. On June 2 Khomeini named the speaker of the majlis, Ali Akbar Rafsanjani, as commander in chief of the military. Rafsanjani was willing to compromise with the Iraqis and on July 18, 1988, Iran accepted a truce with Iraq. A cease-fire took effect in August while United Nations observers were deployed in order to stop any new fighting. The bitter and grudging acceptance of the truce by Khomeini as well as the heavy casualties of the war promised a long and difficult peace-making process.

The Iranian armed forces had surprised Iraq by their determination and willingness to fight despite the chaos caused by the revolution. On several occasions military officers plotted against Khomeini, but these plots were discovered and were followed by widespread purges. Recruits and draftees were thoroughly indoctrinated in the regime's Islamic values, and Islamic Republican party ulema supervised all soldiers. Non-Muslims and Sunnites have not usually been promoted to high ranks, while Persian-speaking Shiites have benefited greatly from the new situation. By 1985 the total Iranian armed forces had increased to nearly one-half million, including the regular military, the Revolutionary Guards, and the volunteer martyrs. The Revolutionary Guards also took over internal security, and they have been a power base for the ulema against various opponents.

The course of the war in 1987–1988 hinged not only on large-scale battles but also on other aspects of the two countries' confrontation. Aerial exchanges of bombs and missiles intensified. Relations with the superpowers, the tanker war in the Gulf, United Nations mediation efforts, and the roles of Kuwayt, Saudi Arabia, and Afghanistan increasingly preoccupied the leaders of Iran and Iraq.

THE FOREIGN POLICY OF THE ISLAMIC REPUBLIC

Negative equilibrium was the key concept of Iranian foreign policy under Prime Minister Mosaddeq in the early 1950s and, with some changes, it also became the basis of foreign policy under the Islamic Republic. According to this concept, Iran should keep both superpowers out of Iran's domestic affairs and not ally with either of them. Khomeini added the view that the United States and the Soviet Union were satanic, and that of all the nations of the world only Iran had a Godly political system. He envisioned this system inevitably spreading elsewhere, both to nominally Muslim countries nearby, and eventually to the whole world. Nationalism was not the key to Iranian policy, but rather Islam was the determinant. The foreign policy of Iran led in part to Iraq's attack on Iran in 1980 and also embroiled Iran in repeated clashes with the United States. Two American presidents, Carter and Reagan, were substantially affected by Iranian-United States problems.

One of the first signs of the foreign policy of the new regime came when the building occupied by Israel's mission in Tehran was turned over to the Palestine Liberation Organization. Far more significant was the loss of power of Iranian moderates, such as Prime Minister Bazargan, which was caused in part by radical revolutionaries who accused them of truckling under to the United States. Massive anti-American rallies were organized. The admission of Muhammad Reza Shah to the United States for medical treatment on October 22, 1979, led to the seizure of the U.S. embassy in Tehran on November 4 by pro-Khomeini hard-line students and others. The Americans captured inside the building became hostages. Documents seized there were used to discredit Iranians who had had contacts with the embassy.

President Bani Sadr and his associates made arrangements for the release of the Americans with President Carter on several occasions, but these deals collapsed because the formal Iranian government did not control the persons holding the hostages. The radicals, with the support of Khomeini, did not want to see tensions eased with the United States. Instead, they used the hostage crisis as a way of bringing down their domestic opponents and humiliating the United States for its past support of the shah. Even the Soviet invasion of Afghanistan in late 1979 was not enough to alarm the radical revolutionaries, who demanded that the U.S. deliver the shah to them. An exasperated Carter authorized an American military rescue mission of the hostages in April 1980, but this mission failed, largely because of technical problems. Muhammad Reza Shah died in Cairo in July, and the hostages were at last released, after arrangements had been made to release Iranian assets frozen in the United States. The hostages arrived back in the United States on the inauguration day of the new president, Ronald Reagan, in January 1981.

With the resolution of the hostage crisis, Iran's attention turned toward the increasingly bitter internal power struggle. After the ulema crushed the leftist guerrillas, Iran accelerated its attacks on oil tankers. It seemed possible that ships of neutral states might be stopped from exporting any oil from the Persian Gulf. The oil-exporting Arab countries of the Gulf, and Europe and Japan (who imported most of that oil), became very concerned, despite high oil production worldwide. The United States navy supported freedom of navigation in the Gulf, and, joined by other nations, patrolled just outside the entrance to the Gulf to demonstrate its ability to intervene with massive force. In 1987, the United States placed its flag on reregistered Kuwayti oil tankers and it provided direct protection for convoys of these vessels as they went to and from Kuwayt. The Soviet Union also assisted Kuwayt by leasing some of its tankers. Attacks on shipping by Iraq and Iran nevertheless increased remarkably over previous years, and numbered 178 in 1987.

The U.N. Security Council on July 20, 1987, unanimously passed a resolution calling for an end to the war. Iraq was willing to accept the terms of the cease fire, but Iran rejected key sections until July 18, 1988, when Khomeini surprisingly accepted it. Secret attempts by the United States to reach an accommodation with the Iranian regime in 1986 also failed. Those contacts were designed to help bring about peace; other goals included the strengthening of the relatively more moderate factions inside the Iranian government and the release of Americans held hostage in Lebanon by pro-Iranian Shiite groups. As the details of these contacts became known in the United States, and particularly after the sale of American (and Israeli) weapons to Iran and the diversion of the resulting profits to Nicaraguan "Contras" was discovered, a major internal political debate erupted in America. The consequences for Iran included the foreclosure, at least for a time, of more negotiations with the United States. Instead, Iran turned to the Soviet Union to block further U.N. Security Council action, and to China for armaments purchases. In late 1987, and again on April 18, 1988, the United States attacked and destroyed a number of Iranian naval vessels and oil platforms in the Gulf, claiming that Iran was responsible for positioning mines in the waters of the Gulf. These mines were a threat to American and other shipping and had caused damage to some vessels. In a tragic accident, the United States shot down an Iranian civil aircraft on July 3, 1988, killing 290 people.

These events took place in a regional environment fraught with danger from all sides for Iran. Most Arab countries favored Iraq in the war. Only Syria and Libya seemed to be partial to Iran, and Syria's support cost Iran a substantial oil subsidy. Saudi Arabia in particular opposed Iranian expansionism, radicalism, and religious exclusivism. Iranians in Mecca during the pilgrimage of July 1987 rioted and were violently suppressed by the Saudis. Iran threatened Saudi Arabia not only on this occasion, but at numerous other times, saying that the Saudis and others, such as the Kuwaytis, should stop their financial aid to Iraq or suffer the consequences.

Afghanistan, on the other side of Iran, provided through most of the 1980s an even greater potential threat to Iran's security because of the presence there of more than 100,000 Soviet troops. This situation had begun with major internal changes in the Afghan government. In 1973 King Muhammad Zahir was ousted and a reformist republic came into existence. The Communist People's Democratic party and the army seized power in 1978. Internal disputes among the leftists created turmoil, leading to direct Soviet intervention on behalf of one of the factions on December 27, 1979. Iran condemned this Soviet invasion, refused to recognize the new regime, boycotted the Olympic Games in Moscow, and welcomed more than a million Afghans who fled from the ensuing devastating fighting and settled in eastern Iran. The Islamic Republic aided in a limited way various Afghan resistance groups who sought to defeat the Afghan Communists and the Soviet troops who kept them in power. Since the United States and Saudi Arabia were also supporting the Afghan guerrillas, Iran ironically found itself on the same side as nations it was vehemently condemning in regard to other aspects of their foreign policy. On April 14, 1988, the Soviet Union agreed to withdraw its forces from Afghanistan. The future of the Communist government in Kabul appeared bleak, and the Islamic guerrilla movements aspired to gain control of the whole country as Soviet troops completed their pullout in February 1989.

Iran's foreign policy had nearly isolated her, but despite numerous crises the Islamic Republic seemed to be able to overcome its military, economic, and social problems—at least until the challenge to the system posed by the death of Khomeini on June 3; 1989.

REFERENCES

Important readings for this chapter are also found in Chapters 29, 36, and 37. Among the many works published on the subject of Iran since 1945, the following are particularly noteworthy.

Abdulghani, Jasim. *Iraq and Iran: The Years of Crisis.* Baltimore, Md.: Johns Hopkins University Press, 1984.

Akhavi, Shahrough. "Elite Factionalism in the Islamic Republic of Iran." *Middle East Journal* 41 (1987): 181–201. A highly detailed discussion of the subject by an authority.

———. *Religion and Politics in Contemporary Iran: Clergy-State Relations in the Pahlavi Period.* Albany: State University of New York Press, 1980. An excellent treatment.

Bakhash, Shaul. *The Reign of the Ayatollahs: Iran and the Islamic Revolution.* New York: Basic Books, 1986. An excellent general survey; clear and relatively concise.

Benard, Cheryl, and Zalmay Khalilzad. *"The Government of God": Iran's Islamic Republic.* New York: Columbia University Press, 1984. More analytical than most treatments; outstanding.

Gasiorowski, Mark J. "The 1953 Coup D'Etat in Iran." *International Journal of Middle East Studies* 19 (1987): 261–286. Serves as a valuable addition to the account by Kermit Roosevelt cited below; based on British and U.S. sources.

Hiro, Dilip. *Iran Under the Ayatollahs.* London: Routledge and Kegan Paul, 1985. A more balanced approach than most books; clearly written and organized.

Hooglund, Eric J. *Land and Revolution in Iran, 1960–1980.* Austin: University of Texas Press, 1982. The best study of the topic; extremely useful.

Ismael, Tareq. *Iraq and Iran: Roots of Conflict.* Syracuse, N.Y.: Syracuse University Press, 1982. Contains many documents illuminating the origins of the 1980 war.

Joffé, George, and Keith McLachlan. *Iran and Iraq: The Next Five Years.* London: Economist Publications, 1987. In addition to speculation about the future, this book also contains insights into the recent past.

Katouzian, Homa. *The Political Economy of Modern Iran: Despotism and Pseudo-Modernism, 1926–1979.* New York: New York University Press, 1981. Highly critical of Muhammad Reza Shah; economic data are informative.

Keddie, Nikki, and Eric Hooglund, eds. *The Iranian Revolution and the Islamic Republic.* Washington, D.C.: Middle East Institute, 1982. Essays on the economy, clergy, change in rural areas, ideology, the role of women, the opposition to Khomeini, and foreign policy.

Khadduri, Majid. *The Gulf War: The Origins and Implications of the Iraq-Iran Conflict.* New York: Oxford University Press, 1988. Valuable for its detailed coverage of events from 1979 onward, as well as an excellent introduction to earlier happenings. Presented largely from the Iraqi point of view.

Khomeini, Imam. *Islam and Revolution: Writings and Declarations of Imam Khomeini.* Translated by Hamid Algar. Berkeley, Calif.: Mizan Press, 1981. Includes lectures on Islamic government and on Islam, as well as speeches and interviews. This is the best source in English to learn about the views of Khomeini.

Limbert, John W. *Iran: At War With History.* Boulder, Colo.: Westview, 1987. A useful general introduction to the geography, history, and recent developments in Iran.

Mohammadi-Nejad, Hassan. "The Iranian Parliamentary Elections of 1975." *International Journal of Middle East Studies* 7 (1977): 103–116. Shows the futility of elections under the shah.

Nashat, Guity, ed. *Women and Revolution in Iran.* Boulder, Colo.: Westview Press, 1983. A wide variety of articles that demonstrate the richness of research being undertaken on a subject previously ignored.

Pahlavi, Mohammad Reza, Shah of Iran. *Answer to History.* New York: Stein and Day, 1980. The late shah's own account of his reign and his downfall.

Ramazani, Rouhollah K. *Iran's Foreign Policy, 1914–1973: A Study of Foreign Policy in Modernizing Nations.* Charlottesville: University Press of Virginia, 1975. Shows the emergence from the desperate 1941–1946 period to the power and position of 1973.

————. *Revolutionary Iran. Challenge and Response in the Middle East.* Baltimore, Md.: Johns Hopkins University Press, 1986. Concentrates on Iranian foreign policy and the reaction to it in the Middle East.

————. *The United States and Iran: The Patterns of Influence.* New York: Praeger, 1982. Another fine work by an outstanding scholar; covers the subject up to 1979.

Roosevelt, Kermit. *Countercoup: The Struggle for the Control of Iran.* New York: McGraw-Hill, 1979. The dramatic story of the Central Intelligence Agency and the overthrow of Mosaddeq; should be read in conjunction with the Gasiorowski article cited above.

Rubin, Barry. *Paved With Good Intentions: The American Experience and Iran.* New York: Penguin Books, 1981. Concentrates on the American side of Iranian-American relations; excellent.

Sanasarian, Eliz. *The Women's Rights Movement in Iran: Mutiny, Appeasement, and Repression from 1900 to Khomeini.* New York: Praeger, 1982.

Schahgaldian, Nikola B. *The Iranian Military Under the Islamic Republic.* Santa Monica, Calif.: Rand Corporation, 1987. Based in part on interviews with former officers in the Iranian armed forces; especially useful for its discussion of the Revolutionary Guards.

Smith, Anthony. *Blind White Fish in Persia.* New York: E. P. Dutton, 1953. An excellent study of village life in Iran.

Zabih, Sepehr. *Iran Since the Revolution.* Baltimore, Md.: Johns Hopkins University Press, 1982. Traces internal struggle for power.

————. *The Mossadegh Era: Roots of the Iranian Revolution.* Chicago: Lake View Press, 1982.

Zonis, Marvin. *The Political Elite of Iran.* Princeton, N.J.: Princeton University Press, 1971. An in-depth view of the most powerful political decision makers in Iran.

40

Oil and Saudi Arabia

The collapse of the Ottoman Empire and the withdrawal of Turkish forces from the Arab provinces following the Mudros armistice in 1918 created in the Arabian peninsula a partial political and power vacuum. Within two years, the French took over Syria and the British occupied Palestine, Transjordan, and Iraq in accordance with their prearranged agreements. For the Arabian peninsula the situation was quite different. London did not doubt that it was to be a British sphere of influence.

Long before World War I the Persian Gulf had become an English lake; official British residents and agents controlled the foreign affairs and advised the rulers of the small states on the eastern coast of the Arabian peninsula from Kuwayt to Muscat. On the southern shore of Arabia Britain held her colony of Aden and protected or had treaty rights with the various sultans, imams, and amirs. And even Abd al-Aziz, the Saudi ruler of Nejd, admired the British. But along the western coast communications from Istanbul by sea via Suez, by land routes from Damascus, and by the Hijaz railway enabled the Ottoman Empire to maintain more than a shadow of control. From this coast and from Syria and Iraq the Porte found it profitable and possible to keep a hand on the precarious balance among the Arab tribes of the interior deserts and to sway decisions favorable to the Ottomans.

SHARIF HUSAYN OF MECCA

In essence the British inherited the Ottoman role in 1916, when they subsidized Sharif Husayn of the Hijaz on the western coast and recognized and subsidized Abd al-Aziz in central and eastern Arabia. Sharif Husayn was given nearly $1 million in gold each month and supplied with arms to captain the Arab rebellion against the Ottomans. Husayn proclaimed himself king of the Arabs, and was promised a united Arab state at the end of the war. When the mandate system was established and Syria, Palestine, and Iraq were taken by France and England, he was disillusioned and provoked. In 1921, after the Cairo Conference, the British proposed a treaty that recognized Husayn as the sovereign of the Hijaz, and continued his subsidy indefinitely. Yet, he refused; his pride and honor would not permit him to accept the clauses that mentioned Britain's "special position" in Palestine. The payments of gold ceased and Husayn was on his own, although negotiations were attempted in 1923 and again in 1924.

Without British protection and assistance Sharif Husayn of the Hijaz, even though he styled himself king of the Arabs, reverted to being only an independent Arab ruler, and by no means the strongest. His position was not enviable. He had taken the lead in the discussions with the British regarding Syria and Iraq; now, the onus of failure was his, even though he always acted as if his sons Abd Allah and Faysal in Transjordan and Iraq were only his viceroys in those "Arab provinces." Unfortunately for his son Ali, heir in the Hijaz, his viceroys had taken with them most of the veteran army built up during the Arab revolt in World War I.

Husayn was not an Arab of the desert. Having lived in Istanbul at the court of the Ottomans for fifteen years, he looked down upon such individuals as Abd al-Aziz, the Wahhabi leader, as uneducated Bedouins, and certainly he did not know how to talk with them. They, for their part, considered Husayn to be a protégé of the British.

In addition, Husayn was a poor administrator. Almost the sole income of the Hijaz was derived from the annual pilgrimage. Husayn mismanaged it, offended the Egyptians over ceremonials, and permitted pilgrims to be fleeced by the merchants until it became a scandal throughout the Muslim world. His final mistake was the assumption of the title of caliph in 1924 after the Turkish Republic abolished the Ottoman caliphate and exiled the last one.

Abd al-Aziz boiled in rage that that "sinful man" should so desecrate the position held by Abu Bakr and Umar. Moreover, Abd al-Aziz had several old scores to settle with Husayn and he needed the income from the pilgrimage. Most important of all, however, was Ibn Saud's inclination to unite the Arabian peninsula under his own rule.

IBN SAUD

Abd al-Aziz ibn Abd al-Rahman ibn Faysal Al Saud, better known in the West as Ibn Saud, was born about 1880 to the Saud family of Riyadh in the Nejd. Since the middle of the eighteenth century his royal family had been the political mainstay of the puritanical sect of Islam originated by Muhammad ibn Abd al-Wahhab, and the Saudis aided in the propagation of Wahhabism throughout Arabia. Ibn Saud's ancestors battled Muhammad Ali of Egypt, who invaded Arabia. In the late nineteenth century, the most serious rivals and enemies of the Saudis were the Rashidi family of the Shammar tribe to the north, centered upon the town of Hail. Abd al-Aziz's father and uncles lost out to the Rashidis in various battles in large part because of an internal struggle for power, and at an early age Ibn Saud lived in exile in Kuwayt and other Arab towns. His father renounced any right to rule, but the son was of a different character. In 1902, against seemingly impossible odds, Ibn Saud, in the kind of derring-do so much loved and admired by the Arabs, led forty young men up tilted palm trunks over the walls and rooftops of Riyadh to recapture the city for himself and his family.

In the years that followed he was able to ward off the declining Rashidis. In 1913, he captured from the Ottomans the province of al-Hasa on the Persian Gulf, not knowing then that the province was practically floating on oil. When World

War I reached the Middle East, Ibn Saud was visited by British officers and agreed to accept a subsidy not to join the Ottomans and not make any foreign commitments without informing the British. Upon the defeat of the Ottoman Empire in Arabia, and with the knowledge of the provisions of the Mudros armistice as well as the Sykes-Picot agreement, Ibn Saud was as anxious to extend his rule as any other Arab potentate. He encountered strong opposition from the Hashimites of Mecca who were also intent on expanding their rule.

In 1919, Abd Allah, Husayn's second son, led a column of armed men to seize the disputed oasis of Khurma. The Saudis fell upon Abd Allah at Turaba and annihilated his army. Abd Allah barely escaped with his life, and the British informed Ibn Saud that he could keep his conquests but must not invade the Hijaz.

When in 1920 and 1921 Britain installed Abd Allah in Transjordan and Faysal in Iraq, Ibn Saud felt surrounded by Husayn and the Hashimite clan. The apparent encirclement spurred the Saudis to move outward. Ibn Saud sent his son Faysal in 1920 across difficult trails to acquire the highlands of Asir and the realm of the Idrisi family south of the Hijaz.

Forging a strong bond of friendship with the Idrisis and obtaining their allegiance, Ibn Saud (whose name was really Abd al-Aziz) settled his family feud with the Rashidis. In a series of swift and daring expeditions, the Saudis captured Hail in the autumn of 1921. A number of the Rashidis then resided as his "guests" at Riyadh, and Ibn Saud became the sole power in the interior expanses of Arabia. A provisional settlement was made with the British with regard to their "protected" areas. Sir Percy Cox in 1922 drew up with Ibn Saud the protocol of Ukair, loosely defining areas and districts. Two neutral zones were set up on the boundaries of Ibn Saud's domain—one facing Iraq and the other next to Kuwayt. These neutral zones served as buffer regions, so that wandering tribes would not create incidents.

The extension of his realm, however, led to serious economic problems. The annual income of the kingdom, which was treated as the king's own personal income, at the time was about $750,000, to which was added a subsidy from the British. For a state that had just doubled its responsibilities, however, this was patently insufficient, and to augment it in Arabia seemed exceedingly difficult. In the winter of 1923, the Eastern General Syndicate was granted an oil concession, for a rental of $10,000 a year. Ironically, only two years' rental was paid; then, upon the advice of geologists who explored the al-Hasa desert, the concession was abandoned.

KING OF SAUDI ARABIA

In the autumn of 1923, Great Britain held a conference at Kuwayt of Arab leaders under her subsidy. They were told that payments would stop at the end of March 1924; a lump sum payment was handed them forthwith.

Abd al-Aziz had hardly reached Riyadh after leaving the conference when Husayn arranged to be proclaimed caliph. The announcement shocked the Saudis who felt that the Holy Places of Islam were being defiled by a presumptuous person. In September, Abd al-Aziz attacked the Hashimites at al-Taif, and in October the Wahhabis occupied Mecca. Husayn fled to Jidda and abdicated in favor of his eldest son, Ali. Husayn then took up residence in Aqaba, until the British conveyed him to Cyprus. He died in 1930 in Amman at the court of his son, Abd Allah. Abd al-Aziz could have pressed on easily and defeated Ali at Jidda, but he realized that this might involve the European powers. Obtaining no aid from Great Britain, Ali surrendered Jidda to Ibn Saud in 1925 and went to Baghdad to live at his brother Faysal's court.

Ibn Saud was now master of most of Arabia, including the Hijaz. He added the title of King of the Hijaz to that of Sultan of Nejd. The Wahhabis, in taking Mecca, destroyed a number of the shrines that they considered the works of the devil, and then Abd al-Aziz refurbished the Holy Places. In 1926 he held an Islamic congress in the Hijaz. This congress brought Islamic leaders of all schools of thought from all parts of the Muslim world to see him and the administration he was inaugurating in the Hijaz. In effect, it legitimized his rule. The congress also indicated that the pilgrimage, now the Saudi's greatest source of income, was again safe.

Abd al-Aziz was a born leader. He inspired confidence. He was just and honorable in his administration and prompt in his decisions and actions. He observed the Wahhabi code; yet social innovations were carefully appraised and judged. The introduction of the telephone and the radio into Arabia, for instance, was bitterly opposed by the arch conservatives among his Wahhabis, who argued that these instruments must be agents of the devil since they could carry the voice so far. Ibn Saud neatly disputed that contention by pointing out that these instruments would bring the word of God and that one would be able to hear the Koran read by worthy ulema. The telephone and the radio thus came to Arabia, and in doing so helped centralize and stabilize the power of the state over all its far-flung territories.

Life around Ibn Saud, whether he was at al-Taif, Mecca, or Riyadh, was simple, democratic, and direct. The business of the government was dispatched with simplicity and efficiency in a patriarchal atmosphere. Abd Allah Sulaiman, the treasurer, on most occasions kept the state's money in his bedroom at the palace in Riyadh. At one time he commented on his anxiety over the risk involved when the balance rose to $50,000 in cash. Other advisers, besides members of the royal family, included Arab political refugees, ulema, merchants, and the British convert to Islam H. St. J. Philby.

The military power of Ibn Saud rested on a combination of groups, including the town militias, tribal units, and the *Ikhwan* (Brotherhood). The founding of Ikhwan communities starting in 1912 proved significant in the Saudi rise to power. The first brotherhood was established around the desert wells of Artawiya, where the fighting Bedouin were settled. Its motive was partly economic. The state provided funds for a mosque, religious schools for reading and writing, wells, agricultural irrigation, arms, and ammunition. The settlement was a religio-socio-military camp and became the prototype of many such towns. From the brotherhoods Ibn Saud received his most devoted soldiers and the necessary stiffening for the regular levies that made his army so feared.

Ibn Saud's power was extended over the bedouin tribes. Traditionally independent, they rebelled against Saudi justice, military control, peace, and taxation.

When the Ikhwan joined the tribes, claiming Ibn Saud was too sympathetic to the British and that he had compromised the Wahhabi cause by settling for peace with Iraq and Transjordan rather than further expansion, a small-scale civil war broke out. This struggle of 1928–1930 ultimately was won by Ibn Saud, who received the backing of the ulema and most of the settled population.

Abd al-Aziz tied the tribes to his rule by the holding of suitable hostages at his court, by judicious marriages for himself and his sons, cash grants, and, if necessary, armed subjugation. In 1932, the official name of the state was changed from the Kingdom of the Hijaz and of the Nejd and Its Dependencies to the Kingdom of Saudi Arabia, a name which reflected the centrality of the dynasty to the state.

After the occupation of Jidda, Ibn Saud in 1925 arranged treaties with Sir Gilbert Clayton which defined on paper the frontiers with Iraq and Transjordan. However, no mention was made of Maan and Aqaba, which Ibn Saud claimed, but which were joined to Transjordan. In 1927, Sir Gilbert returned and the treaty of Jidda was signed. Great Britain recognized Ibn Saud as a sovereign and independent ruler. He pledged to "maintain friendly and peaceful relations" with Kuwayt, Bahrayn, Qatar, and the Oman Coast—all of which were under the protection of Great Britain. The treaty of Jidda set a precedent, and within a few years Saudi Arabia was recognized by, and had similar treaties with, Italy, France, the Soviet Union, Turkey, Iran, and other states.

The problem of Asir troubled Ibn Saud for many years. After the death of Muhammad Idrisi in 1923, his heirs mismanaged affairs and quarreled continually. When Imam Yahya of Yemen supported the Idrisis, hostilities broke out in 1934, Ibn Saud won a quick and crushing victory. In the treaty of al-Taif peace was established magnanimously on the basis proposed before the Saudis attacked. Imam Yahya retained the plain of Tihama and the valuable port of Hodeida. Ibn Saud had shown his authority and his power; he had also proved his leniency, honor, generosity, and wisdom.

DISCOVERY OF OIL

The worldwide depression of the early 1930s upset the Saudi economy. Government depended upon the pilgrimage traffic, which in the late 1920s had amounted to over 100,000 visitors each year. In 1931, however, the traffic dropped to 80,000; in 1932, to 40,000. The Kingdom of Saudi Arabia could no longer meet its bills.

Karl S. Twitchell, an American mining engineer, was employed to search for oil and other mineral resources in Saudi Arabia. His expenses were paid by the American philanthropist Charles R. Crane, of the King-Crane commission fame. While Twitchell was exploring the breadth of the country in 1933, Ibn Saud gave a concession to the Standard Oil Company of California and received an advance of 30,000 gold sovereigns. The concession ran for sixty years, and a royalty of four gold shillings per ton of oil would be paid to Saudi Arabia.

The California Arabian Standard Oil Company (CASOC), owned equally by Standard Oil of California and the Texas Company, was formed. Mapping, geologic surveying, and drilling in al-Hasa province were initiated by engineers who came across to the mainland from Bahrayn, where oil had been found in 1932. With the deepening of well number seven at Dhahran in 1938 oil was found in quantity. The first oil was shipped in November to Bahrayn. Piers were quickly constructed, and the first tanker was filled directly at Ras Tanura in May 1939, Ibn Saud turning the first valve. Exploration spread. Before World War II other producing wells were located north of Dhahran and another forty miles west of Abqaiq. When the war came, 12,000 barrels were going daily to Bahrayn, and Saudi Arabia was considered as a future important oil-producing state. However, oil production was not expanded in Saudi Arabia during the war for lack of men and equipment.

WORLD WAR II

With the outbreak of World War II and the fall of the pilgrimage trade Ibn Saud was reduced to desperate financial straits. In 1940 CASOC advanced several million dollars against future royalties. In 1941 Ibn Saud requested a further advance, declaring that without the sum the state he had built would disintegrate. Since the future of CASOC was obviously at stake, a proposal was made to the American government to grant the sum against future oil deliveries. President Franklin Roosevelt directed the bid to the British, who began advancing sizable sums to Saudi Arabia in 1941. American lend-lease was later made available. Saudi Arabia had not joined the League of Nations, but in 1945 the kingdom declared war on Germany so as to become a member of the new United Nations.

In 1944, the American army requested the building of a refinery at Ras Tanura; compliance strained the finances of the company, which by now had changed its name to Arabian American Oil Company (Aramco). In 1945, an underwater pipeline was built to Bahrayn, enabling the flow of oil in Saudi Arabia to be increased. Royalties paid by Aramco to Ibn Saud began to obviate the need for the subsidies from the West.

The total income of the Saudi government jumped from about $7 million in 1939 to over $200 million by 1953. Because of inadequate banking facilities and Wahhabi views on loans, much of the cash journeyed to Cairo, where it was turned into luxury articles of small bulk that could be easily shipped by small dhows to the Arabian coast. Lavish living and excessive incomes for the family of Ibn Saud and his friends became the custom, and a great part of the income of the state was squandered.

EXPANSION OF OIL PRODUCTION

In the postwar era Saudi Arabia became entirely dependent upon oil royalties. Toward the end of the war the demand for petroleum products in the Mediterranean became staggering, and the need for a pipeline from Dhahran to the Levant coast prompted the American government to suggest that it buy into Aramco and finance the pipeline. Private oil companies raised a violent storm, but it appeared that the European market for oil in the recovery period would be insatiable, and it was imperative that more pipelines be built from the oil fields to the Mediterranean.

Aramco was compelled to seek additional capital for the construction; in 1946 arrangements were made for Standard Oil of New Jersey and Socony-Vacuum to acquire 30 and 10 percent, respectively, of Aramco stock.

Work on the pipeline was started, and steel pipe began to be shipped in 1947. All work on the line ceased during the 1948 Arab-Israeli War. Syria, Lebanon, and Jordan declared that the line would not be permitted as long as the United States supported the partition of Palestine and the creation of Israel. Ibn Saud, however, announced that he would not revoke the American oil concessions, and work was resumed. The oil companies thereupon organized the Trans-Arabian Pipe Line Company. Over half a billion dollars was expended between 1948 and 1953 in constructing the TAP-line and developing new fields and facilities for Aramco. In 1950 the 1,068-mile (1,719-kilometer) TAP-line was completed, and 300,000 to 500,000 barrels a day began to flow from Dhahran to Sidon. New production was brought in every year; by 1955 oil was being produced at a daily rate exceeding one million barrels. In 1943 the daily rate had been 15,000 barrels; in 1950, 500,000 barrels.

As production increased and Aramco profits began to swell, Ibn Saud pressed for greater returns. The Saudis were annoyed to learn that in 1949 Aramco paid more taxes to the United States than royalties to the Saudis. At the end of 1950 a new concession was signed. It gave Saudi Arabia: four gold shillings, at the official $8.25 rate, per ton; a 20 percent tax on Aramco profits before United States taxes; and certain customs duties and taxes or 50 percent of Aramco profits after United States taxes, whichever sum was the greater, an arrangement first devised by Venezuela. Made retroactive to January 1, 1950, the new formula increased the 1950 royalties from $60 million to $90 million. By 1956 the payments topped $250 million annually. The announcement of these terms led to the breakdown of oil discussions in Iran and a change in the rates in Iraq. In fact, the Aramco Saudi Arabia concession terms in 1950 established the general pattern of royalties throughout the Middle East.

For the next several years oil policies and arrangements remained steadfast, except for a 40 percent increase in production in 1951. By 1954, largely as a result of a near shutdown in Iran, oil exports were 75 percent above the 1950 level. The rising income posed many new problems to government leaders who, at this critical juncture, no longer had the accustomed stern hand over them.

An example of this problem was in the area of budgeting. The first budget, of $55 million, was drawn up for the fiscal year 1948, but no budget was published

Abd al-Rahman

|

Abd al-Aziz II (Ibn Saud, 1902–1953)

|

| Saud (1953–1964) | Faysal II (1964–1975) | Khalid (1975–1982) | Fahd (1982–) |

The Later Saudi Rulers

again until 1952. Budgets were not necessarily followed, however, especially since a distinction between the public treasury and the private purse of the king and the royal family had not yet been drawn.

KING SAUD AND KING FAYSAL

Ibn Saud died on November 9, 1953, and was immediately succeeded by the eldest of his thirty-five living sons, Saud ibn Abd al-Aziz. For a number of years the aged Ibn Saud had been afflicted with arthritis and was approaching blindness. In 1933, Prince Saud had been declared heir apparent and began to participate in governmental activities. Other sons shared duties of administration; the most prominent of these was the second living son, Prince Faysal. In the king's last years definite ministries of government were established, and a formal cabinet was organized. The new King Saud served as his own prime minister. Prince Faysal was declared heir to the throne and continued his work in foreign affairs.

Extravagant spending led to government deficits and even foreign borrowing! Corruption spread rapidly, especially in the awarding of contracts. Many Saudi officials were able to buy estates in Egypt or apartment houses in Beirut, and the construction of palaces in al-Taif and other spots in Arabia proceeded apace. Problems of finance, bitter Arab rivalry, internal social upheaval, international politics, traditional nepotism, and the impact of modern living produced such dire conflicts in King Saud's mind that he became unequal to the task of governing. Suddenly, in March 1958, after a family conference in Riyadh, King Saud assumed the role of a "constitutional" monarch. The reins of government were awarded to Prince Faysal, who was generally acknowledged as a firmer and more talented administrator than his brother.

Faysal ibn Abd al-Aziz was born in Riyadh in 1904 and grew up in the household of his maternal grandfather, where he was toughened in the ways of desert warriors. As early as 1919 he undertook various missions for his father, becoming viceroy of the Hijaz and foreign minister in 1926. Though Faysal had traveled widely, he remained austere and simple in his personal tastes. He was known for his fairness, integrity, and dependability.

The question of highest priority for Faysal was how to cope with the ineptness and prodigality of King Saud in a society in which the king's wish was law. Faysal had promised his father many years before that he would never raise a hand against his older brother. When, in December 1960, King Saud reasserted his authority, Faysal dutifully stepped aside. The drastic measures adopted by Faysal to end corruption and waste, to institute efficiency and tighten authority, and to modernize the state and society had irritated many influential figures and depressed the economy. In the struggle against Saud, his brother Faysal was supported by the National Guard, many of the royal princes, the ulema, and those who favored change and reform.

King Saud's return did not meliorate the situation. Numerous pro-Nasser groups were coalescing into substantial factions, and in 1962 Prince Talal and three other brothers left for Beirut publicly censuring King Saud for idleness and mismanagement. The revolt in Yemen in September opened the eyes of even the most conservative elements as to what could happen at home and they called for Prince Faysal to run the government. Refusing to be king, he again took over as prime minister, forming a new cabinet, and removing from office all of King Saud's sons. Faysal outlined a new program calling for the drafting of a body of fundamental law; the organization of a consultative council; the establishment of a ministry of justice; the abolition of slavery (which took place in 1963); and rapid economic and social development. Faysal began to establish a more progressive regime, and Prince Talal and the others returned to Riyadh in 1963, forgiven for their defection.

King Saud failed miserably in a second bid to regain his powers. On November 2, 1964, he renounced his right to rule and left Saudi Arabia, and died in 1969, a pitiful figure. Faysal was recognized as king. In 1965, the popular fifty-two-year-old Prince Khalid, another son of Ibn Saud, was named deputy prime minister, crown prince, and heir to the throne.

For a decade King Faysal managed the affairs of Saudi Arabia astutely. In spite of the billions that began to pour into the treasury in the 1970s and the undreamed of budgetary surpluses, King Faysal stood fast in the conservative management of affairs. Faysal gathered his brothers about him and drew heavily on family talents. In 1967, Minister of the Interior Prince Fahd, a brilliant administrator and facile negotiator, was named second deputy prime minister and second in line to succeed to the throne.

Following the death of Egypt's President Nasser in 1970, King Faysal became the dominant figure among the Arabs as well as the leader of Islamic society. An avowed enemy of communism and Zionism, he was ready to use his influence, power, and resources against both. He was assassinated on March 25, 1975, at the hands of a disgruntled nephew, who three months later was beheaded publicly, as tradition demanded.

KING KHALID AND KING FAHD

Following the assassination of Faysal power continued in the hands of the extremely numerous royal family. The hundreds of royal princes in effect delegated their potential authority to a dozen or so senior princes and especially to the other surviving sons of Ibn Saud. "Politics" for Saudi Arabia was the struggle for influence and position among this small group. Despite widespread discussion and repeated pledges by various rulers, Saudi Arabia has had no constitution or parliament, and there were also no political parties, while the press and other media have been indirectly controlled by the monarchy. The kings appointed some technocrats to the cabinet, but the key posts were reserved for royal princes. Descendants of Muhammad ibn Abd al-Wahhab, the eighteenth-century religious reformer, also occupied prominent places in government. In general, the royal family relied on the ulema for legitimacy and, in return, supported the ulema and their ideas on social and legal policy. The basis of the state was dynasty and religion, not nationalism.

Since the government controlled enormous oil riches, it was able to accommodate most forms of dissent. Rapid economic development, large-scale weapons purchases, personal advancement and high salaries to deserving commoners, economic subsidies to tribes and peasants, and commercial prosperity enhanced the monarchy's popularity with various sectors of society. The kings opted for rapid economic change, but without corresponding political change; this choice excluded most groups from a role in political decision making. A prudent foreign policy also was a hallmark of Saudi Arabia, which managed to avoid direct warfare and the destruction and chaos that often ensued.

Within hours of Faysal's murder the council of royal princes installed Prince Khalid ibn Abd al-Aziz as king, prime minister, and foreign minister of Saudi Arabia. Prince Fahd became crown prince, first deputy prime minister, and minister of the interior; Prince Abd Allah was named second deputy prime minister and commander of the National Guard. King Khalid, now the oldest of Ibn Saud's living sons, was born in Riyadh in 1912. Shunning public life as much as possible and loving the desert, many assumed he would be overshadowed by his aggressive brother, Prince Fahd, but Khalid, extremely popular with the tribes, rapidly learned to wield his power in a quiet but forceful way. However, his poor health made him delegate more and more power to Fahd.

A severe and unexpected threat to the royal rule took place on November 20, 1979, which was the first day of the Muslim year 1400, when some hundreds of armed men seized the Kaaba and the enormous mosque built around it in Mecca. The rebels, most of whom were Sunnite tribal Saudis, declared that one of them was the expected Mahdi or divinely-guided messiah and that they were now entitled to rule the state. They denounced corruption and demanded a moral cleansing of the country. Saudi forces carefully took the mosque in bitter fighting and more than sixty of the rebels were subsequently executed. This event surprisingly caused very few repercussions. There were minor and unrelated Shiite uprisings in eastern Arabia, where that sect was locally numerous, and some administrative changes transpired, but the main effect was to decrease the already small chances of secularization.

King Khalid died of a heart attack on June 13, 1982, and was succeeded by Crown Prince Fahd, who named his brother Prince Abd Allah as the new crown prince.

One of the most notable events of the 1980s involving the Saudi royal family took place well above the kingdom, and even the world, as Prince Sultan bin Salman, a nephew of the king, flew aboard the U.S. space shuttle *Discovery* in June 1985. He thus became the first Saudi, the first Arab, and the first Muslim in space. The ulema dealt with the thorny issue of which direction to face—normally toward the Kaaba in Mecca—for a person praying in space by declaring that one could pray while facing in any direction at all! Royal prestige was convincingly demonstrated on October 30, 1986, when King Fahd dismissed long-time Oil Minister Yamani from that position. Although Yamani had served for twenty-four years, and he had been the single most important figure in OPEC for nearly as long, the king named Hisham Nazir as his replacement and opted for a new oil strategy.

THE OIL BOOM AND OPEC

Each year after 1956 the production of oil increased beyond all predictions. At first a daily average of 1 million barrels was a yearly goal frequently reached; in 1962 it soared to 1.5 million barrels daily; and in 1966 it topped 2.5 million barrels a day, making Saudi Arabia then the fourth largest world producer, after the United States, the U.S.S.R., and Venezuela. Offshore discoveries, added to continuous exploration and new finds, more than maintained the quantities of proven oil reserves, which were 50 billion barrels in 1960, 81 billion by 1967, and 175 billion ten years later. By 1981 new reserves continued to be discovered; Saudi Arabia had about one-quarter of the world's oil!

One of the difficult problems for Saudi Arabia as well as for the oil companies has been the vagaries of supply and demand. These were made more complex by new discoveries of oil in many new regions, and subject to the wish of each nation to be self-sufficient in petroleum products, becoming if possible an exporter to earn foreign exchange. Though increases in world oil consumption have not always kept pace with production, any reduction in exports has hurt Saudi Arabia's budget, since it is tied to oil exports (which often account for over 90 percent of revenues). Moreover, larger exports from one country too frequently meant that the international oil companies would curtail production in another country. The oil-producing countries wished to gain control over their own natural resources and thereby reduce the influence of foreigners on their economies.

To meet these goals, Abd Allah al-Tariki, Saudi director of petroleum affairs, initiated in 1960 at Baghdad the Organization of Petroleum Exporting Countries (OPEC), composed of Iran, Iraq, Kuwayt, Saudi Arabia, and Venezuela. OPEC sought to stabilize world prices, obtain reasonable profits for oil companies, ensure a voice in all oil decisions, guarantee that consumers would not be cut off from supplies, and boycott companies not cooperating with OPEC. Since its formation, Libya, Algeria, Indonesia, Qatar, Nigeria, United Arab Emirates, Gabon, and Ecuador have joined, making it by 1973 a powerful force in the world.

Initially, OPEC attempted to protect its members, each one a weak developing nation, against the machinations of an informal cartel of the international oil companies, sometimes referred to as "the seven sisters." In the mid-1970s, however, the tables were turned. The oil companies, through the nationalization or purchase of oil-producing resources by the host country, had become subservient to the OPEC members, while the petroleum-importing states were reeling from OPEC price fixings and increases that were sucking billions of dollars from their economies into the treasuries of the oil producers.

In 1968 Kuwayt, Libya, and Saudi Arabia joined together in the Organization of Arab Petroleum Exporting Countries (OAPEC), with the stipulation that membership was reserved to Arab states whose oil production constituted a major part of the nation's economy. Because of their almost total dependence upon their petroleum resources, they saw the need to enter into the oil business on their own. Immediately, Shaykh Ahmad Zaki Yamani, Saudi oil minister, pressed for Aramco to accept active participation by Saudi Arabia in producing, refining, transporting, and marketing oil and its derivatives. OAPEC had deemed 20 percent a prudent beginning. Five years later, the Saudi government bought 25 percent of Aramco. In 1974, the government owned 60 percent of Aramco at a cost of $1.2 billion. Negotiations to obtain the remaining 40 percent for an additional $800 million were concluded in 1976 and took effect in 1980. The settlement allowed the former owners of Aramco to market 80 percent of Saudi oil production, receiving a fee of 21 cents per barrel for their services. Furthermore, they would be paid to explore, expand facilities for refining, and ship petroleum.

Except for 1967, when oil revenues faltered because of the Arab-Israeli War, the closing of the Suez Canal, and a temporary freezing of shipments to Great Britain and the United States, Saudi oil production broke one record after another. World economies were prospering and their petroleum requirements mounted. By the end of 1971, output was over 5 million barrels per day and the government budget reached $2.4 billion. Yamani announced in 1970 the ability of Saudi Arabia to produce 12 million barrels per day to supply the needs of the United States. However, Saudi Arabia cut production somewhat during the oil embargo directed by the Arab states against America for her support of Israel after the 1973 Arab-Israeli War. In 1974, Saudi Arabia averaged 8.3 million barrels a day. Despite the record production, proven reserves increased each year as exploration showed new fields.

Oil consumption rose rapidly throughout the world, and demand was outrunning supply. With no end of the seller's market in sight, OPEC raised prices several times in 1973–1974, so at the end of 1974 the average posted price of Saudi Arabian crude oil stood between $11 and $12 a barrel, and the auctioned price often went higher. The quadrupling of prices disturbed world economic and financial relationships, spurring a worldwide recession. With inflated prices, Saudi Arabian budgets escalated, jumping to $32.5 billion in 1976–1977. Foreign reserves invested abroad by Saudi Arabia rose $12 billion or more each year.

In the middle and late 1970s Saudi oil production increased and so did Saudi revenues from it, despite worldwide inflation that decreased the value of payments. Following the Iranian Revolution of 1979 oil production was increased to over 9 million barrels per day, and Saudi Arabia became the second largest producer of oil in the world, exceeded only by the Soviet Union. Output reached almost 10 million barrels per day in 1981 as the price of oil rose to $34 per barrel, while Saudi revenues were more than $100 billion! OPEC oil prices doubled in 1980–1981.

As world demand for oil began to decline in the face of such high prices, and as production by non-OPEC countries increased, prices started to fall. By August 1982 the Saudis cut their output to only 6 million barrels per day. Oil Minister Yamani tried to persuade other OPEC countries to reduce production and lower prices, but the market operated more quickly than Saudi diplomacy. By early 1983, Saudi Arabia produced only 3.6 million barrels per day, and in the same year OPEC cut its official prices, assigned production quotas, and gave the Saudis the "swing" role in production. Since the population of the kingdom was so small, and its oil reserves were so great, the Saudis agreed to vary their production as world demand varied.

While the government budget fell into deficit, Saudi foreign reserves were tapped to provide cash. Yet Saudi Arabia at this time made some progress in reaching at least one of its goals: a Saudi for the first time became president of Aramco in 1984.

Oil production in Saudi Arabia reached a twenty-year low in August 1985 at 2.2 million barrels per day, and the Saudis unilaterally cut their oil prices. They then began to increase output, being tired of the cheating of some OPEC members who produced more than their quotas while leaving the Saudis holding the bag. The Saudi goal was to pressure the rest of OPEC into more equitably applied restrictions on output and pricing. Yamani sharply increased pumping to 5.5 million barrels per day in the middle of 1986. World oil prices fell sharply, to a six-year low, and OPEC agreed to try the Saudi strategy. On November 28, 1988, all OPEC countries agreed upon a quota system for limiting their production at 18.5 million barrels of oil per day, including limits of about 2.6 million barrels each for Iraq and Iran. But while this strategy ultimately was adopted, Saudi revenues were falling; they had been $43 billion in 1984, but were only $22 billion in 1987. Uncertainty within Saudi Arabia was so great the government never issued an official budget for 1986–1987.

Saudi Arabia had a preeminent role in OPEC because it sold about 40 percent of OPEC production, but it has not had complete control, and OPEC itself has not totally dominated the world oil market. In the 1980s only about one-third of world oil has come from the OPEC countries. Each individual member of OPEC has had its own interests and internal disagreements have been deep and varied. Algeria, Libya, Iraq, and Iran have often pushed for higher prices than Saudi Arabia wished. The Saudi position was based on its enormous reserves and a relatively small population which enabled it to take a long-range view of oil issues. The enormous riches of Saudi Arabia gave it a margin enabling variation in pricing policies, while at the same time they posed an alluring opportunity for poorer and ambitious neighbors.

MILITARY FORCES

For all of Ibn Saud's character and personality, he never for one moment forgot that his position rested on military power. Saudi Arabia did not fight in any major wars after 1934 in a substantial way, and Ibn Saud's royal sons also preserved the peace. In fact, the chief purpose of the military and National Guard was to secure domestic order and preserve the regime. Two parallel organizations existed: the regular armed forces had as their rivals the tribally based National Guard. Despite some occasional plots aimed at military coups, the two institutions remained loyal to the government and the monarchy.

In 1951 Saudi Arabia signed a mutual-defense assistance agreement with the United States for various types of equipment, including eighteen tanks. The most powerful military base in that part of the Middle East was located at Dhahran. Here, toward the close of World War II, the United States constructed a mighty airfield and installations from which planes could control much of the Middle East and bomb strategic spots in the U.S.S.R. In 1956, Saudi Arabia requested that the United States pay an annual rental of $50 million for Dhahran; in 1957, during King Saud's visit to Washington, a five-year renewal was authorized. In exchange, the United States promised to train a small Saudi navy, organize and instruct a Saudi air force at Dhahran, and expand the army school at al-Kharj. However, King Saud informed the United States that the lease for the base would not be renewed. In 1962, the Dhahran base was relinquished to Saudi Arabia and another vestige of World War II was removed.

The outbreak of civil war in Yemen in the autumn of 1962 reemphasized the military aspects of life in Saudi Arabia, as the United Arab Republic supported the Yemeni republican forces under al-Sallal while Imam Muhammad al-Badr and the royalists sought protection from Saudi Arabia. In the northeast, Kuwayt looked to Saudi Arabia to help ward off the danger of invasion from Iraq. Jet fighters were quietly invited back from the United States in 1963, American paratroopers participated in training the Saudi Paratrooper Corps, and a British military mission arrived to advise the Saudi army. The military seriousness of the civil war in northern Yemen and Egyptian involvement also in southern Yemen impressed King Faysal, especially as Egypt bombed Saudi border towns.

Saudi Arabia felt weak and vulnerable. This was reinforced with the British withdrawal from the Persian Gulf in 1971. Faysal aided Sultan Qabus of Oman against guerrillas. As Iran, Israel, and other possible enemies acquired vast supplies of weapons, an arms race in the region began. In 1973 Saudi military purchases topped $1 billion.

In 1975–1976 Saudi Arabia spent $4 billion in the United States for military goods, and $4 billion more in the next year. It seemed that the military could escalate its requirements to almost any heights. About one-quarter to one-third of the national budget went in various ways for military expenditures.

By 1979 more than half of all U.S. foreign military sales went to the Saudis. In the 1980s there were several instances, however, when Saudi Arabia wished to buy weapons systems but pro-Israelis in the U.S. Congress objected, fearing such arms would be used against Israel. Saudi Arabia therefore sought to diversify. There ensued a $4 billion purchase of weapons from France in 1984, and sales in 1985 and 1988 by Great Britain that totaled considerably more than $14 billion. Saudi Arabia secretly bought Chinese surface-to-surface missiles that were capable of hitting any targets in the Middle East, and they were installed in 1987–1988.

Pakistan sent an armored brigade of about 10,000 troops to Saudi Arabia in the early 1980s in return for financial arrangements. They were to be withdrawn in 1988 because Pakistan, although willing to have them used against Israel, was not agreeable to their employment against Iran, should a war take place.

SAUDI FOREIGN RELATIONS

The foreign interests of Saudi Arabia have been predicated upon maintaining the status quo in the region through an unofficial alliance with the United States. Saudi kings saw Soviet communism, Zionism, and pan-Arab nationalism and socialism as their chief enemies. This view implied a basic contradiction in Saudi policy, however, for while a close reliance upon American power for opposing Russia was desirable, nevertheless the United States was also the major backer of Zionist Israel. Another basic aspect of Saudi policy pertained to the pilgrimage to Mecca: the Saudis were the protectors of the Holy Places and came to play a major role among the Muslim countries of the world as a result. (The pilgrimage season was highly significant for the government; much of the government moves to Mecca every year at that time.)

Saudi Arabia participated in the deliberations of the Arab League, but it was only in 1973 that she took a leading role in Arab affairs. In 1948, for instance, the Saudis had sent only a nominal force to fight Israel.

In 1953 a serious dispute arose with Great Britain over the possession of the Buraimi oases, which Abu Dhabi also claimed. The question remained unsettled until 1974 when Saudi Arabia and Abu Dhabi divided the area. Saudi borders to the south and east were still largely undemarcated, which led to this sort of problem.

Saudi Arabia during the 1956 Arab-Israeli War supported Egypt. Diplomatic relations with France and Britain were severed. Throughout the union of Egypt and Syria during 1958–1961, and the vagaries of Nasserism, King Saud tended to support Egypt, while King Faysal strongly opposed Nasser. Conservative, monarchical, fundamentalist, rich, and pro-American Saudi Arabia naturally clashed with revolutionary, republican, secularist, poor, and pro-Soviet Egypt. Pan-Arab nationalism was a threat to the Saudi royal family's power and wealth and to the identity of the country.

In 1962 Saud and Faysal, condemning Egypt's intervention in Yemen on the side of the republican regime, broke diplomatic relations with Nasser. Faysal believed that the republican regime in Yemen would collapse within a few hours if Egyptian forces were withdrawn. Faysal initiated costly and decisive steps to strengthen his own military forces to show Nasser he could not be cowed into abandoning his neighboring Arab state. When Great Britain announced in 1966 that her withdrawal from Aden was fixed for 1968, Nasser could not bring himself to pull his troops from nearby Yemen. Faysal maintained that the Yemeni people should determine their own future. Only in the aftermath of the June 1967 Arab-Israeli War was Nasser forced to withdraw his forces and permit a compromise.

Saudi Arabia, however, refused to recognize either the Yemen Arab Republic or the People's Republic of South Yemen. Relations with both remained strained and border incidents kept the frontiers closed until 1970, when agreements were reached with the Yemen Arab Republic and diplomatic relations were established. King Khalid and Prince Fahd, wishing to pacify all Saudi borders, in 1976 normalized relations with the People's Republic of South Yemen and gave that state a grant of $100 million.

In 1968, when Great Britain announced her intention to give up her bases on Bahrayn and Sharjah and her special privileges in the Persian Gulf, Saudi Arabia understood the need to secure the Gulf's stability and peace. She denied Iran's claim to Bahrayn, but after the shah visited Riyadh, Faysal did agree to divide the continental shelf in the Gulf with Iran. The seven shaykhdoms of the Trucial Coast began to discuss forming the United Arab Emirates, and King Faysal urged Qatar and Bahrayn to join. When the United Arab Emirates was launched in 1971 Saudi Arabia maintained cordial relations.

Saudi Arabia's friendship with Kuwayt goes back to the nineteenth century. In 1970, Saudi Arabia and Kuwayt arranged to divide the Neutral Zone equally into what each termed the "Partitioned Zone." In 1975, after King Faysal's assassination, Prince Fahd flew to Baghdad to mediate the border problems between Kuwayt and Iraq and agreed with Iraq on dividing the Neutral Zone between Saudi Arabia and Iraq.

Saudi Arabia began to take an active role in Arab affairs at the Arab meeting in Khartoum in 1967, when she agreed to give $140 million a year to Egypt and Jordan for their expenses as states facing Israel. Faysal declared publicly in 1971 that there could be no peace in the Middle East without Israeli evacuation of Muslim Holy Places in Jerusalem, withdrawal from 1967 conquests, and recognition of Palestinian rights. In 1973 Faysal was one of the leaders of the oil embargo against the United States, reducing Saudi Arabia's production levels and signaling his solidarity with the Arab cause against Israel. Saudi support for Egypt, Syria, and Jordan was continued in 1974, and an extra $300 million was pledged to Egypt. At the Arab summit meeting in Morocco that year Faysal accepted the Palestine Liberation Organization (PLO) as the representative of the Palestinian people and declared again that there could be no peace in the Middle East until the Arabism of Jerusalem was recognized.

Faysal's policies were continued after his death. King Khalid and Prince Saud, his foreign minister, brought Syria and Egypt together in 1976 over the civil war in Lebanon, inducing Egypt, Syria, Lebanon, Kuwayt, Saudi Arabia, and the PLO to agree to the creation of an Arab peacekeeping force of 30,000 in Lebanon. Egypt, Syria, and Saudi Arabia managed also to align their positions on terms for a settlement with Israel, indicating they would accept the existence of Israel if Israel would recognize Palestinian rights, would withdraw to her pre-1967 frontiers, and would accept Arab control of Islamic Holy Places in Jerusalem.

The strong Islamic traditions were preserved by Faysal, who expressed sorrow at the annexation of the Muslim parts of Jerusalem by Israel in 1967 and who repeatedly avowed his desire to pray at the Holy Places there. Believing that the 375,000 pilgrims from eighty countries who came to Mecca in 1969 testified to the strength of Islam, Faysal organized the First Islamic Conference, a summit of all Muslim nations and peoples.

Saudi Arabia broke diplomatic relations with Egypt in 1979 following Egypt's peace treaty with Israel. The Saudis also stopped paying Egypt a subsidy of nearly $1 billion per year. By 1982, however, the Saudi king came to accept Egypt again as a partner in discussions, and resumed formal relations in 1987.

The kingdom proposed its own plan to end the Arab-Israeli dispute in November 1981 at the Arab summit conference, but key elements in the conflict rejected it. Even more pressing than the Arab-Israeli question, at least from the Saudi viewpoint, was the 1980 Iran-Iraq War, in which Saudi Arabia backed Iraq financially and diplomatically. The royal house feared the possible expansion of the war into Kuwayt and Saudi Arabia and repeatedly attempted to encourage a cease-fire and peace.

One way to increase Saudi security was through regional cooperation, and the kingdom on March 10, 1981, joined with Bahrayn, Kuwayt, Oman, Qatar, and the United Arab Emirates to create the Gulf Cooperation Council to coordinate military, diplomatic, and other matters. Another device was the increased purchase of arms, particularly from the United States. President Ronald Reagan assured the Saudis of U.S. military intervention if the royal government was under direct attack, whether from within or without. King Fahd secretly gave millions of dollars to the Nicaraguan "Contras" and other groups at the request of the U.S. government, and Saudi Arabia thus became indirectly involved in the Iran-Contra affair in the United States. And the Soviets were periodically contacted, but Saudi Arabia continued to avoid actual diplomatic recognition of, and the exchange of ambassadors with, the U.S.S.R.

During the Iran-Iraq War, large oil slicks in the Persian Gulf, caused by the bombing of petroleum installations and tankers, threatened the Saudi coast and its desalinization plants, and there were minor skirmishes with Iran in 1984, but Saudi Arabia was usually able to stay out of that nine-year war. As the tanker conflict in the Gulf intensified in the middle 1980s, however, Saudi vessels came under more frequent attack from Iran. And a riot by thousands of pro-Khomeini Iranian pilgrims in Mecca in 1987 was repressed by the Saudis at the cost of 400 deaths.

Saudi Arabia has granted large amounts of its oil wealth to various Muslim countries and groups abroad, and has built mosques, trained preachers, and printed Korans to help spread Islam. The kingdom has helped fund the Palestine Liberation Organization, the Eritrean rebels in Ethiopia, and the Afghan guerrillas.

DEVELOPMENT IN SAUDI ARABIA

The considerable influx of money following World War II generated many plans for the improvement of Saudi Arabia. In 1947, a four-year plan called for the building of railroads, highways, ports, airfields, schools, hospitals, electric-power plants, irrigation systems, and conduits and canals for supplying water to Jidda, Mecca, and other cities. Aramco proved an interested ally in these programs and located able engineers for many of the projects. The railway between Dammam and Riyadh was completed. The port of Dammam was reconstructed, and three small ports on the Red Sea were improved. To serve as a gateway to Medina, the port of Yanbu was developed on the Red Sea; it was opened by Prince Khalid in 1966.

The first secular university was opened in Riyadh in 1957, while the Islamic Sharia College of Mecca had been created in 1949 and other traditional schools were founded. The Petroleum and Mining College at Dhahran graduated its first class in 1972. Several other universities, institutes, and educational centers were built.

Elementary schools appeared in all parts of the kingdom in great numbers; in 1963 alone there were 100 new schools for boys and 62 for girls. About half as many girls attended schools as boys, and they were taught separately. As thousands of Saudis educated abroad returned and Saudi universities also produced many graduates, careers in government and business opened up to them.

New construction radically transformed the appearance of Riyadh; most of the older buildings were torn down and new construction was everywhere. Many government offices were moved there from Jidda. Hospitals were built not only in the capital, but throughout the country. Each year transportation and communications were vastly improved, financed by ever larger budget appropriations, thereby extending the power of the central government over all areas.

Under Faysal economic development had the highest priority, receiving 40 percent of the budget. Surveys revealed sizable deposits of iron, copper, and silver, and the amounts of sulphur obtained from oil were vast. A steel-rolling mill was opened in 1966. A glass industry was established at Riyadh, and plants for producing sulphur, paint, ammonia and its derivatives, fertilizers, and other products were built in Dammam by foreign firms.

In 1975, a second Five-Year Development Plan was announced; it would cost the staggering sum of $150 billion. Allocations were chiefly for infrastructure and social development: roads, housing, harbors, and irrigation. One-sixth of the plan's cost was to go to industrial development.

Starting in the late 1970s, as infrastructure projects were completed, the Saudis turned to the long-range issue of future sources of income other than exporting oil. Natural gas utilization and petrochemicals were obvious choices. A new pipeline linking the Persian Gulf and the Red Sea opened in 1981 and a $12 billion natural gas system was completed later. The new industrial cities of Jubail and Yanbu were opened in the late 1980s. Jubail on the Gulf cost more than $45 billion to complete.

Agriculture also was given attention by the government. In the early 1950s at al-Kharj deep wells were cleaned, pumps were installed, and more than 8,000 acres of land produced crops in great abundance. The scarcity of water hampered agriculture, except in some of the great oases in al-Hasa, and only about 2 percent of the country's land was arable, the rest being desert or mountainous. Saudi Arabia engaged in several desalinization projects. In 1962 there was more drilling for water than for oil. Intensive hydrological surveys were carried out in several areas. The supply of water became critical in Riyadh. Dams were built wherever water resources justified the investment.

In 1970, agriculture was responsible for 70 percent of employment, but by 1980 this fell to only 25 percent. Peasants moved to the cities even though governments paid much higher than world prices for their products. Poultry and dairy farming flourished, and the subsidized wheat farmers have, in the 1980s, produced enough grain to feed the kingdom on their own. The Saudi government helped agriculture by bringing electricity to 2,000 villages in the 1970s.

Agriculture produced only a small part of the Saudi gross national product. Even after oil revenues sharply declined in the 1980s, oil was by far the most important aspect of the Saudi economy. Private companies, especially those engaged in construction, suffered losses, but major projects were completed, while the government became more interested in the full and efficient use of existing facilities than the building of new enterprises.

The sums spent on development were allotted to contractors, many of whom were foreigners, and who needed to hire foreign laborers. Hundreds of thousands of North Yemenis, Palestinians, Egyptians, Pakistanis, Koreans, and others were brought into the kingdom. They often lived apart from the Saudis, but there was inevitably some interaction and diffusion of new ideas, values, and patterns of living. Saudi tourists who traveled abroad also encountered very different life styles than those they were accustomed to at home.

A large gap between high urban and low rural income led many peasants and tribesmen to move to the bigger cities. By 1981, two-thirds of the Saudis lived in cities. They had greater access to educational facilities and other government services than the rural population. Population growth rates were high, and in the 1970s school enrollments almost doubled, and university students' numbers increased four times. Since there were not enough Saudi teachers, the government hired many foreigners to staff all levels of the educational system.

Although wealth was concentrated in the hands of the royal family, many others also became wealthy, and a great deal of money "trickled down" even to the poor. Radios, television sets, automobiles, and consumer goods of all sorts were widely available and purchased. And social services improved greatly in quality and availability.

The new media gave even the rural population access to new items. Radio broadcasts began in 1949, while television service commenced in 1965. Religious programing occupied a substantial proportion of broadcast time. Since public cinemas are not permitted, private rentals of movies and, more recently, video cassettes, have been the means of dissemination of films. The Saudi government in the 1970s sharply increased the number of public libraries to about 40, while the new Department of Antiquities surveyed archaeological sites, opened museums, and sponsored historical research. Youth groups sponsored poetry recitals, musical performances, and literary clubs. Saudi Arabia hosted many Arab, Muslim, and other international conferences and congresses.

In literature Saudi Arabia followed the same trends as in many other Arab countries. Saudi poets shared the modernist versus classical or romantic split in poetry. New forms included the use of free verse, and there has been some following of European examples as well as a good deal of originality. Short stories and novels frequently stressed change and separation, themes widespread in Saudi social life, as well as depictions of local and regional life.

In all these activities women have either no part or a very restricted role. Despite increasing literacy, Saudi women have not been active in public or political life; males run the government, the religious system, courts, and most economic institutions. Sexual segregation in public places is strictly enforced. Women are not allowed to drive automobiles and are sharply restricted as to places where they can work outside the home. The legal system has changed in some ways, particularly in regard to commercial and administrative law, but personal matters have been adjudicated on the Wahhabi interpretation of the Koran and the hadiths or sayings of the Prophet. Therefore, the legal status of women and their dependence on men have continued, without profound changes, as they had been in earlier days.

Continuity in most aspects of public life, despite extraordinary economic and technological changes, has so far marked Saudi Arabia's recent history.

REFERENCES

Significant works for this chapter are also found in Chapters 18, 22, 24, 25, 28, 30, and 31.

Abdalla, Abdelgadir Mahmoud, *et al.,* eds. *Sources for the History of Arabia.* Riyad: Riyad University Press, 1979. 2 vols. The best beginning place for historiographical studies; a mine of information about events as well as sources.

Abir, Mordechai. *Saudi Arabia in the Oil Era.* Boulder, Colo.: Westview Press, 1988.

Almana, Mohammed. *Arabia Unified: A Portrait of Ibn Saud.* Rev. ed. London: Hutchinson Benham, 1982. A colorful and personal account of administration in the days before oil.

Altorki, Soraya. *Women in Saudi Arabia: Ideology and Behavior Among the Elite.* New York: Columbia University Press, 1986. Shows the changes in the patterns of living for urban elite women.

Anderson, Irvine H. *Aramco, the United States, and Saudi Arabia: A Study of the Dynamics of Foreign Oil Policy, 1933–1950.* Princeton, N.J.: Princeton University Press, 1981. Concentrates on the U.S. side.

Armstrong, Harold C. *Lord of Arabia, Ibn Saud: An Intimate Study of a King.* London: Berker, 1934. An early and friendly biography.

Chalabi, Fadhil J. al-. *OPEC and the International Oil Industry: A Changing Structure.* Oxford: Oxford University Press, 1980. An able presentation of the Arab members of OPEC and their views.

de Gaury, Gerald. *Faisal, King of Saudi Arabia.* New York: Praeger, 1967. A perceptive study of a complex ruler.

Dickson, H. R. P. *The Arab of the Desert.* New York: Macmillan, 1949. A classic sociological study of the nomads of Arabia.

Finnie, David H. *Desert Enterprise: The Middle East Oil Industry in Its Local Environment.* Cambridge, Mass.: Harvard University Press, 1958.

Goldberg, Jacob. *The Foreign Policy of Saudi Arabia: The Formative Years, 1902–1918.* Cambridge, Mass.: Harvard University Press, 1986. A perceptive study of the subject.

Habib, John S. *Ibn Sa'ud's Warriors of Islam.* Leiden: Brill, 1978. An examination of the Ikhwan.

Helms, Christine Moss. *The Cohesion of Saudi Arabia: Evolution of Political Identity.* Baltimore, Md.: Johns Hopkins University Press, 1981. An analytical work emphasizing geography and its effects, as well as history and diplomacy for the early twentieth century.

Howarth, David. *The Desert King: Ibn Saud and His Arabia.* New York: McGraw-Hill, 1964. A well-researched, sympathetic, and very readable account of the colorful founder-king. Written from the British viewpoint.

Islami, A. Reza S., and Rostam Kavoussi. *The Political Economy of Saudi Arabia.* Seattle: University of Washington Press, 1984. A critical but balanced appraisal.

Jayyusi, Salma Khadra, ed. *The Literature of Modern Arabia: An Anthology.* London: Kegan Paul, 1988. This massive anthology of poetry and short stories includes Saudi Arabia, the Yemens, and other countries of the Arabian peninsula; a valuable introduction provides an overview of recent literature. Exceptionally important.

Johany, Ali D., *et al. The Saudi Arabian Economy.* Baltimore, Md.: Johns Hopkins University Press, 1986. An excellent treatment of all aspects of the economy and related subjects.

Katakura, Motoko. *Bedouin Village: A Study of a Saudi Arabian People in Transition.* Tokyo: University of Tokyo Press, 1977. Shows the impact of change and the resilience of tradition among tribal villagers near Mecca. Most useful.

Kostiner, Joseph. "Tracing the Curves of Modern Saudi History." *Asian and African Studies* 19 (1985): 219–244. By means of an extended book review the author indicates a new way of interpreting the periodization of Saudi history.

Kramer, Martin. *Islam Assembled: The Advent of the Muslim Congresses.* New York: Columbia University Press, 1986. Deals with the Hijazi congress and other such gatherings in the 1920s and 1930s. Well-researched and well-written.

Longrigg, Stephen H. *Oil in the Middle East: Its Discovery and Development.* 3rd ed. New York: Oxford University Press, 1968. Thorough study of oil development and its effect on politics and life in the Middle East. By one of the individuals involved in the process.

Mani, Muhammad Abdullah al-, and Abd ur-Rahman Sbit as-Sbit. *Cultural Policy in the Kingdom of Saudi Arabia.* Paris: UNESCO Press, 1981.

Mikdashi, Zuhayr. *The Community of Oil Exporting Countries: A Study in Governmental Cooperation.* Ithaca, N.Y.: Cornell University Press, 1972. Traces the evolution of OPEC and OAPEC.

Monroe, Elizabeth. *Philby of Arabia.* London: Faber & Faber, 1973. A vivid picture of the man, the times in which he lived, and the journeys by which he most deserves to be remembered.

Netton, Ian Richard, ed. *Arabia and the Gulf: From Traditional Society to Modern States.* Totowa, N.J.: Barnes and Noble, 1986. Seventeen essays on historical, political, economic, social, and literary themes.

Niblock, Tim, ed. *State, Society and Economy in Saudi Arabia.* London: Croom Helm, 1982. A fine collection of essays on various topics; especially valuable for diplomatic and economic matters.

Ochsenwald, William. "Saudi Arabia," in *The Politics of Islamic Revivalism: Diversity and Unity.* Edited by Shireen T. Hunter. Bloomington: Indiana University Press, 1988.

Philby, H. St. John B. *Arabia.* New York: Scribners, 1930. Philby was a British Muslim who served as adviser to Ibn Saud for several decades and was one of the outstanding Arab scholars of his day. It was Philby who suggested the name "Saudi Arabia" to Ibn Saud. A fine survey of the early period.

———. *Arabia of the Wahhabis.* London: Constable, 1928. Tells of Ibn Saud's conflicts with the Rashids.

———. *Arabian Days.* London: Robert Hale, 1951. An excellent account of the life of Ibn Saud.

————. *Arabian Jubilee.* London: Robert Hale, 1951. An excellent account of Ibn Saud and his dynasty.

————. *Arabian Oil Ventures.* Washington, D.C.: The Middle East Institute, 1964. Philby was the focal point of nearly all the early negotiations between the oil interests and the king. He relates the three oil ventures—two ill-fated attempts followed by the third one by Aramco.

————. *Forty Years in the Wilderness.* London: Robert Hale, 1957. An account of Philby's life and travels in Arabia.

————. *Saudi Arabia.* London: Benn, 1955. A history of that state.

Salibi, Kemal. *A History of Arabia.* Delmar: Caravan Books, 1980. A fine general survey of the whole peninsula's history, including early as well as recent times.

Shwadran, Benjamin. *Middle Eastern Oil Crises Since 1973.* Boulder, Colo.: Westview Press, 1986. Especially useful for the 1979–1985 period.

Szyliowicz, Joseph S. "The Prospects for Scientific and Technological Development in Saudi Arabia." *International Journal of Middle East Studies* 10 (1979): 355–372. An important study of the constraints on development, particularly in science.

Troeller, Gary. *The Birth of Saudi Arabia: Britain and the Rise of the House of Sa'ud.* London: Frank Cass, 1976. Of particular value for the period from 1910 to 1926.

Twitchell, Karl. *Saudi Arabia.* Princeton, N.J.: Princeton University Press, 1953. A fundamental work by a mining and hydraulic engineer who did much of the original work in exploring Arabia.

van der Meulen, Daniel. *The Wells of Ibn Sa'ud.* New York: Praeger, 1957. Rise of the Saudi family and the development of the state.

Vidal, F. S. *The Oasis of al-Hasa.* New York: Arabian American Oil Company, 1955. The geography and economy of this province of Saudi Arabia.

Winder, R. Bayly. *Saudi Arabia in the Nineteenth Century.* New York: St. Martin's Press, 1966. A valuable, comprehensive, well-organized, scholarly study. Indispensable.

Yassini, Ayman al-. *Religion and State in the Kingdom of Saudi Arabia.* Boulder, Colo.: Westview Press, 1985. An excellent survey of the subject.

41

Smaller Arabian States

The great central mass of the Arabian peninsula consists of the Kingdom of Saudi Arabia which also controls al-Hasa facing the Persian Gulf and the eastern shore of the Red Sea from the Gulf of Aqaba southward through Asir to Yemen. All of the other coastal areas of the peninsula are divided into numerous smaller Arab states. On the east, along the Persian Gulf, are Bahrayn, Kuwayt, Qatar, and the United Arab Emirates (formerly the Trucial States of Oman). Oman is on the southeastern and southern shores. In the south and southwest are the former Imamate of Yemen, the British colony of Aden, and the Hadhramaut, all of which are now divided between the Arab Republic of Yemen in the north and the People's Democratic Republic of Yemen in the south.

Most of these states have been sparsely inhabited and have only small amounts of arable land. Some areas of the two Yemens and Oman form an exception to this rule; there one can find substantial agricultural regions and a denser concentration of people. The peoples of the various states share a similarity in language, religion, and culture. Almost all speak Arabic, although there are substantial dialectical differences. A majority are Sunnite Muslims. In Bahrayn, however, there is a Shiite majority, and a substantial Shiite minority resides in other countries as well. North Yemen and Oman have substantial Shiite and Ibadi (Kharijite) communities. With the exception of the two Yemens, the states are monarchies, and the republican form of government in the Yemens is of recent origin. All of the countries were substantially influenced by Great Britain throughout most of the twentieth century, except for northern Yemen, which remained remarkably isolated until the 1960s. The presence or absence of oil has been the chief variable among the various states. Those countries possessing quantities of oil undertook massive social and economic change; the most notable example of this is Kuwayt. Those countries with little oil or which only discovered their oil and natural gas recently have continued to be poor. Southern Yemen since independence has embarked upon a radical political transformation, while most of the other countries opted for either no political change at all or a slow rate of institutionalization and political modernization. In foreign policy, the two Yemens have given much attention to their uniting, but differences have remained great between the two. In the 1980s, the Persian Gulf Arab states were preoccupied with the threat of the Iran-Iraq War spilling over to their territories, and they formed with Saudi Arabia the Gulf Cooperation Council in 1981 to coordinate policies in a number of fields, including military matters.

BAHRAYN

Bahrayn is an amirate composed of several islands totaling about 240 square miles (620 square kilometers) and standing about twenty miles (32 kilometers) off the coast of Saudi Arabia and the Qatar peninsula in the Persian Gulf. Inhabited largely by Arabs and ruled by Iran for more than a century, Bahrayn was taken by Arabs from Iran and became a British dependency through naval action in 1820. Except for pearl fishing, Bahrayn was quite unimportant until the presence of oil was suspected in the 1920s.

In 1930, after three other concerns had held oil concessions, Standard Oil of California and the Texas Company formed the Bahrayn Petroleum Company (Bapco), a Canadian corporation, and obtained the concession. Oil in commercial quantities was discovered in 1932, and Bahrayn oil entered the world markets in 1934. A refinery was constructed to handle Bahrayn's output of 30,000 barrels a day and, later, an additional 125,000 barrels coming from Saudi Arabia by an underwater pipeline. In 1952 Bapco entered into an equal profit-sharing agreement with Bahrayn's ruler, which gave him about $8 million a year in royalties to add to his $3 million income from taxes. Bapco signed an agreement with the amir in 1974, turning over 100 percent of the company to the government in two stages. In 1976, the Bahrayn National Oil Company was formed by the government to hold the oil rights; Bapco, however, continued to manage the business. Bahrayn's oil reserves are limited, but improved production techniques have increased output in the 1970s to about 66,000 barrels daily.

Bahrayn's financial condition remained stationary until oil prices jumped in 1973 and Bahrayni oil revenues topped $100 million a year. Bahrayn became a member of OAPEC, honored the 1973 embargo against the United States and the Netherlands, and participated in the Persian Gulf production slowdown. OAPEC decided in 1972 to spend $250 million to build a tanker drydock in Bahrayn to service ships. In 1969, a £2 million satellite station was built in Bahrayn, which with the OAPEC drydock and a British naval base provided income and more jobs. As oil became less abundant, Bahrayn was the first country of the region to enter the post-oil economic era. It became the banking, communications, and services center of the Persian Gulf Arab states.

Bahrayn has been ruled by the Al Khalifah family for more than a century, the ruler in 1988 being Amir Isa ibn Salman Al Khalifah, who succeeded his father in 1961. The Al Khalifah family has been noted for its leniency. Life on the islands has been secure and not too harsh, and the appeal of political opponents has usually been temporary. A nineteenth-century treaty with Great Britain placed the foreign relations of the state in British hands, exercised from 1926 to 1956 by Sir Charles Belgrave, the ruler's adviser. The period 1953 to 1956 saw sectarian rioting, labor unrest, and a general strike, and pan-Arab nationalism threatened the ruler's power. Bahrayn turned to Saudi Arabia and Kuwayt for protection. After the immediate danger passed, nationalists concentrated on building Arab socialism in Bahrayn. From time to time the Arab Nationalist Movement instigated strikes; trade unions were banned.

Great Britain dropped a bombshell in January 1968 when she announced that her special treaty position with the states of the area would be abrogated at the end of 1971. Bahrayn, Qatar, and the seven small amirates of the Trucial Coast discussed a federation. Encouraged by Saudi Arabia and Kuwayt, numerous conferences were held to draw up the structure of such an entity. To the dismay of Arab leaders everywhere, however, Iran reasserted her old claim to Bahrayn. When a mission from the U.N. in 1970 ascertained that Bahrayn desired independence, Iran indicated that Bahrayni wishes would be honored. After the proposed federation rejected Bahrayn's demand for representation according to population, Amir Isa on August 14, 1971, declared Bahrayn an independent and sovereign state. A treaty of friendship was signed with Great Britain, and Bahrayn's applications for membership in the Arab League and the United Nations were accepted. When the British left in 1971, the United States assumed responsibility for their base and it continued to maintain a small military presence there.

In 1972, the amir convened a constituent assembly, half appointed and half elected. By mid-1973 the constitution was approved by the amir and by popular referendum. It declared that Bahrayn is an Arab and Islamic state; that the amir, not the parliament, appoints the prime minister; that any concessions must have parliamentary approval; that labor unions are sanctioned; and that the government should strive for Arab unity. When elections for thirty seats in the National Assembly were held in December, with only males voting, political parties were banned and the government appointed fourteen ministers as members of parliament. Still, eight young "leftists" were elected, as well as a Shiite religious bloc, and a number of older established figures were defeated. Then, in August 1975, the amir dissolved parliament, refused to schedule the election of a new parliament, and transferred its responsibilities to the cabinet, which he expanded. A number of leftists were arrested, and the parliament has not met since then.

Many Shiites, who constituted a substantial majority of the Bahrayni population, resented the Sunnite control of the political system, the military, and the economy. Shiites were of mixed ancestry; some were Arabs, while others were from Iran. In December 1981, Iran attempted to bring about an Islamic fundamentalist coup, but it was detected and suppressed by the regime. The amir has named Shiites to high government posts and Shiite religious festivals have been declared national holidays. Bahrayn has also created a comprehensive social welfare system including free education and medical care, and subsidized housing in newly built towns. Urbanization has been rapid and literacy high.

Strong security measures and a relatively open society which permitted criticism of the government lessened Shiite opposition. And the opening of a causeway to Saudi Arabia in 1986, physically linking Bahrayn to its much larger, conservative neighbor, plus Saudi financial aid, have helped the Bahrayn government meet the needs of its people. Bahrayn has also bought sophisticated military aircraft from the West, and expanded its small armed forces, fearing the extension of the Iran-Iraq War into the immediate vicinity.

KUWAYT

North of Bahrayn on the mainland of Arabia near the head of the Persian Gulf lies the small principality of Kuwayt. Long a port and the seat of a profitable shipping trade, the city-state of Kuwayt first came to world attention when the British agreed in 1899 to protect Kuwayt against Ottoman expansion. Britain did so in order to stop the building of the last part of the Berlin-to-Baghdad railroad south to the Gulf. Thereafter, Kuwayt lapsed into oblivion, except to the British colonial office, until the end of World War I. The Saudis tried to seize it, but British guns stopped them.

After oil was struck on Bahrayn, the world oil companies sought concessions in Kuwayt. The Kuwayt Oil Company, Ltd. (KOC), a British corporation owned equally by the British Petroleum Company and the Gulf Oil Company, received a concession in 1934 for the entire area of the state. Oil was not found until 1938, when the Burghan field was tapped and proved to be the largest known pool of oil in the world. Commercial production, however, was stalled during World War II and did not begin in earnest until 1946. Even then operations went slowly. In 1950, as troubles loomed in Iran, production was increased rapidly.

The original concession had provided for a royalty payment of 7 cents a barrel; a new agreement in 1951, following the examples of Saudi Arabia and Venezuela, called for equal sharing of company profits. In 1955 production soared over 1 million barrels a day, and royalty payments to Kuwayt's ruler since 1950, Amir Abd Allah al-Salim Al Sabah, exceeded $250 million.

The Kuwayt National Petroleum Corporation (KNPC) was founded, with 60 percent held by the government and the remainder held by Kuwayti nationals. Oil production passed 2 million barrels per day in 1960; royalties stood at $600 million; and petroleum exports at well over $1 billion.

Kuwayt could hardly spend all her oil income; nevertheless, in 1968 the amir urged the oil companies to increase production and royalties, even though KOC had recently paid $90 million to cover back royalties. In the mid-1970s, concerned about the effects of worldwide runaway inflation and fearing that she was depleting her proven reserves too rapidly, Kuwayt began to limit her oil production. To leave much of the oil safe in the ground rather than bring it to the surface had considerable appeal. Though oil at auction brought $12 to $19 a barrel, the government forced production down to 2 million barrels daily in 1975; yet in 1976 oil revenues were nearly $8 billion. In 1975, the assembly voted for full nationalization of oil, with Kuwayt guaranteeing to sell the companies oil for five years.

Revenues were so great that the state and wealthy individuals invested large sums abroad. Kuwayt developed an official stock market and another unofficial, free-wheeling, and extremely risky market for Gulf securities. The crash of the unofficial market in 1982 wiped out $40 billion in real terms. This financial catastrophe plus lower world oil prices and the Iran-Iraq War caused an economic slowdown throughout the 1980s. In 1984, the discovery of new oil reserves, however, sharply increased Kuwayt's future ability to pump oil: there were about 200 years of petroleum in reserve at then current rates of extraction. Kuwayt has had government budget deficits, but foreign monetary reserves were kept. Still, the 1982–1983 budget showed a 40 percent drop in oil revenues compared to the previous year. And in 1987 oil revenues were about $6 billion and from foreign investments Kuwayt gained $4 billion more.

With a population of less than 200,000 before 1950 and about 800,000 by 1977, less than half of whom were native born, the wealth pouring in changed the life of the people rapidly. Amir Abd Allah used half his royalties to build schools, roads, hospitals, electrical plants, and the other requirements of a modern community. Kuwayt University opened in 1966 with faculties in arts, sciences, and education. Because Kuwayt's water resources are negligible, large sea-water conversion plants were built in the 1950s; new plants doubled the supply every decade.

KOC had constructed three oil refineries, and in 1958 construction on modern port terminals was launched. By 1960 Kuwaytis were saying that everything needed had been completed and the city and state had been constructed. But when new building slowed down and government land purchases stopped, everyone complained of a recession. Government leaders realized that continued expansion was essential. Massive five-year plans were devised to stimulate the gross national product, raise the per-capita income, and generate an "equality in distribution" for society. In actuality, income in Kuwayt remained heavily skewed toward the ruling family and wealthy merchants. The surge in oil income beginning in 1973 increased the per-capita income dramatically; by 1976 it reached $11,500, the highest in the world.

In Kuwayt, education is free, from elementary school through university; medical attention and hospital care have been free; there are no taxes; and there are more millionaires per thousand of population than anywhere. Nevertheless, curbs on the press and the dissolution of the National Assembly coincided with the rise of a substantial strain of Kuwayti nationalism. As far back as 1969 foreigners had to have an invitation or a permit. The government began to deport non-Kuwaytis for "subversive acts," and enacted laws making the obtaining of Kuwayti citizenship almost impossible. From 1965 on, Kuwaytis were a minority within their own country; most of the immigrants, who formed the majority, were laborers. They came chiefly from Jordan, Egypt, and other Arab areas.

The city of al-Kuwayt, with the highest per-capita income in the world, became a modern town within a decade, with more automobiles and more hard-surfaced roads per capita and more air conditioners per habitation than any other city in the world. Its wealth attracted people from many parts of the world, especially from other Arab areas. The influx of Egyptians and Palestinians was relatively high, a factor which sensitized most Kuwaytis to Arab nationalism.

Kuwayt was declared free and independent on June 19, 1961, after discussions with Great Britain led to a peaceful termination of the treaty of protection. In less than a week Amir Abd Allah was threatened by Iraq, and called upon Great Britain for protection; three warships and a contingent of marines arrived to stay until August, when troops from Saudi Arabia, Jordan, and the United Arab Republic replaced them. Kuwayt joined the Arab League, but her entry into the United Nations was delayed until 1963 by the U.S.S.R.

New law codes based largely on those of Egypt were adopted. At Amir Abd Allah's behest a constituent assembly drafted a document in 1962 calling for an elected National Assembly. The majority of those elected supported the rule of the Sabah family, and the appointed cabinet became members of parliament; eight, however, belonged to the Arab Nationalist Movement. The amir's brother Sabah al-Salim Al Sabah was named prime minister and heir to the throne, and became the new ruler when Abd Allah died in 1965. The royal family occupied eleven of the sixteen places in the first cabinet. The new amir chose his cousin Jabir al-Ahmad al-Jabir Al Sabah as prime minister and heir to the throne. When Amir Sabah died on December 31, 1977, Jabir was recognized immediately as amir of Kuwayt.

During the 1960s and 1970s there were three more National Assembly elections. Of the members elected in 1975 half had not served before. They were younger, better educated, and less conservative than those they replaced. The new National Assembly chose to be active; this irked the ruling family, so on August 29, 1976, Amir Sabah dissolved it, suspended the articles of the constitution guaranteeing freedom of the press, and declared he would rule by executive decree.

Kuwayt's tremendous wealth and oil resources are constant temptations to aggression. To provide a buffer, Kuwayt's rulers initiated a policy of granting and lending significant sums to other Arab states. In 1962, the Kuwayt Fund for Arab Economic Development (KFAED) was established. By 1977 it had given out more than $1 billion to Arab states for a great variety of enterprises.

After Great Britain announced she would withdraw from the Persian Gulf in 1971, Kuwayt began to buy defensive weapons. In 1973 $1.5 billion was allocated for defense expenditures over the next seven years. But Amir Sabah recognized that a state as small as his could not hope to withstand the armed might of any of the world powers. His only hope was to conduct a foreign policy that would guard his independence and maintain friendly relations with all, offending none.

Kuwayt declared war against Israel in 1967. Later, Kuwayt joined in contributing to Egypt and Jordan. In 1970 Palestinian Liberation Organization leader Yasir Arafat received $14 million, and $180 million in the Kuwayti budget was designated for the support of "Arab steadfastness." In 1973, $344 million was given to the Arab countries fighting Israel. Yet, Palestinians, as foreigners, were not permitted to settle permanently in Kuwayt.

Kuwayt's relations with Iran have been in a delicate balance. An agreement was struck in 1968 on offshore oil rights in the Persian Gulf. Crown Prince Jabir, urging the nine smaller Arab states in the Persian Gulf to unite in some kind of federation, gave his blessing to the new United Arab Emirates in 1971. In 1971, Kuwayt's rulers were also vexed by Iraq's occupation of two nearly uninhabited Kuwayti islands near the mouth of the Shatt al-Arab, which dominate the sea lanes to the Iraqi port of Umm Qasr. The Arab League acted to settle the dispute, and Saudi Arabia sent 15,000 soldiers to protect Kuwayt.

Such foreign policy concerns became far graver in the 1980s with the Iran-Iraq War. Kuwayt was officially neutral, but unofficially it was pro-Iraq. As a result, Iran tried to apply pressure directly and through intermediaries to make Kuwayt reverse its position. One example was in December 1983 when widespread bombing incidents took place; there were also hijackings of airplanes and attacks on Kuwayti oil tankers in 1984. To counterbalance the danger from Iran, Kuwayt cooperated closely with Saudi Arabia and the Gulf Cooperation Council in military matters, and bought quantities of weapons from both the United States and the Soviet Union. Despite these steps, a group seeking the release from prison of those convicted in the 1983 bombings came close to assassinating Amir Jabir on May 25, 1985. In 1987 Kuwayt arranged to have some of its tankers registered as American so as to secure U.S. protection in the Gulf, which was extended by war vessels that escorted convoys of tankers to and from Kuwayt. The amir also persuaded the Soviets to lease some of Kuwayt's tankers, thus preserving a balanced approach between the two superpowers. An Iranian missile hit Kuwayt's main offshore oil terminal in October 1987, and Kuwayt remained very worried about the nearby war.

In domestic matters, Jabir reinstituted parliament in 1981. In the ensuing elections Bedouins and Sunnites were heavily represented, while only a few Shiites, Muslim fundamentalists, and Arab nationalists were elected. Despite lobbying by women's groups, the franchise remained for males only. Economic difficulties following the crash of the unofficial stock market, the fall of the price of oil, internal corruption, and the question of what to do about the Iran-Iraq War all caused severe disagreements among Kuwaytis. Maneuvering inside the royal family for position also led to parliamentary criticisms. And the parliament, intent on securing a cabinet truly responsible to it, was prepared to express "no confidence" in some of the princes who held cabinet rank. Saudi Arabia may also have exerted its influence on the ruler to act against parliament. In July 1986, the amir once again dissolved the National Assembly, and the constitution became moribund as censorship was harshly applied.

QATAR

Under a treaty with the British in 1916 the ruling shaykh pledged to prevent piracy along his coasts and recognized a perpetual truce with Great Britain that virtually controlled all of Qatar's foreign relations. Occupying a barren peninsula of more than 4,000 square miles (11,000 square kilometers) jutting north ward into the Persian Gulf, the amirate has one principal town, Doha, is Wahhabi in religion, and is ruled absolutely by the Al Thani family. The Qatar Petroleum Company, a subsidiary of the Iraq Petroleum Company, held the mainland concession and exploited it starting in 1949. Offshore rights were held by Shell Qatar, which began producing in 1961, and which was reorganized in 1967 to include Ente Nazionale Idrocarburi of Italy. By 1966 Qatar was receiving over $100 million annually in royalties, and production stood at 276,000 barrels daily. A decade later annual income was over $2 billion, oil production had doubled, and the population had increased tenfold to 220,000, about 80 percent of whom lived in Doha. Most of the population were expatriates.

Qatar, admitted to OPEC in 1968, agreed with Abu Dhabi to divide the revenues from the rich Bunduq field that straddled the line separating them. In 1974 a general agreement was initialed by which the government would buy 60 percent of Qatar Petroleum Company and Shell Qatar. In 1977, Qatar Petroleum Company relinquished all control of its oil operations to the government but continued to provide services, managerial assistance, and trained personnel.

The amir gave half of the revenues to his family which, with retainers, was estimated to number 20,000; used one-fourth to cover the expenses of government and the public services; and kept the remainder for himself. A religious scholar of Arab history and Islamic law, Shaykh Ali ibn Abd Allah ibn Qasim Al Thani acceded to rule in 1949. He found the problems of oil development and riches so vexing that he retired in 1960 to his villa in Switzerland, abdicating in favor of his son Shaykh Ahmad ibn Ali Al Thani, who also preferred Switzerland.

The British departure from the Persian Gulf in 1971 gave birth to a federation of Gulf states. As proposed, the first prime minister would have been Shaykh Khalifah ibn Hamad Al Thani, cousin and heir of Qatar's ruler and actual ruler while Shaykh Ahmad was in Switzerland. The plan foundered, and on April 2, 1970, Amir Ahmad ibn Ali Al Thani declared he was independent. He issued a constitution. Khalifah was named prime minister; nine of the other ministers were from the Thani family as well. On September 1, 1971, Amir Ahmad proclaimed Qatar's separation from the British. Later that month Qatar was admitted to the Arab League and the United Nations.

On February 22, 1972, with Amir Ahmad vacationing in Switzerland, Khalifah ibn Hamad Al Thani staged a bloodless coup. He pledged to modernize the administration, cut consumer prices, and raise salaries by 20 percent. He formed an appointive Advisory Council to discuss draft legislation and the budget. Amir Khalifah took an active role in Arab affairs, proposing a Persian Gulf common market. He made loans or grants to Arab states for military preparedness against Israel and for economic development. In addition, he arranged for an earth satellite communications system centered at Doha to carry thirty international telephone lines and TV and radio transmissions. In 1975 per-capita income in Qatar rose to $8,320, behind only Kuwayt and the United Arab Emirates.

Economic growth attracted many expatriates who substantially outnumbered the Qataris themselves. Since the agricultural base was small, and industry limited, the economy was dominated by oil. The government controlled the oil and thereby the economy. Qatar tried to promote a sense of national identity, while values and attitudes changed rapidly, creating strong generational gaps. Because of the need to diversify the economy, after basic infrastructure was built the amir turned to industrial development using natural gas and its by-products. But with the decline in world oil prices Qatar's income by the middle 1980s fell by one-half and government deficits became normal.

Qatar signed a mutual internal security treaty with Saudi Arabia in 1982. And Amir Khalifah turned to the Gulf Cooperation Council for military and economic cooperation to protect Qatar as the Iran-Iraq War became more intense in the Gulf. The Council's powers were somewhat strained as Qatar and Bahrayn quarreled over their borders in regard to islands and regions in the Gulf.

TRUCIAL STATES OF OMAN

Seven Arab shaykhdoms lie along a four-hundred-mile (640-kilometer) strip of the coast of Arabia on the Persian Gulf south from the Qatar peninsula to the

Strait of Hormuz and along the Gulf of Oman to the territory of the sultan of Oman. Since only about 5 percent of the land is arable, for centuries the inhabitants won their livelihood from the sea by pearl diving and commerce. When not thus engaged they raided each other. In 1820 a British naval expedition forced a treaty upon each of the seven rulers by which they agreed not to make war on each other, not to raid shipping, not to traffic in slaves, and not to make treaties with other powers. Great Britain in return agreed to protect them from outside aggression. In 1853 a Perpetual Maritime Truce was signed, and by another treaty in 1892 Britain assumed responsibility for foreign relations. These seven are: Abu Dhabi, Dubay, Sharjah, Ajman, Umm al-Qaywayn, Ras al-Khaymah, and Fujayrah. Each was hardly more than a small coastal town with a desert hinterland, although Abu Dhabi held several of the settlements in the inland Buraimi oases. Multiethnic Dubay was the largest town; Sharjah was the location of the British political resident agent, a small military force, and an airstrip; Abu Dhabi was the largest. In 1960 the total population of all seven states was estimated at 86,000. The seven shaykhs met twice a year in a kind of council, but no formal organization or federation developed.

Pearling reached its peak about 1925, at which time the revenue in the pearl trade for all of the Persian Gulf area including Kuwayt and Bahrayn was about $10 million. Less than a tenth of this came to the seven rulers of the Trucial States. The marketing of cultured pearls hurt the trade, and then the development of even less expensive synthetic pearls, followed by the 1930s depression, finished it off. After World War II, as the total value of the pearling industry in the Persian Gulf dropped to $250,000, the towns of the Trucial States were in the doldrums. Abu Dhabi in 1961 was still insignificant, with a population of about 15,000 and a total revenue of a little under $150,000 for its ruler Shaykh Shakhbut ibn Sultan Al Nuhayyan, who had acceded to his position in 1928.

For more than a decade Petroleum Development (Trucial Coast) Ltd., later named Abu Dhabi Petroleum Company, a subsidiary of Iraq Petroleum Company, held the concessions for the seven shaykhdoms. Oil had been struck in 1960 in commercial quantities in Abu Dhabi. Offshore concessions had been given by Abu Dhabi and Dubay to Abu Dhabi Marine Areas Ltd., two-thirds owned by British Petroleum Company and one-third by Compagnie Française des Petroles, and a strike had been made offshore. In 1962 Shaykh Shakhbut received $20 million in royalties; by 1966 royalties had reached $84 million. Production jumped rapidly to reach 367,000 barrels daily, more than in Qatar. Proven crude reserves were estimated in 1967 to be about 12.5 billion barrels.

What to do with all this money? Shaykh Shakhbut's wants were simple and inexpensive. His major recreation was hawking. He baffled British oil executives by putting off arrangements for a new contract more favorable to him until 1965 when he accepted the fifty-fifty split. Disconcerting changes were everywhere: immigrants brought diseases unknown to the local Arabs; there was an emphasis on rapid change; prices soared; visitors came and left without his knowledge or permission; a new twenty-five-room air-conditioned hotel and water distillation plants were built. He was not convinced all this was for the betterment of his people.

Developments were slow and difficult to wheedle from Shaykh Shakhbut. With British blessings, a family council sent Shakhbut to Bahrayn in 1966, placing his youngest brother, Shaykh Zayd ibn Sultan Al Nuhayyan, in control. Shaykh Zayd, ebullient, lighthearted, and possessed of great physical strength, was brought up in the informal nomadic life of the desert. He announced a $42 million development plan with a British consortium, which would build a covered market, a seawall, sewage works, a dual highway from Buraimi to Abu Dhabi, and water pipelines from Buraimi.

Zayd began with a substantial income of $170 million, more than double that of Shakhbut's last year; ten years later, after production had quadrupled and OPEC had upped the prices tenfold, revenues were nearly $8 billion. At the 1976–1977 rate of production, oil reserves were expected to last for a century at least. Meanwhile, the population had jumped to 100,000, only a third of whom had been born in Abu Dhabi. Zayd arranged with Qatar to delimit their common border in order to divide the Bunduq field, which began producing in 1976. He also settled a long-standing feud with Saudi Arabia over the Buraimi oases, agreeing in 1974 to divide the promising Zararah oil fields.

With other OPEC members Abu Dhabi pressed her oil companies for a transfer of ownership. But little progress was achieved until 1972 when 25 percent was obtained; this was increased in 1974 to 65 percent.

In 1967 the Abu Dhabi Investment Board was established to invest the surplus funds, which each year became greater; in 1976 they were estimated at roughly $6 billion. About $1.5 billion has been given or loaned to less affluent Arab states, to neighboring shaykhs, and to Bedouin chiefs. Still, what to do with the mounting cash balances created a controversy in governing circles.

In 1969 Shaykh Zayd named his eldest son, Shaykh Khalifah, as his heir, and began to assign prime ministerial tasks to him. With the 1971 British pullout and the apparent failure of a Persian Gulf states federation, Zayd declared Abu Dhabi to be an independent amirate. On July 1, 1971, he appointed a full-fledged cabinet, with Khalifah as prime minister. This gave Abu Dhabi the only governmental cabinet among the seven Trucial States, but it withered and was dissolved after the United Arab Emirates became a reality.

Northeast of Abu Dhabi along the Persian Gulf coast toward the Strait of Hormuz lies the small amirate of Dubay. With 120,000 people, Dubay was the most populous of the seven amirates. Based on an estuary of the gulf, Dubay had been the main commercial and smuggling center on the coast for more than a century. Dubay's ruler, Amir Rashid ibn Said Al Maktum, who succeeded his father peacefully in 1958, had considerable knowledge of foreign trade and international finance, skills acquired from his mother, who was the real power in Dubay for fifty years. Rashid demonstrated great acumen in the political advancement of Dubay, especially within the growing structure of the United Arab Emirates.

Oil was discovered in commercial quantities in 1967 by the Dubay Petroleum Company offshore. Oil was first exported in 1969, at which time Dubay attained membership in OAPEC. By 1977 daily exports neared 300,000 barrels and yearly revenues exceeded $1 billion. Many millions were spent to enlarge the airport to accommodate jumbo jets, to build a new air terminal complex, to construct the biggest deep-water port in the Persian Gulf, and to establish a free port.

When OAPEC decided in 1972 to locate a large drydock in Bahrayn, Dubay, outraged, resigned from OAPEC and spent $225 million to erect one on her estuary, completing it ahead of OAPEC's. Dubay remained the chief business center for the entire coast, and by the mid-1970s twenty banks handling capital from two dozen countries had joined the British Bank of the Middle East, long the sole banking house in Dubay.

The amirate of Sharjah lies contiguous to Dubay on the north and east. Included in Sharjah's territory is the strategic island of Abu Musa in the Strait of Hormuz, with its offshore oil fields. The amirate's fine municipal government, developed over many decades, has served as a model through the entire region.

Until 1971 the British located their military and air bases in Sharjah, which was the headquarters of the Trucial Oman Scouts. Egyptian support of Sharjah's Amir Saqr ibn Sultan Al Qasimi irritated the British, and his flirting with Nasser who was stirring up trouble in Aden was not appreciated. When the British suggested in 1965 to Amir Saqr's six brothers that he be replaced, Saqr retired to Cairo. His cousin Khalid ibn Muhammad Al Qasimi, at that moment successfully operating a paint store in Dubay, became amir.

The day before the British withdrew their forces from Sharjah and before their treaties with the amirs, including Amir Khalid, expired, Iran occupied Abu Musa with no interference or objections. An arrangement was made whereby the inhabitants of the island would remain under Sharjah rule, offshore oil revenues would flow to Sharjah, and Iran paid $7.5 million for the military bases.

Soon thereafter, former Amir Saqr staged an unsuccessful coup with the aid of the Arab Socialist Action party. Khalid was killed but the rebels were captured by troops of the recently organized United Arab Emirates. Khalid's brother Sultan ibn Muhammad Al Qasimi then became the new Sharjah ruler. Sultan was temporarily displaced in 1987 by his brother Abd al-Aziz, but the United Arab Emirates mediated the dispute, reinstated Sultan, and named Abd al-Aziz as heir apparent.

The easternmost amirate, adjacent to the tip of the peninsula, is Ras al-Khaymah. Without any known oil resources until discoveries in 1983, Ras al-Khaymah depended on agriculture, fishing, and shipping for her income. Amir Saqr ibn Muhammad Al Qasimi, who seized power in 1948, is a strong-minded leader, though sensitive to the positions of the wealthy and powerful amirs of Abu Dhabi and Dubay. He objected loudly to the Iranian occupation of his Tunb Islands and has refused to accept their loss.

The other three amirates, Ajman, Umm al-Qaywayn, and Fujayrah, are small—their combined territory is smaller than that of Ras al-Khaymah, the smallest of the larger four—and are sparsely populated. Their incomes will remain meager unless oil is found on or off the shores of their territories.

UNITED ARAB EMIRATES

Early in 1968 the rulers of the nine small states in the Persian Gulf region under British protection began to think about forming a kind of federation as it became clear Britain would leave the Gulf. They sought the reactions of Iran, Iraq, Kuwayt, and Saudi Arabia. Iraq called it a British subterfuge for continued control, but Kuwayt and Saudi Arabia were very encouraging. Iran, claiming ownership of Bahrayn, termed it an intolerable outrage. Abu Dhabi and Dubay then announced that they intended to federate. With the wealthiest and the most populous of the seven smaller amirates leading the way the others found refusal difficult, though Bahrayn, Qatar, and Ras al-Khaymah did decline to join. On July 18, 1971, six (Abu Dhabi, Dubay, Sharjah, Ajman, Umm al-Qaywayn, Fujayrah) of the amirates formed the United Arab Emirates (or Amirates) and accepted the provisional constitution, which allowed other amirates to apply for membership. Officially coming into being the day after the British treaties lapsed, the UAE was within a week admitted to the Arab League and the United Nations. Ras al-Khaymah joined the UAE in 1972.

The UAE constitution recognized the independence of each member, each with her own flag and in full control of local affairs. It provided for a Supreme Council, consisting of the rulers of the states, each of whom had one vote. Decisions on procedural matters were to be reached by majority vote, while substantive issues required a five-vote majority that had to include Abu Dhabi and Dubay. Policies of state, federal laws, budgets and financial reports, decrees, treaties, and the appointment of high officers of the government had to be approved by the Supreme Council.

Amir Zayd of Abu Dhabi was chosen president and Amir Rashid of Dubay vice president, each for a five-year term; both were eligible for reappointment, and they continued to be reelected to those posts. Amir Rashid Al Maktum, the amir of Dubay, was named prime minister. A forty-member council appointed by the rulers consisted of eight members each from Abu Dhabi and Dubay, six each from Sharjah and Ras al-Khaymah, and four from each of the others. The Trucial Oman Scouts were taken over from the British and proved their worth shortly in quelling the coup in Sharjah.

As time passed the UAE government under the amirs of Abu Dhabi and Dubay won the approval of most of the political and business leaders in the area and acceptance by states around the world. The U.S.S.R. accorded it full diplomatic recognition at an early date. In 1973 most local cabinets were disbanded, and education, public works, industry, agriculture, and justice were added to the responsibilities of the federal cabinet, its membership now at twenty-seven. Abu Dhabi's OPEC membership was transferred to the UAE. Except for the rulers of Abu Dhabi and Dubay, however, the heads of state were reluctant to surrender much of their power and revenue or allow any diminution of their prestige. There was an absence of overall planning as the rulers attempted to outdo each other's construction programs. In 1976 agreement could be reached only to extend the interim constitution of 1971 for another five years. Crises in 1979 and 1981 showed a severe split among the rulers existed in regard to the possible increase of federal power.

In the late 1970s and 1980s, the population of the UAE grew to more than 1 million, but only about 200,000 were citizens. Foreign residents included Indians, Pakistanis, Omanis, Iranians, Palestinians, and others. Oil wealth increased urbanization—three cities accounted for 80 percent of the UAE residents—while youths constituted a large proportion of the total population. The National University at al-Ayn graduated its first class, including men and women, in 1982. Sports (such as soccer), radio and television, and plays competed among the young for their attention, while poetry still played a large cultural role.

Oil and natural gas revenues caused the social transformation; they peaked at $20 billion in 1980. Per-capita income for UAE citizens was close to $100,000! Production in the middle 1980s fell, while revenues in 1982–1983 were only $13 billion, although reserves were abundant for the foreseeable future. Each member state controlled pricing and oil production policy, but the UAE presented a common front in OPEC with one representative for all of the states.

The great sums of the 1970s and the more modest revenues of the 1980s built roads, airports, seaports, hotels, and provided the foundation for a social welfare system. This prosperity was threatened by the Iran-Iraq War, whose possible extension to the UAE area caused grave concern. The UAE established diplomatic relations with the Soviet Union in 1985, but the federal government turned mainly to Saudi Arabia for support, and to France for weapons. Its own armed forces included many noncitizens and seemed incapable of defending the federation against attack from a major regional power.

OMAN

The Sultanate of Oman, sometimes referred to as Muscat and Oman (Muscat was the official residential town of the sultan) has been inhabited since antiquity and is situated at the southeastern corner of the Arabian peninsula. By the Treaty of Sib of 1920, the sultan recognized that the tribes of the interior of the country would be governed by an elected Ibadite imam who would have political and religious authority over them. No great difficulties arose until 1954, when Ghalib ibn Ali was elected imam to succeed Muhammad al-Khalili (1920–1954); this selection was against the strong wishes of Sultan Said ibn Taymur ibn Faysal, who had been sultan since 1932. War broke out between the two in 1955, with Sultan Said aided by British troops. For many years the sultan's foreign relations were managed unofficially by Great Britain, a practice obtained through treaties in 1939 and 1951. By 1959 the imam and his followers had been routed from their mountain strongholds and fled into neighboring Saudi Arabia. In the meantime, in 1955, the sultan visited the interior where the imam had held sway—the first such trip by any sultan of the coast since 1886!

Sultan Said was autocratic, vain, and slow to modernize. He feared accumulating a foreign debt, and preserved his rule by dividing the tribes and isolating Oman from most contact with the outside world. Said himself stayed in Salalah and never went to Muscat after 1958.

On July 23, 1970, Sultan Said was overthrown by his English-educated son Qabus (born 1940), who exiled his father to England. Sultan Qabus ended Oman's isolation but preserved power in his own hands. Oman was admitted to the Arab League and the United Nations in 1971. Hampered by the massive expenses incurred in fighting the rebellion in Dhufar, Qabus declared that Oman was not yet prepared for responsible ministerial government.

In 1963, oil in commercial quantities was discovered by Petroleum Development (Oman) Ltd. In 1967 a new agreement was reached with Sultan Said, giving him a percentage of the royalties and splitting the profits on the usual 50-50 basis. Oil production averaged 300,000 barrels through the 1970s. Though not a member of OPEC, Qabus followed it carefully, and government revenues soared from about $6 million in 1966 to $1.4 billion in 1976. In 1974 Oman acquired 60 percent of the oil company, which it retained in subsequent reorganizations.

The greatest problem facing Sultans Said and Qabus over the years was the guerrilla warfare and open rebellion in Dhufar province in the southwest. Drought in the 1950s and the restrictions imposed by Said upon Dhufar increased local unhappiness. Left-wing activists with help from South Yemen formed the People's Front for the Liberation of the Occupied Arabian Gulf (PFLOAG), which clashed with Said's forces. When Qabus became sultan he offered amnesty to the Dhufar rebels who were being trained in Iraq by Chinese officers supplied with Russian arms obtained from South Yemen. Rejecting his offer, they took control of much of the southern regions of Dhufar.

In 1971, King Faysal of Saudi Arabia recognized Qabus' regime and gave him substantial sums. The struggle began to go the sultan's way in 1972, when most of the tribesmen and nationalists gave their allegiance to Qabus. Qabus married King Husayn's daughter in Amman, and arranged for a Jordanian military mission. Much to the annoyance of Arab leaders, Qabus also received substantial aid from Iran, including troops. The Chinese then withdrew and the U.S.S.R. told PFLOAG to go underground. Qabus gave permission to the United States to use Masirah island and other bases under certain conditions; in return, the U.S. agreed to improve these facilities. Oman also established diplomatic relations with the Soviet Union in 1985.

Convinced that the rebellion in Dhufar had been crushed, Qabus in 1976 began to devote more than half of his budget to development. The Supreme Planning Council issued a five-year plan to expend $8.2 billion for education, harbors, roads, and electrification. Qabus built radio and television stations, and the first newspapers appeared. A desalinization plant opened, and education rapidly expanded. In 1970 there were only about 900 students in secular government schools; in 1985 there were 200,000 in 560 schools, mostly staffed with foreign teachers. Qabus University opened in 1986. This development of infrastructure gradually reached the one million Omanis, and it began to affect the lives of most, even though the tribes often remained beyond the reach of government. Peasants tilled the 1 percent of the land that was arable, and most continued to use traditional irrigation methods while raising dates and other crops.

Justice was still based on the shariah. While there was no constitution or parliament, Qabus named an appointed State Consultative Council in 1981 to offer advice periodically on economic, social, and legal matters. The small army became less dependent upon foreigners, except in the area of armaments, most of which were purchased from Britain. The government spent about 40 percent of the gross national product on the military.

Petroleum provided most government revenues. In 1985 and 1986 production was over 500,000 barrels per day and new reserves have been discovered.

Oman helped form the Gulf Cooperation Council in 1981. Another aspect of the sultan's security policy has been a close friendship with the United States and Great Britain. Sultan Qabus did not oppose the Egyptian-Israeli Peace Treaty of 1979, and even relations with the Marxist government of South Yemen became less hostile after agreements were signed in 1982. The two nations exchanged ambassadors in 1985.

Problems of the 1980s included governmental corruption, excessive reliance upon foreigners, potential opposition from Ibadi ulema, the continuing strength of tribalism, lack of a clear successor to Sultan Qabus, and the Iran-Iraq War. Since all power was in the hands of the sultan, he and he alone received the credit for the many accomplishments of the regime as well as the blame for the failures.

ADEN AND THE FEDERATION OF SOUTH ARABIA

The port of Aden is located 700 miles (1,126 kilometers) west of the Dhufar border on a rocky peninsula jutting out from the south coast of Arabia into the Indian Ocean about 100 miles (161 kilometers) east of Bab al-Mandeb, the narrow strait controlling the southern entrance to the Red Sea. Aden has been important for trade between East and West, including Africa, since antiquity. Local shaykhs seized Aden in 1735 and occupied it until the British came in 1839. After the opening of the Suez Canal, Aden grew rapidly into one of the great British coaling stations, a submarine cable center, and, as a free port, a trading entrepôt. From the Crown Colony of Aden the British spread their influence along the entire southern Arabian coast, and by treaties with local rulers established what came to be known as the Eastern Aden and the Western Aden protectorates. The former comprised five independent sultanates and two shaykhdoms; the two largest sultanates together were usually called the Hadhramaut, from which originated many of the prosperous Arab merchants of Indonesia. In Western Aden, which surrounded the city of Aden, there were seven sultanates, six shaykhdoms, two amirates, and one confederation of tribes.

After World War II social and political attitudes in Aden and the protectorates changed markedly. During the war, the mountains of supplies on their way to Middle East theaters of war raised Aden to the third-ranking port, after London and Liverpool, in the British Empire. In 1954 the Anglo-Iranian Oil Company erected a $150 million refinery there and almost overnight created a new city, Little Aden, to support it. The contrast in living conditions and public conveniences with Aden made its residents wish for similar improvements. In the protectorates a new generation of rulers wanted more independence. Aden governors were dependent directly upon London, and the individual princes longed for home rule.

Talks in London led to the creation in 1959 of the Federation of the Arab Emirates of the South, comprising six of the states of the Western Aden Protectorate. Later others joined to make a total of seventeen. The name was changed in 1962 to the Federation of South Arabia. Aden became a member in 1963. A new capital, al-Ittihad, not far from Aden, was completed and occupied in 1961. The federation was governed by a seven-member Supreme Council elected by a Federal Council composed of six members from each state except Aden, which had twenty-four. North Yemen refused to recognize the federation because she had claimed the territory for centuries. In Aden many North Yemeni workers and refugees mounted a Free Yemeni Movement. As long as Imam Ahmad ruled in Sana they did not want a union, but the revolution of 1962 and the birth of the Republic of Yemen (North Yemen) altered conditions. President al-Sallal (North Yemen) claimed Aden and the Federation of South Arabia, and was strongly supported in this demand by Nasser. Leaders of the various states who cooperated with the British or participated in federation matters were subjected constantly to threats of violence and assassination. Great Britain promised independence for 1968, and announced that troops would be withdrawn. Agitation grew as competition developed in Aden and the federation states among Arab nationalists for the role of the successor to the British. One important group was the National Front for the Liberation of Occupied South Yemen (FLOSY), sponsored by Egypt. Among the others only the National Liberation Front (NLF) survived. Through coups the NLF gained control of all the states of the federation, whose officials declared the union to be at an end. As the position of the British grew untenable the date of withdrawal was moved up to November 1967. The NLF appeared to have the upper hand, and Qahtan al-Shabi, the NLF's leader, formed a group that assumed office as the British left.

Extreme radicals and Communists took power in South Yemen because of the great chasms in society: Aden versus the hinterland, class-conscious workers versus "feudalistic" tribal autocrats, a national structure versus petty principalities. The indigenous middle class was small and politically inexperienced, while those who wanted rapid change, complete independence from Britain, and national unity believed that they needed a totalitarian state to achieve those goals and also to preserve themselves in power against their numerous opponents.

PEOPLE'S REPUBLIC OF SOUTH YEMEN

The NLF controlled all the states, but only a small minority of politically minded individuals felt any national pull for South Yemen or any devotion to a socialist society. Rebellions against the NLF and its edicts broke out in every part of the state. Within the NLF there was constant bickering and rivalry over programs and positions. Saudi Arabia refused to recognize the new regime and gave asylum to former rulers of the federation. A score or more of the former leaders of the small states were executed, and FLOSY continued to operate in the Yemen Arab Republic, serving as a magnet for all the malcontents. Though loyalties were not established, attacks originating in Saudi Arabia or the Yemen Arab Republic were repulsed.

Qahtan al-Shabi, the leader of NLF, became the president, prime minister, and commander in chief of the armed forces of the People's Republic of South Yemen. The high command of NLF served as the executive council and a cabinet took office. All were inexperienced in administrative matters. Before the end of 1967 South Yemen had been admitted to the Arab League and the United Nations. The new defense minister hastened to Moscow for aid and arms at the same time as al-Shabi was proposing complete harmony with the Yemen Arab Republic.

The Suez Canal had been blocked just before the republic was formed, and it was not reopened until June 5, 1975. In modern times the chief reason for the development of Aden, and the main source of its income, was the servicing and repairing of ships in connection with the canal. The cessation of traffic produced economic disaster, compelling the new regime to adopt austerity measures, which aroused considerable discontent among the populace. In 1969 young leftists removed al-Shabi, accusing him of "one-man dictatorial rule." A five-man presidential council under the chairmanship of Salim Rubay Ali, with Muhammad Ali Haytham as prime minister, took power. Later, al-Shabi was arrested; he was shot "while trying to escape." The cabal drafted a constitution in 1970, which provided for a People's Supreme Assembly. Salim Rubay Ali remained securely on top, however.

The new administration could not alter the basic difficulty: the collapse of trade and the resulting massive unemployment. Stringent economic measures were adopted, including the raising of tariffs to 300 percent to inhibit imports. The new leaders sought funds in Moscow.

The council purged the government and army of nearly all their officials. Foreign concerns were nationalized, peasants and workers seized control of property, and a complete revolution of society was attempted. About one-fourth of the population fled abroad as the secret police crushed internal opposition. Nearly one-half of the land was redistributed to 26,000 families by government decree and most of the farmland was organized into cooperatives.

PEOPLE'S DEMOCRATIC REPUBLIC OF YEMEN

Late in 1970, after the publication of the draft of the new constitution, the name of the People's Republic of South Yemen was officially changed to the People's Democratic Republic of Yemen (PDRY).

Conditions did not improve. Whereas at least 500 ships a year dropped anchor in Aden harbor before the Suez stoppage there were fewer than fifty in 1972. Higher taxes were imposed on sugar, flour, and other foods, bringing insurrection in many rural areas. With NLF extremism and ineptitude aggravating the economic difficulties and inciting more rebellions, other Arab countries began to question NLF policies and leadership. The government's week-long celebration of Lenin's birthday contrasted against no acknowledgment of Muhammad's birthday engendered dismay.

Poverty did not halt military ambitions. China set up a military mission in Aden alongside Moscow's, which was arming the PDRY forces. The arms often went to PFLOAG'S guerrilla war in Dhufar against Oman; most, however, were used in attacking exiles and FLOSY "mercenaries" in Saudi Arabia and the Yemen Arab Republic (YAR). In 1972 a group of more than forty exiled leaders, invited to a conference with NLF, were shot on arrival. PDRY then lost all her friends except China, the U.S.S.R., and Iraq.

After secret meetings the prime ministers of both Yemens signed a document pledging to halt acts of hostility and to pull back troops from their borders. Over the next two years the negotiations on unity revealed only that each side was ready to absorb the other.

During the October 1973 Arab-Israeli War, PDRY declared the Strait of Bab al-Mandeb a war zone and consented to the stationing of other Arab troops there. PDRY leased Perim island in the strait to Saudi Arabia for ninety-nine years for $150 million. Relations improved with Egypt and Saudi Arabia. Salim Rubay Ali then pronounced a policy of coexistence with all Arab states.

The Suez Canal was reopened for traffic on June 5, 1975, and life began to stir in Aden, but shipping patterns had changed and fewer of the new supertankers now called at Aden. Plans were made to recondition harbor facilities. Relations with Saudi Arabia were normalized, eased by a Saudi grant of $100 million. British Petroleum in 1977 transferred title to its large refinery in Aden to the government, but in subsequent years the refinery often operated at a loss.

Internal disputes repeatedly tore apart the ruling Marxist-Leninist party. In 1978 Salim Rubay Ali and several hundred others were killed during severe fighting, and in 1980 Abd al-Fattah Ismail, the chief of state and head of the party following Ali's death, was deposed. The prime minister, Ali Nasser Muhammad, added the post of secretary-general of the Yemeni Socialist party to his duties and became the chief political figure until the bloody fighting of January 1986, when he was replaced as leader by Haydar Abu Bakr al-Attas, the prime minister. Al-Attas was chosen president and was elected for a five-year term of office on November 6, 1986, following new elections to the People's Supreme Council. In the January fighting more than four thousand people had been killed and a small-scale civil war broke out in Aden. The party leaders in such crises differed about ideology, tribalism, relations with conservative regimes, and personal rivalries for power.

The constitution proclaimed Islam the state religion, while South Yemeni emulation of the U.S.S.R. did not extend as far as atheism, but only to a very cautious secularism. New legal codes were gradually adopted, but Islamic and tribal law remained widely used. Women and men were declared equal in family relations, and women served in the People's Supreme Council. In the first elections for the Supreme Council in 1978 nonparty independents held 40 of 114 seats, but power was in the hands of the party apparatus. The party used education to inculcate Marxist values, expanded the number of students greatly, sent thousands of youths to the Soviet Union for training, and opened the University of Aden in 1975. The government strongly encouraged female education.

In the economic sphere, the regime achieved some limited degree of success for its 2 million people. Agricultural goods had to be sold to the state at prices fixed by it. Production fell following independence, although the standard of living of many of the peasants may have improved. Yemenis living abroad sent remittances back home, and this was the country's largest source of foreign exchange. Redistribution of wealth and particularly the extension of services to the countryside, formerly available only in Aden, were undertaken by the government. The basic poverty of the country, however, remained unchanged, and South Yemen accumulated a large external debt. South Yemen discovered oil and natural gas fields and began in April 1987 to export oil—a promising development for the economy.

In its foreign policy the regime provided access to military facilities and allied itself very closely with the Soviet Union, which in return provided armaments, training, financial aid, and a treaty of friendship signed in 1979. South Yemen opened diplomatic relations with Saudi Arabia, but the Rubay Ali government may have had a hand in the assassination of North Yemen's leader in 1978, which alienated many nearby states. This situation led to a border war between the two Yemens in 1979. Despite periodic meetings and discussions, little real progress toward uniting the very different political and economic systems of the two Yemens was made; such a union seemed less possible than ever as the two societies increasingly diverged.

THE IMAMATE OF YEMEN

The Imamate of Yemen was one of the most remote and isolated spots in the world. In 1934 Ibn Saud had defeated the ruler of Yemen, Sayf al-Islam Yahya Hamid al-Din, and annexed Asir. Charles R. Crane visited the country in the 1930s, and Karl Twitchell built bridges there to connect Sana with ports on the Red Sea. The British had a running quarrel with Imam Yahya over the frontier of the Aden protectorate, somewhat abated by the British-Yemeni treaty of 1934.

In the period between the two world wars the imam turned to Italy for support. A ten-year treaty was signed and a Yemeni mission visited Mussolini to obtain arms and munitions. Yemeni students were sent to Iraq and Egypt for military training. During World War II Yemen remained neutral, but ousted Germans and Italians from her territory. Yemen was admitted to the Arab League in 1945 and to the United Nations in 1947.

Society changed slowly in Yemen; Imam Yahya remained a despot, and Zaydi Shiites dominated the government, much to the displeasure of Shafii Sunnites who lived in the coastal and southern parts of Yemen. Many of the younger generation plotted to remove the imam. In 1948, Imam Yahya was assassinated, and a member of the notable family of the al-Wazirs became imam in his place. However, Yahya's eldest son, Ahmad Hamid al-Din, overthrew the insurgents and many rebels were beheaded as he became imam.

The political development of Yemen proceeded at a snail's pace, and the forces for change attempted a coup against Imam Ahmad in 1955. The revolt was led by his brother Prince Abd Allah, who had represented Yemen at the United Nations. It was crushed by the imam's eldest son, Prince Muhammad al-Badr, who freed his father and executed Prince Abd Allah.

The attempted coup, however, did stir up action in Yemen. Imam Ahmad appointed al-Badr deputy prime minister, foreign minister, and minister of defense. A trade mission from the Soviet bloc arrived in Taizz, the imam's favorite residence and thus the capital, and negotiated trade agreements for the U.S.S.R. and the Eastern bloc. And China signed a five-year trade agreement and provided credits for economic development.

Yemen signed the Jidda pact with Egypt and Saudi Arabia, which established a military alliance. After the formation of the United Arab Republic of Egypt and Syria, Crown Prince al-Badr visited Cairo where he signed a pact in 1958 creating the United Arab States, a vague federation of Yemen and the United Arab Republic.

In 1959 Imam Ahmad went to Italy for medical treatment. He left his son and crown prince, Muhammad al-Badr, as regent. Seizing the opportunity, al-Badr immediately liberalized the regime. Imam Ahmad rushed home, placed al-Badr under house arrest, and beheaded or imprisoned al-Badr's closest partners in the reforms. Yemen remained politically frozen until Imam Ahmad's peaceful death in 1962, whereupon his son became Imam Sayf al-Islam Muhammad al-Badr. The new ruler appointed his friend, Soviet-trained Colonel Abd Allah al-Sallal army chief of staff, and promised that Yemen would begin to advance. A week later, on September 26, a military junta bombarded the royal palace at Sana, declared that Imam al-Badr had been killed, and formed a republic with al-Sallal as leader. However, al-Badr was not dead, and about ten days later he held a news conference in the mountains of northern Yemen.

YEMEN CIVIL WAR: ROYALIST VS. REPUBLICAN

At the very outset al-Sallal arranged a military defense pact with Cairo; between 20,000 and 70,000 Egyptian troops were ultimately sent to Yemen to ensure al-Sallal's position and to solidify control by Nasser over republican Yemen. The modernized Egyptian army, finding it difficult to fight in the mountain areas, restricted its activities to the plains and larger towns. The royalists were supplied with arms and ammunition by Saudi Arabia; their fighting forces were almost entirely made up of Zaydi hill tribesmen who fought willingly against the Egyptian foreigners. Furthermore, they were eager to capture weapons and stores of ammunition. No one doubted that they could conquer the plains within hours after the departure of the Egyptian troops. As the war dragged on Nasser became bogged down in Yemen, as the French did in Algeria. At the same time support for the republic slowly grew in the cities.

Toward the end of 1962, after the Yemen Arab Republic had been recognized by the U.S.S.R. and the United Arab Republic, the United States proposed the withdrawal of all foreign troops from Yemen. On this basis the United States recognized the republican regime, which was admitted to the United Nations. Not until Egypt's setbacks in the June 1967 war with Israel, however, did Nasser give his word to King Faysal of Saudi Arabia that Egyptian troops would depart from Yemen and that support for al-Sallal would be terminated.

Republican Yemen had great difficulty in forming a stable government that could gain the support of the people. As well as being a hard man to please, al-Sallal was in poor health and was forced to remain in Cairo for medical treatments for protracted periods. Amid jealousy and distrust one prime minister after another would be turned out to escape to Cairo with his life, often to return when his replacement fled. After an attempted coup, al-Sallal reassumed the post of prime minister and reestablished his absolute authority. Nasser hoped al-Sallal would hold Yemen until the British departed from Aden, but Nasser had to abandon him. On November 5, 1967, on his way to Moscow, al-Sallal was overthrown in a bloodless army coup.

YEMEN ARAB REPUBLIC

With al-Sallal gone, the last Egyptian troops departing in December, and King Faysal demanding compromise, the civil war lost its drive. The army turned over the government to a group of civilian "Third Force" anti-Egyptian moderate republicans under Qadi Abd al-Rahman al-Iryani and a presidential council. When Saudi Arabia halted the flow of arms and money, al-Badr, with his brothers, uncles, and cousins, gave up the struggle and left.

At the first session of the new republican government in March 1969, Abd al-Rahman al-Iryani declared that the royalists had been defeated and the war was over. The new National Assembly at its first meeting reelected al-Iryani president. Twelve of the fifty-seven seats in the Assembly remained empty, reserved for members from South Yemen, a gesture on the part of the Yemen Arab Republic (YAR) toward union of the two Yemens.

Society in the YAR was in chaos, the economy was in a shambles, famine stalked a land devastated by a three-year drought as well as civil war. The moderately socialist government was staffed by relatively able and earnest people. But governments were only temporary, and no faction could establish general legitimacy. Early in 1970 Muhsin al-Ayni, an experienced politician, took over the leadership of the cabinet and went to Saudi Arabia, the key to peace and economic progress for Yemen. He agreed to discontinue the friction along the frontier, to promote reconciliation among all the factions within northern Yemen, and to accept back all exiles except al-Badr. After thirty royalist leaders returned to Sana, regained their property, and had one of their number elected to the presidential council, Saudi Arabia recognized the YAR and exchanged ambassadors. That autumn it rained for thirty consecutive days, breaking the drought, but not in time to alleviate a famine. With 40 percent of the people near starvation, the United Nations issued a general appeal; it received a generous response.

A border war with the People's Democratic Republic of (South) Yemen superseded all else in 1972 and 1973. In 1972 the prime ministers of the two Yemens approved detailed agreements to unify, the heads of state signed a unification document, and the YAR Consultative Council approved it. Yet, little was done in reality to obtain the popular but elusive goal of unity because the two countries differed sharply in political systems, economic situations, and foreign orientations. In 1973, though the talks with South Yemen continued, so did border raids and assassinations.

One prime minister followed another, until al-Iryani, in poor health and frustrated, resigned the presidency. The next day, June 13, 1974, the army staged a bloodless coup, suspended the constitution, dissolved the assembly, and removed the prime minister and cabinet. Leading the coup was a Ruling Command Council of seven members under Colonel Ibrahim al-Hamdi, who became chairman and head of state. Yemen developed closer ties with Saudi Arabia, which provided budget and development aid. Saudi financing helped Yemen buy weapons from the United States. A sign of national progress was the first census, completed in 1975.

Al-Hamdi was assassinated on October 11, 1977, and his successor, Major Ahmad al-Ghashmi, was killed by a bomb on June 24, 1978. The Constituent Assembly elected Colonel Ali Abd Allah Salih as president on July 17, 1978. Salih conciliated all factions and foreign states, and he managed to establish a more permanent regime. Elections in July 1988 for the Assembly also resulted in the renewal of Salih's tenure. However, the military remained as the only institution that could hold the country together. Foreign policy during the Salih years was designed to secure the approval both of the United States and the Soviet Union.

Border fighting with South Yemen intensified into full-scale war in February 1979. In March a cease-fire was concluded with the withdrawal of troops from the border areas of both Yemens and a reopening of unification talks. Unity continued to be the stated goal of both Yemens, but no real change has taken place in the relations between the two countries.

The YAR concluded economic development and trade agreements with the European Economic Community and the Soviet Union in 1984, and continued to rely on the Arab Monetary Fund and the International Monetary Fund to relieve its persistent budget deficits. Yemeni prosperity and economic growth depended upon the employment situation in Saudi Arabia, where hundreds of thousands of North Yemenis worked, out of the total population of more than nine million. Remittances from Saudi Arabia, and returned workers living again in North Yemen, began to change the Yemeni countryside. Other changes resulted from the discovery and exploitation of oil; exports commenced in 1987. Hopes were raised that the YAR might be able to develop its own resources. Television broadcasting began in 1975, and it also has affected the lives of North Yemenis, especially women, by showing alternatives to strict sexual segregation practices. While most poets have not experimented as radically in form as elsewhere in the Arab world, they have been deeply committed to reforms and the process of change.

Recent social and economic transformations have taken place inside the political tranquility provided by the relatively stable regime of Ali Abd Allah Salih. The military has solidly supported him, but the integration of Shafii Sunnites into the Zaydi-dominated government has taken place only on a small scale and remains an important issue for the future.

REFERENCES

Significant works for this chapter are also found in Chapters 24, 28, 30, 31, 33, 39, and 40.

Allen, Calvin H., Jr. *Oman: The Modernization of the Sultanate.* Boulder, Colo.: Westview Press, 1987. An excellent general survey.

Amin, S. H. *Law and Justice in Contemporary Yemen: The People's Democratic Republic of Yemen and the Yemen Arab Republic.* Glasgow: Royston Limited, 1987. A very useful comparative study, which deals with political and economic factors, as well as legal matters.

Anthony, John Duke. *Arab States of the Lower Gulf: People, Politics, Petroleum*. Washington, D.C.: The Middle East Institute, 1975. An analysis of the political, economic, social, and tribal structure of the amirates by a leading authority.

Belgrave, Charles. *Personal Column, An Autobiography*. London: Hutchinson, 1960. Belgrave was adviser to the shaykh of Bahrayn for many years.

Bidwell, Robin. *The Two Yemens*. Boulder, Colo.: Westview Press, 1983. A comprehensive history of both north and south by an outstanding scholar.

Burrowes, Robert D. *The Yemen Arab Republic: The Politics of Development, 1962–1987*. Boulder, Colo.: Westview Press, 1987. Especially valuable for the Salih years.

Cigar, Norman. "South Yemen and the USSR: Prospects for the Relationship." *Middle East Journal* 39 (1985): 775–795.

Cottrell, Alvin J., ed. *The Persian Gulf States: A General Survey*. Baltimore, Md.: Johns Hopkins University Press, 1980. A massive study with chapters on early as well as recent times; includes Saudi Arabia, Iran, and Iraq as well as the smaller states of the Gulf. Important.

Darwiche, Fida. *The Gulf Stock Exchange Crash: The Rise and Fall of the Souq al Manakh*. London: Croom Helm, 1986. Useful economic analysis.

Dickson, H. R. P. *Kuwait and Her Neighbors*. London: George Allen & Unwin, 1956. A lengthy survey of statistics, history, travel, and life.

Gause, F. Gregory, III. "Yemeni Unity: Past and Future." *Middle East Journal* 42 (1988): 33–47. Shows internal, foreign, and political reasons for lack of progress in unification.

Graham, Helga. *Arabian Time Machine: Self-Portrait of an Oil State*. London: Heinemann, 1978. Extensive interviews vividly show the transformations in people as well as the general society of Qatar.

Hawley, Sir Donald. *Oman and Its Renaissance*. 4th ed. London: Stacey International, 1987. A general survey that is very favorable to Sultan Qabus and is beautifully illustrated.

Hunter, Shireen T. "The Gulf Economic Crisis and Its Social and Political Consequences." *Middle East Journal* 40 (1986): 593–613.

Ismael, Jacqueline. *Kuwait: Social Change in Historical Perspective*. Syracuse, N.Y.: Syracuse University Press, 1982. Treats Kuwayt before and after oil, with an emphasis on economic factors.

Ismael, Tareq Y., and Jacqueline S. Ismael. *The People's Democratic Republic of Yemen: Politics, Economics and Society*. Boulder, Colo.: Lynne Rienner, 1986. A thorough and somewhat favorable view of South Yemen; very useful for the detailed history of internal political struggles.

Khuri, Fuad I. *Tribe and State in Bahrain: The Transformation of Social and Political Authority in an Arab State*. Chicago: University of Chicago Press, 1980. A sociological study up to 1975; subtle and penetrating.

Landen, Robert Geran. *Oman Since 1856: Disruptive Modernization in a Traditional Arab Society.* Princeton, N.J.: Princeton University Press, 1967. An outstanding work on diplomacy, imperialism, and political development.

Makhlouf, Carla. *Changing Veils: Women and Modernisation in North Yemen.* Austin: University of Texas Press, 1979. Discusses upper-class women in Sana, the capital.

Melikian, Levon H. *Jassim: A Study in the Psychosocial Development of a Young Man in Qatar.* New York: Longman, 1981.

Peck, Malcolm C. *The United Arab Emirates: A Venture in Unity.* Boulder, Colo.: Westview Press, 1986. A short but highly informative general survey.

Peterson, J. E. *The Arab Gulf States: Steps Toward Political Participation.* New York: Praeger, 1988. A useful study of recent political history by an outstanding authority on the Arabian peninsula.

————. *Oman in the Twentieth Century: Political Foundations of an Emerging State.* London: Croom Helm, 1978.

————. *Yemen: The Search for a Modern State.* Baltimore, Md.: Johns Hopkins University Press, 1982. Political history and development with a concentration on institutions.

Ramazani, Nesta. "Arab Women in the Gulf." *Middle East Journal* 39 (1985): 258–276.

Rihani, Ameen. *Around the Coasts of Arabia.* London: Houghton Mifflin, 1930. A description of the Arab states in the Persian Gulf region.

Serjeant, R. B., and Ronald Lewcock, eds. *San'a': An Arabian Islamic City.* London: World of Islam Festival, 1983. Excellent scholarly essays on all aspects of Sana, modern and historical.

Soffan, Linda Usra. *The Women of the United Arab Emirates.* London: Croom Helm, 1980.

Stookey, Robert W. *South Yemen: A Marxist Republic in Arabia.* Boulder, Colo.: Westview Press, 1982. An outstanding general survey.

Taryam, Abdullah Omran. *The Establishment of the United Arab Emirates, 1950–85.* London: Croom Helm, 1987. The author, a member of the UAE cabinet, is well informed as a first-hand witness of the events he describes.

Wenner, Manfred. *Modern Yemen.* Baltimore, Md.: Johns Hopkins University Press, 1967. A useful concise history of Yemen.

Wilkinson, John C. *The Imamate Tradition of Oman.* Cambridge: Cambridge University Press, 1987. Valuable for earlier periods of Omani history and especially the struggle of sultans versus imams.

42

The Arab Crescent and the Arab League

FRENCH EVACUATION

The U.S.S.R., China, and the United States recognized the unconditional independence of Syria and Lebanon in 1944. Shortly thereafter, both declared war against Germany and joined the United Nations as charter members.

General de Gaulle understood that French troops would have to be withdrawn, but he evidently hoped to retain a strong French influence in the Levant by means of treaties with Syria and Lebanon that would be at least as favorable as the British treaties with Iraq and Egypt. Naval, military, and air bases for the French would be held indefinitely, and assurances would be given that the Levant would remain a French sphere in economic matters.

Syria and Lebanon indicated a willingness to discuss these points and negotiate treaties, but only after departure of the troops. The landing of additional French soldiers in Beirut was interpreted as military pressure. Open resistance to the French erupted, and the French shelled Damascus in May 1945. This goaded Churchill into serving an ultimatum upon de Gaulle to cease fire and detain his troops in their barracks while British forces restored order. The U.N. Security Council, prodded by the U.S.S.R. and the United States, recommended that foreign troops leave Syria and Lebanon as soon as practicable. French troops departed from Syria in April 1946, but some remained in Lebanon until December. The two countries of the Levant had achieved real independence.

REPUBLIC OF LEBANON

In Lebanon the nationalist-minded leaders who had controlled the quasi-independent regime since 1943 remained unchanged. The confessional aspect of the state was upheld, as was the tradition that the president be a Maronite Christian and the prime minister a Sunni Muslim. At that time the Lebanese chamber of deputies included 30 Christians and 25 Muslims.

The problem of Palestine, the economic detonations resulting from independence, the postwar relaxations, and the East-West crisis gave Lebanese politicians ample opportunity for disagreement. Perhaps the smallness of the country, the paucity of its natural resources, and the diversity of religious affiliations bound together all the political leaders except the extremists. Among themselves they quarreled over favors, prestige, position, and power, but they usually closed ranks on foreign crises. Cabinets changed frequently, but the leaders shuffled the various ministerial posts among themselves. In the three decades following the departure of the French fifteen different men occupied the position of prime minister, many of them on several occasions. President Bishara al-Khuri was overthrown in September 1952 by a bloodless public strike; he was charged with mismanagement, corruption, and arrogance. Camille Shamun was elected president. A new electoral law enacted in 1952 decreed that the chamber be composed of 13 Maronites, 9 Sunnites, 8 Shiites, 5 Greek Orthodox, 3 Druzes, 3 Greek Catholics, 2 Armenian Orthodox, and 1 collectively to the minor groups such as Protestants, Jews, and Roman Catholics.

Fringe parties did not succeed in winning many supporters, but they did have considerable nuisance value and kept the leaders in office more alert to their responsibilities. The largest of these parties—the Nationalist Bloc, at one time led by Raymond Iddah (Eddé)—believed that Lebanon's destiny, and certainly her independence, rested upon close relations with France. This party declined after the French departed. Kamal Jumblat, a Druze, pursued a utopian socialist doctrine, whereas Antun Saada, who refused to accept the partition of Syria, formed the Syrian National party, a pro-fascist group that strove incessantly and often violently for the reunion of Lebanon with Syria.

Beirut and the other Lebanese towns on the coast had prospered greatly during the mandate period, mainly from commerce. During the war Beirut, which served as a port and base for operations in the Levant, became Westernized to a remarkable degree. National independence gave Beirut the opportunity to become one of the great markets in the Middle East. Her merchants proved equal to the responsibility, and Beirut evolved rapidly into an important Middle Eastern commercial and financial center. Beirut became a beautiful and cosmopolitan city, filled with excellent restaurants, cinemas, newspapers, publishing houses, and consumer goods of all descriptions.

The trans-Arabian pipeline, carrying oil from the Saudi Arabian fields to the Mediterranean, had its terminus near Sidon in southern Lebanon. In 1947 Lebanon forced work to cease on the line because of the American support of the partition of Palestine. Construction, however, was resumed in 1949, and oil began to flow in 1950. A refinery was built in Sidon to process petroleum, and a second was erected in 1955. On the coast north of Beirut the Iraq Petroleum Company's (IPC) pipeline touched the sea at Tripoli, and after World War II two new parallel lines were laid to offset the disuse of the Haifa line and to market the increased Iraqi production. The lines and refineries brought very welcome income.

In 1962 IPC built a modern refinery at Tripoli. Although Lebanon had no oil of her own, she began to benefit indirectly from Middle Eastern oil resources elsewhere. As oil prices moved up due to OPEC pressures, Lebanon sought increased payments for the flow of oil across her land, and Lebanese working abroad in oil-producing countries sent home larger amounts of money.

Although the Lebanese had rejoiced over the departure of the French, they were not bitterly anti-French. The many business connections and cultural ties precluded a complete break. And Lebanese-Syrian currency remained tied to the French franc until 1948. In 1964 the charter of the French-owned Banque de Syrie et du Liban expired and the new state Bank of Lebanon was established to take over the issuing of currency and to conduct banking for the government. French control and the mandate period were finally concluded by the termination of this last visible instrument of power.

Every year after World War II Lebanon had a sizable unfavorable balance of trade that was more than redressed by commercial services, tourism, remittances from Lebanese emigrants, and investments of foreign capital. Since banking was one of the leading businesses in Lebanon and the principal occupation of many of the political figures and cabinet members, the security and integrity of banking was a prime concern of the government. In 1958, just a day or two before the formation of the United Arab Republic, large capital sums flowed to Beirut from Syria. Wealthy individuals in Arab countries and from many other parts of the world found Lebanon a suitable haven for their funds. When such moneys were invested in local apartment houses or in new industry, the balance of payments was aided, but it endangered the liquidity of these accounts. The closing of the doors on October 15, 1966, of the Intra Bank of Beirut was a rude shock to the Middle East. A bank holiday was declared; the Bank of Lebanon guaranteed the solvency of all other banks in the country; but it took a full year for the reorganization of Intra Bank.

For some years business and political leaders in Lebanon deplored the nation's dependence on commerce and banking as too uncertain in times of world recession or tension; they advocated taking measures to direct the economy toward industry and agriculture. Difficult as this was where consumer prices were high and natural resources few, considerable progress was achieved. Except for a recession in 1961 each year seemed more prosperous and auspicious until in 1967 the tightening of money, the June Arab-Israeli War, and the closing of the oil pipelines from Iraq slowed the economy.

From 1968 until the civil war in 1975 the Lebanese economy showed growth rates in some years up to 20 percent; in other years it stagnated, especially at those times when the border with Syria was closed or oil stopped flowing through the pipelines from Iraq and Saudi Arabia. Seventy-three percent of the Lebanese economy stemmed from commerce, and any restraint on the movement of goods was felt immediately in most sectors of society. Wealth was piling up in the hands of merchants and bankers while unemployment and poverty were spreading through the cities and villages. Strikes and student demonstrations were manifestations of an escalating revolt against the growing inequities in Lebanese society: the poor countryside versus the rich city, the poor southern districts versus the north, the poor Palestinians and Shiite Lebanese versus the generally richer Maronite Christians.

Rapidly expanding population (about 3 percent a year), limited land resources, and unemployment offered a severe challenge. Lebanon initiated various projects, the most promising being the Litani River irrigation and hydroelectric power plan, which also met some of the need for economic development in the Shiite south.

Lebanon in the main remained a Western-oriented nation although the Muslim majority of the population emphasized instead her Arab history and cultural associations. Relations between Lebanon and the United States generally were cordial until the early 1970s. The American University of Beirut created much good will, as did the presence in the United States of numerous Lebanese emigrants, usually Christians.

By far the greatest difficulty for Lebanese foreign policy after 1945 arose from the partition of Palestine and the birth of Israel. Lebanon joined the Arab League at its inception. She argued in the United Nations against the partition of Palestine and halted work at Sidon on the pipeline. Lebanon's part in the 1948 war was very small, and she suffered only a handful of casualties. Many refugees from Palestine settled in camps in Lebanon. Public demonstrations in Lebanon definitely indicated sympathy for the Palestinian Arabs.

Lebanon, however, found no difficulty in subscribing to the various truces declared in the Palestine war and easily entered into armistice negotiations. Israeli forces withdrew from four Lebanese villages that they had occupied. In 1949, an armistice was signed, recognizing the previous Palestine-Lebanon frontier and adding demilitarized zones on each side. Lebanon refused to recognize Israel and adopted the boycott practices of the Arab League.

LEBANESE POLITICS

The relative calm of post-World War II Lebanese political life was shattered by the 1956 Suez crisis. President Shamun supported Egypt in her nationalization of the Canal, and mass rallies condemning Western pressures on Egypt took place in Beirut. As soon as the 1956 Arab-Israeli War ended, Lebanese leaders engaged in a bitter parliamentary election. A National Union Front announced its opposition to Prime Minister al-Sulh and President Shamun. The front was against a constitutional amendment permitting Shamun to succeed himself as president. Despite clashes the elections were held in July. The government won 50 seats, the National Union Front 8, and the Independents 8. Significantly, Salam, Jumblat, Karami, and other prominent politicians failed to win election, and in August Sami al-Sulh reshuffled his cabinet.

The politicians who found themselves frozen out of office commenced a battle to regain power and discovered eager allies in Syria and Egypt. Arms smuggling from Syria became commonplace, and Lebanese frontier police were shot in their attempts to halt the illicit traffic. Foreign Minister Charles Malik reiterated that Lebanon would side with the Arabs in any dispute with the West involving legitimate Arab rights and aspirations. He warned, however, that Middle Eastern conflicts could not be solved by alliances with Communists.

When the new United Arab Republic increased pressures on Lebanon, her leaders announced immediately that Lebanon would not join it. Arms and men from Syria and Egypt began to flow into Lebanon, but Malik confirmed a report that he had received a promise of unlimited military and economic aid from the United States to maintain Lebanon's independence.

In 1958 political demonstrations and outbreaks of violence erupted in Tripoli and Beirut. Soon designated as rebels, politicians out of office extended independently their sway over specific areas: Salam in Beirut; Jumblat in the Druze mountain area; Karami in the sector north of Tripoli; and others in two or three isolated regions. Syria and Egypt helped the rebels, but matters remained stalemated, as General Shihab refused to commit the army to either political camp and acted only to maintain public order.

When revolution broke out in Iraq, Shamun called upon the U.S. for urgent relief. The landing of American marines in Beirut heightened the quarrel among local politicians to the level of the cold war between East and West. Many blustered, but it was evident that no one would seriously challenge the Americans, who asserted that the marines would be withdrawn as soon as a peaceful solution to Lebanon's political problems could be devised. As was expected, the presidential election resulted in the choice of General Fuad Shihab, and the rebels declared they would be satisfied if and when the American troops left.

President Shihab was inaugurated September 23, 1958; American troops departed a month later; and the United Nations observers were gone by November. Some of the open wounds of the battles began to heal and calmer relations with the United Arab Republic alleviated much of the bitterness. Shihab and Nasser met for a warm exchange at the Lebanese-Syrian border. Prime Minister Karami skillfully avoided involvement in the heated quarrels between Nasser and Iraq, and so satisfied the domestic and foreign policy inclinations of the Lebanese factions that he was able to remain at the helm until the spring of 1960. Then he stepped aside for the formation of a caretaker cabinet in preparation for the summer elections for a new ninety-nine-member Chamber. (The number of members in Lebanon's Chamber was usually divisible by eleven so that the accepted ratio of six Christians to five Muslims could be easily maintained.) No official census had been taken since 1932 as the ruling Maronites did not wish to test this proportion. The membership breakdown, which remained unchanged, was: 30 Maronites, 20 Sunnites, 19 Shiites, 11 Greek Orthodox, 6 Druzes, 6 Greek Catholics, 4 Armenian Orthodox, 1 Armenian Catholic, 1 Protestant, and 1 other Christian.

Saib Salam formed a large cabinet to try to unite all parties and shades of opinion; but after bitter quarrels he relinquished the post to Karami who skillfully steered a neutral course until the 1964 presidential elections. Charles Hilu, the minister of education, was elected fourth president and took office in September 1964.

When the 1967 Arab-Israeli War broke out President Hilu declared a state of emergency. Lebanon branded Israel as the aggressor and made only one brief air foray over Israel. After the fighting was halted Lebanese politics returned to the usual competition for position, influence, and money.

In January 1969, Rashid Karami was called upon once again to form a coalition cabinet in an attempt to solve the problem of clashes between security forces and Palestinians. Without a representative of Shamun's party in the cabinet, conservative Christians withdrew. Karami offered to resign, but stayed on until after the presidential election in 1970.

Throughout the two terms of Presidents Shihab and Hilu from 1958 to 1970 reforms were undertaken as the state controlled dissent through the internal security forces. Some social services were extended to the poor, and the presidents managed to offend few people while most Lebanese enjoyed prosperity.

The unwritten national pact that the president be a Maronite, the prime minister a Sunnite, and other officials belong to other religious groups was reaffirmed by all leaders, assuring a peaceful election in 1970. Supported by Shamun and Jumayyil, the minister of economy, Sulayman Franjieh, was elected president. He received 50 votes while Ilyas Sarkis, governor of the Central Bank, Karami's candidate, received the remaining 49.

In the late 1960s and early 1970s the Palestinian refugee problem became more pressing. The influx of over 100,000 Arab Palestinian refugees in the late 1940s, mostly Muslims and almost 10 percent of the total population of Lebanon, had injected an explosive factor into that country. The refugees were located in fifteen camps scattered from Tripoli to Tyre. Very few became citizens of Lebanon and they were supported by United Nations grants. They became natural allies of the Lebanese Muslims, the poor, and the pan-Arab nationalists.

From 1968 on, the Palestinian specter jarred Lebanon's precarious equilibrium repeatedly, as the level of violence rose steadily. In December 1968, Palestinian commandos based in Beirut attacked an Israeli plane at the Athens airport, killing one passenger. Two days later the Israeli air force raided the Beirut airport in retaliation.

Already, students had been demonstrating, and after the airport affair 25,000 students struck, protesting the inefficacy of the armed forces and demanding universal conscription in Lebanon. Palestinian actions against Israel were intensified, though the government tried to prevent Lebanon from becoming a base for such attacks. The Lebanese army moved to crack down on Palestinian activities, but guerrilla forces seized control of most of the refugee camps in the country. Bloody riots in Tripoli, Beirut, and other places compelled the government to attempt a cease-fire, the first of many over the ensuing years.

Palestinian guerrilla operations throughout 1970 brought repeated retaliatory raids from Israel. Over 15,000 Lebanese abandoned their homes in the south. Christian and Shiite Muslim leaders demanded that the government act to curtail the Palestinians; Sunnite Muslims supporting the Palestinians called on the government to strengthen the army and urged that outside aid be found. Armed clashes occurred in Beirut between Palestinians and Pierre Jumayyil's Christian Phalangist private army. A nationwide strike drew attention to the need for protection and economic assistance to south Lebanon. Signs of incipient civil war were everywhere.

Palestinian forces poured into Lebanon after their defeat in Jordan in 1970 in such numbers that they took full control of a thirty-five-kilometer strip along the southern border. Martial law was invoked in the entire country. PLO leader Yasir (Yasser) Arafat, headquartered in Beirut, reached an agreement in 1972 with Prime Minister Salam whereby the guerrillas would consult with the government, which would hold ultimate veto power over any action. Large sections of the population, however, subscribed to the Palestinian aims; sympathy strikes were frequent; to many university students Palestinian activists were neither guerrillas nor terrorists but heroic national freedom fighters.

During the October 1973 Arab-Israeli War Lebanon maintained an official neutrality, to the disgust of most Palestinian groups. As clashes multiplied in 1974 and the Palestinian armed forces grew to 10,000, Shamun's National Liberal party and Jumayyil's Phalange formed independent militias. In September, after armed battles and political assassinations, two ministers, followers of Jumblat, resigned, claiming the government was ignoring the issue of law and order and had allowed huge arms shipments for the militias to be landed on the coast.

LEBANESE CIVIL WAR

The causes of the civil war lay in part with the personal and group rivalries and antagonisms endemic in Lebanese political, social, economic, and religious life. Added to this were the growing involvement of Lebanese and Palestinians in each other's affairs, and the inflexibility of Lebanon's political and governmental structures. The war was exacerbated by the participation of foreign powers desiring to determine its outcome.

Most Lebanese supported the aims of the Palestinians and viewed their plight with sympathy, but as Lebanese many did not wish to share directly in the struggle. They refused to accord citizenship to them and hoped they would go away. Above all, the Lebanese abhorred the idea that the Palestinians might somehow have an overriding voice in Lebanon's political future. Thus, they were greatly distressed as the Palestinians increased their use of Lebanon as a base of operations against Israel, fearing especially that Israel might seize south Lebanon up to the Litani River.

The Palestinians for their part saw in Lebanon a staging area for incursions into Israel; they used Beirut as a convenient spot for plotting actions against Israel throughout the world. Christian conservative militants like Shamun, Jumayyil, and Franjieh, finding their government supine in the face of the Palestinian menace, organized to combat them privately. Leftist groups in Lebanon, especially those who were Sunnites, accepted their Palestinian co-religionists as useful allies in the contest against the well-armed and wealthy Christian rightist minority.

Quite apart from the Palestinians, the political structure of Lebanon was askew. No census had been taken since 1932, as those in power were afraid of what it might reveal. Most knowledgeable observers judged that the ratio of six Christians to five Muslims in parliament and the civil service no longer reflected Lebanon's demography; it might even have changed to a ratio of four Christians to six Muslims. Tampering with the original ratios would alter the power lines within the state, and any suggestion of this infuriated Shamun, Jumayyil, Franjieh, and their confreres. Jumblat, the Druze socialist, demanded equal representation of Christians and Muslims and proposed completely secular elections in which religion would be ignored. Furthermore, the Christian rightist minority was considered the party of the wealthy while the Muslim leftist majority was the party of the poor and underprivileged. Separated by religion, political philosophy, and economics, the two sides seeking power had drifted into civil war.

On April 13, 1975, a busload of Palestinians was massacred by Phalange militia, just at the time Prime Minister Rashid al-Sulh was suggesting a reform of the parliamentary representative system to give greater military and political muscle to Lebanon's Muslims. These actions accelerated the polarization of Lebanese society. The Palestinians joined the leftist parties, largely Muslim in composition, while Shamun's National Liberal party cooperated with Jumayyil's Phalange in supporting President Franjieh, to form a Maronite-dominated coalition of the Christian right. The experienced Karami formed a six-man Christian-Muslim cabinet, omitting followers of Jumayyil and Jumblat. But calls to end the national pact ensured the continuation of the civil war.

Bitter fighting continued through 1975 and most of 1976. The Lebanese army, which for a time had remained aloof, entered the war in September 1975 in the battle between the Muslims of Tripoli, Karami's home, and the Christian town of Zgharta, Franjieh's residence. The bloodshed spread to Beirut, where house-to-house fighting devastated sections of the city. It was calculated that $3.4 billion in damages was incurred in 1975–1976, as 3,500 businesses were bombed, burned, or looted. Though a half dozen cease-fires were agreed upon, none lasted more than a few days. Muslims and others called repeatedly upon President Franjieh to resign.

After a short lull intense fighting was resumed in December 1975; by March 1976 it was reported that between 15 and 20 percent of the heart of Beirut had been destroyed and perhaps 10,000 people had died. Franjieh continued to refuse to step down and the Lebanese army began to experience massive defections. The perplexing situation in the army was that most of the 18,000 men and many of the junior officers were Muslims, while the senior officers were almost all Christians. Franjieh had hesitated to call upon the army, fearing that the men might shoot their officers. Then, army defectors formed the Lebanese Arab Army and united with leftist Muslims and Palestinians. Franjieh and Karami, deeply concerned, met with Syria's President al-Assad in February 1976 to initial the Damascus Agreement. In it, al-Assad pledged to withdraw the Syrian-based Palestine Liberation Army and Franjieh promised to call for an equal number of seats in parliament for Christians and Muslims, to revise the electoral law to give genuine representation to the people, and to provide real social reforms. Back in Beirut he announced the "new foundation," which would modify the national pact.

As the fighting wore on it began to look as if victory for the leftist Muslim-Palestinian coalition was only weeks away. Then, on March 29, 1976, al-Assad cut off all supplies going from Syria to the Palestinians. He switched sides perhaps because he did not relish the idea of a Palestinian-dominated Lebanon that could involve him in a war with Israel at a time he did not choose. He may not have wished to see the Maronites crushed in Lebanon, since he and many of his colleagues also belonged to a distinct minority in Syria, the Shiite Alawites. Also, many of the leftists were members of the Iraqi branch of the Ba'th party, bitter enemies of the Syrian branch. Al-Assad certainly did not wish his country to be squeezed between Iraq and Lebanon. All seemed to add up to the old adage of divide and rule.

The Christian militias and the Syrian army were now aligned against the Palestinians and Muslim leftists. Neither side was prepared to compromise. Syrian troops entered Lebanon in April, and opposed victory for any Lebanese party.

Throughout the spring of 1976 maneuvering for the election of a successor to Franjieh consumed the attention of all the factions. Syria obtained the necessary votes for Ilyas Sarkis, who had lost out by only one vote six years earlier. Elected in May, Sarkis assumed office on September 23, 1976, but the war continued. When Syria ordered the bombing of refugee camps, Iraq shut off the flow of oil to Syria. The strain of the military operation began to tell on the Syrian economy, especially when Saudi Arabia and other Arab states cut off aid. At the same time, Israeli naval units were preventing arms shipments from reaching the Muslim leftists and were supplying arms to the Christian militias. By October, there were more than 20,000 Syrian troops in Lebanon, occupying nearly half the country.

With the internationalizing of the Lebanese civil war the Arab League called for a joint Arab force to police a cease-fire. Major resistance ended when the Tel al-Zaatar refugee camp fell to Syrian and Christian guns. Meeting in Riyadh under pressure from King Khalid, Egypt, Syria, Kuwayt, the PLO, Lebanon, and Saudi Arabia called for an Arab peacekeeping contingent of 30,000, under the command of President Sarkis. Composed mainly of Syrian troops, the Arab force was warned by Israel not to enter the area south of the Litani River. The war was not over, however, for the shelling, bombing, ambushing, and killing continued, although at a reduced rate. Many international companies moved their headquarters from Beirut to Athens, Amman, Cairo, or Dubay. Beirut ceased to be the financial center of the Middle East.

The fundamental causes of the civil war in Lebanon are difficult to resolve until an overall peace settlement in the Arab-Israeli dispute can be reached, for local political and economic problems were exacerbated by foreign intervention and the issue of the Palestinians. The violence continued, as was seen in the assassination of Kamal Jumblatt in March 1977. By October the Christian and Muslim militias were larger than ever and public recruitment had lifted their numbers to 45,000, ten times the size of the Lebanese army. No parliamentary election was held in 1976 (or subsequently) as required by the constitution, and the question of representation, one of the roots of the civil war, was not resolved.

Most of the fighting occurred in the sensitive area south of the Litani River along the Israeli frontier where Muslim and Maronite villages and enclaves are juxtaposed in an irregular pattern. Israel had already advised Arab peacekeeping forces not to enter the region; without the presence of the Lebanese army there, battles between Palestinian forces and Christian militias resumed. Early in 1977 the Christians were receiving Israeli support in the southern region and also in their enclave north of Beirut. The Israeli-Lebanese frontier was opened; supplies and armed forces moved back and forth. Israel declared it would not tolerate attacks on Lebanese villages near the Israeli border. Long-range artillery duels erupted, the Palestinians supported by Syria and the Christians by Israel.

On March 11, 1978, eleven Palestinian commandos landed on the Israeli coast with the intention of entering Tel Aviv, seizing hostages, and demanding the release of some of their brethren. They were apprehended, however, and most of them were killed; but thirty-one Israelis were also killed in the incident. Three days later, in retaliation, the Israeli army in its largest engagement since 1973 invaded south Lebanon to a depth of six miles, hesitated briefly, and then occupied nearly all of Lebanon south of the Litani River. U.N. peacekeeping forces (UNIFIL) were assembled quickly and began to take up positions there on March 22. Considerable fighting continued in scattered areas between Israelis and Palestinians and between Lebanese Christian militias and Lebanese Muslim and army groups. World opinion obliged the Israelis to pull back, which they did in stages; insisting that Palestinian forces be controlled before withdrawal, the Israelis completed their operation in mid-June. Israel turned over a narrow but long strip of Lebanese territory along the Israeli border to Major Saad Haddad and his pro-Israeli Lebanese militia, who retained this area thereafter. Meanwhile, several hundred thousand Lebanese villagers, many of whom were Shiites, had become refugees, and any hope for internal peace in Lebanon was pushed far into the future.

In the late 1970s, the youthful Bashir Jumayyil, son of the veteran Lebanese politician Pierre Jumayyil, brutally consolidated the rightist militias under the name of the Lebanese Forces. With secret Israeli and American help, he was strong enough to complete his control over the Maronite enclave stretching through East Beirut northward along to the coast to south of Tripoli and inland into Mount Lebanon. The leftists, on the other hand, disintegrated, as Kamal Jumblat's son Walid proved unable to keep that disparate grouping in West Beirut and the south together. President Sarkis, presiding over what remnants of a government still endured, was ineffectual—in large part, because he was perceived as the tool of Syria, which would not, or could not, deliver sufficient force to impose its will on all the Lebanese factions. Also, the central government could no longer tax most imports which instead were subject to the militias' illegal tariffs.

Despite this chaos, Lebanon's economy began to recover from the devastation of 1975–1976. Some income was derived from Lebanese working abroad, whose remittances were substantial. Various Arab and other governments aided different Lebanese factions and groups, and the PLO's infrastructure benefited local traders. The Lebanese currency remained relatively stable in value until 1982, while a local black market flourished.

THE 1982 WAR

Israel was under the leadership of Prime Minister Menachem Begin in 1977; and with the aid of President Jimmy Carter, Begin concluded a series of arrangements culminating in the peace treaty with Egypt in 1979. In accordance with the exchange of land for peace, Israel returned all of Sinai to Egypt by the spring of 1982; in return, Egypt guaranteed Israel that it would not go to war. Since Israel's southern border was now safer, Begin and Defense Minister Ariel Sharon hoped to destroy the PLO in Lebanon and to impose a peace treaty on Lebanon.

On June 6, 1982, Israel invaded Lebanon with overwhelming force. The stated goal of the Israelis was to clear the PLO guerrillas from a security zone north of Israel. Bypassing UNIFIL troops, Israel fought PLO forces and pushed rapidly north in a "leapfrog" pattern toward Beirut. An enormous land and air battle between Syria and Israel for control of Lebanon then ensued. Israel shot down around 100 Syrian airplanes and destroyed Syrian surface-to-air missile batteries while pushing Syrian troops back toward the Beirut-Damascus road.

By June 13 Israel had reached the outskirts of Beirut. There it linked up with Bashir Jumayyil's Lebanese Forces in East Beirut. Egypt and the other Arab states did nothing but protest while Israel cordoned off the PLO and some Syrian forces in West Beirut and bombarded them by land, sea, and air. The 600,000 or so civilians and the thousands of combatants in the Lebanese capital's western half then underwent a siege, with water and electricity supplies turned off, and the television cameras of the world turned on extraordinary images of modern warfare devastating an already-damaged city.

On August 21 the PLO started to evacuate West Beirut according to conditions agreed upon by the United States and other parties. By September 1 the Palestinian fighters had gone, leaving behind their heavy armaments and their families, the latter under the protection of a pledge of safety from the multinational force of U.S., French, and Italian troops. In the meantime, a new president of Lebanon was elected under Israeli aegis; on August 23 Bashir Jumayyil reached this goal, and the victory of the rightist and Christian side in the civil war finally seemed to be definitive.

The violence of the times robbed Lebanon of whatever feeble chance of peace and national reconciliation this situation might have allowed, for on September 14 Bashir Jumayyil was assassinated. Israel then moved into West Beirut, and the Lebanese Forces killed hundreds of Palestinian civilians living in their refugee camps in that area. Bashir's older brother, Amin Jumayyil, a more moderate figure and a member of parliament, was then elected president of Lebanon on September 21, as the multinational force returned to West Beirut. The Israelis pulled out of that part of the city, and the Lebanese desperately hoped the carnage might somehow end.

SYRIA REGAINS LIMITED PREEMINENCE IN LEBANON

The United States in late 1982 tried to increase the strength of the Israeli-backed central government of Lebanon and its army. The Americans sent arms, trainers, and money to help Jumayyil. This seemed a feasible policy since many groups in southern and central Lebanon had initially been amenable to Israel's invasion, welcoming the Israelis as a better alternative than the PLO, whose control had grown increasingly oppressive. However, Jumayyil's appointments of Phalangists to high offices, his purges of the army and judiciary, and the actions of the Lebanese Forces soon alienated these groups. First the Druzes, then the Shiites, and eventually other Lebanese came to want the Israelis out of their country, and the Shiites especially were vigorous in launching attacks against Israel and the multinational forces. The latter seemed intent on supporting the rightists in a total victory over the leftists—a victory based on arrogance and vengeance rather than a policy of national reconciliation.

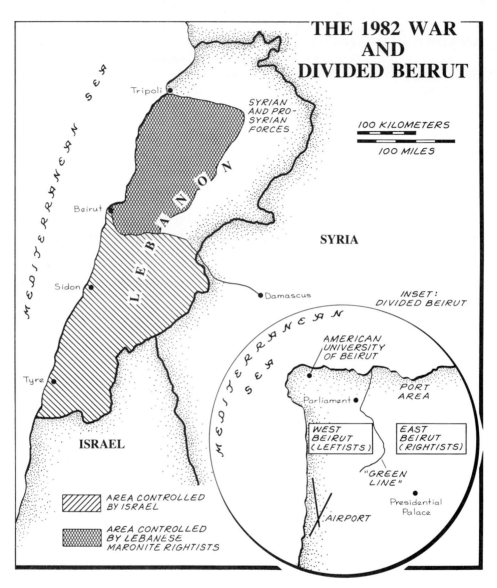

THE 1982 WAR AND DIVIDED BEIRUT

MEDITERRANEAN SEA

Tripoli

SYRIAN AND PRO-SYRIAN FORCES

100 KILOMETERS

100 MILES

LEBANON

Beirut

SYRIA

Sidon

Damascus

INSET: DIVIDED BEIRUT

Tyre

ISRAEL

MEDITERRANEAN SEA

AMERICAN UNIVERSITY OF BEIRUT

Parliament

PORT AREA

WEST BEIRUT (LEFTISTS)

EAST BEIRUT (RIGHTISTS)

"GREEN LINE"

Presidential Palace

AIRPORT

AREA CONTROLLED BY ISRAEL

AREA CONTROLLED BY LEBANESE MARONITE RIGHTISTS

Jumayyil signed a quasi-peace treaty on May 17, 1983, with Israel. This agreement called for a termination of the state of war, an Israeli withdrawal, a special security region in southern Lebanon, and liaison offices to coordinate relations between the two countries. Syria strongly opposed this agreement, and so did many Lebanese, such as Jumblat, Karami, and Franjieh; so Syria helped the Shiites and Druzes as they battled the central government army and the U.S. navy in September for control of West Beirut and central Lebanon. When guerrillas attacked the U.S. barracks in Beirut on October 23 and killed 241 marines the American administration finally secured Jumayyil's agreement on Geneva talks among the Lebanese leaders aimed at compromise and peace. These talks failed, the Muslims in the central army in West Beirut deserted, and in February 1984 President Reagan ordered the withdrawal of American forces from Lebanon. The Shiites of the Amal ("Hope") organization now controlled West Beirut, and they suppressed the Sunnite militia and tried to do the same to the Palestinians. President Jumayyil turned to Syria for help, thereby demonstrating his own remarkable flexibility and bringing Lebanon back to the situation that had existed before the 1982 war. Rashid Karami became prime minister in a cabinet that included the leaders of the Phalangists, the Druzes, and the Shiites.

Israel retreated southward, finishing its own withdrawal from most of Lebanon in June 1985. This left most of Lebanon under the control of Syria. The Israeli-Lebanese agreement of 1983 was abrogated by Lebanon. It became clear that Palestinian forces supported by Syria were staying in Lebanon. Syrian-backed Fatah rebels had ousted Yasir Arafat from northern Lebanon in December 1983, and the PLO was internally split, but it still had a resident base for further action in Lebanon against Israel.

In the middle and later 1980s many Lebanese groups suffered internal schisms as political society deteriorated even further. The Maronite Lebanese Forces rejected President Jumayyil's leadership over whether to accept a large role for Syria. Amal and the Shiites split internally as they battled over Iranian influence, theocracy, hostage-taking, and the acceptability of compromise with other Lebanese groups. The leftist Lebanese of various stripes battled the PLO so as to stop it from establishing its forces once again in Beirut, the refugee camps, and southern Lebanon.

Despairing of a compromise among the old politicians, Syria in December 1985 engineered an agreement among the militia leaders, but President Jumayyil disrupted this initiative. Under such circumstances Lebanon floundered and the economy disintegrated. In 1987 inflation reached almost 500 percent.

Culturally, Lebanon in the 1980s continued to be so diverse as to be without any real national unity. In radio and television broadcasting, in newspapers, in education, and even in language (Arabic versus French as the language of high culture), the various confessional and political groups and factions each had its own choice. While the Shiites clearly replaced the Maronites as the largest and most important element in Lebanon's mosaic, they were too divided to provide a generally accepted philosophy that could make a new and united Lebanon work. Instead, drastic inflation and unemployment increased; kidnappings, especially of foreigners, became frequent; and anonymous and highly destructive car bombings were the symptoms of Lebanon's collapse. According to the Lebanese police nearly

130,000 people were killed in Lebanon from the beginning of the 1975 civil war to the middle of 1987.

The June 1, 1987, assassination of Rashid Karami, the able Sunnite leader from Tripoli, who had so often served as a focus of compromise while prime minister, epitomized the degradation of Lebanese politics and the Lebanese polity. President Jumayyil's term of office expired September 22, 1988, but parliament could not agree on electing his successor. Instead, the incumbent Sunnite prime minister was challenged by Jumayyil's appointment of Maronite General Michel Aoun as head of a caretaker cabinet. Lebanon seemed to be sinking into partition.

REPUBLIC OF SYRIA

When World War II ended, the Syrian political leaders who had battled for complete independence in the mandatory period were in control and had the satisfaction of forming the first fully sovereign Syrian republic. Shukri al-Kuwatli held the presidency, Jamil Mardam was prime minister, and a new chamber of deputies was elected in 1947.

National feelings in Syria ran high. The actions of the French had been more drastic in Damascus and the interior provinces of Syria than in Beirut. Three times in recent memory the French had wantonly shelled Damascus, which had been the site of the Arab congresses as well as the capital of Faysal's short-lived Arab kingdom in 1920. All French schools in Syria were closed in 1945, and when France devalued the franc in 1948, Syria issued her own separate Syrian pounds.

The dream of a united Arab state to include Lebanon, Syria, Transjordan, Palestine, and Iraq had not died in Syria. As Syria emerged independent at the close of the war, the value of union appeared greater than ever; many Syrians regarded it as almost a necessity. Each state separately was weak; together they would have strength. Yet, an arrangement to accomplish even partial federation required political genius of a high order. Fertile Crescent unity was not a new idea, but after the area had been divided between England and France unification had been impossible.

The fall of France in 1940 whetted Abd Allah's ambitions to join Syria to Transjordan. But in 1947 President al-Kuwatli of Syria publicly stated that in any uniting Transjordan would be annexed by Syria. Syrian political leaders had no intention of being governed from Amman. Indeed, they did not relish the thought of surrendering position and power in Syria to any group or person. Others within Syria looked forward to the merger of Iraq and Transjordan, the two Hashimite kingdoms, and the eventual inclusion of Syria and Lebanon. Leaders in Iraq and Syria discussed the union of their two states into a Fertile Crescent union. The Syrians believed that they possessed a more advanced population and that though slightly smaller, they would dominate Iraq. On the other hand Iraqis recognized that their country contained greater wealth, both developed and potential, and felt certain that Iraq would lead the combined state.

Syria played an active part in the formation of the Arab League, attended its conferences, and promised to cooperate militarily against the formation of a

Zionist state. In 1947, the Palestine liberation committee obtained over 27,000 volunteers in Syria. In the spring of 1948 various Syrian army officers, including Colonel Adib Shishakli, participated in the war, but in the actual fighting Syrian forces proved to be ineffective. There was no great enthusiasm for shedding Syrian blood so that Abd Allah in Transjordan or Faruq in Egypt might have more territory to rule.

On March 30, 1949, Chief of Staff Husni Zaim carried out a bloodless coup d'état. Learning that President al-Kuwatli was planning his dismissal, Zaim arrested the president and the leading political figures. The public approved for a number of reasons: the war in Palestine was a failure; corruption was not reduced; the constitution had been amended to permit the president to succeed himself; and al-Kuwatli opposed the Fertile Crescent unity plan. A new cabinet was formed; Zaim as prime minister also held the portfolios of defense and interior. Political parties were outlawed, and a new constitution was planned. Husni Zaim started out strongly, arranging a cease-fire agreement with Israel and obtaining assurances from Nuri al-Said that Iraq would come to the assistance of Syria if attacked by Israel. Syria proposed unity with Iraq "on the basis of a full autonomous state for each country," and military figures journeyed between Damascus and Baghdad. Fearing Hashimite rule in Syria, Egypt and Saudi Arabia rushed diplomatic and financial support to Zaim, causing him to abandon unionist policies and become president of a new Syrian republic. Worst of all, he showed an inclination to restore to France some aspects of her cultural influence. French, for instance, became an official language, along with Arabic. In June Zaim, "The Leader," was elected president; on August 14 General Sami al-Hinnawi arrested Zaim and had him shot.

Upon the execution of Zaim, a constituent assembly was elected and women voted for the first time. Meanwhile, discussions with Iraqi officials produced a draft framework for a common regime. But the Republican Bloc, enemy of union, stirred the army to move. On December 19, 1949, Colonel Adib Shishakli arrested al-Hinnawi, who was charged with treason and conspiracy with a foreign power (Iraq).

Colonel Shishakli did not at first rule directly. The constituent assembly declared Syria to be a republic, and Hashim al-Atasi was elected president. No one, however, doubted who was the real power in the government. A liberal constitution adopted in 1950 contained articles with respect to education, labor, land ownership, and the rights of the citizen. The new constitution and the new government did not alter the fundamental weakness of Syria or usher in a new flourishing economy. The major area of growth was in the agriculture of the northeastern part of the country. Thanks to increased production there, the wheat grown in Syria in the 1940s had doubled, and in the 1950s it increased by another 50 percent. The Bedouin tribes increasingly became sedentarized.

In 1951 Colonel Shishakli jailed the cabinet, President al-Atasi resigned, political parties were outlawed, and plans for a new government and a new constitution were initiated. The new constitution was not presented until 1953, at which time Shishakli became president and prime minister. He arrested many leading political figures and declared martial law in Damascus and Aleppo.

But Shishakli had overreached himself. The army revolted, forcing him to flee. Hashim al-Atasi became president again; the 1950 constitution was reinstated; and the 1949 chamber of deputies was recalled until a new parliament could be elected. Khalid Baqdash, leader of the Communist party, became the first Arab Communist duly elected to an Arab parliament on a Communist party ticket. Ex-president Shukri al-Kuwatli returned from five years of exile in Egypt and was elected president in August 1955. A succession of prime ministers battled with the complex problems of Syria, but none found a constructive program, largely because of virulent nationalism and the political turmoil created by a rivalry for influence in Syria among Egypt, Saudi Arabia, and Iraq.

The political instability in Syria in the decade after World War II was extremely detrimental to economic planning and development. Excellent plans for the division and distribution of large tracts of land among poor and landless peasants were enacted into law, but were not implemented to any great extent. Moves in that direction antagonized the large landowners and led in part to the demise of the Shishakli regime in 1954.

Raids and counterraids occurred frequently on the border of Israel. In 1955 Israeli forces mounted a massive attack on Syria. Since the Western powers, and particularly the United States, were identified with the foundation of the Zionist state, the West bore the onus of the Syrian defeat and frustration. Only then did the Syrian political leaders turn more directly to the Soviet bloc and begin to put into effect the old axiom that my enemies' enemies are my friends.

The signing of the Baghdad Pact in March 1955 moved Syrian politicians into the Egypto-Saudi camp. The Syrians were already suspicious of the series of treaties of friendship among Turkey, Iraq, and Transjordan in 1946; the Baghdad Pact, especially after the ready adherence given to it by Britain, was anathema to Syrian nationalists and incited most of them to join the Egyptian camp.

Shukri al-Kuwatli, who was elected president in 1955, had lived in exile in Egypt from 1949 to 1954, where he had witnessed the exciting successes of Colonel Nasser. In Damascus any role other than that of a friend to Egypt was unpardonable and impossible, since the new, young army staff officers were ardent supporters of Nasser and his revolution. Thus, when Nasser nationalized the Suez Canal in 1956, Syrian demonstrations were more open and enthusiastic than those of other Middle Eastern states. Syrian spokesmen swore that the oil pipelines would be sabotaged should the West commit aggression against Egypt. After Israel, Britain, and France invaded Sinai, Syria did not permit the repair of the pipelines until Israeli forces withdrew from the Gaza Strip.

To distract the attention of the masses from internal political sniping, a running series of plots, accusations of treason, scandals, and political witchhunts were offered in Damascus. Israel, the United States, Iraqi royalty, Turkey, and Shishakli were the most convenient whipping boys. Incidents such as these abetted the drift toward the left.

The regime needed arms to prevent an internal coup, to strengthen Syria's position vis-à-vis Israel and Iraq, and to influence affairs in Jordan. Furthermore, the army was moving rapidly into the political arena and had a natural desire for quantities of improved weapons. Following Nasser's example, Syria applied to

Moscow and received about $60 million in tanks and other matériel in 1956. Each setback drove the Syrians further to the left, strengthened Soviet bargaining, and emboldened the pan-Arabists. It also brought to a head a rivalry brewing in the army for a decade. The young army graduates of the Homs Staff College were fiery Arab nationalists who pointed to the defeats in Palestine and the weakness of Syrian policies as proof of the senior officers' incompetence. Lt. Col. Abd al-Hamid Sarraj, chief of army intelligence, emerged as the leader of the junior officers.

SYRIA AS THE NORTHERN REGION OF
THE UNITED ARAB REPUBLIC

Meanwhile the hope of uniting Syria and Egypt germinated. In 1956 Syria appointed a committee to negotiate a federal union with Egypt, and the various steps toward the union's consummation were outlined. To drown all possible opposition in a bath of emotional nationalism, conspiracies jeopardizing national integrity were unearthed and ordinary frontier incidents involving opium smugglers and cattle rustlers along the Turkish border were magnified into crises. Turkish acts of aggression were imputed to the machinations of Western imperialists.

The resulting tension not only silenced internal opposition but also served as a screen for the arrival of Egyptian troops to forestall a likely coup d'état of the 1949 variety. The insubstantiality of the crisis was disclosed, but the Egyptian regiments remained in Syria. In February 1958, the union was officially declared by the Syrian government and Nasser, though Nasser was somewhat cool to the haste in which the union was effected. A few days following the announcement, Khalid Baqdash, leader of the Arab Communist party, left Damascus with his family for Moscow. There was also considerable flight of capital to Beirut. Nasser became president and al-Kuwatli vice president of the United Arab Republic, which was divided into two regions, Egypt and Syria.

To effect the union of two sovereign states has always been a most difficult, perplexing, and sometimes painful experience. In the case of Egypt and Syria, with no common frontier, separated by nearly 600 miles (966 kilometers), and with such disparate economies and social customs, it was a daring step but one that had to be rigorously enforced. In a few weeks Syrian foreign affairs were thoroughly submerged by Egyptian policies. Nasser as president of the United Arab Republic directed all activities and appointed all officials. Trade and economic measures were to conform as soon as possible, and in each case Egyptian patterns were to be imposed upon Syria. Unity in other matters moved more deliberately. Budgets, finances, and currency were to remain separate for at least five years. Egypt's austere economy of the post-Sinai War period was imposed on Syria, and all imports were rigidly licensed. Merchants grumbled and permits for expensive luxury goods were denied. Egyptian land reform ideas were extended to Syria.

All this might have been acceptable had there not been severe droughts and crop failures in 1958, 1959, and 1960. Syria's barley crop was wiped out in 1958, and there was only a 40 percent yield of wheat in 1959. Famine was avoided by shipments of grain from the United States in 1959 and 1960, all for nontransferable

Syrian pounds. Export trade with Lebanon, Syria's best customer, was shattered in part by the difficulties and border closing of 1958, in part by the shift to Soviet orientation and Egyptian controls, and in large part by the scarcity of commodities. Syria survived by receiving Egyptian budgetary support, aid from the United States, a credit from the International Monetary Fund, development loans from the U.S.S.R., and by having relatively normal cotton crops.

It was not possible politically to govern Syria like an Egyptian province. Nasser announced the appointment of the first United Arab Republic cabinet in March 1958 and named four vice presidents, two of them from Syria. Most regular cabinet posts had two heads, one for Syria and one for Egypt. All political parties in Syria were dissolved; political figures lost their power bases and found themselves isolated in Cairo or eased out of position, sometimes not so gently. With political parties and leaders gone and the Syrian army immobilized and demoralized by control from Cairo, real power in Syria fell to Colonel Abd al-Hamid Sarraj and his intelligence forces.

The major weakness of this arrangement was the lack of sufficient authority to crack heads together and get things done. To remedy this, Nasser in 1959 sent Field Marshal Abd al-Hakim Amer to Damascus as chief of government. The Syrian military resented his presence and looked to Colonel Sarraj as the leader of Syrian factions. A year later Sarraj assumed the chairmanship of the executive committee. As head of the executive, the police, and military intelligence Sarraj's position in Syria rivaled that of Nasser in Egypt.

In the economic field, the Rastan Dam on the Orontes River was completed in 1961, and the great Euphrates Valley Project, to cost nearly $300 million, was initiated. A dam was to be built to add to cultivation, avert disastrous floods, and produce enough electric power to satisfy the needs of the country for the foreseeable future.

The new social and economic forces at work in Syria freed the imaginations of Syrians who had been suffocated by politics since the end of World War I. However, the better-established groups and families involved in land, trade, finance, politics, and the army discovered that the union relegated them to less prominent positions and infringed upon many of their accustomed prerogatives. Land reform sapped their privileges and power; trade quotas, import licenses, and nationalization hampered their business opportunities; banks were nationalized or "Arabized"; and army officers were frustrated and divided by their loyalties to the uncertain power of Field Marshal Amer and the clandestine intelligence apparatus of Colonel Sarraj.

Acute rivalry and controversy between these two officers quietly waxed through 1961. In Damascus Sarraj called together all governors and important officials to outline future steps in the growth of Syria and to receive their loyalty to him. Amer objected violently; Nasser called them to Cairo to settle the dispute. Sarraj evidently got the worse of it for he resigned his vice presidency and returned to Damascus. However, with both Amer and Sarraj absent for nearly a week, the army, banding together with all the dissident groups, staged a successful coup on September 28, 1961. Nasser's first reaction was to order purely Egyptian cadres of the army to seize the rebels, naval units to occupy Latakia, and paratroopers to drop on Damascus. Informed that these would be unsuccessful, he declared the next day that Arab should not fight Arab and recognized the fait accompli. A month later the Syrian Arab Republic was by unanimous vote readmitted to the Arab League.

THE SYRIAN ARAB REPUBLIC

Perhaps if Nasser had granted regional autonomy to Syria within the United Arab Republic, Syrian nationalism and pride would not have been so outraged at being ruled by Egyptians. Syrian officers resented their second-rate positions, and the stifling of political activity was more than the Ba'th party leaders had bargained for. The military council placed a civilian group at the head of the government. It pledged to reverse the nationalization process launched that spring and to reestablish a free economy although it declared that the land reform measures would stand. (Land reform did, in fact, continue, and by 1972 about 40 percent of the total land under cultivation had been redistributed to about one-fourth of all the farm families.) Activity on the part of political parties was prohibited. Amer escaped to Egypt the morning of the coup and Sarraj was arrested and imprisoned four days later. Syria was readmitted to the United Nations.

National elections were held for a parliamentary body that would serve until the constitution was readied. Moderate conservatives held a majority in this body. However, officers of the armed forces overthrew the government on March 28, 1962. Four days later there was a countercoup in Aleppo by officers who appealed to Nasser for intervention. The army resolved the impasse: President Nazim al-Kudsi resumed his office, the rebellious officers left Syria, and a new cabinet ordered some renationalization.

Every successive coup made the government weaker and more imperious and deepened the rifts within the body politic. The Ba'th party with each change profited from its better organization and from its well-defined and articulated objectives. Ba'th ("Renaissance") developed during World War II by Michel Aflaq, a French-educated Christian Arab, and Salah al-Bitar, a Sunnite Muslim; it stressed nationalism, unity, and socialism as the three forces Arab society should embrace in order to rejuvenate the Arab world. Most of the Ba'th party members were students, educators, professionals, civil servants, and soldiers. Among the latter, persons from the provinces and from the Muslim religious minorities were especially numerous; they welcomed the secular ideology of the party.

The Ba'th's main opposition was lodged in the pro-Nasser elements of the army and among those who believed that only under his leadership could the cherished dream of Arab unity be achieved. Nasserite and Ba'thist ministers in the cabinet quarreled repeatedly, and when a Ba'thist coup in Baghdad on February 8, 1963, took place, a similar blow was expected in Damascus. It came on March 8. This important revolution subsequently established the Ba'th party's army officers as the new ruling elite in Syria. The Sunnite large landowners and merchants were replaced as the ruling class by the sons of the lower middle class and the sons of peasants. These army officers were young, locally educated, and most of them were Alawite Shiites.

Salah al-Bitar became prime minister and he announced on March 14 that steps were being taken to form a tripartite union with Iraq and Egypt. Conferences were held in Cairo and, with much fanfare, on April 17 a charter uniting the three states was proclaimed. It was dead, however, before it was published, because Syria and Iraq insisted upon equal votes whereas Nasser demanded that voting should depend upon population, probably because Egypt's population was greater than that of the other two combined.

Real power in Syria was held by General Amin al-Hafiz, a staunch moderate Ba'thist who alternated with al-Bitar as prime minister until they were ousted by a radical left-wing branch of the Ba'th party on February 23, 1966. As long as the Ba'thists dominated the government in Iraq the two states cooperated in many affairs, and the pan-Arab executive of the Ba'thist party directed policies. Syria sent 5,000 soldiers to help Iraq quell Kurdish revolts; in 1963 an Iraqi-Syrian Supreme Defense Council was created. Syria also joined with Lebanon, Jordan, and Egypt in plans for diverting water from the Banyas River to the Yarmuk and thence to Jordan. Nationalization, industrialization, and economic development proceeded rapidly. In 1965 al-Hafiz nationalized all major manufacturing and processing plants, public utilities, domestic and foreign oil companies, and many export-import firms. But al-Hafiz was too conservative for some, too radical for others, too cool toward Nasser, or too friendly.

In early 1966 General Salah Jadid and the extreme army wing of the Ba'th party arrested and imprisoned the moderates. Jadid became the chief executive of the party and chairman of the National Revolutionary Council; Nur al-Din al-Atasi, chief of state; and General Hafiz al-Assad (born 1930), minister of defense. Jadid and al-Assad were members of the Alawite Muslim minority group of north Syria, a group numbering about one-eighth of the total population of Syria.

This faction declared that it wanted to maintain a "permanent struggle" on all fronts, and coupled Nasser with "traitors in the Arab world" who compromised with imperialism and reaction. The new regime sought aid from the Soviet bloc countries. The arrangement with West Germany for the Euphrates Dam was dropped, and in 1966 the U.S.S.R. granted $157 million for the first stage of the dam that would, it was hoped, double the cultivable area of Syria.

Border incidents on the Israeli frontier increased in number and seriousness in 1966, especially as action on the water-diversion plans commenced. In July Israel attacked in considerable force the earth-moving machinery employed and some of the foundations of the project. In January 1967 acts of violence became so numerous that the United Nations brought about a temporary cease-fire. Raids that included mine explosions and the shooting of Israeli soldiers and police were frequently carried out by members of al-Fatah, a society of Palestinians dedicated to the regaining of their homeland. Many units of this society were based in Syria, but raids often came from Lebanon or Jordan. In November 1966, Israel attacked and destroyed the village of al-Samu in Jordan to warn that al-Fatah raids should be stopped. Syria called for the deposing of King Husayn for not having prevented the raid or retaliating in like measure. A crisis flared in May 1967, when Syria believed that she had evidence that Israel was preparing an attack in such depth that even Damascus might fall. Sensing that this might be similar to the Israeli war on Suez in 1956, Syrian leaders called on Egypt and the other Arab states to make good on their pledges to come to her assistance and protection.

THE AFTERMATH OF THE JUNE 1967 WAR

When the Arab-Israeli War broke out on June 5, 1967, the main fighting occurred in Sinai and Jordan, and not until the fourth day did Syria feel the full brunt of the Israeli forces. By the time the cease-fire became effective Syria had lost the Golan (Jawlan) Heights above the Sea of Galilee and the Israeli army had occupied the city of al-Quneitra as tens of thousands of Syrians fled the area and became refugees in Syria. To regain the Golan Heights now became Syria's chief foreign policy goal. Despite the defeat General Jadid and General al-Assad retained their hold on government and party affairs.

Through 1969 and 1970 General al-Assad moved carefully into a position of dominance in the Ba'th party. Less concerned than Jadid with doctrinaire ideology, al-Assad stressed the Arab and nationalist aspects of Ba'th principles. He urged more cooperative ventures with Iraq and Egypt, pushed preparations for another war with Israel, but demanded greater independence from the U.S.S.R. At a stormy Ba'th party congress al-Assad took charge and arranged compromises favorable to his positions. Al-Assad was still only defense minister, but as "regional" (that is, Syrian) commander of the Ba'th party he was the most powerful person in the government.

Following a Ba'th party congress in October 1970, al-Atasi resigned as prime minister and al-Assad seized control in a bloodless coup. Hafiz al-Assad, now prime minister, at this time was about forty years old; he was born near Latakia, the son of a peasant. As an Alawite he had found an opportunity for education and advancement only in the military. As a leading officer and minister of defense he had visited the Soviet Union and many of the countries of Europe. Early in 1971, a constitutional change made the president the highest official of the state, and al-Assad was sworn into this office in March. He asserted he would return the Ba'th party to the masses. Michel Aflaq, one of the founders of the Ba'th, Amin al-Hafiz, and others were tried *in absentia* and given death sentences, which al-Assad commuted to life imprisonment.

A People's Council of 170 members was appointed: 85 Ba'thists, 12 Socialist Union Movement members; 12 Arab Socialist Unionists; 8 Arab Socialists; 8 Communists; and 45 representing trade unions, peasants, doctors, lawyers, artisans, and religious men. The new cabinet had members from several political parties, and in 1972 the regime was able to consummate a National Progressive Front. Only the Ba'th party, however, had the right to engage in political activity in the army!

The permanent constitution was approved by the council in March 1973. It stated that Syria was democratic and socialist, with sovereignty belonging to the people, and that laws were to be based on the shariah. The Ba'th was declared to be the leading political organization; the economy was socialist; personal and religious freedoms were supposedly guaranteed; the president, who dominated the whole government, was elected to seven-year terms; and the legislature was to consist of a National Assembly, with at least one-half of its members to be workers and peasants. In May 1973 elections the Ba'th party obtained 70 percent of the vote, and al-Assad was chosen president. The Ba'th party subsequently increased in size to around 150,000 members.

The defeat in the 1967 Arab-Israeli War and the loss of the Golan Heights did not greatly injure Syrian economic life. The destruction of war matériel was significant, however, and the influx of persons displaced from the Golan added to problems. Good crops during these years eased the situation considerably. The government in 1968 moved the first earth for the Euphrates Dam, which was intended to irrigate fertile lands and, with eight giant turbines, would create 800,000 kilowatts of electric power. As the first stage of the dam was completed in 1973, the dam made available irrigated land that proved very expensive to reclaim, and while later stages were finished, the Syrian government turned its attention toward more pragmatic and smaller-scale agricultural improvements. Once in use the dam also brought acute problems with Turkey and Iraq over amounts of water flow.

Al-Assad benefited from the beginnings of Syrian oil production. Largely on her own, Syria organized the General Petroleum Organization (GPO) to exploit oil resources discovered in the northeastern areas of the country. In 1968 oil began to flow and in the 1970s Syria was a net exporter of small amounts of oil. Syria was admitted to OAPEC in 1972. Prices for Syrian oil followed those of OPEC, but since Syria had developed the fields and brought the oil to market without the participation of the international oil companies, she found selling it difficult until 1973, when other producing nations began to dispose of their oil at auction.

In 1970 all large industrial firms that had not yet been nationalized were taken over. The economy, however, was not booming, for Syria was experiencing difficulties in selling oil, sagging cotton production, and trade deficits. A sweeping economic liberalization program was instituted; individuals were encouraged to participate in and stimulate the private sector of the economy.

Syria had broken diplomatic relations with the United States and several western European countries at the time of the June 1967 war, and they remained severed for a number of years. Lines to the U.S.S.R. were open and strengthened. Soviet arms shipments of all types continued to arrive and were the only source of weapons. The Soviet Union moved her Mediterranean fleet base from Egypt to Latakia in 1972, and transferred to Syria massive quantities of arms, including surface-to-air missiles.

The July 1968 coup in Baghdad placed Ba'thists unfriendly to the Syrian regime in control of Iraq. Baghdad began to give sanctuary to Syrian Ba'thists out of favor in Damascus, and al-Assad castigated the Iraq Ba'thists for murdering progressives. He worked in 1969 to establish a joint command among Syria, Iraq, and Jordan, but King Husayn's bloody contest with the Palestinians in 1970 and eviction of the PLO aborted the collaboration. Syrian tanks rushed to support the Palestinians but had to be recalled five days later when al-Assad refused them air support.

The Federation of Arab Republics, consisting of Egypt, Libya, and Syria, became an official body in September 1971, organized to coordinate policies and to merge at some distant future date.

The most immediate tasks facing al-Assad, however, were what to do with the Palestinians within his borders and how to regain the Golan area. When Syria had become a haven for Palestinian commando groups the Syrian army helped train one, al-Saiqah. The cease-fire line with Israel stayed relatively quiet until 1969 when air clashes occurred frequently with Israeli planes penetrating deeply. The first half of 1970 saw tank battles, massive air actions, and an Israeli attack on a Syrian army camp. Though al-Assad spurned a cease-fire the combat subsided considerably. Al-Assad then ruled that Palestinian groups must not involve Syria in their operations. Eventually he curbed al-Saiqah's independence and placed it under Syrian army control. Al-Assad may have been planning war with Israel, but he had no intention of giving al-Saiqah or any other body the opportunity to select the place or time.

THE ARAB-ISRAELI WAR OF OCTOBER 1973

In conjunction with Egypt, Syria launched a massive attack upon Israel on October 6, 1973. With more than 1,000 tanks, the Syrians crossed the Golan cease-fire line, captured Mt. Hermon, and encircled the town of al-Quneitra. Israel counterattacked, bombed key military and economic targets throughout Syria, and by October 10 had pushed to within twenty-five miles (forty kilometers) of Damascus, thereby going even further into Syrian territory than had been the case in the 1967 war. Egypt deserted Syria: before the war began their leaders had agreed to act jointly during the fighting, but Egypt's President Anwar al-Sadat withdrew from the war first. Israel destroyed a new electric power system, the oil refineries at Homs and Banyas, much of the port facilities at Latakia, and various industrial plants. The cost of war damage to Syria was set at $2.4 billion, but in this war, unlike 1948 and 1967, the Syrian armed forces performed very well, even though they were ultimately defeated.

Within two weeks after the beginning of the war immense quantities of arms and munitions were being airlifted to Syria from the Soviet Union. After a trip to Moscow by American Secretary of State Henry Kissinger, the two great powers forced a cease-fire upon the three belligerents on October 23, under the auspices of the U.N. Security Council.

In May 1974, Syria and Israel, acting through the United States, agreed to limited disengagement by the establishment of a U.N. neutral zone on the Golan Heights, which included giving to Syria the town of al-Quneitra and the area newly taken by Israel in the recent fighting. The U.N. force was to remain for six months, when a more permanent settlement was expected, but its mandate was renewed periodically by the United Nations and it continued on the Golan Heights indefinitely. Al-Assad's stand continued to be that Israel must give up all the lands Israel had taken in 1967. Israel extended its law to the Golan Heights of Syria in December 1981, thereby in effect annexing the region.

The longer President al-Assad retained power in the 1970s the more stable the economy became. Evidence of economic growth was everywhere. Oil exports grew, cotton crops were excellent, and trade with neighboring countries was improving. A generous five-year trade agreement with the Soviet Union was signed in 1976. Syria's gross national product jumped 25 percent between 1973 and 1975.

The shifting sands of Arab diplomacy, however, created a constant challenge for al-Assad. He denounced President Sadat after Egypt signed a disengagement pact with Israel in 1975. Al-Assad led the drive among the Arabs at Rabat to recognize the PLO as the sole legitimate representative of the Palestinians. Although at first he mildly favored Palestinian aspirations in Lebanon, by the spring of 1976 he began to understand that the victory of any faction in Lebanon could well be a hollow one. Al-Assad sent thousands of troops into Lebanon, and about 20,000 usually remained in that country permanently. Syria expended much of its wealth on subsequent developments in Lebanon and hundreds of thousands of Syrians who had been residing in that unhappy country had to return to their homes, increasing even more the financial burden of Syria. One of al-Assad's continuing concerns was to dominate Lebanon by a policy of divide and rule. Syria however took great care to avoid stationing Syrian forces close to the Israeli borders, fearing their presence in large numbers might invite a full-scale Israeli invasion. Even in 1978, during the Israeli incursion into south Lebanon, Syrian units were ordered not to confront the Israelis.

CONTINUITY IN THE 1980S

President al-Assad, his family, and the Alawite army officers retained their power into the 1980s, but their popularity has diminished as some of their policies seemed to fail. Pan-Arabism became only a fiction, as conflicts with Ba'thist Iraq and Syria's alliance with non-Arab Iran demonstrated. In Syria the Alawite minority control of all power increasingly alienated many in the Sunnite Muslim majority, and especially the fundamentalists among them. Elections in 1977 and in 1981 to the People's Assembly saw a low voter turnout. Many people within Syria accused the regime of corruption, oppression, and torture of prisoners. Assassinations of Alawite officials and military cadets led the government to attack Hama in 1982; in that central Syrian city a general insurrection by the fundamentalists was crushed as military forces caused many casualties.

Despite such opposition, al-Assad provided remarkable stability to Syria by ruling for such a long time in a country that had been famous for its political volatility. Al-Assad was reelected president in plebiscites held in 1978 and 1985, even though he was in bad health in the 1980s. There has been no clearly recognized principle of succession, and members of the president's family and entourage have on occasion intrigued against each other for positions in the military and security forces that would command power in the event of al-Assad's death or removal from office.

Much of the regime's energies continued to be devoted to foreign policy issues, especially Lebanon. The 1982 war with Israel in Lebanon saw a marked defeat of the Syrian armed forces, although they were soon resupplied by the Soviet

Union. The subsequent course of events in Lebanon brought Syria a victory of sorts: Israel and the United States withdrew; President Jumayyil at least temporarily accepted Syrian guidance; Syria occupied much of the country even including West Beirut; Syria's allies, such as the Amal groups, overcame their local foes; and the Syrian-backed faction within al-Fatah gained the upper hand in much of the northern part of Lebanon. Syria was predominant in chaotic Lebanon, but its troops and its economy paid a heavy price. Another less successful but very bitter rivalry for Syria was with the fellow Ba'thists who ruled Iraq. During the Iran-Iraq War beginning in 1980, Syria backed Iran despite all the claims of Arabism, socialism, and secularism that might have inclined it toward Iraq. Iran granted Syria oil—some free and some at special rates. This policy, plus Syrian closeness with Libya's erratic leader Mu'ammar al-Qadhdhafi, made Syria somewhat of an outcast among the Arab states. Syria was especially cool toward Egypt and Jordan, and al-Assad strongly opposed U.S. and Egyptian attempts to bring Jordan and the mainstream of the PLO into peace talks with Israel.

With the Soviet Union, on the other hand, Syria retained very close ties during the 1980s. The October 1980 treaty of friendship and cooperation was supplemented by Soviet shipment of arms and Soviet diplomatic support of Syria, all this despite Soviet feelings that Syria should settle its differences with Iraq and lessen its forward policy in Lebanon. Relations with the United States have usually been very tense, in part because of strong differences between the two countries in regard to Israel, the Palestinians, and Lebanon, but also because of Syrian involvement in kidnappings, hijackings, and bombings directed against American and other Western targets. In 1988, however, U.S. Secretary of State George Shultz carefully included Syria in his renewed drive for an Arab-Israeli peace conference. The United States hoped Syrian troops who entered West Beirut in February 1987 would eventually locate and help free American hostages being held there by pro-Iranian Lebanese Shiites.

Earlier trends in the economic and social areas have also continued into the 1980s in Syria. An example has been the growth of population and the concentration of persons in the cities. From 1945 to the early 1980s the population increased from 2.5 million to more than 9 million as the death rate fell, and half the people now lived in cities. New apartment buildings were everywhere, and new roads helped bring rural dwellers into the urbanized areas. This happened despite government efforts to encourage development of the small towns and villages by providing them with schools, electricity, and health care. Education increased remarkably; in the 1980s there were more than 2 million students at all levels, including those attending the four universities. Female students attended schools in record numbers and the status of women in public life changed rapidly under the Ba'th regime. Women played a prominent but not leading role in the party, the People's Assembly, commercial offices, and the professions.

In the general economy increasing world prices for cotton in the 1980s did not compensate Syria for the fall in the value of its oil, the chief export. Natural gas discoveries and increased exploitation of them provided a new source of income, but the Syrian balance of trade was negative.

Syria's obligations to the Soviet Union (perhaps as much as $15 billion), and to Iran, the World Bank, and various Western countries alarmingly increased in the 1980s. One source of help for the Syrian economy was foreign aid from the oil-rich Arab states such as Saudi Arabia, but this help was conditional on their approval of Syria's foreign policy. When Syria acted in ways these countries approved, as when Syria approved the November 1987 Arab summit meeting call for peace in the Iran-Iraq War, the Saudis and others would give money to Syria. On the other hand, when Syria broke from the Arab ranks, most of such aid would be frozen. A union with Libya in 1980, although only symbolic, secured financial aid from that source.

One cause of the economic downturn in the 1980s was the heavy continuing drain on the economy resulting from military expenditures which took one-half of the budget. As Syria sought military equality with Israel the Syrian people paid for it—electricity was rationed and shortages of food appeared in 1986. The army's size expanded, but the goals of security and regaining the Golan Heights seemed more distant than ever.

KINGDOM OF IRAQ

From the declaration of war against the Axis in January 1943 until the revolution of 1958, Iraq underwent twenty-one changes of prime minister, with thirteen different men holding the office. On six different occasions Nuri al-Said occupied it; and at all times he was the most powerful political leader in Iraq. When he was not prime minister, he served as minister of defense or from his seat in the senate pulled the strings to direct the policies followed by others.

In 1939, when King Ghazi was killed in an automobile accident at the age of twenty-seven, the throne had passed to his four-year-old son Faysal II. King Ghazi's cousin Abd al-Ilah became regent and heir to the throne. The authority of the palace was prescribed by the constitution; yet the regent's influence was felt in all quarters through the difficult years of World War II and the 1948 Arab-Israeli War. In 1953 King Faysal II reached his eighteenth year and nominally assumed full power.

The experience of the British with the Rashid Ali episode during World War II opened their eyes to the necessity of revamping their attitude toward Iraq. Iraqi leaders, indirectly encouraged by growing American interest in the area, pressed for a new treaty to replace the one of 1930. Negotiations led to the signing of an Anglo-Iraqi treaty at Portsmouth, England, in 1948, wherein Britain retained the right to send troops in case of war or threat of war. Almost immediately bitter riots broke out, and the regent declared that the new treaty did not "realize the national aims of Iraq." The treaty was never ratified, and the 1930 treaty remained in force until Britain joined the Baghdad Pact.

In 1947, Senator Nuri al-Said tried to bring about a union with Transjordan. In the end he settled for a treaty of friendship and brotherhood providing for mutual consultation in matters of foreign affairs. Although criticized in parliament, it was ratified in June and served as the basis for joint operations in the 1948 war. In 1947

Iraq protested the partition of Palestine and sent nearly 20,000 soldiers to fight alongside the Arab Legion of Transjordan.

Although the geographical position of Iraq precluded any appreciable number of Arab refugees from Palestine locating there, sympathy for them ran high. Iraqi officials declared they would not open any negotiations with Israel until the plight of the refugees was relieved. Ill feeling toward the Jews of Iraq mounted in proportion to the misery of the refugees and the general disillusionment over the war's outcome. In March 1950, a law was passed permitting Jews to renounce their Iraqi citizenship and their property, and in the following months thousands left for Israel. Before 1951 was out almost all of Iraq's Jews had left, creating a gap in the economy soon filled by an emerging Shiite middle class.

Frustration and unrest mushroomed in Iraq. This was especially true in Baghdad, whose population was expanding rapidly. In the countryside where the peasants were brutally oppressed and degraded by the landlords there was also widespread unhappiness with the regime. A few families owned most of the land: four-fifths of the population owned no land at all in 1958, while 2,500 people possessed one-half of all the arable land. Since the landlords were very influential in the parliaments, basic land reform was impossible. Other grievances included lack of full independence from Great Britain, the loss of the 1948 war, political corruption, nationalization of oil in Iran and the new 50-50 profit-sharing arrangement in Saudi Arabia, the high cost of living, poor harvests, and the disastrous annual flooding of sections of Baghdad. Grass roots participation in government was quite absent. Instead, elections for the chamber of deputies were usually managed by Nuri al-Said. All political parties were dissolved in 1952 and again in 1954. These moves were instigated to force parties to reapply for licenses, some of which might be denied. The Communist party remained underground and worked assiduously through other groups and parties. In Iraq the Communists found their following in the educated youth of the lower middle class in the large cities, in those who adhered to the Rashid Ali movement from 1935 to 1941, among Shiites and the religious minorities, and among some workers.

The lid was clamped on political disturbances in 1952, but professional politicians were frightened and realized that reforms of some kind had to be initiated. Fortunately, new financial resources were at hand. Oil production, because of a closedown in Iran, had been expanded; more important, the Iraq Petroleum Company agreed in 1952 to a new schedule of royalties, increasing them to 50 percent of the profits before taxes. The treaty was retroactive to 1951; as world petroleum requirements spurted, royalties mounted until in 1955 they were estimated at $250 million.

By a law passed in 1950, 70 percent of all oil royalties were devoted to economic development, especially flood control and irrigation projects on the Euphrates, the Tigris, and the Diyala rivers. Aided by a loan in 1950 from the International Bank, the development board began flood control and irrigation works at Samarra on the Tigris and at Ramadi on the Euphrates. Completed in 1956, the Samarra barrage prevented serious flooding in Baghdad in 1956, and the waters from the lake created made it possible to reclaim valuable land by irrigation.

Other programs cleared vast slum areas in Baghdad and built public-housing projects. Schools were extended to push down illiteracy rates and the University of Baghdad opened in 1957, but the peasants in the countryside remained illiterate. While many Shiites went to secular schools and some became integrated into Iraqi society on the national level, most Kurds remained untouched by the changes of the late 1940s and 1950s. Short-story writers, journalists, poets, painters, and other artists and intellectuals strongly criticized the regime and described the plight of the poor. Despite this opposition, many Sunnite Iraqi leaders saw in the future a great and prosperous Iraq, if there was internal peace and no attacks from the Soviet bloc. Others were extremely impatient and believed that the government of Nuri al-Said moved too slowly, too inefficiently, and too indifferently to achieve a better life for Iraqis.

Because of the proximity of the U.S.S.R. Iraqi leaders had a discerning respect and fear of Russian power. In 1955, Iraq signed the so-called Baghdad Pact with Turkey. In general, this pact repeated the terms of the earlier treaty of friendship, but it added military cooperation and coordination. Britain adhered to the pact by signing an important agreement with Iraq. Among other things, this agreement wiped out the treaty of 1930, provided for Britain to evacuate her troops and air force, and gave fuller sovereignty and independence to Iraq. An improvement over the draft treaty of 1947, this instrument brought Britain into the Baghdad Pact and gave Iraq her wishes. Soon Iran and Pakistan joined the Baghdad Pact, making a chain of allied states separating the Soviet bloc from the strategic areas of the Middle East. Although the United States did not join the pact, she sent military missions to the area, provided military equipment for member states, and affiliated officially with the pact's military and economic committees.

Egypt viewed the Baghdad Pact as a threat to her control over the Arab League and her leadership in the Arab world. Nuri al-Said was accused of being the tool of Great Britain and restoring colonial status to Iraq. Iraqis who were Arab nationalists or who favored neutrality in the cold war between the United States and the Soviet Union strongly opposed the Baghdad Pact. Calling Nasser a dictator and declaring that the Baghdad Pact was Iraq's concern, Nuri al-Said held firm to his course. He was confident that peace and security from fears of Russia, as well as economic development, a higher standard of living, and a cultural and social renaissance would create in Iraq a life and society to parallel the modern rejuvenation of Turkey combined with the medieval splendor and wealth of the days of Harun al-Rashid.

Although Nasser was regarded as his rival for leadership in the Arab world, Nuri al-Said stated that Western threats of force when Nasser nationalized the Canal violated the United Nations Charter. When Israel, France, and England invaded Egypt in 1956, Iraq was in an embarrassing position. Her army, poised on the Jordanian border to counter an Israeli military buildup, entered Jordan; and she broke diplomatic relations with France. There was great clamor in Baghdad against Great Britain, and from November 1956 to March 1957 Iraqi officials boycotted meetings of the Baghdad Pact in which Britain was represented. Syria complained so insistently over the presence of Iraqi troops in Jordan that they were recalled. A semblance of normalcy was not attained until March 1957, when the oil pipelines in Syria were repaired.

As the United Arab Republic began to form, political tension in Baghdad mounted. The possibility of a union between Iraq and Jordan had been discussed for many years, and the annexing of Jordan had been openly proposed in 1956. The union of Syria and Egypt forced the issue in Jordan. In February 1958 Iraq's King Faysal went to Amman, and after visits there by Nuri al-Said and Crown Prince Abd al-Ilah, the real power in Iraq, an Arab federation of Iraq and Jordan was proclaimed. King Faysal was recognized as chief of state and King Husayn as second in leadership. Defense, foreign affairs, finance, and education were consolidated, but the treaties, laws, budgets, and local administrations of each state retained their validity and were not binding upon the other. In March a federal council was named and a constitution was drafted and proclaimed. In Iraq Nuri al-Said resumed the post of prime minister.

Upon hearing the news Nasser congratulated the two kings; in a few weeks, however, his remarks turned into condemnations and open invitations to Arab nationalists in each state to remove the kings, by assassination if necessary.

REPUBLIC OF IRAQ

Iraqi troops were ordered in July to march into Jordan to be ready to safeguard the Hashimite monarchy there. But the Iraqi commander, General Abd al-Karim Qasim, in a swift coup d'état on July 14, 1958, overthrew the king and Nuri al-Said, both of whom were massacred in the revolution. Mobs in Baghdad became delirious with excitement. Order, however, was quickly attained.

General Qasim proclaimed the Republic of Iraq and became prime minister of the state. Oil production did not stop; the pipelines were undamaged. Neutrality was pronounced the policy of the state. Qasim declared that Iraq would honor her international obligations, and did not formally resign from the Baghdad Pact. When King Husayn of Jordan announced he was assuming the position of chief of state of the Arab federation, Qasim renounced the union.

The completeness of the revolution and its full acceptance by the general populace throughout the state amazed only those unfamiliar with Iraq's social and national conditions. Nuri al-Said was thoroughly disliked and the crown prince was hated. The same government had been in power too long and had failed to satisfy the aspirations of the majority. Land reform, poverty, and the low standard of living, Israel, social advances for the urban masses, and the depressed state of the educated middle class were but a few of the problems the people of Iraq felt pressing upon them, and the belief was widespread that Nuri al-Said and the Hashimites had not tried to cope with them adequately.

In the minds of the populace the old regime had built too many palaces and had allocated too much of the oil royalties to dams and less useful capital works. Many of these were still in the construction stage and their returns were yet to be enjoyed by the public. General Qasim announced that a new development board would receive 50 percent of the royalties and would work to establish Iraq as a welfare state based on practical socialism. Under a five-year agricultural program, holdings would be expropriated and distributed to landless peasants. The actual effect of this program was that much land was confiscated but uncertainty over distribution meant relatively few peasants had benefited by 1963, while agricultural production sharply declined. Tribesmen were placed under the same law codes as other Iraqi citizens, women received greater rights, and spending on education doubled.

Coming so soon after the birth of the United Arab Republic, General Qasim's revolution in the same year raised expectations of an immediate fulfillment of Arab unity by joining Iraq to Egypt and Syria. Colonel Abd al-Salam Muhammad Arif, second in rank among the revolutionaries and assistant commander in chief of the armed forces, led the group that soon came to be called Nasserites. Watching the trend in Syria, Qasim and other leaders, however, had no desire to be puppets of Cairo. The fundamental Iraqi nationalism of these leaders forced Qasim to dismiss Arif as deputy prime minister and to designate him as ambassador to West Germany. A revolt by his regiment was crushed, and he was arrested on the charge of having attempted to murder Qasim. At a trial in 1959, he was found guilty and sentenced to death; at a later date the death sentence was lifted.

Until Qasim was overthrown and executed in a coup in 1963, his primarily Sunnite regime was constantly beset by a three-way struggle among Communists and pro-Communists on one side, Nasserite pan-Arab nationalists on another, and Iraqi Ba'thists on the third. There was street fighting in Baghdad at the slightest provocation. In 1959, a revolt broke out in Mosul led by the anti-Communist army officers and pan-Arabists. Blaming the United Arab Republic for plotting it, the army loyal to Qasim crushed the revolt with the aid of Kurdish forces. Qasim increasingly turned to the Communists for support.

In 1961 Qasim laid claim to Kuwayt. Because of the return of British forces and the quick adverse reaction by other Arab states, Qasim did not press this claim. Iraq walked out of the Arab League meeting that admitted Kuwayt to membership, and broke relations with states recognizing her independence. Qasim generally remained isolated from other Arab states, but became much more friendly with the Soviet Union, Iraq's chief source of weapons.

Iraq had had persistent difficulties with the Kurds in northern Iraq since the end of World War I. The Kurdish tribes wanted independence or at least autonomy in a federalized or decentralized Iraq. The British and Nuri al-Said discussed, negotiated, fought, and left the Kurdish problem unsolved. Under the leadership of Mulla Mustafa Barzani, Kurdish resistance increased in 1961. Although temporarily subdued, it exploded in 1962 into a full-scale revolt, placing all of northeastern Iraq, except for the cities and towns, entirely in Kurdish hands. Because major oil resources of the state were in this region the government was unwilling to tolerate secession or total local control. The army had attempted to subdue the Kurdish provinces but had never succeeded. Each time a government in Baghdad hinted at some accommodation with Barzani the generals showed their disaffection. The people in Basrah and Baghdad, on the other hand, chafed at the continuing conflict and the percentage of the national budget consumed in the struggle.

Added to the factionalism brought by Nasserism, communism, and Iraqi nationalism, the Kurdish dilemma set the stage for a successful Ba'th party coup on February 8, 1963. Qasim lacked charisma; he had been unable to articulate an appealing ideology. Iraqi Ba'thists, who were dominated by the pan-Arab executive of the Ba'th party, mostly from Damascus, engineered the coup in collaboration with the army, immediately organized a Revolutionary Command Council, and executed Qasim. Colonel Arif was appointed president and General Ahmad Hasan al-Bakr became prime minister. A roundup of Communists and subsequent murder of hundreds of them indicated the nationalist orientation and ruthlessness of the Ba'thists. From his redoubt in the north Barzani welcomed the Ba'th coup. Little changed, though. The new regime, pressed by the soldiers, resumed Qasim's campaigns, remaining at odds with the Kurds, the Communists, and Nasser. The Ba'th leaders canceled ambitious development plans as being ineffective and drew up their own.

The U.S.S.R. protested vigorously to Prime Minister al-Bakr about the treatment that Communists were receiving from the Ba'thists, and Nasser began to assail the Baghdad regime for treachery to the Arab cause. In May most of the non-Ba'thists were ejected from the cabinet and a small Nasserite revolt was broken ruthlessly while talks for complete economic union with Syria were in progress. The problems facing Baghdad and the continuous discussion within the Ba'th hierarchy deterred unanimity of purpose. By autumn Iraqi nationalists in Ba'thist circles resented the domination of the Syrian Ba'thists in every policy dispute. In November 1963, all non-Iraqis were forced out of positions of influence, and President Arif assumed power. Two months later Arif removed all extreme Ba'thists from office and went on to form his own political group. A Ba'thist coup in 1964 was foiled while cabinet shifts added Nasserites.

The government nationalized all banks, insurance companies, and some industries. It also gained control of imports. Iraq turned toward state planning and direction of the economy.

From 1963 to 1968 Iraq was under the personal rule of one or another of the Arab Sunnite Arif brothers. When Abd al-Salam Muhammad Arif lost his life in a helicopter crash on April 13, 1966, his elder brother, General Abd al-Rahman Arif, was elected president, and carried on with the same fundamental program and political orientation.

From the time the Ba'thists established themselves in Baghdad, Barzani had refused to bargain for anything short of Kurdish autonomy and a statement in Iraq's constitution that "Iraq is a federative state of Arabs and Kurds." With the inability of the first Arif to meet this condition Barzani asserted *de facto* autonomy for Iraqi Kurdistan and established a parliament and a legislative supreme revolutionary council. The fighting continued, and in 1966 the second Arif launched an offensive with 65,000 troops and coordinated heavy bombing by the air force. The offensive failed, and the Kurdish forces (with help from Iran) scored some notable victories over the Iraqi armies. For many months Iraq's prime minister had been advocating a moderate stand on Kurdish rights; when the military approach failed again, as he had predicted, he announced that the government was prepared to recognize "Kurdish nationality, language, and tradition." Kurdish delegates were received in Baghdad and a twelve-point program for the Kurds was announced. Among other things, it promised general amnesty for Kurdish rebels; recognition of Kurdish cultural and political autonomy; decentralization of the government; proportionate Kurdish representation in the cabinet, the army command, and the diplomatic corps; economic redevelopment in the north; and the appointment of Kurdish officials in Kurdish areas. Barzani accepted these proposals, but pan-Arabs and the army were so incensed at the implied surrender to the Kurds that President Arif was pressed into appointing a general as prime minister.

The following spring students at Baghdad University went on strike, criticizing Arif for ineffectual leadership and accusing the prime minister and others of incompetence and corruption. They demanded immediate elections and a constitutional regime. Even retired army officers joined the protests. Arif refused to comply, and on July 17, 1968, was removed by a coup and packed off to London.

Inter-Arab relations, particularly those with Cairo, always had been difficult for Iraqi leaders. When Colonel Arif was first in command under Qasim, he was ousted for being too pro-Nasser. As a figurehead in 1963, President Arif showed no public inclination toward Egypt. When he became president in his own right, he approached Nasser for a reconciliation and made cabinet shifts to bring in more Nasserites. Most of these resigned in 1963, charging Arif and his ministers with being dilatory in implementing Arab socialism and in effecting a union with the United Arab Republic. At the onset of the 1967 Arab-Israeli crisis Arif sent 30,000 Iraqi troops to Jordan, to reinforce and encourage King Husayn to take a firmer posture toward Israel and the Western powers. Arif maintained a middle course in the debates of the Arab summit meetings at Khartoum. As it turned out, Nuri al-Said, Qasim, and the two Arifs all experienced similar problems with other Arab states in the period after World War II.

BA'THIST RULE IN THE 1970S

The July 1968 coup was plotted by a group of young, secularist, Arab nationalist army officers in collaboration with the right wing of the Ba'thist party. They coalesced temporarily under a group of leaders called the Revolutionary Command Council (RCC). Controlled by the Ba'th, it named General Ahmad Hasan al-Bakr president, prime minister, and commander in chief of the armed forces. Restrictions against Communists were relaxed; a wave of political arrests followed; and a new provisional constitution was promulgated giving all power to the RCC.

Political existence was so dangerous for the new rulers that they constantly saw themselves confronted by spies, saboteurs, and plotters. In the first eight months of 1969 at least six public hangings occurred, in which fifty-four people were executed for spying for the United States, Israel, or Iran, or for seeking to overturn the administration. Arrayed against the regime were conservative forces on one side and ardent Communists and left-wing Ba'thists supported by Syria on the other. In addition, the Kurds in the north constantly were fighting for full local autonomy, while Shiites in the south sought religious support from the ulema in Iran. Although the Shiites of Iraq were a majority of the population, no Shiite served on the RCC from 1968 to 1977, and even thereafter real power was entirely in the hands of Sunnite Arab Ba'thists.

In the late 1960s a new strong man appeared, Saddam Husayn al-Takriti (born 1937), an Arab Sunnite, who became assistant secretary-general of the Ba'th party, vice-chairman of the RCC, and vice president of Iraq. There were constant rumors that al-Bakr was not well, and it was clear that Saddam Husayn was gradually gaining more and more control of the government and party. The political clout of the military wing of the Ba'th party ebbed rapidly. For the next several years there were no major challenges to the Ba'th party's power.

Since the end of World War II the economy of Iraq had been linked to oil. Under al-Bakr and the restored Ba'thist rule the importance of oil to the general economy increased in the 1970s. With royalties and taxes raised from 50 to 55 percent, Iraq garnered substantial oil income: $914 million in 1971. And with Czechoslovakia building and financing a refinery near Basrah, Hungarians and INOC drilling new wells, and the strength of OPEC, Iraqis harbored justifiable expectations of swelling treasury receipts.

Following OPEC policy, Iraq's oil minister in 1971 demanded acquisition of 20 percent of IPC and received an affirmative reply early in 1972. However, a cut in IPC production during the first half of 1972 led to bitter arguments, and Iraq nationalized IPC on June 1, 1972. After nine months of bargaining, an agreement was reached whereby IPC would pay Iraq $367 million in back taxes and arrears on royalties, Iraq contracted to deliver to IPC at Mediterranean terminals 50 million barrels of crude in 1973 and 60 million in 1974, IPC waived all claims on the North Rumayla fields and agreed to increase production in the Basrah field. New oil fields were discovered near Baghdad in 1975, and the Basrah Petroleum Company was fully nationalized. Volume continued to mount, bringing in unbelievable sums—$9.25 billion in 1976. An oil pipeline from the Kirkuk area northward and then across Turkey to a terminal near Iskenderun was completed in 1977, and its capacity was increased between 1980 and 1984. With the pipeline to Fao it gave Iraq outlets on the Persian Gulf and through Turkey, Syria, and Lebanon, assuring her multiple access to world markets. As oil wealth mounted, inflation increased and Iraq brought in hundreds of thousands of foreign workers, especially Egyptians. Oil production in 1979 grew to more than 3 million barrels per day and oil revenues rose to about $30 billion.

Iraq's other economic concern, after petroleum, was agriculture. Under Nuri al-Said great emphasis was laid on irrigation projects and dams, since a large majority of the population won its livelihood from the land. Though the new regimes were more concerned with finding income for the inhabitants of the teeming slums of Baghdad, the several five-year plans also carried development programs for irrigation. In 1971 the World Bank lent $27.5 million and the U.S.S.R. advanced $20 million to dig and equip the twenty-five mile Tharthar Canal, which linked the Tigris River to the Euphrates and channeled surplus water to irrigate central Iraq. With the completion in 1973 of Syria's Euphrates Dam, peasants in Iraq began to grumble about low water levels; in 1975 70 percent of the winter crops were ruined, cultivation in some areas being reduced to 4 percent of normal. Iraq stepped up her schedule for the great dam being built on the Euphrates near Haditha. Begun in 1966, largely under the supervision of Soviet engineers, its cost was estimated at $709.8 million. It was supposed to supply 80 percent of the irrigation and industrial needs of the region, and electric power produced from the dam would exceed 1.5 billion kilowatts annually. Salinization annually created new problems as land was lost to farmers; reclaiming land formerly farmed became a major priority of the agricultural sector.

Land reforms by the late 1970s had led to the government farming one-third of the land. The Ba'th party initially encouraged both the formation of collectives, along the model of Soviet agriculture, and also state cooperatives, with a greater degree of peasant rights. In the 1980s collectives were nearly abolished as inefficient.

The regime also greatly expanded the educational system as the number of students more than doubled between 1968 and 1983. About one-third of the students were women. Urban areas grew rapidly in population since their standard of living was higher than in rural districts. By 1965 a majority of the people lived in cities, and by 1981 more than two-thirds of Iraqis dwelled there. Baghdad's population swelled to more than 4 million, about one-quarter of the population of the whole country.

The Kurds continued to press for independence. Mustafa Barzani led sporadic military actions in 1969, often against IPC installations at Kirkuk. In the autumn Baghdad launched a full-scale military campaign against Barzani. In 1970 al-Bakr guaranteed that Kurdistan within the Iraqi state would become an autonomous area where Kurdish would be the official language and that in Iraq as a whole Kurds would enjoy proper proportional representation in the army, the civil service, the national legislature, and the cabinet, including a Kurdish vice president. Five months later Barzani accused the government of inaction and bad faith. Serious fighting resumed and lasted until 1974. The leftist Kurdish Revolutionary party, which fought with the Ba'th against Barzani, merged with the Kurdish Democratic party to form an alliance with the Ba'th to counter Barzani. Barzani's forces maintained a stout resistance, supplied with arms and funds from Iran, Israel, and the CIA. The detente arranged in 1975 between Iran and Iraq spelled disaster for the Kurds. Iran abandoned them and drove out most of the 100,000 Kurds who had fled to Iran as refugees, while the Iraqi army mounted an offensive that killed many Kurds and gave Baghdad control of the areas of the north. The government uprooted thousands of Kurds from their homes and scattered and transplanted them in the south.

Relations with Iran during most of the period after 1968 had been bad. Besides the Kurdish irritant, the two states quarreled over the Shatt al-Arab and the Persian Gulf. Iraq refused to renegotiate the 1937 treaty, insisting in 1969 that Iranian ships using the Shatt strike their colors and not carry Iranian navy personnel. The Iranian ambassador was expelled from Baghdad in 1970; the next year diplomatic relations were cut when Iran occupied Abu Musa and the Tunb Islands. Over the years numerous Iranians had visited the Shiite pilgrimage holy places in Iraq, many residing indefinitely. In 1972 more than 60,000 pilgrims were deported to Iran, causing a horrendous uproar. At last, in March 1975, at an OPEC meeting in Algiers, the shah and Saddam struck a reconciliation. In a formal treaty of detente signed in June in Baghdad, Iraq relinquished exclusive control of the Shatt and the shah deserted the Kurds. Subsequently, Iraq consented to visits by 12,000 Iranians a year to the Muslim shrines in Iraq.

The regime acted to enhance relations with the U.S.S.R., which generally supported Iraqi interests and policies and supplied large loans for the Euphrates Dam and other undertakings. When a fifteen-year treaty of friendship was signed in April 1972, a number of Arab states objected and likened the treaty to Nuri al-Said's Baghdad Pact. Iraq offered Basrah as a port for Soviet warships, and that summer the U.S.S.R. sent a naval squadron on an official visit to Umm Qasr, where it was agreed that the Soviet navy would have priority bunkering and resupply rights.

Iraq took a very hard line position against Israel and against any Arab state that might be willing to compromise with her. In the 1973 war Iraq sent an armored division to help Syria, but the hostility and rivalry between Iraqi Ba'thists and Syrian Ba'thists was so extreme that Iraq quickly withdrew its forces after the end of the fighting. In following years Iraq helped the Palestinian cause by financial and diplomatic support. When it appeared in 1981 that Iraq might be altering a civilian nuclear power plant near Baghdad for the production of fissionable material to produce a nuclear weapon, Israel bombed the Iraqi reactor. Saddam Husayn denounced the Egyptian-Israeli Peace Treaty of 1979, but in 1987 Iraq reestablished diplomatic relations with Egypt since Egypt was aiding Iraq in its war against Iran.

SADDAM HUSAYN AND THE WAR WITH IRAN

President al-Bakr resigned on July 16, 1979, and he was immediately succeeded by Saddam Husayn, who also became chairman of the Revolutionary Command Council, secretary-general of the Ba'th party regional (Iraq) command, and head of the armed forces. Saddam Husayn then conveniently discovered a plot which made it necessary for him to execute his chief rivals and consolidate all power in his own hands. A personality cult centered around Saddam Husayn made his image familiar to all Iraqis, while a semblance of democracy was created. After a lapse of twenty-two years an Iraqi parliament met once again: the National Assembly was first elected in June 1980. It included a substantial Shiite as well as female membership. New elections took place in 1984. The Assembly, however, lacked any substantial power and was completely subordinate to Saddam Husayn and the Ba'th party. The latter group grew in size in the 1980s and was put in charge of all the key positions in trade unions, the schools, and the government. The party even had its own militia, a counterbalance to the regular armed forces.

Opponents were ruthlessly persecuted by the internal security forces, who executed a large number of persons in the 1980s. The government secretly killed the Iraqi Shiite religious leader Baqir al-Sadr, and the Ba'th militia destroyed an underground pro-Iranian fundamentalist organization. The regime also used the carrot as well as the stick—the government built roads, schools, and refurbished mosques in Shiite southern Iraq and in Kurdish northern Iraq, while it also subsidized Shiite and Kurdish leaders who would cooperate with the Ba'thists. Saddam Husayn appointed more Shiites to the RCC in 1982. Kurdish nationalists became divided after the death of Mustafa Barzani in 1979 as they split along various ideological and leadership lines. By 1980 the Iraqi rulers seemed in complete political, economic, and military control of that once chaotic country.

This optimistic evaluation by Saddam Husayn led him to invade Iran, a grave decision whose repercussions affected all aspects of Iraqi history in the 1980s. The causes and course of the war were more fully discussed in Chapter 39; the most important events included the outbreak of hostilities, the initial Iraqi successes, a period of stalemate followed by Iranian advances, and then Iraqi counterattacks as international involvement in the conflict increased.

Saddam Husayn chose to attack Iran in 1980 chiefly to advance his own desired prestige as leader of the Arab world, to crush any danger posed to his leadership of Iraq by Iranian fundamentalists, and to win a definitive victory on the border question. By March 1981 Iraq had seized much of southwestern Iran but Iraq had many limitations that subsequently gave Iran an advantage in the fighting. These included Iraq's smaller population; limits placed on Iraqi exports of oil by Syrian and Iranian actions; the surprising strength of the Iranian government, despite its internal struggle for power, a struggle ultimately won by people who seemed incapable of compromise; and most importantly, the fact that while Iraq was unable to ever conquer and hold all of Iran, Iran could aspire to conquer at least southern Iraq and possibly even take Baghdad. Iraq had some advantages in the war, including its superior armaments. Once Iran invaded Iraq in many areas in 1984, Arab Iraqis, both Sunnites and Shiites, fought with great enthusiasm for their country, putting nationalism ahead of religion.

Iraq tried to stop Iran's oil flow and thereby severely injure Iranian ability to fight. Iraq repeatedly bombed Iranian ports, refineries, and vessels, and Iraq also tried to destroy foreign vessels carrying Iranian oil. While pursuing this course of action Iraq accidentally attacked an American war vessel, the frigate *Stark,* in May 1987, killing 37 American sailors. Iran stopped the export of Iraqi oil through the Persian Gulf, but Iraq did export its petroleum through the Turkish pipeline. Saddam Husayn was given billions of dollars of aid by Saudi Arabia, Kuwayt, and other Arab countries, but Iraq's economy slowed down as it proved impossible to pay for the war and maintain regular civilian expenditures at the same time. From 1981 through 1985 Iraqi oil production averaged slightly more than 1 million barrels per day and income from oil was about $10 billion per year. OPEC excluded Iraq from its oil production quotas in 1986, thereby allowing her to produce as much oil as she could. Iraq opened a second pipeline through Turkey in August 1987.

In 1983, nonessential imports were barred, austerity measures taken, and debt repayments to European countries rescheduled. A shortage of civilian workers led to the employment of women in greater numbers. In 1987 the regime reorganized the state-owned sector of the economy and increased the role of private entrepreneurs in industry. Iraq also turned ever more to the Soviet Union for help, although Iraq did reestablish full diplomatic relations with the United States in 1984, and received substantial direct or indirect assistance from Jordan, Egypt, and Turkey. France was her second most important source of weapons after Russia.

Iraq in 1985 and 1986 lost territory in the south to Iran, and Iran helped unite several Kurdish factions who then gained Iraqi territory in the mountainous north.

The military situation appeared desperate for Iraq, but Saddam Husayn persevered, and in 1988 his armed forces regained the Fao peninsula and the Majnun oil islands as well as some Kurdish districts. Iraq continued to be willing to accept a cease-fire, which Iran finally agreed to on July 18, 1988.

Saddam Husayn and the Ba'thists have sought to maintain their power through repression of opposition, great caution in the use of troops so as to decrease casualties, and seeking foreign allies—all this while welcoming the new change of policy and leadership in Iran. The end of the war may well determine the immediate future of Iraq and its government, but the most important long-range issues facing the country remain those of national integration of ethnic and religious groups in a diverse society.

THE ARAB LEAGUE

The notions of Arab unity, cooperation among Arab states, even one federated or national Arab country were not novel when Anthony Eden, British foreign minister, said in 1941 that Britain would give "full support to any scheme that commands general approval." In 1942 Nuri al-Said circulated his "Blue Book," which suggested the "reuniting" of Syria, Lebanon, Palestine, and Transjordan into one state (Syria) and the formation of an Arab League to include any Arab states that might desire to join. Egypt and Saudi Arabia were lukewarm, fearing the Greater Syria embodied in his idea. In 1944 a committee representing the Arab states, including Palestine, presented the Alexandria Protocol to the various Arab governments. In essence it was the draft charter of the Arab League. Following discussions within each Arab government, representatives of Iraq, Syria, Lebanon, Transjordan, Saudi Arabia, and Egypt signed the Arab League pact at Cairo in March 1945. Other members joined later: Yemen, 1945; Libya, 1953; Sudan, 1956; Morocco, 1958; Tunisia, 1958; Kuwayt, 1961; Algeria, 1962; South Yemen, 1967; Bahrayn, 1971; Qatar, 1971; Oman, 1971, United Arab Emirates, 1971; Mauritania, 1973; Somalia, 1974; Palestine Liberation Organization, 1976; and Jibuti, 1977. The pact provided for a council, composed of a representative of each member state, and a secretariat-general, whose permanent seat was to be in Cairo.

The purpose of the league was to seek cooperation of member states in economic, cultural, social, and health affairs, in communications, and in matters affecting nationality. It embodied a guarantee of the sovereignty of each member and a promise to respect the systems of government established in other member states and to abstain from any interference in internal affairs of other member states. No collective-security or mutual-defense articles were included in the pact; no separate defense arrangement developed until 1950, when a loosely constructed security pact was accepted.

The Arab states found in the league a promise of unity against the partition of Palestine and the birth of a Zionist state. In this connection six Arab rulers pledged their cooperation in opposing Zionist claims to Palestine. To implement the promise, the Arab League council in extraordinary session voted to send notes to Great

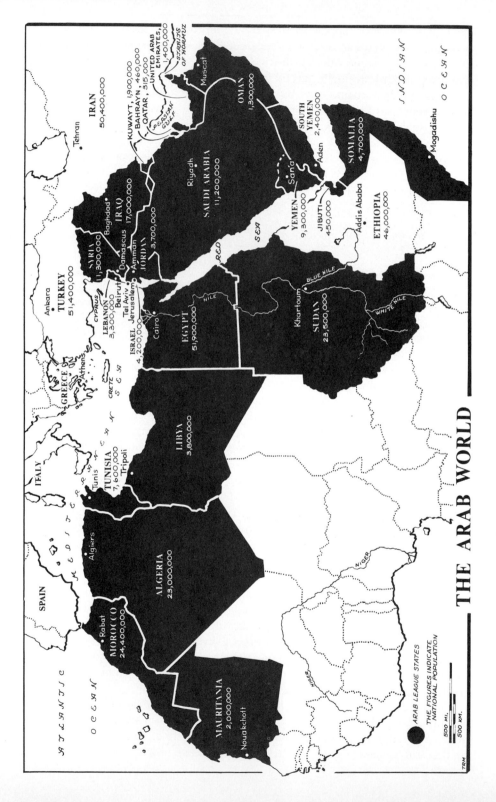

THE ARAB WORLD

Britain and the United States protesting the recommendations of the Anglo-American committee of inquiry.

Egypt, Saudi Arabia, and Iraq each wanted the Arab League based in her country. From the league's inception, however, Egypt had the upper hand. The league's second and longtime secretary-general was Abd al-Khaliq Hassunah, former Egyptian foreign minister. When the partition of Palestine became certain, the league urged its members to resist and later exhorted them to go to war against Israel. Saudi Arabia and Yemen, however, gave only token aid; Syria and Lebanon proved ineffective; and the Egyptian army was poorly equipped and mismanaged. Only Abd Allah's forces of Transjordan, the Arab Legion, and the Iraqi troops showed any capacity to fight, and only on their center front was there any success. Although each Arab state signed an accord that no part of Palestine would be annexed to another Arab state, none intended to uphold that agreement. Agents of the Arab League refused arms to other Arabs in Palestine if they were supporters of Arab families known to be inimical to Hajj Amin al-Husayni, the ex-mufti of Jerusalem who looked upon himself as the future ruler of Arab Palestine.

As defeat was experienced in Palestine, the Arab League declared that any member who made peace with Israel would be expelled. It also voted to oust Jordan, which annexed most of the remaining Arab portions of Palestine. In 1950 a treaty of joint defense and economic cooperation was inaugurated, obligating all to take up arms if any one became the victim of aggression. Actually designed to prevent the Fertile Crescent unity program, but purporting to strengthen the Arab states against Israel and satisfy the clamors of Arab nationalists in the streets, the treaty was signed by five states. Two more states, Iraq and Jordan, acceded to it in 1951 and 1952, respectively.

Beginning in 1950 the Arab League expanded its activities. An Economic Council was created to coordinate and unify economic policies, commerce, trade, and financial developments. An Arab common market consisting of Iraq, Jordan, Libya, Mauritania, Syria, and South Yemen (Egypt was suspended in 1979) eliminated mutual customs duties by 1971. It helped establish a number of joint ventures in such fields as cement manufacturing, pharmaceuticals, and leather industries, but political differences precluded full economic integration. In 1964, the league also set up an office in Brussels to serve as a liaison with the European Economic Community (EEC or Common Market). The EEC signed cooperation agreements with Egypt, Jordan, Lebanon, and Syria in 1977, and with the Yemen Arab Republic in 1984. Councils and federations for education, science, communications, public relations, labor, the practice of law, and aviation were also formed. Conferences and congresses were sponsored on a wide variety of subjects such as medicine, Islam, Arab history, banking, chemistry, pharmacy, law, dentistry, tourism, and engineering. Ministers and high officials met with their counterparts from Arab League countries to correlate policies and to formulate plans for joint ventures of every kind. These meetings and similar activities were valid steps in the direction of real unity and effective means of drawing leaders in Arab society together for the exchange of ideas. Yet, mutual distrust and the resistance of particular groups and states to many of the suggestions often proved strong, as the participants found it difficult to surrender their own national interests and special advantages.

International diplomacy and politics, however, were the Arab League's under-pinnings. The league declared its sympathy for Arab independence struggles in Morocco and Algeria, supplied funds to nationalists there, granted asylum to the leaders, and urged that economic measures be taken against France. When Morocco and Algeria had acquired independence they were duly admitted to full membership in the league. Egypt was supported in her struggle with Britain over Suez Canal bases; Yemen and Saudi Arabia were aided in their disputes with Britain over Aden and the Buraimi oases; and West Germany was invited to reconsider her reparations agreement with Israel. In 1965 the league asked all Arab states to recall their ambassadors from Bonn after West Germany exchanged ambassadors with Israel; some Arab states went on to recognize East Germany. After Lebanon, Algeria, and the Sudan recognized West Germany in 1972, the Arab League voted to nullify its stand.

The United Nations in 1960 officially accepted the Arab League as a regional organization, which facilitated agreements between the league and such U.N. bodies as the World Health Organization. Furthermore, it made possible the opening of Arab League offices with full diplomatic status in non-Arab capitals.

Early in 1955, when Iraq announced her intention to enter into a military arrangement with Turkey, the Arab League almost foundered. Egypt threatened to resign from the "Collective Security Pact," and Saudi Arabia and Yemen promised to follow Egypt into a new pact that would exclude Iraq. After the signing of the Baghdad Pact, however, Egypt did not walk out.

The Arab League became weaker in the late 1950s and 1960s as pan-Arabism seemed likely to unite the Arabs through other means than the cooperation of independent states. When the United Arab Republic of Egypt and Syria split up in 1961, and still later, as the failure of Ba'thism and Nasserism to bring about real unity became apparent, the league seemed one of the few avenues for fruitful cooperation. However, with the resurgence of Islamic fundamentalism and the rise of oil wealth, the secular ideal of pan-national union and integration generally faded in the 1970s and 1980s.

In intra-Arab affairs the league tried to use its good offices to keep peace but usually acted only after one or both parties to an argument invited it to do so. In 1972 the league's representatives were stationed on the border between Oman and the People's Democratic Republic of Yemen; later the league appointed a committee to observe the frontier between the two Yemens to prevent armed incursions. Neither league venture proved very successful, and the hostilities were resolved in other ways. In 1975 the league was asked to mediate at a technical but not at a political level the Euphrates water dispute between Iraq and Syria. Within a few weeks, however, Syria withdrew from the talks, preferring a settlement arranged by Saudi Arabia.

In addition to the meetings of the Arab League there have also been numerous gatherings of Arab heads of state who made mutual commitments and decisions in summit conferences. The first such conference was held in 1964. Another Arab summit meeting was held in Khartoum in the summer of 1967 to assess the disastrous Arab-Israeli War of that year. The conferees pledged to unify their diplomatic and political actions "to ensure the withdrawal of Israeli forces from the occupied Arab territory," as well as to speed the liquidation of foreign bases, to consolidate military preparedness, and to employ oil policies as a weapon to achieve these goals. Saudi Arabia, Kuwayt, and Libya agreed to give financial aid to Egypt and Jordan to ease their war losses. Another summit was held in Rabat in 1974, where the important decision was reached to make the Palestine Liberation Organization the sole legitimate representative of the Palestinian Arabs.

The Arab boycott of Israel was shaped at summits and Arab League meetings. Each country was pledged to cease trade and all dealings with firms and individuals in all countries that had financial, business, or personal connections with Israel. Pressure was applied, at first with little effect, to obtain the cooperation of foreign firms, and a regular "blacklist" was maintained.

The Arab League drew up a plan for an Arab Investment Bank, but it was modified in 1968 to become the Arab Development Bank. Its loans in the 1970s and 1980s were allotted in particular to agriculture and transportation development. An Arab Bank for social and economic development in Africa, with a capital of $200 million, was incorporated in 1974. By 1986 it had a paid-up capital of about $1 billion; aid was usually given in conjunction with other international agencies, and it was used especially for the development of agriculture, industry, and energy. The Arab Monetary Fund, headquartered in Abu Dhabi, was created in 1976, with a capital of $875 million to cover balance-of-payments problems among the Arab states. This organization's help was much in demand, and its capital was substantially increased in the 1980s. In addition to helping commerce, the fund made available loans to countries that had poor agricultural seasons.

Undoubtedly the best-known and certainly the most influential Arab alliance is the Organization of Arab Petroleum Exporting Countries (OAPEC), formed in January 1968 by Saudi Arabia, Kuwayt, and Libya. Prior to this several Arab Petroleum Congresses had been held. OAPEC's structure includes a council of ministers, an executive bureau, a secretariat, and a court; its purpose is to "determine ways and means of safeguarding the legitimate oil interests of its members." Algeria, Abu Dhabi, Dubay, Qatar, and Bahrayn were accepted as members, with the last four having no votes. When Iraq asked for admittance in 1970 the debate within OAPEC was furious, for Iraq was considered a radical state that in policy decisions would probably vote with Libya and Algeria against Saudi Arabia and Kuwayt. After many heated arguments Iraq, Syria, Egypt, and Oman were allowed to join in 1972, and OAPEC's charter was altered to permit membership to any oil-producing Arab state, not just to those whose oil income constituted more than 50 percent of its total revenues, as had been the case. When oil prices began to double and quadruple in 1972 and 1973 OAPEC and OPEC worked in tandem. OAPEC in the 1980s sponsored many conferences on such subjects as mineral resources, new techniques in petroleum production, and the petrochemical industry.

The Arab League played a role in Lebanon's civil war. When it seemed the country was about to be destroyed, the league, opposed to any partitioning of Lebanon, held a meeting in Cairo in June 1976, at which Saudi Arabia suggested organizing Arab peacekeeping forces to supervise a cease-fire. At a partial summit meeting in Riyadh in September, attended by the heads of state of Saudi Arabia, Syria, Egypt, Jordan, Kuwayt, and Lebanon, and the leader of the PLO, arrangements were made for a cease-fire policed by an Arab military presence composed of contingents from several Arab states, though most were Syrian soldiers already in Lebanon. It was financed by contributions from various Arab states, and was to remain in Lebanon for six months so that Lebanese officials could reestablish the authority and legitimacy of government. The force remained on when the six months expired, but Syria was in control as other Arab countries withdrew their forces later.

Arab unity was severely strained by the 1979 peace treaty between Egypt and Israel. In March 1979, Egypt's membership in the Arab League and associated groups was suspended. The league headquarters moved to Tunis from Cairo and most Arab states broke diplomatic relations with Egypt. The seeming widespread support for these actions gave way to fraternal bickering over what positive steps could be collectively taken in regard to the Arab-Israeli dispute. Arab summit conferences in 1980 and 1981 accomplished little, and the peace plan proposed by Saudi Arabia and adopted at the 1982 summit conference met little success. In 1984, Egypt regained membership in the Islamic Conference Organization. This was followed by the reestablishing of diplomatic ties with many Arab countries. Syria, Algeria, South Yemen, and Libya strongly objected to this process which, they felt, endorsed the 1979 peace with Israel. On May 22, 1989, Egypt was readmitted to the Arab League.

Syria and Libya also supported non-Arab Iran in its war against Arab Iraq, causing another major problem for the Arab League. Despite this and other difficulties, in November 1987 all of the members of the Arab League met in Amman and condemned Iran for actions taken by its pilgrims in Mecca, expressed "solidarity" with Iraq and Kuwayt, urged a peace in the interminable Gulf war, and spoke in favor of a United Nations-sponsored Arab-Israeli peace conference. Despite the willingness of Syria, Libya, and Algeria to accept these conclusions, major disputes still faced the Arab League: the Palestinian-Israeli impasse remained, and the intellectual and political dispute over pan-Arabism versus local state national identity was unresolved.

REFERENCES

Important references for this chapter are also found in Chapters 23, 28, 30, 33, and 37.

Abu Jaber, Kamel S. *The Arab Ba'th Socialist Party: History, Ideology, and Organization.* Syracuse, N.Y.: Syracuse University Press, 1966. A descriptive and analytical study gathered from printed material in Arabic and English.

Batatu, Hanna. "Some Observations on the Social Roots of Syria's Ruling Military Group and the Causes for Its Dominance." *Middle East Journal* 35 (1981): 331–344. Very useful.

Bengio, Ofra. "Shi'is and Politics in Ba'thi Iraq." *Middle Eastern Studies* 21 (1985): 1–14.

Birdwood, Lord. *Nuri al-Said: A Study in Arab Leadership.* London: Cassell, 1959. A political biography.

Boutros-Ghali, B. Y. *The Arab League, 1954–1955.* New York: Carnegie Endowment for International Peace, 1955. Historical background followed by sections on political and nonpolitical activities.

Brown, Michael. "The Nationalization of the Iraqi Petroleum Company." *International Journal of Middle Eastern Studies* 10 (1979): 107–124. A detailed look at an important topic.

Cobban, Helena. *The Making of Modern Lebanon.* Boulder, Colo.: Westview Press, 1985. An excellent general survey that shows historical continuity underneath the surface pattern of events.

Conrad, Lawrence I. "Culture and Learning in Beirut." *The American Scholar* 52 (1983): 463–478. One of the very few studies of recent cultural developments in Lebanon.

Devlin, John F. *The Ba'th Party: A History from Its Origins to 1966.* Stanford, Calif.: Hoover Institution, 1976. A detailed account of origins, doctrine, and political fortunes of the Ba'th.

Entelis, John P. *Pluralism and Party Transformation in Lebanon: al-Kata'ib, 1936–1970.* Leiden: Brill, 1974. A comprehensive study of the best-organized political grouping in Lebanon.

Faksh, Mahmud A. "The Alawi Community of Syria: A New Dominant Political Force." *Middle Eastern Studies* 20 (1984): 133–153. A recent study of this important community in Syria that has provided the leadership of the army and Ba'th party.

Farouk-Sluglett, Marion, and Peter Sluglett. *Iraq Since 1958: From Revolution to Dictatorship.* London: KPI Limited, 1987. A highly critical study with an emphasis on economics; very detailed up to 1980.

Ghareeb, Edmund. *The Kurdish Question in Iraq.* Syracuse, N.Y.: Syracuse University Press, 1981.

Gilmour, David. *Lebanon. The Fractured Country.* New York: St. Martin's Press, 1983.

Gordon, David C. *The Republic of Lebanon: Nation in Jeopardy.* Boulder, Colo.: Westview Press, 1983. A general survey of geography, history, and politics; very good.

Haddad, George M. *Revolutions and Military Rule in the Middle East.* Vol. 2. *The Arab States.* New York: Robert Speller & Sons, 1971. Discusses the thirty-nine coups in Syria, Iraq, Lebanon, and Jordan between 1936 and 1969. Best on Syria.

Helms, Christine Moss. *Iraq: Eastern Flank of the Arab World.* Washington, D.C.: Brookings Institution, 1984. Contains especially useful chapters on the Ba'th party and the war with Iran.

Hudson, Michael C. *The Precarious Republic: Political Modernization in Lebanon.* New York: Random House, 1968. A fine analysis of governmental institutions.

Ismael, Tareq Y. *The Arab Left.* Syracuse, N.Y.: Syracuse University Press, 1976. Covers the Ba'th, the Arab Nationalist Movement, Nasserism, and the "New Left" after 1967.

Keilany, Ziad. "Land Reform in Syria." *Middle Eastern Studies* 16 (1980): 209–224. A good study of an important topic.

Kerr, Malcolm H. *The Arab Cold War: Gamal 'Abd al-Nasir and His Rivals, 1958–1970.* 3rd ed. London: Oxford University Press, 1971. A subtle and profound analysis of the confusing web of alliances and enmities of the period by a political scientist who became president of the American University of Beirut before being tragically assassinated there.

Khadduri, Majid. *Arab Contemporaries: The Role of Personalities in Politics*. Baltimore, Md.: Johns Hopkins Press, 1973. A survey of the personalities of twelve modern Arab political leaders, including Nuri al-Said, Nasser, Jumblat, Aflaq, and Baqdash.

―――. *Republican Iraq: A Study of Iraqi Politics Since the Revolution of 1958*. New York: Oxford University Press, 1969. Detached and objective, with painstaking attention to detail and accuracy.

―――. *Socialist Iraq: A Study in Iraqi Politics Since 1968*. Washington, D.C.: Middle East Institute, 1978. A continuation of the above.

Khalidi, Walid. *Conflict and Violence in Lebanon: Confrontation in the Middle East*. Cambridge, Mass.: Center for International Affairs, Harvard University, 1980. Especially valuable for its discussion of the Palestinians in Lebanon.

Khalil, Muhammad. *The Arab States and the Arab League: A Documentary Record*. 2 vols. Beirut: Khayats, 1962. A valuable reference work of over 600 documents.

Kliot, N. "The Collapse of the Lebanese State." *Middle Eastern Studies* 23 (1987): 54–74. A general survey of the chasms in Lebanese society.

Macdonald, Robert W. W. *The League of Arab States*. Princeton, N.J.: Princeton University Press, 1965. An examination of the accomplishments of the league since its inception.

Ma'oz, Moshe, and Avner Yaniv, eds. *Syria Under Assad: Domestic Constraints and Regional Risks*. London: Croom Helm, 1986. Mostly on Syrian foreign policy and involvements.

Norton, Augustus Richard. *Amal and the Shi'a: Struggle for the Soul of Lebanon*. Austin: University of Texas Press, 1988. Valuable for southern Lebanon; written by an eyewitness.

Penrose, Edith, and E. F. Penrose. *Iraq: International Relations and National Development*. London: Ernest Benn, 1978. This work interlards political and economic matters carefully.

Polk, William R. *The Arab World*. 4th ed. Cambridge, Mass.: Harvard University Press, 1980. A perceptive general essay by an expert on the modern Arab Middle East.

Porath, Yehoshua. *In Search of Arab Unity, 1930–1945*. London: Frank Cass, 1986. Shows that it was Arab politicians and not the British who were chiefly responsible for the idea of the Arab League; good on Iraq and on British policy.

Qubain, Fahim I. *Crisis in Lebanon*. Washington, D.C.: Middle East Institute, 1961. A comprehensive, fair-minded account of the 1958 crisis.

―――. *The Reconstruction of Iraq, 1950–1957*. New York: Praeger, 1958. A picture of change induced by rising oil earnings, by the interest of Nuri al-Said, and by the Development Board.

Rabinovich, Itamar. *The War for Lebanon, 1970–1985*. Rev. ed. Ithaca, N.Y.: Cornell University Press, 1985. The various participants, their motives, and their interactions are examined.

Roberts, David. *The Ba'th and the Creation of Modern Syria*. New York: St. Martin's Press, 1987.

Salibi, Kamal S. *Crossroads to Civil War: Lebanon, 1958–1976*. Delmar, N.Y.: Caravan Books, 1976. Deals well with complex elements.

Seale, Patrick. *The Struggle for Syria: A Study of Post-War Arab Politics, 1945–1958*. New ed. London: Tauris & Co., 1986. Advances the thesis that whoever wishes to dominate the Middle East must control Syria. The new edition has a new foreword and a changed bibliography.

Snider, Lewis W. "The Lebanese Forces: Their Origins and Role in Lebanon's Politics." *Middle East Journal* 38 (1984): 1–33.

Springborg, Robert. "Baathism in Practice: Agriculture, Politics, and Political Culture in Syria and Iraq." *Middle Eastern Studies* 17 (1981): 191–209. One of the few comparative studies that shows the similarities and differences between Syrian and Iraqi Ba'thism in practice.

Suleiman, Michael W. *Political Parties in Lebanon: The Challenge of a Fragmented Political Culture*. Ithaca, N.Y.: Cornell University Press, 1967. A solid, straightforward, and informative work; describes seventeen parties and two quasi-party groups in Lebanon.

Torrey, Gordon H. *Syrian Politics and the Military, 1945–1958*. Columbus: Ohio State University Press, 1964. A thorough study of the various political parties and the position of the military toward and within each.

Van Dam, Nikolaos. *The Struggle for Syria: Sectarianism, Regionalism, and Tribalism in Politics, 1961–1980*. 2d ed. London: Croom Helm, 1981.

Weinberger, Naomi Joy. *Syrian Intervention in Lebanon: The 1975–76 Civil War*. New York: Oxford University Press, 1986. This recent study emphasizes a comparative framework for examining the motives of Syria in intervening in Lebanon.

43

The Partition of Palestine: Israel and Hashimite Jordan

THE JEWISH REFUGEES

The British White Paper of 1939 was intended to place the future of Palestine on ice for the duration of World War II. Land transfers from Arabs to Jews were halted, and total immigration of Jews for the next five years was fixed at 75,000. For the moment the Jewish Agency and the Arab Committee acquiesced to these terms, but few believed that the Palestine problem would not demand a solution immediately at the end of the war. The Jewish Agency and the neighboring Arab states were girding themselves for the eventual struggle.

The official Zionist position was drawn up in 1942 by a Zionist conference at the Biltmore Hotel in New York City. Ratified in Jerusalem by the inner general council of the Jewish Agency, the Biltmore program called for the establishment of a Jewish commonwealth in all of Palestine, and for unlimited immigration under the control of the Jewish Agency.

As the war in Europe drew to a close, the drive to fulfill the Biltmore program was intensified by pressures from all sides. Jews from Germany, Poland, and eastern Europe fled their homes and found temporary refuge in German and Italian displaced-persons camps. World Jewry in the West, in memory of the 6 million Jews massacred by the Nazis, felt a "divine impatience" over the procrastination in finding homes for these displaced persons. The basic argument of Zionism seemed confirmed as the full extent of the dreadful Holocaust in Europe became clear: Jews could be safe only in a Jewish state. Illegal immigration to Palestine multiplied. Crises arose when British authorities would not permit ships carrying Jews to land in Palestine, turned them back, or interned them in Cyprus. All but one of the 769 visaless passengers on an old cattle boat, the S.S. *Struma,* were lost when she sank in the Black Sea. Incidents such as these heightened the irritation at the delay in opening the gates of Palestine to the homeless.

To the new leader of the Jewish Agency, David Ben-Gurion, the refugees, if settled in Palestine, would provide the needed majority to ensure a dominant position for the Zionists. The Jewish Agency, therefore, insisted that the refugees come to Palestine, and urged the continuance of immigration quotas in the United States to prevent their departure for America.

An influx of Jews into Palestine found ready opposition from the Arab governments. Britain, in the midst of war, had her hands full with internal security in the Arab states. Thus, any policies for Palestine had to remain quiescent in order not to incite an Arab uprising, which the British believed to be certain if Jewish immigration stood at a high level. Since the Zionists feared that time might be against them, they urged the attainment of their program in 1945. They rejoiced at the British Labour party's victory at the polls, because Labour leaders, in opposition and out of power, had made promises favorable to Zionist aspirations.

Ben-Gurion had already warned that the reply to the British government, should it return to the 1939 White Paper, would be "bloody terror" and "constant and brutal force" in Palestine. British Foreign Minister Ernest Bevin learned, however, that there was an Arab as well as a Jewish question. Consequently, all the ministries of the government concerned with the Middle East "sang the same refrain…nothing should be done that would further antagonize the Arabs." The Labour government postponed any new departure and left the 1939 White Paper in effect. In the United States, President Truman, who bore no responsibility for the problems of the Middle East, supported the immediate granting of 100,000 immigration certificates requested by Ben-Gurion and entreated British Prime Minister Attlee to act quickly in the matter. To this the British declared that no radical change in policy toward Palestine could be made unless the United States would share in the maintenance of security in Palestine by providing U.S. troops. Attlee knew Truman would refuse to consider this move.

ZIONIST GUERRILLA TACTICS AND TERRORISM

Delay brought terror to Palestine. Ben-Gurion gave his approval of overt actions by the three illegal Zionist armed forces in Palestine. Haganah ("Defense"), with a membership of about 60,000, had been organized in 1920 to defend isolated Jewish settlements from Arab attacks; in the 1930s it spread, with winks from the British, to every Jewish community in Palestine. During World War II it acquired by various illegal means weapons of every description from small sidearms to tanks. In 1945 the "brilliant and biting" Moshe Sneh, aged thirty-seven, assumed command of Haganah and worked out arrangements to coordinate efforts with Menachem Begin, leader of Irgun Zvai Leumi ("National Military Organization"), and Nathan Freidmann-Yellin, leader of the Stern Gang (Lehi; "Fighters for the Freedom of Israel"). All three men had resided together at the Jewish Academicians House at the University of Warsaw. Irgun and the Stern group were right-wing semimilitary expansionist organizations dedicated to obtaining a Zionist political state that would include all of Palestine, in sharp contrast to the Zionists of the Jewish Agency and Haganah, who were more likely to be left-wing and socialist.

The British were caught between urgent Zionist and American demands and a categorical refusal of the Arab states to countenance any abrogation of the 1939 White Paper. Upon the stalling of the Labour government Sneh suggested that "one serious incident" should occur as a warning of what would erupt unless Zionist policies obtained. On October 10, 1945, the Palmach (Haganah commandos) raided a British detention camp and freed 208 illegal immigrants. On the night of October 31 the Palmach sank three small British naval ships and tore up the tracks of the Palestine railway in 153 places; Irgun attacked the Lydda railway station; and Sternists sabotaged the Haifa oil refineries. Although conferences were held between leaders of Irgun and the Jewish Agency every fortnight, Ben-Gurion and Moshe Shertok (later Sharett), head of the political department of the Jewish Agency, denied all knowledge of these affairs.

Upon rumors that British delays would continue until further investigations were made, Zionist leaders reminded all: "Six million Jews died in Europe while we waited for the democratic powers to act. Thousands more of the remnant will die if we sit here with hands folded during the winter, while they investigate again."

ANGLO-AMERICAN COMMITTEE OF INQUIRY

Since Britain hesitated to act because of Arab pressures and since the United States was insisting on action without any willingness to shoulder the responsibility of maintaining order in Palestine, an Anglo-American committee of inquiry was appointed to study the question. The committee was to meet in Washington, London, Europe, Palestine, and the Arab states and recommend steps to achieve a solution. In the early months of 1946, while the committee questioned individuals in Palestine, terrorist deeds continued. Haganah publicly boasted of its participation. The report of the committee recommended granting 100,000 immigration certificates to European Jews. It recognized, however, that hostility between Jews and Arabs made the establishment of an independent Palestine impossible at the moment, and advised that Britain retain the mandate until a trusteeship agreement under the United Nations could be arranged.

British leaders were provoked when President Truman suggested 100,000 visas be given at once. The Labour government was faced with a dilemma. Approval of a loan to Britain was before the American Congress, where the Zionists had many friends; negotiations were in process for a treaty with Egypt; Soviet pressures upon Turkey and Iran were increasing day by day. The cost of maintaining a sizable force—at least 100,000 men—in Palestine was a heavy charge on a tight budget for a state on the verge of bankruptcy. Furthermore, if Britain were to evacuate her troops from Egypt, as seemed likely, the need of a strong base in Palestine became imperative.

As the British cabinet weighed the dilemma, violence spread in Palestine. Munitions thefts, explosions, sabotage, bank robberies, killings of English soldiers, and destruction of bridges were an open declaration of war by the Jewish resistance movement. Jewish leaders in Palestine reasoned that outrages would obtain concessions from a fearful England. As part of the British reaction Jewish Agency leaders were arrested and their offices occupied; members of the Palmach were rounded up; British military authorities imprisoned numerous suspected terrorists; and great caches of arms were seized. In retaliation Irgun, with the help of Haganah, blew up the King David Hotel in Jerusalem, British military headquarters, killing ninety-one people.

To resolve the impasse a new Anglo-American suggestion, called the Morrison-Grady plan, was presented. This plan advocated the creation of separate Arab and Jewish autonomous provinces under a central government that would control Jerusalem and the Negev Desert. Similar provincial autonomy plans had been rejected by the Anglo-American committee of inquiry, and even before that such plans had gathered dust in the colonial office for years. Rejected by both Arabs and Zionists as unsatisfactory, the plan was then modified by the leaders of the Jewish Agency, who by this time had abandoned the Biltmore program and indicated a readiness to accept a separate state in Palestine. It was insisted, however, that the state include the Negev Desert.

Hope for a solution was in the air as Dr. Chaim Weizmann's moderation gained ascendancy—only to be shattered beyond repair by President Truman's announcement in October 1946, just before the congressional and the New York gubernatorial elections, that the United States strongly supported the immediate entry of 100,000 Jews into Palestine. Furthermore, at the world Zionist congress at Basle in December, Weizmann was elected president by only 51 percent of the vote, and the activism of Ben-Gurion carried political resolutions against the moderation of Weizmann.

PALESTINE BEFORE THE UNITED NATIONS

In February 1947, the British made one last desperate offer, but each side rejected it. Consequently, Bevin decided to refer the question to the United Nations.

At British request a special session of the U.N. General Assembly was called to consider Palestine. The U.N. Special Committee on Palestine (UNSCOP) was authorized to investigate any question relevant to Palestine and report by September 1. UNSCOP visited Palestine in June and July, during which time Zionist terrorists attacked the prison in Acre and freed many prisoners. In another incident, the S.S. *Exodus 1947,* boarded at Marseilles by 4,554 Jewish passengers with passports and visas for Colombia, was seized at Haifa by British authorities and turned back to France.

The situation remained tense as all awaited the UNSCOP report being drafted at Geneva. All eleven members agreed that the mandate had proved unworkable. Three approved a binational federal state; the other eight favored a partition plan envisaging an economic union. The report recommended partition lines forming three sections of territory for Jews and three for Arabs, with northern and southern points of intersection and communication. Jerusalem and Bethlehem were to be internationalized. The Arab and Jewish states would become independent only when they signed a ten-year economic union pact compelling the more developed

Jewish state to assist the poorer Arab one. As proposed, 45 to 50 percent of the population in the Jewish state would be Arab, and 1 percent in the Arab state would be Jewish. Referred to as "death by a thousand cuts," the partition plan was as improbable and impractical as the signing of a ten-year economic union between the two was unthinkable. UNSCOP called for establishment of the states before October 1, 1948, while Britain declared her mandate would be terminated May 15 and her troops evacuated before August 1.

The General Assembly reached a vote on the UNSCOP report on November 29, 1947, approving it by a vote of 33 to 13, with 11 abstentions. Both the United States and the Soviet Union voted in favor, while Britain abstained. Several days before the vote was taken it appeared that the partition plan might not obtain the necessary two-thirds majority of those voting, but several postponements gave the Zionists and their sympathizers among United States officialdom opportunity to put pressure on five states that had intended to vote against partition.

THE 1948 WAR

The U.N. partition plan touched off a civil war in Palestine. Thereafter, Haganah, Irgun, and Sternists openly attacked the British when in need of arms, and Arab forces grew in numbers with volunteers and arms coming in surreptitiously from neighboring Arab states. As more and more British soldiers were killed, there arose a clamor from the British public to pull out fully and quickly. Weapons for the Zionists were smuggled in from New York and Czechoslovakia. No day passed without violence. On December 15, 1947, the Palestine government relinquished the policing of Tel Aviv to the Zionists and Jaffa to the Arabs. Attack and counter-attack brought savagery to new heights in Jerusalem and Haifa. Syrian volunteers with a few officers from the Syrian army entered north Palestine in January 1948; by mid-March they numbered about 5,000, under the leadership of Fawzi al-Qawukji, a soldier of fortune and Arab patriot.

The Arab liberation army, augmented by Iraqi and Egyptian contributions and dignified by the blessing of the Arab states, together with detachments of Palestinian Arab units, became engaged in April with the Zionist military organizations in many sectors of Palestine. The Jews took Tiberias and Haifa, which were in the area assigned to a Jewish state by the partition. Heavy mortar attacks by Irgun and the Sternists upon Jaffa and Acre, which had been reserved for the Arab state, accelerated the flight of Arabs from those cities. Arabs threatened the line of communications between Haifa and Tel Aviv and Jerusalem. On April 9 Irgun units attacked the Arab village of Dair Yasin near Jerusalem and killed about 250 villagers. Three days later the Arabs attacked a Jewish convoy bound for beleaguered Hebrew University and Hadassah Hospital on Mount Scopus, killing 77 doctors, nurses, university teachers, and students. As war spread and its outrages multiplied, civilians tried to escape. It was estimated that by the middle of May 1948 Arab civilian refugees from thirty exposed villages and from Tiberias, Haifa, Jaffa, and other occupied cities totaled about 150,000.

On May 14, 1948, at Tel Aviv, in the midst of such anarchy, Ben-Gurion, flanked by his twelve fellow ministers of the national council of the Jewish state, proclaimed the establishment of the Jewish state in Palestine, to be called Israel. President Truman announced *de facto* recognition of Israel by the United States minutes after Ben-Gurion's proclamation in Tel Aviv, and the Soviet Union recognized Israel two days later.

The Arab League had previously declared that it would not recognize the state of Israel and that league members would be encouraged to intervene in Palestine. On May 15, 1948, the war began. Two Egyptian forces entered Palestine. One proceeded along the coast to twenty miles south of Tel Aviv, where it was halted by an Israeli force; the other crossed the Negev, through Beersheba, to Bethlehem and the southern suburbs of Jerusalem. A Palestinian Arab force held the Lydda airfield (Lod; later, Ben-Gurion airport), and an Iraqi force crossed the Jordan and advanced to Tulkarm, ten miles from the Mediterranean. A small Lebanese token force crossed into Palestine from southern Lebanon, and an army of a few thousand Syrians served to pin down a few Israeli forces in the north. The Arab Legion of Transjordan held the center of the line, occupied areas in the Arab portion of Palestine, and defeated Israeli attacks upon Jerusalem.

Although the Arab radio and press claimed victory after victory and described excursions through Arab-held areas as triumphant advances in Palestine, the Arab leaders knew that success had not been theirs. Arab soldiers found their equipment obsolete or defective; officers were incompetent in staff work; the zeal of the Arab soldier was lacking. Moreover, the Arab Legion was under orders not to move into territory awarded to the Jews by the U.N. partition plan. On the other hand, Israeli activity and ardor were highly stimulated. In the early days of the war bitter controversy developed between Haganah and the extremist groups, but Ben-Gurion became official commander in chief of the army, and direct leadership was given to Yigael Yadin and Yigal Allon.

The war distressed the major world powers. On May 20, the U.N. Security Council appointed Count Folke Bernadotte of Sweden as mediator for Palestine, giving him a free hand to bring about an end to hostilities. A truce was arranged that ran from June 11 to July 8, and a second truce began on July 19. In October Israeli forces drove the Egyptians from most of their positions in the Negev, including Beersheba; they cleared northern Palestine; they drove al-Qawukji and his Arab liberation army into Lebanon and Syria; and they occupied fifteen Lebanese villages. In December Israeli mechanized forces drove the Egyptians into a narrow corridor at Gaza and invaded Egyptian territory in the Sinai peninsula, compelling the Egyptian government to sue for a cease-fire arrangement on the promise of agreement to an armistice.

Without question the Israeli army and the leadership of David Ben-Gurion won the 1948–1949 war. To a very marked degree during those months Israel was a nation in arms fighting for her independence and her very existence, and this spirit pervaded the fighting units. Flexibility in tactics, the use of surprise and innovations, speed and outflanking maneuvers all marked the Israeli forces and contributed to their victory. Pride in the courage of the Jewish soldier in the face of great danger aroused soldiers to extraordinary accomplishments. A singleness of

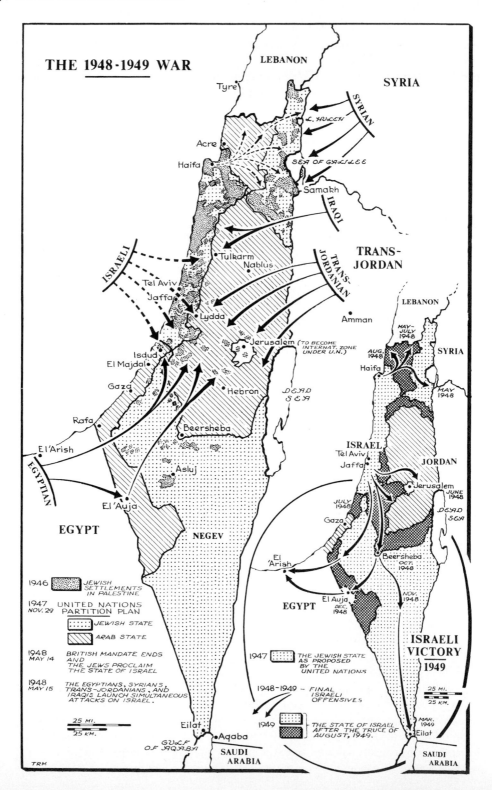

THE 1948-1949 WAR

LEBANON

SYRIA

Tyre

SYRIAN

L. HULEH

Acre

SEA OF GALILEE

Haifa

Samakh

IRAQI

ISRAELI

Tulkarm

Nablus

TRANS-JORDANIAN

TRANS-JORDAN

Tel Aviv

Amman

Jaffa

Lydda

Jerusalem (TO BECOME INTERNAT. ZONE UNDER U.N.)

Isdud

El Majdal

Gaza

Hebron

DEAD SEA

Rafa

Beersheba

El 'Arish

EGYPTIAN

Asluj

El 'Auja

EGYPT

NEGEV

LEBANON

MAY–JULY 1948

AUG. 1948

SYRIA

Haifa

MAY 1948

ISRAEL

Tel Aviv

Jaffa

JORDAN

Jerusalem JUNE 1948

JULY 1948

DEAD SEA

Gaza

EGYPT

El 'Arish

Beersheba OCT. 1948

El Auja DEC. 1948

NOV. 1948

ISRAELI VICTORY 1949

1946 — JEWISH SETTLEMENTS IN PALESTINE

1947 NOV. 29 UNITED NATIONS PARTITION PLAN

JEWISH STATE

ARAB STATE

1948 MAY 14 BRITISH MANDATE ENDS AND THE JEWS PROCLAIM THE STATE OF ISRAEL

1948 MAY 15 THE EGYPTIANS, SYRIANS TRANS-JORDANIANS, AND IRAQIS LAUNCH SIMULTANEOUS ATTACKS ON ISRAEL.

1947 — THE JEWISH STATE AS PROPOSED BY THE UNITED NATIONS

1948-1949 — FINAL ISRAELI OFFENSIVES

1949 — THE STATE OF ISRAEL AFTER THE TRUCE OF AUGUST, 1949.

25 MI.
25 KM.

Eilat

Aqaba

GULF OF AQABA

SAUDI ARABIA

25 MI.
25 KM.

MAR. 1949

Eilat

SAUDI ARABIA

TRM

ISRAEL AND THE SUEZ, 1947, 1949, AND 1967

50 KILOMETERS

50 MILES

LEBANON
Beirut
Sidon
Tyre
GOLAN HEIGHTS
SYRIA
L. TIBERIAS
Haifa

MEDITERRANEAN

SEA

ISRAEL
Tulkarm
Nablus
Tel Aviv
Jaffa
JORDAN
Jericho
Jerusalem
Amman
Bethlehem
Hebron
Gaza
GAZA STRIP
DEAD SEA
Kuruk
Sedom

NILE DELTA
Damietta
Port Said
El 'Arish
Qantara
Misfaq
Auja
Isma'iliya
NEGEV
Khamsa
GREAT BITTER LAKE
Ma'an
Gineifu
El Kuntilla
Cairo
Suez
El Shatt
Nakhl
Eilat
Taba
Aqaba

E G Y P T
UNITED ARAB REPUBLIC
Sudr
Haqal

NILE
SINAI
Mereighat
PENINSULA
SAUDI ARABIA
△ MT. SINAI
GULF OF SUEZ
GULF OF AQABA
Magna
El Tor
RAS NUSNANI
TIRAN IS.
STRAIT OF TIRAN
Gemsa
GULF OF JUBAL
SHARM EL SHEIKH
RED SEA

JEWISH STATE AS PROPOSED BY THE UNITED NATIONS, 1947

ISRAEL AFTER THE 1948 WAR

AREAS SEIZED AND RETAINED AFTER THE SIX-DAY WAR, 1967

TRM

purpose permeated all levels of society and eliminated most problems of discipline. Early in the struggle the independence of the Sternists and Irgun was largely curbed, even with force on several occasions. In contrast, the diversity of aims, personal jealousies, and national self-interest of the Arab states and their leaders deprived the Arab armies of the cooperation and coordination necessary for victory.

In the spring of 1948 the Arab states, taken as a whole, were better supplied and more numerous than the Zionists; Iraq, Transjordan, and Egypt had arms treaties with England. But by the autumn of 1948 the situation was reversed. Numerous shipments of smuggled arms from the United States arrived in Israel, and dollar gifts collected in the United States purchased quantities of arms from Czechoslovakia. Bombers were obtained in the United States and England. The arms embargo to the area hindered the Israeli effort very little, but the Arabs were not so successful in circumventing it. Then, too, truces worked to the disadvantage of the Arabs. Delays gave greater opportunity for the individual ambitions of the leaders to erode the Arab effort.

ARMISTICE

During the first truce Count Bernadotte made several suggestions for a basis on which peace could rest. A fundamental point incorporated most of the Arab portion of Palestine into the state of Transjordan, a development which Israelis rightfully recognized would alter the balance of power in Palestine. The second truce was never well observed, and the Israelis, who conquered three times more Arab territory in the second stage of the war than they had in the first, were difficult to contain. Bernadotte was murdered by a Sternist soldier.

Israel was awarded about 55 percent of the British mandate's territory by the United Nations in 1947; by 1949 it controlled about 77 percent of what had been the mandate.

In the fall of 1948 several cease-fire agreements were arranged. Ralph Bunche, the acting mediator, at his headquarters on Rhodes obtained an armistice between Israel and Egypt in February 1949. The important article pertained to the temporary frontier between the two states: the Gaza Strip was left to Egyptian occupation, but not annexation. The line was drawn so that many Arab villages were separated from their farm lands; the al-Awja area was demilitarized on the Israeli side, and Egyptian forces were withdrawn.

An armistice between Israel and Lebanon was signed in March, and the old frontier was recognized and demilitarized on each side. The question of a settlement with Syria was delayed by the coup d'état of Husni Zaim; in July Ralph Bunche obtained agreement and an armistice. The frontiers remained as they were drawn in 1920; the upper Jordan River and the Sea of Galilee were wholly in Israel, but a small part of the Lake Hulah marsh area was recognized as a demilitarized zone.

With Transjordan the settlement was far more complex. Debates at the U.N. in the autumn of 1948 revealed that the Western powers agreed that Abd Allah of

Transjordan might take over what was left of Arab Palestine, an annexation perfectly agreeable to him. Although such a step was definitely in opposition to the ex-mufti's government-of-all-Palestine plan, proclaimed at Gaza, the main area left to Arab control was occupied by the Arab Legion of Transjordan. Israel refused to consider surrendering her award of the Negev in the partition plan for western Galilee, which she had conquered shortly before the cease-fire. Israeli forces ignored cease-fire agreements in Jerusalem; later they ignored the armistice with Egypt and pushed south, hoping to establish themselves on the Gulf of Aqaba, open a route to the Orient, and bypass the Suez Canal. British troops occupied the port of Aqaba to prevent its fall to Israeli forces, but Israeli troops reached the gulf at Eilat.

In central Palestine the position of the Arab Legion grew precarious. Israeli commanders told King Abd Allah to withdraw or Israel would resume hostilities. Such an expansion was necessary to the state of Israel, as the Arab lines blocked the main road connecting Tel Aviv with Galilee; but for Transjordan it left many villagers destitute since their lands were on the other side of the line. With these concessions the armistice was signed in April between Israel and the new state of Jordan, which had been announced in December 1948. Iraq came under this armistice, since she had declared she would recognize any armistice entered into by her fellow Hashimite ruler.

ARAB REFUGEES

After the several armistices defined the temporary boundaries of Israel, the greatest question remaining was that of the Arab refugees. The number of Palestinian Arabs from the area incorporated in Israel gathered in surrounding Arab states totaled some 700,000 in 1949, while more than 100,000 Arabs remained in Israel. The refugee camps with about 500,000 persons were located in the Gaza Strip held by Egypt, and in Jordan, Syria, and Lebanon. Egypt and Lebanon had serious overpopulation problems; east Jordan was quite barren; and west Jordan (the West Bank), the portion of Palestine annexed to Transjordan, did not have the resources to support a large influx of destitute people. Also, many inhabitants of Jordan were without means of support because the new frontier line had put their lands in Israel. In Jordan and Israel the Palestinians became citizens, but in the Gaza Strip and most other places they were stateless noncitizens.

The refugees had left their homes for a variety of reasons. In some places Arabs were expelled when the Israelis took over. And in a number of Arab villages Israeli forces demolished the houses so the Arabs could not return. The massacre at Dair Yasin, the fear of being involved in the fighting, and the reprisals of previous years frightened the Arabs. Hearing over the radio optimistic broadcasts and news reports that Arab armies would be victorious in a week or two, many Arabs in towns and villages turned the key in the door, pocketed it, and walked away, fully expecting to return shortly.

The refugee question was also a main stumbling block to any peace settlement. Most refugees believed that they wished to return, although very few would have felt at home had they been allowed to do so. Conditions, and even the surroundings, had changed. But lands, buildings, and bank accounts required compensation, if refugees stayed away. Arab leaders had not the political courage to tell the refugees they could not return; and Israel agreed to discuss compensation and aids to resettlement only in an overall peace arrangement with the Arab states.

Late in 1948 the U.N. set up a disaster-relief operation to care for refugees, whose numbers were growing rapidly. The United Nations Relief for Palestine Refugees (UNRPR) was organized January 1, 1949, to operate for nine months until the next harvest. When refugee work appeared to be a long-range rehabilitation task as well as straight relief the United Nations Relief and Works Agency for Palestine Refugees in the Near East (UNRWA) was created. Work-relief projects and reintegration schemes were developed, but the refugee camps continued as an irritant in the Middle East and acted as breeding grounds for frustration and social revolution. Israel remained adamant about not taking back most of the refugees. One positive step to alleviate tension, however, was taken in October 1956, when Israel released 80 percent of the funds in blocked accounts of the refugees.

Most Arab Palestinians came to support the pan-Arab nationalists in the 1950s, and especially Nasser of Egypt. They hoped he could liberate Palestine and allow them to return to their homes.

Another issue of contention was the status of Jerusalem. The partition plan of 1947 had called for internationalization of the Holy City. The armistice between Israel and Jordan left Jerusalem divided with barbed wire cutting across it. (The eastern part and most of the Old City containing the holy shrines were held by Jordan.) Although the United Nations declared that Jerusalem must remain an international zone, it became two cities. Israel refused to demilitarize her sector, asserting that it was surrounded by Arab territory on three sides, and Jordan refused to permit Jews access to their holy places in the Old City. In 1949, a number of Israel's ministries were moved from Tel Aviv to Jerusalem, and in December the *Knesset* (Parliament) met there. In January 1950 it was proclaimed that Jerusalem had been the capital of Israel since her founding. All government offices moved there except the ministry of foreign affairs, which remained in Tel Aviv to keep in touch with foreign diplomats. Many governments, including the United States, forbade their diplomats to move to Jerusalem and refused to recognize it as the capital.

King Abd Allah proceeded formally to incorporate the West Bank Arab portion of Palestine into his state, renaming Transjordan the Hashimite Kingdom of Jordan. An election was held in 1950, and a new cabinet was formed composed of ministers from both parts of the kingdom. Most countries refused to recognize the incorporation of East Jerusalem into Jordan, but the Arab League grudgingly agreed to the annexation of the West Bank and East Jerusalem, even though they had threatened to expel from the league any state that took any part of Palestine.

In 1950 the American, British, and French foreign ministers, meeting in London, signed a tripartite agreement affirming that their states would take action to prevent any violation of frontiers or armistice lines. They also declared that they were prepared to forestall an arms race between the Arab states and Israel. This meant lifting the arms embargo and accepting the armistice lines and the *status quo* in the Middle East.

THE STATE OF ISRAEL

When the state of Israel was proclaimed in 1948 by David Ben-Gurion, a provisional government was organized. In 1949, elections were held for a national parliament and constituent assembly (Knesset). Mapai (Workers' party), a socialist center group, obtained the largest bloc of seats in the Knesset, but not a majority. Although a committee was directed to bring in a written constitution, Ben-Gurion, the prime minister, was predisposed to an unwritten constitution in the British manner, and desired that the constitution be built up law by law. By doing so internal debates about the role of religion in the state could be lessened. One of the very first laws (the Law of Return) provided for unlimited ingathering of the Jewish people, the immigrants becoming Israeli citizens upon their entry.

The Israeli Arab minority could and did vote in parliamentary elections, and some were elected to the Knesset. New anti-Zionist Arab parties were not allowed to be formed. Since most of the Arab leadership had fled, and those who stayed were quiescent and cut off from the political and cultural trends of the Arab world, Israeli Arabs initially tended to vote for Jewish Israeli parties. Israeli Arabs faced security laws which in effect limited their civil rights in a number of ways until 1966. They were not drafted into the Israeli armed forces, although the Druze minority did voluntarily serve. Their greatest problem was existential: what did it mean to be a Muslim or Christian Arab in a Jewish state?

The Knesset, with its Jewish majority and Arab minority, was composed of 120 members elected by proportional representation from national party lists. Elections were usually held every four years, with some exceptions. In every election up to 1977 the Mapai won a commanding plurality and easily formed the government with a coalition of one kind or another. Thirteen parties were represented in the Knesset elected in 1951! If a coalition could not be formed, as in 1961, when Ben-Gurion resigned over the Lavon affair, he called a new election. He then put together a shaky coalition until 1963, when he resigned in favor of Levi Eshkol. Ben-Gurion split from Mapai and formed his own party in 1965, as he came to disagree strongly with Eshkol over policies. Herut, a right-wing party, and the Liberals coalesced for the 1965 election as did Mapai and a few minor parties. Even though seventeen parties presented candidates, Eshkol and his Mapai and associates won forty-five seats.

In addition to the key post in government, the prime ministry, which was determined by the parliament, Israel also had a presidency, an honorific office. Chaim Weizmann was the first person elected to that post, and he served in it until his death in 1952.

Ben-Gurion was prime minister from 1948 until January 1954, when he retired to his home in a kibbutz in the Negev. He was an activist leader, a man of action, and "hawkish" in regard to the Arabs. Ben-Gurion believed in Israeli self-reliance, a view he summed up by the phrase "Our future does not depend on what the Gentiles say but on what the Jews do." He was followed as prime minister by Minister for Foreign Affairs Moshe Sharett, a leader of Mapai. Sharett was cautious, quiet, and more willing to seek a rapprochement with the Arabs than was Ben-Gurion. However, as the situation around Israel became more serious, Ben-Gurion returned to the cabinet as minister of defense and later as prime minister in November 1955. In 1956 Sharett was relieved of the foreign ministry because he did not favor reprisal attacks upon Egypt, Syria, and Jordan. Golda Meir, minister of labor, took his place. After the 1956 war Ben-Gurion remained as prime minister until he resigned in 1963. Levi Eshkol, his successor, had been the minister of finance and a prominent member of the powerful Histadrut, the Israeli Federation of Labor.

The Lavon affair that caused so much turmoil in the government started in 1954. Bombs planted in books in the United States Information Agency library in Cairo exploded killing several persons. Egyptian investigators traced the act to Israeli agents, who were caught and tried. Egypt claimed that the plot had been an Israeli attempt to anger Americans against Egypt and to effect the cutoff of American support for the Aswan Dam. Pinhas Lavon, Israel's minister of defense at the time, was blamed for the act and forced to resign in 1955. In 1960 he was exonerated by the cabinet, which accepted the evidence that Lavon's signature to the documents and orders had been forged.

Although Ben-Gurion had not been prime minister when many of these arrangements were said to have been made but had been closely associated with Moshe Dayan and other individuals involved, he felt the blame was being shifted to him. Ben-Gurion, with the support of Moshe Dayan, formed his own party, Rafi, and presented a slate of candidates for the election of 1965. The majority of Mapai supported Eshkol, and Rafi placed only ten members in the Knesset. Eshkol formed a new coalition cabinet. When the crisis developed in late May 1967 over the Straits of Tiran and war was imminent, Eshkol gave the portfolio of the defense ministry to General Moshe Dayan.

Real authority rested in the hands of the prime minister. He usually held the post of defense minister as well as prime minister; the concentration of power was considerable, especially because there was no effective committee in the Knesset to review affairs of the ministry of defense. Eshkol followed the custom of Ben-Gurion and headed the defense ministry along with the prime ministry. Every cabinet after the first election until 1977 was a coalition centered around the Mapai party which Ben-Gurion and Eshkol headed. Various parties joined with Mapai, and these changed through the years except Mapam, a leftist party that was a constant partner. The National Religious Front consisting of middle-of-the-road parties with a religious basis supported Mapai after 1959 until 1977. Several cabinet crises occurred over Jewish dietary beliefs and the question of women serving in the armed forces. There were important discussions over the question of who was considered to be a Jew. In 1960 it was decided that a Jew is a person born of a Jewish mother who does not belong to another religion or who is a convert according to religious law; still later in 1970 it was ruled that non-Jewish spouses, children, and grandchildren of Jews could come under the Law of Return to become Israeli citizens but they would not be accepted as Jews.

Open immigration into Israel had been the goal of Zionist leaders from the beginning of the mandate. In the first decade after independence at least 800,000 immigrants swelled Israel's population rapidly; 700,000 came in the first four years. Since 55 percent of these postindependence immigrants were Sephardic Jews of Eastern origin, their assimilation presented new problems for Israel. Furthermore, because the birth rate in this group was much higher than in others, in time Sephardic Jews outnumbered the politically dominant Ashkenazi, or European Jews. In May 1958, at the time of the tenth-anniversary celebrations, Ben-Gurion announced that the population of Israel had reached 2 million.

The immigrants had to learn Hebrew, which was, with Arabic, the official language of the state. Although Hebrew was used in religious ceremonies, modern spoken Hebrew had to be learned as a living language. As the decades passed, more and more Israelis came to speak Hebrew, and the *sabras* (native-born Israelis) tended to forget the languages spoken by their immigrant parents. The Hebrew language served to unify the nation and to distinguish it from other countries in the world.

Economic difficulties in Israel, resulting from a widening trade gap, greater military expenditures at the expense of development, and a sharp dropping off of capital investments, reparations, bond sales, and charitable gifts, brought unemployment, devaluation, and belt tightening pressures. Furthermore, more than 40,000 Eastern immigrants were housed in makeshift camps, and riots occurred in Haifa, Beersheba, and other cities over the discriminatory practices of government in housing, jobs, and higher education for the Sephardic Jews. Consequently, Israelis began to emigrate in worrisome numbers. On August 2, 1966, the Law of Return was amended to curb the practice of residing in Israel long enough to acquire citizenship and a passport and then departing.

ISRAELI ECONOMY AND CULTURE

The economy of Israel has been exceedingly precarious ever since her birth in 1948. Many inhabitants expected and obtained a standard of living comparable to that of central Europe, although Israel was a small and poor country of the Middle East. Their standard of living was made possible by gifts and loans from foreign governments and individual Jews in many countries. The United Jewish Appeal set a goal of raising approximately $250 million in each of the early years, which contributed greatly to maintaining a balance in Israeli finances.

Imports for several years ranged from four to five times the value of exports. In the five years from 1961 to 1965, the average yearly unfavorable balance was $371 million, and in the year before the 1967 war Israel had an unfavorable balance of payments of over $600 million. A new economic policy had to be found, as critical reports were issued on the inefficiencies of the kibbutzim (collective villages), the question of agriculture versus industry, planning for the productive employment of immigrants, and the general standard of living. Because Histadrut, the

Israeli Federation of Labor, controlled Mapai, and Mapai dominated the government, there was considerable doubt as to how strong a check Eshkol could maintain on wages, prices, and the standard of living. In 1967, wages and prices continued to rise at their usual rates until the outbreak of war in June when the entire economy was disrupted to such an extent that it marked a watershed in the Israeli economy.

The burden of the immigrants upon the economy hampered capital development in many ways. New houses were built by the tens of thousands, and the newcomers had to be fed and clothed for many months before they were integrated and absorbed into Israeli society. Some Israeli economists suggested that immigration be limited, but such a policy was anathema to leaders who had heard the British and Arabs mouth such proposals for a quarter of a century. In 1950, in anticipation of 600,000 additional immigrants in the following three years, Israel organized a drive to raise $1.5 billion to settle the new people. In 1953 relief came in the form of an agreement with West Germany, whereby Israel would receive $822 million in reparations to be paid over the next fourteen years. After the 1956 war, as the number of new immigrants dropped off, the building trades in Israel suffered a slump, with mass dismissals. The conclusion of German reparations in 1965 and the serious decline in charitable gifts from world Jewry made the economic crisis of early 1967 more acute. One cause of that crisis was frequently attributed to the great mass of immigrants over the previous twenty years, the rapidity of their integration into the economic life of the state, and the lack of any critical evaluation of the productiveness of these immigrants, and usefulness of the work in which they were engaged, and the general criterion used in planning their employment.

During her first ten years Israel received more than $2.5 billion as imports of capital. Much of this foreign exchange had been spent for consumer goods, producing an artificial standard of living that demanded a continuation of this stream of foreign capital to maintain it. The need for capital funds for irrigation projects, industry, communications, and exploration for natural resources exceeded most expectations.

One of the gravest burdens upon the Israeli economy was imposed by the economic boycott by the Arab states. The proclivity of Israelis was for industry or mechanized and specialized production, which would complement the raw materials and agricultural produce of Arab countries. Iraq shut off the flow of oil in the pipeline to Haifa, forcing Israel to buy higher-priced petroleum from Iran and the Gulf of Mexico. This pressure stimulated a drive to become more independent of the Arab states in matters of transport as well as in oil. Eilat on the Gulf of Aqaba was pushed as the gateway to the east. After exploratory talks with Asians and Africans Israeli leaders felt that their industry and commerce had a propitious future in those continents, and Eilat was the key as long as free passage through Suez was denied to them.

Interest in Eilat, however, did not blind the Israeli planners to their dependence upon the West and Mediterranean contacts. In 1960 a loan was negotiated for the construction of a deep-water port at Ashdod, south of Tel Aviv. When the port was completed in 1965 the ports of Jaffa and Tel Aviv were closed, and

Ashdod and Haifa were the only two Mediterranean ports. In the 1967 crisis the closing of the Straits of Tiran by Egypt to Israeli shipping and other flags carrying strategic goods to or from Eilat affected Israel and was a cause for war.

The prospect of irrigating the Negev and utilizing its land inspired Israeli engineers and planners to build gigantic canals from the north, circumventing Jordan, to the barren southlands. Syria and Jordan protested this unilateral use of Jordan waters, but settlement and irrigation in the Negev remained a promising and exciting development in Israel. When water from the Jordan began to flow southward through the channels and pipes on May 5, 1964, it was a day of great celebration.

Other substantial accomplishments included growth in scientific and technical research, urbanization, education, agricultural production, and industry. Israeli universities and research institutes developed strong research agendas in such areas as desalinization of sea water, atomic energy, aeronautical engineering; and Israel spent more on basic and applied research than all of the Arab states combined. Urbanization and the construction industry proceeded rapidly after 1948. At that time about one-fourth of the Jewish Israeli population was rural and three-fourths urban; as time passed Israel became ever more urbanized, ultimately reaching a situation where 86 percent of the population lived in towns and cities. Most of the growth took place in the coastal areas, and Tel Aviv became the dominant city with about 25 percent of all Israelis living there. Educational institutions also grew rapidly, both for the Jewish majority and the Arab minority. While in 1949 only 1,600 students were enrolled in two universities, by 1975 47,000 students attended seven universities and higher institutes. By 1963, Israel spent 7 percent of its gross national product on education. Between 1948 and 1956, the number of Arab children attending Israeli schools more than doubled. Arabic was their language of instruction, and Hebrew was taught as a second language. In agriculture there was also steady growth in production. In 1950, Israel imported one-half of its food, but by the middle 1960s Israel was self-sufficient in staple foods, and agricultural exports, worth about one-third of total exports, expanded beyond citrus to include cotton, peanuts, and winter vegetables and fruits.

Industrial output increased five times between 1950 and 1969, and it nearly doubled again in the following decade. Tourism grew remarkably. The gross national product increased in real terms from 1950 to 1972 at an annual average rate of nearly 10 percent, and output per worker tripled. Unemployment fell steadily, from 10 percent in 1953 to less than 4 percent in 1967, while the standard of living of the average Israeli steadily and dramatically improved. Despite this economic progress, imports exceeded exports, taxes were very high, and inflation was a constant problem.

Partially because of the newness of the country, the diversity of the origins of its people, and the numerous linguistic and intellectual differences among them, a unified Israeli culture was slow to emerge. The Arab minority did not share at all in Jewish Israeli culture. Many cultural trends and institutions from before 1948 continued for the Jewish majority after independence, as in the theater, but there were also changes in various fields. The Israel Philharmonic Orchestra gained an international reputation, while the Israel Museum in Jerusalem became renowned for its archaeological collections. Archaeology was a national hobby and many famous Israelis, such as Moshe Dayan, were amateur archaeologists. Archaeology represented a way of reasserting the historical continuity of modern Israelis with the ancient history of the Jews in Palestine. The same connection existed in painting in the 1940s and 1950s, as some artists sought a primitivism in style and content. Other painters moved toward abstract, universal art, especially in the 1950s. Painting in the 1960s was influenced by American trends, while public sculpture flourished as memorials were built around the country. Architecture tended to follow Brazilian and French influences in the 1950s and 1960s.

Newspapers flourished, and broadcasting was controlled by the state. Television began in 1966. Israel in 1975 was second in the world in the number of books published per person.

In literature the impact of the Holocaust was very strongly felt, and the most famous Israeli writers internationally were those associated with European Jewry. S. Y. Agnon won the Nobel Prize in literature in 1966. The younger generation of writers spoke Hebrew as their first language, were born in Israel, and were more Israel-centered and less interested in the experiences of Jews in the diaspora. In their novels, poetry, and plays they dwelled on Arab-Israeli relations, wars, materialism, and the antihero.

Women participated vigorously in cultural, economic, and political activities. The declaration of independence, Zionist-labor ideology, and the Women's Equal Rights Law of 1951 all emphasized the equality of men and women, although Jewish religious law gave men a superior role, particularly in matters of marriage and divorce. Most women served in the armed forces, while about one-third of Israeli women by the 1970s worked outside the home. Golda Meir was prime minister from 1969 to 1974, but few other women have been prominent in Israeli politics. Attitudes of Jews from the Middle East were against women working outside the home unless it was absolutely necessary; in this, as in many other aspects of society and culture, Israeli Jews of European background tended to hold sharply differing views.

THE EICHMANN TRIAL

On May 23, 1960, Ben-Gurion startled the world by announcing that Adolf Eichmann, head of the German Gestapo Jewish Affairs Bureau during World War II, had been captured and was in Israel, where he would be tried for his war crimes and genocide against the Jewish people. Located in Argentina and abducted by Israeli agents, he had been flown directly to Israel. Eichmann was ably defended by Robert Servatius of West Germany. He declared that the kidnapping of the prisoner in Argentina made the trial illegal, that Israel and Israeli law did not exist during World War II, and that no Israeli court could be objective in this case. Gideon Hausner, Israeli attorney general, as the chief prosecutor, stated that the manner of bringing the prisoner to trial was irrelevant to the legality of the trial; that no court could be objective in view of the enormity of his crimes; and that there was no international or other national tribunal available for the trial.

Eichmann entered a plea of not guilty. The trial ended August 14, 1961, after an almost daily procession of gruesome photographs, letters, diaries, and witnesses portrayed the dreadful events perpetrated against the Jews for which Eichmann was held responsible, either directly or indirectly. He was judged guilty by the court and executed on May 31, 1962.

The extensive publicity given to the trial and the horrible details contained in the evidence and accusations served to remind the world of the terrible suffering experienced by Jews and to bolster flagging sympathy and support for Israel. Within Israel, the trial spurred comfortable and lagging spirits to make greater efforts to build the state.

FOREIGN AFFAIRS

Israel looked to the United States for political and financial support. In the face of mounting armament in Egypt, Syria, and other Arab states Israel turned to the United States, England, and France for arms of the most recent manufacture and type. In 1958 she obtained Mystère jets from France; in 1962 the United States supplied Hawk missiles and in 1966 offensive weapons such as Skyhawk bombers. Since the cost of such weapons if purchased in an open market was prohibitive, Israel urged that arms be supplied at prices more commensurate with her ability to pay. Israeli leaders believed that their favorable press and many sympathetic coreligionists in the United States would make it difficult for any American administration to act for long in a manner unfriendly to Israel. It was largely this support and confidence that gave the Israeli government its courage in the face of the surrounding hostile Arab states.

In the early days of the state of Israel relations with the Soviet bloc were cordial, and sizable shipments of arms from Czechoslovakia in 1948 were instrumental in winning the 1948 war. Maki (the Communist party) was active, and Mapam subscribed to Marxist philosophy. Mapai, the largest party, followed a left-wing political ideology and was not antagonistic to advanced socialist concepts. However, most Israelis were fiery nationalists and found it difficult to subordinate their aims to those of the U.S.S.R. Moreover, Stalin in his last years became anti-Jewish. In 1955, when the Soviet bloc began cultivating the Arabs and arms deals were made, Israeli feelings toward the U.S.S.R. took a sharp turn for the worse. Nonetheless, since the Arab states did not permit their oil to be delivered to Israel, arrangements were concluded in 1956 to import oil from the U.S.S.R., the price being considerably less than dollar oil from Iran or the Western Hemisphere. After the 1956 war the Arab states complained so bitterly to the U.S.S.R. over the oil affair that deliveries were discontinued, but no break occurred.

Relations remained cool, and in the 1960s as Israel looked more to the West for trade and support and sent her technicians to aid developing African and Asian countries, thus competing with Soviet engineers and agents, the U.S.S.R. grew more critical of Israel. In 1964 all outstanding commercial agreements with Israel were canceled, and Israel on her part complained of the treatment of Jews in the U.S.S.R. and the limitations placed on their cultural development as Jews. In the war of 1967 the Soviet delegate to the U.N. Security Council attacked Israel bitterly and severely as an imperialist and a tool of the imperialists and the Soviets severed relations with Israel.

After the armistice agreements came into effect in 1949, hopes for peace remained unsatisfied. The growth of Arab nationalism, particularly in Egypt and Syria, gave Israeli leaders cause to look to the defenses of the state. The most common expression of Arab leaders in this respect was contained in the idea of a "second round" in which the Israelis would be driven into the sea. On the other hand, some political leaders in Israel, frequently of the Herut party, spoke of the need to expand and to take Aqaba to the south and to incorporate all of Palestine, even Transjordan, into the state of Israel. To many Arabs across the frontier the likelihood of expansion being forced upon Israel by the swarms of immigrants seemed very real. Border incidents occurred every few days, and Arab raids from the Gaza Strip into southern Israel were particularly damaging. Israel was not always blameless in these affairs and was censured or reprimanded for several. In 1953 Israeli troops attacked the Jordanian village of Qibya, and killed fifty-three people in reprisal for the murder of three Israelis.

Until 1956 Israel felt considerable security because of the support of the United States and world Jewry. Her military posture with respect to her neighbors was excellent; jealousies and rivalries among the Arab states, notwithstanding the Arab League, appeared to be her salvation. In 1956, however, there seemed some danger that the balance might be changing in favor of Egypt. The Soviet-bloc arms deals of 1955, the inability of the West to act in the face of Nasser's nationalization of Suez, and Nasser's success in aligning Syria, Jordan, and Egypt in a military pact under one command, thus tightening the noose around Israel, led Ben-Gurion to undertake a military buildup in 1956.

THE 1956 WAR

Israel, England, and France, it turned out, all had been harboring grievances against Egypt, and during the summer plotted an attack. The nationalization of the Suez Canal, the denial of its use to Israeli shipping, the Egyptian possession of the Straits of Tiran, and its closure to the Israelis almost strangled Israeli trade with Japan, Asia, and East Africa. A direct attack upon Egypt seemed the only way out, but Ben-Gurion held that such a unilateral move would open Israeli cities to bombing by Egypt, against which he had little defense. Dayan wrote that if they did not succeed at the very outset in surprising the Egyptians, the Israeli plan would fail. Israel needed the collaboration of the British and the French, especially the former with their bombers based on Cyprus. Britain was seriously provoked by the nationalization of the canal, and France was furious over the help Egypt was affording to the rebels in Algeria. At first England and France wanted to make the assault without Israeli participation, but Israel declared they were engaging in the enterprise willy-nilly.

On October 24 or 25 near Paris, Ben-Gurion, with Dayan at his side, signed an Anglo-French-Israeli agreement to attack Suez. The plan was for Israel to start the attack on October 29, 1956, as though it were a typical border-reprisal raid, and for two days her air force with undercover French assistance would confine itself to protecting Israeli skies and ground forces. This ruse was set so that Egypt would consider it a raid and would be caught by surprise by the subsequent escalation. Then, England and France would enter the war, bomb Egyptian airfields, seize the canal, and cut off Egyptian forces in the Sinai peninsula where they could be utterly destroyed. It all went as planned except that the Anglo-French force did not act quickly enough, perhaps in an attempt to conceal the collusion. It gave time for world opinion, and the actions of the U.S.S.R. and the United States, to force the cease-fire and eventual evacuation.

The Israeli army moved quickly, and by November 7 most of the Sinai peninsula had been occupied. Sharm al-Shaykh, guarding the Straits of Tiran and the entrance to the Gulf of Aqaba, was taken. British and French troops then seized the Suez Canal by heavy bombing and captured Port Said and the northern half of the canal on October 31. Israel's announced war objectives were: to weaken the Arab positions and destroy their arms; to unseat Nasser by administering a swift military defeat; to open the Suez Canal to Israeli use; to control the passage of ships into the Gulf of Aqaba; and to free the port of Eilat.

From the very beginning world opinion was so shocked by the action that achievement of the war aims was doubtful. President Dwight Eisenhower had telephoned British Prime Minister Anthony Eden some days before the outbreak to dissuade him from engaging in such measures. The day before the attack Eisenhower had warned Ben-Gurion against war; and immediately after the attack an emergency meeting of the U.N. Security Council denounced the invasion and demanded a cease-fire. England and France entered the fray with the avowed purpose of keeping the canal open for traffic. Egypt, however, found it easy to block the canal by sinking ships in the channel. With the United States, the U.S.S.R., and most of the world ranged against the three invaders, the cease-fire was accepted on November 7. Withdrawal from Suez by the English and French and from Sinai by the Israelis started within a few days. U.N. forces were gathered and came in to prevent incidents. But Israel refused to surrender the Gaza Strip and Sharm al-Shaykh. Finally, in March 1957 Ben-Gurion, in the teeth of violent opprobrium from the Herut, agreed to withdraw from both points on the "assumption" that border incidents would halt and that the Gulf of Aqaba would be open to Israeli shipping. The troops pulled back, Egyptian civil administrators took over in the Gaza Strip, and the U.N. Emergency Force (UNEF) was permitted to patrol only the Egyptian side of the frontier, including Sharm al-Shaykh. In many observers' eyes the situation returned fully to the conditions prevailing before the outbreak of the war.

The aggressive nationalism of Israel was disclosed by the 1956 war, and many Zionist sympathizers the world over were keenly chagrined by the revelation. The Arab states experienced defeat again and, amazed at the might of Israel, felt the urgent need for more military equipment, organization, and cooperation. The Gulf of Aqaba remained open, and though Egypt and Saudi Arabia protested its use, they made no move to block the Straits of Tiran.

That Egypt would not some day seek revenge for this humiliation no one could gainsay, but Nasser's first reaction was to seek greater influence throughout the Arab world and to disregard Israel. When turmoil developed in Jordan later in 1957, Israel warned against Iraqi or Syrian troops occupying Jordan. It was an open secret that Israel would feel compelled to seize all of Palestine west of the Jordan River if Jordan was annexed to another Arab state. When the revolution in Iraq in 1958 shook confidence in the future of Jordan, Israeli leaders again warned that Israel would move to the west bank of the Jordan River if Syrian or Iraqi troops entered Jordan. Questions of permanent frontiers, the fate of the Palestinians, and Israel's influence with the world powers remained to be settled.

ISRAEL AND THE ARABS AFTER THE 1956 WAR

Following the 1956 war, Israel proceeded with her plans to build a nuclear reactor in the Negev to develop an atom bomb, which was achieved ultimately in the 1970s, thereby guaranteeing Israel military superiority over her neighbors who did not possess atomic weapons.

With UNEF stationed on the Egyptian side of the frontier, clashes after 1957 were rare there. Israel would not permit this group on Israeli soil so that UNEF was unable to control Israeli movements. For the most part, Israel's clashes with her Arab neighbors centered on Syria. The border had a neutral demilitarized zone, with both sides asserting the rights of its owners to cultivate it. Each spring there were raids by Arabs upon Israelis who were cultivating land in the demilitarized zone, to which Israel frequently answered with reprisals.

The most serious Israeli reprisal occurred in 1966 against the village of al-Samu, Jordan. The Security Council censured Israel for the deed and King Husayn of Jordan was bitterly criticized by the Arab League and by large numbers of his own subjects for not having replied to the Israeli forces. Some feared he might lose his throne as a result of the incident, and even Israel was worried over this possibility, for any new group in Amman would be less friendly to Israel than Husayn had been. Within Israel there was grave concern lest Eshkol's government had gone too far.

The problem of the infiltration of the Israeli frontier by Arab individuals and guerrillas such as the al-Fatah group, the planting of mines, arson, and the shootings of soldiers, police, and farmers continued. The solution seemed as far away as ever, though some Israelis began doubting that reprisals against the Palestinians they called terrorists were the answer.

Israel was not accepted by its Arab neighbors and it lacked legitimacy in their eyes and also in the views of the Arab Palestinians, many of whom still hoped to create an Arab Palestine with a Jewish minority in the land.

TRANSJORDAN

East of the Jordan River Prince Abd Allah ruled his semidesert domain and people under the tutelage of Great Britain. The strength of his position was anchored to the financial and diplomatic contributions of Great Britain and was buoyed by the Arab Legion and the Transjordan frontier force, the strongest Arab armies in the

Middle East in the 1940s. The British found them useful in Iraq and Syria during World War II. Abd Allah was the staunchest friend of the British in the Middle East.

Abd Allah's rule and his governmental machinery were uncomplicated until 1949. A new treaty was drafted and signed in 1946, recognizing Abd Allah as king of Transjordan and giving him greater independence from Great Britain, which was permitted to keep a military mission and various training facilities in the country. A constitution was promulgated and became effective in 1947, providing for a chamber of deputies consisting of 20 members: 12 Muslim Arabs, 4 Christian Arabs, 2 Muslim Bedouins, and 2 Muslims to represent the ethnic minorities. The other house of the parliament was a council of notables composed of ten members appointed by the king.

King Abd Allah was strongly criticized in the Arab League for agreeing to such a subservient position as the treaty established, and Transjordan's application for membership in the United Nations was blocked by the Soviets on the grounds that Transjordan was not independent. Consequently, another treaty was signed in 1948, specifying "co-operation and mutual assistance" between Transjordan and Great Britain. In new elections only one political party presented candidates for the chamber of deputies, although a few independents were returned. Aside from Abd Allah's relations with the British and the annual subvention received from them, his main attention politically centered not upon Transjordan but rather upon the dream of a greater Syria over which he would rule.

During the 1948 war, the Arab Legion occupied East Jerusalem and the fortress of Latrun against desperate Israeli attacks. Together with Iraqi troops, Abd Allah's forces held the lines from the Gulf of Aqaba to north central Palestine and bore the main brunt of Israeli drives. Abd Allah favored the Nashashibi and other Palestinian families who opposed the al-Husaynis and the ex-mufti Hajj Amin al-Husayni. When the defeat of the Arabs could no longer be denied, Abd Allah acted to incorporate what remained of Palestine into his state, and in 1949 renamed it the Hashimite Kingdom of Jordan.

HASHIMITE KINGDOM OF JORDAN

Almost overnight King Abd Allah's problems became exceedingly complex. The small state of an estimated 400,000 inhabitants suddenly burgeoned into a kingdom of 1,360,000 people. More than half of the Arab refugees flocked into Jordan. Those who had means of support, an education, or a skill either integrated themselves into Jordanian life or migrated to other Arab lands or to the far corners of the earth; nearly 500,000 did not and continued to live in refugee camps.

Grave as the refugee situation was, the most significant aspect of this influx and the annexation of Arab Palestine to Transjordan sprang from a transformation in the character of the state. West Jordanians and refugees after 1950 comprised more than half of the population. On the average they were better educated, more politically minded, more ardent in their Arab nationalism, and more unremitting in their desire to have a "second round" with Israel and regain mastery in their own state. Abd Allah doubled the size of the chamber of deputies in 1950, and half of the members were elected to represent each side of the Jordan. The council of notables was also increased to a membership of twenty, seven of whom were Palestinian. All real power continued to be, however, in the hands of the king.

The Palestinian Arabs, accustomed to blaming their woes on the Zionists and the British, turned their frustration on King Abd Allah. He was a sane and shrewd ruler, as well as moderate and realistic. For these attributes he was despised as too conciliatory toward the Israelis with whom he had many secret contacts. In 1951 he was murdered in Jerusalem by an adherent of the ex-mufti, Hajj Amin al-Husayni.

KING HUSAYN

The king's eldest son, Talal, was proclaimed king. His emotional stability was highly questionable, and in 1952 he departed for Europe, leaving the kingdom to his son Husayn. The latter became king on his eighteenth birthday, in 1953. The post of prime minister became more important, but until 1956 the position shifted from one old-time political friend of the king to another.

Britain continued her support of the Arab Legion and subsidized the government to the extent of several million pounds annually. The signing of the Baghdad and Damascus Pacts in 1955 and the formation of power rivalries in the Middle East placed Jordan in a critical position. Her dynasty belonged to the same family as that of Iraq, and her financial ties to England favored a closer relationship to the Baghdad Pact. But the bitter denunciations of the pact from the other Arab League states, led by Egypt and Syria, warned Jordan of the dangers in allying herself with Britain, Turkey, and Iraq. Furthermore, Palestinian Arabs, in their campaign to regain possession of the whole of Palestine, were very skeptical of a pact that included or was under the patronage of any Western state, for it was generally understood that the West would not permit the destruction of Israel.

Thus, in 1955 when pressure was exerted upon Jordan to join the Baghdad Pact, Saudi Arabia announced her willingness to contribute to the support of Jordan's government and the Arab Legion on the condition that the British be ousted. John Bagot Glubb Pasha, the English head of the Arab Legion, was dismissed summarily in March 1956 and was replaced shortly by Colonel Ali Abu Nuwar, the military aide and long-time companion of King Husayn. Abu Nuwar became chief of staff, head of the Arab Legion, and a contender for complete power in Jordan. Britain continued financial support, but sympathizers of President Nasser rapidly gained in strength and position in Jordan. King Husayn was young and inexperienced. Abu Nuwar, young and exceedingly ambitious, looked upon himself as the Nasser of Jordan, and gathered together a band of young and ardent nationalistic officers seeking power.

JORDANIAN CRISES

With the nationalization of the Suez Canal Company in 1956 Abu Nuwar went from Beirut to Damascus to Cairo, receiving assurances of military assistance in case Jordan were attacked.

With that backdrop for an election campaign, leftist and pan-Arab candidates were assured victory in the relatively free parliamentary elections. The king was too young and inexperienced to control them as had been the case earlier and as was to occur later. About 50 percent of the qualified voters cast ballots, and the National Socialists under Sulayman Nabulsi won eleven seats in the 40-member chamber. Nabulsi's cabinet was installed the day Israel invaded Egypt, and Syrian and Iraqi troops moved in to safeguard Jordan from Israel—and from one another.

Nabulsi frequently suggested that Jordan should ask for arms and aid from the Soviet bloc. Passionately anti-British, he reminded Syria, Egypt, and Saudi Arabia of their offer to assume the annual subvention Jordan received from Great Britain and declared that Jordan was ready to terminate her treaty with Great Britain.

Many Jordanians rejoiced as the British troops departed in 1957. Nabulsi, in collaboration with Abu Nuwar, appeared ready to form a closer political, economic, and military union with Syria. However, King Husayn dismissed Nabulsi, and Abu Nuwar fled to escape arrest. Syrian troops moved to occupy north Jordan. The fate of King Husayn hung in the balance. Showing real courage, Husayn rallied his Bedouin troops about him at Zarka and reestablished peace and his authority. From that point forward, Husayn ruled the country and held all political power in his hands.

Jordan's finances were in serious trouble. Saudi Arabia paid her first installment on the Arab solidarity pact in May, but nothing was forthcoming from Egypt or Syria. Husayn, therefore, asked for aid from Iraq and the United States. Arms from the United States were airlifted to Amman in September. Feeling more secure, Husayn convened parliament in October and denounced U.S.S.R. sympathizers. The Ba'th and Communist parties were outlawed, and the plan to merge Jordan with Syria was driven underground.

The next crisis arose when Syria and Egypt formed the United Arab Republic. Husayn begged his cousin in Iraq to visit Amman and protect Jordan by establishing some type of federal union. As a result the Arab Federation was consummated in February 1958. Provisions were included in its constitution to ensure separate treaty obligations, as Husayn did not believe Syria would countenance his adherence to the Baghdad Pact. King Husayn became an alternate to the chief of state, and procedural steps for closer federation were undertaken.

But still another and more serious crisis fell on Husayn in July 1958, with the revolution in Iraq and the murder of King Faysal, of Arab Federation prime minister Nuri al-Said, and of two Jordanians in the federation's cabinet. Left, technically, head of the federation, Husayn proceeded to assert his authority, but Iraq abrogated the union, abruptly throwing Jordan adrift in a turbulent storm of Arab nationalism. British paratroopers were flown in from Cyprus. The Bedouin troops rallied to Husayn's side, and his throne seemed secure as long as the British troops remained in Jordan.

With Egypt and Syria bound together in the United Arab Republic, with Iraq having ousted the monarchy and destroyed the Hashimite family there, with the Saudi family maintaining its perpetual feud with the Hashimites, with Israeli expansionists talking of annexing all of Palestine west of the Jordan River, with several thousand British soldiers in Jordan causing Arab nationalists everywhere to call King Husayn the tool of the imperialists, and with half of his own subjects wishing for a different state and a different regime, retreating to a villa in Lausanne must have seemed tempting to Husayn. To make matters worse, nearly 75 percent of Jordan's total revenues in 1958 came from grants and subsidies from Great Britain and the United States. Imports were more than eleven times the amount of exports. Local capital was virtually nonexistent and exploitable natural resources were unknown. But King Husayn was tough and tenacious. He enjoyed the loyalty of his army, which was regarded as the best-trained and best-equipped force among the Arabs. The British troops left in November, and Husayn set out to keep his throne. His program consisted of internal economic growth and development, aimed at making Jordan economically self-sufficient; of stabilizing the government; and of steering an artful course among the jealousies, rivalries, ambitions, and ideologies of his Arab neighbors.

In 1959 the Jordan Development Board was established to coordinate and sponsor efforts to increase the productivity of the state. A major project was the East Ghor Canal, which was to channel off water from the Yarmuk River and carry it parallel and east of the Jordan River for more than forty miles toward the Dead Sea to irrigate dry but fertile lands. The first stage was finished in 1961. The banks of the canal would be heightened as more water became available; at two Arab summit meetings in 1964, plans for diverting water from the Hasbani and Banyas rivers to the Yarmuk and for building dams on the Yarmuk were designed to augment the flow into an enlarged East Ghor Canal. The Jordan Phosphate Company received loans from the U.S. government to enlarge its facilities for exploiting the vast chemical deposits in the Dead Sea. Tourism became a growing industry as Jordan began to capitalize on her wealth of archaeological remains, as at Petra.

Despite economic progress the long-range future of the kingdom seemed uncertain as the Arab states voted in Cairo in 1964 to create an Arab political entity for the Palestinians. Known as the Palestine Liberation Organization (PLO), it was to raise an army that would have a separate identity but be a part of the army in each of the Arab host states. In 1966 Husayn agreed that PLO might conduct elections in Jordan for the national assembly, but he refused to accept its armed forces or PLO leader Ahmad Shuqayri's suggestion that the capital of Jordan should be transferred to Jerusalem.

Vilification of Husayn from some Arab capitals continued, and Damascus suggested that the Syrian army would gladly supply arms to those who wished to overthrow him. Yet, in May 1967, at the height of the crisis with Israel, Husayn flew to Cairo where Nasser embraced him at the airport. They proceeded to sign a five-year mutual defense pact, and Jordan pledged her army, should war come with Israel. Husayn believed fully that his throne would be lost and he assassinated if his army did not move promptly and with full vigor on the center front in any Arab-Israeli confrontation.

REFERENCES

The number of books covering this subject is very large and is growing rapidly. Of special significance are items in Chapters 34 and 42.

Abdallah, King. *My Memoirs Completed.* Translated by Harold Glidden. Washington, D.C.: American Council of Learned Societies, 1954. A continuation of the reference edited by Philip P. Graves in Chapter 34.

Abidi, Aqil Hyder Hasan. *Jordan: A Political Study, 1948–1957.* New York: Asia Publishing House, 1965. Scholarly, well-researched and documented, and readable.

Allon, Yigal. *The Making of Israel's Army.* New York: Universe Books, 1970. Allon, who has been deputy prime minister of Israel, was a commander in the Palmach and one of the architects of the Israeli defense forces.

Beaufre, André. *The Suez Expedition, 1956.* New York: Praeger, 1969. Beaufre was the key French officer in the planning and execution of the Suez operation.

Begin, Menachem. *The Revolt: Story of the Irgun.* New York: Schuman, 1951. A fascinating story by the Irgun's leader, a legendary figure who became prime minister in 1977.

Bell, J. Bowyer. *Terror Out of Zion, Lehi and the Palestine Underground.* New York: St. Martin's Press, 1977. The story of Irgun and the Sternists.

Ben-Gurion, David. *Israel: Years of Challenge.* New York: Holt, 1963. An account of the founding of the state and the accomplishments of the first decade.

Bernadotte, Folke. *To Jerusalem.* London: Hodder & Stoughton, 1951. By the U.N. mediator who was assassinated while attempting to bring peace.

Bernstein, Marver H. *The Politics of Israel: The First Decade of Statehood.* Princeton, N.J.: Princeton University Press, 1957. The best study of Israel's early government, administration, and politics.

Brecher, Michael. *Decisions in Israel's Foreign Policy.* New Haven, Conn.: Yale University Press, 1975. It contains an analysis of decision making in Israel on critical issues, including the war of 1956 and the war of 1967.

Buehrig, Edward H. *The U.N. and the Palestinian Refugees: A Study in Nonterritorial Administration.* Bloomington: Indiana University Press, 1971.

Burns, E. L. M. *Between Arab and Israeli.* London: Harrap, 1962. By the Canadian general who headed the U.N. Truce Supervision Organization after 1949.

Collins, Larry, and Dominique Lapierre. *O Jerusalem!* New York: Simon and Schuster, 1972. A lengthy but very well-written account of the 1948 war.

Crosbie, Sylvia Kowitt. *A Tacit Alliance: France and Israel from Suez to the Six-Day War.* Princeton, N.J.: Princeton University Press, 1974. Traces the rise of Franco-Israeli friendship to 1967.

Dayan, Moshe. *Diary of the Sinai Campaign.* New York: Schocken Books, 1967. A first-hand account by the commanding general of the Israeli forces.

———. *Story of My Life.* London: Sphere Books, 1978. Covers the life of this very important Israeli general and politician up to 1975.

Eban, Abba. *Autobiography.* New York: Random House, 1977. A full story of his public life.

Eytan, Walter. *The First Ten Years: A Diplomatic History of Israel.* New York: Simon and Schuster, 1958. By the director-general of the Israeli Foreign Office.

Flapan, Simha. *The Birth of Israel: Myths and Realities.* New York: Pantheon Books, 1987. A careful examination, based on Israeli archives, by a prominent revisionist Israeli scholar.

Glubb, Sir John Bagot. *A Soldier with the Arabs.* New York: Harper, 1958. The memoirs of a professional soldier with experience in Iraq and Jordan who served as chief of staff of Jordan's Arab Legion until 1956. Indispensable.

Halevi, Nadav, and Ruth Klinov-Malul. *The Economic Development of Israel.* New York: Praeger, 1968. A macroeconomic analysis of the period since 1947.

Harlap, Amiram. *New Israeli Architecture.* East Brunswick, N.J.: Associated University Presses, 1982. General trends as well as many specific examples.

Hazleton, Lesley. *Israeli Women: The Reality Behind the Myths.* New York: Simon and Schuster, 1977. A feminist critique of what the author calls the myth of equality in Israel.

Herzog, Chaim. *The Arab-Israeli Wars: War and Peace in the Middle East.* New York: Random House, 1982. Covers the war of attrition and the 1982 war in Lebanon as well as the other conflicts; a very valuable and detailed account by the president of Israel who was also a major-general in the Israeli army.

Jiryis, Sabri. *The Arabs in Israel.* Translated by Inea Bushnaq. New York: Monthly Review Press, 1976. Deals especially with the effects of the military government on Arab Israelis.

Khouri, Fred J. *The Arab-Israeli Dilemma.* Syracuse, N.Y.: Syracuse University Press, 1985. 3rd ed. A scholarly and comprehensive portrayal of the views, politics, and actions of the contending parties. One of the best sources available on this issue.

Kimche, Jon. *Seven Fallen Pillars.* New York: Praeger, 1953. An account of the 1948 Arab-Israeli War.

Litvinoff, Barnett. *Ben-Gurion: The Biography of a Statesman.* New York: Praeger, 1954. Based largely on interviews with people close to Ben-Gurion.

Love, Kenneth. *Suez: The Twice Fought War: A History.* New York: McGraw-Hill, 1969. A monumental work on the 1956 conflict.

Luttwak, Edward, and Dan Horowitz. *The Israeli Army.* New York: Harper and Row, 1975. One of the best studies of the Israeli military.

O'Ballance, Edgar. *The Arab-Israeli War, 1948.* New York: Praeger, 1957. An excellent military study.

Peretz, Don. *The Government and Politics of Israel.* Boulder, Colo.: Westview Press, 1983. 2d ed. Especially good on the political parties and the actual functioning of government.

Polk, William R. *The Elusive Peace: The Middle East in the Twentieth Century.* New York: St. Martin's Press, 1979. Concentrates on the role of the Palestinians, nationalism, and the

Arab-Israeli dispute; by one of the most thoughtful writers on modern Middle Eastern history.

Qawuqji, Fauzi al-. "Memoirs." *Journal of Palestine Studies* 1: 4 (1972): 27–58 and 2: 1 (1972): 3–33. Extracts from the diary kept by one of the Arab leaders in the 1948 war.

Safran, Nadav. *The United States and Israel.* Cambridge, Mass.: Harvard University Press, 1963.

Segre, V. D. *Israel: A Society in Transition.* London: Oxford University Press, 1971. A sociological study of Israel's development.

Selzer, Michael. *The Wineskin and the Wizard.* New York: Macmillan, 1970. A profound study of what it means to be a Jew, and an explanation of the Jewish mission and its relation to the state of Israel.

Shlaim, Avi. "Conflicting Approaches to Israel's Relations with the Arabs: Ben Gurion and Sharett, 1953–1956." *Middle East Journal* 37 (1983): 180–201. Shows the great differences between the two; based on original and highly informative sources.

Spiro, Melford E. *Kibbutz: Venture in Utopia.* Cambridge, Mass.: Harvard University Press, 1956. An intimate study of a kibbutz.

Wilson, Evan M. *Jerusalem: Key to Peace.* Washington, D.C.: Middle East Institute, 1970. An account of the city from 1945 to 1967 by the American consul general in Jerusalem from 1964 to 1967.

Zahlan, Antoine. "The Science and Technology Gap in the Arab-Israeli Conflict." *Journal of Palestine Studies* 1: 3 (1972): 17–36. Shows some of the reasons for Israeli success over the Arabs were in the accomplishments of Israel in science and technology.

44

Israel, Jordan, and the Palestinians Since 1967

THE 1967 WAR

Israeli cabinet members, under great pressure from the public for action against mines, bombs, and killings, spoke out on the possibilities of a penetration in depth in Syria, which was regarded as the base of al-Fatah operations. The Syrians believed they had evidence that an Israeli move was scheduled for May 1967. Alarmed, they called upon Egypt to make good on her mutual-defense pact. This led Nasser to request the secretary-general of the United Nations to remove its troops from Egypt. This he promptly did—some thought too promptly—and since Israel in 1957 had refused to accept any UNEF troops on her soil the frontier was suddenly alive with military forces on each side. With the U.N. leaving Sharm al-Shaykh, Egypt took over there and announced the closing of the Straits of Tiran to Israeli shipping. Egypt had never renounced her claim that these straits were territorial waters. The loss of free navigation to and from the Gulf of Aqaba was so menacing that Israel declared she would rather fight than acquiesce in this closure. This was the difficult problem facing the Security Council in 1967.

When it became apparent that neither the United States nor the U.N. was able to effect an immediate opening of the Straits of Tiran, and in order to preclude Egypt and its allies from attacking Israel, the Israelis launched an attack upon Egypt. Although Israel warned Jordan and Syria to stay out of the quarrel, they had joined with Egypt to form a united front. Israel believed, however, that the most serious challenge would come from Egypt. Nasser had begun to mobilize his troops in Sinai even before the U.N. withdrawal. Coupled with his bellicose public speeches, the concentration of Egyptian forces east of the Suez Canal forced Israel to act. General Dayan, the hero of the 1956 Sinai campaign, was brought into the cabinet as minister of defense. On June 5, Israel, in a surprise attack, destroyed the air capabilities of Egypt, Jordan, and Syria. With complete mastery of the skies and superb coordination of all branches of the military, Israeli forces within six days occupied the Gaza Strip, all of Sinai to the east bank of the Suez Canal, all of Jordan west of the Jordan River including East Jerusalem, and the Golan Heights of Syria. When they captured the Old City of Jerusalem, Israelis poured into the streets to rejoice at the seizing of their holy places. They then agreed to a cease-fire called for by the U.N. Security Council.

Throughout the summer and autumn of 1967, at numerous sessions of the U.N. Security Council and General Assembly, Israel's Foreign Minister Abba Eban stated repeatedly that there could be no peace until the Arab states sat down and negotiated directly with Israel, even though Eban knew full well that no Arab leader felt sufficiently secure to do this. Israeli demands, in addition to recognition by the Arabs, were the establishment of definite boundaries, the guaranteed use of the Suez Canal and the Straits of Tiran, and the end of raids and terrorism. Within a few days of the cease-fire, the eastern part of Jerusalem was incorporated into the Israeli sector; General Dayan and others categorically stated that this act was permanent and not negotiable. Structures before the Western Wall were bulldozed away so that the many thousands who came there to pray could be accommodated.

Israel said that Arabs living in East Jerusalem now could choose either to be citizens of Israel or of Jordan. Most chose to be considered Jordanians. In the Gaza Strip and the West Bank Israel ruled the Arabs by military force. The Arab Palestinians there did not become citizens of Israel and they had almost no voice in their own governance.

As the summer passed it became doubtful that the Arab leaders would negotiate with Israel, especially after the Arab summit meeting at Khartoum in August where such a step was vigorously condemned. The Israeli government now was faced with the problem of what to do with the occupied territories. Some proposed an autonomous Arab state federated with Israel, while others favored annexation or the return of the land to Jordan in exchange for peace. Each day that no settlement was achieved, the status quo became more difficult to dislodge.

No resolution of the tensions in the Middle East appeared remotely possible. On November 22, 1967, the Security Council passed unanimously Resolution 242, authorizing Secretary-General U Thant to send to the Middle East a special personal representative to negotiate peace between Israel and her Arab neighbors. Resolution 242 implicitly recognized Israel's right to exist, and called for the establishment of permanent borders, withdrawal of Israeli troops from occupied lands, Israeli use of the Suez Canal and the Straits of Tiran, and a just settlement for refugees. Gunnar Jarring of Sweden was appointed for this mission, which had no chance for success because Nasser declared that he would not recognize Israel and that the Suez Canal would not be open to Israel as long as Israel occupied Arab lands. At the same time, Israel repeated that there could be no substitute for direct negotiations. Many believed that Israel's leaders took this stand to avoid having to commit themselves on what they would accept as the state's new frontiers, since they were not sure that the Israeli public would condone any withdrawal from lands won in the 1967 war.

NO PEACE, NO WAR

The expenses of the war and of maintaining the occupied territories left Israeli finances in a weak position. The unfavorable trade gap of $200–$300 million a year was met from gifts and loans by foreign governments and individuals. The expectation of such annual sums made it possible to live with large budgetary deficits, at a time when defense spending took half the entire budget. In 1968 it was estimated that nearly 60 percent of the budget was raised by bond sales in the United States and Canada. Meanwhile, the trade gap did not disappear: in 1969 it was over $700 million; by 1973 it had soared to $1.5 billion. Drives to curb imports, high taxes on all luxury items, tariffs, and liberal gifts from abroad did not seem to suffice. In 1970 the European Economic Community agreed to a preferential trade arrangement that would, over a three-year period, reduce European tariffs on Israeli goods by 50 percent, with the hope of opening up new markets to Israeli producers. But the advent of another war in 1973, followed by worldwide inflation and economic recession, and the quadrupling of energy costs, so altered conditions that the EEC arrangement could not be tested properly. Israel's trade gaps persisted; the military and defense expenditures did not permit otherwise.

During the six-year interlude between the wars of 1967 and 1973 the development and industrialization of Israel proceeded rapidly, though not as swiftly as many wished. However, economic growth did increase substantially, with per-capita income going from $1,011 in 1967 to $2,806 in 1973. Production climbed in most sectors of the economy, and capital investment from overseas was impressive.

Inflation grew rampant. To stem it wage and price controls were tried, but they proved unworkable and ill-suited to an economy in which a preponderance of goods were imported. The budget and that portion of it allocated to defense increased dramatically until 1972 when defense demands fell below 30 percent. Still, enormous defense costs were a crushing burden on Israelis, who accepted them as the price of survival.

In these years cynics began to assert that Israel was losing her special character and becoming like other societies. They cited as evidence a growing materialism. The utopian idealism of the kibbutz, the agricultural commune, was waning. Moreover, there was an astounding rise in the nation's crime rate. Though some spirits did flag, Israel's military victories and ensuing self-confidence generated widespread ebullience and produced advances in business enterprise, art, literature, scientific discovery, and archaeology. Life in Israel in 1973 was vibrant but, as the continual rash of strikes showed, many were dissatisfied with the present. And many were apprehensive of the future.

After the Arab part of Jerusalem was proclaimed an integral part of Israeli Jerusalem, plans were developed to reconstruct the old Jewish quarter inside the medieval walls, evicting Arabs who had lived there since 1948, when the Jewish inhabitants were evicted. In 1969, after a fire raged for two hours in the very holy al-Aqsa mosque in Jerusalem, the Islamic states in a meeting at Rabat accused Israel of careless surveillance. Authorities in Jerusalem apprehended a foreign Christian who was adjudged the arsonist and found to be mentally deranged. Incidents of various kinds occurred repeatedly and Israeli officials reacted by expelling Arabs—teachers, shopkeepers, religious leaders, and notables—to Jordan and sometimes confiscating or bulldozing shops and homes. The physical and economic aspects of the city were greatly enhanced but the Arab inhabitants never felt secure as citizens with rights equal to the others.

In much of the rest of the occupied territories life went on as before. After the Israeli economy had been righted trade between Israel and the occupied lands began to provide a substantial market for West Bank produce; in addition, the previous markets in Amman and on the East Bank remained accessible to the West Bank, as bridges over the Jordan River were reopened. Yet, the Arabs deeply resented having to live under an occupying force. This brought incidents of violence, anti-Jewish reactions, and stern Israeli reprisals.

Soon after the end of the fighting in 1967, Jewish settlers moved into places near Hebron and Jericho from which Jews had been forced to leave in 1948. New settlements were established in the occupied lands as Dayan advocated that new settlements be established in any occupied area from which Israel did not intend to withdraw.

The cease-fires arranged in June 1967 were never fully observed, and Resolution 242, though accepted in principle by all parties, could not be implemented as no agreement could be reached on the meaning and extent of Israeli withdrawal. By 1968 air raids and artillery duels on the Golan Heights and over Suez were commonplace. All semblance of peace disappeared in 1969. In one fifty day period Egypt flew 100 sorties against the Israelis in Sinai and the Israelis countered with 1,000 over Egypt. After an Arab attack on Eilat, Israeli bombers knocked out Jordan's East Ghor irrigation system. Air encounters over Syria and Golan were daily occurrences. In the first three months of 1970 Israel made air raids deep into Egypt; these were curtailed when losses inflicted by newly installed Soviet surface-to-air missiles made the missions too costly. On August 7, 1970, a ninety-day cease-fire between Israel and Egypt arranged by U.S. Secretary of State Rogers went into effect.

The tempo of the war of attrition along the canal never rose to the level of the 1967 war, and it gradually ended. On the Syrian front artillery duels and even tank battles occurred and air engagements often over the Mediterranean kept all on constant alert. One battle in November 1972 lasted eight hours and to many it seemed that all-out war must be imminent. After King Husayn defeated and drove all armed Palestinian forces from Jordan in 1970–1971, they settled in Lebanon and began to harass Israel from south Lebanon, which many began to call "Fatahland." By 1973 peace in the Middle East was as elusive as ever.

In the six years following the 1967 war Israel felt compelled to allocate over $6 billion for defense expenditures; several billion dollars more came in the form of gifts and marked-down sales of matériel from the United States. General Bar Lev, Israel's chief of staff, directed the construction of a strong defense, named the Bar Lev line, east of the Suez Canal to serve as a forward wall against attack.

Israel found herself increasingly dependent on the United States. Her diplomatic relations with many nations, especially in Europe, took on a formal, often frosty, tone; by the end of 1969 Israel found herself isolated at the U.N. and unwelcome in many European capitals.

After the June 1967 war Dayan remained minister of defense; his splinter Rafi party, along with another centrist party, Ahdut Avodah, were gradually reintegrated into Mapai. General Itzhak Rabin, chief of staff and one of the architects of the 1967 victory, was appointed ambassador to Washington in 1968. Though there were significant political divisions on ideas regarding peace, Mapai was united for the election of 1969, joining with Mapam to form a Labor Alignment. Prime Minister Eshkol died on February 26, 1969, and on March 17 the party chose Golda Meir to become Israel's fourth prime minister.

Sixteen parties participated in the October 1969 elections for the Knesset. The Labor Alignment won fifty-six seats, and after much political maneuvering Meir enticed the right-wing Gahal party, the National Religious party, and others to join a coalition commanding ninety-eight seats in the Knesset. Showing great skill in pouring balm on open political wounds, she formed a broad coalition cabinet. To hold together such a galaxy of prima donnas was not easy, and it was said frequently that only Golda Meir had the ability to manage them. In August 1970, Gahal withdrew in protest over the cabinet's acceptance of the American-sponsored cease-fire at Suez. In 1973 Gahal joined Herut and the Liberals to form a new right-wing bloc, Likud, in preparation for the October elections.

THE WAR OF 1973

War broke out again on October 6, 1973, as Egypt and Syria, in a surprise, coordinated campaign, attacked Israel on Yom Kippur, Judaism's Day of Atonement. The war also fell during Ramadan, the Muslim month of fasting. Egyptian forces quickly crossed the Suez Canal, shattering the thinly manned Bar Lev line, while Syrian troops occupied Mt. Hermon and retook much of Golan. Within a few days the highly trained, well-organized, and spirited Israeli forces were able to beat back the attacks and go on the offensive. They contained the Syrian drive and directed air attacks at Latakia, Banyas, Tartus, and Homs, where the oil refinery was destroyed and new industrial plants were leveled. A few districts in Damascus were bombed and Israeli troops reached Sasa, about 22 miles (35 kilometers) from the capital. On the southern front Israeli forces had crossed to the west bank of the Suez Canal and were driving to surround the Egyptian Third Army on the east bank, when a cease-fire was arranged. The quantities of weapons deployed and destroyed on all sides were enormous. Five days after the war started the Soviets were airlifting weapons, tanks, and airplanes to Egypt and Syria in astounding numbers. Israel called upon the United States for help, and began to receive massive shipments on the eighth day of fighting. In all it was estimated that Israel lost 500 tanks and 120 aircraft and suffered 2,400 killed and as many wounded; the Arabs lost 1,500 tanks and 450 airplanes, while their numbers killed and wounded exceeded Israel's. The cost to all the combatants was staggering; it has been estimated that Israel spent $7.2 billion.

The magnitude of the war shocked the world, and when the U.S.S.R. and the United States became indirectly involved as suppliers the full impact of the war was frightening. The U.N. Security Council could do nothing to stop the fighting, so on October 20 Secretary of State Kissinger flew to Moscow and reached an understanding permitting the adoption of U.N. Resolution 338 which called for a cease-fire on October 22. The cease-fire did not hold, and the U.S.S.R. suggested to the United States that the two take action to enforce it. When the United States

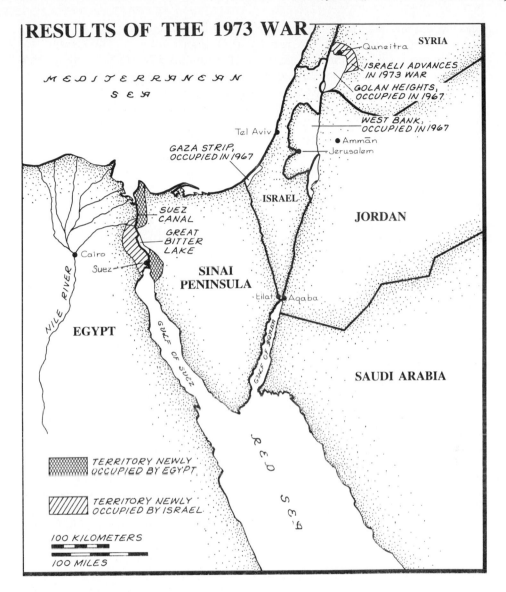

RESULTS OF THE 1973 WAR

MEDITERRANEAN SEA

SYRIA

Quneitra

ISRAELI ADVANCES
IN 1973 WAR

GOLAN HEIGHTS,
OCCUPIED IN 1967

WEST BANK,
OCCUPIED IN 1967

Tel Aviv

GAZA STRIP,
OCCUPIED IN 1967

Amman
Jerusalem

ISRAEL

JORDAN

SUEZ
CANAL

GREAT
BITTER
LAKE

Cairo

Suez

SINAI
PENINSULA

Eilat Aqaba

EGYPT

NILE RIVER

GULF OF SUEZ

GULF OF AQABA

SAUDI ARABIA

RED SEA

TERRITORY NEWLY
OCCUPIED BY EGYPT

TERRITORY NEWLY
OCCUPIED BY ISRAEL

100 KILOMETERS

100 MILES

rejected this the Soviets seemed as if they would intervene unilaterally, where-upon President Nixon ordered a partial alert of American forces. The specter of a world war loomed until the passage of U.N. Resolutions 339 and 340, calling for a cease-fire and providing for a United Nations Emergency Force (UNEF), which began to arrive on the lines between the Egyptian and Israeli armies on October 27.

Tensions eased on November 11 when Israeli and Egyptian officers met on the road to Cairo and signed an agreement freeing the trapped Egyptian Third Army and providing for the immediate exchange of prisoners, an end to the Arab blockade at the southern end of the Red Sea, further negotiations on cease-fire lines, negotiations on an overall settlement, and U.N. enforcement of the cease-fire. A conference on an overall peace settlement was convened in Geneva in December by the United States and the Soviet Union, but it was adjourned after one day. Amid continual cease-fire violations Egypt and Israel, prodded by the United States, signed a disengagement agreement in January 1974. Israel agreed to pull back her troops 20 kilometers east of the canal and allowed limited numbers of Egyptian soldiers to be stationed on the east bank, separated from Israeli forces by UNEF detachments.

The cease-fire on the Syrian front was abrogated repeatedly until May 1974. After Kissinger engaged in several rounds of shuttle diplomacy between Jerusalem and Damascus, all additional territory on the Golan seized by Israel in the 1973 war, as well as the city of al-Quneitra taken in 1967, was relinquished to Syria. U.N. Disengagement Observer Force units were placed between the two antagonists on a three-month, renewable basis.

Rather than return to Geneva, Israel and the United States preferred a step-by-step approach to peace. Kissinger shuttled between Jerusalem and Cairo, with side trips to Damascus, Riyadh, and Amman, until Israel and Egypt signed a Sinai disengagement pact in Geneva in September 1975. Israeli forces withdrew east-ward in Sinai for 50 kilometers, yielding the strategic Mitla and Giddi passes. UNEF units were stationed between the Israeli and Egyptian zones with an early-warning electronic system erected at the passes and manned by 200 American civilian technicians. Israel agreed to return the oil fields in the Sinai to Egypt and Egypt promised to permit nonmilitary cargoes bound for Israel to pass through the canal, which had been reopened in June.

Israel had been preparing for a parliamentary election when the war broke out. The platform of the Labor Alignment had been more "dovish" than before. Postponed until the end of December 1973, the election, in which twenty-two parties and splinter groups presented candidates, diminished strength for the Labor Alignment. It won just under 40 percent of the popular vote, and its seats in the Knesset were reduced from 56 to 51, while Likud, the more "hawkish" coalition, received more than 25 percent of the votes and increased its position from 32 to 39 seats.

Shortly after the elections, the Agranat Commission that had been appointed to investigate the conduct of the war issued its report blaming the army chief of staff, along with Defense Minister Dayan and Prime Minister Meir, for Israel's un-preparedness and early setbacks. Golda Meir resigned, and the Labor Alignment chose Itzhak Rabin to head a new government. He had been chief of staff from 1963 to 1967 and ambassador to Washington from 1968 to 1973.

Meir and Rabin had to deal with the exceptional costs of the war, which dislocated Israel's economy. Then, OPEC's quadrupling of oil prices brought worldwide inflation and recession. Israel's budget moved up to $8.4 billion in 1974, with over 40 percent for defense, and to $15 billion in 1977, $4 billion of which went for defense. The Israeli pound underwent almost constant devaluations. Taxes jumped until it was estimated that Israelis paid about 70 percent of their income to the state. Despite these problems immigration increased, as Jews from the Soviet Union came to Israel by the thousands in the 1970s. However, Israel's domestic problems had an effect on Soviet immigration since about one-half of the immigrants ultimately chose to go to the United States rather than to Israel.

A great boon to the economy was the development and rapid growth of the armament industry. Not only did it help to reduce imports of weapons and dependence upon foreign sources but it also provided export revenues. In this industry Israel showed great skill and ingenuity in redesigning foreign models or in using foreign parts and engines in original Israeli designs.

After the cease-fires and withdrawals stabilized the fronts in Sinai and Golan, at least for the time being, the major point of conflict shifted to the border with Lebanon, where shellings or incursions from one or another side occurred daily. Many Palestinian camps in south Lebanon served as staging areas for raids into Israel. In 1974 Palestinian commandos attacked the towns of Kiryat Shemona and Maalot, killing a great many, and in 1975 Palestinians seized a small hotel in Tel Aviv and killed eighteen before they were subdued. Israel retaliated for these and scores of other raids by shelling the camps and villages where the raiders were based and sending punitive missions of armored detachments, often to a considerable depth into Lebanon, to try to destroy the potential for such actions. The eruption of the Lebanese civil war in 1975 gave Israel a temporary respite on her northern border. Israel assisted Lebanese rightist Christian groups, and asserted that she would never again permit south Lebanon to come under the control of the Palestinians.

Who would control the lands in Gaza, the West Bank, and Golan captured in 1967 became an increasingly troublesome problem for Israeli leaders. The pressure of ultranationalist political and religious groups such as Gush Emunim (Faith Bloc) to establish Jewish settlements in the territories, even in defiance of authorities, was relentless. The U.N., with the United States concurring, condemned such settlements as obstacles to peace. Within the occupied Arab territories and in Arab-inhabited regions of Israel, the respectable showing made by the Arab armies in the 1973 war stirred the population's latent Arab nationalism. Sabotage and internal resistance increased after the war. Added to them were open anti-Israeli demonstrations and incidents in West Bank towns and in Arab areas of Israel. Authorities gave more power and autonomy to West Bank mayors, and in local elections in 1976 for councils and mayors pro-PLO candidates won sweeping victories. In Nazareth, a Christian Arab town, the Communists elected a mayor and took a majority of the council seats. In 1977 about one-half of the Israeli Arabs who voted cast their ballots for the Communists, who were the one available vehicle for a protest vote. Israeli Arabs earned only one-half of Israeli Jews' per-capita income; Arabs were one-sixth of the Israeli population, but they owned no banks or independent newspapers, and had an infant mortality rate twice that of the

Jewish majority. In most socioeconomic indicators, the Israeli Arabs ranked significantly below Israeli Jews. To protest government expropriation of Arab-owned land, Israeli Arabs called for a general strike on "Land Day," March 30, 1976. They came increasingly to identify themselves as Palestinians rather than assimilating into Israeli society.

Another problem facing Israel after the 1973 war was its increased isolation. Cuba and most of the black African nations severed diplomatic relations with Israel. UNESCO ostracized Israel in 1974, asserting that she was altering the historical features of Jerusalem, and in 1975 the U.N. Social Committee declared Zionism to be a form of racism and the General Assembly passed a resolution to the same effect, although the United States government vehemently denounced these stands.

BEGIN'S LIKUD COMES TO POWER

The political timetable in Israel called for the election of the Knesset in the autumn of 1977, but scandals in the government and various challenges to Prime Minister Rabin's policies and leadership forced him to resign and schedule elections for May 17. New parties began to appear. Yigael Yadin, a former general turned archaeologist, founded the Democratic Movement for Change, a party whose position on the Arabs seemed similar to that of Labor, but which advocated massive structural reforms in Israel's government. Remaining as interim prime minister in a caretaker government, Rabin won the leadership of Mapai by a very narrow margin over Defense Minister Peres. A bare five weeks before the election Rabin was forced to withdraw from the leadership position in favor of Peres when it was disclosed that he and his wife kept illegal bank accounts in Washington.

On May 17, 1977, the Israeli voters gave Likud ("Unity") 43 seats in the new Knesset, an increase of only four from the election in 1973; but the Labor Alignment fell from 51 to 32 and thus no longer held a plurality. The law required the president to invite Menachem Begin, head of the Herut party and leader of Likud, to form a government. With the aid of several religious parties and a few independents and the defection of Moshe Dayan from Labor to become foreign minister, Prime Minister Begin welded a coalition of 61 of the 120-member Knesset. Begin was the first non-Mapai prime minister in the history of Israel.

Yigael Yadin, leader of the Democratic Movement for Change, added his party's fifteen seats to the Begin government in October. Yadin became deputy prime minister, an important post in view of Begin's poor health.

Since early in 1976, living conditions in Israel had deteriorated. Inflation was running at 38 percent a year and the annual trade deficit was nearly $3 billion. Business and industry felt shackled by the red tape of a controlled economy. A combination of wealthy entrepreneurs, poor and disenchanted Eastern Jews, right-wing hawks, young people, and discontented shopkeepers threw out the Labor Alignment to support Likud, which had promised to cure the social, economic, and financial problems weighing upon Israel. The 1977 election represented a major upheaval in Israeli politics.

At the end of October, the new government lifted restrictions of the buying and selling of foreign exchange and the freeing of the Israeli pound from controls; its value dropped 40 percent overnight. A conservative free economic system was announced with import and export subsidies ended and many taxes raised sharply. Yet the economic problems of Israel were so embedded in its social, political, and geographic resource systems as to be nearly intractable. Inflation continued, few government corporations were sold, taxes remained exceptionally high, and the basic reform package espoused by Begin was dropped by 1981. Instead, the government, despite its stated desire to curb government, ironically succeeded in extending its role in housing and neighborhood development and in lengthening by three years the tuition-free period of public schooling.

The general economy gained some ground even though the turnover of Egyptian oil fields as a result of the step-by-step peace process initially boosted Israel's import bills. As the price of oil declined in the middle 1980s the Israeli economy was helped. Real per-capita income rose although at a slower rate than in earlier times.

The United States in 1981 and in subsequent years changed its economic assistance entirely to grants that did not have to be repaid. U.S. aid sharply increased in the 1980s: in 1980 it was $1.8 billion and in 1983 $2.5 billion. Inflation, however, became an even greater problem in the late 1970s and early 1980s, rising from 78 percent in 1979 to 145 percent in 1983. The foreign debt per capita was the highest in the world, and was increasing steadily, as the trade imbalance continued.

The limited degree of domestic success enjoyed by the Begin coalition was more than compensated by foreign policy victories, and with the 1981 general election the Likud bloc again managed to form the government. Likud received 37 percent of the vote and 48 seats in the Knesset, a slight gain over 1977, while the Labor and Mapam bloc also had 37 percent of the votes and 47 seats, thus showing a nearly equal split in the electorate. Begin formed a coalition with small rightist parties and particularly with the religious parties, which thereby gained considerable influence on public policy. This coalition endured through the 1982 war in Lebanon, raging inflation, and Begin's own resignation, until the next parliamentary elections were held in 1984.

SOCIAL AND CULTURAL CHANGES

During the late 1970s and 1980s the gap between Eastern and European Jews seemed to steadily widen and sharp clashes emerged between the two communities as already seen in the bitter political rivalry of Likud and Labor. But this new and increasing difference was largely a question of perception, since the communities had been consistently the opposite of each other in many ways since the founding of the state. Now the Eastern Jews emerged in public with new spokesmen and a driving resentment against European Jewish domination of the social order. In actuality, as the decades passed and intermarriage between members of the two groups increased, and even more as they experienced the same environment in a united Jewish state, their extremely different origins came to count for less. The Arabs of Israel, on the other hand, seemed to increasingly feel their close links to the Arabs of the occupied territories—a development that was extremely threatening to the existing order in Israel.

Most aspects of culture reflected these societal and other political concerns. In construction and architecture, for instance, much attention was devoted to new buildings on the eastern outskirts of Jerusalem intended for Jewish settlers. There and in the Old City, esthetic concepts competed against the pressure to erect tall, massive structures that would alter the skyline. Tel Aviv boomed with new high-rise buildings. Painters and sculptors tended to study abroad, while many chose to live outside Israel for a time. Their art generally followed the patterns established in Europe and the United States and used a wide variety of media. Writers often were sympathetic to Labor or smaller leftist parties; many became highly critical of the Begin regime and its policies.

PEACE WITH EGYPT

Prime Minister Begin's foreign policy started with his firm desire to keep control of Gaza and the West Bank. The latter he called Judea and Samaria (as they were called in Biblical times), areas he felt were inseparable parts of Israel that had been liberated from foreign control in 1967. His intransigent stand had been harshly criticized inside Israel and seemed in 1977 to be destined for failure, as first the European Economic Community and then the U.S. and Soviet Union spoke out for the rights of the Palestinians. On October 1, 1977, a joint American-Soviet declaration called for the reconvening of the 1973 Geneva Conference with the statement that the Palestinian problem must be considered. Begin asserted that under no conditions would Israel negotiate with the PLO, nor would Israel ever agree to the establishment of a Palestinian state on the West Bank.

Egypt and Israel both opposed the reinvolvement of the Soviet Union in the peace process, as represented by the U.S.-Soviet note. Egypt's President Anwar Sadat, determined to unfreeze the Arab-Israeli dispute by a bold gesture, flew to Israel on November 19, 1977. In a highly dramatic speech to the Knesset Sadat appealed for a peace based upon complete Israeli withdrawal from the occupied territories, Israeli recognition of the Palestinians' rights, and full peace between the Arab states and Israel. This extraordinary step provided the psychological and moral impetus for subsequent peace negotiations. Between September 5 and 17, 1978, at Camp David in Maryland, President Carter, Sadat, and Begin established what they hoped would be the bases for peace in the Arab-Israeli dispute. One part of the Camp David agreements comprised principles for a separate Egyptian-Israeli peace, and the other part dealt in rather vague terms with the future of Gaza and the West Bank. This part called for "full autonomy" and a "self-governing authority" for the inhabitants of these areas and also posited participation by Jordan, leading eventually to a peace treaty with that country. Jerusalem was not specifically mentioned, nor was the Golan Heights of Syria.

Prime Minister Begin secured by the Camp David accords a great victory for Israel. The effect of a disagreement over interpretation of the accords was to let the present conditions prevail, that is, Israeli control of the occupied territories would persist. Almost immediately Egypt and the United States disagreed with Israel on implementation, as in Israel's building new Jewish settlements in the territories. Later on, Egypt and the United States interpreted such phrases as full autonomy for the Palestinians more widely than did Begin, who essentially wanted to annex or permanently keep control of the West Bank and Gaza, and therefore wished to deny any real autonomy to the Palestinian Arabs.

The PLO, Syria, Jordan, most of the other Arab states, and the Soviet Union denounced the Camp David agreements as a separate peace wherein Egypt deserted its Arab allies and the Palestinians so as to regain the Sinai peninsula. Sadat responded by saying that this was the best compromise he or anyone else could hope to gain, and that Egypt had sacrificed more than any Arab state on behalf of the Arab cause in Palestine.

With extensive new U.S. economic, military, and diplomatic support guaranteed to Israel and Egypt, Begin and Sadat signed the Treaty of Washington on March 26, 1979, and formally established peace between Israel and Egypt. The treaty was long but basically simple in its provisions. it was based upon the exchange of land for peace. Israel returned the Sinai peninsula to Egyptian control in phases extending to 1982, and in return Egypt established normal diplomatic and commercial ties with Israel. Both countries renounced the future use of force in their mutual relations. Israel had open access for shipping through the Suez Canal and the Gulf of Aqaba. Egyptian control in the Sinai was limited in various ways, and a multinational force, including U.S. troops, was stationed there and in a narrow strip of Israeli territory nearby to supervise the agreement. The real proof of the effectiveness of the treaty came in 1982 with the Israeli invasion of Lebanon. This took place after the turnover of Sinai to Egypt was completed by Israel in April. Egypt did not mobilize its armed forces nor did it take any other action except for withdrawing its ambassador from Tel Aviv. Israel thus gained by the peace treaty of 1979 the neutrality of Egypt in subsequent Arab-Israeli wars, which was a tremendous military asset for Israel. Israel also obtained acceptance and recognition of its legitimacy as a nation from its strongest opponent.

After 1979, Israel undertook a number of military, diplomatic, and political measures that severely tested the peace process. In July 1980, the Knesset passed a law declaring Jerusalem to be the united capital of Israel. In June 1981, F-16 Israeli jets bombed Iraq's nuclear reactor in order to stop Iraq from being able to produce atomic weapons. On December 14, Israel extended its "law, jurisdiction, and administration" to the Golan Heights. This amounted to Israeli annexation. Israel built more Jewish settlements on the West Bank, in Gaza, East Jerusalem, and the Golan Heights, expanded the area of existing settlements, and confiscated large amounts of Arab-owned land.

The numbers of Jewish settlers in the West Bank had grown slowly under Labor party governments—by 1977 there were only about 5,000. Likud governments built "bedroom" suburban settlements for Israeli commuters, and by 1982 Jewish settlers in the West Bank area had increased to 25,000, while 65,000 Jews lived in East Jerusalem. Arabs on the West Bank took part in large-scale protests and riots in 1982 against Israeli policies. Ariel Sharon, ex-general and now minister of agriculture, tried to build up rural leagues of Palestinians who would collaborate with the occupation forces, but the rural leagues were extremely unpopular among most Arabs, who objected vehemently to the Israeli attempt to gradually take control of the region.

In all of the formerly Jordanian territory the Arab-Jewish ratio was about 10 to 1, while in all of what had been the British mandate (Israel, Gaza, united Jerusalem, and the West Bank), two-thirds of the population was Jewish and one-third Muslim and Christian Arab.

THE 1982 WAR

Israel had aided the mostly Christian rightists in the Lebanese civil war of 1975–1976. When Syria intervened in Lebanon in 1976, Israel warned her not to send troops into extreme southern Lebanon, an area Israel wished to keep under her own aegis as a kind of security zone. Raids by Palestinians into Israel from that area encouraged the government to invade all of southern Lebanon up to the Litani River on March 16, 1978. Israel then withdrew, hoping United Nations forces and Israel's Christian allies would stop further attacks by the Palestinian commandos. The raids and counterraids resumed, however, until separate but mutual cease-fires by the PLO and Israel were arranged by the United States in July 1981.

As indicated in Chapter 42, Begin and Sharon decided to invade Lebanon in 1982 to achieve several different objectives. Their stated goal was to secure for northern Israel peace from raids, but more important aims probably included destroying the PLO and its headquarters in West Beirut; driving the Syrians out of most of Lebanon; helping to secure the election of Israel's friend, Bashir Jumayyil, as president of Lebanon; and then signing a peace treaty with Jumayyil on the model of the 1979 Egyptian treaty. Israel invaded on June 6, 1982, with about 80,000 troops, and pushed rapidly forward north toward Beirut and the Syrian forces in the Biqa Valley. Three divisions successfully fought the 15,000 outnumbered but well-armed Palestinians. Bypassing the U.N. forces the Israelis took Tyre, Nabatiyah, and Sidon—in large part because of their complete command of the air and the sea. Syria had 40,000 troops available in Lebanon and an extensive missile and aircraft combat force. On June 7 Israel directly attacked the Syrians. In the following days Israel destroyed Syrian surface-to-air missile batteries, between 84 and 100 aircraft, and 400 tanks. Both Israel and Syria accepted a cease-fire on June 11. Syria did not fight in the 1982 war with all its forces. The Syrian navy, for instance, never left port, and no fighting at all took place on the Golan Heights.

In the Beirut area Israel continued to fight the Palestinians and Syrians. On June 13 Israeli forces met their Phalangist Lebanese allies, who already held East Beirut. In this manner Israel completed the encirclement of West Beirut with its civilian population of one-half million people. Israel launched a siege with aerial, naval, and land bombardment designed to force the Lebanese leftists, Palestinians, and Syrians to surrender. This policy was ultimately successful. In short order Israel made Yasir Arafat and 14,000 Palestinian guerrillas leave Lebanon by ship; gained the election of Bashir Jumayyil and then, after his assassination, of his brother Amin Jumayyil, as president; brought about the stationing of an international peacekeeping force (including U.S. troops) in West Beirut; and then Israeli occupation of that area. Israel had won the war, and at what seemed a relatively moderate cost of 340 killed and some 2,200 wounded.

This victory soon turned sour. President Reagan proposed on September 1 an American initiative for peace in the Arab-Israeli dispute that included a freeze on new Israeli settlements, full autonomy for the Palestinians, an undivided Jerusalem, and the association of the West Bank and Gaza with Jordan. This latter point was designed to preclude both an independent Arab Palestine and Israeli annexation. Begin immediately and completely rejected the Reagan initiative. Another dilemma for Israel arose from the behavior of its rightist Lebanese allies who, with the knowledge and implied consent of some Israelis, massacred hundreds of Palestinian refugees in the camps of West Beirut. An Israeli commission of inquiry, whose creation was demanded by 400,000 Israeli protestors and was chaired by Yitzhak Kahan, the head of the supreme court, said indirect responsibility for the massacre fell upon the defense minister, Ariel Sharon, and high-ranking military officers. Even more worrisome to the Begin government was the growing opposition to the war among Israeli soldiers, reservists, and the general public. For the first time a substantial, though minority, opinion among Jewish Israelis opposed the state on a major security-military issue.

Prime Minister Begin and Sharon, now minister without portfolio, remained adamant in pursuit of their goals. They still hoped for a success in Lebanon that would compensate for the casualties, turmoil, and expense of the war. On May 17, 1983, Israel and President Jumayyil of Lebanon signed a troop withdrawal agreement whose provisions were tantamount to an Israeli-Lebanese peace treaty. Despite U.S. support of Jumayyil, strong internal opposition to him and to the Israelis emerged in Lebanon. Syria also opposed the withdrawal agreement. United States troops left Lebanon in February 1984 and Israel slowly withdrew its forces as well, leaving just a few troops and some Lebanese proxies in the southern districts as of June 1985. Jumayyil abrogated the agreement with Israel, Syria gained the upper hand, a pro-Syrian Palestinian group ousted Arafat in 1983 once again from Lebanon, and that unhappy country sank farther into chaos and strife. Out of this situation the Likud could point to the PLO evacuation, the dispersion of the Palestinian fighters, and the loss of prestige and control by Arafat, whose new headquarters in Tunis was now far indeed from Israel. Despite this, the 1982 war in Lebanon was, on the whole, not a success for Israel.

ISRAEL SINCE THE 1982 WAR

On September 15, 1983, Menachem Begin resigned as prime minister. Yitzhak Shamir, the foreign minister, replaced him. Shamir had also been a member of the Irgun, a leader of the Herut party, and a vehement proponent of retaining the occupied territories. He first had to deal with an economic crisis: an inflation rate approaching 400 percent, a stock market collapse, and drastic devaluation of the Israeli currency, the shekel. The painful withdrawal from Lebanon was underway, and in July 1984 the national parliamentary election took place. Labor won 44 seats and Likud 41, but the voters also elected a number of Knesset members who were more conservative than Likud, including one radical who proposed ousting by force all Arabs from the West Bank and even from Israel itself. More than 70 percent of Eastern Jews voted for Likud and more than 70 percent of European Jews voted for Labor.

After much maneuvering Likud and Labor agreed on a joint coalition that represented 97 Knesset members. Despite this large number of votes, the coalition government was deadlocked on most major issues because of the sharp disagreements among its chief parties and their leaders. The two major blocs of Labor and Likud rotated the most important posts of government for two-year terms, as Shimon Peres of Labor became prime minister and Shamir of Likud was foreign minister. In October 1986 the two reversed their posts.

This coalition inherited in 1984 an economic crisis. With a national external debt of about $23 billion, increasing unemployment, a trade deficit of at least $4 billion, rampant inflation, hundreds of thousands of Israelis living abroad, and expenditures of billions of dollars on the war in Lebanon, Israel was in a dire situation. One source of help was increased U.S. aid. Israel now received more U.S. assistance than any other country in the world, almost $4 billion in 1987. The government in 1985 introduced budget cuts, price and wage controls, higher taxes, and a free trade agreement with the United States. Israel needed to export more, and armaments such as the Kfir fighter and the Gabriel missile seemed to be the answer. In 1984 Israel sold weapons worth $1 billion to such countries as Colombia, El Salvador, Zaire, and even to anti-Israeli Iran!

Technical cooperation with the United States in economic and military matters was crucial to Israel. When the United States urged the cancellation of the Lavi jet fighter project because America could supply the same sort of airplane at lower cost, Israel had to eliminate it despite the investment by both countries of $1.5 billion in development costs. The uncovering of Americans who spied for Israel inside the United States did not seriously disturb U.S.-Israeli relations. In June 1988, America committed itself to pay 80 percent of the research costs for a new Israeli missile designed to shoot down Chinese and Soviet missiles possessed by Saudi Arabia, Iraq, and Syria. And Israel was of considerable help to the United States during its secret dealings with Iran, an arms-for-hostages arrangement that became known as the "Iran-Contra" affair. Israel recognized that both Iran and Iraq were its enemies and desired to keep their conflict in a continuing stalemate.

In the middle 1980s a very mixed set of developments took place in Israel. Emigration exceeded immigration even though the Soviet Union allowed more Jews to leave Russia. In 1986 and 1987 the economy once again resumed its growth, although at a modest rate. Debt repayment took one-half of export earnings, but inflation was reduced to a manageable level of under 20 percent by 1987. Imported oil cost less, but revenues from tourism declined.

The power of the Orthodox Jewish groups steadily grew, as could be seen in the law banning the sale of pork. Public controversy over the application of religious precepts by government came to the fore, and occasionally gave rise to violence between religious zealots and secularists. Religious parties again played an important role as potential partners in building a coalition cabinet following the Knesset election of November 1, 1988.

In that contest Likud obtained 40 seats and Labor 39 after a bitter campaign that hinged largely on policy issues relating to the uprising of the Palestinian Arabs as well as future peace talks with the Arab countries. Likud was opposed to an international peace conference with superpower participation, was reluctant to take a risk on the exchange of West Bank and Gaza territory for peace, and proposed more Jewish settlements in the occupied territories. Labor favored an international peace conference followed by direct negotiations and was more receptive to territorial adjustments for peace. Despite these differences, a new government under the leadership of Likud included the Labor party within its coalition.

THE PALESTINIANS TRY COMPROMISE
AND THEN INSURRECTION

In the 1980s, the fragmented structure of the Palestinians was a major hindrance in uniting behind a compromise peace with those Israelis willing to deal with them. The Palestinian Arabs were widely dispersed. The experiences of Palestinians in such differing environments as Kuwayt, Syria, and the United States influenced their behavior. And the Palestinians living in Israel, and after 1967, in East Jerusalem, the Gaza Strip, and the West Bank differed again in their experiences. Ideological chasms also existed among the factions: some were radical Marxists, while others ignored ideology in favor of a united struggle. The leaders and groups were subsidized by various governments that naturally sought to determine policy as well as lend assistance. Yet, despite these variations, nearly all Palestinians had accepted the PLO as their spokesman, and had given Yasir Arafat, its leader, their respect and loyalty.

The catastrophe suffered by Arafat and the PLO in the 1982 war was reinforced by Syria's determination to manage the Palestinians for its own purposes, leading to a split within al-Fatah, the largest military grouping, and a weakening of Arafat's role. Syria forced Arafat out of northern Lebanon in December 1983. He then turned to Egypt and Jordan, hoping to reach with their help a compromise with Israel leading to the creation of a Palestinian "mini-state" of the West Bank and Gaza in a loose confederation with Jordan. The Palestine National Council met in Amman in November 1984, but the repeated attempts then and subsequently to arrange a joint Palestinian-Jordanian delegation for peace talks with Israel foundered. Jordan feared that the United States would not sufficiently pressure Israel; the Israeli Labor party feared the PLO and King Husayn were not sincere, while Likud rejected the whole process; most of the Palestinians feared and distrusted the real motives of their past enemies—Israel, the United States, and King Husayn; and the United States feared the reentry of the Soviet Union into the peace process, should an international conference be convened to discuss peace before bilateral Jordanian-Palestinian-Israeli talks got underway.

Instead of peace, raids and counterraids between Israel and the Palestinians continued, as in the Israeli attack on the PLO headquarters in Tunis on October 1,

1985, and in various incidents of violence by Palestinians against U.S., Israeli, and other civilians. Israel attacked PLO bases in Lebanon as a response to guerrilla raids. In April 1987 the various Palestinian factions papered over their disagreements, but in 1988 full warfare erupted in Lebanon when a pro-Syrian faction defeated Arafat loyalists. Most Palestinians, the Soviet Union, Egypt, and Jordan nevertheless continued to recognize Arafat as the Palestinian leader. Israel assassinated his chief military adviser in Tunis on April 16, 1988.

Within the occupied territories in 1987 demonstrations, arrests, deportations, riots, and physical attacks by Israelis on Arabs and vice versa steadily escalated as the twentieth year of occupation passed with no substantial change in sight. Many Palestinians from Gaza and the West Bank came to support Islamic fundamentalism rather than secular nationalism, but followers of both approaches were united in opposing Israel. Very large-scale Arab demonstrations broke out on December 8, 1987, and they continued for months. Israeli troops killed more than 565 Palestinians while about 36 Israelis were killed. Thousands of Palestinians were arrested and general strikes, commercial boycotts, and violent demonstrations persisted. The uprising gained sympathy among Israeli Arabs and provided clear evidence that Israeli rule was not accepted by the population of the occupied lands. The 1988 peace initiative begun by U.S. Secretary of State George Shultz was designed to show the Israelis and Palestinians that an alternative to repression and violence existed, but it failed.

Basic issues of identity were at the core of the Palestinian-Israeli conflict. Israel's original reason for being was to serve as a haven for Jews, a state where they could be safe and could lead a fully Jewish life. Yet it became clear in the forty years after the creation of Israel that most of the world's Jews would not or, in some cases, could not emigrate to Israel. The rationale for the Zionist state thus came into question. In regard to the aspect of Zionism that called for a safe haven, in some ways Israel in the late 1980s was as safe as, or at least safer than, she had been earlier. The peace treaty with Egypt, Israeli nuclear strength, and the growing acceptance of Israel's existence by many Arab states lessened the possibility of destruction in war. The transformation of the democratic nature of Israel as a result of its oppression of the Palestinians nevertheless opened the door to a number of negative possibilities. Israel's identity was bound ever more closely with the national identity of the Palestinian people and with the fate of the kingdom of Jordan. The way their conflicts would be resolved would be crucial for all three parties.

JORDAN AND THE 1967 WAR

Within a few hours after the beginning of hostilities on June 5, 1967, the Jordanian air force had been destroyed by Israel. Complete mastery of the air over Jordan gave Israel such an advantage that King Husayn's army was ineffective. The entire area west of the Jordan River, including East Jerusalem, was lost, and about 200,000 refugees fled eastward across the river. Most of the Palestinians of the West Bank and Gaza, however, stayed on in their homes.

The most productive part of Husayn's kingdom was gone, his finances were in shambles, and his armed forces were without equipment. Husayn assumed virtual command of all branches of his government. At an Arab summit meeting in Khartoum, Saudi Arabia, Kuwayt, and Libya agreed to aid Jordan financially. Thirty thousand Iraqi troops remained in Jordan to protect the king as well as to strengthen his position against Israel.

The Hashimite Kingdom of Jordan was now confined to the East Bank of the river. Israel was holding some 5,600 square kilometers of Jordan which had had a population of 650,000. During the few days of fighting or soon thereafter more than a third had fled, most ending up in Jordan, and very few ever returned to their homes. Israel for a time permitted the civil administration of the West Bank to remain Arab, and since the salaries of most officials had come from Amman, Husayn continued to pay them.

Jordan served for the next several years as the staging area for Palestinian attacks upon Israel. The Palestinian nationalists now came to understand that their earlier dependence upon Egypt and the other Arab states was futile. If an Arab Palestine would be created, it would have to be done by their own actions, and chiefly, they thought, through a guerrilla war of national liberation similar to that undertaken by the Algerians against the French in the 1950s. This idea was especially strong in al-Fatah, led by Yasir Arafat, the largest military organization within the Palestine Liberation Organization. The PLO overall organization was headed after 1969 by Arafat, but there was no unity of command.

Very soon after the close of the 1967 war, Husayn declared his opposition to any attack upon the occupied areas, reminding all that such incursions would be injurious to their fellow Palestinians living there. He objected strongly to the use of Jordan as a base for training and launching guerrilla actions against Israel—not that he was unsympathetic to the goals. He had no intention of transforming Jordan into a guerrilla state, and he fully supported U.N. Resolution 242 for ending the state of war and bringing peace to the area. His interpretation of 242 required Israel to return all his lost territory to him.

Since more than half of Husayn's subjects were Palestinians, many of them recent arrivals, his policies were condemned by many as traitorous to the Arab people. In any case, throughout 1968, 1969, and 1970 there were countless assaults on Israel, followed by reprisals on Jordan. The Israeli attack on the village of Karameh was particularly grave. Over fifty Jordanians were killed and the U.N. Security Council censured Israel for it. Destructive Israeli retaliation upon Jordan did not deter Palestinian guerrilla deeds on Israel and the Security Council denouncings never dampened the Israeli determination to punish the invaders.

Husayn decreed that the commandos were not to wear Jordanian army uniforms nor to carry arms in Jordan's towns, but enforcing the rule was next to impossible. In general, Jordan suffered more than Israel did in these exchanges. The radical Popular Front for the Liberation of Palestine (PFLP) and al-Fatah were training commandos and launching attacks from Jordan almost at will. Israel's retaliations were crippling Jordan's economy. When Palestinians shelled Eilat the Israeli air force bombed the East Ghor Canal. Through American mediation, Jordan agreed to curtail commando operations and Israel permitted the restoration of the canal.

The forced migration of many "new" personages to the East Bank after the 1967 war brought a growth of radical political parties to parallel the influx of Palestinian commandos and patriots. A National Front was formed in 1968 as an umbrella for the Communists, the Ba'th, the Muslim Brotherhood, the National Socialists, and the Independent Socialists. They united under the leadership of Sulayman Nabulsi, a National Socialist whom King Husayn had dismissed from the post of prime minister in 1957. When Husayn accepted the American proposal for a Middle East cease-fire in July 1970, the Palestinians declared they would not "tolerate such treason" and prepared for a showdown with Husayn. Husayn at this point acted decisively, removing the civilian government, establishing military rule, and personally taking control of his armed forces.

"BLACK SEPTEMBER"

Peace negotiations in New York in August aroused the commandos for battle. Iraq announced she would aid the Palestinians. Then, al-Saiqah, Syrian-based Palestinian commandos, moved into Jordan. On September 6, 1970, Palestinians hijacked three airliners. Two days later a BOAC plane was taken. All were flown to the Middle East; after the passengers were evacuated the four were blown up, three of them in Jordan. A week later Husayn appointed a cabinet made up entirely of military officers. On the following day, September 17, 1970, Husayn launched a full-scale campaign against the commando groups. Syrian tanks crossed the border to support the hard-pressed Palestinians, but withdrew upon warnings from Israel and the United States. After a week Husayn had the upper hand. Under pressure from the Arab League, Husayn and Arafat signed in Cairo a fourteen-point peace agreement. Guerrilla actions in Jordan were clearly defined and attacks upon Israel were not to be launched from Jordan. The Palestinians, angered by their defeat, began to refer to the time as "Black September."

Jordanian officials met in Beirut in 1971 with West Bank leaders and commando officers on the issue of a Palestinian state as Palestinian strongholds in the northern hills of Jordan were being besieged and eliminated. In July the Jordanian army killed about 300 commandos and took 2,500 prisoner. Resumption of hostilities distressed all the Arab leaders, who angrily charged Husayn with violating the Cairo agreement. The nub of that accord was Husayn's acceptance of the clause, "free movement of Palestinians" in Jordan.

Having driven most of the commandos from Jordan to Lebanon, Husayn was freer to arrange his own affairs. In March 1972 he issued a twelve-point plan for peace with Israel. It proposed the creation of the United Arab Kingdom, a federated state of two autonomous regions—the East Bank and the West Bank—with Amman and Jerusalem as the two capitals. Israel was not enamored of the proposal. Arab leaders fumed; many who had not already cut diplomatic ties with Jordan did so, leaving Husayn isolated among the Arab states. By the end of the year, however, relations were partially restored with Syria and Egypt.

The internal strife cut Jordan's gross national product for 1970 by 25 percent. The United States and West Germany together nearly made up Jordan's $25 million budget deficit, though, and the United States promised to replenish Jordan's expended stock of military equipment and to provide aid for reconstruction.

As a crisis atmosphere arose in 1973, Husayn observed that in case war should break out in the area, Jordan would not act "impulsively and naïvely." In September full diplomatic relations were renewed with Egypt, then with Syria; Kuwayt restored her subsidy soon after.

AFTER THE 1973 WAR

Syria and Egypt initiated the war against Israel on October 6; Husayn did not participate, but held his forces on full alert until the 13th, when he sent the 40th Armored Brigade to join the Syrians. They returned to Jordan at the initial cease-fire. In January 1974 Husayn passed to Kissinger a confidential ten-point proposal for disengagement between Israel and Jordan, including the West Bank. The second world Islamic conference, held a few weeks later in Lahore, named the PLO as the sole legitimate spokesman for the restoration of Palestinian rights and territories. Again, at the Arab summit meetings in Rabat in October, twenty kings and presidents reaffirmed the Lahore declaration. Husayn could only acquiesce; Saudi Arabia gave Jordan $300 million to soften the blow, as Husayn agreed that he would be the first to recognize Arafat. Legislation in 1974 stripped the West Bank of its half of the seats in parliament and of its half of the posts in the cabinet. This was a somewhat empty gesture, however, since no parliamentary elections were held in Jordan for seventeen years following the 1967 war.

The 1973 war left few economic traces in Jordan. The immense surge in oil revenues brought untold wealth to the oil-producing Arab countries. The sudden affluence of Jordan's neighbors spilled over. In 1975 aid money from the United States and the Arab countries topped $500 million. From 1973 to 1981 the gross national product of Jordan grew at about 10 percent per year, the value of exports increased twelve times, and Jordanians working abroad sent home about $1 billion in 1981. However, inflation, the trade deficit, and the need to import food for the rapidly growing population also rose. Half the population lived in Amman and their need for greater city services was immense.

When oil revenues elsewhere fell, so did Jordan's economy. Arab aid to Jordan was cut by one-half in the early 1980s, and the country took to foreign borrowing. Many workers returned home, exports fell, and subsidies for maintaining low prices of basic commodities were slashed, an action which produced riots in 1989.

Economic changes particularly affected the Jordanian Bedouins. Most served in the armed forces, where they were strong backers of King Husayn, and many stayed beyond their mandatory service. Another source of income for them was sheepherding, which came in the 1950s and 1960s to include motorized transport of the herds and provisioning of them by water trucks. Very few Bedouins were completely nomadic by the 1970s; nearly all had settled down. Deep wells provided water for agriculture while many tribesmen moved to towns and cities.

Education prospered in the 1970s and 1980s as the number of children and youths attending schools steadily grew. While the population increased at a rate of about 3 percent annually, growth in school attendance was more rapid. In 1966–1968 there were 440,000 students on both sides of the Jordan, including 287,000 on the East Bank. The latter number grew to 460,000 by 1973, with nearly equal enrollments of boys and girls. The University of Jordan in Amman was founded in 1962, the Royal Scientific Society in 1970, and Yarmouk University in Irbid in 1976.

King Husayn inaugurated television broadcasting in 1968; television and radio were both governmentally operated. Jordanian newspapers published in Amman were subject to the influence of the royal government, and occasionally they were suspended by royal decree. Many aspects of culture were dominated by the political concerns of the day, and especially by the drama and tragedy of the Palestinians. Poetry, painting, and fiction have been associated with that history, but folklore and archaeology constituted independent fields of cultural production.

Because of the Lebanese civil war some international companies vacated their offices in Beirut; many moved to Amman, thereby adding to Jordan's revenues. As a member of the World Institute of Phosphates, a sort of OPEC organized by Morocco for phosphate producers, Jordan saw the price of her exports of 1.3 million tons jump from $15 to $60 a ton. Income from tourism also increased sharply. All these revenues, coupled with a growing amount of remittances from Palestinians working in countries throughout the world, produced a boom in Jordan.

Parliament was dissolved in 1974, and Husayn governed without it. After the Rabat decision on the roles of Jordan and the PLO, Husayn postponed elections indefinitely. As long as the West Bank was occupied and its future was unsure, elections from that area to a Jordanian parliament, the king argued, could not be held. Therefore Husayn appointed the National Consultative Council in 1978 so as to coopt leaders and mobilize support for his policies. The Council served many of the functions of a parliament until 1984, when it was dissolved and new partial elections for parliament were held; those elected from the East Bank then selected delegates from the Israeli-controlled West Bank. Women voted for the first time. Israel allowed delegates from the West Bank to attend the opening session of parliament. One-half of the parliament's seats were reserved for West Bankers by the 1986 electoral law.

A JORDANIAN/PALESTINIAN-ISRAELI PEACE?

In 1977, as the civil war in Lebanon wound down, the Palestinians not only were weakened by their losses of men and weapons but were controlled by Syria to some extent. It seemed possible that Husayn might once more have a voice in any settlement between the Israelis and Palestinians. But the Camp David agreements of 1978 between Israel and Egypt, while inviting Jordanian participation, actually seemed to the king to be a trap. From his point of view, Israel under the Begin government would not agree to terms minimally satisfactory to Jordan or to the Palestinians, unless pressured to do so by the United States. If Jordan entered the step-by-step peace process and failed, it might well lead to revolution. Husayn denounced the 1979 peace treaty and waited for better days.

Husayn strongly supported Iraq in the war with Iran, and thereby earned the enmity of Syria, which was aiding Iran. In 1984 Jordan resumed diplomatic relations with Egypt, becoming the first Arab state that had denounced the peace treaty to reestablish contact. Relations with Syria improved somewhat in 1985 as the king sought to bring Syria into the peace process with Israel. Jordan hosted the Arab League conference in November 1987; Husayn's ability to gather together the discordant Arab states was a substantial accomplishment.

In the 1980s King Husayn and Yasir Arafat reached agreement with each other on several occasions for a joint Jordanian-Palestinian delegation and policies for a peace conference with Israel. In secret talks with Israeli Labor party leaders Husayn worked out many of the details for such a conference. And he counted on diplomatic and economic support from Jordan's close friend, the United States. In each case these agreements failed, not because of the king, but rather because of Israeli or PLO opposition. When the king then closed the PLO's offices Yarmouk University students rioted in May 1986. The government suppressed them and other elements of the internal political opposition.

Chagrined by these setbacks and worried about the Iran-Iraq War, Jordan by the late 1980s seemed caught in an impasse. King Husayn saw that Israeli control over the occupied territories was becoming firmer as new Jewish settlements were built, and he also saw a weakening of the already small support of his regime among the West Bank Arabs. Their uprising in late 1987 and its subsequent growth impelled Husayn on July 31, 1988, to sever official Jordanian legal and administrative links and claims to the West Bank. He also dissolved the lower house of parliament and called for the PLO to establish an independent state.

The Palestine National Council voted on November 15 to declare the "establishment of a Palestinian state with Jerusalem as its capital" but the new state had no control over any territory. This symbolic declaration of independence was recognized by the Soviet Union, Egypt, and many other countries. Arafat and the Palestine National Council endorsed U.N. Security Council Resolution 242 of 1967 which implicitly recognized the existence of Israel and its right to live within secure and recognized borders. The Palestinians also continued to assert their right of armed resistance to Israeli control of the occupied territories as well as their right of national self-determination. Israel rejected the Palestinian actions, while the United States barred Arafat from speaking to the United Nations in New York, but then entered into talks with the PLO.

All these matters left Jordan in an ambiguous and awkward position. King Husayn's response was caution, a useful trait that had already saved him on innumerable occasions. He awaited the outcome of developments outside his small country's control.

REFERENCES

References for this chapter are also found in Chapters 34, 42, and 43.

Abu-Lugod, Ibrahim, ed. *The Arab-Israeli Confrontation of June, 1967: An Arab Perspective.* Evanston, Ill.: Northwestern University Press, 1970. Nine essays by Arab scholars.

Ahmad, Hani al-. *Cultural Policy in Jordan.* Paris: UNESCO, 1981. A short official guide to the subject.

Aronson, Geoffrey. *Creating Facts: Israel, Palestinians and the West Bank.* Washington, D.C.: Institute for Palestine Studies, 1987. A detailed, pro-Palestinian interpretation through the events of 1982.

Bernstein, Marver H. "Israel: Turbulent Democracy at Forty." *Middle East Journal* 42 (1988): 193–201.

Cobban, Helena. *The Palestine Liberation Organization: People, Power and Politics.* Cambridge: Cambridge University Press, 1984. An excellent study, especially useful for internal organization.

Heikal, Mohamed. *The Road to Ramadan.* London: Collins, 1975. The causes and nature of the 1973 war as told by the Egyptian journalist and adviser to President Nasser.

Khalidi, Rashid. "The Palestinian Dilemma: PLO Policy After Lebanon." *Journal of Palestine Studies* 15: 1 (1985): 88–103. Analysis by one of the most astute contemporary Arab scholars.

Khoury, Nabeel A. "The National Consultative Council of Jordan: A Study in Legislative Development." *International Journal of Middle East Studies* 13 (1981): 427–439. A careful and sympathetic article.

Lesch, Ann M., and Mark A. Tessler. "The West Bank and Gaza: Political and Ideological Response to Occupation." *The Muslim World* 77 (1987): 229–249. Valuable for developments in the 1980s.

Meir, Golda. *My Life.* London: Weidenfeld and Nicolson, 1975. A vivid and personal account.

Miller, Aaron David. "The Arab-Israeli Conflict, 1967–1987: A Retrospective." *Middle East Journal* 41 (1987): 349–360. A good summary, full of insight.

Mishal, Shaul. *The PLO Under 'Arafat: Between Gun and Olive Branch.* New Haven, Conn.: Yale University Press, 1986.

Mutawi, Samir A. *Jordan in the 1967 War.* Cambridge: Cambridge University Press, 1987. Based on Jordanian military records and interviews; very useful.

O'Ballance, Edgar. *The Third Arab-Israeli War.* Hamden, Conn.: Archon Books, 1972. A fine military account of the 1967 war.

———. *Arab Guerrilla Power: 1967–1972.* Hamden, Conn.: The Shoe String Press, 1973. Follows the Palestinians closely.

Peretz, Don. *The West Bank: History, Politics, Society, and Economy.* Boulder, Colo.: Westview Press, 1986. Short but full of valuable information.

———, and Sammy Smooha. "Israel's Eleventh Knesset Election." *The Middle East Journal* 39 (1985): 86–103. A good examination of the 1984 elections.

Quandt, William B. *Camp David: Peacemaking and Politics.* Washington, D.C.: The Brookings Institution, 1986. Among the various first-hand accounts of Camp David this is perhaps the most important. The author was on the United States National Security Council at the time. Contains the texts of the Camp David agreements and the peace treaty.

Reich, Bernard. *Israel: Land of Tradition and Conflict.* Boulder, Colo.: Westview Press, 1985. An able survey by a leading authority. Includes geography, earlier history, economics, politics, the Arab-Israeli dispute, and relations with the United States.

———. *The United States and Israel: Influence in the Special Relationship.* New York: Praeger, 1984. Deals primarily with the period after 1976.

Sachar, Howard M. *A History of Israel.* Vol. 2. *From the Aftermath of the Yom Kippur War.* New York: Oxford University Press, 1987. A continuation of the excellent volume cited in Chapter 43.

Satloff, Robert B. *Troubles on the East Bank: Challenges to the Domestic Stability of Jordan.* New York: Praeger, 1986. A short and rather pessimistic discussion of recent developments in Jordan.

Sayigh, Yazid. "Israel's Military Performance in Lebanon, June 1982." *Journal of Palestine Studies* 13: 1 (1983): 24–65. A fine evaluation of the Israeli military victory by a Palestinian.

Smith, Pamela Ann. *Palestine and the Palestinians, 1876–1983.* London: Croom Helm, 1984.

———. "The Palestinian Diaspora, 1948–1985." *Journal of Palestine Studies* 15: 3 (1986): 90–108. An outstanding survey that emphasizes the diversity of Palestinian experiences.

Tessler, Mark. "The Political Right in Israel: Its Origins, Growth, and Prospects." *Journal of Palestine Studies* 15: 2 (1986): 12–55. A perceptive study of the Likud bloc, and religious and other parties.

Yishai, Yael. "Israeli Annexation of East Jerusalem and the Golan Heights." *Middle Eastern Studies* 21 (1985): 45–60. Shows how the 1981 decisions were reached in reaction to internal as well as external factors.

45

The Egyptian Republic and the Sudan

ANGLO-EGYPTIAN AFFAIRS

The murder of Ahmad Mahir in 1945 raised Mahmud al-Nuqrashi, second in the Saadist party, to the prime ministership and highlighted the long-standing questions that clouded the relations of Egypt and Great Britain. Having declared war against Germany, Egypt entered the United Nations as a charter member. There she confronted Great Britain with the allegation that the provisions of the Anglo-Egyptian treaty of 1936 infringed upon Egyptian sovereign rights beyond a point tolerable for an independent state.

Egyptians believed that when the new British Labour government came to power the moment for a thorough renovation of relations with England was propitious. Nuqrashi asked England for a reexamination of the treaty. The Wafd and other groups in opposition rioted in February 1946, protesting Nuqrashi's supineness toward the British, and forcing his resignation. King Faruq appointed to the prime ministership Ismail Sidqi, who permitted some demonstrations but clamped down sternly when they seemed to get out of hand.

Negotiations with the British were now a political necessity. Sidqi and the British disagreed on evacuation, joint defense, and the Sudan. Egypt held that the British must evacuate all of Egypt. If war broke out or if Egypt felt threatened, she would call upon England. With respect to the Sudan, the unity of Egypt and the Sudan under the Egyptian crown must be recognized. On the other side, Britain was unwilling to withdraw her forces from Egypt unless there was an alliance specifying terms for the return of troops. Soviet claims against Iran, Turkey, and Greece led London to fear for the safety of the Suez Canal. Treaty revision reached a stalemate after much discussion. The reinstalled Egyptian prime minister, Nuqrashi, took the dispute to the U.N. where in 1947 no proposals could obtain sufficient votes to pass. The British refused to budge on the Sudan, stating bluntly that they did not intend to appease Egypt by compromising the right of the Sudanese to self-determination. Since British troops had departed from Cairo and Alexandria, part of the Egyptian urgency in negotiating no longer pertained.

The future of the Sudan loomed large in the minds of Egyptians. The water of the Nile passed through the Sudan, and the possibility of dams and water diversion frightened Egypt. The Sudan was underpopulated and contained vast areas where the expanding population of Egypt might earn a livelihood. Moreover, cotton culture in the Sudan was considered an unnecessary and threatening competition for the cotton of Egypt. In view of these factors Egypt wanted to control the Sudan and force the Sudanese economy into a role complementary to her own. To foster such a development, Egypt at every opportunity mouthed the cliché: the unity of the Nile Valley and her peoples. Another consideration for Egypt was the utilization of the Nile for electric power and wider irrigation. Egypt's swelling population presented an awesome and relentless specter to her politicians. Industrialization required power, which was available if the Nile could be harnessed.

THE 1948 WAR

Soon after Nuqrashi returned from his futile attempt at the U.N., the partition of Palestine and war against Israel engulfed Egypt and dissipated the resources of the nation. King Faruq prompted the war, hoping to maintain Egypt's leadership in the Arab League and gain a clear dominance among the various Arab states. Egypt sent two forces into Palestine in May 1948. One advanced through Gaza along the coast; the other pushed inland to Bethlehem and the outskirts of Jerusalem. In October the Egyptian forces suffered several reverses from Israeli surprise attacks in the Negev, which left the Egyptians discredited. Egypt signed the armistice in February 1949, leaving her in possession of the narrow Gaza Strip and recognizing the demilitarization of the al-Awja area on the Sinai frontier. The armistice was a humiliation for the leader of the Arab League and an experience the soldiers would not soon forgive the politicians in Cairo, whom they were sure were responsible for the defeat. Over 200,000 refugees were huddled in the narrow, barren Gaza Strip, solemn testimony of the defeat of the Arabs and a vexatious problem for Egypt.

THE MUSLIM BROTHERHOOD

Inflamed nationalism, rampant during the 1948 war, provided the perfect climate for the further growth of the Muslim Brotherhood. Founded in 1929 by Hasan al-Banna, then a youthful teacher in the Suez Canal zone, the Muslim Brotherhood grew under the founder's fiery oratory and positive approach to a personal and social religion. He exhorted his followers to return to the Islam of the Prophet, which meant an acceptance of the Koran as divine revelation and the law of society. He desired to re-create Egypt, as well as other Muslim lands, as an Islamic theocracy and to thwart the trend toward a secular state. But the true strength of the Muslim Brotherhood lay not so much in its ideology as in the energy, devotion, ruthlessness, and singleness of purpose of the leaders and in the tightness of its organization.

In its earlier years the Muslim Brotherhood maintained an active program of social welfare and agricultural cooperatives, but in later years it dedicated its workers in a militant spirit reminiscent of fascism. Its goal became the remaking of so-ciety into a manifestation of Hasan al-Banna's mystical concept of early Islamic life. No compromise from the "right way" could be tolerated. In the 1948 war the fear-lessness of Brotherhood units at the front occasioned many heroic acts, which, however, in no way changed the outcome of the war. Reprisals, pressure, assassi-nation, and armed gangs gave the Muslim Brotherhood power, and its actions at-tracted the youth who yearned for an active course to follow.

The Egyptian government found the Muslim Brotherhood a serious threat and took punitive measures against it. In 1946 fifty-seven members were arrested in Alexandria; in 1948, after the murder of the chief of police, thirty-one were ar-rested in Cairo, and Prime Minister Nuqrashi ordered the Brotherhood dissolved. A few days later Nuqrashi was assassinated by one of the Brethren. In 1949, when Hasan al-Banna was murdered, the government took no serious steps to ascertain his assailants. In 1951 permission was given to reactivate the Brotherhood on con-dition that its semimilitary activities be discontinued. Hasan al-Hudaibi, elected su-preme guide in 1951, did not have the unrelenting zeal of al-Banna, and the move-ment appeared to lose its drive and spirit.

POSTWAR ECONOMY

Postwar Egypt found herself in a curious economic situation. Price levels were still high, employment full, and commodities scarce. But over £E450 million in funds lent to Britain during the war were held in blocked sterling assets in London. For the first time in the memory of man Egypt became a creditor state—and almost overnight. Egypt clamored for machinery, machine tools, industrial and capital goods, and consumer articles. Bankrupt Great Britain could only allow a few pur-chases and promise the rest in the future. Formal negotiations were opened in 1947 over the balances, a schedule for the release of old funds was established, and Egypt left the sterling zone by creating its own independently backed cur-rency. In 1951 Egypt established its own central bank.

But sterling balances only spotlighted the economic needs of Egypt. Schools, health facilities, industry, fertilizers, and better markets for her cotton were re-quired in an increasing volume. Land reform to break up the concentration of ar-able acreage in the hands of a few and revision of the tax structure to increase taxes on income became a necessity. No country in the Arab Middle East was bet-ter prepared to accomplish these changes than Egypt. She had a progressive soci-ety, with an educated group that understood the needs and saw many of the ways in which they could be met. But political power remained in the hands of those who preferred to check the social and economic revolution in Egypt.

FARUQ AND POLITICS

The corruptness and vagaries of King Faruq and his palace entourage made poli-tics unstable in Egypt. With immense wealth in land at his disposal, his political influence was considerable; no one could foretell what might capture his fancy.

For a time he even subsidized Hasan al-Banna and the Muslim Brotherhood. His control of appointments, government contracts, policies of all kinds, land sales, and every aspect of society smothered any political responsibility and tended to corrupt wealthy landowners, ambitious journalists, lawyers, and politicians. Public morals were at a low ebb.

Following the assassination of Nuqrashi, the question of the withdrawal of British troops from the Suez Canal zone dominated the national scene. The relatively free elections held in 1950 revolved around this issue, as they showed Wafd supremacy and the hold of Nahhas upon Egypt. Nahhas assumed the prime ministership again and remained in office until the riots of January 1952.

One clear gain for Egyptian nationalism had already been secured before the elections—the ending of the mixed courts as provided for in the Montreux treaty of 1937.

By October 1950 Nahhas, after innumerable warnings, abrogated unilaterally the Anglo-Egyptian treaty of 1936 and the Anglo-Egyptian agreements of 1899 that established the condominium over the Sudan. This drastic declaration brought forth the British suggestion that Egypt become one of the founders, along with England, France, Turkey, and the United States, of a Middle East defense command similar in scope to the North Atlantic Treaty Organization. Britain announced she was ready, if Egypt would form such a command, to abandon the Anglo-Egyptian treaty of 1936 and her rights therein to military establishments and troop bases in the Suez Canal zone.

Demonstrations, riots, and limited military engagements broke out at several points in the canal zone. Egypt protested that a Middle East defense command could not be accepted, since it would inevitably mean the presence of foreign troops in Egypt. Britain, on her part, stated frankly that troops and officials would remain in the Sudan and in the Suez Canal zone regardless of Egypt's unilateral denunciation of her international commitments. Incidents became more frequent, and on January 25, 1952, an engagement at Ismailia involved 1,500 British troops.

*T*HE 1952 REVOLUTION

The following day, "Black Saturday," Cairo exploded with riots and demonstrations against the British, foreigners, and authority. Damage ran into the tens of millions of pounds and subversive elements tried to overturn the government. Martial law was declared, and Faruq replaced Nahhas with Ali Mahir, directing him to maintain security and order.

On July 23 the government was overthrown by an army coup, ostensibly led by Major General Muhammad Nagib. Announcing the revolution to the nation, Nagib attacked corruption and bribery as the "main reason for our failure in the Palestine war; they are the main reason for troubles in Egypt's political and economic life." He went on to say that his group of officers sincerely believed that steps "were necessary to inspire the Egyptians with a new spirit and determination to go ahead and work toward fulfilling Egypt's national aspirations." King Faruq was forced to abdicate on July 26, 1952, in favor of his infant son, Prince Ahmad Fuad.

The army had refused to shoulder the blame for the defeat in Palestine, contending that the war had been lost in Cairo. When Cairo tried to make the army the scapegoat, the officers revolted, adopting the popular theme that the economy and political life of the state had to be cleansed thoroughly before Egypt could become a modern state or hope to stand up against Israel. Revolution would lead to a full reformation of the state. Ali Mahir was invited to form a civilian cabinet; all civilian titles were revoked; secret political-police sections of the royal and provincial governments were abolished; political prisoners were released; corrupt officials were arrested; censorship of the press was terminated; elections for parliament were announced for February 1953; and a land reform program drawn up by army leaders was submitted to the prime minister.

That measures for land reform came from army sources indicated that the Revolutionary Command Council (RCC), about which little was heard in the first weeks of the revolution, played a powerful role in the events of the day. The RCC assumed that the disproportionate size of landholdings by a few was the primary cause of the abject poverty of the masses. The RCC was comprised of less than a score of officers from various branches of the services. Each officer of the council held the support of other officers, and thus the RCC acted as the governing body of the revolution. The most powerful leader of the RCC was Lt. Colonel Gamal Abd al-Nasser (Jamal Abd al-Nasir), born in 1918; Nasser had graduated from the military academy in 1938, had fought against Israel in the 1948 war, and was the chief organizer of the military revolutionaries.

In September 1952 Ali Mahir resigned as prime minister and Nagib took over. The new cabinet decreed that all political parties be purged of corrupt leaders. At first the Wafd refused to comply, but later arranged to do so by elevating Nahhas to honorary president. Four hundred fifty army officers were dismissed, and a steady house cleaning began in the various ministries. The head of al-Azhar was replaced by a theologian friendly to the revolution. In November Nagib was voted dictatorial powers until January 1953; his powers were then extended another six months.

In September 1952, the cabinet decreed a new agrarian law, restricting land ownership and stating that the government over the ensuing five years would expropriate excess lands, beginning with the largest estates. Ownership of land had been highly concentrated, with 12,000 families owning 35 percent of the farmland while 60 percent of the rural population was landless. The land reform eventually broke the power of the old ruling class and thereby solidified the revolutionaries in power.

REPUBLICANISM AND THE STRUGGLE FOR POWER

It soon became obvious that the RCC had no special plans outlined when the revolution began, even though this revolution became one of crucial importance for Egypt itself and was a model for many others in other parts of the Middle East. Army officers in other countries seized power in a similar way and enacted similar reforms, but the initial changes brought about by the RCC were very pragmatic and gradual.

Believing that if they "turned the rascals out" all of Egypt's troubles would be ended, the RCC soon discovered that vigorous action was necessary to prevent chaos and to accomplish its dream. The revolution in Egypt was three revolutions in one: a "French Revolution," to get rid of a king and form a republic; an "American Revolution," to drive out the British; and a "Kemal Atatürk Revolution," to transform and regenerate the social and economic facets of an old civilization. For purposes of clarity and to avoid a chronological discussion of events on almost a day-to-day basis, each revolution will be examined singly. Yet the interplay of the revolutions and the basic complexity of the situation should never be overlooked in assessing the forces at work in Egypt in the period beginning in 1952.

Once the power of the army was established by the coup d'état, even though it worked through a civilian government, the influence and authority of the king vanished. The deposing and exile of King Faruq were simple matters of informing him that he had to go. A national committee suggested the formation of a republic, which was declared on June 18, 1953. Nagib was acclaimed president and prime minister, and Nasser became deputy prime minister and minister of the interior of the parliamentary Egyptian republic. The RCC announced that it would rule for a transitional three-year period, at the end of which parliamentary government would be established.

The government instituted a new revolutionary tribunal to try enemies of the state and especially Communists, Wafdists, and confederates of the king. Nahhas, his wife, the former chief of the royal cabinet, and others were sentenced to long prison terms.

Extremists, however, did not surrender so easily. In January 1954, serious fighting broke out between a group of the Muslim Brotherhood and the Liberation Rally, the party organization sponsored by the RCC. A six-day state of emergency was declared, the Muslim Brotherhood was dissolved, and seventy-eight of the members, including Hasan al-Hudaibi, were arrested. On February 25, 1954, the first showdown occurred between Nagib and Nasser. It appeared that Nagib was willing to make peace with the Brotherhood and some of the old political groupings, proceed immediately with the calling of parliamentary elections, and reinstitute civilian government. Nasser and his followers believed that such a course would surely return the old crowd to power, defeat the revolution, and hurry the social and economic principles of the new order to an early grave.

Nasser, for the RCC, announced that Nagib had "resigned" from the presidency and the prime ministership "three days ago" and was confined to his house. Nasser became prime minister; but this development did not please the socialists, the Muslim Brotherhood, and the Wafd. On February 27 Major Khalid Muhi al-Din, an avowed socialist, member of the RCC, and commander of the tank corps, appeared before Nasser and demanded that Nagib be reinstated. When Nasser ordered his arrest, the major coolly remarked that his officers at the tank park were at that moment preparing to launch an assault upon the RCC headquarters if their major was not back in their midst with an affirmative response within two hours.

Nasser gave in when an officer brought word that Muhi al-Din was not joking. The tanks were manned, the motors were running, and the ammunition was in place. Nagib returned to the presidency, but Nasser remained as prime minister. Sentiment for a civilian government was very strong, even in the army. Students demonstrated against the military regime; and the Egyptian bar, in a memorandum signed by one hundred leading Egyptian lawyers, asked for a return to civil rule.

Nagib became prime minister again and chief of the RCC, which declared that power would be transferred to a civilian government on July 23, 1954. Nahhas, leaders of the Muslim Brotherhood, and other politicians were released.

At the end of March the RCC threatened to resign, and Nasser and Major Salah Salim absented themselves from RCC meetings. The pressure was on, and Nasser emerged victorious. It was announced that the RCC would not relinquish its power and that elections would not be held until 1956, when the three-year transitional period terminated. In April, after Major Muhi al-Din went to Paris "on business for the RCC," Nasser averred that Nagib had become the tool of dishonest politicians of the old regime. Nasser again became prime minister; he brought eight members of the RCC into the cabinet. In June nine officers of the tank corps were sentenced to fifteen-year prison terms; in September five leaders of the Muslim Brotherhood were stripped of their Egyptian citizenship.

In October 1954, following the signing of the agreement with the British on the evacuation of the Suez Canal zone, Nasser narrowly missed being assassinated by a member of the Muslim Brotherhood. The treaty was not tough enough for them. An angry mob immediately burned the Brotherhood headquarters, and 400 Brethren, including Hasan al-Hudaibi, were arrested. President Nagib was relieved of his office and placed under house arrest; it was charged that he had cooperated with the Muslim Brotherhood and with Communists in the attempt to overthrow Nasser and the RCC. Hasan al-Hudaibi and others went on trial; six were hanged for complicity in the attempt on Nasser's life.

Shortly thereafter, Nasser became acting president. He declared that parliamentary government would be restored as promised in 1956. When that time came Nasser introduced a draft constitution, which was submitted to a national plebiscite. Following its approval, the national assembly met and elected a president as the constitution provided. The public then voted its approval of the president, also as outlined in the constitution. These events transpired without any hitches; President Gamal Abd al-Nasser was duly elected and inaugurated as head of the Arab Republic of Egypt. The constitution contained a full bill of rights and obligations for the individual and guaranteed the economic, physical, legal, and moral welfare of Egyptian citizens. It provided for a national assembly, elected for a term of five years, and a president, who could dissolve the assembly, propose, veto, and promulgate laws, and appoint and dismiss civil, diplomatic, and military officials.

The transition from military rule to constitutional government appeared complete. However, the constitution of 1956 was drawn to place extraordinary power in the hands of the president. Thus, the change altered Nasser's title, but not his power. The popularity of Nasser in his heroic acts of the summer of 1956 belied, at least for some time, doubts regarding the success and permanence of the revolution and the consolidation of all power in the hands of one man.

THE SUDAN AND SUEZ

The second aspect of the Egyptian revolution was, as one American observer aptly phrased it, "Turning out the Redcoats." It had two phases: freeing the Sudan, and obtaining full sovereignty over the canal zone. Prime Minister Nagib was especially favored to accomplish the former. His mother was Sudanese; no one dared accuse him of being negligent in pressing Egyptian interests in the Sudan. In 1952 Nagib held conversations with various Sudanese leaders and signed an agreement approving the establishment of self-government in the Sudan. Great Britain subscribed in principle to Nagib's arrangement, and on February 12, 1953, an Anglo-Egyptian agreement was entered into in Cairo ending the condominium of 1899.

The signing of this Anglo-Egyptian agreement served as a step in solving Suez difficulties. Negotiations with the British were reopened but were broken off summarily, again over conditions upon which British and Allied troops might return. Agreement was reached on four points: an Egyptian would command the bases in the canal zone; his deputy, a technical adviser, would be British and would receive orders from London as well as from the commander; 4,000 British technicians would remain until Egyptians were trained to take over; and the British garrison would depart from the zone eighteen months after full agreement was ratified.

In July negotiations moved to high-level discussions in Cairo. President Eisenhower sent a letter to President Nagib stating that "simultaneously" with the signing of an Anglo-Egyptian accord on the Suez Canal zone the United States would enter into "firm agreements" with Egypt for economic assistance to strengthen the Egyptian armed forces. An agreement in principle was made on July 27, 1954, although the formal arrangement was not signed until October. There were five main points: British troops would be withdrawn by June 18, 1956; the Anglo-Egyptian treaty of 1936 was abrogated; Britain or her allies would be afforded facilities for the entry of troops into Egypt in case of an attack upon Arab League states or Turkey; each party pledged to uphold the Constantinople Convention of 1888 guaranteeing freedom of navigation of the canal; and the duration of the agreement would be seven years. The American role in bringing a settlement between Cairo and London was generally recognized.

ARMS FOR EGYPT

When Egypt entered into the Suez agreement with England, Nasser expected to arm and operate the military establishments in the zone. Modern military machines, however, were so costly that only a nation with a large heavy-industrial capacity could afford the matériel unless purchases could be made at only a fraction of the real cost. Nasser undoubtedly recognized this, for Egyptian officials hoped for an arrangement between the United States and Egypt similar in character and scope to the American program in Turkey, where nearly $1 billion had already been spent by the American government.

Requests for arms aid, specific and general, were forwarded to Washington. But little was forthcoming for the army; Israel and her American friends objected strenuously. Moreover, Nasser was unable for internal political reasons to enter into agreements such as Turkey had with the United States.

Receiving little military aid from the West, Nasser turned to the Soviet bloc. Nasser's power rested on army officers who demanded first-rate equipment. If he could not satisfy them, they would turn to someone else who would promise to get them arms. Unless Egypt had arms of sufficient quantity and quality she could not expect the powers to believe that she could operate the bases along the canal. The solution: Egypt would control and man the defenses of the zone; the powers would furnish the money and matériel.

Nasser announced on September 27, 1955, that an arrangement had been concluded with Czechoslovakia to obtain arms in exchange for cotton. Egyptian and neighboring Arab nationalists rejoiced over the news, since they interpreted the turn of events to mean that they were more independent of the Western imperialist powers and could at their own convenience attack Israel, which they viewed as the satellite of those same powers.

NASSER SEEKS TO DOMINATE THE MIDDLE EAST

Peace between Israel and Egypt remained unattainable under Nagib and Nasser. The pattern of infiltrations, border raids, reprisals, bombings, protests, threats, accusations, and denunciations was unchanged. Israeli boats and ships of other nations laden with cargo for Israel were denied passage through the canal; Egypt asserted that any goods that would aid an enemy could legally be denied transit through the canal insofar as it was a part of Egyptian territory.

The most serious incident occurred on the night of February 28, 1955, when Israelis fell upon Egyptian positions near the outskirts of Gaza, killing thirty-eight. The attack had the effect of forcing Nasser to obtain arms somewhere, regardless of price or strings. This act above all others drove Egypt to the Czechoslovak arms deal.

With regard to the other states of the Middle East Nagib and Nasser looked upon themselves as natural leaders and sought to augment the dominant role of Egypt. Egypt had the largest population and, with the exception of Lebanon, was by far the most Westernized Arab state. Her newspapers, movies, radio, universities, industry, and commerce outstripped those in other Arab countries. Naturally, Arabs turned to Nasser for leadership. "Free Officer" or "RCC" groups sprang up in Syria and Jordan, and Nasser gave their leaders encouragement and assistance.

With the Arab League's headquarters and staff located in Cairo and most of its council meetings held there, the natural tendency of Arab political leaders to gravitate to Egypt encouraged Nasser's stand. The Cairo newspapers and radio exercised a powerful influence throughout the Arabic-speaking world. Nationalism, sponsored and disseminated by those media, always was Arab in scope, rarely Egyptian. In fact, Egyptian nationalism and Arab nationalism were equated; if a Syrian or an Iraqi national proposed a course of action in the interests of his own state that might run contrary to the interests of Egypt, he was immediately branded, even in his own country, as opposed to Arab national interests.

Nasser and the Arab League looked with sympathy upon the actions and aspirations of Arab nationalists in Morocco, Algeria, and Tunisia, and funds were collected and sent to help them achieve their goals. In the Sudan, once the Sudanese attained self-government and release from Great Britain, the experience of freedom was so sweet they hesitated to exchange it for Egyptian control. Political parties favorable to federation with Egypt cooled their ardor, and political leaders enjoyed the prerogatives of cabinet offices. In 1955 no agreement was reached over the division or use of Nile water for power and irrigation, and in the program concerning the construction of the high dam at Aswan, no discussions were undertaken over the creation of the lake that would inundate a considerable area in the Sudan.

Nasser's most caustic wrath was reserved for Nuri al-Said, his archenemy and the architect of the Baghdad Pact. Nuri had aligned with Turkey and the West, and the military aid program he embarked upon would strengthen Iraq. Cairo broadcasts vilified Nuri as a British agent and invited Iraqis to rejoin the Arab nation, which of course meant under Egyptian leadership. This rivalry was a competition for leadership in the Arab world—a competition extending back through history to early Muslim times and into antiquity. Egypt and Iraq, and indeed the whole Middle East, had become more power-conscious than ever before when, with the decline of England and France, the old colonial powers withdrew and the shape of the future balance of power in the region was unclear.

DOMESTIC REFORMS

Many Egyptian leaders under Nagib and Nasser contemplated establishing a more secular government, but they proceeded slowly. Private religious endowments were ended in 1952. Muslim and non-Muslim religious courts in Egypt were abolished in 1956, and cases were heard in secular courts. The decree did not repudiate Sacred Law, but henceforth precepts of Sacred Law were to be interpreted by civil judges.

The revolution also brought benefits in social welfare for the masses. A minimum wage for agricultural workers was set, and relief programs for the destitute were inaugurated. Village schools were built, teacher training extended, health services widened, and many projects for agricultural improvement instituted. In industrial areas social workers were employed to begin the monumental task of aiding new factory workers to make the adjustment from village life to the strange ways of an urban center.

When Nagib announced his coup d'état, he blamed corruption and bribery for the ills that beset Egypt. Inefficient and corrupt officials were dismissed, and a special court was established to try cases of corruption. Much publicity was given to these trials and proceedings, mainly to demonstrate the sincerity and fervor of the revolution and to reduce the natural tendency toward corrupt governmental practices.

The population in Egypt in 1956 numbered about 22 million and was increasing by 500,000 every year. Without a parallel increase in economic output the standard of living remained so low as to constitute a political danger. Thus, the most pressing problems for Nasser were economic.

The new leaders were so eager on the question of land distribution that they rushed forth with land reform measures. Implementation, however, progressed slowly. Landowner opposition and the likelihood of reduced production on broken estates deterred a government already hard-pressed by the realities of politics and economics. But the power of the large landowners, who were the most likely persons to oppose the new regime, was nevertheless broken. And the small peasantry supported the revolution that helped many of them gain some land. In 1961 Nasser entered a new phase of land reform. As a result of changes then and earlier, a total of 12 percent of the arable land was affected. Most of it was distributed to former tenants, while day laborers got relatively little land. Overall yields increased as the reforms took full effect. The state strongly encouraged the creation of government-controlled agricultural cooperatives, and it also subsidized the prices of food for the cities.

The greatest revolutionary project of all, of course, was the great dam at Aswan, which took years to construct, cost hundreds of millions of pounds, and was designed to irrigate millions of acres. It was obvious, however, that the economic situation in Egypt could not wait for the completion of such a long-term project.

Reforms, social measures, expanded government services, strengthening of the army, and irrigation programs increased the size of annual budgets. Income from taxes, though not fully published, obviously fell behind spending. Nasser resorted to loans and artificially low prices paid to peasants for crops rather than drastically increasing tax collections. Money in circulation jumped by 30 percent. Inflation appeared, gold balances dropped, and wealthy Egyptians turned their cash into any goods that could be purchased.

The economic pressures in Egypt, which the old regime largely ignored and which in the absence of any national or moral inspiration brought its downfall, were still present to crowd in upon Nasser and his government. He described himself as a "man in a hurry" and warned that "the longer I take to do things the less time I will have to accomplish them." Many things that Nasser, the RCC, and the dedicated men about them wished to do were long-range affairs requiring twenty or forty years to effect. But the peasants and the poor in the cities would not wait for the better life unless they could have some concrete assurance that it would come; they needed a small down payment on it immediately. Also, the old ex-pashas and wealthy landowners, who found their income diminished, the bulk of their lands seized, the cotton market no longer rigged in their favor, their taxes collected, and their names reviled, opposed the new order.

HIGH DAM AT ASWAN

It behooved Nasser to give an earnest demonstration of the "promised future." Construction of the high dam at Aswan was gloriously pictured as the rational step to revolutionize the Egyptian standard of living. New land would be made available for cultivation and almost limitless kilowatt hours of electricity generated. Upper Egypt would become industrialized and the population pressure would be relieved. Arable land would increase 30 percent. This would give Egypt a balanced and healthy economy.

The Egyptian economy was itself too poor to finance the dam. A charge of $70 or $80 million a year taken from the living of the people would lower the standards beyond endurance. Furthermore, an estimated $200 million in foreign exchange would be required in the early stages of construction to import the necessary equipment and materials. The United States government admitted an interest in 1954, and the possibility of a loan from the International Bank was investigated.

Talks on these subjects were held in Washington in 1955. The arms deal with the Soviet bloc had already been announced and shipments had begun. These events gave rise to fiery denunciations of the West. Nasser defiantly warned that his acquisition of arms must not lead to Western shipments of arms to Israel. At the same time Egyptians and the Arab world were treated to bitter harangues against the Western powers when the Baghdad Pact was signed and the members invited Jordan to join.

Nasser's government already had trade pacts with the U.S.S.R. The West looked upon these as economic necessities for Egypt and regarded Nasser's ranting against Great Britain and the United States as bombast for domestic consumption. In spite of these factors, therefore, the United States offered in December 1955 to grant $56 million and Great Britain agreed to release £5 million to Egypt to strengthen her internal economy, on the assumption that work on the high dam would begin. With the American grant it also became apparent that Egypt's economy would be considered strong enough to warrant a $200 million loan from the International Bank.

At this juncture Nasser appeared to have been triumphant. He had obtained from the U.S.S.R. the arms his soldiers were demanding and was offered approximately $900 million over a ten-year period to build what every educated Egyptian dreamed of. Egypt stood where Turkey had stood in 1947, and the promise of the future was even brighter.

But Nasser failed to grasp the opportunity. His basic ignorance of the West, his inexperience in politics, economics, and foreign affairs, and the weakness of his advisers led him astray. It was announced that the U.S.S.R. was also offering to finance the building of the high dam at Aswan "with no strings attached." Although the authority for this notice became uncertain, Nasser continued to deliver emotional diatribes against the West, complaining of the humiliating "strings" attached by the United States. To the West it appeared that Nasser was courting the Communist bloc in order to increase the grants from the West.

On June 18, 1956, the last contingent of British soldiers departed from Suez in accordance with the treaty of 1954. Foreign Minister Shepilov of the U.S.S.R. was the honored guest of the three-day celebration. In his speeches and those of Nasser opprobrium was heaped upon the West; Shepilov declared that the U.S.S.R. was happy to see the end of political and military imperialism and encouraged Nasser to work to remove economic colonialism—the oil companies—from the Arab world.

These attacks by Nasser, and his embrace of the Soviet bloc, paralleled a further worsening of the Egyptian economy. Expenditures continued to exceed income, charges for sustaining the expanding military establishment mounted, and gold balances dropped sharply. In 1956, when the Egyptian ambassador to Washington returned from Cairo with instructions to notify the American government of Egypt's readiness to accept the American offer to build the high dam at Aswan, Secretary of State Dulles first informed the press, then coldly told him on July 19 that times and conditions had changed and that the United States had withdrawn the offer.

NATIONALIZATION OF THE SUEZ CANAL

The manner in which the notice was given advertised the fact that a calculated rebuff was intended, perhaps to downgrade Nasser's reputation as Washington had downgraded Mosaddeq's in 1953. Nasser struck back by nationalizing the Suez Canal Company on July 26, 1956. He had raised great expectations in Egypt about the building of the dam. Without some dramatic move he was lost. The Suez Canal provided the answer. In his declaration on the canal Nasser stated that Egyptian officials had taken over the company offices in Egypt, ordered all employees to stay on the job, asserted that the canal would remain open and would operate as usual, and explained that nationalization would provide Egypt with a $100 million annual profit to use in building the Aswan Dam. (In 1955, although gross revenues in tolls were nearly $100 million, the figure cited by Nasser, profits were only $31 million; the Egyptian share was only $2,170,000.)

The boldness, excitement, and drama of the action were heady fare for the Arabs and a much-needed tonic for Nasser's prestige. When England and France threatened to use force against Egypt, all the Arab states, as well as the U.S.S.R. and India, rallied to Nasser's support. Workers in Iraq, Kuwayt, Jordan, Syria, and Lebanon pledged to cut the oil pipelines if the West attacked Egypt.

Nationalization of the Suez Canal Company had been contemplated in previous years by other Egyptian governments. According to the terms of the concession, the ownership of the canal would revert to the Egyptian government in 1968, at which time the government would purchase the assets of the company.

The canal had been the subject of the international Constantinople Convention of 1888, in which passage through it was guaranteed in peace and war to all ships. Egypt, however, was held to be the custodian of the canal's security, and Article X stated that the provisions of the convention "shall not interfere" with steps Egypt "might find it necessary to take for security...the defense of Egypt and the maintenance of public order." Until 1954 it was recognized that Great Britain was the protector of the canal; since 1948, however, Egypt, using Article X of the convention, had acted to deny passage of the canal to Israeli shipping, and by inaction on this point the powers condoned the Egyptian interference with Israeli use of the canal.

Reaction in the West, especially in England and France, to the nationalization was precipitous. Naval units were moved to the eastern Mediterranean, troops were readied, and paratroopers were rushed to Cyprus. In London and Paris government leaders pointed out that Nasser by the seizure was assuming a position along the vital artery of world commerce; he would be able to close the route at his whim and thus subject western Europe to economic blackmail. The bulk of the oil consumed in western Europe was Middle Eastern oil, 60 percent of which passed through the canal. It was charged that Nasser violated international treaties and ignored the international character of the canal.

The issue resolved itself into four main points. Paramount was the ability of Egypt at some unforeseen moment to close the canal, raise rates, or deny entry to ships of a single state and thus jeopardize the security and well-being of any nation. As Nasser had been able to do that for quite some time, nationalization of the canal hardly changed the status or the international conditions of the waterway or its transit. Secondly, genuine concern was felt in many quarters over the question of whether Egypt could manage the intricate operations of the canal and maintain its efficiency. A third and very significant factor involved prestige. It appeared to the Western public that Nasser had, with support from the Soviet bloc and neutralist India, gained a diplomatic victory. The fourth and most telling component of nationalization arose from its avowed purpose of obtaining a munificent income and from the invidious inference that the canal company had reaped exorbitant profits. In fact, profits from the canal would not go far in building the high dam.

Under nationalization, operation of the canal continued and ships passed through as usual. Hurriedly, a twenty-four nation conference in London devised a plan whereby Egypt would own the canal, but an international body in accordance with an international treaty would operate and control it. Although agreeing to maritime states advising on the operations of the canal, Nasser politely rejected the proposal and insisted on "the sovereign right of Egypt to run the canal."

As time passed, and the boats were still going through the canal, the opportunity grew for a reasonable settlement. It was illogical to deny that Egypt had the sovereign right to nationalize the Suez Canal Company, and no action was being taken in violation of the Constantinople Convention of 1888. Moreover, as Arab opinion cooled, Nasser became less bold. Iraq, Kuwayt, and Saudi Arabia were suspicious of references in his speeches to "Arab oil" as if it belonged to Egypt. They resented the fact that he took this step without conferring with other Arab League states and were apprehensive lest oil production would be curtailed and their royalties reduced. In October 1956 each side to the dispute brought the matter to the Security Council of the U.N., where agreement was reached on six basic principles for the canal's operation. Accepted by England, France, and Egypt, these six principles were an equitable compromise devised as a face-saving program for all.

THE WAR

The emotionalism aroused by the keen disappointment in the Aswan Dam fiasco and the obvious success in the Suez triumph waned, and diplomats believed that "reason," through the six principles drafted at the United Nations, would prevail. The calm, however, was upset by the Israeli invasion of Sinai on October 29, 1956. Many aspects of this event, including the British and French plot, using the Israelis as a willing foil, have been discussed in Chapter 43. As surprising as was this attack to the world public,

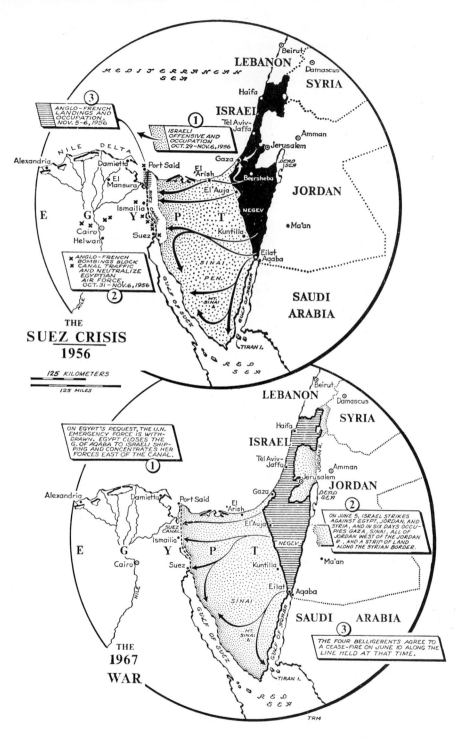

THE
SUEZ CRISIS
1956

THE
1967
WAR

many foreign offices and military intelligence units were well aware that forces were being mobilized by England, France, and Israel, perhaps with the expectation that if they attacked, Nasser's regime would collapse. Britain and France had agreed at their secret conclave to enter the war in not less than four days after the Israeli attack, and the ultimatum that they delivered to Egypt and Israel on October 30 calling for a halt to the war and insisting that each withdraw to positions away from the canal was a ruse, in part to cloak their collusion and in part to enable them to occupy the canal area without Egyptian resistance. Aware of the French air force participation in the war from the start, Nasser early in the war ordered his troops to fall back to positions west of the canal, grounded some of his planes, and sent the rest to bases in Saudi Arabia. Nasser refused the ultimatum and the powers entered the fray. Air attacks on November 2 brought about meetings of the U.N. Security Council, which called for an immediate cease-fire. Cooperation by naval forces and paratroopers brought the fall of Port Said, whereupon the U.S.S.R. warned that she was prepared to use force if need be to obtain the withdrawal of Western and Israeli troops from Egypt. In the face of sharp words from the United States and the U.S.S.R., a cease-fire was ordered on November 7, and U.N. observers entered the canal area the next day. The British and French began their evacuation in December upon the arrival of the United Nations Emergency Force (UNEF), and Israel withdrew from Sinai in January. Only after severe pressure from the United States in March did Israel give up her hold on the Gaza Strip and the Straits of Tiran. U.N. salvage crews cleared the canal, which Egypt had blocked in several places during the war, and shipping was resumed in April.

Upon Egypt the effects of this episode were incalculable. A large part of the arms recently acquired from the Soviets was lost in Sinai, and the Egyptian army was again said to be weak and unprepared. The Western world and the Middle East were blanketed with accounts of the rapidity and apparent ease with which the tough and highly trained Israeli army had occupied Sinai, and much was made of the phrase, "one hundred hours to Suez," without examining the role the expected British and French invasions had upon Egyptian strategy. The destruction in Port Said, the damages in Sinai, and the loss of revenue from Suez operations were severe blows to the national economy. Had not the United States and the U.S.S.R. rescued Egypt, Nasser might have fallen after the British, French, and Israeli attack. Nasser, however, assumed a bold posture and emerged from the disaster stronger than ever. All the Arab nations rallied diplomatically to his side and Nasser grew even more popular with the Arab masses throughout the Middle East.

After Israeli troops left Gaza relations between Egypt and the West improved. During negotiations for compensating the Suez Canal Company shareholders, agreement was reached for a payment of £28 million, and Egyptian authorities operated the canal efficiently.

THE UNITED ARAB REPUBLIC

In Arab politics, the year 1958 was one of remarkable developments. Provisions of the various pacts Egypt had entered into with other Arab governments stipulated that unified military command rested in Egyptian hands. Thus, in 1957 when the Syrian-

Turkish crisis arose, Egyptian troops were sent to Syria. Their presence in Syria ensured a peaceful birth for the United Arab Republic. Certain Syrian groups had long favored a merger with Egypt, and Nasser's Radio Cairo carried to every Syrian village vigorous propaganda for uniting all Arabs. The rush of events carried Nasser pell-mell into the union, obviously more hastily than desired, but he could hardly refuse the fruits of his own propaganda. The United Arab Republic was declared with little deliberation on February 1, 1958, and several days later Nasser presented to a cheering throng in Damascus a program for the new state. He declared that a new assembly would be appointed, composed of 300 Egyptians and 100 Syrians. A cabinet for the U.A.R. was also selected. Significantly, twenty of the thirty-four members were Egyptians, and Egyptians held, among others, the portfolios for defense, foreign affairs, education, and national guidance.

As the months passed, many Syrians acted displeased over the merger. Nasser revealed that Syria was not as rich as he had supposed and that the union would take a number of years to perfect. Nevertheless, its creation upset the balance of power among the Arab states. The imam of Yemen sent his son to Cairo to seal the establishment of the United Arab States. Although only a nominal merger, it gave lip service to the ideal of Arab unity, showed the imam's respect for Nasser's position, and afforded the imam freedom from having Radio Cairo beamed at his country. Movements similar to Nasserism in Iraq, Saudi Arabia, Kuwayt, and Jordan were encouraged, and Jordan and Iraq formed a union. Nasser reacted swiftly to the challenge to his dominance and condemned that federation as the evil doings of "imperialists." Elements in every Arab state looked to him for inspiration and sought to attach themselves to his political coattails. Nasser could hardly disappoint them. Radio Cairo invited Arabs in Baghdad, Beirut, and Amman to revolt against their rulers. Syrians found the Lebanese borders easy to infiltrate, and Nasser's agents abetted the civil disturbances that racked Lebanon in 1958. He inspired the men who led the Iraq revolution in July 1958. Had not American marines and British paratroopers landed in Lebanon and Jordan, those states might have fallen to Nasser's partisans. The amir of Kuwayt and Prince Faysal of Saudi Arabia recognized Nasser's power and hastened to make their peace with him before their dynasties followed the Hashimites of Iraq into oblivion.

The appointed assembly of 400 for the United Arab Republic was looked upon as a preliminary body that would take some of the first steps in consummating the union. Elections in Syria were too normal a process to ignore, and in Egypt elections were a long tradition. The problem was how to bypass the politicians and get through to the people. Machinery for obtaining an elected national assembly had been devised to eliminate political parties and politicians. The Ba'th leaders in Syria were so opposed to it that Nasser dropped Hurani and al-Bitar as vice presidents. President Nasser took his constitutional oath of office, and the fiction was maintained that the people ruled through a hierarchy of committees, councils, unions, and assemblies. A month before, however, an executive council of fifteen had been designated as a kind of super-cabinet to make decisions, but even here most questions of any weight were referred to the Supreme Council of three— President Nasser, Field Marshal and Vice President Amer, and Vice President (Syria) Abd al-Latif al-Baghdadi. In 1961, the skilled, disgruntled Syrian politicians collaborated with disaffected soldiers, merchants, and landowners to lead Syria out of the union.

THE UNITED ARAB REPUBLIC WITHOUT SYRIA

The Syrian secession caused only a slight shock to the Egyptian region of the United Arab Republic because most of the adjusting had been on the Syrian side. President Nasser called for new elections in 1962 for the National Union (sometimes called Congress), which would represent the "genuine popular forces—peasants, workers, artisans, industrialists, etc."—of the nation.

The Arab Socialist Union under Nasser's presidency was launched as the U.A.R.'s sole political party, to gather into its fold all political activists and would-be leaders from the nation's various social and economic sectors. A great deal of hard work at the grassroots level produced sufficient understanding to hold elections for the National Assembly in March 1964. Nasser remained president and was elected to a third six-year term in 1965. Elaborate internal security forces and various secret police organizations were established or strengthened in the 1960s as Nasser became more suspicious and more isolated from his former colleagues.

ARAB SOCIALISM

European communism, because of its emphasis on dialectical materialism and its atheism, had difficulty in making an appeal in Egypt. This foreign ideology, supported by one of the great powers of the world, was an easy target for the deep-rooted Egyptian xenophobia. Governmental control over agriculture and commerce had been traditional in historic times, and in the monolithic structure being devised by Nasser any different pattern was unthinkable. The state held a responsibility for the economic well being and advancement of its citizens, and whether it was called state capitalism or state socialism really made no difference. Arab socialism had all the right connotations, did not conflict with Islam or the past, and with such a name it was a commodity exportable to neighboring states.

Steadily, the government increased its hold over commerce, industry, and finance by nationalizing many types of businesses. By 1961 all banks and insurance companies had been nationalized in what was deftly called "Arabization," and all newspapers and periodicals were placed under the control of the National Union and later the National Assembly. In 1962 estimates showed that 90 percent of all major businesses had been "Arabized," including flour mills, transportation firms, and seventy-seven bakeries in Cairo. In 1963 foreigners were forbidden to own farm land in Egypt. Over $1 billion in property was sequestered when the property of Egypt's richest citizens, "422 millionaires and reactionaries," was confiscated. A highly progressive income tax was enacted, and 25 percent of net profits in all businesses had to be distributed to the employees. The Pan American Oil Company brought in commercially productive wells in the Gulf of Suez and the Red Sea; natural-gas strikes were made in the delta area; and several rich seams of coal were discovered.

The greatest single venture was the building of the new dam at Aswan. At the end of 1958 the U.S.S.R. lent the U.A.R. $100 million to get it under way, and open construction began in 1960. Prime Minister Khrushchev, who attended the celebrations in May 1964, when the first stage was completed, promised to see it through to completion.

The second most dramatic development project was the improvement of the Suez Canal. In 1958 a record number of ships, 17,842, used the canal, but already the size of oil tankers, nearly half of the ships passing through, was increasing to the point where many were unable to navigate the narrow and shallow course. Once shipbuilders reached the tonnage that was too great for the canal, they would likely start building much larger tankers suitable for rounding Africa. Nasser planned to spend $270 million over a ten-year period to enable supertankers to navigate the channel. However, new tankers of 300,000 to 2 million tons aroused concern in the United Arab Republic that even after the completion of the extensive improvements, oil shipments from the Persian Gulf to Europe would not be able to pass through the canal.

Through the years industrial development in Egypt moved rapidly forward. Agreements were reached with Soviet-bloc countries and mainland China for financial and technical aid to industry of every sort. The same was true for Western nations. In this decade the United States gave large amounts of aid, and almost every year shipments of American wheat and other foodstuffs, paid for in nonconvertible currency, arrived at Alexandria.

The continuing problem of the population explosion was a counterbalance to these advances. In 1958, at the time of the formation of the United Arab Republic, Egypt's population was estimated at 24 million; by 1966 it was slightly over 30 million, an increase of 25 percent in only eight years. The annual increase in population was rapidly approaching the 1 million mark, and when the impounded waters of the Aswan High Dam became available to expand the irrigated lands in Egypt, they would hardly feed the numbers added after the project was begun. Any improvement in the standard of living had to come from improved agricultural methods and industrial production.

NASSER AND THE WORLD

Following the Soviet agreement to aid in building the Aswan High Dam, the U.A.R.'s relations with the U.S.S.R. and the Soviet bloc continued on a friendly government-to-government level. Large quantities of military goods were supplied, ostensibly in exchange for future cotton shipments, but arrangements were shrouded as were the actual military deliveries. In spite of the massive aid for the Aswan High Dam and other programs, Nasser actively suppressed Communists. Several hundred were jailed at various times, and special crackdowns were conducted almost yearly, much to the annoyance and embarrassment of Soviet leaders, who admonished Nasser publicly for his treatment of the left. The Soviet Union, nevertheless, upheld its position of general support and in the 1967 war between Israel and the U.A.R., the U.S.S.R. strongly supported Egypt in discussions at the U.N. Security Council.

Nasser's relations with the West were always somewhat fragile because of past European imperialism and the difficulty that Europeans and their governments had in throwing off the concepts on which that imperialism had been based. With Nasser's growing interest in Aden, relations became strained with London. Diplomatic relations were severed in June 1967 over the war in the Middle East. In 1967 President de Gaulle took a neutral stand on the war and would not involve France in the meetings of several maritime powers that were considering the means of forcing the Straits of Tiran. West Germany gave many loans and considerable aid to Egypt for industrial development, and many West German scientists were employed in missile and rocket endeavors.

Relations with the United States fluctuated widely in the period after 1956. Suspicious of the close relations between the United States and Israel and mindful of America's great wealth and power, Egypt was wary in her attitudes toward the United States. In the crisis with Israel in 1967 Egypt was angered by American leadership in trying to break the blockade of Eilat. Accusing the United States of participating with Israel in the war against the Arab states, Egypt broke diplomatic ties with the United States on June 6, 1967.

The greatest role and the greatest hope for leadership of the U.A.R. in the world was in the Middle East and among the Arab nations and peoples. Nasser was cast as the hero of the modern Arabs, and he had a large and devoted following in every Arab country from the southeastern tip of Arabia to Morocco on the Atlantic. His followers kept the political pot boiling in Syria and Iraq, and those who desired a change in Saudi Arabia, Kuwait, Yemen, Aden, and Jordan were in his camp as well. In 1962, at the outset of the revolution in Yemen, Egypt was the first among the Arab states to recognize the republican regime of al-Sallal; Nasser signed a joint defense agreement with al-Sallal and sent 12,000 soldiers to fight against the forces of al-Badr. Egypt sustained the republicans and controlled them to the point where Cairo dictated policies. Estimates were made that Egypt had expended about $1 billion in the effort. After England announced her planned withdrawal from Aden in 1968, Nasser not only decided to stick it out in Yemen but also encouraged his supporters to acts of violence in Aden so as to secure a favorable regime.

The Ba'thist coups in 1963 in Baghdad and Damascus were supposed to be first steps in the establishment of a new United Arab Republic. Conferences to effect these steps proved that Arab peoples might want Arab unity, but Arab leaders were not prepared to sacrifice local interests and personal positions to Egyptian dominance.

Arab leaders recognized that Saudi Arabia, Kuwait, Iraq, and Libya had wealth in oil royalties; they looked to these states for economic leadership. However, Egypt, the most populous, the most modernized in industry, education, and transportation, and, with Soviet aid, the best equipped in modern weapons, was regarded as the natural military leader. Nasser had been successful in standing up to the powers in 1956, and the propaganda effort from Cairo had succeeded in making Nasser the outstanding charismatic figure in the Arab world. With Arab summit meetings in Alexandria and Cairo, with the headquarters of the Arab League located there, it was natural that the Arab states would follow his lead in general world affairs and in matters of joint military action and defense against Israel. President Arif of Iraq joined in a mutual military command in 1964 and Syria followed in 1966. They were pledged to join with each other in a war against Israel, and each agreed to accept Palestine Liberation Organization armies as adjuncts to their own forces.

In May 1967, Syria called upon Nasser to make good his pledge to come to Syria's assistance should Israel attack. Feeling that he would have a serious problem at the Israeli frontier because of the presence of the United Nations Emergency Forces, Nasser requested U Thant to remove these troops from their places along the Gaza Strip, the Sinai peninsula, and the Straits of Tiran. Egypt immediately reinstituted the blockade of Eilat she had enforced up to 1956. Israel reacted angrily. As the tension mounted, and as each side prepared for war, great solidarity appeared among all the Arab states; each one gave her support to Nasser as the strain between Syria and Israel shifted southward toward the Israeli-Egyptian frontier.

THE 1967 WAR

When war came in June, Egypt bore the main brunt of the six days of fighting, but other fronts were opened between Israel, Syria, and Jordan. The cease-fire of June 10, 1967, called for by the Security Council, left Israeli troops holding Sinai and the east bank of the Suez Canal. Egypt lost most of her air force and a large part of her tanks and other war matériel. Several thousand soldiers, mostly officers, remained as prisoners of war in Israeli hands.

Nasser publicly assumed the blame for the disastrous defeat and resigned his office. The general reaction against his resignation was so overwhelming he rescinded his decision. The quality of the military leadership and the lack of organization and commitment were blamed for the infamy, and several thousand officers were relieved of their commands. It was reported that many officers had deserted their posts and men in the face of the enemy and that the planning of offense and defense had been exceedingly faulty. At the time that Nasser went to Khartoum for summit meetings Field Marshal and Vice President Amer was arrested. Shortly thereafter Amer committed suicide, and it was announced that he had been involved in a plot to overthrow Nasser.

As soon as the cease-fire became effective, various Arab leaders indicated the need for a conference of leaders of Arab states to arrive at a unified position. The prime minister of Sudan arranged to have an Arab summit meeting at Khartoum. The meeting's final resolution, announced on September 1, 1967, affirmed Arab solidarity and the necessity for joint efforts to eliminate all traces of Israeli aggression. In addition, the resolution called for liquidating all foreign bases in Arab countries, consolidating military preparedness, considering oil as a diplomatic weapon, and upholding of the rights of the Palestinian people to their land. This included refusing to recognize Israel or to have negotiations with her. At the summit meeting Saudi Arabia, Kuwayt, and Libya promised the equivalent of $100 million to Egypt to offset the loss of revenue from the closure of the Suez Canal.

In addition, Nasser and King Faysal of Saudi Arabia agreed to end their intervention in the Yemeni civil war. This understanding led to the overthrow of al-Sallal in November and so weakened the forces of FLOSY in South Arabia that its rival party, NLF, gained the upper hand and received the power and symbols of government when the British evacuated Aden.

On the international scene the U.S.S.R. supported the position of the U.A.R. at the United Nations and began to replace much of the military equipment lost or damaged in the 1967 war. For the first time Nasser surrendered to the U.S.S.R.'s demands that Soviet military personnel be stationed in Egypt to train officers in the use and maintenance of Soviet equipment and to aid in the organization of a more effective armed force.

CEASE-FIRES AND STALEMATE

When Gunnar Jarring, the Swedish ambassador to Moscow, was appointed special U.N. representative to the Middle East to aid in the negotiation of a settlement as outlined by Resolution 242 that was passed unanimously by the Security Council on November 22, 1967, Nasser was careful not to be too enthusiastic over the terms. There were hopes that Ambassador Jarring, by shuttling back and forth between Cairo and Jerusalem, would be able to implement Resolution 242 and convert the rather ephemeral cease fire into a more permanent accord, maybe even a peace treaty. Both Israel and Egypt subscribed publicly to the resolution, but each interpreted it differently. Nasser, insisting that Israel withdraw from the Sinai and all Arab lands, refused to negotiate face-to-face with the Israelis, as they were demanding, until they had pulled back to the pre-1967 borders; Israel refused to consider doing so until a peace agreement was signed. Jarring made several efforts, but each time he had to announce that the positions of the sides were irreconcilable.

Within days after the cease-fire began, the inevitable incidents along the canal began to occur. Artillery duels and air raids became commonplace. In April 1969 Nasser no longer recognized the cease-fire as being in force. In 1970 the duels in the war of attrition involved such advanced weapons that it appeared that full-scale war would be resumed. An Israeli air raid on an industrial plant near Cairo killed many civilians, which hastened the Soviets in sending and setting up SAM-3s (surface-to-air missiles) in the canal area. Israeli planes could no longer fly over Egyptian territory at will. A six-month truce went into effect on August 8; though each side accused the other repeatedly of violations, the serious shooting stopped. By mid-1970 such large amounts of Soviet war matériel had been received by Egypt that it was estimated Nasser's forces were better armed than they had been in 1967, despite considerable economic damage.

In the last half of 1967 Nasser's friends rallied to his side. Large subsidies from Saudi Arabia, Kuwayt, and Libya kept the economy afloat. Oil from the Sinai was not available, the canal was closed, tourists did not come, and the cotton worm infestation was the worst in fifty years. Blueprints for another deepening and widening of the canal were shelved, but drilling by American companies for oil in the Gulf of Suez and in the western desert proceeded. The Aswan Dam was completed without much fanfare in midsummer 1970, at a time when crops were greatly improved and the forecast of production was rosy indeed. By 1970 Egypt had adjusted from the shock of 1967; recovery was on the way.

ANWAR AL-SADAT

Nasser had assumed the office of prime minister and head of the only political organization, the Arab Socialist Union (ASU). He dissolved the National Assembly and called for new elections in 1969, at which time Anwar al-Sadat, one of the original military officers on the Revolutionary Command Council, became vice president. Many wondered how the 1967 disaster could have left Nasser more popular than ever and his leadership so compelling. The only answer could be that despite his numerous setbacks he was the most charismatic figure to appear among the Arabs in this century. He was, however, to leave them at the age of fifty-two, for on September 28, 1970, Nasser died suddenly of a heart attack. Heads of state and dignitaries from around the world attended his funeral and paid their respects to the creator of the Egyptian republic. Vice President Anwar al-Sadat automatically became interim president. Sadat was nominated president by the National Assembly, elected overwhelmingly by national referendum, and sworn in on October 17.

Sadat was born in 1918 in a village in the Nile delta. Attending a military academy in 1936, he formed a secret group of twelve along with his classmate Nasser to work for the liberation of Egypt from Faruq and the British. Jailed by the British during World War II as a German sympathizer, he participated with Nasser, Ali Sabri, and others in the 1952 coup and acted as its first spokesman. He wrote an account of the coup and held positions as speaker of the National Assembly and secretary-general of the National Union, the first political party of the revolution.

ARAB REPUBLIC OF EGYPT

The name of the United Arab Republic was incongruous since Syria's secession in 1961, and in 1971 Sadat pronounced the formation of the Arab Republic of Egypt, calling it a socialist democracy. Meeting opponents head on, Sadat removed Ali Sabri from the vice presidency and arrested him along with several other high officials, accusing them of plotting a coup. Sadat used a national referendum then (and also other referenda later) to validate his changes. Later, he dissolved the parliament, reorganized the ASU, scheduled new elections for the assembly, and brought forth a new constitution. Under this, Islam was declared the state religion, civil rights were strengthened, seizure of property was banned, and women were given equal rights. Sadat had taken full power in his own administration.

Soviet President Podgorny returned to Cairo in May 1971 to sign a treaty of political, economic, and military cooperation under which the Soviets agreed to provide training for the army and to furnish weapons. On return visits to Moscow Sadat boldly stated Egypt's policy of resistance to communism anywhere in the Arab world; he was not very successful in obtaining more arms.

Within a few weeks, however, Nixon was in Moscow and the Soviet-American policy of détente was proclaimed. Sadat decided that he could no longer rely on Moscow to support him actively in regaining the lands from Israel or on Washington to pressure Israel to withdraw. On July 18, 1972, he ordered all Soviet military advisers and experts to leave Egypt, a move popular with the Egyptian people, who had had many unpleasant experiences with them. By autumn, Sadat began to have second thoughts about alienating the Soviets; through al-Assad of Syria a rapprochement was made and arms shipments were revived, though the number of Russians in Egypt was kept small.

Oil strikes in the Libyan desert not far from the Egyptian border gave hope of finding commercial quantities of oil in Egypt. New discoveries in 1971 and 1972 helped Egyptian production to rise to over 200,000 barrels daily and enabled Egypt to become a member of OAPEC. The Egyptian economy was sustained only by the regular remittances from Saudi Arabia, Kuwayt, and Libya, plus occasional one-time grants such as $250 million from the Persian Gulf states and 260,000 tons of wheat from the United States.

Sadat's relations with other Arab states were not easy. More conservative than Nasser, he steered a course further to the right, especially after Ali Sabri's attempted coup. The coordination of policies with the more radical leaders of Syria proved difficult, leading to the early demise of the Federation of Arab Republics. With the foundering of the federation, Sadat and Libya's al-Qadhdhafi made plans for a merger of their two political movements. But before long that idea was dead and Libya had closed her embassy in Cairo. Sadat broke diplomatic relations with King Husayn of Jordan after Husayn made proposals for peace with Israel and for a Palestine-Jordan federation. To the south, Sadat had so many controversies with Sudan that he requested Sudanese troops to leave the Suez Canal battle area. In 1973 Sadat mended his fences, smoothed over differences with the Sudan, and diplomatic relations were restored with Jordan. Several months earlier Sadat had taken over the positions of prime minister and military governor-general, placed Egypt on a war footing, and announced a war budget. As the days passed and as Sadat drew closer to his Arab allies, tension mounted.

THE 1973 WAR

Early in 1973 Sadat, no longer able to tolerate the stalemate with Israel, sent his national security adviser to Washington and then to Moscow. His reception was cool. Without any advance toward the return of territory, Sadat coordinated military operations with Syria and they jointly attacked Israel and the occupied territories. Sadat sent Egyptian forces across the Suez Canal on October 6, 1973, in the midst of Ramadan, the Muslim holy month of fasting, and Yom Kippur, the Jewish Day of Atonement. The main battles terminated on October 25 with a temporary cease-fire on October 22, as called for by the Security Council. Egypt insisted that the Israelis return to the October 22 cease-fire line before prisoners could be exchanged.

Egypt was defeated in the war, as Israel now occupied portions of both banks of the Suez Canal, and had an Egyptian army surrounded and in an untenable position. Israel had also defeated Egypt's ally, Syria; the latter blamed Sadat for leaving the battle without a joint agreement on actions. On the other hand, Sadat could and did portray himself on enormous billboards in Cairo as "the hero of the crossing," that is, since Egyptian troops had crossed the canal, and were now in occupation of portions of both banks, Sadat could claim some element of victory from the war. Egypt had also fought with considerable ability in the early days of the war, and for that reason as well Egypt could boast of some success.

After the exchange of prisoners Sadat accepted an American invitation to attend a peace conference in Geneva in December, but it lasted for only a day. After many trips by Kissinger between Jerusalem and Cairo or Aswan, an interim withdrawal was agreed upon on January 18, 1974; Israel pulled back her forces east of the canal, Egypt was allowed limited armed units on the east bank of the canal, and U.N. Emergency Forces patrolled the area between.

A *NEW EGYPT*

Sadat's exuberance at Egypt's initial successes in the war, though dampened by the Israeli counterthrusts, left him confident enough to modify the severity of his control over Egypt's political processes. Former powerful military, political, and press figures were released from jail in 1974. He instigated the formation of two groups within the Arab Socialist Union, a leftist one and the Social Democratic Platform, whose goal was the encouragement of industrial development and the investment of foreign capital. Sadat was reelected in 1976 to another six-year term as president. In the elections for the People's Assembly, many of the seats were contested; embryonic political parties could be seen, though they were tightly circumscribed: There were centrists, rightists, leftists, and independents in the new body.

In 1978, the old Wafd party was allowed a brief reappearance, but it was soon forced by Sadat to disband as it seemed likely that it might become a strong and viable opposition. A few leftist critics won election to parliament as well, but generally speaking Sadat kept power in his own hands and increasingly curbed any visible opposition.

Egypt's war losses since 1967 were calculated at $38.8 billion; her needs seemed astronomical. In 1974 Sadat received millions from Iran, West Germany, Japan, France, the United States, and the World Bank, $1.7 billion from Saudi Arabia and the Persian Gulf states. In June 1975, the Suez Canal was officially opened to traffic, a peace gesture that did not go unnoticed in Jerusalem. Though rates were double what they had been when the canal was closed in the 1967 war, usage reached the 1967 level by autumn.

As debate became somewhat freer in Egypt in the 1970s the Aswan High Dam turned out to be a favorite topic for disagreement. The direct costs of the dam and power station were about $800 million, but far more was ultimately spent on other aspects of the project. Its electric power generation had fallen short of what had been promised; a number of land reclamation projects had failed; each year many tons of rich silt were being blocked from the Nile delta and profitable fishing was being ruined in the Mediterranean; and new currents were causing severe erosion along the coast. Evaporation of water increased, and drainage in the delta was neglected. On the other hand, defenders of the dam pointed out that electric power had been quadrupled; rice production rose; flooding had been curtailed; productivity increased; and the water supply and control system had saved crops in 1972, when water levels in the Nile, without the dam, would have been ruinously low.

The increase in world oil prices resulted in economic growth in addition to that caused by the Aswan Dam. A powerful demand for Egyptian professionals and skilled laborers was created in the oil-producing states of the Middle East. At the same time, higher prices for wheat, and domestic and foreign pressure for economic liberalization, pushed the regime to loosen economic controls. This opening to foreign investment and domestic capitalism was a substantial ideological change from the socialism of the Nasser years. Remittances from Egyptians working abroad, petroleum exports from Egypt itself, aid from the United States, tourism revenues, and Suez Canal tolls all helped compensate for the relative stagnation of agricultural revenues. Egypt's population dramatically rose, from 33 million in 1970 to 39 million in 1976, and the government looked increasingly to industry to overcome the inertia of agriculture.

CULTURAL AND SOCIAL CHANGES

The revolution of 1952 led to a great increase in the number of students attending government schools. Between 1952 and 1970 enrollments tripled, and in universities they increased almost fivefold, thus causing considerable overcrowding. By 1980 there were over 4 million students in elementary schools, but this represented only slightly more than one-half of the eligible age group. Classes were so crowded that teachers and professors often could not devote much attention to the individual student. Many faculty members left Egypt for employment elsewhere, thereby accentuating the problems of overcrowding for those left behind. After 1962 the government guaranteed every university graduate a job, if necessary with the bureaucracy. The famous al-Azhar became a modern university, teaching secular as well as theological subjects under government control. Literacy rates improved, so that by 1976 about 55 percent of men were literate, while only about 29 percent of women could read and write.

The educational system, newspapers, broadcasting, and some of the arts were placed under fairly rigid government control between 1956 and 1964. Television broadcasts began in 1960 and rapidly became highly popular. The regime encouraged the production of films, some with a social realism or patriotic approach; many were commercial successes that were often boisterous melodramas, farces, or musicals.

The status of women improved in the years following the revolution. Middle- and upper-class urban women especially benefited from the expansion of educational opportunities. More women worked outside the home in the 1960s than in the 1950s, but this was still a far lower proportion than was the case for males.

Even though the National Charter of 1962 specifically called for equality between men and women, government employed fewer women than did private businesses.

Women gained the right to vote and to be elected to parliament in 1956, and by 1967 one million women had registered to vote. Women were appointed to the cabinet. In 1979 the Sadat government reserved 30 seats in parliament for women and made legal changes favorable to women, but some of these policies were later reversed.

Changes in the Egyptian economy in the 1970s and 1980s made it possible for more women to find employment in the service sector, in fields such as banking and tourism, as well as taking positions vacated by Egyptian men who were working abroad. About one-third of those working overseas were themselves women. Many women also participated in the Islamic fundamentalist revival by dressing in a more conservative fashion. Calls for limits on women working outside the home have been made in the 1980s as unemployment increased with the decline of oil revenues and the return of workers to Egypt. Muslim fundamentalists also strongly criticized the role of women in Egypt, claiming that the limited steps made toward their equality with men were contrary to Islam.

In cultural matters a very great chasm continued to exist between the high culture of the elite and the folk culture of the masses. To a certain extent the cinema, radio, and television helped to transcend this difference, particularly since Egypt after World War II was a major producer in all three of those media. Oral folk poetry was closely associated with religious festivities while painting and sculpture in the Western tradition were purchased by the upper classes. The Egyptian government sponsored conservation of the folk tradition, as in Egyptian Arabic music, while the singer Umm Kulthum (d. 1975) became the most famous performer in the Arab world, holding millions of people spellbound via her radio performances. Much of literature, poetry, and drama was preoccupied with political events, and particularly the issue of social justice for the poor and the 1967 defeat of Egypt by Israel. Najib Mahfouz, the preeminent novelist of the Arab world, who won the 1988 Nobel Prize for literature, had turned inward and pursued a personal vision. Political patronage encouraged writers to express support of the state, while censorship restrained dissident opinions unless they were carefully disguised.

SADAT VEERS TOWARD THE WEST

In 1975 Sadat met President Ford to serve notice of his earnest desire for peace. Kissinger, taking heart from these conversations, as well as from the opening of the canal and earlier disengagement agreements, succeeded on September 4 in getting Egypt and Israel to sign an interim agreement. Israeli forces withdrew additional kilometers, surrendering the strategic Mitla and Giddi passes and giving up the Abu Rudeis oil fields. Egypt agreed that Israeli nonmilitary cargoes might pass through the canal. The U.N. accepted a larger buffer zone, and the United States consented to monitor an early-warning electronic complex and to relay the signals received to both sides. This 1975 agreement infuriated Syria's al-Assad, who likened Sadat to a traitor for freeing the Israeli enemy to concentrate all her power on the Syrian front. Sadat quietly protested that Egypt's economy was woefully weak and that the country's miserable standard of living demanded peace.

Relations with Libya fluctuated month by month, but usually they were not pleasant; Qadhdhafi looked upon Sadat as a weak reed. Sudanese ties were much warmer; tentative joint-defense plans were drafted, though the idea of any union was shelved.

As early as 1974 Sadat announced that Egypt would not rely solely on the U.S.S.R. for arms, though he did concede that Soviet friendship would be an active factor in Egyptian policies. More Soviet fighter planes arrived in 1975, but Sadat looked for military goods elsewhere. He obtained bombers in France, and Saudi Arabia purchased arms from Great Britain for Egypt.

Sadat abrogated the Soviet-Egyptian Treaty of Friendship on March 14, 1976. Part of Egypt's problem was the huge debt of more than $14 billion to the Soviets and others. In 1977 Sadat postponed indefinitely all debt payments. Sadat was convinced that the United States, not the Soviet Union, held the cards for peace, and he therefore turned to the United States and away from the Communist bloc.

Because of the debt, constant unfavorable balances of trade, and a burgeoning population, Sadat pressingly needed peace, loans, credits, and capital for development. The oil-rich Arab states, western Europe, and the United States were his best hope. In 1977 he obtained grants and promises of about $2 billion in American aid, and he also gained $140 million from the International Monetary Fund following riots in Cairo over food price increases. Saudi Arabia and other Arab oil states came up with $2.5 billion, assuring Egypt sufficient financial security to remain independent of the Soviets, but, of course, dependent upon them.

Even with such massive foreign aid, ends just did not meet. One-half of the rural population owned no land at all in 1972; their standard of living was deplorable. Sadat tried belt tightening in the cities. When prices were increased on basic commodities the worst riots since 1952 broke out in January 1977 in Cairo. They were quelled only with difficulty by the militia. The cries of the people calling, "Nasser, Nasser," must have sent chills through Sadat. Removing the bread subsidy might well bring revolution. Even though Sadat backed away from this, there was no doubt that he had moved away from Nasser's path. The middle classes and the rich were now the beneficiaries of government, while the workers, peasants, and the poor generally were disregarded. Sadat favored a more open economy in place of a highly centralized regime; his eye looked first to Egypt rather than to pan-Arab nationalism; his policies veered to the right, not to the left; and his ear was attuned to Riyadh and Washington instead of Moscow and New Delhi.

SADAT'S PEACE OFFENSIVE

Sadat astonished the world by flying to Jerusalem on November 19, 1977. Greeted at the airport by Prime Minister Begin, and all important Israeli leaders, Sadat was showered with warm enthusiasm on the drive to Jerusalem. In his speech to the

Knesset on the following day Sadat boldly announced that he recognized Israel as a state in the Middle East and was ready to make peace. He stated that Arab lands seized by Israel in 1967 must be returned and the right of self-determination for the Palestinian people recognized.

By this audacious trip Sadat demonstrated in full view of the world his sincere desire for peace with Israel and gambled that this action would compel Israel to make an equal compromise or show her intransigence to all. Over and over Sadat repeated his stand that he had no intention of making a separate peace, and that self-determination for the Palestinians was the crux of the issue. Despite these assurances, Egypt agreed at Camp David in 1978 and in the peace treaty of Washington in 1979 to a separate peace with Israel and to arrangements for the Palestinians that were exceedingly unlikely to be put into effect, thus leaving them under continuing Israeli control. As pointed out in Chapter 44, Sadat received in return a number of benefits for his country, including the Sinai peninsula, increased U.S. aid and backing, and the cessation of war with Israel. Sadat sought to use the leverage of the United States upon Israel to rectify Israel's military superiority and to apply pressure on Prime Minister Begin to interpret the written agreements in a way conducive to Egyptian national interests. This failed to happen. Instead, Begin embarked upon a series of steps, such as the annexations of East Jerusalem and the Golan Heights, that severely tested Egyptian willingness to abide by the peace treaty. However, Israel did return the Sinai to Egypt in phases, culminating in April 1982, and Egypt did allow Israeli vessels to pass through the Suez Canal, establish diplomatic relations with Israel, and permit a whole host of commercial and cultural ties between the two countries. When Israel invaded Lebanon in 1982 Egypt did almost nothing to show its displeasure, thereby demonstrating that direct Egyptian-Israeli military confrontations were indeed a thing of the past.

As the multinational force oversaw the Israeli withdrawal from Sinai and the implementation of limited Egyptian control, most of the Arab states vigorously condemned Sadat. The Arab League headquarters was moved to Tunis, Egypt's membership in the league was suspended, most Arab governments broke diplomatic relations with Egypt, and the PLO referred to Sadat as a traitor to Arab nationalism. Internal opposition also emerged as many groups saw Sadat's foreign and domestic policies as failures. Islamic fundamentalists particularly objected to Sadat's corruption, his secularism, and his dependence upon the United States. The Muslim Brotherhood was permitted by Sadat to operate with some freedom, since it did not pose a direct danger to the regime, but other, smaller, and more radical groups engaged in violence and murder. On October 6, 1981, Sadat was assassinated by a small fundamentalist organization as he reviewed a military parade commemorating the 1973 crossing of the Suez Canal.

Sadat had accomplished many of his goals by 1981: the basic continuity of the revolutionary regime was preserved while some of Nasser's policies were changed; the 1973 war led to an opening to the United States, peace with Israel, and the return of the Sinai to Egypt; and some economic progress was made, even though daunting problems remained. Despite these accomplishments, Sadat was not loved by the Egyptians as Nasser had been. Nasser was a heroic figure whose successes and failures were on an epic scale. Sadat was a more limited and less emotionally effective leader, although in many ways more successful.

CONTINUITY IN THE MUBARAK ERA

Vice President Husni Mubarak, former commander of the air force in the 1973 war, immediately succeeded Sadat. Mubarak repressed the fundamentalists and promised to continue Sadat's economic and foreign policies. While the basic political structure remained much as it had been under Nasser and Sadat, there were some alterations.

Changes since 1981 included the emergence of genuine political parties in the parliamentary elections of 1984. Using a system of proportional representation for every party that gained more than 8 percent of the vote, the government's National Democratic party (NDP) gained 391 seats with over 70 percent of the vote. The NDP had its greatest strength in the rural areas and especially from the still important rural notables. Copts, Christians who were upset over the growth of fundamentalist Islam, also tended to vote for the NDP. The Wafd (revived yet again!), in alliance with the Muslim Brotherhood, had 57 seats and 15 percent of the vote, and it was the only other party represented in the lower house of parliament. These elections were the most open and free in many years, although there was a low turnout of voters and some government manipulation.

New elections in April 1987 were again fairly open and strongly contested. The National Democrats once more took 70 percent of the votes and 308 seats, while 17 percent and 56 seats went to a leftist and Muslim Brotherhood coalition, 11 percent and 36 seats to the Wafd, and independents took 39 seats. President Mubarak was elected in October 1987 for another six-year term. He clearly controlled the military, which he had purged of possible opponents, and thus he was undeniably in control of the whole state apparatus. Even though violent incidents and assassinations took place, and Muslim fundamentalists were responsible, the government easily arrested them and sentenced them to long prison terms.

Egypt sought to retain a reasonably friendly relationship with Israel and the United States, while at the same time regaining its cooperation with the Arabs and the Soviet Union. In this venture President Mubarak was quite successful. Yasir Arafat, the head of the PLO, met with Mubarak in 1983 after being expelled from Lebanon by Syria. Egypt aided Iraq in its war with Iran, and gradually most Arab states reestablished diplomatic relations with Egypt. In May 1989, the Arab League readmitted Egypt as a full, voting member. Gulf Arab oil states resumed financial aid to Egypt. The erratic ruler of Libya, al-Qadhdhafi, sought to intervene in the internal affairs of the Sudan and Egypt, both of which cooperated closely in various measures directed against him. Ties with Israel in the mid-1980s were strained by Egyptian-Israeli disagreements over Israeli policy in Lebanon, Israel's building of new Jewish settlements in the occupied territories, and a border dispute over a small section of land. After the border dispute was submitted to arbitration in 1986, Mubarak met with Israeli Prime Minister Peres and Egypt once again sent an ambassador to Tel Aviv.

The United States and Egypt maintained a close relationship as the U.S. poured billions of dollars of military and economic assistance into the country. In the 1980s such aid was about $2 billion per year. The two nations also conducted frequent joint military maneuvers in Egypt starting in 1980. Mubarak balanced the United States relationship by restoring close contacts with the U.S.S.R., and in 1987 Egypt and the Soviets concluded their first trade agreement in a decade. By the late 1980s Mubarak had retained the foreign policy benefits of the 1979 peace treaty while overcoming most of its drawbacks.

In economic matters the Mubarak regime has not been as successful as in foreign questions. Government deficits have ballooned, increased food imports became far more expensive, Egypt's own oil exports fell in value, and remittances from the millions of Egyptians living abroad sharply decreased. In 1985 Egypt imported almost $6 billion more than it exported. The foreign debt by 1987 had increased to about $40 billion. Many countries, including the United States, rescheduled payments on the debt owed by Egypt so as to reduce the intolerable burden it posed for the Egyptian government.

A substantial section of the population continued to be extremely poor. The subsidies that kept food prices low helped these people but the subsidies represented a great expense for the state. The subsidy for bread was more than the annual income from the Suez Canal!

Population growth was very high. Egypt's population by 1988 was 50 million or more. Such large numbers of people necessitated ever-growing investments in capital as well as facilities and services. The quality of urban life inevitably deteriorated as crowding became ever more intense. Greater Cairo with 12 million or more people was especially affected as people moved from the countryside to the cities. The urban congestion was slightly alleviated when the first subway opened in 1987, but transportation was still a difficult problem for most Cairenes.

Government development planners, recognizing these difficulties, were more realistic in the middle 1980s than earlier. They sought to encourage agriculture-related industries, reduce dependence on imported food, extend electrical energy production, and concentrate government money on infrastructure. New oil and natural gas discoveries were a cause for some optimism amid the general gloom.

Egypt's withdrawal from the long confrontation with Israel that had consumed so many resources since 1948 opened up the opportunity for a concentrated attack on domestic economic problems. Most of these problems seemed, however, extremely difficult to resolve. The extraordinary stability of the Egyptian political system was remarkable, but the transferral of the benefits of stability to economic growth and increased social equity was a major dilemma.

INDEPENDENCE OF THE SUDAN

During World War II the British, other Allies, and the expanded Sudan Defence Forces had staved off Italian attacks from Ethiopia. The demands by educated Sudanese for British commitment to ultimate Sudanese self-determination were denied.

At the end of World War II the sentiment in Egypt for the unification of the Nile and the absorption of the Sudan left the British unmoved, but it attracted the support of Ashiqqa party leaders in the Sudan, largely because they sought to play Egypt off against Great Britain. In 1947 the British announced that, even without any agreement or confirmation from Egypt, steps would be pursued to form a separate Sudanese elected legislative assembly with an executive council at Khartoum. The new governor-general proceeded slowly, and elections did not materialize until November 1948. The Umma party, which gathered its inspiration from the famed nineteenth-century Mahdi, incorporated in its platform a program of independence and won the election. The Ashiqqa party showed friendship for Egypt and boycotted the election. Both major political parties were religiously based and under the power of sectarian Muslim leaders. All the parties in 1950 demanded that Great Britain and Egypt grant the Sudan the right of self-government and self-determination as early as 1951.

Pressure for independence was not a result of economic causes. In fact, the overall economy was booming as cotton exports grew. From 1941 to 1951 the value of exports increased almost sevenfold. Since the vast majority of the population was engaged in agriculture, they prospered during this period. In the cities, wages failed to increase as fast as food prices, thereby hastening the development of labor unions, particularly among the railway workers. The total population was about 10 million, according to the first systematic national census that was conducted in 1956.

Within a few months after the 1952 Egyptian revolution, Nagib met with many Sudanese leaders. He reached an agreement with the Umma party approving the establishment of self-government in the Sudan by the end of 1952. For a three-year period the administration, police, and army were to be Sudanized, after which time the right of self-determination would be exercised by the peoples of the Sudan. An Anglo-Egyptian agreement was entered into in Cairo ending the condominium of 1899 and accepting the self-government statute formulated by the Sudan government. After it became official on March 21, 1953, preparations for the election of a two-chamber parliament were launched.

Two prominent parties opened their campaigns. The Umma party declared that it favored the founding of a republic. The head of the party was Sir Abd al-Rahman al-Mahdi, spiritual leader of the Ansar sect of Muslims. The Umma group favored a slow process of separation from England; to ardent nationalists, therefore, Umma was a stronghold of the conservatives and the *status quo*. Sir Ali al-Mirghani, head of the Khatmiya sect, served as titular head of the Ashiqqa party, which now took the name of National Unionist party (NUP). The active leader was Ismail al-Azhari, a graduate of the American University of Beirut and teacher of mathematics at Gordon Memorial College in Khartoum, who espoused a close tie with Egypt.

Elections were held in November 1953. Of the ninety-seven seats for the house of representatives NUP won fifty, and Umma twenty-three. Voters were split along regional, sectarian, and economic lines. Ismail al-Azhari became prime minister, and formed a cabinet of twelve. Sudanization proceeded rapidly; in August eight Sudanese became provincial governors, replacing the customary British civil servants. Very few southerners were appointed to posts as the British left; instead, northerners secured the key appointments.

Early in 1955 the NUP started to splinter over the question of the tie to Egypt. Three members left the cabinet to establish a new Republican Independence party, which presented a platform of unfettered sovereignty for the Sudan, but pledged cultural and economic cooperation with Egypt. By June Ismail al-Azhari took the same position and ousted from the cabinet the advocates of union with Egypt.

In August leaders of NUP and Umma requested Egypt and Great Britain to withdraw their troops from the Sudan—which they agreed to do. This action led Sir Ali al-Mirghani and Sir Abd al-Rahman al-Mahdi to effect a compromise. On December 19, 1955, the Sudan house of representatives declared Sudan an independent state and requested recognition from Egypt and Great Britain, which they granted on January 1, 1956; Sudan became the ninth member of the Arab League and was admitted to the United Nations.

Nearly 50 percent of Sudan's trade had been with Great Britain, less than 10 percent with Egypt. Cultural ties with Egypt were firm; a great number of Sudanese were educated in Cairo and Alexandria, where they came under strong Egyptian influences. The problem of the Nile waters was a vital one for Sudan, but doubly so for Egypt. Negotiations between the two states ended in stalemates. With these complex and diverse forces at work upon Sudan, a policy of complete independence and an honest neutralism attracted general support.

Sudan's foreign policy was based on close friendship with the Arab states. The Sudan condemned Britain, France, and Israel for their 1956 aggression against Egypt. The blocking of the Suez Canal hurt Sudan's trade more than that of any other country. When Egypt formed the United Arab Republic with Syria, however, Sudan evidenced no desire to join the federation.

MILITARY GOVERNMENT

Since the cotton harvests in 1957 and 1958 were poor and the world price for cotton fell, Sudan's economy and government encountered serious economic problems.

Another problem arose when Nasser of Egypt publicly asserted that Sudan had violated the 1929 Nile Water Agreement by undertaking the new Managil Project, a plan similar to the Gezira Scheme, whereby a significant part of the Nile's water was to be taken without any prior consultation with Egypt. Fearing a new arrangement with Nasser would move Sudan into the Egyptian camp, General Ibrahim Abboud, commander of the army, in an easy military coup, suspended the constitution on November 17, 1958, turned out the cabinet, dissolved parliament and the political parties, abolished trade unions, and declared a state of emergency. A thirteen-member Supreme Council of the Armed Forces proclaimed that it held constitutional authority and that its president, General Abboud, would exercise all legislative, judicial, and executive powers and remain commander in chief of the armed forces. However, with improved economic conditions and apparent progress in developing resources, political stability induced Abboud to take the first step toward more responsible government. Abboud announced that a Central Council of State would be formed, a majority of whose members would be chosen by elected provincial councils. Six million voters cast their ballots in 1963 to elect rural and municipal councils, which in turn would choose the provincial councils. This exercise in democracy occurred without any widespread disorders, although the response in the three southern provinces was accompanied by the rumblings of nationalist and separatist movements.

Abboud also tackled the long-standing argument with Egypt over the Nile waters; in 1959 he accepted $43 million from Egypt to help resettle those in the Sudan who would lose their lands and homes from flooding caused by the new Aswan Dam. A general agreement was also reached whereby in the future Sudan would be authorized to take 18.5 billion cubic meters of water annually from the Nile, leaving some 55.5 billion for Egypt. There was genuine satisfaction in Sudan over this division, for it was far greater than she had previously.

RETURN TO CIVILIAN RULE AND THE SOUTHERN PROVINCES

On October 23, 1964, rioting and bloodshed erupted in Khartoum as a result of many frustrations, the greatest of which were the continuing unrest and disorders throughout the southern provinces. Sudan's political leaders compelled Abboud to step aside for a civilian caretaker government under an independent who appointed a five-man council to assume the presidential function. Political prisoners were released, censorship ended, political parties legalized, and Khartoum University granted autonomy again. Elections for a constituent assembly, in which women for the first time voted, were called in 1965 but held only in the north. In June 1965, a coalition government of Umma and NUP members was formed by Muhammad Ahmad Mahjub of Umma and Ismail al-Azhari, the NUP leader, who was elected president of the Supreme Council.

In 1966 the assembly voted a censure motion against Mahjub's rule charging corruption and failure, and elected Sadiq al-Mahdi, the new leader of Umma, as prime minister. Sadiq was thirty years old when he took office; he was an Oxford-educated economist and a modernist who had broken with his uncle, the leader of the Ansar sect and descendant of the Mahdi who had thrown out the Egyptians and British in the late nineteenth century. Sadiq, the great-grandson of the Mahdi, advocated neither capitalism nor communism, but a "clear-cut form of socialism" to harmonize the efforts of government capital and individual effort. He also felt that there was a real basis for national cohesion in the Sudan, and the activist southern leaders had more confidence in him than in his predecessors. Sadiq went ahead with the first elections in ten years in the south to fill their seats in the assembly. Umma won fourteen and the Sudan African National Union ten, forming a rather conservative southern bloc in the assembly. In April 1967 Sadiq swayed the vote in a popular referendum on the philosophy of the new constitution, producing a document more secular than Islamic, but his Umma party then fragmented.

When the 1967 war between Israel and the Arab states broke out, Sudan severed relations with Great Britain and the United States. In order to achieve a firmer Arab position, Mahjub called for an Arab summit meeting in Khartoum. The meeting condemned Israel as an aggressor and reaffirmed Arab solidarity. Such emphasis on Arab identity threatened the non-Muslim Sudanese, who objected to any possible union, federation, or close cooperation of the Sudan with the Arab states.

Sudan needed political tranquility, however, and this would depend on Sadiq's skill in solving the southern problem. After the declaration of Sudan's independence and the departure of the British, strife erupted between the pagan and Christian blacks inhabiting the southern provinces and the northern Arab Muslim regions. Self-rule, autonomy within a loose federation, secession, and independence—each of these schemes had supporters who mistrusted the government of Khartoum and the Arab politicians and generals. To centuries of distrust and fear was added the new African nationalism. In 1962 large-scale fighting broke out and it lasted for ten years. Government forces were only partially successful in curbing the uprising, although tens of thousands of rebels fled into other African states. William Deng, leader of the Sudan African National Union, from his exile pleaded the southern cause, but others who believed his organization to be too ineffective organized Anya-Nya, a terrorist society pledged to kill Arabs. A new separatist group, the Azania Liberation Front, was also born, and the stream of exiles and refugees widened. Israel provided some assistance to the southern rebels. Bloodshed in the southern provinces pulled down one cabinet after another.

Mahjub continued to fail to pacify the south. With southerners in the cabinet and amnesty offers to the rebels in 1968, he still could not end the civil war. Fighting in the south involved Zaire and Uganda, where exiles formed a provisional government. At one time government troops opened the roads in Equatoria and secured the towns, but the countryside was fully in the hands of the Anya-Nya guerrillas.

In Khartoum itself, the squabbling of the main political parties and the petty bickering of the chief politicians once again discredited the democratic and parliamentary system.

JAAFAR MUHAMMAD AL-NUMAYRI

On May 25, 1969, Colonel Jaafar Muhammad al-Numayri and a band of young officers seized the government and established a Revolutionary Command Council (RCC) to rule. Numayri's cabinet, composed of officers and Nasserite socialists, offered a policy of "freedom and socialism" and pledged to find a solution for the south. Former leaders were arrested, all salaries and fringe benefits were cut 20 percent, press censorship was abolished, offenders from the old order were tried, and the poll tax was dropped. In the autumn the cabinet was reorganized; civilians were placed in most posts and Numayri became prime minister as well as head of the RCC. Communists were dropped from the RCC and all political parties were outlawed. Numayri sought to align his ideas with those of Nasser, but the Sudan did not join in any meaningful union with Egypt.

Since the rift in the Umma party had been healed, Imam al-Hadi al-Mahdi as Ansar leader and his nephew Sadiq retained considerable power. In March 1970 they tried to overthrow Numayri, but the army easily defeated them. Thousands of their supporters and al-Hadi himself were killed. Then it was the turn of the Communists. Numayri seized their leader and exiled him to Cairo. The Communist party, however, had a very strong and active membership, estimated at between 5,000 and 10,000; denouncing it and punishing its leader hardly rendered it impotent.

Numayri was driven to seek some way out of the impass in the south. The south itself was seemingly so divided that Numayri hardly knew who represented the majority. Numayri extended amnesty to all rebels, announced that a provisional government for the south would be established, developed intensive social, economic, and cultural programs, and began a school to train southerners for leadership roles. Yet, the battles went on. Failing in these schemes, Numayri offered regional autonomy to the three southern provinces, but he could find no hand to grasp. As the most power resided in the leadership of the Anya-Nya National Armed Forces, Sudan launched an offensive against it; the only result was a steady increase in the insurgency.

The revolutionary regime of Numayri inherited a formidable set of economic challenges. Sudan's foreign debt was rapidly increasing, reliance on cotton as the only major earner of foreign exchange continued, strikes by trade unions hampered economic growth, and the railways and Gezira cotton area showed increasing inefficiencies. On the other hand, light manufacturing had increased, and agriculture had expanded both in terms of the amount of land cultivated and mechanization.

In 1970 Numayri produced a five-year economic development plan intended to raise the gross domestic product. All banks and cotton exporting firms and some foreign companies were nationalized. Newspapers had already been taken over. Numayri's brand of socialism meant an end to foreign and domestic private companies of any size. A number of small loans from other nations and international organizations helped Sudan's economy. Numayri, however, needed immediate results, and these would not be forthcoming for a decade or more.

In July 1971 the leader of the Communist party escaped from jail. A few days later, his followers captured Numayri and sixty army officers. A new seven-man RCC was formed, claiming to represent a National Democratic Front, "an alliance of workers, peasants, intellectuals, soldiers, the Free Officers, and national capitalists." They stood for agrarian reform and autonomy for the south. Pro-Numayri organizations were banned and four Communist ones were reactivated. However, two leaders of the coup were in London. When they flew to Sudan their British plane was forced to land in Libya where they were detained. The Sudanese people and the army did not rally to support the Communists, and the army, loyal to Numayri, took control, arrested the instigators of the coup, and reinstalled Numayri on July 22. Fourteen of the coup leaders were tried and executed, and leftists within the government and army were dismissed.

DEMOCRATIC REPUBLIC OF SUDAN

Leaders of the coup had charged that Numayri was squeezing out leftists and Communists and drifting to one-man rule; that the economy was stagnating; that the southern rebellion was dragging on; and that Sudan had not joined Egypt. Numayri recognized the validity of these accusations, and in August 1971 the RCC produced a provisional constitution for the Democratic Republic of Sudan. Numayri ran for president in September and received 98.7 percent of the vote. After his inauguration the RCC resigned and Numayri formed a cabinet with himself as prime minister. He appointed three vice presidents: the general and chief of staff who had rescued him in July; a former leftist civilian chief judge who had been allied with the Communists; and Abel Alier, a loyal and influential southerner.

For twenty years the southern civil war had hampered every action in Khartoum. Numayri realized he could not defeat the rebellion so he opened negotiations in London with Major Joseph Lagu, the Anya-Nya leader, and Abel Alier met in Ethiopia with a southern executive council of the South Sudan Liberation Union. Six separate peace documents were signed in March 1972 in Addis Ababa, giving local autonomy to the south and amnesty to all; arranging for a cease-fire, the return of refugees, and the transition of the guerrillas into the southern army; and paving the way for the higher executive council of SSLU to become the council for South Sudan. By the end of the year the three southern provinces had been united into South Sudan, which had an elected assembly, a chief executive answerable to it, and an executive council responsible for all government except defense, currency, and foreign affairs, which remained under the control of Khartoum. Six thousand guerrillas and a like number of regular soldiers became the southern command under General Joseph Lagu, whose military rank equaled that of Numayri. Abel Alier became president of South Sudan, still holding the rank of vice president for Sudan. One of the greatest problems facing these new leaders was that of resettling the 180,000 refugees returning from Uganda, Ethiopia, and Zaire and the 250,000 who had fled to the bush. Autonomy turned out to be real, as English rapidly replaced Arabic in southern government affairs, though Arabic was supposed to be the official language.

At the end of 1973 Numayri opened the first People's Regional Assembly of South Sudan, an act that finally marked the end of rebellion and the achievement of autonomy from Khartoum. In the 1978 regional elections Alier was defeated and Lagu became head of the regional authority. Most observers, remembering the bitter feuds and the bloodshed of two decades, marveled at the arrival of peace.

Numayri's paramount foreign relations concern was with Egypt and other Arab states, for they exercised the most influence over affairs in the Sudan. Sudanese troops were on their way to Suez two days after the outbreak of war in 1973. The Sudanese Socialist Union, Sudan's sole political party, followed the programs of the Arab Socialist Union in Egypt and even began to cooperate with the Syrian Ba'th party. In 1974 Numayri met with Saudi Arabia's King Faysal and concluded an accord on the minerals on the Red Sea bed, offshore rights in the Red Sea, and the security of that region.

Numayri shifted to the right in domestic politics after the aborted 1971 coup. After the election in 1972 for a new People's Assembly he held the offices of president, prime minister, and minister of defense. A permanent constitution was drafted and the Sudanese Socialist Union took an active role in the task. In May 1973 the new constitution was promulgated. Some groups, fearing Numayri's obvious power, had been opposed to it but the new apparatus for government won popular acclaim; even university students and the Muslim Brotherhood praised it.

In response to the worldwide inflation that also affected Sudan, Numayri raised prices on many consumer goods such as sugar, gasoline, and cigarettes. The protests were so vehement and popular reaction so violent that Numayri resigned. Immediately the masses demonstrated and demanded that he return, which he dutifully did. By 1974 Numayri released large numbers of political prisoners, including most former leaders. Probably this was a mistake as in 1976 Sadiq al-Mahdi, with Libyan backing, staged a coup attempt, which led to bloody riots and over one hundred executions following its suppression. Numayri's susceptibility to this and numerous other attempted coups derived from an inability to institutionalize his support, tolerate dissent, or unite a highly pluralistic body politic.

Numayri's retreat from the left became clear in 1972, when he appointed a committee that recommended denationalization. The regime wanted to attract foreign capital and to open the door to the oil money flowing into the Middle East. In a joint venture with Saudi Arabia an oil refinery was located at Port Sudan. Prospecting for oil was widespread and major discoveries were made at Bentiu in 1979. Oil operations soon became involved in the renewed southern uprising of 1983 and were thus interrupted. Investments in basic infrastructure became urgent: the railway system was revitalized and some all-weather roads were built.

Since the end of the nineteenth century many had seen Sudan's potential as one of the great food producers of the world. In 1904 the British proposed cutting a channel for the White Nile to bypass the Sudd swamp area, where every August the Nile floods. Such a bypass canal would save some 4 million cubic feet of water. Called the Jonglei Canal, it would be about 224 miles (360 kilometers) long. In 1975 a French consortium was contracted by Egypt and Sudan to build it at an estimated cost of $175 million. Estimates were that it would eventually open a vast area to cultivation. Numayri hoped that such projects, oil money, and Western technology would develop the Sudan into a "food power."

SOCIAL AND CULTURAL DEVELOPMENTS

The extraordinary diversity of the people of the Sudan continued with little change throughout the period after independence. The population increased to 22 million. More than 100 languages were spoken by fifty ethnic or tribal groups, although Arabic has been by far the most widespread. Storytelling, pottery, poetry, and music reflected this diversity. Written cultural expressions were mostly in Arabic. About 40 percent of the population considered themselves to be Arab in ancestry and language, but a larger proportion spoke the Arabic language itself. A new generation of Sudanese Arab poets flourished in Egypt after World War II and demonstrated the strength of the Arabic tongue in the Sudan. The post-World War II generations of poets in the Sudan sought to find, define, and express a national identity that would include African as well as Arab elements. In the southern third of the country English served as a common language to be used for communication by the speakers of the many regional languages.

Religious diversity often coincided with regional and language factors, as Muslims were overwhelmingly the majority in the northern two-thirds of the Sudan but were only a small minority in the south. About 5 percent of the total population was Christian and 30 percent believed in tribal and animist faiths. The cultural unity of the Sudan was further weakened by the relatively small proportion of the citizenry that lived in urban areas. Two-thirds of the Sudanese lived in the countryside where they were widely separated from each other in an enormous nation one-quarter the size of the continental United States. Literacy was low, as only about 20 percent of the adults could read and write, thereby limiting the effectiveness of newspapers as a unifying factor. In addition to language, religion, ethnic, and regional differences, there were also remarkable variations in attitude and behavior between the rich and the poor, the educated and the uneducated, and men and women.

THE LAST YEARS OF NUMAYRI

By 1977 Numayri had stabilized his regime to the extent that he sought to conciliate his opponents. Sadiq al-Mahdi and the head of the Muslim Brotherhood returned from exile and accepted the framework of government. Numayri especially appealed to the Brotherhood as his regime adopted an Islamic fundamentalist tone in the 1980s. This latter step brought the greater application of Islamic law based on the shariah, even for non-Muslims, in all parts of the country in 1983. Numayri showed his growing egotism by requiring military officers to swear allegiance to him in 1984 as the imam, the leader of the faithful. He proposed amendments to the constitution that would transform Sudan into an Islamic republic, extend the term of the president to life, and make the shariah the sole source of legislation.

In the south political and tribal infighting among local leaders allowed the central government in Khartoum great leeway. Numayri played the leaders off against each other and then divided the south into three distinct regions with separate governments. This step, plus the Islamic policy and the inefficient dictatorship of Numayri, ultimately united the sentiments of the southerners against the northern-dominated government. The civil war emerged again, after a ten-year lull. Colonel John Garang led the Sudanese Peoples Liberation Movement in victories over the hapless central government armed forces and by 1986 he controlled most of the south. The civil war stopped the two-thirds completed Jonglei Canal.

The Jonglei Canal was a major part of Numayri's development plans. Sudan needed, he felt, to diversify its agriculture. In the 1970s cotton production fell and other crops were encouraged. The results of this and other measures were a foreign debt that grew to $9 billion or more, a devaluation of Sudan's currency, an increase in corruption, and an inflation rate of around 60 percent per year. Imports by the early 1980s were three times the value of exports. The precarious economy was further affected by the famine and drought that hit the Sudan and neighboring Ethiopia in the middle 1980s. The Sudan's own severe problems were exacerbated by the need to feed hundreds of thousands of starving Ethiopians who fled their country. Perhaps as many as 500,000 Sudanese died as a result of starvation and malnutrition—a disaster that Numayri denied or whose importance he sought to minimize.

Sudan's foreign policy in the last years of Numayri was allied closely with that of Egypt. The two countries signed a mutual defense pact in 1977. Numayri supported Sadat's peace initiative with Israel and Sudan was one of the few members of the Arab League that did not break diplomatic relations with Egypt upon its signing of the peace treaty with Israel in 1979. Sudan and Egypt also established coordinating committees that dealt with such matters as immigration and trade. Because of a perceived threat from Libya, the Sudan and Egypt acted closely together to formulate joint steps against al Qadhdhafi. Sudan was especially concerned about Libya's ambitions in Chad, so Numayri backed Chadian leaders opposed to those favored by al-Qadhdhafi.

As Sudan adopted a more conservative domestic economic policy and an alignment with Egypt and Saudi Arabia, it tended to ally itself more frequently with the United States. In return, the United States provided strong economic and military support to Numayri against both Libya and Communist Ethiopia.

CIVILIAN CONTROL RETURNS

On April 6, 1985, General Abd al-Rahman Siwar al-Dhahab, the minister of defense, announced an armed forces coup and the ousting of Numayri. The causes of the coup included the resumption of the civil war in the south, foreign pressure, economic catastrophe, famine, Numayri's growing isolation as he suppressed even the Muslim Brotherhood, and popular unhappiness with the removal of government food subsidies. Large-scale riots and demonstrations broke out in March while Numayri was in the United States. Trade unions and professional associations had led the call for the overthrow of Numayri, and the army then joined the civilians at a later stage.

Siwar al-Dhahab dissolved the Sudan Socialist Union party and pledged the military to turn over power to civilian authority. He suspended the constitution and announced power was in the hands of a transitional military council. Political prisoners were released and the security police was disbanded. The provisional constitution of 1956 as amended in 1964, with added provisions for southern autonomy, was adopted, and elections to a constituent assembly took place in April 1986. Numayri's shariah legislation of 1983 was retained, much to the displeasure of the southerners. The civil war, which persisted despite the new situation, precluded elections in some of the southern districts. Since the Umma was the largest single party, even though it lacked a majority, it formed a coalition with other groups and Sadiq al-Mahdi became prime minister. The Muslim Brotherhood emerged as the leading element within the opposition, while a member of the Mirghani family became the head of state. The army actually did turn over effective power to the civilians, much to the surprise of many observers.

The new regime had to deal quickly with the dreadful famine, which had been exacerbated by locusts. Luckily, the harvests of 1985 were sufficient for most of the country, but the civil war and famine continued in the south. Inflation rapidly increased as the weak and unsure government resumed subsidies and resisted austerity measures suggested by the International Monetary Fund, which declared the Sudan to be bankrupt in 1986. Flooding devastated the Sudan in 1988.

Sadiq al-Mahdi sought friendship with all countries and particularly with Numayri's enemies, Libya and Ethiopia, which had supported the southern insurgents in the civil war. Libya then dropped this support as its ties with the new government warmed, but Ethiopia continued to aid the rebels. The Sudan claimed Israel was also aiding Garang's forces. Assistance from the United States was endangered by Sudan's increasingly pro-Libyan atmosphere, while ties with Egypt were somewhat strained for the same reason and because of other suspicions and uncertainties.

The southerners were promised a "revision" of the shariah laws and the central authorities did offer amnesty and limit their fighting to defensive actions, but there was little agreement among the northerners about what steps to take and how far to go to meet the demands of the south. Little progress seemed possible in the late 1980s on the key issues of the south, the economy, and the political system. Indeed, the whole issue of national identity remained open and unresolved. The appropriate balance among language groups, religions, ethnicities, and regions was unclear as the military once again seized power on June 30, 1989.

REFERENCES

Important references for this chapter are also found in Chapters 22, 27, 35, 43, and 44.

Abd al-Rahim, Muddathir, et al., eds. *Sudan Since Independence: Studies of the Political Development Since 1956*. Aldershot, Eng.: Gower, 1986. Fifteen essays by political scientists who were associated at various times with the University of Khartoum.

Allen, Roger. "Contemporary Egyptian Literature." *Middle East Journal* 35 (1981): 25–39. An excellent short survey for 1952 to 1980.

Aly, Abd al-Monein, and Manfred W. Wenner. "Modern Islamic Reform Movements: The Muslim Brotherhood in Contemporary Egypt." *Middle East Journal* 36 (1982): 336–361. A comprehensive sketch of this important movement and the political reactions to it.

Ansari, Hamied. *Egypt, the Stalled Society*. Albany: State University of New York Press, 1986. Valuable for discussions of rural notables.

———. "Sectarian Conflict in Egypt and the Political Expediency of Religion." *Middle East Journal* 38 (1984): 397–418. Deals with the Sadat years and includes Copts and fundamentalist Muslims.

Bechtold, Peter K. *Politics in the Sudan: Parliamentary and Military Rule in an Emerging African Nation*. New York: Praeger, 1976.

Dekmejian, H. Hrair. *Egypt Under Nasir: A Study in Political Dynamics.* Albany: State University of New York Press, 1971. The product of considerable scholarly research and close attention to the Egyptian scene.

Esposito, John L. "Sudan's Islamic Experiment." *Muslim World* 76 (1986): 181–202. A thorough discussion including the political ramifications of religion.

Faksh, Mahmud A. "The Consequences of the Introduction and Spread of Modern Education: Education and National Integration in Egypt." *Middle Eastern Studies* 16 (1980): 42–55.

Glassman, Jon D. *Arms for the Arabs: The Soviet Union and War in the Middle East.* Baltimore, Md.: Johns Hopkins University Press, 1975. Emphasizes the periods of 1956, 1967, and 1973.

Heikal, Mohamed H. *Cutting the Lion's Tail: Suez Through Egyptian Eyes.* New York: Arbor House, 1987. The Egyptian perspective on the 1956 war by the journalist, editor, and adviser to Nasser.

———. *Nasser: The Cairo Documents.* Garden City, N.Y.: Doubleday, 1973. An account by a confidant of Nasser.

Hinnebusch, Raymond A., Jr. *Egyptian Politics Under Sadat: The Post-Populist Development of an Authoritarian-Modernizing State.* New York: Cambridge University Press, 1985.

Hopkins, Harry. *Egypt: The Crucible: The Unfinished Revolution in the Arab World.* Boston: Houghton Mifflin, 1969. The revolution of 1952, Arab socialism, the newly emerging society, and the Palestinian problem.

Hopwood, Derek. *Egypt: Politics and Society, 1945–1984.* 2d ed. Boston: Allen & Unwin, 1985. A good text that covers politics, economics, ideology, and culture.

Hussini, Mohez M. El. *Soviet-Egyptian Relations, 1945–85.* New York: St. Martin's Press, 1987. The author, a commodore in the Egyptian navy, concentrates on naval matters as well as a general review of the subject. An unusual and interesting perspective.

Lacouture, Jean. *Nasser: A Biography.* New York: Knopf, 1973. By a distinguished French journalist.

Lesch, Ann Mosely. "Confrontation in the Southern Sudan." *Middle East Journal* 40 (1986): 410–428. A penetrating study by a leading authority on the contemporary Middle East.

Mabro, Robert. *The Egyptian Economy, 1952–1972.* New York: Oxford University Press, 1974. Fine survey of land reform, the Aswan Dam, and industry.

Manzalaoui, Mahmoud, ed. *Arabic Writing Today: The Short Story.* Berkeley: University of California Press, 1968. An anthology of short stories, mostly from Egypt, that paints a sharp portrait of Egypt and Egyptians.

Mayer, Thomas. "Egypt's 1948 Invasion of Palestine." *Middle Eastern Studies* 22 (1986): 20–36. The author emphasizes the role of King Faruq in bringing about Egypt's involvement in the war.

Nasser, Gamal Abd al-. *Egypt's Liberation.* Washington, D.C.: Public Affairs Press, 1955. A blueprint of the revolution. First issued in Cairo under the title *The Philosophy of the Revolution.*

Neff, Donald. *Warriors at Suez: Eisenhower Takes America into the Middle East.* New York: Linden Press, 1981.

Neguib, Mohammed. *Egypt's Destiny.* London: Gollancz, 1955. By the Egyptian general who headed the revolution in 1952.

Sadat, Anwar el-. *In Search of Identity: An Autobiography.* New York: Harper and Row, 1977.

————. *Revolt on the Nile.* New York: John Day, 1957. Sadat's description of the events leading to the 1952 revolution.

Safran, Nadav. *Egypt in Search of Political Community.* Cambridge, Mass.: Harvard University Press, 1961. A very well written analysis of the political thought that shaped modern Egypt.

Shazly, Saad el-. *The Crossing of the Suez.* San Francisco: American Mideast Research, 1980. An anti-Sadat account of the 1973 war by the chief of staff of the Egyptian army at that time.

Shibl, Yusuf. *The Aswan High Dam.* Beirut: Arab Institute for Research and Publishing, 1971. A very useful account, with tables and a good bibliography.

Stephens, Robert. *Nasser: A Political Biography.* New York: Simon and Schuster, 1972. A thorough biography by a British correspondent.

Sullivan, Earl L. *Women in Egyptian Public Life.* Syracuse, N.Y.: Syracuse University Press, 1986.

Vatikiotis, P. J. *Nasser and His Generation.* London: Croom Helm, 1978. A highly critical and comparative biography.

Voll, John Obert, and Sarah Potts Voll. *The Sudan: Unity and Diversity in a Multicultural State.* Boulder, Colo.: Westview Press, 1985. An excellent short survey that covers economics, geography, history, modern politics, and culture.

Wai, Dunstan M. *The Southern Sudan: The Problem of National Integration.* London: Cass, 1973. Covers the wide spectrum of views on the Sudanese conflict.

Waterbury, John. *The Egypt of Nasser and Sadat: The Political Economy of Two Regimes.* Princeton, N.J.: Princeton University Press, 1983. A thorough study of class, foreign affairs, and political factors.

————. *Hydropolitics of the Nile Valley.* Syracuse, N.Y.: Syracuse University Press, 1979. Concentrates on water, ecology, and the political and economic impact of the Nile River on Egypt and the Sudan.

46

Trends Since 1945

*F*ollowing World War II nationalism became the chief force in the Middle East as nationalists won many victories over Britain and France, the retreating imperial powers. The independent nation-state was the victor in the historical process. Most of the history of the time since 1945 has, therefore, been told in regard to each country, but certain trends and themes affected the whole region so broadly and generally that they can best be seen in a separate discussion. These trends include, among others that could be cited, the decline of the old great powers, the increasing importance of the new superpowers, the rise of religious fundamentalism, the working out of the implications of pan-Arab nationalism, growing militarization and terrorism, and the widening gap in scientific and technological areas between the Middle East and the West.

THE DECLINE OF THE OLD POWERS

After World War II the world at large became greatly concerned with the affairs of the Middle East. The advent of the state of Israel and the enormous flow of oil focused attention upon the area and emphasized its importance in matters of politics, transportation, communications, religion, culture, markets, military strategy, imperialism, and nationalism.

Until the summer of 1956, the British enjoyed the dominant role in the Middle East. Great Britain had held sway consistently; and her ambassadors, merchants, and navy exerted a profound influence wherever they went.

British involvements in the Middle East were various and comprehensive. Paramount solicitude, however, had revolved around the fact that the Middle East lay astride the route to India, which the British regarded as the jewel in the crown of the empire.

The British used every device to maintain their imperial position in the Middle East. Officials and colonial agents, both in London and the Middle East, regarded the inhabitants as "natives" in the Kipling sense and believed that the best way in which to preserve peaceful and proper relations was to cooperate with the native ruler. Support was given to strengthen him with his people. Where possible, however, a constitution was introduced. Such a government, created in the image of the British government, was expected to function in a friendly and peaceful manner within the British family of nations.

In any case, the British by economic, financial, military, and ideological means fully intended to retain their dominant position in the Middle East. However, weakened at home by losses in World War II, Great Britain found the retention of the Middle East beyond her means in the face of rising nationalism and growing economic strength and determination among Turks, Arabs, Israelis, and Iranians. Withdrawal of the British, partial though it was in the 1950s, led to a realignment of the power and position of foreign states and internal factions. Readjustment of these forces gave rise to uncertainty and feelings of insecurity, evidences of which were particularly noticeable in the controversies surrounding the issues of oil in Iran, Cyprus, the Suez Canal, the 1958 revolution in Iraq, and the various pacts, unions, and federations among the Arab states. Britain intervened in Jordan in 1958 and in Kuwayt in 1961 to protect those allied regimes, but these interventions were the last direct attempts to show military strength.

The eclipse of British power in the Middle East became nearly complete in the 1960s, when the British pulled out of the Gulf and southern Arabia.

Never able to match the power of England and plagued by miserable governments in Paris, French empire builders, except for their brief success in Syria and Lebanon between World Wars I and II, devoted their energies to spreading and establishing French culture among the elite of the local peoples. Cabinets and governments might come and go in the Middle East, as they did in France; but if the people were imbued with French culture and spirit and thus wedded to French civilization, a lasting sympathy for France would be generated. Such an understanding would be translated into trade, concessions, successful diplomacy, and allies in international conflict and wars. These were the true sinews of empire. However, the utter defeat of France in World War II and the weakness of her economy dispelled most of the prestige held by France in the Middle East. Admiration for French manufactures and French ways largely vanished in the postwar period, even though the French language remained popular as a means of communication in cultured circles—a fact which over a longer period of time might substantiate the French claim to the permanence of their civilization in the Middle East.

In 1956, greatly agitated by Nasser's aid and encouragement to Algerian leaders in their drive for independence, France, along with Great Britain and Israel, attacked Suez. In subsequent years France supported Israel in various ways, but in the 1967 crisis de Gaulle maintained a neutrality, which to the Arabs appeared to be a friendly and sympathetic position in sharp contrast to British and American attitudes.

In the 1970s and 1980s Great Britain and France still played a role in the Middle East, although it was much less prominent than formerly. They both sold weapons on a large scale to such countries as Jordan, Saudi Arabia, Oman, and Iraq. Both countries were members of the European Economic Community and the EEC undertook a multitude of diplomatic and economic actions that affected the Middle East. Trade with the area increased, and a great deal of oil revenue was invested by Middle Eastern governments in European banks and industries. Greek membership in the EEC as of 1981 and the tangled and troubled relationship between Greece and Turkey were of major concern to those Turks who saw the future of their country lying in Europe. The Venice Declaration of June 1980 put the

EEC on record in support of "the legitimate rights of the Palestinian people" as well as of Israel.

Britain and France participated in the multinational force in Beirut following the 1982 Israeli invasion, and also, with more success, in the Sinai observer force after 1979, and in the fleets that stood outside the Persian Gulf in the 1980s ready to intervene to protect shipping. France vigorously and directly backed those forces in Chad opposed to Libya's al-Qadhdhafi. Britain under Prime Minister Margaret Thatcher closely cooperated with United States actions in the Middle East.

THE NEW SUPERPOWERS

After the 1956 war the most important external powers for the Middle Eastern countries were clearly the United States and the Soviet Union.

United States goals in the area were chiefly strategic. However, the welfare and security of Israel evoked greater concern in the United States than any other Middle Eastern issue, although American devotion to Israel fluctuated somewhat. It was more difficult to obtain approval of the Congress for aid to the Arab states than for Israel. American oil investments in the area were very extensive, but they were purchased by the oil-producing countries in the 1970s. The U.S. supported pro-Western regimes in Turkey and Iran against Soviet pressures. When the United States strongly supported Israel, as in the 1967 war, American prestige suffered enormously among the Arabs. Such moves had a tendency to throw the Arabs into ready and waiting Soviet arms and to augment East-West competition and conflict in the Middle East.

Soviet Russia's aim has been to secure the friendship and sympathy of Middle Eastern peoples for the way of life in the Soviet bloc and to win the cooperation of their governments with that of the U.S.S.R. Attainment of these objectives has been sought by a mixture of pressure and inducement upon political figures to pursue Soviet policies and by the steady exploitation of every incident and disturbance to keep society in a constant ferment of unrest and uncertainty. Skillfully, Soviet envoys and agents played upon the fears and aspirations, defeats and disappointments, and the emerging nationalism of the Middle East in order to turn the people, especially the leaders, away from the West and toward the Soviet bloc.

Beginning in 1955 Soviet arms were supplied in ever-increasing quantities to Middle Eastern Arab states as a further move to draw them closer to the Soviet orbit and free them from susceptibilities to Western pressures. Complementing these arms were sizable developmental grants and loans for such important and visible items as the Aswan High Dam, the Euphrates Valley project in Syria, and innumerable factories, roads, harbors, and industrial complexes.

The Israeli-Arab crisis and the 1967 war were harsh testing experiences for the Soviets, but the initial results brought them favor among the Arabs. Replacement from the Soviet bloc of the arms lost and expended in the disastrous war was a reassuring gesture giving courage to the Arab military and their leaders.

The two superpowers dramatically increased their involvement in the Middle East after 1967. The United States continued to maintain its military commitment to the defense of Turkey as part of NATO, despite conflicting views over the actions of Turkey in Cyprus. President Richard Nixon assigned to the shah of Iran a role as policeman of the Persian Gulf, as a sort of surrogate for direct United States involvement. Iran was able to purchase enormous quantities of sophisticated weapons from America. U.S. foreign policy in regard to both Turkey and Iran was predicated on the desire to contain the Soviet Union while, at the same time, avoiding situations that might lead to nuclear war.

Another basic ingredient in United States foreign policy was support of Israel. In 1971 aid to Israel was increased fivefold. During the 1973 Arab-Israeli War the United States went to the brink of nuclear conflict with the Soviet Union, causing a shock that impelled Secretary of State Henry Kissinger to throw himself into the search for peace in the region. Throughout the following dramatic developments—disengagement, step-by-step withdrawals, the 1978 Camp David agreements, and the peace treaty of Washington in 1979—it was the United States that provided the diplomatic energy, the pressure, and the financial and other guarantees that permitted Egypt and Israel to bring about a mutual peace. The flaws, as well as the successes, in that peace process were also partially the responsibility of the United States, including the highly unsatisfactory situation that resulted for the Palestinian Arabs in the West Bank and Gaza.

United States commitment to Israel became even stronger in the 1980s. The Reagan administration tacitly approved Israel's invasion of Lebanon in 1982 and its subsequent support of a pro-Israeli Lebanese government. The United States directly and actively supported the new Lebanese administration and then underwent the humiliation of being forced out of Lebanon; Israel rejected the carefully constructed Reagan peace initiative of 1982. The United States accepted numerous actions by Israel that were generally opposed by nearly all the countries of the world. American financial, military, and diplomatic aid to Israel continued at extraordinarily high levels in the 1980s.

In other parts of the region the United States faced grave threats to its predominant role. Two of the chief purposes of U.S. diplomacy were to maintain access for itself and its allies to Middle Eastern resources, especially oil, and to secure a general stability in that part of the world. Both purposes seemed threatened by the 1978–1979 Islamic fundamentalist revolution in Iran, the ensuing Iran-Iraq War that began in 1980, and the potential involvement of other Persian Gulf countries in the fighting. Presidents Carter and Reagan became closely involved with Iran and they were substantially hurt by their failures to effect changes in Iranian foreign policy. On the other hand, the United States and other countries were successful in keeping open the sea lanes for the shipment of oil. America was publicly committed to the defense of Saudi Arabia in particular and to the freedom of navigation for neutral shipping in the Gulf in general. At the same time, the United States sought to curb Soviet domination in Afghanistan following Russian invasion of that country in 1979.

Soviet policy in the Middle East in the 1970s was oriented primarily toward the extension of Soviet influence through alliances and cooperation with friendly, non-Communist regimes. In 1967, the Soviets broke diplomatic ties with Israel and did not resume them thereafter. Instead, the U.S.S.R. aided Egypt and Syria in their

1973 war with Israel, and provided arms to Iraq. Between 1967 and 1973 the Soviet Union supplied $3 billion in arms to the Middle East, including almost $2 billion to Egypt. Soviet influence in Egypt was then lost, as President Sadat turned to the United States. As the conservative monarchies in the Gulf region gained wealth they tried to diminish the appeal of Soviet aid by providing an alternative source of assistance. Saudi Arabia helped Egypt, Syria, Jordan, Lebanon, Iraq, the Palestinians, North Yemen, and others. In some cases these countries and groups continued to accept Soviet aid, but in other instances they left their prior relationships with the Soviets.

The only Communist government in the Middle East, that of the People's Democratic Republic of Yemen, was quite dependent upon the Soviet bloc. Internal government structures were modeled upon the Soviet system, but South Yemen was not a total satellite, as was shown in the 1986 coup.

In the 1980s the Soviet Union vacillated over what course of action to take in the Iran-Iraq War, but it usually sided with Iraq. The Soviets also had close ties with Syria and the Arafat-led majority of the PLO; however, the mutual antipathy of Assad and Arafat posed continuing problems to Moscow. The Soviet Union was consistent in opposing the United States' step-by-step peace process; instead, the Russians called for the major world powers to provide the venue and the pressure for a comprehensive peace conference to resolve the Arab-Israeli dispute.

Soviet influence in the Middle East has, on the whole, diminished in the 1980s, and the appeal of Marxism Leninism has steadily declined. The Soviet withdrawal from Afghanistan in 1988 was a further indication that Russian leaders had a more realistic appraisal of where their true interests lay, as well as an acknowledgment of the failure of communism in the face of a nationalist and Islamic resistance.

THE FUNDAMENTALIST CHALLENGE

From the perspective of many Muslims, Jews, and Christians in the Middle East after 1945, both secular nationalism and Marxism were failures. The leaders of the secular nation-states seemed to want to modernize and transform their societies into carbon copies of the United States or the Soviet Union. Usually they were unable to do so. The small oil-rich states were successful to a degree, but they were only beginning the process of transformation, while the larger and relatively poorer countries had considerable experience in Westernization and modernization but with questionable results. The nationalists promised far more than they were able to deliver, so that rising expectations were disappointed, thereby creating a potentially revolutionary situation. In those societies where the desire to imitate other countries was at least partially realized, many of the lower classes were either unaffected or alienated by the transformation. Many intellectuals wondered if either the West or the Soviets were really worth imitating. Instead of such mimicking, they said, it was time for one of those periodic waves of reform and renewal that had so often revived the religious communities in the past. Muslims argued that revitalization of Islam would address the severe stress and dissatisfaction with prevailing norms that permeated most developing societies. Development in the Middle East had often led to an abandonment of the national past, the loss of newly gained independence to neo-imperialism, and most importantly, it left religious systems and values in favor of secular law, individualism, and materialism. The rich in such societies got much richer while the poor were given platitudes about social justice, land reform, and national glory. Even the most modern and autocratic secular rulers were unable to secure many of the basic goals and needs of the population, examples being the failure of Nasser's Egypt in wars against Israel, and the uninvolvement of Iran's villagers in oil prosperity. Islam seemed the only channel by which radical changes that worked could be made.

As a result of all these factors, religious fundamentalism grew in appeal, particularly in the 1970s and 1980s. The most spectacular case showing this trend was the Islamic Republic of Iran, where the ulema who had led the mass struggle against the shah in 1978 gained power and created a theocratic state. But in many other countries fundamentalism or communal parties, movements, and ideas increased their followings. Christians in Egypt became more conscious of their separate communal existence, while Lebanese Maronites led one side in the civil war that devastated their country. In Israel fundamentalist Orthodox Jews helped gain power for the Likud bloc and they strongly influenced policy on domestic matters as well as on the question of retaining the occupied territories.

In some places the fundamentalists seemed to have only a very small following. Saudi radical fundamentalists seized the Kaaba in Mecca in 1979, but they were soon repressed. The assassination of Sadat in Egypt in 1981 proved to be an isolated act. Iraqi fundamentalists were easily isolated, executed, or coopted. In these and other cases, however, the national governments found it desirable to adopt symbolic gestures showing a greater commitment to Islam, thereby defusing any possible mass appeal for the fundamentalists.

The controversy created by the fundamentalists in 1988–1989 over Salman Rushdie's novel, *The Satanic Verses,* illustrated the symbolic side of their movement. Rushdie was an Indian Muslim writer who had become a British citizen. His novel contained passages concerning the prophet Muhammad that many Muslims found deeply offensive; a number of countries, including Egypt, banned the book. Iran went beyond this, as the Ayatollah Khomeini on February 14, 1989, called for Rushdie's assassination as punishment for blasphemy, apostacy from Islam, and slander against Muhammad. Despite Rushdie's apology, Iran subsequently broke diplomatic ties with Britain since the British government refused to ban sales of the novel. The European Economic Community governments withdrew their top diplomats from Tehran as a sign of their disapproval of Khomeini's extremist position. The Salman Rushdie affair gained worldwide publicity and attention for the fundamentalist cause.

The fundamentalists, however, wanted far more than symbols. Their goals included the establishment of an Islamic moral order; the banning of sinful behavior; social and legal justice for all, irrespective of wealth; the greater application of religious precepts to all areas of life; struggle to remove Western imperialism, both direct and indirect; and the search for pan-Islamic unity. The fundamentalists were strongly antinationalist. Many of them adopted a strident tone, deeply offensive to most other Muslims. Koranic literalism, impractical utopianism, and political demagoguery also limited the appeal of many of their leaders. On the other hand, fundamentalism seemed to present an opportunity to overcome the deep schisms between elites and masses in culture, values, and identity.

While the Islamic revolution in Iran remained the sole example of fundamentalists seizing total control, religious fundamentalism became an important element in the ongoing debate in the Middle East about political system legitimacy, social identity, and the ultimate meaning of life for individuals and for groups. In some countries the consequences of intellectual fundamentalism were devastating in these subjects, as in the Sudan, where the fall of Numayri and the resumption of civil war were in part due to non-Muslims who objected to the emphasis on shariah.

One reason for the relatively slow spread of fundamentalism in the 1980s was that the Iranian experience had shown several problems that resulted from the actual implementation of fundamentalist ideals. The sovereignty of God, as interpreted by the ulema, conflicted with popular sovereignty, which was the theoretical basis upon which most nation-states were founded. Harsh internal actions, repression of domestic opposition, and an unwillingness to compromise with Iraq so as to bring about peace (until finally doing so in 1988), discredited Iran's regime in the eyes of many Muslims. The Iranian and other fundamentalists were also unclear in their own minds about a number of economic issues. Land reform, banking, the role of women in society, education, technology and science, and the adaptation of shariah to new circumstances were only a few of the matters which were still being debated among fundamentalists.

The Soviet Union and the United States opposed the spread of fundamentalism and the Iranian revolution to other countries. The United States vehemently objected to Iran's taking of U.S. diplomats as hostages and Iranian backing of terrorism in Lebanon. It also became clear to the kings, generals, and politicians who controlled politics in the Middle East that the victory of fundamentalism could only come about following their own ouster.

FAILURE OF PAN-ARAB NATIONALISM

From 1945 to the late 1960s Arab states sought to gain or expand their independence from Great Britain and France. In addition to international recognition of sovereignty, this struggle included several other goals—expelling all foreign troops, nationalizing major enterprises owned by foreigners, selecting political systems attuned to the perceived needs of the nation, advancing local culture, and lessening cultural borrowing from abroad. Arab nationalists also sought to spread the basic concepts of nationalism to groups whose political values were not yet nationalistic. These groups included the masses of society and especially the poor, as well as ethnic, linguistic, and religious minorities. Most Arab nationalists during this time also favored the goal of Arab unity. They argued that the Arabs constituted one ethnic unit and that separate political categories such as Jordanians, Iraqis, and Egyptians were artificial and should give way to one large, powerful, and united people living in one state. Such a political entity would have the ability to accomplish many things that each separate government could not hope to do.

Many of these goals, hopes, and dreams were accomplished. By the 1980s nearly all the Arab states were clearly independent, sovereign, free of unwanted foreign troops, in control of their own natural resources, and energetically spreading nationalist values through education. Most had political systems that differed from earlier liberal parliamentary forms of government. Cultural borrowing was still widespread, but the Arabic language was predominant and governments could freely alter the pace and direction of such borrowing.

While some members of minority groups were willing to accept Arab nationalism and were starting to identify themselves as Arabs, others opposed that ideology. The latter included some of the Kurds in Iraq, the Lebanese Maronites, and the southern Sudanese. Where religion, language, and ethnicity overlapped in one geographical region such opposition to centralizing nationalist governments was especially strong.

The primary problem for Arab nationalism was that of pan-Arab unity. This was an ironic result of the very successes of the nationalists, for as each country gained independence its leaders and many of its people savored the benefits of a separate existence while coming to fear and distrust union with another Arab country. The failure of the Egyptian-Syrian union of 1958–1961 showed this trend.

Repeatedly various Arab governments announced their intention to unite, but these unions were only on paper, and were not real or thorough. In fact, the pressure for union became a cause for disunity, since the various leaders and parties sharply disagreed with each other over methods of achieving union and who should control a united state once established.

Arab politics evolved then on a country-by-country basis. Even when regimes were supposedly committed to unity, they often actually opposed each other, as in the case of Ba'thist Syria versus Ba'thist Iraq in the 1970s and 1980s. Egypt under Sadat put its own national interests first while making peace with Israel. The Palestinians wanted to have their own country, not to be part of a greater pan-Arab nation. Saudi Arabia opted for pan-Islam rather than pan-Arabism. Rich oil states financially helped their fellow Arabs in a number of ways but with no abdication or lessening of their separate sovereignties. Technocrats in the oil states were bored with nationalism; instead, they turned to economic development as a panacea for the questions about identity.

As the decades passed, national borders that had been created by the European powers and that had been regarded by the pan-Arab nationalists as unreal, offensive, and impractical took on an air of permanency. Only Israel seemed able to alter Arab borders!

The desire for Arab cooperation and for the close coordination of military and foreign policy, however, still ran deep among the Arabs of the Middle East in the 1980s. The issue was how to obtain such cooperation among sovereign states that were very different, ranging from such countries as Marxist South Yemen to conservative monarchies in the Gulf to military-dominated socialist Syria.

The Arab League was weakened by suspending Egyptian membership in 1979. Many Arabs turned instead to local regional cooperation, taking as models the

United Arab Emirates, the Gulf Cooperation Council, the attempted merger of the two Yemens, and the cooperation of Sudan and Egypt. Such local measures did not provide much help for the Palestinians who sought a nation-state of their own, nor did they help end the tragic fighting in Lebanon, but regional cooperation was more realistic and more likely to bring immediate results than grandiose pronouncements about pan-Arab unity.

MILITARIZATION AND TERRORISM

The many conflicts in the Middle East since World War II led to a steady growth in the importance of the military in the governments of most of the countries involved, a dramatic increase in the amounts spent on armaments, more reliance on foreign sources of weapons and military assistance, and an exaltation of military values at the expense of civilian goals.

Most countries other than Israel saw the military seize power, as in Egypt, Syria, Iraq, Sudan, North Yemen, and Turkey. The Pahlevi dynasty in Iran came to power in a similar fashion in the 1920s. In other cases the armies tried to seize power but were defeated. The reasons for their actions depended in part upon specific conditions in each country, but they also resulted from such general factors as their monopoly of legitimate power, the desire to win wars and the feeling that military governments might prosecute wars more efficiently, the tendency for the military to be the most efficient and modernized sector of society, and the incompetence and corruption of many civilian governments.

The pattern of events following the military seizures of power varied sharply. In some cases the military returned rule to civilians after a relatively short period of time, for example, in Turkey. On the other hand, in Egypt after 1952, and Syria after 1970, the military or leading personalities within it retained power indefinitely. The actual accomplishments of each military regime also varied quite substantially. Occasionally the military would fall from power through sheer ineptitude, as in the Sudan.

While the evaluation of military rule was the subject of much debate, it was clear that far more was being spent on weapons in the 1980s than in the 1950s. The size of most armed forces grew greatly: Egypt's army went from 60,000 to more than 300,000. In constant 1982 dollars, military expenditures in the Middle East increased from $24 billion in 1973 to $61 billion in 1983, for a total of $542 billion in ten years. Military spending took about one-quarter of government expenditures in the 1980s. The Middle East bought close to one-half of total world weapons imports! These extraordinary amounts were spent by societies that ranged from a few extremely wealthy countries that could perhaps afford such expenses to some of the poorer nations on the planet, where the diversion of large sums meant real deprivation for already desperately poor people.

The militarization of society contributed indirectly to the growth of terrorism, that is, to violent attacks or kidnappings directed against innocent civilians by nonofficial organizations for political purposes. Persons engaged in these acts viewed themselves as freedom fighters and used the pejorative label "terrorist" for their enemies, not for themselves. Terrorists saw their own cause as absolutely correct and good and their enemies as absolutely wrong and evil; any kind of action could be moral under such circumstances. Often the terrorists had been psychologically and physically brutalized as children. The terrorist groups justified their actions by pointing to their goals, cited their frustration arising from the seeming impossibility of securing those goals by peaceful means, and showed their anger against injustices of a type whose results were said to be more damaging than any harm they might inflict on their own victims.

Terrorism became an obsession for the United States in the 1970s and 1980s, because so many terrorist acts were undertaken against Americans. Other special targets of terrorists included Palestinians, Israelis, Turks, Lebanese, and non-Middle Easterners residing in Lebanon. The chaotic situation of Lebanon following the 1975 civil war allowed terrorist groups to operate in relative safety; often these bands became simple bandit gangs seeking cash and masquerading behind ideological, nationalist, and religious rhetoric.

A small number of Muslims, including the Shiite leaders of revolutionary Iran, argued that struggle against the enemies of Islam through the use of terrorism was justifiable. Some Israelis and Armenians said that reprisals against perpetrators of violence were justified because of past injustices against their communities. They also wished to achieve future expansion, more security, or statehood. Palestinians who attacked Israeli civilians generally used nationalistic arguments. In many of these cases many members of the groups and countries involved opposed random violence, individual assassinations, collective punishments, bombings of civilian settlements, kidnappings, and similar events.

THE SCIENTIFIC AND TECHNOLOGICAL GAP WIDENS

Following 1945 a number of social and economic trends created both problems and challenges for the Middle East. Population, particularly in the cities, grew at such a rapid pace as to make necessary the creation of millions of new jobs. At the same time, the highly unequal concentration of wealth in the hands of small elites and the control of resources by governments often worked against the interests of the poor and the rural population. There was a clear and pressing need for balanced economic growth in industry, agriculture, and services. Scientific and technological advancement seemed to be one of the main keys to obtaining such development.

Middle Easterners had come to understand after World War II that there was a decided gap between scientific and technological knowledge, education, and application in the Western bloc and the Soviet Union on the one hand, and the Middle East on the other. This gap was most clearly shown in military technology. It also appeared in the ceaseless stream of new discoveries and inventions that enabled the more developed societies to boost their standards of living. In order to obtain an improved position in science and technology most countries in the Middle East increased the size and sophistication of their educational institutions; encouraged students to study abroad, especially for advanced degrees; and sought to allocate resources for local research and development projects. Foreign aid also helped develop science and technology. These measures resulted in great progress being made in some cases, but the even more rapid rate of advances in the developed world was such that the scientific and technological gap grew, except perhaps in the case of Israel.

Technology and science flourished in Israel, originating at the Haifa Technion, and the Weizmann Institute of Science, which conducted research in the natural sciences. Teachers in such fields as aeronautical engineering, nuclear physics, medical technology, and computer sciences trained scientists and engineers who directly helped Israel's military efforts. Many scientists sought advanced degrees abroad, and Israel by the middle 1970s had 15 percent of its work force with academic credentials. The need for scientists and technologists increased in the late 1970s and 1980s because of Israel's economic difficulties. Persons who specialized in dry farming techniques, solar energy, medical imaging devices, electronic software, and especially armaments research and development helped the Israeli economy through increasing exports. Science and industry cooperated closely as high technology seemed the best hope for Israeli economic development as well as a key ingredient in Israeli military superiority over its Arab enemies.

In the cases of Iran and Turkey, the two governments followed basically similar policies until the Iranian Revolution of 1979. Under Muhammad Reza Shah, Iran undertook an ambitious expansion of universities and scientific institutes, including an atomic energy program. The transfer of technology from foreign firms, particularly United States companies, ran into a number of problems including the sometimes inappropriate technology being transferred as well as a shortage of trained Iranian technicians. Vocational education in Iran was often poor in quality and inadequate in comparison to demand. The revolutionary government of Iran since 1979 reorganized the educational system and commissioned the writing of new textbooks. Science policy has been aimed at rural development and indigenous industrial research, presumably involving the development of a more religious approach to science and technology. Turkish scientific growth has been directed by the Science Policy Unit of the Scientific and Technical Research Council, created in 1963. The Science Policy Unit has emphasized technology transfer from the West and has spent research funds on such fields as local geology, ecology, agronomy, and medical and engineering studies. Particular attention was devoted in Turkey to documentation services so that Turkish scientists could stay up to date with scientific research done elsewhere using other languages than Turkish.

In the Arab world higher education expanded dramatically after 1945. By the early 1980s there were over 50 universities, with an enrollment of about 1 million students. The universities were generally teaching institutions—research budgets were very low. Scientific periodicals showed a growth in numbers. However, the gap between Israeli and Arab research, as measured by various quantitative factors, persisted, and remained roughly constant. In the 1950s Egypt dominated scientific publishing among Arab countries. There and elsewhere in the Arab world most scientific research centered initially around medicine. By the middle 1970s medicine and agriculture were the two primary topics, and most published research dealt with local applications and field research. Egypt, Lebanon, Sudan, and Iraq dominated research but political and military developments in Iraq and Lebanon later decreased the opportunities for research.

Many Arab governments developed institutes, councils, and committees to promote science and technology. Most were national in scope, but some included cooperation with the United Nations or involved persons from several countries in the region. The Kuwayt Institute for Scientific Research, one example of a national coordinating institution, was founded in 1967. By the middle 1970s it had 35 researchers, several with specializations in solar energy, who produced numerous publications, conducted tests of solar energy equipment produced elsewhere, and studied the adaptation of various techniques and scientific principles to local circumstances. Another example was the International Centre for Agricultural Research in the Dry Areas, established in 1977 in Aleppo. The Centre has studied successfully planting seasons, herbicides, planting patterns, and disease-resistant plant varieties. The two chief difficulties such institutes faced were in maintaining high standards and in linkages with government so that discoveries could be practically applied.

There was little original research conducted in most parts of the Middle East, and the quality of applied technology also remained fairly low. Reasons for this included the poverty of many countries; the dependence upon foreigners for large projects; the underdevelopment of local high-technology industries; the newness of scientific and technological programs in some of the wealthier states; the inadequacy of many libraries and laboratories; and the intolerance of higher authorities toward criticism and dissent among scholars. Thousands of scientists and engineers moved to Western countries and to the oil-rich countries of the Middle East, thereby creating a massive "brain drain" that further hampered creativity in the poorer nations. Another problem was the issue of which languages to use in scientific education. Arab nationalists pushed for the use of Arabic in the classroom and the coinage of Arabic words for scientific concepts, even though English was the language most often used in international scientific exchange of information.

Despite these and other difficulties, some major research and engineering projects aimed at economic development or military security were underway in the 1980s. Saudi Arabia invested in solar energy research through its own universities and in the United States as well. Turkey, Iran, Israel, and other countries developed plans for atomic energy plants to reduce the need for oil or coal. Israel had developed the ability to produce atomic weapons at an earlier time. The Arab Satellite Communications Organization's permanent communications satellites were launched by the United States and France in 1985. However, dependence upon Western science and technology remained considerable in order to achieve most of these undertakings.

The peoples of the Middle East sought success in scientific and technological development as in the quests for complete national independence, resistance to great power domination, and military strength. Frustrations in these areas increasingly impelled scientists and others toward their own cultural roots and particularly toward fundamentalist religious values, structures, and institutions. Dependence upon other societies and states was a grave threat both to fundamentalism and nationalism. The search for religious, ideological, and military independence and separateness conformed to the long historic identity of the Middle East. It remained to be seen how decisively growing world interdependence would influence the various national and religious loyalties of the Middle East and the peoples who so strongly believed in them.

REFERENCES

Ajami, Fouad. *The Arab Predicament: Arab Political Thought and Practice Since 1967.* Cambridge: Cambridge University Press, 1981. A fine analysis of the decline of pan-Arabism.

Ashegian, Parviz. "Technology Transfer by Foreign Firms to Iran." *Middle Eastern Studies* 21 (1985): 72–79. Deals with education, research, and technology in the prerevolutionary period.

Ayubi, Nazih. "The Egyptian 'Brain Drain': A Multidimensional Problem." *International Journal of Middle East Studies* 15 (1983): 431–450.

Be'eri, Eliezer. "The Waning of the Military Coup in Arab Politics." *Middle Eastern Studies* 18 (1982): 69–81. An excellent and influential study.

Brown, L. Carl. "The Middle East: Patterns of Change 1947–1987." *Middle East Journal* 41 (1987): 26–39. A superb overview of general trends.

Chaliand, Gerard. *Terrorism: From Popular Struggle to Media Spectacle.* London: Saqi Books, 1987. Although covering the whole world, this interesting work has much on the Middle East written by a first hand observer.

Cordesman, Anthony H. "The Middle East and the Cost of the Politics of Force." *Middle East Journal* 40 (1986): 5–15. The best short work on the subject; the author is an outstanding writer on the military and the Middle East.

Enayat, Hamid. *Modern Islamic Political Thought.* Austin: University of Texas Press, 1982. Discusses the connections between nationalism, democracy, socialism and religion; particularly valuable for discussion of Sunnite and Shiite points of view.

Esposito, John L. *Islam and Politics.* 2d ed. Syracuse, N.Y.: Syracuse University Press, 1987. A good coverage of early history, modernization, nationalism, and a country-by-country survey of the Islamic revival.

Farah, Tawfic E., ed. *Pan-Arabism and Arab Nationalism: The Continuing Debate.* Boulder, Colo.: Westview Press, 1987. Among the several valuable chapters Fouad Ajami's essays and various discussions of surveys on attitudes should be mentioned.

Findley, Carter V., and John Rothney. *Twentieth-Century World.* Boston: Houghton Mifflin, 1986. An outstanding world history with a particularly good section on the Middle East.

Haddad, Yvonne Yazbeck. *Contemporary Islam and the Challenge of History.* Albany: State University of New York Press, 1982. Shows how fundamentalists have viewed history; most of the examples are drawn from Egypt.

Ismael, Tareq Y. *International Relations of the Contemporary Middle East: A Study in World Politics.* Syracuse, N.Y.: Syracuse University Press, 1986. Includes chapters on western Europe, the United States, Soviet Union, China, and Africa.

Kuniholm, Bruce R. "Retrospect and Prospects: Forty Years of US Middle East Policy." *Middle East Journal* 41 (1987): 7–25. An excellent survey of goals and accomplishments.

Piscatori, James P. *Islam in a World of Nation-States.* Cambridge: Cambridge University Press, 1986. Perceptive discussions of international relations, territorial pluralism, nationalism, and development.

Rahman, Fazlur. *Islam and Modernity: Transformation of an Intellectual Tradition.* Chicago: University of Chicago Press, 1982. Emphasizes role of education; by a great Muslim scholar.

Reich, Bernard, ed. *The Powers in the Middle East: The Ultimate Strategic Arena.* New York: Praeger, 1986. In addition to the U.S. and U.S.S.R., also talks about Britain, France, and the EEC.

Sardar, Ziauddin. *Science and Technology in the Middle East: A Guide to Issues, Organizations and Institutions.* London: Longmans, 1982.

Taylor, Alan R. *The Islamic Question in Middle Eastern Politics.* Boulder, Colo.: Westview Press, 1988. A clear and concise review of neofundamentalism.

Voll, John Obert. *Islam: Continuity and Change in the Modern World.* Boulder, Colo.: Westview Press, 1982. An outstanding book that deals with the whole Muslim world; the discussion of the relationship between current fundamentalists and earlier periods is exceptionally important.

Wright, Robin. *Sacred Rage: The Wrath of Modern Islam.* New York: Linden Press, 1985. A study by a very perceptive journalist.

Zahlan, A. B. *Science and Science Policy in the Arab World.* London: Croom Helm, 1980. A full account of the subject by the leading authority.

Index